Praise for

Life Beyond the Classroom, Fourth Edition

"This book should be required reading for professionals supporting students with disabilities in making the transition from high school to adult life. It's an invaluable resource on research-based practices, effective program models, and transition planning strategies."

—**David R. Johnson, Ph.D.**
Professor and Director
Institute on Community Integration
University of Minnesota

"Families of young people with disabilities need all the help we can get to assure their rights and full participation in 21st-century America. We count on professionals to bring us the best ideas. *Life Beyond the Classroom* will help caring professionals support us to let go, and learn to let our son or daughter take the lead and find their rightful place in the heart of our communities, no matter what their disability. This book recognizes the good intentions of families and gives professionals the concepts and tools they need to turn these intentions into reality. The world can change, one student at a time."

—**Sue Swenson**
Executive Director
The Arc of the United States

"Comprehensive, covers areas that other transition books overlook. Includes cutting-edge strategies embedded in practical and research-based approaches. A great book that will enable educators to provide students with disabilities opportunities to develop strong transition plans and experiences to increase their postschool success."

—**James Martin, Ph.D.**
Zarrow Endowed Professor in Special Education
Zarrow Center for Learning Enrichment
The University of Oklahoma

Distributed By:
Program Development Associates
5620 Business Ave. Suite B
Cicero, NY 13039
www.disabilitytraining.com
1-800-543-2119

"In a tight, crisp style, covering all the key issues, Wehman and his colleagues have produced the ultimate transition handbook. Paul looks at curriculum, community, and unique aspects of disability, leaving no stone unturned. I only wish I had such a text when I was entering the field."

—**Al Condeluci, Ph.D.**
CEO
United Cerebral Palsy of Pittsburgh

"If I could buy only one book on transition, *Life Beyond the Classroom* would be my choice. Paul Wehman has put together a comprehensive and cutting-edge masterpiece that can help professionals and parents connect the dots from research to practice and from high school to a successful life."

—**Cherie Takemoto**
Executive Director
Parent Educational Advocacy Training Center (PEATC)
Springfield, Virginia

"This book is *the* definitive and comprehensive resource on transition. This up-to-date volume is a must for any individual or professional, no matter the role, interested and involved in assisting youth with disabilities to prepare for life after secondary education. It covers everything one needs to know about transition."

—**Richard G. Luecking, Ed.D.**
President
TransCen, Inc.

"As a professional involved in transitioning students with disabilities to the world of work, I am reserving space on my 'must have' bookshelf for *Life Beyond the Classroom*. The comprehensive coverage of major transition issues, practical and usable examples, extensive, up-to-date reference list, and chapter-ending study questions make this an excellent resource for students in training to become special educators and practicing professionals. Very well done!"

—**John A. Nietupski, Ph.D.**
Director
The High School Super Senior Transition Program
Grant Wood Area Education Agency
Cedar Rapids, Iowa

"Witnessing the accomplishments of youth with disabilities pushes us to re-examine the systems designed to support them but, more importantly, challenges us to expect more than what has ever been imagined. Thanks to Wehman and colleagues for updating the stories and the possibilities."

—**Caren L. Sax, Ed.D., CRC**
Professor
Department of Administration,
Rehabilitation, and Postsecondary Education
San Diego State University Interwork Institute

"For educators who wish to reduce the unnecessary unemployment, poverty, and social isolation of youth and adults with disabilities, you would be wise to read and implement the rich information and practical strategies provided in *Life Beyond the Classroom, Fourth Edition.*"

—**Diane Nelson Bryen, Ph.D.**
Professor and Executive Director
Institute on Disabilities
Temple University

"The search for a comprehensive resource on effective transition planning strategies for youth with disabilities stops here! Wehman's *Life Beyond the Classroom, Fourth Edition* is the biggest and best—providing critical information transition stakeholders need for effective, positive adult outcomes for youth with disabilities."

—**Thomas P. Golden, M.S., CRC**
Associate Director
Employment and Disability Institute
School of Industrial and Labor Relations
Cornell University

"Yet again, Dr. Wehman has provided all of us with a comprehensive, thorough, and up-to-date edition of *Life Beyond the Classroom.* This book is an excellent resource for practitioners, government, and students."

—**David Mank, Ph.D.**
Director, Indiana Institute on Disability and Community
Professor, School of Education
Indiana University

Life
Beyond
the
Classroom

Life Beyond the Classroom

Transition Strategies for Young People with Disabilities

FOURTH EDITION

by

Paul Wehman, Ph.D.
Virginia Commonwealth University
Richmond

with invited contributors

Baltimore • London • Sydney

Paul H. Brookes Publishing Co.
Post Office Box 10624
Baltimore, Maryland 21285-0624

www.brookespublishing.com

Typeset by Barton Matheson Willse & Worthington, Baltimore, Maryland.
Manufactured in the United States of America by
The Maple-Vail Book Manufacturing Group, York, Pennsylvania.

Some individuals described in this book are composites or real people whose
situations are masked and are based on the authors' experiences. In these instances,
names and identifying details have been changed to protect confidentiality.

The source for Table 10.1 (p. 275), Disability: Dispelling the Myths, was
funded by the Workforce Innovation Networks (WINs) through a grant from
The Ford Foundation and the Annie E. Casey Foundation. WINs is a partnership
among the Center for Workforce Preparation, an affiliate of the U.S. Chamber
of Commerce; the Center for Workforce Success, an affiliate of the National
Association of Manufacturers; and Jobs for the Future. Opinions expressed in this
publication do not necessarily represent the policies or views of the funders or the
WINs partners.

Library of Congress Cataloging-in-Publication Data

Wehman, Paul.
    Life beyond the classroom : transition strategies for young people with disabilities /
    Paul Wehman.—4th ed.
        p.   cm.
    Includes bibliographical references and index.
    ISBN-13: 978-1-55766-752-6
    ISBN-10: 1-55766-752-7
    1. People with disabilities—Vocational guidance—United States.   2. Youth with
    disabilities—Employment—United States.   3. Youth with disabilities—United States—
    Psychology.   4. School-to-work transition—United States.   I. Title.
    HV1568.5.W43   2006
    331.3'4087—dc22   2006009993

British Library Cataloguing in Publication data are available from the British Library

Contents

About the Authors

Paul Wehman, Ph.D., Professor, Department of Physical Medicine and Rehabilitation; Chairman, Division of Rehabilitation Research; Director, Virginia Commonwealth University, Rehabilitation Research and Training Center (VCU-RRTC) on Workplace Supports and Job Retention; Virginia Commonwealth University, 1314 West Main Street, Post Office Box 842011, Richmond, Virginia 23284

Dr. Wehman is Professor of Physical Medicine and Rehabilitation, with joint appointments in the Department of Special Education and Disability Policy and the Department of Rehabilitation Counseling at VCU. He pioneered the development of supported employment at VCU in the early 1980s and has been heavily involved in the use of supported employment with people who have severe disabilities, such as those with severe mental retardation, brain injury, spinal cord injury, or autism spectrum disorders. Dr. Wehman is also Director of the VCU-RRTC on Workplace Supports and Chairman of the Division of Rehabilitation Research. He has written extensively on issues related to transition from school to adulthood and special education as it relates to young adulthood. He has published more than 180 articles and 30 book chapters, and he has authored or edited 33 books. He is a recipient of the Joseph P. Kennedy, Jr. Foundation International Award in Mental Retardation; was a Mary Switzer Fellow for the National Rehabilitation Association in 1985; and received the Distinguished Service Award from the President's Committee of Employment for Persons with Disabilities in October 1992. Dr. Wehman was recognized as one of the 50 most influential special educators of the millennium by a national survey coordinated by the *Remedial and Special Education* journal (December 2000), and he received the VCU Distinguished Service Award, 2001 (September 6, 2001). He is also Editor-in-Chief of the *Journal of Vocational Rehabilitation.*

Amy J. Armstrong, Ph.D., Assistant Professor, Virginia Commonwealth University (VCU), 1112 East Clay Street, McGuire Hall, Richmond, Virginia 23298

Dr. Armstrong has been involved in advocacy and employment issues related to individuals with disabilities for more than 21 years. She has extensive experience providing personnel training nationally on disability-related issues, employment of marginalized populations, and distance education. She has been involved in providing distance education, in both synchronous and asynchronous formats, since 1989. Dr. Armstrong has held a variety of community agency positions, including both direct service and management at the local, regional, and national levels (including United Cerebral Palsy and the Rehabilitation Research and Training Center on Supported Employment/Workplace Supports). Her interest areas include the employment of individuals with significant disabilities, advocacy, welfare and poverty issues, disability policy and systems issues, and distance education. She received a master's in rehabilitation counseling from Michigan State University and a doctorate in education from VCU.

Lori W. Briel, M.Ed., Research Associate, Virginia Commonwealth University, Rehabilitation Research and Training Center (VCU-RRTC) on Workplace Supports and Job Retention, 1314 West Main Street, Post Office Box 842011, Richmond, Virginia 23284

Ms. Briel is a research associate at the VCU-RRTC on Workplace Supports. She has extensive experience with career development, resource coordination, and identifying compensatory strategies for individuals with significant disabilities. Ms. Briel is working with colleges and universities to replicate a comprehensive career development model for college students with disabilities.

Her specific research and career interests include transition from higher education to employment, internship supports, and career development for people with disabilities. She has presented nationally and has co-authored several journal articles and book chapters in these areas.

Valerie Brooke, M.Ed., Director of Training, Virginia Commonwealth University, Rehabilitation Research and Training Center (VCU-RRTC) on Workplace Supports and Job Retention, 1314 West Main Street, Post Office Box 842011, Richmond, Virginia 23284

Ms. Brooke is a faculty member at VCU and has been working in the field of employment for people with disabilities since 1979. She is the Director for Training for the VCU-RRTC on Workplace Supports and the Project Director for the Social Security Administration's Regional Benefits Planning, Assistance, and Outreach Technical Assistant Center. Ms. Brooke is nationally recognized for her personnel training programs and technical assistance work at the local, state, and federal levels. She has authored numerous book chapters, journal articles, newsletters, and fact sheets on transition and employment for people with disabilities. Her areas of interest include creating business partnerships, systems change, and self-advocacy leadership.

Elin Cortijo-Doval, M.Ed., Special Education Consultant and Advocate, Elin Doval and Associates, 3221 Skipwith Road, Richmond, Virginia 23260

Ms. Cortijo-Doval is an international consultant in the areas of education, transition, leadership empowerment, and advocacy for people with disabilities and their families. She has a creative and positive perspective on how to support people with autism and their families. She is the mother of two sons, the younger of whom has autism and is in his early 20s. In addition to her extensive experience in the field of family dynamics and autism, she regards her sons as her best teachers and most valuable source of inspiration. Her philosophical approach is based on many years of experience with positive behavior supports from a person-centered and self-determination approach. In addition to her private practice and consulting business, Ms. Cortijo-Doval is a very active advocate for individuals with disabilities and their families at the local, state, and federal levels. She has a master's degree in counseling/education from Virginia Commonwealth University (VCU) and is presently enrolled in the doctoral program at VCU under the Disability Policy and Leadership track. She also holds a mediation certification from The Center for Mediation Key Bridge Foundation, Washington, D.C., and she is a graduate from the Leadership Metro Richmond and Partner in Policy Making programs of Virginia.

Sandra Embler, M.Ed., Faculty Research Assistant, University of Maryland, 4619 Ripley Manor Terrace, Olney, Maryland 20832

Ms. Embler is a doctoral candidate and Faculty Research Assistant in the Institute for the Study of Exceptional Children and Youth at the University of Maryland, College Park. Her area of concentration is special education policy, with a particular focus on large-scale assessments and accountability policies for students with disabilities. Ms. Embler is currently involved in two research projects at the University of Maryland. One is investigating the policies and practices in high-performing rural schools in the Mid-Atlantic region, and the second is a training grant for doctoral students and postdoctoral fellows in using large-scale data for policy research for students with disabilities. Ms. Embler holds an undergraduate degree in special education from Appalachian State University and a master's degree in special education from the University of South Carolina. She has more than 17 years of classroom experience teaching students with disabilities in grades K through 12 with a range of disabilities.

Lori Eshilian, M.A., Assistant Principal of Student Support Services/Guidance, Whittier Union High School District, 12417 Philadelphia Street, Whittier, California 90601

Ms. Eshilian has been a teacher of students with significant challenges for 25 years. She has coauthored chapters in five books, presented at numerous state and national conferences, and taught at both California State University–Los Angeles and California State University–Long Beach as a visiting lecturer over the last 15 years. She has provided independent consultation to family and school districts working toward inclusive education. Ms. Eshilian was department chair of special education at Whittier High School and pioneered inclusive education at the secondary level for 8 years. She continues to work collaboratively with general education teachers, administrators, and families to develop individualized educational services that best support the academic and social success of all students. Ms. Eshilian is currently Assistant Principal at Los Nietos Middle School, responsible for curriculum and programming including education of students with disabilities in an integrated setting.

Mary A. Falvey, Ph.D., Director of Student Services, California State University–Los Angeles (CSULA), 5151 State University Drive, Los Angeles, California 90032

Dr. Falvey is a coordinator of credentials and master's programs in special education at CSULA. She teaches courses in each of these programs as well as the doctoral program, which is a joint program with University of California, Los Angeles and International TASH Board of Directors. She has been a teacher and administrator of programs for students with and without disabilities, and has worked with numerous schools and school districts in developing inclusive educational services and programs. She is one of the Least Restrictive Environment (LRE) Consultants for the Chanda Smith Consent Decree with the Los Angeles Unified School District. She has lectured at more than 200 international, national, state, and local conferences as well as taught courses at numerous universities throughout the United States, Canada, Peru, and New Zealand. She has written, edited, and contributed chapters to more than 12 books. Her most recent book is *Believe in My Child with Special Needs! Helping Children Achieve Their Potential in School* (Paul H. Brookes Publishing Co., 2005).

William Edward Fuller, Ph.D., Housing Officer, Virginia Housing Development Authority, 601 South Belvedere Street, Richmond, Virginia 23236

Dr. Fuller is a housing officer with the Virginia Housing Development Authority, where he is responsible for designing and implementing the Commonwealth housing policies affecting people with disabilities. He also serves as Vice Chairman of the Governor's Olmstead Implementation Team and serves on the Board of Directors of the Virginia Housing Coalition. He has published several articles in the area of housing policy and related issues on disability. Dr. Fuller also publishes a statewide newsletter on housing policy for people with disabilities.

Elizabeth Evans Getzel, M.A., Director of Postsecondary Education Initiatives, Virginia Commonwealth University, Rehabilitation Research and Training Center (VCU-RRTC) on Workplace Supports and Job Retention, 1314 West Main Street, Post Office Box 842011, Richmond, Virginia 23284

Ms. Getzel is the VCU-RRTC Director of Postsecondary Education Initiatives at Virginia Commonwealth University in Richmond, Virginia. She has considerable experience conducting research, evaluation, and training in the areas of transition planning for secondary students with disabilities, postsecondary education for students with disabilities, and career planning/employment for individuals with disabilities. She has published extensively in the areas of transition, postsecondary education, and disability.

Stelios Gragoudas, M.A., Research Associate, Beach Center on Disability, University of Kansas (KU), 1200 Sunnyside Avenue, Room 3136, Lawrence, Kansas 66045

Mr. Gragoudas is a research associate at the Beach Center on Disability at the University of Kansas and a doctoral student in the KU Department of Special Education. His areas of research interest and expertise involve youth leadership, self-determination, self-advocacy, and transition. He recently completed a term as the student representative to the Council for Exceptional Children's Division on Career Development and Transition.

J. Howard Green, M.S., Instructor, Virginia Commonwealth University, Rehabilitation Research and Training Center (VCU-RRTC) on Workplace Supports and Job Retention, 1314 West Main Street, Post Office Box 842011, Richmond, Virginia 23284

Mr. Green is an instructor and business liaison in the Rehabilitation Research and Training Center on Workplace Supports at VCU-RRTC. He has more than 30 years of experience in the rehabilitation field and tremendous experience in working with businesses on national, state, and local levels. He is a strong advocate for people with disabilities and has worked with individuals and organizations to promote the full employment and active citizenship for individuals with disabilities. Mr. Green continues to provide training and technical assistance to businesses, rehabilitation providers, and rehabilitation agencies on issues related to disability and business. Over the past several years, he has co-authored and contributed to several articles and book chapters relating to the employment of people with disabilities. In addition, Mr. Green has taught or assisted with many on-line and on-campus classes at VCU.

Cary Griffin, M.A., Senior Partner, Griffin-Hammis Associates, LLC, 5582 Klements Lane, Florence, Montana 59833

Mr. Griffin is Senior Partner at Griffin-Hammis Associates, a full-service consultancy specializing in building communities of economic cooperation, creating high-performance organizations, and focusing on disability and employment. He maintains a strong relationship with the Rural Institute at the University of Montana, where he served as director of training and now conducts special projects. He is the former Executive Director of the Center for Technical Assistance and Training (CTAT) in Denver. Mr. Griffin provides training to administrative and direct service–level professionals in the rehabilitation field; consultation to businesses and rehabilitation agencies regarding the employment of individuals with significant disabilities, field-initiated research and demonstration, family and consumer case consultation, resource development, and organizational development. Recently, he has been instrumental in designing self-employment protocols and training for individuals, agencies, and states. Mr. Griffin speaks on an international basis, with an emphasis on leadership and community employment. He is on the editorial board of the *Journal of Vocational Rehabilitation* and the *Journal of Mental Retardation.* His latest book, co-authored by Dave Hammis, is titled *Making Self-Employment Work for People with Disabilities* (Paul H. Brookes Publishing Co., 2003).

John J. Gugerty, M.S., Researcher, Center on Education and Work, University of Wisconsin, Madison, 964 Educational Sciences Building, 1025 West Johnson Street, Madison, Wisconsin 53706

Since 1975, Mr. Gugerty's professional life has focused on improving career and employment options for youths and adults with disabilities. Since 1977, he has collaborated with Center on Education and Work staff and professionals in higher education, state agencies, local agencies, community-based organizations (including parent advocacy groups), local 2-year colleges, and secondary schools from around the country on 18 multiyear federally funded projects and numerous state-funded efforts designed to improve career aspirations, preparation, and employment outcomes for individuals with disabilities.

Pamela Luft, Ph.D., Associate Professor, Department of Special Education, Kent State University, 405 White Hall, Kent, Ohio 44242

Dr. Luft is an associate professor of special education at Kent State University in the Deaf Education and Multiple Disabilities programs. She received her master's in deaf education from Western Maryland College, her master's in computer technology from The Johns Hopkins

University, and her doctorate in transition services from the University of Illinois at Urbana-Champaign. She has been a deaf educator for more than 20 years in public, private day, and state residential schools. She has worked as a teacher, a resource consultant, and an administrator for both academic and dormitory programs. Her students have ranged from elementary through graduate school, and included deaf with multiple or mild additional disabilities, deaf, and gifted deaf.

Margaret J. McLaughlin, Ph.D., Professor, Department of Special Education, University of Maryland, College Park, 1308 Benjamin Building, College Park, Maryland 20742

Dr. McLaughlin has been involved in special education all of her professional career, beginning as a teacher of students with serious emotional and behavior disorders. She earned her doctorate at the University of Virginia and has held positions at the U.S. Office of Education and the University of Washington. Currently, she is the Associate Director of the Institute for the Study of Exceptional Children, which is a research institute within the University of Maryland, College of Education. Dr. McLaughlin currently directs several national projects investigating educational reform and students with disabilities, including the national Educational Policy Reform Research Institute (EPRRI), a consortium involving the University Maryland, The National Center on Educational Outcomes, and the Urban Special Education Collaborative. EPRRI is studying the impact of high-stakes accountability on students with disabilities. Dr. McLaughlin is also directing a national research project investigating special education in charter schools and a policy leadership doctoral and postdoctoral program in conducting large-scale research in special education. She also has worked in Bosnia, Nicaragua, and Guatemala, developing programs for students with developmental disabilities. Dr. McLaughlin has consulted with numerous state departments of education and local education agencies on issues related to students with disabilities and the impact of standards-driven reform policies. She co-chaired the National Academy of Sciences (NAS) Committee on Goals 2000 and Students with Disabilities, which resulted in the report *Educating One and All*. She was a member of the NAS committee on the disproportionate representation of minority students in special education. Dr. McLaughlin teaches graduate courses in disability policy and has written extensively in the area of school reform and students with disabilities.

Shannon McManus, M.Ed., Research Associate, Virginia Commonwealth University, Rehabilitation Research and Training Center (VCU-RRTC) on Workplace Supports and Job Retention, 1314 West Main Street, Post Office Box 842011, Richmond, Virginia 23284

Shannon McManus is a faculty member with the VCU-RRTC. With the VCU-RRTC, she has been involved in many activities that promote self-determination, academic success in postsecondary education, and effective transition services for students with disabilities. Her research areas of interest include students with disabilities making the transition from high school to postsecondary education, identifying educational interventions that support students with learning disabilities in postsecondary education, and exploring assistive technology options for students with disabilities.

Lucy A. Miller, B.S., Training Associate, Virginia Commonwealth University, Rehabilitation Research and Training Center on Workplace Supports, 708 Cherokee Woods Road, Louisville, Kentucky 40206

Ms. Miller currently serves as Trainer and Technical Assistance Liaison for Social Security Administration (SSA) Region 4 with Virginia Commonwealth University's Benefits Assistance Resource Center (BARC). In this capacity, she provides work incentive training, technical assistance and consultation to SSA-funded Benefits Planning, Assistance, and Outreach projects in six southeastern states. Before joining VCU BARC, Ms. Miller served as the Vice President of Development for Career Resources, Inc., a nationally recognized leader in One Stop and

Welfare-to-Work services in the greater Louisville metropolitan area. Prior to this, she worked for more than 10 years at Seven Counties Services, the regional planning authority for mental health, mental retardation, and chemical dependency services. She has more than 17 years of experience in supported employment implementation and management for adults with the most severe disabilities in both urban and rural settings. A dynamic public speaker, Ms. Miller has presented on diverse career and workforce development topics, including job development strategies for people with severe disabilities, strategies for serving people with disabilities in One Stop centers, and Social Security disability benefits management and work incentives.

Devon Monson, M.S., Whittier Union High School District, 12417 Philadelphia Street, Whittier, California 90601

Ms. Monson completed her master's in school counseling at University of LaVerne. She has been employed as a dropout prevention specialist for a large Los Angeles County school, as a special education vocational counselor at another high school district, and currently is counselor for the comprehensive, 2,400-student Whittier High School. She is completing a master's in educational management and administrative credentials. She is an active member of Guidance Advisory for the Los Angeles County Office of Education and the California Association of School Counselors.

Susan O'Mara, B.S., Project Coordinator, Virginia Commonwealth University (VCU), Rehabilitation Research and Training Center Youth Transition Project, 2116 Wake Forest Street, Virginia Beach, Virginia 23451

Ms. O'Mara has more than 20 years of experience in providing education, work incentive counseling, and employment assistance to individuals with disabilities. From 1983 to 1988, she provided benefits counseling as a component of supported employment services in Virginia. Since 1988, Ms. O'Mara has provided leadership as a state and national consultant, providing direct benefits assistance to people with disabilities as well as national resource and curriculum development, training, and technical assistance to employment providers, rehabilitation and benefits counselors, beneficiaries, and their families. Her direct counseling and education experience includes extensive work with beneficiaries and recipients while developing and coordinating a statewide work incentive support project, as well as benefits consultation provided in support of Social Security Administration's Project ABLE. Ms. O'Mara currently serves as coordinator of training and technical assistance for the VCU Benefits Assistance Resource Center. She is also a member of the VCU National Project Office team, providing technical assistance, monitoring, and evaluation to State Projects under the Social Security Administration/Rehabilitation Services Administration State Partnership Systems Change Initiative. Other previous experience includes serving as a regional marketing specialist for the Virginia Department of Rehabilitative Services, coordinating training and assistance on workplace supports to the business community and workforce development entities, and experience as a job coach, program manager, and consultant on Virginia's Supported Employment Systems Change Grant.

Cynthia E. Pearl, Ph.D., Project Coordinator, University of Central Florida, College of Education, Department of Child, Family, and Community Sciences, Post Office Box 161250, Orlando, Florida 32816

Dr. Pearl is currently employed at the University of Central Florida as the Coordinator for Project ASD (Preparing Teachers to Work With Students With Autism Spectrum Disorders), a personnel preparation grant funded by the Office of Special Education Programs, U.S. Department of Education. This federal project is designed to increase the number, qualifications, and diversity of special education teachers prepared to work with students with autism spectrum disorders. Dr. Pearl received her master's and doctorate from the University of Central Florida. Her 23 years as a special educator include 5 years in higher education and 18 years as a special education teacher. She held the position of behavior specialist within five Central Florida Public Schools and has had teaching experience in the areas of learning disabilities, emotional handicaps, and varying exceptionalities. In the summer of 2003, Dr. Pearl completed a public policy internship at the Council for Exceptional Children in Washington, D.C.

W. Grant Revell, M.S., M.Ed., Research Associate, Virginia Commonwealth University, Rehabilitation Research and Training Center on Workplace Supports and Job Retention, 1314 West Main Street, Post Office Box 842011, Richmond, Virginia 23284

Mr. Revell conducts research in the areas of state systems change and funding of competitive employment outcomes. He is training manager for the Training and Technical Assistance for Providers, a project funded by the U.S. Department of Labor to reduce the use of subminimum wage certificates. He has worked for more than 30 years in the area of building competitive employment opportunities for individuals with disabilities.

Richard L. Rosenberg, Ph.D., Lead Vocational Coordinator, Whittier Union High School District, 9401 South Painter Avenue, Whittier, California 90605

Dr. Rosenberg received his doctorate from the University of Wisconsin–Madison in Behavioral Disabilities and Educational Administration. He has had more than 25 years of teaching and administrative experience. He is a faculty member at California State University–Los Angeles. He is the Lead Vocational Coordinator for Whittier Union High School District's Career Connection. This special education administrative position coordinates vocational and career support for all students with special education needs for the seven high schools, two continuation schools, and a number of middle schools with the WorkAbility project. In addition, Dr. Rosenberg provides technical assistance for Community Advocates for People's Choice adult agency providing supported employment and supported living services. He has worked for a number of years with Interagency Systems Change grants linking education, rehabilitation, and developmental disabilities services at the local, state, and national levels.

Phillip D. Rumrill, Jr., Ph.D., Professor and Director, Center for Disability Studies, Kent State University, 413 White Hall, Kent, Ohio 44242

Dr. Rumrill is a professor of rehabilitation counseling at Kent State University in Ohio. He also serves as director of the Kent State University Center for Disability Studies. Dr. Rumrill earned his bachelor's and master's degrees at Keene State College in New Hampshire and his doctorate at the University of Arkansas. His research interests include the career development implications of disability, psychosocial adjustment to chronic illness, and consumer implementation of the Americans with Disabilities Act of 1990.

Carol Schall, Ph.D., Executive Director, Virginia Autism Resource Center at Grafton School, 4100 Price Club Boulevard, Richmond, Virginia 23112

Dr. Schall is the Executive Director of the Virginia Autism Resource Center at Grafton School. She provides on-site training technical assistance and consultation to individuals with autism, their family members, educational and support team members, and administrators across the state of Virginia. Her research and teaching interests include understanding challenging behavior, the prevalence of psychotropic medication use among youth with autism, the use of positive behavior support for individuals with autism and transition planning for individuals with autism and with Asperger syndrome. In addition, Dr. Schall teaches as an adjunct professor at Virginia Commonwealth University.

Karrie A. Shogren, M.A., Project Coordinator, Beach Center on Disability, University of Kansas, 1200 Sunnyside Avenue, Room 3136, Lawrence, Kansas 66045

Ms. Shogren is the project coordinator on a National Institute on Disability and Rehabilitation Research–funded study of the impact of the use of cognitively accessible technology on self-determination and transition outcomes for high school students with intellectual impairments. She is also a doctoral student in the Department of Special Education at the University of Kansas. Her areas of research interest and expertise are self-determination, health care access for people with developmental disabilities, and technology use and self-determination. Ms. Shogren is the 2005 recipient of the American Association on Mental Retardation Outstanding Student Award.

Kim Spence-Cochran, Ph.D., Coordinator of Educational and Training Programs, University of Central Florida (UCF), Center for Autism and Related Disabilities (CARD), 12001 Science Drive, Suite 145, Orlando, Florida 32826

Dr. Spence-Cochran received her undergraduate degree in Secondary English Language Arts Education, her master's degree in Varying Exceptionalities, and her doctorate in Special Education from UCF. She is currently a Coordinator of Educational and Training Programs for CARD at UCF. Prior to joining the staff at CARD in 1999, Dr. Spence-Cochran worked for 10 years within public and private school settings as a teacher, behavior specialist, and a student assistance coordinator. She holds a professional teaching certificate in the state of Florida with several endorsements, is a published author, and consults nationally on issues germane to individuals with disabilities. Currently, Dr. Spence-Cochran is on the state board of the Council for Exceptional Children's Division on Developmental Disabilities and a member of the Project ASD (Preparing Teachers to Work With Students With Autism Spectrum Disorders) Grant Advisory Committee.

Pam Sherron Targett, M.Ed., Director of Employment Services, Virginia Commonwealth University, Rehabilitation Research and Training Center (VCU-RRTC) on Workplace Supports and Job Retention, 1314 West Main Street, Post Office Box 842011, Richmond, Virginia 23284

Ms. Targett is a collateral faculty member at the School of Education at VCU and Program Manager for the Employment Services Division at the RRTC on Workplace Supports, which provides supported employment services to people with severe disabilities. Over the years, she has overseen a number of employment demonstration projects. Ms. Targett has authored or co-authored journal articles and book chapters and has served as a guest editor for the *Journal of Vocational Rehabilitation*.

Colleen A. Thoma, Ph.D., Associate Professor, Virginia Commonwealth University (VCU), 1015 West Main Street, Post Office Box 842020, Richmond, Virginia 23284

Dr. Thoma is an associate professor in the Department of Special Education and Disability Policy in the School of Education at VCU. She coordinates the graduate program in teaching students with cognitive disabilities and teaches courses in that program including curriculum, transition planning/secondary education, and characteristics of students with cognitive disabilities. Her research interests include self-determination in transition planning, transition assessment and postsecondary education for students with cognitive disabilities. Dr. Thoma coauthored a book on transition assessment with Dr. Caren Sax titled *Transition Assessment: Wise Practices for Quality Lives* (Paul H. Brookes Publishing Co., 2002), in addition to authoring book chapters, articles, and conference presentations on transition-related topics. She is a member of the executive board of the Council for Exceptional Children's Division on Career Development and Transition and is currently Vice President of the division.

Michael L. Wehmeyer, Ph.D., Associate Professor, Department of Special Education; Director, Kansas University Center on Developmental Disabilities; Associate Director, Beach Center on Disability, University of Kansas, 1200 Sunnyside Avenue, Room 3136, Lawrence, Kansas 66045

Dr. Wehmeyer is engaged in teacher personnel preparation in the area of severe, multiple disabilities and directs multiple federally funded projects conducting research and model development in the education of students with intellectual and developmental disabilities. He is the author of more than 170 articles and book chapters and has authored, co-authored, or co-edited 19 books on disability and education-related issues, including self-determination, transition, universal design for learning and access to the general curriculum for students with significant disabilities, and technology use by people with cognitive disabilities. He is a past president of the Council for Exceptional Children's Division on Career Development and Transition and is Editor-in-Chief for the journal *Remedial and Special Education*. In 1999, Dr. Wehmeyer was the inaugural recipient of the Distinguished Early Career Research Award from the Council for Exceptional Children's Division for Research. In May 2003, he was awarded the American Association on Mental Retardation's Education Award. Dr. Wehmeyer holds undergraduate and master's degrees in special education from the University of Tulsa and a master's degree in experimental psychology from the University of Sussex in Brighton, England, where he was a Rotary International Fellow. He earned his doctorate in Human Development and Communication Sciences from the University of Texas at Dallas.

Michael D. West, Ph.D., Associate Professor, Virginia Commonwealth University, Rehabilitation Research and Training Center (VCU-RRTC) on Workplace Supports and Job Retention, 1314 West Main Street, Post Office Box 842011, Richmond, Virginia 23284

Dr. West is an assistant professor at VCU and is also a research associate with the VCU-RRTC on Workplace Supports. His research projects have included national surveys of supported employment policies and practices, a study of students with disabilities in higher education in Virginia, and states' use of Medicaid Home and Community Based Waivers to fund employment services. Dr. West also is involved in research and demonstration efforts related to Social Security disability reform at the VCU-RRTC on Workplace Supports.

Satoko Yasuda, Ph.D., Research Associate, Virginia Commonwealth University, Rehabilitation Research and Training Center (VCU-RRTC) on Workplace Supports and Job Retention, 1314 West Main Street, Post Office Box 842011, Richmond, Virginia 23284

Dr. Yasuda has been involved in examining return to work for individuals with traumatic brain injury and spinal cord injury, and she has published numerous journal articles and book chapters. Her other interests include disability management and students with disabilities in higher education. Dr. Yasuda has also examined the cultural differences in the perception of mothers with children with disabilities.

Preface

The education and employment of young adults with disabilities in the United States is a leading national priority. The education of individuals with disabilities is critical to the foundation of adult adjustment and success in work and the community. Without an education that focuses on the development of personal competence, life skills, and employment opportunities, young adults with disabilities are greatly handicapped in the complex modern society in which we live. In this fourth edition of *Life Beyond the Classroom*, the contributors and I emphasize the importance of independent living skills, assistive technology, high-stakes testing, and post-secondary education, along with employment. Job carving, customized employment, self-employment, and community-based instruction are all focused on in detail. The field of transition has expanded dramatically, and these topical areas, in their own way, will influence employment, postsecondary education, and community living.

Getting into college, gaining employment, and starting one's own company are more challenging and competitive than ever. Therefore, this book focuses heavily on the outcomes associated with the transition process. Competitive employment is the most desirable alternative for young adults with disabilities and may take place in many different types of businesses, industries, and settings. Some individuals will choose to become self-employed, others will choose to work part time and continue school, others will go on to technical schools, and still others will enter the work force full time with the help of job coaches and other technological aids, such as voice-recognition devices and computers. We believe, however, that all students must work in real jobs before they leave school. We believe strongly that paid employment before exiting school is highly correlated with successful adult employment.

In *Life Beyond the Classroom*, unlike other books related to the transition field, we focus on people with disabilities who have different strengths and weaknesses. We specifically dedicate chapters to the best methods of transition planning and intervention for youth with intellectual, physical, emotional, and learning disabilities. People labeled with traumatic brain injury, sensory impairments, and autism spectrum disorders are also included. These chapters were developed in order to meet the unique needs of a wide variety of students.

Having high aspirations for success can influence the actual outcomes of people with disabilities—a major theme of this book. We live in a rapidly changing society, both politically and technologically, and it can become easy to feel inept or overwhelmed. However, positive self-esteem and confidence can directly affect one's level of success. There are substantial doubts on the part of many in society about the quality and credibility of education for young people with disabilities. We believe that the only way to change these views is for young people with disabilities to demonstrate their competence on college campuses, in community malls, in recreational centers, and in the workplace. Societal attitudes only change when everyone can see the successful behaviors of individuals with disabilities—many of whom have never been given the opportunity to perform well.

Whatever the political climate, there will always be young adults in need of education and work opportunities. In addition to the emphasis on evidence-based academic research and high-stakes testing, inclusive employment will continue to be the targeted outcome. Transition from school to adulthood has remained a major priority of state legislatures, as well as the U.S. government, primarily because intelligent and informed people know that the country's future rests on the education and employment of its young people, thousands of whom have specialized needs or disabilities. As society becomes more complex and as technology and jobs become more specially designed, upgraded equipment and facilities, as well as a more sophisticated approach to training, will be required. Greater work experiences in the community, more intensive apprenticeships, greater use of business mentors, and employment during school all constitute a more successful approach to transition planning, according to observations made since 1980.

The issues that face high school–age youth with disabilities and their families as they prepare and plan for completion of special education are the same in this edition of *Life Beyond the Classroom* as in previous editions. These issues have, however, become more complex, complicated, and challenging as our society demands greater levels of knowledge and competence in young people. Educators at the high school level must therefore be informed about postschool services, especially postsecondary college outlets, because they will be the major source of information to concerned parents and their teenage students about what awaits them after they finish school.

The information and assistance needs identified by parents point to two primary issues facing the secondary-level educator in relating to the adult community, both as a place where the youth with a disability will live and work and also as a potential resource for services and supports. First, to have true and lasting meaning, education programs must help prepare youth with disabilities to live, go to school, and work in the community with confidence and value. To accomplish this goal, the educational program must provide consistent opportunities for students with disabilities to go to school with nondisabled peers. The curriculum also must be functional and community referenced and must involve the increasing participation of community representatives such as case managers. Second, for many secondary school–age youth with disabilities and their families, the special educator is frequently the primary person they turn to with their questions about education, training, work, social and recreational opportunities, and resources. The educator must be able to respond to these questions accurately and confidently by identifying and/or drawing on needed information and referral contacts within the adult community.

The services available through the assistance of the vocational rehabilitation counselor and other adult services resources are most effective if the school program aggressively incorporates transition planning into middle school and secondary-level activities. This planning may include, for example, the family of a young adolescent with a disability signing up for service coordination assistance from local mental health/mental retardation services programs as early as possible in the student's school career. The service coordinator is then invited to attend selective individualized education program meetings to assist with services such as living arrangements, respite services, and recreation.

As early as middle school, the process of situational or formal vocational assessment can be initiated as a starting point in vocational planning. Vocationally oriented student résumés are started at this level. In the first years of high school, the student can secure a picture ID and begin vocational exploration placements. During the last several years of high school, the state vocational rehabilitation counselor helps the student and family make plans for placement after graduation. By spreading these activities over a number of years, the school system helps students and their families to plan gradually for life after secondary education. Following set time lines prevents students and families from failing to make long-range plans. These procedures also make students aware of the different agencies that have services to assist them in the transition to adult life.

Many youth with disabilities and their families experience a sense of isolation from the community. A primary example of this isolation is the limited participation of youth with disabilities in work and work-related activities. By encouraging and supporting middle and secondary school–age youth with disabilities to obtain ID cards, develop and maintain résumés, and to seek out work opportunities, school programs can expand student involvement in the community, knowledge of work requirements, and awareness of individual interests. These activities provide a firm base of information for the transition committees to use in assisting individual students in planning for postsecondary interests and services needs.

As we move farther into the new millennium, we can point to wonderful progress that has been made in the education and employment of young people with disabilities over the past 20 years. There is an unfortunate disparity among communities in successfully helping their young adults. In this fourth edition of *Life Beyond the Classroom*, we continue to provide individualized examples of how person-centered planning can be fused with transition planning in order to give the reader more specific and concrete illustrations of how students can collaboratively plan for meaningful outcomes. The strong focus on person-centered planning, business partnerships, and career development imparts a clear message: Unless businesses and industry are involved in a more direct fashion, those training activities generated exclusively in the school environment are doomed to fail because they are largely ungeneralizable.

We believe that this fourth edition of *Life Beyond the Classroom* will successfully touch the lives of thousands of university students and professionals who wish to accumulate more information and knowledge in the important areas of education and employment for young people with disabilities. The challenge is greater than ever. There is a critical need for professionals to take a more significant leadership role in the community on behalf of people with disabilities. Advocacy and involvement are essential to making transition work in a community. This book is based on the notion that any community can have a successful transition program, but individuals with disabilities and their families and advocates must be actively involved and committed to envisioning successful employment and community outcomes for students after high school.

Acknowledgments

I am grateful to many people in the development of this fourth edition of *Life Beyond the Classroom*. Many individuals with whom I have worked have taught me a great deal about what I do and think every day. It is difficult to know where to start, because there are so many who have very much influenced this work. I am so fortunate to work with some wonderful people at the Rehabilitation Research and Training Center on Workplace Supports at Virginia Commonwealth University. Many of these people have willingly and generously shared their written material and wonderful expertise with me to help complete this text. Teri Blankenship, Valerie Brooke, Doug Erickson, Susan Evans, Elizabeth Evans Getzel, J. Howard Green, John Kregel, Jennifer McDonough, Lucy A. Miller, W. Grant Revell, Pam Sherron Targett, Colleen A. Thoma, Ed Turner, Darlene Unger, and Michael D. West have been critically important to my work. They have given me insights as to the future direction of transition for young people with disabilities. I also want to thank other important university colleagues for their support of my work, including Bill Bosher, Dave Cifu, Jeff Kreutzer, Bill McKinley, and Brian McMahon. They have greatly enriched this effort.

In the past 5 years, my children, Brody, Cara, Blake, Ragan, and Peyton, have grown to 15–22 years old—all transition age! Their experiences and their feelings about disability and being with people with disabilities have helped me write parts of this book more insightfully. Many of their life experiences, successes, trials, and tribulations helped shape my writing, especially Chapter 1. My wife, Lele, has been my biggest supporter and biggest fan and is always for the underdog, always for the person who needs a boost. She has been a truly wonderful companion and person to be with every day and has influenced my thoughts about the importance of self-esteem in young people with disabilities.

Next, I feel compelled to acknowledge the parents, individuals with disabilities, and advocates who have continually shown us the way in terms of their wishes, demands, requests, and so forth. They have asked us, as professionals, to be responsive to their needs. I only wish that more of us could be more responsive and hear them more clearly. It is from this group of young people and families, and attending conferences such as the National Down Syndrome Society each year, that I have learned what topics matter the most. Listening to the concerns of families and students tells us what is most important.

Finally, I want to strongly acknowledge and dedicate this book to Jeanne Dalton for the technical development and typing of the manuscript. She has spent hundreds of hours helping me improve this book by tracking down references, obtaining permission releases, and communicating with contributors on my behalf. This is thankless work, but it is crucial for the text to be professionally and thoroughly completed. I could not have finished any of the first three editions of this book without her willing and positive help, especially in providing me with chapter after chapter of clean manuscript. She has literally made this a better book. I want to dedicate this book to her again.

I also want to recognize Rebecca Lazo, my editor at Paul H. Brookes Publishing Co., and her assistant, Steve Peterson. They spent many hours to make this a highly successful manuscript, especially with the significant revisions that have been necessary. I sincerely thank them for doing such a nice job.

We believe this book will have a positive impact on thousands of university students as well as on professionals who are looking to amass more information and knowledge in the important areas of education and employment for young people with disabilities. We need them to be the next generation of leaders to help advocate for youth with disabilities. We know that youth is where hope resides. It begins with the young ones. There is a critical need for more students in training to take a more significant leadership role in the community on behalf of people with disabilities. Advocacy and involvement are essential to making transition work in a community.

To Jeanne Little Dalton—
for all of her incredible labor on this book

I

Transition
Planning

1

Transition

The Bridge from Youth to Adulthood

Paul Wehman

AFTER COMPLETING THIS CHAPTER, THE READER WILL BE ABLE TO

○ Describe the major societal challenges that face young adults as they make the transition into adulthood

○ Describe the requirements that are placed on educational systems by the Individuals with Disabilities Education Act (IDEA) Amendments of 1997 (PL 105-17) and the Individuals with Disabilities Education Improvement Act of 2004 (PL 108-446) regarding transition

○ Discuss the roles of violence, drug abuse, poverty, and chronic unemployment in the lives of people with disabilities

○ Discuss the role of the Internet in enhancing the employment of young people with disabilities

○ Describe the role of the economy and local business in the employment outlook for young people with disabilities

○ Describe the major themes involved with helping young people with disabilities grow up and achieve their life goals

○ Describe the major research evidence and findings in transition research

This is a story of transition. Sara Ruh[1] is 18 years old. She has Down syndrome, red hair, a brother named Kevin, and a boyfriend named Justin. Sara's favorite person in the world is her Dad (just ask her). Sara is currently in the 12th grade at Patrick Henry High School and about to go to the state vocational rehabilitation (VR) supported transition program for a 10-day evaluation.

Sara started high school in the special education class of students with moderate intellectual disabilities. Well, at first her parents were not sure if Sara should be in this class. They felt that academically she should be in a higher-functioning class, but this class had fewer students, a better teacher–student ratio, and Mrs. Bailey, who was a dream of a teacher.

However, Mrs. Bailey set the bar high and introduced Sara to some creative ways to help her with her reading, math, and writing skills. Sara began high school at a high first-grade level in her reading and writing, but she continues to strengthen her skills.

During the beginning of 10th grade, Sara's vocational assessment was conducted as a bagger at a large grocery store in town. Jennifer, the vocational teacher, felt that Sara did well

Sara Ruh is clearly a success story to date. This is a case study of how young people begin to go through the transition process. It is important because it shows how parent advocacy coupled with teacher collaboration can truly work. Sara is on track to be a star, the type of young person whose parents can indeed be proud. But there are millions of young people in this country and other countries as well who are not benefiting from this type of home, school, and community leadership. This book is about how to reach these young people, their parents, and the community and school personnel who serve and support them. There are millions of young people with disabilities in the United States, and a signifi-cant number of them are in middle and secondary schools. Table 1.1 shows the distribution of these children in 2000–2001 across disabilities: when compared with 10 years earlier, there has been an increase of 28.4% in the number of students in special education. Throughout the country, these young people with disabilities are leaving the public schools and looking for postsecondary opportunities in community colleges and the work force, searching for their rightful places in the community. Table 1.2 shows the number and percentage of students with disabilities ages 14 and older who exited school during the 1999–2000 school year.

DEFINING TRANSITION

Much was written about transition in the 1980s and 1990s (e.g., Blackorby & Wagner, 1996; Hughes, 2001; Hughes & Carter, 2000; Knott & Asselin, 1999). *Transition* may be defined as the life changes, adjustments, and cumulative experiences that occur in the lives of young adults as they move from school environments to independent living and work environments. Examples of transitions include changes in self-awareness, body, sexuality, work and financial needs, and the need for independence in travel and mobility. Successful transitions also increase success, confidence, and competence in one's work skills (Benz, Lindstrom, & Yovanoff, 2000).

One of the better early definitions of transition, which still has merit today, was given by the Council for Exceptional Children's Division on Career Development and Transition in 1994: *Transition* refers to a change in status from behaving primarily as a student to assuming emergent adult roles in the community (deFur, Todd-Allen, & Getzel, 2001). These roles include having employment, participating in

---

[1]The story of Sara Ruh is a true story, one that she and her family are proud of and want to share with all. It is one student's journey through the school system into transition age.

on her assessment at Ukrop's grocery store, but there were some concerns with speed and safety in the parking lot. For the next assessment, Jennifer took Sara to Wendy's to try out a dining room attendant's job. Sara had an excellent assessment at Wendy's. The restaurant was extremely busy, but Sara did not get overwhelmed or frustrated. After the assessment at Wendy's, the manager reported that there was a position available from 11 A.M. to 2 P.M. Monday through Friday. Jennifer felt Sara would be an excellent candidate for the job. The school would provide transportation on school days but we would be responsible for transportation on nonschool days. The parents talked about it and he really wanted Sara to get this opportunity as much as she did.

What really surprised all about her experience working at Wendy's was how her independence and confidence grew. Sara's parents were not expecting the intangibles that she got from her work experience. She would come home and say we had three buses come to Wendy's today and we were slammed. Sara bonded with her managers, co-workers, and the customers. Several customers say they come in several times a week just to see Sara. Sometimes Sara even gets tips from customers.

postsecondary education, maintaining a home, becoming appropriately involved in the community, and experiencing satisfactory personal and social relationships. The process of enhancing transition involves the participation and coordination of school programs, adult agency services, and natural supports within the community. The foundations for transition should be laid during the elementary and middle school years, guided by the broad concept of career development. Transition planning should begin no later than age 14, and students should be encouraged, to the full extent of their capabilities, to assume a maximum amount of responsibility for such planning (Halpern, 1994). This definition continues to have good fundamental utility and merit for school personnel and families.

Implications of the Individuals with Disabilities Education Act Transition Requirements

The Individuals with Disabilities Education Act of 1990 (PL 101-476), which has been subsequently updated in 1997 (PL 105-17) and 2004 (PL 108-446), reauthorized the Education for All Handicapped Children Act of 1975 (PL 94-142), which first mandated a free appropriate public education (FAPE) for all children regardless of disability. IDEA 1990 extended the requirement for education for children with disabilities and required transition services for all children with disabilities.

> The purpose of this part is
> 1. To ensure that all children with disabilities have available to them a free appropriate public education that emphasizes special education and related services designed to meet their unique needs and prepare them for employment and independent living; this should culminate into an individual education plan.
> 2. To ensure that the rights of children with disabilities and their parents are protected. (PL 101-476, § 300.1)

The explicit statement that special education and related services are intended to prepare students for employment and independent living makes it clear that educators, parents, and students must consider adult outcomes as they plan for students' school experiences. The definition that is used in Section 300.29 follows:

> As used in this part, transition services means a coordinated set of activities for a student with a disability that
> 1. Is designed within an outcome-oriented process, that promotes movement from school to postschool activities, including postsecondary education, vocational training, integrated employment (including supported employment [SE]), continuing and adult education, adult services, independent living, or community participation

2. Is based on the individual student's needs, taking into account the student's preferences and interests
3. Includes
   - Instruction
   - Related services
   - Community experiences
   - The development of employment and other postschool adult living objectives
   - If appropriate, acquisition of daily living skills and functional vocational evaluation

Transition services for students with disabilities may be special education, if provided as specially designed instruction, or related services, if required to assist a student with a disability to benefit from special education. David Johnson (2005), who is one of the eminent national leaders in transition, has analyzed the differences between the 1997 IDEA and the 2004 reauthorization (see Chapter 1 Appendix). There were relatively few substantive changes.

At a minimum, the individualized education program (IEP) should address each of these areas, including instruction, community experiences, and development of employment and other postschool adult living objectives. In many cases, each of these areas, and possibly some others, will be included in students' IEPs; however, transition services may be provided by the education agency or, as outlined in Section 300.348 of the regulations, by agencies outside the school. Steere and Cavaiuolo (2002) provided functional examples of how outcomes, goals, and objectives can be tied together (see Figure 1.1). Furthermore, there is an increasing interest in providing self-determination, self-advocacy, and financial management objectives. Whatever

Table 1.1. Number of students ages 6–21 served under IDEA during 1991–1992 and 2000–2001

Disability	1991–1992	2000–2001	Percent change in number
Specific learning disabilities	2,247,004	2,887,217	28.5
Speech or language impairments	998,904	1,093,808	9.5
Mental retardation	553,262	612,978	10.8
Emotional disturbance	400,211	473,663	18.4
Multiple disabilities	98,408	122,559	24.5
Hearing impairments	60,727	70,767	16.5
Orthopedic impairments	51,389	73,057	42.2
Other health impairments	58,749	291,850	396.8
Visual impairments	24,083	25,975	7.9
Autism	5,415	78,749	1,354.3
Deaf-blindness	1,427	1,320	−7.5
Traumatic brain injury	245	14,844	5,958.8
Developmental delay	—	28,935	—
All disabilities	4,499,824	5,775,722	28.4

Note: Reporting in the autism and traumatic brain injury categories was optional in 1991–1992 and was required beginning in 1992–1993. Data from 1991–1992 include children with disabilities served under the Chapter 1 Handicapped program.

From U.S. Department of Education. (2002). *Twenty-fourth Annual Report to Congress on the Implementation of the Individuals with Disabilities Education Act* (p. II-22). Washington, DC: Author; adapted by permission.

Table 1.2. Number of students age 14 and older exiting special education during the 1999–2000 school year

State	All disabilities				
	Graduated with diploma	Received a certificate	Reached maximum age	No longer receives special education	Died
Alabama	1,252	2,077	216	607	29
Alaska	413	18	10	273	6
Arizona	2,290	—	104	604	21
Arkansas	2,176	185	8	361	14
California	9,962	4,689	811	9,913	147
Colorado	2,348	154	82	1,562	31
Connecticut	3,223	37	46	2,608	19
Delaware	267	37	2	88	3
District of Columbia	45	132	4	47	0
Florida	5,516	4,140	6	3,257	99
Georgia	1,913	2,077	0	1,325	30
Hawaii	480	468	195	12	4
Idaho	866	17	22	567	9
Illinois	7,772	165	575	2,908	99
Indiana	4,539	398	50	922	46
Iowa	2,501	57	46	861	22
Kansas	2,241	—	31	1,022	21
Kentucky	1,947	305	13	837	21
Louisiana	1,090	1,769	40	185	46
Maine	1,108	61	25	687	10
Maryland	3,088	458	85	1,357	23
Massachusetts	6,164	—	205	3,012	49
Michigan	5,000	596	302	3,520	97
Minnesota	4,396	—	27	14	19
Mississippi	749	1,549	40	244	38
Missouri	4,391	313	172	915	44
Montana	512	20	21	143	8
Nebraska	1,246	40	47	611	13
Nevada	454	653	1	162	29
New Hampshire	1,230	54	29	173	16
New Jersey	9,599	—	378	995	54
New Mexico	803	22	2	454	13
New York	9,749	4,558	673	3,418	129
North Carolina	2,988	1,420	136	1,372	35
North Dakota	532	8	7	275	1
Ohio	9,709	—	1,227	3,029	40
Oklahoma	3,449	—	10	436	28
Oregon	1,130	246	144	1,433	22
Pennsylvania	6,941	39	89	1,432	55
Puerto Rico	553	368	296	463	27
Rhode Island	899	10	41	317	6
South Carolina	1,033	988	106	771	28
South Dakota	409	23	15	152	2
Tennessee	2,369	3,001	160	2,650	60

(continued)

Table 1.2.   *(continued)*

State	All disabilities				
	Graduated with diploma	Received a certificate	Reached maximum age	No longer receives special education	Died
Texas	17,406	—	54	6,982	83
Utah	1,598	97	79	673	23
Vermont	403	11	14	266	6
Virginia	4,218	1,155	95	1,192	62
Washington	2,702	270	0	0	19
West Virginia	1,618	107	12	284	12
Wisconsin	4,666	129	52	1,537	52
Wyoming	386	8	21	264	8
American Samoa	8	5	1	20	0
Guam	36	—	0	4	0
Northern Marianas	10	4	0	1	0
Palau	2	—	0	2	0
Virgin Islands	22	33	3	18	0
Bureau of Indian Affairs	163	18	8	49	4
U.S. and outlying areas	162,580	32,989	6,838	67,286	1,782
50 states, District of Columbia, and Puerto Rico	162,339	32,929	6,826	67,192	1,778

Please see data notes for an explanation of individual state differences.

Washington State data based on previous year's data.

Data based on the December 1, 1999, count, updated as of August 30, 2001.

U.S. Department of Education, Office of Special Education Programs, Data Analysis System (DANS).

From U.S. Department of Education. (2002). *Twenty-fourth Annual Report to Congress on the Implementation of the Individuals with Disabilities Education Act* (pp. A286–A287). Washington, DC: Author; adapted by permission.

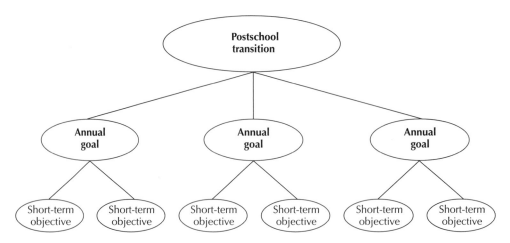

Figure 1.1.   Relationship of postschool outcomes to annual goals and short-term objectives. (From Steere, D.E., & Cavaiuolo, D. [2002]. Connecting outcomes, goals, and objectives in transition planning. *Council for Exceptional Children, 34*[6], 54–59; reprinted by permission.)

the case, these objectives must be written into the IEP and the responsible agency noted. IDEA and its reauthorizations require that transition services be provided to students by the time they are 16 years old.

2004 HARRIS POLL: LIMITED PROGRESS FOR
PEOPLE WITH DISABILITIES ON EMPLOYMENT, QUALITY OF LIFE

The 2004 Harris Survey on disability trends, commissioned by the National Organization on Disability (NOD, 2004), surveyed people with disabilities and compared their attitudes and participation with other Americans. The results document trends affecting the more than 54 million Americans with disabilities. This survey also showed that Americans with disabilities are at a critical disadvantage compared with other Americans in 10 key areas of life that the Harris Poll has tracked since 1986.

- Only 35% of people with disabilities reported being employed full time or part time, compared with 78% of those who do not have disabilities.

- Three times as many people with disabilities live in poverty, with annual household incomes below $15,000 (26% versus 9%).

- People with disabilities remain twice as likely to drop out of high school (21% versus 10%).

- They are twice as likely to have inadequate transportation (31% versus 13%) and a much higher percentage go without needed health care (18% versus 7%).

Not surprisingly, given the persistence of these gaps, life satisfaction for people with disabilities also trails people without disabilities, with only 34% saying they are very satisfied compared with 61% of those without disabilities.

Regarding employment, the survey found little progress since the 1986 Louis Harris Poll (U.S. Employment Rates, 2004/2005) in employment participation. The employment rate further deteriorates with the severity of disability. Only one in five people with severe disabilities had at least a part-time job in 2004. In fact, people with severe disabilities have much greater disadvantages in all the quality of life areas surveyed.

GALLUP POLL EMPLOYER RESULTS: THE NEWS IS NOT ALL BAD

In another national study (Siperstein, Romano, Mohler, & Parker, 2006), The Gallup Poll conducted a major survey of what people in the United States feel about people with disabilities in the workforce. Employers' negative attitudes and fears have long been a barrier to the employment of individuals with disabilities (Unger, 2001b). Accordingly, attitude literature on the employment of people with disabilities has focused almost exclusively on employers. However, due to their influence over business practices, the successful employment of people with disabilities is also heavily contingent on the views of the consumer. Consumer attitudes toward companies that hire individuals with disabilities were assessed through a Gallup Poll of 803 persons. The findings also indicated that most respondents (75%) had direct experience with people with disabilities in a work environment and that these experiences were very positive. More information from this study is presented in Chapter 12.

Nick, a 14-year-old student who has bipolar disorder, often has "up or down" extremes with his emotions. Nick comes home from school every day, watches television, and then has dinner with his mother or father before watching more television. He has no chores and no job, does not participate in any extracurricular activities, and does not have any specific goals. Nick's parents are extremely busy with their careers and have been unable to help him structure his future. Should it be surprising that Nick is beginning to get progress reports from teachers indicating that he has been doing poorly in class, has withdrawn, and is noncommunicative? Should it be surprising that Nick is becoming listless around the house and indifferent to the authority of his mother or father? Should it be surprising that Nick does not want to go to school any more and has no interest in going to college? Thousands of young people who have disabilities face these problems. The issue is not that these students lack potential; it is that they do not have goals. There is not a plan in place to help them move into adulthood. **Life beyond the classroom requires a blueprint for navigating the waters of the community, workplace, finances, personal life, and home.** These are the challenges young people with disabilities face—in fact, all young people face them. How well they are prepared and can exercise their free will to implement their blueprint and embark on their journey separates those who are happy and successful from those who will run into continual trouble, problems, and failures.

These findings present dramatic new evidence of how American society values individuals with disabilities, not only as coworkers, but also as providing a reason to do business with a company that employs persons with disabilities.

MAKING THE JOURNEY TO ADULTHOOD: THE IMPORTANCE OF SETTING GOALS

One of the most important aspects of helping young people attain happiness, success, and competence is the process of helping them set goals (Copeland & Hughes, 2002). The ability to help a child understand the importance of identifying and meeting goals in his or her life can make all the difference in the world to the transition from living at home to becoming established in the community with a job and friends.

For example, a 16-year-old who has never worked before and is afraid of being alone in the work environment might set a goal of working 3 days per week for a total of 15 hours in a familiar environment. As one *Wall Street Journal* article noted, even menial summer jobs can really pay off for students: "Even in the new economy, basic work at a classic summer job can't be beat for teaching responsibility, resourcefulness, and empathy" (Stout, 1999, p. B1). This target would be meaningful in the sense that it would allow the child to develop work skills, follow instructions from a supervisor, interact with co-workers, and, above all, develop a work ethic and have a day-to-day purpose. Establishing goals is a learning process. Very few children or teenagers are able to set goals without some guidance from a parent, teacher, mentor, or someone else whom they respect and who can give them realistic direction about what are appropriate actions to take under different circumstances. Remember Sara's story at the beginning of the chapter—without her mom and her heavy involvement in IEP goal setting, Sara would not have been included in school events and work (e.g., Myers & Eisenman, 2005). Setting goals is a critical process and an inherent aspect of the transition process. Essentially, transition planning is planning for the future, and, in order to plan for the future, one must have some sense of what goals make sense and what goals do not make sense. Copeland and Hughes (2002) noted:

> Goal setting instruction typically requires teaching people to (a) select an appropriate behavior to target, (b) set a desired level of performance for that behavior, (c) develop a plan to meet the performance standard, (d) monitor their performance by evaluating it in relation to the preset standard, and (e) adapt their behavior, if needed, to accomplish the goal. (p. 40)

What are the ways to help young people with disabilities transition into the community? Most parents know from experience that the best way to help their children obtain a higher level of achievement is to set goals in a stair-step fashion. The IEP is an educational program mandated by law (most recently IDEA 2004) that states the goals, objectives, and timeline of activities necessary for educational program implementation. An IEP is developed for each student with disabilities; it is highly specific only to the student it is designed for. The IEP should also provide a plan for making the transition to adult life which some have referred to as a *transition IEP* (Wehman, 2002a). During the 1990s, though, educators learned that no amount of paper programs, interagency agreements, or even new teaching techniques will help a teenager grow into a successful adult without transition planning and follow through. Ongoing reinforcement by educators, parents, and others in the community for doing positive activities is very important for students making the transition from youth to adulthood. Once again, these goals need to be performed in a successful way over an extended period of time. Functional life skills are an important consideration and this is discussed in depth in several chapters which follow (Wehman & Kregel, 2004).

Many teachers wonder what they can do to help a child at home or in the community. What influence do they really have? The answer is: their influence is enormous. Students who have a purpose in their lives, who know how to set goals, and who have been reinforced for those goals are much more likely to succeed in the world of work and living in the community. Teachers, guidance counselors, coaches, and other staff in the high school environment can have as much or more affect on their students than parents do during this critical developmental period. Many young people rebel against parental authority and are not interested in advice from their parents; high school staff may be able to help in a less emotional way to carve out goals in the areas of community service, academic performance supports, or other activities that will help develop and create a sense of self-esteem. Can you think of someone you know who has been rebellious, oppositional, or unwilling to respect authority? What impact does that person have on his or her class or family? Highly effective educators in middle schools and high schools look beyond the classroom to identify ways to elevate their students' abilities.

TRANSITION FROM SCHOOL TO EMPLOYMENT: WHAT DOES THE RESEARCH SAY?

This chapter is based as much as possible on research that provides true empirical support for excellent practice. Since the 1990s, there have been somewhat more concentrated efforts to determine the efficacy of transition.

For example, Williams and O'Leary (2001) presented an analysis of the extent to which states and entities implemented the transition services requirements during the 1993-1994 through 1996-1997 monitoring cycles based on monitoring reports from the U.S. Department of Education. Their study reviewed the status of implementation prior to IDEA 1997, which added the requirements for a statement of transition service needs. Their article offers recommendations for policy changes to ensure that students receive the required transition services consistent with IDEA's statutory and regulatory provisions (see Appendix). They made the following recommendations for change:

1. Professional and technical assistance: The study findings dictate that professional development and technical assistance activities provided at the preservice and in-service levels include all stakeholders responsible for designing and implementing the transition services requirements. Institutions of higher education; federal, state, and local education agencies; technical assistance and dissemination providers; parent training and information centers; and others conducting training must involve all stakeholders and provide the same information to them.

2. Monitoring: Monitoring is the second area in which to make recommendations to ensure that the transition services provisions are implemented within every school in the country. We view monitoring or oversight by the federal, state, and local education agencies as complementary to the provision of professional development and technical assistance. This oversight is the vehicle through which it is possible to determine whether the professional development and technical assistance activities have been effective in accomplishing full implementation of the transition services requirements. We recommend that monitoring activities focus on the transition services requirements as a measure of accountability for improved results for students.

Kohler and Field (2003), two of the best researchers in transition, indicated that since 1985, there has been an increased focus on improving transition education and services for youth with disabilities. Three specific initiatives characterize this development: 1) federal special education and disability legislation; 2) federal, state, and local investment in transition services development; and 3) effective transition practices research. Outcomes of these initiatives include 1) an expanded perspective concerning transition education and services and 2) identification of practices that apply this perspective to individual student needs. Kohler and Field (2003) described effective transition practices in five areas: student-focused planning, student development, interagency collaboration, family involvement, and program structures. Developing specific interventions and service arrays for individual students within each of the transition practice areas is essential for postschool success.

In a classic paper, Furney, Hasazi, Clark/Keefe, and Hartnett (2003) conducted a longitudinal policy analysis in four schools. Their purpose was to explore the degree to which positive outcomes associated with a 1990 state policy on education reform had been sustained in the context of subsequent policies emphasizing standards-based reform and school accountability. The shifting policy context supported the sustainability of initial positive outcomes, such as increased use of educational support systems and teams, but was associated with increases in referrals to special education and the use of more restrictive special education placements. Findings suggested a need to recognize shared as well as competing goals among educational policies and to explore a variety of approaches to expanding the capacity of general education to support students within the context of standards-based reform.

One research-based transition model that is working is described by Luecking and Certo (2005). The Transition Service Integration Model initially described by Certo et al. (2003) integrates resources and expertise of the three primary systems responsible for transition from school to adulthood for individuals with significant support needs. These entities are local public schools, the rehabilitation system, and the developmental disabilities system. The model involves school districts forming a partnership directly with private nonprofit agencies that typically serve adults with significant support needs. Through this partnership, personnel from the school district and private agencies work together during a student's last year in pubic school (i.e., typically 21 years old) to develop a paid direct-hire job and a variety of inclusive community activities to engage in when not working. In doing so, they provide SE services and job accommodations that enable individuals with significant support needs to secure gainful employment in inclusive job settings and stable access to other integrated community environments prior to graduation, and a seamless transition to a person-centered and self-determined adult lifestyle by securing funding to continue these services after school exit from the rehabilitation and developmental disability systems. In many ways this model extends with data the earlier model described by Wehman, Kregel, and Barcus (1985).

The amount of prospectively designed large-scale transition from school to work studies is minimal. This is partially because of the complexities of designing and maintaining the controls necessary longitudinally to measure employment changes for young people still in school. The identification of appropriate community living and adjustment variables has also been problematical.

However, Wittenburg and Maag (2002) did examine data sources of at least 250 observations from a large state or national study that evaluated economic outcomes of youth with disabilities. They drew on multiple data bases from Social Security, VR, and special education. Many of the studies that were relied on in shaping the conclusions of the authors provide information for transition planning and practices discussed not only in this chapter but throughout the book.

RELATED DISABILITY LEGISLATION

In order to promote transition practices in schools, Congress has enacted a number of related laws, in addition to the IDEA 1997, that influence the transition from school to adulthood for young people with disabilities. Together, they form an important foundation for understanding the transition process.

Rehabilitation Act Amendments of 1998

The Rehabilitation Act Amendments of 1998 were signed into law as a part of the Workforce Investment Act (PL 105-220). The Rehabilitation Act governs the VR Program, the federal and state cooperative effort that provides employment services nationally for working-age individuals with disabilities. The VR Program works cooperatively with local education authorities to serve youth with disabilities during their transition from secondary education; it is the primary employment support resource for adults with disabilities. The Rehabilitation Act Amendments of 1998 provide federal dollars, matched by state dollars, to all 50 states to give people with disabilities the opportunity to obtain employment and independent living assistance as needed. The Rehabilitation Act Amendments of 1998 also provide new opportunities for people with disabilities to gain access to VR services and to choose the specific services needed for them to achieve their individualized employment goal. For example, the amendments require that a trial work experience in the most community-integrated setting possible be made available to certain individuals with significant disabilities in order to help identify the services and supports necessary for them to achieve an employment outcome. Also, recipients of VR services have control over the contents of their individualized plans for employment (IPE) and have information made available in order for them to make informed choices about specific services they will receive. This information includes the cost, duration, and accessibility of potential services; consumer satisfaction with these services; qualifications of potential service providers; types of services offered by potential service providers; and the degree to which services are provided in integrated settings (Federal Register, 2000).

A major provision of the Rehabilitation Act is known as Section 504. Section 504 of the Rehabilitation Act of 1973 (PL 93-112) is major federal legislation that affects entities that receive federal funding. It is civil rights legislation for people with disabilities that is designed to prevent any form of discrimination based on disabilities. Individuals with disabilities who are otherwise qualified are protected.

The role played by Section 504 in schools has increased dramatically in recent years; schools can no longer ignore this legislation (Miller & Newbill, 2005). As parents and advocates for children with disabilities learn more about Section 504, schools are having to respond to requests for protections and services. There are several reasons why Section 504 has begun to more directly affect services for children with disabilities, including the following:

- The Americans with Disabilities Act (ADA) of 1990 (PL 101-336) mandated nondiscrimination on the basis of disabilities nationwide:

- Certain disabilities not automatically resulting in eligibility for special education under IDEA, such as attention-deficit/hyperactivity disorder (ADHD) and oppositional defiant disorder (ODD), have gained more parental and professional attention.

- Parents' awareness that Section 504 can be used to provide certain protections for children who may not be considered eligible for special education under IDEA has increased greatly.

- School personnel are more aware that some students who are not eligible for services under IDEA may be eligible for services under Section 504.

Regardless of the specific reason for the increase in attention to Section 504, the reality is that more parents are beginning to present requests to schools for services and protections under this legislation. As a result, school personnel must be able to respond accordingly by understanding the legal requirements of the act, implementing an effective eligibility process, and providing appropriate services, which are required for students who are determined to have a disability as defined under Section 504.

The two federal acts that most affect public schools and students with disabilities are Section 504 and IDEA. Section 504 also affects students with disabilities in college; IDEA does not. There are many similarities and differences between these two acts. As previously noted, one of the areas that is significantly different is the definition of disability and, therefore, the requirements for eligibility. The definition of disability and eligibility requirements are much more restrictive in IDEA than they are in Section 504. This will likely result in more children being eligible for protections and services under Section 504 than under IDEA.

Americans with Disabilities Act of 1990

On July 26, 1990, President George H.W. Bush signed the ADA into law, and many have hailed the act as a civil rights law for all people with disabilities. In the past, laws to end discrimination against minority groups did not specifically include individuals with disabilities. The intent of the ADA was to end discrimination toward people with disabilities throughout society. This act was followed exactly 1 year later by a comprehensive set of regulations that provided for accessibility; nondiscrimination; and greater access to workplaces, community facilities, public transportation, and telecommunications. The law went on to state that individuals with disabilities continually encounter various forms of discrimination including outright intentional exclusion; the discriminatory effects of architectural, transportation, and communication barriers; overprotective rules and policies; failure to make modifications to existing facilities and practices; exclusionary qualification standards and criteria; segregation; and relegation to lesser services, programs, activities, benefits, jobs, or other opportunities. Before this law, people with disabilities had no legal recourse against those discriminating against them. The ADA was intended to break down a wide array of artificial barriers that were unnecessarily and unfairly limiting the employment participation of individuals with disabilities.

In order to promote the employment of individuals with disabilities, the United States has developed specific, protective policies and regulations designed to promote the employment of individuals with disabilities that are very different from those used in most parts of the industrialized world. In the United States, civil rights laws, specifically the ADA and Section 504, protect individuals by prohibiting discrimination in employment on the basis of disability.

Under the ADA, employers are prohibited from discriminating against otherwise qualified individuals with disabilities during recruitment, hiring, evaluation, promotion, or any other facet of employment. Employers are further required to provide reasonable accommodations to enable individuals with disabilities to successfully perform their jobs, when accommodation can be provided without an employer sustaining an undue hardship. Reasonable accommodations may include such things as restructuring jobs or work schedules, modifying equipment, providing assistive devices, providing an interpreter or reading aids, or improving the overall accessibility of the worksite. Employers found to be in violation of the law face the same legal penalties as those found guilty of discrimination based on gender or race (see also the appendix to Chapter 8). The relationships between the ADA, IDEA, and Section 504 are very important to understand as they each provide certain guidelines and restrictions for services (see Figure 1.2).

Workforce Investment Act and One Stop Career Centers

The Workforce Investment Act (WIA) of 1998 (PL 105-220) was the first major reform of the nation's job training system since 1982. WIA, which supersedes the Job Training Partnership Act (JTPA) of 1982 (PL 97-300), includes the following key

	K–12: IDEA, Section 504, ADA	College/university: Section 504, ADA	Employment: Section 504, ADA
Requirements of the laws	No discrimination based on disability Free appropriate public education in the least restrictive environment	No discrimination based on disability Modifications, aids, and services (accommodations) to ensure equal educational opportunities	No discrimination based on disability Reasonable accommodations to ensure equal employment opportunities
Covered entities	Public elementary and secondary schools; certain private schools that receive money from the federal government	Private and public colleges/universities that receive money from the federal government	**Section 504:** Employers who receive money from the federal government. **ADA:** Public employers and private employers with 15 or more employees.
Types of disabilities	**IDEA:** Students with disabilities in specified categories who require special education services Not all students with disabilities are eligible **Section 504/ADA:** Physical or mental impairment that substantially limits one or more major life activities; record of such an impairment or regarded as having such an impairment	Physical or mental impairment that substantially limits one or more major life activities; record of such an impairment or regarded as having such an impairment	Physical or mental impairment that substantially limits one or more major life activities; record of such an impairment or regarded as having such an impairment
Who is covered	Generally, students ages 3–21 or until graduation	Applicants and students who meet the college's or university's academic and technical standards	Applicants and employees who, with or without reasonable accommodation, can perform essential functions of the job
Services provided	**IDEA:** Special education and related services (including services that can be provided in regular classroom) **Section 504/ADA:** Regular or special education and related aids and services	Elimination of barriers that would prevent full participation in programs/services offered to other students—generally through provision of accommodations	Reasonable accommodations
Funding	**IDEA:** Funding statute: schools receive federal funds to provide services **Section 504/ADA:** Nondiscrimination statutes: no additional funds to provide services	Nondiscrimination statutes: no additional financial support to provide accommodations	Nondiscrimination statutes: tax incentives available for businesses that incur costs to make work environment accessible

	IDEA	Section 504/ADA	ADA
Evaluation/documentation	School district is responsible for identifying and evaluating students with disabilities Parents generally must consent to evaluations and placement decisions Evaluations are the responsibility of the school and are performed at no expense to the student or parent	Applicant/student must self-identify as having disability and must provide adequate documentation of disability and its impact Student, not parent, has responsibility for advocacy Evaluation/documentation of disability is student's responsibility and at student's expense	Employee must self-identify as having disability and, at employer's request, must provide adequate documentation of disability and its impact Documentation of disability is employee's responsibility and at employee's expense
Identification of services	**IDEA:** Individualized education program (IEP) developed with parents, teachers, and other specialists **Section 504/ADA:** Decisions to be made by team of people knowledgeable about student, disability, and placement options; usually reflected in 504 Plan.	Disability Services Coordinator and student work together to identify needs and develop accommodations	Employee and employer work together to identify needs and develop accommodations
Placement	Placement must be in the least restrictive environment; may be special classrooms, resource, or regular classroom	Courses are with students without disabilities	Can vary

Figure 1.2. Requirements of the Individuals with Disabilities Education Act (IDEA), Section 504 of the Rehabilitation Act, and the Americans with Disabilities Act (ADA). (From Virginia Higher Education Leadership Partners. [2005]. *Requirements of the Individuals with Disabilities Education Act [IDEA], Section 504 of the Rehabilitation Act [Section 504], and the Americans with Disabilities Act [ADA].* Unpublished document. Virginia Commonwealth University at Richmond; reprinted by permission.)

components (Social Security Administration [SSA], Government Accountability Office [GAO], 2005):

- Streamlining services through a one-stop service delivery system
- Empowering job seekers through information and access to training resources
- Providing universal access to core services
- Ensuring a strong role for local workforce investment boards and the private sector
- Improving youth programs

With the passage of WIA, local service delivery areas across the country that formerly operated job training programs under JTPA are teaming with other employment and workforce development partners to establish a One Stop Career Center system. Some locations have brought in new partners and expanded on career centers that were already in operation (Bader, 2003).

Contained within the WIA are four principles that guide the implementation of One Stop Career Centers: universality, customer choice, integration of services, and accountability for results.

Universality   The intent of the WIA is for all services available through a One Stop Career Center to be accessible to everyone who uses them. For example, it is hoped that people with disabilities will be able to use the same information resources and services as their peers. In a similar way, citizens who do not speak English will be able to gain access to the services without language being a barrier.

Customer Choice   Under the WIA, individuals are empowered to obtain the services and skills they need to enhance their employment opportunities. Through self-directed use of available core services and being able to choose the qualified training program that best meets their needs, customers of One Stop Career Centers, including those with disabilities, have increased control of the planning and implementation of their employment and training programs (SSA, GAO, 2005).

Integration of Services   Under the WIA, all of the career and vocational services are presumed to be integrated in order to make it easier for those with disabilities to utilize these services. Vocational evaluation, career planning, job placement, and employer contacts are among the services to be integrated.

Accountability for Results   The WIA specifically identifies performance standards that One Stop Career Center operators and training service providers must meet to continue to receive funding. These indicators include job placement rates, earnings, retention in employment, skill gains, and credentials earned (SSA, GAO, 2005). Chapter 4 provides more information on how One Stop Career Centers operate.

No Child Left Behind

The No Child Left Behind (NCLB) Act of 2001 (PL 107-110) was signed into law on January 8, 2002. This bill reauthorized the Elementary and Secondary Education Act

(ESEA) of 1965 (PL 89-10), which is the federal government's largest investment in public education.

NCLB is based on education reform principles that include provisions requiring schools to make genuine progress in closing the persistent achievement gaps between students who are disadvantaged or disabled and their peers. This law has created significant confusion and consternation among educators working with students with disabilities (e.g., Ysseldyke et al., 2004), because not all states have school districts that have the capacity to meet NCLB standards for students with significant needs (Nolet & McLaughlin, 2005).

The accountability system must be the same for all public schools and agencies in the state, and time lines must be put in place to ensure that all students will meet or exceed the state-determined proficiency level (this is expressed as the percentage of students the state projects will be at or above grade level) no later than the 2013–2014 school year. All educators must work closely together to implement this law, which has been wide reaching and controversial, for students with disabilities who are educated under IDEA and/or Section 504 (e.g., Mooney, Denny, & Gunter, 2004; Sitlington & Neubert, 2004). The U.S. Department of Education issued "nonregulatory guidance" to states in March 2003 outlining and clarifying NCLB assessment requirements for students with disabilities.

First, the state's assessment system must be designed to be valid and accessible to students with disabilities under IDEA and Section 504. Assessment accommodations must be determined by the student's IEP team, must be based on individual student needs, and should be in place when students take classroom tests and assessments.

The U.S. Department of Education (2002) has defined *accommodation* as "changes in testing material or procedures that ensure that an assessment measures the student's knowledge and skills rather than the student's disability." This is different and broader than the notion of adapting instruction or the accommodations contained in IDEA. No matter how broad the definition, however, out-of-grade-level testing is not an acceptable means for meeting either the assessment or accountability requirements of NCLB.

Browder and Spooner (2003), in a synthesis of the complex issues associated with NCLB and services to students with disabilities, indicated the following:

> NCLB can promote general education curriculum opportunities for all students. Ideally, the provisions of NCLB will promote opportunities for students to learn skills from the general curriculum in typical classes. As teachers focus on state standards in reading/language arts, math, and science, they may find it more efficient and effective to collaborate with general education to address these skills. Hopefully, this will give further impetus to inclusion efforts. NCLB does not let any program for students with significant disabilities ignore the need to create access to general curriculum. Even self-contained schools for students with significant cognitive disabilities must address their states' academic content standards and complete alternate assessments. (p. 14)

What About Life Skills Instruction?   Many teachers are concerned about the priority of life skills instruction. Students' need for instruction in functional, life skills has not disappeared just because of the new focus on academics. The best way to address these two priorities for instruction may be to find ways to incorporate the two where

possible. Academic skills will often be learned more readily when they relate to real-life activities.

Although Browder and Spooner (2003) are hopeful that NCLB will be able to help students with disabilities, they are also concerned that this may not be the case. They suggested:

> NCLB could simply target meaningless IEP goals that comply minimally with the need for measures of reading/language art and math and could further stigmatize students with disabilities when schools fail to meet adequate yearly progress. The potential advantages of NCLB are not assured. Educators must work towards responding to this legal mandate in ways that not only promote but also achieve access to the general curriculum. (p. 17)

The Ysseldyke et al. (2004) paper addressed many of these issues in more detail as does Chapter 7.

The Ticket to Work and Work Incentive Improvement Act of 1999

The Ticket to Work and Work Incentive Improvement Act (TWWIIA) of 1999 (PL 106-170) was designed to ensure that many of the country's 9 million adults with disabilities receiving Medicare and Medicaid keep their benefits after they obtain remunerative jobs. Until the law went into effect, many people with disabilities faced losing federal benefits that they needed to cover their medical costs if they went to work. Some feared that by taking any jobs that paid even a minimal income, they would no longer receive benefits that are vital to maintaining the quality of their lives.

Removes Limits on the Medicaid Buy-In Option for Workers with Disabilities
TWWIIA lets states remove the income limit of 250% of poverty-level income (approximately $21,000) for people with disabilities who receive Medicaid funds, allowing states to set higher income, unearned income, and resource limits. This important change allows people to buy into Medicaid if they earn more than minimum wage but do not have access to private health insurance.

Creates the Option for People with Disabilities to Retain Medicaid Coverage
TWWIIA allows people with disabilities to retain Medicaid coverage even when their medical condition has improved as a result of medical coverage. This act also provides $150 million over 5 years in health care infrastructure grants to states to support people with disabilities who return to work.

Creates a New Medicaid Buy-In Demonstration   TWWIIA provides $250 million to states for a demonstration to assess the effectiveness of providing Medicaid coverage to people whose condition has not yet deteriorated enough to prevent work but who need health care to prevent that level of deterioration. For example, individuals with muscular dystrophy, Parkinson's disease, or diabetes may be able to function and continue to work with appropriate health care, but such health care may only be available once their conditions have become severe enough to qualify them for SSI or Social Security Disability Insurance (SSDI) and Medicaid or Medicare. This provision would provide new information on the cost-effectiveness of early health care intervention in keeping people with disabilities from becoming too disabled to work.

Extends Medicare Coverage for People with Disabilities Who Return to Work
TWWIIA extends Medicare Part A premium coverage for people on SSDI who return to work for another 4.5 years. Although Medicare does not currently provide prescription drugs that are essential to people with disabilities, this assistance will be available nationwide, even in states that do not take the Medicaid options.

Creates a "Ticket to Work" Program The Ticket to Work Program will enable SSI or SSDI beneficiaries to obtain VR and employment services from their choice of participating public or private providers. If the beneficiary goes to work and achieves substantial earnings, then providers will be paid a portion of the benefits saved. In the Ticket to Work program, more than 10 million tickets have been made out to Social Security recipients, and there are more than 1200 employment networks approved to take tickets. Approximately 80,000 people have gone to work using the Ticket. The program has had a very limited impact to date and further efforts are underway for improvement.

OPPORTUNITIES THAT EMPOWER YOUTH WITH DISABILITIES

As we move into the new millennium, more opportunities exist than ever before to help young people be successful. An extraordinary number of positive changes have opened the door for much greater social and vocational possibilities for young people in the United States if they have access to resources and choose to draw on them. There are more jobs, more opportunities to travel, more opportunities to go to college, and more diverse and exciting ways to have fun than ever before for those who have the capacity and drive to take advantage of these opportunities. The following sections discuss some of these opportunities in more detail.

Internet and Technology

When we first wrote about the Internet in earlier editions of *Life Beyond the Classroom*, discussion was related primarily to assistive devices that could be used to help people with disabilities. The Internet has become much more than an assistive technology (AT) tool. It has now become a prime form of electronic communication, often compared in magnitude with the Industrial Revolution of the late 18th century. It is the way that people in business, home, and community increasingly communicate with each other. The amount of information flowing between people with e-mail is dramatic, indeed. The Internet allows people to send and receive electronic mail, make travel reservations, find jobs, meet new people, and learn new skills both academically and vocationally. Devices such as Palm Pilots have been shown to facilitate communication in inclusive classroom (Bauer & Ulrich, 2002). As children, the baby boomers used the Encyclopedia Britannica to do their research; the youth of today use the Internet. Companies such as America Online and Google currently play a major role in the lives of millions of people, and the number of handheld devices that have Internet applications, such as cellular telephones and pagers, is increasing. Now even telephone communication is occurring over the Internet, along with instant messaging. Furthermore, businesses now use the Internet to communicate and trade with each other at a rapid speed. All young people need to know how to use the Internet with proficiency. Computer skill is imperative.

The Internet is also a way to improve homework communication and completion (Salend, Duhaney, Anderson, & Gottschalk, 2004). The case study in Figure 1.3 shows how Ms. Anderson, an English teacher, was able to enhance homework completion through the Internet.

Why is this so important for people with disabilities? As manufacturers of software and hardware devices begin to realize that people with disabilities are users and consumers, these companies will make increasing numbers of application devices that help individuals with cognitive, physical, and emotional disabilities to become more independent. The Internet can be a significant equalizer for somebody who wants to start a business and yet is in a wheelchair and needs to telecommute or for a person who has dyslexia. Voice recognition software can be a compensatory strategy for college students with learning disabilities (Roberts & Stodden, 2005).

As part of her efforts to prepare her students for the state tests, Ms. Anderson, an English teacher, increased her use of homework assignments. However, despite frequent reminders to her students, she was disappointed by their inconsistency in completing their homework. To remedy the situation, she decided to send a letter to her students' families explaining the importance of homework and asking them to make sure that their children completed their homework.

Several family members responded, and one parent suggested that Ms. Anderson e-mail the assignments to families. Ms. Anderson mentioned this request to Ms. Taylor, the school's instructional technology (IT) specialist, who told Ms. Anderson that it was a good idea and that she would work with her to create a homework web site.

Sensing Ms. Anderson's concerns about her technology skills and the time demands of creating and maintaining the site, the IT specialist told her that they would start slowly. They began by creating a web site called the Homework Assistance Center (HAC) that contained a welcome, an index, and a menu of the content of the site. It also included homework policies, homework assistance recommendations, and ways to contact Ms. Anderson.

When the web site was created, Ms. Anderson sent a note home to families introducing them to the site and explaining how to gain access to it. The teachers also invited families to attend a meeting where Ms. Taylor and Ms. Anderson explained the web site and showed the families how to use it. They provided students and their families with guidelines for evaluating web-based information

At the meeting, the students and their families asked many questions, which the teachers answered. The teachers also posted some of these questions and their answers on the Frequently Asked Questions section of the web site.

As students and families felt comfortable using the site, Ms. Anderson added homework assignments, models, and rubrics. Although she noted an improvement in her students' homework completion and an increase in her communication with families, Ms. Anderson also had some concerns. She worried about those students who did not have access to the Internet, which put them at a disadvantage. In addition, she observed that some students and families were misusing the system and inundating her with e-mail.

Ms. Taylor suggested that they establish rules regarding the nature of the messages to be sent, the approximate time period with in which a response to an e-mail may be expected, and the type of assistance that Ms. Anderson would be providing to families or students to complete assignments.

Ms. Taylor then suggested that Ms. Anderson add a digital suggestion box so that students and families could provide feedback and make recommendations about how to improve the site. The feedback was positive and discussed the possibilities of adding new features, including guidelines for helping children complete their homework, links to online resources for specific assignments, and homework assistance sites.

Figure 1.3. Case study. (From Salend, S.J., Duhaney, D., Anderson, D.J., & Gottschalk, C. [2004]. Using the internet to improve homework communication and completion. *TEACHING Exceptional Children, 36*[3], 64–73; reprinted by permission.)

The question is, are administrators, local government agencies, and teachers ready to purchase this equipment, train personnel how to use it, and maximize its utility for students with disabilities? If the answer is yes, then it will be a tremendous instrument for empowering students with disabilities.

Better Research About Learning and Performance

There is no doubt that more is now known about helping people who have physical disabilities requiring extensive support with employment, getting about in the community, and becoming more physically independent through the use of personal assistance and technological advances. More is known about helping individuals who have cognitive and emotional disabilities requiring extensive support to become more capable in the competitive workplace. More research has been published on helping people learn; on developing instructional environments; on helping people perform at a higher rate; and on generalizing knowledge from one environment to multiple environments, often with the help of AT devices such as headphones in work environment (Post, Storey, & Karabin, 2002). The federal government has invested millions of research dollars in these areas. Significant investment has also been made in the use of different medications to help people overcome ADHD and emotional disabilities and to enhance the hearing and visual abilities of people with sensory disorders. These research and clinical advances are available only to those who go to school in environments in which teachers are knowledgeable and in communities in which doctors can provide this help. However, when one compares the 1980s with today, the amount of information that is now available is staggering and this can only be considered positive.

New Models of Collaborative Instruction

Perhaps one of the most useful applications of the original school "mainstreaming" concept has been collaborative teaching (Snell & Janney, 2005). In this approach, a special education teacher or paraprofessional works collaboratively in the general education classroom with the regular education teacher. This collaboration can take place in a tutoring mode, a team teaching mode, or any set of collaborations that may benefit the students with disabilities or special needs who are in the classroom. There are many models of collaborative teaching. For example, Walsh and Jones (2004) identified and developed four different models that can work with youth:

1. Collaborative Scheduling A: Special educator splits class time between two different classes

2. Collaborative Scheduling B: Special educator splits time between two different classes on different days of the week; the schedule is modified on the basis of the needs of team members

3. Collaborative Scheduling C: Special educator's schedule is set weekly on the basis of activities planned for each class; the special educator serves as a resource for the team and does not have a rigid schedule

4. Collaborative Scheduling with a teacher's assistant: Teacher's assistant represents the special educator in co-taught classes as directed.

Keefe, Moore, and Duff (2004) discussed the challenges involved with collaborative teaching, despite its many options.

> The nature of high schools present greater obstacles for co-teachers because of the emphasis on content area knowledge, the need for independent study skills, the faster pacing of instruction, high-stakes testing, high school competency exams, less positive attitudes of teachers, and the inconsistent success of strategies that were effective at the elementary level. (p. 36)

Despite these points, the fact is that collaborative teaching opens up the doors for students to have many more opportunities to interact with students without disabilities and general education teachers. This means higher expectations of students with disabilities, higher aspirations by parents, greater access to activities and, in general, much richer opportunities for enhanced self-esteem and adjustment (Murawski & Dieker, 2004).

However, collaborative models do require significant planning to be successful. One model that specifically merits attention is the model of Applied Collaboration developed at the University of Minnesota. Intended to be both interactive and dynamic, Applied Collaboration is a professional development training model in which teams of general and special educators work together to identify mutual goals and use negotiation skills to address the needs of students with disabilities. An important aspect of the training is that it is always delivered by a training team consisting of a general educator and a special educator.

Within the general framework of the training, teams are provided with 1) collaborative strategies to increase communication and facilitate cooperative working relationships between special education and general education staff and 2) instructional strategies in which teams learn about various teaching strategies (e.g., differentiated instruction, shared classroom management) that are "practiced" in the classroom setting. The model is quite simple and kept intentionally so: it relies on a few effective, yet easily implemented, collaborative and instructional strategies.

Parent Power

Parental involvement is perhaps the most significant factor in the transition outcomes for students from youth into adulthood (Grigal & Neubert, 2004). Involvement means informed knowledge about what school and employment options are available and then the willingness to deal with the frequent oppositional or recalcitrant behaviors of high school youth. Why is it that students such as Sara Ruh are doing well? Clearly, her mother and father have played a major role, not only in facilitating decisions and advocacy, but also in staying the course over long periods of time and not giving up.

In a word, good parents are awesome. They *do* make a difference with their values and their contacts in the community and workplace, and the family and extended family all play a role (Taunt & Hastings, 2002). The transition to adulthood is both an exciting and challenging time for young adults and their families. Although this period is critical for all individuals, for people with significant cognitive disabilities, development of appropriate supports during the transition process is crucial. Indeed, individuals with significant cognitive disabilities may be described by the supports they need in relation to the demands of specific environments (Thompson et al., 2002). For example, these individuals may have support needs in areas of intellectual functioning, adaptive skills, motor development, sensory functioning, health care, or communication (Turnbull, Turnbull, Shank, Smith, & Leal, 2001), which necessitate identifying strategies and supports that will assist these individuals in being successful and achieving desired outcomes.

Parent power is underutilized by schools and community agencies. Parents have the most knowledge of their children. Parents have a deeply vested interest—they *love* their children and will do anything for them. They are not transient, they are not passing, and they do not forget when they go home at night. Parent power provides transition specialists a tremendous opportunity to capitalize on a resource that can problem solve many issues related to student's transition. Unfortunately, this resource is underutilized. Chambers, Hughes, and Carter (2004) conducted a study on parent and sibling perspectives on transition. Eight parents and eight siblings of high school students with significant cognitive disabilities completed questionnaires addressing transition outcomes. Results indicated that parents and siblings believed that they lacked knowledge with respect to postschool options, and parents reported assuming more active roles in the transition process than did siblings. Although future employment and independent living were important to respondents, both parents and siblings anticipated that after high school, their family member with a disability would work in a segregated employment setting and would live in the parent's home.

In sum, the majority of parents want to help and be involved and aspire for their children to succeed. This is a resource that must be brought to the table early on in the process not just because it is the right thing to do but because it is the smart thing to do.

CHALLENGES THAT AFFECT YOUTH WITH DISABILITIES

Despite the many wonderful and positive events that have occurred since the 1980s, numerous challenges are still present. Special education services for young people with disabilities have all too often been considered in a vacuum. One only has to look at children as they leave elementary school and move into the world of middle and high school to begin to understand the multiple pressures that are affecting the way they behave.

Violence in the Public Schools and the Community

One of the most critical social issues facing all Americans is safety in the community. Violence is in many homes, in many communities, and, regrettably, in many schools. At the time that we wrote the first edition of *Life Beyond the Classroom*, this type of violence would have never been thought likely or possible except in the most unusual or high-risk environments within urban areas. Violent events are increasingly common and are bound to have an adverse effect on the psychological outlook of children.

Thousands of young people with behavior disorders are already at risk for greater likelihood of inappropriate social behavior or even violent behavior and, when placed in schools and communities that allow this type of behavior to occur, are more inclined to further engage in such activity. IDEA 2004 is supposed to supply school personnel with guidelines for how to manage these students; yet, as Smith (2000) noted, this has been an ongoing and major challenge not yet successfully met. Understanding the importance of this negative societal development simply cannot be avoided, and violence must be combated with the use of greater communication, safety procedures, anger management classes, counseling, and psychological help. Students who come from homes and neighborhoods where there is a regular level of verbal and physical violence must be identified early in the educational process for help and support. Guetzloe (1999a) wrote eloquently on this topic:

> On April 20, 1999, the entire population of our country was shocked by the massacre in Littleton, Colorado. All across the continent, parents, educators, mental health professionals, and lawmakers are asking, "Why?" and "How can such a thing be prevented?"
>
> Even worse, on September 11, 2001, an extraordinary devastating event occurred when two airplanes crashed into the Twin Towers in New York City instantly killing almost 3,000 people and launching the U.S. into a worldwide war on terror. This has been followed by long difficult wars in Afghanistan and Iraq, events that have clearly affected the lives, safety, and transition outlook of many youth in America. This level of violence has become an inescapable part of how youth grow up in America today.
>
> The number of murders committed by adolescents in the United States has increased in the last decade from approximately 1,000 to 4,000 each year. In many of these cases, there are certain similarities—situations and factors that are known to be risk factors associated with violent and suicidal behavior. To many, the most horrifying part of the murders is the killers' total disregard for the value of human life—and their apparent enjoyment of the act of killing others (as if they were involved in a violent video game). It has been said that such young people need a complete emotional overhaul—a restructuring of their emotional development (Clark & Davis, 2000).
>
> Of course, the school alone cannot effect these changes. Effective interventions must address the multiple determinants of such behavior, including cognition, neurophysiological problems, and physical health as well as factors related to family, peers, school, community, and the greater society.

Access to Alcohol and Other Drugs

Americans face the increasing ease of access to alcohol and other drugs for children of all ages. This problem is not new but is one that definitely impinges on the productivity, performance, and safety of young people with disabilities. The use of alcohol and illegal drugs is not appropriate for any young person, but the risk goes up dramatically for those with disabilities because they may be on other medications, they may not have the social competence to understand how they may be taken advantage of, and they may form habits and addictions that will further impair their vocational and social competence. Once again, early identification of alcohol and drug use, communication with appropriate social agencies, and vigilant school administration policies can all help to reduce this problem.

Emphasis on High-Stakes Testing

With the passage of NCLB, state governors and education leaders have put a rising emphasis on testing competence in core academic areas, such as science, civics, foreign language, mathematics, and language arts (see Chapter 7). As well intentioned as this powerful state- and federal-mandated emphasis on school reform and testing is, it has often placed undue hardship on thousands of students with disabilities who need reasonable accommodations to take tests and, more important, who need a different area of focus than the core academic areas (Nolet & McLaughlin, 2005; Ysseldyke et al., 2004). For example, students with cognitive disabilities requiring significant support may not need to know algebra and will not perform very well on algebra and geometry competency tests. They would benefit more from functional math skills to be successful in the community and in the workplace. However, if they do not pass these tests, they will not have the ability to receive a high school diploma in many states. Educational reform as it is constituted by NCLB has been a major barrier for thousands of teachers who are trying to empower students to be more independent in the community (Browder & Spooner, 2003), despite the hopeful tone of Wehmeyer, Field, Doren, Jones, and Mason (2004) who believed that school reform efforts will provide an opportunity to infuse instruction in self-determination into programs for all students.

Continual Poverty and Chronic Unemployment

Despite the significant efforts of thousands of rehabilitation professionals, well-meaning advocates, and legislators, over the past decades, 65%–70% of people with disabilities remain unemployed as noted by the Louis Harris and Associates poll (NOD, 2004) outcomes noted earlier in this chapter. McMillan (2000) noted:

> Only three out of 10 people with developmental disabilities have jobs—meaning that the unemployment rate is 70% for the 1.2 million Americans of working age who have a developmental disability, compared with a U.S. national average of 5.1%. The rate is higher for those with developmental disabilities that typically involve some type of mental retardation and possibly physical problems, such as with cystic fibrosis. (p. 1)

A majority of people with disabilities are poor, including asset poor. The welfare and disability policies in this country do not allow individuals who rely on public benefits to accumulate assets or save. Although there are efforts underway to reverse this situation, major changes will be required in federal laws and policy.

This problem has occurred despite the fact that the unemployment rate has hovered around 5%–6% nationally, and more jobs were created during the 1990s than in any other decade in American history. Some have suggested this problem is due to job discrimination (McMorris, 2000), but the issue is too complex for only one reason to be identified. Much of this book will be devoted to discussing ways to resolve this problem, but whether it is discrimination, perceived incompetence, policy issues, transportation issues, or all of the above, the fact remains that this is a major societal barrier—there is no protracted history of individuals with disabilities gaining access to the work force in a meaningful way, and, subsequently, any progress is going to require a significant change in attitude and policy. Many of the chapters in this book discuss this issue, particularly Chapters 8 and 9.

Peer Pressure

A final area to consider is one that all children have coped with—peer pressure. As children become older, there is increasing emphasis from their peers on how they look; how they talk; who they spend time with; what skills they possess; how much money their families have; and, in general, what type of person they are perceived to be. As children move into middle school, this need for peer affiliation really begins to show itself, and, by the time high school and college arrive, the self-esteem that is derived from this type of peer relationship is either significantly developing or has not developed. Young people with disabilities have consistently had poor self-esteem, and one reason for that is poor peer relationships. A 14-year-old with a reading disability and dyslexia who may have some mild speech dysfunction might be ridiculed during lunch by children who are in his or her class. This teasing is not uncommon, and the issue is not whether it will occur—because it will—but rather how well the student is able to manage his or her anger toward the teaser and to find other friends who will be more positive. One way to approach and manage peer pressure for people with disabilities is social integration into inclusive settings. For example, Boutot and Bryant (2005) suggested that students with autism in inclusive settings are accepted, visible members of peer groups, including peers without disabilities and those with other disabilities.

TRANSITION TO ADULTHOOD FOR YOUTH WITH DISABILITIES

Young people with disabilities face many types of transitions that must be successful in order for them to move into stable adulthood. Youth with disabilities face seven common transitions:

1. Employment

2. Living arrangements and community participation

3. Getting around the community

4. Financial independence

5. Making friends

6. Sexuality and self-esteem

7. Having fun

Employment

Most young people, regardless of disability, have concerns about what they will do after they finish high school. Not knowing how to find a job and lacking specific vocational skills are added sources of anxiety for people with disabilities. Without some form of employment, departing students are immediately dependent on their parents or society, in the form of Social Security allowances (Mank, Cioffi, & Yovanoff, 2003; Wehman, Revell, & Brooke, 2003). In addition, studies show that U.S. businesses greatly value attitude, communication skills, and work experience when deciding to hire young people leaving high school—assets to which many students with disabilities are never exposed.

Unfortunately, as noted earlier in the Harris Poll (NOD, 2004), we have a long way to go. For example, McGlashing-Johnson, Agran, Sitlington, Cavin, and Wehmeyer (2003) indicated:

> Despite focused efforts at federal, state, and local levels to ensure successful transition outcomes for youth with disabilities, unemployment, financial dependence, and limited social relationships remain outcomes experienced by many individuals with disabilities (Greene & Kochhar-Bryant, 2003; Wehman, 1996), particularly individuals with more severe disabili-

ties. For example, Blackorby and Wagner (1996) reported that 25% of youth with mental retardation were competitively employed when out of school less than 2 years, and that this
figure rose to 37% 3 to 5 years after leaving school. In addition, the competitive employment rate was only 15% for youth with multiple disabilities out of school less than 2 years
and 17% 3 to 5 years after leaving school. (p. 194)

The ability to be employed after leaving school, therefore, is important for at least
three reasons: 1) working in competitive employment provides an opportunity to receive wages and benefits that lead to greater independence and mobility in the community at large, 2) being productive on a daily basis in a meaningful vocation is critical for one's self-esteem and dignity, and 3) establishing new friendships and networks
of social support in the community is facilitated by having a job.

Hence, the first aspect of transition that teachers, service providers, rehabilitation
personnel, family members, and others should focus on is reducing students' anxiety
over unemployment and economic insufficiency by effective occupational training.
This should occur through real jobs (i.e., paid employment in local business and industry) while the students are still in school. White and Weiner (2004) have clearly
demonstrated that the community-based model of vocational instruction is effective.

Living Arrangements and Community Participation

The second aspect of transition that most individuals concern themselves with involves
their postschool living arrangements and participating in the community. They ask
questions such as, "Must I always live with Mom and Dad?" and "Will I have to live in
a room by myself?" These are very important questions that significantly influence the
way people look at themselves and the types of friends they choose. We have already
discussed the trend to move back in with one's parents. Therefore, a crucial aspect of
home and community living is personal competence.

The importance of acquiring functional community skills to promote transition is
essential. These include skills such as shopping, purchasing, travel and mobility, banking, and participating in recreational activities. The ability to gain access to restaurants, including fast food, "sit down," and family restaurants, is also reported as functional and meaningful for a person with disabilities and is a skill that can be used
repeatedly and across multiple environments. A number of important subskills are necessary when using a restaurant, including ordering, paying, eating, traveling, attending
to safety, and learning social etiquette (Mechling, Pridgen, & Cronin, 2004).

There are many examples of successful living and community participation in the
literature. Learning laundry skills (Taylor, Collins, Schuster, & Kleinert, 2002), cooking skills (Graves, Collins Schuster, & Kleinert, 2005), and food preparation skills (Fiscus, Schuster, Morse, & Collins, 2002) are just a few illustrations of personal competence. For more detailed information, Belva Collins at the University of Kentucky has
proven to be a national leader and resource in this area.

Getting Around the Community

A third aspect of transition is mobility; getting around school independently is important as well (Agran et al., 2005). The ability to move around both within the community and in and out of the community is often taken for granted. Most people drive

Kirk is a 16-year-old student with an emotional disturbance and mental retardation requiring intermittent support. He has only recently been re-enrolled in a public school after completing a year of court-ordered therapy in a private rehabilitation setting for his outbursts of anger. Academically, Kirk reads on a beginning third-grade level and does math on the fourth-grade level. He has visual impairments and experiences great difficulty in reading charts, schedules, or graphs.

Kirk has experienced many failures in his prior educational programs. On his return from his out-of-school placement, he was anxious to begin a job training program. The school's Education for Employment (EFE) teacher helped Kirk locate a job training program at a local restaurant. The restaurant manager participated as a member on Kirk's IEP team, along with Kirk's parents, the EFE teacher, a VR counselor, Kirk's probation officer, and Kirk.

Kirk's duties at the restaurant include making coffee and cleaning. He has mastered the basic skills, likes his job, and is well liked by his fellow workers. The primary obstacle has been transportation to and from work; initially, the EFE instructor provided transportation, but this arrangement could not continue indefinitely. The IEP team convened to resolve the problem. After considering several possibilities and the limitations that each posed, the team arrived at a workable plan:

- Kirk's supervisor would fix Kirk's work schedule at 5 days a week, 7:00 A.M. to

automobiles, have access to public transportation, or have friends who can help them to get around. Independent movement in the community is critical for going to movie theaters, convenience stores, grocery stores, parks, church, and work, as well as for feeling independent (West, Wittig, & Dowdy, 2004). One of the great difficulties that people with disabilities face is a lack of independent mobility. In addition, the ability for students to seek help if they are lost is an important skill that was recently trained to students with intellectual disabilities (Taber, Alberto, Hughes, & Seltzer, 2002; Taber, Alberto, Seltzer, & Hughes, 2003).

Mobility and travel refers to movement both *within* and *between* environments. Assisting students to move about in the school, workplace, home, stores, or other public areas would be mobility within environments. "Between environments" refers to getting from one environment to another, such as from the home to school, work, or shopping centers.

Both aspects of mobility are essential components of educational planning and instruction. Increasing a student's mobility within environments increases the likelihood of achieving successful educational outcomes. Being able to maneuver about and locate specific areas within an environment increases the student's competencies and independence in that particular setting and increases the likelihood that the student will be successful there. For example, instructing a student in work-related skills will be more likely to result in successful employment if the student is also able to move about within the building, locate work areas, or gain access to common areas such as rest rooms, cafeterias, break rooms, and conference areas.

Lack of mobility can be caused by ambulation problems or inaccessibility of public places. More often than not, however, lack of mobility is caused by having a limited number of friends who are able to drive, an inability to drive an automobile, or an inability to obtain a driver's license. Lack of mobility may also reflect living in an area without public transportation.

Financial Independence

Economic self-sufficiency is a major goal that most citizens desire and individuals with disabilities are no different. Unfortunately, education does not help students learn financial planning, investment strategies, or the basic knowledge necessary to evaluate the quality of retail sales and merchandising. Not surprising is that individuals with disabilities are among those most vulnerable to scams and unfair marketing practices.

2:00 P.M., to limit transportation difficulties.

- Kirk would carpool with the manager of a video store next door to the restaurant to get to work each morning.

- Kirk would require training to walk independently from his home to the carpool pickup point approximately three blocks away.

- The EFE teacher and Kirk's mother would collaborate on this training, gradually fading their presence as Kirk showed that he could walk to the pickup point safely.

- His stepfather's work schedule enabled him to pick up Kirk at the end of his work shift to take him home.

Financial security transition goals should rank in importance just behind employment and postsecondary education transition goals, especially when considering that the majority of money spent on disability in the United States goes toward Social Security payments and medical assistance. A large number of people with disabilities live in poverty (Stapleton, O'Day, Livermore, & Imparato, 2005). Individuals with disabilities need to be educated in their rights and entitlements to these payments. Although the details of Social Security regulations are almost too complex to understand, an individual should know how to get help and resolution to specific questions. In Chapters 4 and 15, much more detail is presented on the important topic of benefits counseling and planning. See also Virginia Commonwealth University's *Desktop Reference Guide for SSA Youth Transition Waivers* (2005), which is an excellent resource available for students who need information on Social Security.

Financial planning and income security involve a range of issues from straightforward topics, such as money management, saving money, and making purchases, to more complex topics, such as estate planning, using credit, or long-term financial planning. For example, consider Laura, a 21-year-old woman whose parents have saved $250,000 for her. They may decide, after discussion with the education team, that an annual structured annuity payout over the next 40 years is most advantageous to Laura. The transition plan should reflect this type of specificity. The plan needs to sufficiently integrate all major aspects of the student's life.

Making Friends

Peer relationships and making friends are a fifth aspect of transition. Beginning in the late 1980s, the transition literature has increasingly stressed the importance of and need for friendships in the lives of people with disabilities (Geisthardt, Brotherson, & Cook, 2002). In addition, there must be sensitivity to the changing nature of peer relationships as students move from middle school to high school and then out of high school into adult environments. Once in adult environments, young people are expected to be increasingly independent in identifying friends, socially networking with people, and initiating social activities (Kennedy, 2004; Kraemer, McIntyre, & Blacher, 2003). Obviously, some people are better and more successful than others in developing such relationships. This is clearly a cause of stress and anxiety for many people with disabilities who do not yet have a network for meeting people (Pottie & Sumarah, 2004). Gilson and Gilson (1998) described a case study about two women, which is summarized in the case study on p. 32.

Joblessness, substandard living quarters, and restricted mobility are factors that can inhibit peer relationships. Developing new friendships, maintaining old friendships, and meeting the challenge of changing peer relationships are critical aspects of transition for all people with disabilities. David Pitonyak (2004), a national leader when it comes to

MARTHA AND JENNY

Martha and Jenny have work stations next to each other. They are both in their 20s, are fashion-conscious, and have personal mementos decorating the space around their computers. Both have been hired as part-time workers to do data entry. During breaktime conversations, the two women have found that they share a passion for finding bargains when shopping for clothes and are both waiting for "Mr. Right" to come into their lives. On Saturdays, Martha and Jenny often meet at the mall, shop for a few hours, and then eat lunch at the food court. Jenny then goes home to her apartment, which she shares with a roommate and two cats. Martha goes home to a building that she shares with 99 other people who have varying degrees of physical, sensory, and cognitive disabilities. When each of the young women was asked who she considers her friends to be, both Martha and Jenny, without hesitation, named each other first.

positive behavior supports and understanding the role of friendship in life adjustment, noted the following:

> Many people who experience disabilities live lives of extreme loneliness and isolation. Many depend almost exclusively on their families for companionship. Some have lost their connections to family, relying on people who are paid to be with them for their social support. Although paid staff can be friendly and supportive, they frequently change jobs or take on new responsibilities. The resulting instability can be devastating to someone who is fundamentally alone.
>
> In my view, most people served by the human services industry are profoundly lonely. Loneliness is the central reason why so many are unhappy and distraught. It is not because our instructional strategies are ill-informed or because our planning processes are inadequate. It is not because our medications are in-potent or because staff are untrained. Their suffering results from isolation.
>
> For years, the human services profession has been preoccupied with questions such as: What's wrong with you? What do we do with you if we can't fix you? I believe these are the wrong questions. The central function of our human services system, in my view, should be to help people who experience disabilities to develop and maintain "enduring freely chosen relationships." The field is now moving toward a much more promising set of questions: What are your capacities and gifts and what supports do you need to express them? What works well for you and what does not? What are your visions and dreams of a brighter future and who will help you to move toward that future? (p. 1)

Sexuality and Self-Esteem

The development of sexuality and self-esteem is a sixth aspect of transition. As teenagers grow into adulthood, they begin to establish their own values. Their confidence levels and how they choose to interact with people who they are interested in are very important in establishing good self-esteem. People express sexuality, both on dates and in groups, through their clothes, hairstyles, and recreational activities. Several resources are available for parents and teachers; Schwier and Hingsburger (2000) discussed sexuality training programs for youth with intellectual disabilities and listed many books, magazines, and organizations that are useful for helping young people cope with puberty and adult sexuality. Too little attention has been paid to this important transition, but with increased focus in this area, some of the other transitions will fall into place more smoothly.

Having Fun

Finally, simply having fun and appreciating life constitute the seventh aspect of transition; yet, Schwartzman, Martin, Yu, and Whiteley (2004) noted that this is not often the case for many people with disabilities. Fortunately, there are many wonderful materials and curricula that reflect age-appropriate leisure activities (Chandler & Pankaskie,

2004; Moon, 1994; Schleien, Meyer, Heyne, & Brandt, 1995). The key to selecting appropriate recreation goals hinges on the following criteria.

- What recreational interests does the student demonstrate, and are these interests consistent with his or her intellectual and physical capabilities?

- What opportunities are available in the home and local community to actually enjoy this leisure activity?

Participating on the swimming team, serving as the manager on the junior varsity soccer team, walking or jogging, working out in an aerobics class, taking an arts and crafts class, or learning a game that other friends play (e.g., video games) are some examples of leisure goals. Usually, these goals are facilitated through local parks and recreation specialists instead of in the classroom. With insight and creativity, an educational team can find scores of activities in which students can participate; however, planning will be necessary to make leisure options a reality. The use of adaptations for the leisure program or materials can also play a major role in identifying viable recreation goals.

Frequently, materials and equipment used in a recreational activity act as barriers to participation because they are usually designed for individuals without disabilities and do not take into account the possible physical or sensory impairments of those with disabilities. Therefore, it is often necessary to adapt or modify the equipment or materials to eliminate these barriers to recreation.

THEMES FOR SUCCESS

As one considers the cornerstones of success for young people as they grow up, one must look at why some adults are so successful and others consistently have difficulties and fail. Clearly, many skills contribute to success, but we repeatedly come back to several themes that seem to characterize people who do well in life compared with those who do not. Doing well is not necessarily earning the most money in the highest status job or being the most famous or popular. Success is a very personal issue and relates to how happy one feels about oneself and the impact of one's life on others. To this end, we stress five major themes in this book. These are personal responsibility, self-determination and self-advocacy, social competence, vocational competence, and postsecondary education.

Personal Responsibility

Personal responsibility is important for all young people to learn, particularly young people with disabilities. Personal responsibility involves, for example, self-control around people whom one may be attracted to. Financial habits and the ability to save money that one has earned represent another area of responsibility. Arriving to work on time and accepting criticism from a supervisor are yet more illustrations of personal responsibility. Educators must work in collaboration with other members of the educational team and should not concentrate exclusively on the instruction of selected academic skills. They should infuse habits and patterns of personal responsibility into the curriculum for youth with disabilities. Certainly, teachers cannot take the role of parents, but they can influence the direction in which students are headed.

Self-Determination and Self-Advocacy

Self-determination is the capacity to choose and to act on the basis of those choices (e.g., Wehmeyer, Lance, & Bashinski, 2002). The emphasis on self-determination for people with disabilities can be traced to the independent living and self-advocacy movements that emerged in the 1970s. Most people develop self-determination in childhood and adolescence as they receive greater responsibilities and freedom from their parents and teachers (Nerney, 2005; Williard & Dotson, 2005). Individuals cannot self-advocate if they have not developed self-determination skills. Self-advocacy will, ultimately, be the way for young people to navigate the challenges they face.

Self-determination requires that the young person be provided with the knowledge, competency, and opportunities necessary to exercise freedom and choice in ways that are valuable to him or her (Agran, Alper, & Wehmeyer, 2002). Little doubt remains that those people who are self-directed have the initiative to be successful, have ambition, and practice a reasonable degree of work ethic inevitability do better in life than those who do not. There is, of course, room for debate regarding how much the schools are able to instill these important skills. Whose Future is It Anyway?, a self-advocacy program developed by Wehmeyer and Kelchner (1995a), which is described in Chapter 2, and *The Transition Handbook*, developed by Hughes and Carter (2000), are good tools for helping teachers get started in teaching this process. Likewise, papers by Wood, Karvonen, Test, Browder, and Algozzine (2004) and Test, Browder, Karvonen, Wood, and Algozzine (2002) do an excellent job of guiding teachers and students through the self-determination process when developing IEPs. Self-determination is related to personal attributes as well. This is true whether a person has mental retardation requiring extensive support and works in the back of a kitchen or whether the individual is recovering from a spinal cord injury and is considering a career in computer engineering.

Social Competence

Many believe that getting along with people, interpersonal skills, and social competence in a variety of environments are the most important features of success in life. Unfortunately, many young people with disabilities are ultimately unable to achieve this level of competence. Using effective social skills and knowing how to behave in a variety of challenging social situations can make the difference in successful outcomes in the workplace as well as at home and in the community. Young people who get into fights will not make friends. Young people who are verbally abusive will not end up with effective social relationships. Many of the precipitating factors that lead to violence or similar types of behavior in the classroom are predicated on poor social skills. Part of the resolution of this issue within the schools is a tighter administrative structure, but much of the problem is that some students simply do not know the socially appropriate way to behave. Role playing, counseling, and targeted instruction on certain social skills can go a long way toward overcoming this problem. This is an important theme that we repeatedly come back to throughout the book.

Vocational Competence

Vocational capacity, employment, and the opportunity to advance in a career is a major underpinning of success in American society (Wehman, 2001b; Wehman, Revell, & Brooke, 2003; Wehman, Inge, Revell, & Brooke, in press). Individuals are defined by earning ability, the type of work that they do, the regularity with which they are employed, the type of environment that they work in, and long-term work potential. The United States is a capitalist society. It is a country that expects people to be productive in work. The use of the Internet, automation, greater efficiency in the workplace, and technology all empower workers. Individuals with disabilities must become competent. They must take courses, improve themselves continually, and be highly persistent to secure employment. Schools have emphasized academic skills too much and employment not enough. This must change so that individuals with disabilities can take their rightful place in American society.

Postsecondary Education

A final theme that continually emerges throughout this book is the need for ongoing education and lifelong learning (Getzel & Wehman, 2005; Grigal, Neubert, & Moon, 2002). Many individuals with disabilities have difficulty in the workplace throughout their lives. They also have difficulty with social skills and personal self-esteem. One way to overcome that is education. Earning an associate's degree or a bachelor's degree from a 4-year college will be an outstanding asset to add to one's résumé, but being able to take courses and assimilate new information can also make a significant difference (Fisher & Eskow, 2004). Adding new skills to one's knowledge base; identifying new interests, hobbies, and avocations; and making new friends are all mediated in a very effective way through postsecondary education and lifelong learning experiences. Significant opportunities for individuals with disabilities to try different areas of learning are increasingly available, even to those with significant intellectual disabilities (e.g., Schmidt, 2005).

Madaus (2005) noted:

> The transition from high school to college can be a confusing and overwhelming time for students with learning disabilities (LD), their families, and the secondary-level professionals who assist them. In addition to the challenges that all students face when transitioning to college, additional obstacles confront students with LD. Chief among them is the move from the familiar model of special education services at the high school level to very different services at the college level. Not only does the scope of these services change considerably from high school to college, but there can also be a great deal of institutional variation in the way that these services are provided. Additionally, at the college level, significant changes occur in the legal rights of students, and there is a sharp reversal of parental and student responsibility. (p. 32)

CONCLUSION

A new generation of teachers who fully comprehend the importance of transition in the special education curriculum and the adult services system is needed to empower young people with disabilities. This book proposes several basic tenets for professionals:

1. The student or family (i.e., the consumer) is usually right. Listen to the student. Listen to the family. What are they saying? What hints are they giving about what they need? These ideas are the critical features of a student-oriented transition program.

2. It is essential to look closely at what businesses and industry require of their work force. The new generation of teachers will examine daily curricula and evaluate whether the skills, objectives, and activities they are currently emphasizing have direct relationships to what local employers need in order to maintain a dependable work force. These teachers will also determine whether their curricula are being influenced by what businesses say is required and needed or by objectives generated by bureaucrats.

3. All young people with disabilities should have the opportunity to be included in the workplace and schools. Special schools, segregated work activity centers, and programs that are designed only for people with disabilities must become institutions of the past. People with disabilities consistently perform better in typical work environments and natural community environments. Perpetual segregation hinders transition. Integration must be an outcome, not a process, that educators, parents, and professionals work toward together.

This chapter has discussed a legislative and philosophical framework for promoting school to adulthood transition. Strategies for enhancing transition services for young people with disabilities are developed in subsequent chapters.

STUDY QUESTIONS

1. List four societal challenges that affect the transition process and describe ways to help students with disabilities overcome each of the challenges that are identified.

2. Give examples of how IDEA objectives can positively affect the transition planning and employment outcomes of youth with disabilities.

3. Describe three disability related laws, aside from IDEA, and how they affect employment of people with disabilities.

4. Describe three opportunities that help to empower youth with disabilities.

5. What do current research findings say about transition outcomes for youth with disabilities?

Appendix

Key Provisions on Transition:
IDEA 1997 Compared to H.R. 1350 (IDEA 2004)

On December 3, 2004, President George W. Bush signed H.R. 1350 (IDEA 2004) into law. This document identifies the major changes between IDEA 1997 and H.R. 1350 (IDEA 2004) concerning transition services (**bold** text indicates language changes from IDEA 1997).

Individuals with Disabilities Education Act Amendments of 1997	H.R. 1350: Individuals with Disabilities Education Improvement Act of 2004
Part A: GENERAL PROVISIONS	
Section 601: SHORT TITLE; TABLE OF CONTENTS; FINDINGS; PURPOSES	Section 601: SHORT TITLE; TABLE OF CONTENTS; FINDINGS; PURPOSES
(d) PURPOSES. The purposes of this title are—	(d) PURPOSES. The purposes of this title are—
(1)(A) to ensure that all children with disabilities have available to them a free appropriate public education that emphasizes special education and related services designed to meet their unique needs and prepare them for employment and independent living	(1)(A) to ensure that all children with disabilities have available to them a free appropriate public education that emphasizes special education and related services designed to meet their unique needs and prepare them **for further education,** employment, and independent living
Section 602: DEFINITIONS	Section 602: DEFINITIONS
(30) TRANSITION SERVICES. The term "transition services" means a coordinated set of activities for a student with disability that—	(34) TRANSITION SERVICES: The term "transition services" means a coordinated set of activities for a **child** with a disability that—
(A) is designed within an outcome-oriented process, which promotes movement from school to post-school activities, including post-secondary education, vocational training, integrated employment (including supported employment), continuing and adult education, adult services, independent living, or community participation;	(A) is designed to be **within a results**-oriented process, **that is focused on improving the academic and functional achievement of the child with a disability to facilitate the child's** movement from school to post-school activities, including post-secondary education, vocational **education,** integrated employment (including supported employment), continuing and adult education, adult services, independent living, or community participation;
(B) is based upon the individual student's needs, taking into account the student's preferences and interests; and	(B) is based on the individual child's needs, taking into account the **child's strengths,** preferences, and interests; and
(C) includes instruction, related services, community experiences, the development of employment and other post-school adult living objectives, and when appropriate, acquisition of daily living skills and functional vocational evaluation.	(C) includes instruction, related services, community experiences, the development of employment and other post-school adult living objectives, and when appropriate, acquisition of daily living skills and functional vocational evaluation.

(continued)

Individuals with Disabilities Education Act of 1997	H.R. 1350: Individuals with Disabilities Education Improvement Act of 2004

Part B: ASSISTANCE FOR EDUCATION OF ALL CHILDREN WITH DISABILITIES

Section 614: INDIVIDUALIZED EDUCATION PROGRAMS

(c) ADDITIONAL REQUIREMENTS FOR EVALUATION AND REEVALUATIONS

(5) EVALUATIONS BEFORE CHANGE IN ELIGIBILITY—A local educational agency shall evaluate a child with a disability in accordance with this section before determining that the child is no longer a child with a disability.

Section 614: INDIVIDUALIZED EDUCATION PROGRAMS

(c) ADDITIONAL REQUIREMENTS FOR EVALUATION AND REEVALUATIONS

(5) EVALUATIONS BEFORE CHANGE IN ELIGIBILITY—

(A) IN GENERAL—**Except as provided in subparagraph (B),** a local educational agency shall evaluate a child with a disability in accordance with this section before determining that the child is no longer a child with a disability.

(B) EXCEPTION—

(i) IN GENERAL—The evaluation described in subparagraph (A) shall not be required before the termination of a child's eligibility under this part due to graduation from secondary school with a regular diploma, or due to exceeding the age eligibility for a free appropriate public education under State law.

(ii) SUMMARY OF PERFORMANCE—For a child whose eligibility under this part terminates under circumstances described in clause (i), a local education agency shall provide the child with a summary of the child's academic achievement and functional performance, which shall include recommendations on how to assist the child in meeting the child's postsecondary goals.

Section 614, INDIVIDUALIZED EDUCATION PROGRAMS

(d) INDIVIDUALIZED EDUCATION PROGRAMS

(1) DEFINITIONS

(A) INDIVIDUALIZED EDUCATION PROGRAM

(vii)(I) beginning at age 14, and updated annually, a statement of the transition service needs of the child under the applicable components of the child's IEP that focuses on the child's courses of study (such as participation in advanced-placement courses or a vocational education program);

(II) beginning at age 16 (or younger, if determined appropriate by the IEP Team), a statement of needed transition services for the child, including, when appropriate, a statement of the interagency responsibilities or any needed linkages; and

(III) beginning at least one year before the child reaches the age of majority under State law, a statement that the child has been informed of his or her rights under this title, if any, that will transfer to the child on reaching the age of majority under section 615(m); and

(viii) a statement of—

(I) how the child's progress toward the annual goals described in clause (ii) will be measured; and

(II) how the child's parents will be regularly informed (by such means as periodic report cards), at least as often as parents are informed of their nondisabled children's progress of—

Section 614, INDIVIDUALIZED EDUCATION PROGRAMS

(d) INDIVIDUALIZED EDUCATION PROGRAMS

(1) DEFINITIONS

(A) INDIVIDUALIZED EDUCATION PROGRAM

(VIII) **beginning not later that the first IEP to be in effect when the child is 16, and updated annually thereafter—**

(aa) appropriate measurable postsecondary goals based upon age appropriate transition assessments related to training, education, employment, and, where appropriate, independent living skills;

(bb) the transition services (including courses of study) needed to assist the child in reaching those goals; and

(cc) beginning **not later than** 1 year before the child reaches the age of majority under State law, a statement that the child has been informed of the child's rights under this title, if any, that will transfer to the child on reaching the age of majority under section 615(m).

(ii) RULE OF CONSTRUCTION—nothing in this section shall be construed to require—

(I) that additional information be included in a child's IEP beyond what is explicitly required in this section; and

(II) the IEP Team to include information under 1 component of a child's IEP that is already contained under another component of such IEP.

[Note: The following text appears in Part B, Section 614 (d)(1)(A)(i), as part of the definition of what an IEP includes.]

Individuals with Disabilities Education Act of 1997	H.R. 1350: Individuals with Disabilities Education Improvement Act of 2004

(aa) their child's progress toward the annual goals described in clause (ii); and	(II) a statement of measurable annual goals, including **academic and functional goals,** designed to—
(bb) the extent to which that progress is sufficient to enable the child to achieve the goals by the end of the year.	**(aa)** meet the child's needs that result from the child's disability to enable the child to be involved in and **make** progress in the general education curriculum; and
	(bb) meet each of the child's other educational needs that result from the child's disability;
	(III) a description of how the child's progress toward meeting the annual goals described in subclause (II) will be measured and when periodic reports on the progress the child is making toward meeting the annual goals (such as through the use of quarterly or other periodic reports, concurrent with the issuance of report card) will be provided;
(3) DEVELOPMENT OF IEP—	(3) DEVELOPMENT OF IEP—
(A) IN GENERAL—In developing each child's IEP, the IEP Team, subject to subparagraph (C), shall consider—	(A) IN GENERAL—In developing each child's IEP, the IEP Team, subject to subparagraph (C), shall consider—
(i) the strengths of the child and the concerns of the parents for enhancing the education of their child; and	(i) the strengths of the child;
(ii) the results of the initial evaluation or most recent evaluation of the child.	(ii) the concerns of the parents for enhancing the education of their child;
	(iii) the results of the initial evaluation or most recent evaluation of the child; and
	(iv) the academic, developmental, and functional needs of the child.
(6) CHILDREN WITH DISABILITIES IN ADULT PRISONS—	(7) CHILDREN WITH DISABILITIES IN ADULT PRISONS—
(A) IN GENERAL—The following requirements do not apply to children with disabilities who are convicted as adults under State law and incarcerated in adult prisons:	(A) IN GENERAL—The following requirements **shall** not apply to children with disabilities who are convicted as adults under State law and incarcerated in adult prisons:
(i) The requirements contained in section 612(a)(17) and paragraph (1)(A)(v) of this subsection (relating to participation of children with disabilities in general assessments.)	(i) The requirements contained in section 612(a)(16) and paragraph (1)(A)(i)(VI) (relating to participation of children with disabilities in general assessments).
(ii) The requirements of subclauses (I) and (II) of paragraph (1)(A)(vii) of this subsection (relating to transition planning and transition services), do not apply with respect to such children whose eligibility under this part will end, because of their age, before they will be released from prison.	(ii) The requirements of items (aa) and (bb) of paragraph (1)(A)(i)(VIII) (relating to transition planning and transition services), do not apply with respect to such children whose eligibility under this part will end, because of **such children's age, before such children** will be released from prison.

From the National Center on Secondary Education and Transition (2005). *Key provisions on transition: IDEA 1997 compared to H.R. 1350 (IDEA, 2004).* Minneapolis, MN: Institute on Community Integration, University of Minnesota; reprinted by permission.

2

Self-Determination, Student Involvement, and Leadership Development

Michael L. Wehmeyer, Stelios Gragoudas, and Karrie A. Shogren

AFTER COMPLETING THIS CHAPTER, THE READER WILL BE ABLE TO

- Define *self-determination* and identify component elements of self-determined behavior that contribute to its development

- Identify why promoting self-determination is important to the education of students with disabilities

- Identify and utilize existing methods, materials, and instructional strategies that promote self-determination in the transition years

- Discuss how efforts to promote self-determination contribute to student involvement with and progress in the general education curriculum

- Define student involvement, discuss federal policy dictating active student involvement, and identify why students need to be involved in educational planning and decision making

- Identify and utilize existing methods, materials, and strategies that promote student involvement in transition planning and decision making

- Discuss leadership development and the role it plays in the transition process

SELF-DETERMINATION, STUDENT INVOLVEMENT, AND LEADERSHIP DEVELOPMENT

Promoting and enhancing the self-determination of youth with disabilities has become best practice in transition services. In 1998, the Council for Exceptional Children's Division on Career Development and Transition issued a position statement on self-determination (Field, Martin, Miller, Ward, & Wehmeyer, 1998), noting that a focus on self-determination is important to enable students to "be more successful in education and transition to adult life" and "holds great potential to transform the way in which educational services are planned and delivered for students with and without disabilities" (p. 125). The 2003 report of the President's Commission on Excellence in Special Education stated that efforts to promote self-determination are necessary if students with disabilities are to achieve successful results.

This chapter defines *self-determination* and examines its importance to successful transition-related results. It then describes methods, materials, and strategies to promote self-determination and to support active student involvement in educational planning and decision making and youth leadership.

SELF-DETERMINATION IN TRANSITION

What Is Self-Determination?

The historical roots of self-determination for people with disabilities can be found in the normalization, independent living, disability rights, and self-advocacy movements and in legislative protections ensuring equal opportunities for people with disabilities (Ward, 1996). Promoting self-determination emerged as an instructional focus area in special education as a result of efforts to improve transition-related outcomes for youth with disabilities, and the U.S. Department of Education's Office of Special Education Programs (OSEP) has made a substantial investment in the development of methods, materials, and strategies to promote self-determination (Ward & Kohler, 1996) and to achieve active student involvement in transition planning (Wehmeyer & Sands, 1998). As a result, there are numerous frameworks that can serve as a basis for instructional design, as well as specially designed instructional methods, materials, and strategies to promote self-determination (Wehmeyer, Abery, Mithaug, & Stancliffe, 2003; Wehmeyer, Agran, & Hughes, 1998).

Although these frameworks propose different definitions of the self-determination construct, there is a general consensus in the field as to what characterizes *people* who are self-determined.

> [Self-determined people] know how to choose—they know what they want and how to get it. From an awareness of personal needs, self-determined individuals choose goals, then doggedly pursue them. This involves asserting an individual's presence, making his or her needs known, evaluating progress toward meeting goals, adjusting performance, and creating unique approaches to solve problems (Martin & Marshall, 1995, p. 147).

Our own work to promote self-determination, and the framework that guides our presentation of relevant interventions in this chapter, has been based on a functional model of self-determination (Wehmeyer, 1998, 1999, 2001a) in which *self-determined behavior* is defined as "acting as the primary causal agent in one's life and making choices and decisions regarding one's quality of life free from undue external influence or interference" (Wehmeyer, 1996, p. 24). Within this model, self-determined behavior refers to actions that are identified by four *essential characteristics:* 1) the person acted *autonomously,* 2) the behavior(s) are *self-regulated,* 3) the person initiated and responded to the event(s) in a *psychologically empowered* manner, and 4) the person acted in a *self-realizing* manner. These four essential characteristics describe the *function* of the behavior that makes it self-determined or not. That is, it is the function that the behavior serves for the individual that defines it as self-determined, not any specific class of behaviors themselves.

The concept of causal agency is central to our perspective. Broadly defined, *causal agency* implies that it is the individual who makes or causes things to happen in his or her life. One frequent misinterpretation of self-determination is that it simply means "doing it yourself." When self-determination is interpreted this way, however, there is an obvious problem for people with more severe disabilities, many of whom may have limits to the number and types of activities they can perform independently. However, the *capacity to perform* specific behaviors is secondary in importance to whether one is the causal agent (e.g., caused in some way to happen) over outcomes such behaviors are implemented to achieve. Thus, people who have severe physical disabilities can employ a personal assistant to perform routine activities and, if such functions are performed under the control of that person (e.g., person with disability), it is really a moot point whether the person physically performed the activity. Likewise, a person with a severe cognitive impairment may not be able to "independently" (e.g., alone and with no support) make a complex decision or solve a difficult problem. However, to the extent that supports are provided to enable that person to retain control over the decision-making process and to participate to the greatest extent in the decision-making or problem-solving process, he or she can become more self-determined.

Self-determination emerges across the life span as children and adolescents learn skills and develop attitudes that enable them to be causal agents in their lives. The *essential characteristics* that define self-determined behavior emerge through the development and acquisition of multiple, interrelated *component elements* (see Table 2.1).

Table 2.1.   Component elements of self-determined behavior

Choice-making skills

Decision-making skills

Problem-solving skills

Goal-setting and attainment skills

Independence, risk-taking, and safety skills

Self-observation, evaluation, and reinforcement skills

Self-instruction skills

Self-advocacy and leadership skills

Internal locus of control

Positive attributions of efficacy and outcome expectancy

Self-awareness

Self-knowledge

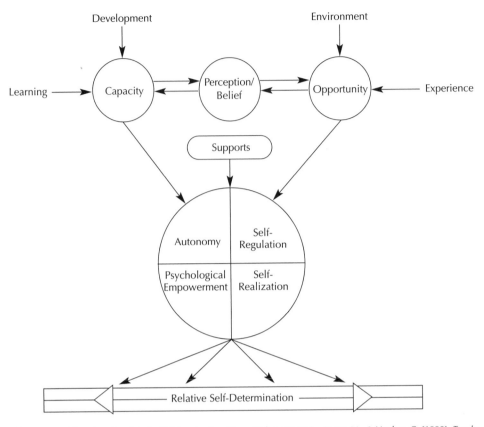

Figure 2.1. A functional model of self-determination. (From Wehmeyer, M.L., Agran, M., & Hughes, C. [1998]. *Teaching self-determination to students with disabilities: Basic skills for successful transition* [p. 18]. Baltimore: Paul H. Brookes Publishing Co.).

Although not an exhaustive list, these component elements are particularly important to the emergence of self-determined behavior. The functional model is depicted in Figure 2.1 (Wehmeyer, Agran, & Hughes,1998).

Self-Determination, Disability, and Empowerment

The role of educators in promoting self-determination is to teach students the knowledge and skills they need to become causal agents in their lives. However, it is important that educators not forget that the self-determination focus in disability services, including special education, emerged from deeply held convictions pertaining to the rights of people with disabilities to control their own lives. Within the context of the disability rights and advocacy movement, the self-determination construct has been imbued with an empowerment and "rights" orientation. *Empowerment* is a term usually associated with social movements and typically is used, as Rappaport (1981) stated, in reference to actions that "enhance the possibilities for people to control their lives" (p. 15). People with disabilities (Kennedy, 1996; Ward, 1996) have been unequivocal in their understanding of self-determination as a form of empowerment.

Is Self-Determination Important to
Transition Outcomes for Students with Disabilities?

The emphasis on promoting self-determination was introduced in response to findings that transition-related outcomes for youth with disabilities (e.g., employment, independent living, community integration) were not as positive as desired, as well as to calls from people with disabilities for greater control in their lives. The proposal that self-determination is an important outcome if youth with disabilities are to achieve more positive adult outcomes is predicated on an assumption that self-determination and positive adult outcomes are causally linked. The hypothesis that self-determination is important for more positive adult outcomes has support from the literature in two ways; first, by examining the contributions of component elements of self-determined behavior to more favorable school and adult outcomes and, second, by examining studies that tested this hypothesis directly.

A comprehensive review of the impact of component elements of self-determined behavior on adult outcomes is beyond the scope of this chapter, but a brief overview should adequately make the point that there is abundant evidence that promoting the component elements listed in Table 2.1 can result in more positive adult and transition outcomes, including improved employment, community living, and community integration outcomes for students with disabilities. So, for example, providing opportunities for making choices and enhancing the capacity of youth and young adults with disabilities to express preferences has been linked to multiple outcomes of benefit to transition. There is an emerging database showing that incorporating choice-making opportunities into interventions to reduce problem behaviors of children and youth with disabilities results in improved behavioral outcomes (Shogren, Faggella-Luby, Bae, & Wehmeyer, 2004). Cooper and Browder (1998) found that teaching young adults to make choices improved outcomes of community-based instruction. Watanabe and Sturmey (2003) found that promoting choice-making opportunities in vocational tasks for young adults with disabilities increased engagement in the activity.

Teaching effective decision-making and problem-solving skills also has been shown to enhance positive transition outcomes for youth and young adults. Teaching young women with intellectual disabilities to make more effective decisions improved their capacity to identify potentially abusive social interactions (Khemka, 2000). Datillo and Hoge (1999) found that teaching decision making to adolescents with cognitive disabilities in the context of a leisure education program improved their acquisition of socially valid leisure knowledge and skills. Limitations in social problem-solving skills has been linked to difficulties in employment, community, and independent living situations for people with developmental disabilities (Gumpel, Tappe, & Araki, 2000). Storey (2002) reviewed the empirical literature pertaining to improving social interactions for workers with disabilities and determined that problem-solving skills contributed to more positive workplace social interactions. O'Reilly, Lancioni, and O'Kane (2000) found that incorporating instruction in problem solving into social skills instruction improved employment outcomes for supported workers with traumatic brain injuries. Finally, as described subsequently, several studies (Agran, Blanchard, & Wehmeyer, 2000; Palmer, Wehmeyer, Gipson, & Agran, 2004; Wehmeyer, Palmer, Agran, Mithaug, & Martin, 2000) show that teaching students with disabilities a self-regulated problem-solving process enables them to self-direct learning and to achieve educationally relevant goals, including transition-related goals.

Similarly, there is research linking enhanced self-management and self-regulation skills to the attainment of positive adult outcomes. Teaching students self-monitoring strategies has been shown to improve critical learning skills and classroom involvement skills of students with severe disabilities (Agran et al., 2005; Gilberts, Agran, Hughes, & Wehmeyer, 2001; Hughes et al., 2002). Grossi and Heward (1998) showed that teaching young adults with developmental disabilities goal-setting, self-monitoring, and self-evaluation strategies improved work productivity. Browder and Minarovic (2000) taught workers with intellectual disabilities self-instruction strategies to self-initiated job tasks in work environments, resulting in enhanced performance and employer satisfaction. Finally, Woods and Martin (2004) found that teaching supported employees to self-manage and self-regulate work tasks improved employers' perceptions of the employee and improved work performance.

Research on these component elements of self-determined behavior provide strong, though indirect, evidence that youth who are *more self-determined* achieve more positive adult outcomes. There are a few studies that provide direct evidence of the relationship between self-determination and transition outcomes. Wehmeyer and Schwartz (1997) measured the self-determination of 80 students with learning disabilities or mental retardation and then examined adult outcomes 1 year after high school. Students in the high self-determination group were twice as likely (80%) as youth in the low self-determination group to be employed (40%) and earned, on average, $2.00 an hour more than students in the low self-determination group who were employed. There were no significant differences between groups on level of intelligence or number of vocational courses taken. Wehmeyer and Palmer (2003) conducted a second follow-up study, examining adult status of 94 students with cognitive disabilities 1 and 3 years postgraduation. One year after high school, students in the high self-determination group were disproportionately likely to have moved from where they were living during high school, and by the third year, they were still disproportionately likely to live somewhere other than their high school home and were significantly more likely to live independently. For employed students, those scoring higher in self-determination made statistically significant advances in obtaining job benefits, including vacation, sick leave, and health insurance, an outcome not shared by their peers in the low self-determination group.

Sowers and Powers (1995) showed that students with disabilities involved in instruction using the TAKE CHARGE materials (described subsequently) to promote self-determination increased their participation and independence in performing community activities. Finally, Wehmeyer and Schwartz (1998) examined the link between self-determination and quality of life for 50 adults with intellectual disabilities. Controlling for level of intelligence and environmental factors, they found that self-determination predicted group membership based on quality of life scores. That is, people who were highly self-determined experienced a higher quality of life; people who lacked self-determination appeared to experience a less positive quality of life.

In summary, there is an expanding base of evidence suggesting that higher self-determination and increased capacity in the component elements of self-determined behavior results in better transition-related outcomes for youth and young adults with disabilities. The obvious next issue is how to achieve this important outcome.

METHODS, MATERIALS, AND STRATEGIES TO PROMOTE SELF-DETERMINATION

Efforts to enhance the self-determination of youth with disabilities should involve multiple, parallel activities focused on teaching skills related to the component elements of self-determined behavior and promoting active involvement in educational planning and decision making. We have already described how such interventions can positively impact transition-related outcomes for youth and young adults with disabilities. Research has shown that students with disabilities can, in fact, acquire skills and knowledge pertaining to the component elements (Algozzine, Browder, Karvonen, Test, & Wood, 2001) and learn to self-regulate learning and improve overall self-determination (Wehmeyer, Palmer, et al., 2000).

Prior to describing specific strategies and models to promote self-determination, it is important to note that the educational climate in which efforts to promote self-determination occur has changed since the early 1990s when the self-determination initiative was launched. The Individuals with Disabilities Education Act (IDEA) Amendments of 1997 (PL 105-17) included requirements that the individualized education programs (IEPs) of all students with disabilities contain statements regarding how the child's disability affects involvement with and progress in the general education curriculum and measurable goals and program modifications to ensure such involvement and progress (Wehmeyer, Lance, & Bashinski, 2002; Wehmeyer, Lattin, & Agran, 2001). These requirements, referred to as the "access to the general educaton curriculum mandates," were intended to align special education practice with standards-based reform and school accountability efforts codified in the federal No Child Left Behind (NCLB) legislation.

Although the self-determination initiative was introduced within the context of U.S. Department of Education efforts to promote transition services and influence outcomes for students with disabilities, the access to the general education curriculum initiative was introduced within the context of efforts to align special education practices with prevailing reform efforts, primarily standards-based reform, and to impact student performance in core content areas. This emphasis on core content areas has been amplified by the steady progression of the implementation of assessment-based accountability mechanisms aligned to state and local standards. This is accompanied by an increased emphasis on the importance of evidence-based practices to improve instruction in core content areas such as reading and math. Wehmeyer, Field, Doren, Jones, and Mason (2004) identified two ways in which promoting self-determination will, in fact, promote access to the general education curriculum.

First, state and local standards frequently include goals and objectives that pertain to component elements of self-determined behavior. By identifying where in the general curriculum all students are expected to learn skills and knowledge related to the component elements of self-determined behavior, teachers can promote self-determination and promote progress in the general education curriculum. Second, model processes that identify how to promote access to the general education curriculum emphasize the importance of curriculum modifications, adaptations, and augmentations that enable students to interact with curricular content. Teaching students the skills that enable them to be more self-determined, such as goal setting and attainment, problem-solving, self-regulation and self-management, self-directed learning, coping and organizational, and leadership and teamwork skills, will also enable them to more effectively interact with the general education curriculum.

Infusing Instruction to Promote
Self-Determination in the General Education Curriculum

Infusing instruction on component elements of self-determined behavior (Table 2.1) into instruction across content areas provides the first focus for promoting self-determination. This section briefly identifies some key strategies to achieve this instructional outcome.

Goal Setting   Goal setting and attainment skills are critical to students with disabilities becoming more self-determined. Goals specify what a person wishes to achieve and act as regulators of human behavior. If a person sets a goal, then it increases the probability that he or she will perform behaviors related to that goal (Latham & Locke, 1991). The process of promoting goal-setting and attainment skills involves teaching students to: 1) identify and define a goal clearly and concretely, 2) develop a series of objectives or tasks to achieve the goal, and 3) specify the actions necessary to achieve the desired outcome. At each step, students must make choices and decisions about what goals they wish to pursue and what actions they wish to take to achieve their goals. Goal-setting activities can be easily incorporated into a variety of transition-related activities and across multiple instructional areas, as well as in the educational planning process, including through student-directed planning activities such as those discussed subsequently.

Research has suggested some general strategies to follow to make goals both meaningful and attainable for students with disabilities. First, goals should be challenging for the student. They should not be so challenging that the student cannot attain them, as this will lead to frustration and withdrawal from participation, but they must provide enough motivation for the student to work to attain them. If goals are too easy, then there is neither motivation to engage in the work necessary to attain them, nor is there a feeling of accomplishment after achieving them. Although it is preferable for students to participate in setting their own goals, at whatever level is appropriate given the nature of their disability, if this is not possible and goals need to be set by teachers, then the student's preferences and interests should be incorporated into the goal to increase the student's motivation to pursue the goal. Goals that have personal meaning are more likely to be attained (Doll & Sands, 1998).

Choice Making   Choice making (e.g., the expression of a preference between two or more options) has received considerable attention in the self-determination literature. One of the early impetuses for the educational emphasis on self-determination in the disability field was the increasing recognition of the lack of choice-making opportunities available to people with disabilities (Dunlap, Kern-Dunlap, Clarke, & Robbins, 1994; Stancliffe & Wehmeyer, 1995) and the negative impact this had both on behavior and development.

Promoting choice making has several benefits. First, research has found that when students with disabilities are provided opportunities to make choices, reductions in problem behavior and increases in adaptive behaviors are observed (Shogren et al., 2004). Second, by making choices, students, particularly younger children, learn that they can exert control over their environment. For students to fully understand the process of choice making, including the various effects of making certain choices, choices need to be real and meaningful for students. Some students may need to learn how to make choices, particularly if the student's previous opportunities to do so have been restricted. To do this, picture cues can be used to teach students to choose between two or more depicted activities, with the selection of an activity followed immediately by performance of the activity (Bambara & Ager, 1992). A variety of adaptive equipment, ranging from picture communication systems to computer technology, can be used to support students with more severe disabilities to indicate their preferences. Such strategies may be particularly helpful for students with autism, given their preference for information in a concrete, visual form.

Choice opportunities can and should be infused through the school day. Students can be provided opportunities to choose within or between instructional activities. They can also choose with whom they engage in a task, where they engage in an activity, and if they complete an activity (Brown, Appel, Corsi, & Wenig, 1993).

Problem Solving A problem is an activity or task for which a solution is not known or readily apparent. The process of solving a problem involves: 1) identifying and defining the problem, 2) listing possible solutions, 3) identifying the impact of each solution, 4) making a judgment about a preferred solution, and 5) evaluating the efficacy of the judgment (D'Zurilla & Goldfried, 1971). Developing effective social problem-solving skills is central to the process of becoming self-determined. These skills are central to a student's capacity to interact with other people and to cope with problems that arise in social contexts.

A number of strategies to promote problem solving have been evaluated for students with disabilities. Bauminger (2002) developed a curriculum to teach students with autism social and interpersonal problem-solving skills. Students were taught about social concepts, such as starting a conversation, and then presented a vignette of a student having difficulty implementing the skill. Students went through an 8-stage problem-solving process with their teacher in which they: 1) defined the problem, 2) discussed the emotions associated with the problem, 3) defined the alternative social actions, 4) considered the consequences of each alternative, 5) made a decision about the best alternative, 6) role-played the solution with their teacher, 7) received homework to practice the social skill covered in the lesson at home with peers, and 8) received feedback from the teacher on the homework. After 7 months, students generated more appropriate solutions to problems faced in social situations and initiated more social interactions with their peers.

Bernard-Opitz, Sriram, and Nakhoda-Sapuan (2001) developed a computer program to teach students with developmental disabilities social problem-solving skills. The program first presented pictures or videos of people experiencing social conflicts. The program guided students through an animated problem-solving process in which they were asked to generate alternative solutions. After identifying an alternate solution, a video clip of the actors resolving the problem was presented. As students had repeated experience with the program, they generated more alternative solutions. The increase in the generation of solutions observed in both of these studies is important, as research suggests that generating more solutions to a problem often leads to a better resolution of the problem (D'Zurilla & Nezu, 1980).

Decision Making   A decision-making process involves coming to a judgment about which solution is best at a given time. Making effective decisions typically involves: 1) identifying alternative courses of action, 2) identifying the possible consequences of each action, 3) assessing the probability of each consequence occurring, 4) choosing the best alternative, and 5) implementing the decision (Beyth-Marom, Fischhoff, Quadrel, & Furby, 1991). Although the ability to engage in this process develops with age, research has shown that young children can engage in a systematic decision-making process, often by reducing and simplifying the steps in the decision-making process, although they are not as effective as older students (Crone, Vendel, & van der Molen, 2003). Thus, working to promote systematic decision-making skills is best addressed at the secondary level, whereas at the elementary level, a focus on choice making and problem solving can support the development of effective decision-making skills later in life.

Studies have shown repeatedly that adolescents with disabilities can effectively participate in the decision-making process (Taylor, Adelman, & Kaser Boyd, 1983, 1985; Wehmeyer & Lawrence, 1995). In addition, research has suggested that students with disabilities want to be involved in decisions related to their life. For example, Ruef and Turnbull (2002) conducted a qualitative study of the perspective of adults with cognitive disabilities and/or autism on their problem behavior and found that participants repeatedly said they wanted to have a "voice" in their lives and be actively involved in decisions related to their supports, their living arrangements, and their employment. They also wanted to learn skills that would enable them to exert control over these processes.

To support students with disabilities to acquire decision-making skills, a number of strategies can be implemented throughout the student's educational career. Early on, students should be provided a wide array of choice opportunities and receive instruction regarding how to make effective choices, as discussed previously. As students age, they should be provided overt instruction in the decision-making process. A number of curricular approaches have been developed to promote decision-making skills (see Baron & Brown, 1991), all of which can be individualized based on a student's learning and support needs. When teaching decision-making skills, opportunities to make decisions should be imbedded in the curriculum. By supporting students to make decisions in "real-world" situations, they will better develop their ability to conceptualize and generalize the decision-making process.

Self-Regulation and Student-Directed Learning   Each of the aforementioned areas are important to enable students to self-regulate their behavior and their lives. Self-regulation is the process of setting goals, developing action plans to achieve those goals, implementing and following the action plans, evaluating the outcomes of the action plan, and changing action plans if the goal was not achieved (Mithaug, Mithaug, Agran, Martin, & Wehmeyer, 2003). The skills associated with self-regulation enable students to examine their environments, evaluate their repertoire of possible responses, and implement and evaluate a response (Whitman, 1990). A lack of ability to self-regulate one's behavior has been identified as one of the greatest problems facing students receiving special education services (Agran, Martin, & Mithaug, 1989).

Student-directed learning strategies involve teaching students strategies that enable them to modify and regulate their own behavior (Agran, King-Sears, Wehmeyer, & Copeland, 2003). The emphasis in such strategies is shifted from teacher-mediated and directed instruction to student-directed instruction. Research in education and rehabilitation has shown that student-directed learning strategies are as successful, and often more successful, as teacher-directed learning strategies, and these strategies are effective means to increase independence and productivity. A variety of strategies have been used to teach students with disabilities how to manage their own behavior or direct learning. Among the most commonly used strategies are picture cues and antecedent cue regulation strategies, self-instruction, self-monitoring, self-evaluation, and self-reinforcement. These are briefly introduced next (see Agran et al., 2003, for a comprehensive treatment of student-directed learning strategies).

Picture cues and antecedent cue regulation strategies involve the use of visual or audio cues that students use to guide their behavior. Visual cues typically involve photographs, illustrations, or line drawings of steps in a task that support students to complete an activity that consists of a sequence of tasks. Audio cues include prerecorded, taped directions or instructions that the students can listen to as they perform a task. Emerging technologies, such as handheld computers, provide new and potentially powerful vehicles to deliver visual or auditory cues to learners. Picture cues and antecedent cue regulation strategies have been used to teach individuals with intellectual disability complex work task sequences (Bambara & Cole, 1997; Wacker & Berg, 1993) and to promote on-task behavior and independent work performance (MacDuff, Krantz, & McClannahan, 1993; Mithaug, Martin, Agran, & Rusch, 1988).

Self-instruction involves teaching students to provide their own verbal cues prior to the execution of target behaviors. Students and adults with intellectual disabilities have been taught to use self-instruction to solve a variety of work problems (Agran & Moore, 1994; Hughes & Rusch, 1989), to complete multistep sequences (Agran, Fodor-Davis, & Moore, 1986), and to generalize responding across changing work environments (Agran & Moore, 1994). Graham and Harris (1989) found that a self-instructional strategy improved the essay composition skills of students with learning disabilities. Agran, Salzberg, and Stowitschek (1987) found self-instructional strategies increased the percentages of initiations with a work supervisor when five employees with mental retardation ran out of materials or needed assistance.

Self-monitoring involves teaching students to observe whether they have performed a targeted behavior and whether the response met whatever existing criteria were present. Several applications were reported in the research literature, including the effects of self-monitoring on facilitating job task changes (Sowers, Verdi, Bourbeau, & Sheehan, 1985) and evaluating how often a task was completed (Mace, Shapiro, West, Campbell, & Altman, 1986). Self-monitoring and self-recording procedures have been shown to improve the motivation and performance of students with disabilities. McCarl, Svobodny, and Beare (1991) found that teaching three students with intellectual disabilities to record progress on classroom assignments improved on-task behavior for all students and an increase in productivity for two of the three. Kapadia and Fantuzzo (1988) used self-monitoring procedures to increase attention to academic tasks for students with developmental disabilities and behavior problems. Lovett and Haring (1989) showed that self-recording activities enabled adults with intellectual disability to improve task completion of daily living activities. Chiron and Gerken (1983) found that students with intellectual disabilities who charted progress on school reading activities showed significant increases in reading level.

Self-evaluation involves teaching the student to compare his or her performance (as tracked through self-monitoring) with a desired goal or outcome. Schunk (1981) showed that students who verbalized cognitive strategies related to evaluating their study and work habits had increased math achievement scores. Brownell, Colletti, Ersner-Hershfield, Hershfield, and Wilson (1977) found that students who determined their performance standards demonstrated increased time on-task when compared with students operating under imposed standards.

Self-reinforcement involves teaching students to administer consequences to themselves (e.g., verbally telling themselves they did a good job). Self-reinforcement allows students to provide themselves with reinforcers that are accessible and immediate. Given access to self-administered reinforcement, behavior change may be greatly facilitated. Lagomarcino and Rusch (1989) used a combination of self-reinforcement and self-monitoring procedures to improve the work performance of a student with mental retardation in a community setting. Moore, Agran, and Fodor-Davis (1989) used a combination of student-directed activities, including self-instruction, goal setting, and self-reinforcement, to improve the production rate of workers with mental retardation.

Self-Advocacy Students with disabilities need to learn the skills to advocate on their own behalf. To be an effective self-advocate, students have to learn both how to advocate and what to advocate for. There are ample opportunities for students to practice and learn self-advocacy skills within the context of the educational planning process. Too often, students' perspectives have been lost because they have not had the opportunities or the skills to express their perspective within the IEP, transition, or general educational planning meetings. A first step to enabling students to express their wants and needs during these meetings is educating students about their rights and responsibilities in these areas. They can be educated about their educational rights and responsibilities under IDEA; about their civil rights under the Americans with Disabilities Act (ADA) of 1990 (PL 101-336); or, more generally, about the rights available to citizens. Instructional strategies have been developed for teaching such knowledge to students with disabilities (see Wehmeyer et al., 2003).

When teaching students how to advocate for themselves, the focus should be on teaching students how to be assertive, how to effectively communicate their perspective (either verbally or in written or pictorial form), how to negotiate, how to compromise, and how to deal with systems and bureaucracies. Students need to be provided real-world opportunities to practice these skills. This can be done by embedding opportunities for self-advocacy within the school day, by allowing students to set up a class schedule, work out their supports with a resource room teacher or other support provider, or participate in IEP and transition meetings.

Perceptions of Efficacy and Control People who have positive perceptions of their efficacy believe they can perform the behavior required to achieve a desired outcome (Bandura, 1977; Bandura & Cervone, 2000). Furthermore, individuals also have efficacy expectations, which are beliefs about the probability of the performance of a given behavior leading to the desired outcome. These two constructs are both necessary for the performance of the skills discussed previously. For example, if a student does not believe that he or she can perform a given behavior, then he or she will not engage in it (i.e., if a student with a disability does not believe he or she has the requisite skills for communicating with his or her peers, then he or she will not make attempts to communicate). However, even if a student does believe he or she can perform a given behavior, but holds low expectations for the attainment of the desired result from the behavior because previous attempts to engage in the behavior have been ignored or disregarded, then he or she is still likely not to perform the behavior.

Research has shown that students with disabilities tend to have less adaptive perceptions of efficacy and outcome expectations than do students without disabilities (Wehmeyer et al., 2003). The same has been found concerning the perceptions of students with disabilities about their ability to exert control over their environment. People who believe they have the ability to exert control over their lives and outcomes tend to be described as having an internal locus of control; whereas people who perceive that others are largely controlling their lives and outcomes are described as having an external locus of control (Rotter, 1954, 1966). Research has shown that students' perceptions of control and efficacy interact with academic, social, and behavioral outcomes, with students who have more adaptive perceptions of their abilities in each of these areas experiencing more positive outcomes (Hagborg, 1996; Ollendick, Green, Francis, & Baum, 1991).

Students must be provided with opportunities to develop adaptive perceptions of their efficacy in performing given behaviors and their ability to exert control over their lives. By enabling students to engage in problem solving, goal setting, choice making, and decision making, they can learn that they have control over their outcomes and develop confidence in their ability to perform these behaviors and achieve their desired outcomes. Both teacher and classroom characteristics can influence students' perceptions of efficacy and control. Overly controlling environments can diminish students' perceptions of their ability to exert control and engage in actions that enable them to develop adaptive efficacy expectations. It is important for teachers to work to empower students to be active participants in their classrooms.

Self-Awareness and Self-Knowledge

For students to become more self-realizing, they must possess a reasonably accurate understanding of their strengths, abilities, unique learning and support needs, and limitations. Furthermore, they must know how to utilize this understanding to maximize success and progress. However, like perceptions of efficacy and control, self-awareness and knowledge are not things that can simply be taught through direct instruction. Instead, students acquire this knowledge by interacting with their environment. Unfortunately, students with disabilities often learn to identify what they *cannot* do instead of what they can. This skews students' perceptions of themselves and influences how they interact with people and systems they encounter.

Thus, it is important to promote *realistic* self-awareness and knowledge in students with disabilities. For example, Faherty (2000) developed an approach to guide children and youth with autism spectrum disorders through the process of developing an understanding of their strengths, their abilities, and the impact of autism on their lives. The process has a number of activities that encourage students to think about their strengths and abilities and contains activities to support students to develop and reflect on how they learn, their sensory experiences, their artistic and technological abilities, their social and communication skills, their thoughts, and why they sometimes feel upset. It also helps students reflect on the people in their lives, including their school experiences

Self-Determined Learning Model of Instruction

Like all educators, special education teachers use a variety of *teaching models*, which is defined as "a plan or pattern that can be used to shape curriculums (long-term courses of study), to design instructional materials, and to guide instruction in the classroom and other settings" (Joyce & Weil, 1980, p. 1). Such models are derived from theories about human behavior, learning, or cognition, and effective teachers employ multiple models of teaching, taking into account the unique characteristics of the learner and types of learning. A teacher may use the role-playing model to teach social behaviors, social simulation and social inquiry models to examine social problems and solutions, assertiveness training to teach self-advocacy skills, or a training model to teach vocational skills. Likewise, special educators employ more traditional, cognitively based models of teaching, such as the concept attainment model to teach thinking skills, the memory model for increasing the retention of facts, or inductive thinking and inquiry training models to teach reasoning and academic skills. The teaching model most frequently adopted by special educators is the contingency management model, drawing from operant psychology.

The common theme across these teaching models is that they are teacher-directed. Although they provide direction for strategy and curriculum development activities that can teach components of self-determination, none adequately provide teachers a model to truly enable young people to become causal agents in their lives. The *Self-Determined Learning Model of Instruction* (*SDLMI;* Mithaug, Wehmeyer, Agran, Martin, & Palmer, 1998) was developed to address this problem and is based on the component elements of self-determination, the process of self-regulated problem solving, and research on student-directed learning. It is appropriate for use with students with and without disabilities across a wide range of content areas and enables teachers to engage students in the totality of their educational program by increasing opportunities to self-direct learning and, in the process, to enhance student self-determination.

Implementation of the model consists of a three-phase instructional process depicted in Figures 2.2, 2.3, and 2.4. Each instructional phase presents a problem to be solved by the student. The student solves each problem by posing and answering a series of four Student Questions per phase that students learn, modify to make their own, and apply to reach self-selected goals. Each question is linked to a set of Teacher Objectives. Each instructional phase includes a list of Educational Supports that teachers can use to enable students to self-direct learning. In each instructional phase, the student is the primary agent for choices, decisions, and actions, even when eventual actions are teacher-directed.

The Student Questions are constructed to direct the student through a problem-solving sequence in each instructional phase. The solutions to the problems in each phase lead to the problem-solving sequence in the next phase. Teachers implementing

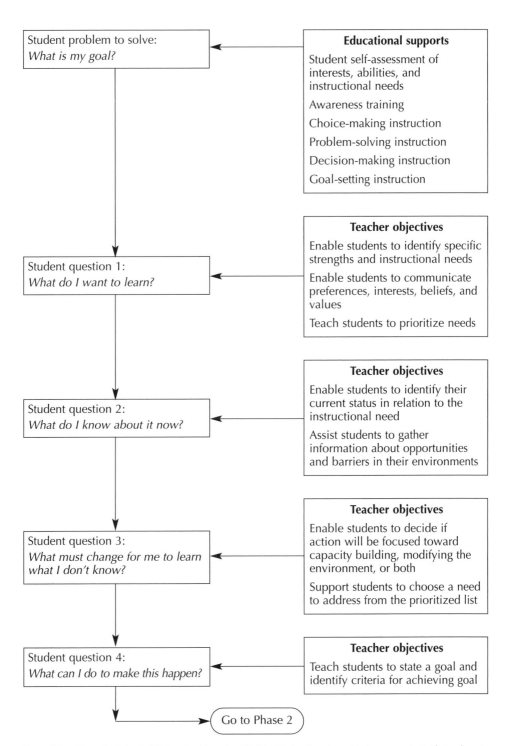

Phase 1: Set a goal

Student problem to solve:
What is my goal?

Educational supports

Student self-assessment of interests, abilities, and instructional needs

Awareness training

Choice-making instruction

Problem-solving instruction

Decision-making instruction

Goal-setting instruction

Student question 1:
What do I want to learn?

Teacher objectives

Enable students to identify specific strengths and instructional needs

Enable students to communicate preferences, interests, beliefs, and values

Teach students to prioritize needs

Student question 2:
What do I know about it now?

Teacher objectives

Enable students to identify their current status in relation to the instructional need

Assist students to gather information about opportunities and barriers in their environments

Student question 3:
What must change for me to learn what I don't know?

Teacher objectives

Enable students to decide if action will be focused toward capacity building, modifying the environment, or both

Support students to choose a need to address from the prioritized list

Student question 4:
What can I do to make this happen?

Teacher objectives

Teach students to state a goal and identify criteria for achieving goal

Go to Phase 2

Figure 2.2.   Phase 1 of the *Self-Determined Learning Model of Instruction.* (From Wehmeyer, M.L. [with Sands, D.J., Knowlton, H.E., & Kozleski, E.B.]. [2002]. *Teaching students with mental retardation: Providing access to the general curriculum* [p. 246]. Baltimore: Paul H. Brookes Publishing Co.)

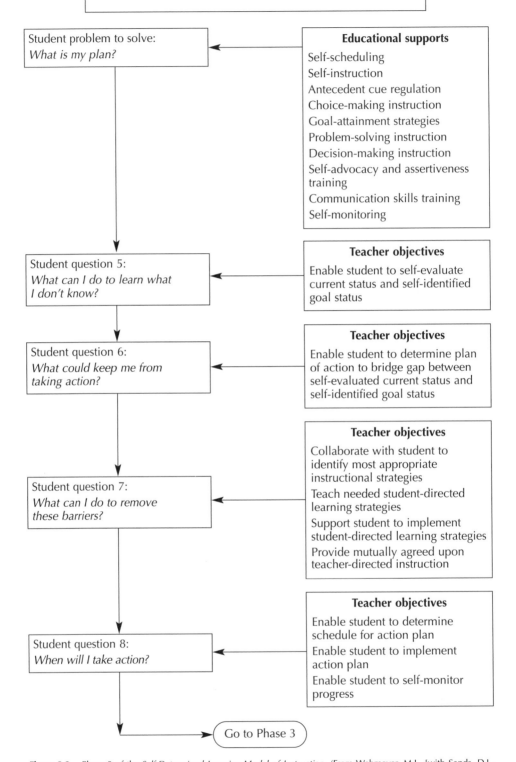

Figure 2.3. Phase 2 of the *Self-Determined Learning Model of Instruction.* (From Wehmeyer, M.L. [with Sands, D.J., Knowlton, H.E., & Kozleski, E.B.]. [2002]. *Teaching students with mental retardation: Providing access to the general curriculum* [p. 247]. Baltimore: Paul H. Brookes Publishing Co.)

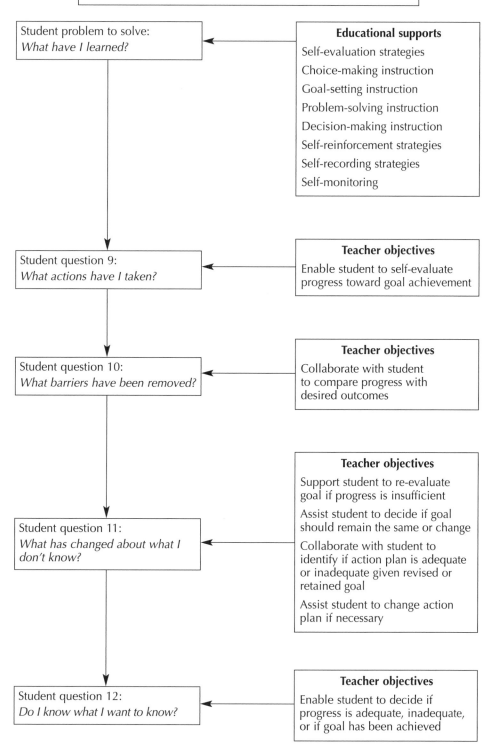

Phase 3: Adjust goal or plan

Student problem to solve:
What have I learned?

Educational supports
Self-evaluation strategies
Choice-making instruction
Goal-setting instruction
Problem-solving instruction
Decision-making instruction
Self-reinforcement strategies
Self-recording strategies
Self-monitoring

Student question 9:
What actions have I taken?

Teacher objectives
Enable student to self-evaluate
progress toward goal achievement

Student question 10:
What barriers have been removed?

Teacher objectives
Collaborate with student
to compare progress with
desired outcomes

Student question 11:
*What has changed about what I
don't know?*

Teacher objectives
Support student to re-evaluate
goal if progress is insufficient

Assist student to decide if goal
should remain the same or change

Collaborate with student to
identify if action plan is adequate
or inadequate given revised or
retained goal

Assist student to change action
plan if necessary

Student question 12:
Do I know what I want to know?

Teacher objectives
Enable student to decide if
progress is adequate, inadequate,
or if goal has been achieved

Figure 2.4. Phase 3 of the *Self-Determined Learning Model of Instruction.* (From Wehmeyer, M.L. [with Sands, D.J., Knowlton, H.E., & Kozleski, E.B.]. [2002]. *Teaching students with mental retardation: Providing access to the general curriculum* [p. 248]. Baltimore: Paul H. Brookes Publishing Co.)

the model teach students to solve a sequence of problems to construct a means-ends chain—a causal sequence—that moves them from where they are (an actual state of not having their needs and interests satisfied) to where they want to be (a goal state of having those needs and interests satisfied). Its function is to reduce or eliminate the discrepancy between what students want or need and what students currently have or know. We construct this means-end sequence by having students answer the questions that connect their needs and interests to their actions and results via goals and plans.

To answer the questions in this sequence, students must regulate their own problem solving by setting goals to meet needs, constructing plans to meet goals, and adjusting actions to complete plans. Thus, each instructional phase poses a problem the student must solve (*What is my goal? What is my plan? What have I learned?*) by, in turn, solving a series of problems posed by the questions in each phase. The four questions differ from phase to phase but represent identical steps in the problem-solving sequence. That is, students answering the questions must: 1) identify the problem, 2) identify potential solutions to the problem, 3) identify barriers to solving the problem, and 4) identify consequences of each solution. These steps are the fundamental steps in any problem-solving process and they form the means-end problem-solving sequence represented by the Student Questions in each phase and enable the student to solve the problem posed in each instructional phase.

Because the model itself is designed for teachers to implement, the language of the Student Questions is not written to be understood by every student, nor does the model assume that students have life experiences that enable them to fully answer each question. The Student Questions are written in first-person voice in a relatively simple format with the intention that they are the starting point for discussion between the teacher and the student. Some students will learn and use all 12 questions as they are written. Other students will need to have the questions rephrased to be more understandable. Still other students, due to the intensity of their instructional needs, may have the teacher paraphrase the questions.

The first time a teacher uses the model with a student, he or she will read the question with or to the student; discuss what the question means; and then, if necessary, change the wording to enable that student to better understand the intent of the question. Such wording changes must, however, be made so that the problem-solving intent of the question remains intact. For example, changing Student Question 1 from *What do I want to learn?* to *What is my goal?* changes the nature of the question. The Teacher Objectives associated with each student question provide direction for possible wording changes. It is perhaps less important that actual changes in the words occur than that students take ownership over the process and adopt the question as their own, instead of having questions imposed on them. Going through this process once, as the student progresses through the model, should result in a set of questions that a student accepts as his or her own.

The Teacher Objectives within the model are just that—the objectives a teacher will be trying to accomplish by implementing the model. In each instructional phase, the objectives are linked directly to the Student Questions. These objectives can be met by utilizing strategies provided in the Educational Supports section of the model. The Teacher Objectives provide, in essence, a road map to assist the teacher to enable the student to solve the problem stated in the Student Question. For example, regarding Student Question 1, *What do I want to learn?* Teacher Objectives linked to this question comprise the activities in which students should be engaged in order to answer this question. In this case, it involves enabling students to identify their specific strengths and instructional needs; to identify and communicate preferences, interests, beliefs, and values; and to prioritize their instructional needs. As teachers use the model, it is likely that they can generate more objectives that are relevant to the question, and they are encouraged to do so.

The model's emphasis on using instructional strategies and educational supports that are student-directed provides another means of teaching students to teach themselves. As important as this is, however, not every instructional strategy implemented will be student-directed. The purpose of any model of teaching is to promote student learning and growth. There are circumstances in which the most effective instructional method or strategy to achieve a particular educational outcome will be a teacher-directed strategy. Students who are considering what plan of action to implement to achieve a self-selected goal can recognize that teachers have expertise in instructional strategies and take full advantage of that expertise.

We have conducted research with students with disabilities to determine the efficacy of the model. The fundamental purpose of any model of instruction is to promote student learning. Teachers use models of instruction to drive curriculum and assessment development and to design instructional methods, materials, and strategies, all with the intent of improving the quality of the instructional experience and, presumably, enhancing student achievement. Thus, the first requirement of any model of instruction is that teachers can use the model to "teach" students educationally valued skills or concepts.

Wehmeyer, Palmer, et al. (2000) conducted a field test of the *SDLMI* with 21 teachers responsible for the instruction of adolescents receiving special education services in two states who identified a total of 40 students with mental retardation, learning disabilities, or emotional or behavioral disorders. The field test indicated that the model was effective in enabling students to attain educationally valued goals. In addition, there were significant differences in pre- and postintervention scores on self-determination, with postintervention scores more positive than preintervention scores.

Agran et al. (2000) conducted a study using a single subject design to examine the efficacy of the *SDLMI* for adolescents with severe disabilities. Students collaborated with their teachers to implement the first phase of the model and, as a result, identified one goal as a target behavior. Prior to implementing the second phase of the model, teachers and researchers collected baseline data on student performance of these goals. At staggered intervals subsequent to baseline data collection, teachers implemented the model with students, and data collection continued through the end of instructional activities and into a maintenance phase. As before, the model enabled teachers to teach students educationally valued goals. In total, 17 of the participants achieved their personal goals at or above the teacher-rated expected outcome levels. Only two students were rated as indicating no progress on the goal.

Wehmeyer, Lattimore, et al. (2003) modified the *SDLMI* for use specifically with people in the vocational rehabilitation (VR) process and found that VR consumers were able to self-set and achieve vocational goals and achieve more positive VR outcomes.

Student Involvement in Transition Planning and Leadership Development

Another important component of enhancing self-determination is promoting active involvement in transition planning. Test et al. (2004) conducted an extensive review of the literature pertaining to student involvement and determined that students across disability categories can be successfully involved in transition planning, and a number of programs, including those mentioned subsequently, are effective in increasing student involvement. Martin, Marshall, and Sale (2004) conducted a 3-year study of middle, junior, and senior high school IEP meetings and found that the presence of students at IEP meetings had considerable benefits, including increasing parental involvement and improving the probability that a student's strengths, needs, and interests would be discussed. Research (Mason, Field, & Sawilowsky, 2004; Wehmeyer, Agran, & Hughes, 2000) has found that teachers value student involvement, though they fall short of actually implementing practices to promote this outcome.

Involvement in education planning, decision making, and instruction can take many forms, from students generating their own IEP goals and objectives, to tracking their progress on self-selected goals or objectives, to running their own IEP meeting. It is important to emphasize that it is not what the student does in the meeting that is critical, but, instead, the degree to which the student is an equal partner in and, to the greatest extent possible, in control of his or her planning. Students with severe disabilities can be involved in their educational program every bit as much as students with less severe disabilities. Student involvement may look very different in these cases, and students with more severe disabilities may not be able to make independent decisions or solve problems, but that is not the criteria by which we should judge student involvement. It is, instead, the degree to which the student is actively engaged in his or her planning and education program.

There are multiple advantages to student involvement. Test and colleagues (2004) reviewed studies examining efforts to promote student involvement and concluded that there was clear evidence that such efforts enhanced student involvement in educational planning. Research has shown that student involvement in goal setting and decision making results in enhanced performance and motivation (Doll & Sands, 1998; Wehmeyer, 1998). Similarly, student involvement in instruction can enhance educational goal achievement and support positive adult outcomes (Agran et al., 2003). Student involvement in the educational process is a good way to teach and allow students to practice skills important to self-determination (e.g., goal setting, decision making, negotiation), self-advocacy, leadership, and teamwork.

There are several programs designed to promote student involvement, and space restrictions allow only a brief description of several resources.

ChoiceMaker Self-Determination Transition Curriculum and Program The *ChoiceMaker Self-Determination Transition Curriculum* (Martin & Marshall, 1995) consists of three sections: 1) Choosing Goals, 2) Expressing Goals, and 3) Taking Action. Each section contains from two to four teaching goals and numerous teaching objectives addressing six transition areas. Included are: 1) an assessment tool; 2) Choosing Goals lessons; 3) the Self-Directed IEP, and 4) Taking Action lessons. The program includes a criterion-referenced self-determination transition assessment tool that

Table 2.2. Steps for transition planning from the *Choice-Maker* program

Step	Activity
1	Begin the meeting by stating the purpose.
2	Introduce everyone.
3	Review past goals and performance.
4	Ask for others' feedback.
5	State your school and transition goals.
6	Ask questions if you don't understand.
7	Deal with differences in opinion.
8	State the support you will need.
9	Summarize your goals.
10	Close meeting by thanking everyone.
11	Work on IEP goals all year.

Source: Martin & Marshall (1995).

matches the curricular sections. The Choosing Goals lessons enable students to learn the necessary skills and personal information needed to articulate their interests, skills, limits, and goals across one or more self-selected transition areas. The Self-Directed IEP lessons enable students to learn the leadership skills necessary to manage their IEP meeting and publicly disclose their interests, skills, limits, and goals identified through the Choosing Goals lessons. Rather than be passive participants at their IEP meetings, students learn to lead their meeting to the greatest extent of their ability. These lessons teach students 11 steps for leading their own staffing (see Table 2.2).

The Taking Action materials enable students to learn how to break their long-range goals into specific goals that can be accomplished in a week. Students learn how they will attain their goals by deciding: 1) a standard for goal performance; 2) a means to get performance feedback; 3) what motivates them to do it; 4) the strategies they will use; 5) needed supports; and 6) schedules. There have been four studies examining the efficacy of the *ChoiceMaker* materials (Allen, Smith, Test, Flowers, & Wood, 2001; Cross, Cooke, Wood, & Test, 1999; Snyder, 2002; Snyder & Shapiro, 1997) documenting positive effects on student self-determination, skills in goal setting and leadership, and student involvement in educational planning.

Whose Future is it Anyway? A Student-Directed Transition Planning Program

Whose Future is it Anyway? (Wehmeyer, Lawrence, et al., 2004) consists of 36 sessions introducing students to the concept of transition and transition planning and enabling students to self-direct instruction related to 1) self- and disability-awareness; 2) making decisions about transition-related outcomes; 3) identifying and securing community resources to support transition services; 4) writing and evaluating transition goals and objectives; 5) communicating effectively in small groups; and 6) developing skills to become an effective team member, leader, or self-advocate.

The materials are student-directed in that they are written for students as end-users. The level of support needed by students to complete activities varies a great deal.

Some students with difficulty reading or writing need one-to-one support to progress through the materials; others can complete the process independently. The materials make every effort to ensure that students retain this control while at the same time receiving the support they need to succeed.

Section 1 (Getting to Know You) introduces the concept of transition and educational planning; provides information about transition requirements in IDEA; and enables students to identify who has attended past planning meetings, who is required to be present at meetings, and who they want involved in their planning process. Later, they are introduced to four primary transition outcome areas (employment, community living, postsecondary education, and recreation and leisure). Activities throughout the process focus on these transition outcome areas. The remainder of the sessions in this first section discuss the topic of disability and disability awareness. Students identify their unique characteristics, including their abilities and interests. Participants then identify unique learning needs related to their disability. Finally, students identify their unique learning needs resulting from their disability.

In the second section (Making Decisions), students learn a simple problem-solving process by working through each step in the process to make a decision about a potential living arrangement and then apply the process to make decisions about the three other transition outcome areas. The third section (How to Get What You Need, Sec. 101) enables students to locate community resources identified in previous planning meetings that are intended to provide supports in each of the transition outcome areas. Section 4 (Goals, Objectives, and the Future) enables learners to apply a set of rules to identify transition-related goals and objectives that are currently on their IEP or transition planning form, evaluate these goals based on their own transition interests and abilities, and develop additional goals to take to their next planning meeting. Students learn what goals and objectives are, how they should be written, and ways to track progress on goals and objectives.

The fifth section (Communicating) introduces effective communication strategies for small-group situations, such as the transition planning meetings. Students work through sessions that introduce different types of communication (e.g., verbal, body language) and how to interpret these communicative behaviors, the differences between aggressive and assertive communication, how to effectively negotiate and compromise, when to use persuasion, and other skills that will enable them to be more effective communicators during transition planning meetings. The final section (Thank You, Honorable Chairperson) enables students to learn types and purposes of meetings, steps to holding effective meetings, and roles of the meeting chairperson and team members. Students are encouraged to work with school personnel to take a meaningful role in planning for and participating in the meeting.

Students are encouraged to work on one session per week during the weeks between their previous transition planning meeting and the next scheduled meeting. The final two sessions review the previous sessions and provide a refresher for students as they head into their planning meeting. These materials have been field tested and validated for use with students with cognitive disabilities (Wehmeyer & Lawrence, 1995, in press) and shown to impact student self-determination, self-efficacy for educational planning, and student involvement.

Next S.T.E.P.: Student Transition and Educational Planning A third student-directed transition-planning program is the *Next S.T.E.P.* curriculum (Halpern et al., 1997). The curriculum uses video and print materials developed for specific audiences (students, teachers, family members) to help students become motivated to engage in transition planning, self-evaluate transition needs, identify and select transition goals and activities, assume responsibility for conducting their own transition planning meeting, and monitor the implementation of their transition plans.

The curriculum consists of 16 lessons, clustered into 4 instructional units, designed to be delivered in a 50-minute class period. These lessons include teacher and student materials, videos, guidelines for involving parents and family members, and a process for tracking student progress. Unit 1 (Getting Started) introduces and overviews transition planning, which enables students to understand the transition planning process and to motivate them to participate. Unit 2 (Self-Exploration and Self-Evaluation) includes six lessons that focus on student self-evaluation. Students work through activities that identify unique interests, strengths, and weaknesses in various adult-outcome oriented areas. At the end of this unit, students complete the student form of the *Transition Skills Inventory*, a 72-item rating instrument assessing how well the student is doing in four transition areas: 1) personal life, 2) jobs, 3) education and training, and 4) living on one's own. The student's self-evaluation of these areas are combined with similar evaluations by his or her teacher and a family member to form a basis for future transition planning activities. Students are encouraged to discuss differences of opinion between the teacher or family member evaluations and their own self-evaluation and to resolve these discrepancies either before or during the transition planning meeting.

Unit 3 (Developing Goals and Activities) includes five lessons regarding transition goal identification in the four areas comprising the *Transition Skills Inventory*. Students identify their hopes and dreams, then select from a range of potential goals in each area, narrowing the total set of transition goals to four or five goals that they prefer. In addition, students choose activities that will help them pursue the goals they have selected. Unit 4 (Putting a Plan into Place) includes three lessons that prepare students for their transition planning meeting. The lessons emphasize the implementation of their plan and work with students to ensure that they monitor their progress and, if necessary, make adjustments. Zhang (2001) examined the efficacy of the *Next S.T.E.P.* materials and found implementation significantly impacted student self-determination.

The Self-Advocacy Strategy for Education and Transition Planning Van Reusen et al. (2002) developed a procedure that stresses the importance of self-advocacy to enhance student motivation and that is "designed to enable students to systematically gain a sense of control and influence over their own learning and development" (p. 1). Students progress through a series of lesson plans focusing on seven instructional stages. Stage 1 (Orient and Make Commitments) broadly introduces education and transition planning meetings, the program itself, and how participation can increase student power and control in this process. Stage 2 (Describe) defines and provides detailed information about transition and education meetings and advantages students experience if they participate. In this stage, the I PLAN steps of student participation are introduced. These steps provide a simple algorithm that students can use to chart their participation in planning meetings.

In Stage 3 (Model and Prepare), the teacher models the I PLAN steps so students can see the process in action. Students complete an Inventory, Step 1 in the I PLAN process, resulting in information they can use at their conference. In Stage 4 (Verbal Practice), students are asked questions to make sure they know what to do during each step of the I PLAN strategy and then verbally rehearse each of the steps. In Stage 5 (Group Practice and Feedback), students participate in a simulated group conference (after they have mastered the I PLAN steps). The student receives feedback from the teacher and other students, and the group generates suggestions on where the student might improve. The simulated conference is audio- or videotaped for future reference.

Stage 6 (Individual Practice and Feedback) allows the student to meet independently with the teacher for practice; feedback; and, eventually, mastery. The audio- or videotape from the previous stage is reviewed, and students provide a self-evaluation of their performance. The student and instructor work together to improve areas of self-identified need and engage in another simulated conference that is also audio- or videotaped and used to document improvement and reevaluate performance. Stage 7 (Generalization) is intended to generalize the I PLAN strategy to actual conferences. This stage has three phases: 1) preparing for and conducting the planning conference, 2) preparing for other uses of the strategy, and 3) preparing for subsequent conferences. Van Reusen and colleagues (1989, 2002) have shown that the I PLAN strategy can be successfully implemented with students with disabilities and results in increased motivation and participation.

TAKE CHARGE for the Future   *TAKE CHARGE for the Future* (Powers et al., 1996) is a student-directed, collaborative model to promote student involvement in educational and transition planning. The model is an adaptation of a validated approach, referred to as *TAKE CHARGE*, to promote the self-determination of youth with and without disabilities (Powers et al., 1998). *TAKE CHARGE* uses four primary components or strategies to promote adolescent development of self-determination: 1) skill facilitation, 2) mentoring, 3) peer support, and 4) parent support. For example, *TAKE CHARGE* introduces youth to three major skills areas needed to take charge in one's life: 1) achievement skills, 2) partnership skills, and 3) coping skills. Youth involved in the *TAKE CHARGE* process are matched with successful adults of the same gender who experience similar challenges, share common interests, and are involved in peer support activities throughout (Powers et al., 1996). Parent support is provided via information and technical assistance and written materials.

TAKE CHARGE for the Future uses the same set of core strategies to enable learners with disabilities to participate in their planning meeting. Students are provided self-help materials and coaching to identify their transition goals; to organize and conduct transition planning meetings; and to achieve their goals through the application of problem solving, self-regulation, and partnership management strategies. Concurrently, youth participate in self-selected mentorship and peer support activities to increase their transition focused knowledge and skills. Their parents are also provided with information and support to promote their capacities to encourage their sons' or daughters' active involvement in transition planning. Powers, Turner, Matuszewski,

Wilson, and Phillips (2001) conducted a control-group study and found that the *TAKE CHARGE* materials had a positive impact on student involvement.

Student-Led IEPs: A Guide for Student Involvement McGahee, Mason, Wallace, and Jones (2001) developed a guide to student-led IEPs (available on-line at http://www.nichcy.org/stuguid.asp) that introduces students to the IEP process, the purpose of an IEP, and suggestions for writing an IEP. Mason, McGahee-Kovac, Johnson, and Stillerman (2002) showed that students who used this process knew more about their IEP and showed enhanced self-confidence and self-advocacy.

Leadership Development Larson (2000) suggested that the youth of today do not appear to be leaders in their own lives, that they seem to be "bored and unexcited about their lives" (p. 170). One reason for this, according to Larson, is that adults do not provide opportunities for young people to experience leadership. Instead of providing them with instances to lead, parents and other figures of authority tend to shelter youth. Although they do this to protect young people from harm, they may also be depriving them from acquiring the attributes necessary for them to become more independent and self-determined.

Imada, Doyle, Brock, and Goddard (2002) noted that becoming a good leader involves understanding and being able to demonstrate the building blocks of leadership. According to Imada et al., the first step in leadership development involves issues of self-knowledge and self-awareness, also important to self-determination. These include assessing one's personal values, strengths, and weaknesses, as well as likes and dislikes. The next step is developing a vision for the future. Students should be encouraged to dream about their future and what they want it to be like. Once students have developed a vision, the next step is constructing a plan to achieve the vision.

Though students may benefit from instruction to enhance leadership skills during the school day, and through the types of IEP-linked activities discussed previously, after- or out-of-school programs can be an important way to enhance the skills that students are learning in school (Froschi, Rousso, & Rubin, 2001). One visible effort in which issues of youth leadership development are brought to the forefront involves the Youth Leadership Forums (YLF) held around the country. There are numerous goals for YLF activities, including building a network of peers and mentors for students with disabilities, enabling youth to explore positive and negative aspects to living with a disability or handling discrimination, promoting career exploration, and informing youth of civil and legislative rights and advocacy. In addition, there are self-advocacy groups—consumer organized and controlled organizations that focus on self-advocacy—in most states, and teachers can be instrumental in linking youth with cognitive disabilities to these groups.

Infusing Self-Determination into 18–21 Programs

Students with more severe disabilities will likely receive educational services through the age of 21. It is important that high-quality 18–21 programs ensure a strong focus on self-determination. To that end, we have been engaged in the development and evaluation of a multistage model called *Beyond High School* (see Figure 2.5) to infuse

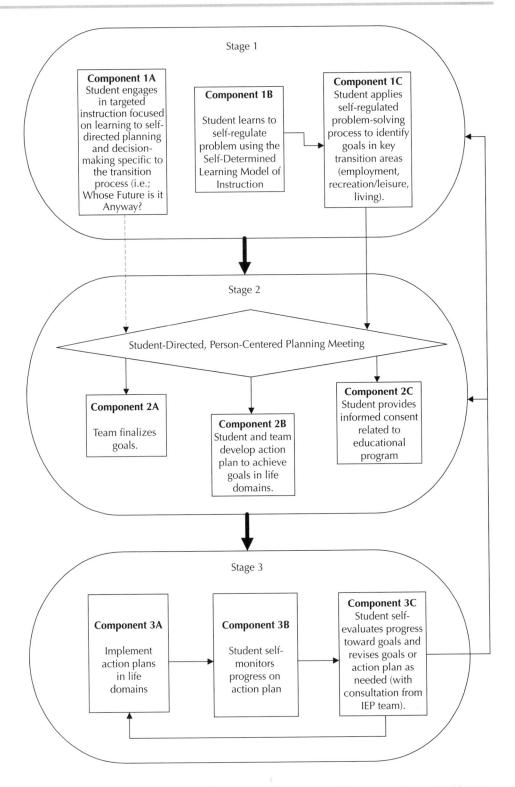

Figure 2.5.   *Beyond High School* 18–21 model to promote self-determination. (Adapted from Wehmeyer, Bolding, Yeager, & Davis, 2001.)

self-determination into quality 18–21 services and supports and to promote active student involvement (Wehmeyer, Garner, Lawrence, Yeager, & Davis, in press).

Beyond High School: Stage 1　This first stage of the *Beyond High School* model is designed to enable students to establish short- and long-term goals based on their own preferences, abilities, and interests. First, students are involved in targeted instruction teaching them to self-direct planning and decision making specific to the transition process. This could be accomplished through multiple informal or formal strategies and methods that prepare students to participate in or direct their educational planning process, such as those discussed previously. Next, students were taught to self-direct the transition goal-setting, action planning, and program implementation process using the *SDLMI*, again discussed previously. Once students learn this self-regulated learning process, they apply the first part of the *SDLMI* (*What is my goal?*) to identify goals in key transition areas, including employment, independent living, recreation and leisure, and postsecondary education.

Beyond High School: Stage 2　The second stage of the model involves convening a student-directed, person-centered planning meeting that brings together other stakeholders in the instructional process to work with students to refine goals, as needed, to support the student as he or she implements the second phase of the *SDLMI* (*What is my plan?*) and to enable the student to provide informed consent with regard to implementation of the instructional program. This meeting is not intended to be the mandated IEP meeting, although these activities certainly can occur at an IEP meeting. Instead, the meeting bears a closer resemblance to person-centered planning process in which stakeholders come together on a more frequent basis to identify hopes and dreams, natural supports, and so forth (Holburn & Vietz, 2002). This meeting varies from traditional person-centered planning meetings in scope, intent, and process. First, it is intended that this is the student's meeting. The teacher or person-centered planning facilitator should support the student, who will use the skills he or she acquired in the first phase of the model to present the goals he or she has generated. The second difference is that these student goals provide the foundation for the meeting's purpose and direction. Other stakeholders are encouraged to help the student refine the goals, more clearly define the goals, or identify objectives to reach the goals, but not to criticize or replace the goals. These goals will form only a subset of the total goals on a student's IEP, but the intent is that students have a forum to discuss their goals and gather the support of parents, family members, teachers, and others to make those goals achievable. This is also an opportune time to consider how each stakeholder can support and contribute to the student's efforts to attain those goals.

Beyond High School: Stage 3　During the final stage of the model, the student, with supports identified from the second stage, implements the plan, monitors his or her progress in achieving the goal, and evaluates the success of the plan, making revisions to the goal or the plan as warranted. This is accomplished using the strategies and questions comprising the third phase of the *SDLMI*.

Students involved in the field-test of the model were successful at achieving self-set transition goals across multiple domains (Wehmeyer et al., in press) and increased perceptions of their autonomy after involvement in the process. Anecdotal information provides further evidence of the degree to which students benefited from the process. One student completed the recreation and leisure goal he had set (to contact a volunteer center to find out how to volunteer) and then followed up on that to identify a specific volunteer situation related to his preferences, applied for the position, underwent orientation, and began the volunteer experience. Another student had as her goal to identify a list of questions and then interview a friend to determine if she would make a good roommate. This student and her family had long-term plans for her to room with this friend. In completing this goal, she recognized the need for her friend to interview her and then to discuss their mutual compatibility and did so. This student decided, in the end, that her friend might not be a compatible roommate for her or that there were issues they would need to resolve before that arrangement was made.

CONCLUSION

Promoting self-determination and student involvement in educational planning has become best practice in the education of students with disabilities, particularly with relation to transition planning and services. Students with disabilities who leave school as self-determined young people achieve more positive adult outcomes. Moreover, promoting student self-determination provides, as it were, a gateway to the general education curriculum for students with disabilities and can result in enhanced leadership skills. This chapter overviewed the methods, materials, and strategies to achieve the outcome that students with and without disabilities can become more self-determined. If educators are to achieve the outcomes envisioned by the transition mandates in IDEA, then they will need to ensure that students with disabilities are provided sufficient opportunities to learn these skills and strategies and to use them to play a meaningful role in their educational program, from planning to implementation.

STUDY QUESTIONS

1. Interview three parents of young people with disabilities who are in the IEP process. Discuss with them and write up how self-determination objectives could be infused into each IEP.

2. Interview two teenage students with disabilities and two without disabilities about their vocational aspirations and dreams. Compare and contrast their *different* views.

3. Pick one student with a disability and study his or her problem-solving strategies. Write this up as a short case study.

4. Self-advocacy is a very important skill for young people with disabilities. Give three examples of how self-determination instruction facilitates self-advocacy skills.

5. Select one student and implement the *Next S.T.E.P.* curriculum. Write a brief case study describing how well this curriculum worked to help this student.

RESOURCES

The *ChoiceMaker* materials are available from Sopris West Educational Services (http://www.sopriswest.com/swstore/product.asp?sku=629).

The *Whose Future is it Anyway?* materials can be ordered by contacting the Beach Center on Disability (http://www.beachcenter.org/).

The *Next S.T.E.P.* program is available from PRO-ED Publishing Company (http://www.proedinc.com/store/index.php?mode=product_detail&id=9265).

The *Self-Advocacy Strategy* materials are available from Edge Enterprises, Lawrence, Kansas (http://www.ku-crl.org/iei/sim/strategies/advocacy.html for more information).

TAKE CHARGE for the Future can be obtained by contacting the Oregon Health Sciences University Center on Self-Determination (http://cdrc.ohsu.edu/selfdetermination/).

3

Individualized Transition Planning

Putting Self-Determination into Action

PAUL WEHMAN

AFTER COMPLETING THIS CHAPTER, THE READER WILL BE ABLE TO

○ Describe person-centered planning values and how they have an impact on transition

○ Describe how person-centered approaches can be used for individualized transition planning and individualized education programs (IEPs)

○ Describe the role of the family in transition IEPs

○ Identify the basic steps that are involved in accomplishing person-centered transition IEPs

○ Know how to develop a transition IEP with a person-centered emphasis

In the previous chapter, the power of self-determination was described in detail. For adolescents and young adults, the ability to demonstrate self-determination skills will separate the successful from the unsuccessful. The ability to have self-determination skills will empower access to community inclusion. The ability to have self-determination skills will distinguish inclusive employment from sheltered employment. Self-determination leads to individual power for decision making and a sense of control over one's life, something that has not characteristically been in place for a person with disabilities.

However, in order to make this journey to community inclusion with a feeling of personal competence, a well-designed blueprint of transition from school to adulthood needs to be written and implemented. This blueprint must be generated from the student, his or her family and friends, and the significant educators and community personnel in the student's life. This chapter explains how to integrate person-centered planning and transition planning into a meaningful blueprint with the student's self-determination as the engine.

GOALS OF INDIVIDUALIZED TRANSITION PLANNING

Adolescence is a time of decision making and goal setting in areas such as sexual and reproductive health, nutrition, fitness, finances, vocational planning, employment, transportation, postsecondary education, and independent living. One of the most important things that adults can do is to help young people learn about themselves in each of these areas, how to make decisions and set goals, and how to plan and organize their futures. When it is done correctly and comprehensively, individualized transition planning assists students in learning about themselves, developing statements of their future goals, and negotiating with their IEP team members for a plan of objectives and activities that are necessary to accomplish their goals. When it is not done correctly or not at all, the student will flounder, will drift from idea to idea, and will have no meaningful purpose, thus resulting in negative behavior such as antisocial behavior, excessive drinking and drug use, and low self-esteem.

Individualized transition planning has two goals. The first goal is to identify the outcomes desired and expected by students and their families along with the services and supports desired and needed to achieve these outcomes. Cameto (2005) provided *National Longitudinal Study 2* data on students' post–high school goals as well as the active participants who provide the most effort with transition planning. She indicated that although 58% of students provide some input to their transition planning, only 12% take a leadership role. In similar fashion, Katsiyannis and colleagues (2005) studied transition planning and role of supports for students with mental retardation, finding approximately 60% of these students nationally had planning started at 14 years old. To accomplish desired outcomes, the transition planning process must provide IEP teams with an understanding of what students want and need, along with jointly created plans or blueprints on how to get there. This process draws on a person-centered planning approach, which becomes the gold standard to follow (Holburn, 2002). The second goal is to use these needs data to drive local systems-change efforts. The purpose of this chapter is to address the first goal by discussing person-centered practices that may be used by IEP teams to more fully individualize the transition process and outcomes.

It is important to note that we visualize student-directed IEPs as being a very important aspect of the overall person-centered planning process. Agran (1997) has done an outstanding job of outlining the key instructional strategies essential in empowering students with the capacity to direct their own IEP. Wehmeyer (2002) notes the close association between person-centered planning and student-directed planning and notes that these two approaches may appear synonymous. With that said, Wehmeyer (2002) notes: ". . . person-centered planning emphasizes the role of significant others, whereas student-directed planning processes emphasize building student capacity . . ." (p. 77)

In this chapter we will focus more on person-centered planning. We believe that the student can only direct his or her IEP effectively, if there is important input gathered from significant others. We do not see this as necessarily "either/or" between person-centered and student-directed; rather, it is our position that student-directed IEPs *must* have a person-centered philosophy.

PERSON-CENTERED PLANNING: VALUES AND TRANSITION

The goal of all person-centered approaches is to learn about people with disabilities in more effective and efficient ways to plan and create supports that can assist them in participating in and experiencing self-directed lives (O'Brien, 2002). A related goal is to place individuals with disabilities in respected positions and even leadership positions during the assessment, planning, and service delivery process. To accomplish these goals, all person-centered approaches share some common values or beliefs. For example, Schwartz, Holburn, and Jacobson (2000) identified eight hallmarks of person-centered planning in Table 3.1.

Table 3.1. Hallmark of person-centered planning

1. The person's activities, services, and supports are based on his or her dreams, interests, preferences, strengths, and capacities.

2. The person and people important to him or her are included in lifestyle planning and have the opportunity to exercise control and make informed decisions.

3. The person has meaningful choices with decisions based on his or her experiences.

4. The person uses, when possible, natural and community supports.

5. Activities, supports, and services foster skills to achieve personal relationships, community inclusion, dignity, and respect.

6. The person's opportunities and experiences are maximized and flexibility is enhanced within existing regulatory and funding constraints.

7. Planning is collaborative and recurring and involves an ongoing commitment to the person.

8. The person is satisfied with his or her relationships, home, and daily routine.

From Schwartz, A.A., Holburn, S.C., and Jacobson, J.W. (2000). Defining person-centeredness: Results of two consensus methods. *Education and Training in Mental Retardation and Developmental Disabilities, 35*(3), 238; reprinted by permission.

Table 3.2.   Person-centered interdependent planning

1. The person and his or her family are informed.

2. They choose services and supports.

3. The person and his or her family choose and attain their goals.

4. The person and his or her family exercise their rights.

5. The person and his or her family have economic resources.

6. The person and his or her family are satisfied with their services.

7. The person and his or her family are satisfied with their life situation.

From Kim, K., and Turnbull, A. (2004). Transition to adulthood for students with severe intellectual disabilities: Shifting toward person-family interdependent planning. *Research and Practice for Persons with Severe Disabilities, 29*(1), 54; reprinted by permission.

Person-Centered Approaches Are Driven by the Individual, Family, and Friends

When used to individualize the transition process, person-centered approaches place the student in the driver's seat, which is why the self-determination skills described in the previous chapter become crucial. Person-centered approaches encourage IEP teams to define an active, participative role for the student with a disability and the student's family and friends. Kim and Turnbull (2004) expanded the concept of person-centered and family-centered planning to person-family interdependent planning (see Table 3.2). Everson and Reid (1999) have drawn more heavily on the person-centered approach than family, but they also capture many of these same themes (see Table 3.3).

TOOLS AND STRATEGIES ASSOCIATED WITH PERSON-CENTERED TRANSITION APPROACHES

In order to organize transition services in a person-centered manner, all IEP team members, including students and family members, must be knowledgeable about and skilled in the tools and strategies associated with person-centered approaches. When used together and effectively, these tools and strategies can enhance the quality and

Table 3.3.   Seven core values of person-centered planning models

1. Driven by the individual and family

2. Focus on an individual's gifts and capacities

3. Visionary and future-oriented

4. Dependent on community membership and commitment

5. Emphasize supports and connections over services

6. Enable individualized plans to be developed

7. Change services to be more responsive to consumers

From Everson J.M., and Reid, D.H. (1999). *Person-centered planning and outcome management: Maximizing organizational effectiveness in supporting quality lifestyles among people with disabilities* (p. 27). Morganton, NC: Habilitative Management Consultants; reprinted by permission.

Table 3.4. Guidelines for developing person-centered individualized education programs (IEPs)

1. Identify members of each student's personal network.

2. With support from members of each student's network, create personal profiles and future vision or dream maps for each student.

3. Bring the maps to IEP meetings and post them on the wall. Use the maps to open the meetings by asking the student and family to summarize their dreams, wants, and needs.

4. Encourage the student, family members, and other IEP team members to discuss the maps.

5. Discuss themes, things that work well, and things that do not work well.

6. For each transition outcome area, discuss the student's dreams. What programs, places, experiences, services, and supports are in place to support them? What gaps exist? What programs, places, experiences, services, and supports does the student want and need in order to fulfill future dreams?

7. Develop IEP/statement of transition services goals and objectives. Use the future vision or dream map as a checkpoint: Will the articulated goals move the student toward desired dreams? Will mastery of these goals assist the student in leading a more community-inclusive adult life? If the answer is no or if there is uncertainty, then the team should discuss and possibly reconsider the identified goals.

From Everson, J.M., and Reid, D.H. (1999). *Person-centered planning and outcome management: Maximizing organizational effectiveness in supporting quality lifestyles among people with disabilities* (p. 28). Morganton, NC: Habilitative Management Consultants; reprinted by permission.

quantity of transition outcomes for individuals with disabilities and their families. Table 3.4 summarizes the guidelines associated with person-centered transition planning.

To understand the variety of tools and strategies used in person-centered approaches, it is helpful to picture a large toolbox. Within the toolbox, there are a number of odd and unfamiliar tools. Each tool has a different purpose. Once IEP teams become familiar with each tool, many of these tools can be used in a variety of ways to accomplish specific tasks. Others may need to be modified to meet the needs and preferences of individual students and to fit the settings and materials that are idiosyncratic to a given school, adult services agency, or community. When faced with especially complex and unfamiliar desired transition outcomes and support needs, however, IEP teams must be competent in the use of many, if not all, of the tools. In addition, they must be prepared to use all of them to accomplish the systems-change tasks that may be necessary.

At first, the tools and strategies of person-centered approaches will seem strange and unfamiliar. As a result, IEP teams are frequently uncomfortable using person-centered tools and strategies and may try to fit them into a model with which they are more comfortable. As familiarity and experience with each tool increases, IEP teams usually develop an understanding of how the tools work together. In addition, they learn to modify many of the tools to suit their needs and preferences and the needs and preferences of their students.

The person-centered toolbox includes a number of tools and strategies that are common in all person-centered approaches. They may be called various names by different authors of the specific approaches, but, essentially, all person-centered approaches share four common tools and strategies: assessment tools, planning tools, collaborative teaming and action-planning strategies, and circles or networks of formal and informal supports.

Assessment and Planning Tools

Assessment tools discover the unique preferences, experiences, skills, and support needs of individuals with disabilities. These tools are frequently referred to as *maps*. Like all assessment tools, each map will provide a unique type of data about a student's background, preferences, connections to people and places, communication style, medical and health behaviors, hopes, goals, and fears. Specific frameworks exist for developing each assessment map, and each map requires between 15 and 30 minutes to create. Assessment maps do not take the place of traditional assessment tools but instead offer capacity-building data about those students for whom traditional assessment tools typically provide more data on deficits than abilities. Maps can be used by teachers to build the self-determination skills and behaviors of students by guiding them through a self-discovery process.

Maps can also be used as planning tools. They provide IEP teams with a vision of the individual's desired future or goals. They can be created by students prior to participating in their IEP meetings, shared with family members and peers as appropriate for feedback, and then shared at the beginning of the IEP meeting. These maps provide a unique picture of a student's dreams for life after school. Once again, there are specific frameworks for developing planning maps, and each one typically requires 15–30 minutes to create. Planning maps provide IEP teams with an individualized focus for each student and a foundation on which to write and prioritize every IEP goal, objective, and activity. One example of a planning map would be to assess the lifestyle satisfaction of a person. Consider Angie, a young adult with a severe disability who developed a map of her life outcomes (see Figure 3.1). In this example, the people who know Angie best have identified four words to describe satisfaction in her life: *comfort, attention, humor,* and *relationships.* Each of these areas is more clearly defined by providing examples of what each means to Angie as illustrated in the center ring. The outer ring of the circle is used to identify activities that would enhance the opportunities for Angie to experience quality of life outcomes in those four key areas. When Angie experiences one of those activities, people who are responsible for her supports are asked to evaluate how satisfied they think Angie was using the Likert-type scale shown at the bottom of the figure. This method of looking at activities and events in Angie's life is not intended to be free of bias, but rather to be a focal point of discussion about how community experiences can bring satisfaction to Angie's life as observed by the people who know her best.

Collaborative Teaming and Action-Planning Strategies

Collaborative teaming and action-planning strategies are used to develop and pursue short- and long-term IEP goals and objectives for the student and to identify interagency linkages, responsibilities, and time lines. Teaming and action-planning strategies are also used to monitor and evaluate progress and to solve problems and create solutions.

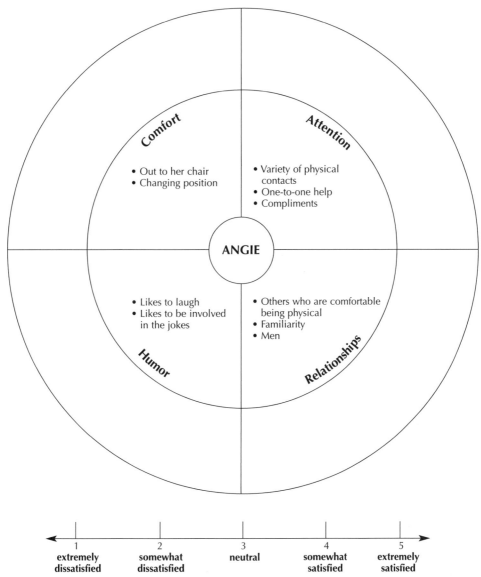

Figure 3.1. Four quality of life outcomes for Angie and how these outcomes are individually defined from her sense of satisfaction. Activities and supports are entered in the outer circle and a level of satisfaction is obtained from Angie's perspective. (From Davis, P.K., & Pancsofar, E.L. [1999]. Living in the community. In P. Wehman & P. Sherron-Targett [Eds.], *Vocational curriculum for individuals with special needs: Transition from school to adulthood* [p. 125]. Austin, TX: PRO-ED; reprinted by permission.)

Coordinated Circles or Networks of Formal and Informal Supports

A coordinated circle or network of formal and informal supports is created around each transition-age student. To be most effective, each student must have a network that includes several teams, each operating both independently and interdependently. For example, the IEP team provides one team, operating within the mandates of educational legislation. This team is responsible for writing and implementing the IEP according to mandates and policies. Students may have another team or circle of support consisting of peers, high school friends, and classmates. This circle provides students with comfortable opportunities to refine goals, explore interests and strengths, practice self-determination behaviors and skills, and receive invaluable peer feedback. This circle operates within the culture of high school settings and rituals of adolescence. Students may have yet another circle of support consisting of parents and other family members, adult mentors, neighbors, church members, co-workers, and employers. This circle provides students with additional opportunities to refine goals, explore interests and strengths, practice self-determination behaviors and skills, and receive equally invaluable feedback from experienced adults. This circle operates within the various cultures of family homes, workplaces, neighborhoods, and other community environments. The common member across each of these teams is, of course, the student. Some students will naturally and easily develop all of these networks, communicate and behave effectively within them, and use all of the opportunities they offer to pursue transition goals. Most students with disabilities, however, will need help building their circles, communicating and behaving appropriately within the circles, and using all of the opportunities they offer to pursue their goals.

Community Resource Mapping

Community mapping is an effective professional development activity for all types of teachers who use a contextualized teaching and learning approach. Mapping can acquaint teachers with the target community's culture, resources, transition assets, and needs. Community mapping is best done in small groups of three or four students whenever possible to ensure a variety of perspectives and insights.

When educators engage in community mapping, they explore such things as resources, housing, businesses, social services providers, recreational facilities, religious institutions, neighborhood history, and public opinion about local issues. For transition planners, the objective of the exploration is to develop baseline knowledge about the community's current issues and assets that will become an intrinsic part of their transition planning. This experience also allows teachers to explore career opportunities that may be relevant to their students' goals and interests.

The challenges facing every IEP team are selecting and modifying the tools, such as community mapping, that are most appropriate for individual students and that the settings and materials are idiosyncratic to a given school, adult services agency, or community. An additional challenge is remaining person-centered when facing the realities of largely systems-centered programs, environments, and processes. The remainder of this chapter presents a step-by-step process for using person-centered values and practices to accomplish person-centered transition IEPs.

WHAT ARE THE BEST STEPS TO IMPLEMENT
PERSON-CENTERED INDIVIDUALIZED TRANSITION PLANNING?

Generally, person-centered approaches require teams to follow six basic steps that fit within the traditional model used by most IEP team members:

1. A team must be convened around each transition-age student, and leadership roles that the student can assume within his or her team must be identified.

2. The team reviews assessment data and conducts additional assessment activities.

3. The team develops service and support plans, in this case IEPs or statements of transition services.

4. The transition team implements plans and evaluates resulting accomplishments.

5. The transition team updates the IEP or transition IEP annually and implements follow-up procedures.

6. The team holds an exit meeting for the student during his or her last year in school.

The steps are grounded in the values discussed in this chapter and facilitate the use of the tools and strategies that make agencies and transition planning activities person-centered. The following sections describe the six-step process in sequence and include the activities that are necessary for developing person-centered and individualized statements of transition services within IEPs. Suggestions are also offered regarding responsible personnel and time lines for completion of each step. Many excellent transition planning manuals are available that have been developed for specific states and localities (e.g., Goodson, 1995; Storms, O'Leary, & Williams, 2000). These manuals provide specific and tested guidelines for transition IEPs that can be adapted to the unique needs of individual students in specific communities. This chapter is somewhat unique in that it provides IEP teams with specific examples of how person-centered tools and strategies can be combined with these guidelines to make transition services more person-centered and ultimately more individualized.

Step 1: Convene IEP Teams, Individualized Around the Wants and Needs of Each Transition-Age Student

Initiating transition planning for students with disabilities is the responsibility of the local education agency (LEA) because the school is the primary provider of services to youth during the transition planning years. However LEAs should not be solely responsible for individualized transition planning; they require the cooperation of local adult services providers, families, and students. Communitywide transition activities, documented in a local interagency agreement, are a critical tool that enables school systems and community core teams to initiate, implement, and monitor interagency transition planning processes.

Identify All Transition-Age Students   Formal transition planning must begin for all students who receive special education services when they are 16 years of age. By the time that the student is age 16, a statement of the transition services needs of the student must be included under the applicable components of the IEP, and it must be updated annually. This statement must focus on the student's course of study (e.g., advanced placement coursework, career education). By the time the student is age 16, a statement of needed transition services must be included within the IEP, and it must

Table 3.5.   What does a transition coordinator do?

1. Intraschool linkage
2. Interagency/business linkages
3. Assessment and career counseling
4. Transition planning
5. Education and community training
6. Family support and resource
7. Public relations
8. Program development
9. Program evaluation

From Asselin, S.B., Todd-Allen, M., and deFur, S. (1998). Transition coordinators: Define yourselves. *TEACHING Exceptional Children,* 14; adapted by permission.

also be updated annually. This statement must include needed transition service in the areas of instruction; related services; development of employment and other postschool adult living objectives; and, if appropriate, acquisition of daily living skills and functional vocational evaluation. This statement must also include (as appropriate) interagency linkages (e.g., referrals to supported employment [SE] providers or university offices of student affairs) or responsibilities (e.g., job placement activities of vocational rehabilitation [VR] counselors, a college course for which a sign language interpreter is needed).

A teacher, social worker, guidance counselor, or other designated personnel typically assumes the role of transition coordinator. This person operates within the procedures that have been determined by the LEA and the community core team (and in many communities, documented in a local interagency agreement). The transition coordinator is responsible for compiling the list of transition-age students and overseeing the remaining steps in the transition planning process.

Asselin, Todd-Allen, and deFur (1998) developed an outstanding paper on transition coordinators, their functions, and roles. They described a strategy that targets critical skills needed to be an effective transition coordinator. Table 3.5 lists nine of these functions, but the reader is encouraged to review the entire paper for a more in-depth look at the numerous functions of the transition coordinator.

Identify Appropriate School Service Personnel   School personnel (e.g., teachers, therapists, counselors) who have been involved with individual students targeted for transition planning should be identified to participate in the individualized transition planning process. When enlisting school personnel for involvement, the transition coordinator should be careful to solicit input from staff in all relevant disciplines who have had recent and meaningful contact with the student. However, the number of participants actually attending the IEP meeting should be kept to a minimum so that teams are not too large to work productively as a group.

Identify Appropriate Adult Services Agencies   Needed and desired adult services agencies should be contacted when their services can be used best in order to avoid overloading them when they cannot be active participants. Arrangements should be made (and once again documented in a local interagency agreement) for representatives to participate in the transition planning process for students in their final 2 years of school. In some cases, it may be desirable to involve representatives before the final 2 years of school; however, transition coordinators should be aware of the very large caseloads of adult services workers and should refrain from requesting earlier involvement unless it is required for certain students. Instead, typically during the early secondary years, adult services providers will assist IEP teams best in an informal consultative role and through their participation as community core team members.

During the crucial, final transition years, adult services representatives can provide valuable information about the available and most appropriate programs and placements for a particular student as he or she leaves the school program. Adult services areas from which representatives may be drawn include mental health, intellectual disabilities, VR, social services, and other local organizations such as The Arc (formerly Association for Retarded Citizens of the United States) and the United Cerebral Palsy Association (UCP). The likelihood that the student will benefit from an agency's participation or will be using its services in the future determines that agency's involvement. When the transition coordinator is knowledgeable regarding the functions and service capabilities of adult services providers and agencies, he or she is better able to identify appropriate agency representatives for participation in transition planning meetings.

Identify Appropriate Members of the Student's Networks   To truly function as an individualized transition planning team, the members of the team must, by definition, vary from student to student depending on the vision that the student and his or her family have for the future. When person-centered values and practices are applied to transition planning, one is reminded that students will need to rely on a network of people to make their dreams a reality. Thus, the approaches suggest that people other than paid professionals and service providers be identified. With the help of individual students and their families, transition coordinators must identify these people and define roles for them to play in the transition planning process. For example, one student may want extended family members to attend all or parts of the IEP meeting to support the student's articulation of his or her goals and to describe their roles in supporting the student's accomplishment of the goals. Another student may want an employer or co-workers to attend part of the meeting in order to support the student's articulation of interests, skills, experiences, and dreams. Yet another student may not want to have a specific member of the traditional IEP meeting attend because the person has not supported the student's preferences and goals in the past.

Thus, person-centered approaches require that transition coordinators and systems must begin to identify the unique networks around each student, ask the student and family about their comfort with various potential team members, and respond to the student's and family's wants and needs in putting together an individualized planning team. Developing a relationships map is one way of identifying these individuals (Holburn & Vietz, 2002; Mount, 1997). Another way is to simply ask the student and his or her family to develop a list of people they want and need, define roles for them to play, and invite them to attend the appropriate meetings or parts of meetings. Questions to consider in identifying appropriate members and the roles they might play include

- Who knows you best?
- Who do you trust and feel comfortable around?
- Who do you look to for advice and support?
- Who would you like to help you plan your transition from school to adulthood?
- How can these people best help you (e.g., by giving you letters of recommendation, by helping you create a dream map, by attending your IEP meetings and helping you communicate, by sitting in on your meeting and hearing how you will learn best when you go to college)?

At a minimum, the student, his or her family, and a special education teacher must be included as IEP team members. Typically, a general education teacher and a vocational educator will also be members. In addition, a VR counselor and one or more representatives from other adult services agencies will be included. As person-centered values and practices begin to be embraced, other family and community members become involved.

Students

- Attend IEP/transition IEP meetings
- Share personal preferences, interests, skills, goals, support wants and needs (with support, as needed)
- Ask questions and provide information to the team on various issues that the student and family want to address, such as sexual, wellness, medical, social, financial, or guardianship issues (with support, as needed)
- Negotiate wants, needs, and goals with professionals and family members (with support, as needed)
- Assume responsibility for completing agreed-on goals, objectives, activities, and action steps

Family Members

- Attend IEP/transition IEP meetings
- Share the student's and family's preferences, interests, skills, dreams, support wants and needs
- Negotiate the student's and family's wants, needs, and goals with professionals
- Focus the team's planning on the student's and family's wants, needs, and goals
- Provide informal home and community experiences and training, if possible
- Ask questions and provide information to the team on various issues that the student and family want to address, such as sexual, wellness, medical, social, financial, or guardianship issues

Special Educators

- Target names of students eligible for transition planning and coordinate data collection and management
- Organize and attend IEP/transition IEP meetings
- From the student's vision, identify referral needs and ensure that referrals are made to appropriate adult services agencies
- Coordinate the writing and implementation of IEPs/statements of transition services
- Ensure that the student's and family's wants, needs, and goals are articulated, understood, and used to drive transition planning

General Educators

- Attend IEP/transition IEP meetings for all students who receive general education services
- Consult with the IEP team on regular education opportunities, graduation requirements and assessments, and the student's progress and support needs
- Help identify and analyze postsecondary education opportunities and needs
- Provide instruction in general education classrooms and environments
- Assist the IEP team in inclusion activities

Vocational Educators

- Attend IEP/transition IEP meetings for all students who require vocational training or placement
- Consult with the IEP team on vocational opportunities, local employment trends, and specific skills required for jobs
- Help identify and analyze community-based vocational training sites
- Provide instruction at community-based vocational training sites as necessary
- Assist students in creating a vocational résumé and portfolio
- Provide leadership roles in job placement activities for students during their last years of school

Vocational Rehabilitation Counselors

- Serve as consultant to the IEP/transition IEP team throughout the student's secondary education years
- Coordinate the identification and delivery of VR services (e.g., vocational assessments/evaluations, postsecondary training, job placement, SE) through the development of an individualized plan for employment (IPE)
- Provide leadership roles in job placement activities for students during their last years of school

Other Adult Services Providers

- Share responsibility for assessment of students' wants and needs as necessary

- Conduct home visits and case management as needed or appropriate

- Attend IEP/transition IEP meetings for students in their last years of school or for students at high risk of dropping out

- Provide follow-along services once students have been placed in supported living or SE programs

Other Family and Community Members

- Attend IEP/transition IEP meetings as appropriate

- Share information on the student's and family's preferences, interests, and dreams, along with evidence of skills, support wants, and needs

- Assist and support the student and family in negotiating wants, needs, and goals with professionals

- Focus the team's planning on the student's and family's wants, needs, and goals

- Provide informal home and community experiences and supports, if possible

- Ask questions and provide information and support to the team on various issues that the student and family want to address, such as sexual, wellness, medical, social, financial, or guardianship issues

Step 2: Review Assessment Data and Conduct Additional Assessment Activities

IEP teams typically have available to them a great deal of educational, psychological, health and medical, behavioral, and vocational data on adolescents with disabilities. Unfortunately, much research focuses on deficits (i.e., what a student cannot do) or problems (i.e., what a student can but should not do). During the transition planning process, it is essential to move beyond traditional ways of describing and assessing students with disabilities. The time has come to think about students' dreams, their preferences, their gifts and capacities, what they can contribute to their communities, and what they need to accomplish their dreams and make their contributions. For most, if not all, transition-age students, traditional assessment data will need to be supplemented with person-centered assessment tools and strategies in order to respond to these areas.

The goal of all person-centered assessment activities is to get to know individuals with disabilities as people with unique personalities, hopes, dreams, and support needs. Person-centered assessment tools require an initial focus on abilities and then a subsequent focus on support wants and needs. Person-centered assessment tools remind IEP teams that each student has a set of experiences, networks of people, and a set of preferences that make the student unique. The tools likewise remind IEP teams that every adolescent has dreams and fears and that every family has dreams and fears for their family members.

Effective use of person-centered assessment tools requires IEP teams to leave behind preconceived notions of disability labels and test scores. Team members should ask themselves: What do we need to know about this student that traditional evaluations do not tell us? Only when teams know a student as an individual should they go back and use traditional assessment tools and data (as necessary) to identify disability labels, test scores, and deficits. But supplementing the data with the results of person-centered assessments is always important.

The crucial task in conducting person-centered assessment activities is to identify the appropriate individuals as members of the assessment team. In traditional, systems-centered agencies and organizations, assessment activities are conducted by a multidisciplinary or interdisciplinary planning team. Individuals with disabilities and their families may be invited to attend these meetings, but they are seldom viewed as equal members of the team or as experts. Extended family, friends, neighbors, co-workers, church members, and other people who serve as natural supports are almost never invited to participate. In contrast, person-centered assessments bring to the table people who 1) know the student well, 2) support or potentially can support the student during the transition process, and 3) are chosen by the student or family to participate in assessment activities. Thus, person-centered assessments are as likely to involve restaurant co-workers, members of softball leagues, and real estate agents as they are school psychologists. Direct support staff, personal care attendants, and peer tutors who interact daily with the student are as likely to participate in the assessment process as are physical therapists who see the student weekly or itinerant vision teachers who see the individual biweekly.

To help illustrate the important and unique role that groups of people can play in the life of a student with disabilities, various person-centered planning approaches refer to groups called circles of support or circles of friends (Holburn & Vietze, 2002; Mount, 1997). These individuals are drawn from the student's and family's networks and may play various and highly individualized roles during the transition planning process. Some may be members of the IEP team; many others will not be members. A circle may be initiated by a student, by a family member, by a friend or advocate, by a teacher, by a transition coordinator, or by anyone else who is interested in guiding the assessment and planning activities being conducted by the IEP team.

To accomplish person-centered assessment activities, a circle might meet once, twice, quarterly, annually, or on some other as-needed schedule. A circle typically meets at the student's home or other comfortable setting before the team meeting to guide the IEP's development and after the team meeting in order to support its implementation. The tools and strategies used by the teams as well as the meeting schedule are dictated by the unique nature of the student's desired outcomes and by the characteristics of the agencies targeted to serve and support the adolescent as he or she makes the transition from school to adult life. The circle's goal at this step in the transition process is to ensure that the student and other IEP members have all the data necessary to write a person-centered and comprehensive transition plan. Ultimately, once the assessment phase is completed, all circle members will have to make some hard decisions about the time, energy, and other resources they are willing to contribute to assist the adolescent in attaining his or her goals.

Mapping person-centered models offers some unique assessment tools that assist circles and IEP teams in thinking about and discovering the student's gifts, capacities, and support needs. Group graphics, also know as mapping, is one of the most unique tools associated with person-centered planning approaches (see previous section on assessment and planning tools). Mapping uses color, symbols, words, and pictures to gather and record information about people. Information is collected using an interactive group process and recorded on large sheets of paper for the entire team to view and discuss. Research has demonstrated that the group process can be a reliable and valid assessment approach that successfully includes students, families, and support personnel in the assessment and planning procedures (Holburn & Vietze, 2004; Reid, Everson, & Green, 1999; Whitney-Thomas et al., 1998).

According to each person-centered model, a team begins the assessment process by creating a set of maps, typically known as a personal profile. Suggested maps to include in a personal profile vary from approach to approach and by the preliminary goals, wants, and needs of the individual. (For more details on mapping, see Baird & Everson, 1999; Mount, 1997; Mount & Zwernik, 1988.) For example, the Individual Service Design model (Yates, 1980) suggested focusing group graphics around three basic questions: 1) Who is the person? 2) What does the person need? and 3) What will need to happen to meet the person's needs? The Personal Futures Planning model (Mount & Zwernik, 1988) suggested completing five assessment maps: 1) relationships; 2) places; 3) background; 4) personal preferences; and 5) dreams, hopes, and fears. The dreams, hopes, and fears map may alternatively be referred to as a future vision map. The Personal Futures Planning model also suggested that teams consider developing other optional maps such as a health map or communication map as needed. Expanding on these basic frameworks, the Essential Lifestyle Planning approach (Smull & Harrison, 1992) includes a nonnegotiable map, and MAPS (Vandercook, York, & Forest, 1989) includes a nightmare map (which asks what is the worst possible thing that can happen). As circles become proficient in using mapping, they can choose specific maps or create their own maps to include in a personal profile on the basis of the wants and needs of the student they are getting to know and the type of services and supports the student wants and needs.

Whatever maps are chosen, circles and IEP teams should consider getting to know these things about transition-age students with disabilities:

- People in the student's life, both paid and unpaid

- Where the student spends his or her time

- Things that people see as contributing to the student's positive reputation

- Things that people see as contributing to the student's negative reputation

- Choices the student makes

- Preferences (i.e., things that motivate the student and create happiness)

- Nonpreferences (i.e., things that do not work for the student, that create frustration and unhappiness)

- Personal goals and dreams

- Most important priorities to work on now (2–12 months) and in the future (1–5 years)

- Opportunities (i.e., things or people that can help the student achieve personal goals and dreams

- Obstacles or barriers (i.e., things or people that are getting in the way of the student's achieving personal goals and dreams)

- Strategies to help the student overcome obstacles or barriers and achieve personal goals and dreams

In sum, assessment maps can be created by circles and teams before IEP meetings to guide the development of statements of transition services. Alternatively, maps can be created by students as part of classroom self-determination activities provided by teachers. Many of the commercially available self-determination curricula (e.g., *Next Step, Steps to Self-Determination, TAKE CHARGE for the Future, Whose Future Is It Anyway?*) use mapping or similar self-discovery activities to encourage teenagers to get to know themselves in order to be more active and informed participants in their transition planning process.

Regardless of whether assessment maps are created by circles, by IEP teams, or by students themselves, students must be encouraged, prepared, and supported in sharing what they have learned about themselves at the beginning of their IEP meetings. Much of the systems centeredness surrounding the development of IEPs can be minimized by making the student with a disability the focus of assessment activities. For example, consider asking students what assessment information they would like to find out about themselves. Circles and self-determination activities are excellent tools and strategies for making transition planning more person-centered and individualized. When these practices are adopted, together, the student and family, professionals, and community members can let go of old assumptions and begin thinking about adolescents with disabilities in new and different ways. Deficit-finding assessment activities must be eliminated as a part of individualized transition planning. Instead, people with disabilities must be viewed with respect, as people who are capable and prepared to build goals on their strengths, unique talents, and interests.

Step 3: Teams Develop IEPs/Transition IEPs

Schedule the IEP Meeting Transition planning meetings for eligible students should be scheduled so that they are concurrent with their IEP meetings. Meetings must be scheduled for each eligible student so that the student, his or her parents or guardians, school personnel, adult services representatives, and community members can attend. The student should always be included in the scheduling and planning of the transition meeting so that he or she can play an active and informed role in planning his or her future.

Before the IEP meeting, the transition coordinator should identify any need for cross-agency sharing of information about transition-age youth and should ensure that release forms can be signed by the appropriate people. These arrangements are essential because the LEA is prohibited from releasing confidential information on students in special education programs without the signature of a parent, a guardian, or the student if the student has reached the age of majority.

Conduct the IEP Meeting Development of the transition IEP should be conducted as the opening component of a student's IEP meeting. In this way, IEP goals and objectives can be written to reflect the transition IEP. A transition IEP addresses desired adult outcomes along with the desired services and supports necessary in order

DELINDA

Delinda is an outgoing and active young woman who is eager to experience living on her own. She would like to move from her parents' home into an accessible apartment within the next 2 years. Her team envisions her living with one other woman in which she would have 24-hour supports for meals, housekeeping, and daily living care. Delinda's family and occupational therapist agree that she should be fully independent in her daily self-care routines as long as her bathroom and bedroom are fully accessible. Delinda's family indicate that, although she likes to spend time in the kitchen, she needs a lot of support to prepare meals. They also note that she does not enjoy housekeeping tasks and finds many tasks physically challenging.

to achieve and maintain these desired goals. In contrast, an IEP identifies skill and behavioral impairments and remediation strategies. An effective transition plan matches the specific strategies and behavioral objectives of the IEP with desired employment goals, postsecondary education goals, living goals, and so forth.

The meeting format outlined and discussed in the following sections is based on a typical transition planning strategy used in LEAs in many states. Following these procedures will help team members develop transition plans that include 1) clearly defined and expected adult outcomes, 2) selection of desired and appropriate services and supports to achieve those outcomes, and 3) delineation of skill and behavioral objectives that must be met to arrive at the outcomes.

Open the IEP/Transition IEP Meeting The transition coordinator or the person conducting the meeting should welcome and introduce all meeting participants. An informal atmosphere is recommended so that the student and his or her parents will feel as comfortable as possible. The professionals have the responsibility to encourage honest and open participation from everyone in attendance.

As specified previously, the student or family, with support from other team members as needed, should open the meeting by articulating a future vision statement—a statement of desired outcomes. Consider the case examples (Delinda, Harold, and Tyrone) of future vision statements.

The articulation of a student's dreams or desired outcomes requires important decisions on the part of an IEP team who is attempting to operate in a more person-centered manner. In particular, team members must ask themselves, "Can we support this student's desired outcomes?" and more specifically, "Do we believe this student can and should accomplish these outcomes, and do we have or are we willing to develop the capacity necessary to support this student's accomplishment of these outcomes?" An important part of the transition planning meeting during this step is listening to and ensuring understanding of desired and expected outcomes as articulated by the student and family. Following this, the entire IEP team must agree to support all of the student's desired outcomes, some of them, or none of them and, in some cases, negotiate with each other until the entire team reaches consensus on a future vision statement. Next, the team must begin to discuss specific outcomes that can be attained through IEP and transition goals, objectives, linkages, and responsibilities.

Generate a Discussion of Desired Outcomes and Available Support Services
Following articulation of the student's future vision or dreams, the remainder of the transition meeting should progress through stages to ensure that delineated goals and objectives are specific enough and person-centered enough to achieve the desired outcomes. A comprehensive transition plan should address all of the student's and family's

HAROLD

Harold is an intelligent, soft-spoken, and self-determined young man. He would like to live at home next year and attend the state university as a part-time student. He plans to study child psychology and ultimately earn a doctorate. Because he uses a ventilator to breathe, he and his mother want his VR counselor and a representative from the university to be actively involved in choosing appropriate assistive technology for school work and medical care along with touring the university for necessary physical accommodations. Harold also hopes to live in a dorm on campus during his junior and senior years of school and become involved in university social life. His mother is fearful of this aspect of Harold's dream; she worries about his safety and medical needs.

desired and expected wants and needs. Typically, a comprehensive plan addresses expected outcomes and desired services and supports in the following areas:

- Employment opportunities
- Postsecondary education opportunities
- Living opportunities
- Financial and income needs
- Friendship and socialization needs
- Transportation needs
- Health and medical needs
- Legal and advocacy needs

For each outcome area, the team should consider the following five questions:

1. What is the student's dream?

2. What skills or behaviors does the student need to learn to attain this dream?

3. To what locally available programs, services, and supports should referrals be made to support this dream?

4. What responsibilities must education, adult services, student, and family team members assume to make this dream a reality?

5. What program, service, and support gaps and barriers exist that must be addressed by community core teams and/or family and student-initiated circles of support?

The IEP team must acknowledge that schools and adult services may not be able to provide all of the services and supports necessary for the student to attain all desired outcomes. For example, an IEP team may support one student's dream of owning his own home but may also recognize a local lack of the services and supports necessary for the student to attain the dream. In this case, the team may agree to support the dream and identify the IEP skills and behavioral goals and objectives the student needs to attain the dream. The team may also identify the interagency linkages necessary to initiate the dream, such as a referral to VR for employment services or a referral to the local mental retardation agency for supported living services. Next, the team may suggest that the family assume responsibility for contacting a local bank and nonprofit housing organization to determine availability of affordable housing loans. Then, the team might ask a case manager to contact a program in another community to determine the next steps in attaining the dream. Last, the team might share the student's future vision statement with the community's local core team and ask them to review the student's dream and consider expansion of local services and supports to assist the student. Likewise, students' dreams and preferences should be strongly emphasized along with these five questions in the establishment of transition goals for all desired outcome areas.

Tyrone is a shy and gentle young man who enjoys spending time alone or with small groups of people. His team would like Tyrone to be more physically active. After exiting school next year, Tyrone plans to move into a two-bedroom apartment. He wants to have his own bedroom, to choose a roommate to share his apartment, and to have a desk with a rocking chair. Currently, Tyrone spends a lot of his free time watching television and sleeping. Tyrone enjoys cooking, taking walks, and going to coffee shops. He wants to do these activities when he moves into his new apartment. His team would like Tyrone to experience a variety of activities that allow him to choose some additional preferred leisure options.

Many desired programs, services, or supports will not be available in some communities. However, in a person-centered environment, IEP teams will assume responsibility for providing community leaders with valuable ongoing needs assessment information. Specifically, the transition coordinator is responsible for compiling information from students' future vision statements into a report at the conclusion of each year's transition planning activities and submitting it to the community core team or to administrators of the appropriate agencies. Table 3.6 presents an example of how services might be arranged for two students, Lee and Pam.

Identify Transition Goals Having discussed and agreed on desired outcomes, the IEP team must now consider long-term goals in all desired outcome areas. A goal should include the desired outcome (e.g., full-time employment) and the appropriate service delivery model to achieve the goal (e.g., a supported competitive employment approach). Wehman (2002a) developed a transition planning manual with over 40 sample transition plans. Each of these plans had important life and work goals that were seen by teachers and families as crucial in life success. These plans reflect real students' goals and provide illustrations of blueprints for success. The typical goal areas included vocational training, employment, postsecondary, financial, self-advocacy, independent living, and so forth. Some examples for transition goals to consider include

- Full-time employment with time-limited VR services for job development and job interviewing assistance
- Part-time employment in a group enclave model with two or three co-workers
- Part-time college attendance with an interpreter and note-taking assistance from the college's office of student affairs
- Part-time community college attendance with Braille books and audiobooks provided by the college's office of student affairs
- Community living in a supported living apartment program with two roommates and 24-hour supports
- Participation in an integrated recreation program (e.g., beginners' swimming at the YMCA) with support from a local peer-advocate program
- Enrollment in a local health club with facility accessibility and staff in-services provided by a local hospital occupational therapy center
- Community access with training on use of the public transportation system provided by the high school program
- Estate planning with services provided by a pro bono law clinic

Table 3.6. Sample high school transition services

Population	Service delivery	Planning	Competencies	People/professionals involved
Lee, age 14	Intensive support services	Lee wants to be included in community activities (volunteer work and leisure) and to participate as best as he can with life at home with his family.	Communicates with an augmentative communication device Prepares a meal through the principle of partial participation Volunteers at a community agency or business twice a week	Speech-language therapist Vocational rehabilitation specialist Family members Community agency personnel Business personnel Special educator Physical therapist Recreation and leisure therapist
Pam, age 17	Time-limited support services	Pam wants to work full time as a registered nurse. She wants to live in an apartment, have a family, and volunteer at the local fire department.	Completes a child and family care class Completes consumer and homemaking classes Volunteers at the local fire department Participates in the Tech Prep program for health	Course instructors Special educator Fire department personnel School nurse Guidance counselor Tech Prep teachers

From Repetto, J.B., and Webb, K.W. (1999). A model for guiding the transition process. In S.H. deFur and J.R. Patton (Eds.), *Transition and school-based services: Interdisciplinary perspectives for enhancing the transition process* (p. 434). Austin, TX: PRO-ED; reprinted by permission.

Each goal should also include

- The projected date for achievement of the goal, specifying completion before or after graduation

- Delineation of the agencies responsible for attaining this particular goal

- The people primarily responsible for seeing that the goal is achieved by the date set for completion

Determine Objectives and Steps to Accomplish Goals   The IEP team must also identify the objectives and sequence of steps needed to accomplish each transition goal. Typically, objectives should be written for those skills and behaviors that a student needs to learn in order to attain his or her goals. Thus, mastery of designated objectives is the responsibility of the student. Objectives should be written according to the LEA's policies and procedures on developing IEPs and should include all appropriate components (e.g., level of present performance, modifications or accommodations needed in regular class). Typically, actions should be identified for all interagency linkages and responsibilities (i.e., those actions to be assumed by students, family members, teachers, adult services providers, and other members of the IEP team). This can

RICHARD

Richard is an 18-year-old man who lives with his adoptive father since the divorce of his adoptive parents. He had been residing with them and his biological sister since removal from the custody of his biological parents at age 4. Richard was diagnosed with ADHD, mild intellectual disabilities, and depressive disorder. He is far below grade level academically; his reading and math skills are equivalent to those of the third to fourth grade. He occasionally has discipline problems at school related to skipping classes and smoking. He has held, and lost, a couple of part-time jobs. He rides his bike to school and around his small, suburban neighborhood.

be done in much the same way as writing a task analysis, the step-by-step delineation of all activities from beginning to end that are necessary for accomplishment of a desired goal. Action steps should also include the responsible team members and time lines for completion.

Devise a Services Referral Checklist   Actions beyond those listed in the IEP, the statement of transition plan objectives, or the "steps to accomplish goals" may be necessary to effect a smooth transition. On the basis of the needed goals and services as identified by the transition planning meeting participants, agency representatives should be designated as responsible for beginning the formal referral and application processes that will initiate the appropriate adult services. Application and referral forms must be completed by each of the adult services representatives who are identified as having a role in the student's postschool life. These may include, for example, representatives from the VR agency, social services, community mental health and intellectual disabilities services, the local Social Security office, the local supported employment program, local recreation center, or a local college or university.

End the Meeting   At the end of the meeting, all participants should sign the IEP or transition IEP. The school liaison should send copies of the IEP/transition IEP to all participants as soon as possible. Information describing adult community services should be given to the parents or the student at this time.

Step 4: Implement the IEP or Transition IEP

Operating under the terms of an interagency agreement, those agencies that are responsible for goals or specific steps in the transition plan should implement the plans as prescribed. Most of the transition planning goals will require cross-agency involvement. Some services may be needed immediately, whereas other services may be needed over a period of several school years and may even extend beyond graduation.

Thinking about assessment in new and different ways and creating IEPs with goals that reflect the goals and needs of students lay the foundation for agencies to function in a person-centered manner. However, writing person-centered IEPs represents only one component of person-centered planning. Once IEP teams have developed personal profiles and have written IEPs for students, the teams are then ready to tackle the discussion, planning, and systems-change activities necessary to implement the plans in a truly person-centered manner. At this point, most agencies will have a very clear idea of desired consumer outcomes—and most likely, a very unclear idea of how the agency can support consumers in attaining their desired outcome.

Agencies that are sincerely invested in person-centered approaches must actively take on the challenging role of assisting consumers in reaching their goals. Such a role requires the creation of new relationships with consumers and family members as well as new relationships with community members. This role also requires the revision of existing services and the creation of new service directions. Finally, to be successful, the role requires an effective and coordinated working relationship among all agency personnel including executives, middle managers, and direct support staff.

With the values and tools associated with person-centered planning in place, educators must turn to managing the actual logistics of transition plan design. For students to attain their dreams, successful implementation of the IEP requires the commitment and energy of people in all of the student's various networks. The IEP team must implement a set of objectives and activities as specified in the IEP/transition IEP. The student must pursue skill and behavioral objectives as specified in the IEP/transition IEP. For many students, a circle of support or circle of friends, either meeting regularly and formally or working informally, will also work on behalf of the student to supplement the efforts of the IEP team and the student. Typically, circles will dedicate themselves to activities such as creating assessment maps, making telephone calls to verify terminology and eligibility procedures, writing letters to appeal decisions or plead cases, providing informal behavioral and skill training experiences to supplement what is offered in the IEP, accompanying the student and family on site visits to interview and choose desired programs, helping the student prioritize wants and needs, supporting the student by attending IEP meetings, and other person-centered activities. The role of the circle is to assist the student in setting goals, developing strategies, and solving problems. The circle members make a commitment to act on behalf of the student and do whatever they can to help the student accomplish his or her goals. As they develop the personal profile, the circle of support should also discuss strategies for working with the IEP team, supporting the goals and activities of the transition IEP, and problem solving any barriers to desired services and supports.

Step 5: Update the IEP/Transition IEP Annually and Implement Follow-Up Procedures

As the student nears graduation and the school is preparing to end its involvement in the transition plan, adult services agencies should increase their involvement with the student. At this point, the school should concentrate on transferring its information and services to these agencies. One of the agency liaisons should be designated to follow up on the progress of the transition plan as the student exits school. This may mean calling the transition coordinator to check on the status of individual goals or items. Follow-up should occur at least quarterly to ensure completion of all steps and, thus, increase the likelihood of achieving goals. Follow-up also may involve organizing and scheduling another meeting of IEP team participants if goals are not being achieved as planned. Annual or more frequent revisions of the original IEP may be required.

Step 6: Hold an Exit Meeting

Toward the end of a student's last year in school, the school liaison and adult services representatives should plan an exit meeting with graduating students and their parents to finalize plans for the transition from school to work. At this time, any final needs relevant to the transition process can be addressed. The group should examine goals that have and have not been achieved by their scheduled completion dates and verify goals that are scheduled for completion shortly after graduation. Those goals that have not been achieved as scheduled and those scheduled for postgraduation should be reviewed by the group for acquisition and relevancy. Achieved outcomes should also be discussed to determine how the student and his or her family are faring with the new activities.

In an excellent summary of how the school-based transition process occurs, Izzo and Schumate (1991) delineated seven steps, summarized here, that show how the IEP is used as the administrative vehicle overriding the transition plan:

1. Prepare for the student's transition from school to work. Obtain or update information on the student's vocational skills, including the use of the following:

   - Vocational interest inventory

   - Formalized vocational assessment

   - Informal assessment, including behavioral observation

2. Establish a transition file for each student:

   - Obtain or update information concerning the student's disability, including medical and psychological evaluations.

   - Gather or update information about public and private agencies and individuals, including family members, that may be involved in the student's eventual transition, placement, or support.

   - Collect information from the bureau of employment services and local chamber of commerce regarding local labor market needs.

3. Establish the transition team:

   - The IEP chairperson reviews updated student information to determine individuals and agencies necessary to implement a successful school-to-work transition.

   - The IEP chairperson ensures that agencies will have entered into a working interagency agreement with the school system.

   - The IEP chairperson convenes the first full transition meeting.

   - The IEP chairperson assigns a transition coordinator as the student advocate who will monitor the transition process.

   - The transition coordinator completes referral forms to adult services agencies and monitors services provided by adult agencies to ensure a well-coordinated transition process.

4. Set broad transition goals via the IEP/transition IEP:

   - The team determines the type and nature of the school and community placement that will be the context for the student's transition.

   - The team determines appropriate community living goals, including living arrangements, medical needs, estate planning, social options, and so forth.

- The team determines appropriate short- and long-term employment goals, including job training and employment options.

- The team writes the goals on the IEP/transition IEP.

5. Establish the transition objectives:

- Attach objectives with specific initiation and completion time lines to each of the goals specified on the transition IEP.

- On the transition IEP, write the name of the individual assigned to be responsible for monitoring each objective.

- Affirm the transition IEP team coordinator's role in monitoring the objectives with each team member throughout the year.

6. Update the transition plan based on the student's progress:

- Reconvene the transition IEP team at least once to evaluate progress on the plans, goals, and objectives.

- Modify or update the transition IEP based on reports by team members responsible for transition objectives.

7. Establish follow-up and follow-along services:

- Determine scope and nature of follow-up.

- Establish agency or individual responsibility for follow-up and follow-along.

- Forward information gathered during the course of the transition IEP process to the follow-up coordinator.

- Update school and agency files to reflect changes in the student's plans.

CONCLUSION

As is seen in this chapter, there are a number of tools and strategies that IEP teams and, specifically, classroom teachers and transition coordinators should consider adopting in order to more fully individualize the transition planning process:

1. Invite students, their families, and other community members to attend IEP meetings and share their stories and experiences as part of the assessment data.

2. Devote classroom time to having students pursue self-determination activities, develop maps, and receive peer and family feedback.

3. Support students in developing dream maps or future vision statements and presenting their visions at the opening of their IEP team meetings.

4. Modify IEP forms to include space to write a future vision statement.

5. Use the future vision statement to drive the identification and prioritization of all IEP goals, objectives, and activities.

6. Encourage students and families to identify and use their networks or circles of support throughout the multiyear transition process to supplement IEP team actions.

7. Encourage other IEP team members to recognize the importance of a student's networks and expand responsibility for transition actions to networks of people beyond the traditional IEP team.

8. Develop a mechanism to share IEP future vision data with community core teams so that person-centered systems-change activities can be pursued.

Three factors are critical to the successful implementation of a transition IEP:

1. The involvement of IEP members who are knowledgeable about the availability of local services

2. A process that ensures the identification of all desired outcomes within the least restrictive service options

3. The ability of community agencies to provide or procure the needed services

Communities with well-written interagency agreements, a wide array of community service options, and a collaborative plan to address service needs will have the best chances of achieving desired outcomes for each student.

STUDY QUESTIONS

1. Describe the seven approaches that reflect person-centered planning values in transition.

2. Provide a detailed discussion of the assessment tools used in person-centered planning.

3. Describe the steps in implementing person-centered individualized transition planning.

4. Discuss the roles of identifying and establishing a coordinated circle or network of formal and informal supports for a transition student.

5. Describe six different types of nonstandardized assessment instruments that can be used in the transition planning process.

4

Transition Planning in the Community

Using All of the Resources

Valerie Brooke, J. Howard Green, W. Grant Revell, and Paul Wehman

AFTER COMPLETING THIS CHAPTER, THE READER WILL BE ABLE TO

○ Identify at least six community agencies that support youth in transition

○ Describe the critical elements in community-based transition

○ Describe the important role of interagency planning in transition

○ Discuss the importance of benefits planning as a component of transition planning

○ Understand the potential support available through community programs in the areas of case management, employment services, and funding

○ Describe the role of business and industry in transition

This chapter addresses transition planning from a community perspective. It builds on the earlier chapters' overview of the governing legislation and the critical issues involved in high-quality transition planning, particularly a specific focus on self-determination and strategies to promote student involvement. The involvement of key community agencies and organizations is vital to the success of all transition planning. This school-to-community connection must be made to ensure such outcomes as post-secondary training, educational outcomes, employment opportunities, residential services, and leisure/recreational possibilities. Specifically, this chapter presents the vast array of community partners potentially involved in the transition planning process and the roles, functions, and benefits of each partnership.

COMMUNITY AGENCIES: ROLES, RESPONSIBILITIES, AND IMPACT

High-quality transition planning requires that a major emphasis be placed on strong community participation in the transition process. Yet, all too frequently, transition individualized education programs (IEPs) fail to effectively involve community resources. A major reason for this inconsistency is that many educators, students, and family members of individuals with disabilities do not recognize that most adult services are eligibility driven. In comparison, special education is an entitled service, and local school systems are the single agency that coordinates education services. This single point of service coordination does not exist in adult services. Instead, postsecondary education, counseling, rehabilitation, therapy, residential, and recreational services all have their own individual eligibility system that must be met prior to acceptance into an individual program. A variety of laws as well as state and agency policies govern each of these programs. Consequently, students with disabilities and their family members must develop a strong understanding of these community programs to ensure a smooth transition using a results-oriented process that is emphasized in the 2004 reauthorization of the Individuals with Disabilities Education Improvement Act (PL 108-446), Section 614(34)(A).

In assisting students with transition planning, it is important to look at resources within the school *and* to also target community agencies and organizations that can provide support. Each of these organizations will play a unique and vital role in the successful transition from school to work and independence in the community. Successful youth with disabilities will receive services and support from a variety of public and private programs. However, the exact mix of programs will vary depending on the needs of each student, his or her family's economic resources, and each program's eligibility requirements (Wittenberg, Golden, & Fishman, 2002).

Planning for transition must involve the entire community. An extensive analysis of the community must be completed to ensure that all programs and services are identified. Community organizations that are important transition resources include the Benefits Planning, Assistance, and Outreach (BPAO) projects, the federally funded state vocational rehabilitation (VR) program, community rehabilitation service providers, social services, community colleges, Social Security Administration, Centers for Independent Living, One Stop Career Centers, community service boards, and local businesses. Each of these community agencies brings its own unique set of services and supports to students with disabilities as they plan for and consider preparing for a productive life in the community. Many have entrance eligibility and prerequisite criteria

Table 4.1. Community organizations that support youth in transition

Community organizations/agencies	Role and functions
Local rehabilitation services	Determines eligibility, provides assessments, guidance and counseling, and job placement services under an individualized plan for employment (IPE)
Community rehabilitation providers	Provides assessments, counseling, job placement, and follow-up services
Social services	Assists with housing, financial, health, and transportation issues
Community colleges and technical schools	Provides assistance with application and financial aid and information on accessibility during training
Social Security Administration	Financial assistance with Supplemental Security Income as well as other work-related benefits (e.g., Plan for Achieving Self Support [PASS], Impairment Related Work Expense [IRWE])
Centers for Independent Living	Provides information for self-advocacy, understanding one's rights, as well as training programs dealing with money management, sexuality, leisure activities, and socialization
One Stop Career Centers	Assists students with career and vocational counseling, helps with occupational training and job placement
Local community service boards	Provides case management services and assistance for counseling, family planning, nutrition, health care, and transportation
Local businesses	Assists with mock interviews, job-seeking skills, career information, and work experience opportunities
Benefits Planning, Assistance, and Outreach (BPAO)	Provides financial analysis and information on work incentives and disability benefit programs operated under the Social Security Administration

necessary to gain acceptance to these programs and services. Table 4.1 identifies a variety of typical community organizations and the purpose of each organization. The role and function of the agencies listed in Table 4.1 and how these agencies can support successful transition will be discussed in detail in this chapter.

The programs listed in Table 4.1 provide a snapshot of the typical options that are available to provide assistance in the transition planning process. It is important to involve these community agencies early in the process so the entire transition team can learn and become familiar with the resources that are available from the specific agencies (Wehman, 2001a). Without continual involvement, planning, and collaboration from key community agencies, the potential for a successful transition from secondary education to the community will be greatly diminished for students with disabilities.

Critical Elements in Community-Based Transition

A meaningful transition includes postsecondary educational opportunities such as admission to a community college program or employment in real work. It also includes moving toward postsecondary residential independence and individual competence in community living. Transition does not simply mean being placed onto a waiting list or having a referral made on one's behalf. Clearly identified community-based outcomes such as work or school are essential.

The Need for Parents and Students to Be Stakeholders

As noted in Chapters 2 and 3, students and families play a critical role in transition planning. Parents must take a proactive role in the planning for their children during secondary school and adult years. Students and families must be the focal point of services. If this principle is ignored, then service providers will begin to plan curricula and services around what they think is necessary rather than what students and families consider important. Families must not only participate in the educational planning but must also be involved in the community for their children to have viable living and work opportunities. The responsibility for locating a community or 4-year college with learning disability services cannot fall exclusively on the school counselor—parents need to be involved.

The Need for Functional Community-Referenced Skills

Students need to acquire community-referenced skills while they are in high school. This tenet has been frequently described (Wehman & Kregel, 2004) and is discussed in considerably more detail in Chapter 16. In fact, most researchers have concluded that these skills are critical in order for students, especially those with severe disabilities, to effectively make the transition to adult living. A functional curriculum fosters instruction that focuses on developing needed skills and experiences based on objectives drawn from career exploration and individual assessment (Wehman & Targett, 2005). It emphasizes the most important activities that the student will need to perform independently or with supports in vocational, residential, and community environments.

Selecting the most necessary skills in which an individual student needs instruction involves the student, teacher, and others who either know the student well or know the environments well in which the student will most likely participate after leaving school. Continued use of an individualized functional curriculum provides the opportunity for the student to make incremental improvements in job-related skill areas, mobility about the community, and the ability to interact appropriately in a variety of circumstances with the public and with co-workers without disabilities.

The Need for Connections with Adult Services and Vocational Rehabilitation

Helping youth with disabilities successfully negotiate the transition from school to work and community life requires innovative, effective, and enduring partnerships among a variety of key stakeholders. The VR system is identified consistently as a fundamental partner in any collaborative transition effort because of its ability to help youth develop vocational skills, obtain employment, and advance the opportunity to live independently. Systematic efforts must be undertaken to address the barriers that historically have prevented school and VR staff from working together effectively on behalf of youth with disabilities and their families.

Benz, Lindstrom, and Latta (1999) suggested that collaboration between schools and VR agencies is far from commonplace and is limited largely to the basic referral of students to VR. They indicated that the two general barriers to school and VR collaboration cited most often include: 1) poor or inaccurate perceptions of VR by school staff, youth, and parents, and of schools and youth in transition by VR staff; and 2) nonexistent or ineffective procedures to structure collaboration by school and VR staff across the referral, eligibility determination, planning, and service delivery process.

Developing effective school and VR collaborations appears especially problematic for youth with cognitive disabilities (i.e., youth identified by schools as having a learning disability or an emotional disability) and for youth who reside in rural communities (Cimera & Rusch, 2000). The transition planning team is responsible for establishing and maintaining relationships with adult services and funding agencies, a job that is easier said than done. Little doubt exists that all students and their families would like to know that a planning team is available at school or within the community that will take care of all matters that affect transportation, accessibility, community recreation, and nondiscriminatory employment—important goals that all transition models should embrace. (See later in this chapter for some of the ways to create these interagency agreements that allow planning teams to be more effective and less restrained by bureaucracy.)

The Need for Work Before Graduation The availability of paid community employment after graduation is a major outcome that must be established in all communities (Johnson, 2004). This was discussed and recommended by Wehman (2002b) in his testimony to the President's Commission on Excellence in Special Education. Full employment for all people with disabilities who want to work must be a national goal. This goal will not be attained unless the schools actively promote employment, ideally while the student is still in school. Local planning teams must be involved in planning for job placement because few rehabilitation counselors will have the resources or the time to place every student. Brown, Farrington, Suomi, and Ziegler pointed out that:

> Confining instruction to school grounds inhibits or even prohibits too many students with disabilities from learning to function effectively in integrated non-school work and related settings. Particularly if almost all who attend those schools: are from marginalized minority groups; are from depleted neighborhoods or concentrated poverty that countermand almost any kind of healthy human development and achievement; have access to few, if any, effective public services; are not taught to switch to the communication, behavior, dress and other codes critical for success in integrated environments; have not been taught to get to and from important places on time or to produce consistently; and, are perceived as evil, not job ready, untrustworthy and/or dangerous by employers. Maybe some schools cannot be desegregated until neighborhoods are. However, students with disabilities can be at least partially desegregated by teaching them meaningful skills, attitudes, and values in integrated non-school work and related settings during school days and times. Further, regardless of where educational and related services are provided, the generalization/transfer of training difficulties of many individuals with disabilities are devastating. Thus, quality instruction that results in behavioral competence in integrated and respected non-school work and related environments and activities are critical for success therein. (1999, p. 6)

Participation in community-based work helps the student with a disability to build work and work-related skills and also to explore a variety of work settings as a tool in career awareness and exploration. Community-based work experiences can involve unpaid activities in a variety of job areas (Brown et al., 1999). This type of training can take the form of vocational exploration, vocational assessment, or vocational training (Simon, Cobb, Norman, & Bourexix, 1994). Community-based work experiences can also include a variety of paid activities including work experience and on-the-job training. The Bridges Model, developed by the Marriott Corporation (Luecking, Fabian, & Tilson, 2004; Tilson, Luecking, & Donovan, 1994), is an excellent example of a formal community-based work experience program in which students are placed in 4- to 6-month paid internships in positions matched to their interests and skills (Inge, 1991). The range of community-based options available provides the student who has a disability with exposure to real-work settings and experience in interacting with a variety of people and situations.

The Need for Business Alliances with the Schools   Education and business need to learn how to work together and how to understand each other in order to create successful school-to-work partnerships (McMahon et al., 2004). To get business involved with education, a starting point is necessary—a place of access that makes it possible for employers to understand the experiences of the children and young adults who will one day become employees in the work force. Employers can become involved with the school-to-work system in many different ways. Opportunities can range from minimal investment to intense, long-range involvement. The key is to ask, "What is most important to this employer?" and to be flexible in opportunities for the employer's involvement.

Employers can offer many opportunities that help students understand what business and industry offer and the connection between what they learn in school and what is needed in the work force. The Employer Participation Model, published by the National Employer Leadership Council (1996), presents the following examples of opportunities that are invaluable to students and that offer employers a range of levels of investment, from minimal through intense:

- *Career talks:* Visit the classroom and share information about the business or industry (minimal).

- *Career fairs:* Attend special events to allow students to meet with employers and ask questions about different industries (minimal).

- *Workplace and industry tours:* Host student visits during which they talk to employees and observe workplace activities (minimal).

- *Job shadowing:* Arrange for students to follow an employee at a business to learn about a specific occupation or industry (moderate).

- *Job rotations:* Arrange for students to transfer among a variety of positions and tasks requiring different skills and responsibilities to understand all of the steps in a product or service (moderate).

- *Internships:* Employ students for a specified period of time so they can learn about a specific industry or occupation (intense).

- *Cooperative education:* Arrange for students to alternate or coordinate their high school or postsecondary studies with a job in a field related to their academic or occupational objectives (intense).

- *Youth apprenticeships:* Combine school- and work-based learning over multiple years in a specific occupational area or cluster designed to lead directly into a related postsecondary program, entry-level job, or registered apprenticeship program (intense).

- *Mentoring:* Pair students with employees who instruct the students, critique performance, challenge them to perform well, and who work in consultation with teachers (intense).

The Need for College Opportunities Involvement in colleges and universities has been limited for young people with disabilities, but this is all changing (Getzel & Wehman, 2005). Movement into postsecondary institutions of higher education is critical. Several strategies should be implemented.

- Greater efforts should be made to educate faculty, staff, and other students regarding disabilities, accommodations, services, and the legal rights of students with disabilities.

- Appropriate action should be taken against instructors or professors who repeatedly refuse to make course or examination modifications and other accommodations for students with identified disabilities.

- Postsecondary schools should initiate more creative measures to advertise disability-related services to prospective students in need.

- Support groups and clubs, if not organized in particular schools, should be encouraged and supported by postsecondary schools.

- Students with disabilities should be included in formulating disability-related policies and services.

- Consistency should be developed both within and among postsecondary schools regarding the types of services and accommodations that are available to students with disabilities. At present, too much ambiguity exists in availability and delivery of services, which limits the access of students with disabilities to services and accommodations.

Interagency Planning in Community Transition

In order for interagency cooperation to occur and tangible goals for individuals with disabilities to be achieved, state and local community leaders must follow federal examples of leadership. Terms for cooperation must be designed and written for local-level agencies, and staff and participating agency resources must be committed to accomplishing transition-related outcomes. Plans must be developed and implemented to provide for regular and frequent face-to-face interaction of interagency teams at the service delivery level (Everson, Rachal, & Michael, 1992).

Interagency Cooperation at the State Level For state-level interagency collaboration to bring about changes in local-level activities, the leaders must have a strong and visible commitment to common missions. This sense of mission is necessary in order to focus the activities of an organization (Foley, Butterworth, & Heller, 1999). Service provision is the mission for most agencies serving individuals with disabilities.

The purpose of providing educational programming to children and youth with disabilities is to maximize their independence as adults. Education should prepare children and youth for adulthood. In contrast, adult services providers do not begin their service provision to individuals with disabilities until these individuals are adults. The goal of service provision is the same for schools and adult services providers; it is their deadlines for accomplishing the goal that differ. In order to use time more efficiently, adult services providers look for more immediate and varied means to accomplish their goal. Because their missions are the same but different approaches are being used by these agencies, the methods of each agency should be examined and efforts should be coordinated. Gaining a better understanding of how and why the different agencies operate as they do will improve efficiency and reduce instances of duplicated services.

One example of duplication is the repetition of expensive diagnostic evaluations because one state agency does not accept the records of another state agency or because an agency is required to conduct its own evaluations as a part of eligibility determination. Yet, some agencies continue to complete diagnostic evaluations in advance, assuming they will meet the receiving agency's eligibility requirements. This duplication, however, is senseless. Individuals who have received services while in public school special education programs must have been determined eligible for those services because of a disability; procedures for eligibility determination are carefully prescribed in the regulations specified by the Individuals with Disabilities Education Act (IDEA) of 1990 (PL 101-476), the Amendments of 1997 (PL 105-17), and the reauthorization of 2004 (PL 108-446). The existence of an IEP or a transition IEP, as required by law for each student with disabilities, should therefore be sufficient documentation that there is a disability and that the individual is eligible for adult services for individuals with disabilities.

Programs with similar service provision goals for people with disabilities include the vocational education program (Workforce Investment Act [WIA] of 1998, PL 105-220) and developmental disabilities programs. In order to demonstrate how these service providers are similar in mission, it is necessary to restate or reexamine each agency's mission and to recognize common goals. This process is also a useful tool for initiating interagency cooperation. Once a common mission is identified across agencies, the purpose of formalizing interagency collaboration and efficient provision of services becomes clear and logical.

After recognizing that interagency cooperation is advantageous, the leader at the state level must work with agencies to commit staff and resources to initiating the transition process. For example, designating middle-level management personnel to develop interagency activities is a logical starting point. Management liaisons from the different agencies must come together as a core team to examine the need for interagency cooperation by conducting state- and local-level needs assessments to define necessary changes.

One approach to assisting state-level transition coordinators has been advanced by Stodden, Brown, Galloway, Myrazek, and Noy (2004) with an instrument called the Essential Tool. The Essential Tool is designed to assist state-level transition coordinators and others responsible for forming, conducting, and evaluating the performance of interagency transition teams that are focused on the school and postschool needs of youth with disabilities. It guides the coordination efforts of people working at the grassroots level up through the state government. This Essential Tool will assist state interagency transition teams to understand their roles and responsibilities while providing problem-solving strategies and evaluation techniques to ensure that the process is operating in an efficient and successful manner. Ultimately, the Essential Tool will help guide the work toward the primary purpose of an interagency transition team: to improve postschool outcomes for youth with disabilities who are transitioning from secondary school to adult living.

The Essential Tool will help state-level transition coordinators and other current or potential interagency team facilitators learn:

- Why it is valuable to form and use an interagency transition team

- The purpose of an interagency transition team

- What an interagency transition team does

- The roles and responsibilities interagency transition team leaders/facilitators and members need to follow to fulfill their duties

- Who should serve on an interagency transition team and how to select members

- The most opportune times for interagency transition teams to do their work

- Where various interagency transition teams fit into state, district, and local systems

- How to solve problems regarding typical transition issues encountered within the team

- How to evaluate the activities, actions, and values of an interagency transition team

In sum, negotiating the array of adult services and programs can be at best disjointed and at worst completely overwhelming. If youth with disabilities and their families are ultimately going to achieve a smooth transition from school to the full community, then strong relationships need to be built. Several states, including Arizona, Connecticut, Colorado, and Pennsylvania, serve as models for evidence-based practice in interagency transition teams (Stodden et al., 2004). Although all of community resources presented here are important, there are three relationships in which transition teams need to concentrate their efforts: 1) Social Security benefits planning, 2) VR and community rehabilitation agencies, and 3) relationships with business. If one of these three relationships is missing from a student's transition planning from school, gaps in needed services will likely occur. The remainder of this chapter provides in-depth information on why these three partners are so important and illustrations of successful models.

BENEFITS PLANNING ASSISTANCE AND OUTREACH

Since the 1980s, several exciting legislative reforms have occurred aimed at assisting people with disabilities in gaining access to competitive employment. Yet, none of these reforms holds more promise than the Ticket to Work and Work Incentives Improvement Act of 1999 (TWWIIA; PL 106-170). Although TWWIIA contains several different components and strategies aimed at removing barriers to employment and creating greater choice for individuals with disabilities, the most significant component for youth in transition is the National Benefits Planning, Assistance, and Outreach (BPAO) initiative. Lack of understanding of the complex requirements for gaining access to Social Security work incentives and Medicaid benefits available under the Social Security Act are major barriers contributing to the unemployment of youth with disabilities. The BPAO program, contained in Section 121 of the TWWIIA, addresses this barrier.

The BPAO program comprises 117 projects nationally. The goal of each of these projects is to provide information and direct individualized benefits analysis assistance on how Social Security Administration (SSA) benefit programs and work incentives interface with work. As a result, each SSA recipient is better able to make informed choices about work. These services are available to all individuals receiving Supplemental Security Income (SSI) and/or Title II disability benefits who are between the ages of 14 and 64.

During the transition planning process, students and families often express concerns about the potential impact of earnings from competitive employment on their existing federal benefits. Generally, these concerns are related to a potential loss of Social Security income benefits and/or medical benefits. The benefits specialists employed by a BPAO project recently implemented by the SSA provide a resource through which individuals receiving a Social Security benefit can gain access to benefits counseling to determine the impact of employment on the specific benefits they receive. These highly trained benefits specialists provide informational resources as well as conduct intensive benefits analysis that is specific to the individual's unique circumstances through a written benefits analysis. Once this benefits analysis is complete, the individual with a disability is able to make an informed decision regarding employment. The results of this analysis identify the true impact of employment on the person's SSA benefits and on other federal benefit programs. Because there are unique work incentives that are available to students, a local BPAO program should be contacted for all students with disabilities who receive a SSI or a Social Security Disability Insurance (SSDI) benefit and are interested in employment. The following is a summary description of key Social Security benefits and work incentives that are potential resources for youth with disabilities in the transition process.

SSI Program Basics

A benefits specialist working with students who are receiving or who may be eligible for a Social Security benefit known as SSI can help students and their families to clearly understand four key points about this program:

1. Students will always have more money working than by not working when they receive SSI.

2. There are several "work incentives" that may help SSI recipients pay for items that are necessary in order to work.

3. There is a special work incentive targeted to students that makes employment highly desirable while attending school.

4. Students can keep Medicaid until they earn as much as nearly $40,000 annually in some states.

To understand how all of these features of the benefits program work, benefits specialists would first introduce the basics of the SSI program, which is designed to supplement any income a person with a disability may already have to meet the minimum needs for food, clothing, and shelter expenses such as rent and utilities. A person can be eligible for SSI if he or she is a United States citizen or is able to meet the necessary requirements for noncitizens under the law. In addition, he or she must have a disability serious enough that it substantially limits the individual from engaging in the activities that other students often perform. Furthermore, to gain eligibility for SSI, the individual must have a limited income and very few resources. The bottom line is that the more income and resources an individual has, the less the benefit will be. Because SSI has income criteria for eligibility, an individual will not be eligible for a benefit if he or she has too much income.

The first question that teachers, students with disabilities, and families typically ask is when should a person apply for SSI. An individual with a disability can apply for SSI at any time. It is important to know that if SSA turns down an application, the family should keep that record, and if circumstances change, a new application can be submitted. There are a variety of ways to apply. Applications can be made by contacting the local SSA office by telephone, calling the SSA's toll free number at 1-800-772-1213, downloading the application from their web site at http://www.ssa.gov, or by making an appointment at the local SSA. There is a variety of paperwork that SSA will request at the time of application, so being prepared can save everyone a lot of time. A list of documents that should be prepared is presented in Table 4.2. The list includes such items as a social security number, school background medical and work history, and financial records.

When SSA makes a decision about whether an individual qualifies for SSI, it will send a letter to directly inform the new beneficiary. If eligible, the first monthly check will include the 3–6 months that the applicant waited during the application process. This check can be automatically deposited into a personal bank account. If SSA has found that the individual is not eligible for a benefit, then an explanation will be provided. It is important to know that this SSA finding can be appealed, and the letter from SSA will include information on how to initiate an appeal process.

IMPACT OF EMPLOYMENT ON SUPPLEMENTAL SECURITY INCOME BENEFITS

The SSA wants beneficiaries to attempt employment and provides multiple opportunities for this to occur without the beneficiary losing his or her cash benefit. The benefits specialist with the local BPAO program can carefully analyze how employment will impact SSI, Medicaid, and other federal benefits. The benefits specialist will explain the multiple employment supports and SSA work incentives that are available to the SSI recipients. Taking advantage of these work incentives will allow a beneficiary to continue to receive his or her SSI check and/or Medicaid while maintaining employment. The SSI incentives that are reviewed here include:

- 1619 (a) and (b)
- Earned Income Exclusion
- Student Earned Income Exclusion
- Impairment-Related Work Expense
- Blind Work Expense
- Plan for Achieving Self-Support

Table 4.2.   Records for Supplemental Security Income (SSI) application process determination

Personal identification information of applicant

Name

Address

Social Security number

Medical history

Names and addresses of physicians

Names and addresses of medical and/or treatment facilities where services have been provided

Names and addresses of health care professionals

Names and addresses of facilities and a record of treatment

Educational history

Names and addresses of schools attended

School records

Names and addresses of the most recent teacher and/or school counselor

Vocational rehabilitation (VR) history

Names and addresses of VR services center

VR records

Name and address of the most recent VR counselor

Employment history

Names and addresses of current and previous places of employment (if applicable)

Summary of work history tasks

Legal records

Birth certificates

Adoption papers

Marriage certificates

Divorce papers

Immigration or naturalization papers

Financial records

Latest tax bill

Property statements

Rental agreements

Proof of utilities

Proof of food expenses

Insurance policies

Name and address of bank

Recent bank/credit union statements to include checking and savings accounts

Resource and assets records

Car registration

Bank book

Insurance policies

Parents/family financial history

Record of parents' income if under 18 years of age

1619 (a) and (b)

The SSA has a relatively new law that protects individuals receiving SSI and Medicaid who want to attempt work. Once employed, SSA will count less than half of gross wages when they calculate the amount of the SSI cash benefit. As long as the individual still qualifies for even one penny of the SSI benefit when the calculation is performed, then he or she is protected under the first part of the law known as 1619 (a). Essentially, this means that the SSI beneficiary will always have more money by working than if he or she was solely dependent on the SSI benefit. The SSA simply reduces the SSI check by about $1.00 for every $2.00 earned, and Medicaid continues for as long as the beneficiary remains in 1619 (a).

If the individual continues on his or her career path and earns so much income that the SSI check ultimately gets reduced to $0.00, then protection is available under the second portion of the law known as 1619 (b). This guarantees that SSA will keep a beneficiary's file open in case employment hours are reduced or if there is a loss of employment. Furthermore, 1619 (b) protects Medicaid eligibility for all SSI recipients, even those living in states where an individual's income level may be too high to receive a Medicaid benefit. These individuals cannot have more than $2,000 in resources, but they can earn more than $25,000–$30,000 in most states and not worry about losing Medicaid. Recipients who choose to accept medical insurance coverage provided by their employer are still covered by 1619 (b).

Earned Income Exclusion

As further proof that SSA wants SSI recipients to attempt employment, SSA disregards most of the income that was earned when they calculate the amount of the SSI check. The first $65.00 of wages in any month is not counted, and if there is no other income, SSA excludes $85.00 rather than $65.00. Once this calculation is completed, SSA will then only count half of the remaining wages. Therefore, if Mathew was receiving a $603 monthly SSI check and then went to work for a home improvement store earning $600 a month as a stock clerk, the following calculation would be performed to determine total monthly income.

Mathew working as a stock clerk earning $600.00 per month and receiving a $603 monthly SSI benefit from SSA.

$600.00 (wages)
–$ 85.00 (exclusion)
$515.00 / 2 = $257.50 (wages counted by SSA)

$603.00 (amount of SSI check if there are no wages)
–$257.50 (wages counted by SSA from employment)
$345.50

New monthly amounts
$600.00 (wages from stock clerk job)
$345.50 (amount of SSI check)
$945.50 (total monthly income plus no loss of Medicaid)

Student Earned Income Exclusion

This particular work incentive is designed exclusively for young people under the age of 22 who are attending school and are not married or considered the "head" of household. To qualify, an SSI recipient must be regularly attending school. In addition, one of the following must apply to the student's individual situation: 1) attending college for at least 8 hours per week, 2) attending junior or senior high school at least 12 hours per week, or 3) attending a vocational training program for least 12 hours a week (intern program for at least 15 hours per week). Less time may be needed in these programs if it is the result of student illness. If a student qualifies for this incentive, then he or she can go to work and SSA will count even less of total earning when calculating the SSI benefit.

In the case of Mathew, a benefits specialist would help him and his family to understand that while Mathew was in school and earning $600 in wages, a Student Earned Income Exclusion (SEIE) would apply and SSA would not count any of his wages from his job at the home improvement store. Therefore, without the job at the home improvement store, Mathew would simply be receiving a monthly SSI check for $603. Applying the SEIE, Mathew continues to receive the $603 from SSI along with $600 in earning from employment, resulting in a total monthly income of $1,203.00.

Mathew working as a stock clerk earning $600.00 per month and receiving a $603 per month SSI benefit from SSA.

$ 600.00 (wages from job)
$ 603.00 (amount of SSI check)
$1,203.00 (total monthly income plus no loss of Medicaid)

A benefits specialist would further explain that if Mathew decided to work full time in the summer (June through August) while he was on school break, the SEIE would make it possible for him to keep his earnings from his paycheck while maintaining his SSI check of $603.00. So, if Mathew earns $1,000 a month from his summer job, his total monthly income, including his SSI check of $603, would be $1,603. Clearly, Mathew is doing much better working that if he was just receiving an SSI check.

Impairment-Related Work Expense

Another SSA work incentive known as an Impairment-Related Work Expense (IRWE) can be used to pay for items that are necessary to work and are incurred due to the individual's disability. The benefits specialist would explain that this work support can be used in any month while work is occurring for the total length of employment tenure. A "credit" is given for expenses that meet the following rules:

- The item or service must directly assist the individual to maintain employment
- The item or service is needed because of a disability
- The item or service is directly purchased by the SSA beneficiary

- The cost for the item or service is "reasonable" using a standard cost in the community

A benefits specialist is not able to approve an individual for an IRWE, only an SSA claims representative is able to make this determination. It will be the SSA claims representative that determines if the previous criterion apply. Examples of items or services that some people have had approved as an IRWE expense include specialized transportation, assistive technology (AT), medications to control a disability, attendant care, and job coach services. Talking with a benefits specialist prior to employment can assist in identifying possible expenses that may qualify for an IRWE.

Mathew, who earns $600.00 each month from his job is paying $200 each month from his wages to receive door-to-door transportation because of his disability. Once an SSA claims representative approves Mathew's transportation cost as an IRWE, this ultimately will have a positive effect on his total monthly income, allowing Mathew to recover half of the expense that he pays for transportation.

Blind Work Expense

A Blind Work Expense (BWE) is limited to those individuals who receive SSI and are blind. Unique to this population, SSA deducts all work expenses, whether they are due to an individual's disability or not. A benefits specialist would be able to demonstrate how students who are blind are able to receive a higher SSI check when they go to work than other people on SSI. In order to receive a BWE, the work expenses must have been paid for by the individual beneficiary and the expense must be deemed reasonable by SSA. The BWE will continue throughout an individuals tenure of employment and as long as the employment expense is still present. Unlike the IRWE, the BWE includes a much broader range of work expenses to include, but not limited to, taxes, union dues, parking fees, transportation, AT, reader services, meals eaten during work, and guide dog expenses.

Plan for Achieving Self-Support

Most benefits specialists would describe SSA's Plan for Achieving Self-Support (PASS) as a tremendously flexible work incentive. This particular incentive allows an SSI recipient to save money to pay for expenses that are necessary to reach a stated career goal. For example, if a certification, degree, or a car are necessary to achieve a career goal, then a PASS could be written to help pay for the expense. The development of a PASS and how it excludes earned income, unearned income, and/or resources to allow a beneficiary to use financial resources now or in the future for approved expenses must be related to a stated career goal.

In order for a PASS to be approved, it must meet the criterion presented in Table 4.3. Although a benefits specialist can assist an SSA beneficiary in the development of a PASS, it is the sole responsibility of the SSA to approve the PASS. Typical expenditures that have been approved by SSA for a PASS include equipment, supplies, operating capital and inventory required for starting a business, supported employment (SE) services, costs associated with advanced education or vocational education, dues and publications for academic or professional purposes, child care, attendant care, and

Table 4.3.   Nine steps for writing a successful Plan for Achieving Self-Support (PASS)

Steps	PASS
1	The plan must be individualized and designed for a specific individual.
2	The plan must be in writing on the established form—SSA-545.
3	The plan must have a clearly stated career goal that is feasible for the individual to obtain.
4	The plan must include a milestone and/or time frame for when the career goal will be reached.
5	The plan must show the expenses that will be incurred to reach the career goal and which expenses will be paid for by the beneficiary.
6	The plan must document the resources that will be used to pay for the expense related to the career goal. These resources cannot be from a Supplemental Security Income (SSI) benefit.
7	The plan must show how financial resources will be set aside to pay for the expenses (e.g., an individual bank account).
8	The plan must be submitted to the Social Security Administration (SSA) for approval before the PASS can be initiated.
9	The plan must be reviewed by SSA on a regular basis to update progress.

uniforms. The development of a PASS can be a complex process, and some frequently asked questions regarding PASS are presented in Table 4.4.

In the past, teachers, VR counselors, advocates, social workers, and employment support personnel have included benefits planning as part of their existing job responsibilities. However, because this was typically an add-on job duty to an ever-expanding job description, students and adults with disabilities would often get inaccurate information regarding the impact of work on their Social Security benefit as well as the other federal benefit programs. Therefore, in order for true reform to take place, the United States needed practitioners dedicated to providing high-quality benefits planning to SSA recipients with disabilities. SSA truly understood that concern and created the BPAO program. To date this community resource has served approximately 200,000 SSA beneficiaries. To find the location of BPAO programs across the country go to http://www. vcu-barc.org. Youth with disabilities in transition and their families who have a clear understanding of the impact of earnings on benefits are well prepared to make decisions about employment and to select appropriate community programs and services.

TRANSITION AND COMMUNITY TRAINING, EMPLOYMENT, AND SUPPORT PROGRAMS

The Rehabilitation Act Amendments of 1998 (PL 103-569) defined *transition services* as follows:

- Transition services means a coordinated set of activities for a student designed within an outcome-oriented process that promotes movement from school to post-school activities, including postsecondary education, vocational training, integrated employment (including SE), continuing and adult education, adult services, independent living, or community participation.

- The coordinated set of activities must be based upon the individual student's needs, taking into account the student's preferences and interests, and must include

Table 4.4. Frequently asked questions regarding Plans for Achieving Self-Support (PASS)

Question	Response
Who can have a PASS?	Anyone that receives Supplemental Security Income (SSI) or could be eligible for SSI can have a PASS plan. PASS plans are designed to help individuals set aside income/resources for a specified time period for a work goal. The intent of the PASS program is to assist people in achieving self-sufficiency and reduce their dependency on Social Security Administration (SSA) benefits.
Who can help set up a PASS?	Anyone can help set up a PASS plan, including Benefits Planning, Assistance, and Outreach (BPAO) project personnel (benefits planners), teachers, rehabilitation counselors, consultants and advocates, and SSA personnel. SSA PASS Specialists and Employment Support Representatives (ESRs) will play a major role in both the application process and the review process. Both PASS specialists and ESR personnel can be reached via toll-free telephone numbers and are located around the country in regional and local SSA offices. Specific locations and contact information can be found through the SSA web site at www.ssa.gov/work.
Can students under the age of 18 establish a PASS to assist with the transition process?	Students younger than age 18 can establish a PASS if they have earned/unearned income or resources of their own or have deemed income or resources from an ineligible parent to set aside.
Does an individual need to be determined eligible for SSI prior to establishing a PASS?	The two processes typically occur simultaneously for people interested in establishing a PASS that are currently not eligible for SSI. These individuals will have to go through the SSA application process to determine eligibility prior to the PASS, resulting in the SSI cash benefit being issued. Individuals already receiving SSI will not be required to meet initial SSI eligibility.
Can wages be excluded under a PASS in determining SSI eligibility?	One of the criteria to determine SSI eligibility is that the individual is either currently not working or if working, earning under SGA. Although income/resources that are set aside in a PASS are not counted in the SSI eligibility determination process, wages that are set aside in the PASS cannot be deducted from gross wages for SGA determination.
How are a PASS and an Impairment-Related Work Expense (IRWE) different?	The PASS work incentive allows an individual who is receiving SSI or could be found eligible for SSI to set aside income and/or resources for a specified period of time to purchase items and/or services necessary to achieve a work goal. The IRWE work incentive allows individuals to deduct certain impairment-related items and/or services that are necessary to maintain employment from their gross earnings on an ongoing basis as needed.
Is it possible to use a PASS and an IRWE at the same time?	It is possible and allowable to have a PASS and also use an IRWE at the same time for ongoing expenses not included in the PASS. For concurrent beneficiaries, it is also possible to use the same expense as a PASS for the purpose of SSI and simultaneously claim it as an IRWE for the purpose of the SSDI, assuming that the expense meets the requirements of the two work incentives. In addition, during the SSI eligibility process, an individual could use an IRWE that is also included as a PASS expense to reduce gross monthly countable income below SGA. Only during SSI eligibility determination may the same expense be counted as an IRWE and included in the PASS simultaneously.
Would an individual be penalized if he or she did not reach the work goal at the end of the PASS?	An individual would not be penalized if he or she did not reach his or her work goal at the end of the PASS if he or she: • Followed the PASS steps to reach the work goal as established and/or revised • Spent the income and/or resources that were set aside as outlined in the PASS • Kept records of the expenditures, including receipts • Actively sought employment at the end of the PASS

Source: Benefits Assistance Resource Center, Plans for Achieving Self-Support Briefing, 2004, Virginia Commonwealth University.

instruction, community experiences, the development of employment and other post-school adult living objectives, and, if appropriate, acquisition of daily living skills and functional vocational evaluation.

• Transition services must promote or facilitate the achievement of the employment outcome identified in the student's individualized plan for employment. (Federal Register, January 17, 2001, p. 4389)

In relation to the adult service community, this definition of transition services emphasizes an outcome-oriented process focused on postsecondary education and vocational training, employment, independent living, community participation, and/or other adult services as needed by each transitioning youth. This range of potential services encompasses a variety of programs with distinct roles, eligibility criteria, service guidelines, and funding requirements. In approaching agencies and programs in the adult services system, it is most helpful if youth with disabilities in transition and their families understand the core general role and function of each agency in the following areas: 1) service coordination, including case management services; 2) direct service provision; and 3) potential for gaining access to funds to use in acquiring services. The following description of the role of programs and agencies in the adult services community in supporting transition will be framed around these three areas.

State Vocational Rehabilitation Services

Individuals with disabilities may qualify for federally supported state VR services if the individuals' disability presents a barrier to obtaining competitive employment or maintaining employment. The Rehabilitation Act of 1973 (PL 93-112), as amended, provides states federal grants to operate comprehensive programs of VR services for individuals with disabilities. VR is a federal/state cooperative program that exists in all 50 states and the U.S. territories.

A rehabilitation counselor will process an application for services and make a determination of eligibility for VR services. Eligibility is based on the presence of a disability that is an impairment to employment and an expectation that the provision of VR services will assist the individual to achieve an employment outcome. VR services can provide an array of services and supports prior to and after graduation. Once eligibility has been determined, an individualized plan for employment (IPE) must be developed in connection with the completion of high school. Driven by the IPE, and specifically the work goal of the individual with a disability, a host of services and supports are then made available. Rehabilitation counselors are an excellent resource for schools as they plan for the transition of students with disabilities.

Case Management Through Vocational Rehabilitation   Each applicant for VR services is assigned a rehabilitation counselor who is responsible for determining eligibility for VR services and assisting the individual in completing the IPE. The counselor is positioned to provide information and referral on a variety of community services and can incorporate a variety of services into the IPE if those services specifically support the identified employment outcome. Case management through VR continues until the case is closed. Case closure can occur after a minimum of 90 days of employment in a job consistent with the employment objective established in the IPE. A case can also be closed if the individual is not making progress toward achieving an employment outcome.

Employment and Related Services Available Through Vocational Rehabilitation

There are a variety of services potentially available through a VR agency. These services include, but are not limited to, the following.

- Assessment for determining eligibility for VR services

- Vocational counseling, guidance, and referral services

- Physical restoration and mental health services

- Vocational and other training, including on-the-job training

- Maintenance services such as meals and housing

- Interpreter services for individuals who have hearing impairments

- Reading services for individuals who have visual impairments

- Personal assistance services, including training in managing and directing a personal assistant

- Rehabilitation technology services

- Job placement services and SE services

A VR agency directly provides services such as counseling, guidance, and job placement assistance, and it will usually arrange with other community providers to acquire services such as rehabilitation technology, physical and mental restoration, and SE. The ability of a VR agency to reach out into the community for individualized services is one of the key potential strengths of the VR system.

Funding Available Through Vocational Rehabilitation
VR counselors have access to case service funds that can be used to purchase services from authorized vendors. If the service supports the employment goal established on the IPE, then VR funds can be used to purchase services such as postsecondary education and training, SE, transportation, tools and uniforms, and a variety of other services. VR counselors are also usually very familiar with other funding sources that can be used to complement VR funding. Critical considerations in advocating for VR funding is that the service being considered for funding clearly supports the employment goal and is not available from another funding source.

VR counselors can serve as an information resource about community services for transition teams during the early planning stages in the transition process. As the youth with a disability nears completion of his or her secondary education program, the rehabilitation counselor should become actively involved with the youth so that an IPE is in place prior to the student exiting the school program. VR agencies are well positioned to serve as the service coordination hub for employment-oriented community services for eligible youth with disabilities transitioning from secondary-level programs.

Self-Determination and Vocational Rehabilitation
Self-determination is important for VR clients for several reasons. First, as mentioned previously, promoting

choice and self-determination is mandated by federal disability policy and legislation. Second, people with disabilities have been unequivocal in their demands for enhanced self-determination (Kennedy, 1996; Ward, 1996). Third, there is compelling evidence from the special education literature that enhanced self-determination status leads to more positive adult outcomes. Wehmeyer and Schwartz (1997) measured the self-determination status of 80 students with mild mental retardation or learning disabilities in their final year of high school and then 1 year after high school. Students with higher self-determination scores were more likely to have expressed a preference to live outside the family home, have a savings or checking account, and be employed for pay. Eighty percent of students in the high self-determination group worked for pay 1 year after graduation, whereas only 43% of students in the low self-determination group did likewise. Among those who were employed after high school, youth who were in the high self-determination group earned significantly more per hour ($M =$ \$4.26) than their peers in the low self-determination group ($M =$ \$1.93).

Wehmeyer and Palmer (2003) conducted a second follow-up study, examining the adult status of 94 young people with cognitive disabilities (mental retardation or learning disability) 1 and 3 years postgraduation. These data replicated results from Wehmeyer and Schwartz (1997).

Finally, there is a growing body of evidence in the field of VR that enhancing choice opportunities leads to better VR-related outcomes. For example, Farley, Bolton, and Parkerson (1992) evaluated the impact of strategies to enhance consumer choice and involvement in the VR process and found that consumers who were actively involved in VR planning enhanced their vocational career development outcomes. Similarly, Hartnett, Collins, and Tremblay (2002) compared costs, services received, and outcomes achieved for people served through the typical VR system and people involved in a "Consumer Choice Demonstration Project" in Vermont. They found that the Choice group was two times more likely to have completed rehabilitation, and their mean income was 2.7 times higher.

Community Rehabilitation Providers

A typical community will often have multiple community rehabilitation service providers with an agency mission of assisting people with disabilities to obtain and maintain competitive employment. Many of these service providers work closely with the state VR service agency. Specific services offered by providers will vary, with many offering counseling, assessments, benefits counseling, job placement, and supported employment (SE) services designed to assist students to live independently in the community. Community rehabilitation programs providing employment related services for individuals with a disability can operate as for-profit or as nonprofit businesses. However, it is important to note that these programs do usually provide services based on contract or fee-for-service arrangements. Therefore, access to their services will frequently require a funding authorization from an agency such as VR.

Case Management Services Through Community Rehabilitation Providers The employment support staff for community rehabilitation providers is usually called employment consultants/specialists, job coaches, or other job titles linking their work closely to employment outcomes. Some community rehabilitation providers have con-

tracts with their local developmental disabilities agency, for example, to provide case management services. Usually, case management assistance involving identification of potential resources in the community and coordination with other service providers is provided in response to individual support needs critical to employment success. For example, an employment consultant might seek out benefits counseling assistance, child care options, mental health services, or other supports needed for a consumer who needs this type of assistance. The case management role of community rehabilitation providers is most frequently time-limited and situational, with staff coordinating its services with the funding agency such as VR and/or addressing individual support needs critical to employment success.

Employment and Related Services Available Through Community Rehabilitation Programs Community rehabilitation programs provide a variety of employment related services such as helping the youth with a disability explore potential job and career options through, for example, situational assessments at competitive job sites and job tryouts. A variety of job preparation, job development, and job placement services are also provided. These services might include mock job interviews, job seeking skills classes, résumé preparation, guided job searches, and negotiations with employers. For example, an employer has a job with multiple job duties. Some of these duties match well to the abilities of the job applicant with a disability; other features of the job responsibilities are a poor match for the applicant. The employment consultant, with the permission of the applicant, might work with the employer to negotiate a job carved out of the original job description that is a good match for the individual with a disability. Once the job match is completed, the employment consultant can assist with training at the job site, help the worker with a disability adjust to job demands, and provide ongoing support as needed to help maintain the job or to potentially assist with job change (Johnson, 2004).

Funding Available Through Community Rehabilitation Programs Community rehabilitation programs are usually not a primary source of funding because they usually work under contract/fee arrangements to cover the cost for their services. However, these programs are frequently quite familiar with the funding resources in a community and can assist in identifying funding resources. Community programs combine the funding received through contracts/fees with funding available to an individual consumer, such as the PASS plan. Successful community rehabilitation programs create a diversified funding base that brings together a variety of funding options (Brooks-Lane, Butterworth, Ghiloni, & Revell, 2004; Brooks-Lane, Hutcheson, & Revell, 2005).

Community rehabilitation programs are a very important resource for youth in transition. These programs can offer specialized services that match well to the needs of individuals with specific types of disabilities; with specific training and support needs; and/or more time-intensive, prescriptive service requirements that are beyond the capacity of public agencies serving large numbers of people. Youth with disabilities and their families need to review information on the providers in their community before committing to a specific program. This review should potentially include personal interviews with the representatives of the programs. Funding agencies such as VR should have information on the outcomes achieved by these programs, including satisfaction reports from their consumers (O'Brien, Revell, & West, 2003). Before selecting a community rehabilitation program, the following questions should be researched:

1. What are the general characteristics of the program (e.g., location, contact information, program model, availability of transportation to the program)?

2. What kinds of jobs do consumers get?

3. How stable and supportive is the job coaching staff likely to be?

4. What level of hours, pay, and benefits can a consumer expect?

5. How likely is a consumer to get a job, and how long will it take to get one?

6. How satisfied were other consumers with the services of the provider?

Social Services Agencies

The local social services office can play a vital role in the transition process. Social services agencies manage programs such as Temporary Aid to Needy Families (TANF), the Food Stamp program, Medicaid, foster care, and Child and Adult Protective Services. Case managers with these programs should be aware of the available community resources and entrance criterion for each program. Support can be found for such services as housing, financial assistance, health, transportation, employment, Child and Adult Protective Services, and child care.

Case Management Services Available Through Social Services Agencies   Social services agencies can help coordinate services that would assist the student in the transition process. Youth in transition will frequently be eligible for assistance through a social services agency as a part of a family unit receiving services (e.g., as a part of a TANF eligibility in a Welfare to Work program). A youth in a foster care program or as a part of a Child Protective Services program could be eligible on his or her own. Many foster care programs include help with the transition process from foster care to independent living in the community. Social services agencies differ from state to state and community to community. The type of case management assistance available through social services will be dependent on the specific services for which an individual is eligible.

Employment and Related Services Available Through Social Services Agencies Social services agencies are not a primary source of direct employment support in areas such as job leads, job placement assistance, or on-the-job training. However, these agencies can help with key employment related services such as child care, transportation, food and medical assistance, and crisis services. In the TANF Welfare to Work program, the TANF plan managers can be an information and referral resource for assistance in career exploration and job placement activities.

Funding Available Through Social Services Agencies   Social services agencies are the primary access point to food stamp grants, Medicaid health benefits, and other benefits that are based on income-eligibility guidelines. Social services agencies can also have funds to purchase certain employment related services. For example, within the TANF Welfare to Work programs, some social services agencies have special grants or other funds that can be used to purchase a variety of job preparation, job placement, and postemployment support services from community programs.

Although the core programs, such as Medicaid and food stamps, are governed by federal regulations, there is substantial variation across states and communities in many of the programs and services provided by social services agencies. Youth in transition, their families, and the key stakeholders supporting the transition process in their community need to work closely with the social services agency to understand eligibility guidelines and the case management, service, and funding resources potentially available locally.

Local Community Service Boards/Agencies

Local agencies that provide services in the mental retardation/mental health/ developmental disabilities/substance abuse service area operate under a variety of different names. In some communities, these services are managed by local community service boards. Some states operate these services under direct state supervision as local agencies. Eligibility for these services are based on the presence of a disability that meets specific state guidelines, and these eligibility criteria will vary from state to state. The services from these local community service board/agencies are a core potential resource for youth with disabilities in transition that meet the eligibility guidelines.

Case Management Services Available Through Local Community Services Boards/ Agencies Case managers with the local community mental health/mental retardation/ substance abuse office are excellent resources for the transition planning process. Generally, case managers are available to serve as a coordination hub with very specific knowledge of services for the youth as well as for family members. Case managers will be knowledgeable about resources for community housing and supported living, for example, and can help the youth and family identify and gain access to a variety of services funded through the Home and Community Based Services (HCBS) Medicaid Waiver, which will be discussed later in this chapter. Case managers can attend transition meetings, both as resources for information and referral and also to help plan for specific transition support services needed by an individual.

Employment-Related Services Available Through Community Service Boards/ Agencies These programs can provide an array of services that include counseling, family planning, training, nutrition, personal health care, and consultation. Many community service boards operate or contract for community housing and supported living programs, a critical need for many youth with significant disabilities in transition as they seek to live separate from their families (or in fact do not have the option of living with family). For individuals with a mental health-related disability, these programs are the primary source of public mental health clinical and support services, including medication management and therapeutic counseling. There is substantial evidence that the integration of mental health and employment services increases the expectation for successful employment outcomes for individuals with a severe mental illness (Bond, 2004a). Therefore, it is critically important that transition plans and services include close coordination with the local mental health agency for youth in transition with mental health-related issues.

Funding Available Through Community Service Boards/Agencies   Depending on state and sometimes local laws and policies, the populations served by individual community service boards/agencies can vary widely. Some serve a wide range of individuals with a disability; others serve a much more limited population. Unlike state VR agencies discussed earlier, community service boards/agencies are not operated under a specific set of federal laws. The disability-related service areas these agencies serve can include, but potentially are not limited to, mental health, mental retardation, developmental disabilities, and/or substance abuse services. Therefore, because public funding is frequently categorical in nature and targeted to specific disability groups, the funding resources available through community service boards/agencies can vary widely from state to state and across communities. It is critically important that youth with disabilities in transition, their families, and key stakeholders take the time to become fully informed regarding the target populations and related funding resources and priorities

Community service boards/agencies have access to a variety of funding resources. Funding is frequently available to assist with acquiring housing and supported living services, as well as employment supports. A primary funding source is the HCBS Medicaid Waiver, which provides services in the community for individuals who, without these services, would need to live in an institutional setting because of the significant nature of their disability and resulting support needs. In June 2002, 77.4% of combined HCBS and Intermediate Care Facilities for the Mentally Retarded service recipients were receiving HCBS, compared with approximately only 30% in 1992 (Larkin & Gaylord, 2003). Medicaid Long-Term Support Services funding for individuals with an intellectual disability/developmental disability has grown from $11.4 billion in fiscal year (FY) 1993 to $25.6 billion in FY 2003 (Larkin, Prouty, & Coucouvanis, 2005).

The Balanced Budget Act of 1997 (PL 105-33) opened up funding for SE through the HCBS Medicaid Waiver (West et al., 2002). It is important to note that HCBS Medicaid Waiver and other Medicaid funding continues to be used predominantly for prevocational activities and other types of day habilitation services that do not involve competitive employment services. For example, in FY 1998, federal Medicaid funding for SE totaled $35 million compared with $514 million for day program services that did not include supports to people in competitive employment. From 1998 to 2002, the funding for SE grew to $108 million, and the funding for day programs dropped slightly to $488 million. However, $4 dollars continues to be spent for services that do not support competitive employment outcomes for every $1 spent on SE services that do support competitive employment outcomes (Braddock, Hemp, Parish, & Rizzolo, 2002; Braddock, Rizzolo, & Hemp, 2004).

Each individual state submits applications for HCBS Medicaid Waivers that define specific target populations and designate specific services. There are states that place a premium on competitive employment outcomes (Wehman, Revell, & Brooke, 2003). For many youth with significant disabilities transitioning into the adult services community, the HCBS Medicaid Waiver is a critically important funding source because of its flexibility and potential responsiveness to individual need (Larkin & Gaylord, 2003). However, funding for the HCBS Medicaid Waiver is drawn from federal funds matched with state dollars. Youth who are transitioning out of school and living in states experiencing difficulties in HCBS Medicaid Waiver funding face the potential of waiting lists, limited services, and/or narrowly defined target populations that result in gaps and limitations in services.

Community Colleges and Other Vocational and Technical Schools

Many postsecondary schools offer their services to assist with the transition from high school into postsecondary education and training opportunities. Community colleges serve as a gateway to eventual movement to a 4-year bachelor's degree program after completion of an initial course of college-level study. Community colleges also offer trade and vocational programs that are reflective of the local economy and job market. These programs can be responsive partners as a part of community training initiatives that might have particular value to youth with disabilities in transition in learning how to live and work in the community. Vocational and technical schools also offer curriculum reflective of the local job market. In working with these programs in transition planning prior to enrollment, the youth with a disability, with support as needed by his or her transition team members, should gather information about employment outcomes achieved by individuals who completed the training programs offered.

Case Management Services Available Through Community Colleges and Other Vocational and Technical Schools Staff from these schools will provide assistance with entrance requirements and the application process. Generally, there is a separate office that will provide guidance for financial aid. Community colleges sometimes offer information on housing and other community supports, including access to VR services. A critical case management service offered by many community colleges is information and support in the area of programs to assist students with disabilities. This assistance could involve information on how to self-advocate in working with instructors in requesting needed accommodations related to the presence of a disability and how to gain access to specific technology (e.g., adapted computer equipment).

Employment Related Services Available Through Community Colleges and Other Vocational and Technical Schools Many community colleges and vocational and technical schools have advisory boards made up of local employers. These boards can serve as links to the local community by providing information on careers that are in high demand. These colleges and schools offer job fairs and other recruitment activities that offer the possibility for youth in transition to talk with employers, submit résumés, and set up exploratory visits to job sites. Some of these programs have employment support personnel on staff that can help identify job openings and provide training in job seeking skills.

Funding Available Through Community Colleges and Other Vocational and Technical Schools Funding assistance would primarily be for information on grants, scholarships, and loans to pay for the costs involved in attending the college or school. The financial aid office at the school would provide information on how to apply for these funds. There are a variety of potential funding sources in addition to standard financial aid for youth with disabilities, including funding through the VR agency. Youth can gain access to grants or loans through the community college or vocational school for a particular piece of adaptive equipment.

Centers for Independent Living

Centers for Independent Living are a great resource for local transition teams (Wehmeyer & Gragoudas, 2004) because they can provide a wealth of information for students and their families. Centers for Independent Living staff can assist in helping the student to build his or her advocacy skills as well as understanding his or her rights. Most Centers for Independent Living provide general information about resources in the community and will also offer classes in areas such as financial management, socialization, sexuality, leisure activities, peer counseling, and self-advocacy.

Case Management Services Available Through Centers for Independent Living

Centers for Independent Living place an emphasis on hiring people with disabilities to be on staff (Usiak, Stone, House, & Montgomery, 2004). These staff have personal insights into the challenges and opportunities in the local community involved in living and working with a disability. The staff offer information and referral assistance, peer counseling, and self-advocacy training, as well crisis intervention assistance. Centers for Independent Living frequently serve as a community hub for information, services, and support for individuals with disabilities and can help significantly in transition planning and in implementing transition plans.

Employment Services Available Through Centers for Independent Living

Employment services available through Centers for Independent Living can vary substantially from program to program. The most frequently available service is helping train individuals with their job-seeking skills. Some Centers for Independent Living do provide direct employment supports in helping consumers locate jobs. Centers for Independent Living place a premium on self-advocacy and independence, so a part of the peer counseling service is to help job applicants represent themselves effectively to employers. The peer education might also provide information and guidance on how to approach an employer about a disability, particularly in situations where there is a need to negotiate a job accommodation.

Centers for Independent Living have long been in the business of providing community-based support services to people with disabilities (Wilson, 1998). However, the provision of transition services to youth and young adults has, mostly, been the responsibility of school systems. Lattin and Wehmeyer (2003) documented that Centers for Independent Living can and, increasingly, do serve an important role in supporting youth with disabilities to transition from secondary education to adulthood. In a national survey, Lattin and Wehmeyer found that Centers for Independent Living provided an array of transition-related supports, including job training and coaching, benefits advocacy, transportation training, and training to empower youth and promote self-determination.

Despite the potentially important role Centers for Independent Living might play in supporting the transition of youth with disabilities, Lattin and Wehmeyer (2003) found that fewer than half of Centers for Independent Living had any focus on this population and most had only minimal contact with youth. This is likely due to the fact that transition services are the responsibility of public schools. It is also the case that Centers for Independent Living and public schools have, historically, operated under differing philosophies. The independent living movement emerged from a strong empowerment and self-determination emphasis, whereas education has historically been aligned with medical models and/or a deficits-reduction focus.

However, the seeds for more meaningful collaboration between Centers for Independent Living and school districts were sown in 1990 when Congress reauthorized the IDEA (PL 101-476), the federal legislation that mandates a free appropriate public education for all children with disabilities. IDEA required, for the first time, that needed transition services be addressed in every student's IEP when they reached the age of 16. The intent of the transition mandate was to ensure that all students received educational programming that adequately prepared them for adulthood.

Funding Available Through Centers for Independent Living   Many Centers for Independent Living receive federal funds that include purchase of service dollars that can be used to acquire goods or services for individuals. These independent living services funds are usually very limited but are a potential resource that should be explored. The Centers for Independent Living also have targeted state or local dollars that can sometimes be used for services such as transportation, personal assistance services (at home and/or in the workplace), and training. As a community service hub, a major strength of Centers for Independent Living is the strong partnership arrangements these programs have with other community service agencies. Frequently, the Centers for Independent Living can help an individual with a disability obtain funding support from these partner agencies.

One Stop Career Centers

The WIA of 1998 created One Stop Career Centers as a key employment resource in the community. They have core services that are available to anyone in a community who needs help in locating employment. These core services mainly involve access through self-directed job searches to an information center that contains information on available job openings in the community. For those individuals who meet the criteria for eligibility for more intense service through One Stop Career Centers, a variety of more individualized services are available. Youth and young adults with disabilities are targeted for services through One Stop Career Centers, which can play a significant role in the delivery of transition services. One Stop Career Centers can be a tremendous resource for both students and the school's transition team in developing a plan for transition. One Stop Career Centers have an exciting information and referral mechanism through which they can connect their customers with disabilities to a large variety of community resources. Specifically, youth with disabilities can take advantage of their career guidance program and competitive employment services.

Case Management Services Available Through One Stop Career Centers   One Stop Career Centers staff include plan managers who can assist in planning employment related services through the center and can also reach out into the community to help identify and acquire other needed transition services (Bader, 2003). Some One

Stop Career Centers have "program navigators" to help individuals with a disability match up with the most appropriate service within the center and the community. By design, One Stop Career Centers frequently serve as a home base for many community partners who co-locate staff within the center setting. VR and social services are two of the partner agencies that participate in the One Stop Career Centers program and offer additional case management support for eligible participants.

Employment Services Available Through One Stop Career Centers

One Stop Career Centers have job listings identifying available employment opportunities. Information from interest inventories can help guide a job search. For individuals who need accommodations to gain access to job information through, for example, computerized job search resources, work stations are frequently equipped with accessibility kits that accommodate a variety of disabilities. (Gervey, Gao, & Rizzo, 2004). One Stop Career Centers offer job clubs in which an individual looking for employment can get the support and information from peers and a group facilitator. Some One Stop Career Centers have more customized employment resource staff that will represent the job interests of an individual with a disability to a potential employer and help negotiate a job opportunity. Additional employment services of potential value to youth in transition include paid and unpaid work experiences, occupational skills training, job placement, and follow-up services after employment to help with job retention and career development.

Funding Available Through One Stop Career Centers

If an individual is eligible for intensive work force investment services through the One Stop Career Centers, then he or she can gain access to individual training accounts. On an individual prescriptive basis, the individual training accounts can be used to purchase services such as training, adapted equipment, or SE. The main funding strength of One Stop Career Centers is its direct links with the other community agencies that fund employment services, such as VR and community service boards/agencies.

Summary of Transition and Community Training, Employment, and Support Programs

Youth with disabilities in transition have potential access to a variety of community training, employment, and support programs. These programs offer an array of case management assistance, employment services, and funding possibilities. However, these programs operate under a wide assortment of federal, state, and local laws, regulations, policies, and service arrangements. The key to a successful transition outcome is early involvement with these programs during the planning process. Becoming fully educated regarding the resources and service relationships that characterize community training, employment, and support programs specific to the youth in transition is a critical first step. The next step is identifying the primary community agencies and work to incorporate these programs into the transition plan. Identify the primary case management/service coordination resource among the community agencies. This role might be taken on by different agencies for different youth in transition depending on the nature of the disability, core service needs, and/or local eligibility requirements. For example, one person might need VR services, and another person might need service coordination through a case manager at a community services board or a plan manager at a One Stop Career Center. Early transition planning can help establish these key relationships with community agencies and establish the primary and secondary level participation needed by each to support a successful employment and community living outcome.

PROMISING TRANSITION MODELS

There are several models of community-based transition that have been discussed since the 1980s (Wehman, Kregel, & Barcus, 1985; Will, 1984), but they have lacked empirical evidence. However, two models have emerged that hold promise.

The first model is called the Transition Service Integration Model developed by Luecking and Certo (2005), Condon and Brown (2005), and Certo et al. (2003). This model integrates the resources and expertise of the three primary systems responsible for transition from school to adulthood for individuals with significant support needs—local public schools, the rehabilitation system, and the developmental disabilities system. School districts form a partnership directly with private nonprofit agencies that typically serve adults with significant support needs. Through this partnership, personnel from the school district and private agencies work together during a student's last year in public school (i.e., typically when the student is 21 years old) to develop a paid direct-hire job and a variety of inclusive community activities to engage in when not working. In doing so, they provide SE services and job accommodations that enable individuals with significant support needs to secure gainful employment in inclusive job settings and gain access to other integrated community environments prior to graduation. There is a seamless transition to a person-centered and self-determined adult lifestyle after high school because of the funding secured from the rehabilitation and developmental disability systems.

The second model is the Transition Supports Model developed by Hughes and Carter (2000). In this approach, large numbers of field-tested support strategies were developed with youth with disabilities. The emphasis was completely on *transition supports*. In this model, practical examples, case studies, visual displays, and reproducible forms are provided to illustrate the use of more than 500 easy-to-use secondary transition strategies. This approach provides a model of support for secondary students that may improve their outcomes after high school. A unique feature of *The Transition Handbook* (Hughes & Carter, 2000) is that it contains only transition support strategies that are both research based and teacher tested. Although the type and intensity of support that students need to make a smooth transition to adult life will differ according to individual needs, such as a personal care attendant for a person with quadriplegia or a communication book for a student who is nonverbal, there are strategies appropriate for every student.

PUBLIC/PRIVATE PARTNERSHIPS: THE ROLE OF BUSINESS

As previously discussed, the business community is a natural partner for school programs interested in assisting students who will be transitioning with job shadowing, mentoring, work study programs, and competitive employment. However, business is frequently either overlooked or taken for granted in the transition process. School programs and businesses need to do a better job of establishing strong working relationship. Businesses should see a partnership with a local school program as a rich source of potential labor and therefore a good investment of time to nurture these relationships. Schools, however, must also understand that they are creating a value to community employers and must be willing to commit the necessary resources that will yield productive relationships. This type of relationship building, in which school personnel are actively marketing their potential labor source to the local business community, will mean a drastic departure from current practices.

Given the growing demands for labor in this country and the dwindling number of available workers, school programs must be prepared to initiate this new marketing approach to business. The Herman Group reported that the private sector is facing a a labor shortage of 10 million people by 2010, and there is a need to actively recruit from untapped labor pools (Herman, Oliva, & Gioia, 2002). New public/private partnerships with the schools can answer this labor shortage if school programs will actively participate in the community, collect data about the business community needs, and employ this newly acquired information to satisfy these personnel shortages (Wehman, Brooke, & Green, 2004).

The key to this marketing approach is satisfying the needs of businesses through an exchange process in which each party receives some value from the relationship. Often, school programs do not see themselves as adding value to the business community. Yet, many businesses already recognize their labor shortage needs and are actively looking for interested school programs and rehabilitation agencies for assistance. Businesses are telling the public sector that they want to know more about the issues facing people with disabilities as they relate to employment. Businesses also want to know how rehabilitation programs can benefit their operations (Green & Brooke, 2001). They want to know what value rehabilitation and school programs bring to the relationship and how that will help impact the bottom line for the businesses.

School programs need to develop a clear and simple message to businesses regarding the value they bring to the business relationship. It is important to develop a full range of services that can be provided to the business community and to market how they benefit business. Like any relationship, a business partnership needs to be nurtured in order to grow and stay healthy. The qualities that make most relationships successful (e.g., trustworthiness, honesty, commitment, perseverance, and reliability) apply to any business partnership that a school forms. It is in the best interest for all involved (i.e., school agency, employer, students) that the school program lives up to promises and commitments made to the business community. For example, a school program should not promise an employer a qualified worker if no one is available who can meet the employer's needs. In the same respect, it would not be appropriate to promise a student a job with a specific employer if a job opening does not exist (Wehman, Brooke, & Green, 2004).

School professionals cannot be complacent. Teachers, transition coordinators, and other school personnel need to learn more about current trends in employment and the latest AT. It is important to join business-led organizations and become active members of the community. They must ask for business assistance and demonstrate that they have something of value for the employer.

In 1998, Erin Riehle, clinical director of the emergency room department at Cincinnati Children's Hospital, had a revelation. She had been struggling to solve a performance problem that plagued the efficient operation of the emergency room department. It involved restocking supplies in a timely and dependable manner. Filling these entry-level jobs with students and other part-time workers hoping to pursue careers in health care professions was not the problem. However, turnover was continuous due to the repetitious nature of this task. Though critically important, restocking the supplies was a task neither valued nor reliably performed by her current staff pool.

Erin saw that the hospital had adopted a policy statement from the American College of Healthcare Executives that reads, "Healthcare organizations must lead their communities in increasing employment opportunities for qualified people with disabilities and advocate on behalf of their employment to other organizations." She recognized that virtually every child with a disability living in that community is a customer at the hospital at some point in his or her life. Yet, when she looked around, these customers encountered almost no role models with disabilities among the staff providing services.

Putting these factors together, Erin realized that the solution to her staffing problem could also help fulfill the diversity mission of her hospital in a more complete way. She came up with the idea for Project SEARCH to provide employment for individuals

Business Partnerships that Are Working

Partnerships with the business community are essential. There are many examples of excellent public-private partnerships throughout the country. These partnerships have been established because both parties were able to build a trusting relationship with each other. Businesses will realize the value of this approach, which leads to a win-win situation for employers, students, and school programs. The corporate example (sidebar) describes one partnership that continues to yield great jobs for students with significant disabilities, a competent work force for the business, and an outstanding employment training site for students who may be interested in this particular career path.

A number of other businesses are getting involved with local schools through special education and vocational education programs to bring students with disabilities into the workplace to enable firsthand learning about career opportunities. These companies are recognizing that not only do they need to focus on recruiting from adult untapped talent pools, but they also need to begin recruiting with youth who represent the future of the work force. Businesses can offer many opportunities for school programs across the country. A partnership was developed between Bergen County Vocational-Technical Schools in New Jersey, Cornell University, and the Wakefern Food Corporation/Shoprite (1990) to implement supermarket skills training programs. The ultimate goals of the program included preparing students with learning disabilities for career alternatives in the supermarket industry, placing them in unsubsidized employment, and heightening public and corporate awareness of the value of individuals with disabilities as reliable and stable employees. Another productive partnership occurred between San Marcos, California, employers, Disabled Student Programs and Services, and Student Placement Offices at Palomar College (Palomar College, 1992). This unique partnership enabled students with disabilities to enter employment mainstream and establish a safety-net support system within the work environment. The active 35-member advisory board included representatives from both the college and business community and stimulated a true partnership between the project and the business community that resulted in 21 students achieving employment.

Work force issues and the need to hire good workers has become a major focal point for businesses. This concern is not just a business concern. It has direct impact for educa-

whose disabilities had been a significant barrier to employment. The target group would include individuals with multiple disabilities, as well as people with severe learning challenges. Erin immediately realized that the hospital would need community partners to achieve her goal of bringing people with significant developmental disabilities into the emergency room department to fill open positions as productive employees. Two collaborating partners were identified: the Great Oaks Institute of Technology and Career Development and the Hamilton Country Board of Mental Retardation and Developmental Disabilities (MR/DD). Both organizations proved to be a rich source of potential labor. Great Oaks served 36 school districts and prepared more than 6,000 youth in full- and part-time programs per year. Hamilton County Board of MR/DD provided countywide educational and residential programs to adults and children with mental retardation and other developmental disabilities and served more than 10,000 individuals.

The partners committed personnel to this project who were charged with the responsibility of becoming truly knowledgeable about the work culture, site responsibilities, and work tasks at the hospital. Furthermore, there was a commitment to provide training and support services designed to enhance the carefully selected and motivated candidates to perform the necessary functions of identified jobs successfully and reliably.

"The key to our program is having the professionals from Great Oaks and Hamilton County Board of MR/DD working on site," Erin explains. "All the managers know them and they know the jobs and what

Table 4.5.   Examples of collaborative activities for building business partnerships

Meet with community business people to clarify the role you want business to play in the transition process.

Seek the advice of business people regarding curriculum training programs, marketing materials, and other items that are targeted toward the business community.

Get business involvement in joint newsletter articles regarding success stories.

Request that business people sit on focus groups to identify program strengths and weaknesses.

Seek a commitment from business people to participate in career exploration activities at school.

Share information regarding disability-specific issues such as the Americans with Disabilities Act (ADA).

Schedule joint speaking opportunities to community groups such as the Lions Club, Rotary Club, local Chamber of Commerce, and the local Society for Human Resource Management (SHRM) chapter.

Seek opportunities for students to take part in tours and information interviews at the work sites.

Request possible internships and mentors for students involved in transition.

Develop opportunities for businesses to recruit and interview students with disabilities.

tional systems across the country. By coming together at a local level, businesses and schools have the opportunity to build a partnership that has direct economic benefits for both parties. If school transition programs expect businesses to work together, then it is important for schools to recognize the need for an ongoing collaborative partnership. There are many ways a business can interact with youth with disabilities while they are still attending schools. Table 4.5 provides a range of ideas that schools could utilize to build business partnerships. Businesses are concerned about the educational and economic issues in the communities where they conduct their work. In order to grow and make a profit, they need young people coming out of the schools ready to engage in work activities that will meet their skill demands. Being involved with a school-to-work transition program allows the business to invest first hand in making sure that youth with disabilities will meet their labor demands.

CONCLUSION

This chapter has emphasized that effective transition planning involving movement from secondary education into the community involves integrating the input and resources of a variety of key partners. First, youth with disabilities and their

it takes to succeed in each position." All of the employed individuals report to their department supervisors, like traditional employees. But individuals associated with Project SEARCH have follow-along support services to aid the employee in resolving problems and adapting to changes that may seem minor or embarrassing for supervisors to address (e.g., scheduling special transportation, dealing with co-worker requests, maintaining hygiene). These problems can lead to termination for these workers if effective and knowledgeable support is not provided.

To date, Project SEARCH has resulted in more than 70 people with significant developmental disabilities working as employees of the hospital, with two staff providing on-the-job support services to these individuals. On average, these individuals have been employed for 5 years and earn an average wage of more than $8 per hour. Most are working approximately 32 hours per week and receive the full benefits package of other hospital personnel. These employees work in a wide range of positions, often overlooked for people with development disabilities. Many of these require mastering complex functions, yet they are routine in nature, such as sterilization technician, department sticking, lab courier, and clinical support staff. "Our program uses a business model," explains Erin. "We provide a single conduit for organizing and delivering employment services, in collaboration with the community, and deliver them in an effective and accountable way as an integrated part of the work site. It is an appealing model to employers, and it works."

families and key stakeholders need to be fully educated on the impact of employment and disability benefits. The BPAO projects now provide a critically important resource for obtaining benefits-related information and assistance. Second, there are a variety of community training and employment support programs that can serve as resources in planning and providing transition services. These services vary considerably across states and communities. Early involvement with these services will help a youth in transition become known to the case management, employment services, and funding support resources most needed to support his or her plan. Finally, successful employment outcomes depend on employer involvement. Work experiences and job internships while a youth with a disability is completing his or her secondary program expands job and career awareness and helps target postsecondary training and employment interests. Access to information about benefits, involvement of key community programs, and employer participation in the transition process are the cornerstones of effective community involvement in the transition of youth with disabilities from school to living and working in the community.

STUDY QUESTIONS

1. Describe the major roles of at least six community programs in supporting transition.

2. Describe the six critical elements in community-based transition.

3. Explain the importance of benefits planning as a component of community-based transition.

4. Identify and describe at least four work incentives offered through the SSA available to recipients of SSI.

5. Describe and discuss the case management, employment services, and funding opportunities offered by at least three community service agencies for youth in transition.

6. Identify five questions that should be researched before selecting a community rehabilitation program.

7. Describe six examples of collaborative activities for building business partnerships in support of youth with disabilities in transition.

II

Facilitating and Supporting Transition

5

Moving Toward Full Inclusion

Kim Spence-Cochran and Cynthia E. Pearl

AFTER COMPLETING THIS CHAPTER, THE READER WILL BE ABLE TO

○ Gain a historical perspective on the movement to integrate or merge general and special education resources, personnel, methods, and curriculum

○ Understand the importance of working collaboratively with students, families, and a variety of professionals to enhance successful inclusion

○ Gain an awareness of the arguments and the critical issues related to the implementation of inclusion

○ Develop a personal position on the issues surrounding inclusion

○ Recognize practical strategies for achieving successful inclusion in school and community settings

○ Recognize crucial transitional supports to facilitate inclusion across the age span

RENEWING OUR COMMITMENT TO INCLUSION

Volumes have been written on the issues surrounding the inclusion of students with disabilities in school and community settings. Authors have discussed at length why students should be included, which students should be included, where students should be included, and how students should be included (e.g., Fuchs & Fuchs, 1991, 1994, 1998a; Kauffman & Hallahan, 1995; Salisbury & Chambers, 1994; Waldron & Mc-Leskey; 1998; Zigmond, 1995, 2003). Foreman, Arthur-Kelly, Pascoe, and King (2004) identified the range of perceptions that have been aired by various stakeholders as falling between two polarized positions—those who contend that all children should be educated together with the necessary resources or services provided in the general education classroom and those who argue that an appropriate educational experience for some students, particularly those with complex and severe disabilities, is only possible with the infrastructure of a special school or unit. In examining the rhetoric, the reader is encouraged to determine his or her own position regarding best inclusive practices (see Figure 5.1).

Despite varied opinions on the best educational placements for students with disabilities, there is general agreement that our highest aspiration should be the inclusion of students in integrated school and community settings, to the fullest extent possible, with the appropriate individualized supports necessary for a successful educational experience. This is the position supported in the Individuals with Disabilities Education Improvement Act of 2004, passed by Congress on November 19, 2004. This legislation represents a renewed commitment to provide a free appropriate public education (FAPE) for students with disabilities and moves beyond questions of why and where students should be included to focus attention on how, as a nation, we can come closer to attaining the goal of full inclusion for individuals with disabilities not only in school settings, but also in their communities and ultimately in the world of work.

Envisioning the future, the National Council on Disability (2005) maintained, "The United States of America will be a stronger country when its 54 million citizens with disabilities are fully integrated into all aspects of American life" (p. 12). The need to facilitate inclusion across the age span is highlighted in U.S. Census 2000 data revealing that people between the ages of 16 and 64 were less likely to be employed if they were disabled (U.S. Census Bureau, 2003). Data showing that only 13% of students with significant support needs were competitively employed 2 years after high school (National Council on Disability, 2000) is particularly troubling. "Significant barriers to achieving the goals of independence, inclusion and empowerment for all persons with disabilities still remain" (National Council on Disability, 2005, p. 12).

In an effort to address these barriers, IDEA 2004 requires that a plan for transition to postsecondary activities be in place beginning no later than the first individualized education program (IEP) to be in effect when the child is 16. Kohler (1998) promoted an even more comprehensive approach identified as transition-focused education. This perspective recognizes that transition planning should not be viewed as an additional activity to be introduced when students with disabilities reach age 16, but rather as a foundation from which educational programs and activities are developed. Long-range planning for transition should provide students with disabilities with opportunities to learn alongside peers without disabilities throughout their schooling. In inclusive set-

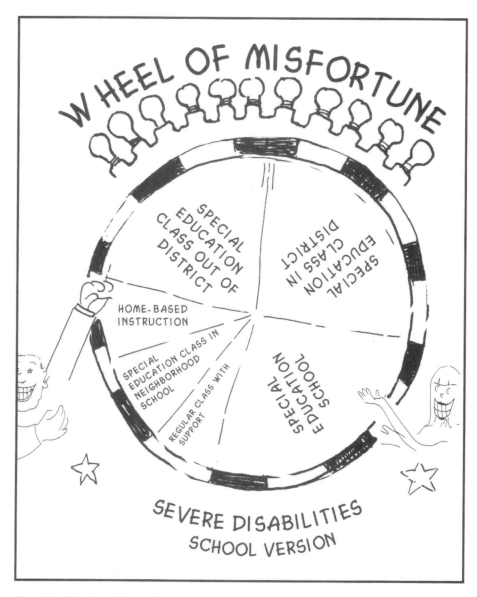

Figure 5.1. Wheel of misfortune. (From Giangreco, M., & Ruelle, K. [1998]. *Ants in his pants: Absurdities and realities of special education* [p. 21]. Minnetonka, MN: Peytral Publications; reprinted by permission.)

tings, they can begin to develop academic, social, and functional skills necessary for eventual independence and participation in society (Foreman et al., 2004). These skills are further developed when inclusion in school settings is paired with community-based instruction (CBI) aimed at the acquisition of independent living and job-related skills (Lawrence-Brown, 2004). Certo et al. (2003) made a strong point in favor of inclusive education. In their words, "It is difficult to imagine that students with significant support needs, who have been fully included through high school, and their families, will continue to accept less than full inclusion into typical adult life after graduation" (p. 3).

**LEE AND
SCHOOL**

Table 5.1. Reflecting on the educational experiences of Lee and Tammy

Questions for reflection

After reading about the educational experiences of Lee and Tammy, reflect on the following questions.

1. Why are the educational placements of these students so markedly different?

2. What is your opinion regarding the marked differences in the experiences of these two students?

3. What are the supports that facilitate Lee's inclusion in school and classroom activities?

4. Do you think it would be possible to include Tammy at the same intensity as Lee?

5. Education benefit is an important consideration in the placement of students with moderate and severe disabilities. What are the benefits and concerns of Lee's full inclusion?

6. Which of these students do you think is most likely to be employed in an integrated setting following graduation from high school? Why?

At 16 years of age, Lee stands six and a half feet tall. Over the years, he has been diagnosed as having a pervasive developmental disorder (autism), mental retardation, obsessive-compulsive disorder, attention-deficit/hyperactivity disorder (ADHD), and bipolar disorder. Despite an extensive history of physically aggressive behavior and a tendency to leave an assigned area when frustrated, Lee was fully included at his neighborhood high school and received a regular diploma at graduation. Multiple supports were provided to facilitate his successful inclusion in general education classrooms. Within his regular classes, Lee received language and occupational therapies and social skills instruction every week. A full-time support assistant worked closely with Lee and was available to assist other students. Lee's peers were prepared to provide support when he encountered difficulty in any school setting. A comprehensive behavior plan was in place to assist and instruct him during times of frustration, as well as provide the staff with support while maintaining safety. Lee uses a computer to communicate with others because he is nonverbal. After school and on weekends he participated in the school's computer club and was an active member of the student government. Lee rode the regular school bus to and from school, receiving assistance from designated peers when necessary.

The cases (see sidebars) describe the high school experiences of two students with disabilities. They illustrate how our progress toward full inclusion must be measured on a student-by-student basis. Unfortunately, it seems that for every student like Lee, whose educational experience illustrates how far we have come toward the inclusion of students with disabilities in schools and communities, there is another student like Tammy to demonstrate how little has changed over the years. Even though these two students are within the same school district, their daily educational experiences are completely different. After reading about Lee and Tammy, reflect on the questions in Table 5.1.

A HISTORICAL PERSPECTIVE ON INCLUSION

On May 17, 1954, the historic *Brown v. Board of Education* decision struck down the "separate but equal" doctrine that had prevailed for 58 years. Chief Justice Warren concluded, "We come then to the question presented: Does segregation of children in public schools solely on the basis of race, even though the physical facilities and other 'tangible' factors may be equal, deprive the children of the minority group of equal educational opportunities? We believe that it does." The *Brown* decision was the catalyst that led to the broadening of education for all people. Prior to the enactment of the Education for All Handicapped Children Act of 1975 (PL 94-142), half of all children with disabilities had only limited access to the education system, and

LEE
TODAY

Lee currently works in a family-owned hardware store located 7 miles from his home. He works 25–30 hours per week, Monday through Friday, and utilizes the public transportation system or his bicycle to get himself to and from work each day. Lee has successfully worked at this store in a supported employment (SE) situation for the past 2½ years. He is supported in a variety of jobs by two young men he met in general education classes prior to high school graduation, one of whom Lee has been friends with since the beginning of middle school. Lee's family members alternate taking him to private counseling sessions and social skills instructional groups each week, both of which have increased in frequency and intensity since he graduated from high school. Lee still lives at home with his family, although plans are underway for him to move into an apartment with his older brother, his friend, and his co-worker from the hardware store. Most recently, Lee has expressed his intention to work full time at the hardware store, as well as a desire to get his driver's license.

1 million children with disabilities were excluded entirely (U.S. Department of Education, Office of Special Education Programs, 2000). Actions initiated by families, advocacy organizations, and civil rights lawyers culminated in two historic decisions, *Pennsylvania Association for Retarded Citizens (PARC) v. Commonwealth of Pennsylvania* (1972) and *Mills v. Board of Education of the District of Columbia* (1972). The Commonwealth of Pennsylvania and the District of Columbia were ordered to 1) provide a free appropriate public education to all students with disabilities, 2) educate students with disabilities in the same schools and basically the same programs as students without disabilities, and 3) put into place certain procedural safeguards so that students with disabilities can challenge schools that do not live up to the court's orders. Three years later, the Education for All Handicapped Children Act of 1975 was enacted, guaranteeing the right of students with disabilities to a free, appropriate public education and providing federal money to assist states in paying for special education. Since the 1970s, key amendments to the Education for All Handicapped Children Act of 1975 have expanded on its support for equality of access and quality programs and services for children with disabilities. Via legislation, Congress has clearly and consistently supported the intention that educational outcomes for individuals with disabilities mirror those of their peers without disabilities. Now known as IDEA 2004, this law has provided the major impetus to the movement of students with disabilities away from segregated settings. The concept of least restrictive environment (LRE) is central to IDEA 2004. Federal law states

> To the maximum extent appropriate, children with disabilities, including those children in public and private institutions or other care facilities, are educated with children who are not disabled, and special classes, separate schooling, or other removal of children with disabilities from the regular educational environment occurs only when the nature or severity of the disability is such that education in regular classes with the use of supplementary aids and services cannot be achieved satisfactorily. (IDEA 2004 [Part B, Sec 612 (a) (5)])

PHILOSOPHICAL APPROACHES TO INCLUSION

Although few dispute the moral and ethical basis of the LRE concept, its implementation has been the focus of continued debate (Kochhar, West, & Taymans, 2000). Three widely recognized terms—*mainstreaming, inclusion,* and *full inclusion*—refer to different approaches to the placement of students with special needs in general education classrooms. In the 1970s and 1980s, the placement of students with special needs in general

TAMMY

Tammy spent her entire educational career in self-contained special education classrooms. She is diagnosed as having mild cerebral palsy, mental retardation, a hearing impairment, and an eating disorder. By age 17, she had been placed in 10 different schools: five elementary schools, three middle schools, and two high schools. Frequent school moves were the direct result of an ongoing disagreement between the school district and Tammy's parents regarding the "most appropriate" and "least restrictive" classroom placement. During her final high school placement, she received all of her special education services within a segregated high school for students with emotional disturbances and behavioral disorders. This meant all of her daily instruction, including her lunch, was provided within one classroom. When Tammy became angry or frustrated or did not care to complete the repetitive worksheets she was often asked to complete, she became physically aggressive to others and often engaged in self-injurious behavior. Despite having a teaching assistant assigned to her for the majority of her school career, Tammy's school records reflect little documented progress. Her IEP goals included objectives that were repeated for several years due to lack of mastery. There were few opportunities for Tammy to interact with her typical peers during the school day due to the nature of the segregated classrooms and schools she attended. She rode a special education school bus, with an attendant, for 2 hours each day (1 hour to and from school) during her final year of high school.

education classrooms was referred to as *mainstreaming*. This term was largely replaced when the terms *full inclusion* and *inclusion* became popular following the Individuals with Disabilities Education Act (IDEA) of 1990 (PL 101-476) mandates for increased participation of general education. Lewis and Doorlag (1999) noted, "It is important to determine what each speaker and writer means by the term inclusion because there are basic philosophical differences between the approaches of full inclusion and mainstreaming" (p. 5).

Mainstreaming refers to the selective placement of special education students in one or more regular education classes. These placements are based on the assumption that students with disabilities have earned opportunities to participate in the mainstream by demonstrating the ability to "keep up" with the other students (Rogers, 1993). Essentially, mainstreaming refers to a part-time placement of students with disabilities in general class settings and is associated with the belief that, although these students visit the mainstream, they remain the responsibility of special education (Mastropieri & Scruggs, 2000). Although many professionals have adopted the term *inclusion* in referring to this practice, the basic philosophy of mainstreaming is still prevalent in the field.

Inclusion is conceptually similar to mainstreaming, albeit a critical difference between the two definitions exists. This difference represents a significant paradigm shift requiring only that the child will benefit from being in a general education class with no demands that he or she "keep up" with other students (Rogers, 1993). According to Udvari-Solner and Thousand (1996),

> Inclusive education is a process of operating a classroom or school as a supportive community and, thus, is qualitatively different from integration or mainstreaming efforts of the past, which attempted to "fit" a particular category of students (e.g., students with severe disabilities) into a standardized education mainstream in which uniformity and conformity were valued over personalized learning. (p. 183)

In the case of inclusion, although a student may leave the classroom for special education services, that student remains the responsibility of the general educator. The inclusion model enlarges the role of general education but also acknowledges the need to maintain a continuum of special education services. Educational programs ranging from hospital and homebound services to special schools to full-time placement in general education should be specifically and effectively tailored to meet the needs of individual students. The

TAMMY TODAY

Tammy exited high school in December 2004, just before her 22nd birthday. She "graduated" with a special diploma, very few functional skills of independence, and no vocational training or experience. During the day, while her parents are working, Tammy attends a specialized adult day care where she watches television and movies, completes directed crafts, or walks around the facility with staff. Recently, Tammy required increased staff supervision due to an increase in her aggressive and self-injurious behaviors, as well as substantial weight loss due to her refusal to eat during the day. Managing Tammy's maladaptive behavior has proven considerably more challenging than the day care staff had anticipated, or generally allow. Tammy's parents are very concerned she may soon not be allowed to attend this specialized adult day care facility and are frantically attempting to hire a behavior analyst to assist the day care staff with Tammy's challenging behavior. She continues to live at home, relying completely on her family for support in all aspects of her life. If Tammy has any dreams or desires for her life outside of the adult day care setting or home, then they are unclear and unexplored at this time.

Council for Exceptional Children (CEC; 1993) released the *CEC Policy on Inclusive Schools and Community Settings* supporting the concept of inclusion as a meaningful goal to be pursued in schools and communities. The CEC position recommended the availability of a continuum of services, but maintained, "Children, youth, and young adults with disabilities should be served whenever possible in general education classrooms in inclusive neighborhood schools and community settings" (p. 1).

Those who advocate for full inclusion, including TASH and Schools Are For Everyone (SAFE), reject the CEC (1993) "whenever possible" caveat for placement of students with disabilities in general education classrooms. They do not acknowledge the need for a continuum of services and maintain instead that full-time placement in a general education classroom is appropriate for all students with disabilities including those with severe disabilities. In a full inclusion model, special education is imported into the general education setting. Support is provided in the regular classroom and students do not leave for special education services. Lee is an example of a student who was fully included. He did not leave the classroom to receive special education services. Language therapy, occupational therapy, and social skills instruction were provided in his general education classroom.

In reviewing the evolution of the term *inclusion* and looking to the future, Kochhar et al. (2000) predicted that schools will continue to review inclusion practices in an effort to assess the quality and effectiveness of educational programs for students with disabilities. They identified the trend for 2000 and beyond as *full participation* and *meaningful educational benefit*. These terms represent an approach that emphasizes not only maximum opportunity for inclusion, but also positive outcomes for students with disabilities. This trend is in keeping with the focus in the No Child Left Behind Act (NCLB) of 2001 on accountability for results and proven educational methods. Under NCLB, states are currently working to close the achievement gap to ensure that all students achieve academic proficiency.

SPECIAL EDUCATION SERVICE DELIVERY

Despite a lack of consensus on the issue of inclusion, increasing numbers of children with disabilities have moved and continue to move away from segregated schools and classrooms to general education settings (McLesky, Henry, & Axelrod, 1999). Data for the number of children ages 6–11 served in different educational environments under IDEA, Part B, for the December 1, 2003, count were released July 31, 2004, by the

U.S. Department of Education, Office of Special Education Programs. In 2003, 60.28% of students with disabilities spent less than 21% of the school day in segregated settings (see Table 5.2).

Learning disability is the most common type of disability represented in general education classrooms (Austin, 2001). McLeskey et al. (1999) found the numbers of students with learning disabilities educated in less restrictive settings had increased steadily over the prior 6 years, though placement practices varied from state to state. According to the U.S. Department of Education, Office of Special Education Programs (2003), progress toward less restrictive settings is seen across all age groups, though elementary students are more likely than older students to be served in the regular classroom. Furthermore, the U.S. Department of Education noted that students with high-incidence disabilities are also more likely to be served in the general education classroom than are those with low-incidence disabilities. Although McLeskey et al. noted an "emerging consensus that students with LD should spend most of the school day in general education classrooms" (p. 56), data suggest that there is less support for the inclusion of students in some of the other disability categories. Table 5.2 reveals considerable variation in educational placements across disability areas. The placements of students with mental retardation, multiple disabilities, autism, and deaf-blindness run counter to the trend toward less restrictive environments found in other disability categories. This difference is most marked in the case of students with mental retardation. Figures 5.2 and 5.3 illustrate the differences in educational environments for students with mental retardation compared with students with all disabilities. Tammy's placement in self-contained special education classrooms in elementary and middle school, followed by placement in a separate high school, is a prime example of this difference. Although her placements were highly restrictive when compared with Lee, they are actually very similar to those of other students with mental retardation, the majority of whom spend 60% or more of the school day in educational environments outside of the general education classroom.

All disabilities							
< 21%	21%–60%	> 60%	Public separate facility	Private separate facility	Public residential facility	Private residential facility	Home hospital environment
60.28	22.24	15.34	1.01	0.70	0.10	0.11	0.22

Figure 5.2.   Percentage of children ages 6–11 in all disability categories served in different educational environments.

Mental retardation							
< 21%	21%–60%	> 60%	Public separate facility	Private separate facility	Public residential facility	Private residential facility	Home hospital environment
14.66	30.33	51.34	2.72	0.53	0.05	0.08	0.28

Figure 5.3.   Percentage of children ages 6–11 with mental retardation served in different educational environments.

Table 5.2. Percentage of children ages 6–11 served in different educational environments under IDEA, Part B, by disability

Disability category		Different educational environments						
	< 21%	21%–60%	> 60%	Public separate facility	Private separate facility	Public residential facility	Private residential facility	Home hospital environment
All disabilities	60.28	22.24	15.34	1.01	0.70	0.10	0.11	0.22
Learning disabilities	50.90	37.51	11.23	0.13	0.14	0.01	0.03	0.04
Speech and language impairments	90.90	5.02	3.76	0.08	0.17	0.01	0.01	0.05
Mental retardation	14.66	30.33	51.34	2.72	0.53	0.05	0.08	0.28
Emotional disturbance	32.25	20.42	36.38	4.77	3.97	0.36	1.14	0.73
Multiple disabilities	14.46	17.74	48.27	10.51	6.09	0.47	0.54	1.92
Hearing impairments	48.61	16.90	24.09	4.13	2.58	3.34	0.23	0.12
Orthopedic impairments	53.12	18.33	23.84	2.83	0.56	0.05	0.05	1.22
Other health impairments	52.41	29.75	15.73	0.60	0.51	0.04	0.08	0.87
Visual impairments	58.80	16.51	15.68	3.68	1.86	2.62	0.27	0.58
Autism	29.76	17.42	44.24	4.32	3.57	0.04	0.39	0.26
Deaf-blindness	26.17	13.53	38.20	7.67	7.37	4.36	1.35	1.35
Traumatic brain injury	37.73	30.31	26.81	1.91	2.18	0.09	0.18	0.80
Developmental delay	51.19	28.11	18.67	0.61	1.10	0.07	0.03	0.22

Data based on the December 1, 2003, count, updated as of July 31, 2004. From U.S. Department of Education, Office of Special Education Programs. (2004). Retrieved July 19, 2005, from http://www.ideadata.org/index.html.

CHALLENGES OF INCLUSION

Williams and Martin (2001) noted the IDEA "commitment ensuring quality teaching, learning, and educational outcomes for students with disabilities in the general education curriculum offers exciting opportunities and significant challenges to all educators" (p. 60). General educators approach their expanded roles in the planning and implementation of programs for students with disabilities with various levels of preparation, experience, and skill (Dennis & Ryan, 2000; Dorn & Fuchs, 2004; Miller, Wienke, & Savage, 2000). Few general educators receive teacher preparation in the area of special education or the necessary skills to adapt their instruction for students with special needs (Boudah et al., 2000; Coombs-Richardson & Mead, 2001; Singh, 2002). Ansell (2004) found that only 14 states and the District of Columbia required that general education teachers complete coursework in special education for licensure, and only nine states required preservice teacher preparation related to special education.

According to Loveland, McLeskey, So, Swanson, and Waldron (2001), 80% of general education teachers without inclusion experience and 90% of general education teachers with inclusion experience agreed that students with disabilities have a basic right to receive their education in the general education classroom. However, when Gilmore, Campbell, and Cuskelly (2003) surveyed 538 experienced teachers in regard to the inclusion of students with Down syndrome, they found that although the majority recognized the educational, social, and emotional benefits of inclusion, only 20% identified the regular classroom as the best setting for these children. Teacher perception surveys have revealed a number of specific general educator concerns regarding inclusion. Boudah et al. (2000) reported pervasive general educator perceptions that students with disabilities held back the class and limited the teacher's ability to do as many activities and cover as much content. Austin (2001) noted that a "preeminent reservation" (p. 8) of general educators was concern that inclusion of students with disabilities for the purpose of socialization did not take into account disparity in academic achievement between the student with the disabilities and general education peers. Teachers also expressed concerns regarding the potentially disruptive effects of some students with disabilities. There is evidence suggesting that negative teacher attitudes may be associated with resistance to change and lack of experience with well-designed programs (Jallad, Schumm, Slusher, & Vaughn, 1996; Loveland et al., 2001). Loveland et al. found that teachers with experience in inclusive school programs showed significantly more positive perspectives regarding inclusion than teachers who had not been in inclusive programs. However, even in these well-designed inclusive programs, general education teachers' concerns included 1) need to maintain special education resources, 2) behavior of some students with disabilities, 3) influence on students without disabilities, and 4) teacher skills required to meet the needs of students with disabilities. Unfortunately, the *Federal 2000 Schools and Staffing Survey* found fewer than 4 in 10 general education teachers agreed they were given the support they needed to teach students with special needs (National Center for Education Statistics [NCES], 2000).

PREPARING FOR SUCCESSFUL INCLUSION

Successful implementation of inclusion requires that school administrators and teachers make changes in the ways in which they assign students to classrooms, schedule classes, set up teams, allocate resources, design curriculum, deliver instruction, and assess student progress. However, it is important to recognize that real change is deeply imbedded in the systemic structure of an organization; it goes beyond reallocation of resources and implementation of new teaching methods (McGregor & Vogelsberg, 1998; Villa & Thousand, 1992). Though programs and materials support change, it is primarily about the beliefs and actions of individuals. As schools take on the challenges of inclusion, those working for change must recognize that it is a process that occurs slowly and requires that all stakeholders make a long-term commitment to provide ongoing support and address problems as they emerge (Walther-Thomas & Bryant, 1996).

Assessing Readiness for Inclusion

The first step in preparing for successful inclusion is to assess school and personnel readiness for the changes ahead (Kochhar et al., 2000). Increasing the quantity and quality of inclusive education in schools requires comprehensive and collaborative efforts for system-wide planning, implementation, and ongoing evaluation (McGregor & Vogelsberg, 1998). Bauwens and Hourcade (1995) developed the *Collaboration Readiness Scale*, an instrument that assesses the overall readiness of educators to move into collaborative ventures in schools. Items on this scale focus on 1) a common understanding and awareness of purpose and need, 2) involvement and incentives for stakeholders, 3) district and administrative support, and 4) effective planning. In the case of inclusion, key stakeholders must address district, building, and classroom-level planning issues (Walther-Thomas & Bryant, 1996). Kochhar and colleagues (2000) identified several areas for evaluation when assessing inclusion readiness: 1) readiness for student evaluation and assessment, 2) readiness of the educational environment, 3) readiness of the physical and support services environment, 4) readiness of the attitudinal culture and environment, 5) readiness for school and community involvement, 6) readiness for individualized planning and student and parent involvement, 7) readiness for professional development and teacher in-service training, 8) leadership and resources, and 9) data collection, evaluation, and continuous improvement. Table 5.3 describes specific considerations and strategies to facilitate planning and implementation of inclusion derived from the change literature (McGregor & Vogelsberg, 1998).

Administrative Support

Administrative support has been identified as a meaningful variable associated with successful inclusion (Mastropieri & Scruggs, 2001; Walther-Thomas & Bryant, 1996). Administrators at the district and building level can provide leadership and vision to effect school change. Kennedy and Fisher (2001) found that teachers were more willing to consider alternate service delivery models when administrators created an atmosphere that was supportive of inclusive education. Administrative involvement can ensure that the inclusion planning team consists of willing and capable participants who are representative of all of the key stakeholders, including general and special education teachers, resource and related services personnel, and families (Villa & Thousand, 1992). Administrators also play an important role in addressing many of the issues that arise with inclusion such as the allocation of resources, teaching assignments, student assignment, scheduling of classes and planning time, and assignment of paraprofessionals (Kamens, Loprete, & Slostad, 2000).

Table 5.3. Strategies to facilitate inclusion derived from the change literature

Consideration	Implications to facilitate inclusion
Rationale	The rationale for inclusion must be developed in collaboration with general educators and communicated in terms relative to the needs and benefits of all students. Inclusion must be a professional value that encompasses *all* students. Support and acceptance of student diversity must be a common goal. Anticipated benefits to students who are not in special education should be emphasized.
Scope	Inclusion is a fundamental change, but the inclusion of students with disabilities is often initiated incrementally, beginning with one or two students. Support issues are resolved with these students to demonstrate positive outcomes and gain full school support. Unless this initial effort addresses existing structures, roles, and resources, these small steps are not likely to lead to large-scale change.
Pace	The pace of change must fit the setting. Placing all students with disabilities in general education classes too rapidly will leave staff unclear about their new roles and expectations. In contrast, moving too slowly can lead to criticism about the lack of visible outcomes. Collaborative planning is necessary to set and review the pace, accelerating it or decelerating it to fit the setting.
Resources	The move to inclusion must be supported with resources to gain full team commitment. Resources in the form of release time, technical assistance time, and substitute time are especially important to assure adequate planning. Inclusion should not mean a decrease in special education or related services supports. It does mean that resources are used differently, including in different locations. Dedicated and creative teams can find and develop resources others might not recognize.
Commitment	The commitment to inclusive schooling practices must be broad-based. This is not just a special education initiative; efforts require the entire school facility. Planning, rationale, scope, pace, and resources must be developed through the collaboration of a broad spectrum of school personnel and families.
Key staff	The impetus to include students with disabilities often originates with special educators. This can lead to a situation in which inclusion is viewed as a single person's "project." Collaborative teaming, involving administrators, families, students, general educators, and special educators, must be recognized as necessary and supported components of successful inclusion. Key staff from all areas of the school must be involved in the implementation of this innovation.
Parents	Parents of both general and special education students should be involved in discussions and planning about inclusion so that misunderstandings are minimized and concerns are addressed from the beginning.
Leadership	Administrative support and leadership are crucial for schoolwide adoptions of inclusion. Successful leaders recognize the power of team collaboration and use these structures to guide the implementation of inclusive schooling practices.
Relationship to other initiatives	Inclusion fits well with many current educational initiatives to improve the learning outcomes for all students. Rather than being viewed as a separate initiative, issues relative to students with disabilities should be considered within the context of the other instructional and organizational agendas of the school.

From McGregor, G., and Vogelsberg, R.T. (1998). *Inclusive schooling practices: Pedagogical and research foundations* (p. 12). Baltimore: Paul H. Brookes Publishing Co.; reprinted by permission.

Identifying Opportunities for Inclusion

Dorn and Fuchs (2004) identified four questions to consider when identifying appropriate settings for students with disabilities:

1. Where can the student learn specific skills?

2. Where does the student feel better?

3. Where can the student socialize?

4. Where do current skills of teachers fit the needs of the student?

The general education classroom is often the most appropriate answer to these questions; however, in considering these questions, it is important to bear in mind that inclusion opportunities are not limited to the general education classroom. Figure 5.4 is a questionnaire that helps to identify inclusive opportunities beyond the classroom. This is especially critical for students with severe disabilities, such as Tammy, who spend most of their school day in segregated settings. Schools must consider the participation of students with disabilities in all aspects of school and community life whether they occur before, during, or after school. These include school transportation, breakfast and lunch in the school cafeteria, extracurricular activities, field trips, and special schoolwide and community events (Stainback & Stainback, 1985). All too often, students with disabilities are excluded from these activities for reasons of convenience. Students eat lunch in their classrooms or in some cases with the school nurse simply because the logistics of arranging for a student to eat in the school cafeteria poses difficulties that require additional planning and special supports. Even though schools are prohibited from excluding students with disabilities from extracurricular activities, they are less likely to participate without the added encouragement and support of school staff and peers.

When identifying inclusion opportunities, it is important to recognize that inclusion is not about a place. Zigmond (2003), reflecting on a review of 35 years of efficacy research on the settings in which special education services are delivered, stated, "We know that what goes on in a place, not the location itself, is what makes a difference" (p. 198). Physical placement of a student with a disability in an inclusive setting does not guarantee that that student will be included. Dorn and Fuchs (2004) observed situations in which students with developmental disabilities were given very different tasks and in which teachers were not assisted in dealing with difficult behavior problems. They noted that, in such circumstances, "these children served primarily as classroom mascots and problems, not peers" (p. 64).

To be fully included, the student with a disability must have access to the natural supports available to all students (Fisher, Sax, & Pumpian, 1999). This includes access to general education peers who are not specifically designated as peer tutors or buddies. A growing body of research suggests that the excessive physical proximity of paraprofessionals can have negative social effects. Paraprofessional training to increase awareness of practices that may isolate students with disabilities from their peers and to teach strategies to facilitate peer interactions is needed (Causton-Theoharis & Malmgren, 2005). Although Lee had the extra support of a paraprofessional and peers who were specially trained to assist him in times of need, it was also important that he was provided with opportunities to interact and develop relationships with peers independently. Figure 5.5 is a helpful tool for identifying possible barriers to natural support networking (Vandercook & York, 1990).

Effective General Teaching Skills

CEC worked in collaboration with the Interstate New Teacher Assessment and Support Consortium (INTASC; 2001) to develop a comprehensive set of standards for general and special educators. The INTASC Special Education Committee based their work on the premise that "all teachers are responsible for providing an appropriate education to students with disabilities" (2001, p. 1). In 2001, INTASC released *Model*

Directions: After reading each question, put an "X" under the category that best reflects how many students with disabilities engage in the specified activity or environment.					
Do students with disabilities...	All (100%)	Most (> 50%)	Some (~ 50%)	Few (< 50%)	None (0%)
1. Ride the same school buses that students without disabilities ride?					
2. Have special education classrooms that are located throughout the school building with general education classrooms?					
3. Attend school assembly programs with peers in general education?					
4. Eat lunch in the school cafeteria during the same time as peers without disabilities?					
5. Eat lunch at the same tables in the school cafeteria with peers without disabilities?					
6. Share recess (or recreational times) with peers without disabilities?					
7. Go on school field trips with peers without disabilities?					
8. Participate in extracurricular activities such as school clubs, sports, special events, and school parties, with peers without disabilities?					
9. Participate in homeroom with peers in general education?					
10. Use the same bathroom as peers without disabilities?					
11. Use the school hallways at the same time as peers without disabilities?					
12. Share one or more classes with peers without disabilities?					
13. Have their school pictures interspersed with their peers without disabilities throughout school publications (e.g., yearbook, newsletter, displays)?					
14. Share the same school jobs and responsibilities with peers without disabilities?					

Figure 5.4. Identifying opportunities for inclusion. (From Stainback, W., & Stainback, S. [1985]. *Integration of students with severe handicaps into regular schools* [pp. 30–31]. Reston, VA: Council for Exceptional Children; adapted by permission.)

Directions: Record a "Y" for yes and an "N" for no on the blank preceding each item. If the answer to any of the items is "no," then your team may wish to consider whether any changes should be made and what those changes might be.

Going with the flow

_____ Does the student enter the classroom at the same time as classmates?

_____ Is the student positioned so that he or she can see and participate in what is going on?

_____ Is the student positioned so that classmates and teachers may easily interact with him or her (e.g., without teacher between the student and his or her classmates, not isolated from classmates)?

_____ Does the student engage in classroom activities at the same time as classmates?

_____ Does the student make transitions in the classroom at the same time as classmates?

_____ Is the student involved in the same activities as his or her classmates?

_____ Does the student exit the classroom at the same time as classmates?

Acting cool

_____ Is the student actively involved in class activities (e.g., asks or responds to questions, plays a role in group activities)?

_____ Is the student encouraged to follow the same classroom and social rules as classmates (e.g., hugs others only when appropriate, stays in seat during instruction)?

_____ Is the student given assistance only as necessary (assistance should be faded as soon as possible)?

_____ Is assistance provided for the student by classmates (e.g., transitions to other classrooms, within the classroom)?

_____ Are classmates encouraged to provide assistance to the student?

_____ Is assistance provided for the student by classroom teachers?

_____ Does the student use the same or similar materials during classroom activities as his or her classmates (e.g., Tom Cruise notebooks, school mascot folders)?

Talking straight

_____ Does the student have a way to communicate with classmates?

_____ Do classmates know how to communicate with the student?

_____ Does the student greet others in a manner similar to that of his or her classmates?

_____ Does the student socialize with classmates?

_____ Is this facilitated?

_____ Does the student interact with teachers?

_____ Is this facilitated?

_____ Do teachers (e.g., classroom teachers, special education support staff) provide the same type of feedback (e.g., praise, discipline) for the student as for his or her classmates?

_____ If the student uses an alternative communication system, do classmates know how to use it?

_____ If the student uses an alternative communication system, do teachers know how to use it?

_____ Is the system always available to the student?

Figure 5.5. Inclusion checklist. (From Vandercook, T., & York, J. [1990]. A team approach to program development and support. In W. Stainback & S. Stainback [Eds.], *Support network for inclusive schooling* [pp. 117–118]. Baltimore: Paul H. Brookes Publishing Co.; adapted by permission.)

(continued)

Figure 5.5. *(continued)*

Looking good

_____ Is the student given the opportunity to attend to his or her appearance as classmates do (e.g., check appearance in mirror between classes)?

_____ Does the student have accessories that are similar to his or her classmates (e.g., oversize tote bags, friendship bracelets, hair jewelry)?

_____ Is the student dressed similarly to classmates?

_____ Is clothing that's needed for activities age appropriate (e.g., napkins instead of bibs, "cool" paint shirts)?

_____ Are personal supplies or belongings carried or transported discreetly?

_____ Is the student's equipment (e.g., wheelchair) kept clean?

_____ Is the student's hair combed?

_____ Are the student's hands clean and dry?

_____ Does the student change clothing to maintain a neat appearance?

_____ Does the student use chewing gum, breath mints, or breath spray?

Standards for Licensing General and Special Education Teachers of Students with Disabilities. Forty-nine standards for general educators were identified to represent appropriate and pedagogically sound teaching practices essential to the provision of equal access to quality learning for students with disabilities. Particular emphasis was placed on abilities to do the following:

1. Set realistically high expectations for students with disabilities

2. Demonstrate knowledge and understanding of disability legislation and special education policies and procedures

3. Demonstrate knowledge of the general characteristics of the most frequently occurring disabilities

4. Demonstrate basic understanding of ways that disabilities impact learning and development

5. Make accommodations, modifications, and/or adaptations to the general curriculum

6. Use a variety of instructional strategies and technologies

7. Work collaboratively with special education teachers

8. Promote positive social relationships among students with disabilities and their age-appropriate peers in the learning community

9. Foster independent engagement, self-motivation, and independent learning

10. Incorporate accommodations and alternate assessments into the ongoing assessment process of students with disabilities

Collaborative Teaming

Of the 10 essential general educator abilities identified by INTASC, the seventh ability, "work collaboratively with special education teachers," is pivotal to the accomplishment of the other nine. Few general education teachers feel prepared to integrate students with disabilities in their classrooms (Kamens et al., 2000; Singh, 2002). Although there is a critical need for general educator preparation to work with students with disabilities (Ansell, 2004; Boudah et al., 2000; Coombs-Richardson & Mead, 2001; Snell & Janney, 2005), even highly skilled general educators require the support of other professionals to work effectively with students with disabilities in general education classrooms. LRE provisions in IDEA 2004 support the "use of supplementary aids and services" in order that "education in regular classes" may be "achieved satisfactorily" (IDEA 2004 [Part B, Sec 612 (a) (5)]). Services that focus on general and special educator collaboration are often critical to the success of students with disabilities in inclusive settings. Friend (2000) maintained

> Virtually every treatise on inclusive practices, whether conceptual, anecdotal, qualitative, or quantitative, concludes that inclusion's success in large part relies on collaboration among staff members and with parents and others, and that failures can typically be traced to shortcomings in the collaborative dimension of the services to students. (p. 130)

In developing standards for special educators, the INTASC Special Education Committee paid particular attention to the wide range of roles assumed by special education teachers and the "differential knowledge, skills, and dispositions that each of these roles requires" (2001, p. 6). Special educators participate in a variety of collaborative structures in an effort to increase instructional options for students with disabilities in general education settings. Consultative models with the special educator as consultant and the general educator as "consultee" were widely used in the 1970s and 1980s. However, the role of the special educator as expert was not well received by many general educators (Pugach & Johnson, 1989). In 1986, Idol, Paolucci-Whitcomb, and Nevin introduced *Collaborative Consultation*, a model that focuses on parity between participants with equal partnership and shared expertise. According to Idol et al., collaborative consultation is an interactive process in which people with diverse expertise generate creative solutions to address mutually defined problems. The multidisciplinary team is a model that expands the number of participants in the collaborative consultation process validating the capabilities of all educators, support personnel, and families in planning and evaluating services provided to students with disabilities in inclusive settings. (Dettmer, Thurston, & Dyck, 2002). According to Friend and Cook (2003), effective models emphasize four defining characteristics of collaboration:

1. It is voluntary

2. It requires parity among participants

3. It is based on mutual goals

4. It depends on shared responsibility for participation and decision making

Providing Supports in General Education Classrooms

Collaborative efforts should emphasize curriculum and instructional practices that are responsive to students with varied educational needs (Udvari-Solner & Thousand, 1996). Administrators, general educators, special educators, and families must work together to develop individualized supports tailored to the specific needs of students with disabilities. Fisher (2000) identified formalized supports for students with disabilities in general education classes in three major areas: 1) personal support, 2) curriculum accommodations and modifications, and 3) assistive and instructional technology. Figure 5.6 depicts Fisher's *Triangle of Support*. Individual students vary in the types and levels of support that they require in each of these areas to be successful. According to Fisher, Sax, and Pumpian (1999),

> Each class and each lesson is unique, and teachers must plan accordingly. Overutilization of supports constitutes restrictive intervention for the student and a situation in which the student learns little. Underutilization of these supports constitutes "dumping" and a situation in which the student may be set up to fail. (p. 59)

Personal Supports   A variety of personal supports may be employed to increase the participation of students with disabilities in general education classrooms (Fisher, Sax, & Pumpian, 1999). Specialized support staff including special educators, related services personnel, paraprofessionals, and peers can be used on a full-time, part-time, or as needed basis to assist students in inclusive settings. Lee is an example of a student who required a high level of personal support to function successfully in the general education classroom. A full-time paraprofessional and trained peers were available to help him as needed throughout the school day. He also received assistance from a speech-language therapist and an occupational therapist within the general education classroom.

Special educators may provide support to students in general education classrooms through consultation, support facilitation, or co-teaching service delivery models. Consultation between that general and special educator can help to identify instructional and curricular accommodations and modifications to be implemented by the general

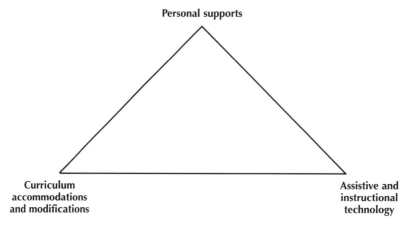

Figure 5.6.   Triangle of support. (From Fisher, D. [2000, March]. Curriculum and instruction for all abilities and intelligences. *High School Magazine, 7*[7], 22; National Association of Secondary School Principals. www.principals.org; reprinted by permission.)

Student course selection and special education services worksheet

| Student name: Michael Johnson | | | | Grade: 10 | |

Subject area courses	Low support ⟶		Moderate support ⟶		High support
	Consult only	Support facilitation	Co-teaching	Resource room	Self-contained
Math				✗	
English			✗		
History		✗			
Life science		✗			
P.E.	✗				
Elective 1	✗				
Elective 2	✗				

Figure 5.7. Personal supports across subject areas. (From Florida Inclusion Network [2004]. *Student's course selection and services worksheet.* Tallahassee, FL: Florida Department of Education, Bureau of Instructional Services and Community Support.)

education teacher (Idol et al., 1986). As a support facilitator, the special educator provides the appropriate level and frequency of in-class support or engages others, including paraprofessionals and peers, to provide additional support in the general education classroom (Stainback, Stainback, & Harris, 1989). Peer-mediated instruction, partner learning, and cooperative group learning provide academic support for students with disabilities in general education settings (Udvari-Solner & Thousand, 1996). Increasingly, special educators and related services providers are leaving resource settings to work with students in inclusive settings. Co-teaching is a model that has steadily gained popularity as a way to increase access to the general education curriculum for students with disabilities. The special education teacher provides additional support in the classroom and supplements the content area knowledge of the general education teacher with knowledge and expertise related to teaching students with disabilities (Rea, McLaughlin, & Walther-Thomas, 2002). This expertise includes an understanding of how disabilities impact academic performance as well as knowledge of specific instructional practices, accommodations, and enhancements to increase access to the general education curriculum for students with disabilities (DeBoer & Fister, 1995). The need for consultation, support facilitation, or co-teaching varies across students and across activities. To avoid the problems associated with under- or overutilization of these supports (Fisher, Sax, & Pumpian, 1999), the implementation of personal supports must be tailored to the individual needs of the student. Figure 5.7 provides an example of the services provided to a student with a learning disability.

Curriculum Accommodations and Modifications Proven teaching methods that promote the achievement of individuals with wide differences in abilities within general education classrooms have been identified. Universal Design for Learning (UDL) is based on multiple and flexible methods of presentation, expression, and engagement (Rose & Meyer, 2000). The term *universal* indicates these are not disability-specific practices, but rather best practice for all students. Therefore, it is recommended these methods be promoted for all classrooms. Differentiated instruction addresses the needs of diverse learners and emphasizes a variety of methods. Tomlinson (2001) identified three elements of the curriculum that could be differentiated: 1) content (concepts, principles, and skills students must learn), 2) process (a variety of instructional groupings), and 3) products (ongoing formal and informal assessments). Differentiating content is an element that allows students with a wide range of abilities to be included in a single general education classroom. Lawrence-Brown (2004) identified several ways to differentiate content based on individual needs, including 1) goal adaptations (only parts of the general curriculum are included in the student's instructional goals), 2) prioritized instruction (student participates in general curriculum while accomplishing very different content or curriculum goals), and 3) authentic instruction (additional goals for students with severe disabilities are addressed by changing the emphasis and presentation of large-group lessons). When students with more significant disabilities are working toward different goals (IEP goals or alternate learning outcomes) than their peers in the general education classroom, the practice is often referred to as a *modification;* whereas changes in teaching methods and materials for students working toward the same goals and standards as the rest of the students in the general education classroom are frequently referred to as *accommodations.* Table 5.4 provides a side-by-side comparison and outlines associated teaching methods.

Table 5.4.   Curriculum accommodations and modifications

Accommodations	Modifications
Changing *how* the student gains access to information and demonstrates knowledge or skills. Instruction and assessment incorporates multiple means of representation, expression, and engagement. Instructional level, content, or performance criteria are not changed.	Changing *what* the student is expected to learn and/or demonstrate. Subject area remains the same, but course content is modified. Students work on individualized objectives within the context of the general education classroom.
Examples:	*Examples:*
Representation	Streamlined curriculum
Flexible curricular materials	Reduced number of items
Multimedia	Modified assignments
Digital formats	Reduced content
Audiotaped textbooks	Individualized goals
Video description and captioning	Multilevel curriculum
Graphic organizers	Curriculum overlapping
Advance organizers	Functional curriculum
Scaffolding	Life skills
Strategies instruction	Social skills instruction
Expression	Infused skills
Word processing software	Alternate assessment
Multimedia presentations	Authentic assessments
Oral tests	Performance-based assessments
Engagement	Portfolio assessment
Peer-mediated instruction	
Peer tutoring	
Cooperative learning groups	
Learning partners	
Computer-based instruction	

Assistive and Instructional Technology Assistive technology (AT) frequently brings to mind visions of complicated, high-tech equipment and is perceived as unmanageable by many professionals within education (Langone, 2000; Mirenda, Wilk, & Carson, 2000). AT devices include a range of items, pieces of equipment, or product systems that may be used to increase, maintain, or improve the functional abilities of children with disabilities (Galvin & Phillips, 1994; Lahm & Nickels, 1999; Parette, 1997; Schneider, 1999). AT includes any type of tool that could be used on a daily basis with the potential to increase the functional abilities of children with disabilities (Galvin & Phillips, 1994; Parette, 1997). In practice, AT devices can range from very simple to quite complex and generally fall into two categories: low-tech and high-tech. Low-tech devices tend to be simple, have few moving parts, and are relatively inexpensive. They are easy to manipulate and require little training for effective use (Lahm & Nickels, 1999; Parette, 1997; Schneider, 1999). Conversely, high-tech devices tend to be more complex, often have an electronic component, are generally more expensive, and usually require more training for staff on proper use (Lahm & Nickels, 1999: Parette, 1997; Schneider, 1999).

Frequently, people with severe disabilities require increased supervision and instruction within community-based job sites. Consequently, their performance is often dependent on a job coach, teacher, or other type of support person. Job coaches provide specific training and extended support, such as instruction of new tasks, retraining of previously taught skills, and the systematic training of skills for new job acquisition (Lee, Storey, & Anderson, 1997; Nuehring & Sitlington, 2003). The absence of these support personnel often results in poor skill demonstration and/or overall poor job performance by people with significant disabilities. Research indicates the use of AT increases competency and independence of individuals with severe disabilities in community-based settings. Furthermore, AT increases their probability of success in self-management skills in community work settings (Langone, 2000; Post & Storey, 2002; Smith, Belcher, & Juhrs, 1995; Wehman, 1997b). Lee's use of AT lends support to the immense capacity of technology to support students with significant limitations in all settings. Specifically, his experience demonstrates the importance of AT access for all students with disabilities. A promising new technology in relation to a specialized project (*MISSION POSSIBLE*) that further illustrates the power of AT as an instructional methodology is discussed later in this chapter.

TRANSITION AND INCLUSION

During transition, students leave the ranks of high school programs to actively join local adult communities. The metaphor of a vehicle is often used to describe the metamorphosis that takes place during this period (Nuehring & Sitlington, 2003) and is frequently described as a car reaching an intended destination. The provision of inclusive activities within the community during transition preparation and implementation should be considered in order to plan appropriate instruction, systems of support, and activities for all students with disabilities.

Although inclusion in general education is an important goal for students with disabilities, there is a critical need to prepare high school students with severe disabilities for transition and the world of work (Conley, 2003; Frank & Sitlington, 2000; Kiernan, 2000; Kraemer, McIntyre, & Blacher, 2003; Neubert, Moon, & Grigal, 2002;

Nuehring & Sitlington, 2003; Wehman & Gibson, 1998) within environments similar to those where they may seek future employment. Because little empirical evidence exists illuminating how schools are preparing individuals with severe disabilities for the world beyond school or the type of outcomes targeted for these students when they exit high school (Cooney, 2002; Grigal, Test, Beattie, & Wood, 1997; Kraemer & Blacher, 2001; Pearman, Elliott, & Aborn, 2004; Snell & Brown, 2000), it would be useful for teachers to collect and maintain appropriate instructional outcome data. Unfortunately, young adults with disabilities continue to experience high school failure, low employment rates, low participation in postsecondary education, and low satisfaction with their adult lives (Halloran & Simon, 1995; Unger, 2002; Wehman & Gibson, 1998; Wehman & Revell, 2002).

Compounding the difficulty of implementing inclusive transition activities, the quality of transition goals defined within IEPs are often inadequate and contain vague references to critical outcome expectations for students. Several studies indicate a considerable number of transition plan goals for students with disabilities are difficult to identify and translate into meaningful practice (Frank & Sitlington, 2000; Grigal et al., 1997; Halpern, 1994; Wehman, 1992). As a result, several well-documented barriers to inclusive transition planning have been consistently cited within research literature. Among these are inadequate preservice training, insufficient resource incentives, poor coordination of multiagency involvement, failure to seek or achieve consensus among stakeholders, and inconsistent resource allocation in state and federal transition practices (Blackorby & Wagner, 1996; Burgstahler, 2003; Cooney, 2002; deFur & Taymans, 1995; Derer, Polsgrove, & Rieth, 1996; Frank & Sitlington, 2000; Katsiyannis, deFur, & Conderman, 1998; Noyes & Sax, 2004). Research further illustrates inclusive transition planning often centers on student disabilities, rather than student needs (Cooney, 2002; Grigal et al., 1997; McDonnell, Mathot-Buckner, & Ferguson, 1996; Wehman & Gibson, 1998). This type of stereotyped service delivery, one based on type or label, occurs within many settings to the detriment of students (Noyes & Sax, 2004; Wittenburg & Maag, 2002).

Facilitating Transition with Functional Curriculum

Historically, instructional programs for students with moderate to severe disabilities included a multitude of nonfunctional tasks (Iovannone, Dunlap, Huber, & Kincaid, 2003; Sternberg, 1994; Wehman, 1997b, 2002a), such as inappropriate paper and pencil assignments and a lack of community focus (Nietupski, Hamre-Nietupski, Donder, Houselog, & Anderson, 1988; Sternberg, 1994). Instruction over objectives poorly suited to individual needs was most often provided within segregated settings. In addition, the instruction provided within these noninclusive settings was at skill or developmental levels that were not appropriate for individual students. With the increased acceptance of the normalization movement in the late 1970s (Perske, 2004), questions began to surface regarding the efficacy of merely providing instruction within segregated school-based environments to students with severe disabilities. Educators and parents expressed concerns about nonfunctional skills identified as irrelevant to individuals with severe disabilities and recommended independent functioning within communities as a main priority and goal for instruction. Due to these global concerns, many educators began to focus on the development of chronological, age-appropriate skills within the inclusive environments that students would be living and working in as adults (Fisher & Pumpian, 1998; Neubert et al., 2002; Nietupski et al., 1988; Nuehring & Sitlington, 2003; Perske, 2004; Sternberg, 1994). Although functional curriculum is important when preparing students with disabilities for the world of work, it is often challenging for general education teachers to provide appropriate functional curriculum within their classrooms. Careful team planning and collaboration between special and regular educators is necessary to ensure student goals are meaningfully addressed and that the mastery of necessary postsecondary skills may be achieved. One method of providing specialized instruction during general education classes is through the use of an infused skills grid. An infused skills grid clearly illustrates where identified skills will be taught during a student's day and which team members have identified particular skills for targeted instruction (Fisher, Sax, & Pumpian, 1999). Many variations of the infused skills grid exist, demonstrating its power as a useful planning tool. Table 5.5 is an actual planning tool used by Lee's team for IEP objective planning purposes.

Community-Based Instruction for Inclusion

Although students with severe and moderate disabilities receive educational benefit from interacting with their peers without disabilities during school and classroom activities and instruction, they also benefit from inclusive opportunities within the com-

Table 5.5. Plannning matrix for Lee

IEP objectives	Homeroom	English I	Algebra I	Computer science	Lunch	P.E.
When frustrated, Lee will ask for assistance from staff or a peer(s).	Yes	Yes	Yes	Yes	Yes	Yes
Lee will maintain an appropriate boundary of a least one arm's length when interacting with others.	Yes	Yes	Yes	Yes	Yes	Yes
If noise levels become too loud, Lee will notify staff or peers verbally or by signaling.	Yes	Yes	Yes	Yes	Yes	Yes
Lee will initiate one conversation with a typical peer per hour.			Yes	Yes	Yes	Yes
Necessary support staff	General education teacher, peers, teaching assistant	General education teacher, resource teacher, peers, teaching assistant	General education teacher, occupational therapist, peers, teaching assistant	General education teacher, peers, teaching assistant	Assistant principal, cafeteria staff, designated peers, teaching assistant	General education teacher, occupational therapist, peers, teaching assistant

Student: Lee   Week of: February 10–14, 2003   Domain focus: Social skills

From Beninghof, A. (1993). *Ideas for inclusion: The classroom teacher's guide* (p.). Longmont, CO: Sopris West; and Fisher, D., Sax, C., and Pumpian, I. (1999). *Inclusive high schools: Learning from contemporary classrooms* (p. 67). Baltimore: Paul H. Brookes Publishing Co.; adapted by permission.

munity. Specialized vocational instruction is especially critical for students with significant disabilities (Grossi, 1998; Noyes & Sax, 2004; Nuehring & Sitlington, 2003; Pearman et al., 2004; Wehman, 1992). Traditionally, vocational instruction has been conducted inside simulated classroom settings or sheltered workshops. Alternatively, CBI is a more inclusive approach to vocational instruction because it provides students with opportunities to receive vocational instruction within the communities in which they are likely to seek gainful employment (Noyes & Sax, 2004; Nuehring & Sitlington, 2003; Patton, 1999; Wehman & Revell, 2002). The element of CBI, in the real world, is particularly important for students with disabilities due to their difficulty in generalizing instruction between settings and functional instruction (Grigal et al., 1997; Post & Storey, 2002; Wehman & Gibson, 1998). Unfortunately, few schools offer sound community-based programs for students with severe disabilities (Grigal et al., 1997; Moon & Inge, 2000; Neubert et al., 2002).

When an increase of CBI and inclusive transition programming for students with all types of disabilities occurred during the late 1980s, researchers intently began to study best practices for students with severe disabilities (Grigal et al., 1997; Wehman & Gibson, 1998). As a result, literature on transition practices increased dramatically. Several studies outline the following characteristics as necessary to successful inclusive transition planning for positive student outcomes: early planning; interagency collaboration; individualized transition planning; focus on integration; community-relevant curriculum; community-based training; business linkages; job placement; ongoing staff development; and program evaluation, including identifying specific individuals involved, identifying the role of each person involved, and identifying the time that services should begin (Garcia-Villamisar, Ross, & Wehman, 2000; Grigal et al., 1997; McDonnell, Hardman, Hightower, Keifer-O'Donnell, & Drew, 1993; Morgan, Gerity, & Ellerd, 2000; Neubert et al., 2002; Smith et al., 1995).

The importance of CBI is delineated by the reality that most students with moderate to severe disabilities have great difficulty generalizing skills learned within their classroom to actual job sites within the community (Iovannone et al., 2003; McDonnell et al., 1996; Moon & Inge, 2000; Nietupski et al., 1988). Moreover, numerous studies indicate the need for students with severe mental retardation to be educated within the settings they will likely become employed after high school (Kraemer & Blacher, 2001; Nietupski et al., 1988; McDonnell et al., 1996; Smith et al.,1995), demonstrating evidence of a specific need to design instructional practices for these students that will meet the expectations and realities of specific postschool settings, such as work or SE (Chadsey-Rusch & Gonzalez, 1996; Kraemer & Blacher, 2001; Moon & Inge, 2000; Wehman, 1997b; Westling & Fox, 2000). The use of curriculum emphasizing employment, personal management, and leisure activities has had significant impact on the development and implementation of high school programs for students with severe disabilities, including those with mental retardation and autism spectrum disorders (Iovannanone et al., 2003; McDonnell et al., 1993, 1996; Nietupski et al., 1988; Moon & Inge, 2000; Westling & Fox, 2000).

Given this knowledge, it is incumbent on educators to design instructional programs containing specialized vocational instruction within school and community-based settings. Because learning in school differs from learning in community-based settings (Chadsey-Rusch & Gonzalez, 1996; McDonnell et al.,1993), there is a need for students with severe disabilities to receive CBI on actual job sites. Furthermore, it is important for students to have opportunities to engage in school experiences in preparation for meaningful work within community environments (Chadsey-Rusch & Gonzalez, 1996; McDonnell et al., 1993; Nietupski et al., 1988).

Technology has become an essential tool in nearly every educational, employment, and community environment (Burgstahler, 2003). For people with severe disabilities, access to such equipment potentially maximizes their independence and participation within a myriad of community-based settings. As these individuals continue to participate in integrated community settings, the need continues for researchers and practitioners to identify effective and socially acceptable methods of intervention and instruction (Alberto, Taber, & Fredrick, 1999).

MISSION POSSIBLE: AN INCLUSIVE COMMUNITY PROJECT

Mission

Implement an instructional strategy in an inclusive, community-based job site using an advanced technology support system.

Mission Specialists

Janice Dolan: Classroom teacher

Susan Lerschlolarn: Speech-language pathologist

Kim Spence-Cochran: Research lead

Mission Participants

Five high school students with the dual diagnosis of autism and mental retardation (see Figure 5.8).

Purpose

Teach students with autism and mental retardation to use hand-held computers to complete various authentic jobs in a community-based setting.

Mission Technology

The *Visual Assistant* program was used to illustrate individual task analyses for specific jobs. It is a multimedia training program designed to run on the Windows CE platform of a hand-held computer (AbleLink Technologies, 2005; Davies et al., 2002). It enabled students to view step-by-step pictures paired with auditory instructions on a hand-held computer screen to complete authentic work at their own pace. Pictures and voice prompts were loaded into hand-held computers (see Figure 5.9) by the research team to illustrate the correct sequence of specific work tasks.

Location

The project took place at a department store located 2 miles from the students' high school. This site, developed by two members from the research team, was first approved

Figure 5.8.   Using the palmtop computer to complete an authentic job in the community. (Copyright © 2005 K. Spence-Cochran and C. Pearl. Used by permission of Vanessa McClaugherty.)

Figure 5.9.   Example of a personal digital assistant (PDA).

by one of the assistant store managers. An informal meeting with the assistant store manager yielded a preliminary approval, then the team requested and received permission from the regional manager prior to commencing project activity. The support and cooperation of the store staff was critical to the success of the project.

Mission Description

Prior to implementation in the community, students were systematically taught to accurately use the hand-held computers within their classroom. Instruction with the computers continued until each participant could independently demonstrate proficiency and independent job completion and task performance. Once in the community and on the job site, staff provided minimal instruction to participants and then a prompt for the students to begin completing an authentic novel job with the hand-held computer. Jobs were selected by the assistant department store manager, who also determined individual job accuracy criterion for each task. For each job, research staff gave the following verbal prompt, "Watch, I am going to show you how to do a job," followed by a demonstration of scrolling through the first three to five steps of the task (according to a predesignated task analysis) with the student looking on. While scrolling through jobs with the computer, research staff provided necessary verbal instructions to students. Next, staff would verbally identify each item the participant would be interacting with during task completion (i.e., colors, shapes, hangers) and in each area where participants would be working. Finally, staff issued the verbal prompt, "Now it is your turn to do this job with the computer," and the hand-held computer was relinquished to the participant for task completion.

Excerpt from Slipper Wall Task Analysis

Steps in task analysis	Task completion
1. Place the cream slippers on a peg on wall 1	Yes___ No___
2. Place the cream slippers on a peg on wall 1	Yes___ No___
3. Place the leopard slippers on a peg on wall 1	Yes___ No___
4. Place the red slippers on a peg on wall 1	Yes___ No___
5. Place the red slippers on a peg on wall 1	Yes___ No___
6. Place the pink cat slippers on a peg on wall 2	Yes___ No___
7. Place the cream, woman and dog slippers on a peg on wall 2	Yes___ No___
8. Place the green dragonfly slippers on a peg on wall 2	Yes___ No___
9. Place the cream, woman on a couch slippers on a peg on wall 2	Yes___ No___
10. Place the cream, cool cat slippers on a peg on wall 2	Yes___ No___
11. Place the red, woman and dog slippers on a peg on wall 2	Yes___ No___
12. Place the red, woman on a couch slippers on a peg on wall 2	Yes___ No___
13. Place the black, woman on a couch slippers on a peg on wall 2	Yes___ No___
14. Place the black, woman and dog slippers on a peg on wall 2	Yes___ No___
15. Place the fuzzy purple slippers on a peg on wall 3	Yes___ No___
16. Place the fuzzy black slippers on a peg on wall 3	Yes___ No___
17. Place the fuzzy leopard slippers on a peg on wall 3	Yes___ No___

Criterion for this Task Each pair of slippers should be hung properly on a peg. Similar types of slippers should be placed on designated pegs and should not be mixed with other types of slippers. Slippers should hang in a straight row and look neat. Types of slippers should be hung on their designated walls (e.g., wall 1, wall 2, wall 3).

Mission Outcome

Five participants accurately completed nine authentic novel job tasks during the course of the project. The lowest level of measured accuracy for any participant during any of the nine jobs was 93%, demonstrating a high level of proficiency. Percent correct (or accuracy) was determined by identifying correct and incorrect responses within the context of a designated task. The store manager determined specifications and job criteria for the novel job tasks according to acceptable corporate standards for job accuracy and completion. These were recorded with the use of a distinct task analysis for each job. Independent observers determined which of the specific responses or steps within the tasks were correct or incorrect to determine the percent correct per task. *Correct* referred to the correct completion of one part or step of a designated task analysis per novel job task. *Incorrect* referred to a missed step or an incorrect completion of one part or step of a designated task analysis. Overall percent correct of an individual's responses per task was calculated with the following formula: number of cor-

Figure 5.10. Regional manager Eric Bass and one of the study participants on the research site. (Copyright © 2005 K. Spence-Cochran and C. Pearl. Used by permission of D.J. and E.B.)

rect responses divided by the sum of correct responses, added to the number of incorrect responses, multiplied by 100% (Richards et al., 1999). The average number of steps for each of the tasks was fairly consistent.

Demonstrated accuracy levels from this project provide evidence of a highly acceptable vocational instructional methodology for the accuracy of work-related activity by students with severe disabilities. Accuracy, a requirement in all job settings, is frequently difficult and time-consuming to teach to students with severe disabilities (Grossi & Heward, 1998; Post & Storey, 2002). Study results support the use of hand-held computers in community-based settings and demonstrate the potential to advance the vocational instructional repertoire of high school personnel across the nation (see Figure 5.10).

Notable Mission Findings

Of particular interest, two participants independently discovered how to restart task analyses on the hand-held computer when they made errors or were missing items that obviously needed to be placed within a specific area. All participants were taught to use the computers after research staff had initiated an assigned task on the touch screen by double clicking the corresponding task icon. They were not taught to manipulate individual screens, programs, or icons on the hand-held computer. The revelation that individual participants were able to independently manipulate the computer in a purposeful manner, without any staff instruction for several specific functions, indicated they had the capacity to operate the computers with greater independence than had been originally assessed by the research team.

Mission Summary

High school students with significant disabilities urgently need preparation for transition and potential employment opportunities. This urgency is compounded by the fact that many transition activities do not occur with regularity or success. Students must be afforded opportunities to engage in vocational preparatory activities with the use of socially and empirically validated methodologies. It is vital for students with severe disabilities to receive sound instructional programming that will adequately prepare them to successfully work and function within their communities. Specialized technology holds great promise for individuals with autism and mental retardation who desire full inclusion within their community. The ability to successfully operate and manipulate a hand-held computer for the purpose of managing a schedule, completing job tasks, or self-monitoring behavior could assist individuals with severe disabilities in the realization of desired life goals. In addition, these types of skills have the potential to provide support to individuals who benefit from elaborate support systems for successful community integration and functioning.

This project contributes to an existing body of knowledge illustrating the vast potential specialized technology holds for individuals with autism and mental retardation by demonstrating the tremendous capability people with significant challenges possess. For individuals who have traditionally experienced segregation in all aspects of their lives, hand-held computers present teachers, parents, and community providers with a legitimate option for the provision of ongoing support to work and participate within their communities. This type of technology purports a dignified support option for people who may otherwise be unable to complete work within community-based settings (see Figure 5.11).

CONCLUSION

McLeskey et al. (1999) concluded that a dual system of special and general education was becoming less and less feasible. Since then, there has been no evidence of a reversal in the movement away from segregated settings. However, effective inclusion of students with disabilities in general education is dependent on the innovation and perseverance of professionals who 1) value and support collaboration between general and special educators (Weiss & Lloyd, 2003), 2) recognize barriers and engage in joint problem solving (Pugach & Johnson, 1995), 3) share responsibilities and accountability (Friend & Cook, 2003), and 4) maintain focus on the implementation of best practice in teaching partnerships (Villa, Thousand, & Nevin, 1996). In 1985, Lieberman cautioned:

Figure 5.11. Tyrell enjoying community inclusion and the opportunity to work with his nondisabled peers. (Copyright © 2005 K. Spence-Cochran and C. Pearl. Used by permission of Elaine Murry.)

> We cannot drag regular educators kicking and screaming into a merger with special educa-
> tion. . . . This proposed merger is a myth, unless regular educators, for reasons far removed
> from "it's best for children" decide that such a merger is in their own best interests. This is
> something that we will never be able to point out to them. They will have to come to it in
> their own way, on their own terms, in their own time. How about a few millennia? (p. 513)

Fortunately, progress since the 1980s has not borne out Lieberman's prediction. It has
not been "a few millennia" and yet increasingly the perceptions of educators reflect the
emerging consensus that most, if not all, students with disabilities should spend the
school day in general education classrooms. The essential flaw in Lieberman's reasoning is the assumption that the reasons why a merger of special and general education
is "best for children" could possibly be "far removed" from the "best interests" of
teachers. Such a merger will occur when it is fully understood by all stakeholders that
the reasons why inclusion is "best for children" are inextricably entwined with the reasons why it is best for teachers. Inclusion is "best for children" when it provides students with access to the general education curriculum and opportunities to interact in
meaningful ways with peers without disabilities within general education settings and
when it is individually planned, specialized, intensive, goal-directed, research-based,
and guided by student performance (Heward, 2003). Inclusion is in the "best interests"
of teachers when professional development and follow up is provided, when it is carefully planned and evaluated on an ongoing basis, and when it involves differentiation
and parity in general and special educator roles and responsibilities.

Half a century has passed since the *Brown v. Board of Education* decision. Parents and educators have gone forward to meet the challenges of full implementation of IDEA. As a group, the majority of children with disabilities are now being educated with peers without disabilities in general education classrooms in neighborhood schools. Lee's educational experience illustrates the progress that has been made. Unfortunately, Tammy's case offers a reminder that the stigma of categorical segregation persists. IDEA 2004 requires a renewed effort to build on past successes to ensure that all students with disabilities, including those with severe disabilities, are taught in the LREs. This will require highly qualified general and special education teachers who are skilled in individualized approaches that allow students with disabilities to gain access to the same educational environments and curriculum as students without disabilities. It will also require teachers with a vision of the future who use sound instructional programming to afford students opportunities to engage in vocational preparatory activities that will adequately prepare them to successfully work and function within their communities. In summary, it will require educators with an expanded view of IDEA 2004's "whenever possible" as it applies to the inclusion of students with disabilities.

Addressing the need for systems change and the community integration of individuals with severe disabilities, Brown and York (1974) stated, "It seems that we now have an opportunity to create humane, tolerant, developmentally sound, and existentially relevant social and emotional environments that can replace oppressive, rejecting, undignifying, and intolerant systems so long in operation" (p. 10). These words exemplify a modern need to change systems that continue to relegate individuals with severe disabilities to segregated settings. Moreover, they lend credence to a belief system that encourages the inclusion of all individuals within a community and offer hope to those wishing to conduct their lives in a dignified and meaningful manner.

STUDY QUESTIONS

1. List three barriers to inclusion and outline a plan for overcoming each.

2. Imagine that you have been given the responsibility of explaining to a group of classroom teachers why inclusion is occurring and how it might be accomplished. What would you say?

3. What do you think might be the major argument against merging special and general education? What are the key arguments for the merger of special and general education?

4. Ask a friend, roommate, or fellow student if he or she would have a friendly discussion or debate with you about what Walter Lippmann said more than a half century ago. He stated:

   If a child fails in school and then fails in life, the schools cannot sit back and say: you see how accurately I predicted this. Unless we are to admit that education is essentially impotent, we have to throw back the child's failure at the school, and describe it as a failure not by the child but by the schools. (Quoted in Block & Dworkin, 1976, p. 17)

5. One of the best ways to learn about people with disabilities is to interact with and get to know them. Thus, one activity to further your knowledge about students with disabilities and inclusion might be to volunteer to serve as a buddy or on a circle of friends for a student with disabilities. Many public schools have recently started this or are considering it. Ask your instructor, a teacher you know, or someone else connected with the schools if it would be possible for you to do something like this.

6. How would you feel about being put into a special class in which all the children had disabilities?

7. What do you think the major agenda items might be for a schoolwide inclusion task force?

8. How do you think the parents of children without disabilities would feel about children with severe disabilities being in their child's general classes? Present your brief oral arguments for both sides of this opinion.

9. Research the major changes made to IDEA in its most recent reauthorization. How do those changes relate to the issue of inclusion?

10. Develop a statement that articulates your position on the inclusion of students with disabilities in general education.

6

Facilitating and Supporting Transition

Secondary School Restructuring and the
Implementation of Transition Services and Programs

Mary A. Falvey, Richard L. Rosenberg, Devon Monson, and Lori Eshilian

AFTER COMPLETING THIS CHAPTER, THE READER WILL BE ABLE TO

○ Understand the concept of inclusive education and transition services for students with disabilities and why inclusive education has become the recommended practice

○ Understand and describe the role of the Individuals with Disabilities Education Act (IDEA) Amendments of 1997 (PL 105-17) and the Individuals with Disabilities Education Improvement Act of 2004 (PL 108-446) in promoting inclusive education

○ Describe characteristics of inclusive schools that utilize effective transition services

○ Identify and describe specific systems-change efforts that can result in inclusion and effective transition programs and services

○ Describe the role of educators in implementing inclusive education and secondary school restructuring

○ Describe authentic assessment and the different types of options that can be available to students in a restructured secondary school environment

The title of this book, *Life Beyond the Classroom*, implies that, at some point, life involves time in the classroom. This chapter discusses critical issues and essential characteristics of secondary school experiences that prepare students for life beyond. During the 19th century, the economy in the United States changed from agrarian to industrial, with significant effects on culture and opportunities. This resulted in the majority of schools, which were one-room schoolhouses, being replaced by large schools that used factory-line technology engineered to yield standard results. This Industrial Age factory model school, still dominant in many locations throughout North America, is gradually being replaced by schools that reflect the Information Age and the needs of all students, rather than the demands of bureaucracies (American Youth Policy Forum, 2000).

Schools have been engaged in restructuring efforts since the 1970s. These restructuring efforts have been based on the recognition that public schools must and can effectively teach a heterogeneous population of students, including those with and without disabilities. Specifically, these restructuring efforts have been designed to

- Make schools more responsive to all students' needs

- Hold all students to high standards while recognizing that learning and development do not occur at the same rate for all students

- Provide students with the skills to effectively participate in work and other aspects of life

- Teach students the critical skills of collaboration and cooperation through modeling and experience

This chapter covers these concepts and discusses the value, philosophy, and actions of restructuring at the secondary level.

Elementary schools have been engaged in restructuring efforts longer than secondary schools, although many restructuring efforts in the 1990s specifically targeted secondary schools (e.g., Sizer, 1992). Traditional secondary schools have been designed to prepare students for factory work through their organizational structures and expectations of students. The organizational structures of traditional schools generally result in students sitting in desks that have been placed in rows (Brentro, Brokenleg, & Van Bockern, 1990). Typically, the students sit for 40- to 60-minute periods for each subject. They are rarely given opportunities for honest collaboration (Kohn, 2004). After the period is over, the students move to another room with a different teacher, different subject matter, different students, and different expectations. This process continues throughout the day, often totaling six or seven periods. The teachers generally do not collaborate and, therefore, each class's material has no relationship to materials in other classes. The students are taught to memorize in a rote fashion, often stifling creative problem-solving abilities. The teaching in these schools is generally didactic and discourages discourse among students and between students and teachers.

TRADITIONAL SECONDARY SCHOOLS

The results of traditional secondary schools have caused educators, parents, and students to rethink and restructure their experiences while in school. The school dropout rate, although lower than the 50% rate of the 1950s, continues to be problematic; 5

out of every 100 students leave school without a high school diploma (National Center for Educational Statistics, 2003). For students with disabilities, the dropout rate is estimated at 28.9% (U.S. Department of Education, 2005). In addition, with the advent of state and federal mandates for schools to show progress in proficiency (e.g., the No Child Left Behind [NCLB] Act), as well as the implementation of high school exit exams (e.g., California High School Exit Examination [see http://www.cae.ca.gov/ta/tg/hs/overview.asp]), students with disabilities face an even greater risk of not earning a high school diploma than students without disabilities (U.S. Department of Education, 2005). In addition to failing these students, the traditional schooling system is not adequately preparing them for the world of work. For example, high school dropouts today have less than one chance in three to get a job, and if they do get a job, their earnings are equivalent to less than half as much as they would have earned in the 1970s (American Youth Policy Forum, 2000).

Many of the changes in secondary schools have come as a result of these undesirable student outcomes. In addition, for students with disabilities, the traditional secondary school is often inaccessible and inconsistent with their learning needs. The impersonalized high school that relies on lectures for delivering information and on factual multiple-choice exams is not an environment in which most students' learning is optimized, particularly students with disabilities (Falvey et al., 1997).

As secondary schools have restructured their learning environments to reflect more personalized settings that meet the needs of all students and the community, students with disabilities are included in more meaningful ways. The traditional secondary school is making way for schools that have created smaller student–teacher ratios so that secondary teachers can develop more personalized relationships with all of their students (Toch, 2003). Student–teacher ratios in secondary schools were often 180 students per teacher. In smaller learning communities, this ratio is often 30–60 students per teacher. In addition, teachers are working in more collaborative ways with one another and integrating the curriculum to a much greater extent than before (Villa, Thousand, & Nevin, 2004). The teaching process has become more active for the learners. Rather than teachers lecturing to students, students are more engaged in self-discovery and working in collaborative and cooperative teams. Students are expected to learn about information and how to obtain additional information rather than relying on memorization of isolated facts. Schools are holding students to high standards but recognizing that the means for obtaining these standards will vary as the students vary themselves. Students are demonstrating their accomplishments and knowledge in multiple ways, not through one standardized method of assessment and evaluation. The climate in these restructured schools is one of trust and open and honest communication among teachers, administrators, parents, students, and the community. Instead of placing all of the emphasis on punitive consequences for rule-violating behaviors, these schools have focused on rewarding student outcomes and behaviors in genuine and positive ways (Kohn, 2004).

INCLUSIVE SECONDARY SCHOOLS

As schools have restructured, an increasing number of them have developed and implemented inclusive educational service delivery models in which students with disabilities attend the same school and classes that they would attend if they did not have a

JOSÉ

José, who participates in the humanities class with all of his friends, uses a wheelchair and does not have a reliable means of communicating verbally or nonverbally. José uses his personality, his skills, and his support staff in order to be an active member in the cooperative group projects. With José's help, students in his cooperative group sometimes present materials by using his wheelchair tray to hold the materials. In addition, José, with the assistance of support staff, uses pictorial sequences to help him acquire knowledge and skills in the humanities class. These pictorial sequences are also available to those students who learn more readily with these materials than through written words. All of the students in José's class are learning some important lessons about valuing diversity, which will undoubtedly assist them in adolescence and adulthood. Similar experiences are occurring throughout the United States, Canada, and other countries as secondary schools welcome all students.

disability. Individualized supports that are needed are identified by students' family, friends, teachers, and administrators and are provided by the schools (Falvey, 2005).

Inclusive education for students with disabilities has gained in popularity for several reasons. First, research studies conducted during the 1990s have demonstrated that when students with disabilities were in inclusive classrooms, they fared better academically and socially, were more likely to form friendships with peers without disabilities, and were more likely to be successful in employment and continuing education (Anderson, Yilmaz, & Washburn-Moses, 2004; Bauer & Brown, 2001; Fisher & Frey, 2003; Kennedy & Fisher, 2001). The true story (sidebar) shows how research is translated into practice.

Second, the precedence established by both legislation and litigation is also a compelling argument in support of inclusive educational practices. In 1954, the U.S. Supreme Court, in a unanimous decision in *Brown v. Board of Education*, ruled that school segregation was immoral and that it would "retard" the educational and moral development of those being segregated. This important ruling is often cited in cases involving protecting the rights of students with disabilities. The Education for All Handicapped Children Act of 1975 (PL 94-142) was replaced by the Individuals with Disabilities Education Act (IDEA) of 1990 (PL 101-476), which was in turn, amended in 1997 (PL 105-17) and reauthorized in 2004 (PL 108-446). It states that all students with disabilities are guaranteed a "free appropriate public education, in the least restrictive environment" (LRE). LRE is defined as an environment in which

[To] the maximum extent appropriate, handicapped children, including those children in public and private institutions or other care facilities, are educated with children who are not handicapped, and special classes, separate schooling, or other removal of handicapped children from the regular educational environment occurs only when the nature or severity of the handicap is such that education in regular classes with the use of supplementary aids and services cannot be achieved satisfactorily. (PL 105-17, § 1412[5][b])

These acts establish the legal framework for the provision of inclusive education. In the early 1990s, two court cases were instrumental in increasing inclusive educational options for students with disabilities: *Sacramento City Unified School District v. Rachel H.* (1994) and *Oberti v. Board of Education* (1993). These cases are important in that the courts, citing the growing knowledge in the area of education of students with disabilities, ruled in favor of inclusive educational options for students with developmental disabilities. In addition, four major class action lawsuits throughout the U.S. have resulted in an increase in inclusive educational options for students with disabilities (*Chanda Smith v. Board of Education Los Angeles Unified School District; Corey H. v. Board of Education of the City of Chicago; Gaskin v. Commonwealth of Pennsylvania; P.J. v. State of Connecticut, Board of Education*).

Third, children and adolescents are more likely to form friendships with their peers if they are in close physical proximity and have frequent opportunity to be together (Falvey, 2005). When children with disabilities are sent outside of their neighborhood to go to schools in order to receive specialized services, they have more difficulty in forming friendships with their peers who live close to them (Falvey, 2005).

Fourth, schools are a microcosm of society and offer students opportunities to learn about how society is organized and what is and is not tolerated. When segregation is permitted through segregated classes and schools for students with disabilities, students without disabilities may believe that excluding people with disabilities is acceptable because the adults in charge of the school are doing it. This can have a very powerful and lasting effect on students without disabilities, making it difficult and uncomfortable to relate to people with disabilities.

A growing number of secondary schools are moving toward inclusive educational practices. The impetus for restructuring often begins with the concerns shared by students, staff, and parents regarding a high dropout rate, low test scores, and low college graduation rates.

Secondary restructuring efforts are often closely linked with the Coalition of Essential Schools movement (Sizer, 1992). The Coalition of Essential Schools is devoted to the principle that all students can learn and that the educational community must develop personalized and meaningful learning experiences so that all students can succeed. The Coalition is committed to placing students at the center of the learning activities so that they are the workers and the teacher is the facilitator. In addition, rather than believing in teaching students to memorize a large number of unrelated facts, the Coalition is committed to the idea that students need to learn more about how they learn and how to conduct research to gain information. Authentic teaching and assessment are also critical elements for the Coalition. Table 6.1 contains a list of the 10 common principles for the Coalition of Essential Schools.

Table 6.1. The 10 common principles of the Coalition of Essential Schools

1. Teach students to learn how to use their minds well: "Encourage habits of the mind."

2. Focus on the mastery of essential skills: "Less is more."

3. Set high goals and standards for every student: "Equity and excellence for all."

4. Reduce teacher–student ratio, and increase student and parent contact: "Personalize the teaching and learning process."

5. Provoke students to want to learn how to learn: "Student as worker, teacher as coach."

6. Provide opportunity for students to demonstrate knowledge and skills: "Authentic assessment and graduation by exhibition."

7. Stress the values of trust, respect, fairness, and tolerance for diversity: "Unanimous expectation."

8. Share a commitment to the entire school, and expect multiple obligations: "Be a generalist."

9. Provide time for collaboration and collective planning: "Value and respect the hard work of teaching."

10. Model democratic and equitable practices.

From Sizer, T.R. (1992). *Horace's school: Redesigning the American high school* (p. 30). Boston: Houghton Mifflin; reprinted by permission.

DEVELOPING A COMMUNITY OF LEARNERS

Establishing and developing a true community of learners is an essential characteristic of an inclusive school. Positive attitudes and reciprocal relationships among students with and without disabilities can be seen in schools where students are positively engaged in learning and relating to one another. Positive interactions can be fostered by ability-awareness in-service programs for students, peer tutoring arrangements, circles of friends, mapping activities, and other specific arrangements designed to facilitate the development of a community and to foster friendships (Falvey, 2005). Inclusive secondary schools reflect a general tone of acceptance of diversity, belonging, and membership within classrooms and throughout the campus. Students no longer observe special education teachers making unnatural arrangements for students to gain access to core curricula or elective classes. All students' names appear on roll sheets, and students with disabilities are in attendance in classrooms from the first day. Pull-out programs or inconsistent attendance of students with disabilities interfere with building relationships and students' understanding what is expected of them.

As secondary schools change from isolated and segregated models to inclusive and collaborative models, the need for building a sense of community is essential. Bauer and Brown (2001) posed questions built from the work of Sergiovani (1994) to guide school teams in their restructuring efforts. The questions relate to

1. How can our school develop a sense of belonging and collaboration?

2. How can our school truly develop a sense of professional community?

3. How can our school develop a means to address parents/families to become a key component in the new developing community?

4. How can positive relationships between teachers, coaches, staff, and students be developed and enriched as the norm of our community?

5. How can teaching environments be more family friendly and trusting?

6. How can schools develop a true sense of kinship, neighborliness, and friendship in the school and community?

7. What are the shared duties, responsibilities, and roles of all stakeholders as our new community evolves?

Many secondary schools offer the opportunity for students to enroll in a school service program that allows them to earn credit. Some schools allow service learning to be done on the school campus where students provide support to those who need assistance in order to participate fully in academic or elective classes. Many students within classes also informally extend support to students with needs. It is not unusual in these schools to observe peers who are supporting students with motor challenges while going from one class to the next class. Students also provide support for peers with disabilities while "hanging out" together in the cafeteria during lunchtime. In one school, a student was observed providing support to help the peer with disabilities by placing a hand on his shoulder as reassurance and a reminder to remain calm during their humanities class, and this relationship grew outside of school. In order to facilitate and create an open learning environment, special education support teachers in collaboration with general education teachers need to develop student profiles that delineate the specific learning needs of each student. Sample student profiles are provided in Figures 6.1 and 6.2. The purpose of such information is that staff are aware of students who have unique learning or behavioral needs who will be fully participating members of their classes.

UNIVERSAL ACCESS TO LEARNING: NEW SOLUTIONS AND STRATEGIES

When designing and delivering effective educational interventions for a group of diverse secondary students, including those with disabilities, school personnel must adopt Universal Design principles (Nolet & McLaughlin, 2005). These principles are designed to eliminate the need for accommodations and modifications whenever possible. All learners in the class are provided with the supports needed that are built into the lesson and instruction rather than an "add-on" to the lesson, which is often the case with adaptations and modifications. When using a universal design framework, teachers must consider the essential effects of their instructional decisions on the learners in the class. The implementation of Universal Design principles does not lower standards for any student, but rather provides access to all students. For example, stairs and ramps get a person to the same place, but the ramps can be used by all students, even though some students do not necessarily need a ramp. Another example would be to provide all students with graphic organizers of the content from the biology chapter they have been assigned to read. These graphic organizers can be used by all students to remember the essential content of the chapter as well as how the information relates to each other. A third example would be to provide students with multiple means to communicate what they have learned. Some students might take a traditional multiple choice test to demonstrate their knowledge base, whereas other students might create a PowerPoint presentation of the material they have learned using the computer, and a third student might represent the information through drawing or illustrations.

Providing universal access is not enough for some students, although it is a great beginning. There has been a tendency in the past to segregate students with disabilities if they were not on grade level as measured by traditional assessment tools (e.g., standardized tests), or even with Universal Design principles in place. Individualized additional supports might be necessary for some students. For example, a student who is a braille reader would need access to the materials in braille in order to meaningfully participate in their learning outcomes. Educators should always begin by making the least intrusive instructional modifications possible for students. For example, a freshman student who reads on the first-grade level is enrolled in an English class and assigned to read *Romeo and Juliet*. This student could listen to the book on tape, view the video of the movie, and learn the basic concepts of vocabulary rather than look at books targeted at a first-grade level.

Several elements are important when planning for students' access to the curriculum, including acquiring academic curriculum skills, developing functional or life skills, developing social and friendships skills, and building on students' developmental skills. Acquiring academic curriculum skills refers to providing students with disabilities access to the same curriculum as students without disabilities. Acquiring these skills helps students with disabilities learn what their typically developing peers are learning while having opportunities to become a member of the class and school communities.

Student Profile

Student Name __Sue Lee_____ Age _15_ Grade _10_____

RSP__ LH _X_ SH___   Support Teacher __Jeff Duncan_____   Extension _1248_

Parent/Guardian__ Bernadette (Mom), Fred (Dad)___ Telephone __555-555-5555__

Class Schedule: Per.1 _____MASS_____ Rm. 214_____

                     Per.2 _____MASS_____ Rm. 214_____

                     Per.3 _____Humanities_____ Rm. 218_____

                     Per.4 _____Humanities_____ Rm. 218_____

                     Per.5 _____PE_____ Gym_____

                     Per.6 _____Keyboarding_____ Tech Lab_____

Grade Equivalent Academic Scores: Math   _4___

                                         Reading   _6___

                                         Written Lang.   _6___

General knowledge, Area of strength/interest __Sue has excellent verbal_____
communication. Her written skills are slow, but she is very neat and accurate._____

Areas needing support __Sue needs to remain focused. She has to be able to follow__
directions that are provided verbally, written, and sometimes in picture format. Sue__
needs support regarding the academic content and her reading skills at times may__
require peer support or books on tape._____

Individualized Educational Objectives __Sue has IEP objectives in the area of math,__
reading, and written expression, and she has an ITP. Her career objectives are to be able__
to work with children._____

Successful Learning Strategies and Modifications/Adaptations Needed _Sue will need_
to utilize with support her Minder Reminder (calendar). A calculator has proven to__
be helpful over the years. She may require additional time as well as reduced quan-__
tity. Sue desires a diploma, therefore, the course content must be verified for each__
of her classes_____

Grading Accommodations _Accuracy is important and the amount of work may be__
reduced. Letter grades are desired; please consult with case worker to identify__
supporter and/or classes that may need to be pass/fail._____

Important Family/Health Information __Parents are separated. Sue has an older_____
brother who also receives special education support services._____

                                              Date: _10/05_____

Figure 6.1.   Student profile/teacher communication form. (From HORACE'S SCHOOL by Theodore R. Sizer. Copyright © 1992 by Theodore R. Sizer. Reprinted by permission of Houghton Mifflin Company. All rights reserved.)

Student Information Sheet

Student's name David Sebastian   **Age** 17

Notes _____

_____

_____

_____

_____

Staff	**Room**
1. Coppes	SC 123
2. Hubbard	A 206
3. Eshilian	Study Skills
4. Bove	L 123
5. Lablin	Vocational Skills
6. Miller	Study Skills

Disability Down syndrome, communication support

Lives with His mother and father. David also has two siblings who live on their own.

Postive Student Profile	**IEP Objectives**
Friendly	Self-regulate for behaviors
Stays with a task	Type or say messages
Good sense of humor	Cope with change
Very motivated	Have more eye contact with
Very artistic	students and adults
	Develop functional math skills
	Initiate conversation
	Develop vocational awareness
	Increase class participation
	Attend and participate in self-
	advocacy support group
	Use public transportation

Management Needs	**Medical Needs**
Needs support to maintain attention	Has had 1–2 seizures per year
Needs support to maintain behaviors in class	(Knows when they are coming)
It is sometimes necessary to help David when he leaves class to go to the Study Skills room or the Guidance Office so that he doesn't interrupt others.	

Grading Accommodations David may need more time, large print, and support from other students for note-taking and support from staff and students in reaching IEP goals.

Other Comments When David disrupts class, he should immediately be helped to the Study Skills room.

Service Coordinator Eileen Mikel   **Extension** 1222

Parent or Guardian Adelaide and Mike   **Phone** 555-555-5555

Figure 6.2.   Student profile/teacher communication form.

Students with disabilities need to develop the academic skills that students without disabilities learn and sometimes need to acquire functional or life skills. Functional and life skills involve those skills that are necessary to participate in life and daily routines (e.g., making purchases at the snack bar, changing after PE, asking for assistance as needed). There are numerous opportunities for students to learn and practice functional life skills within high school without denying them access to the core curriculum. Several examples are listed next.

- Making change when working at the student store
- Making change when selling pizza for the booster club
- Making purchases at lunch
- Utilizing vending machines on campus
- Collecting attendance sheets from classes
- Assisting the teacher with classroom preparation
- Providing assistance in the school office, (e.g. answering the telephone, running copies, delivering messages, summoning other students)

Students with disabilities must have the opportunity to develop and build their social and friendship skills because sometimes they have difficulty forming relationships. These skills are best taught in the context where social and friendships skill opportunities occur (i.e., in settings where numerous socially and communicatively competent peers are present and interactions are occurring).

Finally, considering student's developmental levels helps determine where to begin teaching students in terms of cognitive complexity of the skills as well as how to teach the students academic, functional, life, and social and friendship skills. Building on students' developmental skills allows teachers and parents to emphasize students' strength and skills; however, students' developmental skill levels should never be used to hold students back. For example, when Max, a tenth-grade student with learning disabilities, had not yet memorized his multiplication tables, the special education teacher wanted him to attend a special education math class so that he could continue to learn his multiplication tables. Instead, Max insisted that he remain in the general education algebra class, and his parents insisted that supports be provided for him to learn in his classroom with his peers. The tenth-grade math standards were utilized to assist Max at his present developmental level. Max had a great teacher who brought in real pizza and artificial materials to help him understand algebra in a meaningful manner. This was an excellent teaching tool because pizza was a very highly preferred food for Max and most of his classmates. Max's mother also used incentives to teach him multiplication tables, but he was unable to retain the multiplication facts for more than 3 days at a time.

Max, who is an adult now, uses a calculator to compute multiplication problems. If Max's parents had agreed with the special education teacher to put him in the special education class for remedial math, he would not only be behind in learning his math facts but also would not have received the instruction in algebra that he needed. He would have gotten farther behind and it would have been more difficult being included in general education math classes during his junior and senior years.

EFFECTIVE INSTRUCTION

Active learning strategies increase and improve students' engagement in learning, encourage greater student contributions, and enable students to use higher-order thinking skills and to choose a variety of ways to demonstrate their knowledge and skills. The use of these strategies also encourages more teacher collaboration and team teaching, as professionals share units and develop lessons under these models.

In addition to implementing cooperative groups, teachers have adopted a new view on intelligence, which has helped them to personalize instruction and assessment. In 1983, Howard Gardner challenged the traditional view of intelligence with his pivotal book *Frames of Mind*. According to this book and the subsequent work of others (e.g., Armstrong, 2000, 2003), standardized methods of measuring students' abilities identify only a limited portion of students' talents, focusing primarily on linguistic and logical/mathematical areas of intelligence and ignoring musical, bodily/kinesthetic, visual/spatial, interpersonal, intrapersonal, and naturalistic intelligence. By recognizing students' strengths and intelligences, teachers and staff can more easily create a personalized instructional plan that capitalizes on those strengths to facilitate learning and simultaneously offer instructional opportunities to each student in his or her area(s) of intelligence where the student is not currently strong.

As teachers become more comfortable with using a variety of active learning strategies, they also become more comfortable with multilevel instruction, which is teaching students who are working on different levels. The concept is based on the premise that students do not learn in the same way, at the same time, using the same materials (Falvey, 2005). Once teachers accept this concept, strategies for responding to the students' multiple skill levels can be brainstormed and implemented.

Organizing Heterogeneous Groups

The traditional method of organizing students in secondary programs, often referred to as *tracking*, must be intentionally decreased and eliminated in order for a secondary school to embrace inclusive education. Tracking has been used to create homogeneous groups of students in which students are grouped together in classes according to their perceived ability to achieve. Secondary schools must work to decrease tracking by eliminating what was previously called the *basic track*, the track identified for the students who were the least successful. All students, including those with disabilities, should be able to enroll, participate, and learn in college preparatory courses and career preparation courses throughout their 4 years of high school. The purpose of this is to encourage students to focus on higher academic goals, to help students prepare for postsecondary educational and work opportunities, and to offer all students a solid and comprehensive curriculum consistent with IDEA requirements.

In order to support students with disabilities effectively, faculty must develop a menu of options that can be used for students who need additional support. The support may be necessary for a student with language challenges, a student who is at risk, a student who requires disciplinary action, a student who qualifies for services detailed in Title 1 of the ADA (see the appendix of Chapter 10), as well as a student identified with a disability. A menu of various options for support is listed next.

Total Staff Support   Support staff can either be special education teachers, teacher's assistants, or related services staff people (e.g., speech-language therapists, occupational therapists, physical therapists). They need to remain in close proximity to students and bring materials and supplies to them. Support staff members should also assume responsibility for developing or acquiring support strategies and materials that will increase student success. Students receiving this option of support are receiving full-time, one-to-one support throughout their day.

Daily In-Class Staff Support   Support staff assist many students by moving around the room and providing supports as needed. Staff provide role models for co-operation, collaboration, acceptance, and respect. Staff also assume responsibility for developing or acquiring support strategies and materials that will increase students' success. Staff may supervise or teach small groups in the class as needed.

Part-Time Daily Support   Support staff provide support to students at a predeter-mined time or on a rotating basis. Staff should maintain awareness of the curriculum and assignments in order to encourage students' productivity, successful completion of assignments, and tutorial or organizational support. Support staff may also bring sup-plemental materials for classroom use and suggest cooperative learning group combi-nations among students who may work well together in other classes.

Stop-In Support One to Three Times Per Week   Support staff observe students to determine any possible need for increased support. They assist the general education teachers in setting up peer support for recording assignments or notes. They maintain open communication and accessibility to the classroom teachers and to the students.

Team Teaching   Support staff assume half of the responsibility for teaching the curriculum, as prearranged by both the general education and support staff members. Both staff members assume responsibility for the development of a multilevel curricu-lum, appropriate teaching strategies, grading, the learning environment, and student arrangements that allow for a high level of success for all students.

Classroom Companion (Peer Support)   Students who take the student service class for credit or who agree to assist classmates in academic or elective classes may help them in getting to and from class, carrying or remembering materials, taking notes, completing assignments, facilitating communication, and having role models for social or friendship interactions. These students may also participate in development of support strategies.

Consultation   Support staff meet regularly with general education teachers in order to keep track of students' progress, to assess need for supplemental materials, to solve problems, and to maintain positive and open communication.

Paraprofessionals

The special education support staff includes not only teachers but also paraprofession-als. Paraprofessionals are an integral part of the successful restructuring efforts, and they should be supervised and supported by the special and general education teachers. The duties of paraprofessionals are

- Facilitate the academic, behavioral, and social growth of the students
- Support the classroom teacher
- Monitor and assist students during whole-group and independent learning activities
- Be familiar with and teach to students' individualized education program (IEP) and transition IEP goals
- Become familiar with and be able to facilitate the students' use of augmentative and alternative communication (AAC) devices and adaptive equipment
- Provide personal hygiene assistance when needed
- Keep data and anecdotal information on each student's progress
- Implement curricular adaptations
- Implement behavior plans
- Implement specific teaching strategies
- Facilitate opportunities for friendships
- Model respectful interactions with all students
- Back away whenever possible

Once students with disabilities are enrolled in general core curriculum classes, the support is located within general education classes. The additional supports benefit not only those students identified as needing specialized services but also other students who do not qualify for specialized services and who, nevertheless, experience their own unique challenges in learning. On the basis of students' individual learning needs, the faculty team need to determine the amount and type of consultation and in-class support provided to classroom teachers.

Block Scheduling

Scheduling classes in such a way to facilitate deeper learning is essential in restructured secondary schools. Instead of teachers teaching five periods of 55 minutes each day, teachers might be assigned to blocked periods once a day or several times a week. By scheduling teaching of integrated subject matter in blocks, the student–teacher ratio can be reduced from approximately 180 students per teacher to 90 or fewer students per teacher. Block scheduling can dramatically increase the opportunity for more personalized student-teacher time, and the curriculum becomes more integrated across subjects (Thousand, Rosenberg, Bishop, & Villa, 1997).

In blocked schedules, teachers need to adapt their teaching styles and strategies to accommodate the increased time block (e.g., 2 hours). Teachers can arrange a variety of activities throughout the block—cooperative groups to individual practice, group instruction, and group projects. Research has demonstrated that cooperative groups promote high academic achievement, improve self-esteem, promote active learning and social skills development, and influence peer acceptance and friendships (e.g.,

Johnson & Johnson, 1989, 2000, 2003). Although the benefits of cooperative group learning have received substantial documentation in the literature, much of the emphasis and use has been with elementary-age students. Clearly, the benefits for older students are no less than for younger students, particularly because cooperative learning experiences are designed to teach students the skills to collaborate with others and reach common goals, skills identified by employers as critical for success in the interdependent employment fields of the 21st century (U.S. Department of Labor, 1993).

AUTHENTIC ASSESSMENT

A critical issue related to the inclusion of students with diverse learning needs and ability levels is assessment and grading. Just as traditional didactic teaching strategies fail to meet the needs of many learners, so do traditional assessment materials. The point of assessment is not to teach students how to take a test for the purposes of passing but rather to determine students' growth in knowledge, understanding, and application of knowledge, which are identified as educational goals. Examples of authentic and performance-based assessment are

- Portfolio evaluations
- IEP evaluations
- Real-world problem solving
- Real-world money management
- Family feedback
- Performances
- Productions
- Musical scores
- Artistic presentations
- Work samples

Figure 6.3 reflects one method of assessing students' progress and communicating among teachers if additional support is necessary. Communication among the staff, students, and families is essential.

When students receive supports and/or modifications, educators often struggle with ways to grade students' performance in a fair way. The grading difficulty that educators encounter is not specific to students with disabilities. Inherent problems exist in the traditional grading process instituted in the majority of schools, especially secondary schools. Grades often are interpreted by parents, students, teachers, administrators, and eventually colleges, universities, and employers as objective information about students' actual performance, even though the presumed objectivity of grades is extremely questionable for several reasons (Marzano, 2000). First, there is no one agreed-upon specific criterion that is used across teachers and grade levels or within or across schools and school districts. Second, some teachers consider each student's personal progress when assigning grades, whereas others only consider each student's performance at the time the grade is assigned. Third, the majority of grading involves the assignment of a single grade, even though it is impossible to use a single grade to

Student Class Update

Student _Sue Lee_   **Date** _11/05_

Teacher   **Extension**

Work Habits in the Classroom	Yes	Sometimes	No
Is motivated to work		X	
Follows directions easily, self-initiates assignments		X	
Does homework, completes work independently		X	
Brings materials to class	X		
Is usually on time	X		
Is organized, remembers assignments	X		
Is able to do independent written work			X
Works best within a structured routine	X		
Type of Assistance Needed			
Prompt to get started		X	
Materials read out loud or book on tape	X		
Ability to give information verbally		X	
Support with organizing notebooks, materials, and assignments		X	
Extra time to finish work	X		
Length of assignments reduced	X		
Alternative assessment	X		
Ability to move around occasionally	X		
Daily/weekly work contract			X
Attendance contract		X	
Other:			

Notes

Figure 6.3. Class update sheet.

evaluate all aspects of a student's performance or ability for an entire subject area. These reasons, along with the challenges of grading a student who receives supports or modifications, make grading a huge challenge for educators.

Few would disagree that the entire grading structure and the over-reliance on a gross letter-grade system needs to be examined and modified; however, until such examinations and modifications occur to the existing grading structure, consider the following grading options. If a student receives accommodation, then no notation or modification should be made to his or her grades. If a student receives multilevel instructional modifications, then his or her grades can be modified with a notation indicating that the grades reflect a modified performance standard. When modifying the grading performance standard, rather than relying on a single grade, consider using

- The student's IEP objectives to measure performance rather than grade-level standards

- A pass–fail system

- A student–teacher generated contract and evaluation procedure

- A narrative descriptive of the student that does not rely on a single grade

Each student's IEP team should discuss the issue of grading and making decisions for grading that make sense for the student and those who will be reviewing the grades in the future.

TRANSITION SERVICES AND PROGRAMS

Transition IEPs must be developed and presented during the IEP meeting as a component of the IEP for each student. IDEA 1997 required transition IEPs for students 14 years and older, and IDEA 2004 increases the age requirements to 16 years and older. This does not, however, restrict school and vocational personnel from continuing to work on transition planning at younger ages. School personnel (e.g., special education teachers, counselors, career and transition specialists) must implement and monitor both short-term (e.g., completing driver's training or community transportation training) and long-term transition goals (e.g., enrollment in college or adult services). Acquiring the skills of effective self-advocacy are essential for all students, particularly those with disabilities, in order to successfully transition into the adult world of work and postsecondary education (Test, Fowler, & Wood, 2005).

Students' transition services while enrolled in high schools should complement participation with core academic curriculum. To that end, some schools have developed specific work training opportunities for students with disabilities that do not interfere with their participation in their core academic classes. In addition to their core academic classes, students in their freshman and sophomore years might participate in career awareness activities such as interviewing family members about their jobs, searching the Internet for job possibilities and college options, defining personal interest and goals, and volunteering in various settings within the school and/or the community. In addition to their core academic classes, students in their junior and senior years might participate in a career seminar or elective course designed to create résumés, prepare for job applications and interviews, volunteer or perform paid work in school and/or in the community, gain awareness of adult support services (e.g., adult school, trade technological schools, community colleges, universities), and become knowledgeable about resources and services from adult service agencies (e.g., State Department of Vocational Rehabilitation, Social Security Administration, and Departments of Mental Health and Developmental Services).

Merging the IEP and transition IEP processes and engaging students and their parents (as well as general education counselors, administrators, teachers, special education teachers, vocational coordinators, and appropriate community agency representatives) as active participants in planning is not only good for a student's school life but also for life beyond school. There are several options available for students who do not graduate at the end of their senior year (i.e., that is after 4 years in high school). First, a student who is close to meeting graduation requirements might take additional time to complete the graduation requirements. This can be completed at the high school or a continuing education campus. Second, a student might enroll in a community-based transition program designed to prepare that student for participating in adult activities (e.g., work, recreation, living) within that community. Preparing students for postgraduation life must be a focus of every student's IEP/transition meeting.

CONCLUSION

Restructuring does not have a finishing point; it is an ongoing process to facilitate the best learning environment for all students. Restructuring at secondary schools is essential in order for all students to achieve at higher levels. These restructuring efforts must result in positive outcomes for all students, including those with disabilities.

STUDY QUESTIONS

1. Visit a high school where there are special education classrooms and interview one or more teachers asking them what would be the best way to improve service delivery as students with disabilities plan for adulthood. Consider all aspects of administrative issues that affect restructuring.

2. How have secondary schools changed for students with disabilities as a result of restructuring?

3. What are Universal Design principles and how do they affect students with disabilities?

4. Describe five options that school faculty members can use in order to support students who need additional support.

5. Describe the different types of authentic and performance-based assessment that can affect the way students are evaluated.

6. Describe in detail, using one or more case studies, active teaching strategies and transition services and programs that can affect employment and community integration outcomes for students with disabilities.

7

High-Stakes Accountability and Students with Disabilities

The Good, the Bad, and the Impossible

Margaret J. McLaughlin and Sandra Embler

AFTER COMPLETING THIS CHAPTER, THE READER WILL BE ABLE TO

○ Understand the history of current accountability reforms

○ Explain the rationale for including students with disabilities in state assessment and accountability systems

○ Describe the major provisions of the No Child Left Behind Act of 2001 and the Individuals with Disabilities Education Improvement Act of 2004, specifically those that relate to assessments and teacher quality

○ List the challenges in assessing students with disabilities and including them in high-stakes accountability

This work was produced under Cooperative Agreement #H324P000004 from the Office of Special Education Programs, U.S. Department of Education, and under Subcontract #31-1992-231 from the Institute of Education Sciences of the U.S. Department of Education through a grant to the Laboratory for Student Success (LSS) at Temple University. The opinions expressed do not necessarily reflect the position of the supporting agencies, and no official endorsement should be inferred.

Jack and Tamara are two experienced special education
teachers. They have taught
together at Woodmont High
School for the past 7 years, and
they think they are pretty good
at what they do. Together with
27 other special education
teachers, Jack and Tamara
share responsibility for educating about 250 students in
grades 9–12. Tamara alone
manages transition plans for
about 55 students in vocational
and career education. Some of
her students require extensive
support and spend half of their
school day at job sites in the
community and in school. Jack
teaches English, social studies,
math, and history to special education students. He also provides support to students with
individualized education programs (IEPs) who come to his
room to learn study skills, take
tests, and get help with class
assignments during one period
a day. These two teachers are
proud of the good relationships
they have with their students
and their families. They are also
proud of their students' accomplishments. For example, in past
years, Jack has been able to
help a number of his students
get enough credits to receive
their diploma, while Tamara has
seen students receive their diploma and become employed in
jobs in the community.

The world has changed for Jack and Tamara and their colleagues. In the past several years, they have learned that the
special education students they teach will no longer be able to
graduate unless they *successfully* pass general education
courses in English, algebra, and geometry as well as basic science. This means that they must pass a standardized end-of-
course examination. Jack has also learned that he is no longer
"qualified" to teach core subject matter courses to special education students and that "his" students must be taught by
teachers who are certified to teach English, math, and science. Jack and Tamara are confused, angry, and frustrated.
They don't see how the students they teach will ever be able
to pass the new high school examinations. What is more, they
don't believe that their students should be wasting their time
sitting in these classes when they could be getting job training or learning more fundamental skills. The students and
their families are also scared and confused. They expect that
Jack and Tamara will help them pass the courses or get their
diplomas. After all, aren't children entitled to special instruction and specialized supports to help them graduate and move
into jobs? Both the teachers and the families ask, "Why aren't
special education students exempt from the new requirements? Why do we even have these new requirements?
Won't teachers just teach to the test and instruction will become boring? Won't we lose all of the creative and supportive teachers?"

These are just a few of the questions that special education teachers across the U.S. are asking as the country moves
forward with major educational reforms that include more
challenging curricula, assessments, and increased accountability. Although all special education teachers are struggling
to understand the new requirements, in some ways, secondary level teachers face even more challenges as they attempt
to reconcile two core policy goals. The first goal is to ensure
that each individual student with a disability makes a successful transition to postsecondary employment, education, and
life, whereas the second demands that every student has the
same opportunity to learn challenging content.

In this chapter, we describe the characteristics of the reforms that are dominating today's schools. We also explain
the foundations of these reforms as well as the issues schools face in implementing
these policies with students with disabilities. Finally, we discuss considerations for
aligning accountability requirements with important transition goals.

WHAT ARE THE NEW REFORM POLICIES?

The education of students with disabilities in U.S. schools today is shaped by two very powerful laws: the Individuals with Disabilities Education Improvement Act (PL 108-446) of 2004 and the No Child Left Behind Act (NCLB; PL 107-110) of 2001. Although neither law is new, recent changes to both have created unique demands and expectations for schools. The basic provisions contained in the IDEA have been in federal law since 1975 and guarantee each eligible child with a disability a free and appropriate public education (FAPE) in the least restrictive environment (LRE). Some major changes were made to the IDEA in 1997 to begin to align this law with the larger standards-driven reforms underway in the U.S. The NCLB is the 2001 reauthorization of the Elementary and Secondary Education Act (ESEA) of 1965 (PL 89-10). This law has been a major presence in schools for more than 40 years, but as we discuss next, changes made in the 1994 ESEA reauthorization began to drastically reshape federal (and state) education policies including the IDEA. In the following sections, we provide an overview of the current legal requirements of NCLB as well as the most recent IDEA provisions that are aligning federal special education policy with NCLB.

The Rise of Accountability in U.S. Schools

As noted previously, current reform policies being enacted in U.S. schools had their origins in changes made to ESEA during the 1990s, which in turn evolved from individual states' education policies that began in the 1980s. In 1994, Congress reauthorized the ESEA and renamed it the Improving America's Schools Act (IASA; PL 103-382). The IASA required that in order for states to receive Title I funds, they were to develop challenging content and performance standards in reading and math and adopt yearly assessments to determine how well all children were meeting the states' performance standards. However, unlike previous mandates that allowed states to use a variety of assessments and required no real accountability for results, the IASA required states to develop and implement one statewide assessment and accountability system that covered all students and schools. The IASA stipulated that *all* students should participate in the state assessments and that the results for all students must be publicly reported. In defining *all*, the IASA specifically referred to students with disabilities as well as students with limited English proficiency (34 C.F.R. § 111[b][3][F]).

In order to align policies for students with disabilities with the IASA and the reforms that were occurring within general education, several new provisions were added to IDEA 1997. Language was incorporated that required students with disabilities to have access to the general education curriculum and participate in the state and local assessment systems with accommodations and/or alternate assessments if needed.

Although IDEA 1997 implied that students with disabilities should participate in accountability by requiring their participation in assessments and reporting of scores, the IDEA did not specifically mandate their inclusion in accountability systems (Thurlow, 2004). The IDEA referred to the IEP as the method of accountability and did not require that any agency or person be held accountable if a child does not achieve the goals and objectives listed on the IEP (34 C.F.R § 300.350[b]). The IDEA also did not require states to reward or sanction schools based on the outcomes for students with disabilities. This lack of accountability was cited as a significant problem by a National Academy of Sciences committee (McDonnell, McLaughlin, & Morison, 1997) that noted that the IEP was a form of "private" (p. 151) accountability and inconsistent with the move toward public reporting of student achievement and of holding schools or individual students accountable for that achievement.

In fact, as states implemented their assessment and accountability systems throughout the latter part of the 1990s, students with disabilities were erratically and inconsistently included. For example, in some states, the scores of students with disabilities who received an assessment accommodation were not reported at all or were not included in the accountability formula. Few states reported the assessment results of all of their students with disabilities, and even fewer states had implemented and reported student performance on alternate assessments. In 2001, the reauthorization of ESEA, now the NCLB, changed all of that.

No Child Left Behind Act

In 2001, Congress made sweeping changes to ESEA. Building on the 1994 requirements, Congress mandated new accountability requirements and renamed the law No Child Left Behind. The NCLB now mandates that states hold individual schools accountable for ensuring that all students reach proficiency on state standards in reading, math, and science by 2014. In order to do that, states must administer assessments annually in reading/language arts and math to students in grades 3–8, and at least once in grades 10–12. Beginning in 2005–2006, states must also assess students in science. States must establish three levels of performance—basic, proficient, and advanced—on their assessments. The primary purpose of these assessments is to determine the yearly progress of students and hold schools, districts, and states accountable for helping all students master the content standards (Hanushek & Raymond, 2002; Linn, 2001). Although NCLB requires states to use one other measure in addition to assessments (e.g., attendance, graduation rates), to measure a school's performance, accountability is based primarily on assessment results.

One of the key provisions in NCLB is that schools be accountable for the performance of all of their students, as well as for the performance of specific subgroups, such as students who receive special education services. NCLB parallels IDEA in specifying that students with disabilities receive assessment accommodations, and states must provide an alternate assessment for students who cannot participate in the state assessment. Alternate assessments are intended only for students with the most significant cognitive disabilities. Under NCLB, states and school districts can measure the achievement of these students against alternate achievement standards in reading, math, and science (34 C.F.R. § 200.1[d]) and can count not more than 1% of these students as proficient in the calculation of Adequate Yearly Progress (AYP; 34 C.F.R. § 200.13[c][1][i]). However, in May, 2005, the Department of Education issued a set of new guidelines that offered states additional alternatives and flexibility to implement NCLB. Under the new flexibility option, eligible states may implement short-term adjustments to their AYP decisions to incorporate the need for alternate assessments based on modified achievement standards for students with disabilities up to an additional 2%. This is a separate policy from the current regulation that allows up to 1% of all students being tested (those with the most significant cognitive disabilities) to take an alternate assessment.

Individual states are allowed to define alternate achievement standards as long as they are aligned with the state's academic content standards, promote access to the general curriculum, and reflect professional judgment of the highest achievement standards possible (34 C.F.R. § 200.1[d]).

Accountability Under the No Child Left Behind Act

AYP is the key accountability tool that is used in NCLB. For a school to make AYP, NCLB requires that student performance be calculated separately by grade and subgroups in mathematics, reading/language arts, and science. AYP combines the percent of students who score at "proficient" and "advanced" levels and requires that 95% of the students be assessed. High schools must also meet the state graduation standard. The goal of achieving AYP is to ensure that 100% of each subgroup of students reaches the state standard of proficiency by 2014. This requires that states set annual goals for the percent of students in each subgroup that must reach "proficient" or "advanced" levels. Obviously, the percentage increases each year and schools are required to meet each year's goals.

Schools that do not make AYP for any year or for any subgroup are subject to a mandatory sequence of increasingly serious consequences (see Table 7.1). Any school (specifically those receiving Title I funds) that does not meet AYP goals for 2 consecutive years must be identified for "school improvement." Schools under improvement must devise a school improvement plan that addresses strategies to improve performance and incorporates a mentoring and professional development program. These schools must provide parents with written notice regarding the schools' identification and must offer students the option to transfer to another school. Choice schools for students with disabilities do not have to be the same as choice schools for students without disabilities, but they must be able to offer the special education and related services that the student requires.

If a school fails to meet AYP goals for 3 years, then the school must continue offering parents a choice to transfer their child, as well as supplemental services, which can be tutoring or other services offered in addition to instruction provided during school hours. After 4 consecutive years of failing to make AYP for any one subgroup,

Table 7.1. What happens to schools that do not make adequate yearly progress (AYP)?

Year 1: School choice; 2-year improvement plan; professional development

Year 2: Supplemental educational services to students from low-income families

Year 3: + Local education agency (LEA) intervention

Year 4: + Restructure plan

Year 5: Implement restructure plan

State determines whether consequences apply to all schools or Title 1 schools.

Note: + indicates actions in addition to previous criteria.

districts and states can take "corrective action" with a school and can institute a "restructuring plan" that may include replacing staff, implementing a new curriculum, or changing the internal organization of the school. After 5 consecutive years of failing to make AYP, the local education agency (LEA) must prepare a plan to reopen the school as a charter school, replace all or most of the school staff, or turn the operation of the school over to the state educational agency (SEA). In his "State of the Union Address" to the 109th Congress, President Bush indicated his intention to propose extending the accountability of NCLB into high schools.

Other No Child Left Behind Requirements   Although the new accountability requirements are receiving the most visibility in schools, there are at least two other provisions in NCLB that are noteworthy. Title II of NCLB requires that states assure that their teachers are "highly qualified" by 2005–2006 (34 C.F.R § 200.55[a]). To be considered highly qualified under NCLB, teachers must have a bachelor's degree, full state certification or licensure, and be able to demonstrate that they are knowledgeable about each subject they teach. Teachers in middle and high school must prove that they know the subject they teach by having either a graduate degree or major in the subject they teach, credits equivalent to a major, pass a state-developed test, or possess advanced certification from the state. Some of these requirements have been eased for teachers in rural areas as well as teachers who teach more than one subject.

The Individuals with Disabilities Education Improvement Act of 2004

In December 2004, Congress again reauthorized the IDEA and clearly aligned the educational provisions of this special education law with the requirements of NCLB. The IDEA made changes to the IEP provisions and added new requirements pertaining to special education teachers. Following are the requirements for an IEP that address access to standards and assessments.

- A statement of the child's present levels of academic achievement and functional performance, *including how the disability affects the child's involvement and progress in the general education curriculum*

- Measurable annual goals, including academic and functional goals, designed to enable the child to be involved and progress in the general education curriculum as well as meet each of the child's other unique educational needs

- Short-term objectives or benchmarks for children who will take an alternate assessment aligned to alternate achievement standards

- A description of how a child's progress toward meeting the IEP goals will be measured and reported both annually as well as during specific periods within the year

- A statement of the special education and related services and supplementary aids and services, based on peer-reviewed research to the extent practical, or program modifications that are to be provided that will allow the child to meet IEP goals and make progress in the general education curriculum and participate in extracurricular and other nonacademic activities. Also, there must be an explanation of the extent to which a child will not participate in the regular class or other nonacademic activities.

- A statement of any individual accommodations that will be necessary to measure the academic achievement and functional performance of the child on state- and districtwide assessments. If the IEP team determines that the child will take an alternate assessment on a specific state or district assessment, then the IEP must include a statement that explains why the child cannot participate in the regular assessment and indicate why the particular alternate assessment selected is appropriate for the child

In addition, IDEA 2004 continues to require that at least one general education teacher participate on the IEP team if the child is or may be participating in the general education curriculum. Other provisions require that states report the assessment results of students with disabilities in the manner required by NCLB. States must also establish performance goals that will be publicly reported and which must include assessment results and dropout and graduation rates.

Highly Qualified Special Educators IDEA 2004 also specifically defined, for the first time, the qualifications of special education teachers. Specifically, any public elementary or secondary school special education teacher must have obtained full state certification as a special educator or passed a state's licensure examination allowing them to teach and must hold at least a bachelor's degree. Then, special education teachers must meet the same requirements as all other public school teachers, such as demonstrate that they are knowledgeable about each subject they teach. Special education middle and high school teachers must prove that they know the subject they teach in the same manner described previously under the NCLB.

Special education teachers who are teaching core academic subjects to students who are held to alternate achievement standards as defined under the NCLB must meet the basic certification requirement specified previously and also have knowledge of the subject matter appropriate to the student's level of instruction. The IDEA 2004 and NCLB require that each state determine the level of competency and how that will be demonstrated.

Evolution of Current Accountability Policies

As discussed previously, today's assessment and accountability requirements have evolved over time and resulted from both long-standing frustrations with the lack of success in reducing racial and economic educational inequities and the "educational call-to-arms" that occurred during the 1980s with the publication of *A Nation at Risk* (National Commission on Excellence in Education, 1983). At that time, policy makers at the highest levels began to define a vision for American education that was grounded in the belief that schools must raise educational expectations and performance for all students (McLaughlin & Shepard, 1995). The new vision for education that emerged was referred to as "standards-driven reform" and is based on three elements. The central and most important element is a set of challenging content and achievement standards that establish high expectations for student performance. The *content* standards define the important knowledge and skills that *all students* are expected to learn, and the *achievement* standards define the levels at which students must demonstrate the knowledge and skills. The standards are to be challenging and demand that students learn how to reason with and use the specific knowledge and skills that they learned (McLaughlin & Shepard, 1995). The standards must also apply to all students and be directly linked to curriculum and define what teachers teach and how they teach it (McDonnell et al., 1997; McLaughlin & Thurlow, 2003).

The second and third elements of standards-driven reform are assessments and accountability. In order to ensure that every student meets the challenging standards, individual states and the federal government need to assess student achievement and be held accountable for student performance. Being accountable means that schools, districts, students, and in some instances teachers must face consequences (i.e., rewards and/or sanctions) if they do not meet the standards.

This model of standards-driven reform began to be adopted at the state level beginning in the 1980s. However, it was not until the passage of the Goals 2000: Educate America Act of 1994 (PL 103-227) and the 1994 IASA that the federal government endorsed standards-driven reform and accountability for producing higher levels of student achievement as a driving force in American education.

Accountability Under Standards-Driven Reform

Educational accountability as it has emerged is characterized by one or more of the following factors: 1) district/school approval is linked to student performance rather than compliance with regulations or procedures; 2) the school is the unit for improvement, and improvement is focused on the specific assessments; 3) new school-level assessment data is used to evaluate classroom practices and improve instruction; 4) school-level assessment results are publicly reported; and 5) there are consequences for not achieving certain levels of student performance (Fuhrman, 1999).

Focus on Student Academic Performance   The dominant feature of today's educational accountability is the emphasis on student performance. Accountability rests heavily on assessments and the logic that unless we test students' knowledge, we will not know whether they have met the content standards and if schools are doing their job. In reality, schools and districts also are judged against a number of other factors, such as dropout rates, student attendance, expenditures and use of resources, graduation rates, expulsion and/or suspension, and transition to postsecondary education or employment after high school (Education Commission of the States, 2002).

Special education accountability has traditionally focused on compliance with procedures. But now, states and districts are also being held accountable for student outcomes, such as test performance, graduation rates, and dropout rates. States and districts can also be held accountable for the percent of students with disabilities being educated in general education classrooms and the proportion of minority students being identified as eligible for special education.

School versus District Accountability   Historically, educational policy making has rested with individual states that, to a greater or lesser extent, gave individual school districts in most states great control over their curriculum standards. Moreover, states gave districts great latitude in how to measure the performance of their individual students and schools. This situation began to change beginning during the 1980s, culminating in NCLB, which now requires that states establish one set of standards and assessments for all schools. Now, school-level student achievement, attendance, and graduation data are reported publicly on school report cards. These data are used to sanction or reward individual schools as well as to guide individualized school improvement efforts (Fuhrman, 1999; Linn, 2000; Olson, Jones, & Bond, 2001).

Consequences Attaching consequences to the failure to meet or sustain specific levels of student performance is a critical feature of new accountability systems. In the past, states and districts varied in the use of rewards and sanctions. During the 1990s, public reporting of assessment results was an almost universal feature of individual state accountability, but not all states reported the scores for all students (such as students with disabilities) to all audiences (such as parents; Olson et al., 2001). States also differed in what they required of low-performing schools and districts (e.g., corrective action plans), as well as in the types of sanctions they might use (e.g., reassignment or dismissal of staff, takeover by the SEA, loss of state accreditation, closure or merger of schools or districts; Thurlow, Nelson, Teelucksingh, & Ysseldyke, 2000).

Some states also provided monetary rewards or other tangible recognition to schools that met or exceeded performance targets (Fuhrman, 1999). A few states have created financial awards or college scholarships to high-performing students, and five states provided regulatory waivers to schools or districts that showed positive performance (Olson et al., 2001). Although many of these consequences continue within some states, one of the most dramatic changes to federal law has been the mandatory consequences for low-performing schools.

Student Accountability So far we have been focused mostly on NCLB and school-level accountability. However, when students are held directly accountable for their performance, it has typically been at the high school level and based on coursework completion rather than on direct measures of academic performance (Heubert & Hauser, 1999). But that is changing. In 2004, 20 states required students to pass an examination to earn a standard diploma, and more states are expected to implement high school exit examinations in the coming years. An additional five states have exit examinations but provide options for students who do not pass. Assessments in 10 of the 20 states are based on minimum level competencies. However, by 2008, only three of these states will continue with their minimum competency testing (Quality Counts, 2004).

At least 19 of the 25 states offer special waivers or exemptions, alternate assessments, or alternate graduation criteria for students with disabilities who fail an exit examination after multiple attempts. In addition, 16 states award special diplomas (e.g., IEP diplomas) or certificates of attendance to students with disabilities who cannot pass exit examinations or meet other criteria for a regular diploma (Gayler, Chudowsky, Hamilton, Kober, & Yeager, 2004). Although some states have established standards for their alternate documents, most are based simply on attendance or the judgment of the IEP team (Gagnon, McLaughlin, Rhim, & Davis, 2002). There is also little research on the effects of nonstandard diplomas on postsecondary outcomes (Johnson & Thurlow, 2003).

Tests are also increasingly being used as requirements for promotion from one grade to the next (Heubert & Hauser, 1999). Ten states and an unknown number of districts now require schools and districts to use state standards and assessments in determining whether students should be promoted into specific grades.

LEGAL ISSUES SURROUNDING
HIGH SCHOOL ASSESSMENT OF STUDENTS WITH DISABILITIES

Requiring that students pass an assessment in order to receive a high school diploma has implications for all students. However, exit examinations or assessments raise a number of policy and legal issues for students with disabilities, including the economic and educational consequences of credentials that students are awarded, the stigmatizing effect of the denial of a diploma, the need for adequate notification and appropriate instruction, and the provision of reasonable accommodations and alternate assessments (Karger & Pullin, 2002).

As states increasingly use exit examinations as prerequisites for granting a high school diploma, lawsuits are challenging both the process and the results for students with disabilities. Legal challenges have included constitutional claims brought under the due process and equal protection clauses of the Fourteenth Amendment of the U.S. Constitution and claims under disability statutes, including the mandate for a free appropriate public education; the requirement that a sole criterion not determine an appropriate educational program; the need to provide reasonable accommodations and/or alternate assessments; and the decision to provide alternate exit documents in place of a regular diploma.

Court Cases

Karger and Pullin (2002) cited the following three cases as the legal basis for high school assessments and students with disabilities.

Debra P. v. Turlington is the leading case concerning high school exit examinations. Although this case did not specifically address students with disabilities, it established a model for student challenges to exit examinations, including those made by students with disabilities. In this case, the U.S. Court of Appeals for the Fifth Circuit held that the state could not deprive students of a high school diploma based on an exit examination unless the state could prove that the students received adequate notice about the test, that the test was fundamentally fair, and that it covered material actually taught in the classroom.

The first court case pertaining to students with disabilities and exit examinations was *Board of Education v. Ambach* in New York state. In this case, the New York state trial court held that in general, the state had the power to adopt standards requiring the passing of an exit examination for receipt of a diploma and that the denial of diplomas to students with disabilities was not a violation per se of the Education for All Handicapped Children Act (EAHCA) of 1975 (PL 94-142; the forerunner of IDEA) or Section 504 of the Rehabilitation Act of 1973 (PL 93-112).

In *Brookhart v. Illinois State Board of Education*, the U.S. Court of Appeals for the Seventh Circuit also found that requiring students with disabilities to pass an examination as a prerequisite for receipt of a diploma was not a violation per se of the EAHCA or Section 504. However, the *Brookhart* court also found that the students' due process rights were violated because they received only a year and a half period of notice before the test requirement was imposed.

According to Karger and Pullin (2002), there are a number of issues pertaining to exit examinations and students with disabilities. For one, the denial of a diploma to students with disabilities has a negative effect on future educational and occupational attainment and can thwart the underlying goals of IDEA and the Americans with Disabilities Act (ADA) of 1990 (PL 101-336), which is to help students with disabilities lead active and productive adult lives in the community. Second, decisions about how an individual student with a disability participates in a state or local assessment program must be made by the student's IEP team. Third, students with disabilities and their families must receive adequate notification of the testing requirement and the date of the test to enable their IEPs to be adjusted and to ensure that they receive appropriate instruction in the material that will be tested. Procedural due process requires states to provide students with adequate notice of testing requirements that are prerequisites for receipt of a diploma. But, courts have not set specific time periods that constitute adequate notice, and the sufficiency of notice for a testing requirement will depend on the curriculum and instructional opportunities provided to prepare students for the test as well as whether there are opportunities for retesting and remediation.

In short, students with disabilities must be afforded the opportunity to learn the material covered on exit examinations. Furthermore, an important measure of the fairness of an exit examination is whether curriculum and instruction provided to a student are aligned with what the test measures. As challenges to exit examinations continue, states will have the burden of presenting substantial evidence that the students have actually had the opportunity to learn the material on which an examination is based.

Students with disabilities must also receive appropriate accommodations on exit examinations. IDEA and NCLB require the participation of students with disabilities in state- and districtwide assessments such as exit examinations, with *appropriate accommodations* where necessary. Similarly, Title II of the ADA and Section 504 require states and school districts to provide students with disabilities with reasonable accommodations on exit examinations. Increasingly, the use of accommodations on assessments is being decided in court. In *Chapman v. California Dept of Education*, the judge ruled that the California High School Exit Exam (CAHSEE) violated the rights of students with disabilities under federal law because students were not allowed to use calculators and other accommodations on the assessment. Similar legal challenges in Oregon (*ASK v. Oregon State Board of Education*, 2001) and Alaska (*Noon v. Alaska State Board of Education*, 2004) were settled out of court, with the states in both cases agreeing to both expand the accommodations students are allowed to use and to provide alternate tests for the high school exit examinations. Finally, if an exit examination is not appropriate for a student with a disability, even with accommodations, then the student must receive an alternate assessment.

This overview of current accountability policies provides the context for the following discussion of the issues that impact how students with disabilities will be included in the new accountability requirements. In the following section, we present some of what we have been learning about high-stakes accountability and students with disabilities.

WHAT ARE WE LEARNING ABOUT
STUDENTS WITH DISABILITIES IN HIGH-STAKES ACCOUNTABILITY?

One of the first questions is, "Why are we doing this?" By now you should be aware of the basic protections afforded students with disabilities in assessment and accountability. You also know that there are two types of high-stakes assessments and accountability. One focuses on schools and school systems and is primarily defined by NCLB. The other applies to individual students in those specific states or districts that are using assessments to determine who may receive a diploma or be promoted to the next grade. Although there are some major similarities between the two types (i.e., system, individual) of accountability, there are also some differences in terms of impact for students with disabilities.

With respect to system or school-level accountability, until the passage of NCLB, there was general support for fully including students with disabilities in standards-driven reform initiatives, as long as IEP teams maintained the discretion and power to exempt or modify standards and assessments. Prior to IDEA 1997, students did not have to participate in assessments nor were alternate assessments required. The scores of those students with disabilities who did take achievement tests were not reported separately and those who received accommodations were likely not to be reported at all. Now the scores of special education students must be reported separately at the *school*, *district*, and *state* levels, and schools and districts are subject to consequences if this subgroup fails to make specified levels of progress each year (i.e., AYP). According to data obtained from the National Longitudinal Transition Study 2 (U.S. Department of Education, Office of Special Education Programs [OSEP], 2004b), virtually all secondary students with disabilities (99%) attended schools that administered mandated standardized tests. Among these secondary students with disabilities, 80% took one or more of the mandated tests, 11% were given alternate assessments, and 9% were exempted from testing. In addition, 57% of students with disabilities received an accommodation when they took mandated standardized tests. Has any of this made a difference for students? The answer is that it is too soon to make sweeping generalizations.

Since the passage of NCLB, we have witnessed increased participation of students with disabilities in assessments. However, among the 39 states that reported fourth-grade reading achievement data for students with disabilities in 2003, 30 showed an average performance gap of 30 percentage points between students in general and special education. These gaps increased as students progressed in grades (Quality Counts, 2004).

Yet, some states report significant progress. In Kansas, nearly half of the fifth-grade students scored at the "proficient" level or higher on reading tests, and 58% of fourth-grade students scored at the "proficient" level in math, an increase of 22% over 4 years. The performance of students with disabilities on high school exit examinations also has improved in some states. In Massachusetts, the state reported that 67% of students with disabilities passed the state high school examinations in 2004. In contrast, California reported that only 22% of students in special education in the class of 2004 passed the math portion of the CAHSEE (Quality Counts, 2004), and it is estimated that three fourths of students receiving special education in Alaska will fail that state's high school exit examination.

We are far less certain about the impact of high-stakes graduation testing on dropout rates. Some research has indicated moderate evidence that there may be a relationship, other research has indicated no increases in states that have instituted high school graduation examinations (Greene & Winters, 2004). Students with disabilities have had a history of much lower rates of school completion as compared with students without disabilities (Wagner et al., 1991). But, we do not yet know if dropout rates are related to high-stakes assessments or how high-stakes assessments may affect dropout rates.

Another area in which data are just beginning to emerge relates to the use of alternate assessments. Although policy makers continue to grapple with increasing the participation of students with disabilities in regular assessments through use of accommodations and universal design principles, some students with disabilities are still not able to participate in these assessments. Those students with significant cognitive disabilities may be held to alternate achievement standards, whereas others are expected to meet grade-level achievement standards. However, they may be given alternate assessments that allow them to demonstrate their learning in different ways. The purpose of alternate assessments is to ensure that large-scale accountability systems include all students and provide accurate and meaningful information to schools.

We know that states are using a variety of alternate assessments formats. About 50% of states currently use portfolios or bodies of evidence, whereas 30% use a rating scale or checklist, although the use of portfolios is decreasing (Thompson & Thurlow, 2003). Quenemoen, Thompson, and Thurlow (2003) noted that there is much overlap between the approaches, which run a continuum from unstructured portfolios to paper and pencil tests.

The number of states using out-of-level tests as alternate assessments has risen from 5 states in 1997 to 17 states in 2003 (Quenemoen et al., 2003). Out-of-level testing refers to giving a student a test at grade levels below his or her placement. Out-of-level testing is highly controversial (National Council on Disability, 2004) due in part to fears that too many students with disabilities will be assigned to an out-of-level assessment that is not appropriately challenging in order to avoid accountability consequences (Browder, Spooner, Ahlgrim-Delzell, Flowers, & Karvonen, 2003; Thompson & Thurlow, 2003).

Current evidence also suggests that states are using alternate assessments for different types of students. Based on a nationally representative group of school districts, Schiller et al. (2004) reported that on average, 96.2% of all students with IEPs participated in statewide reading assessments in 2001–2002, with 8.8% of them taking an alternate assessment. At the state level, Browder et al. (2003) found participation to vary widely, with up to 2.5% of the total student population in some states taking an alternate assessment. Participation rates on alternate assessments also varied by disability, ranging from 6.2% for students with learning disabilities to 32.0% for students with autism and 32.6% for students with mental retardation (Browder et al., 2003). Furthermore, Schiller et al. (2004) reported that almost three fourths of the states publicly reported the test scores of students who took an alternate assessment.

States currently provide various forms of guidance for IEP teams in determining which assessment is most appropriate for each student (Lehr & Thurlow, 2003). The most commonly used determinants are the instructional level of the student, whether the student is receiving instruction in the regular curriculum or a more functional life-skills curriculum, parent input, and nonpursuit of a standard diploma (Thurlow, Lazarus, Thompson, & Robey, 2002). Some, but not all, states specifically prohibit the use of disability category and percent of time receiving special education services in general education in making this determination.

ISSUES IN INCLUDING STUDENTS WITH DISABILITIES IN HIGH-STAKES ACCOUNTABILITY

There are a number of assessment-related issues that impact accountability for students with disabilities. Among the challenges are the need to: 1) have valid measures of performance and progress and 2) provide meaningful and timely information about student performance so that policy makers, administrators, and practitioners can improve programs and services. Some of the issues involve assessment design, specifically related to assessment accommodations, and issues over how scores are reported and/or progress is determined (Almond, Lehr, Thurlow, & Quenemoen, 2002; McLaughlin & Thurlow, 2003).

Perhaps the most prominent issue surrounding the assessment of students with disabilities is the use of accommodations. As noted earlier, several federal laws, including the ADA, Section 504, and the IDEA, guarantee students with disabilities the right to assessment accommodations. The IDEA gives the IEP team the right to decide which accommodations are necessary for a student to participate in the classroom and in assessments. The issue is how to treat the scores of assessments when students have used certain accommodations, such as reading aloud a reading test to a student.

Advocates, parents, and legal groups have claimed that it is a violation of students' rights to withhold any accommodation listed on the students' IEP. Others have argued that if certain accommodations are used, then the scores are invalidated, and under NCLB, the students' scores become zeroes or are classified as nonproficient, which jeopardizes a school's performance. However, courts and the Office of Civil Rights have tended to find that accommodations that impact the integrity of the test by altering what is being measured (e.g., reading aloud a reading test) are not required by law and have not been considered appropriate accommodations and do not have to be "counted" (Karger & Pullin, 2002).

OSEP, which is within the U.S. Department of Education, issued a memo in 2001 clarifying the role of the IEP team (http://www.ed.gov/policy/speced/guid/idea/omip.html). OSEP stated that the IEP team has the authority to select individual accommodations and modifications required by a student with a disability in order to participate in state- and/or districtwide assessments. If the IEP team determines that the child will not participate in a particular state- or districtwide assessment of student achievement (or part of an assessment), then the IEP team must state how the child will be assessed (i.e., what is the alternate assessment that will be used). Although the IEP team may select whatever individual assessment accommodations and modifications are needed for a child with a disability to participate in the assessments, the team must base its decision on a full understanding of the possible consequences. For example, it is possible for an IEP team to select individual accommodations or modifications that produce scores that are deemed invalid for purposes of reporting, accountability, or determining student benefits such as promotion or high school diplomas.

However, OSEP also cautioned that states and local districts must make sure that their assessments are valid, reliable, and consistent with professional and technical standards, particularly for assessments that will have important consequences for the student or schools. The states and districts can provide guidelines that provide clear instructions and conditions for how specific accommodations may be used. For example, these guidelines can define the role of the scribe or how to use a reader. OSEP specifically cites the need for IEP teams to give important consideration to decisions regarding assessments associated with high-stakes for the students, such as promotions, diplomas, or access to programs.

School-level accountability requires that we be able to make accurate interpretations about the achievement levels of groups of students from year to year. That is, how do this year's eighth-grade students compare with last year's, and so forth. This requires that the characteristics of the groups be reasonably stable from year to year (Bracey, 2000; Ladd, 2002; Linn, 2001; Ysseldyke & Bielinski, 2002). This year's eighth-grade students with disabilities, for example, are assumed to be similar as a group to last year's eighth-grade students. If the composition of the groups changes significantly from year to year, ". . . then one is really comparing apples to oranges" (Ysseldyke & Bielinski, 2002, p. 2). For students with disabilities, the fluctuations in group characteristics from year to year can be significant. For example, researchers have estimated that 15%–20% of the students with disabilities stop receiving special education services each year and "return" to general education, whereas a similar percentage of students become eligible for special education (Walker et al., 1988; Ysseldyke & Bielinski, 2000). This movement is directly linked to academic achievement, with higher-performing students exiting only to be replaced with lower-performing students (Ysseldyke & Bielinski, 2002).

A second issue about making year-to-year comparisons is the numbers of students that comprise the subgroup of students with disabilities, particularly when a school is judged on the performance of that subgroup at each grade level. NCLB does not require AYP calculations for any subgroup of students in which the number of students in a category is "insufficient to yield statistically reliable information or the results would reveal personally identifiable information about an individual student (34 C.F.R. § 1111[b][2][C][v][II]). States have defined *statistically reliable* to be numbers anywhere from a minimum of 5 students to as high as 200. Clearly, judging a school on the basis of two or three students is not valid, but setting minimum numbers at high levels excludes many schools and even smaller districts from being accountable for a group of students' performance.

SUMMARY OF ISSUES

A number of criticisms have been leveled at the model of standards-driven reform that forms the foundation of current accountability policy. Although there is widespread public and professional support for the need to raise expectations for all students and provide them with more challenging curricula (McLaughlin & Shepard, 1995), there has also been a great deal of concern among general and special educators about the notion of centrally imposed content and achievement standards (McDonnell et al., 1997). Establishing a common set of standards that *all* students are expected to meet ignores the vast differences among schools in terms of resources, quality of instruction, and student characteristics. Yet, proponents of standards rightfully argue that setting lowered standards for some students, such as those in high-poverty schools is neither right nor justifiable under law. In fact, research has shown that when low-performing students are exposed to intensive and sustained instruction in challenging academic content, their achievement dramatically increases. Yet, for students with disabilities, the issues become more complex. These students are entitled to an appropriate education that is defined in part as being individually tailored to a student's unique needs and expected to confer benefit. For many special educators, the concept of common standards flies in the face of the core entitlement in IDEA. However, in the absence of a standard or benchmark against which a students' progress can be measured, there is a real danger that IEPs underestimate what students can do and tend to dumb down curriculum (McLaughlin, 2002).

On another note, both general and special educators have voiced concerns that the focus on standards has diverted attention from more fundamental or critical needs (McLaughlin, Henderson, & Rhim, 1997; McLaughlin & Shepard, 1995). In particular, special education teachers report being caught between the competing priorities of teaching to the standards and trying to teach important life skills. Because standard setting has largely been based on professional opinion and consensus and has not addressed all segments of the student population, many in special education believe that standards ignore important curricular areas such as vocational and career education. Currently, the subject matter content that is being assessed is overwhelmingly academic, and the resulting curricular frameworks, goals, and school improvement efforts are focused on reading, math, and science.

Centralized standards can undermine professional opinion and judgment in determining what an individual student needs to learn. This has been a particular issue for IEP teams, which have traditionally had the right to determine what constitutes an "appropriate" education for a student with a disability and in some cases even determines the "curriculum" for a student. Yet, research has pointed to some serious problems in terms of both the low expectations and lack of consistency of IEPs (Nagle, 2004; Shriner & DeStefano, 2001). Nolet and McLaughlin (2005) noted that the IEPs that are not clearly tied to the general education curriculum tend to focus on discrete skills and ignore the important scope and sequence.

On the positive side, both content and achievement standards provide important guidelines and benchmarks for measuring student progress and setting performance targets. Research conducted at the state and district levels has revealed that special education administrators and policy makers are seeing some positive impacts from the new accountability reforms (Nagle, 2004). In interviews with state-level administrators and parents in four states, all participants identified increased expectations for students with disabilities as a major outcome of accountability. Parents and policy makers agreed that expectations for students with disabilities had been too low and that both special and general education teachers tended to underestimate the abilities of students with disabilities. As one policy maker noted, "I think historically that we underestimate the ability of children with disabilities. We usually set up our instructional program around those expectations. What we want to do is force people to reconsider their expectations and allow children to have opportunities they haven't had before" (Nagle, 2004, p. 15).

In general, special education administrators, practitioners, and parents believe that reporting the assessment results of students with disabilities leads to better programs and better outcomes (Nagle, 2004). In fact, parents and special educators have reported that once scores are made public, schools begin to focus on how to improve instruction and include students with disabilities in school improvement initiatives. Parents also become more informed about what their child's school is doing.

CONCLUSION

How students with disabilities will fare within standards-based reform is still a work in progress. Although we are definitely witnessing some positive effects, a number of challenges remain. Some of these challenges may be addressed in the near future through new assessment and curricular designs that are based on the principles of universal design (Johnson & Thurlow, 2003). Other adjustments to current policies, such as the use of individual student versus cohort progress monitoring may also help deal with some of the issues inherent in annual accountability goals. But, NCLB and the new accountability demands are forcing us to face up to even deeper conceptual and policy issues. For one, we need to reconcile what constitutes an "appropriate" education for a student with a disability with universal standards. Special education programs and practices and standards represent a convergence of two social forces. One is the rights-based movement that provides equal protection and access to individuals with disabilities, whereas the standards movement is a response to society's beliefs about the importance of education as a social tool and a remedy for inequality of social and economic opportunity.

The essence of current policy is that "appropriate" must be considered in relation to an individual child and reflected in an IEP. Appropriate is always subjective and open to dispute. When is some benefit "reasonable?" When is enough really enough? Under what circumstances can we say with confidence that a child has received a sufficient quality and quantity of special education services? Advocates and policy makers push for individualization to ensure that children are not forgotten in regular classrooms and are given needed services. Furthermore, policy makers believe that requiring a team, including a child's parents, to make decisions about what is appropriate would maximize, if not guarantee, the appropriateness of a program.

However, not only has the IEP created enormous bureaucratic inefficiencies, but research also has clearly demonstrated that IEPs are often instructionally irrelevant, only marginally individualized, and only effective as accountability tools when a parent exercises his or her right to disagree (Giangreco, Dennis, & Edelman, 1991; Smith, 1990; Smith & Brownell, 1995). The IEP process becomes one of political bargaining between parents and professionals and "the collective result is considerable momentum against the level of individualization intended by federal law" (McDonnell et al., 1997, p. 64).

Beyond the IEP process itself is the dilemma of defining *appropriate* in the absence of some standard. Yet, what does individualization mean in relation to standards? This question was addressed in a report of the National Research Council (McDonnell et al., 1997) that concluded that standards and the education of students with disabilities "embody potentially compatible goals" (p. 64) but also acknowledged that the concept of common content and performance standards can be troublesome given the heterogeneity of the special education population.

Nevertheless, in order for us to meet the true intent of what constitutes an "appropriate" education for any given student with a disability, we must be able to have an objective measure against which we can compare a student's progress and to judge the adequacy of his or her education. Even so, the practical issue of what is meant by "standards" in the context of an individualized education cannot be ignored. Whether it is feasible or even wise to endorse one *common* set of achievement standards is open to discussion. What is certain is that we need to reconcile what we understand about educating students with disabilities with a standards model if we are to ever achieve the goal of a "free appropriate public education" for every student with a disability.

STUDY QUESTIONS

1. In what ways does the NCLB help students with disabilities? What are the challenges?

2. How does the IDEA support accountability for students with disabilities?

3. Who is considered a "highly qualified" teacher?

4. What are the legal issues concerning requiring students with disabilities to pass one or more assessments in order to receive a high school diploma? What are the possible benefits of these policies? What are the possible consequences?

5. What are alternate assessments?

6. What are three issues in including students with disabilities in the types of high-stakes accountability that is in place in today's schools?

8

Teaching for Transition

Paul Wehman and Colleen A. Thoma

AFTER COMPLETING THIS CHAPTER, THE READER WILL BE ABLE TO

- Understand the concept of access to the general education curriculum
- Define UDL
- List four problems and their solutions in implementing community-based training
- List the components of direct instruction and explain how to implement them
- Explain at least three strategies that classroom teachers can use to assess student learning
- Explain the steps of general case programming

To this point, this book has been devoted to planning for transition, working with other agencies, and designing transition individualized education programs (transition IEPs). Very little attention has focused on individualized instruction for transition or what the teacher should do in the classroom. A number of books are available that provide more in-depth information about assessment, instruction, behavior management techniques, and other types of educational strategies (e.g., Kerr & Nelson, 1998; Sax & Thoma, 2002; Schloss & Smith, 1998). The purpose of this chapter is to discuss what the educator must do to enhance the likelihood of positive transition outcomes from an instructional perspective.

The guidelines for enhancing the likelihood of positive transition outcomes from an instructional perspective have changed a great deal in the past few years with a new emphasis in education on accountability and standards-based education. The change does not mean that special educators should discard the teaching of functional skills, or a focus on outcomes and the postschool goals of individual students. Instead, teaching those skills must be tied to the general education curriculum, fusing the two rather than taking an either/or approach. Therefore, this chapter addresses the following questions:

1. What should teachers teach transition-age students?

2. How should teachers tie transition outcomes to educational standards?

3. What is a Universal Design for Learning (UDL) approach, and how can it be used to ensure access to the general education curriculum for all students?

4. What are some adaptations to the general education curriculum that can be used to improve transition outcomes?

5. What are some augmentations to the general education curriculum that can enhance transition outcomes?

6. How do teachers implement community-based training?

7. What are some principles to follow when choosing alternatives to the general education curriculum?

TEACHING SECONDARY STUDENTS WITH DISABILITIES

A secondary teacher must examine many facets of curriculum development as he or she designs and implements a transition IEP. This section focuses on the development of individualized educational goals within the context of the general education curriculum. Students with and without disabilities will live in a world that is technologically advanced and with greater connection between countries and cultures than ever before. They must leave school with skills that will help them achieve in this world. Teachers are held increasingly accountable not only for teaching curriculum, but also for ensuring that their students can demonstrate what they know in a variety of ways, not the least of which is through the use of standardized tests. Instructional planning must be based in that reality.

Rationale for Selecting Instructional Objectives

There are two issues to address when selecting instructional objectives for transition-age students with disabilities. First, teachers must address the standards that are part of the general education curriculum. Second, the individual needs of students, based on their visions for an adult lifestyle, must be addressed. Each of these is discussed in detail.

Standards and Transition Planning   For many years, the education of students with disabilities, particularly students with significant disabilities, had very little relationship with the curriculum to which students without disabilities were exposed. Instead, a team defined what was appropriate for an individual child. Annual goals were based on information collected from a series of assessments and were focused on deficits and not necessarily tied to what everyone else in that grade was learning. This made progress difficult to monitor and made the inclusion of students with disabilities more difficult to achieve. Teachers might ask why that would be important, why would we care if including students with disabilities in general education classrooms was not possible? Inclusive education is an evidence-based practice that is linked to improved academic outcomes for students with and without disabilities, as Cole, Waldron, and Majd (2004) found. Their research indicated that students without disabilities who received their education in inclusive classrooms made significantly greater academic progress in mathematics and reading. In addition, students with disabilities made academic progress in inclusive settings, particularly those students with learning disabilities and mild cognitive disabilities.

The Individuals with Disabilities Education Act (IDEA) Amendments of 1997 (PL 105-17) and the Individuals with Disabilities Education Improvement Act of 2004 (PL 108-446) changed the process of developing educational programs from a purely individualized approach. This law required that students with disabilities have access to the general education curriculum, the first time that it was necessary that individualized education programs (IEPs) be developed with an explicit connection to the standards to which all other students are held. Access to the general education curriculum does not refer to providing education in inclusive settings, but to making the necessary adaptations and modifications to ensure that students with disabilities can participate in the educational activities and assessments regardless of where the education takes place. IDEA 2004 has kept this focus on access to the general education curriculum, bringing the law even further in line with the No Child Left Behind legislation.

The No Child Left Behind (NCLB) Act of 2001 (PL 107-110) addressed the education of all children in the United States, with an emphasis on ensuring that all states develop academic standards and test students on their progress in learning those standards (Yell, Drasgow & Lawrey, 2005). It also indirectly increased the responsibility for teachers to connect IEP goals for students with disabilities to the general education curriculum. Teachers need to demonstrate that students with disabilities are making Adequate Yearly Progress (AYP) and eventually that they are able to meet the same standards as students without disabilities (by 2013–2014). With this emphasis on teaching academic content, how do teachers also ensure that students with disabilities learn the functional skills that are necessary to achieve their transition outcomes (Rosenberg, Sindelar, & Hardman, 2004)?

Individual Needs of Students with Disabilities   It can be argued that what makes special education different from general education is the focus on *individualized instruction* for students based on their strengths and needs (Scruggs & Mastropieri, 1995). Individualized instruction means that teaching is "tailored to the student's strengths, needs, and individual characteristics" (Rainforth & England, 1997, p. 95). Snell and Brown (2000) further describe individualized instruction as instruction that "reflects the student's stage of learning for a given skill; his or her preferences, priorities, and chronological age; and specific assets or limitations that may require adaptation in materials, environment, or teaching methods" (pp. 123–124).

Although in the last few years the focus in public education has centered on academic achievement, students with disabilities have additional instructional needs. These individual needs often include skill development in areas as diverse as social interactions, language or communication, advocacy, daily living, and/or employment. Although these areas are particularly relevant for students with more significant support needs, their importance cannot be overstated for any student (arguably with or without disabilities).

Many researchers are examining ways to link instruction in these nonacademic skills to state standards. For instance, a recent plan in the state of Virginia includes providing instruction to all ninth-grade students with disabilities in self-advocacy/self-determination skills. To do this without completely revamping the current ninth-grade curriculum, state staff provided information about using the Self-Determined Learning Model of instruction in already existing classes. This model teaches students to use problem solving, a core component skill of self-determination, to solve educational problems and direct their own learning. In addition, state standards that match problem solving or other core component skills were highlighted so that teachers could identify work they were already doing. Table 8.1 includes a list of some examples of Virginia standards that involve the development of self-determination skills. The more creative special educators are, the more likely they will be to find innovative ways to combine academic and nonacademic skill instruction. Figure 8.1 provides an example of a health lesson plan that also provides an opportunity to teach problem-solving skills, a key component skill of self-determination.

Although some researchers advocate for a return to a functional approach to curriculum for students with disabilities (e.g., Bouck, 2004), and some advocate for a completely academic focus at least through the age of 18 (e.g., Fisher & Sax, 2002), we believe that a more effective approach links the two. We need to find ways to meet academic standards by teaching students what they need to know to meet their own goals for their adult lives (Sitlington & Neubert, 2004).

Wehmeyer (2002a) outlined a process for determining an individual student's curriculum, beginning with the general education curriculum and individual student needs. This process is outlined in Figure 8.2 and provides the organizational structure for this chapter. This approach requires that teachers first start with the general education curriculum standards and then make individualized modifications and/or adaptations to them when necessary, based on student preferences and interests as well as their strengths and support needs.

THE GENERAL EDUCATION CURRICULUM

Wehmeyer (2002a) recommended that teachers begin their individualization of a student's curriculum by beginning with the general education curriculum (Nolet & McLaughlin, 2005). The general education curriculum refers to both the formal curriculum (what is taught explicitly) as well as the informal curriculum (what is learned

Table 8.1. Links between common academic standards and self-determination skills

Self-determination skill	Elementary school	Middle school	High school
Choice making	Look for standards in social studies classes such as students learning to identify the choices that people make about lifestyles, employment, and/or freedom.	Look for health standards about making choices among healthy and unhealthy diets and the relationship between those choices and emotional and physical health.	Look for health standards related to making choices about relationships, drug abuse, smoking, and so forth.
Problem solving	Look for math standards that address story and picture problems involving one-step solutions	Look for math standards that address more complex word problems involving multiple-step solutions.	Look for math standards such as consumer math problems related to budgeting for a preferred lifestyle.
Risk taking	Look for health standards that ask students to identify the risks associated with unhealthy lifestyle choices (smoking, obesity, and so forth)	Look for health standards that address the identification of health risks associated with complex behavioral interactions (diet and exercise, food and cholesterol levels, and so forth).	Look for social studies standards that address the interaction between world economies and national decision making (i.e., factors that lead to wars, economic boycotts, rising fuel costs).
Self-advocacy/leadership	Look for English standards that focus on interpersonal conflict resolution and/or understanding and communicating rules.	Look for English standards that address the relationship between verbal and nonverbal messages.	Look for English standards that address the relationship between passive, assertive, and aggressive communication.

PURPOSE: Health SOL 8.2 The student will apply health concepts and skills to the management of personal and family health. Key concepts/skills include

    a. The benefits of using resistance, problem-solving, and decision-making skills for resolving health issues

    b. The importance of developing relationships that are positive and promote wellness

    c. The benefits of developing and implementing short- and long-term health and fitness goals that are achievable and purposeful

PROCEDURE: The procedure consists of three components:

1. Introduction:

    a. Students will learn how to problem solve and use decision-making skills to resolve a personal health issue.

    b. Students will use the Self-Determined Learning Model of instruction to resolve a personal health issue.

    c. The teacher will talk about the fact that he or she needs to get more sleep. Teacher will ask students what ideas they have to help him or her get more sleep. The teacher will write the students' ideas down on a SMART board.

    d. The teacher will introduce the Self-Determined Learning Model of instruction. He or she will apply this model step-by-step to the problem of not getting enough sleep.

2. Development (activities selected to achieve purpose):

    a. Students will use the Self-Determined Learning Model of instruction to problem-solve a health issue. Each student will choose a health issue—emotional, physical, or mental—to work on. They will work on Phases 1 and 2.

    b. In a month, the class members will revisit their Self-Determined Learning Model and evaluate their progress. They will work on Phase 3.

3. Summary (closure to lesson):
Students will share their Self-Determined Learning Model of instruction plan for their health issue. The class will discuss the differences in goals and the plans. Classmates can give suggestions for Phase 3.

RESOURCES: The resources to be used in teaching the lessons need to be identified. These include transparency and copy of the Self-Determined Learning Model of instruction.

EVALUATION: The evaluation can be performed in several ways.

1. Assessment of student learning

    a. Teacher assessment of student learning. The teacher measures student learning through the visual representations of the concept.

    b. Student self-assessment. Students check their own performance of an activity through modeling of the completed activity and the illustration of the concept.

2. Teacher self-assessment. The teacher reflects on success of lesson by analyzing

    a. His or her performance and the value of the lesson as a learning experience

    b. Student reactions during the lesson

Figure 8.1. Lesson plan.

through peer interactions) of the school. Ensuring that students with disabilities have access to the general education curriculum should include both informal and formal aspects of the curriculum. But how can this be accomplished? How can teachers learn to modify the general education curriculum so that each student with a disability can learn? When the instructional strategies for teaching and assessing student progress in the general education curriculum follow the principles of universal design, there is a greater likelihood that students with and without disabilities will be able to benefit from receiving their education in the general education classroom and that adaptations

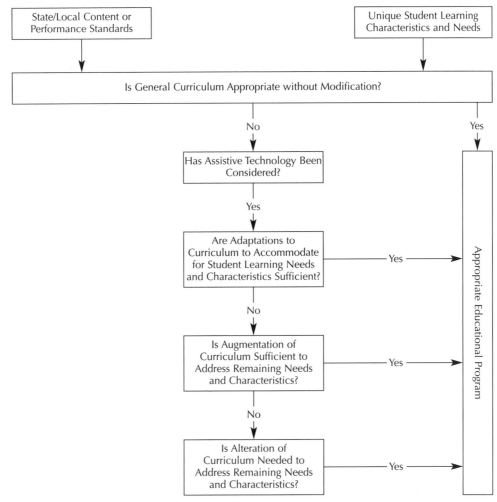

Figure 8.2. A model for ensuring access to the general education curriculum. (From Wehmeyer, M.L. [with Sands, D.J., Knowleton, H.E., & Kozleski, E.B.]. [2002]. Achieving access to the general curriculum. In *Teaching students with mental retardation: Providing access to the general curriculum* [p. 55]. Baltimore: Paul H. Brookes Publishing Co.; reprinted by permission.)

and modifications will not become overwhelming for the general education teacher. Step 1 is to determine the general education curriculum, enhancing it for all.

Universal Design for Learning

UDL provides teachers with an alternative approach to meeting the learning needs of all students. The premise of UDL highlights an educational approach for teaching all learners, regardless of diversity, through designing flexible applications of technology tools, instructional networks, and manipulation of digital content.

UDL has its roots in the field of architecture. With the passage of the Americans with Disabilities Act (ADA) of 1990 (PL 101-336) and its requirement that public spaces be accessible for individuals with disabilities, architects began to look for ways to change what they built so that people with disabilities could gain access to it. Our most common example is the curb cut. This innovation proved to be beneficial for people with disabilities as well as many other members of our society—kids on skateboards or bicycles, mothers pushing their children in strollers, people with broken legs who are using crutches to get around, and elderly people who find it difficult to move quickly. In fact, there are more people without disabilities who benefited from that design change than people with disabilities.

In the late 1990s the UDL approach was applied to school instruction. This was the beginning of some exciting research at the Center for Applied Special Technology (CAST). CAST is a nonprofit organization that works to expand learning opportunities for all individuals, especially those with disabilities, through the research and development of innovative, technology-based educational resources and strategies. Their web site provides information on the latest research on UDL and examples of how to incorporate this approach into classroom instruction. The focus of UDL was on creating new materials to use in instruction, materials that were accessible for all (Bowe, 2000; Rose, Meyer, & Hitchcock, 2005). This approach helped instructors develop accessible web sites, digital written materials, and computers with various input and output methods.

The UDL approach is based on research on how the brain learns, and how some people learn differently (Bowe, 2000). This research supports the success of using a mixture of technologies to enable students with diverse learning needs to become successful in instruction (Orkwis & McLane, 1998). A major theme of UDL proposes that instruction and assessment approaches should include alternatives to make them accessible and appropriate for individuals with diverse backgrounds and varied learning approaches, abilities, and disabilities (Rose, Meyer, & Hitchcock, 2005).

One significant result of incorporating UDL strategies in education is that students with or without disabilities can benefit when a variety of teaching strategies are used by teachers. For example, when teachers use lectures only, they need to make adaptations to adequately provide access to the general education curriculum for students who have disabilities as well as those students who learn best by doing or who are visual learners. On the other hand, a teacher who supplements lectures with hands-on activities, visual cues, or web-based notes that can be printed or accessed electronically will be able to engage students with disabilities while enhancing the education of all students (Connell et al., 1997). Far fewer additional adaptations and/or accommodations will be necessary at that point.

Has Assistive Technology Been Considered?

The second step in the model for ensuring access to the general education curriculum (Wehmeyer, 2002b) is to consider any assistive technology (AT) that might be necessary for an individual student with a disability. Considering AT is a different process from using a UDL approach in that it requires that the needs of individual students be considered as opposed to choosing multiple means of teaching to a group. Of course, individualized assistive technology could conceivably include technology that is offered to all students in a particular lesson.

AT can include either devices or services. IDEA 2004 defines *assistive technology devices and services* as follows:

Assistive technology device means any item, piece of equipment or product system, whether acquired commercially off the shelf, modified or customized, that is used to increase, maintain, or improve the functional capabilities of a child with a disability. (§ 1401, PP1)

> Assistive technology service means any service that directly assists a child with a disability in the selection, acquisition or use of an assistive technology device. (§ 1401, PP2)

AT can have a variety of applications in the classroom and can meet a variety of needs. To benefit from their education, some students with disabilities may require AT for mobility and others may require AT for communication so that they can demonstrate what they have learned. There are many ways to describe AT but most describe it by its degree of complexity and its primary use. *Low tech* refers to devices that are passive or simple, with few moving parts (Mann & Lane, 1991), such as picture communication boards, pointers, and switches. *High tech* refers to devices that are complex and typically contain electronic components (Inge & Shepherd, 1995), such as voice output communication aids, electronic wheelchairs, universal remote controls, and computers. Typically, the complexity of AT devices can be conceptualized as a continuum from low or no tech to high tech.

Considering AT for the transition-age student needs to go beyond those devices and services that can meet purely academic goals. Instead, devices and services also need to help students move toward their transition goals and, therefore, must take into account the needs they have related to work, postsecondary education, recreation and leisure, socialization, community living, and/or personal care. Considering this requires that teachers and transition planning team members know both the students' needs as well as the needs of the environment in which they will need to use the device or service. The Matching Person and Technology process (Craddock & Scherer, 2002) provides guidelines for not only taking individual student preferences about technology into consideration, but also the demands of the environment. For instance, Maria was a young woman whose ability to communicate verbally was very limited. An assistive technology assessment was conducted and a laptop system with voice output was chosen for her. Maria had the intelligence to use the system, but not the desire. She hated the slowness of the computer, and the impersonal nature of this means of communication. Maria preferred to attempt to use her limited speech and have an interpreter who knows her well translate when others did not understand. She was quick to voice this opinion, yet until this model was used with her, assessments continued to point to a higher technology system that would spend more time sitting in a closet than on her desk at school. Table 8.2 outlines the steps in this approach.

ALTERATION OF OR ADAPTATION TO THE GENERAL CURRICULUM

Wehmeyer (2002a) defined curriculum adaptation as "any effort to modify the representation or presentation of the curriculum or to modify the student's engagement with the curriculum to enhance access and progress" (p. 52). Many of the same strategies or techniques that could be used in a universally designed curriculum could also be used to adapt the general education curriculum specifically for one student. The difference between the two is that the techniques for adaptation are used to meet the needs of a small number of students (sometimes just one student with a disability) and are not available to all students.

Table 8.2.   Matching person and technology components of assistive technology usability

Device evaluation: Assistive technology (AT) meets the individual's functional need
  Milieu: Determination of environments in which it will be used
  Person: Discussion of preferences and needs
  AT: Delineation of desired functions and features
Device selection: AT has appeal and is obtainable
  Milieu: Good device/environment fit exists
  Person: Accepts AT use and is psychologically ready for use
  AT: Product is acceptable in terms of cost, delivery date, aesthetics, and usefulness
Device use: AT performance and achievement of the functional goal
  Milieu: Environmental accommodations in place, AT performs adequately in different
    environments
  Person: Satisfaction with use
  AT: Has the desired durability and operability

From Craddock, G., and Scherer, M.J. (2002). Assessing individual needs for assistive technology. In C.L. Sax and C.A. Thoma (Eds.), *Transition assessment: Wise practice for quality lives* (p. 100). Baltimore: Paul H. Brookes Publishing Co.; adapted by permission.

Like UDL, curriculum adaptations can include modifications to instructional materials, the delivery of instruction, the manner in which a student engages in instruction, or the process of assessing what a student has learned (Nolet & McLaughlin, 2000) Because many instructional materials are print-based, adaptations to these materials can include books on tape, braille, computer-based work, audiocassette tapes, videotapes, and CD-ROMs.

Teachers generally deliver instruction verbally through lectures or in written format on chalkboards, overheads, or worksheets. Changes in instructional delivery can make learning more functional through the use of community-based instruction (CBI), hands-on or discovery learning, and authentic learning. For example, instead of teaching algebra through the use of worksheets and textbook-based homework, students can use formulas to determine how much paint they need to buy to paint one room in their house. In addition, they can determine how much money they will need to earn to afford a lifestyle of their choosing, using equations to factor in taxes, insurance, and other payroll deductions. Choosing appropriate adaptations for the transition-age student with disabilities requires examining the where, what, how, and when components of instruction (Cawley, Foley, & Doan, 2003; Downing & Eichinger, 2003).

Adaptations to What to Teach

Instructional objectives must focus on skills that the student will need to function as an adult in his or her preferred setting (Wehmeyer, 2002b). Therefore, the choice of objectives must start with a backward planning process, starting with where the student wants to be (the outcomes of transition planning) and comparing that with where he or she is now. That difference, or discrepancy, provides a focus for planning the individualized curriculum for that student, providing a clear roadmap for where the student is currently and where he or she wants to be, and then developing concrete steps to get him or her there.

The activities and skills that are most conducive to independent performance in postsecondary education and vocational, residential, and community environments must guide the selection of transition objectives. For instance, if a student wants to live alone after high school, then skills related to safety, home ownership, and independence would be the most important to learn. On the other hand, if a student wants to continue to live at home with his family, independence in living might not be as important as academic skills because going to college is what is most important to him. Transition planning must be an open dialogue between the student and family and the school personnel.

In addition to keeping student and family ideas in mind when choosing transition IEP goals and objectives, teachers must be familiar with college entrance requirements because students with mild disabilities frequently plan to attend college (Wehman & Getzel, 2005). The process of determining objectives cannot be conducted exclusively by the teacher but requires ongoing collaboration with the student and family. In fact, in order for a transition IEP team to use a self-determined approach, the student must be the starting point in the plan. This rationale for skill selection continues to be one of the most overlooked aspects of instructional planning and implementation in special education.

Adaptations to Where Teachers Provide Instruction

Increasing numbers of educators are accepting that CBI is best for implementing transition programs for young adults with disabilities (Pierangelo & Giuliani, 2004). Whenever possible, instruction should be provided in the community in which the student lives and in the businesses frequented by the student and his or her family. This will ensure that the student has opportunities to socialize in the community and to learn applicable community skills. Classroom instruction often does not generalize into the community well, which frequently makes instruction nonfunctional. With CBI, however, educational objectives are taught in natural community environments, such as worksites, shopping malls, and restaurants. Regardless of the student's disability or its severity, community-based training experiences appear to be the most functional. These sites can involve vocational training, home-living skills instruction, recreational instruction, and community skills development.

Creative Sites for Community-Based Training Creative teachers who understand that leaving the school campus to go to community sites may not always be possible will identify sites and tasks within the school that can provide authentic learning experiences. Students can help with identifying what they might want to do, and where. Possible sites for work experience in school include the following:

- Main office
- Attendance office
- Library
- Audiovisual room
- Athletic office
- Teachers' work room
- Nurse's office

- Counselor's office

- Cafeteria

- Physical plant and grounds

Authentic Learning Experiences at School   The school provides dozens of opportunities for students to engage in real work. For example, students' attendance information or semester grades can be entered on a computer in the attendance office. In the main office, students can take telephone messages, deliver faxes, and photocopy documents. In the library, checkout cards can be filed, protective covers can be put on new books, and old book covers can be repaired. Health status information can be entered on the computer for the school nurse. In the multimedia room, records of equipment can be maintained, and audiovisual equipment can be delivered to appropriate classrooms. Cleaning and landscaping can be done on the grounds. Table 8.3 provides a description of the variety of potential vocational activities that can be taught throughout a student's educational career. Of course, this list is not all-inclusive, but it can serve as a starting point for teachers wishing to begin to organize their efforts. It is, however, important that these tasks are introduced to students at a young age.

In order to implement any community-based training program successfully, a philosophical commitment to the training must be made. Commitment to training requires not only providing the option of community experiences, but also identifying specific program objectives and the target age and populations of students who should participate. Through this identification process, different types of jobs, community activities, and resources can be selected for specific students. Potential training sites where initial contacts can be made with business owners or employers will then become apparent. These sites can be visited to determine whether a sufficient array of skills and activities could be acquired by the student. Once it appears that the site is appropriate, the teacher should be ready to negotiate for use of the site for training. This usually entails writing a training agreement and asking the employer to sign it.

Community-Based Training Problems and Solutions   A number of chapters and books have been written about the challenges associated with moving from classroom instruction to community-based training sites (e.g., Falvey, 1989; White & Weiner, 2004). Essentially, however, the major problems revolve around staffing and scheduling, transportation, liability and safety, and costs.

Staffing and Scheduling   The first issue for educators designing community-based training programs is locating the staff to manage students who are dispersed throughout the community. Educators should use team teaching and look to volunteers, paraprofessionals, student teachers, practicum students, graduate students, and peer tutors as potential instructors. Student training schedules can be staggered, but students should be grouped heterogeneously so that the students with the most significant support needs are not congregated at one site. An important aspect of coordinating services is using occupational therapists, recreational therapists, and other support personnel in an integrated therapy model. Computers can also be very helpful for scheduling issues, both in providing a mechanism for coordinating schedules, sharing information across staff, and communicating among staff members as well as in providing a mechanism for

Table 8.3. Teaching for transition

Student	Domestic	Community	Leisure	Vocational
Tim (elementary age)	Picking up toys Washing dishes Making bed Dressing Grooming Practicing eating skills Practicing toileting skills Sorting clothes Vacuuming	Eating meals in a restaurant Using restroom in a local restaurant Putting trash into container Choosing correct change to ride the city bus Giving the clerk money for an item he wants to purchase Recognizing and reading pedestrian safety signs Participating in local scout troop Going to a neighbor's house for lunch	Climbing on swing set Playing board games Playing tag with neighbors Tumbling activities Running Playing kickball Playing croquet Riding bicycles Playing with age-appropriate toys Playing volleyball Taking aerobics classes	Picking up plate, silverware, and glass after meal Returning toys to appropriate storage spaces Cleaning the room at the end of the day Working on a task for a designated period Wiping tables after meals Following two- to four-step instructions Answering the telephone Emptying trash Taking messages to people
Mary (junior high school age)	Washing clothes Preparing simple meals (e.g., soup, salad, sandwich) Keeping bedroom clean Making snacks Mowing lawn Raking leaves Making grocery lists Purchasing items from a list Vacuuming and dusting living room	Crossing streets safely Purchasing an item from a department store Purchasing a meal at a restaurant Using local transportation system to get to and from recreational facilities Participating in local scout troop Going to a neighbor's house for lunch on Saturday	Playing checkers with a friend Playing miniature golf Cycling Attending high school or local basketball games Playing softball Swimming Attending craft class at city recreation center	Waxing floors Cleaning windows Filling lawn mower with gas Hanging and bagging clothes Busing tables Working for 1–2 hours Operating machinery (e.g., dishwasher, buffer) Cleaning sinks, bath tubs, and fixtures Following a job sequence
Sandy (high school age)	Cleaning all rooms in place of residence Developing a weekly budget Cooking meals Operating thermostat to regulate heat and air conditioning Doing yard maintenance Maintaining personal needs Caring for and maintaining clothing	Utilizing bus system to move about the community Depositing checks into bank account Using community department stores Using community restaurants Using community grocery stores Using community health facilities (e.g., physician, pharmacist)	Jogging Archery Boating Watching college basketball games Playing video games Playing card games (e.g., UNO) Attending club swimming class Gardening Going on a vacation	Performing required janitorial duties at J.C. Penney Performing housekeeping duties at Days Inn Performing grounds keeping duties at college campus Performing food service at K Street Cafeteria Performing laundry duties at Moon's Laundromat Performing job duties to company standards

presenting some supports to students that do not necessarily require a person to deliver. For instance, instead of needing a staff person to deliver prompts for completing the steps of a job, a student might have a pocket PC provide verbal directions to keep him or her on task. Creativity and organization are the two skills that will help teachers juggle the support needs of students in community-based settings.

Transportation   There are many ways to facilitate movement of students from classrooms to different community sites. Often, the regular bus schedule can be coordinated with the training schedule, and school district vehicles, such as vans, teachers' cars, or other vehicles, can be used throughout the day. School district vehicles are used for many student functions and can also be available for CBI. In schools with limited transportation availability, CBI may need to be the first activity on the classroom schedule. This is particularly true for high school students who are participating in time-limited, nonpaid vocational training placements.

In many school systems, teachers have conveniently transported the students to their worksites and have been reimbursed for mileage. Also, in some urban areas, training sites can be identified that are within walking distance of the school.

Liability and Safety   The local school board must have a districtwide policy agreement regarding liability and safety. Furthermore, specific school or student agreements with participating companies or sites are essential. District liability insurance policies usually cover teachers and students while they are in the community. Students can be insured through school accident funds or employees' policies. If students are being paid, then their worker's compensation insurance will be drawn from their wages. Volunteers can register with a school system volunteer training program for insurance coverage. Although liability and safety issues take time and thought to resolve, they require little attention once they are in place.

Costs   The issue of how to pay for CBI is paramount but, with planning and thought, this problem can usually be solved. For example, most classrooms have supply budgets that can be used for community-based costs as well as classroom supplies. CBI costs should also be included in proposed budgets. Most school districts have career and vocational education funds that could rightfully be used. Furthermore, a number of local businesses and community groups, such as Kiwanis Clubs and Lions Clubs, make donations for specific uses such as bus passes or training. Finally, educators should try to structure training around regular purchases, using the family supply list for funds. Clearly, teacher creativity and resourcefulness as well as school and community resources are key to resolving cost issues. Lastly, many teachers successfully organize school-based businesses to both provide a mechanism for raising money that can be used to supplement limited budgets as well as provide an opportunity for students to learn skills authentically.

General Case Programming

Students with severe cognitive disabilities frequently have difficulty with transferring information learned at one instructional site to another setting (Hickson, Blackman, & Reis, 1995). General case programming provides a framework for increasing generalizability. Although this is not new information for most teachers, it is an evidence-based practice that has been successful, and therefore warrants inclusion in this chapter. The following section is summarized from an ERIC report sponsored by the U.S. Department of Education's Office of Special Education and Rehabilitative Services (1990). It describes the steps of general case programming created by Horner and McDonald (1982) and provides examples of each step.

Identify Appropriate Training Sites in the Community   The teacher should select many sites for teaching specific tasks. He or she should then list the steps required to complete the task (i.e., task analysis). Last, the teacher should make note of environmental cues at each site that tell the student how and when to carry out the steps of the task. For example, the teacher may be teaching the student how to grocery shop. The teacher would first identify as many grocery stores as possible where the training could take place. Then, he or she would list the specific tasks (e.g., entering the store, getting a shopping cart, selecting desired items, going through checkout, paying for groceries, leaving the store, loading the car with groceries, putting the cart in the appropriate location in the parking lot). Environmental cues could include where the doors entering the store are located (e.g., front, side), where shopping carts are located (e.g., inside or outside of the store), how the store is arranged (e.g., produce on the left, bread and baked goods on the far right wall, deli in the back), number of check-out aisles, the presence of a person to bag groceries (or does the customer do it him- or herself), payment options (e.g., check-cashing card, credit card machine), and the presence of an employee to assist the customer in carrying groceries to the car.

Select Training Sites   The teacher determines the number of sites needed to teach all of the variations of the activity. Variations of grocery shopping could probably be provided in three or four different stores. Variations of all environmental cues would need to be represented in the sites as well.

Sequence Sites and Tasks for Instruction   If possible, the teacher should develop a random training sequence so that the student learns to do the activity in many different sites. If this would overwhelm the student, then training may take place at one location only until mastery is achieved, and then the task can be taught at the next store. The sites where mastery was achieved are then randomly selected so that the student does not know where the training will take place that day. The teacher must specify how well the student must perform the activity and how many times the student must perform at that level in order to demonstrate mastery. For example, the student would have to show 100% accuracy for two consecutive sessions without assistance.

Conduct Baseline Probes   The teacher identifies the steps of the activity that the student cannot perform and the level of needed assistance. The teacher then assigns the easiest site for the first session and continues to add sites according to difficulty. Next, the teacher times the trials and uses an increasing-prompt hierarchy, which allows the teacher to progress from the least invasive prompt to more direct prompts when the student makes an error. The hierarchy of prompts is 1) an indirect verbal prompt, 2) a direct verbal prompt or gesture, 3) a model, 4) a physical prompt, and

5) full physical assistance. Using this method, the teacher determines the level of assistance necessary to ensure correct responses for all tasks and the approximate time it will take to train.

Select a Chaining Strategy   Chaining is a technique that links component behaviors into a meaningful sequence of steps (Hickson et al., 1995; Spooner & Wood, 2004). Teachers may present all of the steps at once, or if that is too much for the student to understand at one time, then the teacher may teach one step of the task at a time (i.e., backward chaining). For example, if a task is composed of 10 steps, then the teacher assists with the first nine and the student performs Step 10. Then, the teacher assists with the first eight steps and the student performs Steps 9 and 10. This continues until the student performs all steps without assistance.

Select an Assistance Strategy   The teacher may use the increasing-prompt hierarchy, which allows students to make errors and correct them while the teacher gradually intensifies the prompts until the student accurately performs the step, or a decreasing-prompt hierarchy, which reduces the level of assistance across settings.

Select Correction Procedures   If a student makes an error, then three elements should be included in the correction procedure: 1) provide immediate feedback, 2) provide the student with an opportunity to do the step over, and 3) provide needed assistance to ensure the step is performed accurately. For example, if the student attempted to enter the store without first getting a shopping cart, then the teacher would provide immediate feedback by saying, "No, you must get a shopping cart." The teacher would go back to the previous step in the chain by bringing the student back to the entrance of the store. Then, the teacher would say, "Go get a shopping cart" and point to the carts. The student would then have an opportunity to demonstrate the step.

Organize Data Collection and Monitor Student Performance   The teacher records the date, location, cues used for each step, and necessary prompts. These steps increase the probability that students will generalize skills that are featured in the transition IEP to several settings.

Direct Instruction Techniques

Because students with milder cognitive disabilities frequently plan on receiving academic diplomas, it is necessary for them to succeed in content area classes. Students with moderate disabilities have more functional academic objectives in their transition IEPs (e.g., reading in the workplace, consumer math, how to put coins in a vending machine). Using direct instruction techniques is one method of instruction that has received much attention from practitioners. The following section briefly describes selected teaching techniques that characterize direct instruction (Carnine, Silbert, & Kameenui, 1997). The components were selected because they may be used in classrooms or community-based settings and have been adapted for use in either setting. They include 1) monitoring, 2) diagnosis and correction, 3) motivation, 4) pacing, and 5) wait time.

Monitoring   Teachers must monitor students as they complete steps in community-based settings so that errors can be caught as soon as they are made. For example, a student may be learning how to use a cash register. The teacher monitors closely to ensure that he or she immediately detects and corrects any mistakes that the student may make while at the cash register.

For example, in a classroom science setting, the students may be responding orally. The teacher may ask, "What is the first element in air?" The teacher must watch the students carefully to be sure all students answered, "Water." Individual verbal tests can also be used to verify that students have mastered the skill. Teachers need to provide adequate opportunities for group response before they conduct individual testing so that all students have several opportunities to practice the correct response.

Diagnosis and Correction   Carnine and colleagues (1997) explained that in order to diagnose the cause of a student's error, the teacher must first determine if the error was a result of inattentiveness or lack of knowledge. A student who is looking at the teacher is usually paying attention, but the student who is looking out the window may not be. If the teacher determines that the error was caused from lack of knowledge, then he or she must determine the specific skill deficit. For example, during a geography lesson, the teacher may present several states and ask the capitals of each. The teacher points to the state of Georgia and asks, "Everyone, what's the capital?" Some students answer, "Atlanta," but one student answers, "Tallahassee." The teacher first praises a student who made the correct response, saying, "Good job, John. You gave the right answer: Atlanta." The teacher models the correct answer, "The capital of Georgia is Atlanta." Next, he or she may lead the group in saying the correct answer. "Everyone, say the capital of Georgia with me." Finally, the teacher does individual tests to ensure that all students know the capital.

Motivation   Carnine and colleagues (1997) pointed out that individual students require different reinforcement. Some students may respond to verbal praise, but other students may need more demonstrative methods, such as handshakes, high-fives, or pats. Regardless of individual preferences, students need to feel successful in learning. This can be accomplished through well-designed lesson plans and implementation. Eventually, students need to strive for intrinsic motivation, succeeding because it makes them proud of a job well done.

Pacing   Pacing involves the teacher moving from one task to another in a brisk manner (after mastery has been achieved). It does not mean teachers talk fast or rush through instruction. Teachers need to progress through units of material at a quick pace in order to enhance students' interest and to increase the number of objectives to be covered from the transition IEP.

Wait Time   This technique can be used when a new skill is being taught or when students are having difficulty with answering a given question correctly. The teacher asks, "What is 9 + 3 + 5? Think about it." The teacher waits as long as he or she thinks is appropriate (e.g., 2–3 seconds) and then encourages students to respond. Likewise, when using chaining procedures, the teacher allows enough time for the student to respond on his or her own before providing a prompt.

Instructional Strategies

Direct instruction procedures have been widely documented in studies (e.g., Carnine, 1981; Carnine et al., 1997; Darch & Gersten, 1986) that have suggested its usefulness in teaching students with learning difficulties. In addition to these techniques, other studies have featured tips and strategies to enhance social and academic learning, such as 1) peer buddies, 2) mnemonic strategies, 3) guided notes, 4) concept diagrams, 5) compensatory strategies, and 6) classroom modifications. These and other strategies are discussed in detail in Gore (2004). The next sections describe these strategies.

Peer Buddies   The peer buddy system is a technique that has been used to encourage social skills and friendships among students with disabilities and their peers (Hughes et al., 1999). Students with severe disabilities are paired with students in general education. The peer buddies regularly interact in and out of class by assisting with class projects and introducing their own friends to their partners. Activities that are academically and socially based include 1) vocational classes, 2) academic courses, 3) recreational activities, 4) after-school sports, 5) eating lunch together, 6) visiting each other's homes, and 7) school clubs (Hughes et al., 1999).

Mnemonic Strategies   Typically, students with academic difficulty have trouble retrieving important information. Mnemonic strategies assist students in remembering pertinent steps in skill sequences. Czarnecki, Rosko, and Fine (1998) featured examples and guidelines for teaching such strategies. Guidelines for implementation include 1) conducting a pretest to learn how students are performing; 2) describing the strategy; 3) modeling the strategy; 4) having students memorize the strategy by providing true/false, matching, or fill-in-the-blank exercises and verbal rehearsal; 5) providing practice with prompts and verbal and written feedback on the use of strategy steps; 6) providing a posttest; and 7) promoting generalization by monitoring strategy use in other classes.

Guided Notes   Students taking classes such as science, history, or literature frequently depend on their notes as they review for examinations. Most students sometimes have difficulty listening to lectures and copying notes simultaneously. Consequently, students who perform at a lower level may transcribe pertinent information incorrectly or miss the main idea altogether. Guided notes, which have been used successfully with students in both general and special education classes (Lazarus, 1996), provide a map of the lecture. Students are able to follow along, listening to what is being taught and making notes of important information. Figure 8.3 shows examples of guided notes and accompanying transparencies.

Concept Diagrams   Students with mild learning difficulties often have trouble organizing material. Concept diagrams may help alleviate some of the frustration by providing a blueprint of material to be covered. Teachers create visual maps of the les-

(Student copy of guided notes)

Nutrition

I. The U.S. recommended guide to good eating habits is called the _____ _____.

II. The _____ is made up of _____ levels or groups of food.

    A. The _____ level represents _____ or the least amount of servings you should have per day.

    B. The _____ level represents _____ or the most amount of servings you should have per day.

III. Each level of food groups shows how many servings you should eat every day.

    A. _____ , _____ , _____ group.

        1. You should _____ .

    B. _____ , _____ , _____ group.

        1. You should have _____ servings each day·

    C. _____ , _____ , _____ , _____ , _____ , _____ group.

        1. You should have _____ servings each day·

    D. _____ group.

        1. You should have _____ servings each day·

    E. _____ group.

        1. You should have _____ servings each day·

    F. _____ , _____ , _____ , _____ group.

        1. You should have _____ servings each day·

Figure 8.3. Examples of guided notes for students and accompanying transparency.

(continued)

son's content, which allows students to see the big picture of the lesson so that when they actually read (or hear a lecture on) the subject matter, they know how the material is related (see Table 8.4 for creating and using a concept diagram). Vaughn, Bos, and Schumm (1997) recognized that concept diagrams may help students understand potentially difficult information, such as definitions and characteristics of a particular subject. Figure 8.4 provides an example of a concept diagram used in a science lesson.

Compensatory Strategies Lewis and Doorlag (1999) suggested the use of compensatory strategies for older students with disabilities. A widely used strategy is to replace written language requirements with oral language requirements. Also, electronic

Figure 8.3.   *(continued)*

(Teacher transparency)

Nutrition

I.   The U.S. recommended guide to good eating habits is called the ___food___ ___pyramid___.

II. The ___food pyramid___ is made up of ___6___ levels or groups of food.

    A. The ___top___ level represents ___fats, oils, & sweets___ or the least amount of servings you should have per day.

    B. The ___bottom___ level represents ___bread, cereal, rice, & pasta___ or the most amount of servings you should have per day.

III. Each level of food groups shows how many servings you should eat every day.

    A. ___Fats___ , ___oils___ , ___sweets___ group.

       1. You should ___use these sparingly___ .

    B. ___Milk___ , ___yogurt___ , ___cheese___ group.

       1. You should have ___2 – 3___ servings each day.

    C. ___Meat___ , ___poultry___ , ___fish___ , ___dry beans___ , ___eggs___ , ___nuts___ group.

       1. You should have ___2 – 3___ servings each day.

    D. ___Vegetable___ group.

       1. You should have ___3 – 5___ servings each day.

    E. ___Fruit___ group.

       1. You should have ___2 – 4___ servings each day.

    F. ___Bread___ , ___cereal___ , ___rice___ , ___pasta___ group.

       1. You should have ___6 – 11___ servings each day.

---

aids, such as calculators, and facts tables, have been used by students who have poor math skills. Teachers should note that this is a debatable strategy in that some practitioners believe that students should receive instruction in areas in which they are weak. Others who endorse compensatory strategies believe that it is best to use the student's areas of strength to compensate for those weak areas.

Classroom Modifications   Often, students with mild or severe cognitive disabilities have difficulty with reading and written examinations. Reading modifications proposed by Lewis and Doorlag (1999) included presenting information through other media such as class discussion, movies, audiotapes of material, or presentations from resource people.

Table 8.4. Steps to create and use a concept diagram

Step	Activity
1	Identify major concepts to teach.
2	List important characteristics of the concepts. Think about whether each characteristic is always present, sometimes present, or never present.
3	Locate examples and nonexamples of the concept.
4	Construct a definition of the concept by naming the superordinate concept, its characteristics, and the relationship among characteristics.
5	Introduce the concept diagram to students, using an advance organizer.
6	Elicit a list of key words or ideas that relate to the concept.
7	Explain or review the parts of the concept diagram and their intended use.
8	With students, name and define the concept.
9	Discuss characteristics that are always present, sometimes present, and never present in the meaning of the concept.
10	Link the examples and nonexamples for the characteristics.

From Vaughn, S., Bos, C.S., & Schumm, J.S. *Teaching exceptional, diverse, and at-risk students in the general education classroom* (pp. 469–470). Copyright 2000 by Allyn & Bacon. Reprinted by permission.

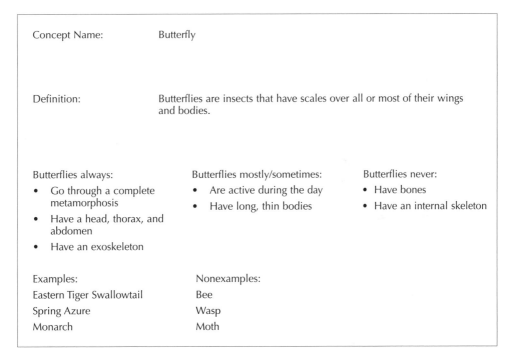

Figure 8.4. Concept diagram.

How Do Teachers Implement Community-Based Training?

After the school has verified that all program operation procedures adhere to U.S. Department of Labor standards, the necessary skills for instruction can be analyzed in detail (Moon, Kiernan, & Halloran, 1990; Simon & Halloran, 1994). Typically, one to three students are assigned to a community site, and detailed schedule and transportation arrangements are made. From this point, systematic instruction procedures (Falvey, 1989) can be developed and implemented, and a means of monitoring students' performance can be designed. It is, of course, necessary to maintain contact with employers, co-workers, and any supportive people at the training site. The appropriateness of the training site should be reviewed at least monthly. At the beginning of such a program, only a limited number of sites should be used until their success is shown. The next sections describe characteristics of training sites as well as potential problems and solutions with community-based training.

Characteristics of Successful Vocational Training Sites

Several characteristics of successful vocational training sites have emerged over the years. First, employers should understand that students are there primarily to receive training and experience, not necessarily to produce large amounts of work. If an employer feels that the main reason the students are there is to complete work, then the program will likely fail. There must be a clear understanding that the work will get done but may require the efforts of several students and the teacher working together.

Second, worksites should offer opportunities for students to perform a variety of tasks. The ideal worksite yields four to six different tasks and allows for interaction with a variety of co-workers—necessary to teach for generalization and to enhance the likelihood of cross-training of skills.

Third, the purpose of work experience is to provide maximal opportunities for individuals to work and interact with employees without disabilities. When analyzing a site, staff should note how much the employees interact with each other and assess the extent to which the assigned task will require them to work with the other employees. The Vocational Integration Index, developed by Parent, Kregel, and Wehman (1992), provided a means of determining the opportunity for physical and social integration.

Alterations to Assessment Procedures

Assessment data are useful for determining the level at which students are currently functioning as well as providing teachers with information regarding instruction. Curriculum-based assessment (CBA) is commonly used to determine how students are progressing through the lesson. Equally important is the process of teachers assessing their own performance.

Curriculum-Based Assessment   CBA is a method of determining if students understand the day's lesson. Strengths of the model are that it identifies those students who did not succeed in the curriculum, and that it is quick, time efficient, and inexpensive (Hughes & Carter, 2002). A teacher instructing students on how to fill out a job application could present a blank job application at the end of the day's lesson to learn if they understood the material covered. If students could not complete the assignment accurately, then the teacher would determine exactly what elements of the application gave students problems and reteach those tasks.

Authentic Assessment   Teachers are rapidly discovering the benefits of using authentic assessment strategies, and nowhere are these techniques more applicable than in assessing a student's progress in meeting transition outcomes. Authentic assessment strategies are those assessment procedures that measure an individual's abilities on real-world tasks. Real-world tasks include tasks that one would perform on the job, at home, in the community, and in recreation and leisure settings, the typical settings to which students transition from school. Students tend to be more motivated to demonstrate their abilities when performing authentic tasks (Wiggins, 1993), which provide much better assessment data.

Multiple measures for determining student abilities and progress toward goals has been described as best practice in transition assessment (Thoma & Held, 2002). Table 8.5 outlines examples of various performance-based assessment strategies.

Teachers Analyzing Their Instruction Plan   The teacher must be continuously mindful of what he or she is doing with the student during instruction, whether instruction takes place in the classroom or in the community. Too many teachers continue an instruction plan for weeks or even months at a time without reviewing the progress that is being made. The teacher must analyze the effectiveness of the training strategy and whether the skill sequence has been individualized sufficiently to match the individual's abilities.

What information can teachers collect to make decisions about instruction? Anecdotal records, rubrics, classroom tests, performance assessment, and curriculum-based measures all provide useful, although different, information for teachers to use in planning instruction. Hughes and Carter (2002) provided a model for making decisions about conducting informal transition assessment that could also include decisions about instructional planning. Hughes and Carter pointed out that "assessment is not an end in itself. Instead, the most important function of assessment is to gather information that will inform and guide instruction, planning, and the provision of supports" (2002, p. 63). They developed an Informal Assessment Model that can guide special educators in choosing assessments that provides information to make decisions. Table 8.6 outlines the Informal Assessment Model.

Anecdotal records "are simple narrative records of what we see and hear as we observe students" (Peterson & Hittie, 2003, p. 242). Such records can provide detailed information about the accomplishments of an individual student or a group of students in a specific lesson or unit. The strength of anecdotal reports is their ability to provide indepth information that was not predicted.

Rubrics are detailed "checklists of specific skills or behaviors" (Peterson & Hittie, 2003, p. 242). Rubrics provide detailed information of expectations and the ability of a student to meet that predetermined criteria.

Classroom tests are paper and pencil assessments that yield information about what a student learned from a particular lesson. They provide information about knowledge, but not about performance.

Performance assessments provide information about what a student or group of students can do. They are particularly helpful for determining students' abilities to apply what they learned in real world settings.

Curriculum-based measures are assessments that measure student progress on specific curricula. They are developed to measure whether students learned what was taught.

Table 8.5. Alternative assessment strategies that work

Strategy	Definition	Example
Portfolios	Collections of formal and informal information about student achievement containing samples of student work in one or more areas. All of the other types of assessment strategies could be included in a portfolio.	Daniel's completed portfolio was used to demonstrate his ability to meet his dreams for a job in the community, living in his own apartment, and being relatively independent in recreation and leisure activities. The works that he collected were chosen to best demonstrate his independence, productivity, and potential.
Demonstrations of mastery	Formal, more or less public performances of student competence or skill that provide opportunities for culminating assessments. These may be tangible products, experimental conclusions, or solutions to practical problems.	Daniel's ability to change oil in a car was assessed by the owner of a local automotive repair shop at the end of his on-the-job training program.
Performance tasks	Tasks, problems, or questions that require students to construct rather than select their own responses	Daniel's long-term dream includes living in his own apartment with minimal supports. The local agency that provides such support requires that adults first live in group homes that provide 24-hour coverage and demonstrate mastery of specific goals. Instead, Daniel's performance in those areas (responding to emergencies, cooking simple meals, and handling finances) was part of his annual assessment process.
Profiles	Ratings, descriptions, and summary judgments produced by teachers, students, parents, and others to give a broad view of student achievement	Daniel's profile focused on all areas of his adult life: his ability to work with cars, live in the community, and take the bus to and from work; his hobbies and recreation interests; and his relationships with others.
Projects	Original, often specialized inquiries devised and undertaken by a student or group of students	Projects for Daniel focused on his desire to live in his own apartment. His project involved collecting the information necessary to determine how this could become a reality for him. His research involved examining the social climate of various apartment complexes; the costs associated with living there (rent, membership fees, utilities); the amenities available; and the proximity to work, recreation, shopping, family, and friends. He also learned how to examine an apartment for problems (insect infestation, rusty plumbing, and structural problems).
Assessment of discourse	An evaluation of what students say. Through language, students indicate their learning by offering evidence of critical thinking or problem solving.	Daniel had a difficult time expressing himself in writing but had no problem telling others what he knew. Instead of taking a written history examination at the end of the semester, he verbally answered a series of questions supplied by his teacher and other students.

From Sax, C., & Thoma, C. (2002). *Transition assessment: Wise practices for quality lives* (p. 84). Baltimore: Paul H. Brookes Publishing Co.; reprinted by permission.

Table 8.6.   Steps of the Informal Assessment Model

1. Determine the purpose of assessment.

2. Identify relevant behaviors and environments.

3. Verify Steps 1 and 2 based on input from student and others.

4. Choose appropriate assessment procedures.

5. Modify procedures as needed.

6. Conduct the assessment.

7. Use assessment findings to identify additional student goals and objectives.

8. Develop curricular plans to achieve goals.

From Hughes, C., and Carter, E. (2002). Informal assessment procedures. In C.L. Sax and C.A. Thoma (Eds.), *Transition assessment: Wise practices for quality lives* (p. 55). Baltimore: Paul H. Brookes Publishing Co; adapted by permission.

AUGMENTING THE CURRICULUM

For some students with disabilities, access to the general curriculum involves more than changing its format, methods of delivery, and engagement. Students may also need augmentation, or instruction in skills that help them succeed. As Wehmeyer (2002a) described, ". . . augmentations do not change the curriculum, but rather, add to or augment the curriculum to provide students with strategies for success" (p. 53). Skills that make up the core component skills of self-determination are necessary augmentations for transition success. In fact, students with high self-determination scores, as measured by The Arc's self-determination scale (Wehmeyer & Kelchner, 1995a), had better adult outcomes than students with low self-determination scores. For example, in the area of employment, they were more likely to be employed and earn higher wages than students with low self-determination scores. In the area of community living, students with high self-determination skills were more likely to live in settings of their choice as opposed to waiting for a place to live and community support services. In the area of postsecondary education, individuals with high self-determination skills were more likely to enter and remain in college. See Chapter 2 for more information about teaching self-determination skills to students with disabilities.

Other augmentations to the general curriculum include teaching students with disabilities how to learn. These educational and learning strategies have been effective in improving the educational success of students with learning disabilities and are beginning to be taught to students with other disabilities as well.

Teaching Adaptive Skills

Many students with disabilities not only need to be taught academic skills, but they also need to learn adaptive skills to help them be more successful in meeting their transition outcomes. This is especially true when students have either emotional/behavior challenges or intellectual disabilities. Students with emotional/behavior challenges obviously need to learn adaptive strategies such as stress management, assertive communication, and/or problem solving. Students with intellectual disabilities by definition have support needs in both academic and adaptive skill areas. They often need a combination of communication, daily living, social interaction, and mobility skill development in addition to a focus on learning academics.

At the beginning of the chapter, we made a distinction between formal and informal curricula. *Informal curriculum* refers to what students learn by interacting with others outside the academic classrooms, including participating in after-school activities; in the lunch room; and during activities such as art, music, physical education, home economics, technical education, and career education. It is important that students with disabilities have access to the informal curriculum so that they can learn social skills, self-advocacy skills, and other such functional skills that will prepare them for life after high school. However, unlike many students without disabilities, it is not likely that they will learn the skills simply by being present in those aspects of the general education curriculum. They often will need to be explicitly taught many of those skills.

There is no dispute that successful adults are those who have good social skills. This is true for individuals with disabilities as well as individuals without disabilities. Students with disabilities have social skill needs that range from behavior control issues to basic communication skill needs to self-determination/self-advocacy skills. These skills can be taught in the general education classrooms, especially those that use cooperative learning strategies in resource rooms or through gaining access to the informal curriculum of after-school activities, lunchroom interactions, and/or special classes such as art, music, theatre, home economics, or technology education.

The use of peers to help teach social skills has been described as an effective strategy (Dopp & Block, 2004). Peers can play an important role in enhancing the learning environment, providing an opportunity for students with and without disabilities learn from each other. This can be a formalized relationship such as the peer buddy model or cross-age buddies and tutors (Girard & Willing, 1996; Sapon-Shevin, 1999). It could also be a more informal arrangements such as Circles of Support (Peterson, Tamor, Feen, & Silagy, 2002) or inviting peers to participate in person-centered planning meetings (Falvey, Forest, Pearpoint, & Rosenberg, 1998).

Selecting Transition Objectives

Many transition objectives can be developed as the student and family draw up a plan for the student's desired future direction. Transition planning involves more than a focus on transition from school to employment, so transition objectives should address the student's long-term goals in all life domains. These objectives can and should intersect with real-life daily environments. For example, Cronin and Patton (1993) provided examples of how 48 target life skills can be infused into daily curricula (see Table 8.7). These activities illustrate how a curriculum can be practical, yet still emphasize selected academic skills such as reading and writing.

The development and use of social skills is also a critical area of competence for transition-age students. Brown and colleagues (1989) developed a series of social relationship objectives to be used in neighborhood high schools (see Table 8.8).

Postsecondary education may be an option for students with milder cognitive disabilities. If a student is considering community college after graduation, then skills required for college entrance must be incorporated into the transition IEP objectives.

Table 8.7. Integrating life skills into the curriculum

Subject	Employment/ education	Home and family	Leisure pursuits	Community involvement	Emotional/ physical health	Personal responsibility/ relationships
Reading	Reading classified ads for jobs	Interpreting bills	Locating and understanding movie information in a newspaper	Following directions on tax forms	Comprehending directions on medication	Reading letters from friends
Writing	Writing a letter of application for a job	Writing checks	Writing for information on a city to visit	Filling in a voter registration form	Filling in medical history on forms	Sending thank-you notes
Listening	Understanding oral directions for a procedure change	Comprehending oral directions about making dinner	Listening for forecast to plan outdoor activity	Understanding campaign ads	Attending lectures on stress	Taking turns in a conversation
Speaking	Asking boss for a raise	Discussing morning routines with family	Inquiring about tickets for a concert	Stating opinion at the school board meeting	Describing symptoms to a doctor	Giving feedback to a friend about the purchase of a compact disc
Math applications	Understanding difference between net and gross pay	Computing the cost of doing laundry in a laundromat versus at home	Calculating the cost of a dinner out versus eating at home	Obtaining information for a building permit	Using a thermometer	Planning the costs of a date
Problem solving	Settling a dispute with a co-worker	Deciding how much to budget for rent	Role-playing appropriate behaviors for various places	Knowing what to do if victim of fraud	Selecting a doctor	Deciding how to ask someone for a date
Survival skills	Using a prepared career planning packet	Listing emergency phone numbers	Using a shopping center directory	Marking a calendar for important dates (e.g., recycling, garbage collection)	Using a system to remember to take vitamins	Developing a system to remember birthdays
Personal/ social	Applying appropriate interview skills	Helping a child with homework	Knowing the rules of a neighborhood pool	Locating self-improvement classes	Getting a yearly physical exam	Discussing how to negotiate a price at a flea market

From Cronin, M., Patton, J.R., & Wood, S.J. (2007). *Life skills instruction: A practical guide for integrating real-life content into the curriculum at the elementary and secondary levels for students with special needs or who are placed at risk, 2e.* Austin, TX: PRO-ED; reprinted by permission.

ALTERNATIVES TO THE GENERAL CURRICULUM

Although the majority of students with disabilities will receive instruction that is based on the general education curriculum, there are a small number whose support needs and transition outcomes require an alternative approach. In addition, students who receive their education past the age of 18 often need an alternative to the traditional

Table 8.8.   Social relationships that can develop between students with and without disabilities

Social relationship	Example
Peer tutor	Leigh role-plays social introductions with Margo, providing feedback and praise for Margo's performance.
Eating companion	Jennifer and Rick eat lunch with Linda in the cafeteria and talk about their favorite music groups.
Art, home economics, industrial arts, music, or physical education companion	In art class, students were instructed to paint a sunset. Tom sat next to Dan and offered suggestions and guidance about the best colors to use and how to complete the task.
General class companion	A fifth-grade class is doing a "Know Our Town" lesson in social studies. Ben helps Karen plan a trip through their neighborhood.
During-school companion	After lunch and before the bell for class rang, Molly and Phyllis went to the student lounge for a soda.
Friend	David, a member of a varsity basketball team, invites Ralph, a student with severe disabilities, to his house to watch a game on TV.
Extracurricular companion	Sarah and Winona prepare their articles for the school newspaper together and then work on the layout in the journalism lab.
After-school project companion	The sophomore class decided to build a float for a homecoming parade. Joan worked on it with Maria, a nondisabled companion, after school and on weekends in Joan's garage.
After-school companion	On Saturday afternoon, Mike, who is not disabled, and Bill go to the shopping mall.
Travel companion	David walks with Ralph when he wheels from last-period class to the gym, where Ralph helps the basketball team as a student manager.
Neighbor	Parents of nondisabled students in the neighborhood regularly exchange greetings with Mary when they are at school, around the neighborhood, at local stores, at the mall, and at the grocery store.

From Brown et al. (1989). The home school: Why students with severe intellectual disabilities must attend the schools of their brothers, sisters, friends, and neighbors. *Journal of The Association for Persons with Severe Handicaps, 14,* 4; reprinted by permission.

academic curriculum, focusing their educational goals on work and/or community living outcomes.

Held, Thoma, and Thomas (2004) described how self-determination was woven into the daily experiences of one student with disabilities. This model is an example of an alternative to the general education curriculum—designing an individualized curriculum for a student with autism who wanted to play drums, find a job, learn more about his disability, and live on his own. To make this a reality for him and for the other students with disabilities in her class, his teacher, Ms. Thomas, changed her classroom-based instruction to a classroom without walls. The students met with her in the morning at the local library where they went over their goals for the week and the day. Ms. Thomas coordinated with teaching assistants and community agency staff personnel to meet the needs of the students in various settings, including job sites, the library, the YMCA, and students' homes. Where students were, and for how long, depended on the goals they needed to meet. Students learned to monitor their own progress and demonstrate their progress to others through videotapes, pictures, work samples, and more traditional data. Other examples of these community-based programs for students with disabilities in the 18–21 age range are described in Gaumer, Morningstar, and Clark (2004).

Creativity in instructional design and assessment are the keys to individualizing curriculum and making it work for students with disabilities. It is important to do more than create experiences for students. Instead, teachers must create experiences that lead students toward their goals for an adult lifestyle and to inclusive outcomes in employment, community living, and recreation and leisure. Brown, Nietupski, and Hamre-Nietupski (1976) outlined a set of principles to help determine and select more appropriate goals for students with disabilities. These principles apply today when discussing an alternative curriculum for students with significant support needs.

Criterion of Ultimate Functioning

Brown et al. (1976) outlined the criterion of ultimate functioning that urged teachers to consider instructional goals that focused on important life skills, including brushing teeth, getting around, communicating, and dressing oneself. Most important, Brown et al. urged teachers to focus on teaching skills that would have the greatest likelihood of improving a student's life at home, in school, or in the community.

Quality of Life Criterion

Pierangelo and Giuliani (2004) urged that teachers consider the quality of life when choosing alternative goals. Teachers should choose goals that help individuals with disabilities make choices for themselves, promote their self-determination, and otherwise allow them to participate meaningfully in the social mainstream. Goals are chosen both objectively and subjectively. Objective choices are those skills that most people agree improve their quality of life, including social interaction skills, communication skills, and the ability to travel in one's own community. Subjective choices are those things that an individual values that others may not. For instance, one student may want to learn to play a musical instrument, and another student may want to learn to take a bus to watch a basketball game.

What Resources Should Teachers Use for Curriculum Development?

After an initial transition IEP is designed, the teacher should obtain direct input from the student and family, members of the community, and others who are interested and concerned about this student's future. The teacher's primary responsibility is to teach those skills that the student will need for a successful future. This does not mean that the teacher purchases a variety of curricula and then teaches all the skills on those curricula, hoping to teach something that the student may be able to use. On the contrary, this "shotgun" approach should be abandoned for a targeted approach that identifies the most essential skills for independence in adulthood. This process is more time-consuming and requires greater thought than simple identification of objectives from a set curriculum or checklist. The teacher must have the intelligence, creativity, and, above all, diligence to work closely with the family in narrowing down those skills that are most necessary and realistic. The strategy for developing a functional curriculum based on the general education curriculum involves identifying and prioritizing key activities. Table 8.9 describes these points and should be followed by teachers who are designing transition programs.

CARMEN

Carmen is a 16-year-old Hispanic student with an IQ score of 56 as measured by the Stanford-Binet Intelligence Scale. Assessment of adaptive behavior skills finds that she has deficits in the areas of social skills, community living, using transportation, and safety as measured by the Adaptive Behavior Assessment System II (Harrison & Oakland, 2003). Her eyesight, hearing, and fine motor skills are unimpaired. Carmen communicates verbally, although she stutters when she is nervous. She takes classes at her neighborhood high school and is included in general education classes for social studies, English, and science. She has difficulty learning math and takes that class in a resource room setting.

Behaviorally, Carmen's teachers described her as "single-minded" and say, "If she wants to do something, she will do it." Her teachers also report that Carmen has few friends, choosing to seek out teachers or other school personnel with whom to talk. Carmen often is teased by other students, particularly for being a "teacher's pet." She will often tell other students what they should be doing, or she simply ignores them. However, she does tell teachers that she wishes she had a good friend and that she "hates it when the other kids pick on me." Carmen's mother reports that outside of school, they spend most of their time together and that Carmen only has one friend with whom she will do things such as go to a movie. Her outside interests include watching movies, cooking, and walking her dog. She is involved with a few afterschool activities, including having roles in the school plays. She

Table 8.9. Establishment of priority activities for instruction

Step	Activity
1	With the student and his or her family, evaluate the student's performance in each of the domain categories and identify desired future environments in which the student will function.
2	Identify activities and skills relevant to the student's current environment and skills necessary to function in projected future environments.
3	Review all relevant current and future activities and indicate those activities that occur in two or more domains and that are age-appropriate.
4	List these activities from most to least frequent in occurrence.
5	From this list, identify activities that are crucial for the student's safety. Next, identify activities critical for functioning independently in the desired future environments.
6	Select for immediate instruction • Activities essential to the student's safety within current environments • Activities that the student must perform frequently in order to function independently within his or her current and identified future environments
7	Select remaining objectives from the list of activities (see Step 4).

From Sowers, J.A. & Powers, L. (1991). *Vocational preparation and employment of students with physical and multiple disabilities* (pp. 30–31). Baltimore: Paul H. Brookes Publishing Co.; reprinted by permission.

PULLING IT ALL TOGETHER

How do teachers pull it all together? This section provides examples for two students, Carmen and Mike, whose IEPs are based on the general education curriculum and have elements of CBI where appropriate. This section provides the reader with instruction on developing unit and lesson plans, the cornerstones of good instruction whether classroom- or community-based, as well as information about making choices about diploma options.

Overall, this was an IEP for Carmen that included general education academic instruction as well as community-based employment instruction. Carmen's educational team found ways to adapt and augment the general education curriculum to design instruction that helped her meet her long range plans.

CBI is a very effective means of implementing a transition program. In fact, teaching for transition is not effective unless at least some instruction occurs in real community environments. Training away from the school takes more planning and time and can be more logistically difficult to implement. However, student interest is heightened, and skill selection is usually more functional.

How Are Units and Lesson Plans Designed?

After deciding what to teach and which resources to use, it is important to organize these components into teaching con-

was a member of a theatre group that went to local elementary schools to teach kids about disabilities. She enjoys both of those activities a great deal.

As for long-range plans, Carmen would like to go to college. She recognizes that everyone else in her family has gone to college, and she would like to do so as well. She would like to work with kids as a teaching assistant or as a child care worker. She would also like to have a job as an actress in movies or television, although she knows that not many people make that a successful career.

Because Carmen wants to go to college after high school, it is important that she be able to finish her high school years and earn a standard high school diploma. To do this, the team decided that she would be included in general education classes for all her academic work. It was believed that she could be included in her remaining English and social studies classes without additional accommodations. However, a laptop computer was identified as an AT device to help her with those classes. The laptop would provide her with an opportunity to do her work electronically and use the spell-check and grammar-check features. It would also provide her with an opportunity to listen to books electronically, using the voice output feature of the laptop.

Carmen would need additional adaptations in the final math class that she needs to meet her graduation requirements. In this class, the special educator and general education teacher worked together to coordinate these adaptations, including adaptations to testing. Carmen was given additional time for tests, as well as having her test read to her. For notetaking in class, Carmen worked

Table 8.10. Examples of units arranged chronologically and conceptually

Chronological arrangement	Conceptual arrangement
American History I	*Settlement of North America*
1. Exploration of North America	1. Exploration of North America
2. Early Settlement of North America	2. Early Settlement of North America
3. Europe and the New World	3. Westward Expansion of North America
4. British Dominance of Eastern North America	*Colonial Society*
5. Colonial Life	4. Colonial life
6. Relationship between Colonies and Great Britain	5. Foundations of American Government
7. American Revolution	*Issues in Colonial North America*
8. Foundations of American Government	6. Europe and the New World
9. Westward Expansion of North America	7. British Dominance of Eastern North America
	8. Relationship of Colonies to Great Britain
	9. American Revolution

From Posner et al. Course Design: A Guide to Curriculum Development for Teachers, 5e. Published by Allyn & Bacon, Boston, MA. Copyright © 1996 by Pearson Education. Reprinted by permission of the publisher.

cepts. Teachers use lesson units and lesson plans to organize important information.

Developing Lesson Units Units are chunks of related instructional material that can be placed into larger groups. (Units and groups are taken from IEP objectives.) They may be arranged chronologically or conceptually depending on what the learner needs to know (Posner & Rudnitsky, 1997). For example, Table 8.10 shows an example of American history being organized in both ways. If the student is expected to know specific events in history and when they occurred, then the chronological sequence would be best. However, if major themes in history is the goal of learning, then the conceptual design would be beneficial (Posner & Rudnitsky, 1997). Notice that in the second example, events are out of order so that they may be categorized into historical themes.

The use of chronological versus conceptual units is also relevant for teachers who are planning instruction for students with mild cognitive disabilities. For example, if students are learning how to get a job, then instructional units would probably be arranged chronologically (e.g., looking for a job, writing a résumé, filling out an application, interviewing, following up).

However, groups of math units may be arranged conceptually (e.g., measuring, whole numbers, decimals, sets of whole numbers). Table 8.11 shows a visual display of math units that may be used by teachers of students with mild

with another student who would
take notes and e-mail her
copies. During the school year,
that general education teacher
learned to use a SmartBoard
that allowed her to record the
steps of a mathematical compu-
tation and save that to a file for
the students in class. This UDL
approach helped both Carmen
and all other students in the
class. Once this was put in
place, the notetaker was not
necessary.

Carmen's teacher arranged
for her to work in the afternoon
at a community child care center
that was nearby to help Carmen
decide whether working with
kids was what she really wanted
to do. An employment specialist
was assigned to teach on-the-
job skills for the semester, which
provided Carmen with an opportunity to learn about the
specifics of a job working in a
child care center, as well as
more general information about
the joys and challenges of work
in this field. At the end of the semester, Carmen would make a
decision about where else she
might want to work or whether
she wanted to continue where
she was.

Carmen used the self-determined learning model of instruction to solve the problem:
What are jobs where I could
work with kids? By using her
laptop to search on the Internet,
interviewing her employer at the
child care center, using career
exploration software, contacting
a community college admissions officer, and talking with a
hospital employment office, she
worked with her teacher to
identify possible postsecondary
educational opportunities to become a certified child development associate. Carmen and
her teacher planned for other
work experiences for the coming year while also keeping her

Table 8.11. Units organized into groups of math concepts

Unit	Concept
Measurement	Time
	Linear measurement
	Area
Fractions	Part–whole relationship
	Rational numbers
	Models for fractions
Whole numbers	Addition
	Subtraction
	Multiplication
	Division
Problem solving	Word problems
	Subject area problems

cognitive disabilities. (For an in-depth look at curriculum development, see Posner and Rudnitsky, 1997.)

Writing Lesson Plans   Lesson plans provide a daily detailed map of exactly how skills from each unit will be taught.
Individual school districts have different approaches to lesson
plan formats. The lesson plan shown in Figure 8.5 includes
1) the goal/objective, 2) task analysis, 3) the set, or how the
lesson will be introduced, 4) instruction, 5) supervised practice, 6) independent practice, 7) closure and summarization,
8) resources and materials, 9) lesson evaluation, 10) reteaching procedures/modifications if lesson objectives are not met,
and 11) option (if time is left at the end of the lesson, how the
teacher will fill it).

Knowing what and where to teach are the first steps of
teaching students with disabilities. However, the next step involves the use of specific teaching instructional methods.
After objectives have been decided (i.e., what to teach)
and documented on the transition IEP, a common question
asked by secondary educators working with students with
more pervasive academic support needs is, "What do I do
next?" The purpose of this section is to provide teachers with
a blueprint for teaching students with disabilities, and it describes procedures that teachers must understand and consider when implementing systematic instruction programs in
community-based settings and classrooms. It has been widely
documented that students with mild cognitive disabilities, as
well as those with more challenging learning problems such
as mental retardation, require more precise and intense systematic instructional techniques (Gable & Warren, 1993;
Kameenui & Darch, 1995). Specific instructional techniques

I.   Identifiers
        Name: Mrs. Hendricks
        Lesson Name: Looking for jobs in the classified ads
        Age/Grade Level: Tenth grade
        Date: October 1, 2004
        Estimated Length: 40 minutes
        Unit/Subject: Getting a Job/Vocational Exploration

II.   Goal/Objective
        The student will learn how to find appropriate job listings in the newspaper. Using the news-
        paper as a resource, the student will identify five potential jobs for which he or she could
        inquire.

III.   Task Analysis (What prerequisite skills must the student have to be successful in this lesson?)
        The student must know how to locate the classified section of the paper, read, write, and
        have some fine motor dexterity.

IV.   Set (How will the teacher introduce the lesson to make it meaningful to students?)
        The teacher will lead students in a discussion of jobs they think would be fun to work in and
        ways they can think of to find out about those jobs. The teacher will explain that the classi-
        fieds are frequently used to find out about job openings.

V.   Instruction (What is the process for teaching this lesson?)
        1. The teacher begins with a concept diagram and student handouts that outline all of the
           component parts of a classified job advertisement.
        2. The teacher models a procedure for finding the job of receptionist in the classifieds.
        3. Students find ads for the job of cashier in their individual copies of classified ads with the
           assistance of the teacher.
        4. Students find the job of telemarketer without the assistance of the teacher (or with least
           intrusive prompts).
        5. The teacher instructs students to list their interests and any job experience they may have
           on a piece of notebook paper.
        6. Through class discussion of each student's interests and experience, students identify five
           jobs that they could search for in the classified ads.
        7. Students use classified sections of the newspaper and circle five potential job ads.
        8. Students copy down the name of the job, phone number or address, and contact person's
           name.

VI.   Supervised Practice (How will the students practice skills with direct teacher supervision?)
        Students will practice the skills in Steps 5–8 of instruction.

VII.   Independent Practice (How will students practice skills without direct teacher supervision?)
        Students will repeat the activities in Steps 5–8 and the closure activity without teacher
        guidance (only if necessary).

VIII.   Closure (How will the teacher review and summarize the lesson?)
        Students will break up into pairs and give their partner a job to find. Students will list the
        name/location of the job, contact person, and address of as many examples of the job that
        they can find.

Figure 8.5.   Sample lesson plan.

(continued)

Figure 8.5. (*continued*)

IX.   Resources/Materials

      Concept diagram worksheets, classified ads, notebook, paper, pencils

X.   Lesson Evaluation (How will the teacher determine if the lesson's objectives were met?)
      The teacher will use CBA by observing and documenting students' performance as they work
      in pairs finding specific jobs in the paper.

XI.   Reteaching Procedures/Modifications (What can be done if lesson objectives are not met?
      OR What modifications are needed for this lesson?)
      A student with cerebral palsy can not use her arms and hands for looking through the paper
      and writing. She will be paired with a student who can turn the pages of the paper for her.
      She will orally report her findings to her partner and the teacher.

XII. Option (What will the teacher do if he or she has 5–10 minutes left at the end of the lesson?)
      Students will play a game of finding the ad the fastest. The teacher will call out the name
      of a job, and students working in pairs will see which team can find the ad the fastest.

---

options open to pursue a community-college education after high school. The teacher was investigating a recreation program in theatre or dance that would provide an opportunity for Carmen to combine her love for working with kids with her interest in performance arts for the next work experience.

Carmen reported that she wanted to live at home with her mother after high school, at least until she finished college. She did require additional instruction in cooking and home management, so her schedule included a home economics class. Carmen's mother was particularly concerned about her safety in the kitchen. The team chose a home economics class that stressed safety, so it was a good fit for Carmen's long-range plan.

Augmenting the general curriculum was necessary to help Carmen make more friends. Carmen participated in an after-school program designed for high school age Hispanic women who were interested in going to college. This program was developed as a support

aimed at students who require more significant supports increase the probability that students will acquire and generalize needed skills.

Diploma Options

Students whose future plans include postsecondary education must meet minimum entrance requirements; these college entrance requirements must be considered when planning ITP goals and objectives. Community college requirements are generally less stringent than the requirements for 4-year universities. For example, one community college requires that students have a high school diploma, occupational diploma, or a GED. Graduates of the program receive an associate's degree, which allows them to transfer to a senior college or university or go to work in a technically oriented field (e.g., automotive mechanics technology, cosmetology, cabinetmaking).

Diploma with Regular Academic Endorsement This type of diploma typically requires students to pass core classes such as math (at least to the level of geometry), science (at least to biology), social studies, and English.

Occupational Diploma Students may receive an occupational endorsement after completing courses in functional curricula. For example, instead of taking algebra, a student would take a math class that teaches practical application of math skills (e.g., how to balance a checkbook, how to count

group for young women to work together and support each other as they made decisions about their lives after high school. It was recommended for Carmen as a way to not only learn about college, but also to learn to speak up for herself in group settings while fostering friendships with others (with and without disabilities) who are preparing for college. Carmen worked with her teacher to identify her learning goals for those meetings, and to develop a plan for increasing her self-determination and socialization skills.

MIKE

Mike is a tenth-grade student who was diagnosed with a learning disability when he was in third grade. He experiences difficulty in reading. Mike goes to a resource room to receive reading, social, and vocational skills training. His special education teacher helps him with his English, math, and social studies using the strategies outlined in this chapter.

Like many other students with learning disabilities, Mike doesn't have many friends and has poor self-esteem. (He was even caught for shoplifting because he was trying to make friends with people from "the wrong crowd.") Currently, he is not involved in any extracurricular activities, but he enjoys playing the guitar. He indicated at the transition IEP meeting that he would like to go to community college after graduation and study music. His parents support his goal of college and would also like for him to improve his self-esteem and social skills.

change after purchasing an item). Other classes typically include life skills, employment training, and career preparation.

Diploma with Advanced Academic Endorsement Students receiving this endorsement are usually required to have coursework in more advanced areas such as upper-level algebra, trigonometry, chemistry, and several years of foreign language.

CONCLUSION

This chapter has provided an overview of what to teach, where to teach, and how to teach students in transition from high school to adult life. Transition planning and implementation consist of far more than instructional plan development and transition instruction because competence in transition skills is necessary for entry into the workplace, independent living, and the community. A number of books and resources delve into this in greater detail (Gore, 2004; Moon, Inge, Wehman, Brooke, & Barcus, 1990; Schloss & Smith, 1998).

The teacher is the "point" person for leading the instruction. All other instructional personnel and transition team members look to the teacher for leadership in the area of critical transition skills. If the teacher is unable to identify the appropriate skills for entry into adulthood, then the student never acquires the appropriate skills for adult competence. Still worse, a number of students with mild disabilities become so disillusioned, disappointed, and bored with school that they drop out. Once these students drop out, they embark on a path of underemployment or no employment. They become potential offenders in the criminal justice system and often end up out of the mainstream of society and community networks.

If the teacher chooses to provide instruction exclusively in the school and the classroom, then there is far greater likelihood that nonfunctional skills or activities will be presented, and the likelihood of high dropout rates and ineffective instruction increases. Teachers who do not understand the most effective instructional practices are unable to equip their students with necessary skills. Therefore, teachers must be aware of the variety of teaching techniques that are reported in the professional literature. Transition instruction must be powerful and precise for students with the most challenging learning and behavior problems; however, all teachers who are working with any students with disabilities must be cognizant of different ways to individualize instruction and be as effective as they can.

With the help of his teacher, Mike found a job at a local family-run music store where he works 4 days per week after school. He is responsible for stringing guitars, ordering items from the catalog, light cleaning such as dusting the merchandise and vacuuming, working the cash register, and referring interested customers to music lessons. Mike and his teacher report that he enjoys working at this store. Currently, his teacher is using a whole task chaining strategy to teach Mike how complete merchandise return procedures.

His general education teachers use direct instruction techniques in the classroom and provide concept diagrams in his math and science classes. His special education teacher uses general case programming to teach him tasks at work. Mike uses the money he earns from work to take group guitar lessons. Mike has shown an increased interest in music and practices his guitar after class with a couple of other students his age. His special education teacher reports that his grades are improving and that he is on course for a diploma with an academic endorsement.

STUDY QUESTIONS

1. What should be the key criterion for selecting transition objectives for students with disabilities?

2. What are the steps for assuring access to the general education curriculum for students with disabilities?

3. What are some ways in which social skills and relationships can be fostered at school?

4. What is CBI, and why is it valuable for students with disabilities?

5. What are some key considerations in establishing and using community-based work experience sites?

6. What are common problems encountered with community-based work programs, and how can those problems be addressed proactively?

7. What are task analysis and chaining?

8. What are the components of general case programming?

9. What is meant by using alternative assessment procedures?

9

Assistive Technology
from School to Adulthood

AMY J. ARMSTRONG AND PAUL WEHMAN

AFTER COMPLETING THIS CHAPTER, THE READER WILL BE ABLE TO

○ Understand the impact assistive technology (AT) may have on the quality of life of individuals with disabilities

○ Identify the role of consumers and considerations when selecting and procuring AT devices and services

○ Explain the benefits of a team-oriented approach to working with individuals who may profit from the use of AT

○ Describe the strategies and/or considerations that may alleviate the risk of technology abandonment

○ Recognize the holistic nature of the use of AT regarding application within multiple life settings and environments

RICK

Rick, who is 22 years old and has experienced multiple sclerosis for 7 years, uses AT daily to perform basic tasks that many individuals may take for granted. He uses a wheelchair due to progressive muscle weakness. He wears a brace on his right hand and wrist for support. Visual aid devices support him to perform his job.

Rick believes that *everyone* uses AT, whether or not they experience a disability. He believes in the concept of universal design—creating access to equipment, buildings, and experiences from which people can benefit. Examples of AT include items such as kitchen amenities that make it easier to prepare food, a television remote that makes it easier to become a couch potato, and a computer that makes it easier to do a job. In Rick's mind, although use of technology by all *is* a matter of convenience, there is a *difference* of convenience. Rick would not be able to work as productively as he does without technology. In addition, without technology, Rick may not be able to work at all because technology empowers him.

IMPACT OF ASSISTIVE TECHNOLOGY ON QUALITY OF LIFE

What may be convenience for many is essential for others. With a television remote control, one can change channels without getting up from the lounge chair. Most people that do not have a disability could get up, walk across the room, and change the channel. It is inconvenient, but possible. An environmental control unit is a small technological advance from the television remote control. This unit, however, allows a person with limited use of the extremities to control the television, lights, temperature, computer, or photocopier.

The absence of technology to the individual without a disability becomes a nuisance that affects *perceived* quality of life. The absence of technology to an individual with a disability is a blow to one's quality of life that can increase dependence. Thus, the acquisition of appropriate AT by a person with a disability increases independence, inclusion, employability, and often access to environments such as college classrooms (Roberts & Stodden, 2005).

The convenience distinction is apparent when speaking of AT and individuals with disabilities (users). It is *not* convenience in the sense of comforts and amenities but convenience in the sense of freedom and accessibility. AT, although perhaps not completely leveling the playing field for many users, does close the gap by increasing quality of life possibilities. Users typically experience greater physical accessibility and accessibility to integrated employment (Morgan, 2003; Morgan & Ellerd, 2005) as well as enhancement of their social skills (Simpson, Langone, & Ayres, 2004).

AT is used in all aspects of an individual's life—home, school, work, social, and recreational. The availability of AT in all aspects of living influences the success of the individual and should not be seen as being a stigma (Parette & Scherer, 2004). Technology can be extremely empowering in all aspects of life. For example, adaptive driving equipment on a van can make transportation to the workplace possible. Mobility equipment, such as a power scooter, can make employment a reality. Devices that assist in daily living skills such as food preparation and hygiene impact independent living. Using these devices to maximize independent living is a necessary first step to community inclusion and employability. With this interdependence acknowledged, this chapter focuses on AT from the user's perspective in the arena of employment. AT most often refers to low and high technology devices and related services that support an individual with a disability, thereby increasing independence.

The promise of technology has never been greater, and its impact will be enormous. The challenge is not only to harness the promise of technology, but also to anticipate the advances in technology that will create new opportunities to develop and adapt devices to guide and direct individuals with disabilities through their daily activities. Medical technology will allow individuals to live longer. Internet technology will make information readily and quickly available. Internet-based distance learning will make training and education available for everyone, anywhere, at any time, and at low cost.

Advances in technology offer great promise, but also concerns. As the Internet is increasingly viewed as the repository of information, lacking access to it may increase isolation for some individuals. It is extremely important to monitor advances in technology that are integrated into daily American life and how they are adapted for individuals with disabilities. Everyone who works to support people with disabilities and their families must remain sensitive to technology gaps and avoid presumptions about ready access to technological advances. Among the emerging issues related to advances in technology are

- Greater access to technology increases expectations of universal access for everyone and threatens to isolate those without access or the capacity to use it.

- Increased use of database technology threatens many people's sense of personal privacy.

- The expanding capability of genetic engineering may shift the traditional focus from support to prevention of intellectual and developmental disabilities.

- The ability to adopt and finance new opportunities to use technology may come slowly to relatively low-tech social services and education programs.

- Advances in medical technology will raise questions about the standards for their application with people with intellectual and developmental disabilities and the relative value of human lives.

- As a relatively "small market," developing and adapting technology for the needs of people with intellectual and developmental disabilities may need more than just the incentives of the "marketplace."

EMPLOYMENT AND ASSISTIVE TECHNOLOGY

Often, for an individual with a disability, a primary barrier to becoming and staying employed is access to, and availability of, AT. Such technology strives to level the playing field in terms of integration and production at the worksite (Carey, Potts, Bryen, & Shankar, 2004). Identifying appropriate physical or social solutions (Carey et al., 2004) is paramount and may include raising a desk or table for a worker with a power wheelchair; changing auditory signals such as a fire alarm to a visual cue of a flashing light or a tactual cue of a vibration; adjusting the slant of a computer keyboard, adding a guiding mechanism onto the paper tray of a copier or Braille next to the copier buttons, or adding a keyboard guide; providing a grounded desktop stamper with a lever for dating invoices received; jigs used for counting items, or a carrying unit for supplies; using existing equipment such as a head pointer to type or a writing splint; lap board to carry supplies; print magnification devices; a TDD; or a shoulder telephone rest.

Prior to seeking employment, the individual with a disability and professionals working with him/her should have some concept of needed technology. That is, need(s) can be anticipated. Such anticipation is useful when looking at specific jobs and tasks or closely examining the educational requirements in a 2- or 4-year college classroom (Sharpe, Johnson, Izzo, & Murray, 2005). Sharpe and Murray used a structured interview approach in which 139 postsecondary graduates were asked to identify instructional accommodations and assistive technologies provided to them in secondary and postsecondary settings. Findings of this study showed that, generally, instructional accommodations and ATs are provided at much higher rates at the postsecondary level. With regard to users of AT, the majority of graduates indicated that they gained access to and learned to use the technology by themselves or with the help of family members. The user of AT must constantly represent his or her respective need(s) and suggestions for possible worksite solutions. To do this, it is helpful to become familiar with legislation, advocacy skills, technology options, and a team approach.

Computer and Assistive Technology Utilization

Computers have been touted as a "great equalizer" for competitive employment. They play an ever-increasing role in our daily lives for activities such as work, socialization, research, communication, and daily living activities. Appropriate computer accommodations for individuals with disabilities will allow for enhanced technical capacities for work and thus improve their ability to compete for gainful employment. The costs of appropriate computer accommodations range from very little to thousands of dollars, depending on individual needs and budget constraints; however the long-term benefit of such expenditures may be significant (Roberts & Stodden, 2005; Sharpe, Johnson, Izzo, & Murray, 2005).

The National Organization of Disability's Employability program reports that by year 2008, there will be 2–3 million more jobs than workers (Sandlund, 2001). At the same time, there are projected to be nearly 4 million unemployed potential workers within the disability community. In addition, today's employers are providing more accommodations to hire workers with disabilities. The U.S. Department of Labor reports that 13–19 million Americans now telecommute at some level in a wide array of positions such as typists, database management, sales, marketing, and accountants (West & Anderson, 2005). Many of these positions require some degree of computer utilization. Telecommuting may help reduce potential barriers such as inaccessible worksites, transportation, and need for personal care assistance by allowing individuals to work from their home.

Kruse, Krueger, and Drastal (1996) reviewed the role that technology plays in employment and suggested that computer training and utilization may be of benefit to individuals with spinal cord injury (SCI). Technology can lessen the impact of mobility limitations that are inherent to those with SCI. Kruse et al. found that 46% of individuals with SCI had used computers in some capacity, although only 22% had received computer training since their date of injury, significantly lower than in the non-SCI population (Sandlund, 2001). Recent statistics from the Disability Statistics Center suggest that this trend continues today. Findings showed that, when compared with individuals without disabilities (ages 15–64), fewer individuals with disabilities had a computer (56% versus 33%), had Internet access at home (34% versus 16%), or used the Internet (42% versus 15%; Kaye, 2000). It seems that although people with disabilities have the most to gain from new technologies and computer use, they have among the lowest utilization rates. As a result, the potential benefits of computers and the Internet to those within the disability community are a long way from being adequately realized.

For example, it is known that individuals with physical disabilities, such as spinal cord injury or severe cerebral palsy, are able to successfully engage in competitive employment if appropriate accommodations are provided (Inge, 2001), including both product-related and worksite modifications. Dowler, Batiste, and Whidden (1998) reported that nearly 75% of individuals required some type of accommodation to improve their productivity and that the utilization of effective AT supports is one of the challenges for successful employment. For people with physical disabilities, the term *jobsite enabling* is used to describe the process of bringing together AT and other factors such as specialized training, ongoing support, and advocacy in the workplace (Targett & Wehman, 2003). Jobsite enabling may involve the negotiation of job duties or requirements, environmental modification, the use of co-workers and personal assistants, or any combination of these and other factors. Therefore, it is important to note that, albeit important, AT is merely one of many factors involved in placing an individual in a work environment where he or she can become successfully employed.

AT provides individuals with physical disabilities with the ability to compensate for functional limitations. Special computer accommodations allow individuals with limited hand function to use a standard computer keyboard. Because there are a variety of adaptive solutions and different manufacturers of computer adaptations, the determination of appropriate accommodations is based on individual needs and should include a computer accommodation evaluation.

Computer accommodation evaluations can assist individuals with disabilities to gain access to computers for educational, vocational, and other activities of daily living needs. This evaluation process should be designed to identify effective adaptive technologies and software for full computer accessibility. Appropriate computer evaluation includes computer access capabilities, computer/hardware options, workstation evaluations, and school/office related tasks (e.g., page turning, faxing, copying). Vocational training and effective use of AT go hand in hand. Training increases a person's knowledge; however, AT gives people the opportunity to practically use that knowledge.

Hand dexterity is essential to fully operate a standard nonadapted computer. An individual with tetraplegia may find this task extremely difficult. Using appropriate AT can provide the adaptive alternative to the physical dexterity necessary for standard computer operations. People with physical, sensory, and/or cognitive impairments that affect their ability to utilize a computer within and across specific environments may benefit from a host of adaptive devices.

The potential costs of AT must also be taken into consideration. Coverage for such items may be available through insurance, federal or state employment programs, and/or from personal resources. Local, state, and federal government programs, along with private companies, may offer loans to subsidize the costs incurred by individuals. Still, these subsidies may not be available or may not be enough to establish the necessary accommodations.

ACQUIRING AND USING ASSISTIVE TECHNOLOGY

The Team Approach

In the past, if someone needed AT, a professional would spend a brief amount of time with the person, make a decision about what was needed ("assessment"), place an order, and finally drop a device off without training or follow-up. Sanctioned dependency instituted by professionals in the guise of protection, accepted by people with disabilities for lack of another option, is outdated and unacceptable. Individual choice and advocacy now empower this process.

In a team approach, the user of technology is the central driving force. He or she leads the process and his or her input and opinion determines the final solution. After all, it is the individual who will develop an intimate relationship with the device(s) chosen. If the solution does not work for the individual, then the device will most likely be abandoned.

Often, abandonment occurs when the user does not drive the team process. The individual may not know how to advocate for him- or herself because he or she has not had the opportunity or experience, or he or she may allow professionals to make the final determination. Allowing others to make critical decisions has often been a lifelong learned behavior. Professionals who cross the path of an individual who does not have the skills of self-advocacy must encourage and teach leadership skills. Wherever that person comes in contact or interacts with the educational, rehabilitation, and/or medical systems, those professionals must begin to educate the user on taking control of his or her own treatment and of getting his or her own AT. A person with a disability learning to take control of the technology process requires reciprocation. It is a combination of the professional teaching the user and the user teaching the professional. It is mutual mentoring, face-to-face, one-to-one.

The professional facilitates opportunities for decision making and assertive communication. Professional mentoring may include teaching the user how to

- Gather information
- Communicate effectively
- Make decisions based on data, preference, and need
- Navigate the system
- Choose a support network

In kind, the user may provide the professional

- Feedback on ability to teach self-advocacy skills
- Individualized insights on specific needs and preferences
- Local community contacts
- Opportunity for a truly team effort
- Opportunity for professional growth

If the individual has difficulty communicating or has a cognitive disability, then the role of the professional and/or advocate is especially critical.

CINDY

Cindy, an elementary school teacher with severe arthritis, identified a work task need and conducted her own research to prepare for determining an appropriate solution with her team. Cindy expressed an interest in using a computer to help her with her lesson plans and other written work. She is exploring all possibilities including modified computer keyboards, software that assists with simultaneous keystrokes, wrist supports, and voice recognition systems. With this information, she expects to obtain a complete computer evaluation before deciding which AT products work best for her. To help achieve her goal, she will chair the team, having identified her need and many possible solutions. Other team members include her physician, an occupational therapist, a computer consultant/evaluator, her employer, and a vendor.

Empowerment, Effectiveness, and Efficiency

Empowerment, effectiveness, and efficiency highlight a team approach. Individuals from a variety of backgrounds and experiences come together to assist the individual in evaluating and identifying the most useful solution. Team members vary depending on the individual and information needs. A team approach is *effective* because it contributes a multitude of expertise and knowledge. Communication and activities are clear, constructive, and outcome oriented. A team approach is *efficient* because team members may have delineated responsibilities that decrease the likelihood of duplication and incompletion and increase the likelihood of procurement in a timely manner (Rust & Smith, 2005).

There is no shortage of the human services professions that may be drawn from, and they have been used for many years as "experts" in their respective fields. However, professionals now assume a role of consultant, providing practical and competent suggestions. A team approach involves *empowerment* when the user actively participates and influences the direction of the process in concert with professionals.

Davies, Stock, and Wehmeyer (2003) reported the evaluation of a software prompting system operating on a Pocket PC model palmtop computer designed to facilitate decision making for individuals with intellectual disabilities. It was hypothesized that such a system would provide measurable improvement in the ability of individuals with intellectual disabilities to navigate decision points in a task more independently. The results provided evidence demonstrating the utility of Pocket Compass, a portable software system that utilizes intelligent audio and visual cues to help individuals with intellectual disabilities navigate through the cognitive process of making appropriate decisions when completing a vocational task. A total of 40 adults with intellectual disabilities participated in a beta test designed to evaluate the effectiveness of the prototype software system. The results demonstrated that the Pocket Compass approach can successfully be used by individuals with intellectual disabilities in a self-directed manner to increase independence and accuracy on vocational tasks. This is a good example of increasing empowerment.

The User's Role

As stated earlier, the user is seen as the "expert" based on his or her needs, comfort level, and preferences. With a customer-driven approach, teams will *always* include the individual with a disability. The user must be involved in the development of his or her own team or support network. Professionals may assist in the development of the team or support network, if requested to do so or if the individual requires assistance.

The team is in place to support and consult with the individual. The rapport with the team should be open, direct, and creative. As the word *team* implies, members are working in concert for the common goal of community inclusion with maximum accessibility to all opportunities offered.

The AT user must ask him- or herself

- Did I assist in the selection of team members?

- Do I have decision-making responsibilities? Am I willing and ready to take on this role?

- Do I have input into the direction of my AT needs and preferences?

- Do I have or want a mentor who can assist me in developing advocacy skills or advocating on my behalf?

The user may have a mentor. If so, the user and the mentor are one unit and may ask these questions in tandem. The user must always ask questions and not rely on one single professional for technology solutions. The team approach strengthens individualized outcomes. See Table 9.1 for examples of additional team members.

Often, there is a distinction between a team and a support network. The team's primary role is to assist in the identification and acquisition of technology. The support network's primary role occurs once the technology is acquired. They assist with the successful implementation and use of the equipment or device. The support network may be ongoing and consist of specific team members as well as family members.

CHOICE BASED ON NEED AND PREFERENCE

In the maze of rehabilitation technology, one can easily become lost. There are so many possibilities in terms of individual need, preference, and potential options. Any acquisition of AT is preceded by a need. A person with a disability wants to be able to perform a specific task; his or her disability may prohibit or limit him or her from doing so. The individual, family member, or professional begin to brainstorm about a device that would assist the individual in performing the task. It may be something as simple as getting a cup off of a shelf or as complex as using a computer to perform job functions. Mull and Sitlington (2003) summarized findings regarding the use of technology in helping students with learning disabilities succeed in postsecondary education settings. The primary purposes of this article were to 1) identify the specific technology recommendations found in the literature, 2) identify issues related to using these recommendations in the transition to postsecondary education, and 3) provide recommendations for planning for the transition to postsecondary education. In addition, Stodden, Conway, and Chang (2003) highlighted the importance of access to postsecondary education for individuals with disabilities and barriers to this access that revolve around the provision of supports, including the provision of technology. In sum, Stodden et al.

1. Described the current status of transition for youth with disabilities from secondary school to postsecondary school

2. Described the current status of disability-related support provision, including the provision of technology in secondary school versus postsecondary school

3. Outlined barriers to transition, including differences in instructional environments and legal mandates, lack of alignment of supports, differences in personal

Table 9.1. Assistive technology team members

Team member	Role
Employment specialist	Assists with job accommodation needs to enhance job performance; may assist with funding issues
Vendors	Offer knowledge on available technology, services, and repairs (usually high-end technology)
Rehabilitation engineer	Assists in development or modification of devices, accommodations, or job redesign
Occupational therapist	Assesses performance in daily living tasks, positioning, and mobility; recommends activities, devices, and adaptations to environment
Recreational therapist	Identifies and assesses social/recreational needs and preferences
Physical therapist	Assesses work capacity—physical strengths and limitations, analysis of workstation; recommends mobility needs, workstation design, and modifications
Employer	May assist with job accommodation needs, input, and approval of workstation modifications
Speech-language pathologist	Assesses language and speech capabilities and recommends specialized communication aids
Educator	Shares knowledge of individual based on experience within school system or community-based instruction sites; provides insight into matching assistive technology to continuing education that may enhance long-term employment opportunities and advancement
Family members	Share knowledge of individual and environments; advocate on behalf of user; demonstrate willingness to acquire knowledge of the device in order to provide in-home support
Rehabilitation counselor	Assists with funding issues and logistics of services to be provided in effort to reduce barriers to employment
Physician	Provides input on medical issues and cognitive and physical abilities of individual; addresses health concerns; provides prescriptions and letters of medical necessity when needed for evaluations and durable medical equipment
Social worker/case manager	May act as coordinator of holistic/community services
Computer consultant	Evaluates computer needs and recommends adaptive computer equipment and training

From Tanchak, T.L., and Sawyer, C. (1995). Augmentative communication. In K. Flippo, K. Inge, and J.M. Barcus (Eds.), *Assistive technology: A resource for school, work, and community* (p. 62). Baltimore: Paul H. Brookes Publishing Co.; adapted by permission.

responsibility, and a focus on legality and cost rather than on individual needs and outcomes

4. Suggested ways to improve transition and access to technology, including increased use of postsecondary supports in secondary school, increased carry-over of technology between secondary and postsecondary environments, better education of secondary students about their responsibilities in postsecondary school, and recognition that the use of technology and other supports are an investment in positive outcomes and productivity.

KATHARINE

Katharine is a young woman with spina bifida (see Chapter 21) who uses a wheelchair and has limited use of her hands. Katharine enjoys her coffee throughout the work day. Although this is not a task specifically related to performance of her work, it is an activity engaged in by many co-workers. Katharine uses a reacher to get her coffee mug from the shelf where she stores it. Most of the time the mug would move down the shelf and slide out before she could get a good grip on it. A team member suggested she put a latex, nonskid lining on the shelf. This was available at Kmart for a little more than $2.00 and it worked very well.

JOSEPH

Joseph works at a restaurant. As a result of a traumatic brain injury (see Chapter 22), he could not read or remember his work schedule and was in danger of losing his job. He frequently did not come to work on time. His rehabilitation counselor contacted the state AT system program, which suggested purchasing a Memo Minder costing about $20.00. Joseph's supervisor records his daily and weekly schedule. Joseph plays it at night and sets his alarm clock accordingly. Joseph has been on time ever since.

One must keep in mind that high tech solutions may not always be needed. When arriving at some technology solutions, one does not have to choose complex; simple may work exceedingly well. That is, when problem solving, look to the low tech technology before moving onto the more involved or elaborate. This strategy, of course, is dependent on the individual and their respective need. If, for instance, communication or mobility is the issue of concern, then one may require a higher tech device such as a Liberator for communication or a powered wheelchair for mobility.

Modified equipment or homemade solutions often meet an accessibility need. The use of switches, Velcro, or grips on existing items often solve an inaccessibility problem. Usually, these low tech solutions fit well into the work environment and will not cause stigma. Creativity is the key to simple, low tech solutions. Katharine's and Joseph's experiences are examples of creative, low tech solutions. Conrad's situation (see sidebar, p. 247) is an example of a core work task accommodation.

Regardless of whether a device or equipment is low or high tech, choice and effectiveness remain the central concern. The user must be comfortable with the AT, and it must satisfy the need. When one makes a major purchase, one may have many options. If an individual is purchasing a sofa, then he or she may sit on many to determine the comfort and fit into his or her home. The user should determine if there are alternatives or options available to a specific device.

If the user has been excluded from the process, or if his or her input has been minimized, the longevity and usefulness of the intended solution is in jeopardy. A user must be vested in the technology and must be trained on how to use the technology; if not, the closet door will open wide.

EVALUATING ASSISTIVE TECHNOLOGY

As a user, it is imperative that the AT being considered is evaluated. Several strategies assist in the evaluation process, including looking at the environment the technology will be used in; trying out the device, equipment or modification; and brainstorming a variety of possibilities. The bottom line is to use it before you choose it.

Looking at the Environment

When considering the use of AT, looking at the environment in which the device or modification will be used is critical. The device or modification must fit with the environment and/or employer, as well as the intended user. To ensure that the optimal

<table>
<tr><td>

CONRAD

Conrad has right side hemiplegia (see Chapter 21) and is receiving supported employment services in a small town. Recently, a recycling company opened in town, and Conrad was hired to crush beverage cans. The volume of cans was such that Conrad would do this activity for the majority of his shift, along with one other co-worker. While wearing gloves, co-workers would crush the cans with their hands and then toss them into a bin. A fellow employer rigged a new device in which Conrad places a can on the bottom holder of the rig, pulls a lever, and crushes the can. With this device, Conrad's production is almost as high as his co-workers. Conrad's experience is a good example of creating a device using a "tinkerer" within the community. Not all devices created need to be developed by professional experts. Users can educate themselves as to who in their community may be helpful with AT solutions.

</td></tr>
</table>

"fit" occurs, the team approach is valuable. Again, the user and the employer provide primary input in the direction of this process. Team members may vary according to the user's needs and the job requirement. An office jobsite evaluation team may include an occupational therapist, a rehabilitation engineer, a computer consultant, and a building maintenance specialist. Clara is an example of a user whose entire workstation was modified with her input.

Functional analysis, or actually using the device or new design within the environment, leads to satisfactory outcomes. Clara was involved in the development of her new office design and was greatly satisfied with the results. When using AT on the job, the user and team must identify the essential functions of the job and barriers to accomplishing those tasks.

Try It Out, Get Training, Use It

Users need to conduct a functional evaluation of AT that they are interested in using. Try out the device within the primary and secondary environments in which it will be used. The environments in which the device will be used should be discussed within the team. Questions that may be asked include: What is the function, role, or purpose of the device? Will it be used in a variety of environments or solely at work?

One would not dream of buying a car unless one had the opportunity to drive it down the street, kick the tires, and haggle with the salesperson. Yet, people with disabilities often get both high and low technology devices chosen for them, without an opportunity to try them out in the environment. If one is unable to try it out and to be trained on using the device, then it can be very discouraging and ultimately expensive. The user must also keep in mind that what has worked for one person may in fact be a horrendous solution for another. Individualized services and devices will be furthered by trying out the proposed solution.

If at all possible, the user should borrow or rent the device. Use it at home, at work, or in the community before making a purchasing commitment. Test the device's capabilities, limitations, and comfort. The device should look good, feel good, and many times create a greater feeling of self-esteem or capability. One user recently ordered a chair that she felt was big, black, and bulky. The chair did not make her feel good, even though it was functional. Another individual who uses forearm crutches has several pairs that represent different functions and settings—bright neon for informal days, a classy bronze for business days, and so forth. If the user of AT feels good about his or her ownership of the device, then he or she will use it to its fullest. If it makes the individual more independent, then it is the right equipment to own.

Training is another key element in properly using the selected equipment. Most likely, the user will have a close, personal, long-term relationship with the device.

Clara experiences postpolio syndrome, with muscle weakness and fatigue. A rehabilitation engineer evaluated Clara's work environment and proposed several changes to increase access and function. Her employer was very supportive. Clara's desk became an L-shaped counter top attached to the wall. This space houses a computer, telephone, and file holders. Open-ended file folder organizers were mounted within her reach on the wall. A file cabinet was purchased that had drawers that could be lifted open and slid back so that they are always open. A reacher is used to gain access to files on a higher shelf. However, Clara's power wheelchair also raises and lowers electronically so that she can reach files in this way. Clara believes the new design is functional, simple, and professional looking. Her work environment suits her needs and preferences as does her power wheelchair.

Replacements are sometimes very hard or impossible to get if an unwise choice is made. An opportunity to try out the device and insistence on training for appropriate use, as well as available features, can mean the difference between success and failure.

Tech Abandonment: The Assistive Technology Closet

As mentioned earlier, if the solution does not work for the individual, then the device most likely will be abandoned. The results of this abandonment are twofold, neither of which is desirable. First, the situation the intended user is attempting to alter is not changed. For example, if an augmentative communication device is purchased, but is discarded because it is too cumbersome on the job, then the person is still without alternative speech. In this situation, perhaps a simpler communication board or other solution is more appropriate. Second, inappropriate devices can be costly. No one wins when the device is abandoned; not the person with the disability, nor the individual who purchased the device.

Technology abandonment is widespread and very expensive. Devices are abandoned because they just don't work for the respective user (Phillips, 1993). Abandonment happens for a variety of reasons—no evaluation, incompetent evaluation, little or no user input, or no training or support.

There are other, rarely recognized reasons for abandonment. One reason is timing and acceptance by the user. A person with a disability must be ready to accept the need and the usage of the device, otherwise, he or she will reject or find excuses for not using it. A second reason is funding. For example, often, third party payers will pay for a manual wheelchair but not a power chair. So, the user gets the manual chair and then can't propel it adequately. The chair goes into the closet to gather dust while the person with the mobility difficulties either stays at home or waits a very long time for funding for the wheelchair he or she needed in the first place.

Devices that end up in the "AT closet" present a challenge. They need to be recycled, but there is little funding. Third party payers rarely pay for a used item. In the future, some method of consistent redistribution needs to be developed to assist in combating technology abandonment.

Selecting a Vendor

The informed user can make a case for using a specific vendor. Selecting a vendor should not be solely based on the product or device chosen. Choosing the ideal product is, of course, a critical component. However, the relationship with the user and the device is only the beginning. The user must "look down the road." There may come a day when the equipment or device needs repairs. This can be a user's worst nightmare, depending on the function the device serves in the user's life. High end technology, such as power wheelchairs and augmentative communication, may be difficult to live without, no matter how temporary. When selecting a vendor, ask

- What services do you offer?

- Do you provide a trial period?

- What will you do for me if this breaks down? (e.g., loan equipment)

- What is your turn-around time for repairs?

- How much do you charge for services and repairs?

Service costs can be enormous. As in any business, customer responsiveness and satisfaction should be a priority for the vendor. If the vendor does not offer to loan a comparable device, or if he or she does not respond with a knowledge of the necessity to get repairs done quickly, then the choice may be made easier for the user.

Training may be a part of the vendor agreement and purchase contingent on receiving immediate and quality training. If a vendor lists services in promotional materials, then the user should look for training, repair, and loans as an indicator of whether he or she will do business with the respective vendor.

The loan aspect is critical to the user who would not have mobility, communication, accessibility, or integration otherwise. Being proactive with anticipated needs and repairs will serve the user well in selecting a vendor. With high end technology, the user, vendor, and device may have a relationship for life. As with all relationships, it should not be entered into lightly.

Funding Issues

Anyone who uses AT knows that funding is often a challenge and a barrier. However, most work accommodations cost very little. According to the Job Accommodation Network (JAN; n.d.), 71% of AT devices cost $500.00 or less. As with identifying technology solutions, creativity and perseverance may be the key to success. An individual may be able to make use of a variety of funding options, including Department of Rehabilitation Services, Medicaid, education, private insurance, Social Security Administration, Veterans Administration, and independent living programs. Each of these sources have eligibility requirements and specific procedures. Nontraditional funding sources may include service, civic, or religious organizations.

Carey, DelSordo, and Goldman (2004) noted that literature on gaining access to AT services and AT funding, as well as literature on gaining access to loans (e.g., mortgages, car loans), has indicated that people from minority populations tend to experience less access to and benefit from these programs. Given these trends, the question they ask is, "To what extent does race affect access to AT through alternative financing programs?" Using a national database of 10 participating states, they explored the impact of race on which people apply for—and succeed in obtaining—alternative financing. The authors then provided an in-depth discussion of Pennsylvania's model outreach program designed to increase access to and use of alternative financing by members of the African American, Latino, and Southeast Asian communities in the commonwealth. This paper does an excellent job of showing the challenges of funding AT for minority populations. It is often possible to blend funding sources (i.e., to use different sources for different devices and services, to use a variety of sources to fund one device or service). The user must become informed about all available funding sources and their respective stipulations. This knowledge provides a "leg up" in the acquisition of AT. Do not rely completely on professionals for this information as their knowledge may vary. Doing one's own research will truly enhance the possibilities.

According to Wallace and Neal (1993), several steps are involved in locating funding. The user must

- Be prepared
- Prove a need
- Match the need with the device or service
- Research prices, providers, and alternatives
- Choose and contact funding sources (identify a specific contact person)
- Be determined and persistent
- Do all of the necessary paperwork
- Keep detailed, written records
- If denied, appeal
- If denied again, move onto another funding option

The Americans with Disabilities Act (ADA) of 1990 (PL 101-336) has created another potential funding option through employers. This, of course, is true as long as the solution is deemed a reasonable accommodation and does not present an undue hardship to the employer. Acquiring funding is a tedious process, one which requires preparation, organization, and perseverance. The user must go in with the attitude that this may take patience, thought, and time.

ADDITIONAL ISSUES

Maximizing Independence in All Aspects

As mentioned earlier, AT must be used to maximize independent living prior to its use to enhance employment opportunities. It can be an important part of the daily living routine of a person with a disability or his or her caregiver. The user needs to be comfortable with his or her activities in the home and community before exploring job opportunities. In simple terms, housing, food, hygiene, medical care, and transportation needs have to be addressed first. Many times, optimal independent living can be achieved by filling these needs with AT services.

Examples of AT devices used for independent living are bath and dressing aids, food preparation aids, lifts, augmentative communication devices, wheelchairs, and low tech items such as reachers, rubber jar openers, grips, and so forth. Individuals may also require home modifications and specialized transportation.

Addressing independent living issues first will contribute to success in the arena of employment. However, not all individuals with disabilities may need to address independent living on the same level, depending on need(s). Devices used in other areas of life may be used on the jobsite as well.

Looking to the Future

Needs change, technology changes, and goals change. The user must be a visionary and look to the future, anticipating physical, medical, and/or career changes. Low tech solutions do not necessarily require a prophetic approach because they are creative, simple, and often inexpensive. However, high end devices, due to funding issues and expense, will require a future-oriented vision. Funding sources may have time frames in which once a device is acquired, they will not pay for another similar device or equipment for a certain period. Thus, it is important for the user to know his or her insurance coverage. The team approach will assist an individual with planning for the future.

CONCLUSION

AT closes the gap between inaccessibility and accessibility. Technology on the worksite continues to be an exciting, integrating opportunity for many individuals with disabilities. The user must be as prepared, as relentless, as questioning as possible to arrive at appropriate solutions. Technology continues to advance and change at a rapid pace, with all members of today's society becoming dependent on and benefiting from its use. Individual advocacy and research in procuring AT on the worksite, as well as other areas of daily living, will continue to increase the independence of individuals with disabilities. It is a matter of convenience in terms of freedom and quality of life.

- She is visually attentive and can turn her head from side to side.
- Susan is labeled severely mentally retarded.

Given that she has multiple physical characteristics that could have an impact on her performance, it was obvious that Susan would need AT to complete the job of stamping books with the library identification number. The team worked closely with a rehabilitation engineer, and a spring-loaded device was designed to assist Susan in completing the task. The first step in the job required personal assistance from a co-worker or project staff member to load the equipment with 10 books for stamping. At that point, Susan was responsible for pressing a switch to drop a book into position. She then would touch another plate that held the heat stamp in order to apply heat to the spine of the book. Susan kept this in place for 10 seconds, finally touching another switch to move the book off the work surface. Intensive systematic instruction was provided by a trainer to assist Susan in learning her job.

STUDY QUESTIONS

1. What does AT include?

2. What is the impact of AT on the quality of life of the user?

3. What is the role of the consumer/user in the acquisition of AT? How can a professional assist in facilitating the realization of this role?

4. What are the benefits to using a team approach when working with individuals to procure AT devices and services? Who may be the individuals who make up such a team?

5. Why is it important to evaluate AT devices across a variety of life settings?

6. What are some of the challenges to locating and gaining access to funding for AT?

7. What does the term *jobsite enabling* mean?

8. What are the emerging issues related to advances in technology?

III

Work and Life
in the Community

10

Finding Jobs for
Young People with Disabilities

Pam Sherron Targett

AFTER COMPLETING THIS CHAPTER, THE READER WILL BE ABLE TO

○ Discuss the role of the employment specialist and skills needed to develop work opportunities for students with disabilities

○ Explain the purpose of the Americans with Disabilities Act (ADA) of 1990 (PL 101-336) and its implications for supported employment (SE) service delivery

○ Describe how to survey the local labor market

○ Discuss how to tap into the hidden job market

○ State some typical employer concerns and explain ways to overcome objections

○ Describe some ways to enhance job development skills

Preparation of this chapter was supported in part by Cooperative Agreement No. H133B9800036 from the National Institute on Disability and Rehabilitation Research (NIDRR), U.S. Department of Education. This support does not constitute official endorsement of the information or views presented here.

The world attempts to exclude people with disabilities, particularly those with the most severe disabilities, from the employment scene. This has been accomplished by isolating individuals with disabilities in segregated settings and regarding them as unemployable or too disabled to work. In addition, many people remain so focused on disability that they fail to embrace the simple truth that with the proper resources and supports, individuals with disabilities can be successful at work (Wehman & Bricout, 2001). For young people with disabilities who are leaving school, competitive work prior to graduation or exit is the best way to negate these poor employment outcomes (Wehman, 2001b; Wehman & Revell, 1997).

All students with disabilities have personal strengths and abilities that allow them to make a meaningful contribution to the work force. Some students will need no or little assistance, whereas others will require more intensive and individualized vocational support services to gain and maintain employment. Assisting students with more significant support needs in going to work is often easier said than done. Dependent on past experiences and staffing, this may initially present a daunting challenge to those responsible for the student's transition from school to work (e.g., transition specialist, special educators, vocational specialist). For example, they must be able to promote relationships with employers and recognize and address their concerns. To complicate matters, every business is different in terms of hiring needs, work requirements, and willingness to provide or create workplace supports. This is further compounded by the fact that each student is unique, with individual vocational strengths and support needs.

This chapter offers some practical information on how transition personnel can assist students with the most significant disabilities with locating and securing employment in their communities. The focus is on ways to facilitate and provide vocational support to those students who are not able to independently conduct their own job search. Specifically, this approach is for students who require advocacy level or SE services to assist them in employment. The job search activities described may be provided by school personnel or purchased from an outside vocational rehabilitation (VR) provider.

This chapter begins with a description of the skills and knowledge needed to assist students with locating work. This is followed by some practical job development strategies that should have employers saying "yes" to hiring young people who just happen to have disabilities. The chapter concludes with some additional tips on ways to enhance job development skills.

VR service providers often refer to the activity of locating work opportunities as *job development*. When using a SE approach, a staff person, sometimes referred to as an *employment specialist* or a *job coach* and, as much as possible, the job seeker with the disability pursue real work for real pay in the local community. A brief description of the individual placement approach to SE follows (Brooke, Inge, Armstrong, & Wehman, 1997; Targett & Wehman 2002).

In SE, prior to initiating job development, the employment specialist should not only have some general knowledge of the business community, but also have a good understanding of the job seeker's abilities, desires, and support needs (Targett & Wehman, 2002). Person-centered and functional assessment activities are conducted to help identify student interests, abilities, and support needs (Brooke et al., 1997; Everson & Reid, 1999).

Some students with disabilities will qualify for existing positions because they are able to perform the essential job functions (major duties) either with or without reasonable accommodation. However, other students may not be able to perform the primary job tasks or myriad duties. Under these circumstances, a position that benefits business is specifically "developed" or created for the student. For instance, some duties from one or more existing staff positions are identified, combined, and then reassigned to create a new job, or someone may be hired to perform work that has often been overlooked or causes the company to accrue overtime expenditures (Brooke et al., 1997; Condon, Enein-Donovan, Gilmore, & Jordan, 2004; Griffin & Hammis, 2002; Inge 2001; Targett & Wehman 2002).

Consider a busy real estate office with eight realtors. Each one is responsible for keeping a computerized database up-to-date and mailing out customer newsletters. These and perhaps other tasks could be taken and combined to form a part-time job. This frees up the realtors to spend more time in the community with their potential buyers and sellers.

A job may also be created by reassigning work that is not getting done to one employee. For example, the waitstaff at a five-star establishment rarely have time to polish the silverware. When the staff do polish the silverware, overtime wages are usually paid. A position may be created by hiring someone who is solely responsible for polishing the silverware. Creating this job helps the restaurant sustain its image as a posh place to dine and cuts cost associated with paying overtime.

No matter how the job is developed, after becoming employed, the newly hired student receives individualized on-the-job supports. For example, the employment specialist may provide the new employee with one-to-one skills training (e.g., using systematic instructional techniques) that extends beyond that offered by the employer while ensuring that the work is getting done. Or, in some instances, the specialist may help the employee select and learn how to use assistive technology (AT; e.g., key guard, reaching device) or compensatory memory strategies (e.g., picture book, checklist; Inge, 2001; Targett, Wehman, & Young, 2004).

Throughout this process, performance data are collected to evaluate the worker's performance. As the employee learns the job and is able to meet the employer's standards, the employment specialist begins to fade from the jobsite until eventually he or she is no longer present on a regular basis. However, the specialist continues to offer periodic follow-up services throughout the individual's employment (Brooke et al., 1997).

These ongoing job retention services are increased as needed. For example, if the employee receives a promotion or is assigned new job duties, then one-to-one skills training may be reinitiated, or if the person cannot solve work-related problems (e.g., unreliable transportation services, being teased at work), then assistance may be provided (Targett, Yasuda, & West, 2001).

While reading this chapter, it is important for the reader to keep the following points in mind. First, although everyone on the school's vocational transition team can provide input and assist with the job search, someone must be responsible for ensuring that the student actually goes to work. Who is responsible will vary from school to school and state to state. It will depend on available resources and funding. Some schools may be rich in resources and have job coaches in-house, whereas others may be very limited and teachers may be expected to conduct such activities. Others may be progressive and have vocational education personnel involved in locating work for all students whether they are disabled or not. And still others may have the state's VR agency actively engaged in this process, especially during the student's last year of school. As illustrated, variability can be quite extensive. Thus, for purposes here, the chapter addresses issues from the perspective that the school has *employment specialists* or *job coaches* on staff who are responsible for ensuring that those students with the most severe disabilities (i.e., those who need intensive supports) will gain and maintain employment prior to exiting school. The term *job development* is used to refer to the pre-employment activities associated with a job search such as meeting with businesses, identifying viable work opportunities, completing the application process, and interviewing for and accepting an employment offer.

Second, when a business contact is made, it should be done with a specific student in mind and never on behalf of groups of people. Instead, the job search should be driven by an individual student's interest, abilities, and support needs. The goal is not to find just any job, but one that allows the student to build on and maximize his or her personal strengths. However, this is a guiding principle and not a hard fast rule because other student job seekers may come to mind after an employment specialist learns more about a particular organization's hiring needs and available work opportunities. But, as a general rule of thumb, an employment specialist should have a specific job seeker in mind when approaching an employer.

Third, to locate meaningful work, employment specialists must look beyond available options and conduct a creative job search. In a traditional job search, employers attract a large number of applicants, screen them, and then pick the best of the pool to interview. In job development, the goal is to avoid the competition by developing relationships with businesses and developing employment opportunities. Richard Bolles first described the creative job hunt in his book, *What Color Is Your Parachute?* (Bolles & Brown, 2001). Instead of looking for jobs in a traditional way (e.g., using the Internet to search for job postings, mailing résumés to employers, answering advertisements announcing vacancies), the creative search involves asking for leads from people you know or just meet, as well as calling and visiting employers whether there is a job opening or not. According to Bolles and Brown, this creative approach has an 86% success rate.

Fourth, instead of revealing to potential employers that the sole intent is to locate a job for a specific student, employment specialists should have some other things to offer to businesses and consider ways to develop strategic partnerships. For example, the employment specialist may give the employer educational materials. Then, in return, the specialist may ask if students can tour the workplace or request a referral to another business, particularly when a job opportunity is not probable in the foreseeable future. This method also helps ensure that the hidden job market is being tapped into, rather than pursuing jobs that are being advertised, and ensures the employment specialist does not leave the meeting empty handed (Bissonnette, 1994).

GETTING STARTED

To conduct a creative job search, employment specialists must know what they have to offer businesses and understand the preferences, abilities, and support needs of the student job seekers who are being represented (Targett & Wehman, 2002). Without this knowledge, employment specialists will not be able to talk intelligently to employers or exude the confidence needed to move toward the primary goal—a job offer. Therefore, before going out and meeting with businesses, employment specialists should understand the program's philosophy, know what services are offered and how this benefits businesses, be able to anticipate typical employer concerns, be familiar with the ADA, as well as know the value that the student job seeker can bring to the workplace (Targett & Wehman, 2002).

Value of Services

An understanding of the program's values and procedures that guide interactions with business is essential. Employment specialists should be able to answer the following questions.

- What is the school's philosophy relating to securing and creating employment opportunities?

- What types of support services are offered to both the student and business (e.g., transportation training, job coaching, payment for accommodations, long-term support), and how is this conveyed?

- What materials will be used to represent the job seeker and/or support services to the business world?

- How will job seeker participation be encouraged in the job search process?

- How will job seekers be represented during initial employer contacts?

This vital information should be readily accessible to staff as part of a policy and procedures manual.

Program Features

Luecking, Fabian, and Tilson (2004) reminded employment specialists to think of employers as customers and give them choices. They recommended preparing a menu of options for employers to consider. For instance, maybe a bigger labor pool is being offered that might help reduce employment cost, or perhaps educational materials or training on disability awareness topics is provided. Even when an employer does not have an immediate work opportunity, employment specialists have the chance to set the stage for a long-term partnership with the school if they can offer something that the business values. For example, reduce recruitment and staffing costs, create new work structures designed to enhance workplace productivity, enhance a diverse workforce, offer new employee training assistance, and offer education and resources on disability- and employment-related topics. Employment specialists should spend some time thinking about their program's features and what they have to offer prior to meeting with business. Considering the following questions may be helpful.

- Why should a business want to work with the school and employ youth with disabilities?

- What services can the employment specialist offer?

- How will this benefit business, the community, and society?

- What concerns will business have, and how will these be addressed?

- What does the school or student expect from a business, and what does the business expect from them?

Although the primary goal of job development is to locate paid work for students, sometimes work is not immediately available. In such instances, employment specialists should consider other things employers offer. For example, perhaps they can serve on an advisory committee, provide expertise and insight about their industry, give feedback or advice on marketing materials and ways to approach employers, or allow student job seekers to tour the business. Whenever a job offer is not on the immediate horizon, employment specialists should consider these and other ways to develop business partnerships.

Employment specialists should keep in mind that not learning about an immediate work opportunity still leaves the door open for building relationships. If an organization is not interested or unwilling to hire at the time, then employment specialists should at least leave the employer with a positive first impression in case they want to reach them at a later date. In this instance, the employer is not necessarily saying that he or she will never consider this, but is saying not right now. Time may be needed to build rapport and gain the trust necessary to form a working relationship that eventually leads to employment opportunities.

Employer Questions and Concerns

Potential employers will want to know what value a student can bring to the business. In addition, they will need to know what types of specialized services are available to assist the business when applicable. Thus, employment specialists should know the nature of the services represented and be well versed in how to respond to potential employer questions or concerns without hesitation (Targett & Wehman, 2002). Employers will be more open to listening to employment specialists who can answer their questions with confidence. Reviewing some typical employer questions and formulating possible responses in advance will not only put employment specialists at ease but will also help them respond without hesitation. For example, consider the following questions.

- What types of services do you offer to assist me in this process?

- What abilities does the job seeker possess that will meet my needs?

- What other businesses have hired students?

- How much is this going to cost in terms of time and resources?

- How successful are the students who go to work?

These concerns and potential responses will be examined more closely in another section of this chapter.

The Americans with Disabilities Act

Employment specialists should also be familiar with the ADA, an important piece of legislation that impacts the employment of people with disabilities (Targett & Wehman,

2002). The law was intended to usher in "a bright new era of equality, independence and freedom" and it gives people with disabilities civil rights much like those held by minorities and women. The ADA is made up of five titles: employment (Title I), public services (Title II), public accommodations (Title III), telecommunications (Title IV), and miscellaneous provisions (Title V).

For the purposes here, the employment provisions, or Title I, of the ADA are reviewed. Title I makes it illegal for employers to discriminate against applicants or workers who have a "known" disability. More specifically, it protects against discrimination from employers with 15 or more employees; so employers with fewer than 15 employees are exempt from this mandate.

The ADA does not require employers to hire people with disabilities, but it does require employers to give individuals with disabilities a chance to compete for jobs and provide reasonable accommodation for them to be successful at work. Discrimination under the ADA covers a wide range of employment related practices and includes hiring and firing, compensation and classification of workers, transfer, promotion and layoffs, recruitment, training and apprenticeships, use of company facilities, pay, retirement plans, disability leave, and other terms and conditions of employment.

The ADA only applies to individuals who are qualified to perform the job in question. This means the applicant with a disability must meet the basic job requirements related to experience, education, skills, or licenses to be covered under the ADA. A person who does not possess requisite skills, experience, education, and other job-related requirements would not be considered a qualified applicant, either with or without a disability.

If the person with a disability is qualified, then he or she must also be able to perform the essential job functions or the primary job duties, with or without a reasonable accommodation. A *reasonable accommodation* is a change in the way things are typically done that allows the person with the disability to participate in all aspects of the employment process. For example, a reasonable accommodation may be necessary to allow a person with a disability to apply for a job, perform job functions, or to enjoy the benefits or privileges of work. Examples of reasonable accommodation include, but are not limited to, making existing facilities used by employees readily accessible, job restructuring, modifying work schedules, providing additional unpaid leave, acquiring or modifying equipment and devices, modifying training materials, and providing qualified readers or interpreters. Please note that at no time is the employer required to reduce his or her expectations (e.g., lower production standards for the employee with the disability). The person with the disability must be able to perform the essential or primary job functions with or without accommodation. Personal items used by the individual with the disability such as eyeglasses, walkers, or hearing aids are not usually covered. An individual who can perform the essential functions with an accommodation is considered a qualified applicant and cannot be screened out on the basis of needing an accommodation.

Employers can expect the applicant or worker with a disability to perform the main job functions of a job either with or without accommodation, but they cannot refuse to hire a person because the disability prevents him or her from performing nonessential or marginal job functions. For example, a store clerk's job functions include greeting and assisting customers throughout the day, stocking, and pricing merchandise. Two times a week the clerk may be asked to assist with unloading a truck and processing newly arriving merchandise. It is very unlikely that "unloading the truck and processing merchandise" is an essential job function. Instead, it is an example of a marginal or nonessential job duty because it is not the primary reason the job exists and does not occur often. However, there are other measures that may come in to play when making a determination about whether a job function is essential. For example, if there was no one else available to perform this function or it created an "undue hardship" due to the cost of hiring another employee to do this, then it is possible that this could be an essential job function. *Undue hardship* is defined as significant difficulty or expense to the employer when taking into account the cost of the accommodation and business resources. An employer cannot make up the cost of providing a reasonable accommodation by lowering the person's salary or paying him or her less than others in similar positions.

Charles (2004) evaluated whether employers had complied with the ADA and examined the impact of accommodations on improved job attachment. Results revealed that the ADA seems to have caused an increase in the incidence of accommodation. However, the increase was only 5% among workers with disabilities, which does not indicate a dramatic improvement in accommodations prior to the passage of the ADA. In addition, accommodations appeared only in time-related adjustments, such as change in schedule, and there was evidence that employers have passed the cost of accommodations to their workers in the form of lower wages. Results also revealed that employer-provided accommodation did not appear to improve labor market attachment among workers with disabilities.

To briefly summarize, under the ADA, a qualified person with a disability is someone who meets the employer's prerequisites in terms of education and training and one who can perform the essential functions of a job. A qualified person with a disability cannot be screened out of an applicant pool simply because he or she is unable to perform nonessential or marginal job functions.

Title I employment provisions are enforced by the Equal Employment Opportunity Commission (EEOC) and/or by state human rights commissions. It is important for employment specialists to have some understanding of the law and be able to locate additional resources if needed because employers or others may have questions or ask for information about the ADA. The appendix at the end of the chapter offers more information on reasonable accommodation, an overview of the potential implications for SE, and resources for additional information.

Student Job Seekers

In addition to being able to present services and how these benefit businesses, employment specialists must also be very familiar with the students represented. Creating a vision of each person's abilities, desires, and support needs will help direct job search activities (Targett & Wehman, 2002). Each student has specific strengths, talents, and support needs. Employment specialists must be able to communicate those abilities to whoever is responsible for making the hiring decision. A careful career planning process should not only identify individual strengths and support needs, but should also lead to ideas about what types of work characteristics and settings would maximize the student's abilities and minimize disability (Callahan & Garner, 1997).

Chapter 3 described how person-centered planning and various activities can be used to identify a student's personal abilities and support needs to create a quality life. Completion of person-centered planning activities, which include career planning, should leave support personnel who are involved with transitioning students with disabilities to work with many ideas on each student's assets and support needs, as well as ideas on how to proceed with the student's job search (Inge, 2001).

These person-centered vocational exploration and assessment activities should give employment specialists a better understanding of what the job seeker expects from work and how this can benefit a business. With this knowledge, employment specialists should be able to identify or create positions that suit the job seeker's preferences and needs (Inge, 2001). Employment specialists who know the job seeker should be able to answer the following questions.

- What are the student's vocational strengths, work preferences, and support needs?

- What approach or combination of approaches will be used to locate work opportunities (e.g., existing work, job carving, self-employment)?

- How will the job seeker be represented, and how will disclosure be addressed?

- How will the job seeker (and family) participate in job development activities?

Efforts that encourage participation in the job search process are likely to improve job retention. The student and family can assist with the job search in a number of ways such as networking with relatives and friends to identify job leads, making initial employer contacts to follow up on, as well as creating marketing tools that highlight the student's abilities or interest, and so forth. This collaboration also gives employment specialists a chance to build rapport with students and their families (Parent, Unger, & Inge, 1997).

Employment specialists should also keep in mind that the job search is usually directed by a number of work-related characteristics, rather than seeking a specific type of job title or position. There may be different types of work that would be of interest to a student if it brings value to the business and meets personal preferences and support needs. Consideration must be given to the type of workplace and job tasks that would match preferences and maximize abilities. Other important considerations may relate to the location or proximity of work to home or school and scheduling for times of day when the student performs best. Certain work environments may be conducive to maximize student ability. For example, does the student tolerate noisy environments and hot temperatures, or does he or she perform best in a quiet, temperature-controlled climate? Does he or she work well as part of a team, or would he or she prefer to work alone? Employment specialists must also remember that the student job seeker does not need to "be ready" to work because the skills needed will be taught at work. These factors and many more contribute to what will culminate into a good job match for the student and business. Thus, work characteristics, interests, abilities, and support needs become the basis for job search activities and drives the process of assisting the student job seeker with not only locating viable opportunities, but also selecting a good one (Targett & Wehman, 2003).

This type of approach helps ensure that work opportunities are specifically developed or created for the student. However, this must be tempered with the fact that finding a "perfect job match" is rare. Instead, the job seeker must be willing to negotiate or give up some expectations in order to receive others. Also, first-time job seekers often need guidance to help them understand how a particular job can serve as a stepping stone toward a future goal.

In summary, assisting students with disabilities with locating work necessitates that employment specialists establish relationships with businesses that can benefit from whatever the job seeker has to offer, as well as negotiate work that suits the student's preferences and skills. Prior to going out and meeting with businesses, employment specialists should:

- Understand the value of services and program features

- Have some ideas on how to respond to typical employer questions and concerns and be familiar with the ADA

- Know the student's expectations, vocational strengths, and support needs

- Have some ideas on ways the student can bring value to business, keeping in mind that skills training and supports will be provided on the job

Employment specialists who are clear on what they have to offer employers, and know the students represented, will be perceived as sincere and send a confident message to businesses. With an understanding of the program's values and features and the job seeker's abilities, expectations, and support needs, employment specialists should forge ahead and actually begin to make business contacts. For some, these skills will come easy, for others, time will be needed to develop and refine their techniques.

IDENTIFYING BUSINESS CONTACTS

There are a variety of ways to target businesses to contact, such as surveying and developing personal networks, using advocate referrals, and conducting informational interviews with companies that are not hiring. However, before choosing businesses to contact, employment specialists should become familiar with their local labor market.

Labor Market Screening

A labor market screening involves canvassing the immediate area to determine what types of businesses and possible jobs are available in the local community. Getting a clear picture of what is going on in the local labor market is a worthwhile activity for a number of reasons. First, it will help employment specialists and job seekers determine what types of businesses to contact. It also helps with employment selection by providing information on whether a specific type of work seems like a good fit for the job seeker in terms of his or her abilities, desires, and support needs. Finally, it provides a foundation for making initial business contacts. Employers are often impressed when someone has researched their company in advance and is familiar with what they do.

Therefore, successful job development begins by understanding the make-up of the local labor market. This involves investigating existing data, as well as surveying the local business community. A local labor market survey may already be in place for review. If so, it should be reviewed, and then employment specialists can conduct some of their own research in order to become better tuned in with the local business world.

If an analysis needs to be conducted, a first step may entail contacting the state's Employment Commission Economic Information Services Division and Chamber of Commerce. Next, business listings in the yellow pages can be reviewed. Additional information is gathered until some of the start-up, established, high- and low-growth industries in the area are identified. It is important to focus on both large and small businesses. Almost two thirds of all nongovernment workers are employed by small business. In addition, small employers create most of the new jobs, thus, they should not be ignored.

After identifying businesses, employment specialists may find it useful to survey a sample of these to glean some additional information. This type of data can be stored in a job bank or database for future reference. Surveys may be conducted by telephone, through the mail, or in person. The goal is simply learn more about a business in general. If a survey is used, then it should be brief and easy to complete. The type of information gathered may include the following.

- Business type

- Number of years in the community

- Types of products or services offered

- Number of employees

- Types of occupations, including entry-level opportunities

- Anticipated labor market needs and hiring trends

Once this information is complete, it should be integrated into any existing organizational labor market survey. Some employment specialists skip over this important activity. Instead, they focus all their energy on locating jobs that are being advertised and see little value in learning more about businesses that are not hiring. They fail to realize that conducting and updating a local labor market screening allows them to tap into the hidden job market (unadvertised jobs) and can lead to job creations.

Employment specialists should not investigate every occupation or business in the area before contacting employers. Instead, they should get a sampling of the business community's makeup. This becomes an ongoing activity that helps employment specialists stay abreast of new business developments and future hiring trends.

In summary, a labor market analysis should leave employment specialists with a better understanding of the types of businesses that make up their local business communities. By becoming more familiar with the business world, employment specialists will be able to make recommendations to job seekers on possible places to look for work. It also should reaffirm that there are vast numbers of potential work opportunities for individuals with disabilities and that businesses are looking for good employees.

Hidden Job Market

Once employment specialists are familiar with services offered, student job seekers, and the local labor market scene, the next step is to identify employers to contact. When choosing businesses to contact, employment specialists should not focus on jobs that are being advertised (Bissonnette, 1994). Although there certainly are exceptions to this rule, generally this is not the best way to develop jobs. For example, consider the fact that when someone applies for an advertised position, he or she is competing with everyone else who decides to apply. This does not necessarily put the odds of being hired in one's favor, unless of course the person is the most qualified applicant. Sometimes, however, it may be acceptable for a job seeker to apply for an advertised job opening, particularly when the student meets the minimal qualifications. However, under such circumstances, competition with other job seekers is inevitable. Sometimes this approach will lead to a job offer, other times it will not.

Generally speaking, this approach should be used sparingly. Instead, employment specialists and job seekers should focus on the hidden job market by arranging to meet with a wide range of employers, not just those who are advertising work. Contacting employers who are not advertising a job opening is typically an excellent way to identify work opportunities.

Most jobs are never advertised in a newspaper. So, to conduct a successful job search, employment specialists should use a combination of strategies, including networking or asking other people about possible leads. Jobs that are not advertised make up the vast majority of all available opportunities.

This also supports the fact that employment specialists need to be out in their communities meeting with employers, developing relationships, and learning about potential and future work opportunities—not waiting for a job opening to be announced. The best time to search for an employment opportunity is before anyone else knows about it. So, employment specialists should position themselves to be one of the first to know. Job search strategies for tapping into the hidden job market include surveying and developing personal networks, informational interviewing, using advocate referrals, and some newer approaches.

Surveying and Developing Personal Networks   Personal connections are a rich source of business leads, and a personal referral network can be easily developed during a person-centered planning meeting or a home visit. For example, during the home visit, everyone can brainstorm the names of people they know such as family and friends, neighbors, church members, social club members, volunteer supervisors or co-workers, professionals (e.g., teacher, hair stylist), and employees in local businesses (e.g., convenience store, dry cleaners). Then, a plan of action to communicate with those identified is devised. For example, one job seeker posted a notice in the church bulletin requesting assistance from the congregation; another person delivered flyers to neighbors in his apartment complex. Whenever anyone has a lead, the aim is to schedule a meeting with the potential employer. No matter the outcome, every contact can be asked for names of others to contact and continue to expand the original referral chain (Ryan, 2000).

A system for obtaining leads from the state VR agency should be established. Many state offices have a marketing coordinator who assists by ensuring that job leads are shared with service providers in a timely manner. Some agencies hold monthly networking meetings in which employers present information on their organization's employment needs and often arrange site tours for interested parties. Social networking through active membership in a business organization or attending community events also provides the opportunity to meet new people and get leads.

Informational Interviewing   Another technique involves conducting informational interviews. This can also be a first step toward job development and will be described in more detail later. This simply involves interviewing an employer or an employee to learn more about the business or a career. In addition to networking, the yellow pages of the telephone book can be used to identify contacts. Review of specialized reference books and periodicals, such as *National Business Employment Weekly* or *Directories in Print*, and published sources of employer information, such as the Chamber of Commerce Directory or newspaper articles, can be useful as well. A drive around the job seeker's community is another way to identify businesses to contact for an interview.

The questions asked during the interview will vary depending on what information is needed. For example, if an employment specialist wants to know more about the employer's goals, concerns, values, and needs, then he or she might ask, "Tell me about your business." If more general information is needed, then he or she may ask, "How do you do what you do?"

Often times the employer will lead the discussion in the direction he or she thinks is important. But being prepared and asking questions is a good way for the employment specialist to show interest and enthusiasm for learning more about the workplace. Many employers are receptive to informational interviews, particularly when scheduled at a time that is convenient for them. Informational interviews can also provide a useful way for some student job seekers to learn more about different types of work options, what employers are looking for in the people they hire, what skills are valued, and what is not so important. Informational interviews are conducted to better understand a business and its needs.

Using Advocate Referrals   The referral approach uses an advocate to provide access to business contacts. An *advocate* is defined as an individual who embraces the idea that people with disabilities can work and who believes in the power of supports. He or she must also have some influence with community business leaders (e.g., business associate, social affiliate, consumer, friend).

In this approach, the first contact with potential employers is made by the advocate, who informs his or her business associate of the benefits of hiring workers with disabilities. The advocate also encourages his or her acquaintance to meet with a SE representative. Once a positive response is received and the introductions have been made, the employment specialist proceeds by contacting the business, meeting with the appropriate representative, surveying business needs, and presenting employment proposals. The advocate usually stays involved in the process and advises the employment specialist on the employer's receptivity. The advocate is also available to assist with problem solving.

Cold Calls versus Referral Model   A study by Nietupski, Verstegen, Reilly, Hutson, and Hamre-Nietupski (1997) documented and compared the effectiveness of two job development models in SE—the cold call model and the referral model. The cold call model used in the study involved looking for work opportunities by contacting employers without having a referral. The three basic methods of initiating direct contact are by telephone, by writing, and by walking into the business unannounced.

Combinations of a letter and a telephone call or a letter and a visit were also used. The method selected was dependent on the style and preference of the job developer and the size and type of the business.

After initial contact was made, an appointment was set to interview an organizational representative in order to learn more about employment options. Next, the job developer surveyed the jobsite in order to gain information for suggesting a suitable job match and to develop a proposal on how the agency and the people represented could assist the business in achieving desired results. These findings were presented to the businesses' decision makers. At this time, the procedures were examined, revisions were negotiated, and a decision for hiring was solicited.

The referral model that was used in the study was similar to the cold call model in that businesses were contacted, surveys were completed, and proposals were presented to solicit hiring decisions. However, in the referral model, two additional steps occurred prior to the business being contacted. First, the job developer identified advocates, including family members of individuals with disabilities, employers who have hired people with disabilities, the staff person's personal acquaintances, and so forth. After identifying advocates, the job developers asked if the advocate would provide access to his or her business acquaintance.

Next, those acquaintances were contacted by the advocate and asked if they would be willing to meet with a SE representative to explore services and the possibility of hiring a person with a disability. If the response was positive, then the advocate introduced the job developer to the businessperson. The advocate often stayed involved to advise the job developer on progress with the lead. Participants were encouraged to use this approach with larger firms.

Twelve SE agencies from Northern Illinois participated in the study, and the results revealed that an average of 10 cold call contacts were needed to obtain a positive decision, as opposed to an average of 2.4 referral contacts. Basically, both approaches worked; however, the referral method led to hiring four times more often than the cold call method.

A similar study was conducted by Williams, Petty, and Verstegen (1998) in which both the cold call and referral models were reviewed for 8 months at four community rehabilitation agencies in Tennessee. The purpose of the research was to improve job development efforts. The results produced a step-by-step process for developing jobs. The four agencies initially participated in a meeting to discuss the approaches and tracking procedures. This was followed by 6 months of data collection and technical assistance. At the conclusion of the investigation, the participants reconvened to debrief and review outcomes.

The cold call approach, as in the previous study, required direct contact with businesses with which the job developer had no prior connection. The steps in the process involved in this study were to identify the consumer's strengths and target potential employers, research the business, make the contact to get an appointment, meet with the employer and provide information, survey the employer's needs, conduct a site survey and meet key people in the company, and present a hiring proposal and follow up.

The referral model or the accepted business model involved contacting businesses through third-party advocates. These advocates contacted employers on behalf of the agencies and encouraged them to explore how hiring people with disabilities may benefit them. The process turned what would have been a cold call into a warm call. The steps in the process were to locate advocates, identify and develop business contacts through the advocates, have the advocates contact the business to obtain a meeting, use the advocates' support to facilitate the hiring decision, maintain contact with advocates, and expand the advocate pool.

The findings revealed that an average of seven cold call contacts were needed to obtain one positive decision. This was compared with the results of the referral model in which an average of three advocates were contacted whose business contacts yielded two placements. As in the previous study, both approaches worked; however, the referral method resulted in fewer rejections. These studies provide programs with a foundation on which job developers can establish goals, expectations, and a basis for comparisons. Comparisons will help identify strengths, weaknesses, and opportunities for improvement.

Job seekers and job developers should not underestimate the power of using referrals to help locate a job (Nietupski & Hamre-Nietupski, 2001; Ryan, 2000). Personal contacts allow the job seeker and developer an opportunity to tap into this hidden job market. Personal contacts may be made through third-party referrals or through a referral chain or networking as described earlier. By using these approaches, the problem of getting one's foot in the door is circumvented. Personal contacts and cold calling are traditional approaches to conducting a job search. Job seekers and developers should keep in mind there are no absolutes in job searches, and different approaches work for different people at different times.

Other Approaches

New and creative ways to approach job development are always evolving. For example, some employment service agencies are approaching businesses and soliciting their interests in making overall improvements in their employment practices by initially reviewing workplace supports for all workers (Wehman et al., 2001). In this approach, the job developer acts as a corporate liaison and offers training and technical assistance to the businesses to support their efforts to make the worksites and employment practices more accessible and appropriate for future and current employees with disabilities.

Mentoring is another concept that is gaining recognition in the workplace (Wehman et al., 2001). Many businesses view their supervisors as mentors to the employees they supervise. A business may wish to formalize this type of relationship by providing specific mentoring training for its supervisors, or the business may wish to develop a mentoring program that assists workers with disabilities throughout the employment process. Using mentoring programs in the broader capacity is an innovative approach, and the corporate liaison is available to assist in developing a program.

Some programs are conducting telephone surveys and inviting interested parties to a forum about the benefits associated with hiring people with disabilities. The training provides the employers with valuable information on disability-related topics and gives the agency a chance for a follow-up meeting with the employer to develop a long-term partnership. Basically, now, the job developer has either met someone who can assist him or her or who can introduce him or her to the appropriate personnel.

Lieshout (2001) presented a national strategy known as the Business Leadership Network (BLN) to advance the employment of people with disabilities. A BLN is an employer-led coalition that works alongside the rehabilitation community, people with disabilities, and employment support programs to promote employment of individuals with disabilities. It can work in both large and small communities. Each are developed on a grass roots level and focus on employer development by identifying and meeting the need of area businesses. Developing strategic partnerships with business service providers can increase employer ownership, participation, and support. This, in turn, will help improve hiring of individuals with disabilities (Rackham et al., 1997).

These and other approaches put a new twist on job development by offering something to the business and focusing on developing an ongoing strategic relationship with the organization, rather than just a one-time meeting about a job placement. The idea of building relationships is more fully explored in Bissonnette's (1994) book *Beyond Traditional Job Development*. She stated that the relationship between an employer and an employment specialist should be dynamic, ongoing, evolving, and altered as either person's needs or interests change. In this capacity, the employment specialist should function as a consultant, focusing on establishing a mutually beneficial relationship.

Using this paradigm, the emphasis shifts from making cold calls to making calls of introduction. As Bissonnette (1994) stated, an introductory call does not seek a "yes" answer from an employer but establishes the rapport needed to develop a creative response to an employer's needs or concerns and offers services. In addition, a one-sided sales pitch becomes a two-way conversation in which the employer can determine the relevance and value of what is being offered. When making introductory calls, there is no failure, only feedback. With a list of employers to reach in hand, the next step is for the employment specialists to contact potential employers.

MAKING CONTACT

Approaching business people requires excellent communication skills, patience, confidence, perseverance, and a positive attitude. Initial employer communications may occur via a telephone call, unannounced personal visit, or written correspondence. No matter which approach is used, employment specialists should be well prepared and should know why the business is being called and the desired outcome of the contact (e.g., to secure an interview for a job seeker, to receive information on the company and future hiring needs, to analyze positions in the organization, to identify job creation or carving opportunities, to gain referrals to similar businesses). The desired outcome can vary depending on whether the employment specialist is looking for a specific type of work for one job seeker or has several job seekers in mind. Over time, some employment specialists may repeatedly lean toward using a certain approach. Their favored approach, however, may not be effective with all employers all of the time. Thus, a variety of contact strategies may be needed in order to find the one that works.

Business Contacts by Telephone

Business contacts can be made by telephone if the employment specialist can speak to the person in charge of hiring. This often requires getting beyond the receptionist, who must decide if the call is valuable enough to forward. Prior to making calls, some employment specialists may benefit from scripting out their approach. In addition, knowing the appropriate contact and confidently requesting to be connected to that person is often effective. For example, to get through, the specialist might say, "Good afternoon. This is Pam Targett from Business Connections, would you please connect me with Ron Sherron?"

Just in case this direct and assertive approach does not work, the employment specialist should be ready to respond to receptionist. For example, if the receptionist replies with, "Perhaps I can help you instead," then the employment specialist could talk slowly and deliberately as he or she recites a long and detailed explanation about who he or she is and what he or she wants to do. If a receptionist is answering a number of telephone lines and feels the caller is long winded, then the call may get forwarded. The specialist can also try using service lingo. Sometimes this may make the receptionist feel unqualified and prompt him or her to forward the call to someone more experienced. Asking a question that can only be answered by the person the specialist wants to reach may also get the desired result.

Another strategy involves calling the person throughout the day. Eventually, a less-experienced relief receptionist may put the call through. If the receptionist indicates the person is not available and asks to take a message, then the specialist should state that he or she will call back later and then ask for the receptionist's name and thank him or her personally for the assistance.

Employment specialists should also be prepared to leave messages on voice mail. Writing down what to say in advance can help eliminate possible pauses and "ums" in the message's content. If the desired contact is repeatedly unavailable or not returning messages, then the employment specialist should attempt to identify the best time of day to reach that person or find an alternative contact.

Once contact is made, the employment specialist should be ready to ask the employer for a personal meeting. This contact should be brief and to the point. The following outline can be used to script the approach.

- Greet the person

- Identify yourself

- Identify who you represent

- Briefly state the nature of the service offered

- Briefly state how the service offered may benefit the employer

- Request an informational interview to learn more about the business or a specific job

Even with advanced preparation, this can be an unnerving event for the novel employment specialists. The following tips might help.

- Calls should be made in a quiet office away from distractions. (Music, talking, or laughing in the background during a telephone call sounds unprofessional.)

- Smiling while talking can give the voice a lift and a cheerful, enthusiastic tone.

- Always be clear and honest about the specific purpose for calling.

- Set aside a block of time each day for making calls.

- Convey to the receiver, through the use of active listening skills, that you understand.

- Performance should be evaluated on an ongoing basis by peer review.

- Be attuned to receivers' reactions.

- Good communication skills are critical; take inventory of existing skills, and, if improvement is warranted, take action to improve ability.

Although not highly recommended, if a position has been identified through the classified advertisements, then the first contact will be by telephone, unless otherwise specified. If the company representative is too busy to meet and requests that an application be dropped off instead, then the employment specialist should inform the person that he or she would like an opportunity to see the job prior to submitting applications to ensure that only viable candidates are referred. If the employer still refuses, then the employment specialist should determine the value of the opportunity and act accordingly.

Drop-In Visits

A drop-in visit has the obvious advantage of getting a "foot in the door"; however, sensitivity must be given to the time constraints placed on an employer who has not set aside time for the visit. This method may be most suitable for the service industry and larger companies that regularly post job leads. Often, an appointment will need to be scheduled at another time. However, employment specialists should be ready to do a presentation on the spot.

Employment specialists should always be on the lookout for opportunities. For example, while out shopping, the need for a service such as bringing in shopping carts from the parking lot or shelving returned merchandise may be noted.

Letters of Introduction

Letters of introduction are an effective way to warm an employer up a future contact. These letters should be no more than one page long, to the point, and keep future follow up in the employment specialist's court. Faxing or e-mailing mass letters of introduction may be sent to a targeted audience of prospective employers. Although e-mail is a less formal method of communication, it has many advantages over other forms of communication. For example, it is faster, goes directly to a reader, and can be sent 24 hours a day. All written communications should be followed up with a telephone call or drop-in visit requesting a personal meeting.

Whether using a letter or placing a telephone call, an employment specialist who is interested in businesswide opportunities may want to begin with the personnel or human resources department. If, however, interest relates to work opportunities within a particular division, then the employment specialist will want to try and reach a departmental manager or supervisor. If pursuing a long-term partnership, then the specialist may need to go for top-down support and contact the company's president or general manager.

Managing Job Development

One of the greatest challenges employment specialists face is how to effectively organize their daily job development activities (Targett & Wehman, 2002). An organizational system is essential, especially when more than one person is involved in making business contacts (e.g., vocational education representative, job coaches, transition specialist). Nothing is more annoying to an employer than to be approached by several individuals from the same school that are essentially offering and looking for the same thing. This makes staff appear disorganized and unprofessional because they do not even appear to know what is going on within their own organization.

There are a number of ways to track business contacts. For example, a telephone log or an abbreviated version of a business contact sheet can be used to record details. The telephone log should have basic contact information such as the telephone number and a brief statement or code related to the results of the call. After meeting with an employer, an entire business contact sheet may be completed with more details on the organization, its hiring needs, procedures for applicants, and future follow-up details.

Regularly scheduled meetings to communicate are often helpful. For example, brief job development meetings can be held first thing in the morning to discuss current and future leads. To be productive, these meetings should be managed in accordance to established rules. For example, staff should come prepared with information on the types of positions or job creations that are being sought, types of businesses being approached, recent employer contact information, and a description of any available job leads. There should also be a set time frame with probably no more than 5-minute slots for each staff member to present his or her information. A meeting facilitator should enforce the rules and make sure everyone has an opportunity to share.

Personal organization is also critical. One possible way to get organized involves establishing and tracking goals and objectives. This helps some specialists stay focused on what needs to be done to reach the desired goal. For example, some students may have a very specific goal (e.g., Jack wants to make pizzas at a restaurant). Or, the goal may not be expressed in terms of a specific job title that is being pursued but instead may speak to different types of situations that may be acceptable to the student. For example, Jose desires to work for a company that offers flexible scheduling, weekends off, health benefits, $6.00 an hour, and is located within a 30-minute bus ride from his home. He is interested in a position that will allow him to work with others and move around throughout the day in a temperature-controlled climate. This does not mean that every aspect of the aforementioned goal will be met through employment, but it does help focus the job search on what is more likely to be acceptable to Jose.

It should be noted that a goal should not stop an employment specialist from informing the job seeker about a particular work option that differs from the stated one. This is because no one will find everything wanted in a particular job. Instead, the job seeker will have to weigh in on and prioritize the most and least important aspects of a particular job opportunity when making a decision about whether to pursue the lead.

Once the goal is established, the steps necessary to achieve it are stated. For example, the employment specialist will meet with at least 30 employers by the end of the month. The employment specialist will make a minimum of 50 telephone contacts a day until 10 employer meetings are set by the 15th of the month. The job seeker and the employment specialist will explore his or her personal network by the 10th of the month. Accompanied by the employment specialist, the job seeker will explore the types of job opportunities available at financial corporations by visiting and touring two local companies. When writing job development goals and objectives, it is important to include a timeline. Then, as time passes, the employment specialist can adjust these as needed.

Once the plan is established, it should be followed. If everything is not accomplished on a specific day, then efforts are increased the next day. The plan becomes a "living" document and is updated as goals are met or revised when a new direction is needed. Also, some employment specialists may feel "down in the dumps" when rejected by employers. Writing a job placement plan of action can help some specialists stay focused. In addition, accomplishing objectives gives reason for celebration, which, in turn, may increase the employment specialists' confidence.

One way to increase the odds of discovering a work opportunity is to make new contacts and follow up with existing ones on an ongoing basis. A tickler file that indicates when to contact employers should be maintained and used to keep the program in the forefront of the employers' mind (e.g., if an employment specialist meets a business on July 20, then he or she enters a note in the tickler file to recontact or send a letter to the business on October 20). Personal schedulers on the computer or a time management software package can be used to integrate contact information with the calendar functions.

The frequency of future contacts will vary from employer to employer depending on the overall goal. For example, the employment specialist may want to stay in touch with some employers on a regular basis and develop long-term partnerships. Other employers may not have expressed an interest in working together, but the employment specialist wants to remain in touch with them in case their needs change. Those who are considering a student for employment must be followed up with regularly. And, of course, there will be some employers that the employment specialist does not wish to remain in contact with at the present time or foreseeable future.

PRESENTATION TO EMPLOYER

Eventually, the time will come to meet face-to-face with prospective employers. The employment specialist should be prepared. This means knowing what he or she has to offer and the job seekers abilities and support needs. It is also important for the employment specialist to project a pleasant, positive, and confident attitude. Employment specialists who are hesitant or lack confidence may send a danger signal to a prospective employer who may then back off. A confident and positive attitude will help reflect personal integrity and indicates that the employment specialist is honest and can be trusted.

Confidence and a Positive Attitude

Personal confidence and attitude will directly affect an employment specialist's success at job development. If a knowledgeable specialist is not seeing results, then he or she may want to consider if any attitudinal barriers are getting in the way. For example,

Table 10.1.   Seven myths to dispel

Myth 1: Individuals with disabilities do not have the right skills for business.
Fact: People with disabilities can develop important critical thinking skills.
Fact: People with disabilities bring unique characteristics and skills to the work force.

Myth 2: Supports in the workplace would be too costly.
Fact: Accommodations are generally not expensive.
Fact: Employers make accommodations daily.

Myth 3: Saying the wrong thing in the workplace will offend employees with disabilities.
Fact: Simple etiquette can avoid relationship barriers.
Fact: People with disabilities appreciate person-first language

Myth 4: Co-workers will be uncomfortable and their productivity will be negatively impacted.
Fact: Workers with disabilities have a positive effect on co-workers.

Myth 5: Getting information on how to hire people with disabilities is time consuming and complicated.
Fact: Help is easy to get and available at little or no cost.
Fact: Employers may be eligible for tax credits and deductions.

Myth 6: Hiring people with disabilities makes businesses vulnerable to litigation.
Fact: Very few businesses experience disability-related claims.

Myth 7: Serving people with disabilities will adversely affect businesses' bottom line.
Fact: Consumers with disabilities represent an enormous market niche.
Fact: Marketing to consumers with disabilities and making appropriate accommodations makes good
      business sense.
Fact: Yesterday's accommodation is today's product innovation.

From Center for Workforce Preparation. (2004). *Disability: Dispelling the myths—How people with disabilities can meet employer needs* (pp. 4–7). Washington, DC: United States Chamber of Commerce; adapted by permission.

employment specialists who believe they have no control will, in fact, have none. One way to overcome this is to get control by refusing rejection. For instance, employment specialists whose mindset is on educating and developing employer relations instead of an immediate payoff of getting a job lead cannot be rejected. Employment specialists can take on a role to educate employers about the benefits of the services and the abilities of people with disabilities. Though inconclusive, O'Hara's (2004) initial research showed that the level of prejudice toward a disability increases the level of discrimination among women with disabilities. He stated that taking action to improve the public's perception of disabilities should help mitigate the effect of discrimination based on prejudice. For example, after meeting with a prospective employer, at the bare minimum, the employment specialist could leave some educational information to help combat prejudice and reduce personal feelings of rejection. Some common myths to dispel about disability are provided in Table 10.1.

This is not intended to imply that employment specialists should simply accept any employer objections, leave educational information, and exit feeling that all is bright and beautiful. But, instead, this technique can be used to help build confidence. The employment specialist is in a win-win situation because under these circumstances an employer has learned more about employment and people with disabilities.

Another practical way to exude confidence is to simply deal with the other person in a way that assumes that he or she will be responsive or receptive to the proposal. The power of suggestion is used by assuming that the other person is going to do what the employment specialist wants him or her to do and communicate this through attitude.

The specialist may also become more self-assured by considering the worst possible scenario. For example, perhaps an employment specialist initially envisions that an employer will suddenly blow up, slam his or her fist on the desk, and call security to escort the employment specialist off of the premises. However, on evaluation, the specialist should recognize that this is very unlikely. Instead, a worse case scenario would be an employer who says, "No, I am not interested" and adjourns the meeting early.

Appearance also affects confidence. Employers will have an immediate impression of the employment specialist and it needs to be a positive one. Employment specialists should ask themselves the following questions to help evaluate their appearance:

- *Is my dress appropriate for the business visit?* Whenever possible, become familiar with what the employees are wearing at the jobsite and then dress a little nicer for the meeting. Dressing in sync with the company's image can give the employment specialist an edge. For instance, a dark suit might be best for a meeting with a law firm, whereas more stylish and colorful clothing is appropriate for a meeting in the fashion industry. Because the employment specialist will likely be meeting with various industries, such a specialized approach to dressing might not always be feasible. Thus, when in doubt, he or she should lean toward conservatism.

- *What does my body language convey?* Employment specialists' body language and nonverbal messages also affect an employer's outlook. Posture should be alert, expressions should convey a pleasant attitude, and eye contact should be comfortable. Walking upright with a smile says, "You want to do business with me." Appearance and body language send messages to employers and influences whether they will consider doing business.

- *Do I look organized and well prepared?* Employment specialists should also have effective marketing tools on hand. At the bare minimum, a brochure and business card are needed. The Office of Disability Employment Policy at the Department of Labor has a number of resources about hiring people with disabilities that can be shared with employers.

Business Meeting Guidelines

In a small business, the employment specialist's goal may be to meet with the owner, and in the service industry, it may be to reach the manager or district supervisor. In larger corporations, employment specialists may have to meet with human resource representatives first before being introduced to the hiring supervisor. Most often, however, the appointment with personnel is more of a matter of protocol than a decision-making point.

To achieve positive results, employment specialists should become skilled at varying their messages, based on what the employer is interested in. In other words, employment specialists should find out what a company wants or needs before offering them anything. This requires employment specialists to be attentive listeners, good conversationalists who speak confidently about what is offered, and convey the message that the employer's needs are understood. Employment specialists must also become skilled at problem solving, be ready to address any employer concerns, and overcome objections.

The goal of the first employer meeting is to have another one in which the employment specialist can learn even more about the workplace and possible job opportunities. The primary objectives are to:

- Build rapport and trust with the employer

- Gain a better understanding about the business by learning about its needs, with an eye toward work opportunities for a specific student

- Demonstrate that the employment specialist can be a valuable business resource

Finding out what a company is interested in will help the employment specialist avoid spending time trying to convince employers to use something that they do not need. So, the employment specialist must first approach a company ready to listen and learn more about a particular line of work and/or the company and its needs. Informational or exploratory interviews that were mentioned earlier can help here.

During the first meeting, the employer is not really asked to do anything more than provide information in his or her area of expertise; therefore, this is not a high-pressure situation. This approach can also lead to future contacts and help establish a partnership with a business that may eventually pay off with a job offer.

Some employers will want a brief, well-organized presentation, whereas others may invite a detailed description of services. Some might be interested in personal accounts of success stories, and others will want to know facts and program statistics. The content of the employer presentation may also vary depending on whether the employment specialist is pursuing an existing position or trying to create a job for a student. The following outline lays a foundation for meeting with an employer and an example of how the conversation might go.

Set the Stage   At the start of the meeting, the employment specialist should explain what he or she would like to achieve. For example, he or she might say,

> Thank you for agreeing to meet with me today. In the next 10 minutes I would like to tell you who we are and what we do and why I think you may be interested in working with us. As I mentioned over the telephone, the school vocational program offers a number of services to employers, including referring students with disabilities for job opportunities. I would like to begin by learning more about your business so I can provide you with the information you need to determine if this service would be beneficial to you. I would also like to establish a protocol for a future relationship in case you do not need services now but may desire them at a later date.

Next, the employment specialist may emphasize the benefits offered rather than just the services. For example, employer benefits include saving time and money on recruitment costs, reducing lag time in filling vacant positions, increasing community involvement, and attracting positive press.

> The goal of this service is to identify ways to help employers meet their business needs and provide a student with a disability an opportunity to work.
>
> As an employment specialist, I am available to refer applicants and help arrange any supports, if needed. These services are highly individualized and may include additional job skills training at no cost to you. If applicable, I will also contribute to getting the job done while the new employee is learning and until he or she is performing the duties independently and to your standards.
>
> Once the worker is able to perform the job to the standards you have set, I will gradually reduce my presence from the jobsite. I will, however, continue to stay in touch and will be available for additional support if needed, such as helping the worker learn a new job duty.

After describing the service, the employment specialist should inform the employer about other businesses he or she has worked with and the available financial incentives, such as the Work Opportunity Tax Credit (WOTC) and tax deductions for making accommodations.

Discuss Business Needs   Next, the employment specialist should request permission to ask questions and discuss the employer's business needs. It may be useful to prepare a list of questions in advance—asking relevant and intelligent questions should help establish credibility with the employer. If an employer feels the employment specialist is genuinely interested in his or her needs and concerns, then it may inspire confidence about establishing a lasting relationship with the program (Owens-Johnson & Hanley-Maxwell, 1999). The following are examples of questions that may help the employment specialist learn more about current business needs.

- Can you tell me about your business?

- How is business going?

- Do you foresee any trends that will affect your industry?

- Can you describe some of the entry-level positions?

- Do you experience a high turnover rate in any positions?

- Have you worked with a SE program in the past?

- Do you feel this service can add to what you are already doing?

Address Concerns and Questions   Not all presentations come off without a hitch. Employment specialists will find that some employers will agree with them up to a point and then come up with an objection. For instance, employers may say, "We cannot do this right now. We are tightening up our budget and can only hire people who we know will help increase our profitability. We train our own people. If the person wants to apply for a job, then ask him or her come in and complete an application. The timing is bad. We are just too busy to focus on it right now. We are trying to deal with a million other things. Maybe we can use your service in the future, but now is not a good time to get started."

When this happens, employment specialist should understand that the reason given is frequently not the real reason (Peck & Kirkbride, 2001). Employers have many questions about the values and the risk of hiring people with disabilities. Many are hesitant to voice their concerns. Some worry about legal liability of what they may ask or not ask. Others do not want to risk appearing ignorant or prejudiced. Therefore, employment specialists must be prepared to uncover the employer's real concerns. Some may be substantiated, whereas others will be based on misconceptions or stereotypes about people with disabilities. Regardless, to be effective, employment specialist must be prepared to address and overcome objections. Some typical types of fears that may surface and some ideas on how to address or offset these follow.

Will this work? This fear is based largely on concern that your service will not function the way you promise. Or, the person who is hired will not be able to do the job. In order to offset this concern, the employment specialist should let the employer know that he or she is representing a number of people with a wide range of abilities and interests and state that he or she wants to learn more about the business needs. The specialist should also reassure the employer that the profitability of the businesses is of utmost importance and will do his or her best to refer appropriate applicants for jobs. Pointing out that other businesses have successfully used the service and hired individuals with disabilities may also help offset this fear. Also, reassure the employer that if the job does not work out for the worker with the disability, then that person can get assistance with locating a more suitable job. Sharing newspaper articles or testimonials from other businesses that have used the service might help.

What will others think? This fear relates to the employer's concern about losing face or status with peer group members. Furthermore, the employer may wonder if hiring a person with a disability will cause discomfort to the other employees or customers. Many people have misperceptions about people with disabilities and need information.

In this situation, providing information such as the *Top 10 Reasons to Hire People with Disabilities* (National Organization on Disability, 2001) may be useful. For example, tips from the book include: people with disabilities have equal or higher job performance ratings, higher retention rates, and lower absenteeism; employees with disabilities can relate better to customers with disabilities, who represent $1 trillion in annual aggregate consumer spending; a person with a disability motivates work groups and increases productivity; or more than three fourths of managers surveyed said that the costs of employing both workers with and without disabilities are about the same.

Relating disability to the employer's personal experiences may be helpful too. For example, the specialist may ask, "Have you ever known anyone with a disability?" or state how one day we will all experience challenges. Mentioning any positive press that other businesses have received may also help alleviate this concern.

Will I lose or spend too much money? The fear of losing money or spending too much money is very common. To counter this, employment specialists should remember to point out that "job coach services" are offered at no cost to the employer. Employers may also be concerned about expenses related to making reasonable accommodations. Unless they can prove "undue hardship," employers are generally responsible for the cost of accommodations.

In such an instance, the specialist should cite data related to cost and, if available, state that cost sharing is possible through state VR agency funds. For example, reports from the Job Accommodation Network (1999, 2000) revealed that 20% of employer accommodations cost nothing, and 80% cost less than $500. In addition, providing examples of simple low or no tech solutions to accommodate individuals may reduce fears. For example, a company may be concerned that a new desk will need to be purchased so a worker who uses a wheelchair can gain access to his or her workstation, when in reality, the desk could simply be raised.

Employers tend to view time as money. The employer may be put at ease by explaining that the new employee is simply treated like any other new hire and any additional skills training needed beyond what the company offers will be provided. In addition, the specialist will make sure the work is being done while the new employee is receiving additional on-the-job skills training. Emphasis is placed on a joint desire for an independent, productive employee. Providing some examples of how this has worked in another business may be helpful. The specialist should also let the employer know that if the job changes or the worker takes on new responsibilities, then additional services are available.

Wrap Up   At the close of the meeting, the employment specialist should ask for what he or she wants. If this is a job placement, then he or she should emphasize the practicality of the idea and explain why it is a no-lose proposition. In addition, he or she should stress that the work is going to be done with little risk. For example, "I would really like to find out more about your operation. Is it possible for me to learn about your overall operation and some of your entry-level positions? I am hoping you will find it worthwhile to interview one of the people I represent, now or in the future."

In addition to conducting an informational interview, a tour is also an excellent way to get firsthand information on the business and its needs. Actually seeing the workplace provides insight in to possible jobs and accommodations. This is also the time when conversations about possible job creations may come up. A job creation involves inventing or customizing a job for a specific student. More information on this important technique will be provided in a later section.

Depending on the situation, during the first meeting or subsequent meetings, a more detailed presentation about a specific job seeker and/or service is provided. At this time, services that help accommodate the student worker can be presented. Sometimes one meeting will lead to a student interview and other times it will be a positive first step in that direction.

If the employer is agreeable, then the employment specialist should arrange to analyze the position and set up times for job interviews. If the employer is not able to grant the employment specialist's request, then he or she should remain open and receptive to getting something else such as mock interviews for students or referrals to another business.

In summary, there is virtually no way to predict in advance which employers will be receptive. Decisions will be based on a number of factors, such as current needs and underlying values. Regardless, employment specialists should try to enhance the odds of being well received by using a professional approach and keeping a positive attitude. Role playing and observing other employment specialists in action can be useful training activities for a novice.

Workplace Analysis   At the close of the meeting, the employment specialist should ask for a time to return to the business to perform a job analysis (Brooke et al., 1997). No two people have the same ability or disability, thus each job seeker presents a need for a unique work situation. Job analysis involves gaining insight into what a position requires and comparing this with the job seeker's skills. The outcome of an analysis is to determine if an existing position suits the job seeker or what positions might be created. During job analysis, the employment specialist should also begin exploring the types of accommodations that would allow the job seeker to succeed in the job.

A tour is an excellent way to get information about a company, and most employers will agree to allow an employment specialist to watch how the business operation performs. Sometimes, this opportunity may immediately follow the initial meeting or at other times during another meeting. In the field, this is referred to as a *workplace analysis*, but when speaking with employers, the employment specialist should simply let the employer know he or she would like to learn more about the business and specific jobs. Again, this is accomplished through interviews with key personnel, reviews of job descriptions, and observations of the work being performed.

The goal is to learn more about various occupations within an organization and try to locate a possible fit between the job seeker and the business. Information from informational interviews and business tours can be used to complement the additional details gained through a workplace analysis. To some extent, all businesses provide support to their employees. This can include formal support, such as employee training programs, supervision, or written rules of conduct. Some are generic to most businesses, whereas others are unique to a particular employer. Learning more about how the business supports its work force offers insight in to whether this would be a good place to work. Some other things to consider might include accessibility, willingness to accommodate job applicants and workers, and employee benefits. Also, exploring how the organization provides supports during the recruitment can be useful. For example, are the applications completed on premises, or can they be taken away to complete? Is any pre-employment testing required and, if so, for what purpose? What type of new employee orientation and training is provided?

Notes on the work setting and environment should also be taken. For example, is the workplace climate-controlled and clean (e.g., a retail store), or is it hot and dusty (e.g., a manufacturer's warehouse)? What do employees wear to work—a uniform or business attire? Is there a lot of background noise, or is it a quiet environment? Does the person work in one area or required to move to different workstations? Does the work require exposure to any unusual fumes or gases?

Specific job tasks or functions also need to be observed. This begins by learning about the position in general. For example, what is the general flow or routine and the goal or outcome of the work being performed? Then, for each job duty identified, investigations on how it is currently being accomplished are conducted. For example, what procedures are followed, and what materials and/or types of equipment are used? Work pace and standards of production should also be considered in addition to the types of interactions required with co-workers. For example, is task completion dependent on others? Do co-workers seem friendly and helpful to one another? A very important, but often overlooked, aspect of this analysis is the informal social interactions and relationships at work. What is the management style? What shared social customs, norms, and expectations exist among the workers that define the workplace culture? Is it positive?

The best way to learn about the workplace is to spend some time making observations and conducting informal interviews in the workplace. Brief, unobtrusive observations, coupled with informal interviews, should provide a wealth of information that is essential when determining what types of work supports a new hire may need to perform the job functions.

Again, although conducting a job/workplace analysis is not a mandatory, it is highly recommended. Allowing this activity will also shed light on an employer's flexibility and willingness to accommodate a worker with disability. It will also likely increase the odds of success and satisfaction at work because the student is advised in advance on how a particular job meets his or her preferences, abilities, and support needs.

Although there is no magical way to ensure a successful job match, making accurate information available to the job seeker can help him or her make an informed decision. However, when creating a work opportunity, job/workplace analysis becomes a critical activity because employment specialists have no idea where to begin or how to proceed with job carving if they do not understand the business operations. Because job creation is highly individualized, this is typically a required or necessary first step. See Chapter 11 for examples of how to carve job opportunities.

In summary, conducting a workplace analysis may be a large or small undertaking depending on the goals and the complexity of the business or the type of work being performed. Even if an employment specialist has experience and knowledge of various types of occupations, an analysis is still recommended because workplaces and the way jobs are performed vary from business to business.

After a workplace analysis, the next step is to find out if the job seeker is interested in the position. As mentioned earlier, when conducting these activities, a person-centered approach should be used. For example, an informal comparison between individual preferences and strengths in relation to a specific job can help indicate possible training needs, accommodations, or supports the person may require should he or she be hired.

Sometimes, employment specialists may discover a potential candidate is not interested or cannot be reasonably accommodated. When that happens, they should try to determine why the individual is not interested. Is it a fear of going to work, transportation concerns, or a dislike of certain job duties? It may take patience and skillful probing to discover the real reasons for not being interested. If an individual has made an informed choice and really does not want to interview for a position, then consider other job seekers and see if they are interested. In such an instance, another informal compatibility analysis can be conducted and other job seekers may be approached. This matching process does not guarantee that a student will succeed at a specific job. However, it can be a useful way of objectively viewing and comparing information on several candidates for a job. If no one wants to pursue the job lead, then employment specialists may be faced with the disappointing task of turning down an interview and potential a job offer. When an individual is interested, the next step is to set up an interview. Depending on the student's abilities, this may be a more formal interview or, at times, much more informal.

SKILL ENHANCEMENT

Locating work opportunities for students with significant disabilities is not always quick or easy. However, with experience, confidence, and determination, success is imminent. Every employer contact provides employment specialists with insight into their present skill level and should help them determine ways to further improve. Some other strategies that may enhance skill development include the following.

- Pair up with colleagues from time to time during an employer meeting in order to get performance feedback.

- Videotape a simulated employer meeting with a supervisor or experienced co-worker playing the role of employer.

- Observe experienced personnel in the field to gain insight on how to strengthen your approach.

- Survey employers for feedback. The survey should be brief, concise, and easy to complete and return.

- Compile data on characteristics of companies that do choose to hire students.

CONCLUSION

Job development approaches must be flexible, creative, and adapted to the employer's needs. To be effective, employment specialists must tap in to the hidden job market and be prepared to allay employer misperceptions or concerns about hiring someone with a disability. Even when a student does not receive a job offer, employment specialists must continue to believe in their power to change nonresponsive attitudes. Education is essential, and no business contact can be perceived as a failure if the employment specialist takes on the educator's role. This chapter examined ways employment specialist can assist students with disabilities with going to work. Information on getting prepared to meet with business, identifying businesses to contact, tapping into the hidden job market, making business presentations, and tips for improving performance was presented.

STUDY QUESTIONS

1. What do employment specialists need to know prior to contacting employers?

2. What is the purpose of the ADA and its implications for SE service delivery?

3. What is the hidden job market and why is it important to tap into it?

4. What techniques can be used to tap in to the hidden job market?

5. What are some typical employer concerns and how are these addressed?

Appendix

The Americans with Disabilities Act

The appendix provides some additional information on reasonable accommodation in the workplace and implications for SE. The reader must remember that the interpretation of the ADA is provided on a case-by-case basis. In addition, state and local laws may apply. Job developers should seek out information for their particular area in order to have a fuller understanding of the rights of the individuals they serve by contacting their local or regional U.S. Equal Employment Opportunity Commission (EEOC) office. ADA information, assistance, and copies of ADA documents are available in standard print, large print, audio cassette, braille, computer disk, and on the Internet at http://www.eeoc.gov.

DEFINING REASONABLE ACCOMMODATION

Although many individuals with disabilities can perform essential functions without accommodations, others are excluded from jobs that they are qualified to perform because of barriers in the workplace. Because of this, the ADA requires reasonable accommodation as a means of overcoming unnecessary barriers that prevent or restrict work opportunities for otherwise qualified people with disabilities. The Rehabilitation Act of 1973 (PL 93-112) and its regulations require reasonable accommodation. *Reasonable accommodation* is defined as "any change or adjustment to a job or work environment that permits a qualified applicant or employee with a disability to participate in the job application process, to perform the essential functions of a job, or to enjoy benefits and privileges of employment equal to those enjoyed by employees without disabilities" (U.S. EEOC, 1997b, p. 2). According to the ADA, if an individual is able to perform the essential functions of a job except for activities that cannot be performed due to barriers or related limitations, then the employer is obligated to identify a reasonable accommodation that would allow the person to perform the function. Employers are only required to make accommodations for the known physical or mental limitations of a qualified applicant or employee with a disability. If an individual does not request an accommodation, then the employer is not required to provide one. Employers are prohibited from lowering an employee's salary in order to make up for the cost of an accommodation (U.S. EEOC, 1997b).

Three aspects of employment that may require reasonable accommodation are the application process, performance of the essential job functions, and ensuring equal employment benefits. A reasonable accommodation must be effective, reduce barriers to employment that are related to a person's disability, and need not be the best accommodation available as long as it effectively serves its purpose. Employers do not need to provide an accommodation that is primarily for personal use, and any adjustments made do not prevent an employer from providing accommodations beyond those required by the ADA. Furthermore, employers are not required to lower their performance standards in order to make an accommodation. The statute and the U.S. EEOC's regulations provide an overview of the common types of reasonable accommodation that businesses may be required to provide, such as

- Making facilities accessible and usable
- Providing assistance with completing applications
- Restructuring the job
- Providing qualified readers and interpreters
- Adjusting and modifying training materials and policies
- Modifying work schedules
- Providing a flexible leave policy
- Obtaining or modifying equipment or devices
- Providing a job coach
- Making the workplace readily accessible and usable by people with disabilities
- Reassigning the employee to a vacant position

When considering accommodation, employers must remember that it is a very individualized process and must be addressed on a case-by-case basis. Two factors that must be taken into consideration are the specific abilities and functional limitations of the job seeker or employee and the specific functional requirements of a certain job. Therefore, many types of accommodations may be appropriate for a particular situation.

A prospective or current employee with a disability should inform the employer that an accommodation is needed. The person does not have to use the phrase "reasonable accommodation" but must let the employer know an adjustment is needed because of a disability. If the person who requests accommodation does not suggest an appropriate one, then the employer and the person should work together. This is where VR professionals can provide a valuable service.

It is also important to keep in mind that people with disabilities have always found methods to compensate in order to maintain or gain independence. All too often the understanding of the idea of accommodation is limited to major structural changes in buildings or costly electronic devices. In fact, accommodations include a full range of adaptations or adjustments. Consider the following examples.

1. *AT:* Sara, an office aide, uses a keyboard guard to reduce typing errors from uncontrollable hand movements. Jack, a receptionist with a spinal cord injury, uses voice recognition computer software to record messages for other employees. Judith, a file clerk with ataxia, uses rubber tips to make turning pages easier.

2. *Compensatory strategies:* Lawrence, a medical supply stocker, uses a checklist to help him remember his sequence of job duties and what tasks he has done. Lisa, a li-

brarian's assistant, uses a memory notebook to record what she has accomplished and what she needs to do. Edith uses a timer to help her keep pace and monitor her productivity as a prep cook.

3. *Job coach:* Raymond, a job coach, accompanies Frank, a houseman at a hotel, to work and provides job-skills training. Gail assists Jennifer, who is blind, with mobility training to allow her to get around her new workplace.

When considering accommodations, the employer should never focus on the disability label. Instead, the employer should consider abilities first and then limitations that require accommodation; job developers should be prepared to assist in this process. The type of accommodation that a person needs will vary depending on personal strengths, functional limitations, and the nature of the job.

Employers are required to provide reasonable accommodation, unless it would result in an undue hardship. *Undue hardship* is defined as "an action requiring significant difficulty or expense when considered in light of a number of factors" (U.S. EEOC, 1997a, p. 3). The determination of whether a specific accommodation will impose undue hardship must be considered on a case-by-case basis as the employer's size, available resources, the nature of the operation, the nature and cost of the accommodation, and its impact on the employer's operation are determining factors. Denial of a job opportunity due to the need for a reasonable accommodation would constitute discrimination under the ADA. Again, this applies to all employment practices, not just hiring.

IMPLICATIONS FOR INDIVIDUALS RECEIVING SUPPORTED EMPLOYMENT SERVICES

It is not possible to fully establish the implications the ADA has on participants of SE programs because interpretation and determination are made on an individualized, case-by-case basis. SE is mentioned in the interpretive guide under the category of reasonable accommodation. It indicates that under certain circumstances, employers may be required to provide modified training materials or a temporary job coach to assist in the training of a qualified individual with a disability as a reasonable accommodation, provided that such a service is paid for by a VR agency.

Job seekers who would require the restructuring of the essential functions of an existing position to fit their abilities in order to perform a task would not be covered. Those protected must be able to perform the essential functions either without accommodations or with reasonable accommodations. Fortunately, although not required under the ADA, many employers are willing to restructure the essential functions of a job in order to create a work opportunity for a person with a disability. Modifications beyond those required under the ADA advance the underlying goal of the act to increase employment opportunities for Americans with disabilities.

It seems reasonable to believe that when an employer chooses to carve or create a position for a job seeker, the new employee would then become covered under the act. Again, it is important to note that all decisions related to the ADA are made on the basis of independent interpretation. Therefore, what will hold true in any individual case cannot be accurately foretold. Whenever an individual is seeking an existing work opportunity (as opposed to a job creation), the employment specialist is a consultant to the job seeker as well as to the business. The employment specialist can provide a variety of functions, such as determining accommodations, identifying funding sources, teaching the person to use the accommodations, and so forth. Employment specialists can use several strategies when discussing the ADA with prospective employers:

- Be prepared to answer questions about the ADA and have written resources available.

- Emphasize your role in assisting the job seeker and the employer with making reasonable accommodations.

- Explain how performing a job analysis is a service that can assist employers with determining the essential functions of the job.

- Be prepared to discuss potential types of accommodations for various positions.

- Point out that there are financial resources, tax incentives, or tax credits available. Federal tax incentives are available to meet the cost of complying with the ADA. Job developers should seek the most current information by contacting the U.S. EEOC and local VR agency.

- Discuss the role of the job coach in assisting the employer with training or arranging accommodations for the new employee free of charge.

- Point out that the ADA only requires effective accommodations, not the most expensive ones.

Several strategies are also available for employment specialists to use to help motivate and empower individuals with disabilities.

- Provide the person with information on his or her rights under Title I of the ADA.

- Make sure the person understands issues related to disclosure and reasonable accommodations and how to speak about this in a positive way.

- Teach the person to talk about his or her attributes, not the disability. If the person has difficulty communicating, then consider alternative means, such as asking questions that can be responded to or preparing a written response in advance that the job seeker can give to the interviewer.

- Assist the person with determining types of possible accommodations, including the use of a job coach, that can be explained to the prospective employer during the interview process.

- Bring out the best of a person's capabilities by helping the person make the best use of his or her own resources and by being a partner. Provide the tools, support, and structure to allow the person to achieve more than he or she might be able to do alone.

Technical assistance on accommodations is also available to all parties from organizations such as the President's Committee on Employment of People with Disabilities, governors' committees on employment of people with disabilities, the Job Accommodation Network, ABLEDATA, and state and local VR agencies.

11

Job Carving and Customized Employment

CARY GRIFFIN AND PAM SHERRON TARGETT

AFTER COMPLETING THIS CHAPTER, THE READER WILL BE ABLE TO

○ Explain the concept of job carving

○ Describe ways employers can take a more active role in the employment of people with disabilities

○ Identify the basic steps involved in the creation of new employment opportunities

○ Discuss various strategies for carving a job

○ Explain the purpose of an employment proposal and its major components

Preparation of this chapter was supported in part by Cooperative Agreement No. H133B9800036 from the National Institute on Disability and Rehabilitation Research (NIDRR), U.S. Department of Education. This support does not constitute official endorsement of the information or views presented here.

This chapter focuses on how to build business awareness about the need for employ-ment among young people with disabilities and job carving without having the "tail wag the dog," so to speak. In traditional employment approaches, jobs are typically identified, and then a job seeker is assisted in applying. Some thought is generally given to the individual's preferences for work, but jobs are often viewed as being in such short supply that choice in employment can be quite limited. Customized em-ployment (CE) addresses this issue by focusing on the individual's needs, skills, talents, and potential contributions to the workplace first, then finding or creating employ-ment, including business ownership, that best represents the ideal conditions of em-ployment for that unique job seeker.

The U.S. Department of Labor definition states that

> Customized employment means individualizing the employment relationship between em-ployees and employers in ways that meet the needs of both. It is based on an individualized determination of the strengths, needs, and interests of the person with a disability, and is also designed to meet the specific needs of the employer.
>
> It may include employment developed through job carving, self-employment or entrepre-neurial initiatives, or other job development or restructuring strategies that result in job re-sponsibilities being customized and individually negotiated to fit the needs of individuals with a disability.
>
> Customized employment assumes the provision of reasonable accommodations and sup-ports necessary for the individual to perform the functions of a job that is individually nego-tiated and developed. (Federal Register, 2002, pp. 43149–43154)

Job carving is a most obvious form of customizing employment. *Carving* is defined by determining the job seeker's skills, interests, and contributions and matching these to a set of duties found in a local workplace. Because such job descriptions rarely appear as a perfect match, carving involves creating a new list of duties that meet both em-ployer and employee needs and which complement the common interests of both.

Getting to know employers and individuals well enough to attempt job carving is a first step. One grassroots effort to develop business partnerships and encourage em-ployers to take a more active role in the employment of people with disabilities is de-scribed here. The process and some of the critical lessons learned are highlighted. Next, various strategies for job carving or breaking jobs down into their key compo-nents and reassigning those pieces in more efficient or understandable ways are pre-sented. Employers understand job carving and regularly re-engineer workplace processes to accommodate new equipment, changing personnel, and variable produc-tion schedules. Business and resource ownership as a variation of job carving is also presented. A number of examples are used to illustrate these concepts. The reader should note that all examples of jobs created began with an understanding of each stu-dent job seeker's abilities, support needs, and employment goals, as well as the busi-ness' needs. Although each student is a unique individual and labor markets and work-site cultures vary drastically by state, county, city, and town, the methods presented here should be generalized.

BUILDING EMPLOYER AWARENESS OF THE NEED FOR JOBS

Understanding the suitability of work from the viewpoint of the person with the dis-ability is always foremost. However, employers have begun taking a more active role in the job search, analysis, placement, and supervision activities necessary in supported employment. In the northern Colorado towns of Fort Collins and Greeley, for instance, the Center for Technical Assistance and Training (CTAT), an organization that promotes employment for citizens with disabilities, and the Colorado Division of Vocational Rehabilitation developed a corporate partnership initiative that is largely directed at a grassroots level by people with disabilities and local businesses.

The Process

As the first step in building employer awareness of the need for jobs, professional staff from CTAT and VR began joining local business and service groups, such as the Chamber of Commerce, Rotary Club, and Kiwanis Club, as active members willing to participate and contribute to products and events (e.g., publicity newsletters, fundraisers). Simultaneously, individuals with disabilities needing jobs and their family members were involved in meeting members of the local business community. In only a few weeks, enough connections were made to form Business Advisory Councils (BACs) in each community, consisting of local employers representing both small businesses and large corporations (e.g., Hewlett-Packard; Sykes Enterprises, Inc.; Bank One; NORWEST Banks; Electronic Fab Tech Corporation; Professional Finance Company; Teledyne; Express Personnel; State Farm Insurance; United Airlines) and people with disabilities, with a few human services and school personnel to explain and manipulate disability systems.

These councils meet monthly, and each member is required to bring at least one employment lead or contact to the corporate initiative manager and the local VR counselors. Consumers enrolled in VR are asked if they have an interest in exploring employment in the contact's business. This contact is then called and given the name of the BAC member who suggested calling, and an appointment is made to discuss employment opportunities. Often, these contacts are suppliers of the BAC member's business, and a natural business relationship already exists that can be leveraged into job development. Often, too, the BAC members find that they have jobs available in their companies and help minimize the red tape and other roadblocks inherent in employment. Because the BACs include the active participation of business and consumers and the expectation that employment outcomes are the absolute priority for all BAC activity, mutually beneficial and respectful relationships form that create a force for job development in the community (Griffin & Hammis, 1994).

This particular BAC took the bold move of adopting as their mission the challenge to make the employment rates of people with disabilities equivalent to that of those without disabilities. In other words, this group sought to lower the unemployment rate for people with disabilities from roughly 70% to approximately 5%. This was a bold stand for the business-dominated council, one that even rehabilitation agencies do not typically aspire to. This mission went on to be accepted by the statewide Business Leadership Network that had strong ties to the Northern Colorado BAC and later showed up in President Clinton's establishment of the National Task Force on Employment of Adults with Disabilities on March 13, 1998. The task force was charged with creating "a coordinated and aggressive national policy to bring working-age individuals with disabilities into gainful employment at a rate approximating that of the general adult population" (President's Committee on Employment of People with Disabilities, 1998). The committee was later reorganized within the U.S. Department of Labor and became the Office of Disability and Employment Policy (ODEP), which takes a lead role in developing best practice in employment by sponsoring CE, transition, and work incentives demonstration projects nationally.

Critical lessons that seem to have universal applicability to all communities are being learned through corporate initiatives across the United States:

1. In order to create employment and act as a representative for people with disabilities, the job developer should be well known in the business community and should have people with disabilities take the lead in creating business and personal relationships.

2. Businesses are particularly concerned about the future of students leaving public schools and most service organizations such as Chambers of Commerce, the Elks, the Rebekahs, local churches, and city and county governments all seem to have committees studying school improvement that welcome contributing committee members and can assist with job development efforts.

3. Do not overlook the public sector as an employment option. There are government jobs in large cities and in the smallest of communities. The Rural Institute recently worked with St. Louis County, Missouri, on restructuring (i.e., carving) jobs, making testing accessible, and developing methods of job training and supervision. The local developmental disability agency, the Productive Living Board, spearheaded the initiative and was welcomed by the county personnel department that oversees 4,000 employees. Jobs are being developed in records, transportation, personnel, and parks departments.

4. The use of Social Security work incentives, such as Plans for Achieving Self-Support (PASS), is especially intriguing to people with disabilities and their families. PASS allows individuals receiving Social Security payments to set aside that income to purchase employment-enhancing assets such as transportation, computers, and training. Typically, citizens with disabilities live in poverty, unable to earn a living for fear of losing medical benefits and unable to own employment-related assets that most people leverage to make themselves employable. A case in point is a mechanic applying for a job. Without a comprehensive set of tools, the mechanic is of little use; but with tools, the employer can exploit this resource in exchange for salary (Hammis, 1994). PASS has allowed a number of individuals working with CTAT to gain employment by protecting benefits while the individuals purchased cars, electric wheelchairs, training, computerized sewing machines, and so forth. Staff formerly from CTAT, now working at the Rural Institute at the University of Montana, have begun writing PASS plans for students under the age of 18, and approvals so far have included purchase of job development and job coaching services.

5. Employers are intrigued by the use of Social Security work incentives and understand that taxpayer savings are an economic resource and that the supports available for purchase through such incentives as PASS help make employment possible for people once considered "too disabled" to work.

6. Employers understand their work force and production needs much better than people who do not work daily in those businesses. Therefore, forging alliances with employers who can assist in job restructuring and on-site training is more efficient and natural than imposing outside human services personnel who typically must first learn jobs, then teach the new worker. In numerous cases, co-workers effectively instruct new workers with disabilities in task performance with employment specialists offering instructional support to the pair or to the experienced worker regarding effective teaching and supervision strategies.

7. Rural communities present unique challenges for job carving. Often, no formal jobs exist, so the strategy is to look for products or services that are needed and create a consumer-run enterprise or help another established business expand through the use of formal partnership agreements.

8. Recent business start-ups include a small engine repair business run as a sole proprietorship but located within another "fix-it shop" in Plains, Montana; a stuffed animal concession at a Nature Center in Red Lodge, Montana, where the Nature Center receives 10% of all sales in exchange for housing the business run by a young entrepreneur with serious disabilities; a soft drink vending business that entails the placement of cola machines in local businesses run by a young man with developmental disabilities; a wildlife photography business supported through the Workforce Investment Act, VR, and a PASS plan from the Social Security Administration; a tie-dyed clothing retail company operated by a young woman in a small town who sells her hand-dyed products through local tourist shops and the Farmer's Market; and a young man recently graduated from special education who works as a carpenter's assistant and who also purchased a used Bobcat earthmover and rents it to his employer as a way of supplementing his income via this investment in a capital asset. The possibilities for self-employment are limitless (Griffin & Hammis, 2002; Hammis & Griffin, 1998; Newman, 2001).

9. Peer marketing—using an employer to influence other employers to hire an individual with a disability—is much more powerful and effective than having a human services representative act as the sole job developer. Employment development can benefit from creative rehabilitation professional expertise, but business people should also work face to face with people with disabilities in need of employment and their peers. Hiring people with disabilities is, unfortunately, still viewed as a business risk. Hearing of successful employment from both business and workers with disabilities provides powerful support to employers who have not hired a worker with disabilities. Human services roles seem most appropriate in the context of getting these constituents together and providing technical and strategic support until a quality relationship is solid.

JOB CARVING

The process of breaking jobs down into their key components and re-assigning those pieces in more efficient or understandable ways is called *job carving*. This strategy is a creative extension of job development that results in job restructuring or job creation (i.e., typical work duties are re-assigned to one or more workers with disabilities or a new job is created to address efficiency needs). Although full-time employment is certainly a reasonable outcome, job carving is typically utilized with individuals in transition from school to work or supported employment (SE) who, for a variety of reasons (e.g., physical disability, psychiatric illness, diminished intellectual capacity, medical fragility, unavailable supports, choice), may not be in the market for full-time employment (Griffin & Hammis, 2002). Care must be taken not to create jobs that devalue people with disabilities by physically separating them from other workers or by having the person perform tasks that are considered bothersome, dangerous, or unpleasant.

Many variables are associated with the job carving process. For instance, the marketing approach in job carving should be deliberate and businesslike. Job developers should approach potential employers as diagnosticians, ready to determine needs and offer solutions to productivity challenges. Another variable is student or adult services consumer employment objectives. No job development effort can take place without a thorough understanding of the type of work that is suitable and acceptable. The attitude of co-workers is also an issue. In creating employment opportunities, the corporate culture (i.e., the unwritten rules of a particular workplace) must be taken into consideration.

For example, a job was once carved for an individual with a psychiatric disability to pick up and deliver parts for an automobile dealership. Employing a designated parts delivery driver as a financially efficient method for this dealership resulted in problems. The dealership's traditional method involved taking a parts order from a local garage and then pulling a parts department, services department, or repair employee from his or her current task to deliver the part. This was very inefficient, but the employees enjoyed it because they got to leave the building for a while and take a break from their regular duties. The job created for a person who wished to work fewer than 30 hours per week did not last because the other employees saw this new worker as taking one of the few benefits associated with their jobs. Careful observation of the worksite culture might have indicated the need for a different employment approach and avoided this job loss.

Observation, in addition to frequent employer contact, is the key to job carving. Without spending time in the actual business setting or one very closely associated with it, the job creation process will not succeed. Every workplace is different in culture, quality standards, personalities, and procedures. To ensure a good employer-employee fit, the job match process must include jobsite research on the basis of consumer desire and employer need.

Steps Involved in Job Carving

Table 11.1 illustrates the steps associated with the creation of new employment opportunities.

Step 1: Determine job seeker needs and desires. This critical step guides efficacious job development based on student choice. Many transition-age students, for instance, have had little exposure to the variety of vocational options found in the employment marketplace. Creating a series of specific work experiences by carving tasks amenable to and manageable by a student can provide valuable information regarding work tolerance, likes and dislikes, learning styles, support needs, and necessary social

Table 11.1. Creation of employment opportunities

Step	Action
1	Determine student needs and desires.
2	Research target businesses, including personnel, training, retention, competition, and technical issues.
3	Visit sample target businesses.
4	Inventory activities of typical workers performing target tasks.
5	Observe corporate culture, including rules and rituals.
6	Task analyze duties and determine consumer capabilities, training, and assistance needs.
7	Negotiate with employer.
8	Teach and refine tasks.
9	Build on typical supports and relationships.
10	Fade.
11	Maintain consultative role.

skills. The teacher or job coach relies on this information when a real first job is considered.

Step 2: Research target businesses that match the job seeker's profile. Once the skills, talents, support needs, and interests of the job seeker are known, a list of possible businesses or types of businesses is assembled. Contacts are sought in order to make an appointment for a tour, an informational interview, or a work trial. Family, friends, school personnel contacts, and various social networks are tapped to find connections to owners, managers, or workers in businesses matching the profile. These connections are critical social lubricants used to gain access to people with hiring authority.

Step 3: Visit the potential employers. Job development is often a formal process based on sales strategy and marketing (Hoff, Gandolfo, Gold, & Jordan, 2000; Luecking, Fabian, & Tilson, 2004). This is a successful approach, but sometimes fails to recognize the common ground so useful in a carving negotiation. For instance, employers, for the most part, relish hiring people. This is the way they give back to their communities (Griffin & Hammis, 2005; Putnam & Feldstein, 2003). Their need to create opportunity dovetails with students' needing to work. By visiting an employer seeking information about pursuing a career in the employer's field of endeavor, the job developer turns the employer into a consultant for the student. Because many people enjoy giving advice, the pressure associated with being asked for a job dwindles and the opportunity to connect as members of a community is realized. Often this technique results in an offer of employment or a work tryout (Griffin, Hammis, & Geary, 2004).

Step 4: Job analysis. The employment specialist usually spends a few hours in the target business to complete a thorough job analysis that details the core duties, identifies natural trainers available to a new hire, and records the work routines that must be taught and reinforced. The employment specialist (or job coach) observes the actions and interactions of workers performing their jobs and designs a training plan based on these data.

Step 5: Observe the corporate culture. The written and unwritten rules of the workplace are discerned though observation and conversation. This allows the employment specialist to prepare for a smooth training and fading period with a minimum of disruption to the work routine or environment. Cultural issues important for

Jim's Texaco is located in a southwestern town of approximately 10,000 people that is slowly becoming a year-round resort due to its proximity to mountains, fishing, hiking, camping, and skiing. Jim has operated the gas station for more than 10 years and usually works alone. He has had part-time help but finds local college students unreliable and hard to supervise.

An employment specialist observed Jim over an 8-hour day. His tasks were recorded, and he was later questioned concerning income, demand for his mechanical repair services, and so forth. The inventory revealed that Jim spent approximately 4 hours a day performing mechanical repairs, for which there was always ample demand. The rest of Jim's day was consumed with the activities listed in Table 11.2. A quick check of these activities and a little behind-the-scenes research, which included calls to the local gaso-

integration into a worksite include attention to dress, humor, general behavior, work ethic, and so forth. A worker that contradicts the dominant culture is less likely to remain employed (Hagner, 2000).

Step 6: Task analyze job duties and determine the job seeker's capabilities. In this step, a job concept or a grouping of job tasks materializes, and the job matching and training plan process should proceed.

Step 7: Negotiation between the job seeker and the employer. The information from the job analysis process is presented to the employer, who has been kept up to date throughout the process, and negotiations of placement, pay, hours, benefits, supports, and supervision are undertaken. The assumption is that the student or adult consumer is an active participant in this process and agrees to the job specifics being explored.

Step 8: Teach and refine work tasks. Once work begins, natural trainers, those who typically assist new hires, are utilized, and the employment specialists assist and consult, offering more powerful teaching strategies as needed.

Step 9: Build on typical supports and relationships. This involves the previous teaching strategy at the jobsite and enlisting co-workers to build supports and relationships for the new employee. Involving the assigned company supervisor in the early phases of training, asking a co-worker to help explain and demonstrate production shortcuts, and making sure that the new employee interacts with other personnel at clock-in and clock-out times and during breaks and lunch are critical to acceptance and job retention.

Table 11.2. An inventory of Jim's duties at his gas station

Jim's inventory (nonsequential)	Efficient and productive for Jim	Valued or useful labor for an assistant
Answer telephones	Sometimes	Yes
Pump gas	No	Yes
Check oil	No	Yes
Troubleshoot	Yes	N/A
Wash windshields	No	Yes
Clean tools	No	Yes
Wash/detail cars	Sometimes	Yes
Make mechanical repairs	Yes	No
Go to post office	No	Yes
Restock shelves/islands	No	Yes
Check-in deliveries	No	Yes
Talk with customers	Sometimes	Maybe
Perform tune-ups	Yes	No/maybe
Fix flat tires	No	Yes
Clean facility	No	Yes

line wholesaler, the National Automobile Dealers Association, and General Motors, revealed that Jim earns $34 per hour when performing mechanical repairs and tune-ups, but only $.05 per gallon when pumping gasoline. However, Jim must sell gasoline to keep the Texaco franchise. The other activities, which account for half the work day, have little direct revenue-generating impact on Jim's business.

Further discussion revealed that Jim takes home approximately $26,000 per year. If Jim was to spend 8 hours per day performing mechanical repairs, which he enjoys and for which there is a waiting market, his annual salary would double to $52,000. By carving out the activities that are vital to the operation of Jim's Texaco and creating a job for an individual with a severe disability, the owner can concentrate on the more profitable activities. The new position might have an annual salary of $12,000 (a reasonable salary for this type of job), thereby reducing Jim's take-home pay to $40,000 per year. This new salary represents a marked increase more than the original $26,000 figure and will appeal to Jim if a cautious, relationship-building sales approach is utilized. The actual job created, of course, depends on consumer choice, competence, and available supports, as well as local market conditions and the general climate of the work environment.

Step 10: Fading. Having the employment specialist leave the work area as soon as possible is critical to integration. Professional human services presence in the worksite carries a stigma that impedes the sense of belonging necessary for the new worker to become a vital participant in the work force (Rogan, Banks, & Howard, 2000). Fading of the trainer or job coach should be planned and systematic. The employer and others in the business should be informed, as appropriate, of the fading process.

Step 11: Maintain a consultative role. The adult services agency that supports the new worker should remain in low-profile contact with the employer. If a business-service approach was used in creating the employment opportunity, then a consultative role with the employer should be maintained. The goal here is not necessarily to develop more jobs for people with disabilities, but rather to assist with advancing the career of the person placed or to refill the position if the person chooses to leave the business. There is a risk of creating worker and employer dependence on the service agency. Hence, care should be exercised to serve unobtrusively in a consultative problem-solving role.

Illustrations of Successful Job Carving

A few examples of job carving follow to illustrate the strategies or approaches employed in developing work experiences and employment options for individuals with severe disabilities.

Business Efficiency and Productivity Strategy
The business efficiency and productivity strategy can be utilized with a variety of service and manufacturing operations.

The business efficiency and productivity strategy, which might seem beneficial to all employers, is not always workable. In a variety of bureaucracies, such as government offices, university departments, and some social services entities, increased efficiency does not have a cash payoff and, therefore, is difficult to engineer.

Shelly, a student, had good interactive and communication skills, could orient well to landmarks, could match and sort items by color, and enjoyed walking. The job developer observed that university department secretaries left their desks at various times in the morning and again in the afternoon to pick up incoming mail and to deliver outgoing mail at the campus post office. The job developer recorded this activity and estimated that approximately 15 civil service secretaries spent more than half an hour per day walking to and from the post office. The developer then checked with university personnel to determine the average salary of a department secretary, broke that down into an hourly wage, and multiplied that by half an hour.

The activity of the 15 secretaries was costing the university approximately $20,000 per year. The job developer reasoned that a 4- or 5-hour-a-day job could be created for the individual with disabilities at $6 per hour, plus benefits and vacation, for under $8,000 per year. This would save the university $12,000 in lost productivity and quell complaints by the secretaries who did not enjoy having to leave their other assigned duties twice each day.

This information was well received by the university vice president. The efficiency increase would benefit staff morale and improve service to faculty and college students; however, the personnel system was such that all available positions were filled, and funding for new positions was restricted by the state legislature. No new positions could be added without significant maneuvering, which would be inconvenient, time consuming, and potentially politically hazardous for the vice president. In short, the rigid employment systems of some bureaucracies may dictate that other approaches or long-term efforts are required to break into these markets.

Consultative/Employment Service Strategy

The consultative/employment service strategy can be utilized with a variety of businesses, especially those that have high personnel turnover or seasonal market fluctuations. Jobs typically having high turnover may not be choice jobs for anyone, however. These positions should not be utilized as dumping grounds for people with severe disabilities and may indeed result in heightened anxiety about work demands, job loss, and employment expectations. These jobs should be approached with common sense and the understanding that such positions can be great first jobs or seasonal jobs and a step on the career ladder. Again, it is important to note the corporate culture and work environment of businesses that appear to have high personnel turnover.

There was a motel that had a high turnover rate, but after a few days of on-site observation, a core group of stable employees became apparent. This group of housekeepers had long-term employment records and shared a highly ritualized culture that was hard to infiltrate. Admission was gained by showing work stamina and a strong sense of insider humor and by contributing to the purchase of donuts, soda, and snacks for team members to share. Failure to understand the culture and take slow, decisive action to fit in led quickly to exclusion. New employees who failed to perceive these rites were left to fend for themselves. In this situation, many workers simply moved on to the next job. A good job developer recognizes these worksite traits and develops strategies to make consumers accepted members of the work force, thus protecting the job and the individual.

In the consultative/employer service strategy, research is performed to find business trends conducive to job development (Griffin & Hammis, 2002). In keeping with the motel example, research was performed in a western city to assist in the creation of a service niche for a local SE agency. The research included the identification of motels near the homes of individuals seeking first and second jobs in housekeeping departments. Calls were made to the owners of a dozen small to moderate-size motels. Almost all of the owners were willing to discuss their turnover, recruitment, and training issues. From these discussions, it was determined that the average moderate-size motel in this area employed five housekeepers, one of whom was the head housekeeper with additional duties, responsibilities, and pay. The average work week for the housekeepers was 40 hours in 6 days, and the average pay was $6.50 per hour with varying benefits. Head housekeepers made $8–$10 per hour. Average annual turnover was approximately 200% with a range of 80%–300%. Turnover varied by city and motel, necessitating case-specific research.

When the housekeeping department terminates the employment of a staff member, the manager or the head housekeeper performs the work or sees that the duties are covered. Head housekeepers get the first option to work extra hours for overtime pay in many cases. Usually, overtime is split between the head housekeeper and the other housekeepers. In any case, the managers or owners view this as a possible time for reduced work quality, poorer consumer service, and additional cost. The search for another housekeeper is vital and is initiated through classified advertisements, a pool of former employees, or word of mouth to friends of the other housekeepers.

Once a new employee is identified, a week is often required for training on company standards. This pulls the head housekeeper away from typical duties and requires more overtime expenditures. When recruitment and training are completed, the expense to the employer can range from $500 to $2,000, largely in hidden costs. If the motel employs five housekeepers and has an average turnover rate of 200%, then the employer stands to lose as much as $20,000 per year in hiring and training costs. The job developer must create a problem-solving relationship with the motel manager or owner and approach the discussion of these costs over time. A rush to accomplish this can cause the owner to feel incompetent or angry, inhibiting employment opportunities.

A job developer can approach the manager with a possible employment service strategy, including hiring, screening, training, and follow up. Charging for this service, on the basis of an analysis of what the employer stands to save by hiring one or two people through the service agency, is also a reasonable business activity. When people get something for nothing, their dedication to it is minimal, and if the provider agency does not value the employment services it offers, then ongoing service accountability to the employer is diminished. Good employment services are worth paying for, and the addition of a market-based price may raise the expectations and accomplishments of all involved parties.

Another strategy is to perform an analysis of housekeeper routines, and, in a fashion similar to Jim's Texaco, carve out unproductive or duplicative efforts to make all workers more productive. This also reduces the inconvenience associated with a team member quitting. Such carved duties at a motel might include stripping beds, emptying trash cans, stocking supply carts, and replenishing towels in towel carts. All of these activities save time and make the workers more productive.

Making people more productive can have the short-range effect of lowering weekly paychecks, however. This event can lead to trouble for the new employee if he or she is viewed by the others as the cause of their misfortune. If this situation occurs, then a strategy should be developed with the employer. Perhaps increased productivity dictates that the next vacancy not be filled, thus guaranteeing full employment for those remaining while securing the need for the newly created assisting position.

Many businesses and offices of all types face similar circumstances and can benefit from consolidating activities into a new core job or jobs. Grease Monkey, a quick oil-change franchise company, has carved a number of duties to speed production and smooth operations. Consumers at Grease Monkey are greeted by an attendant who takes vital information on the service desired. Quickly, an employee begins to vacuum the carpets, while another cleans windows. The vehicle is pulled inside a work bay, and one employee, stationed in the grease pit, drains the oil and lubricates the chassis. Topside, employees check tire pressure, fill fluid reservoirs, and add new oil. The whole process takes less than 15 minutes and costs a little less than typically slower service at a local garage. The labor costs for Grease Monkey can be higher than other companies in the oil-change business because Grease Monkey has as many as four employees working on one car; however, consumer satisfaction, resulting from convenient service hours, short wait periods, and quality service brings an increase in highly profitable, repeat business.

Employment specialists looking for summer employment for students can also find the consultative/employment service strategy useful. One possible avenue to creating employment is to simply walk around the community and note all of the odd jobs that the city or county government has overlooked. This might include painting sign posts or buildings, cleaning and mowing vacant lots, watering flower beds in the city park, or performing maintenance on city vehicles and equipment or tasks predictably overlooked by city officials during the summer due to the activity of road repair, the impact of tourism in some locales, and the shortage of staff due to vacation schedules. By approaching the city manager, the mayor, or the public works director and explaining that there is a waiting work force, temporary summer employment can be created. These jobs represent valuable evaluation and experiential opportunities for transition-age students, teachers, and new job coaches. Towns and cities often use summer youth employment programs operated by entities such as the local Workforce Investment Act (WIA) or One Stop Career Center vendor. Supervision, training, and wage assistance is available and should be utilized by schools, families, employers, and adult services providers.

Interactive Duties Strategy   The interactive duties strategy shares aspects with other strategies but is presented to show how job restructuring can lead to the creation of natural or typical supports. A welding shop operation was observed and inventoried to determine a possible job match for an individual with severe mental retardation. The shop employed four welders who performed all duties associated with business, except accounting, which was handled by an outside agency. In order to create a naturally supportive environment and minimize job coach presence, the inventory of daily activities facilitated the identification of tasks that could be carved for this individual to perform. This also included duties that normally would be accomplished by two welders working together. The sales approach here emphasized that now, instead of having two welders, who each earn $12 per hour, perform a task, one welder and the newly hired assistant, who earns less, can perform the same job at reduced cost and greater efficiency.

This example can be modified to fit many industries. Table 11.3 illustrates the tasks that are performed routinely, possible carved tasks, and the duties that can be performed by the assistant with other workers or performed in the presence of co-workers. The interactive duties strategy decreases job coach presence and stigma, em-

Table 11.3. Job carving at a welder's shop

Welder's inventory (nonsequential)	Carved tasks	Interactive and shared tasks
Clock-in	Yes	Yes
Drink coffee and talk	Yes	Yes
Get work orders	Yes	Yes
Design and trouble shoot	No	No
Weld	No	Maybe
Change welding tanks	Yes	Yes
Sort scraps	Yes	Maybe
Carry scraps to recycling or trash bin	Yes	Sometimes
Clean work area	Yes	Yes
Clean facility	Yes	Maybe
Label stock and supplies	Yes	Yes
Check-in and stock deliveries	Yes	Yes
Talk with customers	No	Maybe
Lunch/breaks: Talk and joke	Yes	Yes
Check-out; ride home	Yes	Yes

phasizes natural supervision and co-worker involvement, and reduces consumer reliance on service systems (Rogan et al., 2000).

White-collar employment also offers diverse opportunities to create employment. In one case, an inventory was performed of an office administrative assistant's duties and interactions. Core duties included answering telephones, word processing, preparing bulk mailings, filing, desktop publishing, bookkeeping, ordering supplies, photocopying documents, running errands, and coordinating company travel logistics. As the business grew, juggling all of these duties became increasingly difficult.

The job developer identified a student interested in office work, contacted several employers, performed job duty inventories by observing and interviewing clerical staff, and approached one of the employers with an efficiency plan. The business manager, consumer, administrative assistant, and job developer created a clerical assistant position that is supervised by the administrative assistant. The individual in this position performs filing, preparing bulk mail, and photocopying. The job is part time, working with a variety of professionals who are well connected in their community, and all of the work is performed with or near co-workers without disabilities. No job coach is necessary on site due to management's commitment to use co-workers in the mentoring process. The employer saw immediate improvement in work quality, consumer service, and office efficiency. The administrative assistant got a helping hand and lessened his work stress.

White-collar employment is available through job carving and creation. Each position that follows had particular duties carved in or out based on the individual's skills, talents, and support needs. Assistive technology and shared job duties were used in several instances to maintain production and quality standards. The general job titles or duties include

- Filing clerk at a large banking company headquarters

- Bar code scanning of active customer files for a multinational insurance corporation

BETH

Beth is a young lady living in the rural south. She has an interest in computers and children. She is graduating with a Certificate of Attendance, cannot read or write very well, and has few options except the local sheltered workshop. Her team considers her interests and proposes that she operate a computer center in a child care center. Unfortunately, no employer will hire her. Her deficits outweigh her talents. The team uses a local Workforce Investment grant through the U.S. Department of Labor and assistance from VR to purchase intuitive children's software and a complete computer and printer tutoring set up. The prospective employer solicits parents who desire individualized computer lessons for their children and signs up 27 students. The employer charges an additional fee for the computer tutoring that Beth provides, thereby creating a new position at the child care center. An agreement is developed that stipulates that Beth's equipment remains in her possession until its useable life is exhausted (about 3 years) and then the employer will pay to replace and upgrade it. With one small investment and a bit of person-centered planning, a job was created that highlights Beth's gifts and that increased the profitability of the host business (Griffin & Hammis, 2003; Sampson, Hermanson, Griffin, & Morton, 2000).

- Pizza delivery call-in center assistant
- Customer service assistant for an international bank
- Make-up artist at a department store cosmetics counter
- Beauty salon receptionist
- Hospital receptionist
- Hotel guest clerk assistant
- Automobile dealer new car check-in clerk
- Cancer clinic biopsy slide technician
- Dry cleaner cashier

Another variation on job carving and job creation is resource ownership (Griffin & Hammis, 2003). The competitive labor market operates on the principle of exploitation. That is, employers hire people with skills, talents, and attributes that are saleable in the greater marketplace. For instance, a mechanic hired at a local garage is expected to bring talent and tools that allow the owner to charge customers a fair price for repair work. The mechanic is paid less than the value of the work, and the owner keeps the remainder to pay operational costs and for profit. Someone with a college education in computer science costing $40,000 or so is hired because of the apparent value of that education. The assumption is that the education benefits the employer through better and marketable ideas and skills, such as computer repair or programming. Without these skills and attributes, such as a college education or mechanics' tools, the individuals are less likely to retain these particular jobs.

Transition-age youth with the most significant disabilities often leave school without skills and talents immediately obvious to employers. Most have a limited résumé consisting of unpaid work experiences in stereotypical jobs such as janitorial work, stocking shelves, and pet care. Such experiences help to demotivate the worker and teach that work is not rewarding (Condon, Moses, Brown, & Jurica, 2003; Griffin & Hammis, 2003). Ownership of exploitable goods can change this outcome.

A note of caution is important here. The purchase of equipment is not solely based on the employer's wishes. The equipment or other resource must fit the job seeker's vocational interests and desires and be used predominantly by the individual. Buying resources for the employer that are not used by the worker in a job of his or her choice betrays the principles of inclusion and respect.

Additional Job Carving Strategies

Edward left school early due to his extreme behaviors. He was clear, however, that he wanted to work detailing cars. Unfortunately, no jobs were readily available in his local community until a job development visit to a local detailing operation revealed the employer did not own a carpet steam shampooer. Upon meeting Edward, the employer agreed to hiring him and training him in the entire detailing process as long as Edward purchased a $2000 carpet steamer. Edward now works daily at the business, makes a wage typical to others employed there, and is on a career path that includes training in all aspects of the business. Two thousand dollars is a minor sum to be paid considering what was spent on 12 years of schooling and what the public tax burden would be if no job was secured upon graduation. The sources for such funds include the school's appropriation for educating Edward, VR, a PASS through Social Security, family funds, Workforce Investment Act dollars, and so forth (Crandell & Brooks, personal communication, September 12, 2003).

Many of the people who benefit from job carving happen to have severe disabilities. They are individuals whom others have deemed "not ready" or "not able" to work. Carving a job to capitalize on the job seekers' unique talents and assembling other workplace supports (e.g., AT, on-the-job skills training, mentoring) can help make work a reality for many. It should come as no surprise that, oftentimes, these job seekers are using SE and the services of an employment specialist or job coach to assist them with gaining and maintaining employment.

The foundation of SE is centered on the ability to tailor job duties and provide supports to maximize an individual's talents while meeting a business's needs (Targett & Wehman 2002). Thus, the importance of using an approach such as job carving to create viable work opportunities for people with more significant disabilities cannot be overemphasized. It is crucial that those charged with this mission learn how to use this powerful technique to develop jobs. Therefore, some additional strategies for job carving and more examples follow.

Job carving, although seemingly logical to some employers, may represent a radical departure from standard operating procedures for others. For example, many employers pack position descriptions with as many duties as possible and seek candidates with the ability to perform many functions. In addition, working with employers to develop or carve jobs will be more complex than simply pursuing existing job vacancies. This is due to the following reasons. First, employers may not even want to talk about work needs if they are not actively hiring personnel. Second, the employment specialist must be able to convince the employer to consider new work structures and recognize the benefits of "creating" work.

Therefore, employment specialists must be prepared to demonstrate the value of carving a job to employers. To start, they should adopt the philosophy that the employer is a primary customer and focus on identifying business needs. And although there are always exceptions to the rule, instead of simply "selling SE services" or representing a job seeker, the goal of the first meeting should center on developing rapport and providing resources that can help the business.

While meeting with employers, employment specialist should listen and keep their eyes open for opportunities to bring up the topic of job carving. Sometimes, the process takes longer or is more complex. For example, an employment specialist may meet with a human resource manager first, then get referred to department heads, and finally to supervisors, only to climb back up the chain of command for job carving

Table 11.4.   Questions to get employers thinking about job creation

Would you be willing to consider some creative ways in which a person with a disability who possesses specific abilities and talents could provide a beneficial service to your organization?

How do you determine when a job description needs to be revised, changed, or created?

Are there any nonessential job functions or duties currently performed by one or more employees that might improve overall efficiency when combined to create a job opportunity for someone else?

Are there any tasks that never seem to be completed or done in a timely manner because, although important, they are viewed as a low priority by other workers?

Have you thought about adding a new service to your business?

Would you be willing to hire someone to do a portion of a job if it would improve the other employee's productivity or free him or her up to do other work?

Source: Hagner & DiLeo, 1996.

discussions and final approval. At other times, the process will be less cumbersome. For instance, during an initial meeting with a manager, mentioning some examples of how other businesses have benefited from this approach can spark some ideas and generate discussions about job carving.

Job carving offers another way to tap into the hidden job market because the work being created is not advertised. Employment specialists must be prepared to guide employers to the conclusion that job carving may be beneficial to their operations. As always, this begins with good understanding of the job seeker's interest, abilities, and potential support needs. Then, when meeting with an employer, the employment specialist should learn about business needs and ask questions to help stimulate thoughts about carving a job (Nietupski & Hamre-Nietupski, 2000). For example, employment specialists may ask questions that encourage employers to think about workflow and help them identify problems. Hagner and DiLeo (1996) suggested that employment specialists find the strategic time to ask questions such as those presented in Table 11.4. Essentially, these questions probe the areas of efficiency, speed, cost, work quality, and morale. The employer's response should give the employment specialist a sense of whether the concept of job restructuring will be well received by the employer.

Hagner and DiLeo (1996) described three typical methods for carving jobs. First, "cut and paste," which involves trading duties between an existing position and a current employee to maximize the talents of both individuals. For example, a small deli staffed by only two employees who usually perform all job functions might restructure one of the positions so that a newly hired student with the disability performs more food preparation while the other person spends more time serving customers.

A second method, "fission," is defined as dividing a single position into two or more jobs. For example, a supermarket's bagger position might be restructured to allow the newly hired student employee to only load customers' cars with groceries, thereby leaving the more complex bagging task to another employee who is not responsible for loading groceries.

A third carving method, "fusion," is the re-assignment of similar functions from several employees to a newly created position. For example, rather than each accounting department clerk vying for time at the copier, an employee could be hired to collect and copy documents for all clerks. This would help reduce downtime spent waiting to gain access to the machine.

According to Hagner and DiLeo (1996), generally, the cut-and-paste method works best when an opening already exists and a filled position contains entry-level duties that could be traded away for more advanced duties from the vacant position. Fission works best when growth in the business makes it difficult for a single employee to perform all the duties previously assigned to the position. Fusion works best when the type and amount of routine work currently distributed across employees could be more efficiently performed by one or more supported employees.

Again, it cannot be overemphasized that when talking to employers about job restructuring or carving, employment specialists should make sure that the individual with the disability is not being devalued. Although what value or devaluation means should come from the job seeker and will vary from person to person, carving jobs that would purposively physically separate the worker with the disability from other workers or creating work that consists of tasks deemed unpleasant by others may exemplify devaluation.

Sometimes, after an idea for work has been developed, a written hiring proposal may be used to communicate the benefits of this to the business. A hiring proposal is a document that describes how the job seeker and SE service provider can assist the business in achieving the benefits of increased efficiency and employee productivity (Nietupski & Hamre-Nietupski, 2000). Proposals are a professional way to demonstrate the effort the employment specialist undertook to learn about the business' needs and care taken to recommend an applicant for the job. Some of the major points to cover in an employment proposal are as follows (Nietupski & Hamre-Nietupski, 2001):

- Start with a description of SE as a business personnel resource and the benefits of interest to the employer.

- Next, the duties and candidate for the position are described. Here, the reasons why the candidate is suited for the position are stated. Personal strengths and support needs should be portrayed in an honest, yet image-enhancing light.

- The hours and wage estimates follow, answering the employer's "bottom line" question of "what will it cost."

- A suggested implementation timeline concludes the proposal, outlining how the program might best be implemented. This may include just the steps and or the projected dates for completion.

Presenting this type of proposal can assist the job applicant with sealing the final deal. With the proposal in hand, the employer will either reject it or let the negotiations begin. Either way, after all is said and done, this approach to "do business with business" should leave the employer with a positive and professional image of those involved.

Here are some more examples of jobs that have been carved.

After meeting with a large retail store manager, an employment specialist learned that the store was no longer hiring cashiers. Instead, all sales staff needed to be on the floor and ready to cashier. When discussing how this impacted operations, the manager indicated it presented a problem. Specifically, this eliminated the staff's ability to go to the supply room to return clothes hangers or get shopping bags. The employment specialist seized the opportunity to recommend hiring someone to do this during peak hours. The store manager liked the idea and agreed to create a part-time job for a student worker to go throughout the store to clean and restock the cashier's stations.

After meeting with a senior partner in a law firm, an employment specialist was referred to the library where attorneys gained access to references and requested copies of material. The librarian had difficulty fulfilling these requests in a timely manner and many times the paralegals were required to copy materials. The employment specialist recommended hiring someone to copy materials. The firm agreed and created a position and hired a student to make copies. This freed up the paralegals to do research, and the attorneys got their copies on time.

During a workplace analysis, an employment specialist noticed that there were stacks of papers in the office of an auto parts store. While talking with the owner, she learned that these were delivery slips from received orders that needed to be filed and verified. The counter workers were supposed to complete this on a regular basis and verify the merchandise when it was delivered. However, they were not able to do so because of an increase in the number of customers who were calling or walking in. The employment specialist and job seeker developed a proposal, and the employer hired the student to check in merchandise and file the invoices on a part-time basis.

An employment specialist met with a large manufacturer and learned they were looking for a front desk receptionist. Unfortunately, the specialist did not know any student who could learn to operate the busy switchboard and other duties. However, during subsequent meetings and a tour of the workplace, the specialist learned there was a delay in getting promotional sales materials out to potential customers. Further investigation revealed that the busy receptionist was paid double time to come in on weekends to create and mail out promotional packets. The employment specialist inquired about hiring someone part time to eliminate these overtime expenditures. Management liked the idea, and a student was hired as a part-time clerical aide who was responsible for distribution of sales materials.

There are several advantages to job carving and restructuring (Hagner & DiLeo, 1996). First, the job seeker is not being judged directly against other applicants. Second, because it is a new job or has not previously been performed, there are no comparisons to other employees or standards that have been used in the past. Thus, the criteria for the worker's performance evaluation are usually individually determined. Third, because this is a position that has been newly formulated or developed, the company is more cognizant of how the employee contributes value to the organization.

CONCLUSION

Progressive vocational service providers understand that offering superior services is essential to the future existence of the company. This is directly tied to the provider's ability to implement a powerful marketing strategy that extends far beyond providing a one-shot, one-time meeting with an employer for the sole purpose of assisting one individual with a disability. It requires a marketing approach that focuses on establishing positive and long-term relationships with businesses in the local community. In turn, this requires vocational specialists to think from a business perspective and find meaningful ways to make a contribution to business, often in the form of or a variation of job carving. Although usually instigated by a vocational transition specialist such as a job developer or employment specialist, both employers and prospective employees must take an active role in the design of individualized job creations. This chapter reviewed ways to build employers' awareness of the needs of jobs, offered strategies on how to carve jobs, and provided various examples on how this has been done to increase the employment of students who just happen to have disabilities.

STUDY QUESTIONS

1. What can be done to help increase employers' awareness about the need for jobs for students with disabilities?

2. How does job carving enhance the employment of students with disabilities?

3. Discuss some strategies for formal and informal job carving.

4. Provide some examples of the types of questions an employment specialist might ask to uncover opportunities to carve a job.

5. Describe an employment proposal.

12

Vocational Placements and Careers

Toward Inclusive Employment

Paul Wehman, Valerie Brooke, and Michael D. West

AFTER COMPLETING THIS CHAPTER, THE READER WILL BE ABLE TO

○ Name four values that should be associated with quality work programs

○ Understand vocational integration and its importance

○ Discuss the process of obtaining vocational rehabilitation (VR) services

○ Present six models of vocational placement and give examples of each

○ Know what supported employment (SE) is and how it differs from sheltered work

○ Discuss the role of natural supports in the workplace

○ Contrast the features of integrated employment with those of segregated employment

○ Describe major aspects of the Americans with Disabilities Act (ADA) of 1990 (PL 101-336)

SARA

Sara is a 19-year-old student with severe mental retardation and autism who lives with her family. She has limited expressive language and communicates primarily through her body language and willingness to participate in activities. She depends on others for her personal and daily living activities. Sara is enrolled in a self-contained high school class. As indicated in her individualized education program (IEP), she participates in a community-based vocational education program that provides SE services. As a result, she has maintained employment in a part-time job at a restaurant as a food preparation worker for more than 1 year. Her job duties include breading ravioli, eggplant, and zucchini sticks and putting loaves of bread in pans for baking. She assists her co-workers with the daily general cleaning by taking all of the dirty pans to the sink area. Her job duties were negotiated and carved from the comprehensive job description for the food preparation worker. She works approximately 22 hours a week as part of her school curriculum and earns $6.25 per hour. Transportation is provided to and from work by the school during the week and by her parents on the weekends.

Sara's daily needs while at work are supported by her co-workers, managers, assistive technology (AT), and her job coach. For example, she receives assistance with taking off and putting on her coat; placing and retrieving items from her locker; clocking in and out; putting on and taking off her hair net, apron, and gloves;

There are thousands of people like Sara in this country who are looking for a job that can lead to career. As most children leave middle school and enter high school, their thoughts turn to college, jobs, careers, and, essentially, what they are going to do with their lives. For young people with disabilities, the questions are as follows: Can I get off a waiting list and into a vocational training program? Will VR find me eligible for services? Can I get a job that pays more than minimum wage? Will I be stuck in the same job for the rest of my life? Will I have to go to an adult activity center or a sheltered workshop? These questions take on even more meaning when one considers that many of these students have been educated with classmates without disabilities (see Chapters 5 and 6). The prospect of not having a real job with co-workers without disabilities is a disheartening prospect, indeed.

The value of work in the United States cannot be overstated. This is a country that wants people to work, expects people to work, and even defines who they are by their type and amount of work. The *Wall Street Journal* (2003) summed it up best in an editorial as they discussed the polls concerning the working public in America:

One employment survey, for example, reports that 33% of workers attest that they like their job and 52% more say they love it or are enthusiastic . . . this simply underscores how remarkably few Americans hate their job. Most Americans seem to truly value work. (p. A8)

So, will there be room in this economy for Sara? What jobs will be available for her? There should be greater vocational opportunities than ever before for young people with and without disabilities (see Chapters 10 and 11). In rehabilitation and other postsecondary agencies, there is an increasingly strong feeling that vocational services should make transition-age students a priority—a feeling that has been intensified by the large investment in resources for special education entitlement programs. This chapter is all about inclusive employment options, careers, and new models for providing vocational services in order to empower young people to enter the work force meaningfully.

Sheltered workshops and adult activity centers are not an acceptable end point for young people with disabilities (Rusch & Braddock, 2004; U.S. Senate, October 20, 2005; Wehman, Inge, Revell, & Brooke, in press). While segregated day programs may be the only placement option for some, most students with disabilities aspire to competitive employment as their first career option and work to achieve

washing her hands; replenishing her work supplies; and going on break. She accompanies her co-workers in setting up her work area for the duties assigned for the day from the food preparation sheet. The manager assigns a co-worker to assist her as a part of the routine. She is provided verbal and physical assistance throughout her work day as needed. Technological assistance has also been incorporated into the routine. As an example, the manager ordered a magnetic scanning card, which eliminated the need to manually enter her employee number into a computer in order to clock in and out. An audio prompting/praising system was developed to provide her with consistent intervention and to decrease her dependence on others for successful work performance. Assistance from her job coach consisted of thorough assessment activities prior to employment, job development activities, the provision of jobsite training with systematic instruction, development of work routines, restructured job duties, identification and arrangement of supports to address her needs, and ongoing observation of Sara's work performance and satisfaction.

that (Wehman, Revell, & Brooke, 2003). Teachers must help these aspirations become realities. If people with disabilities do not view themselves positively and have high vocational aspirations, then the expectations of advocates, family members, friends, and others working on their behalf will reflect that position.

BUSINESS AND INDUSTRY: WHERE ARE THE JOBS?

Many of the world's economies are in increasingly better shape as they are rebounding from the stock market downturn or, as some call it, the stock market bubble (U.S. Department of Labor, November 3, 2005). The September 11, 2001, terrorism attack in the U.S. caused a significant recession and the first loss of jobs in the U.S. since 1929. Yet, despite this fact, the U.S. economy, as well as overseas economies, are rebounding. The inflation rate is lower than it has been since the early 1950s. Interest rates have been low and have not interfered with the growth of the economy, which continues to expand steadily at a moderate rate. Wages and benefits have been rising at a slow pace, primarily because of increased productivity. The evidence is now overwhelming that U.S. businesses are continuing to find ways to gain more output from their workers, their machines, and their technology long after the initial wave of downsizing and cost-cutting. Redesigning products to make them cheaper to produce and re-engineering processes to take out unnecessary costs have become a permanent focus of corporate America. This has been imposed by a competitive marketplace and encouraged through compensation programs at all levels of the company.

At the same time, as a result of outsourcing and a wave of corporate mergers, more economic activity is being shifted out of inefficient firms—or those parts of firms that were inefficient—and into the hands of large, specialized companies that have figured out the best way to do things and can take advantage of the economies of scale. Wessel (2004) noted in the *Wall Street Journal* that there will be continuing changes in the demand for workers in many different fields and that this will be a changing phenomenon. Education and training will be at a premium. Furthermore, innovations such as telecommuting, employee leasing, the increase of temporary work agencies, use of the Internet, computer technology, mobile telecommunication devices, part-time work, and self-employment have also contributed to making companies utilize existing personnel in a more efficient way (Wehman, 2001b).

It would appear that many of the positive attributes of an improved economy should provide significant employment possibilities for people with disabilities. People with disabilities should have greatly expanded work opportunities and their unemployment rate should be rapidly declining. Unfortunately, this does not appear to be the case. As noted previously in Chapter 1, the unemployment rate of people with disabilities still exceeds 65%. Pay is substantially lower for people with disabilities than for those without disabilities (Burkhauser & Stapleton, 2004).

The employment of people with disabilities is important for many reasons. First, working in competitive employment provides an opportunity to receive wages and benefits that may lead to greater independence and mobility in the community at large. Second, extraordinary costs are associated with maintaining people with disabilities on Social Security disability rolls, which is a highly nonproductive and inefficient use of human potential that is now reaching an unacceptable level. This high level of entitlement leads to greater federal deficits and ultimately fosters the incorrect perception that people with disabilities are dependent on public support and incapable of active lives that include competitive employment (Burkhauser & Stapleton, 2004). Third, being productive on a daily basis in a meaningful vocation is critically important to one's self-esteem and dignity. Finally, establishing new friendships and networks of social support in the community is almost always facilitated by having a job within a career path.

So, will there be jobs for people with disabilities as the new millennium unfolds? The answer is a resounding yes. There will be a coming job boom as baby boomers (i.e., people now between the ages of 45 and 65) move into retirement. Consider what Eisenberg (2002) said:

> Though the average retirement age is creeping up—and growing share of Americans, by choice or necessity, are planning to work at least part time well past 65—demographers say there still will not be enough qualified members of the next generation to pick up the slack. So with 76 million baby boomers heading toward retirement over the next three decades and only 46 million Gen Xers waiting in the wings, corporate America is facing a potentially mammoth talent crunch. Certainly, labor-saving technology and immigration may help fill the breach. Still, by 2010 there may be a shortage of 4 million to 6 million workers. (pp. 41–42)

Table 12.1 provides an excellent overview of where jobs are expected in this decade. The question then is, what can professionals, advocates, the business community, and individuals with disabilities do to help increase meaningful employment? This chapter is devoted to discussing obstacles to employment and creative solutions for resolving unemployment.

BARRIERS TO EMPLOYMENT COMPETENCE

Unfortunately, numerous barriers exist in attaining employment competence for people with disabilities. These barriers are societal, programmatic, attitudinal, and physical. It is usually realistic to overcome one obstacle, but many people with disabilities contend with more than one of the barriers listed in the following sections.

Power and Influence

One of the first barriers that must be considered for people with disabilities is their collective inexperience with gaining control over key events in their lives (O'Brien, 2002). The American culture is rooted in a set of values that are strongly tied to power, control, and influence. Bookstores, newspapers, and magazine articles are filled with feel-

Table 12.1. Jobs by category: Biggest gainers and losers

Top 15 jobs with the largest projected increases, 2000–2010	
1. Food preparation and service workers, including fast food: Think Starbucks—as fast-food chains grow, so will their jobs.	673,000
2. Customer service representatives: Some jobs have moved abroad, but growth of Internet commerce will boost demand.	631,000
3. Registered nurses: The biggest occupation in a burgeoning health field stimulated by an aging population	561,000
4. Retail salespeople: With 4 million workers, currently the largest occupation growing with the total population	510,000
5. Computer-support specialists: Requires only a couple of years of college, and the pay is decent; growth is sure to stay strong.	490,000
6. Cashiers (except gaming): In lockstep with retail and restaurant expansion. It is still mostly a minimum-wage job.	474,000
7. Office clerks, general: The job is being redefined, combining more and more diverse tasks into one.	430,000
8. Security guards: Involves minimal training and low pay (about $17,000), but terrorism fears have boosted hiring.	391,000
9. Computer-software engineers, applications: As long as computer upgrades remain constant, so will the jobs.	380,000
10. Waiters and waitresses: High turnover and the expectation that people will continue to eat out more means lots of job openings.	364,000
11. General and operations managers: As new companies start up and old ones branch out, the need for managers will expand.	363,000
12. Truck drivers, heavy and tractor trailer: As the economy grows, so does the amount of freight carried by truck.	346,000
13. Nursing aides, orderlies, and attendants: Booming mostly in response to the increasing emphasis on rehabilitation and long-term care of the elderly	323,000
14. Janitors and cleaners: Needed to meet the growing demand in new office complexes, schools, and hospitals	317,000
15. Postsecondary teachers: Includes teaching and research for colleges and universities and trade and technical schools.	315,000

From Thottam, J. (2003, November 23). Health kick: Why one industry always has more good jobs than it can fill. *Time*, p. 55; reprinted by permission.

good stories about self-made millionaires, powerful CEOs of large corporations, and gifted athletes from humble backgrounds signing multimillion-dollar contracts. Americans have a great fondness for these stories because they are about people who take control of their lives, accept risks, make difficult decisions, set goals, and, most important, become successful.

Historically, individuals with disabilities have been denied access to the very events that would provide them with the opportunity to take risks, make decisions, and ultimately experience these highly prized American values of power, control, and influence (Wehman et al., in press). Furthermore, because of a lack of economic resources or a loss of specific skills, many people with disabilities are vulnerable and depend on a human services system in which they are stereotyped and stigmatized (Condeluci, 1991). Among medical and human services professionals, people with disabilities are viewed as recipients of services with very little to contribute. Consequently, systems are created and service practices are institutionalized that contribute to the disempowerment and dependency of people with disabilities.

For many individuals with disabilities, the seeds of disempowerment and dependency are planted when the person is still very young. In many communities, young children attending special education classes continute to ride a different school bus than other children living in the same neighborhood and attending the same school. Typically, these special school buses pick up students attending special education classes in front of their homes instead of the regular bus stop where the other children wait. As these young people grow into adolescents, they begin attending special disability-only scout programs, dances, and other leisure programs. These seeds of dependency and segregation continue to grow as many young people reach adulthood and begin attending highly structured sheltered workshops in which professionals are in charge, and the opportunity for people with disabilities to make decisions, develop positive attitudes, and achieve self-determination is greatly diminished.

Health Care Benefits and Social Security Administration Policies

Perhaps the most imposing barrier to employment for people with disabilities is the potential loss of income assistance and health care through programs administered by the Social Security Administration (SSA) and the Centers for Medicare and Medicaid Services (CMS). The two major SSA disability programs are Supplemental Security Income (SSI) and Social Security Disability Insurance (SSDI). Although the two have different eligibility criteria, under both programs, individuals with disabilities must prove themselves to be incapable of engaging in substantial gainful activity (SGA), currently determined as earnings of more than $500 per month to be eligible for benefits.

For many individuals with disabilities, full-time employment with health benefits is not an option because of low levels of job skills, local labor market conditions, limitations in stamina or endurance, or the need to commit substantial amounts of time to personal care needs or treatments. Yet, if they obtain part-time employment, they risk losing cash and other benefits, particularly medical coverage under Medicaid (in most states linked to eligibility for SSI) or Medicare (linked to eligibility for SSDI). This economic disincentive persuades most beneficiaries to limit their earnings to less than SGA or, more commonly, not to enter the labor market at all despite the fact that those utilizing Medicaid waivers can do well in the work force (West et al., 2002).

The impact of economic disincentives for SSA beneficiaries to return to work has become all too clear to SSA, the Congress, and the American public (Gerry, 2002). The primary causes for this growth are 1) increasing numbers of applications, particularly from younger individuals and those with mental impairments; and 2) very low rates of return to the work force for those who become beneficiaries (Burkhauser & Stapleton, 2004). Much more detailed information will be presented in Chapter 15 on the different incentives that SSA has implemented to reduce the risks of employment for beneficiaries.

Employer Reluctance to Hire

Businesses rarely admit the real reasons that keep them from hiring people with disabilities. However, looking behind the excuses given, it is possible that the primary reason is concern, fear, or anxiety that people with disabilities cannot work successfully. This may not be politically correct, but we have to examine all possible reasons for this disconnect. Peck and Kirkbride (2001) noted some of these concerns.

Concerns of the Costs Associated with Hiring   The first concern that may limit the employment opportunities of people with disabilities is the fear of potential unknown costs such as accommodations. Although the ADA has helped level the playing field for people with disabilities, there is still an education gap in the workplace. Many employers jump to the conclusion that they will be required to spend tens of thousands of dollars bringing their business up to ADA standards if they were to hire someone with a disability. Few businesses would be willing to invest that kind of money just to bring a new employee on board. The good news is that rarely would companies need to spend that kind of money to meet ADA requirements. In reality, the Job Accommodation Network (JAN; n.d.) reported that 20% of employer accommodations cost nothing and 80% cost less than $500.

Concern About Additional Supervision and Loss of Productivity   A second concern is the perceived effect a person with a disability would have on the workplace culture. This is much more subtle and can be more difficult to overcome than other employment-related concerns. The major components of this fear are best viewed as twofold. First, employers are concerned about the special attention that may need to be devoted to employees with disabilities. They are concerned about the amount of time the supervisor would need to commit to a worker with a disability and subsequently keep him or her from his or her other duties. The second component is the concern regarding the productivity of the employee with a disability. The question foremost in the business person's mind is, "Will I need to make productivity concessions for this employee?" The employer's concern is often a perceived requirement to have different productivity standards for two employees doing the same job.

Consider the following example of a young woman with a developmental disability who was hired by a major retail chain. This young woman was hired to be a greeter. Initially, the employer for this company assured the rehabilitation professional that he or she would take care of all the training. It was soon obvious that no training had been given except for a few cursory instructions. The new employee with a disability needed structured instruction to get her work performance up to company standards. After several meetings, the company allowed the rehabilitation professional to teach the employer these training techniques, and 7 years later, this employee is still employed. Helping the employer make the effort to train this employee took more time up front for the company. However, the money saved in training and recruiting in the high turnover greeter position proved to be an enormous saving to this business.

Concern of Not Being Able to Terminate Employment   The third concern that many businesses experience is likely the fear that causes the most concern for employers—what happens if the job doesn't work out? Will the employer be stuck forever paying a substandard employee? It seems that many employers feel that people with disabilities are a protected class. There is a general feeling that if they hire someone with a disability, then it will be difficult to terminate the working relationship even if the new employee cannot perform the essential functions of the job.

For example, SafeCard hired a person with a cognitive disability to work in their cafeteria. The job involved dishwashing and general cleaning. The service provider supplied a job coach for the 2 weeks of the employee's tenure. After the job coach left, the employee had trouble keeping up with his schedule. The new employee's supervisor posted a schedule to help the employee keep up with his duties. This action resolved the issue and everything went well for a couple of months. Then the employee began showing up late for work. The supervisor emphasized the importance of arriving to work on time. After a couple of months of continued late arrivals, the employee was terminated. In this case, the employer was willing to make reasonable accommodations by posting a work schedule and providing repeated reminders. It was the inability of the employee to perform an essential part of the job, showing up on time, that led to the job termination. People with disabilities should be treated like any other employee in matters such as this. If an employer would fire a worker without a disability for this same behavior, then an employee with a disability should not be treated differently.

Concern that People with Disabilities Are Not Competent   Most employers take action on business proposals because it makes good business sense to do so. As a general rule, employers do not look for the charitable side when contemplating a business proposal. Companies do not want to be involved with things that risk the profitability of the business. When businessmen talk about hiring people with disabilities, they may mention that they hire from a particular recruitment pool because it's the right thing to do. They make this statement because they understand the business reasons for hiring people with disabilities; they are not referring to a noble cause or crusade they have undertaken. It is therefore critical that the placement professionals market the assets of people with disabilities. The potential employer needs to understand that he or she is being offered a qualified candidate that can do the job. If appeals are made to the employer's charitable side for the placement, then the chances for success are limited. A company will not be willing to hire an individual with a disability if they feel that the person lacks competence to fulfill the job.

What Does the Research Literature Say About Employer Attitudes?[1]

The previous concerns are not well supported by the research literature, which tends to show much more positive relationships between employers and workers with disabilities (Blanck, Hill, Siegal, & Waterstone, 2004). Unger, Kregel, Wehman, and Brooke (2002) did the most exhaustive review of the employer attitudes literature to date and analyzed 24 studies to see why employers do not hire. Existing findings derived from quantitative research on employers' attitudes toward people with disabilities were most often drawn from descriptive or correlational research. Several of the reviewed studies investigated employers' perceptions across various combinations of factors (Blanck, 1998; Thakker, 1997).

Less than a third of people with disabilities in the U.S. are in the labor force, but more than three fourths of people without a work disability have jobs.[2] Why the discrepancy? Dixon, Kruse, and Van Horn (2003) went directly to employers for answers.

---

[1]This section draws heavily on Unger, D. (2001). *National study of employers' experiences with workers with disabilities and their knowledge and utilization of accommodations.* Doctoral dissertation, Virginia Commonwealth University, Richmond.

[2]The Bureau of Labor Statistics Current Population Survey (CPS) tracks people with work disabilities. In 2001, the CPS found that 9.6% of people between the ages of 16 and 64 had a work disability. Of those, 29.4% were in the labor force, compared with a labor force participation rate of 82.1% for those without a work disability.

In the survey, employers described a workplace in which people with disabilities are woefully underrepresented, despite the significant number of people with disabilities who can and want to work. In fact, only one fourth (26%) of employers said that their company employed at least one worker with a physical or mental disability.

The lack of training programs at a majority of U.S. businesses represents a major barrier to people with disabilities enjoying free access to the labor market. Meanwhile, the positive record of training at companies that do hire people with disabilities shows that the employer does not regret these decisions (McMahon et al., 2004; Morgan & Alexander, 2005).

One of the critical shortcomings with the existing research on employers' perceptions toward workers with disabilities is that the majority of the studies surveyed employer representatives who may have been responsible for hiring or supervising but who did not necessarily have actual, firsthand experience in working with employees with disabilities (e.g., Olson, Cioffi, Yovanoff, & Mank, 2001). Furthermore, employer representatives who had previous experience in supervising or managing workers with disabilities expressed fewer concerns about hiring applicants with disabilities and reported more favorable perceptions of workers with disabilities.

Summary of Employer Attitude Research Findings   Despite the identified limitations in the methodology used by previous researchers, several key points can be highlighted from Unger's (2001) research on employers' perceptions of people with disabilities in the workplace and these findings are supported by Morgan and Alexander (2005) and Hernandez, Keys, and Balcazar (2000). These findings include the following:

- The type and severity of disability may affect the extent to which people with disabilities are included in the work force. For instance, employers expressed more concern with hiring individuals with mental or emotional disabilities as compared with individuals with physical disabilities. This finding may have direct implications on the willingness of applicants or workers with "hidden" disabilities to disclose them or request accommodations.

- To some extent, employers appear willing to sacrifice work performance or work quality in exchange for a reliable, dependable employee. However, it is unclear the extent to which other factors, such as economic conditions, might influence an employer's willingness to support or sustain a worker with a disability who may be perceived as less productive.

- Employers report several concerns surrounding the work potential of employees with disabilities that may be derived from existing myths and misconceptions and not from their direct experiences with workers with disabilities. These myths and misconceptions may frequently result in an applicant or employee with a disability not being recognized as a "qualified employee with a disability" under the provisions of the ADA.

- Increasingly, there appears to be a renewed emphasis on employers' recognizing the significance of employing workers with disabilities in an effort to enhance their image in the community (e.g., Nietupski, Hamre-Nietupski, VanderHart, & Fishback, 1996; Olson et al., 2001), to strengthen their commitment to corporate social responsibility (e.g., Pitt-Catsouphes & Butterworth, 1995), or increase the diversity of their work force so that it reflects that of the general population.

- An overwhelming majority of studies of employers' attitudes toward workers with disabilities have been completed with managers who have the capacity to hire or supervise. Very few studies were conducted with frontline supervisors or employer representatives who had actual experience supervising or evaluating the work performance of employees with disabilities.

Such viewpoints and prejudices among employers are a significant impediment to the employment of people with disabilities.

In closing, there is one national study recently conducted by the Gallup Poll (Siperstein et al., 2006) which should be mentioned as well. This study is one of the most affirming of how American society views those businesses who hire individuals with disabilities. Most of the 800+ respondents in the national sample indicated they had direct experience with people with disabilities in a work environment. For example, about 75% of the participants have at some point worked directly with someone with a disability and/or received services as a customer by a person with a disability. Overall, 92% of the participants were "more favorable" toward companies that hire people with disabilities.

The respondents also had strong positive beliefs about the value and benefits of companies who hire people with disabilities. Most (83%) felt that companies do not take advantage of their workers with disabilities nor do people with disabilities create problems in the workforce. In fact, most believed that hiring people with disabilities is important for the individual with a disability. Almost all those surveyed (96%) shared the belief that companies who do hire people with disabilities help those individuals lead more productive lives.

Finally, and most important, almost all of the public agreed that they would prefer to give their business to companies that hire people with disabilities. In fact, over one-third of those asked strongly agreed with the statement, "Companies that hire those with disabilities are companies that you would prefer to give your business to." This finding was consistent across gender, age, and level of education.

Transportation

The lack of available, affordable transportation is an employment barrier that cuts across virtually all disability groups (West, Hock, Wittig, & Dowdy, 1998). For many individuals with disabilities, such as those with epilepsy, visual impairments, mental retardation, or severe physical impairments, driving is restricted by law or by individual limitations. Financial restraints may prohibit automobile ownership for individuals with other disabilities, such as psychosocial impairments, who are unemployed. In either case, the result is that many individuals with disabilities must rely on either public transportation or alternative modes of transportation in order to enter the job market.

The ADA mandated that public transportation facilities and vehicles, including buses, vans, and rail cars, be accessible to people with disabilities (Architectural and Transportation Barriers Compliance Board, 1994). Although much progress has been made in improving access to transportation systems, many individuals with disabilities

MARK

Consider Mark and his transportation problems. One day at 5:00 P.M., Mark exited from the office building where he was employed as a customer service representative into the cold rain and waited for his ride home. As he waited for his ride, he thought about how fortunate he was to have a job, which helped him bear the cold and wet weather.

Ten years earlier, at the age of 21, Mark was in an automobile accident that left him with a spinal cord injury. His life had changed dramatically. He depended on others to help him with activities of daily living (ADLs), such as putting on his clothes, cooking, and eating. Over time, Mark made great progress. Last year, he moved out of an adult home and now lives in an apartment by himself. An aide comes in every morning and evening to assist him with the things he is not able to accomplish alone. As Mark waited for his ride, he reflected on how life keeps improving. One month ago, he was offered a position at an insurance company. After 6 years of looking for a suitable work opportunity, he finally found an employer who was willing to hire him. The job offered decent wages and good benefits, which would give him the chance to be self-sufficient and no longer depend on the monthly public assistance that he received.

Mark watched as his co-workers, many of whom were friends, left the building and drove away. It was becoming colder, and the rain was steady. Mark stared down at his digital

have not been affected because of 1) the lack of voluntary compliance or overall cut-backs on routes in response to the ADA or 2) the absence of transportation systems in their communities (National Council on Disability [NCD], 1997; Weller, 1994).

In the absence of public transportation, creative solutions to transportation barriers must be found, particularly in rural areas or situations in which individuals may be unable to move closer to their jobs. Some of these options include

1. Using a personal assistant, friend, or family member to assist with transportation

2. Ride-sharing with a co-worker, possibly with reimbursement for expenses

3. Arranging for transportation through paratransit services or other human services agencies

4. Locating jobs within companies that offer employee transportation for those in need (e.g., hospitals, nursing facilities)

5. Assisting individuals with disabilities to locate work-at-home jobs, such as self-employment, online data entry, child care, and so forth

Unfortunately, Mark's situation is not unusual. Around the world, people with disabilities are frequently without the transportation services and supports that they need in order to be included into the work force and community.

VOCATIONAL OPTIONS: WHAT ARE THE CHOICES?

Although the vocational options for people with disabilities have been limited, this is beginning to change (Wehman, Revell, & Brooke, 2003). Those who were diagnosed as having disabilities were referred to rehabilitation counselors, and, if the counselors could place them, they were considered lucky. In the 1960s and 1970s, the number of sheltered workshops and assorted types of day program arrangements increased dramatically, which increased the options for rehabilitation counselors but left people with disabilities with the same poor quality of choices for competitive jobs (Weaver, 1994). Furthermore, as Weaver observed, many rehabilitation services are not competitively offered. Since the 1990s, however, inclusive work opportunities in competitive employment arrangements have become the highest goal and vocational option of choice (Wehman, Revell, & Brooke,

watch, which was mounted on the arm of his wheelchair. It read 6:00 P.M.—he had been waiting for an hour. A security guard patrolling the parking lot stopped and asked Mark if he needed help. He requested that the guard call the paratransit service that was supposed to pick him up. As the guard was calling, the van pulled up to the building. Mark was wheeled to the lift by the van driver, who offered no apology for the late arrival. Mark felt very angry about being subjected to the incompetence of others and frustrated because this was his only option. He was further saddened and frightened by the fact that he might have been left outside in the cold the entire night. The next day Mark had to go to the local emergency room because he felt very ill, and he was eventually diagnosed with pneumonia. Two months later, Mark was well again, and, fortunately, his employer allowed him to return to his job.

2003). There is an increasing recognition that individuals with disabilities need to be heavily involved in planning their own futures (see Chapter 2). The following sections review different vocational options that are available in some communities in the United States. Some communities have more vocational options and models from which people with disabilities can choose. In addition, some of these communities have limited or stopped the development and expansion of the less desirable choices, such as large adult day activity centers. So what are these choices? What different work and employment opportunities are available to young people?

Figure 12.1 lists the numerous types of options that are increasingly available to young people with disabilities as they exit school. The figure provides a spectrum of choices, and what follows in a large part of this chapter is a description of these choices. It is very important to note that many communities do *not* offer all of these choices, and in some communities, the choices are not well developed. It is also important to note that some of these choices have richer, higher quality outcomes associated with them such as real work compared to sheltered work.

The VR program, mandated through the Rehabilitation Act Amendments of 1998 (PL 105-220), is the primary program through which people with disabilities apply for VR assistance. However, this program is not an entitlement, meaning that some people with disabilities are not accepted into the program. Eligibility requirements vary from state to state.

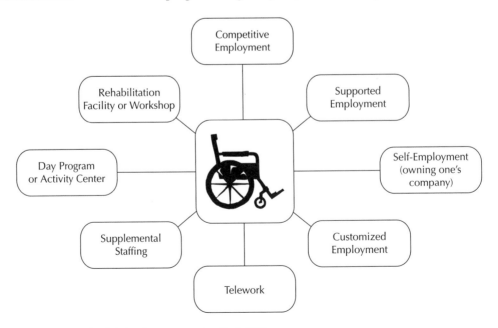

Figure 12.1.   Vocational choices for young people with disabilities.

Day Programs and Sheltered Workshops

In the United States, approximately 5,000 adult activity centers or day programs serve people with mental, physical, and emotional disabilities (Braddock, Rizzolo, & Hemp, 2004). These programs are sponsored by The Arc, United Cerebral Palsy, local churches, and other community organizations. The bulk of community funds for mental health and mental retardation are still allocated to these types of local arrangements for people with developmental disabilities. Usually, these programs offer skill training, prevocational training, make-work vocational activities, field trips, recreation, and other types of special education–related curricula that people with severe cognitive disabilities are assumed to require.

Generally, these programs operate from 9 A.M. to 3 P.M. Often, transportation is provided, and as many as 50–75 or up to several hundred people congregate in one center. Studies have repeatedly shown that people who are placed into these centers do not leave them and never graduate to workshops or into competitive employment (Buckley & Bellamy, 1985). They are, in effect, day care programs with very limited instruction for progression into real-life activities. Staffing ratios tend to be unfavorable, and staff generally work year round for low salaries. Although staff in these programs tend to be very committed to delivering the best services they can, the general concept of the adult day program is flawed.

Traditionally, the philosophy of the adult day program is that adults with severe disabilities should learn skills in center-based programs and, ultimately, generalize those skills into competitive employment and independent residential life. This notion is essentially based on a medical model of training, which aims to fix someone's disability to make him or her well enough to successfully enter the real world. Although it may be a nice idea, this does not work and proves grossly inefficient when compared with providing support to people with disabilities in natural work environments and real home-living environments.

In fact, there are very few positive endorsements for the large-scale maintenance of adult day programs and most recently notable U.S. Senators have publically questioned the value of these programs (U.S. Senate, October 20, 2005). Most agree that they should be shut down or phased out and that funds should be transferred to providing support to people in more productive and dignified community pursuits (DiLeo, Rogan, & Geary, 2000; Murphy, Rogan, Handley, Kincaid, & Royce-Davis, 2002; Wehman, Revell, & Brooke, 2003). People with disabilities can perform quite nicely with help and support and do not need to be segregated on the basis of their diagnosis. Kregel and Dean (2002) presented an in-depth comparison of sheltered work versus SE, the latter which will be discussed in depth later in this chapter. SE is real work but with the assistance of supports for individuals who need extra help to be successful on the job.

The term *sheltered employment* is often used to refer to a wide range of segregated vocational and nonvocational programs for individuals with disabilities, such as sheltered workshops, adult and work activity centers, and day treatment centers. They differ extensively in terms of their mission, services provided, and funding sources.

Sheltered workshops and other segregated employment settings formed the core of the U.S. system of vocational training for adults with significant intellectual disabilities throughout the 20th century. The majority of these adults still are placed into segregated day program settings, as opposed to integrated settings in the competitive labor force.

The U.S. Department of Education's decision (2001) to focus the use of VR funds on the achievement of integrated employment outcomes is the most recent episode in a long and contentious debate over the appropriateness of sheltered employment for people with cognitive disabilities.

Despite the continued existence of segregated/sheltered programs, critics consistently have questioned their effectiveness. For example, sheltered employment

- Fails to provide individuals with meaningful employment outcomes

- Offers low or inconsequential earnings, forcing individuals to remain dependent on federally funded benefit programs

- Isolates individuals from the rest of their community, which contributes to lowered expectations and negative public attitudes

- Allows very few people to progress into competitive employment

- Provides a minimal long-term positive impact on the productivity and community integration of individuals with disabilities

In reaction to these criticisms, SE has emerged as an alternative to sheltered employment. SE is paid employment in a real job in a business within the community, usually utilizing a job coach, teacher, or employment specialist to help provide initial help and support.

Although the relative merits of sheltered employment and SE have been debated widely, little empirical evidence existed that directly compared the outcomes generated by these programs until Kregel and Dean (2002) completed a major study. In this report, they compared the characteristics and long-term employment outcomes of 877 individuals with intellectual disabilities placed into sheltered employment versus SE by one state rehabilitation agency (Virginia). Their findings are summarized here:

1. People in SE statistically were more likely to earn more in each of the 3 years prior enrollment in VR than their counterparts in sheltered employment.

2. In those years after a client was in SE, earnings immediately increased by approximately 50% and then stabilized in the range from $3,600 to $3,800 annually. After program participation, the sheltered employment group's earnings increased by approximately 10% to 20% and then stabilized between $2,000 and $2,500 per year.

3. Mean cumulative earnings of the SE group across the entire 7-year postclosure were $18,945 compared with $8,364 for the sheltered employment cohort.

4. Finally, people with mild cognitive disabilities have the highest reported earnings in every period, followed by the individuals with moderate cognitive disabilities and people with severe cognitive disabilities. But the amount of annual earnings varies little across the three SE groups. The total earnings for 7 years range from $21,000 to $19,000 to $15,000, respectively, for these subgroups.

As community service providers become more skilled at the technical aspects of vocational program development, job development, AT, and working with business and in-

Mick has been diagnosed as having severe mental retardation. His parents are anxious for him to enter the local sheltered workshop even though his teachers, among others, feel that he might benefit from a competitive employment or SE program. But Mick's parents have already spoken with the director of the local facility, and arrangements have been made for Mick to go to the facility each morning during his last year of school.

At the facility, Mick boxes folders for the manufacturing company in town. He is responsible for doing 100 boxes per day. He is paid 50 cents for every box he completes, which are then sold to a local vendor. Mick is surrounded by people with mental retardation or physical disabilities. Most of them are nonverbal or only marginally verbal. Mick's placement has no fringe benefits, no room for advancement, and there is only limited likelihood that Mick will be placed in competitive employment. If he is placed in competitive employment and support is not available, then Mick cannot be expected to generalize any skills that he has learned into a newer, faster-paced competitive environment because he has not been trained.

dustry, there should be less interest in segregated day program services especially in light of studies such as that by Kregel and Dean (2002).

Rehabilitation Facilities

Rehabilitation facilities are usually more comprehensive in work services offered and employment options available then the traditional day program or sheltered workshop. These tend to be quite large programs with some day program aspects, some sheltered work, piece work, group vocational placements in the community, as well as some competitive and SE. These facilities are multidimensional and offer many services but usually slant toward segregated employment.

Mick and his parents (see case study) chose the local sheltered workshop, which will lead to a path of segregated employment and, subsequently, a dependent vocational lifestyle. Service providers, advocates, special education teachers, and families must ask themselves whether they have made the right choice when people like Mick are placed in segregated facilities. Is this the best we can do for people with significant disabilities like Mick in America? Is this the best that Mick can hope for? What kind of employment and career future will Mick have with making boxes all of his life? And, is this a self-fulfilling prophecy, meaning is this what Mick and his parents come to expect of him?

A survey conducted in 50 states found that approximately 20% of all facilities were planning or had already converted or redirected many of their resources into inclusive employment activities (Wehman, Kregel, & Revell, 1991). Unfortunately, more energies and effects need to be redirected in this way. More money should be spent on placing people with disabilities into real jobs and less will then be spent on adult activity center supervision (Block, 1997).

The divisiveness between sheltered and integrated employment can be attributed to differences in values, beliefs, or organizational philosophy. Advocates of integrated employment would expect each other to share in a set of beliefs and values that drive decisions to close sheltered workshops. However, decisions of this type are not always agreed to by professionals, consumers of service, relatives of consumers, community members, or policy makers who consider sheltered workshops to be viable service options. A decision to close a sheltered workshop and convert to a SE system can be met with resistance, hostility, and public criticism (Block, 1997, p. 275).

Before closing this topic, it will be helpful to examine yet another study that looked at people in sheltered work who then moved to SE (Rogan et al., 2002). This is one of the few studies that tracked the same people (291) across disabilities in 40 workshops. Table 12.2 shows the significant differences in wages between SE and sheltered work. It would appear that SE and other inclusive employment options offer a richer set of economic opportunities for young people with disabilities. This is especially the case given the movement in schools toward full inclusion classrooms (see Chapter 6).

As a final note on the relative value of sheltered work consider the testimony in Table 12.3 provided by Robert Lawhead, a parent and professional from Colorado on October 20, 2005 to the United States Senate. In this testimony Lawhead calls for closure of sheltered workshops.

Table 12.2. Disability label and wage and hour outcomes

	Average hours worked per week		Average hourly and monthly wage ($)			
Disability	Sheltered work	Supported employment	Sheltered work		Supported employment	
Mental retardation/ developmental disabilities (9)	22	23	2.56	209.87	5.74	458.97
Mild mental retardation (168)	26	22	2.16	170.22	5.71	468.44
Moderate mental retardation (69)	25	18	2.34	159.06	5.58	391.99
Severe mental retardation (7)	29	18	1.04	149.41	6.24	555.99
Profound mental retardation (1)	30	2	0.25	29.94	5.15	41.20
Autism (1)	20	5	1.96	156.93	6.00	125.00
Mental illness (19)	14	18	3.58	158.35	5.61	352.53
Brain injury (1)	20	30	2.99	59.80	5.75	518.19
Physical disability (5)	28	21	1.91	138.87	6.70	496.91
Visual impairment (5)	31	40	4.10	517.00	8.08	1,292.60
Hearing impairment (1)	19	15	2.30	141.41	5.15	166.80
Seizure disorder (1)	16	20	3.55	285.63	5.83	437.23
Other health impairment (3)	27	24	0.94	110.38	6.13	604.07

From Rogan, P., Grossi, T., Mank, D., Haynes, D., Thomas, F., and Majd, C. (2002). What happens when people leave the workshop? Outcomes of workshop participants now in supported employment. *InfoLines, 13*(4), 1, 3, 6; adapted by permission.

Table 12.3. Robert A. Lawhead, M.A., and The United State Senate, October 20, 2005

Mr. Chairman and Members of the Committee:

Good afternoon. I am pleased to be here today to discuss the issue of pervasive segregation within federally-funded employment programs for people with disabilities. My nine-year-old son, Jess, has Down syndrome. I hope my testimony will result in Jess and other young people with disabilities having regular, integrated jobs when they grow up. My career providing employment services to people with severe disabilities has spanned three decades. Between 1976 and 1996 I managed sheltered workshop programs in both Ohio and Colorado. Over the past ten years I have served as Executive Director of an employment agency which works with businesses throughout the Denver metro area to employ people with severe disabilities.

Sheltered employment refers to a range of segregated programs including sheltered workshops, adult activity centers, work activity centers, and day treatment centers. These kinds of programs have expanded over the last few decades because it was previously assumed that employers would not hire people with severe disabilities without intensive pre-employment training. Sheltered workshops congregate and segregate people within production and/or warehouse-like facilities to complete sub-contract work. Pay is typically based on a piece rate which allows for low compensation, far below the federal minimum wage. When the U.S. Department of Labor (DOL) studied sheltered workshops it was found that these programs did little to assist people in learning the skills needed for placement into real work. In fact, this data showed that a person entering a sheltered workshop upon high school graduation would get their first job at age sixty-five or later. It is estimated that more than one million people with severe disabilities languish in these kinds of segregated day services in the U.S. today.

In the late seventies and early eighties, professionals developed a process for employing people with very significant disabilities within the regular workforce. This process has been refined over the past 25 years and is referred to as "supported employment" which is defined as integrated paid work, within businesses and industry, with ongoing support. Presently it is estimated that nearly 200,000 people with severe disabilities are employed within our business communities through supported employment and similar strategies such as supported self-employment and customized employment. There is a significant body of evidence supporting the enhanced benefit to people with disabilities of these efforts, including increased compensation, social inclusion, marketable work skills, and the dignity that comes from being a contributing community member. This is especially true for individual job placement, as opposed to congregate group placements. Research has also shown that people with severe disabilities prefer community employment to segregation in the workplace. People with disabilities and their families are often told by well-meaning professionals that sheltered employment is the best or only option open to them. This is simply not true.

Evidence-based research completed over the last twenty-five years shows that employment programs placing people into business and industry represent a good tax-payer investment. When one public dollar is spent on supported employment service costs, tax-payers earn more than a dollar in benefits through increased taxes paid, decreased government subsidies, and foregone program costs. Further, this positive cost-benefit relationship for community employment holds true for people with the most significant disabilities and is stronger when people are employed individually as opposed to within group models of employment. On the other hand, segregated employment does not use public dollars efficiently, always running at a deficit year after year.

Over the past fifteen years I have assisted agencies serving urban and rural areas within approximately twenty states to convert their services from segregated sheltered employment programs to programs providing community employment outcomes. It is currently estimated that 275 agencies around the U.S. have changed their missions and are engaged in change-over efforts, with as many as 15% of them completing this activity. It is my experience that once an agency begins this process to change it does not decide to go back to the segregated employment model because the people they serve experience a better quality of life and those people and their families express higher levels of satisfaction with the service. The change-over process and successful examples of agency conversion are well documented within the professional literature.

In summary, we know how to assist people with disabilities to achieve individualized job outcomes within the business community. People with disabilities clearly prefer to work alongside non-disabled co-workers when given choice and individualized support. When public dollars are used for employment programs that place one person at a time within local businesses, those dollars are used more cost effectively then with the dominant segregated program model. And yet, it has been very difficult to break the hold congregate programs have on public funding. We know in 1999 that 75% of the public funding available for on-going employment supports was used instead for segregated programs. There is little evidence that this trend is changing, and this fact leaves very few resources available for individualized integrated employment options. Federal law, federal policy and the present administration support integrated employment and we now have experience in changing the current service system, agency by agency and state by state. We exist at a time when federal policy could be implemented to correct the national shame of our ongoing segregation of workers who experience a severe disability.

Mr. Chairman, I commend this Committee for exploring these issues and thank you for the opportunity to share my perspectives with you today. I hope your leadership will result in real change due to the large number of individuals who have been waiting for far too long to take their place in the workforce.

Lawhead, R.A. (2005). Hearing on Opportunity for Too Few? Oversight of federal employment programs for people with disabilities. Testimony before the Health, Education, Labor & Pensions Committee, U.S. Senate, October 20, 2005.

Mitchell is 20 and is diagnosed with attention-deficit/hyperactivity disorder (ADHD), learning disabilities, and neurological impairments. He has multiple auditory and visual learning disabilities, represented by his inability to read and compute as well as his disorganized memory and planning skills. Mitchell was referred to a rehabilitation counselor by his vocational and special education teachers. His rehabilitation counselor recently completed a special course on adults with learning disabilities and spent several hours counseling Mitchell about vocational options. Specifically, the counselor wanted to know what Mitchell liked most about work and what his ideal job would be.

Mitchell's father is a bank vice president and Mitchell wanted to work in a similar environment. Therefore, a concerted effort was made to find a placement in a community financial institution. A major bank in town had a job opening for a service specialist in the car loan department. This job entailed entering all loan payments in the general ledger system and checking them against the correct account numbers. Because much of this job was automated, the supervisor had to work specifically with Mitchell for a number of weeks. Because of Mitchell's motivation and prior interest in his father's work, however, Mitchell was able to perform this job successfully without specialized on-site help. Within 3 months, Mitchell was very pleased with his employment.

Initially, the bank gave Mitchell only 20 hours of work per week, questioning his ability to do the job quickly enough. He has since been elevated to 40 hours per week and has even been working overtime. The major reasons for the success of this placement were: 1) Mitchell's interests were given careful consideration, 2) his father's background in the field had a positive family influence, and 3) the counselor communicated frequently with the employer to verify Mitchell's progress.

Job Placement and Sample Careers

For years, the preferred vocational option for people with disabilities has been job placement in the competitive employment market. Employment is typically gained in one of two ways. The first is use of rehabilitation counselors who are located in most cities and towns through state and federal VR programs and funded primarily by the federal government through the Rehabilitation Act Amendments of 1998.

Rehabilitation counselors usually have bachelor's and master's degrees in counseling, work adjustment, evaluation, or placement services. They are expected to understand all disabilities and handle very large caseloads (e.g., 100–200 individuals at a time). Subsequently, it is very difficult for counselors to provide the individualized service coordination and specialized placement services that increasing numbers of people with severe disabilities require. Furthermore, most counselors are unable to provide the extended follow-up and on-site services—such as regular visitation, telephone contact, and training—that are required to help some people with disabilities maintain employment. A major aspect of rehabilitation counselors' jobs are to help people with disabilities develop careers, which is increasingly occurring through the use of Centers for Independent Living (Stock, Davies, Secor, & Wehmeyer, 2003; Wehmeyer et al., 2003).

Rehabilitation counselors have come under fire because of these heavy caseloads and their subsequent inability to handle the most challenging cases. In fact, several older studies (Hasazi, Gordon, & Roe, 1985; Hess, Kregel, & Wehman, 1991; Wehman, Kregel, & Barcus, 1985) indicated that a family-and-friend network—the second method of job placement—is often a more valuable way of quickly getting jobs for people with disabilities. This evidence has been reinforced by Luecking, Fabian, and Tilson (2004). The family-and-friend network reflects an increasing reliance on people in the community—that is, employers, friends, and other individuals not involved in the VR system who are willing to try to find jobs for people with disabilities. These contacts have resulted in many job placements for people with disabilities in local businesses. Many possible careers and types of jobs are available for people with disabilities to consider. The *Dictionary of Occupational Titles* (1991) offers some sense of how rehabilitation counselors can identify possible careers (see Figure 12.2).

Job placement for young people can and should be a reality before they exit the public school systems. Once students leave school, it becomes more difficult for them to enter the work force. Whether they acquire jobs through the rehabilitation system or through their families and friends, these students need to be directed into the mainstream work force and taught marketable skills before they become so discouraged that they choose not to work.

Self-Employment

Traditionally, people with the most significant disabilities have been overlooked as candidates for self-employment, a topic discussed in great detail in Chapter 11. However,

---

0/1. Professional, Technical, and Managerial Occupations (001.061-010 to 024.364-010) . . . concerned with the theoretical or practical aspects of such fields of human endeavor as art, science, engineering, education, medicine, law, business relations, and administrative, managerial, and technical work. Most of these occupations require substantial educational preparation.

2. Clerical and Sales Occupations (201.162-010 to 219.362-046) . . . encompasses two occupational fields: Clerical (Div. 20–24) which includes occupations concerned with compiling, recording, communicating, computing, and otherwise systematizing data; Sales (Div. 25–29) which includes occupations concerned with influencing customers in favor of a commodity or service. Includes occupations closely identified with sales transactions even though they do not involve actual participation. Excluded from this category are clerical occupations primarily associated with a manufacturing process.

3. Service Occupations (301.137-010 to 362.687-018) . . . concerned with performing tasks in and around private households; serving individuals in institutions and in commercial and other establishments; and protecting the public against crime, fire, accidents, and acts of war.

4. Agricultural, Fishery, Forestry, and Related Occupations (401.137-010 to 461.684-018) . . . concerned with propagating, growing, caring for, and gathering plant and animal life and products. Also included are occupations providing related support services; logging timber tracts; catching, hunting, and trapping animal life; and caring for parks, gardens, and grounds. Excluded are occupations requiring a primary knowledge or involvement with technologies, such as processing, packaging, and stock checking. Managerial occupations in agriculture, fishery, and forestry are included in Group 180.

5. Processing Occupations (500.131-010 to 519.585-014) . . . concerned with refining, mixing, compounding, chemically treating, heat treating, or similarly working materials and products. Knowledge of a process and adherence to formulas or other specifications are required in some degree. Vats, stills, ovens, furnaces, mixing machines, crushers, grinders, and related equipment or machines are usually involved.

6. Machine Trades Occupations (600.130-010 to 613.132-010) . . . concerned with the operation of machines that cut, bore, mill, abrade, print, and similarly work such materials as metal, paper, wood, plastics, and stone. A worker's relationship to the machine is of primary importance. The more complicated jobs require an understanding of machine functions, blueprint reading, making mathematical computations, and exercising judgment to attain conformance to specifications. In less complicated jobs, eye and hand coordination may be the most significant factor. Installation, assembly, repair, and maintenance of machines and mechanical equipment and weaving, knitting, spinning, and similarly working textiles are included.

7. Benchwork Occupations (700.130-010 to 713.684-018) . . . concerned with the use of body members, handtools, and bench machines to fit, grind, carve, mold, paint, sew, assemble, inspect, repair, and similarly work relatively small objects and materials, such as jewelry, phonographs, light bulbs, musical instruments, tires, footwear, pottery, and garments. The work is usually performed at a set position in a mill, plant, or shop, at a bench, worktable, or conveyor. At the more complex levels, workers frequently read blueprints, follow patterns, use a variety of handtools, and assume responsibility for meeting standards. Workers at the less complex levels are required to follow standardized procedures.

8. Structural Work Occupations (800.662-010 to 821.361-018) . . . concerned with fabricating, erecting, installing, paving, painting, repairing, and similarly working structures or structural parts, such as bridges, buildings, roads, transportation equipment frames and structures, cables, girders, plates, and frames. The work generally occurs outside a factory or shop environment, except for factory production line occupations concerned with fabricating, installing, erecting, or repairing structures. Tools used are handtools or portable power tools, and such materials as wood, metal, concrete, glass, and clay are involved. Stationary machines are frequently used in structural work occupations, but the worker's relationship to machines is usually secondary in importance as compared to use of handtools and portable power tools. Workers are frequently required to have a knowledge of the materials.

9. Miscellaneous Occupations (900.683-010 to 921.683-046) . . . concerned with transportation services; packaging and warehousing; utilities; amusement, recreation, and motion picture services; mining; graphic arts; and various miscellaneous activities. Occupations concerned with activities listed above and involving extensive record keeping are found in Cat. 2. Occupations concerned with hoisting and conveying of logs are included in this category. Other logging occupations are found in Cat. 4.

Figure 12.2. Sample careers for employment. (From U.S. Department of Labor. [1991]. *Dictionary of occupational titles,* 4th ed. Washington, DC: Employment and Training Administration; reprinted by permission.)

support systems can help many people operate their own businesses, limited partnerships, or businesses within businesses (Griffin & Hammis, 2003; Ispen, Arnold, & Colling, 2005). The key to success is support, which gives the entrepreneur a chance to compete in the open market.

The myriad supports necessary for a small business owner typically include accounting services, business planning, access to capital (e.g., loans), marketing consultation, and training in product or service production. The same needs are evident for individuals with disabilities, but sometimes the manner in which the needs must be met is different. For instance, a typical entrepreneur has a credit history that a bank officer can review in structuring a start-up loan. In many cases, small business hopefuls with disabilities have little credit available and few savings because of long-term reliance on Social Security benefits. Support from rehabilitation personnel may be necessary to gain access to VR resources, to determine useful assistive or universal technology, to apply for local low-interest loan funds, or to develop a PASS through Social Security in order to self-finance.

Existing personnel who are paid to help individuals with disabilities find success in the realm of employment will need new skills, and new staff may need specific personality traits in order to best serve their consumers. Effective staff need many of the traits required of entrepreneurs in order to identify and facilitate supports that an entrepreneur with significant disabilities needs in order to flourish.

Since the beginning of the 21st century, there has been great interest in self-employment for people with disabilities (Ispen, Arnold, & Colling, 2005). Even more recently, small business development opportunities have been extended to people with more challenging disabilities, including mental retardation, autism, psychiatric disabilities, and severe physical disabilities. Table 12.4. describes the story of Keith, who created his own employment near Atlanta, Georgia.

Many disability advocates have welcomed this trend. They note that there were many barriers to people with disabilities who wanted to start their own business. Studies have identified lack of supports, discouragement from rehabilitation professionals, and obstacles in planning and financing.

In a 1998 U.S. government report, self-employment options for people with disabilities were cited as often overlooked by employment programs. In 1996, only 2.6% of 225,000 VR consumers with successful closures became self-employed or started a small business. This compares with approximately 18% of people nationwide who choose to work for themselves.

Advantages to Self-Employment As the movement toward greater self-determination has grown, so has the idea that those people who want to start their own business should be given the support to do so. Consider the following reasons why people with disabilities should consider self-employment:

- It is difficult to become employed if you have a disability. Self-employment allows a person with a disability to avoid having to wait for acceptance by an employer.

- By working at home (or a location of the person's own choosing), transportation, often a challenge or limitation to employment, can become controllable.

Table 12.4. Resource ownership and job carving give a man the job of his dreams

A chance trip to Home Depot with one of his customized employment team members led to the job of Keith Woodall's dreams. Woodall, 33, had recently been laid off from his job as a dishwasher and was passing time at NewDirection, a day center for people with developmental disabilities in Douglasville.

"We were picking up wood at Home Depot for our woodworking class, and Keith saw some construction workers picking up supplies, and he said, "I would like to do that kind of work— a man's work," recounted Wanda Standridge, who leads Woodall's customized employment team as the disability navigator.

"NewDirection had just moved from a warehouse to a new business park," explained Nancy Brooks-Lane, who also serves on Woodall's team, to the Cobb-Douglas Community Service Board. "Wanda contacted the construction company that built their new building and asked them if they would consider Keith for a job."

While working with that company, Woodall, who has Down syndrome, met Troy Aquila. When Aquila decided to start his own construction company, Troy Aquila Construction, he hired Woodall.

As an added incentive to Woodall's employment, his customized employment team used $10,000 from a U.S. Department of Labor grant to purchase a piece of earth-moving equipment (i.e., Bobcat) his employer could use. The plan was for Woodall to rent the Bobcat to other construction companies when his company wasn't using it, helping him earn extra money.

"We found out if Keith rented the Bobcat out, it would have a negative consequence on his benefits because it would be unearned income," team member Doug Crandell of the Bobb-Douglas Community Service Board said. "So now, Troy rents it out for him and pays Keith a bonus for it."

The customized employment team negotiated the terms of Woodall's employment with Aquila, who agreed to pay for the insurance and maintenance on the Bobcat and to train Woodall to use it, though his main responsibility is to help get sewer pipes to the right location. "Troy is a wonderful natural support for Keith," Brooks-Lane said.

Woodall enjoys his job. "My dad does the same thing as me and Troy," he said. "I like working with Troy." Woodall works up to 20 hours a week, and Aquila drives him to and from the construction site. The two have developed a friendship beyond typical employer–employee as a result of working together.

"Hiring Keith was the greatest thing I've ever done. I didn't know I'd get so close to him," Aquila said. Although the Bobcat is a nice addition to his company, Woodall's contribution are far more important to Aquila. "Keith will work for me forever even if he didn't have the Bobcat."

From Buxton, V.S. (2004, Summer). Customized employment makes dreams come true. *Making a Difference,* 21; reprinted by permission.

- Within the financial limits of the business, a person with disabilities can create his or her own accommodations, whether they are related to equipment, flexible work times, defining the job to fit abilities as well as disabilities, or having appropriate assistance and support.

- Along with other life skills, people with disabilities bring the skills that they learned accommodating their lives to live successfully with disabilities. They learned how to use both their own abilities and outside resources to live a meaningful life and will do the same with their business.

There are still more advantages. For example, Hagner and Davies (2002) also pointed out that

- Self-employed individuals can be in less danger of losing public medical benefits because a business owner readily can take advantage of work incentives such as PASS and also can control how much personal income is drawn from a business.

- Self-employment also can allow for the accumulation of assets and can help counter the stereotype of dependency and impoverishment faced by individuals with disabilities.

- Self-employment encompasses some types of work not found in existing job opportunities.

TELEWORK

An alternative work arrangement of particular interest to people with disabilities is telecommuting, also called telework (West & Anderson, 2005). Telework is work performed at a distance using information and communication technology (ICT), such as computers, telephones, videophones, and faxes. To be considered telecommuting, an individual must spend at least 1 full day of each work week engaged in paid telework (Pratt, 2000). Telework differs from traditional work in its location: telework takes place either in the home, at a centralized location known as a "telecenter" or "telecottage" or, alternatively, "on the move"—so-called "mobile" workplaces (Lindstrom, Moberg, & Rapp, 1997). For people with significant disabilities, home-based and telecenter-based telework are most accessible. Home-based teleworkers are the focus of Lindstrom, Moberg, and Rapp's work, which reports the experience of a program in Minneapolis. With respect to work contract and employment status, there is a great range among teleworkers, who include full-time and part-time workers, independent contractors, and company employees. This range is implied in the range of job titles held by teleworkers, including software engineer, data entry clerk, and graphic artist (Nilles, 1998).

Telework has emerged as an increasingly prevalent alternative work arrangement in the United States (Dannhauser, 1999; Pratt, 2000). The number of workers who telecommute from home has been estimated at 19.6 million in 1999, up from 4 million in 1990 (Dannhauser, 1999; Pratt, 1999). A study by Wirthlin Worldwide in 1998 estimates that about 2.8 million Americans with home-based offices are teleworkers (Dannhauser, 1999).

For a variety of reasons, many people with disabilities are interested and have capabilities to work from their homes. These individuals, many with good job skills and a strong work ethic, constitute a hidden labor pool. For people with significant disabilities, the increasing prevalence of telework offers the possibility of an accessible, barrier-free workplace, flexible scheduling, and the elimination of disability-related bias or discrimination (Cassam, 1995; Cleaver, 1999; Hesse, 1995; Woelders, 1990). By one estimate, telework for unemployed individuals with a disability in the United States alone would save employers between $48 billion and $96 billion annually (Eaton, 1998).

SUPPLEMENTAL STAFFING

The use of supplemental staffing firms (e.g., Manpower, Kelly) is another potential source of employment for people with disabilities. A company such as Manpower is enormous in size and outreach and has tremendous knowledge in screening personnel, training, and, most important, contacts with business and industry. Wehman, Hewett,

Tipton, Brooke, and Green (2005) did a study that looked at outcomes and people with developmental disabilities going to work using Manpower resources and support. Workers earned 50% higher wages on average than when in SE.

Temp-to-perm workers agree to work at firms temporarily for a set amount of time (e.g., 90 days) with the expectation they will be hired full time if both sides are happy. Conventional temps often work for an unspecified amount of time without the expectation of being added to the payroll.

There were 2.6 million U.S. temporary workers in November 2004, up more than 10% from a year earlier and the most in nearly 4 years. Although there is no way to know how many of those workers were in temp-to-perm jobs, staffing firms, often watched as leading indicators of the overall job market, say the numbers are rising (Hagenbaugh, 2004).

Romanos, President of Miami-based CareerXchange, cited in Hagenbaugh (2004), reported that the number of workers hired from temporary positions arranged through her firm was up 27% in 2004 versus all of 2003. This does not include people currently in temp-to-perm jobs that have not been added to the payroll. Traditionally, about 30% of temporary workers are hired full time by the firms where they are working, according to the American Staffing Association.

One Stop Career Centers

There has been increasing frustration among people with disabilities as well as employers that employment services are spread across so many different agencies. These agencies often give different answers, use different language, and have different funding requirements. This has made it very difficult for people with disabilities and their families to locate the appropriate services to help meet their unique needs (Gervey, Gao, & Rizzo, 2004). Each agency has certain rules for eligibility for services. Consequently, in some states in the United States, as well as in countries around the world, there is a move toward consolidating services into what are called One Stop Career Centers that are funded by the Workforce Investment Act (WIA) of 1998 (PL 105-220; U.S. GAO, 2003).

Special educators and transition practitioners have the opportunity to expand their effectiveness by using the resources of the One Stop Career Centers programs to assist youth in their career development. The WIA system offers several potential advantages for youth with disabilities, no matter what their stage of career development. WIA offers resources that can boost the options available as youth, families, educators, and community service providers plan for transition. In fact, WIA programs themselves are important collaborators in interagency efforts to assist youth with disabilities. Table 12.5 describes points about how transition can be enhanced through One Stop Career Centers.

The advantages offered by WIA will not be established without the careful and active participation of professionals knowledgeable of the circumstances of youth with disabilities. It is for this reason that individuals or agencies serving youth with disabilities might consider becoming actively involved and associated with WIA programs. Not only will their participation benefit the transition outcomes for youth with disabilities, but also the WIA system itself. Table 12.6 describes how customer-driven services can be generated through One Stop Career Centers.

Table 12.5. Transition enhancements offered through the Workforce Investment Act

1. Additional and convenient sources of career development information
2. Expanded opportunities for work-based learning and jobs
3. Access to mentoring and other youth services
4. Access to generic career development and employment training services
5. Indefinite, lifelong access to career development assistance
6. Reduction of stigma
7. Individualized assessment that builds on the concept of self-determination and individual empowerment
8. Coordinated involvement of vocational rehabilitation
9. Convenient and continuous access to specific vocational and adult service programs
10. Customized job training and career support services

From Luecking, R.G., and Crane, K. (2002). Addressing the transition needs of youth with disabilities through the WIA System. *Information Brief, 1*(6), 2; reprinted by permission.

Table 12.6. One Stop Career Centers provide customer-driven services

Since the mid-1980s, the philosophy of providing vocational rehabilitation (VR) services to people with disabilities has changed dramatically. Until that time, the VR provider frequently took the lead in selecting the type of services offered to clients when pursuing employment. The Rehabilitation Act Amendments of 1986 brought substantial changes, giving VR clients the right to choose and direct their services. The philosophy behind customer-driven services is to maximize employment potential by using a service or employment model that acknowledges a customer's career desires and objectives. Some examples of customer-driven employment services may include:

Workplace personal assistance: Directing or supervising a personal assistant at work on how to do specific job tasks

Supported employment services: Directing an employment specialist on the best methods to meet ongoing training needs

Job development services: Directing a provider to pursue career choices preferred by the customer

Training services: Directing a provider to authorize training activities that will best meet the needs of the customer

One Stop Career Centers have been set up to reduce the instance of going from agency to agency. Although there is a lot of progress still to be made (Bader, 2003), there is reason for hope. One Stop Career Centers consolidate a variety of employment options and training programs to form a delivery system for people who are seeking jobs, as well as for employers who are seeking employees. The philosophical and theoretical foundation is providing a common source of information and services that can serve a universal purpose no matter what the consumer's needs are. The goal of these centers is to provide convenience and to cut down on consumers having to go to several different locations to receive different services.

Supported Employment: 20 Years Later

SE was defined for the first time in the Developmental Disabilities Act of 1984 (PL 98-527) as

(i) paid employment for persons with developmental disabilities for whom comprehensive employment at or above minimum wage is unlikely and who need ongoing support to perform in a work setting, (ii) is conducted in a variety of settings in which persons without disabilities are employed, and (iii) is supported by any activity needed to sustain paid work including supervision, training, and transportation. (p. 2665)

For more than 2 decades, SE has been associated with innovations such as natural supports, business leadership, new methods of job development, modern marketing techniques, transition from school to work, expansion of choice, self-determination, person-centered planning, AT, and co-worker training. These areas have surely contributed to the large increases in the numbers of individuals with significant disabilities involved in integrated employment (Revell, Inge, Mank, & Wehman, 1999; Wehman, 2001b; Wehman et al., in press). Work crews and enclaves (Mank, Rhodes, & Bellamy, 1986) were a part of the initial alternatives to activity centers and segregated workshops for people with severe disabilities as SE emerged nationwide. Although these approaches were improvements, it soon became clear that wages and integration were not reaching the desired levels and that individual placements were more likely to produce greater outcomes.

New approaches evolved. Employers have become more involved in the working lives of people with disabilities (McMahon, Wehman, Brooke, et al., 2004). Employers may support people with disabilities through their employee assistance programs, supervisors, and co-workers. When the Rehabilitation Act Amendments of 1992 (PL 102-569) included natural supports as an "extended service option," it became firmly rooted in what would be described as best practices or quality services (Parent, Wehman, & Bricout, 2001). Demonstrations of job choice and selection of providers of service have improved job matching, greater individualization, and the responsibility of people with disabilities to determine how resources are used (Rogan, Hagner, & Murphy, 1993). The importance of the job developer in the initial interview with employers has been recently reported (Gervey & Kowal, 2005). Numerous articles about the importance of workplace supports have been published (e.g., Wehman, Bricout, & Kregel, 2000).

The 1990s ended with a new array of vocational services for people with significant disabilities. Essentially, the old practices of the 1970s and 1980s continued while SE was added onto the traditional rehabilitation services options. People with severe disabilities can now choose from a variety of vocational alternatives depending on where they live (see Figure 12.1). These alternatives range from day treatment services, which are facility-based and generally nonvocational in design, to SE, which includes real jobs in the local labor market with assistance and support in obtaining and maintaining community-integrated competitive employment, as well as many other inclusive employment options, most which require some kind of support. There are nine values that have guided SE efforts since the early 1980s (see Table 12.7).

There are nine best practices that encompass SE. The consumer being in control is central to the concept of SE. The role of the employment specialist is to assist the consumer in reaching his or her career goals. The best practices form the foundation for the consumer-driven approach to SE. High-quality SE service providers will incorporate these practices into their daily activities of implementing SE services.

Table 12.7.   Supported employment values

Values	Values clarification
Presumption of employment	A conviction that everyone, regardless of the level or the type of disability, has the capability and right to a job.
Competitive employment	A conviction that employment occurs within the local labor market in regular community businesses.
Control	A conviction that when people with disabilities choose and regulate their own employment supports and services, career satisfaction will result.
Commensurate wages and benefits	A conviction that people with disabilities should earn wages and benefits equal to that of co-workers performing the same or similar jobs.
Focus on capacity and capabilities	A conviction that people with disabilities should be viewed in terms of their abilities, strengths, and interests rather than their disabilities.
Importance of relationships	A conviction that community relationships both at, and away from, work leads to mutual respect and acceptance.
Power of supports	A conviction that people with disabilities need to determine their personal goals and receive assistance in assembling the supports necessary to achieve their ambitions.
Systems change	A conviction that traditional systems must be changed to ensure customer control which is vital to the integrity of supported employment.
Importance of community	A conviction that people need to be connected to the formal and informal networks of a community for acceptance, growth, and development.

From Brooke, V., Wehman, P., Inge, K., and Parent, W. (1997). Supported employment: A customer-driven approach. In V. Brooke, K.J. Inge, A. Armstrong, & P. Wehman (Eds.), *Supported employment handbook: A customer-driven approach for persons with significant disabilities* (Monograph). Richmond, VA: VCU-RRTC; reprinted by permission.

Choice   The opportunity to make choices concerning employment, living arrangements, and recreation has been limited or nonexistent for many individuals with disabilities. It has become increasingly evident that the powerlessness and lack of direction frequently felt by people with disabilities are related to the attitudes and practices of service providers, caregivers, funding agencies, and society, rather than the result of any true physical, cognitive, or mental limitation. For example, some individuals have never had an opportunity to make choices. Decision-making skills have not been taught or encouraged, and adequate information about alternatives has not been available. Many people with disabilities have voiced their concerns that all too frequently decisions are made by professionals who feel that they know best and that self-assertion is often ignored, underestimated, or seen as a "challenging behavior."

Control   Control is a broader category than choice. The ability to exert control ultimately leads to self-determination. Consumers of SE must be in a position not only to choose their service provider and employment specialist but also to have a measure of control over the services that they seek.

Career Development   Career development is an important consideration for any adult who is seeking employment. However, many SE service providers gauge success by the length of time that an individual remains in the same employment position. In addition, service providers often put too much emphasis on the number of placements that they make rather than on consumer satisfaction with an employment situation. These practices continue to occur for a number of reasons, including inaccurate interpretation of federal and state rehabilitation policies, which results in failure to use funds for job advancement, and limited employment expectations for people with disabilities among service providers, which directs consumers into dead-end positions.

Full Community Inclusion   The concept of full community inclusion calls for a vision of society in which all individuals are viewed in terms of their abilities and are welcomed into the mainstream of community life. The whole notion of community inclusion stresses formal and informal relationships and business and social relationships. Yet, a segment of the general public has the impression that people with disabilities are better served when they are with other people with similar disabilities. This faulty notion persists, in part, because of the creation of special services for people with disabilities and by not adequately representing or connecting people with disabilities to formal and informal social structures.

Long-Term Supports   SE provides for the necessary supports to assist an individual with long-term employment retention (Conley, 2003). By federal definition, SE includes at least two visits per month at the jobsite unless the consumer requests otherwise. The long-term support component is an extremely unique feature among rehabilitation services. Unlike other services, the entire notion of service termination is never addressed. The intention behind this feature of SE is the realization that individuals, as well as businesses, are fluid. Individuals do not simply get a job in a local business and then stay there for the rest of their lives. Although the likelihood of remaining in the same occupation has remained constant, staying with the same employer or even in the same industry has declined significantly since 1986 (National Alliance of Business, 1996).

Community and Business Supports   As stated previously, the whole notion of support has been vital to the national expansion of SE. The individualized nature of SE in the delivery of needed assistance in conjunction with an employment specialist is the major reason why SE is widely accepted and promoted by people with disabilities. As the consumer-driven approach evolves, the employment specialist must develop the necessary skills to ensure that the consumers of the service are directing the process (see Figure 12.3).

Understand how I want to live.

Understand the role of work in my life.

Learn about my dreams/desires, gifts, and capacities.

Do not "place" me, offer me a job that you think will make sense for me.

Do not try to make me "independent."

Help me become part of my workplace.

Be there if I need help because of challenges in other parts of my life, or changes at work.

Keep listening to my words (and behavior) for requests for change—a change in responsibilities, supervision, pay, or where I work.

Help me find new jobs as I want/need them.

Figure 12.3.   What people with disabilities would want their job coach/employment specialist to know.

Continuous Quality Improvement   The concept of continuous quality improvement is known by many different terms and variations, including *total quality control*, *total quality improvement, total quality*, and *managing for quality*. There are striking similarities between these terms that generally refer to an approach that can be used by a service delivery provider to constantly re-evaluate quality. Continuous quality improvement calls for service providers to focus their time and energy on improving the process, the product, and the service. The key to continuous improvement is driven and defined by the consumer.

Assistive Technology   Since the early 1970s, AT or rehabilitation technology has emerged and opened unlimited employment opportunities for people with disabilities (Louis Harris and Associates, 2000). Individuals who at one time faced enormous barriers concerning accessibility, communication, and mobility can now optimize their intellectual and physical capabilities. With the use of voice synthesizers, people are able to express their wants and desires. Computers can be operated by a human voice or a simple gaze. This new technology is unlocking doors and providing opportunities for a greater number of people to obtain and maintain employment.

Person-Centered Planning   SE has always been about assisting one person at a time in achieving employment satisfaction. Yet, over time, some people continue to be excluded from SE. Person-centered planning seeks to support the contributions of each person in his or her local community by building a support group around the individual. This support group or community network functions together to assist the focus person in obtaining his or her goals and aspirations. Group members commit to regular meetings designed to solve problems, develop strategies, and make commitments to act on behalf of the focus person with a disability. Please see Chapter 3 for more information about person-centered approaches.

CONSUMER-DRIVEN APPROACH TO SUPPORTED EMPLOYMENT

Many individuals with disabilities have characterized human services and rehabilitation professionals as paternalistic or as having a "professionals know best" attitude. This general air of condescension toward individuals with disabilities has many negative and far-reaching implications that ultimately affect the ability for them to direct their own lives and become fully integrated into their communities. When professionals view people with disabilities as helpless, then employees, family members, and the general public accept this same attitude. The result is the continuation of negative attitudes and stereotypical images of people with disabilities throughout the general public. This same paternalistic attitude exists in the field of SE. Many rehabilitation counselors, case managers, job coaches, and program managers have been delivering SE services and engaging in practices that directly or indirectly transmit a message to people with disabilities that "we, the professionals, are in charge." Lavin (2000) developed a series of indicators showing the relationship between program outcomes and program stress (see Table 12.8).

The most exciting feature that is consistent throughout the consumer-driven approach to SE is the clear shift of control from the service provider to the consumer.

Table 12.8. Outcome performance indicators for supported employment programs

Program outcomes	Outcome performance indicators
People will obtain competitive or supported employment.	Number of people who obtain competitive or supported employment.
	Percent of people served who obtain competitive or supported employment.
People will achieve increased levels of economic self-sufficiency.	Average hourly or monthly earned wages of people before and after obtaining competitive or supported employment.
	Average number of hours worked by people after job placement. Number of or cash value of employee benefits obtained by people placed (i.e., health and dental care, retirement, vacation and sick leave).
	Number of people obtaining increases in earned wages.
	Percent of people who advance to career ladder jobs with increased earned wages.
	Average change in earned income after 1 year in integrated employment.
People will increase social interaction and inclusion with nondisabled peers/co-workers.	Percent of supported employees who interact with at least two co-workers/peers on the job daily.
	Ratio of employees with and without disabilities in the immediate work environment.
	Number of employees who participate in social events outside of normal business hours with co-workers.
People will increase self-esteem.	Percent of people who report satisfaction with their jobs, duties, wages, and services.
	Percent of people who report positive changes in attitudes, daily living routines, social relationships and overall quality of life after obtaining integrated employment.

From Lavin, D. (2000). *Reach for the stars!* (p. 12). Spring Lake Park, MN: RISE; reprinted by permission.

Historically, the service provider has had many titles such as employment specialist, job trainer, job coach, SE training specialist, and trainer advocate. For the purposes of this book, the direct services position in SE will be referred to as the *employment specialist* or *job coach.*

Employment Specialist

Within a consumer-driven approach to SE, the employment specialist's job functions are linked to major components of the support service: 1) consumer profile, 2) career development, 3) employment match, 4) jobsite training and supports, and 5) long-term supports/extended services. However, the specific activities that the employment specialist actually performs within these categories will vary depending on the needs of the individual who is requesting services. To perform each of these functions adequately, the employment specialist must move comfortably in and out of a variety of roles. There are five distinct roles that SE direct services personnel perform within each of the functions associated with a consumer-driven approach to SE: planner, consultant, head hunter, technician, and community resource.

The five roles described in this section share the same level of importance. A good employment specialist would not, for example, focus solely on his or her role as

a consultant or a planner to the exclusion of other roles. Rather, a well-trained employment specialist must be prepared to serve in many different capacities to effectively
meet the needs of individuals with significant disabilities who seek SE services.

Planner   An employment specialist acting as a planner would analyze the services
that a SE consumer was seeking and then assist him or her in developing a plan to
achieve the identified goals. The planner develops a consumer profile in which desirable career options and community supports are identified. Mapping out activities,
identifying potential supports, scheduling meetings with organizations, and identifying resources would be important functions of the planner.

Consultant   An employment specialist must be prepared to enter into a consultant relationship with consumers of SE services. As with any consultant relationship,
the expectations related to this role would be to provide recommendations on the basis
of the consultant's knowledge and expertise. A specific example of the consultant's role
would be to provide recommendations to the consumer regarding employment selection, jobsite organization, use of compensatory strategies, technology, and potential
support that would assist in getting and keeping a job.

Head Hunter   The employment specialist also engages in a variety of marketing
activities, ranging from the development and dissemination of promotional information about SE services to the identification of strategies for an individual to market
him- or herself to a prospective employer. A head hunter would remain current with
the community labor market and local economic development opportunities, and this
role would include job responsibilities such as tracking data on primary and secondary
labor markets within a community, conducting labor market surveys, and participating
in business advisory boards.

Technician   An employment specialist is required to perform the role of a technician, which requires many technical skills and abilities. He or she must be well versed
in the latest high and low rehabilitation technologies that would help an individual
enter the world of work, maintain a current employment position, or obtain a career
advancement. The technician's role also requires the employment specialist to be able
to identify appropriate strategies to teach needed skills, provide training as needs arise,
and to fade assistance in a systematic process that ensures acquisition and maintenance
of a skill. A typical example of the technician's role performed by an employment specialist is providing instruction to a consumer on how to use public transportation. The
consumer assists the technician in identifying a desirable training option and possible
supports.

Community Resource   The community resource role requires the employment
specialist to have a thorough knowledge of the community by conducting regular community analysis activities that investigate potential support resources. These resource
areas are not limited to the business community but rather cover the entire range of
community supports to include organizations and agencies for transportation, recreation, social activities, housing, and independent living.

Natural Supports in the Workplace

In order to help workers with disabilities retain their jobs and maintain employment, special help and support is usually necessary (Ohtake & Chadsey, 2001; Test & Wood, 1996). Thus, there has been a move to emphasize the use of community and workplace supports in addition to job coaches (Hagner, Butterworth, & Keith, 1995). The notion underlying the natural supports approach reflects an increased recognition of the ability of employers to accept and accommodate a diverse array of employees; the potential role of family members in locating jobs; and the willingness and ability of co-workers to provide training, assistance, and support (Ohtake & Chadsey, 2003; West & Parent, 1995). Before turning to the research literature to evaluate the effectiveness of the natural supports, let's look at two of the most popular examples of natural supports: 1) the employer or supervisor as a training mentor and 2) co-worker assistance.

Employer or Supervisor as Training Mentor For a number of individuals with severe disabilities, the immediate employer or supervisor will be the best trainer for a number of reasons (e.g., Fabian & Luecking, 1991). In some cases, the job is simply too complex or specialized for a job coach to grasp without an extended learning period. Sometimes, companies simply prefer to use their own personnel for training. Other companies are committed to affirmative action hiring but do not wish to have noncompany personnel on the premises.

A particular benefit of this approach is that the employer/supervisor feels additionally empowered to handle difficulties that may arise on the job. A job coach or rehabilitation counselor still may be involved in the initial framing of the training, assist with a behavior management plan, or be available for troubleshooting, but the primary responsibility is assumed by the supervisor or employer.

Co-worker Assistance The co-worker assistance approach is increasingly being documented in the research literature as a critical component in job retention (Cimera, 2001). The co-worker's roles include trainer, observer, and advocate for the individual within the workplace, including the education of other staff about a person's specific cognitive assets and impairments. This typically leads to co-workers who are more cooperative and supportive of the person. The PACER Center in Minneapolis, Minnesota, developed an excellent table for how to be an advocate for natural supports (see Table 12.9).

Ohtake and Chadsey (2003) also examined facilitation strategies used by job coaches. Co-worker perceptions of facilitation strategies provided by job coaches and needed by co-workers and discrepancies between facilitation strategies provided by job coaches and those perceived as being needed by co-workers were analyzed in relation to the types and frequency of problems reported to be exhibited by supported employees ($N = 83$). The results of this preliminary investigation indicated that when the frequency of work problems was low, the majority of the problems resulted in the need for and provision of less intensive facilitation strategies. Co-workers perceived they needed either a low or mixed level of support, not a high level of support, even when the frequency of work problems was high, except when the problems were related to challenging behaviors such as self-injury and property destruction. The most intriguing finding

Table 12.9. Be an advocate for natural supports

If you are an employer	If you are a parent	If you are a teacher	If you are an adult employment provider
Be open to include people with moderate and severe disabilities; focus on people's strengths.	Advocate in general for inclusion of natural supports in your own workplace or in other organizations to which you belong.	Involve the employer in training, supervising, and supporting students at work sites.	Use your resources as a supplement to, not a substitute for, employers' resources.
Build your capacity for Work Force 2000 and increased diversity.	Do regular career planning for your daughter or son to provide information on skills, interests, preferences, and support needs to help when it comes time to choose the right job.	Prepare students for employment and community life, not the adult service system. Focus on communication skills, adaptive technology, and supports each person needs to participate in the community.	Keep in mind that your expectations shape employers' attitudes and that companies have the will and skill to hire and support workers with moderate and severe disabilities.
Promote hiring people with disabilities among other employers.	Be part of the network for job leads or job support for a person with a disability.	Develop a network for job leads and support. Involve members of a student's broader community in planning meetings.	Change your job development process to always include employers in identifying work place supports.
Be involved in job search and support networks for persons with disabilities whom you know.	Help your daughter or son find a job by approaching employers yourself.		

From *Natural supports: The emerging role of business in employment of people with moderate and severe disabilities* (p. 25). (1997). Minneapolis: MN: The PACER Center; reprinted with permission from The PACER Center, (612) 827-2966.

was that job coaches generally used the level of facilitation strategies that matched co-worker needs.

Training Consultant Model   Weiner and Zivolich (2003) described 12 years of the natural support training consultant model for three individuals with significant disabilities. A private country club committed their own employees as initial trainers and long-term supports in a variety of positions within their organization. A full range of placement and support services were provided by the corporation, including job development, on-the-job training, jobsite modification, job sharing, job matching, development of special aids, family communication, case management, and other work-related support services. Although the program achieved significant qualitative success, the corporate partner was prepared to train and employ a larger number of employees with disabilities than were referred by the local developmental disability agency. The participants, compared with job coach-supported consumers, experienced superior work benefits for natural supports in the areas of job tenure, gross wages, and hours worked per week.

For most programs, the use of natural supports contributed to the overall success of SE programs; however, about two thirds of the programs using natural supports indicated that they had experienced problems in the implementation of natural support strategies. These problems overwhelmingly fall into two areas. First, employers are unwilling to implement the natural support strategies recommended by the SE program and resist the notion that they should assume sole responsibility for the training, supervision, and support of the employee with a disability. Second, local programs are having a difficult time identifying staff members with the skills necessary to implement natural support strategies and providing training to current staff members in the use of natural support techniques.

It makes little sense to discuss the benefits and drawbacks of job coaches as opposed to support facilitators because the job coach model has enabled more than 400,000 individuals to gain and retain competitive employment (Braddock et al., 2004; Rizzolo, Hemp, Braddock, & Pomeranz-Essley, 2004). Efforts are only now underway to determine fully the effectiveness of natural support approaches. Framing the argument in a dichotomous "either–or" manner, however, trivializes the real problems and hides the fact that SE needs to move beyond all current models. Support is necessary in most of the vocational options described in Figure 12.1. New strategies that empower consumers must be identified so that all individuals with significant disabilities can benefit from employment. To do this, the best components of the job coach model and natural support strategies must be combined with AT, person-centered planning, compensatory strategies, personal assistant services, and many other strategies and approaches. Mank (1994) eloquently noted,

> Millions of individuals continue to be denied access to high quality employment programs that would enable them to take charge over their careers. The ADA continues to be assailed as an "unfunded federal mandate" which places burdensome constraints on well-meaning businesses. Finding solutions to these challenges will require a renewal of the spirit of innovation and risk-taking which has been a defining characteristic of supported employment since its inception. (p. 37)

Perhaps the most significant question to ask is, how do we find excellent employment specialists, train them, and retrain them? Wehman and Targett (2002) noted that identifying excellent personnel within a business is perhaps the single largest problem in implementing quality integrated employment programs that lead to long-term careers. Identifying who the best people are for competencies required is crucial to an organization's success.

A number of specialized employment programs for individuals with disabilities have emerged over the years. Some have flourished; others have not. SE is one of the few specialized programs in the Rehabilitation Act that has expanded to a degree that it has the potential to make a national impact on the hundreds of thousands of people with disabilities who are still unemployed. SE is specifically designed to assist people with the most significant disabilities with locating and maintaining employment. SE first received public funding through the Rehabilitation Act Amendments of 1986 (PL 99-506). It has steadily increased in popularity and has documented positive outcomes (Mank, O'Neill, & Jansen, 1998; Revell, Wehman, Kregel, West, & Rayfield, 1994).

Today, staffing becomes even more important as more community-based organizations convert from segregated day programs to integrated competitive employment programs and emphasize improving services through the use of natural supports, expanding employer capacity, and self-instruction. Effective staff will translate into better outcomes for people with disabilities. Ineffective staff will result in poor employment outcomes for its customers or, at best, a disproportionate investment of time, energy, and fiscal resources dedicated to training and monitoring those personnel (Pamenter, 1999; Shilling, 1998). Therefore, program managers are wise to invest the necessary time, energy, and resources into the staff recruitment and selection. Figure 12.4 contains a well-detailed program guide on how to establish community and workplace supports. This form can be helpful to employment specialists as they design programs.

WORKPLACE SUPPORTS

All workers, not just individuals with disabilities, require different types, levels, and intensity of supports in their workplaces. Businesses provide supports to their employees and offer them a wealth of resources during the normal course of business. However, some employers may need additional assistance in creating workplace cultures that are supportive of individuals with disabilities. The goal is to work with employers so that businesses can increase their capacity to support workers with disabilities. The following sections list some of the key issues in implementing workplace supports.

What Are Workplace Supports?

Workplace supports typically exist in a business and are available to all employees (Luecking et al., 2004; Wehman, Bricout, & Kregel, 2000). They may include but are not limited to such things as a co-worker mentor who assists an employee in learning

---

Community and Workplace Support Form

Date: _____   Provider ID: _____
Consumer Name: _____   Employment Specialist: _____
SS#: _____   ID Code: _____
Currently Employed?   yes _____   no _____
    Company Name: _____
    Street: _____
    City, State, ZIP: _____
    Date of Placement: ____ /____ /____ (month/day/year)

Please answer the following questions for each support need. Complete a separate form for each area of need that is identified regardless of whether it is new or one that has been previously addressed.

1. What type of support is needed or desired? (check only one)
    _____   1. Determining job choices
    _____   2. Developing a résumé
    _____   3. Finding a job
    _____   4. Learning how to do the job
    _____   5. Remembering how to do the job
    _____   6. Orienting around the workplace
    _____   7. Completing all regular job duties
    _____   8. Being able to perform infrequent duties associated with the position
    _____   9. Arranging work schedule/hours
    _____ 10. Signing in/out at work
    _____ 11. Calling in sick or late
    _____ 12. Attending company meetings
    _____ 13. Taking lunch and/or breaks

Figure 12.4. Community and Workplace Support Form. (From Parent, W., Gibson, K., Unger, D., & Clements, C. [1994]. The role of the job coach: Orchestrating community and workplace supports. In P. Wehman & J. Kregel [Eds.], *New directions in supported employment* [pp. 12–18]. Richmond, VA: VCU-RRTC on Supported Employment, Natural Supports Transition Projects; reprinted by permission).

_____ 14. Receiving a raise or increased benefits
_____ 15. Getting along with co-workers
_____ 16. Developing friendships
_____ 17. Participating in social activities during work hours
_____ 18. Finding transportation to and from work
_____ 19. Finding transportation not associated with work
_____ 20. Getting a learner's permit or driver's license
_____ 21. Using public transportation
_____ 22. Learning how to use public transportation (e.g., taxi, bus, subway)
_____ 23. Using specialized transportation
_____ 24. Making ride arrangements (e.g., co-worker, volunteer, friend, family member)
_____ 25. Meeting people outside of work
_____ 26. Pursuing recreational interests
_____ 27. Purchasing/selecting/maintaining uniforms or clothing for work
_____ 28. Arranging volunteer opportunities
_____ 29. Attending social outings after work hours
_____ 30. Participating in programs/activities offered by community or civic organizations
_____ 31. Locating a place to live
_____ 32. Learning independent living skills
_____ 33. Getting up and/or ready for work
_____ 34. Picking up/cashing a paycheck
_____ 35. Managing money/paying bills
_____ 36. Using money/making purchases
_____ 37. Applying for SSI, SSDI, or other government subsidy
_____ 38. Handling SSI or SSDI issues
_____ 39. Using Social Security work incentives (e.g., PASS, IRWE)
_____ 40. Taking care of personal hygiene and grooming
_____ 41. Dealing with substance abuse issues
_____ 42. Changing something about the job
_____ 43. Attending school/college
_____ 44. Addressing sexual issues
_____ 45. Pursuing career advancement opportunities
_____ 46. Learning how to do something new at work
_____ 47. Finding a different or a second job
_____ 48. Addressing communication issues
_____ 49. Dealing with aggressive, disruptive, or problem behaviors
_____ 50. Handling family issues
_____ 51. Handling legal matters
_____ 52. Addressing/monitoring medical or medication issues
_____ 53. Requesting time off from work
_____ 54. Addressing fatigue or stamina issues
_____ 55. Arranging follow-along job coach services
_____ 56. Recording and monitoring work schedule/hours
_____ 99. Other

2. a. Has this support need been addressed previously while being served by this program?
　　　_____ 1. Yes
　　　_____ 2. No

　　b. If yes, what type of assistance was received? (please describe briefly)

　　c. What is the reason for developing another support option? (check only one)
　　　_____ 1. Consumer handled on own and now would prefer outside assistance
　　　_____ 2. New/additional supports were identified/needed
　　　_____ 3. Consumer no longer needed assistance/issue reoccurred

_____

(continued)

Figure 12.4.   *(continued)*

_____ 4. Consumer chose to stop using the support/has changed mind
_____ 5. Consumer preferred to find a different means of support
_____ 6. Person providing support was no longer willing/able to continue
_____ 7. Support was not successful/did not meet individual's needs
_____ 8. Support was too costly/funding no longer available
_____ 9. Support or assistance no longer available/situation changed
_____ 10. Support was not available/could not be located
_____ 99. Other

3. What is the status of this support need? (check only one)
_____ 1. Critically needed immediately
_____ 2. Critically needed in the future
_____ 3. Possibly needed/desired sometime
_____ 4. Not needed but desired immediately
_____ 5. Not needed but desired in the future

4. a. What support resources have been identified to address this need? (check all options)
Finding a Job
_____ 1. Family/friends assisting with identifying job leads or getting applications
_____ 2. Consumer pursuing job leads and/or picking up applications
_____ 3. Assistance from community employment agencies with résumé writing, job leads, getting/completing applications (e.g., State Employment Commission)
_____ 4. Employment specialist assisting with job development activities
_____ 5. Job placement assistance by members of the community, volunteers, civic organizations (e.g., JayCees)
_____ 6. Job placement assistance by school personnel, human services agencies (e.g., vocational rehabilitation, mental health/mental retardation [MH/MR] services)
_____ 98. Consumer accompanied to different businesses to find out about the type of job and/or company
_____ 99. Exploring interests and experiences/talking with the consumer and others (e.g., family, rehabilitation counselor, teacher, job coach)

Learning How to Do the Job
_____ 7. Co-worker mentoring
_____ 8. New employee training provided by the company (e.g., orientation, videos)
_____ 9. Supervisor training and/or prompting
_____ 10. Employment specialist training
_____ 11. Observing workplace personnel perform the job (e.g., co-workers, supervisor)
_____ 12. Retired person/company employee providing training
_____ 13. Standard company training procedures expanded/modified/extended
_____ 14. Restructuring job duties, making accommodations, developing compensatory strategies
_____ 15. Co-worker training and/or prompting
_____ 16. _____

Assistance with Completing the Job
_____ 17. Co-worker assisting, training, and/or prompting
_____ 18. Modifying job duties/arranging a work routine
_____ 19. Purchasing something to make job easier/better (e.g., toys, lock, raincoat)
_____ 20. Employment specialist training
_____ 21. Modifying/changing work hours
_____ 22. Utilizing a self-monitoring strategy (e.g., checklist, flip cards, diagram)

_____ 23. Consumer handling it on his/her own (e.g., asking, using natural cues)
_____ 24. Utilizing external cues (e.g., pictures, color code)
_____ 25. Supervisor assisting, training, and/or prompting
_____ 26. Making job accommodations, utilizing compensatory strategies/assistive technology

Addressing Work-Related and Non–Work-Related Issues

_____ 27. Consumer doing it on his/her own (e.g., making arrangements, self-monitoring)
_____ 28. Employment specialist assisting, training, arranging, and/or supporting
_____ 29. Family members assisting, arranging, monitoring, and/or supporting
_____ 30. Supervisor/employer arranging, prompting, training, monitoring, and/or supporting
_____ 31. Company providing and/or managing (e.g., direct deposit, programming timeclock)
_____ 32. Community or civic organization providing assistance and/or information
_____ 33. Human services agency providing assistance, information, and/or services (e.g., vocational rehabilitation, independent living center, MH/MR services)
_____ 34. Friend or advocate assisting
_____ 35. Self-managing behavior, walk away, re-direct anger
_____ 36. Member of the community or volunteer assisting
_____ 37. Training or classes through a school or human services agency (e.g., residential services, MH/MR, independent living center, technical center)
_____ 38. Establishing/modifying work hours, job duties, and/or break routine
_____ 39. Residential staff prompting and/or assisting
_____ 40. Arranging a flexible work schedule/hours and/or time off
_____ 41. Co-worker prompting, assisting, training, and/or monitoring
_____ 42. Utilizing an external cue (e.g., alarm watch, color code)
_____ 43. Utilizing a compensatory strategy (e.g., list of names and numbers, letter with blanks, posting schedule, contract, calendar book)
_____ 44. College or university students assisting/tutoring
_____ 45. Training and/or advocacy with co-workers, employers, the community, etc.
_____ 46. Training and/or role-playing with the consumer
_____ 47. Help from a paid personal assistant
_____ 48. Counseling (e.g., individual/family, private/public)
_____ 49. Consultant or specialist assisting (e.g., private company, independent business, Social Security specialist)
_____ 50. Receiving medical treatment/services (e.g., physician, neuropsychologist)
_____ 51. Receiving legal assistance/services (e.g., lawyer, public defendant)
_____ 52. Participating in peer and/or community support groups
_____ 53. Training or classes through a community or civic organization
_____ 54. Participating in community activities/events
_____ 55. Exploring interests, opportunities available, and support resources
_____ 56. Enrolling in college or university courses/program
_____ 57. Teaching personal hygiene and/or grooming
_____ 58. Purchasing something (e.g., extra keys, alarm clock, radio, razor)
_____ 59. Contacting people, friends, others with similar interests
_____ 60. _____

Arranging Transportation

_____ 61. Family member or relative drive
_____ 62. Walk
_____ 63. Take a taxi
_____ 64. Friend, neighbor, community member, volunteer/hired person drive

(continued)

Figure 12.4.   *(continued)*

_____ 65. Use specialized transportation
_____ 66. Carpool or ride with a co-worker
_____ 67. Ride a bus
_____ 68. Drive self
_____ 69. Ride a bicycle
_____ 70. Attend driving school
_____ 71. Family member train and/or assist
_____ 72. Employment specialist train, assist, and/or drive
_____ 73. Receive assistance with purchasing or repairing a car
_____ 74. Utilize a compensatory strategy (e.g., list of phone numbers, availability)
_____ 75. Assistance and/or services from a community or civic organization
_____ 76. Assistance and/or services from a human services agency

Other

_____ 77. _____
_____ 78. _____

b. Which support resources has the consumer chosen to use? (place corresponding number of the support resource identified in above question in the blank beside primary choice of the consumer and any other options being used concurrently or as an alternative or back-up support option)

_____ 1. Primary
_____ 2. Concurrent or alternate/back-up
_____ 3. Concurrent or alternate/back-up
_____ 4. Concurrent or alternate/back-up
_____ 5. Concurrent or alternate/back-up
_____ 6. Concurrent or alternate/back-up

5. What type of support option has been selected? (check only one)

_____ 1. *Employer or workplace support* (e.g., assistance provided by the consumer, employment specialist, or workplace personnel to address work or work-related issues at the job)
_____ 2. *Community support* (e.g., assistance provided by the consumer, employment specialist, or community to address work-related or non–work-related issues outside the workplace)
_____ 3. *Transportation support* (e.g., assistance provided by the consumer, employment specialist, workplace, or community to address transportation issues to and from work or not related to work)
_____ 4. *Recreation and social integration support* (e.g., assistance provided by the consumer, employment specialist, workplace, or community to address social and recreational issues with co-workers or persons outside the workplace after work hours)
_____ 5. *Personal and independent living support* (e.g., assistance provided by the consumer, employment specialist, workplace, or community to address personal, independent living, and residential issues outside the workplace)

6. Who has primary responsibility for arranging or obtaining the support? (check only one)

_____ 1. Consumer
_____ 2. Parent/family member
_____ 3. Friend/acquaintance/neighbor
_____ 4. Employment specialist
_____ 5. Rehabilitation counselor
_____ 6. Case manager
_____ 7. Teacher
_____ 8. Workplace personnel
_____ 9. Residential staff
_____ 99. Other: _____

7. a. Does the support require someone to function in the role of provider?
   _____ 1. Yes
   _____ 2. No
   b. If so, who is the primary person? (check only one)
   _____ 1. Consumer
   _____ 2. Supervisor
   _____ 3. Co-worker
   _____ 4. Other workplace personnel
   _____ 5. Parent/family member/spouse
   _____ 6. Friend/acquaintance/neighbor
   _____ 7. Member of the community
   _____ 8. Student
   _____ 9. Volunteer
   _____ 10. Tutor
   _____ 11. Retired person
   _____ 12. Consultant/specialist
   _____ 13. Rehabilitation counselor
   _____ 14. Teacher
   _____ 15. Case manager
   _____ 16. Employment specialist
   _____ 17. Community/civic agency representative (name: _____)
   _____ 18. School
   _____ 19. Business
   _____ 20. Residential staff
   _____ 21. Human services agency representative (name: _____)
   _____ 99. Other: _____

8. What has been the role of the employment specialist in addressing this support need? (check all that apply)
   _____ 1. Identifying support options
   _____ 2. Contacting support resources
   _____ 3. Assisting consumer with choosing type of support
   _____ 4. Helping/training consumer to obtain/use the support
   _____ 5. Advocating
   _____ 6. Training person providing support
   _____ 7. Working together with the consumer and support provider
   _____ 8. Overseeing the support arrangement
   _____ 9. Ongoing monitoring of support
   _____ 10. Providing additional support as needed
   _____ 11. Providing the support (continued)
   _____ 12. Employment specialist not involved
   _____ 13. Making support arrangements
   _____ 14. Making alternative arrangements if support breaks down
   _____ 99. Other: _____

9. a. Are any costs associated with providing the support?
   _____ 1. Yes
   _____ 2. No
   b. If so, what is the approximate amount? (Round off to the nearest dollar)
   $ _____
   c. Who is the primary funding source for the support? (check only one)
   _____ 1. Supported employment program
   _____ 2. Employer
   _____ 3. Consumer or his/her family
   _____ 4. Vocational rehabilitation

(continued)

Figure 12.4.   *(continued)*

```
_____  5.   School
_____  6.   Private business (other than the employer)
_____  7.   Community or civic organization/agency (name: _____ )
_____  8.   Social Security work incentives (e.g., PASS/IRWE)
_____  9.   Human services agency (name: _____ )
_____ 99.   Other: _____
```

10.   Who is primarily responsible for overseeing the ongoing monitoring of the support? (check
      only one)

```
_____  1.   Consumer
_____  2.   Parent/family member/spouse
_____  3.   Friend/acquaintance/neighbor
_____  4.   Employment specialist
_____  5.   Rehabilitation counselor
_____  6.   Case manager
_____  7.   Teacher
_____  8.   Workplace personnel
_____  9.   Support no longer needed/short-term
_____ 10.   Residential staff
_____ 99.   Other: _____
```

the job, a supervisor who monitors work performance, a co-worker who assists the new worker in developing social networks, or making maximum use of orientation training. This also could include other company-sponsored training events, programs, and benefits such as an employee assistance program. Workplace supports also may be specifically designed to assist a particular employee with his or her job performance. This could include modifications to the work environment, adjustments to employment policies or practices, and/or changes in the way certain job functions are performed that allow the employee to get the job done successfully.

What Are Examples of Workplace Supports that May Already Exist in a Business?

Three major categories of workplace supports that may already exist in a business are environmental, procedural, and natural. *Environmental supports* are defined as physical structures, surroundings, or objects present in the business that make the jobsite more accessible for current or future employees. For example, automatic door openers may be available when entering the building, or signage on the walls may help employees successfully navigate from one department to another. *Procedural supports* are actions or activities that employers provide to assist potential or current employees with performing their jobs and job-related functions. For instance, flextime may be offered to allow employees to work within the hours that are more conducive to their personal lives. *Natural supports* exist in any workplace and are informal supports that are typically available to any employee. This might include workers sharing rides to and from work or a senior staff member helping a new co-worker get the job done when he or she needs extra assistance.

How Will Staff Know What Workplace Supports Are Needed?

Sometimes, job selection can reduce support needs. For example, a job that is negotiated to highlight a person's strength and accentuate abilities may help eliminate need for adding workplace supports. Initially observing what a worker can do can also help determine what, if anything, is needed. At times, an individual's support needs will be obvious. For example, a person who uses a wheelchair for mobility will need an accessible workplace or modifications to the existing environment. Other times, the necessary support may not be readily apparent. Worker behaviors that may signal the need for providing additional workplace supports are failing to initiate an activity, not switching job tasks, difficulty performing a duty, inability to meet established production standards, repeatedly asking for assistance, or making the same mistakes over and over again.

Can Individuals with Disabilities Gain Access to Workplace Supports on Their Own?

The person with the disability may already know or have some ideas of what he or she needs. At other times, the individual may need guidance. Taking advantage of the support resources that are available in a workplace may not automatically occur for many individuals with disabilities.

Even if a resource exists, the individual may not know how to gain access to or benefit from its use. He or she may be unaware of the potential support, how to choose among the support alternatives that are available, or how to gain access to a desired resource. In addition, a company may have varying levels of resource options. For instance, one company may have an intensive orientation and training program, whereas another has none. The existing workplace supports within any company must be analyzed to determine if they meet the needs of the individual with a disability who has been hired.

Are Workplace Supports the Same Thing as Reasonable Accommodations?

Workplace supports and *reasonable accommodations* are sometimes used synonymously; however, there are differences. Some employers may be more open to hearing about "workplace supports" because "reasonable accommodation" may conjure up unwarranted fears about complying with the law and costs associated with accommodations. Under the ADA, employers must provide reasonable accommodations to a qualified individual with a disability. A qualified individual with a disability is someone who can perform the essential functions of a job with or without reasonable accommodations. Many businesses will have a policy in place on how a request for accommodation should be handled.

Some examples of workplace supports that might be useful to an employee with a disability include having a co-worker prompt him or her to take a break, having an employment specialist provide additional job skills training, creating a quiet work area, giving an employee a written list of job duties to perform at the start of each shift, replacing a manual stapler with an electronic one, or allowing a change in the usual work schedule. Support needs vary from person to person. Thus, it should not come as a surprise that workplace supports must be tailored to the particular situation on hand. What works for one employee in one workplace will not necessarily be effective for someone else in another business.

Are Workplace Supports Expensive?

Workplace supports do not have to be expensive. An exemption from or modification to an existing workplace policy is not costly. For example, a simple change in an existing

workplace policy that requires employees to work every other Saturday may be modified for a worker who, due to the nature of the disability, has no access to transportation
on this day of the week. Co-worker support also results in no charge. For example, a co-
worker may work alongside another worker and model the pace needed to meet the employer's production standard. Other simple strategies are not costly, such as a warehouse
worker using a computer printout to remind him or her of what stock to pull and where
to locate various items.

When supports are purchased or fabricated, the cost will vary depending on what
is needed. However, most often, supports are not expensive. For example, an office
worker may need to have the regular computer mouse replaced with a track ball
mouse, which costs around $50.00. Or, an upholstery worker may need tactile cues
made of Velcro placed on the surface of a table to give information on the size of material to cut that cost about $4.00.

In any of these examples, the worker may need the additional assistance of an advocate to assist in the negotiation process and the customization of workplace supports. This could require additional funding supports that are available through the
One Stop Service Delivery System, VR services, Social Security Work Incentives, and
so forth.

What Is the Most Effective Type of Workplace Support?

The most effective type of workplace support is the one that works for the individual.
For every support need that is identified, a variety of support resources may be available. All of the generated ideas should be discussed with the individual including an explanation of what using the specific support would entail. The availability of the support option, the pros and cons of each, and the level of interest expressed by the
individual can be explored at the same time. Assessing these factors also can provide a
direction for job selection. For example, one position offers orientation training; another provides co-worker mentoring; and a third job informally supports employees on
an individualized basis. The varying levels of support offered by these employment settings combined with other characteristics of the job, such as hours, wages, co-workers,
and location, will influence an individual's decision about where he or she would prefer to work.

CONVERSION FROM DAY PROGRAMS TO COMMUNITY-BASED EMPLOYMENT

With so much discussion on the effectiveness of SE, national supports, and workplace
supports as ways to empower people with disabilities, the questions then is, why aren't
more people working? Conversion of day programs to support employment outcomes
is the answer, but it's hard to do.

Much research and interest has been devoted to conversion issues. First, federal
funding of systems-change projects has resulted in a substantial number of rehabilitation facilities converting staff and other resources (to some degree) in order to increase
SE opportunities (Wehman & Revell, 1996). It is remarkable that more than one third
of the respondents to the study by Wehman and Revell (1996) have been able to shift
a significant amount of their resources to SE in a relatively short time period and during a very difficult fiscal period. Still, as others have noted (Mank, 1994; Novak,

Rogan, Mank, & DiLeo, 2003; Wehman & Kregel, 1995), the degree of change has not been as great as was hoped for in the 1980s. Segregated vocational services continue to be the predominant mode of service for individuals in need of extended employment support (Braddock et al., 2004). Although the numbers of SE consumers and providers have increased dramatically since the inception of the program (Wehman & Revell, 1996), so, too, have those for facility-based programs. These initiatives may have resulted in new providers offering only SE; regardless, in most communities, existing facilities are the only avenue of access to SE, and, for the most part, they remain committed to segregated services.

Second, the findings suggest that systems change is an evolution rather than a revolution. Many families, rehabilitation facilities, and communities have invested deeply, financially, and emotionally, in segregated programs, and they resist efforts to downsize or eliminate them. For those facilities, the movement toward competitive employment as the option of choice will be long and arduous and, for many, even unattainable. Achieving this goal for consumers requires a much greater overhaul in the way that programs deliver services. True systems change may come about from an influx of new stand-alone SE providers and new consumers coming into the system who, along with their families, want and expect more than a slot in a workshop or day support program. Rogan and Walker (2003) noted:

> It is nearly 2004. The disabilities support field has demonstrations of thousands and thousands of individuals over the past two decades who are engaged in meaningful supported employment and supported living. People with very high support needs are living, working, and actively participating in their local communities. Research has shown that quality of life outcomes are better for those in supported employment and typical community living settings compared with their counterparts in segregated day and residential services.
>
> Despite this growing body of evidence supporting integrated and individualized outcomes, most people with developmental disabilities remain in congregate, segregated day services and many remain in congregate living situations. (p. 9)

Most agencies have chosen to add SE and supported living to their continuum of services, providing both integrated and segregated services. A relatively small number of organizations have undertaken the process of change from facility-based to community-based services. Fewer agencies have been able to accomplish an overall organizational shift from totally facility-based services to individualized community-based supports. Why is this? Why has true systems change been so slow to occur? If some organizations can do it, then why can't or won't others?

The process of organizational change is complex, difficult, and rewarding. It involves a period of operating dual systems (the old and the new) simultaneously, changing staff attitudes and skills, marketing a new organizational image, interfacing with businesses, assisting people with disabilities to pursue their dreams and develop work skills, and so forth.

Finally, the findings suggest that new methods for increasing SE systems capacity may be needed. Systems-change funding has resulted in some change, but in order to reach the next plateau, new initiatives will probably be required. For example, it has been suggested that state VR agencies can promote conversion to SE through such strategies as fiscal incentives, caps on segregated program slots, changes in licensure and regulatory standards, and increased training and technical assistance (Mank, 1994;

McGaughey, Kiernan, McNally, Gilmore, & Keith, 1995; Wehman & Kregel, 1995). Each of these strategies has been initiated in limited numbers of states with limited results. However, as Weiner and Zivolich (1995) wrote,

> Individuals with disabilities should no longer have to wait in segregation, unemployment, welfare, and poverty, if [facility] management personnel cannot make the required behavioral and managerial changes to implement integrated employment services. . . . People with disabilities consistently have stated that they want jobs. Why do they continue to wait, 20 years later, for the segregation industry to hear and respond to this request? Why do we continue to provide "changeover" consultation for sheltered workshops to help them sort through their own perceived barriers to SE integration? (p. 311)

Weiner and Zivolich (1995) suggested that the changeover strategy has reached the limits of efficacy and cost-effectiveness. They offered an alternative method that focuses on funding for establishing SE in for-profit businesses. We offer other strategies that might spur true systems change.

Strategies for Organizational Change

Despite these many barriers to organizational change and to providing individualized services and supports, many organizations have successfully shifted to totally community-based services. Among numerous factors that these organizations attributed to their success, all reported leadership as the single most important element (Gowdy, Carlson, & Rapp, 2004). Although leadership most often came from the Executive Director/CEO and top-level managers, it was essential that leadership ultimately filter throughout the staff in order for the change efforts to be successful (e.g., via participatory management and shared decision making). Others strategies that have proven effective include those cited by Rogan and Walker (2003):

- Articulating a clear mission, vision, and values among staff and other stakeholders

- Involving key stakeholders from the start in the planning and decision-making process in order to get buy-in

- Listening to and acting on the desires of people with disabilities and their families

- Using individualized, person-centered planning approaches and a "one person at a time" process

- Hiring, training, and supporting a quality staff

- Promoting a learning organization that embraces change and is willing to take risks

- Securing high-quality jobs and typical, desirable homes

- Terminating facility admissions and backfilling after people leave

- Gaining access to external consultants to help guide the change

- Working to flatten the organizational structure with most staff providing direct services

- Using a team structure to support staff and meet the needs of individuals

- Changing job description from specialists to generalists

- Changing the agency's image through marketing and public relations

- Sharing success stories

- Building business and other community partnerships

- Investing in buildings and equipment

- Redirecting existing funds to community services and pursuing flexible and alternative sources of funds

- Connecting with others undergoing changeover

CONCLUSION

This chapter describes available vocational placements and models and the values associated with responsive and quality employment programs. Case studies of young people with disabilities working in the different vocational arrangements illustrate the strengths and weaknesses of each model. As national data indicate, the range of vocational models in place for people with disabilities is increasing (Shafer, Wehman, Kregel, & West, 1990); however, there must be a greater focus on career development and upward mobility into more challenging jobs for people with disabilities.

STUDY QUESTIONS

1. Describe the major barriers to vocational competence for students with disabilities and how to overcome them.

2. How do employers perceive people with disabilities in the workplace?

3. Why is transportation critical when considering employment? Describe options when people with disabilities do not have access to public transportation.

4. List five vocational options for students with disabilities and the advantages and disadvantages of each.

5. Describe the best practices that encompass SE.

6. Describe the different roles of the employment specialists in SE.

7. Explain how natural supports can help workers with disabilities maintain their employment.

8. Describe the major issues to consider when implementing workplace support.

9. What can be done to help more people work in community-based employment?

13

Pursuing Postsecondary Education Opportunities for Individuals with Disabilities

Elizabeth Evans Getzel and Lori W. Briel

AFTER COMPLETING THIS CHAPTER, THE READER WILL BE ABLE TO

○ Describe the challenges involved in gaining access to postsecondary education for people with disabilities, including specific transition issues

○ Identify the skills needed by students for a successful transition to college

○ Discuss the importance of accommodations and assistive technology (AT) devices in a college environment

Increased numbers of students with disabilities are entering postsecondary education to obtain further skills and knowledge as a result of a combination of legislative, academic, and social changes (Gilson, 1996). Students with disabilities seeking access to colleges, universities, and vocational-technical programs, in particular 2-year colleges, have increased as potential transition goals for students with disabilities across disability categories, income, and gender (Wagner, Cameto, & Newman, 2003). Students with disabilities attending 4-year universities and colleges comprised 6%–8% of the student population from 1988 to 2000 (Henderson, 2001). Students are seeking advanced degree programs as a means to enhance their chances of 1) obtaining and maintaining employment, 2) earning a higher annual income, and 3) creating a means for lifelong independence and a greater quality of life (Fairweather & Shaver, 1991; Stodden & Dowrick, 2000; Wilson, Getzel, & Brown, 2000).

POSTSECONDARY TRANSITION CONSIDERATIONS

Preparation for postsecondary education includes learning those skills necessary to deal both with the academic and social challenges presented by college. Educators, family members, and students may assume that if a student is academically capable of participating in higher education settings, then systematic preparation for college is not needed (deFur, Getzel, & Trossi, 1996; Getzel, Briel, & Kregel, 2000; Getzel, McManus, & Briel, 2004). Unfortunately, without effective planning and preparation, students with disabilities can become overwhelmed and unable to adapt to a postsecondary environment. Therefore, the transition to college must begin early in their education experience. Pre–high school activities could include taking challenging courses in English, math, science, history, or foreign language. Exploring course options among high school programs is also important so students can learn more about their academic and career interests. In addition, students need to work on developing strong study skills and learning strategies (Virginia Department of Education [VADOE], 2003).

Although many postsecondary education programs are increasing in the attention and support given to students with disabilities, success in these settings, for the most part, remains dependent on the individual qualities of the student (Brinckerhoff, Shaw, & McGuire, 2002; deFur et al., 1996; Getzel et al., 2004). Students are responsible for a number of activities that are provided by secondary schools. In higher education, students with disabilities are responsible for documentation of a disability, assessment information, programming, advocacy, decision making, and transition planning (Brinckerhoff et al., 2002; Getzel et al., 2004). However, the stigma attached to identifying oneself as needing special services or supports drives some students to elect not to disclose their disabilities in order to avoid being labeled as needing specialized services (Lynch & Gussel, 1996; Wilson et al., 2000). Unfortunately, students who fail to identify themselves as having disabilities are often unable to gain access to many of the supports designed to get them closer to having equal (rather than special) access to education (Getzel et al., 2004; Gordon & Keiser, 1998). To help students with disabilities prepare for their transition to higher education, six primary areas of consideration emerge when creating a planning process: exploring postsecondary educational settings, preparing academically for college, preparing for standardized admission testing, identifying financial aid resources, identifying skills needed by students for a successful transition, and setting career goals. This section of the chapter discusses these areas and suggests planning activities.

Exploring Postsecondary Educational Settings

Postsecondary educational programs are offered in a variety of settings including trade or business schools, vocational-technical schools, community colleges, and specialized training in business and industry (Wille-Gregory, Graham, & Hughes, 1995). It is important for students to explore a variety of postsecondary options to determine what best meets their educational and training needs. There are program considerations that include whether the program meets the student's career goals; the level and type of support services provided; the level of academic coursework required; and general atmosphere, size, diversity of student body, and campus accessibility. When assessing a college or university, it is important to look comprehensively at the programs, college environment, and general feel of the campus, and then look specifically at the disability-related supports and services needed. General background information about colleges or universities can be obtained from a college's web site or a web site that is designed to provide information on a number of colleges (e.g., http://www.petersons.com). Resource books are available either for purchase or developed by a state's department of education about postsecondary schools located in that particular state. However, in-depth research is needed to obtain specific information about the programs and supports that will meet an individual's need. If possible, individuals with disabilities should visit potential schools and find out more about available support services and the school's physical accessibility. Individuals who are considering a particular school should talk with students with disabilities who attend that school about their experiences. According to Wilson et al. (2000), some suggested areas to consider when visiting a program or reviewing information about it are

1. Campus climate: Is the campus atmosphere generally accepting of students with differences in learning styles? Are students considered in the planning process and encouraged to participate fully in a variety of campus-life activities?

2. Program philosophy: Is there a specialized area of emphasis associated with the services? Is there an emphasis on learning strategies, remediation, or social skills?

3. Awareness and support: Are the school administration and faculty aware of the needs of students with disabilities and the adjustments that will help meet these needs? Is there good communication between all parties on whom the student will rely for support?

4. Academic adjustment: How are academic adjustments coordinated? Are there specialized accommodations such as notetakers, real-time captioning, and readers/scribes for examinations?

5. Waivers and substitutions: What are the procedures for waivers and substitutions, and is assistance available with these procedures? What kind of documentation is required? What is the probability that waivers and/or substitutions are granted?

Table 13.1.   Transition support activities

Local activities to assist in transition planning	Brochures with information on specific campus services
	College fairs spotlighting campus disability supports and services
	Presentations at high schools by college support staff about college services
	Student speakers' bureaus made up of college students with disabilities
	Campus visits by high school groups, including tours guided by college students with disabilities
Transition programs to assist in campus adjustment	Summer orientation programs on college campuses for high school juniors and seniors
	Workshops for high school students to develop skills
	Summer orientation for all entering students
	Additional summer orientation programs specifically for students with disabilities
	Freshmen orientation classes provided for the general student population
	A special section of freshmen orientation designed to address disability-specific needs

From Scott, S.S. (1996). Understanding colleges: An overview of college support services and programs available to clients from transition planning through graduation. *Journal of Vocational Rehabilitation, 6*(3), 223; reprinted by permission.

6. Course load and graduation time: Is it possible to maintain a reduced course load? Do students with disabilities generally take longer to complete the requirements for graduation? Is priority registration available for students with disabilities?

7. Tutorial support: Is it scheduled or on an as-needed basis? Is tutoring provided by peers or professional staff? What is the student–tutor ratio? Does the staff receive continual professional development?

8. Student support activities or groups: Are there ongoing groups that meet to talk about issues or concerns related to their experiences on campus? Are there specific activities that are designed to assist students with disabilities to network with other students on campus? Are there student leadership/mentoring programs to help students feel connected with other students with disabilities on campus? Is there a campus disability advocacy or advisory group that students can join to provide input concerning issues on campus?

Another excellent resource to help students with disabilities with the transition from high school to postsecondary educational settings is college support personnel. Often, these representatives have very little involvement during the transition process (deFur, Getzel, & Kregel, 1994); however, these individuals can provide an important link to postsecondary environments. Scott (1996) suggested some activities that college personnel can provide to support students with disabilities during the transition process and once students have arrived on campus (see Table 13.1).

Preparing Academically for College

Students with disabilities must be able to demonstrate that they have met the academic requirements to enter postsecondary education programs. It is critical that students are enrolled in college preparatory classes during high school to build a foundation of knowledge to not only enter college but also to have the academic preparation to remain in school (Brinckerhoff et al., 2002; Eaton & Coull, 1999).

Students with disabilities are often accepted into a college but face meeting course requirements to graduate. In particular, students with disabilities can experience difficulties in meeting a college's language requirement to earn an advanced degree. Prior to selecting a college, students need to be aware of policies that the college or university has concerning course substitutions. It cannot be assumed that because course substitutions for a foreign language were provided at the secondary level that a college or university follows this same policy (Madaus, 2003). Decisions on secondary foreign language coursework must be carefully weighed with the student's potential career goals and what type of postsecondary education program would best meet these goals. Foreign language requirements for graduation vary among the different programs of study offered, and consideration must be made as to the policies and procedures for course substitutions at a specific college and the requirements for degree programs within the college that interest a student (Madaus, 2003).

Preparing for Standardized Admission Testing

Prior to applying for college, students with disabilities will need to take a standardized admission examination—the Scholastic Aptitude Test (SAT) and/or the ACT. If a student is going to request accommodations for the examination, then ample time is needed prior to the date of the test to request these accommodations. SAT and ACT have very specific rules for qualifying for accommodations (Fuller & Wehman, 2003). It is important that students and family members work closely with the transition team to provide the necessary information to request testing accommodations. Since 2003, the SAT and ACT do not indicate if an examination was taken using accommodations. Students with disabilities will need to determine with the assistance of teachers or other education professionals their personal test-taking strategies (Fuller & Wehman, 2003). Strategies that students can use include practice sessions using questions from the test in order to learn the design and format of questions and relaxation techniques (Foster, Paulk, & Dastoor, 1999).

Identifying Financial Aid Resources

A large number of students seeking a college education will need additional financial resources beyond what their families can provide (Heath Resource Center, 2005). Students with disabilities and their family members will need to explore what types of financial assistance are available, whether it is disability-related expenses or general college expenses that need to be covered. Financial assistance may be needed to help cover the cost of tuition, room and board, transportation, or other college-related expenses. Researching financial aid resources from both public and private entities can often be a complicated process as a result of changes in legislation, eligibility requirements, or policies (Heath Resource Center, 2005). It is recommended that students and their families complete the Free Application for Federal Student Aid (FAFSA), which is located online or available through the student's guidance office or the school's career center. Other potential resources for students with disabilities may be available from the state Vocational Rehabilitation (VR) Agency or from the Social

Security Administration (SSA). Students should review several sources of information to determine what financial aid, grants, or scholarships might be available (Heath Resource Center, 2005).

Identifying Skills Needed for a Successful Transition

A growing consideration in transition planning has been how to support the development and use of student self-determination skills. *Self-determined behavior* is defined as "acting as the primary causal agent in one's life and making choices and decisions regarding one's quality of life free from undue external influence or interference" (Wehmeyer, 1996, p. 24; see also Wehmeyer, 1998, 2001b; Wehmeyer, Abery, Mithaug, & Stancliffe, 2003). Students with disabilities who have successfully made the transition to postsecondary schools exhibit 1) an awareness of their strengths and weaknesses both academically and socially in addition to use of compensatory strategies; 2) an ability to discuss their accommodation needs with faculty and staff; 3) an awareness of services and supports available to them; and 4) an ability to gain access to information, services, or supports when needed (Aune, 1991; Bursuck & Rose, 1992; Durlak, 1992; Virginia Commonwealth University, 2004).

In the past, students with disabilities were often unaware of the goals established in their individualized education programs (IEPs) or saw little connection to their education and future goals (Lovitt, Cushing, & Stump, 1994; Morningstar, Turnbull, & Turnbull, 1995). Johnson and Sharpe (2000) reported that more youth are attending their IEP transition meetings than in previous years, but that active participation by the student is still minimal. In fact, administrators representing 50 states reported that teachers mostly used information from student assessments (79%) or represented the student's views at the IEP meetings (68%) and that the least practiced strategy was to have students lead the meeting (8%). Active participation in the IEP process is essential to developing self-determination skills, directing the meeting itself, and helping establish the goals and required services. The IEP process offers students the opportunity to practice applying skills of self-advocacy and choice in a safe environment, and it provides an opportunity for them to develop an awareness of their strengths and needs (deFur et al., 1996). Each of these is critical to developing self-determination. Many times, well-intentioned teachers and family members protect youth with disabilities from making mistakes and refrain from discussing the details and impact of the student's disability (Bremer, Kachgal, & Schoeller, 2003). Exercising personal choice options allows students to know themselves, understand their disability, and understand how it may affect academic learning, relationships, employment, and participation in the community. Directing the IEP also empowers and enhances a willingness to persevere.

As a part of the self-determination process, each student must be prepared to make disclosure decisions in a variety of environments. Disclosing a disability is optional in both the postsecondary setting and the employment arena. Students need to become familiar with the Americans with Disabilities Act (ADA) of 1990 (PL 101-336) and the policies and procedures on campus to disclose disability. Discussions should occur about what students think about this issue and how they will deal with it once they enter a college or university. Students need to explore their comfort level with disclosing their disability and what methods would be best for them (Ettinger, 1995; Virginia Commonwealth University, 2004). In addition, role-playing actual disclosure scenarios can build students' skills and improve the decision-making process.

Setting Career Goals

A number of college students with disabilities have high career aspirations but low expectations of ever accomplishing these goals (Babbitt & Burbach, 1990). Students with disabilities tend to exhibit a greater uncertainty about their career choice than their peers without disabilities. These students may be uncertain about their strengths and limitations and how these fit with different career choices. With postsecondary education as a primary transition goal, secondary transition planning may neglect the attention needed for career guidance (deFur et al., 1996). Career guidance services can help students to better understand what postsecondary options can best meet their needs. Career planning for individuals with disabilities requires partnerships among the student, educators, and community-based service providers, including VR.

School guidance counselors play an important role as members of the IEP team. Programs offered at specific colleges and the advice and support of teachers and guidance counselors have been identified as extremely important factors in helping students with disabilities decide which college to attend (Henderson, 1999). School counselors can help students to determine career interests and assess postsecondary opportunities, and they can work with students, families, and special education staff to develop career goals to help develop a framework for postsecondary education plans. Without an overall context provided by a career objective, a student's ability may be limited in the identification of specific supports and services needed to achieve his or her goals (Briel & Getzel, 2001; deFur et al., 1996). Students with disabilities have similar career development needs as their peers without disabilities; however, students with disabilities have additional factors that need to be considered during the career development process (Ettinger, 1995). Some areas that counselors can address with students include

1. Exploring career goals: There are many acceptable ways to begin exploring career goals. Keep in mind that approximately 80% of all college students change their majors at least once and 50% change more than once (Hughes, 2004). Students with disabilities often lack exposure to the variety of career options and the skills that are required. If a student is unable to articulate his or her general career interests, then an interest inventory may be a good tool to use to begin this process. A review of school records will indicate areas of academic strength and weakness. Promoting participation in volunteer work and extracurricular school activities are methods to discover and define potential interests. Family, friends, and teachers can be very helpful in identifying further strengths. Discussing any experiences that may have influenced the student's interests is also very important. Together with the student, determine several career areas to research. Students need to find out what the academic requirements are for specific careers and what are the typical daily skills and proficiencies that would be expected for an employee. Encourage students to gain access to career information online, use interactive software to communicate with individuals in a specific field, watch educational videos and CD-ROMs, and talk with their family and friends about their jobs, their likes, and

their dislikes. Ideally, students with disabilities will have actual work experience during high school to further explore vocational interests (Reiff, Ginsberg, & Gerber, 1995). These opportunities will assist students in better determining their postschool goals and what type of postsecondary educational setting can best meet their needs.

2. Develop a plan to address affects of disability: After a career direction has been established and the student is familiar with some of the expectations of the field, a discussion should occur with the student on projecting how the disability may affect work performance and what potential strategies could be used to compensate. Students with disabilities must be able to understand their strong points and how their disability affects their learning (Brinckerhoff et al., 2002; Getzel et al., 2004) and performance. This process is best accomplished through personal experiences; having role models; networking with other individuals with the same disability; and talking with teachers, family members, disability specialists, and guidance counselors. Connecting with VR services is recommended for further information, resources, and input to ensure successful career planning. For students with disabilities, this means they must understand and accept their disability and acknowledge their strengths and limitations not only related to learning but also performance as well. Preliminary discussions to identify potential accommodations or compensatory strategies and to gain access to disability-specific adult resources and supports in the community may be timely. For example, a student with a traumatic brain injury interested in engineering may connect with the National Brain Injury Association to learn about specific memory enhancing strategies or organizational supports.

3. Career exploration in college: Employers are not only seeking candidates with production skills but also with qualities that are often referred to as "soft skills" (Gerber & Price, 2003; National Association of Counselors and Employers, 2004). For example, exhibiting effective communication, interpersonal, and teamwork skills and demonstrating motivation, initiative, and a strong work ethic are desirable qualities for employees in a majority of careers. When choosing a postsecondary setting, students should assess the degree to which career exploration and development activities are supported. Does the school or career center offer internship or work co-op opportunities? What student organizations are available to develop teamwork and leadership skills? Are there service-learning courses available that connect students with agencies in the community where the content or skills learned in the course benefit people served by the agency? Hands-on work experiences not only confirm and define career direction but also help students to identify support needs and better prepare the candidate for the competitive job market upon graduation (Briel & Getzel, 2001). Students with disabilities have a number of decisions to make when selecting a postsecondary education program. It is important that students make informed choices about the postsecondary setting that best meets their needs. Gathering specific information about educational programs and the level of support they provide, along with talking to other students and visiting programs, are just some examples of the processes involved in making this decision.

ADJUSTING TO POSTSECONDARY EDUCATION ENVIRONMENTS

Learning about Supports and Services at College

Colleges and universities vary in the types of supports and services provided to students with disabilities. Typically, some of the most commonly requested supports by students include textbooks on tape, notetakers, extended time on tests, distraction-free environments for test taking, use of calculators, and permission to tape lectures (Deschamps, 2004; Getzel & Kregel, 1996; Thomas, 2000). Students also need to explore services that are available on campus for all students (e.g., counseling services, writing or math labs, study skills or time management classes offered either through a counseling center or other entities on campus). There is a full range of services on campus to assist all students to successfully meet their academic coursework, and students with disabilities should take advantage of these services along with any specialized services they are receiving.

One of the biggest differences between high school and college concerns the receipt of services for students with disabilities. Most college campuses have a specific office to handle the request for accommodations or specialized supports for students with disabilities. Usually these offices are called Disability Support Services, or DSS offices. Once these students enter postsecondary environments, they are no longer "entitled" to disability-related services and supports, but must meet "eligibility" requirements through the documentation of a disability. Students with disabilities and their family members need to understand the implications of moving from services and supports provided under the Individuals with Disabilities Education Improvement Act of 2004 (PL 108-446) to the ADA. Unlike the IDEA, in which student services and supports are designed to meet specific educational goals, the supports and services provided in college are designed to ensure access to programs and activities offered on campus. How are students with disabilities determined to be eligible for these services? Colleges and universities have documentation policies or procedures in place to determine eligibility, and it is important for students to inquire about the documentation process on specific campuses they are exploring. Table 13.2 provides a series of questions (Deschamps, 2004) that can be used by students and families as they visit campuses or review information about specific colleges and universities. Knowing about the services and supports prior to applying for college can assist students to gain access to what is needed before academic problems occur.

Table 13.2. Questions to ask concerning services and supports

What specific documentation does your campus require to be eligible for services?

What types of support services are typically provided to students (e.g., learning disability, attention-deficit/hyperactivity disorder, low vision)?

Is new documentation required every year to remain eligible for services?

Are there orientation classes available that address disability-specific issues?

What is the process for gaining access to these support services?

How are instructors notified of a student's disability?

From Deschamps, A. (2004). Traveling the road from high school to college: Tips for the journey. *Transition Times, 9*(1), 1–2; adapted by permission.

Using Assistive Technology

Recently, there have been tremendous advances in the area of AT to enable individuals with disabilities to read, write, communicate, and work with greater ease and efficiency (Langton & Ramseur, 2001). *AT* can be broadly defined as any technology with the potential to enhance the performance of individuals with disabilities (Lewis, 1998). Significant growth in both assistive and instructional technology provides an important link to promoting access to information and learning for students with disabilities (Michaels, Pollack Prezant, Morabito, & Jackson, 2002). Screen readers, speech-to-text software, graphic organization software, word prediction, personal digital assistants (PDA), digital recorders, and handheld spellers are only a few of the products that assist students with disabilities to compensate for their disability. In postsecondary settings, the use of AT benefits students by providing access to previously unavailable academic and social opportunities; providing alternative methods of responding; increasing learner independence; and increasing the ability to cope, compensate, and accept their disability (Bryant, Bryant, & Reith, 2002).

Students who will be using AT need to have access to technology that promotes positive academic and career outcomes and need to learn how to use the technology *before* entering a higher education program (Burgstahler, 2003). All too often, students with disabilities are entering postsecondary education unaware of existing technology (Getzel et al., 2004). Understanding what technology is available is a critical need that can make a tremendous difference in students' ability to perform effectively in college. Students with disabilities who begin working with devices while in high school are able to determine what technology is most effective, prioritize AT requirements that they will need after high school, and explore postsecondary programs to determine which devices can be used to gain access to information (Burgstahler, 2003; Getzel, Flippo, Wittig, & Russell, 1997). Some colleges and universities have begun to address this issue by including presentations about technology during college fairs or other special college programs. College students with disabilities are invited to speak to students about the use of technology and what is available on local campuses. These types of activities, along with continuing to educate college faculty and staff on the uses of technology in their instructional setting, can help individuals with disabilities to benefit from available technology while in college (Fichten, Barile, & Asuncion, 1999; Getzel et al., 2004).

Self-Management Skills

By far, abilities in self-management are the most critical skills that all students attending postsecondary programs need. Larger projects, assignments, and academic loads combined with reduced daily structure challenge all college students to organize their day, break down assignments, and monitor the work flow. This is especially true for students with disabilities who often enter programs with inadequate organizational and study skills (Virginia Commonwealth University, 2004). Students often struggle trying to manage their academic studies with the variety of social opportunities on campus. Self-management such as time management becomes a lifeline to success and a critical skill to help students balance their academic studies and social activities.

TED

Ted is a 24-year-old transfer student who has completed a semester at two separate community colleges. He experienced a traumatic brain injury (TBI) several years ago and had little understanding of how his injury affected his life. Ted elected to live on his own in an apartment near campus. He was not certain about his career goal but thought he wanted to become a journalist and planned on majoring in English. He felt it was important that he attend a 4-year college program.

At the university, Ted registered with the DSS Office and requested accommodations from his instructors. These included notetakers and extended time for assignments and examinations. During the course of the semester, Ted discovered he had difficulty with reading and keeping up with his assignments. It was a challenge to write an essay for an examination or a paper for an assignment. His time-management skills were inconsistent, and sometimes he did not remember when an examination was scheduled or arrived late for class.

After completing his first semester, Ted was placed on academic probation. His advisor told him about the Students with Disabilities Association on campus. He went to a meeting and met a student who also experienced a TBI. This student was able to talk with Ted about his coping strategies and share information about other resources on campus. Ted was connected to the university writing center and learned about regularly scheduled mini-workshops on topics such as test-taking strategies, time management, and maximizing memory skills. He also was informed about the university career center and decided to complete some interest assessment instruments and participate in individual career counseling.

Strategies for managing time in postsecondary programs focus on techniques that encourage students with disabilities to monitor their study habits and to understand the types of resources or supports they will need in order to meet their course load requirements (Dillion, 1997; Hildreth, 1995; Manganello, 1994; Peniston, 1994; Vogel, 1997). Dillion suggested a checklist of strategies that students with disabilities can use to self-monitor their time-management skills in college. Students should check to see if they are

1. Creating a semester schedule, assessing and planning their work load each week, adjusting their plan daily, and evaluating their schedule regularly.

2. Locating a place to study that is suitable to their learning style and using this location on a consistent basis

3. Asking for assistance at the reference desk in the college library

4. Locating tutoring services on campus, if needed

5. Studying an average of 2–4 hours daily

6. Reviewing the syllabus and taking advantage of instructor office hours to get their questions answered about course content or assignments.

Building a Network of Supports

College students with disabilities were asked to identify the self-determination skills that were essential for high school students to possess to be successful in college (Virginia Commonwealth University, 2004). Students felt that forming ongoing relationships with college personnel and classmates was very important. It was recommended that students establish positive associations with their instructors (e.g., greeting instructor by name, participating in class, engaging in occasional short conversations after class). Also, getting to know the DSS coordinator was suggested. By establishing rapport with at least one student in each class, students can assist each other to understand the course content, confirm due dates for assignments, or review for a test. In addition, being aware and willing to use campus support services such as the writing lab, supplemental instruction sessions, and peer tutoring were considered a great advantage.

It is also important for students to develop a network of supports in postsecondary environments because of the changing role that family members will play in their lives. Entering college, perhaps one that is away from home, is a major change and adjustment for all families. This is especially true for families of students with disabilities who have served as their children's advocates throughout their educational experience. There are many legal differences in what information can be shared with families and the delivery of services and supports between postsecondary education and secondary education. It is important that students with disabilities and their families work together to better understand these differences and to begin working on shifting the responsibility of managing one's education more to the student prior to exiting secondary education.

Enrolling in a postsecondary program involves a series of decisions that include identifying academic programs that can meet the personal, educational, and career goals of students with disabilities (Henderson, 1999). Ted should have coped with several decision and planning issues prior to entering a university, which would have helped him in his adjustment to college life. However, he was able to locate individuals and resources on campus to help him meet some of the challenges that he faced. Once students have made their decision and have started their advanced degree program, they must be prepared to face new challenges as they adjust to a different environment and educational process. Postsecondary students with disabilities are in an environment in which classes meet less frequently, the services and supports they need are their responsibility to obtain, and there is typically less student-instructor contact (Brinckerhoff et al., 2002; deFur et al., 1996; Getzel et al., 2000). Although much adjustment depends on a number of factors that are difficult to plan for, students with disabilities can increase their chances of successfully adjusting to college life if they are adequately prepared.

CONCLUSION

For individuals with disabilities, an advanced degree from a university, community college, or technical school can significantly affect their vocational options and financial success. Individuals need to make a series of decisions about which program best meets their academic and personal needs. Students who are making the transition to postsecondary education must make informed decisions on the basis of information gathered from a number of resources. Students with disabilities who are able to successfully enter and complete postsecondary education will have an increased chance of fulfilling their long-term employment potential in careers of their choice.

STUDY QUESTIONS

1. Describe ways to help young people with disabilities prepare to enter college and supports that can be helpful for them to be successful once they enter college.

2. What are some of the areas to consider when students with disabilities are in the process of selecting a postsecondary institution to attend?

3. Identify skills that are necessary for a successful transition to college.

4. What are some of the career goals for successful transition planning for college?

5. Describe strategies for successful adjustment to college.

14

Housing and Community Living

MICHAEL D. WEST AND WILLIAM E. FULLER

AFTER COMPLETING THIS CHAPTER, THE READER WILL BE ABLE TO

○ Describe key differences between continuum-based residential models and models based on individualized supports

○ List at least three nonfacility options for supporting individuals where and with whom they wish to live

○ Briefly describe federal housing programs for individuals with disabilities and how they can be accessed for transition

○ List the steps for identifying and utilizing community and workplace supports

○ Describe community resource mapping and how it can be used with students in transition

○ Provide an overview of person-centered services and how this process can assist individuals with disabilities to live in the community

○ List at least three options for providing transportation support to individuals living in the community

○ Describe behavioral supports and give an example of how individuals with challenging behaviors can be supported in the community

Beth and Robert live in the same city. Both have mental retardation, and both are employed. They are very similar in their behaviors, their learning capacities and limitations, and the adaptive skills they have developed, such as bathing, grooming, dressing, cooking, housekeeping, and attending to other personal needs. Robert lives in a group home with five other individuals with mental retardation—they have three 8-hour shifts of supervision. He wants to live in his own apartment, but the staff of the agency that runs his group home do not believe he is ready for such independence. Beth lives in an apartment with a roommate without mental retardation who helps Beth in many ways, although she is not a paid staffperson. How is it that Beth is ready to live in her own apartment but Robert is not, despite their comparable levels of functioning and skill development?

CHANGING PARADIGMS OF INDEPENDENT LIVING

Beth and Robert's cases illustrate two different organizational views of independent living for people with disabilities. Robert's agency maintains that different types of residential settings require different skill levels or competencies. They organize their residential programs along a continuum that might include large congregate facilities, small-group homes, clustered apartments, and semi-independent or independent apartment living. Their service recipients are expected to progress through this continuum as they acquire more skills and, in the process, gain greater independence, achieve community integration and participation, and enjoy a more normalized lifestyle. This paradigm is often referred to as a *readiness model* because individuals must prove themselves "ready" to function in increasingly integrated environments.

In a critique appropriately titled *Caught in the Continuum*, Taylor (1988) described a number of logical and ethical dilemmas posed by this model:

- It confuses the types and extent of services that individuals need with the locations in which they are provided, as if services were necessarily linked to particular types of residences.

- It makes it virtually impossible for individuals with more severe disabilities to move out of the most segregated and least normalized settings.

- It supports the primacy of professional opinions over people's choices of where they would like to live, work, or socialize.

- It forces people to move as they develop and change, thereby disrupting relationships with family, friends, and neighbors.

The readiness model is perhaps best exemplified by Siperstein, Reed, Wolraich, and O'Keefe's (1990) study of 477 residential program staff members who were asked to identify those skills they considered essential for adults with mental retardation to function in different residential situations. Table 14.1 presents the capabilities that at least 80% of the respondents agreed were essential for functioning in supervised and unsupervised apartments. Although there were no skills considered essential for functioning in a group home setting, eight were identified as essential for supervised apartments and 21 as essential for unsupervised apartments.

These lists of "essential skills" give rise to some speculation. If an individual needs help with dressing and toileting, then does that mean that apartment living is an unachievable goal? Must an individual avoid an unsupervised apartment in an area where there are no bus lines if other means of transportation can be arranged? Are individuals who are nonverbal due to deafness or motor delay—and, therefore, unable to perform three of the essential skills—inappropriate candidates for independent living?

Table 14.1.   Essential skills identified by residential specialists for living in supervised and unsupervised apartments

Skill	Supervised	Unsupervised
Drink from a cup unassisted	✓	✓
Dress and toilet independently	✓	✓
Eat with utensils	✓	✓
Follow a one-step command	✓	✓
Act appropriately toward strangers	✓	✓
Anticipate hazards	✓	✓
Recognize traffic signs	✓	✓
Use a lock and key	✓	✓
Address two people by name		✓
Join in a simple conversation		✓
Indicate symptoms verbally		✓
Choose appropriate clothes to wear		✓
Tell time		✓
Make change for a dollar		✓
Use public transportation		✓
Find way in unfamiliar surroundings		✓
Use pay telephone		✓
Schedule daily activities		✓
Budget for monthly expenses		✓
Cook a meal		✓
Do own laundry		✓

From Siperstein, G.N., Reed, D., Wolraich, M., and O'Keefe, P. (1990). Capabilities essential for adults who are mentally retarded to function in different residential settings. *Education and Training in Mental Retardation, 25,* 48–50; adapted by permission.

Even proponents of the readiness model would have to agree that the answers to these questions are an unequivocal "no." Many individuals with severe disabilities are already living contented and fairly independent lives with personal assistants who help them with dressing and toileting or other personal needs. Many individuals with disabilities walk; carpool with co-workers, family members, or friends; or use specialized transportation services to jobs or recreational activities. Even those who are nonverbal can communicate with other members of their communities through gestures, word or picture cards, or communication devices. In fact, there are numerous ways to reconcile the absence of "essential skills" (e.g., through training, adaptation, or support) while the individual resides in the more integrated and independent setting.

Consider the example of Beth. The staff members working with Beth understand that community living is not an all-or-nothing proposition—if one fails to meet certain preselected criteria for "independent" living, then congregate living is the only alternative. They understand that no one, with or without disabilities, truly lives independently, but that all members of a community are interdependent, conducting their individual affairs through mutual reliance on one another (Klein, 1992; O'Brien & O'Brien, 1992). They believe that a person with severe disabilities can be a valued and contributing member of an interdependent community. They understand that the lines between "independent," "semi-independent," "supported," and "supervised" living are rapidly becoming blurred and irrelevant and perhaps even detrimental to service consumers. Instead of putting their efforts into operating different types of facilities or programs, an increasing number of service providers are adopting a new orientation that focuses on the preferences, strengths, and support needs of every individual (O'Brien, 1994). Ferguson, Hibbard, Leinen, and Schaff (1990) wrote the following:

> A one sentence summary of this new orientation states the goal simply: People, regardless of their disabilities, should live in the community where they want, with whom they want, for as long as they want, with whatever supports they need to make that happen. (p. 18)

This orientation can open up an array of residential options for individuals with disabilities, options that are common and readily available to people without disabilities. For example, once residential service staff have identified the community or area in which an individual desires to live, they can creatively explore such options as roommates, housing cooperatives, boarding with families, living with friends or family members, and even home ownership (Racino & Taylor, 1993).

This chapter describes methods to assist individuals with disabilities in living "where they want and with whom they want." It presents a model for identifying and utilizing community support needs through a planning process that emphasizes the needs and desires of the individual with a disability. A number of key areas in which planning should occur are also presented. Throughout the chapter, case studies detail the lives of individuals with severe disabilities who are being supported in the neighborhoods and homes of their choice.

IDENTIFYING AND FILLING COMMUNITY SUPPORT NEEDS

Support can be very broadly defined as "an array, not a continuum, of services, individuals, and settings that match the person's needs" (Luckasson & Spitalnik, 1994, p. 88). Using a broad array of support technologies, such as training, adaptations and modifications, assistive technology, personal assistance, and family and friends, offers consumers more options from which to choose how their community living needs will be met.

Parent, Unger, Gibson, and Clements (1994) presented a systematic process for identifying support needs and utilizing community and workplace supports that has proven useful for meeting both work-related and non–work-related support needs. First, the effectiveness of a method of support is determined by 1) whether the support actually fulfills the need and 2) whether the consumer is comfortable and satisfied with the support method. Second, ongoing monitoring of support mechanisms is crucial to maintain levels of independence because relationships and circumstances change over time. For example, a friend who gladly provides transportation to an individual with a disability may eventually find it burdensome. Also, as an individual becomes part of a social network within the community, new sources of support begin to emerge that may be more convenient or comfortable. Several elements are critical to the successful implementation of this model including relationship building, person-centered services, circles of support, and total community involvement.

Relationship Building

Taking time to become acquainted with the individual and develop a trusting relationship is the basic foundation of and essential first step in the service delivery process. It is likely that most individuals with disabilities have had some unpleasant or disappoint-

GINA

Gina, a young woman with cognitive disabilities, found a job with assistance from a job coach but had no way of getting to and from work. Short-term provisions were put into place for the duration of the training, with the job coach driving her to work and a family member picking her up. Meanwhile, alternative arrangements were explored that resulted in the following outcome: Gina chose to walk if weather permitted, to use a taxi when running late or during inclement weather, and to ride with a specific co-worker after completing late-night shifts. The job coach assisted by making the arrangements, writing down pertinent information about each option, posting the contact information beside the telephone for quick reference as needed, and implementing ongoing monitoring provisions by the supervisor and family to ensure that the plan was working as intended.

ing experiences with professionals and may be hesitant to open up to yet another service provider. This hesitation is sometimes interpreted as noncompliance or lack of motivation. Spending time with the individual and learning more about him or her, such as past experiences, present lifestyle, hobbies or interests, interpersonal relationships, community connections, and desired goals, will clear up misconceptions and provide valuable insight for planning community supports. Meeting in an informal, comfortable location of the individual's choosing (e.g., the individual's home, school, job, day program, or clubhouse; a restaurant) provides an excellent opportunity for establishing rapport and gathering essential information.

Person-Centered Services

The type of supports that are utilized, the manner with which they are provided, and the frequency of their use should be determined by each individual's support needs and preferences. One method for determining these needs and preferences is Personal Futures Planning (PFP; Mount, 1991, 1994), which emphasizes positive images of individuals with disabilities, maximizes their gifts and talents, and provides for informed choices that truly reflect their preferences. The steps involved in PFP include 1) developing a "circle of support" for an individual with disabilities (this concept is described further in this section), 2) describing a desirable future for the individual, and 3) developing and implementing an action plan.

PFP meetings are attended by the individual with disabilities, family members, friends, current or future service providers, and others who are involved with the individual in some way on a consistent basis (e.g., landlord, employer, co-worker). During the planning meetings, it is important for all participants to offer ideas about any possible resources, to keep an open mind about the potential options, and to collectively brainstorm for creative ways to provide support. Rather than assuming that a desired goal cannot be accomplished due to a perceived lack of support, it is much more productive to develop supports that can assist in achieving the desired outcome.

Circles of Support

During the course of establishing a relationship with the consumer and facilitating community involvement, a variety of support resources are likely to be identified and put into place even if they are not needed at that time. Being prepared to respond to a particular need often reduces its intensity and minimizes its consequences. Just knowing that assistance is in place and available if needed can be a tremendous support in and of itself.

Luckasson et al. (1992) presented supports as a "constellation," or concentric circles of support, with the individual at the center. The closest circle would consist of the individual's family and friends. Unpaid support providers, including co-workers, neighbors, church, or community groups, make up the next circle. The next support circle involves generic services—supports and formal services that are available to all members of the community—such as public transportation, housing assistance, and company-sponsored employee assistance programs. The outermost circle includes specialized support services, which are formal services developed primarily for use by individuals with disabilities, such as vocational rehabilitation, mental health services, and counseling. Typically, the circles of support closest to the individual are the least stigmatizing and obtrusive and should be given preference; however, consumer choice should be the ultimate factor in choosing a support source.

Total Community Involvement

Central to the "circles of support" model is the need for a coordinator or facilitator (Luckasson & Spitalnik, 1994). In many disability service systems, that may be a case manager or service coordinator. This individual needs to be knowledgeable about service provider agencies across many different areas (e.g., employment, housing), groups, and other types of organizations that might provide formal supports.

There are multitudes of people and organizations within communities that can be utilized as sources of support for individuals with severe disabilities. Table 14.2 provides a list of some of the support options that can be developed to facilitate independent living for participants.

Community Resource Mapping for Support Planning

Students with disabilities and their families experience many barriers in making the transition to adulthood, not the least of which is a lack of understanding of the adult services system, the resources that are available, or the demands and expectations that will be encountered (Benz, Lindstrom, & Latta, 1999). This is an area often overlooked in teacher training programs, and thus teachers cannot deliver this information to families or use it effectively in transitional planning.

Most students with disabilities will need some type of postschool support services. The U.S. Department of Education (1996) estimated that 80% of students with disabilities require case management to achieve their postschool employment, independent living, and continuing education goals. *Case management* by definition involves coordination of services and supports across agency lines based on individual needs. Where can the student and family go to obtain information about the effects that employment might have on the student's Supplemental Security Income (SSI) benefits or Medicaid? Which agencies can help the school system plan for needed employment supports? Where are integrated, community-based recreational and social opportunities? Students and families look for guidance from school personnel, who often don't have the answers.

Locating service providers is only the beginning of the collaboration process. Teachers, students, and their families are often unprepared for the realities of the adult services world. A study of families' transition experiences in Massachusetts (Timmons,

Table 14.2. Examples of support resources

Transportation supports	Personal and independent living supports
Taxi	Roommates/housemates
Carpool with co-worker	In-home support staff
Walking	Budgeting assistance
Bicycle	Personal security systems
Parents	Private counseling
Public transportation	Housing assistance
Driving	College students
Community supports	**Recreational and social integration supports**
Cooperative Extension Service	Volunteering
Independent living center	Jaycees
State assistive technology systems	YMCA/YWCA
Planned Parenthood	Neighborhood community association
Neighbors	Employer-sponsored social activities
Red Cross safety courses	Parks and recreation programs
Auto club driving school	
Employment Commission	
Community-sponsored child care courses	

McIntyre, Whitney-Thomas, Butterworth, & Allen, 1998) bears this out. Most families involved in this study found adult services difficult to negotiate, lacking in coordination and continuity with their children's school programs, and unresponsive to their needs and concerns.

As Timmons and colleagues (1998) found, parents and students often have difficulty adjusting to this new service landscape. They are often surprised to learn that most adult services, unlike special education, are not entitlement programs. They may be unaware of eligibility requirements or financial participation on the part of the student or family. They may also be unaware that most adult services have waiting lists, and therefore employment, housing, and other support services may be many months or even years away.

One means for accomplishing this is through *community resource mapping*, also referred to as *asset mapping*. Although there is no universally accepted definition for *resource mapping*, it has been broadly defined as a methodology to link community resources with a common vision, goals, strategies, and expected outcomes (Crane & Skinner, 2003).

The mapping process seeks to identify and catalog resources that are currently available within a defined geographic region to fulfill a specific purpose. Because resource mapping focuses on what's available rather than what's needed, it is especially useful in areas that do not have a wealth of resources to catalog (Beaulieu, 2002). This is because the resource mapping process provides a framework for users to identify assets and resources that a community has, even if they are delivered informally or through unconventional venues, as often occurs in rural or economically depressed areas.

Mapping can be conducted at the state, local, school, or even individual student level. The types of information that is collected include 1) the name, address, and telephone number for an organization; 2) the name and contact information for an individual who serves as the principle contact for transitional planning; 3) information regarding the services offered; 4) eligibility criteria; 5) catchment areas served, including field offices; and 6) fee scales or limitations based on the income of the student or family.

There are several different methods for conducting the mapping process, but the typical result is a resource directory, desktop guide, or a database that can be used by the transition planning team or the transition coordinator to locate organizations, agencies, and other community entities to assist in meeting specific student needs as described in the remainder of this chapter. For individual students, the map can be a list of appropriate resources or a graphical map that will assist the student and family in locating community resources or favorite places.

TYPES OF SUPPORT NEEDS

Although there are specific areas in which support planning should occur, no specific list of supports exists. All individuals have unique skills, characteristics, and needs that influence the types of support needs that must be addressed, among them housing options, transportation, social and recreational activities, shopping and financial management, health and safety, and behavioral support.

Housing Options

A home is more than a place to eat, sleep, and relax. It is a place where people can exercise personal control, express individuality, and experience a sense of ownership (O'Connor & Racino, 1993). *Personal control* means that the individual decides not only where and with whom he or she lives, but also who enters the home and for what reasons, what activities will take place there, and daily routines and "house rules," among other aspects of occupancy. *Individuality* means that the person decides how the home is decorated, including the placement of personal effects such as pictures and mementos. *Sense of ownership* refers to feelings of security and confidence that one will not be forced to move at some arbitrary point.

Many service agencies focus on providing "home-like facilities" or "housing" rather than helping people find and maintain homes (Racino & Taylor, 1993). Nothing is inherently wrong about operating group homes or apartments solely for people with disabilities, unless people are forced to accept only that option and no attempts are made to give people choices or to customize their services for individual preferences.

Upholding the principle that people should live "where they want and with whom they want . . ." involves much more than just having residential programs. It also means creating individualized housing supports, such as the following:

- Providing support services to people living in their own apartments

- Matching individuals with disabilities to roommates without disabilities or with families that may be compensated for providing needed assistance

- Supplying in-home supports to people with disabilities and their families who choose to remain intact

- Assisting people with disabilities to become homeowners via housing cooperatives, federally backed home loans, low-interest loans, or low-cost homes through the U.S Department of Housing and Urban Development (HUD), family trusts, and other options

Solving housing for people with disabilities is more than just finding places for them to live. Where and how an individual lives should be a matter of personal choice and self-determination. Individuals should have the freedom to select from an array of housing alternatives, define their own house rules and lifestyle, and experience the rights and responsibilities of a household. To truly exercise that freedom, support services and assistance may be necessary either within the home or within the immediate community and under the control of the individual with disabilities. Because housing is such a critical need, and helps to shape other areas of independent living, it would be instructive to provide an overview of public programs that provide housing support for individuals with disabilities.

Overview of Federal and State Housing Programs
Public policy affecting housing for people with disabilities has historically been coupled with housing policy addressing the needs of the elderly. In the disability arena, public policy has focused almost exclusively on work and income supports. HUD received much criticism over housing policies that create segregated communities expressly for housing the most severely disabled and economically depressed people with disabilities.

Since the mid-1990s, a loosely defined strategy has emerged regarding housing policy for people with disabilities mainly through the advocacy work of select consumer groups. The separation of the supported housing for people with disabilities from the traditional elderly housing (Section 202 of the National Affordable Housing Act of 1990) is one example of such evolution, as is the development of a Mainstream voucher program that will be described further in this section.

The new awareness of the housing needs of people with disabilities is beginning to focus attention on the unique and varied housing requirements for differing populations of people with disabilities. Probably more than any other minority, the housing needs of people with disabilities require a micro-level solution that emphasizes the uniqueness of differing disability groups. People with impaired mobility require substantially different housing supports than people with cognitive or sensory impairments. Coming to grips with this realization has been difficult for national housing policy makers who historically have preferred a "one size fits most" solution to low- and moderate-income housing. Without doubt, as people with disabilities become ever more present in the policy debate, the issues of choice and self-direction will diversify both the array and magnitude of housing available for people with serious disabilities.

Housing Choice Vouchers
Perhaps the most significant change in housing policy for people with disabilities came from the Experimental Housing Allowance Program in 1970, through the consolidation of the Section 8 certificate and voucher programs

Carrie is an 18-year-old student who attends a rural high school where she has just completed her sophomore year. Carrie has resided with a foster family since she was 3 and has no contact with her natural family. A Department of Social Services service coordinator serves as her guardian and Social Security payee. Carrie has an active case with the local Community Services Board (CSB) and is eligible for all services, which include service coordination and vocational and residential placement. Carrie recently was employed in her first job with the assistance of supported employment (SE). In planning her most recent individualized education program (IEP), participants discussed goals for her future, whether Carrie was benefiting from classroom instruction, and if she should continue in school until age 22. Her foster placement ends upon graduation; therefore, additional concerns were raised as to where Carrie would live.

Carrie currently has no independent living skills and wishes to continue living with her foster family. The foster family, although willing to have her stay, is not sure if this is allowed and wishes to have her live as independently as possible. They do not want to hold her back. Her CSB service coordinator is willing to put her on a residential waiting list for the local group home, but Carrie's Social Services service coordinator is in a different locality and Carrie may need to change jurisdictions, thereby ending her involvement with her current CSB.

in the Quality Housing and Work Responsibility Act of 1998 (PL 105-276). As of 2000, the program had grown to serve a wide variety of people by providing long-term rent subsidies for various classes of people. The classes include conversion vouchers, family unification vouchers, homeownership vouchers, project-based vouchers, tenant-based vouchers, vouchers for people with disabilities, and welfare-to-work vouchers. A full discussion of each of these classes is far beyond the scope of this writing, but several of these classes have a direct impact on families and individuals with disabilities. Mainstream vouchers are exclusively for people with disabilities and are the only class of vouchers that can be administered by entities other than Public Housing Authorities (PHAs).

Housing Choice Vouchers have done an excellent job at placing choice and self-determination into the hands of people who receive them. Most vouchers are portable, meaning that people with disabilities can choose where they live. This represents a vast improvement over the certificate program that required people to live in a specific development to receive the rent subsidy in order to lessen the risk on developers.

PHAs are the administrative agent for these rent subsidies. In localities where no PHA is present, the state financing agency or the state department of housing and community development may administer the program through local administrative agents. This bifurcated administration of the program has lead to complex and difficult-to-understand rules that constantly plague the program. Waiting lists are often years long, and turnover can be excruciatingly slow. Perhaps the greatest downside of the Housing Choice Voucher program is that it addresses such a very small segment of the entire need for such supports.

Low Income Housing Tax Credits   The Tax Reform Act of 1986 (PL 99-514) created the Low Income Housing Tax Credit (LIHTC). This program has evolved into the largest source of capital for the creation of low-income housing. The states were authorized to issue federal tax credits for the acquisition, rehabilitation, or new construction of low-income rental housing. Investors who owned a majority of the partnership-based companies (but held subordinate management positions) could use the credits to offset taxes on other unrelated income. The developer uses the investors' capital to increase equity, reduce debt service, and consequently make the units affordable to low-income families.

Carrie decided to stay in school and continue her employment. She will stay with her foster family but be placed on the group home waiting list. In the interim, she will work on independent living skills at school. More information will be gathered regarding the logistics of her potential move for future planning and referral to other necessary agencies. In addition, other community living arrangements will be explored such as continuing to live with her foster family, renting her own apartment, utilizing a paid companion, applying for an auxiliary grant for a low-income apartment or adult home, and utilizing a Social Security Plan for Achieving Self Support (PASS) to purchase employment-related residential assistance such as readying for work, which might include personal hygiene, laundering uniforms, or preparing her breakfast and lunch.

MARY

Mary is a 23-year-old woman with mild mental retardation and autism who currently resides in a group home. When she was referred to a SE program to obtain a clerical job a year after graduation from high school, transportation to and from work was a critical need. After considerable brainstorming of the different transportation possibilities with Mary, her co-workers and support staff developed a transportation support plan. Her group home staff now take Mary to work, and two co-workers share the responsibility of giving her a ride home.

To qualify for credits, a project must set aside a specific number of units for low-income families. The rents for these units cannot exceed 30% of the families' qualifying income. The credits are calculated based on development costs and the number of units set aside for low-income families. Credits are provided to the owner company and flow through to the partners at a rate based on the needs of occupants with disabilities. Although the LIHTC program is targeted to housing developers as opposed to occupants, many states offer LIHTC loan programs to individuals with disabilities or their families who want to develop multifamily units that would meet their own housing needs.

Section 811 Section 811 of the Housing Act of 1959 (PL 86-372) was originally passed to provide low-interest loans to nonprofit organizations for construction of rental housing. The loans encouraged sponsors to build Section 202 housing by offering very low-interest loan rates over long terms that sometimes reached 50 years. The Housing and Community Development Act of 1974 (PL 93-383) brought more emphasis on programs and housing to serve people with disabilities. Although Section 811 grants are not intended for individuals with disabilities themselves, this resource can be accessed through creative means. For example, families of transitioning students may go through an existing nonprofit organization, or form a nonprofit organization themselves, to apply for funds to purchase, build, or renovate an apartment building or home for their children to rent as adults.

Transportation

Transportation is a critical consideration in all areas of independent living, including work, continuing education or training, recreation, social activities, friendships, shopping, and use of community resources. Safe, affordable, and reliable transportation opens up options in all areas of people's lives, thereby enabling them to lead the lifestyle of their choice (West, Barcus, Brooke, & Rayfield, 1995). Without reliable and affordable means of getting about, many individuals with disabilities are forced into segregated schools and workplaces, social and physical isolation, and economic dependence (Piepmeier, 1992).

Unfortunately, far too many individuals with disabilities lack transportation, which limits their community participation and often bars employment. Many disabilities preclude driving as an option or require such extensive supports to

Frank has cerebral palsy that affects his limb movement and speech, but he can ambulate short distances with a walker. He is a sports fan and spends much of his free time watching sports on television. Frank's service coordinator assigned a leisure coach to him to help develop more social and recreational outlets, and sports seemed a logical place to start.

Frank's city has a minor league baseball team. At the start of the season, the leisure coach purchased season tickets for Frank and himself. Because season ticket holders keep the same seats for the season, they encountered the same individuals repeatedly, individuals who were also avid fans. The leisure coach began to facilitate contacts between Frank and the other fans based on their common interests. The leisure coach also served as an intermediary when the others could not understand Frank's speech. One group of fans in particular took an interest in Frank and invited him to their homes to watch the team play away games as well as other types of sports.

Frank's leisure coach does not go with him to his new friends' homes. He was careful to allow Frank's friendships to develop naturally and then withdrew when he was not needed anymore. Also, because Frank wants to be actively involved in sports, the leisure coach will be getting him involved in a bowling league, perhaps using a portable ramp or other adaptation to send the ball down the lane.

drive (e.g., lift van, customized automobile) that the possibility is financially unfeasible. Despite the mandates for accessibility under the ADA, public transportation remains largely inaccessible because of route limitations (particularly in rural or suburban areas) or the absence of any public transportation.

One solution is to encourage people to relocate in urban areas. This is not always the best approach, however, and sometimes creative solutions are needed to transport people with disabilities. Within the work arena, co-workers can be solicited for rides to work and back. In fact, some companies encourage and sponsor carpooling among employees, and these companies can be targeted during job development. Apartment bulletin boards, public service announcements, or volunteer exchanges can also be used to advertise for purchasing or locating rides to work. Many human services agencies (e.g., The Arc, Red Cross, elderly services) run van or bus routes for their consumers and may be willing to let someone with a disability who lives and works on or near the route purchase a seat. In addition, training in the use of public transportation (or even driver's education) can be explored. These strategies can be utilized for social or recreational outlets as well.

Social and Recreational Activities

As noted by Dattilo and Schleien (1994), social and recreational services for people with disabilities tend to focus on a narrow range of stereotypic activities such as bowling, swimming, and arts and crafts. In addition, most formal programs to increase social participation tend to focus on segregated, disability-only activities instead of assisting individuals to develop the skills and have the opportunities to participate in activities of their own choosing (Dattilo, 1991). Programs that force people to engage in activities in which they have little or no interest disregard the primary purpose of leisure activities: to do things we like to do, with people with whom we enjoy doing them.

Although there has been considerable focus in recent years on developing integrated housing, education, and employment options for individuals with disabilities, inclusive social and recreational activities are often lacking, particularly for those with severe disabilities. As noted in the newsletter *Impact* (Institute on Community Integration, 2003), published by the Institute on Community Integration at the University of Minnesota, inclusive recreational and social ac-

ERICA

Erica lives in an apartment with two other women who, like Erica, have cognitive disabilities. Support staff take the women shopping for clothing and food and assist them with paying rent and utilities. Yet, Erica wanted and needed to learn to make small purchases on her own, such as at the neighborhood convenience store and fast-food restaurants. Her support staff attempted to teach her to count dollars and coins, but she could not count out the correct amount of money in response to a verbal prompt.

Erica can, however, count to 10. Because it would be unlikely that Erica's purchases would ever total more than $10, her support staff have her carry 10 $1 bills when she goes out and have taught her to make purchases using the "next-dollar" method. Beginning in the apartment and then moving to nearby stores, they instructed Erica to attend to only the number of dollars told to her by the clerk or counter person. She then counts out that many dollars plus one more. For example, if the clerk says, "That will be $5.15," then Erica counts out five dollars and one more, then waits for her change. Staff have also taught her to discriminate the rare occasions when a purchase totals an even number of dollars and to eliminate the step of giving the clerk the next dollar. Erica can now make small purchases independently and naturally, and she always has plenty of change for the snack machines at her job.

tivities not only can increase social skills of participants, but also enable mutually beneficial relationships. Some examples of inclusive settings that can be accessed by individuals with disabilities might include the following:

- Neighborhood yards, play areas, and parks
- Educational and recreational programs for youth and adults
- Sports leagues
- Faith communities
- Special interest clubs (e.g., gardening, computer users, books)
- Cultural centers
- Community arts and theatre organizations
- Recreation and fitness centers
- Youth centers
- Nature centers
- Support groups (e.g., singles, parents, survivors)

The following are some practical guidelines for helping individuals with disabilities develop and experience leisure activities of their own choosing:

- Because of lack of experience in integrated leisure activities, some people with disabilities may need to experiment with different types of recreational pursuits and social events in order to develop their preferences.
- Targeted leisure activities should include an array of both solitary and group activities.
- When looking for leisure supports for people with disabilities, it is important to remember that they do not necessarily have to be good at something to enjoy it or to participate with individuals without disabilities. Likewise, individuals do not necessarily have to engage in activities in the ways that people without disabilities do but can use adapted equipment or rules without meeting any objections from their teammates.
- Individuals may choose to participate in segregated activities; however, they should also be able to engage in similar activities with people without disabilities. A support person, often called a "leisure coach," can facilitate those opportunities.

ART

Art, age 21, has a significant psychiatric and learning disability. When he was 18, his doctor recommended that he not reside at home with his mother because of dependency issues. At that time, he and his mother sought alternative housing. Art was offered a vacancy at a nursing home facility that had a young adults section. Given his difficulty managing his medication and his lack of independent living skills, he was willing to reside there. Art was also referred to a Center for Independent Living (CIL) for skills training and other assistance, but he withdrew from the center because he did not like being around other people with disabilities.

However, Art began receiving SE and soon found a job. He had several life needs that required assistance and training: time management, personal hygiene and grooming, money management, care of his uniform and laundry, transportation, medication management, and meals. Art and significant people in his life addressed each need by exploring all options available and utilized the resources of Art's choice. He devised a routine that fit comfortably with his lifestyle pattern. His preference was to sleep late and stay up late; therefore, he worked evenings. Because he was unable to judge when to bathe and how much time to allow for eating and travel, his time was structured. The schedule was monitored by facility staff who would prompt him when he needed assistance. To assist with money management, he and his mother worked out an agreement in which she would

Volunteerism

Volunteering can be individually rewarding as well as beneficial to the community at large. For individuals with disabilities, volunteerism can also lead to the development of friendships and relationships and help to dispel myths and fears regarding people with disabilities. Three areas of volunteerism have been defined by Shoultz and Lakin (2001):

1. Voluntary service, giving willingly of one's time and abilities to achieve goals deemed valuable by the giver

2. Community service, voluntary or involuntary giving of one's time and abilities to help meet the needs of the community and not the giver

3. Service learning, using community service as a means of achieving learning objectives

When assisting and supporting volunteerism for youth and adults with disabilities, it is important to differentiate between these three types of activities. Personal values will dictate appropriate voluntary service opportunities far more than community service or service learning opportunities. When searching for opportunities in any of these three areas, Shoultz and Lakin (2001) warned that teachers and support providers may encounter "gatekeepers" who may not be open to youth and adults with disabilities and may need education regarding the value that they can bring to an organization.

Shopping and Financial Management

Many individuals with disabilities, particularly cognitive impairments, need assistance with household budgeting, shopping, locating income supports (e.g., Social Security, housing assistance, cash subsidy programs), obtaining credit, and paying bills. This type of assistance is critical for ensuring that individuals with disabilities are able to maintain their homes and improve their quality of life. In many cases, these supports can be provided by family and friends or paid staff members. There are also organizations that provide this type of assistance to anyone in need, such as a credit counseling agency, Cooperative Extension Agency, church, or business organization. Requiring assistance with shopping or financial management should not preclude community living.

Health and Safety

Perske (1972) first wrote of the dignity of risk for people with mental retardation and other developmental disabilities. Liv-

assist him with safely picking up his check and depositing it at a bank; prior to working, she was accustomed to bringing him a weekly allowance, so this replaced that activity.

Art left the nursing facility and moved into an apartment with a friend. He took his medication independently with the help of a pill box that held a week's supply by days and times of dosage. He also referred to a written medication schedule. His friend replaced the staff prompting for preparing for work and assisted with meal selection and preparation. His mother continued the money management assistance. Art chose to leave his job and applied for food stamps. He sought other assistance through volunteers with the Cooperative Extension Service, university students, and a paid personal assistant.

Art is moving to his own efficiency apartment as he no longer wants a roommate and has gained the skills to live independently. He will continue to utilize his current supports and will explore additional supports as they are needed.

ing in the community brings risks of rejection, disappointment, and potential harm. Recognizing risk and emphasizing personal control, however, does not mean that unhealthy or unsafe practices are ignored or tolerated; rather, potential risks are balanced against the benefits of participation in integrated environments, and areas that seem "too risky" for a particular individual receive some form of intervention. Table 14.3 presents areas of safety and health that may need to be addressed in planning independent living supports and services.

Behavioral Support

Individuals with disabilities sometimes exhibit inappropriate or stigmatizing behaviors that can limit their participation in integrated living, work, or social activities. The methods of altering or eliminating these behaviors have primarily evolved from the science of behaviorism (Skinner, 1953), which argues that changes in behavioral response rates routinely occur in the presence or absence of either reinforcements or punishments. Behavior management procedures attempt to manipulate individuals to either increase desired behaviors or decrease undesired ones. Typical procedures for reducing rates of undesired behaviors include shaping, fading, extinction, and differential reinforcement strategies for increasing the rates of alternative, incompatible, and appropriate behaviors (Gast & Worley, 1986; Kazdin, 1980).

An emerging application of support technology involves positive behavior support in community settings (Horner et al., 1990; West, Rayfield, Clements, Unger, & Thornton, 1994). Horner et al. listed aspects of a behavioral support program:

Table 14.3. Health and safety issues for independent living

Handling stress	Avoiding unsafe areas
Home cleanliness and clutter	Avoiding unsafe relationships
Home security	Avoiding victimization
Nutrition	Electrical hazards
Personal hygiene	Emergency preparation
Proper lighting	Exercise
Sexual precautions	Family planning
Substance abuse	Fire safety
Traffic safety	First aid
Use of medication	Food storage

ROGER

Roger is a young man with profound deafness and mild mental retardation. He lives in an apartment complex operated by a community services agency. Roger is employed but has some behaviors that are causing problems at work and in the community. After using a public restroom, he restores his clothing while he is exiting, which sometimes results in "flashing" his co-workers or complete strangers. He also sometimes offers to shake hands with others (particularly women), but after taking the other person's hand, he will sometimes grab it and move it to his chest or groin. His support staff feel that these behaviors may cost him his job and his chances at making friends in his neighborhood.

Because Roger's bathroom behavior at home is identical to that in public, his staff hypothesize that it may be a result of poor learning. Roger came to his community services agency from a state institution, where in all likelihood his bathroom behavior was not a high priority. Rather than use a behaviorist model of rewards and punishments for the behavior, staff instituted a functional training program to model appropriate fixing of one's clothes after using the restroom and using the mirror to make a final check before exiting.

Although Roger's bathroom behavior might initially have been a result of poor learning,

- The success of a behavioral support program depends on positive lifestyle change in addition to behavior change. Behavior change is of no value in and of itself but should increase the individual's access to preferred settings, people, and activities.

- Emphasis is placed on determining the function that a behavior fulfills for the individual (i.e., functional analysis) and using that determination to drive intervention.

- Although behaviorism seeks to direct a specific intervention at a specific behavior, behavioral support utilizes multicomponent interventions as part of an overall plan that may address a number of similar behaviors.

- Whereas behaviorism emphasizes the manipulation of immediate antecedents and consequences of behavior, a program of positive behavior support will emphasize instruction in adaptive behaviors and the manipulation of environments and precipitating conditions as means of eliminating the individual's need for the undesirable behaviors and the opportunities for exhibiting them.

- Positive behavior support minimizes the use of punishments and instead emphasizes the use of interventions that promote the dignity of the individual.

CONCLUSION

A growing movement in disability-related services and legislation is self-determination, a belief that the power to choose and have choices is the predominant factor in the progress of one's life (Wehmeyer, 1992). Everyone, with or without disabilities, should have the same opportunity to make decisions about where and with whom he or she lives and socializes. In contrast to the traditional continuum of residential facilities and services, the emerging service paradigm focuses on supporting individuals with disabilities where they choose to live instead of where facilities or programs are located.

the shocked responses he was receiving were undoubtedly reinforcing it. Staff also hypothesized that his behavior of putting others' hands in inappropriate places on his own body were his efforts to gain attention as well. Given the fact that Roger could not communicate with those around him, staff speculated that he was a very lonely man and preferred the negative attention he was receiving to no attention at all. His support staff began to explore ways in which Roger could interact appropriately with those around him and gain the social contact and attention he wanted and needed. They began to teach some of Roger's repertoire of simple signs to co-workers, neighbors, and others with whom he comes in contact regularly. They also began to explore ways of integrating him into recreational outlets where he could associate with people without disabilities. Thus far, Roger's problem behaviors are decreasing as his circle of friends grows.

STUDY QUESTIONS

1. What are some criticisms of the readiness model presented by Taylor (1988)?

2. What does *interdependence* mean, and how does it relate to community living for people with disabilities?

3. What are the steps for identifying and utilizing community and workplace supports for people with disabilities?

4. What is community resource mapping and how can it be used to identify community supports?

5. What are the four circles of support, and how can they be utilized in community living for people with disabilities?

6. What are some federal housing programs for individuals with disabilities?

7. What are three ways of locating transportation support?

8. What are four guidelines for assisting someone with disabilities to engage in recreation and social activities?

15

Social Security Disability Benefit Issues Affecting Transition-Age Youth

Lucy A. Miller and Susan O'Mara

AFTER COMPLETING THIS CHAPTER, THE READER WILL BE ABLE TO

O Describe the Social Security benefit issues affecting transition-age youth and their families, particularly issues that arise when youth turn 18 years of age

O List effective strategies for increasing knowledge about and understanding of Social Security Administration (SSA) disability benefits and associated work incentives

O Explain what the Student Earned Income Exclusion (SEIE) is, and why it is important to transition-age youth interested in employment

O Describe what parent-to-child deeming is and how it affects SSI recipients under the age of 18

O Explain what a Plan for Achieving Self-Support (PASS) is and why it is important to transition-age youth interested in employment

O Describe the Supplemental Security Income (SSI) age 18 redetermination process and why it is important to transition-age youth and their families

O Describe the benefits of Section 301 provisions for youth who are determined ineligible for SSI after the age 18 redetermination

O Describe how SSA rules apply to child support payments

This chapter addresses critical Social Security benefits issues as they relate to the transition planning process. The material presented here builds on the foundation that was developed in Chapter 4, which described the basics of the Supplemental Security Income (SSI) program authorized under title XVI of the Social Security Act and the SSI work incentives applicable to transition-age youth. This chapter provides an introduction to the disability benefits authorized under title II of the Social Security Act, which is less familiar to youth, parents, school personnel, and other disability professionals because it is received less often than SSI. This chapter also offers an in-depth examination of the major Social Security disability benefits issues facing transition-age youth with disabilities coupled with specific information on ways to effectively manage these issues. Teachers will find this information useful because many students with disabilities receive or will be eligible to receive Social Security disability benefits. These same individuals may also be eligible for special incentives designed to encourage paid work (Berry, 2000). This chapter is also designed to help benefits specialists or other disability professionals who perform benefits counseling better understand the unique issues faced by transition-age youth who receive Social Security benefits. As benefits counseling becomes increasingly included in the transition planning process (as it should be), professionals who perform this service will need to become better versed on identifying and managing the public benefits issues facing youth in transition from school to adult life.

Despite the fact that Social Security benefits are one of the most important economic impacts on people with disabilities, very little is understood about how these programs work, or how they may be affected by paid employment. Educators and other school personnel are especially uninformed due to the fact that much of their personnel preparation does not cover this topic (Dreilinger & Timmons, 2001). Although this oversight is attributable to numerous factors, it represents a significant "missed opportunity" to educate students with disabilities and their families. Social Security benefits serve as a valuable resource to eligible students as they make the transition from school to adult life (Berry, 2000). These benefit programs offer not only cash payments and health insurance, but also include numerous work incentives specifically designed to increase employment and earnings capacity during and after secondary education. Failure to focus on Social Security benefits during transition is not only a missed opportunity, but may also cause harm when students and family members are not educated about nor prepared for the effect of earnings on cash benefits and medical insurance (Burkhauser & Wittenburg, 1996).

If Social Security benefits counseling is such an important aspect of successful transition from school to work, why is it not consistently included in the transition planning process? The answer to this question is multifaceted and is due to breakdowns in several service systems; not only education but also vocational rehabilitation (VR) and others (Schuster, Timmons, & Moloney, 2003). First, school system personnel are typically not aware of benefit issues and often do not consider this life domain to be within the scope of their responsibility. In addition, special educators seldom ever receive training on Social Security benefits and work incentives (Dreilinger & Timmons, 2001). Because this is a complex subject matter, school personnel may feel unprepared to address this issue with students and family members. Limited budgets and lack of resources are also problematic issues that frequently occur in schools that ultimately lead to deficiencies in the transition process. Many schools simply do not have the money or the personnel to adequately address important transition issues, including benefits counseling.

School systems are not solely responsible for the failure to include benefits counseling in the transition planning process. State VR agencies also neglect to focus on this critical service, generally for the same reasons as schools. Again, VR personnel are not fully trained on the complex effects of employment on Social Security benefits and may not be able to counsel students in this area. Most VR professionals will only meet individually with a transitioning youth during the final year of school, which results in too much planning and overall work to be completed in too short a period of time. Even worse is the fact that if a student chooses to withdraw from school, it is then the sole responsibility of the youth and his or her family to make contact with a VR representative. These individuals likely will "slip through the cracks" and not receive the services that they are entitled to receive.

Schuster and her colleagues (2003) conducted a study that examined barriers to transition faced by young adults with disabilities receiving SSI and their families. Interviews were conducted with 12 transition-age students and 10 of their parents/ guardians. Obstacles to transition planning that were unrelated to the receipt of SSI included: 1) poor match between students' interests and current jobs; 2) perceived lack of partnership between families and schools; 3) impact of disability on employment, social supports, and continuing education; 4) preoccupation with the present barriers associated specifically with receiving Social Security, including difficulty managing the receipt of SSI; and 5) unawareness of the supports available through the SSI system. The article concluded with a discussion of strategies to ease the transition planning process.

Despite the benefits of the monthly cash assistance it provides, receipt of SSI may function as an additional barrier to a successful transition for young adults, especially in terms of employment. That is, maintenance of health insurance is a primary concern for many SSI recipients, and despite protections that maintain health insurance while allowing recipients to work, the fear of losing benefits has prevented some from doing so. For example, an examination of data from the 1994 and 1995 National Health Interview Survey on Disability Supplement (NHIS-D; Berry, 2000) indicated that the percentage of young adult SSI participants ages 18–29 who reported having worked was substantially lower than for individuals with disabilities who do not receive SSI (66% versus 93%). In addition, both the mean number of hours worked per year and the mean monthly income were significantly less for employed SSI participants than for working individuals with disabilities who were not receiving SSI (Berry, 2000). Burkhauser and Wittenburg (1996) also found that transition-age SSI participants were less likely to work than nonparticipants with disabilities and that the odds of employment were reduced by more than one half for SSI participants. (*Note:* SSI is a needs-based program that provides a monthly stipend and medical benefits for individuals with disabilities who have limited income and resources. To be eligible for SSI, children and adolescents must meet financial and disability eligibility guidelines.)

Since the passage of the Ticket to Work and Work Incentives Improvement Act of 1999 (PL 106-170), there has been a major effort by the SSA to implement a national system of Benefits Planning, Assistance and Outreach (BPAO) services. Since the beginning of the BPAO initiative in early 2000, hundreds of trained disability benefit specialists have been working throughout the United States. Nevertheless, these benefits specialists are simply not reaching the transition-age youth population. According to the National BPAO Data Collection Report (2005) as of May 31, 2005, more than 13,229 people ages 14–22 had received BPAO services. This represents only 7.5% of the total population served by BPAO projects and represents a relatively low penetration rate with the total transition-age population.

For those benefits specialists who are reaching the transition-age population, the counseling provided often is generic in nature rather than custom designed to meet the unique needs and interests of students and their families. The purpose of this chapter is to discuss the numerous Social Security issues unique to this population. It is our hope that this chapter will add value to benefits planning for transition-age youth by highlighting the critical issues relevant to this group and provide some technical information necessary to provide competent advisement on these matters. Because many of the terms used in this chapter are technical, only those who are familiar with Social Security will understand them. Table 15.1 lists a glossary of terms and their definitions.

CRITICAL ISSUES FOR TRANSITION-AGE YOUTH UNDER 18

Issue: Parents and students are usually very uninformed about SSA disability benefits and associated work incentives and fear that employment will cause ineligibility for benefits.

A major concern among parents of school-age children with severe disabilities is related to the process of establishing or maintaining eligibility for the SSI program and Medicaid (Golden, O'Mara, Ferrell, & Sheldon, 2000). Although the need for an SSI cash payment is of paramount importance for some of these families, most will tell you that the Medicaid coverage is their most critical need. Many children with severe disabilities have significant medical involvement requiring expensive treatments, services, and medications. Often, these medical interventions are not covered by private insurance, or the existing coverage involves high premiums, co-payments, or deductibles that families can ill afford. The quest for affordable health insurance that covers needed services is often the driving force behind the desire to establish SSI eligibility for school-age youth.

Because SSI is a "means-tested" program in which eligibility is based on meeting specific financial limits, many children with severe disabilities are not found eligible due to excess parental income or resources. In other cases, families have trouble obtaining the evidence needed to facilitate a positive disability determination. Either way, benefits specialists must recognize that a great deal of time, energy, and effort may have been expended to secure the student's SSI benefit. Parents who have fought a long, exhausting battle to establish SSI eligibility are particularly loath to risk benefits, and *paid employment is viewed as a significant risk*. The risk of employment is felt even more acutely by parents with children in application status. Before the final eligibility determination is rendered, many families will refuse to even consider allowing the student to participate in paid employment for fear that it will result in a negative determination. In some cases, the family will have been advised by an attorney not to permit the student to work for pay.

Table 15.1. Glossary of basic Social Security terms and definitions

Terms	Definitions
Blind Work Expenses (BWE)	When determining a blind student's SSI and Medicaid eligibility and payment amount, SSA does not count earned income that a student may use to meet expenses in earning the income.
Break-even point	This is the dollar amount of total countable income (after applicable exclusions and deductions are applied) that will reduce the SSI payment to zero, and it is the point at which you are eligible for continued Medicaid under 1619(b) protection.
Countable income	The amount of money left after SSA has subtracted all available deductions from your total gross income. They use this amount to determine a student's continued eligibility for SSI and to decide your cash benefit amount.
Deeming	The process of considering some of the income and resources of a student's parent, spouse, or sponsor (if you are an alien) to be considered income and resources when applying for or receiving SSI.
Gross income	Income received from work before taxes or any other deductions are made
Impairment-Related Work Expenses (IRWE)	SSA deducts the cost of items and services that you need to work because of your impairment (e.g., attendant care) when they calculate your SSI cash payment amount.
Income	Income could be earned income (money received from wages, including from a sheltered workshop, self-employment, and certain royalties) or unearned income (money received from all other sources such as gifts or prizes). Income includes cash, checks, and other noncash items you receive such as food, clothing, or shelter.
Medicaid	Medical coverage provided to a person by the state title XIX program. You must be disabled and financially needy for the type of Medicaid protection offered by 1619(b).
Plan For Achieving Self-Support (PASS)	Under an SSA-approved PASS, you may set aside income and/or resources over a reasonable time that will enable you to reach a work goal to become financially self-supporting. You then can use the income and resources that you set aside to obtain occupational training or education, purchase equipment, or establish a business. Money set aside under a PASS is not counted when SSA decides SSI eligibility and payment amount.
Resources	This is something you own, such as a bank account, stocks, savings bond, or real property, that you could use for your own support and medical expenses. Some resources are not counted, such as your house you live in, your car you need for going to work or medical appointments, or things you need in order to work. An individual may own no more than $2,000 of countable resources and still be eligible for SSI.
Substantial Gainful Activity (SGA)	SSA and Medicaid evaluate the work activity of people applying for or receiving disability benefits. They use earnings guidelines to evaluate work and determine if it is "substantial" and whether you can be considered disabled under the law. Earnings averaging more than $780 a month generally demonstrate substantial gainful activity. After you are already receiving SSI, SGA does not matter.
Social Security Administration (SSA)	This is a federal administration that takes your application for SSI and also helps you to manage changes in your SSI over time.
Supplemental Security Income (SSI)	This is funded by federal income tax and is a minimal monthly payment to people with disabilities or aged who are financially needy.

Social Security disability benefits information and/or misinformation among the parents/caregivers of transition-age youth is a powerful force. Unfortunately, most of the information shared among families about Social Security disability benefits is incorrect or, at best, incomplete. To make matters worse, this misinformation is often inadvertently reinforced by school personnel, VR counselors, and even SSA claims representatives (Brooke & O'Mara, 2001). Families are often so uninformed about Social Security benefits that they do not know which of the various disability payments their child receives, what the eligibility guidelines for that program are, or even the amount of the monthly payment. When families are this insecure in their understanding of very basic benefits concepts, it is unreasonable to expect them to grasp the complex effects of employment.

Strategies for Success

One effective way to minimize the problems described previously is to be proactive in providing information about SSA disability benefits and the work incentives to youth and families who are in application status and for those who have yet to apply. The earlier benefits specialists can intervene in this process the better so that misinformation can be avoided and unnecessary fears prevented before they start. Benefits specialists are encouraged to conduct seminars about the various Social Security disability benefits programs and discuss eligibility factors in detail. Don't neglect to invite families with children as young as middle school age or even elementary school age.

Benefits specialists need to spend sufficient time explaining Social Security benefits basics before they launch into lengthy explanations of the work incentives. Social Security knowledge is built cumulatively. A person must grasp simple concepts before higher-order information can be understood. Use a developmental approach when providing information or training to students, families, and school personnel. It may also be necessary to discuss work incentives numerous times and offer documentation from the SSA that the information being provided is correct before parents are willing to consider paid employment for the student. Use visual aids such as SSI calculation sheets to show how wages would affect the SSI check.

Benefits counseling for SSI recipients should always emphasize the SEIE, which is a work incentive that allows certain SSI recipients who are under age 22 and regularly attending school to exclude a specified amount of gross earned income per month up to a maximum annual exclusion. The SEIE decreases the amount of countable earned income, thus permitting SSI recipients to keep more of the SSI check when they work. In many cases, the SEIE allows students to test their ability to work without experiencing any reduction in the SSI cash payment with no change in medical benefits (Section 1612[b] of the Social Security Act, 20 C.F.R. 416.1112, SSA POMS SI 00820.510, SSA Publication No. 64-030 2005; Miller, O'Mara, & Ferrell, 2005).

When working with families in application status, keep in mind that most families do not realize that students may have countable earned income up to the current Substantial Gainful Activity (SGA) guideline and still be found eligible for benefits (both SSI and Title 2 Childhood Disability Benefits). In addition, remember that some work incentives such as Impairment-Related Work Expenses (IRWE), Subsidy, and Plan for Achieving Self-Support (PASS) may be applied during the initial application period in order to reduce countable earnings under the SGA guideline. Students who are blind per the SSA definition are exempt from the SGA test entirely during initial eligibility. *Timely information about work incentives can be used to help a student establish eligibility for Social Security benefits while they are employed.*

Finally, an especially effective strategy for easing employment risk aversion is to have families talk to one another about their experiences with employment and SSI. However, it is important that benefits specialists pair a new family with one that had a positive experience with employment. Word of mouth is a powerful tool for families with school-age children—use it to your advantage. In addition, benefits specialists should reach out to attorneys who handle Social Security cases and provide training and support to them on work incentive issues. Developing a collaborative relationship with these attorneys can be beneficial for both parties.

Issue: Application of parent-to-child deeming rules for SSI recipients under age 18

When SSA determines the eligibility and amount of payment for an SSI recipient, the income and resources of people responsible for the recipient's welfare are also considered. This concept is called "deeming" and is based on the idea that those who have a responsibility for one another share their income and resources. Because SSI is a means-tested program, the portion of parental income/resources shared with the child is "deemed" by Social Security as being available to that child for the purposes of SSI eligibility and when calculating the amount of the SSI payment (Social Security Act, § 1614[f][2][A]; Regulations, 20 C.F.R. 416.1165, SSA POMS SI 01320.000–SI 01320.984). Determining how much of the parental income or resources to count against the child is called "parent-to-child deeming." It does not matter if money is actually provided to a child who is eligible for SSI for deeming to apply.

Families of school-age children with disabilities really struggle with the concept of parent-to-child deeming. Deeming rules and calculations seem inscrutable to families and are often perceived as "unfair" because they cause so many children with severe disabilities to be ineligible for both SSI cash payments and Medicaid coverage. Because deeming rules are so complex, school personnel, VR staff, and even benefits specialists are often at a loss to explain the deeming process in a way that is understandable. Parents end up feeling frustrated and powerless. This sense of helplessness contributes to the fear of benefit loss and aversion to the potential risks of paid employment (Hammis & Miller, 2005).

Strategies for Success

Although parent-to-child deeming is certainly complex, the general rules are not beyond the understanding of the average layperson. It is true that benefits specialists cannot determine the exact amount of parental income or resources deemed to a child, but a trained benefits specialist can explain broad deeming concepts and how the process works. The most important message to pass along to parents is that not all income or resources count—there are myriad deductions and exclusions. Parents should never assume their child is ineligible without completing the application process, nor assume that ineligibility is a permanent condition. Only the SSA can determine how much parental income is actually deemed.

Deemed income from a parent to an eligible child is treated like unearned income when determining the SSI payment amount. For this reason, children with deemed income have a lower "break-even point." The break-even point is the point at which total countable income causes the SSI cash payment to be reduced to zero. Benefits specialists must discuss this effect with parents but should always point out that use of work incentives such as the SEIE in combination with the general and earned income exclusions and the SSI one-for-two reduction often causes earned income to be completely disregarded. Students receiving SSI always come out ahead by working.

Benefits specialists must also remember that because deemed parental income is counted as a particular type of unearned income for SSI, it may be used to fund a PASS. PASS is a work incentive under which individuals with disabilities may set aside income and/or resources to be used to achieve a specific occupational goal. A PASS can be established to cover the costs of receiving an education, training, starting a business, or buying support services and equipment needed to work. Funds set aside in an approved PASS do not count when determining SSI eligibility or SSI payment amounts (Social Security Act Amendments of 1972, § 1612[b][4][A] and [B], § 1613[a][4]; Social Security Independence and Program Improvements Act of 1994 [PL 103-296], § 203; Code of Federal Regulations No. 16, Subpart K, §§ 416.1112, 416.1124, 416.1161, and 416.1180–416.1182, Subpart L, §§ 416.1210, and 416.1225–416.1227, and SSA POMS SI 00870.001). *A student with deemed parental income actually has an advantage when it comes to writing a PASS because he or she has income and/or resources to set aside in the PASS without even going to work.* For students under age 22 without any unearned income (e.g., deemed income from the parents), a PASS can be difficult to use because most if not all earned income will be already be excluded by the SEIE.

Using deemed income in a PASS is not difficult. Simply verify the amount of income SSA has determined to be deemed and have the parent(s) contribute that amount of income into the PASS account each month. Deemed resources may be treated in the same manner. Rather than viewing parental deemed income as something to be avoided, benefits specialists need to see it as a potential opportunity to help students achieve long-term career goals. Keep in mind that a PASS may also be used to help a student become initially eligible for SSI. If deemed income has precluded eligibility in the past, then this income can be set aside in a PASS and thus disregarded during the SSI eligibility determination. Assuming all other SSI eligibility criteria are met, benefits specialists can use work incentives to reduce countable income and/or resources, thus allowing the student to receive SSI and Medicaid.

Supplemental Security Income and Child Support Payments

Some parents of children receiving SSI pay court-ordered support payments. The court-ordered support payments are not counted as part of the parents' income and, therefore, not part of the income deemed from parents to children. Child support payments received for a child are counted as direct unearned income for the child who receives SSI. This rule applies whether the child support is paid in cash or in-kind. *In-kind support* is a phrase the SSA uses to describe goods or items other than money that are given to the eligible child or custodial parent to provide food, shelter, or clothing.

If the eligible child is under age 18, then the SSA deducts one third of the value of the cash support before applying the amount received in the benefit calculation formula. If the eligible child receives in-kind items (food, clothing, shelter) from an absent parent, then SSA applies the one third child support exclusion to the value of the in-kind items, compares this with the Presumed Maximum Value, and counts the lesser amount as the child's income. The Presumed Maximum Value is one third of the SSI federal benefit rate plus $20.00.

If the eligible child is over 18 and no longer meets the definition of a child (adult child), then the support payment is counted the same as other types of unearned income for the eligible individual. This rule also applies if the support payment represents arrearages and the eligible individual is paid directly or paid to a parent that gives the arrearage to the eligible individual. If the parent does not give the arrearage payment to the adult child, then the support arrearage is unearned income to the parent that received the payment. For an adult over 18, the full value of in-kind support is considered unearned income, subject to the Presumed Maximum Value rule.

Issue: Transition-age youth receiving Title II benefits

There is a common misconception that all students with disabilities receiving cash benefits from the SSA are getting SSI. Although most students with disabilities would be receiving SSI payments, by no means does this apply to *all* students. A small percentage of transition-age youth will be receiving disability benefits established under title II of the Social Security Act, such as Social Security Disability Insurance (SSDI) or more commonly Childhood Disability Benefits (CDB), whereas others receive a Social Security child's benefit that is completely unrelated to disability. Once again, the problem with this confusion is that neither parents nor school personnel understand that different Social Security benefit programs exist, nor that these benefits vary widely in how they function. Let's take a look at these programs, how students are found eligible, and the differences in how these benefits work.

Title II Child's Benefits

Title II child's benefits have nothing to do with being disabled, but rather are paid to dependent children of certain insured workers. Even if the child has a disability, the child receives regular child's benefits until the age of 18. Child's benefits may be paid to multiple children and, in some cases, a caregiving parent up to family maximum. To be entitled to Title II child's benefits, an individual must have filed an application for child's benefits and must be

1. The child of an insured worker who is deceased, retired and collecting Social Security retirement benefits, or disabled and collecting SSDI

2. Dependent on that insured worker

3. Unmarried (with some exceptions)

4. Under age 18; or if age 18 or over, a full-time elementary or secondary school student under age 19

Eligibility for child's benefits hinges primarily on how SSA defines the words *child* and *dependent*. The regulations surrounding the SSA's definition of a child are very complex, covering situations such as adoption, stepchildren, grandchildren, illegitimate children, and numerous other convoluted familial relationships. Dependency is also defined very precisely and is related to where and with whom the child lives and how much financial support is provided. It is impossible for benefits specialists to make determinations on these matters. Only SSA personnel have the authority to decide when an individual meets all the requirements to be eligible for a Title II child's benefit (SSA POMS RS 00203.000–RS 00203.090).

Benefits specialists do need to know when a transition-age youth is receiving a Title II child's benefit. This can be verified by sending a signed release of information form to the SSA. The reason for knowing this is that the effect of earned income on Title II benefits is completely different than for SSI, SSDI, or CDB, and is described briefly next.

Annual Earnings Test People who receive Title II Social Security benefits not based on disability are subject to an Annual Earnings Test (AET) that determines if they were eligible for all of the cash benefits they received in a year. Each year, an "exempt amount" is established. Only countable earnings over the exempt amount will affect the beneficiary's Social Security payments. The exempt amount of gross earnings (or net earnings from self-employment) is fairly high when compared with earnings limits under the Title II disability programs. The AET never applies to SSI benefits (SSA POMS RS 02500.000–RS 02510.999 for all rules governing the application of the AET).

If a youth generates earned income that exceeds the AET, then the SSA should be notified. SSA will recover $1.00 of child's benefits for every $2.00 of earned income over the exempt amount. In most cases, this will result in entire benefit checks being withheld until any overpayment has been recovered. Because it is unlikely that school-age youth would earn more than the AET, we will limit further discussion of overpayment recovery.

Social Security child's benefits and CDB are completely different programs. A child's disability cannot be established prior to age 18 for Social Security CDB purposes. For youth with disabilities under the age of 18, the AET would apply because the Social Security program received would be child's benefits, not CDB. Once the youth turns 18 and the disability determination is made, the AET would no longer apply because the benefit received would be CDB. From this point forward, the youth could gain access to the Title II disability work incentives. Keep in mind that Title II child's benefits may continue up to the age of 19 years and 2 months if the beneficiary fails to meet the disability criteria and is attending elementary or secondary school on a full-time basis.

Childhood Disability Benefits

Social Security childhood disability beneficiaries are adults with disabilities who do not have sufficient work credits for insured status, but receive a Title II benefit based on a parent's insured status. To be eligible for CDB, individuals must be at least 18 years old; disabled by SSA's definition before the age of 22; the child of an insured worker who is either deceased, retired and collecting SSA benefits, or disabled and drawing an SSDI benefit; and unmarried (with some exceptions). Some things to remember about CDB benefits include

- A person receiving Title II child's benefits up to the age of 18 must apply for CDB and complete the disability determination process to get CDB payments. If eligible, the individual will be switched from child's benefits to CDB as soon as the he or she turns 18.

- Unlike SSDI, there is never a 5-month waiting period for disability benefits under the CDB provisions.

- The 24-month Medicare Qualifying Period (MQP) applies to CDBs. This means that Medicare coverage cannot begin until the beneficiary is 20 years old, or 24 months after the 18th birthday.

- Benefits will stop if the individual marries, unless the spouse is also someone who receives a Title II Social Security benefit (except a child's benefit). Keep in mind that SSI is not considered a Social Security benefit. If the spouse only receives SSI, then the CDB benefit should stop the month of marriage.

- If an individual becomes ineligible for CDB for reasons other than engaging in SGA, then that individual must become re-entitled within 7 years of termination or the person loses the possibility of being entitled on that parent's work record. With the passage of the Social Security Protection Act of 2003 (PL 108-203) re-entitlement is permitted after the current 84-month period, to CDB benefits for those individuals whose initial eligibility terminated as a result of SGA.

- The same work incentives apply to all people receiving a Social Security benefit due to disability, whether that benefit is SSDI, Disabled Widow(ers) Benefits, or CDB.

- It is possible to collect a Title II benefit on two work records simultaneously: SSDI on your own record and CDB on an insured parent. This is known as being "dually eligible."

Social Security Disability Insurance

The SSDI program provides monthly cash benefits for former workers, under age 65, who become disabled. Individuals may receive an SSDI payment if they meet SSA's definition of disability, have sufficient work credits to be fully insured as a former worker, and be insured for disability status (this last requirement does not apply to individuals who are blind). The SSDI cash benefit received by an individual is related to how much that person earned and how long the person was employed. Unlike the SSI program, unearned income and resources are not considered and have no bearing on eligibility or payment amount (SSA POMS DI 001–DI 900).

There is a common misconception that young people under the age of 18 may not receive an SSDI benefit. In fact, there is no age limit within the SSDI program. Establishing eligibility for SSDI can happen quite quickly for younger people because fewer "work credits" are needed for those who become disabled before the age of 24.

Concurrent Beneficiaries

A *concurrent beneficiary* in Social Security parlance is someone who receives Social Security Title II benefits such as SSDI, CDB, or child's benefits and also a reduced SSI payment. Concurrent beneficiaries receive two separate checks each month (one for the Title II benefit and one for the SSI), as well as both Medicare (after the 24-month MQP) and Medicaid.

A concurrent beneficiary may begin as an SSI recipient who subsequently becomes eligible for a Title II payment. An example of this would be when a parent dies, retires, or becomes disabled and starts to collect Social Security that could trigger eligibility for CDB. In this case, the student would get a CDB payment that would count as unearned income for SSI. The SSI check would be reduced or eliminated depending on the amount of the CDB payment. A concurrent beneficiary may also be created when a youth who is receiving Title II payments subsequently meets the eligibility criteria for the SSI program. An example of this might be a student on child's benefits whose parents become unemployed, thus lowering the amount of deemed income that previously prevented the child from receiving SSI.

In all concurrent cases, Title II benefits take precedence because these are entitlement programs. Once the Title II benefit has been determined, eligibility for SSI is assessed. The Title II payment benefit is considered unearned income for the purposes of determining both eligibility for and the amount of the SSI benefit. There is no choice when determining which benefits a beneficiary will receive because SSI is the payer of last resort in all cases. If there are any other benefits available, then those must be accessed first and will be taken into consideration when determining SSI eligibility. If a youth is potentially eligible for a Title II benefit, then he or she must apply or risk losing SSI eligibility. The concurrent beneficiary must also meet all applicable income and resource tests for the SSI cash benefit.

Strategies for Success

Benefits specialists must never assume that all transition-age youth will be receiving SSI benefits. A surprising number will be getting Title II payments (child's benefits, CDB, or SSDI) or Title II in combination with SSI. Case-specific advisement on work incentives should never be provided until benefit types and amounts have been verified by the SSA. If this is not done, then students and family members will be given inaccurate or incomplete information about the effect of earnings on benefits.

Benefits specialists must learn the specifics of how earnings affect the various Title II programs and be prepared to share this information with students, family members, teachers, and VR counselors. It is not enough to understand the work incentives for SSI and Social Security disability programs when serving transition-age youth. It is important that benefits specialists constantly stress the fact that numerous Social Security programs exist and that they function very differently from one another.

Students who are concurrent beneficiaries need to have extra attention paid to their situations. More time will be needed to discuss the various Social Security benefit programs and work incentives and more time may be needed to help monitor benefits after employment begins. In addition, benefits specialists should remember that concurrent beneficiaries are natural PASS candidates because they have a source of unearned income to fund the plan prior to employment. The advantages of PASS should be discussed in detail with transition-age youth who are concurrent beneficiaries.

CRITICAL ISSUES RELATED TO THE 18TH BIRTHDAY

Issue: The SSI age 18 redetermination

Parents of children with severe disabilities who are awarded SSI benefits and Medicaid are generally relieved when this eligibility is established. They believe that a major hurdle has been cleared and think that they have secured a lifelong benefit for their child. Unfortunately, this perception is wholly inaccurate. Because the adult definition of disability for SSI is different than that for children, individuals who are found eligible for SSI under the childhood disability definition are required to go through a full disability "redetermination" after reaching the age of 18. The SSA calls this process the *age 18 redetermination*. Parents must be aware that SSI benefits are not "for life" and are not an "entitlement." The sooner the facts are realized, the easier it is to prepare for the age 18 redetermination.

The age 18 redetermination process was created when PL 104-193, Personal Responsibility and Work Opportunity Reconciliation Act of 1996 was amended by the Balanced Budget Act of 1997 (PL 105-33). This new law changed the childhood definition of disability for SSI recipients and required that all disability beneficiaries who were eligible as children in the month before the month of their 18th birthday have their eligibility redetermined under the adult standards for initial claims within 1 year of their 18th birthday. SSA's policy is that any individual who attained age 18 on or after August 22, 1996, and who was entitled as a child in the month before the month of attainment of age 18, will be subject to an initial disability redetermination instead of a CDR if a disability determination under the adult standards had not been completed after attainment of age 18 (see 20 C.F.R. 416.1414–416.1418 and SSA POMS DI 33025.075—Age 18 Re-determination Cases Under PL 104-193).

The age 18 redetermination will occur at some point after the 18th birthday. It may occur at a regularly scheduled continuing disability review (CDR) or at another point as determined by the SSA. In general practice, the age 18 redetermination usually occurs within 12 months after the 18th birthday, although this is not required by regulation. An individual who is *not* determined eligible for SSI benefits as an adult will be entitled to receive 2 more months of payments after the date of determination (i.e., the date on which the recipient is notified of the outcome of the age 18 redetermination). Overpayment may be considered if an ineligible individual continues to receive payments after the 2-month grace period. For individuals found ineligible under the adult rules, the SSA does *not* seek recovery of all SSI payments received after the birthday month, but only those received after the determination is made and the 2-month grace period is over.

A significant problem related to the age 18 redetermination is that SSI recipients and their families typically have no idea that this process occurs or how it differs from the regularly scheduled CDRs. Unfortunately, the age 18 redetermination has negatively affected many young adults, particularly those with respiratory, endocrine, and cardiovascular disabilities. Overall, Social Security estimates that 37% of all young adults who are redetermined fail to meet the adult disability standards. This ineligibility causes the loss of SSI cash payments and associated Medicaid coverage. Failure to establish SSI eligibility at redetermination also means losing access to valuable work incentives at a critical transition point for youth. In addition, when eligibility ends, a student no longer has access to the Ticket to Work program.

Strategies for Success

Benefits specialists can have a huge impact if they focus their efforts on early planning and preparation for the age 18 redetermination during the transition process. First and foremost, students, families, school personnel, and VR staff should be given detailed, understandable information about the redetermination process during the earliest stages of transition planning. Specifically, the benefits specialist must discuss how information will be gathered that contributes to the part of the redetermination that examines the recipient's future ability to earn income through paid employment. In addition, a contingency plan must be developed in case SSI eligibility is lost. This plan must include strategies for meeting the youth's support needs for work and community living and for securing appropriate medical insurance.

Fear of the age 18 redetermination process creates significant uncertainty regarding the impact of work/earnings on the disability determination. Many families are under the mistaken impression that SSI recipients must not be working at any level when the redetermination occurs. *In fact, the SGA step of the sequential evaluation process does not apply to these disability redeterminations* (SSA POMS DI 23570.020—Development and Evaluation of Childhood and Age 18 Disability Redeterminations). This means that a transition-age youth may be employed above the SGA guideline and still be found eligible for SSI under the adult rules during the age 18 redetermination as long as the disability standard and all other SSI eligibility criteria are met. Benefits specialists must stress this point repeatedly with all concerned parties. There is no reason to hold back on paid employment until after the student successfully completes the age 18 redetermination. There is no reason not to engage in paid employment before, during, or after the redetermination. This fortifies the previously stated point that if all SSA rules and regulations are followed correctly and all incentives are utilized correctly, then pre-adult SSI recipients should not be penalized for working and earning money.

Benefits specialists must remember that SSI benefit payments may continue even though the student is not found to meet the adult definition of disability if eligibility can be established for "Section 301" status. Until recently, continued payment of benefits under Section 301 was highly restrictive. In order to qualify for Section 301 payments, the previous regulations required that the beneficiary be actively participating in an approved VR program prior to the disability determination. In addition, the completion or continuation of the VR program had to satisfy a test of increasing the likelihood of the individual's permanent removal from the disability rolls. Finally, the individual was required to continue to meet all other SSI eligibility criteria such as the income and resource limits. Needless to say, continued payment of SSI benefits under Section 301 was rarely applied to youth who were found ineligible after the age 18 redetermination for several reasons. First, most students are not engaged in a VR program prior to age 18 because state VR agencies often do not initiate services until the final year of school. Second, although Section 301 has been part of Social Security law and regulation since 1980, awareness of the Section 301 provisions among SSI recipients, family members, teachers, VR professionals, and even SSA personnel is minimal. Because Section 301 payments are not automatic and must be requested, lack of awareness meant that very few Section 301 requests were ever processed. Finally, the previous requirement that the beneficiary pass the "likelihood" test was problematic. SSA personnel without any training in disability issues or VR were required to evaluate and determine whether completion of a specific VR program would result in the likelihood that the individual would be permanently removed from the disability rolls. Suffice it to say that few young people who lost SSI due to inability to meet the adult disability standard ever had benefits continued through the Section 301 provisions in the past.

On June 24, 2005, the SSA published the final revised regulations governing Section 301 payments (*Federal Register*, Volume 70, No. 121, pp. 36494–36509). SSA amended the rules to encourage young people with disabilities to stay in school and complete their educational and vocational training and to encourage the families of students with disabilities to support them in preparing for employment and self-sufficiency. These changes were made due to results documented by the National Longitudinal Transition Study conducted by the U.S. Department of Education showing that students with disabilities who stayed in school and completed their education and vocational training experiences had consistently better employment outcomes than did their peers who did not stay in school. In addition, the amended rules were more consistent with the New Freedom Initiative signed by President George W. Bush in February of 2001. This initiative promotes the full inclusion of people with disabilities in all areas of society by increasing access to assistive technology, expanding educational and employment opportunities, and promoting full access to community life.

The new Section 301 regulations expand the definition of an approved program of VR by utilizing the phrase "an appropriate program of VR services, employment services, or other support services." Under this broader definition, for students ages 18–21, an individualized education program (IEP) developed under policies and procedures approved by the Secretary of Education for assistance to states for the education of individuals with disabilities under the Individuals with Disabilities Education Improvement Act of 2004 (PL 108-446) would now qualify as an approved program. The new regulations go even further to provide that if a student age 18–21 is receiving services under an IEP or similar individualized education program or plan, and if the student's disability ceases as a result of a CDR or an age 18 redetermination, then SSA will consider that the student's completion of or continuation in the IEP will increase the likelihood that he or she will not have to return to the disability rules. This means that SSA will *assume* that continued participation in the IEP with suffice as passing the "likelihood" test without requiring the student to prove anything further. Finally, SSA defines participation in the IEP merely to mean that the student is taking part in the activities and services outlined in the IEP or similar plan.

Benefits specialists need to understand that most VR counselors and school personnel are completely unaware of the Section 301 provision and the benefits it provides. Students at risk of termination due the age 18 redetermination need to receive information about Section 301 continuation of benefits after medical recovery early on. The new Section 301 regulations offer a powerful incentive for students with disabilities to remain in school and to participate in VR programs. The benefit specialist will undoubtedly need to offer substantial training and support around this rather complex provision—especially now that the new regulations are in place—and may need to act as a coordinator to facilitate a successful Section 301 determination because the local SSA field office may not have experience with these rather rare cases and the other involved parties (state VR agency, private VR provider, and school) may not know this provision exists. *Keep in mind that individuals receiving benefits under Section 301 are not eligible for a Ticket from the Ticket to Work program.*

Issue: Parent-to-child deeming stops

Although we have already covered the issue of parent-to-child deeming, it is important to recognize that the 18th birthday marks the end of "deeming" from ineligible parents to eligible SSI recipients. In-kind support and maintenance (ISM) consists of food and shelter that is provided to an SSI eligible individual. ISM counts as unearned income if the eligible individual does not pay for it. When deeming applies to a child under age 18, food and shelter provided by the parent to the child is not counted as income. When deeming ends, the food and shelter is counted as income if the child does not pay for his or her share of the these items. Once a student turns 18, the income and resources of the parents are no longer considered in making SSI eligibility determinations or in calculating the amount of the SSI payment. At this point, only the income and resources of the eligible individual are considered. Some youth may now become eligible for SSI who were not eligible before due to deemed parental income and/or resources. Transition-age youth who were denied SSI as children should be encouraged to reapply when they turn 18. Receipt of an SSI benefit can aid in the transition process by providing the student with cash resources, Medicaid coverage, and access to valuable work incentives.

Although parent-to-child deeming ends at the age of 18, another important SSI concept known as "in-kind support and maintenance," or ISM, begins at this point. Basically, in-kind support and maintenance is unearned income attributable to the eligible individual in the form of food or shelter that is given to the individual or received because someone else pays for it. In-kind support may be provided by someone who resides in the same household as the recipient (such as a parent), or by someone outside of the household. ISM can cause a person to be ineligible for SSI benefits, as well as reduce the amount of benefits paid. SSA uses two rules to determine the value of the ISM an individual receives:

1. The Value of the One Third Reduction (VTR) rule is applied when the eligible individual lives in another person's household for a full calendar month and receives both food and shelter from that person and pays nothing toward his or her fair share.

2. The Presumed Maximum Value (PMV) rule is applied when an eligible individual receives ISM and the VTR rule does not apply (see SSA POMS SI 00835.300).

These two rules are mutually exclusive. When the VTR rule applies in any one month, the PMV rule cannot apply. Social Security carefully assesses an SSI recipient's living arrangement to determine whether ISM is being received, and if it is being received, whether the ISM is to be valued under the VTR rule or the PMV rule. Because of this, an SSI recipient's living arrangement can be a critical factor in determining both eligibility and cash payment amount. Living arrangement and ISM determinations are detailed and complex and final determinations may only be made by SSA personnel (POMS SI 00835.000–SI 00835.900 Living Arrangements and In-Kind Support and Maintenance).

Strategies for Success

Benefits specialists should actively encourage transition-age youth who were unable to establish eligibility for SSI due to deemed parental income to reapply for benefits after their 18th birthday. It is important to remind students and families that the SGA test will apply during the initial application process, so students earning more than the current SGA guideline will not be found eligible. However, once eligibility is established, the SSI work incentives enable eligible students to work with very little negative impact on benefits. In almost every instance, SSI recipients come out financially ahead by working. Although these issues may not seem relevant until after SSI benefits are attained, the SSI work incentives should be discussed as early as possible for any student who may establish eligibility in the future.

The end of parent-to-child deeming can also have a significant impact on transition-age youth who already are receiving SSI. For these students, turning 18 may mean that the SSI check will increase—sometimes substantially. Benefits specialists should identify students affected by parent-to-child deeming and encourage their families to contact the SSA for a reassessment of countable income and resources immediately after the 18th birthday. A higher SSI check also means a higher break-even point allowing more income to be earned before cash benefits are reduced to zero. This higher break-even point often helps families and students feel more comfortable about working.

Benefits specialists need to offer clear and concise information about the change from deeming to ISM calculations and the VTR/PMV rules. Most recipients and their families have little or no understanding of these concepts. It is common for SSI recipients to experience a one third reduction of the SSI due to incorrect application of the VTR rules. This happens because families do not correctly answer questions SSA poses about whether the youth is paying anything toward his or her fair share of the household expenses. Parents often think that having the eligible child make a financial contribution to household expenses is not permitted by the SSA. In fact, if the parents do not ask the child to contribute, then SSA will conclude that ISM is being provided and will apply the VTR rules. This will result in a full one third reduction of the current SSI federal benefit rate. In these situations, a little bit of information supplied at the right time can make a significant difference in the SSI monthly payment. Again, the importance of this correction is to gain a higher base benefit, thus raising the break-even point.

Issue: Eligibility for CDB may begin at age 18

As mentioned previously, turning 18 can also have implications related to Title II eligibility. Students on Title II child's benefits may lose cash payments entirely unless eligibility for CDB can be established. In addition, SSI benefits may be reduced or lost entirely due to establishing eligibility for CDB. In many instances, SSI recipients establish eligibility for additional CDB payments and become concurrent beneficiaries. All of these changes are triggered by the 18th birthday, and none of them can be readily avoided. In the overwhelming majority of cases, parents and students are completely unaware of these potential changes and are ill-prepared to deal with them.

Strategies for Success

Although change can be frightening and stressful, not all Social Security benefit changes are "bad." Benefits specialists can do a great deal to minimize the uncertainty by providing information about the various disability programs, their eligibility requirements, and associated work incentives well in advance. Although SSI may be more "work friendly" than the Title II disability programs, CDB certainly does have some advantages—not the least of which is the potential for a monthly payment higher than the SSI FBR. Benefits specialists should not present these potential changes in a negative light—they are not necessarily events to be feared by students and their families. The best strategy is to portray these changes in a neutral manner, fully explaining both the positive and negative features. Once again, the earlier these discussions take place, the better for all concerned.

It is not uncommon for benefits specialists to characterize becoming a concurrent beneficiary as something to be avoided at all costs. This is unfortunate. Although concurrent beneficiaries certainly have more complicated benefit situations when they go to work, they do have access to all work incentives, without exception. Concurrent beneficiaries can apply the various work incentives in myriad combinations; some work incentives can be applied to both SSI and Title II disability programs simultaneously. In addition, a concurrent beneficiary has a form of unearned income (Title II payment) that can be set-aside in a PASS to help achieve a future occupational goal. This is a very positive feature that should be emphasized during counseling.

Benefits specialists must not forget to talk to students and families about the possibility of establishing eligibility for SSDI benefits by working—even working part time. This is particularly important for SSI recipients as it will generally cause these youth to become concurrent beneficiaries. As stated previously, although this potential should not be feared, it is something to be aware of and planned for. Parents often will ask a benefits specialist to predict when SSDI eligibility will occur, which is an impossible task. Benefits specialists should not even attempt to make this prediction. It is best to refer the family to SSA for assistance with this task, although most SSA employees will also resist trying to determine this because so many inter-related factors are involved. There is one fact that a benefits specialist can discuss with the family: working consistently over the current SGA guideline will cause an SSI recipient *not* to establish eligibility for a Title II benefit. *In this case, working more, not less, will help the student avoid becoming a concurrent beneficiary or being switched entirely over to a Title II benefit (either SSDI or CDB).*

Finally, transition-age youth and their families often fear that establishing eligibility for Title II benefits can cause the complete loss of SSI and, more important, Medicaid. This is a legitimate fear if eligibility is established for SSDI and the resulting benefit exceeds the current unearned income limit for SSI. Fortunately, this instance is extremely rare for transition-age youth because they typically have not earned enough work credits to result in such a high benefit payment. However, the loss of SSI benefits due to establishing eligibility for CDB does occur within the transition population. *Fortunately, there is a special extended Medicaid provision for individuals who lose SSI eligibility due to entitlement for or an increase in CDB after July 1, 1987.* This special Medicaid protection is widely unknown to education or VR professionals. Benefits specialists need to stress this critical provision in training on benefit issues for transition-age youth and may need to offer support to families to make certain the provisions are applied properly. In some states and locales, the agency administering Medicaid programs routinely fails to identify eligibility for this special category (SSA POMS SI 01715.015—Special Groups of Former SSI Recipients; Uttermohlen & Miller, 2004).

Issue: Legal adulthood and representative payeeship

The 18th birthday marks the beginning of legal adulthood in our society, regardless of whether an individual has a disability. Social Security beneficiaries and SSI recipients who are 18 or over are viewed by the SSA as their own legal guardians with full legal power to sign documents, enter into contracts, vote, and enjoy all other rights and responsibilities afforded to adults. Unfortunately, parents of young adults with disabilities often do not understand that this is the case. Many parents of young adults without a disability resist believing this transition occurs at age 18. It can be an even stronger sense of resistance for those parents of 18 year olds who do have a disability. In many instances, parents assume that a young adult with severe disabilities is not afforded adult status, but continues to be the legal dependent of the parent indefinitely. Unless the parent has gone to court and established formal legal guardianship over the young adult, that individual is viewed as an adult. Family members also tend to confuse legal guardianship with representative payeeship. These two concepts are completely unrelated.

Representative Payees

A *representative payee* is someone who receives and manages Social Security or SSI benefits on behalf of another person. A representative payee may be necessary due to either incapacity or to the youth of a beneficiary. Representative payees have authority only over the distribution of the individual's benefit checks—it is a status assigned by the SSA solely for the purpose of managing the beneficiary's benefits. Payees are not legal guardians and are not authorized to be representatives in any area other than Social Security or SSI payments.

Representative payees must report annually how they have used the beneficiary's money. They should retain receipts for expenditures to demonstrate that the money was used for the beneficiary. Payees are responsible for reporting all relevant changes to the SSA that may affect the individual's entitlement to benefits or payment amount. The payee must not merely act as a conduit or use funds improperly (i.e., not for the beneficiary). If the payee misuses funds, then the payee is liable to repay the money to the beneficiary. If there is money left over, then the payee must invest or conserve it for the use of the beneficiary.

For children under the age of 18, the need for representative payeeship is assumed by Social Security (an emancipated youth could assume responsibility for managing his or her own benefits under certain circumstances). When an individual turns 18, SSA will review payeeship status to see if changes are needed. This review takes place at the time of the age 18 redetermination or CDR. If the beneficiary wishes to become his or her own payee, or wishes a different representative payee, then the request for the change should be made in the local Social Security office. The SSA will evaluate the situation and will assign a new payee if that appears to be in the best interest of the beneficiary. If an adult who has had a payee wishes to become his or her own payee, then the person may need to provide medical evidence that the beneficiary is now able to be responsible for his or her own payments.

Strategies for Success

As with so many issues in transition planning, the key to success is starting early and keeping at it. The same holds true with guardianship and payeeship issues. Benefits specialists should begin talking to transition-age youth and their parents about the rights and responsibilities associated with adulthood as early as possible. Families need to have very specific information about the different options available and should be encouraged to start thinking about supporting the student to become as independent as possible. Schools need to include both basic financial management skills and benefits management skills in the core curriculum offered to transitioning students. Benefits specialists can help reinforce this skill development process by offering short seminars on various benefits management subjects to both young adults and their family members. Just talking about these issues informally is not sufficient to get the job done. Formal skill training is essential.

Benefits specialists need to fully understand the process SSA uses to make and change payeeship decisions and should counsel students and families about these issues. Unfortunately, the idea of young adults with disabilities managing their own benefits and finances is still viewed as a radical notion to many parents, teachers, and VR counselors. Once again, time and energy needs to be expended on helping transition-age youth develop the skills necessary to become their own payees, whenever possible.

A big mistake benefits specialists make is assuming that families understand the responsibilities that come with serving as a representative payee. In addition, students who receive their own benefits often have no understanding of what they must report to the SSA. This ignorance is not just unfortunate, but dangerous. Failure to report relevant information to SSA often causes substantial overpayment of benefits that can take many years to pay back. Benefits specialists, in collaboration with schools and VR counselors, should provide formal training on reporting responsibilities and how best to communicate with the SSA about benefits. By doing this, benefit specialists, school personnel, and VR counselors will make their jobs easier and ultimately make the jobs of SSA personnel easier as well. Also important is the fact that this will help to quell the all-too-common belief of families and payees that SSA is unfair in their actions. As one can imagine, avoiding overpayments and subsequent paybacks go a long way in strengthening SSA's relationship with its beneficiaries.

CONCLUSION

As this chapter illustrates, Social Security benefits information is complex and can be confusing if one does not have a good understanding of the rules and regulations. However, these benefits have enormous impact on the transition and employment outcomes of youth with disabilities, and they must be considered seriously. Teachers and rehabilitation counselors will be unable to do all of this work. That is why trained and experienced benefits specialists will be necessary to help.

SSA has made a sincere and serious commitment to improve school-to-work transition for students with disabilities who are receiving monetary benefits. It is imperative that other entities (e.g., family members, school personnel, VR specialists, community-based organizations) share in and assist with this challenging process in order for these students to realize their full potential and to take advantage of the incentives that SSA has put in place for their benefit. The better one is educated on the intricacies of SSA policy, protocol, and guidelines, the more knowledge can be passed on to transition-age youth, the individuals who are directly affected. By working in concert with one another and sharing information, it is inevitable that more and more youth will realize a successful transition from school to work, and it will be an enjoyable and rewarding stage in their lives. Positive results and experiences such as this will pave the way for other youth to write their own successful transition stories. See Table 15.2 for supplementary information in the area of SSA program rules and work incentives for youth with disabilities.

Table 15.2. Web sites that offer information and resources on Social Security benefits for transition-age youth with disabilities

Resource	Web site
Academy for Educational Development	http://www.aed.org
Federal Maternal & Child Health Bureau	http://www.mchbhrtw.org
Institute for Child Health Policy	http://www.ichp.ufl.edu
Michael Walling and Associates, Inc.	http://www.wallinginc.com
National Youth Leadership Network	http://www.nyln.org
Special Education News	http://www.specialednews.com
Social Security Administration	http://www.ssa.gov
Social Security Administration Red Book on Employment Support	http://www.ssa.gov/work/ResourcesToolkit/redbook.pdf
Ticket to Work	http://www.ssa.gov/work http://www.yourtickettowork.com
United States Department of Education	http://www.ed.gov/index.jhtml
Virginia Commonwealth University Benefits Assistance Resource Center	http://www.vcu-barc.org
Virginia Commonwealth University Rehabilitation Research and Training on Workplace Supports and Job Retention	http://www.worksupport.com

STUDY QUESTIONS

1. Describe three major SSA benefit issues affecting transition-age youth with disabilities and their families.

2. For each of the identified SSA benefits issues, list two strategies for addressing the issue.

3. Describe SSA's SEIE and four associated benefits to transition-age youth interested in employment.

4. Explain the importance of deemed income and why this is vital when determining the SSI benefit for SSA recipients under the age of 18 years of age.

5. Describe the basics of PASS and provide an illustration of how this work incentive would be applied for a transition-age youth interested in employment.

6. Provide a brief explanation of how SSA rules apply to child support payments.

7. List and define five common SSA terms.

IV

Designing and Implementing Individualized Transition Plans

16

Applications for Youth
with Intellectual Disabilities

Paul Wehman

AFTER COMPLETING THIS CHAPTER, THE READER WILL BE ABLE TO

○ Identify several characteristics of students with intellectual disabilities

○ Understand challenges that parents, students, and schools face when trying to provide educational services for students with intellectual disabilities

○ Describe and develop learning objectives using the ecological inventory method of curriculum development

○ Describe the benefits of community-based instruction (CBI)

○ Describe how to establish a CBI program

○ Understand the team approach to transition planning and identify the players in the process

○ Describe supported employment (SE) programs and outcomes for transition-age youth

SANDRA

Sandra is an 18-year-old recent graduate of Sandston High School with mild intellectual disabilities. She has a strong desire to work; her smile glows with eagerness, but her face cannot hide her apprehension about finding a "real job." Sandra is the youngest of five girls and has two older sisters who have disabilities.

Sandra has previous employment experience at a McDonald's restaurant. This work experience was positive but ended abruptly when her family moved. Approximately 1 year later, she faced obtaining a new job in her field of choice. Sandra had taken a class in school that had sparked her interest in the clerical field. Although her long-term goal was nursing, she decided that she wanted to work a part-time clerical job while she attended a special community college program that assists individuals with disabilities to further advance their career goals in a specific area.

She had many questions. Could she obtain a job in a field where she had very little training? Would an employer accept her to do clerical work with low reading and writing levels? Who would support her and help her at work when she needed it? Sandra asked an employment specialist to inquire about possibilities in the clerical field. Would she be able to work around her school schedule? She preferred a position that involved filing and possible computer work. Sandra's teacher indicated that this type of position would be excellent for her. Her teacher and

People with intellectual disabilities like Sandra and Rick (see sidebars) have tremendous potential to contribute to the community, the economy, and their families (President's Committee on Intellectual Disabilities, 2004). These individuals were once housed in institutions with the perception that they were highly incompetent. Fortunately, since the 1970s, more and more people with intellectual disabilities are becoming active members of their communities. The support that they receive from a key circle of people in their lives is an important factor and influences their community adjustment.

Although individuals with intellectual disabilities do not usually learn as quickly as the average student, many limitations in vocational performance, residential living, and social adjustment can be successfully overcome with well-placed help and support. With this assistance, many people with intellectual disabilities are becoming competitively employed and living independently (Wehman, Revell, & Brooke, 2003).

This chapter describes ways to help people with intellectual disabilities manage the challenges inherent in any community and make a successful transition from school to the world of adulthood.

WHO ARE INDIVIDUALS WITH INTELLECTUAL DISABILITIES?

Supports are a key aspect of helping people with disabilities achieve their goals and succeed (e.g., Polloway, 2004), and they are a guiding principle of this book. Supports also are a significant way that people with intellectual disabilities are defined. In 2002, the American Association on Mental Retardation (AAMR) further changed its definition of *mental retardation* to incorporate the concept of supports and how they are provided. This definition reflects philosophies espoused in recent years that reflect that the success of people with intellectual disabilities is directly based on the availability and quality of supports in their homes, communities, and workplaces (e.g., Getzel & Wehman, 2005; Wehman, 2001b; Wehman, Revell, & Brooke, 2003); it is a serious departure from the way services have been traditionally provided and provides a new vista of hope. In the 2002 AAMR definition, the following assumptions are considered essential:

1. Valid assessment considers cultural and linguistic diversity as well as differences in communication and behavioral factors.

2. The existence of limitations in adaptive skills occurs within the context of community environments typical of

her rehabilitation counselor both contributed information that could assist in the search for the right job match for Sandra. Within a short amount of time, Sandra successfully interviewed at the Richmond Police Department and was hired there as a part-time file clerk.

The employment specialist helped Sandra on her first day to organize the documents and determine a system for filing. Sandra needed verbal prompts to use the system consistently. On the third day of employment, Sandra was doing so well that she was asked to answer the telephones for an hour while the receptionist went to lunch. Sandra was initially very nervous about answering the telephones. Although that was not one of her initial job duties, she adapted well to the change. During that hour, she was responsible for answering the telephones and directing calls, greeting office visitors, directing inquiries, and other duties as requested by office personnel. Indirect verbal prompting was needed to remind Sandra to use her name when answering the telephone, and lists were created to assist her in forwarding calls to the correct individuals or departments.

Sandra received support from her mentor and all office staff. The employment specialist was able to begin fading after 1 week of full-time job coaching. Relieving the receptionist during lunch became an everyday part of Sandra's duties. She was responsible for checking her watch and, at 2:00 P.M. every day, answering telephones for an hour. Sandra has done so well in learning new tasks that she has an-

the individual's peers and is indexed to the person's individualized need for supports.

3. Specific adaptive limitations often coexist with strengths in other adaptive skills or other personal capabilities.

4. With appropriate supports over a sustained period, the life functioning of a person with mental retardation will generally improve (Luckasson et al., 2002).

These are critically important assumptions that reflect the research of the 1980s and 1990s. They establish the fact that some people with intellectual disabilities may eventually acquire sufficient competence through supports that they may no longer be considered as having a disability.

The 2002 AAMR definition provides four levels of supports as guideposts in determining how much help a person with intellectual disabilities may need:

1. Intermittent: Special help that an individual might need only periodically, perhaps upon losing a job

2. Limited: Supports that occur somewhat frequently but are less intense, such as time-limited job training

3. Extensive: Help that occurs regularly in a person's life, such as living in a group home with a 24-hour counselor

4. Pervasive: Support that is all-encompassing in a person's life and very expensive (e.g., extended medical care, behavioral support)

These supports are considered in conjunction with 1) the diagnosis of intellectual disabilities and 2) the description of the person's adaptive skills and intellectual functioning to form the initial basis of the classification system. Although there is some question regarding how well this new definition is being fully accepted and implemented by the states (Denning, Chamberlain, & Polloway, 2000; Polloway, 2004; Polloway, Smith, Chamberlain, Denning, & Smith, 1999), conceptually and programmatically, this definition remains a national beacon for service providers to follow in designing programs. The AAMR (2003) has released the *Supports Intensity Scale* (SIS), a tool to help assess the level of support individuals with intellectual disabilities will need to be successful. The SIS fills a niche not addressed by any other assessment measure in the market today, including adaptive behavior scales and other measures of personal competence. The SIS measures exactly what practical supports it takes for a person with mental retardation to be proficient in 57 key life activities in seven areas of competence, including results clearly ranked by frequency

swered the telephones all day on two occasions. She has also had training on collating packets of information and using the photocopy machine and the fax machine. Sandra was also asked to assist in the training of the summer clerks who were hired. She showed them the file room and the organizational system used.

Sandra has needed indirect verbal prompting at times to answer the telephone correctly and to prioritize tasks. She is very confident about her job and takes a lead role in completing all duties. She is well-liked by her co-workers and has received compliments from individuals on how personable she is in the office and over the telephone. She has been given the flexibility to adjust her schedule to accommodate her personal needs. She was permitted to come in to work earlier on days of extreme heat because she takes the bus. She has also been informed that she can change her schedule if necessary to accommodate her school schedule.

(how often support is needed), daily support time (when support is required on a typical day), and type of support (what kind of support is needed—verbal, physical, and so forth). Although other scales of personal competence identify skills deficits in an individual, SIS tells you what specific hands-on supports a person requires to perform tasks in seven core areas of living, including home living, community living, lifelong learning, employment, health and safety, social interaction, and protection and advocacy.

This definition accounts for the likelihood that the individual can and will change over time. It is formulated to broaden the conceptualization of intellectual disabilities, prevent the assigning of a disability label based on IQ score, and determine the appropriate support on the basis of an individual's needs. Furthermore, it strongly supports the expectation of individual potential and growth (Schalock et al., 1994). It also recognizes that not all people with intellectual disabilities will have the same limitations, which is important for young adults with intellectual disabilities, giving them a tremendous opportunity to successfully blend into society without odious labels.

Polloway (2004), one of the long-term national leaders in the field of intellectual disabilities, astutely noted:

> The traditional conceptualization of mild mental retardation was based on the presumption of high prevalence rates in programs for school-age children. Not uncommonly, the cited rate in the 1970s was approximately 2.5%–3% for mental retardation, with the majority (more than 2%) being considered to have mild retardation. With prevalence came significant attention. Individuals identified as having mild retardation were participants in much of the groundbreaking work in learning theory, which provided a foundation for many productive directions in contemporary practice. (p. 17)

WORK AND SCHOOL ISSUES FOR INDIVIDUALS WITH INTELLECTUAL DISABILITIES

People with intellectual disabilities can succeed in most aspects of their lives on the basis of the availability and quality of supports in their home, community, and workplace. Specific functional skill limitations can coexist with strengths in other adaptive skills or other personal capabilities. Some individuals with intellectual disabilities have greater support needs and will require specialized help. These supports may be as simple as government policies prohibiting job discrimination against people with disabilities. For example, as noted in Chapters 10 and 12, the passage of the Americans with Disabilities Act (ADA) of 1990 (PL 101-336) and its enforcement by the U.S. Equal Employment Opportunity Commission (U.S. EEOC) provided an important support for people with intellectual and cognitive disabilities to enter the workplace using different accommodations such as job coaches (McMahon, Edwards, Rumrill, Hursh,

RICK

Rick is 22 years old, and he graduated from the local special education program last year. He also has a diagnosis of intellectual disabilities with an IQ score of 35, has a secondary diagnosis of hearing and behavior disorders, and requires extensive support. He has a long history of getting his own way by acting out when he gets upset. On occasion, this behavior has been directed at teachers when they have attempted to intervene. Typically, however, his aggressive behavior is limited to temper tantrums.

Rick lives at home with his parents, who hope that he will be able to work soon. Until recently, his parents thought that his only alternative was a sheltered workshop or an activity center. Rick assists his family in household chores such as cleaning, laundry, and lawn work. He participates in a men's club with his father and other retired men in his community.

After graduation from school, Rick was referred to the vocational rehabilitation (VR) program, which arranged for him to receive a vocational evaluation. This testing indicated that Rick had a short attention span and performed poorly on routine, manipulative, and sorting tasks. Rick was able to follow simple directions when they were specific and when prior demonstration had occurred. However, he became uncooperative and noncompliant after working on a task for several minutes.

2005; McMahon, West, Shaw, Waid-Ebbs, & Belongia, 2005; Unger, Campbell, & McMahon, 2005).

EEOC provides a framework to prevent job discrimination and unfair termination. Recent actions by the EEOC have culminated in a settlement for a 45-year-old supported employee with intellectual disabilities against Dollar General. The woman claimed she was fired because of intellectual disabilities (*EEOC v. Dollar General*, U.S. District Court, Middle District of NC, March 2003). Similarly, EEOC filed a lawsuit against Home Depot alleging failure to accommodate an employee with intellectual disabilities (*EEOC v. Home Depot*, U.S. District Court, ED, NY, Civil Action Number 03-4880). As more and more people with intellectual disabilities enter the competitive labor market, it is inevitable there will be claims of alleged discrimination. For example, Paul Miller (1999) of the U.S. EEOC pointed out

> People with intellectual disabilities are only just beginning to assert their rights under the ADA, and there is still much ground to cover. People with intellectual disabilities generally do not file charges with the EEOC. This is not because they do not face job discrimination. Rather, it may be remarkably difficult for someone with intellectual disabilities to understand their rights and then to seek out the EEOC for help in enforcing those rights when violated. Job coaches and employment agencies may be hesitant to file charges against employers who have hired people with intellectual disabilities out of their concern of making it more difficult to place future clients. But the rights of people with intellectual disabilities must not be trampled on. These individuals have the same rights to a discrimination-free workplace as do any other employee, and where discrimination occurs, rights must be enforced.

Following up on the work capacity of people with intellectual disabilities, several researchers have examined the relationship among customer characteristics, VR services, and employment outcomes for a person with intellectual disabilities (i.e., Moore, Alston, Donnell, & Hollis, 2003; Moore, Flowers, & Taylor, 2000; Wehman, Gibson, Brooke, & Unger, 1999). In addition, Gilmore, Schuster, Timmons, and Butterworth (2000) reported that 34,408 (48%) of people with mild disabilities, 19,605, (27.6%) with moderate, and 4,120 (5.8%) with severe/profound intellectual disabilities were classified as *closed rehabilitated cases* (i.e., maintained a job for a minimum of 90 days). One year later, Moore et al. (2003) reported, however, that VR consumers with mild/moderate intellectual disabilities who were provided business/vocational training, on-the-job training, job placement, transportation, and maintenance were more likely to be successfully closed than those who did not receive such services.

Moore et al. (2000) also found that consumers with mild/moderate intellectual disabilities who received job-placement services were significantly more likely to achieve employment success. In a more recent investigation, Moore et al. (2003) found that Social Security Disability Insurance (SSDI) beneficiaries with mild intellectual disabilities who were provided with job-placement services were significantly more likely to achieve success when compared with those not receiving such services. Other factors, such as family support, well-trained employment personnel, arrangement of appropriate work supports, and the opportunity for developing work competences on the jobsite, have also been cited as contributors to successful competitive job placement (Wehman et al., 1999).

School Participation

Since the 1980s, there has been a substantial change in the characteristics of students who attend classes that were once provided exclusively for individuals with intellectual disabilities—these students are decreasing in number but possess more severe and varied additional disabilities. Before the 1980s, students in special education classrooms were usually male, from racial or cultural minority groups, often from single-parent homes, and they often exhibited problems with adaptive behavior and academic achievement (Lilly, 1979; MacMillan, 1977). These students now constitute a very heterogeneous group (U.S. Department of Education, 2002).

Two factors in particular have contributed to the changes in those students who are diagnosed with intellectual disabilities, especially mild disabilities, both of which contribute to an increase in more suitable placements of students. The first factor to consider is litigation. Litigation has allowed parents and professionals to challenge the placement of a disproportionate number of students belonging to cultural minorities in special education programs (MacMillan & Reschly, 1998; Wehman, 2005). Although these numbers remain high, school officials are being more cautious about the identification procedures used in student placements. Patton (1998), in a now classic article on the disproportionate representation of African American students in special education, noted

> The overrepresentation of African Americans in certain special education programs has been a persistent problem negatively affecting large numbers of African Americans and their families, the field of special education, and society at large. The fact that disproportionately large numbers of African Americans are being persistently diagnosed as disabled and placed in special education programs constitutes a problem—for many of these students are inappropriately placed. The consequences, however, of such misidentification, classification, and placement are often deleterious. As an example, this problem is exacerbated by the fact that many African American youth today fail to receive a quality and life-enhancing education in precisely those special education programs in which they are often inappropriately placed. (p. 25)

Legislation protects students from being miscategorized due to assumptions about race or culture, and, through litigation, more and more families are ensuring that students are taught using curricula that are appropriate to their needs and abilities.

CHALLENGES OF WORKING WITH YOUTH WITH INTELLECTUAL DISABILITIES

When one considers the problems and challenges that young people with intellectual disabilities face, one should also consider the widespread problems that youth without disabilities face in America. Given the range of issues such as domestic violence, the sensationalizing of inappropriate actions in the media, unsupervised periods after school, substance abuse, and teenage pregnancy, among others, it is not surprising to see that young people with intellectual disabilities have some very substantial barriers to overcome. One of the problems that professional educators have in trying to help this group of young people is stereotyping their potential on the basis of labels such as *mentally retarded, slow learners, borderline retarded,* and so forth. The best way to help each student is to look at his or her specific situation. Each student has his or her own set of family circumstances, educational history, supports that are necessary, financial needs, and self-esteem issues. It is simply impossible to construct a meaningful education and transition plan without considering all of the factors that are unique to that particular person. The practice that occurs all too often in many school districts is that transition plans are constructed in an identical or close to identical fashion for large numbers of students who have the same label. This is a prescription for certain failure. Each plan needs to be individualized.

Parents and students, therefore, are increasingly frustrated with the curricula for youth with intellectual disabilities as they too often resemble that of students in the general classroom. Yet, with increased demands from society for more rigorously educated students, the conflict in setting curriculum goals is ongoing. Curricula that combine general and special education requirements are beneficial if the students are on an academic track but can be detrimental if more functional skills training is needed.

Many students, parents, and professionals are confused about what specifically should be included in the curriculum. Students' diagnoses are usually considered only in determining formative school placement, although these individuals possess functional problems that carry over into adult life. Clearly, many students with intellectual disabilities do require special services, such as community-based training, vocational education, and career planning. The key to infusing life skills into the curriculum has been delineated in an outstanding text by Patton, Cronin, and Wood (1999), who listed the infusion technique as including four elements:

1. Familiarity with the comprehensive set of knowledge and skills needed in adulthood (i.e., life skills)

2. Identification of places in the existing curriculum that can be associated with real-life topics

3. Planning life skills infusion activities

4. Actual instruction of life skills during ongoing lessons

Many of the barriers to work that students with intellectual disabilities face can be mitigated through behavior intervention and appropriate learning goals. At times, students with intellectual disabilities exhibit problem social behavior; however, as Reitman, Drabman, Speaks, Burkley, and Rhode (1998) showed, problems such as inappropriate sexual and social behaviors in the workplace can often be remediated by effective behavior intervention. Most of these students also will need the opportunity to earn an occupationally oriented diploma through a program that teaches functional academic skills and helps develop paid work skills. Occupational and career orientations in middle and secondary school are absolutely imperative for this group of students. Unfortunately, many students reject specialized, outcomes-oriented curricula because they are often implemented in stigmatizing ways. This is particularly difficult for students with intellectual disabilities whose disabilities are only recognized among educators and not among the general community (Cartwright, Cartwright, & Ward, 1989). In other cases, these students follow schedules and curricula that closely resemble those used in general classrooms without being afforded the necessary individualization and support services, thus causing them to fall further and further behind both academically and vocationally.

School Reform

Consistent with issues related to curriculum and level of school participation, school reform and high-stakes testing become the single biggest threat to improving community integration and vocational outcomes for youth with intellectual disabilities (see Chapter 7). During the 1990s, there was a significant move to upgrade the quality and intensity of the general education curriculum so that students without disabilities are better prepared in the so-called "hard" academics of mathematics, science, language arts, fine arts, and so forth (Vanderwood, McGrew, & Ysseldyke, 1998). This has been continued in the 2000s as well (Nolet & McLaughlin, 2005). Although this is commendable and essential to help young people without disabilities, it has had a somewhat deleterious effect on the opportunity for young students with intellectual disabilities to learn real-life functional skills, especially when a quality work-based learning model is utilized (Luecking & Gramlich, 2003).

Choice and Empowerment

Many people with intellectual disabilities have not been allowed to participate in deciding the direction of the services they receive, how they are administered, or what their outcomes should be (Brotherson, Cook, Cunconon-Lehr, & Wehmeyer, 1995). All too often, both providers and recipients seem to believe that people with intellectual disabilities should feel grateful simply to get into a program; however, the notion that consumers should gain power over human services, and, in the process, gain or regain power over their own lives is becoming increasingly popular.

This type of *self-determination* or *empowerment* can be broadly defined as the transfer of power and control over the values, decisions, choices, and directions of human services from external entities (e.g., government agencies, service providers, social forces) to the consumers of services (i.e., the individuals with disabilities themselves). This is likely to give consumers increased independence, greater motivation to participate and succeed, and a greater degree of dignity.

Inclusion Experiences

Choice, self-determination, and empowerment are enhanced when there are opportunities for regular inclusion with youth without disabilities. Youth with significant intellectual disabilities need the opportunity to be educated alongside students without disabilities (Janney, Snell, Beers, & Raynes, 1995; McDonnell, 1998; Weiner, 2003). This may be at a vocational technical center in an after-school photography club, during physical education class, or in any of a number of meaningful school experiences (Hunt & Goetz, 1997).

Weiner (2003) reviewed the importance of teacher training on the likelihood of inclusion:

> The data on teacher's beliefs about inclusion students and gains on standardized academic testing for special and general education students suggest that:
> - Staff development personnel working regularly in inclusion classes can help teachers to create optimum learning environments for all students.
> - Students who were previously in self-contained special education classes can be fully participating members of inclusion classes who make significant and educationally meaningful academic gains.
> - General education students can achieve academically as well as or better than their counterparts in non-inclusion classes.
>
> For teachers and schools in a "resistant" stance (Level I), these findings help dispel the myths that general education students will be "held back" by including lower performing special education students in their classrooms and that special education students "can't handle" a rigorous academic environment. (p. 17)

Hughes and her associates (1999, 2000) presented an outstanding program that evaluates the efficacy of peer buddies in high school inclusion experiences. They discussed some of the complex issues associated with enhancing inclusion in general education such as block scheduling periods and working across academic courses. They discussed a highly successful program in Nashville, Tennessee, that provided one perspective from a peer buddy without a disability and how he feels about the experience (see Figure 16.1).

Hello, I'm Corie and I'm a senior at McGavock High School. I heard about the Peer Buddy Program from my guidance counselor and because I really didn't have another class for one of my class periods, I decided to take it. I was kind of interested in it anyway, because I had been a peer tutor in seventh and eighth grade, and I wondered how I could get into it again.

I learned a lot about different people and different aspects of disabilities. I really liked just sitting in the classroom and hanging out with everybody. That was my favorite part. All of my friends said,"Man, that's so cool. I wonder how I could do that." But it was too late because all my friends were seniors and they couldn't do it again.

My second semester as a Peer Buddy I spent mostly with Kim in Ms. Dye's room. And that girl—whew! She was a handful. When I first got into the classroom, she would just sit there and either sleep all day or cry about something. Or kind of just wander around with her eyes and look and not do anything. After my first semester, I noticed how she wouldn't deal with anybody. She was just always by herself. So I would go over there and tickle her and, all of a sudden, she just livened up! It was like someone had to just talk to her one time, and she burst out with life. When I first started talking to her, she really didn't have many words that she could say. Mostly she just said "Milk" if she wanted milk, or if she had to go to the bathroom, she would tell us. That was about it. Then I got to talking to her; and toward the end of the year, she developed more language and everything. We played games like hand-slap games and tickled each other. The bean bag chair was the best because she just loved that thing. Kim would just lay on it and wallow all over the floor and just laugh. It was so cool!

Well, that's Kim! She's cool now.

Corie Byers
McGavock High School
Nashville, Tennessee

Figure 16.1. A peer buddy's perspective. (From Hughes, C., Guth, C., Hall, S., Presley, J., Dye, M., & Byers, C. [1999]. "They are my best friends": Peer buddies promote inclusion in high school. *TEACHING Exceptional Children, 31*[5], 35; reprinted by permission. Copyright 1999 by the Council for Exceptional Children.)

ASSESSMENT OF YOUTH WITH INTELLECTUAL DISABILITIES

Individual students with disabilities continue to be identified and placed in school programs on the basis of their general intellectual functioning. Intelligence tests are presumably used to set the guideline by which students are placed in special classes and programs and to what extent they are served. Commercially prepared, standardized norm-referenced tests have been used for evaluating and classifying students academically and vocationally. Achievement tests have been used to determine students' levels of mastery in basic academic skills, such as reading and math.

The major purpose of vocational assessment has been to measure a student's ability to master skills associated with real work settings (see Table 16.1). This testing is designed to determine who is eligible for services and which services are appropriate for specific individuals with disabilities in the rehabilitation field. Some critics, however, suggest that the purpose of vocational assessment may be unrelated to the identification of specific training needs. Determinations of low IQ scores or poor aptitude do not provide practitioners with clear instructions about what should be included in the curriculum for vocational training. When testing procedures do not provide training-related information, they serve little purpose in the educational setting.

CURRICULUM STRATEGIES FOR YOUTH WITH INTELLECTUAL DISABILITIES

Many individuals with intellectual disabilities experience problems with employment, independent living, and community access—problems that began when they were students. Johnson, Stodden, Emanuel, Luecking, and Mack (2002) do an excellent job of highlighting these challenges. Historically, these students have been educated through workbooks, ditto sheets, and blackboard work instead of training for practical community-related skills, such as driver's education, substance abuse education, sexually transmitted disease (STD) education, job-seeking skills training, and socialization skills training (Smith & Puccini, 1995). These skills must be introduced to students early in their educational careers. Forgan and Gonzalez-DeHass (2004) noted the importance of infusing social skills training into literacy instruction:

> Although research tends to support the effectiveness of social skills instruction and teachers recognize the value of social skills training for students, teachers often report that allocating time to teach social skills is problematic. Many teachers feel pressure to prioritize academic achievement over students' social success given today's environment of high-stakes testing and often feel time for teaching social skills is limited (Cartledge & Kiarie, 2001). One way to overcome this dilemma is to infuse social skills instruction into the academic curriculum (Cartledge & Milburn, 1995) and literacy instruction, in particular (Anderson, 2000; Cartledge & Kiarie, 2001). (p. 25)

Downing (2005), long a national leader in education of those with significant disabilities, has developed a wonderful resource for teaching literacy to students in inclusive classroom. In Table 16.2 of her book, she provides an excellent example of how a tenth grader with severe intellectual disability can benefit from literacy instruction.

Thoma (1999) provides excellent strategies to help with transition planning (see Table 16.2). Krom and Prater (1993) indicated that few career and vocational education efforts are begun in middle school. Furthermore, they noted that teachers write individualized education program (IEP) goals that are based on their own curriculum, not student needs:

Table 16.1. Purpose of vocational assessment

Topic	Questions to consider
Preferences	What types of jobs are preferred and disliked?
	What type of work setting does the student prefer?
Capabilities	What are the students' responses to others in the work setting?
	What work-related values has the student acquired?
Workplace supports	What training strategies promote new learning?
	What types of accommodations can enhance vocational success?
	Who can provide supports to enhance the student's vocational success?
	What is the anticipated level of intervention needed to promote success?
Planning for the world of work	What are some of the existing jobs in the community that the student can learn to do?
	What are some of the work tasks that could be carved or created for the student to do in the community?
	What area businesses may have a need for a service that the student could provide?
	What are the names of businesses where the student would like to work?
Student evaluation and curriculum development	Where is the student in terms of vocational awareness, and is additional career exploration needed?
	What work skills can be taught in order to improve functioning and promote a successful vocational future?
	What workplace values can be taught in order to improve functioning and promote a successful vocational future?

Although the teachers in this study stated they used students' present levels of functioning to determine IEP goals, all of them also reported that they wrote annual goals to fit the content of the curriculum they taught. At the intermediate level, teachers may be confronted with the dilemma of whether to meet students' needs or to meet watered down general education course requirements. The trend to require higher academic standards for receipt of a high school diploma may force special educators to emphasize academic curricula and spend less time on career and vocational experiences (Al Otaiba & Hosp, 2004). Postsecondary outcomes of students with intellectual disabilities indicate that waiting until high school to provide students with life skills may be too little, too late. Preparing all students in systematic and deliberate ways for their adult future must commence early in their schooling. (1993, p. 36)

Table 16.3 lists curriculum recommendations for youth with disabilities.

Most curriculum guides present activities in general terms, but good teachers can design creative ways to involve members of the community in the learning process, especially for instruction in vocational, community, and recreational domains. Table 16.4 contains an example of what questions one might ask to generate a student profile that could help in setting transition goals. Bouck (2004) observed that students with mild intellectual disabilities are often a forgotten group.

Table 16.2. Strategies for effective transition planning

Strategy	Rationale	Example	Resources
1. Hold high expectations for students.	Students truly shine when working on goals that matter to them. If our perceptions of students' abilities are based on their performance on goals unrelated to their own visions for the future, then we need to understand that these perceptions are probably not accurate. When a student says that he or she wants to work in a particular career field, or have a home of his or her own, we need to expect the best because we most likely have not seen what the young person is capable of achieving.	When Elaine shares her dreams for the future, they include a desire to go to college. Most of her teachers were quick to believe that this was an unrealistic goal for her because her performance on most achievement and aptitude tests determined that she had a moderate cognitive disability. Elaine's mother, however, believed that Elaine could go to college. Through the efforts of the coordinator in the Office for Students with Disabilities, she was accepted on a provisional basis. The accommodations that were put in place allowed her to succeed in a way that others had not expected.	For more information about alternative ways to assess student performance, see Wiggins (1993) and Herman, Aschbacher, and Winters (1992).
2. Prepare students for their transition planning meetings.	Student presence does not necessarily ensure student involvement in the individualized education program (IEP) or individualized transition plan (ITP) process. Students need to understand their roles in the process. They need opportunities to role-play, to participate in the information gathering that takes place before these meetings, to discover their options, and to talk with possible support providers.	Jack's transition coordinator met at his home with Jack and his mother before the IEP/ITP meeting. They discussed Jack's plans for his future and the ways that he could discuss those issues during the meeting. They assigned priorities to the goals that Jack wanted to accomplish in the coming year, so that he could talk about those that were most important to him. They brainstormed possible objections to working on these chosen goals, as well as Jack's rebuttals to those objections. The role playing even helped him redefine certain goals when his mother or the coordinator provided additional information. Jack was well-prepared to discuss his own goals and not answer, "I don't know" when asked these questions during the meeting itself.	For more information on how to help students prepare for their transition planning meetings, some of the self-determination curriculums could be useful. Some examples include ChoiceMaker Curriculum (Martin & Marshall, 1995), Learning with a PURPOSE (Serna & Lausmith, 1995), and I PLAN (Van Reusen & Bos, 1990).

| 3. | Allow students to make important decisions about the IEP/ITP planning meeting, including who should participate, where the meeting should be held, and at what time. | Allowing students to be part of making decisions about the meeting sends the message that the meeting is really the student's meeting, not just an adults' meeting about the student. | Barbara talks about the differences between her planning meeting this year and the one she participated in the previous year. Her teacher this year discussed the meeting preparation with her, allowing her to decide where the meeting should be held (her apartment), at what time (7:00 P.M., so that her father could also attend), and whom they should invite (they jointly developed a list of eight people). Barbara arranged for refreshments at the meeting and purchased a new tablecloth that she had admired on a shopping trip with her mother. At the meeting, participants were relaxed, and everyone felt comfortable in contributing to the discussion—but the work still was accomplished. | Some examples of person-centered planning models include Personal Futures Planning (Mount & Zwernick, 1988), Making Action Plans (formerly MacGill Action Planning System) (Forest & Lusthaus, 1987), Essential Lifestyle Planning (O'Brien, 1987), and Group Action Planning (Turnbull & Turnbull, 1996). |
| 4. | Expand your own ideas about what is possible. | Too often, adults make decisions for students with disabilities based on their own experiences, preferences, and ideas about what is possible. It's human nature to do so; but if we want to support student self-determination, we need to understand what is important to the student—his or her preferences and ideas about what is possible, not our own. | Kathleen was someone who liked being a leader. When given an opportunity that matched her desires, she was eager to pursue it. Her mother and her teacher were not comfortable being leaders, and instead felt more comfortable in watching others try something new first, and then deciding if they wanted to pursue it. To paraphrase Robert Frost, they preferred the road well traveled, while Kathleen preferred to cut a path where one did not previously exist. Kathleen had many people interested in helping her meet her goals, and she had an opportunity to be the first student with Down syndrome to earn her final high school credits on a university campus. A professor there was willing to work with other college students, the university office for students with disabilities, and her high school teacher to adapt, support, and modify college classes so that Kathleen could meet her dream of attending college classes. Her teacher and her mother needed to attend to Kathleen's desire to take advantage of this opportunity, rather than hold back because of their own preferences or styles of learning. | For more information on what parents and teachers can do to facilitate self-determination, see Davis and Wehmeyer (1991) for a list of suggestions, such as "Walk the tightrope between protection and independence" (p. 1). See Kennedy (1996) for a description of the trust factors that are essential for self-determination. |

(continued)

423

Table 16.2. *(continued)*

Strategy	Rationale	Example	Resources
5. Involve community members as participants on transition planning teams.	The planning for students' transition from school to adult life should involve identifying necessary supports that will ensure that students' dreams become a reality. Who would be better able to provide information about what supports are already available than someone who is already a member of the community?	Amy was interested in helping others and wanted to find an agency that would accept the help she was offering. An employee at the local United Way office was invited to attend Amy's transition planning meeting. Amy called her, introduced herself, and told her what she would like to do. The employee offered to call some of the agencies that she thought might need the help Amy was offering, so that she could bring that information to the planning meeting. At the meeting, she shared information with Amy and the team members about three local agencies, and Amy was able to make a decision about which met her needs.	For further information on promoting community partnerships, see National Center for Research in Vocational Education (1998), Hanley-Maxwell and Millington (1992), and Benz, Lindstrom, and Halpern (1995).
6. Encourage students to attend transition fairs or other information-gathering events and help them prepare for their participation.	Students need information about adult support agencies and the types of supports they provide to make a truly informed choice regarding which agency will provide support to them after high school. Transition fairs provide an opportunity for students to begin to collect information about different agencies because representatives from most adult support agencies participate. Preparation could take the form of helping students decide what questions to ask, role playing the questioning of adults, and brain-storming ways to ask for clarification or follow-up questions.	Duane's mother was determined that he make decisions about his adult life now that he was 18 years old. Before the transition fair, she talked with him about possible agency supports he might need to make his dreams a reality. Duane did not know what supports were available to help him obtain his own apartment after graduation, nor did he know what supports he would need for living on his own. Duane and his mother developed a list of questions to ask agency representatives to first determine what supports each agency provided. Duane went to the fair and spoke directly with representatives for all agencies that provided supports for community living, asking questions and writing down answers.	For further information on helping students learn about community resources and make choices about them, see Powers, et al. (1996) and Wehmeyer, Agran, and Hughes (1998).
7. Use a portfolio-based assessment process to document student achievement.	A portfolio assessment process can accomplish two important goals: It allows students to demonstrate what they know and have learned in a manner that best demonstrates that knowledge, as opposed to trying to make assumptions about student progress based on his or her ability to take a test.	Sue wanted to go to college and learn skills to be a teacher or teaching assistant. Her writing ability was not very good, which might prevent her from being admitted to a college program. She and her team worked with an admission counselor to determine what skills she needed to be accepted into the college, and the team then discussed Sue's strengths to determine how to demonstrate that she had these	For further information on the use of portfolios, see Choate (1993), Herman et al. (1992), and Poteet, Choate, and Stewart (1993).

424

It provides an opportunity for the student to be a more active participant in the meeting if he or she shares the portfolio with team members as a way of addressing current level of performance.

8. Focus on supports rather than programs.

When transition planning focuses primarily on matching students with pre-existing programs, the possibility of students attaining their adult lifestyle goals decreases dramatically. By determining first what a student's goals are, and then the level of supports necessary to make that a reality, teams can find new possibilities emerging.

competencies. She took the Scholastic Aptitude Test (SAT), like other college applicants, but she also included a portfolio of her best work from school. This portfolio included a videotape of Sue from school-sponsored work experience in teaching a group of first graders in a church-sponsored religion instruction class.

Steve knew that he wanted to be an auto mechanic, like all the other men in his family. There was a class based at the local vocational/technical school that helped prepare other students who had that career goal, but this class had never accepted anyone with a disability—and Steve had a disability. Instead, students with disabilities entered a community transition program, and they were taught on-the-job in various fast food restaurants and retail store settings near the high school. His transition planning team determined that the physical disability would not prevent his participation in the auto-mechanics class. His upper body strength allowed him to transfer himself in and out of his wheelchair, and he could use tools once he was under the car. His limited reading ability meant that he would need modifications to the written manuals, as well as the written tests that were currently part of the program. The auto-mechanics teacher agreed to work with the special education teacher to make such modifications, and Steve became the first student with a disability to enter a vocational education program in that large urban school district.

For further information on the principle of normalization, see the classical works by Nirje (1972) and Wolfensburger (1972), both of whom advocated that people with disabilities should have lives that follow the same rhythms as people without disabilities. Nirje's work came from Swedish law, and Wolfensburger has been credited with bringing this concept to the United States.

Schwartz (1992) described a "conceptual revolution" in the way that society perceives people with disabilities and, consequently, in the way that the community supports them. This book is a good reference for understanding the difference between supports and programs.

(continued)

Table 16.2. *(continued)*

Strategy	Rationale	Example	Resources
9. Provide opportunities for students to explore their communities and career interests.	Students need exposure to lots of experiences to make informed choices regarding their dreams for an adult lifestyle. Until they know what choices are available, they may make a decision that is based on limited information.	John wanted to be a pilot because whenever he flew on an airplane, he heard the pilot's voice. John did not know about the numerous other jobs that were possibilities at an airport or in working for an airline company. A family friend who was a pilot arranged to give John a tour of an airport one day and introduced him to many other people who worked for the airport or an airline company. They answered John's questions, showed him what they did, and gave him a clearer picture of the job possibilities, as well as the education and other requirements necessary to obtain a job and keep it. John realized that being a pilot was not the best decision for him. He was convinced that he would like a job based at an airport, so that he would not have to travel with work, but could still be associated with the travel world. He secured a part-time job at the airport, helping to refuel airplanes and load customer baggage, which provided him with additional hands-on experiences to help him make a more definite career decision.	For further information, see descriptions of job shadowing, mentorships, and other innovative programs to help students learn about careers (e.g., Callahan & Garner, 1997; Rusch & Chadsey, 1998).

From "Supporting student voices in transition planning" by C.A. Thoma, *TEACHING Exceptional Children*, *31*(5), 1999, pp. 4–9. Copyright 1999 by the Council for Exceptional Children. Reprinted by permission.

426

Table 16.3. Curriculum recommendations for children with disabilities

Dos

1. Ask each student the types of activities and skills that he or she would like to work to develop during part of every day.
2. Actively involve students in career education and job-seeking activities.
3. Invite outside speakers from different careers to come into the classroom and share information about their jobs. Encourage students to visit different jobs to gain an understanding of what is involved in holding a job.
4. Teach students how to complete job applications.
5. Teach skilled students how to develop résumés.
6. Make sure every student has a Social Security card.
7. Teach students how to look for jobs in the classified advertisements.
8. Teach students how to find different recreational activities and events in the newspaper. Take them to some of these activities and events and teach them to involve themselves in community activities.
9. Teach students how to get around town using public transportation or learning how to identify a network of people who will give car rides.

Don'ts

1. Do not rely heavily on workbooks, which are essentially simulations of what the real work activity is.
2. Do not rely on large volumes of ditto sheets and desk work.
3. Do not try to simulate regular education academic-based curricula.
4. Do not spend extensive time doing blackboard work.
5. Do not let students repeatedly fail tasks or activities. Instead try to modify the tasks or make them easier or more interesting.
6. Do not segregate the more capable from the least capable students in class. Slower students can learn from more capable students. Also, it is not necessarily true that because students are slow in one area that they will be slow in another area or that they will stay slow in a given area.
7. Do not plan curricula on the basis of a curriculum guide or book that comes from a state agency or book publisher. Plan curricula around the students' needs and interests.
8. Do not arrange teaching environments so the teacher does all the teaching and the students do all of the listening. Design environments where students are heavily involved in the learning process.
9. Do not mass duplicate IEPs.

It is also essential that each student has a personalized IEP, not a program that has been mass produced for all of the students in a class as has been beautifully noted by Wood (2006) and Smith, Polloway, Patton, and Dowdy (2005). Although this is initially more costly in terms of personnel time and planning, it would cost more in the long run not to individualize these programs. Community-referenced skills training that stimulates students' need for independent living must take the place of nonfunctional curricula, which has limited community integration value (Branham, Collins, Schuster, & Kleinert, 1999; McGlashing-Johnson, Agran, Sitlington, Cavin, & Wehmeyer, 2003).

Consider Michael's case. Two possible scenarios can be unfolded for Michael depending on what type of help and support he receives. In Michael's case study, each of these concepts is illustrated. Readers should pay careful attention to the differences in student outcomes as the old and new modes of teaching are demonstrated.

It cannot be emphasized enough that flexible, empowering, outcome-oriented curricula planning is needed. In Michael's case, the second scenario proved successful because of two important factors. First and most important, the family and student had an equal and active role in the decision-making process. Second, the student could take ownership and pride in his schedule because it was independently tailored to meet his needs. Community site trainings were not field trips; rather, they were strategies

Table 16.4.   Questions to generate student profile data

Interests and preferences	What are _____(student's name)_____'s favorite things to do at home?
	What does _____(student's name)_____ dislike doing at home?
	Describe your dream job for _____(student's name)_____.
Skills and abilities	What type of chores does _____(student's name)_____ perform?
	When _____(state home activity)_____ how long does _____(student's name)_____ stay on task before needing a break?
	How long is the break?
	How quickly does _____(student's name)_____ do it; would you say at a slow pace, average pace?
	What are _____(student's name)_____'s skills and abilities?
	How do you see _____(student's name)_____'s talents being used in a work setting?
	What equipment or tools does _____(student's name)_____ use at home?
	Related to learning something new, what are _____(student's name)_____'s greatest accomplishments?
	How long did it take _____(student's name)_____ to learn it?
	How was s/he taught?
On-the-job supports	What accommodation(s) does _____(student's name)_____ use at home?
Ideas for future work (These questions are most suitable for students in their last year of school.)	Name businesses where you would like to see _____(student's name)_____ employed and do you have a connection at any of these businesses?
	What days of week and times of day is _____(student's name)_____ available to work?
	What type of transportation options are available to assist _____(student's name)_____ with getting to and from work?
Student evaluation and curriculum development	Does the student have insight into what type of work s/he would like to perform?
	What skills can be taught or practiced to promote a successful vocational future?

used for goal attainment. Michael's IEP was not photocopied from a standard master; it was an individualized legal and binding document that was produced through collaboration.

Michael's experience points to the need for a plan and structure. His experience also supports research that underscores the importance of youth gaining employment skills as part of the school experience. As illustrated by Table 16.5, Patton, de la Garza, and Harmon (1997) presented an excellent series of 13 instructional units and lessons that teachers can utilize that emphasize work over academics. These units, when combined with direct hands-on experiences suggested by Branham and colleagues (1999) in community-based training, provide a very contemporary approach to curriculum development.

The ultimate goal of education is to prepare students to function in their future environments. Therefore, schools should analyze the demands of these environments and organize curricula that prepare students to function with as much independence as possible. The curricula must provide principles and generic skills that are applicable

Michael is a 16-year-old student in an eighth-grade special education program. He attends a classroom for students with intellectual disabilities. Michael has been in similar classrooms since he was tested and found eligible for special education placement 6 years ago. Before that time, Michael attended general day care in his community and general kindergarten and first-grade classes. Michael's first-grade teacher referred Michael for testing because he was not mastering his basic skills at the same rate as other students. He also displayed some signs of aggression toward other students and figures of authority. Michael experienced more and more frustration as time passed. By the end of first grade, Michael had been labeled with a behavior problem and as a poor learner.

Michael's mother, Ms. Chen, was contacted sporadically about her son's progress and problems. She was asked to come to school only to give her permission for testing and other administrative procedures. The teachers did not make any effort to include Ms. Chen as a part of Michael's planning team. It was assumed that his behavior was typical for a student from a low socioeconomic status and a broken home (Michael's older brother had also utilized special education) and that his parent did not want to be involved in the process.

Michael had an IEP that looked like every other student's IEP in the class. It included objectives pertaining to the mastery of academics, such as sentence dissection,

for solving problems and meeting challenges in adult life (Chadsey-Rusch, DeStefano, O'Reilly, Gonzalez, & Collet-Klingenberg, 1992).

COMMUNITY-BASED INSTRUCTION: DEFINITION AND RATIONALE

In discussing curriculum strategies for youth with intellectual disabilities, one must also consider the impact of CBI, especially for those students with greater support needs. CBI is a proven effective means of helping students learn functional curriculum skills (see Dymond, 2004; White & Weiner, 2004).

CBI is defined as the involvement of instructors, therapists, paraprofessionals, and other personnel teaching instructional objectives in natural environments such as nonprofit agencies, restaurants, shopping malls, recreation centers, worksites, and other age-appropriate settings in the neighborhood and community. These objectives are established for the purpose of fostering and promoting social and community inclusion consistent with contemporary philosophy and statutes. Gaumer, Morningstar, and Clark (2004) noted:

> Community-based transition (CBT) programs are designed as an option on the continuum of services offered to students with disabilities. They are not designed to replace inclusive education for high school students but, instead, expand this inclusion to age-appropriate community settings for young adults (Fialka, n.d.). Thus, CBT programs provide an opportunity for students to receive the best of both worlds—inclusive education during the traditional high school years and a comprehensive community-based program after commencement but before official graduation (Izzo, Johnson, Levitz, & Aaron, 1998). Specifically, community-based settings allow students to expand social relationships with age-appropriate peers, ongoing educational experiences, recreation and leisure activities, and work experiences (Grigal, Neubert, & Moon, 2001, pp. 132–133)

Functional community skills are typically taught in the community. Research has repeatedly demonstrated that systematic instruction in the community leads to learning and retaining new skills better than in a facility (see Gee, Graham, Sailor, & Goetz, 1995; Inge & Dymond, 1994; McDonnell, Hardman, Hightower, Keifer-O'Donnell, & Drew, 1993; Sowers & Powers, 1995; Wehman & Kregel, 2004). Learning skills in the community allows individuals to use the actual materials involved with the activity and to learn skills within the context of the normal sights, sounds, smells, lighting, and distractions that are associated with the natural environment.

American history, civics, and algebra. Michael was not interested in school or his studies. He fell further and further behind academically. He started to miss a lot of school and was always in the principal's office for one thing or another.

Under pressure from the central office to produce "good" statistics, Michael was promoted to the next higher grade one year but then retained the following year for no apparent educational rationale. The teacher completed and mailed his IEP home, and Michael's mother was required to sign it and mail it back to school. Michael and his mom were not involved in any functional curricula or individualized planning for classroom activities or community transition training.

By 16 years of age, Michael was very streetwise, had no regard for figures of authority, intimidated other students, and did not attend any classes or engage in any constructive learning when he went to school. At this point, Michael's mother refused to go to the school for a conference because she felt that the school system had failed her child. Initially, she felt that a special placement was in his best interest and would allow him to catch up in school and afford him some good survival skills. She felt helpless and suspicious about why her involvement was solicited at this late stage. Michael's teacher was contacted 1 week later. Michael had been arrested for murder. Before the school year ended, Michael was sentenced to 99 years in jail.

Many individuals are unable to generalize skills learned under simulated conditions (i.e., ones that use artificial materials and settings that approximate the real thing) to the actual environments and situations where they are normally performed. For example, an instructor in a classroom that houses a mock grocery store may find that students learn to grocery shop appropriately in the classroom but fail to use the skill correctly when taken to an actual grocery store. A CBI model overcomes this problem by teaching skills in the location where they are expected to be performed. Therefore, the main rationale and benefits of a CBI approach are

1. Teaches skills that allow the individuals to more fully participate in activities outside the adult day center setting with peers and family members

2. Exposes individuals to a variety of experiences, thus broadening the choices available to them and increasing their ability to affect their environment

3. Provides opportunities to learn social skills with members of the greater community (not just family, training center staff, and other customers)

4. Enhances quality of life by increasing community inclusion, independence, and participation

5. Prepares individuals for adulthood by teaching skills that will have longitudinal usage

6. Raises the family's expectations for their family member with a disability

7. Increases the community's expectations for individuals with disabilities

8. Helps day center staff and other team members to determine preferences and plan for community-based opportunities that reflect those preferences

Functional Community Skills

Functional community skills are skills that are immediately applicable to daily life. Some of the key qualities that define a functional skill include the following:

- It is performed within the context of a "real" activity.

- The activity is meaningful to the individual.

- People without disabilities believe the activity serves a purpose.

Michael is a 16-year-old student in a secondary special education program. He is placed in a classroom for students with intellectual disabilities but spends most of his time in the community where he is employed as a bus boy in a local restaurant. At school, he attends general elective classes, such as physical education and woodworking. He is also involved in functional academics and community training activities. Both Michael and his mother, Ms. Chen, have been very active in Michael's curricula planning. They are very satisfied with his class placement and work training.

Even though Ms. Chen is a single parent and once attended a similar class, she feels that she can manage her son's education and assist in making sound educational and vocational decisions for him. As a matter of fact, Ms. Chen has signed an agreement with the school to be responsible for making sure that Michael is picked up from work because he gets off work after school hours. In turn, the school's aide, Mrs. Jefferson, drops Michael off at his job in the morning on her way to the community training sites.

Michael and his mother have decided that he will stay in school until he turns 18. He will then receive a special diploma and leave the school system with a transition plan in place for entry into the work force.

- If the person is unable to perform the skill for him- or herself, then it will need to be completed by another individual.

- The skill will be utilized throughout the individual's life.

Functional skills also include those activities that show individuals how to participate in future environments. Post, Storey, and Karabin (2002), for example, showed how a man with intellectual disabilities could perform functional work skills using a simple auditory prompt system delivered via headphones.

The definition of *community skills* has evolved with time. Like many other functional skills, there is no *one* set of curricula that identifies the critical skills that all individuals must learn. The skills that are addressed depend on the activities available in one's community and the individual needs and preferences of the person and his or her family. As a result, most discussions regarding the content of community skills instruction focus on the types of environments or activities where skills may be addressed to facilitate participation in the community. The major goal areas of community skills instruction include travel, community safety, grocery shopping, general shopping, eating out, and using services.

White and Weiner (2004) described a study that looked at the relationship between community-based training and transition outcomes. The participants of the 3-year study included 104 students with severe disabilities in the Orange County, California, public school system who exited school at 21 or 22 years of age. The variables that predicted successful integrated employment at the time of transition (a paid job with co-workers without disabilities at graduation) were duration of community-based training, which included on-the-job training, and age-appropriate physical integration with peers without disabilities. Mental ability as measured by IQ score, behavior problems, physical disability, and participant demographics did not correlate with integrated employment outcome. Transitioning students in integrated age-appropriate school settings, receiving CBI and on-the-job training, demonstrated a 69.2% integrated employment rate postgraduation.

Table 16.6 provides an updated and expanded view of the types of community activities in which individuals engage in their communities. The first three categories (*restaurants/ eateries, grocery stores, retail stores*) focus on places people go to purchase tangible items such as food, clothing, and other necessities. *Services* refer to assistance typically received from specially trained individuals, whereas *public facilities* emphasize services typically provided by the government or nonprofit

Table 16.5. Employability skills instructional units

Unit 1: Preparing To Look For a Job
Lesson 1: Orientation to the Course
Lesson 2: Obtaining Documentation
Lesson 3: Key Parts of a Resume
Lesson 4: References
Lesson 5: Preparing a Resume
Lesson 6: Learning about Job Applications
Lesson 7: Completing a Job Application

Unit 2: What Kind Of Work Would I Like?
Lesson 1: Why Should I Work?
Lesson 2: Finding Out about Different Kinds of Work
Lesson 3: What Am I Interested In?
Lesson 4: What Conditions Would I Like To Work In?

Unit 3: Finding Out About Job Openings
Lesson 1: Job Leads
Lesson 2: Organizing Job Lead Information
Lesson 3: Locating and Using Classified Want Ads
Lesson 4: Reading Classified Want Ads
Lesson 5: Using the Yellow Pages as a Resource
Lesson 6: Using the White Pages as a Resource

Unit 4: Contacting Employers
Lesson 1: Making a Good First Impression
Lesson 2: Practicing Telephone Skills
Lesson 3: Telephoning Employers
Lesson 4: Visiting an Employer

Unit 5: How Do I Interview For a Job?
Lesson 1: Preparing for a Job Interview
Lesson 2: Dressing for a Job Interview
Lesson 3: Preparing for Interview Questions
Lesson 4: Practicing Job Interviews
Lesson 5: Following Up a Job Interview

Unit 6: Handling Paperwork
Lesson 1: Understanding Key Parts of Your Paycheck Stub
Lesson 2: Understanding Deductions from Your Pay
Lesson 3: Reading a Work Schedule
Lesson 4: Reading and Completing a Timecard
Lesson 5: Becoming Familiar with State and Federal Tax Returns

Unit 7: What Makes a Good Employee?
Lesson 1: Positive Worker Traits
Lesson 2: Starting a Job
Lesson 3: Dressing and Grooming Appropriately on the Job
Lesson 4: Taking Initiative on the Job

Unit 8: Getting Along With Others
Lesson 1: Understanding the Role of a Supervisor
Lesson 2: Accepting Criticism from a Supervisor
Lesson 3: What Makes a Good Co-worker?
Lesson 4: Social Skill, "Greeting Your Co-Workers"
Lesson 5: Dealing with Customers

Unit 9: What If I Can't Make It to Work?
Lesson 1: The Four Rules of Good Attendance
Lesson 2: Who to Notify and When
Lesson 3: Notifying Your Supervisor When You Must Be Absent
Lesson 4: Being on Time

Unit 10: How Will I Get to Work?
Lesson 1: Telephoning for Bus Route Information
Lesson 2: Reading Maps and Schedules (Location to Location)

Lesson 3: Reading Maps and Schedules (Reading Time Schedules)
Lesson 4: Selecting a Bus or Trolley Route
Lesson 5: Planning to Transfer
Lesson 6: Safe and Appropriate Behavior When Using Public Transit
Lesson 7: Problem-solving Transportation Problems

Unit 11: Managing Your Personal Finances
Lesson 1: Banking Services
Lesson 2: Choosing a Bank
Lesson 3: Opening a Savings Account
Lesson 4: Making a Deposit
Lesson 5: Withdrawing Money from Your Savings Account
Lesson 6: Reading Your Bank Statement
Lesson 7: Using Your Automated Teller Machine (ATM)

Unit 12: Making Positive Job Changes
Lesson 1: Positive Ways to Handle Stress and "Bad" Days at Work
Lesson 2: Ending a Job in a Positive Way
Lesson 3: Giving Written Notice of Your Resignation

Unit 13: What Are My Goals For the Future?
Lesson 1: Thinking About Your Future
Lesson 2: Guidelines for Setting Goals and Making a Plan
Lesson 3: The Individualized Transition Planning Meeting
Lesson 4: Being an Effective Self-Advocate

From "Employability skills + adult agency support + family support + on-the-job support = successful employment" by P.L. Patton, B. de la Garza, and C. Harmon, *TEACHING Exceptional Children, 29*(3), 1997, p. 6. Copyright 1997 by the Council for Exceptional Children. Reprinted by permission.

Table 16.6. Activities in the general community

Restaurants/eateries	Grocery stores	Retail stores	Services	Public facilities	Recreation facilities	Volunteer work	Transportation
Fast-food restaurants	Convenience grocery stores (e.g., 7-11, small stores associated with gas stations)	Clothing store	Bank	Library	YMCA	Meals on Wheels	School buses
Sit-down restaurants (informal)	Stand-alone grocery stores (e.g., IGA, Wegmans, Price Chopper)	Drug store	Barber shop/hair salon	Church	Recreation center/fitness center	Red Cross	Public buses
Sit-down restaurants (formal)	Grocery stores within mega-stores (e.g., Wal-Mart, K-Mart)	Sporting goods store	Nail salon	Recycling center	Parks	United Way	Taxis
Food courts		Music store	Dry cleaner	Post office	Museums	Food bank	Train/subway
Sidewalk carts (i.e., mobile food stands that set up on the street to sell hot dogs, sandwiches, etc.)		Video store	Laundromat	Department of Motor Vehicles	Skating rink	Nursing homes	Bicycle
Restaurants that deliver		Pet store	Doctor/dentist	Social Security office	Movie theaters	Humane Society	Walking
		Toy and hobby store	Veterinarian	County offices (e.g., voter registration office)	Arcades	Salvation Army	Riding/driving a car
		Mail-order shopping					

Table 16.7.   Sample skills

Skill	Community-referenced instruction
Dressing	Putting on a coat to go into the community; taking off a coat after arriving at the community location (if appropriate); trying on clothes in a department store; changing clothes at the YMCA.
Purchasing	Purchasing items at the drugstore; paying for a game of bowling; purchasing a soda at a restaurant; buying stamps at the post office.
Communicating/understanding pictures	Locating items in the store from a picture grocery list; ordering in a restaurant using a picture menu; presenting a picture to a store clerk to determine the location of a bathroom.

organizations. *Recreation* describes the places where we may choose to spend our leisure time. Activities that allow us to give back to our community through helping others are classified as *volunteer work*. The last category, *transportation*, addresses the methods one might use to gain access to the activities in his or her community.

Table 16.7 lists sample skills that can be taught in community settings.

What Are Major Principles of Community-Based Instruction?

There are four principles that an effective CBI model utilizes:

1. Individualized and person centered

2. Functional or practical

3. Adaptive

4. Ecologically oriented

Individualized and Person-Centered   The concept of person-centered planning has become increasingly popular and is frequently suggested as an approach to promoting individualized service planning. In person-centered planning, environments, services, and supports are tailored to the individual's dreams, wants, and needs. The individual, family, and friends drive person-centered approaches.

Functional or Practical   The second principle of CBI is that objectives be both functional and practical in nature. No matter how good the quality of instruction, how sophisticated the equipment, or how excellent the sites, if the individual is being offered inappropriate skills, then he or she loses the opportunity to benefit from a more useful experience. Common sense suggests that they need to be learning skills that will allow them to be competent at home and in the community rather than spending day after day with, at best, marginal success on a skill that does not build on their strengths or respond to their most pressing needs. Assessment activities and planning will address the following key question: What activities does this person need to perform to be an effective and competent human being in the weeks and months ahead?

Adaptive   In addition to being person centered and functional, CBI must adapt to the specific goals and capabilities of a given individual. It should be obvious that to provide an individual with a functional curriculum, adaptations will be necessary. If the team agrees that a modified objective makes sense, then the goal should be changed. It is unethical and much more problematic to continue providing instruction to people who are not learning because the objective is inappropriate. For example, it may very well be that functioning independently in the community is appropriate as the general area of curriculum, but riding a bus is not the right target objective at this point; instead, crossing the street might be more appropriate.

Ecologically Oriented An ecologically oriented program requires the individual, instructor, and family/residential staff to sit down and discuss the individual's high-priority activities for each of the major living environments. For example, what are the individual's main activities at home and in his or her immediate neighborhood? What are the major activities that the individual performs or wishes to perform in the community (e.g., going to church, shopping for groceries, visiting the mall)? What are the individual's major recreational activities or activities in which the individual has interest? Many potential environments, or subenvironments, can be analyzed for different activities. These activities then provide the foundation for the curriculum objectives. Therefore, if an individual goes with his father to church every Saturday morning to participate in a men's brunch, then the individual might need to place high priority on learning how to perform cleanup activities. The individual could then help the father and participate with other adults in a meaningful activity. An example of a partial ecological inventory for a community grocery store is provided in Figure 16.2.

These four principles of effective CBI design are the glue that hold community training together.

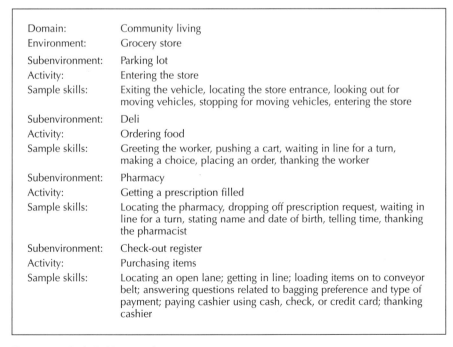

Domain:	Community living
Environment:	Grocery store
Subenvironment:	Parking lot
Activity:	Entering the store
Sample skills:	Exiting the vehicle, locating the store entrance, looking out for moving vehicles, stopping for moving vehicles, entering the store
Subenvironment:	Deli
Activity:	Ordering food
Sample skills:	Greeting the worker, pushing a cart, waiting in line for a turn, making a choice, placing an order, thanking the worker
Subenvironment:	Pharmacy
Activity:	Getting a prescription filled
Sample skills:	Locating the pharmacy, dropping off prescription request, waiting in line for a turn, stating name and date of birth, telling time, thanking the pharmacist
Subenvironment:	Check-out register
Activity:	Purchasing items
Sample skills:	Locating an open lane; getting in line; loading items on to conveyor belt; answering questions related to bagging preference and type of payment; paying cashier using cash, check, or credit card; thanking cashier

Figure 16.2.   Ecological inventory for grocery store.

Program Design of Community-Based Programs

Community-based training must reflect the community in order to prepare individuals with severe disabilities to function more independently. There must be a specific way to gain access to community sites and connect all of the logistics together. A continual assessment of the local community settings helps determine sites in the community. The steps in developing community-based training sites include 1) conducting a community site analysis, 2) identifying profit and nonprofit organizations with the targeted activities and contacting a person such as the Director of Volunteer Services for a community agency, 3) selecting and analyzing appropriate activities for community-based training, 4) scheduling CBI, and 5) designing individualized instructional programs to reflect these activities in different settings in conjunction with case managers.

Conducting a Community Site Analysis   In order to identify different sites, one utilizes staff networks and different companies and agencies in the community, as well as the neighborhood of the student. The telephone directory, newspaper, want ads, follow-up with school graduates, as well as contacting adult services agencies to determine viable community placements, are other strategies. Some potential community contacts include the following:

- Colleges and universities
- State Economic Development Office
- Chamber of Commerce
- Trade associations
- Better Business Bureau
- City and county offices
- Department of Labor
- Telephone book/newspaper classifieds
- Hospitals and retirement centers
- Civic clubs and organizations
- Friends and associates

Once a list of businesses has been generated, initiate contact with the agencies to identify available activities.

Identifying Agency with the Targeted Activities and Contacting the Director of Volunteer Services   Once the local economy has been assessed to determine the possible community settings for individuals with severe disabilities, the instructors must determine where instruction will occur. Initial information to identify potential activities within a setting will be obtained from the personnel director or director of volunteers. Often, this individual will be able to provide written descriptions that can be useful in identifying activities.

Insurance   The transition specialist will discuss insurance coverage and liability issues, as well as the development of a training agreement with the agency. Prior to the implementation of training, the school system should review the insurance policy and ensure that individuals are covered if an accident occurs on a jobsite.

Selecting and Analyzing Appropriate Activities for Community-Based Training

Activities during this phase of establishing a community-based training site include observing others performing similar activities available, selecting tasks that are appropriate to the people who will be receiving training, and actually working the selected activities. A tentative schedule of the activities that they will be performing should be developed, as well as task analyses for skills targeted. Both of these may need modification once specific individuals are assigned to the worksite. Finally, the trainer should negotiate times for the trainees to be on site and a start date. The appendix at the end of this chapter outlines the steps for designing a sample duty schedule that can be utilized for program implementation at the site.

Scheduling Community-Based Instruction

Creative use of school personnel can be used to schedule and transport individuals for CBI. Transportation is always a challenge for administrators and building personnel. Staffing solutions can include using consultants, paraprofessionals, possible volunteers and graduates, staggered training schedules, and utilization of support personnel providing integrated therapy services.

Designing Individualized Instructional Programs

Once the community sites have been identified and a schedule for placement is determined, the instructor must design instructional programs that outline how each person will be taught the activities. Included in the design will be 1) specific training objectives, 2) individualized task analyses, 3) data collection guidelines, 4) instructional strategies, 5) reinforcement procedures, and 6) program modifications.

U.S. Department of Labor regulations must be consulted to guarantee that students are behaving as trainees, rather than as employees, among other issues (see Table 16.8). Only at the end of community-based vocational training, when a student is placed in paid employment, does a change in status from trainee to employee occur.

The goal of community-based vocational training is assessment and instruction, not development of proficiency in a single job. One of the issues of concern is whether this benefits the business training site. In fact, many assert that community-based vocational training with its legal requirements mandated by the Fair Labor Standards Act of 1938 (PL 75-718; see Table 16.8) may actually impede the functioning of the business for the following reasons:

- Students usually train with employees, which may impede the employees from completing their job responsibilities.

- Students do not perform up to usual employee expectations, and there is a reduced production rate or increased instances of materials being ruined, which causes waste for the business training site.

Table 16.8. Vocational trainee legal requirements

The Fair Labor Standards Act (1938) defines situations in which students with disabilities may be considered "trainees," rather than "employees," while participating in community-based vocational training. The act states that each of the following six criteria must be met in order for the student to be considered a trainee:

1. The training, even if it includes the actual operation of the employer's facility, is similar to that given in vocational schools.
2. The training is for the benefit of the trainees.
3. The trainees do not displace regular employees but work under their close supervision.
4. The employer providing the training derives no immediate advantage from the activities of the trainees, and on occasion his or her operation may actually be impeded.
5. The trainees are not necessarily entitled to a job at the conclusion of the training period.
6. The employer and the trainees understand that the trainees or students are not entitled to wages for the time spent in training.

- New students are continuously starting with various job titles in a business and training program—a turnover that impedes business.

- Students do only portions of employees' full job descriptions.

- This model of programming operates on a zero-reject basis, so students of all ability levels are on the sites.

- Collection of data concerning independent performance is critical to documenting maintenance of trainee status. The U.S. Department of Labor's position is that if a student can perform a job description independently, from that point on, the student is providing a benefit to the business. Documentation of students' progress toward independence is provided through regularly collected data in the areas of level of supervision, work adjustment behaviors, specific task acquisition skills, and production rates. School personnel should keep anecdotal data or descriptive notes at the end of each instructional session concerning work quality, type of support needed, and incidents of maladaptive behavior.

- There should be a clear understanding on the part of the employer that there is no guarantee of work to be performed or completed by the students. This should be noted in the agreements between the businesses and the school districts.

- Differentiated training sites and potential employment sites must be maintained. If employers are seen as using the community-based vocational training program as a training ground from which to hire employees, then the employer is benefiting from the process. The U.S. Department of Labor usually asks each employer how many students he or she has hired in order to determine if the employer is using the program as a market to find new employees, thereby overriding the training purposes of the program. If a business is located in a rural area where there are limited employment options, however, then a student may be hired for a paid position in a training site, which is acceptable as long as this does not become a regular practice.

- If a student holds a part-time job outside of school hours, no job training may occur within the same job title for which he or she is employed.

- Student trainees are not to supplant usual employees or to cause employees to have reductions in work hours. While at the site, students may complete a variety of tasks; however, these should not equal the job description of a usual worker. Students often perform parts of jobs, rather than complete jobs. At times, students may be paired so that two individuals "job share" in order to perform tasks. No employee's job description changes as a result of the training program. The training program, therefore, does not alter the crew structure of the business.

Clearly, the U.S. Department of Labor's regulations are complex. All personnel involved in community-based vocational training, including administrators, teachers, and paraprofessionals, should have a clear understanding of the issues before they implement community-based vocational instruction.

IMPLEMENTING INDIVIDUALIZED TRANSITION
PLANS FOR YOUTH WITH INTELLECTUAL DISABILITIES

During the 1980s and early 1990s, much attention was focused on the postschool adjustment of special education students—a movement that stems from the discouraging patterns of postsecondary employment of youth with disabilities.

As a result of these concerns, federal initiatives are being implemented to ensure structured, formalized planning for postsecondary outcomes of students with disabilities. The Individuals with Disabilities Education Act (IDEA) Amendments of 1997 (PL 105-17) and 2004 (PL 108-446) include transition planning as one of the services that should be accessible to all special education students. *Transition services* are defined as coordinated sets of activities for students designed with an outcomes-oriented process that promotes smooth movement from school to postschool activities.

In transition planning it is particularly important that these students be included in all of the planning stages. In many cases, these students have distinct opinions about what they want to do vocationally, socially, academically, and residentially. However, students sometimes have unrealistic views about the types of jobs they can perform. The teacher's role is to help these students to understand the requirements and expectations of various jobs and to identify realistic goals by including career exploration in the curriculum. While helping the student to develop realistic job expectations, teachers should also take into consideration the types of jobs about which the student exhibits interest or distaste. For example, many students find work in fast-food restaurants to be stigmatizing and demeaning but are very comfortable working in hotels because they are less likely to run into their peers while working. Implementing career exploration goals into IEPs can help target appropriate vocational and community training objectives and alleviate unrealistic expectations about job choices.

Social skills training should also be a part of the transition planning process for students with intellectual disabilities, many of whom have problems with managing their behavior appropriately (Crites & Dunn, 2004). Transition planning goals should reflect the teacher's effort to work with students to develop coping strategies and to identify community services that may further alleviate problems.

Finally, postsecondary education is a realistic outcome of transition training for some students with intellectual disabilities (Getzel & Wehman, 2005). For cases in which the student and his or her family have chosen higher education as a transition planning outcome, vocational and community-referenced skills should continue to be

Peter is a 19-year-old senior labeled with mild intellectual disabilities. He has a full-scale Wechsler Adult Intelligence Score of 66. Peter's family transferred from Kansas to Virginia last summer. His adoptive parents are professionals and have given him many advantages. Peter was adopted at the age of 8. His mother was a behavioral technician at a group facility for people with disabilities when she met Peter. His father is a lawyer. Peter's biological mother had intellectual disabilities and was only 15 when he was born.

Peter has a driver's license and works part time stocking shelves at Toys R Us. He will be 20 when he graduates from high school. His parents would like to see him go to VoTech or to a VR sponsored program for training. His mother has done a wonderful job of training Peter for independent living: he cooks, cares for his own clothes, irons, cleans, and shops. Peter uses a calculator for math and is ready for more sophisticated computations. This past year he was an assistant trainer for football, ran track, and also belonged to the Nautilus Club. Peter's parents think he will eventually live independently with support and are in no hurry to see him move out. A trust was established when Peter was adopted to provide for him when his parents have passed on. There are no siblings, and other relatives are distant.

taught; however, academic preparation is very important. Teachers must be sure that students are prepared to take minimum competency and other tests that are offered in general classrooms.

The most important thing to remember while working with students with intellectual disabilities is that they can and should make their wants and desires known (Thoma & Getzel, 2005). Professionals must know how to draw out the best in each student as he or she makes decisions, acquires new skills, plans, and resolves conflicts.

Once a student's wishes and desires have been obtained, an interagency transition team should be formed to design a transition plan. These representatives should be from the local school division (e.g., administration, special and vocational education); VR; mental health and mental retardation agencies; private rehabilitation facilities; postsecondary education institutions; and parents, students, and employers. Individuals with intellectual disabilities usually require these resources, or at least some of them, during the transition planning process.

Each education team member has a role in planning transition. The roles interact, resulting in a collaboration of ideas and resources with each role being equally important. The special education teacher is responsible for the provision of functional school- and community-based training, retrieval and analysis of data, and serving as the educational consultant to the team. The rehabilitation counselor's role is to provide funding for adaptive equipment and transportation needs related to employment and to participate in the assessment process. The school administrator's role includes facilitating CBI and transportation and promoting parent, personnel, and public awareness training programs. The role of the service coordinator involves providing follow-along services after graduation; advising all parties about policies associated with Social Security benefits, medical benefits, and employment incentives; and working closely with families throughout the transition process. The role of the vocational education teacher includes providing specific training skills, locating job training sites, and assisting in the collection and analysis of data from vocational evaluations. The employer provides input regarding business community needs and access to job training sites. All of these representatives of various agencies work together to plan and project the most efficient and productive outcomes for students and their families (Sarkees-Wircenski & Wircenski, 1994).

The student and his or her family are the most important partners in the transition planning process. With foresight and planning of transition services, students with disabilities can look forward to brighter futures. Students should provide information about the jobs they want, how they want to spend free time, and how they wish to spend their money (Wehman & Kregel, 2004). Parents' and students' responsibilities to the planning team include conducting home training, advocating for full community integration, and participating in the selection of IEP transition planning process.

As the evaluation is completed, professionals, parents, and students should feel that something special has been accomplished in the entire planning process (see Chapter 3). These visions need to take into account the different ways to include youth with intellectual disabilities into the mainstream of school activities as well as classrooms. Inclusion must be planned—it will not happen by chance.

EVALUATING TRANSITION OUTCOMES FOR YOUTH WITH INTELLECTUAL DISABILITIES

The most common method of evaluating transition outcomes is to conduct a follow-up study of graduates, school dropouts, and people who "age out" of high school (Sitlington & Frank, 1998). For individuals with significant intellectual disabilities, follow-up studies indicate high levels of unemployment and underemployment, low enrollment in postsecondary training, and continued dependent family living (Bove, Nevin, Paolucci-Whitcomb, & McNeil, 1991; Wehman, Kregel, & Seyfarth, 1985). Frank, Sitlington, Cooper, and Cool (1990) conducted a survey of recent graduates with intellectual disabilities in Iowa and found that slightly more than 8% of the total group interviewed met their criteria for being successful as adults. Individuals are leaving educational programs and exiting to waiting lists and an adult services system unprepared for the quality or quantity of needed services (Sitlington & Clark, 2006; Sitlington & Frank, 2003).

The majority of postschool outcome assessments analyze the employment, postsecondary school enrollment, and residential status of individuals with disabilities (Wittenburg & Maag, 2002). Most employment surveys ask questions regarding employment status, current wages, hours worked, benefits received, and employment history. Independent living outcomes are measured by where and with whom the individual lives. Postsecondary education questions center on enrollment in courses and completion of degree and certificate requirements. For individuals with significant intellectual disabilities, these measures should be expanded to include an analysis of the quality of life and the community integration of the individual. Only then can the success of transition be truly assessed.

In the area of employment, workplace inclusion is critical (Wehman, 2003), and the following questions must be answered during outcome evaluation: Are individuals with significant intellectual disabilities merely working alongside co-workers without disabilities or are they truly socially integrated into the culture of the workplace? Do individuals with significant intellectual disabilities have the opportunity to develop friendships and establish social networks? Is the employment environment conducive to the development of such relationships? What effect does inclusion have on individuals, their co-workers, and the business? Do individuals with disabilities have friendships and supports outside of the workplace? Answers to these questions need further research and would be useful in developing future programs and priorities.

For individuals with intellectual disabilities, integration in community living should not be measured by independent living (Condeluci, 1996), as most individuals with significant intellectual disabilities require lifelong support in this area (Nisbet, Clark, & Covert, 1991). Instead, questions should be asked about participation in decision making and choices (Newton, Horner, Ard, LeBaron, & Sappington, 1994; Newton, Olson, Horner, & Ard, 1996). These questions include the following: Who decides how income is spent? Who does the grocery shopping? To which environments outside the home do individuals with significant intellectual disabilities have access? How frequently do individuals participate in outside activities? With whom do they spend the majority of time? Do they have friends? Do they spend time with friends without disabilities? Are recreational activities planned by others? Are the recreational activities ones in which the general community participates, or are they planned specifically for individuals with disabilities?

Consider a rapidly spreading national program called Best Buddies. Best Buddies Colleges pairs people with intellectual disabilities in one-to-one friendships with college students. Without friends and family, we are alone. In the past, individuals with intellectual disabilities have not had the opportunity to have friends outside of their own environment. By becoming a College Buddy, volunteers offer a buddy the chance to explore a new way of life (West, Wehman, & Wehman, 2005).

Best Buddies Colleges is the premise on which the international organization of Best Buddies began. Social experiences and relationships are a part of life; unfortunately, individuals with intellectual disabilities have historically been excluded from many of the social opportunities that most people enjoy. College chapters are active in more than 360 campuses worldwide. Each chapter is a registered student organization on its college campus and is led by a college buddy director.

HELPING INDIVIDUALS WITH INTELLECTUAL DISABILITIES ENTER INCLUSIVE EMPLOYMENT

For a more in-depth analysis of transition outcomes, it is useful to explore the competitive or supported work potential of people with intellectual disabilities, which has become an increased reality. Supported employment (SE) is one program specifically designed to assist people with the most significant disabilities to achieve competitive, community-integrated employment. SE first received public funding through the Rehabilitation Act Amendments of 1986 (PL 99-509). It has enjoyed steadily increasing popularity since its inception and has achieved carefully documented positive outcomes (Wehman, Revell, & Brooke, 2003; Wehman, Revell, & Kregel, 1998), although in recent years there has been a market slow down from segregated to integrated work options (Braddock, Rizzolo, & Hemp, 2004). The major premise of an SE program is that many people with significant disabilities need some additional support at the jobsite to work successfully. Cimera's research (1998) even showed that SE for workers with intellectual disabilities is more cost-effective than sheltered employment. Through the use of employment specialists, mentors, co-workers, and employers, the

Community based	
Community-based network	**Integrated employment**
A program in which individuals engage in recreational, skill-training, or volunteer activities in settings where most people do not have disabilities (e.g., community integration, community participation services).	A community-based job in which most people do not have disabilities (e.g., supported or competitive employment).
Facility-based network	**Facility-based work**
A program in which primary faocus is skill-training activities of daily living, recreation, and/or professional therapies (e.g., occupational therapy, physical therapy), in a setting where most people have disabilities (e.g., day activity, day habilitation).	Employment that takes place in a facility where most people have disabilities, with continuous job-related supports and supervision (e.g., extended employment, sheltered workshops, work activity).

Nonwork ——————————————————————————————————— Work

Facility based

Figure 16.3. Community- versus noncommunity-based activities. (From Dreilinger, D., Gilmore, D.S., & Butterworth, J. [2001]. National day and employment service trends in MR/DD agencies. *Research to Practice*, 7[3], 1; reprinted by permission.)

impediments to employment that prospective workers face are reduced, and their abilities and work potentials are emphasized through supports designed at the workplace (McDermott, Martin, & Butkus, 1999).

Figure 16.3 presents community- versus noncommunity-based activities and how one might characterize the different outcomes that are experienced by many people with intellectual disabilities. However, it is becoming increasingly clear to many in the field (Olson, Cioffi, Yovanoff, & Mank, 2001) that business and employer support is the answer to solving the unemployment of people with disabilities. Olson et al. (2001) examined the attitudes of employers of people with intellectual disabilities through a survey distributed nationally. Employers of all sizes have favorable experiences in employing people with intellectual disabilities and value the training provided by SE service providers. Common accommodations to employees with intellectual disabilities included extra supervision time, providing flexible hours, and using the services of a job coach. These accommodations are perceived to be of minimal cost to the company. In terms of human resource management, employees with intellectual disabilities are viewed as costing companies the same or less than employees without disabilities, except in the area of supervision and training.

CONCLUSION

Transition planning benefits all parties involved. It benefits the individual with intellectual disabilities because it ensures that appropriate adult options and support mechanisms are in place before the individual graduates so that an integrated lifestyle can be maintained. The school district benefits because graduates attain productive and satisfying lives—one of the goals of public education. Transition planning benefits the service delivery system by examining the effectiveness of current programs and by becoming the driving force for the development of new opportunities for individuals with intellectual disabilities. Without transition planning, there is a higher probability that the individual will exit into waiting lists, sheltered workshops, and segregated living options without the appropriate services or supports.

Implementing transition for individuals with intellectual disabilities is both challenging and complex. Conducting futures planning activities prior to the development of ITPs is one of the ways in which local school districts can begin to address the process. However, the development of an ITP alone does not ensure that students with intellectual disabilities will exit into integrated community lives as adults. School districts still must provide appropriate curriculum, vocational training in community settings, integrated age-appropriate school environments, and interagency linkages in order for transition planning to be successful. Most important, parents and individuals must be empowered with the skills and knowledge to make the best decisions (Fullerton, 1995; Nozoki & Mochizuki, 1995; West, 1995). Only then will the vision of full participation in the community for the individual with intellectual disabilities become a reality.

STUDY QUESTIONS

1. Describe the guidelines when developing a comprehensive curriculum for students with intellectual disabilities.

2. What are some of the obstacles that impede students with intellectual disabilities from achieving successful community integration and vocational outcomes?

3. What are some advantages and disadvantages to community-based vocational instruction as opposed to school-based vocational instruction for students with intellectual disabilities?

4. What considerations should be made when developing a transition plan for students with intellectual disabilities?

5. Describe critical issues that must be addressed in follow-up surveys for students with intellectual disabilities.

6. What strategies can be used to help individuals with intellectual disabilities enter inclusive employment?

Appendix

Sample Community-Based Training Schedule

Community-based training site: Discount clothing store, stock room

Area supervisor: Mrs. Mary Miller

Teacher completing form: Stacy D.

[X] Daily   [ ] Varies day to day

(Training tasks remain the same from day to day)   (If checked here, then complete a separate form for each day's schedule)

If above box is checked, then indicate day for which this form is completed:

   [ ]   [ ]   [ ]   [ ]   [ ]

   Mon   Tues   Wed   Thurs   Fri

Vocational training tasks	Approximate time
Punch in, set up work area	1:00 P.M.–1:15 P.M.
Open clothing boxes	1:15 P.M.–1:30 P.M.
Put clothes on hangers	1:30 P.M.–2:00 P.M.
Break in employee lounge	2:00 P.M.–2:15 P.M.
Unpack boxes, fold items, put on shelves in stock room	2:15 P.M.–3:00 P.M.
Punch out, go to McDonald's, return to school	3:00 P.M.–3:30 P.M.

Comments: Trainees should wear dark blue pants and a white shirt for this training site. Report to Mrs. Miller on arrival. If she is not in the stock room, then call ext. 75 and report to security. Customers will work with Bill and Laura (co-workers) on all tasks.

Signature/Title: _____ Date: _____

17

Applications for Youth with Sensory Impairments

Phillip D. Rumrill, Jr., and Pamela Luft

AFTER COMPLETING THE CHAPTER, THE READER WILL BE ABLE TO

○ Describe some demographic characteristics of youth with sensory impairments

○ Discuss some of the unique learning and behavior characteristics of youth with sensory impairments

○ Identify assessment strategies and processes for youth with sensory impairments

○ Describe effective teaching and instructional strategies for youth with sensory impairments

○ Discuss developing effective individualized transition plans (ITPs) for youth with sensory impairments

○ Identify critical questions to ask in assessing the quality of transition services

○ Identify and understand the major technologies available to help youth with sensory impairments

○ Describe community travel strategies for youth with visual impairments

Some of the material presented in this chapter was used with the kind permission of Susan Lehman Griffin, who wrote this chapter for the first two editions of *Life Beyond the Classroom*. The authors also wish to thank Courtney Vierstra of Kent State University for her clerical and editorial assistance in developing this chapter.

CAROLYN

Carolyn is a 17-year-old high school student with profound deafness and mental retardation requiring intermittent support. She lives in a suburban area with her parents, and she attends a public high school. Carolyn is included in general classes with her peers without disabilities for about half of the school day, where she uses an interpreter to help her with spoken information and class participation. Carolyn also uses a teacher's aide to assist her with content learning.

For the other half of her school day, Carolyn is enrolled in a vocational training program sponsored by her school district. She works as a food service assistant in a local hospital cafeteria, and she is accompanied by a job coach. Her supervisor at the cafeteria is fluent in sign language, which enables her to provide direct feedback as Carolyn receives on-the-job training.

Carolyn is described as a pleasant but shy individual who gets along well with her classmates and co-workers. Communication with her hearing peers is often limited, even when an interpreter is present. Carolyn rarely initiates social contact, but she is eager to respond when approached by another person. She is able to read lips on a very limited basis, and her preferred modes of communication are sign language and rudimentary handwritten notes.

Carolyn has several friends who attend her state's school for the deaf, but she is not active in the local Deaf community. She

Individuals with sensory impairments (i.e., hearing and visual impairments) make up a heterogeneous group of people with challenging transition needs. The functional limitations associated with visual or hearing impairments—coupled with the frequent coexistence of other physical, cognitive, perceptual, or medical disabilities—present significant obstacles for young people in both educational and work arenas. A hearing or vision loss can be a highly disruptive experience in a child's development, but young people with hearing or visual impairments (and especially those with dual sensory impairments, who are described as deaf-blind) remain underserved by rehabilitation and other social service programs (Frank, 2003; Rubin & Roessler, 2000).

Why is this? First, the processes by which sensory impairments are identified are often imprecise. Because of interagency discrepancies in eligibility criteria, assessment procedures, and personnel resources, many people with visual or hearing impairments are misdiagnosed as having perceptual disabilities, mental retardation, or behavior/communication disorders. Moreover, if a person has both a visual and a hearing impairment, then chances are high that only one impairment will be detected during an agency's often cursory initial evaluation.

Second, sensory impairments constitute low-incidence disabilities, which are infrequently observed by educational professionals. Students with visual impairments constitute only 0.04% of the United States' school-age population, students with hearing impairments represent 0.11% of school-age Americans, and 0.002% of that population is deaf-blind. In other words, only about 1.5 out of every 1,000 school-age children in the United States have a visual impairment, a hearing impairment, or both (Twenty-Fourth Annual Report to Congress, 2002). It is also noteworthy that racial and ethnic minorities are overrepresented within sensory impairment populations. Nearly 17% (16.77%) of the American school-age population of students with visual impairments are African American, and African Americans represent 15.8% of the hearing impaired population and 14.1% of the deaf-blind population. Similarly, Hispanics comprise 15.39%, 18.37%, and 17.5% of school-age visually impaired, hearing impaired, and deaf-blind populations, respectively (Twenty-Fourth Annual Report to Congress, 2002).

Third, there is a shortage of trained professionals to meet the needs of people with sensory impairments. Low-

enjoys swimming, arts and crafts, and bicycling. She independently uses public transportation to travel to and from familiar locations, including the mall and the hospital where she works. Carolyn's short-term and immediate goals are to graduate from high school, to move from her parents' house into a group home and eventually into her own apartment, and to secure employment in the food service field. She also wishes to expand her network of friends and acquaintances, both within and outside of the Deaf community.

Another one of Carolyn's goals is to increase her technology skills. She sometimes uses a teletypewriter (TTY) to communicate via telephone, and she is learning to operate the cash register at the cafeteria. She does not have typing or other computer skills, but she has expressed an interest in learning to use the Internet (especially e-mail).

vision specialists, orientation and mobility specialists, rehabilitation engineers, sign language interpreters, audiologists, speech-language pathologists, and rehabilitation counselors for the Deaf (RCDs) remain in short supply in many parts of the United States (Baer & Rumrill, 2001). Particularly lacking is the availability of these professionals in inclusive settings. Because blindness and deafness services in education and rehabilitation have historically been provided in specialized venues separate from those in which people with other disabilities are served (Rubin & Roessler, 2000; Schriner, Rumrill, & Parlin, 1995), coordinating integrated services with those offered by sensory specialists can be an unwieldy task.

Existing transition, education, and rehabilitation literature documents the difficulties that youth with sensory impairments have in establishing their careers after high school. Students who are blind or have visual impairments experience problems related to literacy and technology (Hartz, 2000; Lueck, Dote-Kwan, Senge, & Clarke, 2001; Miller, 1997), a lack of cooperation between parents and adult services professionals (Frank, 2003), linkages between child and adult services (Gartin, Rumrill, & Serebreni, 1998; Marks & Feeley, 1995), securing initial employment after vocational training has been completed (de la Garza & Erin, 1993; Nagle, 2001), and procuring reasonable accommodations in the workplace (Frank, 2003; Rumrill, 1999). Students who are deaf or hard of hearing have reported transition obstacles in the areas of communication and self-advocacy (Garay, 2003; Luft, 2000), academic achievement and socialization (Bullis, Davis, Bull, & Johnson, 1995), and access to postsecondary education (Stodden, Whelley, Chang, & Harding, 2001; Wilson, Getzel, & Brown, 2000). Conspicuous by their absence in contemporary literature are the descriptions and evaluations of model transition programs to help youth with visual and/or hearing impairments bridge the services gap between secondary school and independent adult living (Luft et al., 2001).

A recurring theme in contemporary research is the lack of preparation of special educators and rehabilitation professionals to work together in providing seamless transition services for these low-incidence and, so far, underserved populations (Bullis et al., 1995; Cook & Rumrill, 2000; Everson, 1995; Hayden & Abery, 1994; Luft, 2000; Luft et al., 2001). Accordingly, this chapter focuses exclusively on the transition process for young people with sensory impairments, with particular emphasis on youth with singular impairments (either vision or hearing) and no other coexisting disabilities. These are precisely the people who are falling through the cracks in today's educational and rehabilitation systems, and they deserve services grounded in a thorough understanding of their highly individualized needs.

WHO ARE INDIVIDUALS WITH VISUAL IMPAIRMENTS?

Defining visual impairment is a complicated task because of the wide range of symptoms that people with visual impairments experience. There are many levels and types of visual impairments, most of which leave the person with some residual vision. In fact, only about 10% of people with visual impairments nationwide are completely blind (American Foundation for the Blind, 2005).

The terminology used to describe the range and level of visual impairments varies widely. The generic term *blindness*, as used by the general public, implies that the person receives no information through vision and learns mainly through touch or listening. The term *legal blindness* is quite different. It is used by many agencies and educational systems to determine whether an individual qualifies for services and/or benefits. People who are considered legally blind have a visual acuity of less than 20/200 with the best correction (i.e., they can see at 20 feet what a person with normal vision can see at 200 feet) or a field of vision of less than 20 degrees. Although a person whose visual acuity is 20/200 has difficulty distinguishing fine details, he or she can typically recognize gross objects and may learn a great deal through vision. Many people with legal blindness are visually oriented learners, whereas those who are blind have little or no usable vision.

Several terms are used to describe vision that is significantly different from that of a typical person. The term *low vision* describes a person who is "still severely visually impaired after correction but who may increase visual functioning through the use of optical aids, nonoptical aids, environmental modifications and/or techniques" (Corn, 1980, p. 3). In some regions of the country, the term *partially sighted* refers to a person who has a relatively mild visual impairment that falls within the corrected range of 20/70 to 20/200 and does not qualify the person for services as legally blind.

Regular unbiased assessments are needed to make decisions about appropriate interventions to enhance the student's academic performance and determine the effectiveness of previous instructional strategies. A systematic method of utilizing whatever residual vision the student has (often enhanced by magnification) and providing alternative formats (e.g., braille, voice) for information that the person cannot gain access to visually enables the educational system to maximize the development of learning. Coupling this approach with orientation and mobility training, technology training, social skills instruction, vocational skills training, and career exploration activities can provide a well-rounded and age-appropriate transition program for a student with a visual impairment.

WHO ARE INDIVIDUALS WHO ARE DEAF OR HARD OF HEARING?

Hearing loss is classified according to sensitivity to sound at various frequencies. These frequencies are termed hertz (Hz) and are measured according to loudness or decibel (dB) levels. An individual is considered to have typical hearing if he or she is first able to detect sound at 25dB or lower. Hearing within the 25–40dB range is considered to be a mild loss; within the 40–55dB range, a moderate loss; within the 55–70dB range, a moderately severe loss; within the 70–90dB range, a severe loss; and more than 90dB, a profound loss (Moores, 2001). An audiogram provides a graphic representation of the person's hearing levels in both ears and visually notes the decibel level across several frequencies.

Another important variable is the ability to understand speech and language, which is measured by the speech reception threshold (SRT) and a speech discrimination score. Both of these are reported on the audiogram, usually next to or below the graphic notation of hearing loss. A high SRT indicates that the person needs speech to be amplified in order to understand it correctly. A low discrimination score indicates that regardless of amplification level, the person is unable to understand common spoken words. Such a person is likely to have substantial difficulties in communicating with others. This may occur despite a hearing loss level within the mild or even normal range of hearing.

Several terms are used to describe people with hearing loss according to the amount of loss and their preferred communication modalities. This may have little to do with the audiometric measurement of their hearing loss. Instead, it may reflect their learning preferences in using auditory or visual information and their preferences for identifying themselves as members of either the hearing world or the Deaf world (Lane, Hoffmeister, & Bahan, 1996; Moores, 2001). These terms are defined as follows.

1. *Deaf:* A person who is deaf has a loss of hearing ranging from severe to profound, and he or she does not generally learn speech and language through the auditory mode, with or without the use of hearing aids. A person with a hearing loss who chooses to identify with the Deaf community will describe him- or herself as Deaf. A Deaf person subscribes to values that define the Deaf community as a cultural minority that uses a unique language, American Sign Language (ASL). The Deaf community also shares a unique history including a strong oral history, sense of community, and shared experiences.

2. *Hard of hearing:* A person who is hard of hearing has a hearing loss in which speech and language are learned through the auditory mode, with or without the use of hearing aides. This person usually feels more comfortable with the typically hearing world than with the Deaf world and uses auditory (i.e., residual hearing) and visual (i.e., speech reading) information to communicate successfully in most situations.

3. *Hearing impaired:* This is a culturally offensive term, according to the Deaf community, because it labels individuals with hearing loss as a disability group with implications of a diminished quality of life.

4. *Person with a hearing disability:* This is appropriate person-first language, but the Deaf community does not use this phrase, just as a Mexican-American person would normally not identify him- or herself as a "person of Hispanic ethnicity" (Lane et al., 1996; Moores, 2001).

WHO ARE INDIVIDUALS WHO ARE DEAF-BLIND?

Individuals with both visual and hearing impairments rarely have complete loss of both sensory pathways (Desch, 2000). Often, there is residual hearing or residual vision that the person can use for learning and communication. Depending on which sense is most intact, these individuals may be educated and learn primary communication strategies in the same manner as a person with singular sensory loss. Instructional strategies may include braille and speech or ASL, with an emphasis placed on utilizing whatever residual hearing or vision the person has.

For individuals who cannot learn and communicate in these ways, a number of alternative communication systems are available. For some, sign language–based communication is effective, including signing and fingerspelling in the palm of the hand or placing one's hands over the hands of the person signing to him or her. Other systems include tactual spelling or a variety of visual-display communication boards and computer-based communication boards. Orientation and mobility training needs also depend on the amount of residual vision and may not be needed at all by people with relatively mild visual impairments (Wynn, 1995).

In the case of progressive conditions, when near-total deaf-blindness does occur, the individual will need support and assistance in establishing (or re-establishing) contact with the world and integrating (or re-integrating) into adult activities. The individual may need to adjust to the importance of touch, the inability to know immediately what is happening in the environment, and not understanding communication of those around him or her (Reyes, 1993).

CHARACTERISTICS OF YOUTH WITH SENSORY IMPAIRMENTS

The Deaf and blind communities are widely known for their strong group advocacy efforts. Strategic planning, attraction of media attention, and tenacity among people who are blind have garnered provisions in rehabilitation services for that group that are not available to other disability groups. These include preferential ownership rights to vending operations on state and federal property, a separate division of vocational rehabilitation (VR) services in most states, and blindness-specific tax benefits in the United States Internal Revenue code (Schriner et al., 1995). Similar advocacy efforts can be noted on the part of the Deaf community, including the universal adoption of telephone relay services under Title IV of the Americans with Disabilities Act (ADA) of 1990 (PL 101-336). Acts of self-assurance and advocacy, however, do not necessarily come naturally to youth with sensory impairments; these abilities must be taught by educators, rehabilitation professionals, disability advocates, friends, and family members. With that in mind, the following paragraphs highlight the social, vocational, and academic issues that can confront youth with sensory impairments.

Social Competence

Many of the behaviors seen in youth with sensory impairments occur as compensation for or in reaction to their underlying visual or hearing impairments. Whether the loss is visual or auditory, the common feature is a limited input of information. This limited input presents the student with a different view or sense of the world than is available to his or her peers (Frank, 2003; Luft et al., 2001). It is difficult for seeing and hearing people to imagine the profound loss that can accompany the partial or total diminution of a sense. That lack of identification with the person's circumstance often manifests itself in discomfort around people with visual or hearing impairments. Therefore, youth with sensory impairments are all-too-often isolated from their peers who can hear and see, excluded from normative social activities, and left to socialize primarily with those who have similar disabilities. On the one hand, this exclusion has led the blind and Deaf communities to "stick together" in formulating effective consumer advocacy initiatives (Frank, 2003; Rumrill, 1999). On the other hand, for youth with visual and hearing impairments who have not yet developed sophisticated self-advocacy skills, social isolation can lead to mistrust of others, loneliness, diminished self-esteem, and a lack of self-confidence.

Youth with sensory impairments are usually born into seeing and hearing families. Thus, social isolation can begin at an early age. Given that youth with sensory impairments often have limited interaction with their peers who do not have disabilities, a premium must be placed on transition services emphasizing social skill development. Having role models within and outside the blind and Deaf communities is an important part of social development, as is providing structured opportunities to interact with a wide variety of people in different social settings.

Vocational Competence

Because of social isolation and related barriers, communication problems, and inadequate vocational training, youth with sensory impairments (even those who complete college or other postsecondary training) are often underemployed or unemployed (Frank, 2003; Rumrill, 2001). Luft (2000) noted that communication barriers often relegate deaf employees to semi-skilled or unskilled jobs, even when they possess sophisticated vocational skills. El-Khiami's (1993) study of deaf college graduates revealed a similar pattern of respondents being overqualified for the jobs that they held. In a 1993 study, de la Garza and Erin reported an unemployment rate of nearly 70% among recent graduates of the Texas School for the Blind. Rumrill and Scheff (1997) attributed the difficulties that blind workers have in obtaining employment after high school to a high incidence of employer discrimination in the hiring process. Rumrill, Roessler, Bettersby, and Schuyler (1998) found that even those blind workers who do secure employment experience significant difficulties in maintaining their careers—mostly resulting from transportation barriers, poor access to assistive technology (AT) and other on-the-job accommodations, and secondary effects of the conditions that cause visual impairments (e.g., diabetes, neurological disorders). In a comprehensive study of the impact of the ADA and other civil rights legislation on the employment of individuals who are blind, Frank (2003) identified persistent employer discrimination, coupled with limited ability on the part of blind workers to advocate for themselves in the workplace, as primary reasons for the job acquisition and retention barriers that confront Americans who are blind. He recommended self-advocacy training grounded in the regulations of the ADA as a way to increase confidence and improve outcomes among people who are blind with regard to requesting and receiving needed accommodations in the workplace.

Academic Competence

Youth with sensory impairments generally do not perform as well in academic and vocational courses as their peers without disabilities. Communication barriers (both written and oral) are generally regarded as the most common problems for deaf or hard-of-hearing students, whereas graphic, numeric, and spatial learning is generally most difficult for students who are blind or have visual impairments.

Other Common Characteristics

For all of the differences that are observed among youth with sensory impairments, many share common characteristics that cut across the type of sensory loss. Decreased social participation is typical, primarily as a result of hurdles related to communication and access to information (Frank, 2003; Luft et al., 2001). Interaction between youth with sensory impairments and their peers without disabilities requires effort by both parties; therefore, it is unfortunate but not surprising that youth with sensory impairments often find it easier to interact with peers who have similar disabilities or to remain alone. This restricted range of social experience often leads youth with sensory impairments to underestimate their prospects for academic and career success, and their low aspirations are all-too-frequently realized. Underachievement, then, becomes an outgrowth of the subtle and not-so-subtle messages these youth receive concerning their "differentness" (Rumrill, 1999).

UNIQUE LEARNING CHALLENGES PRESENTED TO PROFESSIONALS BY YOUTH WITH SENSORY IMPAIRMENTS

Perhaps one of the most unique challenges presented by youth with sensory impairments lies in helping them overcome barriers related to communication and access to information. Communication issues—which vary according to the degree of disability, type of sensory impairment, and the individual's compensatory skills—are quite complicated. People with singular sensory impairments (i.e., either visual or hearing) may skew information that they receive from the other major senses without benefit of accompanying verbal or auditory stimuli. For example, people who are blind are likely to misinterpret conversations when the speakers rely heavily on body language.

People with profound, dual sensory impairments (i.e., deaf-blindness) receive little information from the outside world, and preventing social isolation is an ongoing challenge when working with this population. Teachers and adult services providers must, therefore, be prepared for and skilled in communicating with youth who have all kinds of needs (Kauffman, Mostert, Trent, & Hallahan, 1998).

Professionals must also understand the disability's etiology (e.g., whether it was congenital, early onset, or occurred later in childhood) and progression, both of which can influence the student's learning style and, thus, the professional's teaching style (Kauffman et al., 1998). Professionals and paraprofessionals must always remember that no two individuals are alike. Two students may share similar degrees of deafness, but one may have congenital deafness, whereas the other's deafness was the result of an accident at age 12. Those students would almost certainly have different instructional needs in terms of speech development, language reception, and literacy. One student with a visual impairment might prefer to tape-record instructional information, whereas another with similar visual acuity might opt for braille materials or a reader. These individual preferences must be assessed, discussed, and, to the extent feasible, implemented in classroom and other career preparatory activities.

Another prominent challenge for professionals working with students with sensory impairments is ensuring that instruction and interventions foster the highest possible degree of generalizability and adaptability (Luft et al., 2001; Rumrill, 2001). Because people with sensory impairments receive only partial information in one major mode of reception, generalizing from task to task is sometimes difficult. Although instructions or interventions designed specifically for one task or event may be easier to implement on a case-by-case basis, they are not beneficial to students in the long run because the primary indicator of postschool employment success is adaptability of vocational skills to a variety of work settings (Luft & Koch, 1998). The goal of transition is to help youth become as independent as possible. Therefore, programs should be designed to allow students the greatest control and highest applicability across situations.

Professional competence is essential to deal with the challenges presented by people with sensory impairments and to ensure the success of each individual's transition. Communication, access to information, adaptability, and independence issues arise frequently during assessment, instruction, and vocational planning. Having a dual sensory impairment creates a more-than-additive impact on a person's access to information and ability to communicate with others. The interactive effect of deficits in both hearing and vision, which are often used to compensate for one another by individuals with singular sensory impairments, can result in profound social isolation and academic underachievement if professionals do not provide comprehensive instructional and transition services tailored to the student's individual needs.

Assessment Issues for Youth with Sensory Impairments

The transition coordinator or ITP team leader is responsible for bringing essential assessment information into initial meetings. From this information, the transition team makes decisions in terms of additional assessments needed in accordance with students' skills and preferences. A complete battery of standardized tests may not be appropriate to the needs and expected transition outcomes of the student and may provide the team with little useful information (Sitlington, Neubert, Begun, Lombard, & Leconte, 1996).

The communication issues for young adults with sensory impairments often compromise the use of standardized assessment tools (Kleinwaks, 1996), so professionals should become familiar with ecological and situational approaches to assessing students' individual needs. The frequently limited experiences that these students have with occupationally relevant tasks may render standardized vocational assessments invalid (Hershenson & Szymanski, 1992; Koch, 2001; Szymanski & Hershenson, 1998). Many skill-based assessments and interest inventories presume a minimal familiarity with career issues that students who have sensory impairments may lack. In addition, the vocational assessment specialists used by a school district may have limited experience and expertise in providing accommodations for these students (e.g., allowing sufficient exploratory practice trials before taking data). Career planning and vocational adjustment are always intertwined with the individual's values; to the extent that values are culturally bound, unique social environments such as those encountered by youth with sensory impairments can greatly affect values and, thereby, the career planning process (Koch, 2001).

Instead of basing transition planning on the use of standardized assessments, a complete functional assessment should be conducted to provide specific information that is relevant to possible outcomes and potential future environments for the student (Sitlington et al., 1996). The team needs to acquire all obtainable information to assemble a comprehensive transition profile for the student, including information on etiology, educational background and successes, career development experiences, independent living skills, and self-determination (Luft, 2000; Sitlington et al., 1996). For students with sensory losses, the assessment data should also include the following components: 1) a full medical evaluation, 2) a functional assessment of residual capabilities, 3) observational and interview data concerning the student's functional abilities, 4) pertinent scholastic records, and 5) student interview information.

A number of team members may have expertise in performing certain functional assessments. Team leaders who work with adolescents who have visual impairments can use the expertise of an orientation and mobility specialist or rehabilitation teacher in performing such assessments (Baer & Rumrill, 2001). The orientation and mobility specialist determines how the student can move most efficiently and effectively around his or her key environments, performs a functional vision examination, and begins a training program to teach needed orientation and mobility skills (Moore, Graves, & Patterson, 1997). The rehabilitation teacher can help with assessing how the student uses natural and artificial cues in learning tasks and with designing instructional programs for any of the following domains: work, social and leisure, residential, and community participation.

Team leaders who work with deaf or hard-of-hearing students frequently use the services of a speech-language pathologist or an audiologist. Many of these students can speak or speechread certain key words. These specialists can assess a student's oral communication abilities and functional abilities, if the student wishes to use those skills. An audiologist can assist in assessing and recommending particular hearing aids or assistive listening devices to meet specific individual needs and environmental conditions.

Full Medical Evaluation

Several conditions that cause vision and hearing loss can also affect other organs and systems of the body. For example, a student with either vision or hearing loss may also have heart or kidney dysfunction or diabetes (Batshaw, 2002). Progressive deaf-blindness can occur as the result of genetic syndromes or other etiologies; therefore, complicating or coexisting conditions should be ruled out or identified prior to any transition planning. Underlying medical conditions can have serious effects on the lifestyles that students will lead as adults (e.g., type of job, residence, physical/recreational activities). Transition teams need recent medical reports and may require the assistance of medical personnel to help with determining likely prognosis and assistive devices (Biehl, 1996).

Functional Assessment of Residual Hearing or Vision

Transition teams are often presented with detailed medical reports that list numerical sensory limits and categories. However, these provide little information regarding how the student is able to use his or her residual abilities for learning and communication.

Table 17.1. Functional assessment for work potential

Vision	• Analyze lighting source for high or low illumination with light source on side of the "better eye." • Check height and angles of work surfaces and reduce reflective areas as necessary. • Determine if enlarged print, colors, symbols, or pictures can be used for direction/work supplies. • Assess usefulness of tactual clues added to materials, equipment, or environment to focus consumer's residual vision on key aspects.
Hearing	• Note noise level within work environment and determine if work station needs to be repositioned. • Determine if sound discrimination is a critical factor of the job. • Analyze work area to assess employee's need to localize the origin of sound (e.g., fire alarm).
Orientation and mobility	• Determine systematic methods of traveling across or between landmarks to reduce complicated orientation patterns. • Analyze methods of maintaining direction regardless of environmental obstacles. • Critically review all environmental safety factors affecting this area (e.g., fire drills, crowds).
Modifying task requirements	• Check the availability of support to include both natural and artificial systems. • Determine how other senses might be used. • Identify job components that lend themselves to technology solutions that will meet consumer needs.

Source: Ferguson, 1995.

A functional evaluation of residual hearing and vision might contain statements such as "can distinguish a human voice over minimal background sound" and "has an 80% occlusion in the middle of right visual field; surrounding vision is limited to shadows." This type of information about remaining vision and hearing abilities helps the team to determine appropriate future environments and interaction strategies more accurately. The functional assessment should also contain information about visual or hearing aids and devices that the student currently uses or has been tested to use, indicating how well the student functioned with each device and his or her ultimate preference in use of these devices. Ferguson (1995) provided a schema for examining functional capabilities for work and employment that focuses on the individual's strengths (see Table 17.1).

Appropriate assessment is critical not only to general transition planning but also in making determinations regarding appropriate AT. The Helen Keller National Center (1994) recommended performing a functional assessment of 1) general skills including physical and cognitive abilities and 2) the impact of progressive sensory or other ability losses. The environments should be evaluated in terms of the tasks that the individual needs or wants to perform, and a discrepancy analysis should be conducted for current skills and abilities. Searches for the appropriate technology should include both environmental and homemade strategies, with special consideration given to the individual's preferences. Assistive devices should be purchased only after consulting with a trained professional from that specialty area.

Observational and Interview Data Concerning the Student's Functional Abilities

A number of summary and checklist forms are available to assist with gathering functional information about students' abilities across their primary environments (Inge, Dymond, & Wehman, 1996; Sitlington et al., 1996). Regardless of how assessment data are summarized, the transition team leader should make certain that information regarding a student's functional abilities is obtained across these critical current and potential future environments—including home, school, vocational training settings, community recreation sites, and potential worksites (Bradfield, 1992). Information should be gathered regarding the student's work habits, tardiness or timeliness, physical capabilities, instructional needs, reinforcement needs, AT needs, coping abilities, social skills, resource development skills, and adaptability (Gajar, Goodman, & McAfee, 1993; Sitlington et al., 1996). If information is collected across settings, then it is more reliable. Care should be taken to stress the person's abilities and to note the areas in which intervention might be necessary.

If a summary form—preferable for ease of team discussions—is used, it can often be "matched" with a job analysis form, which should be completed when the student is seeking employment (Bradfield, 1992). Although this process of matching skills to job requirements gives the counselor or employment specialist some idea of how the student might perform in a given job and where interventions might be needed, it should not replace the professional's skilled intuition or the student's preferences.

Several comprehensive planning strategies can assist the team in compiling a transition profile of the student and the support people in his or her environment. MAPS and Personal Futures Planning allow student-centered planning with input from other key stakeholders, family, and friends in the student's life (Luft et al., 2001). The *Choosing Outcomes and Accommodations for Children*, 2nd edition (COACH) curriculum also includes data collection forms for comprehensive planning (Giangreco, Cloninger, & Iverson, 1998).

Pertinent Scholastic Records

Scholastic records can assist team members as they make transition plans by presenting academic or vocational areas in which the student excelled as well as those that the student found troublesome or did not like. Scholastic records may also show which learning strategies worked best for the student in the classroom (e.g., taping sessions, using a reader, having an interpreter).

Student Interview Information

None of the assessment strategies described in this section should stand alone as a complete assessment. An assessment is not complete until information is obtained directly from the student and his or her family regarding their aspirations for the student's adult life. Questions to address before the first ITP meeting include the following: Where does the student want to live? What kind of housing arrangement does he or she desire? What are his or her preferred modes of transportation? Does he or she want to go to college? What kind of job does he or she want? Would he or she be comfortable with the assistance of an employment specialist? These questions also need to be asked of the family, who provides much of the emotional and physical support that the student needs in order to accomplish the goals of the transition plan. The *COACH* curriculum (Giangreco et al., 1998) offers structured interview questions for both the student and the family.

TEACHING STRATEGIES FOR YOUTH WITH SENSORY IMPAIRMENTS

Many of the instructional strategies used with students who have sensory impairments are specialized and may be highly individualized. Because of the frequently limited exposure to occupational and adult living opportunities, instruction for transition should begin during early childhood years when perceptions about adulthood are being formed. Instruction should become increasingly focused on realistic transition outcomes as the student progresses through his or her school years.

Integrated Instruction

Research is mixed in terms of the benefit that students achieve in segregated versus integrated educational settings (Bullis et al., 1995; Moores, 2001). Individuals who identify with the Deaf community may show a strong preference for segregated settings to prevent social and communication isolation (Lane et al., 1996; Luft et al., 2001). Other individuals prefer to be integrated for their educational experience. Teachers in these integrated settings will need adequate preparation and training to accommodate students' needs and to ensure social, and not just physical, integration with peers. Regardless of these preferences, at some point the transition team needs to plan for working and living in the world at large. Therefore, whether the student 1) attends a specialized school for the blind or school for the deaf or 2) receives specialized services in an integrated classroom, career exploration activities should center on integrated worksites.

Focus on Adaptation and Coping Skills

Individuals with sensory losses must learn general coping, adapting, and problem-solving skills to be successful at work and independent living (Allen, Rawlings, & Schildroth, 1989; Luft et al., 2001; Moore et al., 1997). Traditionally, vocational and independent living training has focused on discrete skill acquisition, such as typing, sewing, cooking, and so forth (Rubin & Roessler, 2000). Instead, teaching should be focused on skills that can be generalized across multiple areas of adulthood (Kauffman et al., 1998; Luft et al., 2001).

Community-Based Instruction

Community-based instruction (CBI) integrates the skills that the student learns at school with those necessary for home, employment, and community environments (Hanley-Maxwell & Szymanski, 1995). Community-based, or off-site, instruction should begin several years prior to graduation for 1 to 2 half-days per week, gradually increasing as the student ages. CBI is more effective when sites are rotated because the student with sensory impairments learns to generalize orientation and mobility, communication, social skills, and vocational skills across a variety of settings. Given that today's teenagers can expect to change career fields an average of four to six times during their work lives (Rumrill, 2001), the ability to generalize skills across community settings is critically important.

Table 17.2.   An example using the four basic travel skills necessary for an independent adult life

Resource development	Problem-solving ability	Self-advocacy	Social skills development
Cane to get to the lunch room	Which method is most efficient?	Can student talk to person with him or her?	Can student locate assistance if he or she walks alone?
Sighted guide	Which method does the student like?	If the co-worker and student do not want to sit together, how do they part ways?	How should student explain the sighted-guide approach to co-workers?
Walk independently	Can the student get help from a friend?		
	What should a friend do if chosen method does not work?	Will it benefit the student to talk with co-workers?	
	How much time does the student have?		

Instructional Procedures

Instruction should occur in natural surroundings, if possible, and should utilize natural cues and reinforcers. Such strategies foster independence and social interaction. Students, whether they learn from systematic instruction, tactual teaching, or counseling, should learn to 1) expect natural consequences from their behaviors, 2) develop problem-solving and self-monitoring behaviors, and 3) receive and respond to feedback from peers and supervisors (Kauffman et al., 1998; Luft et al., 2001). These are strategies used constantly in adult life and can ease the transition process considerably. Table 17.2 provides an example of the generalizable skills that a student with a disability develops during the transition process.

As important as effective and reliable assessment procedures are, new advances in technology can have a dramatic impact on all individuals with disabilities and especially those with sensory impairments. Teachers, counselors, and others involved in the transition team must stay current with regard to new and potentially beneficial technologies that meet individual student needs.

ASSISTIVE TECHNOLOGY AND ACCOMMODATIONS FOR YOUTH WITH SENSORY IMPAIRMENTS

In the classroom and in the world of work, youth with sensory impairments can benefit from a number of technological devices and accommodation strategies that help them perform expected functions. Braille labels, audiotaped text, and handrails on stairways are examples of inexpensive modifications that can improve productivity for a student or worker with a visual impairment. For youth with hearing loss, vibrating pagers can be rented through a telephone paging service for approximately $20 per month. There are many of these and other types of assistive devices and accommodations that can be used with young adults with hearing impairments. Figure 17.1 provides guidelines for determining accommodations for youth who are deaf or hard of hearing. Listed next are examples of AT and accommodation strategies that can help youth with sensory impairments in classroom and vocational settings:

Can students use their interpreter well? Do they have the facilities for effective use of the interpreter in the classroom (e.g., understand signs well and/or read lips well)? Is the student able to understand the instructor without the aid of an interpreter?

If students are able to understand the instructor, with or without the aid of the interpreter, are they able to take their own notes in the classroom? If so, how good are their notes? Are they helpful to them in their study sessions?

If students are not able to take a complete set of notes, is it possible for them to just jot down their own thoughts, concepts, or key terminology that can help them to study and compare them with other sets of notes provided by a trained note-taker or someone else?

What kind of note-taking assistance would be most appropriate for students? Would a trained note-taker be required, or would a volunteer note-taker be sufficient? Would the student be satisfied with the notes provided by the instructor, if any?

Do students use their notes or notes from someone else as one of the primary study sources? Do the students compare the notes from a trained note-taker or someone else with their own jotted notes, if any, and rework the notes?

If students are not able to use an interpreter and none of them are able to understand the instructor, would notes provided by a trained note-taker help? Would they need a tutor? Is it the best way to provide a service to the students? If not, what are some alternatives?

What additional services are needed for the students? For instance, do the students have reading problems? Are the students academically prepared for the course? Do the students have any other problems (e.g., emotional, social) that may be hindering their academic progress in the classroom in spite of the services being provided? Can a tutor effectively help the students to develop study skills and classroom participatory skills?

Figure 17.1. Accommodations for people with hearing impairments in postsecondary environments. (*Source:* Technology and Disability, 1993.)

1. Sign language: A visual, gestural language used predominantly by those closely connected with the Deaf community; includes ASL and signed English

2. Tactual signing: Signs are made while individuals face each other and hold hands to feel the movement

3. Fingerspelling (i.e., manual alphabet): Words are spelled using a series of finger positions, each representing a single letter

4. Print-on-palm: Tracing capital block letters in person's palm using index finger

5. Speechreading (i.e., lipreading): People with good residual vision may use this method; however, only 30%–40% of spoken English can be understood using this method alone.

6. Tadoma Method: Rarely used method of speechreading using touch in which the person places his or her thumb on lips of the speaker, with fingers on throat

7. Gestural systems: Include natural gestures; behavior showing likes, dislikes, and choices; and touch cues or tactual prompts

8. Pictures/symbols: Use of pictures and symbols to communicate

9. Written notes: Use of a black pen and glare-free paper to communicate expressively and receptively

10. Prewritten cards: Useful for predictable everyday occurrences and basic wants and needs

11. Raised alphabet cards: Useful for predictable everyday occurrences and basic wants and needs

12. Tellatouch: Portable typewriter-like machine enabling a speaker to type a message that the other person receives in braille

13. Tactile speech indicator (TSI): Enables a person with good speech to communicate on the telephone

14. Electronic devices: Include devices to magnify print, computers with programs to enlarge print and give large print or braille output, and telecommunications devices (e.g., telecommunications device for the deaf [TDD]). Also include voice-output (i.e., screen reader) programs that synthesize computer text into vocal information and voice-activated computer equipment for people with visual and motor impairments.

15. TTYs: Enable a deaf person to communicate through typing over the telephone. Relay systems mandated in every state (see Title IV of the ADA) allow deaf and hearing people to communicate with each other, 24 hours per day. There is a nationwide access number: 1-711. TTY options include regular display with 1) print-out options on some models, 2) large visual displays (LVD) but no print out, 3) telebraille, and 4) cell phone connections. (Access to wireless services is an emerging issue. For more information see Ultratec Co., http://www.ultratec.com.)

16. Digital hearing aids: Designed to provide more frequency-specific amplification than is available with standard hearing aids. Ultimately, they can be modified to meet the individual's specific hearing loss profile.

17. Cochlear implants: Implantation of a series of wires through the mastoid process of the skull and into the cochlea to enhance acquisition of gross auditing signals for people with profound hearing loss. New developments are increasing the number of wires being implanted to be increasingly sensitive across multiple frequencies. The user wears a computer-based unit that sends signals to the implant.

18. Digital television: May allow users to modify the size of captioning available. Deaf advocacy groups are watching to ensure the move to digital television includes rules to continue toward the goal of 100% captioning in all televisions sold in America (Strauss, 1999).

19. Video relay interpreting: Uses a computer or television with video capabilities to relay information (through a trained operator) between deaf and hearing users. Advantages over standard TTY usage include shorter conversations and the ability to convey information through visual expressions and gestures.

20. Laser cane: Small, hand-held device with sensors that detect objects in a blind person's path. Signals of obstacles are transmitted via audible beeps or vibrations.

21. Voice-activated hearing aids: Internal hearing device that activates to voice when noise of a predetermined volume is present in the environment. This enables the

user to engage in noisy situations while focusing amplifications on nearby voices (rather than machines and crowd noise).

22. Computer-assisted real-time transcription (CART): Captioning system that uses a transcriber to translate speech into text for display on a screen. This system is used for classes, meetings, and conferences.

23. CapTel: Communication assistant revoices what the caller says (using voice recognition software), producing a transcript that is displayed on the caller's Cap-Tel device. This results in near-instant captioning of speech with an average speed of up to 140 words per minute.

24. ICommunicator system: Laptop computer that translates a speaker's or instructor's speech into text, as well as into ASL, on a word-for-word basis. The software saves a copy of the text so that it can be replayed later.

For additional information regarding AT and accommodations for youth with sensory impairments, contact your state's AT technical assistance program.

Internet Resources Related to Youth with Sensory Impairments

The use of the Internet for interpersonal communications and information resources has dramatically affected the lives of many professionals and their students with disabilities, not to mention society at large. Most school classes have access to computers, either in the classroom or in centralized computer labs. Students and teachers have asynchronous access to a multitude of interactive and informational resources (e.g., e-mail, bulletin boards, listservs, search engines). Table 17.3 provides a list of web sites related to the needs of youth with sensory impairments in five areas: blindness, deafness, deaf-blindness, transition for people with disabilities, and AT.

DESIGNING AND IMPLEMENTING INDIVIDUALIZED TRANSITION PLANS FOR YOUTH WITH SENSORY IMPAIRMENTS

Many wonderful technological strategies are available to help people with sensory impairments and other disabilities, but these devices are of little value if the student does not have access to them. Transition planning can play an important role in enhancing students' opportunities to interact with quality technology and receive other important services.

Professional literature in rehabilitation and education is filled with articles about the necessity of transition planning for youth with disabilities (Baer & Rumrill, 2001; Bullis et al., 1995; Everson, 1995; Gartin et al., 1998; Luft et al., 2001; Rumrill, 2001; Stodden et al., 2001). These articles range from citing career and social development theories to identifying vocational programming as the backbone of transition planning. Virtually every published work on the subject cites interdisciplinary, person-centered planning as the crux of any successful transition from school to adulthood. The process of designing and implementing a transition plan is much like combining the ingredients of a recipe. If all the ingredients are combined in the correct order and in the right measures, then the transition is most likely to be successful. If elements are combined out of order or in incorrect amounts, however, then the transition is destined to

Table 17.3. Selected Internet resources

Resources on blindness

The RRTC on Blindness and Low Vision	http://www.blind.msstate.edu
American Foundation for the Blind	http://www.afb.org
A Blind Net	http://www.blind.net
National Federation of the Blind	http://nfb.org
American Council of the Blind	http://acb.org
Blind Childrens Center	http://www.blindcntr.org

Resources on deafness

Laurent Clerc National Deaf Education Center	http://clerccenter.gallaudet.edu/InfoToGo
Deaf World Web	http://www.icdri.org/dhhi/dww.htm
National Center on Deafness	http://ncod.csun.edu

Resources on deaf-blindness

DB-Link	http://www.tr.wou.edu/dblink
The Arizona Deafblind Project	http://www.azdb.net
The Vermont State Project for Children and Youth with Deafblindness	http://uvm.edu/~cdci/programs/iteam/itdb.html
The National Technical Assistance Consortium for Children and Young Adults who are Deaf-Blind	http://tr.wou.edu/ntac
Deafblind Children home page	http://geocities.com/Heartland/Meadows/5939
Helen Keller National Center for Deaf-Blind Youths and Adults	http://www.hknc.org
A-Z to Deafblindness	http://www.deafblind.com

Resources on transition for people with disabilities

CEC Information Center on Disabilities and Gifted Education	http://ericec.org
National Dissemination Center for Children with Disabilities	http://www.nichcy.org
Regional Resource & Federal Center Network	http://www.rrfcnetwork.org
National Center on Secondary Education and Transition	http://www.ncset.org

Resources on assistive technology

ABLEDATA	http://www.abledata.com/
Alliance for Technology Access	http://www.ataccess.org
Communities of Power	http://www.copower.org

deviate from the plan. This section describes the elements and conditions of transition planning that ensure positive and expected outcomes for people with sensory impairments, according to these seven basic steps:

1. Organize educational and vocational planning teams for all transition-age students.

2. Organize the circle of people, including students, who can craft visions of successful transition.

3. Identify the key activities needed to create these visions.

4. Hold an initial transition planning meeting as part of the annual individualized education program (IEP) meeting.

5. Implement the ITP through secondary school and adult services providers.

6. Update the ITP annually.

7. Hold an exit meeting when the student is preparing to graduate from or otherwise leave public school.

As mandated in the Individuals with Disabilities Education Act (IDEA) Amendments of 1997 (PL 105-17) and the 2004 reauthorization (PL 108-446), transition planning for students with disabilities should begin at no later than 14 years of age. The dropout rate for students with sensory impairments, particularly those with singular sensory impairments, is high (Twenty-Fourth Annual Report to Congress, 2002). According to the IDEA, all students who participate in annual IEP meetings are required to participate in transition planning. Teachers, parents, and administrators should be conscious of the tendency to concentrate on students with more severe or multiple disabilities and should adjust screening and implementation processes to compensate.

Once the teams are organized, a variety of individuals will be invited to participate as the circle of people who help the student identify the vision for the future. Once this vision is crafted and activities are generated, it is then time to advance to the more formal school-based transition plan. The activities reflect a period of brainstorming in which many difficult ideas are put forth by the circle of friends. Core members of this group tend to be the student, the parents, the school transition coordinator (if one is designated), the school-based rehabilitation counselor (if one is available), the school administrator and/or teacher (if the student attends a resource class or segregated classroom), and the state VR counselor (if one has not been placed within the school setting). Additional members are usually called as needed or as the student approaches his or her graduation date. Typical consulting members for students with visual impairments include an orientation and mobility specialist and rehabilitation teacher (Baer & Rumrill, 2001). A rehabilitation engineer or technologist might also be invited. For students who are deaf or hard of hearing, consulting members might include a speech-language therapist or an audiologist. Students with dual sensory impairments may utilize any or all of these consultants to varying degrees. Additional consulting members for youth with sensory impairments can include physicians, low-vision specialists, psychologists, and independent living professionals.

Particularly in rural communities, people other than agency personnel may be formally used to assist the student in transition. These paraprofessionals often serve as links among the school system, adult services agencies, and the community in general. Paraprofessionals may be parents, concerned business leaders, church representatives, or civic group representatives who become to some degree responsible for activities such as career development, community orientation, CBI, transportation, and/or organized recreation.

After the transition team membership has been determined for each student with sensory impairments, planning for the initial meeting can occur. Typically, the initial meeting occurs as a part of the student's IEP meeting (Luft et al., 2001). The meeting should be scheduled at a time when all of the core members of the planning team can be present, but it is most important that the student and his or her parents attend. It is preferable that the meeting occur on a weekday when consulting members can be reached by telephone during the meeting. An initial part of the IEP/ITP plan will be determining when and where the student should receive school services. Services in

1. Find out who is available to help you. (Also, learn what their titles mean and what they do.) One very important person who typically works with students with visual impairments is the itinerant teacher. Itinerant teachers move from school to school working with individual students, and usually translate students' classwork into Braille. Students may also receive training from an orientation and mobility instructor, who will teach them to move independently.

2. Learn how to adapt and modify materials and instruction. (The changes you make might also help other students.) Teachers face a wide variety of students with diverse abilities, styles of learning, and cultural and linguistic systems, as well as disparate economic situations, family structures, and value systems. The good news about the variety in the classroom is that teachers' efforts at individualizing instruction and materials for students with the greatest difference may result in adaptations that will benefit all students.

3. Learn as much as you can, and encourage the professionals you work with to do the same. One of the key ingredients for successful inclusion of students with disabilities is adequate education and support of the professionals who work with students who have disabilities.

4. Find out about training that may be available and ask to go. Often in-service training will be provided by your local school district, a regional service center or co-op, a nearby university, or a regional or national conference. Get your name on the mailing list of organizations whose focus is on visual impairments.

5. Suggest that others become informed, especially students, who may have access to programs like the "Kids on the Block" puppet shows that teach about disabilities. Use your local library and bookstores to find print material that you can read and share.

6. Call parents and ask questions when you do not understand terminology, equipment, or the reasons for prescribed practices. Then, keep an open mind.

7. Teach other students to assist in social as well as academic settings. Most young children are able and willing to help students with disabilities as they adjust to their new situation in a general classroom. Students can offer assistance at lunch, on the playground, and in fine arts classes, where there is less structure and routine.

Figure 17.2. Tips for inclusion of youth with sensory impairments.

neighborhood high schools are preferable for students who are learning how to function in the community. Figure 17.2 provides several tips for inclusion of students with visual impairments into general education classrooms.

The transition coordinator or school-based rehabilitation counselor is responsible for organizing the transition meeting and for gathering all available pertinent information about the student prior to the meeting. The team leader should be able to quickly summarize key information regarding the student's educational history; medical, educational, and vocational assessments; and past activities and interests. Up-front organizational efforts by the team leader ensure more actual planning time for the transition team.

Typically, the transition coordinator or school-based rehabilitation counselor serves as the team leader during the transition planning in an IEP meeting. The leader makes certain that all members know each other and encourages open, honest communication within the group. The team leader is also responsible for discussing the ground rules for participation and decision making in the planning process. One of the most important ground rules is that the student and family always provide input and make the final decision about the student's participation in an activity.

The team leader is also responsible for initiating discussion about transition outcomes and possible support services available to the student. The student with a sensory impairment should decide which outcomes are most important in the following domains: employment and higher education, social and leisure activities, community participation, and residential options. The rest of the group members should generate a checklist of support services to be used during the planning process and a checklist of adult support services that can be used to assist the student in attaining the chosen outcomes postgraduation. Figure 17.3 lists adult support services available to people with varying degrees of sensory impairment. The major benefit of such checklists is to prevent the team from excluding or forgetting potential sources of support for the student. The team leader should encourage all members of the group to voice opinions or concerns about potential outcomes or support services during the ITP meeting rather than allowing a decision to be made without the full support of the group. The student's ITP should at least consider all 10 of the following goal areas:

1. Employment

2. Vocational education/training

3. Postsecondary education

4. Financial/income needs

5. Independent living

6. Transportation/mobility

7. Social relationships

8. Recreation/leisure

9. Health/safety

10. Self-advocacy/future planning

The core and consulting members of each ITP team have numerous responsibilities. Most teams and team leaders find comfort in utilizing a services referral checklist (Wehman, Moon, Everson, Wood, & Barcus, 1988) to initiate and monitor referrals to the various adult services agencies. The checklist does not need to be elaborate; it only needs to convey services to which the student has been referred, the referral date, the name of the contact individual, and the dates by which the services are expected to begin and end.

Each team member should leave the initial ITP meeting with a sense of satisfaction that the student's interests have been fully examined and that actions have been taken to address those interests. Members should also know what their responsibilities are in the actual implementation of the plan. If any issues have not been resolved (e.g., remaining vision, an assistive device must be assessed), then team members should set another meeting time to discuss the results of further investigation and to finalize the

Employment/higher education
  Vocational rehabilitation (VR) (Many states have specialized agencies for vision and hearing.)
    Interpreter services
    Reader services
    Brailling
    Transportation (usually time-limited during job training)
    Counseling
    Evaluation for employment, orientation and mobility, and assistive technology
    Job placement (transitional)
    Job development and supported employment
    Sheltered employment
    Higher education or trade school
    Note: VR for people with blindness is "birth through death"; therefore, some services are
      not time-limited.

Residential
  Vocational rehabilitation through independent living services
    Location of Section 8 housing
    Assistance with housing or roommate search
    Evaluation for and provision of assistive technology devices
    Rehabilitation testing of domestic skills
    Counseling and assistance with home management
    Assistance with Social Security benefits
  Mental retardation/developmental disabilities agencies for students with sensory impairments
    Group home or ICF/MR placement
    Supervised apartment placement
    Location of Section 8 housing
    Service coordination
    Attendant care (if needed)

Recreation
  Vocational rehabilitation (blind services)
    Counseling on finding recreational options
    Assistance in networking
    Updates on recreational options available
    Orientation and mobility instruction
  Mental retardation/developmental disabilities agencies for students with sensory impairments
    Sponsored recreation programs
    Individualized instruction and support for participation
    Service coordination

Community participation
  Vocational rehabilitation through independent living services
    Interpreter services
    Brailling (Library for the Blind)
    Orientation and mobility instruction
    Adaptations and assistive technology
    Rehabilitation teaching
  Mental retardation/developmental disabilities agencies for students with sensory impairments
    Service coordination
    Instruction
    Structured programs for participation

Figure 17.3.   A sample checklist of adult services available to people with sensory impairments.

FRANK

Frank is an 18-year-old student who has a severe visual impairment resulting from juvenile onset diabetes. He must take insulin injections three times per day, and other symptoms of his illness include fatigue and occasional ulcers on his feet. Frank can see large objects and obstacles in his path with adequate lighting. He can read print with a closed-circuit magnification machine, and a voice synthesizer/screen reader program enables him to gain access to a wide variety of computer applications.

Enrolled in a public high school college preparatory program, Frank is entering his senior year. After graduation, Frank has plans to attend college and study business and finance. He would like to be a financial planner and investment broker. Frank is assessed to have above-average intelligence. He tends to be a bit shy, and he maintains a small circle of friends. His best friend, whom he met in a summer job program for students with disabilities, attends the school for the blind in Frank's home state. They communicate regularly via e-mail.

Frank ambulates independently in familiar environments. When traveling to the large city 15 miles from his home, he uses a white cane. He lives with his parents and two sisters, ages 13 and 15. Frank's hobbies include "surfing" the Internet, writing poetry, and watching sports on television.

ITP. A key to good planning is never to leave loose ends without a plan to resolve them. The reader should keep in mind that the ITP presented in Figure 17.4 is only an example. Other students may have similar goals and/or service needs, but no two plans should be identical.

Community Integration for Youth with Sensory Impairments

Along with issues related to education and employment, a comprehensive transition plan for a student with a sensory impairment must involve careful consideration of the supports that he or she will need to successfully integrate into the community as an adult. Discussed in the following section, these community integration issues include enhancing travel skills, public transportation resources, use of public transportation, and dog guides.

Enhancing Travel Skills   The transition team and the student should consider many different forms of travel when planning for the transportation needs of students with visual impairments. Depending on the person's mobility and expressed needs, the orientation and mobility specialist in cooperation with relevant team members might consider teaching the individual a safe walking route to and from the local recreation center. For some individuals, solo foot travel to and from work is possible. If the person chooses this means of transportation, then the orientation and mobility specialist should monitor the individual's applicable safety techniques and use of his or her other senses. If the orientation and mobility specialist determines that the individual's safety is in jeopardy, then various long cane techniques may be taught to assist the individual in locating curbs and objects in the foot path. In addition to acting as a bumper, the long cane alerts drivers that the individual has a visual impairment. This is usually helpful at street crossings where there is moderate to heavy traffic.

Other types of mobility devices such as electronic travel aids, AT, and low-vision devices (e.g., telescopes) may also be useful in assisting an individual with a visual impairment to travel to and from the work setting. These devices can be expensive, however, and may require extensive training for successful use. The transition team must evaluate whether the individual would benefit from such instruction. Figure 17.5 gives an example of how a girl who is deaf-blind ambulates around her community.

An alternative to these technical devices is to teach the individual with a visual impairment the safe method for walking with a sighted individual. In the sighted-guide

INDIVIDUALIZED TRANSITION PLAN

Description of Student's Future Vision

It is Frank's dream to attend college and study business/finance. He wants to work as a financial planner and investment broker. He also wants to expand his social network and engage in more community activities.

Students Name: *Frank*   School: *Roosevelt*

Birthdate: *7-24-82*   ITP Conference Date: *9-8-00*

Student's Identification Number: *OX4-24-3480*

Participants

Name	Position
Frank	*Student*
Sue and Mike	*Parents*
Barb	*Transition Coordinator*
Hugh	*Guidance Counselor*
Ted	*Vocational Rehabilitation Counselor*
Linda	*Stockbroker*

Career and Economic Self-Sufficiency

Employment Goal: *Frank will gain employment as a financial planner.*

Level of present performance: *Frank worked as a unpaid summer intern at an investment brokerage firm. He has no paid work experience in this area, but he worked for 2 summers as a building maintenance assistant.*

Steps needed to accomplish goal: *1) Enroll in 4-year college program in business and finance, 2) participate in summer co-op programs, 3) continue apprenticeship at brokerage firm.*

Date of Completion: *June 2005*

Person(s) responsible for implementation: *All team members*

Postsecondary Education/Training Goal: *Complete a 4-year college degree in business and finance.*

Level of present performance: *Frank is a B+ student in college preparatory courses.*

Figure 17.4. Sample individualized plan for Frank.

Martin Campbell, a college student, uses many different types of assistive technology in a typical day, to make his activities—including a job search—run smoothly.

Martin is 20 years old, and he is deafblind. He has optic neuropathy, and his best corrected visual acuity is 20/200 in his left eye and 20/300 in his right eye. He does not see objects or people clearly, especially in his central field. His hearing loss is moderate to severe in both ears. He hears some speech and most environmental sounds— cars, trains, planes—if there is no background noise.

Martin attends a small state college in his home town, where he is a sophomore majoring in accounting. He works part-time at a pizza restaurant. Martin shares an apartment with three of his friends from the public high school he attended.

Martin uses a closed-circuit television magnification machine to read written documents and large-print computer software for e-mail, the Internet, and his studies. In his college classes, Martin uses a tactile interpreter who signs into his hand, and a notetaker.

Martin uses a cane to travel in unfamiliar settings. He also uses a global positioning system (GPS) with large-print and voice output, scope, and a portable electronic magnification device. He uses public transportation, both fixed-route buses and the paratransit system, and he has several friends and family members who are willing to transport him as needed.

Some people who don't know Martin well have a hard time understanding his voice. Most of them don't know American Sign Language, so if an interpreter is not with Martin, he uses a handheld electronic communication device with large-print and voice output. He can preprogram emergency or help messages, and people can type their responses for him to read in large print. For spontaneous messages, Martin types them directly into the handheld device, and he and the other person pass the electronic device back and forth to read typed messages.

In combination, Martin uses a folding cane with a marshmallow tip, the handheld device, the GPS, the portable electronic magnification machine, the closed-circuit television magnification machine, and large-print computer software. All of these devices, except the closed-circuit television and his computer, are portable and can be used to aid in Martin's mobility. He chooses technology aids based on the activity, on where he is going, and on how familiar the situation is to him.

Last week, Martin had an interview for a part-time job with a local accounting firm. His mobility instructor reviewed the bus route with him. Martin located the bus with his scope and activated a message on his handheld device to the driver before sitting down. Martin sat at the front of the bus, and the driver tapped his hand to let him know when the bus reached his stop, just as Martin had requested in the message on his handheld device. Once he got off the bus, Martin used his GPS and a scope to cross three low-traffic streets and his cane to cross two high-traffic streets. Martin found the directions to the building using his GPS, walked to the building using his cane, and identified the address with his scope.

On entering the building, Martin used his handheld device to ask the receptionist for directions to the office where the interview was being held. Martin's interpreter met him at the office.

Not only was Martin's trip to the job interview a success, the firm called him three days later and offered him the job!

Figure 17.5. Profile of Martin, a college student who is deafblind, and how assistive technology helps him in his daily life.

technique, the individual who is blind grasps the sighted guide's arm directly above the elbow, forming a 90-degree angle with his or her arm. The individual walks one half-step behind and to the side of the sighted person. In this position, the individual can feel the guide's movements and react to turns, proceed up and down stairs, and pass through doors and narrow areas safely. Sighted-guide skills are often used in combination with other mobility devices.

When evaluating a potential worksite, it is important to consider whether the individual's work schedule includes evening duties and responsibilities. If so, the orientation and mobility specialist will need to plan accordingly for potential instruction in night mobility (e.g., a long cane in conjunction with a wide-angle mobility nightlight).

Public Transportation   Some destinations will be too far for the individual with a visual impairment to travel on foot, and alternative methods of transportation will need to be employed. Public transportation may be chosen as the best method for traveling to and from the work setting.

When preparing to use public transportation, certain questions need to be considered by the orientation and mobility specialist: What public transportation systems are available in the community and useful to the individual? Is the transportation schedule consistent enough to match the individual's work or social schedule? Are there adequate sensory landmarks at the pickup and destination points to assist the individual in locating and distinguishing those places? Is the individual capable of using that system? Is there a paratransit system (e.g., vans, taxi vouchers) for people with disabilities who cannot gain access to general transportation services?

Using Public Transportation   To gain access to the public transportation system, the individual with a visual impairment must get to the bus stop or subway station platform, identify the correct bus or car, board and pay the fare (and possibly ask for a transfer), locate a seat, and exit at the proper destination. The orientation and mobility specialist should teach the individual how to obtain information over the telephone regarding schedules, the amount and type of fare, location of pickup and destination points, and whether transfers are needed. Not only does this get the person where he or she is going, but it also teaches him or her solicitation skills that are generalizable to other settings in the community.

Of all the transportation options listed previously, travel on buses and trains requires the greatest orientation and mobility skill. Using minibuses and taxis requires less travel ability, and many people with visual impairments choose these options over travel by foot or on general-access public transportation. In the case of the scheduled minibuses and taxis, which are often offered through paratransit programs, the individual has to telephone the paratransit office and schedule a pickup time and destination point. Usually, reservations must be made in advance. Unlike the scheduled minibus, taxi pickup is usually more flexible in scheduling, but fares are generally more expensive than either minibuses or general-access buses and trains—even if the paratransit program subsidizes the user's fares.

Dog Guides   The use of dog guides, which dates back to the 19th century, is yet another possible method of travel. Systematic mobility training of dog guides began in Germany toward the end of World War I. In 1929, The Seeing Eye, Inc., became the first dog guide training facility in the United States. Initially, airlines, restaurants, hotels, bus lines, and schools were reluctant to allow the dog and the individual with a visual impairment entrance. Because of the ADA and more accepting public attitudes, people with dog guides now have access to all facilities open to the general public, including public transportation. To enhance a student's placement prospects, the teacher may recommend that the student use a dog guide for travel purposes. Training usually takes up to 6 weeks, so adequate time must be included in the placement schedule.

The ultimate decision regarding modes of travel is the responsibility of the student and the orientation and mobility specialist. Weighing the possibilities of available transportation systems and matching those options with the individual's travel abilities require a complete and thorough analysis of the risks and hazards involved in traveling in and around the community.

EVALUATION OF INDIVIDUALIZED TRANSITION PLAN OUTCOMES FOR YOUTH WITH SENSORY IMPAIRMENTS

An ITP is functionally and practically worthless without monitoring, evaluation, and follow-up. In the past, many transitional IEPs and standard IEPs have been written to comply with federal and state regulations and suggestions; however, they were never acted on to a sufficient degree as mandated by IDEA (Luft et al., 2001).

The best evaluation of transition outcomes includes a variety of measures. These measures are both qualitative and quantitative and occur at several different levels. At the planning level, the evaluator should ask the following questions:

- Are interventions and services designed to be maximally under the control of the individual with the disability?

- Do the interventions, programs, and services encourage independence, problem-solving abilities, self-assurance, and needed social skills (Sacks & Wolffe, 1992)?

- Are naturally occurring cues and consequences used first so that human services intrusiveness is kept to a minimum?

- Are interventions designed for generalizability and the promotion of problem solving?

- Are monitoring points built into the plan so that feedback can be obtained from the service providers and the student with sensory impairments?

At the implementation level, the evaluator should continue to monitor the issues outlined previously and add these questions:

- Are the parents and the student periodically consulted to discuss progress and areas that need further attention?

- As a result of planning and progress toward independence made in each domain, is the student able to achieve other personal goals above and beyond those listed?

- Is the student able to wean from assistance and rely more heavily on self-help?

- Is the student building lasting, nonpaid friendships?

- Can the student, at any point during the process, call a meeting and change the transition plan to better suit his or her needs?

At the exit level, the evaluator should examine the following issues:

- Have all transition goals been met or changed for a better outcome?

- Does the student know who his or her service provider contacts are after graduation?

- Does the student have a stable, integrated place to live?

- Is the student employed or enrolled in a postsecondary educational program?

- Does the student have friends, and is he or she involved in recreational activities within his or her community?

- Are the student and his or her family happy with the transition outcomes?

These measures should not be answered with simple "yes" or "no" responses. They are intended to be the basis for further exploration in each domain and for the overall ITP.

CONCLUSION

Youth with sensory impairments comprise a diverse, heterogeneous group of individuals who often have significant transition needs. Barriers that students with visual or hearing impairments face as they move from public school programs to adult life roles include communication difficulties, limited access to information, social isolation, and the secondary effects of conditions that cause blindness or deafness. By developing proactive, interdisciplinary transition services, structured by a student-centered plan, transition specialists in both special education and rehabilitation can assist this all-too-often disenfranchised population of deserving students in the pursuit of rewarding, productive lives beyond the classroom.

STUDY QUESTIONS

1. Why are youth with sensory impairments underserved by rehabilitation and other service programs, and as a result, faced by challenges in both school and employment?

2. What are the differences among the diagnosis of blindness, legal blindness, low vision, and partially sighted?

3. What are the differences among the terms *deafness, hard of hearing,* and *hearing impaired*?

4. What are some common social, vocational, and academic characteristics of youth with sensory impairments?

5. Describe some of the challenges that teachers experience with students with sensory impairments.

6. What are the components of a functional assessment of youth with sensory impairments?

7. Describe AT that can help students with sensory impairments.

8. Describe the transition planning process for students with sensory impairments.

9. What are some methods for improving travel and mobility for individuals with sensory impairments?

18

Applications for Youth with Learning Disabilities

ELIZABETH EVANS GETZEL, JOHN J. GUGERTY, AND SHANNON McMANUS

AFTER COMPLETING THIS CHAPTER, THE READER WILL BE ABLE TO

○ Explain the different definitions of learning disabilities

○ Describe the perceptions and feelings of young people with learning disabilities

○ Identify three cognitive challenges that individuals with learning disabilities face

○ Understand techniques for assessment of transition planning for youth with learning disabilities

○ Describe teaching strategies that can be useful for young people with learning disabilities, including ways to help visual learners, auditory learners, and tactile learners

○ Understand how to work with students with multiple cultural backgrounds

Learning disabilities (LD) can be viewed from at least three perspectives: definitional, data, and individual experience. A working knowledge of definitions and a familiarity with aggregate data are key tools in the effective professional's repertoire; however, professionals who wish to develop a more accurate understanding of LD and the manifestations of LD in personal, social, and work situations must develop and internalize an understanding of the effects on the lives of real people. In doing so, it becomes apparent that those with LD, even in mild forms, face severe problems in developing and maintaining employment, independence, and interpersonal relationships.

DEFINING LEARNING DISABILITIES

Addressing the needs of students with LD is an important component of American education, but as a service category, it is characterized by inconsistency and disagreement (Gregg, Scott, McPeek, & Ferri, 1999; Siegel, 1999; Stanovich, 1999). Differences in the identification of LD have also been shown to be related to disciplinary or professional perspectives and techniques, to the specific formula used for determining a discrepancy between ability and achievement, to the techniques and measures used in diagnosis, and to a variety of institutional or organizational constraints (Gregg & Scott, 2000).

Studies that have reviewed the history and status of diagnostic and classification practices (Raskind, Gerber, Goldberg, Higgins, & Herman, 1998) have cautioned that LD screening and diagnostic activities are sometimes flawed and technically inadequate. Algozzine and Ysseldyke (1986) concluded that resources should be redirected toward corrective and preventive educational interventions. They saw no reason to believe that observed trends in screening and diagnosis would improve programs for individuals with LD and thus recommended that resources used for screening, diagnosis, and classification be diverted to making all education more special.

Nonetheless, the diagnosis, classification, and program design controversies continue unabated (Bender, Marshall, & Wehman, 1997; Gordon, Lewandowski, & Keiser, 1999; Haager, 1997; Miller, 1990; Rispens, van Yperen, & van Duijn, 1991; Siegel, 1999; Stanovich, 1999). Hammill (1990) reviewed efforts made since 1962 to define *learning disabilities*. He quoted 11 widely known and historically influential definitions, compared and contrasted their content, and concluded that the field could and should form a consensus around the National Joint Committee on Learning Disabilities (NJCLD; 1990) definition:

Learning disabilities is a general term that refers to a heterogeneous group of disorders manifested by significant difficulties in the acquisition and use of listening, speaking, reading, writing, reasoning, or mathematical abilities. These disorders are intrinsic to the individual, presumed to be due to central nervous system dysfunction, and may occur across the life span. Problems in self-regulatory behaviors, social perception, and social interaction may exist with learning disabilities but do not by themselves constitute a learning disability. Although learning disabilities may occur concomitantly with other handicapping conditions (for example, sensory impairment, mental retardation, serious emotional disturbance) or with extrinsic influences (such as cultural differences, insufficient or inappropriate instruction), they are not the result of those conditions or influences. (p. 6)

Work by Levine (1989, 1990) and Viadero (1989) supported the role of neurobiological factors in LD. At the postsecondary level, Brinckerhoff, Shaw, and McGuire (1993) supported the NJCLD definition for the following reasons:

- It has a broad base of support, including that of the Association on Higher Education and Disability (AHEAD).

- It is consistent with the concept of intraindividual differences in a range of areas, including reasoning.

- It clearly specifies that LD exist throughout the life span.

- It does not require identification of central nervous system (CNS) etiology.

- It recognizes that problems with related psychosocial skills may exist but does not include them as part of the definition.

- Although it acknowledges possible concomitant disabling conditions, it deals with LD as the primary condition.

- It does not rule out the possibility that LD can occur in people with otherwise superior intellectual functioning.

Bateman (1994) recommended a three-stage identification process for students suspected of having LD who are in kindergarten through twelfth grade. This process examines discrepancy, causality, and the need for special education in a way that is consistent with all legal requirements. It also improves on the too common practice of relying on a mathematical formula, which reduces the child to two test scores and falsely equates learning disabilities with discrepancy.

Although varying opinions and viewpoints exist concerning the classification and diagnosis of a learning disability, researchers appear to have generally agreed on a few broad areas (Sitlington, Clark, & Kolstoe, 2000). In particular, researchers have found that there are specific tasks that students without LD can perform that students with LD are unable to do "in spite of the basic integrity of their senses, cognitive ability, emotional state, or lack of opportunity to learn" (Sitlington et al., 2000, p. 79). Students with LD represent a very heterogeneous group; however, Sitlington and colleagues summarized some of the more frequent difficulties associated with students with LD. These difficulties include discrimination, sequencing, affect, auditory activity, sensory integration, language, self-concept, memory, impulse control, motor behavior, visual-motor functioning, conceptual and abstract reasoning, spatial orientation, and body image.

EXPERIENCES OF INDIVIDUALS WITH LEARNING DISABILITIES

A great deal of literature exists in which people with LD have portrayed their own unique experiences in secondary and postsecondary school settings.

Secondary School Experiences

Some high school students with LD describe their experiences in vivid and colorful language:

"My head is just like a television set except it has no channel selector. So I get all the programs on my screen at the same time."

"When I sit in class, I keep having these 'mind drifts.' I never know when my mind is gonna drift away so I lose what's happening."

"I like to move around a lot. When I sit still, I get tired. I get bored. I need action."

"I think I'm a "busticator." A busticator is someone who busts things up all the time. He doesn't mean to. He's real fast and keeps getting into trouble for not thinking. You know it's not really his fault that he does things fast, but I guess he has to take the blame when he causes trouble or bothers someone. Anyway that's me. I'm a real busticator."

"I was looking at the bulletin board. I noticed that there were seven thumbtacks in the bulletin board but only six of them were being used. I wondered about the seventh thumbtack. Why was there nothing underneath it? Maybe someone had pulled something off, or maybe it had fallen off. I thought about pulling the thumbtack out of the bulletin board. I thought it might even be cool to put it on the seat of the kid in front of me. I noticed that this thumbtack was red and all the others were either blue or green. I wondered why the red thumbtack was the one with nothing under it. Maybe there was a reason for it. I tried to think of some reasons. Then, all of a sudden, the teacher called on me, and I realized I had no idea what had been going on in the classroom. The teacher was telling us important stuff while I was busy with that dumb thumbtack. That keeps on happening to me. I'm so distractible. All kinds of things pull me off track."

Many individuals with LD develop ways to mask or cope with their painful school experiences. Karen Campbell (1988) described her situation:

> Memories of my early childhood are filled with frustration, pain and occasions of constant failure. I always knew I was different from the other kids and I was reminded of it every day. I couldn't remember which hand to raise to salute the flag even though instructions had just been given me. In every attempt at writing something, my letters came out backward and I can remember that heat of tears as I struggled to do the simplest task and failed all too often.
>
> I was really quite verbal so I learned how to get by in classroom discussions, but when it came time to read, my mind would dance away and I couldn't remember what I had just read. I couldn't spell the simplest words. I learned how to write poorly, and to clown around or get defensive about my writing and my trouble carrying out instruction. . . . I had come into the world with a disability that would make learning a struggle, and a tremendous challenge. Not everyone recognized it as such. In school, it had always been the same story, 'Karen's such a bright, attractive girl. Her mind just seems to wander. She doesn't pay attention, nor does she seem to want to try.'
>
> Despite my problem, I was able to get through elementary, junior high and high school with minimal difficulty because I know how to drop classes, copy papers, get into study groups with better students, and cheat. I never felt good about any of that, but I knew I had to go to college to please my parents, and it was the only way I knew to get through." (pp. 42–43)

College Experiences

Amazingly, some individuals do not discover or understand their LD until they are in college or even later. Carolee Reiling is one such individual. As a freshman at Stanford University, she heard another student with LD describe his experiences:

All of a sudden, my mind clicked. It was as if someone had turned on the light in the dead of night. . . . As I tried to resist, each illustration that Andy gave of his learning disability pierced further into my mind. The extreme feeling of sickness before every exam or other measure of ability; the lack of reading comprehension; the inability to communicate thoughts and ideas; the sense of isolation. These difficulties came back to haunt me once more. But weren't these problems common to most people? I had always assumed so because I knew no differently. I realized that I studied more than my friends and that I was a slower reader, but I idealistically had considered them to be the exceptions. I did not consider myself to have weaknesses, but rather my friends to have strengths. It soon dawned on me that it was me who was the exception. . . .

I do not think that I have ever felt so alone in my whole life. Even though essentially nothing in my life had physically changed, it was ironically as if everything in the whole world had changed. My self-confidence seemed to vanish into thin air. I instantly found myself, who was once so secure in my friendships, unable to relate to anyone, including my parents. . . . If I could not even understand and accept this situation that was my own, how could I expect others to do so?

As a result, I set out on a sole expedition to find and conquer these problems which caused me to be identified as learning disabled. Since I had always carried around the idea that I might be learning disabled in the back of my mind, I thought that it would be a great relief for me to be diagnosed. It explained many hardships in my life and allowed me to direct many past criticisms on my inability in certain areas from myself to the disability. However, this was a very painful process since it brought out many unhappy memories from the past.

As I continued to reflect on my past, I also connected my disability with my poor performance in and great dislike for English. At least now there was something to explain why I could read and comprehend an English assignment one night and then the next morning could fail a simple quiz to see if you had read. . . . And yet even though there was now an explanation for many of my difficulties, I was not ready to accept it. . . . Furthermore, it meant accepting this condition as one of my inherent characteristics with which I was to spend the rest of my life. And the scary part was that there was not a single thing that I could do to cure myself of it. I could compensate for it, as I had already innately been doing, but it would always be lurking and hiding, ready to surprise me at any given moment. "I am not disabled," I would think to myself. "I may need a little help once in awhile. I may be a little slow. I may be a little stupid. But I will tell you right now that I am not dyslexic."

These thoughts were quickly contradicted once I went through the evaluation process and the reality of my learning disability was established. And yet to what extent? I had mustered up all of my effort throughout high school and had put everything in the whole world that I had towards getting into Stanford. And I was not going to be conquered after I had succeeded. As a result I wanted to know what I was up against, who my opponent was. I wanted to know which problems, errors, and frustrations I could attribute to the disability and which to my own carelessness and stupidity.

My excitement mounted when I received a thick letter from the Morrissey/Compton Educational Center, Inc. I thought that finally the long awaited end to my anxiety had arrived. I was expecting to find out precisely how disabled I was or wasn't and how exactly I compared with everyone else. But all that I found was that I have "significant disabilities of the dyslexic type." Rather than answering my questions and concerns, this statement served to arouse new ones. How does one characterize the "dyslexic type"? Where does "significant" place me in relation to everyone else? Exactly how significant is "significant"?

As a result, I have endeavored to evaluate the degree to which I am afflicted by my learning disability. For 10 days, from Wednesday, February 28, 1990, to Friday, March 9, 1990, I have monitored and kept track of my errors, difficulties, and frustrations which are generally attributed to the presence of a learning disability. This was a very difficult process because it brought me face to face with the effects of my disability. However, I feel that I have learned a lot more about myself and my thought process. . . . While it was a very awakening and almost disheartening self-evaluation, it was also very interesting.

   Throughout the 10-day time period, I monitored my problems and errors as they corresponded to a learning disability characteristics summary and I also had a log in which I recorded my academic frustrations. The statistical summary, while very informative, is far from as accurate as I would like it to be because often my mistakes and difficulties would be so numerous that I did not include many of them. I rather attributed them to anxiety, lack of careful attention, or just general incapabilities like in reading or writing. The general areas in which my difficulties exist are writing, reading, spelling, testing, concentration, speech, orientation, memory, foreign language, and everyday manifestations such as feelings of stress, isolation, and inadequacy. (1990, pp. 1–4)

Reiling (1990) used an outline of LD manifestations to structure her self-monitoring exercise. Due to space limitations, only selected descriptions of her experiences are presented.

Writing

- Tendency to work out specific parts of the paper laboriously instead of focusing on the paper as a whole: "Once again since it is hard for me to conceptualize the overall idea of papers and so contributes greatly to their lack of organization. . . . I averaged 12.2 times a day, with a high of 22 and a low of 3, depending on how much time I spend on my paper that day" (p. 4).

- Freezing up when trying to write: "I have difficulty taking class notes, writing letters, and of course writing papers. Writing is something that for some reason has always seemed to be very forced for me. It is not natural for me to express myself through writing" (p. 5).

- Sentences seem to vanish before being written down: "This is a problem that contributes greatly to my problems with writing because often when I finally think of a good way to express something, it is a race for me to get it written down before it disappears, never to come back. This also happens many times every day in trying to take class notes. It is really frustrating because I will get the first part and then just put a bunch of question marks for the second part" (p. 5).

Spelling

- Reversals are common (e.g., *b* instead of *d*, *freind* instead of *friend*, *probadly* instead of *probably*, 0137 instead of 0317): "This is a difficulty that I always have seemed to possess, but previously I just thought it was because I was not paying enough attention to what I was doing" (p. 7).

- Frequently dropping, adding, or reversing letters and word parts (e.g., *now* instead of *know*, *dab god* instead of *bad dog*): "This is a very broad category and embodies a lot of the mistakes that I make. I averaged about 31.2 times doing this a day, with a low of 20 and a high of 62" (p. 7).

Testing

- Seldom able to complete examinations in class: "This generally would be the case with me, but now I take all of my exams for extra time. The time that I use is usually up to me. For example, on my last Chemistry midterm, there were so many numbers involved that I spent 2 hours on what was a 50-minute test. . . . I feel bad about this, but it is the only thing that allows me to have a fair chance at doing well in my classes" (p. 8).

- Difficulty with multiple-choice questions; difficulty filling in the bubbles on forms: "This is something that I could never seem to do, but I thought that it was that way for everybody. By the time I even located the correct bubbles, I had forgotten which one I was supposed to fill in" (p. 8).

- Misinterprets directions or questions on examinations: "This is something that I seem to do on every test without fail. It ends up costing me a lot of time and usually a lot of points. On my Physics 61 midterm last quarter, I wasted about 45 minutes of a 2-hour exam by misreading just a couple of words, which completely changes a problem. . . . But by [the] time [I realized my mistake,] I was so flustered and frustrated that the test just went downhill for me from there. I have now gotten into the habit of also rereading the questions when I am checking my work because often I instead give answers for things that were not asked or I will forget to do a second or third part of a question" (p. 8).

- Extreme test anxiety: "I know that everybody gets nervous before tests, but I always knew that there was something wrong with me. I cannot count the number of tests that I have literally almost thrown up before. I usually start shaking and get very short of breath. I can't talk to anybody because my mind is so focused on the ordeal ahead of me. My hands get sweaty and my adrenaline rises to such a height that it is like I am getting a workout while just sitting in one place" (p. 9).

Concentration

- Focusing requires extraordinary effort: "It has always been extremely hard for me to concentrate completely, especially when reading, studying, or listening. I have the attention span to read about 3–4 pages. I constantly have to set goals with myself, like saying after I read 5 more pages I can take a short break. . . . I intersperse reading with math, which helps break up the monotony and dread of reading. I can never stay focused in my classes, but if I get the notes I can understand the rest later" (p. 9).

- Easily distracted by noise and movement: "This is a problem that I always associated with my inability to focus for periods of time. . . . Noises that really bother me a lot are ticking of clocks or people making noises like flicking their pens because of nervous habits. . . . Movement also does not allow me to concentrate. For some reason, when people next to me in class are nervously doing something with their hands or legs, it never fails to catch my attention. When someone is doing that I have to move or else I cannot concentrate on lecture or even take notes" (p. 9).

Speech

- Difficulty in communicating ideas clearly: "I often say something exactly the opposite of how I should have said it. (e.g., 'Does the dog have the ball?' = 'Does the ball have the dog?'). I have gotten into the habit of going over in my head what I have just said hoping to catch stuff like that, and sometimes I do. . . . I also have problems conveying my ideas to others even if I say them how I meant to. This is why I am terrified of public speaking or even talking to a group of peers" (p. 10).

Orientation

- Directions, map reading, and navigating difficulty: "Nothing will make you feel more stupid than getting lost in Meyer Library trying to follow their stupid map. When I was trying to get books for my CIV research paper, it took me forever to find where my book should have been. . . . I finally decided to start over and try again and it was then I realized that I was on the wrong floor" (p. 11).

- Feeling lost in a familiar setting; becoming disoriented easily: "I always seem to get lost. . . . I cannot count the number of times that I have gotten lost running. One afternoon first quarter I was out for 1 hour and 45 minutes because I got lost and could not figure out how to get back. I finally had to ask someone and they showed me the road I was looking for was about 300 feet in front of me" (p. 11).

Memory

- Difficulty recalling familiar things such as one's telephone number, address, age, names of friends, and so forth: "I am the worst person on this whole world with names. . . . Ages are also very difficult for me. By the time I learn mine it seems that it is the next year and it changes. . . . As far as my phone number is concerned, I did not learn it until about half way through winter quarter. I have it posted big on my desk and so it is reinforced in my memory about a hundred times a day. However, when people asked me what it was, I could not remember. Whenever I am on the phone and I need to leave it, I can't remember" (pp. 11–12).

Everyday Manifestations

- Feeling constantly behind: "Even if I am caught up on all my work, I never find myself at a loss for something to do. Just because I read the chapter once doesn't mean that I remember any of it" (p. 14).

- Isolation resulting from fear of being misunderstood: "I have a very difficult time communicating my thoughts, especially when I am speaking to more than just one person and all of the attention is on me. . . . Needless to say, I feel very isolated when ideas that are all so clear in my mind cannot be made understandable to others. I often get a similar feeling when things that others say go so far above my head that they are beyond my reach" (p. 15).

- Feeling inadequate because of difficulty doing tasks that others find easy: "I feel that this statement summarizes for me the primary difficulty of being learning disabled. Even though my slow reading rate has become a joke with all my friends and myself, it still really hurts my self-image. I cannot help being jealous of the ease with which they read, understand, write, speak, remember, and concentrate. It is so easy to feel inadequate and get a low esteem of oneself. Even though I know that I am not stupid because of my learning disability, sometimes I feel that there is no other word with which to describe my incapabilities" (pp. 15–16).

These quotes from Reiling (1990) illustrated what it is like to go through life when one cannot rely on the accuracy of what one reads or expresses either in speech or in writing. It documents the anxiety and stress that an individual with LD experiences and the energy that he or she must expend to cope with tasks that most people perform automatically, accurately, and with minimal effort. Her story also pointed out that the term *dyslexia* does not do justice to the complexity of the experience, the effort required to compensate and cope, or the many other aspects of life that are affected by LD.

It is important to note that the evaluation report that Reiling (1990) received explained nothing, especially omitting the implications of her situation for daily life, academic life, and future employment. Few individuals with LD are able to analyze themselves as thoroughly as Reiling did. In the absence of assistance from knowledgeable professionals, many individuals with LD—even those who were identified in primary or secondary school—have a very incomplete understanding of their disabilities, few use self-monitoring or compensatory strategies, and most have little awareness of how their disabilities influence their abilities to obtain employment and perform successfully on the job. Yet, Reiling made many references to the long-standing nature of several of her problems—reversals, omissions, misperceptions, direction problems, memory problems—and the fact that she completed high school without any of the staff noticing manifestations of what was later diagnosed as a severe LD.

Reiling's situation reflects what Shaywitz and Shaywitz (1990) found when they studied more than 400 Connecticut children from 12 towns who were in kindergarten through third grade. Using some of the same kinds of testing instruments that the school used, the researchers tested each child for reading disabilities and contrasted those findings with the number of students the schools identified as having reading disabilities. After testing each second grader, the researchers found 17 of 198 boys and 15 of 216 girls to have reading disabilities; in contrast, the schools had identified 27 boys but only 7 girls with reading disabilities. By the third grade, the researchers found 18 of 199 boys and 13 of 215 girls with reading disabilities; the schools identified 20 boys, but only 9 girls. In contrast, Shaywitz and Shaywitz (1990) theorized that such imbalances occur because girls typically exhibit more acceptable classroom behavior and are usually not as active or inattentive as boys. Therefore, boys are often inaccurately identified, and girls with difficulties may be overlooked. "Our data indicate that school-identified samples are almost unavoidably subject to a referral bias" (p. 3).

UNIQUE CHALLENGES PRESENTED BY YOUTH WITH LEARNING DISABILITIES

Learning disabilities have often been called the "hidden" disabilities. The number of students served under the category of Specific Learning Disabilities in the IDEA has increased 34% between 1990 and 2000 (National Center for Learning Disabilities [NCLD], 2002); however, because these disabilities are not readily visible, students with specific LD often report that it is difficult to make others understand and accept the problems they experience. As a result, educators form inaccurate perceptions of students with LD, which leads to inadequate preparation and planning for transition from school to the community (Brinckerhoff, McGuire, & Shaw, 2002; Dunn, 1996). To illustrate this lack of understanding and the misconceptions about students with

LD, one student commented, "I have constantly run up against misunderstanding and the unwillingness to accept learning disability as a disability. The typical response I get is that everyone has trouble with learning, which is totally an inadequate response and narrow one" (Board for Rights of Virginians with Disabilities Technical Assistance Project [BRVD-TAP], 1991, p. 20).

The impact of LD on an individual's life can be devastating (Tallal, 1999). In a report presented to the Congressional Biomedical Research Caucus, Tallal noted that 35% of youth with LD drop out of high school at twice the rate of their peers and that 62% are unemployed a year after graduating. Without proper educational planning and intervention, 56% of those students with LD who do drop out will be arrested. It is essential that educators understand the pervasive impact of this disability on the lives of individuals and the need for appropriate accommodations and supports to enable them to successfully make the transition into the community with the skills to pursue employment or higher education.

Understanding One's Disability

The correlation between postsecondary success and self-determination skills is an important one, especially given the fact that other researchers have linked postsecondary education with improved employment outcomes for individuals with disabilities (Stodden & Dowrick, 2001). Therefore, teaching self-determination skills to students with LD is a critical component that will allow them to gain a greater understanding of themselves and learn how to communicate their strengths and accommodation needs both in school and in the community. Adults with LD have identified making the decision to take charge of one's life and making the necessary modifications to achieve one's goals as important keys to success (Reiff, Ginsberg, & Gerber, 1995; Virginia Commonwealth University, 2004). Students with LD who are able to understand their skills, effective learning strategies, and how to acquire information or services are able to obtain a sense of control over their lives (West et al., 1999; Wille-Gregory, Graham, & Hughes, 1995; Virginia Commonwealth University, 2004). Incorporating self-determination skills as part of a student's learning experience is critical. In secondary schools, accommodations may be part of the students' experience, but in most postsecondary or employment settings, the student or worker with disabilities is part of the mainstream and must self-advocate to obtain accommodations (Brinckerhoff et al., 2002; Getzel, McManus, & Briel, 2004; Gugerty, Tindall, Gavin, & Gribbon-Fago, 1993; West et al., 1999).

Wehmeyer (1992) defined *self-determination* as "acting as the primary causal agent in one's life free to make choices and decisions about one's quality of life, free from undue influence or interference" (p. 302). Hoffman and Field (1995) conceptualized self-determination as "one's ability to define and achieve goals based on a foundation of knowing and valuing oneself" (p. 136).

Wehmeyer, Agran, and Hughes (1998) described 12 component skills that are important to the emergence of self-determined behavior. Those elements are: "choice-making; decision-making; problem-solving; goal setting and attainment; independence, risk-taking, and safety skills; self-observation, evaluation, and reinforcement skills; self-instruction; self-advocacy and leadership skills; internal locus of control; positive attributes of efficacy and outcome expectancy; self-awareness; and self-knowledge" (Wehmeyer et al., 1998, p. 11).

It is clear that the goal of transition planning is to prepare students with disabilities for their lives after high school by teaching skills they will need in the new settings. Parents, teachers, friends, and other significant individuals should foster the personal growth and independence of individuals with LD throughout the individual's life (Goldberg, 1991; Ward, 1991). Strategies that have been found effective with students in their overall development include 1) capitalizing on the student's strengths, 2) providing high structure and clear expectations, 3) providing opportunities for success in a supportive atmosphere to build self-esteem, and 4) providing positive reinforcement of appropriate social skills at school and home (LD Online, 2000).

An important method for assisting students with disabilities to take ownership to achieve their goals is through the development of a transition plan as part of their individualized education program (IEP). All too often, students are not active members in their IEP meetings, even though they attend them (Lovitt, Cushing, & Stump, 1994; Morningstar, Turnbull, & Turnbull, 1995). Students with LD need to become active participants in the IEP process by thinking about what they want for the future, communicating their ideas and feelings with parents and teachers to determine realistic goals, and showing responsibility by following up on objectives that they are responsible for completing (Lerner, 2003).

Educators can incorporate self-determination activities into their curriculum to assist students with LD to develop the skills to help them become more active participants in their IEP and transition planning meetings. Examples of two curricula that have been identified as effective for students with LD (Field & Hoffman, 1996; Martin & Marshall, 1994; Wille-Gregory et al., 1995) are described in the following list:

- *The Education Planning Strategy: I PLAN* [revised version is called Self-Advocacy]: I PLAN (Van Reusen et al., 2002) is a megacognitive strategy focused on developing effective planning and communication skills in preparation for participation in the IEP meeting. The strategy can be taught to students in upper elementary and higher grades in about 6 hours over a 1- to 2-week period. With minimal modification, the I PLAN strategy can be used to prepare students to participate in a variety of planning or problem-solving meetings with teachers, employers, or co-workers.

- *The ChoiceMaker Self-Determination Transition Curriculum: Self-Directed IEP*: This curriculum (Martin & Marshall, 1995) teaches students how to manage their own IEP meetings in 11 steps. The methods and materials can be used with a broad range of students, including those with mild to moderate learning and behavior problems.

Problem-Solving and Decision-Making Skills

Students with LD need skills that enable them to identify problems or tasks that must be completed, to list the choices or options involved with problems or tasks, to determine possible outcomes or consequences, and to select the best course of action. The amount of practice and hands-on experience that these students receive in accepting environments increases the likelihood that they will use these skills in all areas of their lives (Izzo, Pritz, & Ott, 1990; Virginia Commonwealth University, 2004; Wehmeyer et al., 1998).

Students with LD may have difficulties managing their time. They may miss appointments or other scheduled events. Even if they have clocks or calendars, they may forget to look at them or may misread what they have written. On the job, they may schedule a number of activities in a row, not allowing enough time to complete each one (Gavin, Tindall, & Gugerty, 1990; Getzel, Briel, & Kregel, 2000; Getzel et al., 2004; Szymanski, Gugerty, Tindall, & Schmidt, 1989). They may also have difficulties with jobs that require tasks to be completed in certain amounts of time and in required sequences.

Setting priorities is another challenge for students with LD. Although these students may appear organized if they keep lists or other techniques to organize their activities (Gavin et al., 1990; Getzel et al., 2000; Szymanski et al., 1989; Virginia Commonwealth University, 2004), they are often unable to determine what to do first. They spend a great deal of time on relatively insignificant tasks and do not focus on the essentials. Many students with LD have difficulty with final decisions and obtaining closure for issues. Teaching self-management skills while in secondary school in the areas of problem identification, goal setting, self-monitoring, self-evaluation, and self-reinforcement can be a method to encourage student participation in learning and to help develop skills that can be generalized to other settings (Snyder & Bambara, 1997; Getzel et al., 2004).

Another issue confronting many students with LD is the ability to remember something that has been taught previously, even on a daily basis. Often these students have been labeled as passive learners, meaning they are not actively involved in the learning process (Izzo et al., 1990; Torgesen, 1982), which is necessary for acquiring problem-solving skills. Short-term memory problems can also contribute to difficulties in remembering information over a period of time. Izzo and her colleagues (1990) identified two basic criteria for instruction that are particularly helpful for people with LD: 1) connecting the instruction to the learners' prior knowledge, which helps students to link new information with what they already know; and 2) using real-life and employment situations to encourage learners' motivation and ability to apply new skills.

Social and Communication Skills

Social skills can present particular challenges to people with LD (Lerner, 2003). As a result of perceptual difficulties, these individuals may have problems understanding others. They may not be able to differentiate between a stare and a thoughtful glance. They may appear to be rude by breaking into conversations or making inappropriate remarks. Individuals with auditory problems may have problems telling the difference between angry and excited voices (Brown, 1982; Price, 1990, 1997). They may also find that they must concentrate so intently on what is said that they miss the nonverbal messages that accompany spoken words (Brown, 1982; Ness & Price, 1990; Price, 1997). Because of this, they may respond incorrectly. In addition, individuals with LD may appear inattentive because they are easily distracted or maintain poor eye contact with the person who is speaking.

Because of the inability to socialize with their peers, these students tend to isolate themselves, which delays social development and can result in immature social skills development. Students need feedback about behaviors that create problems for them if they are to learn creative ways to overcome communication obstacles (Deshler, Ellis, & Lenz, 1996; Lerner, 2003). One method for providing this kind of support is through the use of mentors. Students or adults who are mentors can offer advice on how to interact with others in employment or school settings. If students understand the impact they have on others and know how to improve their skills, then they will be able to increase their self-esteem—an essential asset for pursuing goals (Whelley, Radtke, Burgstahler, & Christ, 2003).

Vaughn and La Greca (1993) suggested that social skills training focus on the areas of communication, social perception (i.e., how behavior is interpreted to understand the thoughts and feelings of others), and social problem solving. They recommend that social interventions be developed for those students with LD who have been identified as having specific sociobehavioral problems.

ASSESSMENT FOR TRANSITION

Assessments of all kinds are part of the transition experience for youth with identified LD. School personnel who are responsible for arranging or conducting assessments can enhance their value by keeping the following points in mind:

1. Do not assume that an individual has a thorough, accurate understanding of his or her disability or its ramifications. Support staff at many postsecondary schools have discovered that students with previously identified LD cannot articulate what having a learning disability means or describe its implications to others (deFur, Getzel, & Trossi, 1996; Getzel et al., 2000, 2004).

2. Explain using specific terms so that the individual can understand why more tests are necessary, what will happen, and what can be learned from these tests. Remember that individuals with communication difficulties may need several explanations, presented in different ways. (Assurances of understanding must be verified.)

3. After all testing has been completed, review the results with the individual. Again, remember to accommodate any perceptual and communication difficulties. Do not accept assurances of understanding without verifying that the individual does, in fact, comprehend.

4. If you purchase assessments from other agencies or independent professionals, discreetly check that the person performing the assessments understands testing accommodations that must be made for the individual. Advanced degrees alone do not guarantee that understanding. In addition, some private testing organizations and professionals actually have psychometricians or paraprofessional staff members administer the assessments while the highly credentialed and highly paid professional reviews the results and writes the reports. Sometimes the importance of appropriate testing accommodations and environments is not fully appreciated by those actually carrying out the assessment.

   It is also important to check the testing environment, in person if necessary, to see that it is free of distractions. A surprising number of testing environments are noisy or contain visual distractions (e.g., ceiling fans, intricate wallpaper, large windows overlooking busy streets). Validity, and thus relevance, of assessments requires that all involved pay close attention to the details of test administration, the details of an individual's known strengths and weaknesses, and the details of the environment in which the assessments occur.

5. Many individuals with LD perform well in the quiet, orderly, systematic environments of classrooms but fail in the noisy, hectic environments of jobs. These latter environments may be replete with interruptions, incomplete or overwhelmingly extensive information, and fluid (i.e., fluctuating, changing) responsibilities. Understanding the conditions under which tasks must be performed is a critical component for success of many individuals with disabilities in the work world.

6. Because it is very possible that other members of the individual's family may also experience LD, take great care to ensure that the purpose, procedures, results, and implications of assessment are conveyed completely and accurately to the individual's parents. Do not rely on the individual to do this unless no other option is possible. When an individual with perceptual or communication problems communicates with others (e.g., parents) who may also have perceptual or communication problems, serious misunderstandings may occur. Preventive actions may result in good working relationships with families and few hostile confrontations.

7. Be sure to address social and interpersonal skills in assessments for transition planning purposes.

> People with positive self-concepts tend to persevere toward their goals, and those with negative concepts tend to avoid tasks they consider difficult. In like manner, social relationships are affected by feelings and beliefs about ourselves. Students with learning disabilities are found to have more negative self-concepts than their classmates when they are asked to rate their academic performance, though not when scales are used that assess feelings of self-worth. Moreover, these negative academic self-concepts do not seem to respond to teachers' attempts to improve perceptions through failure-free instruction and nongraded classrooms, and they extend beyond the school years into young adulthood. Because students' self-concepts are the products of their own experiences, observations, and messages from others, effective interventions involve not just the student but significant others in students' lives. Research findings have indicated that individuals with learning disabilities also have problems gaining social acceptance. . . . Such was the case even at the kindergarten level before the LD child was identified. In a recent study of youngsters with LD, it was found that over half were socially rejected or neglected, and that the rejected tended to become aggressive and disruptive while the neglected became shy and withdrawn. . . . Finally, some studies have found that females with learning disabilities are at greater risk than males. (Bryan, 1990, p. 6)

Review the eligibility criteria for adult services agencies and comply whenever possible in order to minimize repetitive and unnecessary testing. Rehabilitation agencies, for example, require recent diagnostic information from professionals with specific credentials. If these requirements are met as part of a multidisciplinary team process, then the individual is saved from another, frequently onerous, testing situation; the service delivery process is more efficient; and cooperating agencies' resources are used more efficiently.

Assessment Reports

Assessments are only as good as the information they generate, and reports are useful only to the extent that they contain information that guides the design of transition programs and implementation of services. Assessment reports should include a description of the individual's functional strengths and limitations in executive processing skills, a description of how the individual learns or acquires information, coping and compensation strategies used by the individual, demonstrated basic and vocational skills (including the conditions under which performance was measured), social and interpersonal skills, self-advocacy skills, and the vocational implications of all of these items.

A standard assessment package is inappropriate because assessments should be individualized to meet the person's needs and tailored to be useful to those providing services. The following examples, however, are worthy of consideration as parts of transition assessment packages. The first of these, the Specific Learning Disabilities (SLD) Behavior Checklist (see Figure 18.1), was developed by staff at the Vocational Rehabilitation Center of Allegheny County in Pittsburgh, Pennsylvania. Educators can use this checklist to determine how accurately a student with LD understands his or her strengths and difficulties and whether the individual requires additional counseling about his or her LD or practice in explaining strengths and difficulties effectively.

Individuals with LD can use the checklist to develop a complete functional statement of their strengths and difficulties. This functional description could be used when describing one's LD to people without a technical background in the field, such as supervisors or co-workers.

The second instrument, the Functional Skills Inventory (see Figure 18.2), was developed by staff from the Wisconsin Division of Vocational Rehabilitation, the Learning Disabilities Association of Wisconsin, and the Vocational Studies Center at the University of Wisconsin–Madison as part of a project funded by the U.S. Department of Education, Office of Special Education and Rehabilitative Services (OSERS). This inventory is designed to provide rehabilitation counselors with detailed functional information about each individual with LD who seeks vocational rehabilitation services. The questions on the inventory address many functional skills that have a profound impact, by their presence or absence, on an individual's chances for success in the work world. Thus, parents, educators, and other professionals can use this inventory as a means to develop training content for a student's IEP.

The third instrument, the Work Personality Profile (see Figure 18.3), was developed by Bolton and Roessler at the Arkansas Research and Training Center in Vocational Rehabilitation at the University of Arkansas. Educators and other professionals could use this to assess students' performance in work-study or other community-based employment training programs. The resulting profile of work-related skills and difficulties can form the basis of a training plan designed to improve students' on-the-job performances and thus enhance the likelihood of their employment success as adults.

SETTING TRANSITION GOALS

Many youth with LD leave secondary education with insufficient vocational, functional, or academic skills to be successful in either career entry jobs or postsecondary education (Briel & Getzel, 2001; deFur et al., 1994; Getzel et al., 2004). Improved transition planning while the students are in high school is critical to ensure that they

---

SLD Behavior Checklist

Name: _____ Date: _____

Instructions: Ask the client the following questions and have him or her state one of the following responses: NO, NOT AT ALL; YES, JUST A LITTLE; YES, PRETTY MUCH; or YES, VERY MUCH. Hand the client a reminder in order to help him or her remember the four possible answers.

Questions	Not at all	Just a little	Pretty much	Very much
Auditory comprehension				
1. Do you have problems following spoken directions?	___	___	___	___
2. Do you have problems remembering what you heard?	___	___	___	___
Spoken language				
3. Do you have problems telling stories so that people understand?	___	___	___	___
4. Do you have problems recalling the exact word you want to use?	___	___	___	___
5. Do you have problems remembering the names of people or things?	___	___	___	___
Orientation				
6. Do you lose track of time?	___	___	___	___
7. Do you have problems keeping to a schedule?	___	___	___	___
8. Do you get lost?	___	___	___	___
9. Do you have problems judging distances?	___	___	___	___
10. Do you have problems judging weights?	___	___	___	___
11. Do you have problems concentrating on your work?	___	___	___	___
Motor coordination				
12. Do you have trouble walking?	___	___	___	___
13. Do you have trouble running?	___	___	___	___
14. Do you have trouble climbing?	___	___	___	___
15. Do you have trouble playing sports?	___	___	___	___
16. Do you have trouble keeping your balance?	___	___	___	___
17. Do you have trouble using hand tools?	___	___	___	___
18. Do you have trouble writing so that people can read what you wrote?	___	___	___	___
19. Do you have trouble seeing clearly?	___	___	___	___
20. Do you have trouble drawing pictures?	___	___	___	___
Personal and social behaviors				
21. Do you dislike your present job?	___	___	___	___
22. Do you have problems keeping friends?	___	___	___	___
23. Do you avoid social functions (parties, dances, etc.)?	___	___	___	___
24. Do other people have problems understanding you?	___	___	___	___
25. Do you have problems understanding other people?	___	___	___	___
26. Do others have problems getting along with you?	___	___	___	___
27. Do you have problems getting all of your work done?	___	___	___	___
28. Do you make many mistakes?	___	___	___	___
29. Do you need help from others?	___	___	___	___

Figure 18.1. Specific learning disabilities behavior checklist. (From Goyette, C.H., & Washburn, C. [1984]. *Vocational rehabilitation of learning disabled adults, participants manual* [pp. 13–14]. Pittsburgh, PA: Vocational Rehabilitation Center of Allegheny County; reprinted by permission.)

30. Do you get upset easily? _____ _____ _____ _____

Visual comprehension

31. Do you have problems remembering what you saw? _____ _____ _____ _____
32. Do you have problems reading maps? _____ _____ _____ _____
33. Do you have problems reading newspapers? _____ _____ _____ _____
34. Do you have problems doing math? _____ _____ _____ _____
35. Do you have problems when someone shows you how to do something? _____ _____ _____ _____
36. Do you have problems using directions to put something together? _____ _____ _____ _____

Comments

Please describe the client's observed work performance using the five options listed below to complete the 58 behavioral items.

(4) a definite strength, an employability asset
(3) adequate performance, not a particular strength
(2) performance inconsistent, potentially an employability problem
(1) a problem area, will definitely limit the person's chances for employment
(x) no opportunity to observe the behavior

1) _____ Sufficiently alert and aware.
2) _____ Learns new assignments quickly.
3) _____ Works steadily during entire work period.
4) _____ Accepts changes in work assignments.
5) _____ Needs virtually no direct supervision.
6) _____ Requests help in an appropriate fashion.
7) _____ Approaches supervisory personnel with confidence.
8) _____ Is appropriately friendly with supervisor.
9) _____ Shows pride in group effort.
10) _____ Shows interest in what others are doing.
11) _____ Expresses likes and dislikes appropriately.
12) _____ Initiates work-related activities on time.
13) _____ Accepts work assignments and instructions from supervisor without arguing.
14) _____ Improves performance when shown how.
15) _____ Works at routine jobs without resistance.
16) _____ Expresses willingness to try new assignments.
17) _____ Carries out assigned tasks without prompting.
18) _____ Asks for further instructions if task is not clear.
19) _____ Accepts correction without becoming upset.
20) _____ Discusses personal problems with supervisor only if work-related.
21) _____ Accepts assignment to group tasks.
22) _____ Seeks out co-workers to be friends.
23) _____ Responds when others initiate conversation.
24) _____ Conforms to rules and regulations.
25) _____ Maintains satisfactory personal hygiene habits.
26) _____ Changes work methods when instructed to do so.
27) _____ Pays attention to details while working.

(continued)

Figure 18.1 *(continued)*

28) _____ Maintains productivity despite change in routine.
29) _____ Recognizes own mistakes.
30) _____ Asks for help when having difficulty with tasks.
31) _____ Comfortable with supervisor.
32) _____ Gets along with staff.
33) _____ Works comfortably in group tasks.
34) _____ Appears comfortable in social interactions.
35) _____ Initiates conversations with others.
36) _____ Displays good judgment in use of obscenities and vulgarities.
37) _____ Arrives appropriately dressed for work.
38) _____ Maintains improved work procedures after correction.
39) _____ Maintains work pace even if distractions occur.
40) _____ Performs satisfactorily in tasks that require variety and change.
41) _____ Initiates action to correct own mistakes.
42) _____ Performance remains stable in supervisor's presence.
43) _____ Supportive of others in group tasks.
44) _____ Joins social groups when they are available.
45) _____ Listens while other person speaks; avoids interrupting.
46) _____ Listens to instructions or corrections attentively.
47) _____ Expresses pleasure in accomplishment.
48) _____ Moves from job to job easily.
49) _____ Needs less than average amount of supervision.
50) _____ Offers assistance to co-workers when appropriate.
51) _____ Is sought out frequently by co-workers.
52) _____ Expresses positive feelings (e.g., praise, liking for others).
53) _____ Displays good judgment in playing practical jokes or "horsing around."
54) _____ Transfers previously learned skills to new task.
55) _____ Handles problems with only occasional help.
56) _____ Assumes assigned role in group tasks.
57) _____ Expresses negative feelings appropriately (e.g., anger, fear, sadness).
58) _____ Controls temper.

WORKSHEET

Scale		Total	Average
S1	1 __ 12 __ 13 __ 24 __ 25 __ 36 __ 37 __ 46 __ 53 __ 58 __	S1	
S2	2 __ 14 __ 26 __ 38 __ 47 __ 54 __	S2	
S3	3 __ 15 __ 27 __ 39 __	S3	
S4	4 __ 16 __ 28 __ 40 __ 48 __	S4	
S5	5 __ 17 __ 29 __ 41 __ 49 __ 55 __	S5	
S6	6 __ 18 __ 30 __	S6	
S7	7 __ 19 __ 31 __ 42 __	S7	
S8	8 __ 20 __ 32 __	S8	
S9	9 __ 21 __ 33 __ 43 __ 50 __ 56 __	S9	
S10	10 __ 22 __ 34 __ 44 __ 51 __	S10	
S11	11 __ 23 __ 35 __ 45 __ 52 __ 57 __	S11	
F1	2 __ 3 __ 5 __ 14 __ 17 __ 18 __ 26 __ 27 __ 28 __ 29 __ 30 __ 38 __ 39 __ 40 __ 41 __ 42 __ 47 __ 48 __ 49 __ 54 __ 55 __	F1	
F2	9 __ 10 __ 22 __ 23 __ 34 __ 35 __ 43 __ 44 __ 46 __ 50 __ 51 __ 52	F2	
F3	4 __ 12 __ 13 __ 15 __ 16 __ 21 __ 33 __ 56	F3	
F4	11 __ 19 __ 20 __ 24 __ 36 __ 45 __ 53 __ 57 __ 58	F4	
F5	1 __ 6 __ 7 __ 8 __ 25 __ 31 __ 32 __ 37	F5	

Functional Skills Inventory

Name of person being rated _____

Rater _____

Date _____ Phone _____

Independence

1. Will need parental support to arrange and complete interviews
   with DVR counselor   yes _____   no _____
2. Follows a schedule if someone else prepares it.   yes _____   no _____
3. Prepares and follows own schedule.   yes _____   no _____
4. Can tell time to the minute.   yes _____   no _____
5. Meets new people easily. If "no," please explain:

   _____

   _____

6. Accurately *states* his or her:
   - Social Security number   yes _____   no _____
   - Phone number   yes _____   no _____
   - Complete mailing address   yes _____   no _____

Reading

7. Can read, understand, and interpret a single-sentence statement
   or question.   yes _____   no _____
8. Can read, understand, and interpret a paragraph-length
   statement or question.   yes _____   no _____
9. Can read, understand, and carry out instructions that are:
   - Typed   yes _____   no _____
   - Handwritten   yes _____   no _____
   - In paragraph form   yes _____   no _____
10. Can read and understand a job application.   yes _____   no _____
11. Can read and understand newspaper articles.   yes _____   no _____
12. Summarize this individual's reading skills. Be specific in relation
    to the individual's career goals and expected achievement in
    postsecondary education and/or job performance.

    _____

    _____

    _____

    _____

Math

13. Counts to 100 accurately.   yes _____   no _____
14. Performs the following accurately 99%–100% of the time:
    - Adding whole numbers   yes _____   no _____
    - Adding fractions   yes _____   no _____
    - Subtracting whole numbers   yes _____   no _____
    - Subtracting fractions   yes _____   no _____
    - Uses a pocket calculator correctly   yes _____   no _____
15. Can make correct change for purchases under $20.   yes _____   no _____

(continued)

Figure 18.2.   Functional skills inventory. (From Wisconsin Division of Vocational Rehabilitation Counselors, Wisconsin Association of Children and Adults with Learning Disabilities, and Vocational Studies Center. [1988]. *Best practices: Successful vocational rehabilitation of persons with learning disabilities* [pp. 133–138]. Madison: University of Wisconsin–Madison; reprinted by permission.)

Figure 18.2.   (*continued*)

16. Summarize this individual's math skills. Be specific in relation
     to the individual's career goals and expected achievement in
     postsecondary education and/or job performance.

     _____

     _____

     _____

     _____

Writing
17. *Accurately* writes his or her:
     - Social Security number   yes _____   no _____
     - Phone number   yes _____   no _____
     - Complete mailing address   yes _____   no _____
18. Can correctly fill in an application for a job, a school, or a
     training program.   yes _____   no _____
19. Has prepared a complete résumé.   yes _____   no _____
20. Summarize this individual's writing skills. Be specific in relation
     to the individual's career goals and expected achievement in
     postsecondary education and/or job performance.

     _____

     _____

     _____

     _____

Physical coordination and orientation
21. Has this person been observed to have any physical coordination
     problems?   yes _____   no _____
     Describe how this might limit the individual's employment
     possibilities.

     _____

     _____

     _____

22. Has this person been observed to have any directionality problems?
     not observed _____   no _____   yes _____
     The problems are:

     _____

     _____

     _____

Health and hygiene
23. Practices good grooming and hygiene.   yes _____   no _____
24. Implements good health practices:
     - Balanced diet   yes _____   no _____
     - Exercise   yes _____   no _____
     - Medical checkups   yes _____   no _____
     - Dental checkups   yes _____   no _____
25. Missed more than 4 days of school per year.   yes _____   no _____
26. If yes, why?

     _____

     _____

     _____

Travel

27. Uses public transportation. If yes, describe type(s) used.   yes _____   no _____

_____

28. Possesses valid driver's license.   yes _____   no _____
29. Knows route to:
    - Place of work   yes _____   no _____
    - DVR office   yes _____   no _____
    - Grocery store   yes _____   no _____
    - Bank   yes _____   no _____
    - Laundromat   yes _____   no _____
30. Can determine routes to new locations without assistance.   yes _____   no _____
31. Can follow verbal directions to a new location.   yes _____   no _____
32. Can follow written directions to a new location.   yes _____   no _____
33. Must be "walked through" route to a new location in order to learn it.   yes _____   no _____

Employment

34. Can use telephone directory to obtain addresses and phone numbers of potential employers and social services agencies.   yes _____   no _____
35. Will need assistance and encouragement to arrange and complete successful job interviews.   yes _____   no _____
36. Determines appropriate time to arrive at work or other scheduled events (not too early nor too late).   yes _____   no _____
37. Once at work, finds own work station.   yes _____   no _____
38. Asks questions of supervisor if he or she does not understand work assignment.   yes _____   no _____
39. Reacts well to changes in work assignment.   yes _____   no _____
40. Learns and follows safety procedures.   yes _____   no _____
41. Can read and understand technical manuals.   yes _____   no _____
42. Understands that work can result in earning money.   yes _____   no _____
43. What does this individual do if assigned work is finished?

_____

_____

_____

_____

44. If work is completed ahead of schedule, uses unassigned work time appropriately.   yes _____   no _____
45. Works cooperatively in a group of three or more.   yes _____   no _____
46. Works appropriately alone.   yes _____   no _____
47. Behaves appropriately during work breaks.   yes _____   no _____
48. Behaves appropriately during lunch breaks.   yes _____   no _____
49. Handles criticism from fellow workers appropriately.   yes _____   no _____
50. List the work history of this individual and state how he/she obtained these jobs.
    Jobs performed in the school setting: _____

_____

_____

    Jobs performed in the community: _____

_____

_____

(continued)

Figure 18.2.   (*continued*)

51. Can accurately describe *verbally* what he or she did on these jobs.	yes _____	no _____
52. Can accurately describe in *writing* what he or she did on these jobs (e.g., when asked to fill out a job application).	yes _____	no _____
Other skills		
53. Understands and follows three-step verbal directions.	yes _____	no _____
54. Can explain how he or she learns best.	yes _____	no _____
55. List other skills that this individual has (e.g., musical, athletic).		
Learning style and strategies		
56. Needs extra time to answer questions		
• Verbally	yes _____	no _____
• In writing	yes _____	no _____
57. Gets distracted by sounds (e.g., people talking).	yes _____	no _____
58. Gets distracted by visual stimuli not related to the task at hand (e.g., people, birds).	yes _____	no _____
59. What approaches work best if this person needs to learn or practice a new skill that involves eye/hand/body coordination?		

_____

_____

_____

Learning style/strategies

60. What approaches work best when teaching this person information that he or she does not know?

_____

_____

_____

61. Describe this individual's attitudes and abilities in regard to his or her career choice. Include work habits, initiative, teacher comments, and so forth.

_____

_____

_____

Personal statement

62. Attach a paragraph written by this individual that explains: 1) why he or she is seeking DVR assistance, 2) his or her career objectives, and 3) why he or she feels that he or she will be successful in that career.

exit school with the necessary skills and knowledge to acquire the needed supports and services (Brinckerhoff et al., 2002; deFur et al., 1996). Establishing transition goals helps to provide a framework for the curriculum that students with LD will pursue while in high school and to identify independent living skills that students will need in the community. It is critical that the students are actively involved in this process by discussing their interests and postschool goals and planning activities with the IEP team that will assist students in identifying outcomes that will help them reach these goals (Steere & Cavaioulo, 2002).

TEACHING STRATEGIES

Several factors should be considered when determining appropriate teaching strategies for students with LD. These factors can be divided into three categories. The first area focuses on the student. The development of specific teaching strategies is based on the

REPORT

Name ______ Sex ______ Age ______ Race ______

Education ______ Disability ______

Employability ASSET 4 3 2 Employability PROBLEM 1	Percentile Equivalent %		
0 9 8 7 6 5 4 3 2 1 0 9 8 7 6 5 4 3 2 1 0 9 8 7 6 5 4 3 2 1 0			
	______	S1	Acceptance of work role
	______	S2	Ability to profit from instruction or correction
	______	S3	Work persistence
	______	S4	Work tolerance
	______	S5	Amount of supervision required
	______	S6	Extent trainee seeks assistance from supervisor
	______	S7	Degree of comfort or anxiety with supervisor
	______	S8	Appropriateness of personal relations with supervisor
	______	S9	Teamwork
	______	S10	Ability to socialize with co-workers
	______	S11	Social communication skills
	______	F1	Task orientation
	______	F2	Social skills
	______	F3	Work motivation
	______	F4	Work conformance
	______	F5	Personal presentation

Critical employability deficits (i.e., behaviors rated "1" or "2")

"1" Problem areas	"2" Problem areas
______	______
______	______
______	______

Figure 18.3. Work personality profile. (From Bolton, B., & Roessler, R. [1986, December]. *Work personality profile* [p. 212]. Fayetteville: Arkansas Research and Training Center in Vocational Rehabilitation; reprinted by permission.)

unique learning characteristics of the student as identified through formal or informal assessments (Deshler et al., 2001). The cultural backgrounds of the students and their effects on learning should also be considered (Black, Mrasek, & Ballinger, 2003; Lerner, 2003).

The second category concerns the transition and postschool goals of the students. For some students with LD, further education in a postsecondary setting is a goal. Others may seek employment after leaving school. Teaching strategies and the emphasis on what these students must know differs depending on their transition goals. No matter what their goals are, however, many students need assistance with daily living skills so that they can live independently in the community (Getzel et al., 2004).

The classroom environment is the final category to consider when selecting teaching strategies. Helping students to feel motivated to learn is especially important for students with LD (Scanlon, Deshler, & Schumaker, 1996). Many of these students have not had positive experiences in school and, by the time they reach high school or postsecondary settings, are likely to have negative self-images and poor self-concepts and lack motivation (Lerner, 2003; Sarkees-Wircenski & Scott, 1995). Creating an atmosphere that reinforces the strengths of the students and helps them to feel comfortable with learning is not an easy task. However, by enabling these students to feel that they can achieve in certain academic or vocational areas, teachers can help them gain invaluable tools to cope with the many decisions they will make as they move from school to the community.

INSTRUCTING STUDENTS

It is important to determine the student's strongest learning mode(s) to understand how he or she can effectively learn. Assessing the learning styles of students can assist in obtaining a better understanding of their learning difficulties (Lerner, 2003; Vail, 1992). The three primary learning modes are visual, auditory, and tactile (i.e., hands-on) learning. Information about how the student learns can be gained by asking the student directly; interviewing the student's family or guardian; and analyzing formal or informal assessment results, psychological reports, and school records. The first step in determining appropriate teaching strategies is focusing on the learning styles of each student and adapting the curriculum accordingly. The second step is for educators to conduct self-assessments of their teaching styles to determine whether changes are needed to teach students with a variety of learning modes. The curriculum does not always require alterations, however. By offering students a variety of ways to learn material, all students may learn more effectively (Getzel & Finn, 2005; Heron & Jorgensen, 1995).

Visual Learners

The techniques discussed here are only a small selection of the many methods that can be used to instruct students with LD. Instructing a student whose strongest learning mode is visual essentially means assisting the student to turn spoken words into pictures. The student must learn how to "visualize" the information that is presented in lecture format. Whenever possible, lectures should include visual cues to help the student to understand the information that is being presented. Giving students lecture outlines or PowerPoint presentations before class helps them to prepare for class and review the material after it is presented. When presenting class material, a variety of visual aids should be used to reinforce information. Examples of techniques include 1) software programs that diagram information; 2) using PowerPoint presentations that are highly visual, incorporating maps or graphs; 3) incorporating video clips into lessons; and 4) providing demonstrations of skills, concepts, and ideas (Getzel et al., 2004). Students should also be encouraged to complete assignments with graphs or drawings to illustrate their comprehension of the material.

When students are reading class materials, they should be encouraged to underline or highlight key points. They should also be taught how to take notes that clearly separate different concepts using a color coding system. Students who are visual learners should get into the habit of using a planner with assignment due dates, testing dates, important meetings, and other important class related information. In addition, students should be encouraged to develop flashcards in order to enhance memory (Getzel et al., 2004).

Auditory Learners

Gavin and colleagues (1990) suggested several techniques for instructing students who are auditory learners. Teachers should emphasize sound when presenting material and speak slowly and clearly. Students should be taught to listen for cues when information is given. For example, phrases such as, "The most important point is . . ." or "To summarize, we have discussed . . ." are cues that extra attention should be given. Students should be permitted to tape-record information presented in class to review what was presented. Visual cues, such as maps, charts, or overheads, can also be used as long as the information is accompanied by a clear explanation.

Auditory learners may benefit from oral tests or role play (Gavin et al., 1990; Gregory, 1994; Sarkees-Wircenski & Wircenski, 1994; Thompson & Bethea, 1996). In role play, students present information to other class members and answer questions they may have. This technique is helpful because the student verbalizes obtained information (Getzel et al., 2004). Students should be encouraged to join or form study groups to reinforce material learned in class. This will also help to identify areas of confusion about the material, which can be later addressed in class. For students who have difficulty with memory, students can use a digital or tape recorder to input ideas or important dates to have immediate access to this information. In order to enhance time management skills, students with auditory strengths should be encouraged to use personal digital assistants (PDAs). Students can input important dates and tasks and set up auditory prompts as reminders. In addition, the use of text-to-speech software provides students with the ability to convert digital text into computerized speech. This type of software is also very helpful for students who are visual learners.

Tactile Learners

Students who learn best through hands-on experiences are tactile learners. For them, instructors should structure learning situations to include a variety of activities (Gregory, 1994). These students need to be highly involved with class materials using such techniques as highlighting information, developing flashcards, or demonstrating acquisition of information through the development of projects. Students who are involved in training programs should begin to use tools or equipment as soon as possible (Gavin et al., 1990).

General Techniques and Strategies

In addition to specific techniques utilized for each type of learner, several general techniques should be considered when teaching students with LD. These common strategies may assist teachers as they develop and organize classroom materials (Gavin et al., 1990; Sarkees-Wircenski & Scott, 1995; Thompson & Bethea, 1996):

- Use concrete examples when presenting material. Abstract concepts can confuse and frustrate students with LD.

- Try to make all printed materials clear and readable. Materials that are not clearly reproduced will add to the students' difficulty with comprehension.

- List assignments in steps. Too much information or direction given at once can confuse students with LD. It is easier for them to follow one step at a time.

- Allow more time, if necessary, for students to complete activities.

- Use a multisensory approach including visual, auditory, and tactile strategies. These techniques can be helpful to all students in the class, not only students with LD.

ASSISTIVE TECHNOLOGY

The use of assistive technology (AT) in the classroom can be an invaluable support to students with LD. AT can provide a method for coping in a variety of settings (Raskind, 1994) and can help students to capitalize on their strengths (Lewis, 1998). Laptop computers, pocket-size spellcheckers, digital and tape recorders, talking calculators, and personal data managers can be easily taken from one setting to another. For example, computers in school settings can help students complete assignments by offering a multisensory approach to learning and can give them immediate feedback on how well they are doing and where errors are occurring. Digital and tape recorders can be used to assist students in listening to books or lectures. Personal data managers with a calendar can help individuals keep track of class schedules, deadlines for assignments, and examination dates. Software can also enable students to compensate for any challenges that may occur. Examples of the types of software that students with LD should be exploring include text-to-speech, speech-to-text, word prediction, and graphic organization. It is important that students with LD have access to available AT to determine the best match that utilizes their strengths and compensates for their learning needs.

Creating Positive Learning Environments

By the time students with LD reach the secondary school setting, they are often discouraged about school, have negative self-concepts, and lack motivation for learning (Bender et al., 1997; Deschler et al., 1996; Thoma & Wehmeyer, 2005). These feelings typically result from a series of negative experiences associated with school. It is important for teachers to create classroom environments that are nonthreatening and to build on the strengths and capabilities of the students. Some examples of how educators can help to create a supportive environment include 1) serving as good role models, 2) being prepared and organized, 3) developing equitable grading policies, 4) using varying teaching styles, and 5) encouraging teamwork among students to develop skills (Gugerty & Gavin, 1991).

    Creating an environment that enables students with LD to feel motivated about learning and that builds their self-esteem is important. To increase their chances of success in the community, students with LD need many opportunities to learn and practice appropriate behaviors before and during the transition process. If students are given these opportunities in settings that allow them to feel comfortable with making mistakes, asking questions, and acquiring new skills, then they will be interested in and excited about preparing for their transitions into the community. The attitudes and beliefs of teachers regarding their students is fundamental for developing positive learning settings (Fuchs, Fuchs, Hamlett, Philips, & Karns, 1995), as one teacher commented when analyzing positive learning environments:

> In the final analysis, my experience has convinced me that the main ingredient in developing a positive learning environment in the classroom is the teachers' unconditional love for their students. I'm further convinced that none of my motivational gimmicks or techniques would have worked if my students didn't feel or sense the positive regard I had for each of them. (Colby, 1987, p. 33)

INSTRUCTING STUDENTS IN A MULTICULTURAL CLASSROOM

When discussing teaching strategies, it is important to consider working with culturally diverse students with LD (Harry et al., 1995). Careful and comprehensive evaluations should be performed to ensure that these students are not incorrectly identified as having LD as a result of language differences or other cultural influences (Graham, Harris, & Reid, 1990). When assessing the needs of students who are members of cultural minority groups, information should be gathered concerning all of the developmental domains, cultural and linguistic influences, and family and community data (Black et al., 2003; Walker, 1988). Suggestions for assisting students with limited English proficiency in the classroom include the following (Inestroza, 1990):

- Allow students to provide information nonverbally (e.g., pointing to answers on graphs or charts).

- Use synonyms and antonyms, or paraphrase to convey classroom material. Redundancy is allowable when instructing these students.

- Use demonstrations and visual cues when instructing. Concrete examples are better than pictures.

- Respond to students' intended meaning when answering questions. The instructor can rephrase what the students have said to enable them to hear how to state an answer correctly. The instructor should build on the information already provided by the students.

- Do not correct a student's pronunciation more than three times consecutively. Excessive correction may make the student afraid to speak. Correction of grammar is best done through writing.

- Do not change students' names to make them sound more American. Doing so deprives students of their cultural identities.

PREPARING FOR TRANSITION

Postsecondary Settings

To ensure that students with LD are prepared to enter postsecondary education programs, teachers should focus on transition planning by actively working with students with LD to help promote their success in higher education. Students must be prepared to academically meet the required course work by taking challenging courses in high school that not only prepare them to enter college, but to progress through their program of study. In addition, planning efforts must also include direct skills instruction in self-advocacy, independent living, decision making, and working with students to identify career goals to help them establish a career and make future choices for education and training (Aune, 1991; Briel & Getzel, 2001, Getzel et al., 2000; Mull, Sitlington, & Alper, 2001; Sitlington & Frank, 1990). Because of the importance of postsecondary education as a transition goal for students with disabilities, Chapter 10 provides a thorough discussion on working with students to help them successfully make the transition from secondary to postsecondary education.

EMPLOYMENT

Students with LD face employment challenges due to a lack of regular job preparation and networking skills, and a lack of understanding concerning the impact of their disability on daily life, communication, and job performance (Briel & Wehman, 2005). Several studies have reported that students with LD exiting schools experience higher unemployment or underemployment, more dissatisfaction with employment, and a greater dependency on family members (Dunn, 1996; Lichtenstein, 1993; Sitlington, Frank, & Carson, 1992). As Lemke (1991) stated, people with LD are employed, but most face a high job turnover rate. They may be unable to keep jobs, unable to find jobs that maintain their interest, or they may do things that cause them to lose their jobs. Many are also underemployed and commonly complain that they do not get the same promotions that their peers do.

One of the primary reasons that individuals with LD lose their jobs is not the skill level required by the job but the individual's lack of organizational, self-monitoring, and self-correcting skills, all of which result from faulty executive functioning. "It is easy to measure reading and math levels but difficult to measure executive functioning because it is very subtle and sophisticated" (Goodman, 1988, p. 88).

Theis defined the *comparable executive processing* as "those cognitive functions that are responsible for organizing, coordinating, and directing mental activity and behavior" (as cited in Bosch, 1991, p. 37). Executive processing includes attention, formulation of goals and plans to achieve those goals, monitoring and evaluating behavior, and correcting behavior as needed to continue toward the goals. This involves appreciating the situation, managing time, and controlling actions. The flexibility required to evaluate and change behavior, a necessity for attaining goals, is one of the most difficult areas for adults with LD. They cling to routine because of the amount of energy required to learn new tasks.

Gerber and colleagues (1990) studied the persistence of LD in 133 adults categorized as highly or moderately successful in employment. Findings showed that both groups deteriorated markedly in the areas of functioning typically, including in diagnostic and remediation efforts. On every item (i.e., listening, speaking, reading, writing, spelling, math, visual perception, auditory perception, coordination, impulsivity, distractibility, hyperactivity, attention span), roughly a quarter or more of all of the respondents with LD reported increasing difficulties in adulthood.

It is very possible that developmental deficits are exacerbated by increasing demands in adult-hood. . . . The reported persistence of problems by the subjects may also stem from increasing demands of their work and daily routines. The added complexity of tasks in adult life may highlight a multiplicity of self-perceived problems or inadequacies in their lives. . . . It must be kept in mind that, while the population studied may be typical in some respects, the subjects are skewed in the direction of successful to highly successful vocational functioning. . . . The data presented in this study directly support the notion that learning disabilities is a lifelong problem. (Gerber et al., 1990, p. 572)

Unfortunately, many individuals with LD cannot be characterized as successful in their career development efforts (Lerner, 2003). Tomblin (1999) found that in spite of the fact that employment rates for high school graduates with LD were relatively good, a high number of individuals were employed part time in low-status jobs and were not able to live independently.

For students who wish to obtain employment after exiting school, it is important to provide them with numerous opportunities to explore career options throughout their secondary school experience. This will help them to set realistic goals about occupations to pursue. Students working cooperatively with their transition team members and other school staff should consider the following points (Briel & Getzel, 2001; Wille-Gregory et al., 1995):

- Develop an awareness of the range of career opportunities and the requirements for those careers.

- Create opportunities for career exploration and work experience during high school, even for students who are planning to attend a postsecondary school.

- Obtain part-time employment or volunteer experiences to help develop work habits, enhance social skills, and explore vocational interests.

Strategies can be incorporated in the curriculum that include academic and vocational educators working together to incorporate academic competencies into vocational courses or to make academic curricula more vocationally relevant by using vocationally oriented examples when teaching academic subjects. Cooperation among school personnel is essential to ensure that students' academic and vocational skills are integrated. This can be challenging with the increase focus on high-stakes testing and meeting performance standards in which greater emphasis is now placed on academic content, making it difficult to incorporate more vocationally related classes into students' course schedules.

CONCLUSION

This chapter has presented a number of experiences from the perspective of the individual with LD. Readers should understand the complexity of the problems and issues that these individuals face and how their disabilities can affect all aspects of their lives. A number of transition alternatives have been discussed for use when working with these students and their families as they move from school to the community. Individuals with LD are too often viewed in terms of what they are unable to do and not provided the opportunities to develop their skills and talents. Through appropriate services and supports and a shared commitment, these students can pursue their dreams and aspirations as they enter their adult lives.

STUDY QUESTIONS

1. How can LD affect a student's life?

2. Why is having self-determination skills critical in achieving successful transition into adulthood?

3. Describe curricula that have been found to be effective for students with LD.

4. Describe the most useful types of assessment strategies and reports that can be helpful to parents and educators of students with LD.

5. Describe the major issues involved in preparing for transition into postsecondary setting such as college. Be sure to include issues related to employment and career advancement.

19

Applications for Youth with Emotional and Behavior Disorders

Paul Wehman

AFTER COMPLETING THIS CHAPTER, THE READER WILL BE ABLE TO

○ Understand the mental health needs of students with emotional and behavior disorders

○ Describe six characteristics of students with emotional and behavior disorders

○ Understand how work experience and employment can benefit youth with disabilities

○ Discuss the role of student choice in transition planning and vocational placement

○ Be aware of several types of self-control and techniques for teaching self-control

○ Understand the Transition to Independence Process (TIP) system and nine guidelines

○ Discuss supported employment (SE) outcomes for individuals with emotional and behavior disorders

JAMES

James is a 20-year-old man who was diagnosed with anxiety and depression while in high school. Even though he followed his medication schedule, James experienced debilitating mood swings. At times he had difficulty getting up in the morning or getting out of the car at various destinations. When James would begin to feel under stress, he would often manage his stress by leaving a situation, saying that he did not feel well. His one previous job at a grocery store ended after a public outburst.

James elected to pursue a college education and majored in health and community wellness. He did not disclose his disability to the Services for Students with Disabilities Office but self-accommodated by completing two classes per semester and finishing his academic requirements in 8 years. The final requirement for graduation was to complete a 400-hour internship at a community health club. James's mother initiated an appointment with the university career education program, which was designed to assist college students with disabilities with individualized career planning and placement. James preferred part-time hours and felt that he would work best in the morning. He had visited several clubs without success. It was determined that he needed direct job development assistance in order to secure an internship.

Several local athletic clubs were contacted before one agreed to work with the Career Connections Program. The fitness director, James, and program staff initially met to develop a work schedule that gradually

There are many young people in this country like James (see sidebar) who have challenging emotional and behavioral support needs. In fact, children and youth who are classified as having behavior disorders represent the third largest category of students with disabilities in the United States, following only those with speech impairments and learning disabilities (U.S. Department of Education, NCES, 2002). The problems for young people with behavior disorders are complex and at times can appear insurmountable (Karpur, Clark, Caproni, & Sterner, 2005). One of the greatest obstacles to providing transition services is that 51% of these students drop out of school (Sitlington & Neubert, 2004). These percentages are close to twice as great as those for all students with disabilities. Many of these problems begin for children at a young age when help is essential (Hocutt, McKinney, & Montague, 2002) because addressing meaningful educational and adult transition goals in a student's IEP is impossible when the student is no longer attending school. On a positive note, Rylance (1997) found that youth with behavior disorders who received school-based counseling and vocational education had significantly higher graduation rates than students with behavior disorders who did not receive these services.

For many youth, acquiring and maintaining a job is a step to independence and gaining control over one's life that affords them a sense of self-worth and self-esteem. Frank, Sitlington, and Carson (1995) reported, however, that unemployment rates for youth with emotional and behavior disorders (EBD) ranged from 42% to 72% during the first 5 years after exiting high school. Equally disconcerting were findings from the National Longitudinal Transition Study (NLTS) that indicated that youth with EBD lag far behind their peers across many adult domains (Blackorby & Wagner, 1996). These authors found that 41% of youth with EBD were employed 2 years after high school as compared with 59% of youth without disabilities. Additionally, youth with EBD tend to secure lower-paying jobs as compared with students with other types of disabilities (Bullis, Morgan, Benz, Todis, & Johnson, 2002; D'Amico, 1995).

There is increasing research literature available on how students with behavior disorders learn in school, despite the inevitable measurement problems that exist in the evaluation of level of inclusion into general education classrooms (Simpson, 2004). For example, Vaughn, Moody, and Schumm (1998) indicated very little difference between instruction provided in special education classrooms for students with behavior disorders versus instruction provided in general education classrooms. In addition, Levy and Vaughn (2002) found that even

increased in days and hours. The groundwork was laid to assess and identify effective learning strategies and stress management techniques with the assistance from program staff. On the second day of work, James told the fitness director he was not feeling well and went home early. Program staff came on-site on the third day to further assess the work environment and assist with identifying stress management strategies. Preliminary assignments included observing fitness evaluations, orienting to weight machines, and reading the policy manual. More specific duties were identified that could be completed by James throughout the day, such as helping at the front desk or cleaning equipment. These tasks were identified to help James fill any unstructured time.

Program staff talked with James about what helps him to relieve stress. He identified doing exercises, taking a break, and reading. With assistance, James initiated a discussion with the fitness director about his disability and his need for an accommodation when he is feeling stressed. He selected excusing himself for a few minutes and walking outside in the parking lot as one of his primary strategies. This strategy also proved effective for having James get out of the car in the morning when he and his mother arrived at the jobsite.

As James neared completion of his internship, he decided to apply for services with the Department of Rehabilitative Services to secure a job coach. Informational interviews were arranged and conducted with employers at health clubs, YMCAs, and recreation centers. Successful strategies used at

in a special education setting, reading instruction often failed to reflect validated instructional procedures.

This chapter will endeavor to show how students with behavior disorders can be provided significant and meaningful transition experiences.

WHO ARE YOUTH WITH EMOTIONAL AND BEHAVIOR DISORDERS?

The Individuals with Disabilities Education Improvement Act of 2004 (PL 108-446) defines students as being *seriously emotionally disturbed* when any one of the following characteristics occurs over a long period of time to a marked degree and adversely affects educational performance.

- An inability to learn that cannot be explained by intellectual, sensory, or other health factors

- An inability to build or maintain satisfactory interpersonal relationships with peers and teachers

- Inappropriate types of behavior or feelings under normal circumstances

- A general pervasive mood of unhappiness or depression

- A tendency to develop physical symptoms or fears associated with personal or school problems

In addition, the definition includes children who have schizophrenia but excludes those who are socially maladjusted unless they also have serious emotional disturbances (Guetzloe, 1999a). Mooney, Denny, and Gunter (2004) noted:

> Students identified with emotional or behavioral disorders (E/BD) have, by definition, educational difficulties resulting in "an inability to learn which cannot be explained by intellectual, sensory, or health factors . . ." (Individuals with Disabilities Education Act § 300.7 [b] [91]). The educational difficulties of these students, whether a product of their undesirable social behaviors or the cause of them result in their generally experiencing a lifetime of less than desirable social and economic outcomes. (p. 22)

Young people with behavior disorders can be overwhelmed by demands in the community and the workplace, making the transition from school to adulthood particularly difficult (Ford, 2001). These are not typical children who have periodic behavior problems at different points in their lives. Their problems (e.g., disruptive, withdrawn behavior) tend to present themselves over the long term with significantly higher frequencies of occurrences than those seen in children

the internship site and potential job leads were shared with the job coach at an informal meeting with the student and the program staff. Through an informational interview, James was able to secure a part-time position as a program assistant at a YMCA near his home. Effective strategies identified during the internship placement were modified to fit the environment at his new job in the aquatics department.

without behavior disorders. For a more detailed discussion of psychiatric disorders information for teachers see Forness, Walker, and Kavale (2003).

The most important challenge for the majority of these youth is the ability to better control their behavior, specifically impulses to do unusual or bizarre things. Reactions to anxious or stressful situations usually lead to behavior that is inappropriate and viewed negatively by peers or adults.

There are additional behavioral characteristics associated with young people with emotional or behavior disorders. These are described by Ford (2001) and others (e.g., Clark & Davis, 2000).

Learning and Performance Issues

Difficulty Processing Information Cognitive difficulties are one of the most common employment obstacles for people with some types of mental illness, particularly schizophrenia, which typically causes difficulty in screening input, sorting out what's important and what isn't, and taking action on the input. This causes problems with following directions, sequencing tasks, and making decisions.

Trouble Initiating Action Slowness in initiation or reluctance to initiate action causes people to look like they are not motivated. This may be due to difficulty processing the information available in the environment—missing or misunderstanding cues. Trouble with initiation can also be due to a fear of making mistakes, fear of failure or success, or preoccupation with internal ruminations or hallucinations.

Difficulty Concentrating and Distractibility This may be a symptom of an illness or a side effect of the medications that are taken to treat the illness. It may be due to hallucinations or delusions experienced by the individual and demanding attention or a result of difficulty in sorting through and prioritizing environmental input. Changes in distractibility levels can be important feedback for the worker and/or employment specialist to give the medical consultant regarding levels of medication or possible decompensation. Additional structure and/or stronger cues may be needed for the individual to be successful on the job.

Interpersonal Issues

Social Isolation and Alienation from Feelings An appearance of apathy, slovenliness, emotional dullness, and nonmotivation is a common residual symptom of mental illness. People may also feel anxious in the presence of others and resist interpersonal involvement. This anxiety may interfere with task completion in that the worker may appear distracted and perform poorly because he or she is focusing on how uncomfortable it makes him or her to have to interact with others. Students and workers who are socially isolated also miss out on important information regarding the (usually unwritten) behavioral rules of the classroom and workplace.

Variability of Functioning Level   Students with mood disorders generally have periods of at least relative stability between episodes of illness. The frequency of these episodes must be taken into account when helping people select employment. For example, a person who generally becomes ill every spring but who otherwise is able to maintain stability with medication and counseling may need to take a week or two off every year to deal with the illness, but not need a lot of other accommodations. Another person who experiences rapid cycling and many more residual symptoms may need flexibility in the classroom.

UNIQUE CHALLENGES AND ISSUES FOR YOUTH WITH EMOTIONAL AND BEHAVIOR DISORDERS

The challenges and issues for youth with behavior disorders are at times overwhelming (Katsiyannis & Yell, 2004). Millions of children and youth experience significant psychological and behavior problems (Zhang, Katsiyannis, & Herbst, 2004). The most revealing evidence about the difficulties that these youth experience comes from the evaluations of disciplinary exclusions of all students with disabilities. Zhang et al. (2004) noted:

> Students with disabilities are more likely to commit offences resulting in exclusion because of poor social skills, judgment, and planning as well as being less adept in avoiding detection (Leone, Mayer, Malmgren, & Meisel, 2000). According to Leone and colleagues, data from various sources, including Gun-Free School reports and individual states (i.e., Kansas, Kentucky, Maryland, Delaware, Minnesota), revealed that students with disabilities were disproportionately represented in disciplinary exclusions: While approximately 11% of all students ages 6 to 21 receive services under IDEA, close to 20% of students who are suspended are students with disabilities. The data sources, however, did not involve nationally representative data and only occasionally reported exclusions by disability. (p. 37)

Only recently have structured programs begun to emerge that are targeted at the prevention of drop-outs or helping drop-outs get back into school (e.g., Hoover & Stenhjem, 2003; Sinclair, Christenson, Evelo, & Hurley, 1998). Only 17% of students with behavior disorders attend postsecondary school programs as compared with almost 50% of students without disabilities (Knitzer, Steinberg, & Fleisch, 1990; Unger, in press). And perhaps one of the most telling statistics of all is that only 40%–50% of adults with behavior disorders are employed—a stark contrast to the 85% employment rate for the general population of adults and students (National Organization on Disability, 2004).

Work as a Way to Manage Disability

The first major challenge that educators and counselors must face in working with these students is helping them to obtain both paid and nonpaid work experiences while still in school. We know that productive work is therapeutic, meaning it can help manage depression, anger, and frustration (Bond, 2004a, 2004b; Ford, 2001). It is critical that individuals with behavior disorders are not kept from work because of behavior problems but instead are supported at the jobsite with appropriate behavioral interventions (Wehman, Inge, Revell, & Brooke, in press). Improved postschool employment outcomes for students with disabilities who have participated in work-based training have been reported by many researchers (e.g., Blackorby & Wagner, 1996; Krupa, 2004). Owens-Johnson and Johnson (1999) wrote an excellent summary on the post-school prospects for students with behavior disorders. They noted that the American dream of education, employment, and responsible citizenship is likely to be an elusive proposition for students who have not developed the necessary skills to be successful in school, let alone on the job. Successful employment outcomes for this population are positively correlated with variables such as vocational education coursework (Aspel, Bettis, Test, & Wood, 1998).

Positive Behavior Support

The second challenge that educators and counselors face is providing humanistic, non-aversive behavioral and psychological interventions in natural environments for young people with behavior disorders. Training in the community, instructing in the work-place, and teaching mobility within the community are essential elements for promoting transition. Also, use of typically developing peers to avoid behavior problems (Smith & Daunic, 2004) is another strategy that is therapeutic and constructive. Often, however, designing and implementing behavioral interventions in natural environments is preempted for training in controlled environments, such as classrooms or institutions. Zuna and McDougall (2004) observed:

> One of the most frequent concerns expressed by teachers and administrators is how to manage behavioral problems in the classroom (Langdon, 1999). Behavior that disrupts instruction is problematic for teachers and students, in part, because we have known for quite some time that the amount of time students engage actively in academic tasks is positively correlated to how much they learn (Black, 2004). Functional assessment and positive behavioral support (PBS) are two management approaches that are extensions of applied behavior analysis. Unlike some classroom management practices that rely heavily on aversive consequences, these approaches use more proactive techniques to manage challenging behavior and increase students' active engagement in learning. (p. 18)

Lohrmann-O'Rourke and Zirkel (1998) identified legal boundaries and protections for students through a review of the case law on aversive interventions in five categories: electric shock, noxious substances, corporal punishment, restraints, and time out. They found that despite the emergence of positive interventions, qualified support for the use of aversive interventions continues to exist.

Horner and colleagues (1990) were among the first to provide a description of positive behavior support. Since then, leaders such as Reid and Parsons (2003) have extended positive behavior support with extensive curricula. There have been many additional compilations of applied literature and practical applications of positive behavior support (e.g., Carr et al., 1994; Crimmins & Woolf, 1997; Jackson & Panyan, 2004; Koegel, Koegel, & Dunlap, 1996; Lucyshyn, Dunlap, & Albin, 2002; Luiselli & Cameron, 1998). These works, along with the emergence of a journal specifically devoted to positive behavior support (i.e., *Journal of Positive Behavior Interventions*), can be argued to constitute evidence of a field that has emerged from that of applied behavior analysis. This latter point was discussed further by Carr and colleagues (2002), who described positive behavior support as the "evolution of an applied science" (p. 4), one that has emerged primarily from applied behavior analysis, the normalization/inclusion movement, and person-centered values.

Table 19.1. Student recommendations on effective teaching

Rich curriculum
- Allow for more group activities and projects.
- Show enthusiasm when teaching.
- Allow for more discussion and expression of students in class.
- Relate the information to your students' lives (current and future).

Embracing positive behaviors
- Hold high expectations.
- Explain the "rules" clearly and provide consistent consequences regardless of labels or race.
- Encourage students to do their best regardless of their label or race.

Weaving student-centered connections
- Understand issues students face today.
- Get to know students and their families.
- Get to know students in and out of school.
- Communicate with students at their level.
- Identify and connect students with services within and outside the school setting.

From Owens, L., and Kieker, L.A. (2003). How to spell success for secondary students labeled EBD: How students define effective teachers. *Beyond Behavior, 3;* reprinted by permission.

Individualizing Curricula

A third challenge is individualizing curricula to meet the unique and specific psychological and educational needs of students with behavior disorders (Kline & Silver, 2004). Teachers must be able to address the psychological needs of each student in conjunction with his or her educational and vocational needs, ideally with concrete instruction in real-life environments. Instead of trying to solve and eradicate the student's underlying problems, time is better spent developing an array of competent vocational and community skills, especially for those with autism, as the limited data on this population show. Regardless of disability, it is critical that teachers understand and follow this approach in transition planning (Wehman, 2002a).

Owens and Kieker (2003) developed a unique paper that examines how students with behavior disorders look at their teachers and evaluate what is important in their teaching abilities. Table 19.1 lists "rich curriculum," "positive behaviors," and "student-centered connections."

Drop-Out Issues

Results of surveys tracking students for 6 years following high school graduation indicate that a large disparity exists between postsecondary plans and postsecondary outcomes (Rylance, 1997). Approximately half of graduates obtained either 2- or 4-year college degrees; the other half either left college or entered the work force directly after high school. Consider these data for students with disabilities as reported in the Twenty-Fourth Annual Report to Congress on the Implementation of the Individuals with Disabilities Education Act:

> Overall, 30% of students with disabilities who had been enrolled in ninth through twelfth grades left school by dropping out. This dropout rate was particularly high for youth with specific learning disabilities or serious emotional disturbance. Of youth with specific learning disabilities who started the ninth grade, 29% dropped out, as did 51% of students with

serious emotional disturbance. As might be expected, dropouts were less likely to enroll in postsecondary vocational, or academic programs. (2002, p. II-20)

Despite these outcomes, secondary schools continue to implement academic curricula and allocate resources as if to prepare students exclusively for college rather than employment. This is much further complicated by the demands for high-stakes testing success (see Chapter 7; also Sitlington & Neubert, 2004). For many students, particularly those with disabilities, to make a successful transition from school to work, educators must provide them with vocational training and meaningful work experiences. Vocational success depends on three types of skills: job-related academic skills, job-related vocational skills, and job-related social skills (Schoen & Nolen, 2004).

Sinclair and colleagues (1998) listed four ways to reduce drop-outs.

1. Establish a strategy for systematically tracking alterable behaviors associated with dropping out, such as absences, course failures, and out-of-school suspensions.

2. Consider alternative staffing patterns for some school personnel (e.g., assign monitors to a caseload of students rather than to a school building and follow the same students throughout the district).

3. Ask school staff to frequently examine the rationale for punitive discipline policies and practices and to consider situational factors before administering standard consequences.

4. Encourage efforts to increase the relevancy of the high school curriculum, geared toward a variety of postschool endeavors.

Increasingly, alternative schools are becoming utilized in many communities as places to "keep" students with behavior disorders. The growth of alternative schools in many states raises questions about their characteristics and use. A commonly accepted definition of alternative schools is not currently available and a review of state-level legislation/policy suggests that considerable variation exists in definitions across states. *The Common Core of Data*, the U.S. Department of Education's primary database on public elementary and secondary education, defines an *alternative education school* as "a public elementary/secondary school that addresses needs of students that typically cannot be met in a regular school, provides nontraditional education, serves as an adjunct to a regular school, or falls outside the categories of regular, special education or vocational education" (U.S. Department of Education, NCES, 2002, p. 55).

In their review of the literature, Lange and Sletten (2002) found that alternative schools are generally characterized as having small enrollment, one-to-one interaction between teachers and students, supportive environments, opportunities and curriculum relevant to student interests, flexibility in structure, and an emphasis on student decision-making (Barr, 1981; Gold & Mann, 1984; Morley, 1991; Natriello, McDill, & Pallas, 1990; Young, 1990). Most educators, researchers, and policy makers do seem to agree that alternative schools are designed for students at risk of school failure (Raywid, 1994). As alternative schools continue to evolve and play a more prominent role in response to educational political, economic, and social forces of today, the need to collect current information about these settings and the students they serve grows.

Juvenile Justice

More and more students with behavior disorders are finding their way into the juvenile justice system. They are having to go into the courts for consequences associated with inappropriate or illegal community behavior. Juvenile detention homes function like jails, providing secure confinement for youths awaiting trial who are at risk to themselves or to the community. According to the Coalition for Juvenile Justice (*Richmond Times Dispatch*, 2004), between 300,000 and 600,000 young people cycle through juvenile detention each year. The length of time they spend incarcerated ranges from 1 day to several months.

Some youth are incarcerated because they have failed to appear for their court hearing or didn't comply with the rules imposed by the judge or probation officer. Consider the case of Lawrence who is 15. He was convicted of petty larceny, stealing from a clothing store with his friends. He attended only one group session to which he was ordered and has been irregular in his school attendance. His absences, not the theft, led to his first incarceration.

Some youth are confined awaiting a permanent placement outside their homes; occasionally some are detained simply because they have no other place to go. Lucinda, for instance, has been in and out of foster care; she is currently waiting for a space in a group home. At 15, she is a chronic runaway; the last time she left she stole her step-father's wallet. Both Lawrence and Lucinda are troubled but hardly dangerous. They require consequences that will change their behavior positively; incarceration most likely will have the opposite effect.

Once youngsters are confined, their parents frequently let them linger there, as they are often overburdened and relieved to have them off the streets. While in detention, these youths are exposed to—and often intimidated by—those charged with crimes that range from car-jacking to assault to murder. Like any adolescent, they seek to fit in, and they begin to develop a new sense of identity influenced by the maladaptive norms and social pecking order of a correctional institution (Lane, Wehby, Little, & Cooley, 2005a, 2005b).

Bullying: An Increasing Problem

Bullying is most commonly characterized by aggressive behavior or intentional harm (Keenan, 2004). It is carried out repeatedly, and over time it occurs within an interpersonal relationship characterized by an imbalance of physical or psychological power (Hoover & Stenhjem, 2003). Bullying is a learned behavior, evident as early as 2 years of age, and is the most common form of violence—3.7 million youth engage in it, more than 3.2 million youth are victims of bullying each year, and 1.2 million youth are both victims of bullies as well as bullies themselves. Since 1992, there have been 250 violent deaths in schools, and bullying has been a factor in almost every school shooting. Direct physical bullying increases in elementary school, peaks in middle school, and declines in high school. Verbal abuse remains constant across the primary through secondary school years (Hoover & Stenhjem, 2003). Consider the Minnesota School shooting that occurred in March 2005 in which bullying was seen as a possible factor. Boyles noted:

> The extent to which bullying played a role in last week's horrific Minnesota school shooting that left 10 people dead may never be known. Relatives told reporters that the troubled gunman was often teased by schoolmates, and pundits speculated that bullying may be the root cause of most episodes of school violence.
>
> It is also more common than most people realize, according to new research from UCLA. Almost half of the sixth graders surveyed in a study reported being bullied at least once over a five-day period.
>
> Children who were bullied were more likely to report depression and other emotional problems and physical symptoms such as frequent headaches and stomachaches, according to another report from the same research team. (2005, p. 1)

The majority of youth are neither bullies nor victims, but may be present during a bullying incident. Though not directly involved with the incident, the bystander may experience such negative feelings of fear, guilt, and helplessness.

Research has shown that the presence of friends helps to buffer children from bullies (American Medical Association [AMA], 2002; Baugh, 2003). Olweus (1993) stated that experts must encourage students to demonstrate leadership in recognizing bullying, refusing to participate, and coming to the aid of victims skillfully and nonviolently. However, to do so, we must promote a safe, caring environment in which youth feel comfortable in speaking out against bullying, and adults must, therefore, respect youth's voices and perspectives on their personal experiences with bullying.

Today, schools typically respond to bullying, or other school violence, with reactive, punitive measures. However, metal detectors, cameras, or hiring police have no tangible positive results. "Zero tolerance" policies rely on exclusionary measures (suspension, expulsion) that have long-term negative effects. Instead, researchers advocate schoolwide prevention programs that promote a positive school and community climate. Such programs require the participation and commitment of students, parents, educators, and members of the community. Effective school programs include early intervention, parent training, teacher training, and a positive school climate.

DISCIPLINE AND FUNCTIONAL ASSESSMENT

Discipline and functional assessment is a key aspect of required skills and services for youth with emotional and behavior disorders. IDEA 2004 addressed functional behavior assessment for students with special behavior needs after much discussion.

The debate surrounding the 2004 reauthorization of IDEA testifies to educators' growing concerns about the rights of students with disabilities as they relate to school discipline (Gable, 1999; Skiba & Peterson, 2000). It appears that as schools increase the number of students with disabilities in general education settings (U.S. Department of Education, 2002), they also exclude them rather quickly for misbehavior (Smith, 2000). In response to the reported rise in youth violence (Bender & McLaughlin, 1997; Walker & Gresham, 1997), local school boards and state legislatures frequently mandate school discipline programs that focus on the reduction of violent or aggressive behavior through punishment (e.g., expulsion, suspension, time out; Butera et al., 1996; Webber, 1997). As a result, schools must increasingly balance the provisions of school disciplinary codes with students' rights to a free and appropriate public education as detailed in IDEA 2004. Skiba and Peterson (2000) noted that:

The key importance of school discipline in preventing school violence has been highlighted by data demonstrating the relationship between day-to-day school disciplinary disruptions and more serious violence. In the recent National Center for Educational Statistics report, *Violence and Discipline Problems in U.S. Public Schools: 1996–1997* (Heaviside, Rowand, Williams, & Farris, 1998), a clear relationship emerged between low-level school disruption and serious school violence. Among schools reporting at least one serious discipline issue, 28% also reported at least one crime; in contrast, only 3% of schools with minor or no reported discipline problems reported the presence of crime. These less dramatic, but more frequent school and classroom disruptions, may also play a part in shaping perceptions about the safety of schools. (p. 336)

As a way to assess behavior of students with behavior disorders, functional assessment was included originally in the IDEA 1997 as well as IDEA 2004. Despite some concerns about the validity of this approach for public policy decisions (Nelson, Roberts, Mathurs, & Rutherford, 1999), the law requires schools to recognize the relationship between student behavior and classroom learning. This legislation compels education authorities to deal positively with the discipline, invoking the behavior of students with disabilities. Functional assessment is enhanced through functional analysis of behaviors. The term *functional analysis* is used to describe the systematic manipulation of antecedent and/or consequence events that are hypothesized as being related functionally to the occurrence of the problem behavior. Functional analyses are done most often under controlled experimental conditions rather than in applied (i.e., clinical, educational) contexts. Functional assessment is the process of identifying established operations, antecedent variables, and consequent events that control target behaviors. In other words, a functional assessment identifies when, where, and why problem behaviors occur and when, where, and why they do not occur (Sugai, Horner, & Sprague, 1999).

Literature regarding functional behavior assessment (FBA) in general education environments has been critical of the paucity of research in such settings, given the complex and often time-consuming nature of FBA. Less complex team-based FBA processes have been suggested as a realistic alternative for general education environments. Scott, McIntyre, Liaupsin, Nelson, and Conroy (2004) described an informal team-based FBA process implemented with 39 school-based teams who hypothesized behavioral function for students who had been referred. Data from these meetings was then supplied to three national FBA experts who attempted to generate hypotheses from the same information. Results indicate little agreement between teams and experts or between the experts themselves. Analysis of these data prompt a discussion of the possible effect that information sources, individual perceptions, and personal experiences play in the development of functional hypotheses.

THE NEED FOR HIGHLY QUALIFIED TEACHERS

Cook, Landrum, Tankersley, and Kauffman (2003) stated that "there is little or no systematic, institutionalized support for teachers attempting to implement effective practices" (p. 353). Available research appears to question the current capacity of teachers in the field to implement and sustain effective instruction procedures within the general education setting (Abbott, Walton, Tapia, & Greenwood, 1999; Fuchs & Fuchs, 1998b; Vaughn, Klingner, & Hughes, 2004). In addition, Wehby and colleagues (2003) noted that there is a growing body of evidence to support the significant academic and social benefits gained when teachers display more competence in the instructional procedures utilized. For example, Sutherland, Alder, and Gunter (2003) indicated that teacher instructional behavior could be improved by providing regular feedback regarding critical teaching behaviors to the teacher and then having the teacher observe data representing the rate of performance of those behaviors. These data were subsequently graphed at the rate at which those behaviors were observed.

Smith and Daunic (2004) discussed the merits of prevention research in the behavior disorder field. They are underway with a major study to examine how peers without disabilities can influence positive behavior in students with behavioral challenges. They observed:

> Teaching students with EBD alongside typically functioning peers can minimize stigmatization, facilitate monitoring and social skill reinforcement, and maximize generalization throughout the school day. Using a theoretically based, randomized, controlled prevention trial approach, we are studying the effects of a universal cognitive-behavioral intervention designed to help students develop positive solutions to social problems in anger-provoking situations. Our research, however, requires a blend of requisite social science with practical considerations. (2004, p. 72)

Most teachers and education personnel who work with students with behavior disorders possess experience and training only in special education. Furthermore, most educators are not trained well enough to know how to help these students. A national survey of 556 teachers of students with behavior disorders was conducted to identify special educators' beliefs about maltreatment and abuse among the students they taught (Oseroff, Oseroff, Westling, & Gessner, 1999). The respondents reported that they believed approximately 38% of their students had been abused physically or sexually, 41% had been neglected, and 51% had been abused emotionally. The teachers reported that the behavior of their students, student reports, physical signs, and reports from others led them to believe that abuse or neglect had occurred. Furthermore, they reported that their students displayed many personal and behavioral characteristics often identified as indicators of maltreatment. Of the teachers surveyed, 82% related that they had reported maltreatment and that their reports were made most often to school administrators and least often to the abuse and neglect hotline. Many of these students are filled with rage or are depressed or continuously unable to learn or perform effectively at job sites and often suspended or expelled from school. It is critical to realize that many of students' mental health issues can be significantly ameliorated with effective counseling, selected medication, community training with real work activities, and supported education (Collins, Bybee, & Mowbry, 1998; Frankie et al., 1996).

How special education teachers are trained is also important. For example, Nougaret (2002) examined the teaching behavior of teachers with limited preparation.

> In this investigation, it was seen that first-year teachers who had participated in a traditional education program greatly outperformed first-year teachers with emergency provisional licensure on observational ratings of planning and preparation, classroom environment, and instruction. The present findings support earlier studies that reported higher levels of competence in traditionally prepared teachers and extend the findings to the field of special education. (p. 30)

The study illustrates the importance of systematic training in developing special education teachers who are highly qualified in pedagogy as well as content.

In a national e-mail survey conducted by the Council for Exceptional Children (2003a), teachers expressed serious concerns regarding the "highly qualified" requirements of the No Child Left Behind (NCLB) Act of 2001 (PL 107-110). One of these concerns was the possibility that more teachers would leave the field due to additional licensing demands. This reaction, coupled with the already well-documented findings that the majority of teachers of students with behavior disorders enter the teaching professional without being fully certified (Billingsley, 2001), creates a major concern about the available pool of qualified teachers. They also "burn out" at a higher level than any other group of teachers (e.g., George, George, Gersten, & Grosenick, 1995). These factors worsen the "constant confusion of new teachers who probably lack the expertise to effectively deal with both the behavior and the academic needs" (Wehby et al., 2003, p. 196) of these students.

Richardson and Shupe (2003) addressed the crucial importance of teachers self-awareness when working with students with behavior disorders. They listed five very important questions that teachers need to ask.

1. Am I taking proactive steps to identify and defuse my own "emotional triggers"?

2. Am I paying attention to what I need to pay attention to?

3. Am I using effective strategies to reduce burnout and nurture my own mental health?

4. Am I using an appropriate sense of humor to build relationships, diffuse conflict, engage learners, and manage my own stress?

5. Do I regularly acknowledge significant ways I (and others) are making a difference in the lives of students?

TRANSITION ASSESSMENT

The philosophy of assessing the vocational and transition needs of youth with behavior disorders is similar to that of all students with disabilities (Clark, 1998). The focus must be on a community-referenced approach to assessment that specifically asks students about their career and vocational goals. Because of difficulties with the reliability of their responses, it is important to ask about career goals several times and, more important, to observe what their preferences seem to be. Figure 19.1 lists questions that teachers and vocational counselors can ask students; their answers should be shared with parents or guardians. Positive vocational experiences can lead to positive adjustments in the transition process as job motivation and interest are key factors in job satisfaction, which can improve many negative behaviors.

After determining each student's career and vocational interests, teachers must ascertain each student's community living, mobility, recreation, and personal goals. Assessing curriculum targets within these areas is the key to designing good secondary special education programs and effecting positive transitions. Without such an assessment, disgruntlement, boredom, and exacerbation of the student's problems are likely to occur, which often leads to suspension, expulsion, or dropping out.

What jobs can you do now?

What jobs do you think you might like to do in 2 years?

What jobs do you think you might like to do in 10 years?

To do the jobs you want 2 years from now, what skills will you need to improve?

To do the jobs you want 10 years from now, what abilities will you need to improve?

What are your biggest problems with the jobs you can do now?

What problems do you have getting a job now?

What can you do about these problems?

Figure 19.1.   A sample career planning questionnaire. (From Donald D. Hammill, Nettie R. Bartell. Teaching Students with Learning and Behavior Problems, 5e © 1990. Published by Allyn & Bacon, Boston, MA. Copyright © 1990 by Pearson Education. Reprinted by permission of the publisher.)

After making a reliable determination of students' choices and needs, efforts should be channeled into vocational situational assessments. Situational assessments (i.e., the objective quantitative evaluation of student performance in different work settings) are valuable for determining work responses under varied conditions. By varying the stress conditions of the work assessments and modifying the nature of commands and tasks, work performance data can be compiled and potential can be determined. Assessments include observations of students both in school and in the community at various worksites; on-the-job tryouts; classroom performance examples; tests to measure interests, aptitudes, or learning styles; and work samples (i.e., simulated tasks of particular jobs; Clark, 1998). Utilization of standardized vocational evaluation testing for this population, however, has not been promising except in unique circumstances such as determining aptitudes for computer, health care, and automotive repair occupations. Instead, real-life situational assessments yield more practical information.

Vocational assessments should help to obtain information about a student's aptitudes, interests, work habits, socialization skills, work attitudes, and work tolerance (Clark, 1998) and can also be used to help structure students' planning and preparation for further postsecondary training. Vocational assessments provide information in response to the following questions.

- Where is the student in the vocational awareness, exploration, or preparation process?

- In what occupational area does the student show the greatest interest?

- In what occupational area(s) does the student show aptitude and ability?

- Are there specific learning requirements that will need to be incorporated into a student's educational program to help him or her prepare for a particular occupation?

Table 19.2. Recommendations for transition assessments

1. Select assessment instruments and procedures first on the basis of how they address these key questions in a student's individual transition planning: Who am I? What do I want in life, now and in the future?

2. Make transition assessment ongoing.

3. Use multiple types and levels of assessments.

4. Make 3-year psychoeducational reevaluations count for all students.

5. Think of assessment procedures in terms of efficiency as well as effectiveness.

6. Develop a transition assessment approach that is not only fair but also enhanced in terms of gender, culture, and language.

7. Organize assessment data for easy access in IEP planning and instructional programming.

8. Someone in the school needs to take primary responsibility for arranging and coordinating various kinds of assessments and evaluations for transition planning.

From Clark, G.M. (1998). *Assessment for transition planning: Transition series* (pp. 72, 73, 74). Austin, TX: PRO-ED; reprinted by permission.

Table 19.2 lists eight recommendations for transition assessment that the educator needs to consider when planning for transition.

TEACHING FOR TRANSITION

Many teachers who work with youth with behavior disorders focus their curricula and instructional efforts exclusively on academic skills, neglecting career and vocational education curriculum. The following list of units of instruction provides teachers with ideas for developing opportunities to participate in community activities.

- Financial and legal aspects of employment

- Attitudes and skills that may lead to promotion

- Job applications and interviews

- Requirements of different occupations

- Occupational interests

- Private and other employment agencies

- Managing time and activities

- Getting along with co-workers

- Coping with frustration and failure at a job

- Identifying different sources of employment

- Understanding employer and supervisor expectations

Creative teachers turn these units into real-life experiences for students, using guest speakers, such as students with disabilities who are working effectively in the community and panels of professionals. The optimal way to teach these skills, however, is through placement in paying jobs. Concrete actions and practices are particularly important for students with behavior disorders. These students usually have the necessary skills to determine whether an activity is real or simulated. For example, a 3-day internship at a dry cleaning shop, in which a teacher can help the student to manage his or her frustrations and develop work motivation, is far more useful to students than viewing videos or Power-Point presentations in the classroom. Students learn best when they experience repeated practice and reinforcement, especially when learning how to manage their own behavior. It is essential that teachers, job coaches, counselors, aides, volunteers, or university students provide frequent on-site communication with employers and students.

Regan (2003) discussed the use of dialogue journals in the classroom for students with behavioral disabilities on improving their writing skills. A major part of gaining work confidence and competence for these students was establishing a relationship with the teacher.

Economic self-sufficiency and greater independence in controlling personal finances should be tackled after the student is performing reasonably well in his or her job. Examples for lessons in this area include 1) managing money through budgeting, 2) learning how to shop using catalogs, 3) understanding costs of goods and services, 4) considering price versus quality factors when shopping, 5) comparing prices of different brands or sizes, 6) grocery shopping, 7) understanding sales, 8) reading advertisements, 9) making simple home furnishing purchases, 10) caring for personal possessions, 11) understanding banking services, 12) understanding credit and bank loans, 13) understanding and selecting insurance, and 14) saving money—skills necessary for competent and well-adjusted transitions. Because many students with behavior disorders are not intellectually slow or delayed, they can acquire many of these skills. They must, however, be taught in a stimulating and creative fashion with an emphasis on competence, not process. Worksheets, ditto sheets, blackboard work, and extensive bookwork will not elicit optimal learning from students with behavior disorders. Verbal instruction, modeling, ample feedback, and other reinforcements will enhance curriculum and instruction efforts.

Teaching Self-Control and Self-Management Strategies

Self-control training can take place in the community, where the process of independent living presents many decision-making situations. Self-control may be required in the following activities: 1) maintaining a balanced diet, 2) staying on a regular work schedule, 3) washing and caring for clothes, 4) managing money, and 5) using discretion in choosing friends and deciding whom to trust. Situations that arise in public places where frustration tolerance may be low are perfect opportunities to practice self-control, such as riding crowded buses, waiting in lines, following directions, dealing with cab drivers, and interacting with hostile service clerks.

Self-management strategies can also be utilized in the workplace (Furlong, Jonikes, Cook, Hathaway, & Goode, 1994). For vocational adjustment, self-control should be used in task performance and social skills. Social behavior, such as the proper use of breaktime, being prompt, and giving appropriate social greetings, can be incorporated into curriculum objectives. It may also be appropriate to allow students to determine their own work criteria in conjunction with their employer and then self-administer some form of reinforcement. Frequent self-reinforcement for gradually doing more work shapes improved performance.

Martin et al. (2003) conducted an important study to determine if secondary-age students could use self-determination contracts to regulate the correspondence between their plans, work, self-evaluations, and adjustments on academic tasks. The authors examined the impact of these contracts on the plan, work, evaluation, and adjustment behaviors of eight secondary-age students with severe emotional/behavior problems. The students completed daily self-determination contracts to schedule their work on academic tasks, plan for work outcomes, evaluate progress, and adjust for the next day's activity. One-way repeated measures *(ANOVAs)* yielded 15 significant effects for the correspondence between plan and work, between work and evaluation, between evaluation and adjustment, and between adjustment and the next day plan. Pre- and postassessment found significant academic improvement.

Self-management is driven by self-determination (see Chapter 2) and usually entails instructing the student to independently self-monitor by facilitating natural cues or adding external cues and prompts, compensatory strategies, assistive technology devices, and so forth. Instruction can be provided by co-workers, friends, family members, or the employment specialist, depending on the student's needs. For instance, a family member may assist the student in learning how to check off days on a calendar to determine when he or she goes to work. A co-worker may assist the individual by telling him or her when it is lunchtime, and the employment specialist may train the worker to use a timer and external cues to monitor production.

In vocational settings, employment specialists, rehabilitation counselors, employers, and family members may all help the individual with a disability to develop a plan appropriate to a particular situation. To be effective, however, the designers should be competent in the development of behavior management programs and involve the individual who will be implementing the program.

Teaching Social Skills

Most students with behavior disorders lack social skills. Teachers working with these youth must teach these skills in addition to academic and vocational skills. Social skills should be taught in a variety of community settings as well as in inclusive high schools in interactions with peers without disabilities. Table 19.3 gives tips for inclusion that can be infused into the curriculum resources listed next.

There are a number of curriculum packets for social skills instruction. An extremely popular program called the ACCEPTS Program uses scripted lessons and a videotape that emphasize using proper social interactions, making new friends, and getting along with others, particularly in mainstream general education settings (Walker et al., 1983).

A second program called Skill Streaming uses a structured learning approach for teachers engaged in modeling, role playing, and direct feedback (Goldstein, Sprafkin, Gershew, & Cline, 1980). Content areas include coping with feelings while managing aggression, alleviating stress, and planning.

Transition to Independence Process (TIP) System

Clearly, the field of emotional and behavior disorders continues to look for the most effective evidence-based intervention programs that truly work. Relatively few long-term interventions exist for these youth with EBD, yet there is one program that

Table 19.3 Tips for inclusion of youth with behavior disorders

Instructional strategy	Description	Advantages	Disadvantages
1. Modeling	Exposing target student to prosocial behavior	Easy to implement	Not sufficient if used alone
2. Strategic placement	Placing target student in situations with other students who display prosocial behaviors	Employs peers as change agents, facilitates generalization, is cost effective	Research data inconclusive when used alone
3. Instruction	Telling students how and why they should behave a certain way and/or giving rules for behavior	Overemphasizes norms/expectations	Not sufficient if used alone
4. Correspondence training	Positively reinforcing students for accurate reports regarding their behavior	Facilitates maintenance and generalization of training, is cost effective	Very little documentation of effectiveness
5. Rehearsal and practice	Structured practice of specific prosocial behavior	Enhances skill acquisition	Not sufficient to change behavior if used alone
6. Positive reinforcement or shaping	Prosocial behaviors or approximations followed by a reward or favorable event	Strong research support for effectiveness	Maintenance after treatment termination is not predictable
7. Prompting and coaching	Providing students with additional stimuli/prompts that elicit the prosocial behavior	Particularly effective after acquisition to enhance transfer to natural settings	Maintenance after treatment termination is not predictable
8. Positive practice	A consequence strategy in which student repeatedly practices correct behavior	May produce immediate increases in prosocial behavior	Long-term effectiveness not documented; less restrictive approaches should be used first
9. Multimethod training packages	Multicomponent instructional package that incorporates several behavioral techniques	Greater treatment strength and durability, applicable to a range of children and settings	

From Carter, J., and Sugai, G. (1989). Social skills curriculum analysis. *TEACHING Exceptional Children, 22,* 38. Copyright 1989 by the Council for Exceptional Children; reprinted by permission.

appears to show great promise (Clark, 2004). The Transition to Independence Process (TIP) system has been in place with ongoing data being collected since the late 1990s. The TIP system prepares youth with behavior disorders for transition to employment, educational opportunities (college), living situations, and community life functioning.[1]

Theory and Research Underlying the TIP System

TIP System Mission Statement The mission of a service delivery system for transition-age youth and young adults (14–25 years old) with emotional and/or behavior difficulties (EBD) is to assist them in making a successful transition into adulthood, with all of them achieving, within their potential, their personal goals in the transition domains of employment, education, living situation, personal effectiveness, and community life functioning. To accomplish this service system goal, personnel at the prac-

---

[1]The material in this section was graciously contributed by Dr. Hewitt B. "Rusty" Clark, Professor at the Florida Mental Health Institute of the University of South Florida.

Table 19.4. Transition to Independence Process (TIP) system guidelines

1. Engage young people through relationship development, person-centered planning, and a focus on their futures.

2. Tailor services and supports to be accessible, coordinated, and developmentally appropriate, and build on strengths to enable young people to pursue their goals across all transition domains.

3. Acknowledge and develop personal choice and social responsibility with young people.

4. Ensure a safety net of support by involving a young person's parents, family members, and other informal and formal key players.

5. Enhance the competencies of young persons to assist them in achieving greater self-sufficiency and confidence.

6. Maintain an outcome focus in the TIP system at the young person, program, and community levels.

7. Involve young people, parents, and other community partners in the TIP system at the practice, program, and community levels.

From Clark, H.B. (2004). *TIP system development and operations manual* (pp. 8–10). Tampa, FL: University of South Florida, Florida Mental Health Institute. http://tip.fmhi.usf.edu and http://ncyt. fmhi.usf.edu; reprinted by permission.

tice, program, and community levels work closely with the young people and their families and other informal key players (e.g., friend, foster parent, aunt).

The Transition to Independence Process (TIP) system was developed to engage youth and young adults in their own futures planning process, provide them with developmentally appropriate services and supports, and involve them and their families and other informal key players in a process that prepares and facilitates them in their movement toward greater self-sufficiency and successful achievement of their goals related to each of the transition domains. The TIP system is operationalized through seven guidelines and their associated elements that drive the practice-level activities and provide a framework for the program and community system to support these functions. These seven guidelines are presented in Table 19.4 and form the foundation for this program.

Supportive Research Findings The complex challenges of the transition period for these young people with EBD and their unique needs pose major hurdles to parents, practitioners, educators, administrators, policy makers, and researchers. This situation presents a compelling argument for designing transition systems around a solid framework of promising strategies. Research findings regarding the best practices currently used by a number of promising transition programs in some communities across the nation are supportive of the TIP system and its guidelines (Bullis & Fredericks, 2002; Bullis et al., 2002; Cheney, Hagner, Malloy, Cormier, & Bernstein, 1998; Clark, Pschorr, Wells, Curtis, & Tighe, 2004; Cook, Solomon, Farrell, & Koziel, 1997; Karpur, Clark, Caproni, Sterner, & Whitfield, 2003). Each of these studies report improved progress and/or postsecondary outcomes for the young people who were served using the TIP system or a variation of it incorporating most, if not all, of the TIP guidelines.

In addition to these encouraging research findings, each of the guidelines and their elements have either empirical support or broad professional consensus indicating that these are promising practices for use with young people with EBD and their families. As encouraging as this is regarding the TIP system, it is important for the reader to remember that the TIP system is currently a promising practice and that more research is being performed to further refine its practices and system strategies.

Documentation of the Research   A detailed description is provided on the research finding regarding the TIP system and its guidelines in a section of the web site titled, *Theory/Research Base.* The TIP web site address is http://tip.fmhi.usf.edu. The quality or fidelity with which the TIP system is being applied in a community can be measured using the TIP Case Study Protocol for Continuing System Improvement (Deschenes, Gomez, & Clark, 1999), and a description of this instrument is also available through the web site noted above.

In order to understand better how the TIP system works, consider the case of LeVan. This is a young man in strong need of a well-planned intervention program.

LeVan was 16 years old and had had more than a lifetime of trouble. High school consisted of special education classes, absences, increasing disciplinary referrals, and hanging with other neighborhood youth who were in trouble. Having been in out-of-home placements for the past 9 years, he moved around a lot and changed schools frequently. LeVan had been in his current foster home for the past 18 months, the longest he had been in any placement, and he seemed to get along well with his foster mother although he did not comply with the home rules and was often in trouble with the foster father who tried to discipline him. LeVan was arrested with other youth when they robbed a grocery store of several hundred dollars in cash and several six-packs of beer. He was now doing community service.

LeVan, a handsome African American, was typically gentlemanly with those adults whom he felt respected him. He felt his foster mother and his high school math teacher/basketball coach were his only adult key players. Although LeVan had been on the basketball team last year, he failed to maintain his grade level to qualify for the team this year and was acting out more and possibly experiencing ADHD and/or bouts of depression. His coach/teacher referred LeVan to the TIP system, which operated out of the community mental health center. Jennie, the "transition facilitator" assigned to LeVan, approached him in a novel way using a series of "strength discovery" conversations to learn from him, his foster mother, and his teacher/coach about LeVan's interests, strengths, needs, and dreams. Although Jennie had a busy schedule, LeVan felt she always made time for him and was the only person with whom he was completely comfortable in talking with about whatever was troubling him or when he needed guidance. Through the strength discovery conversations, Jennie had learned that LeVan was interested in and did pretty well in math, science, and athletics; did best in his studies when he had a tutor at a previous school; used to enjoy bicycling when he had a trail bike (which was stolen); liked to play sports but didn't have access to such in his neighborhood; and dreamed of playing on the Lakers or other basketball pro team. In talking with LeVan about the pros, it became clear that for him the "pros" meant playing ball, having a neat uniform, earning money, being around sports activities, and being respected. Jennie talked with LeVan and with the help of his coach/teacher and his foster mother they were able to use the principles of the TIP system to work with LeVan in setting up an array of supports and services that built on his strengths and interests and addressed his needs and supported his goals.

The plan involved LeVan 1) interviewing for a job as a Sports Event Security Apprentice so he could attend several sporting events a week and earn some money; 2) securing a tutor to assist him in his studies; 3) getting a membership at the local YMCA so he could participate in sports of his choice when he had time after school and on weekends when he was not working; and 4) purchasing a bicycle to give him the means to get around to all of these locations as he needed to. The TIP system flex funds assisted LeVan in setting his plan in motion. Although there were occasional set backs, LeVan's school situation improved, he got back on the basketball team in his junior and senior years, and he went on to pursue a degree in exercise physiology to work with athletes, employees, and others on the prevention and treatment of injuries.

TIP System Definition

The TIP system was developed to engage youth and young adults in their own futures planning process, provide them with developmentally-appropriate services and supports, and involve them and their families and other informal key players in a process that prepares and facilitates them in their movement toward greater self-sufficiency and successful achievement of their goals related to each of the transition domains—employment, career-building education, living situation, personal-effectiveness and quality of life, and community-life functioning.

The TIP system is operationalized through seven guidelines and their associated elements that drive the practice level activities and provide a framework for the program and community system to support these functions.

Key Aspects of the TIP System

Transition Facilitators To ensure the continuity of planning, services, and supports, the TIP system is implemented with the assistance of *transition facilitators* who work with the young people, their parents, family members, and other informal, formal, and community supports.

- The term *transition facilitator* is used to emphasize the function of *facilitating* the young person's future, not directing it.

- Different sites and service systems use similar terms such as transition specialist, resource coordinator, mentor, transition coach, TIP facilitator, service coordinator, or life coach.

Independence and Interdependence The TIP system promotes independence. However, the concept of "interdependence" is central to working effectively with young people. This concept nests the focus of independent functioning (e.g., budgeting money, maintaining a job) within the framework of young people learning that there is a healthy, reciprocal role of supporting others and receiving support from others (i.e., social support network for emotional, spiritual, and physical support).

Self-Determination The concept of *self-determination* is one that the fields of education and psychology have defined in various ways (e.g., Field & Hoffman, 1996; Martin & Marshall, 1995; Rusch & Chadsey, 1998). In order to operationalize this concept as much as possible, it can be defined as the ability to: 1) set goals that are likely to improve one's quality of life, 2) formulate alternative strategies, 3) choose among the strategies to find the most viable ones for achieving each goal, 4) implement the selected strategies, and 5) evaluate one's progress in achieving the goals.

Some of the personal skills associated with self-determination are: choice clarification, decision making, goal setting, creativity, delayed gratification, self-advocacy, assertiveness, self-monitoring, self-evaluation, and self-reinforcement.

Transition Process Values   Whether they are explicit or implicit, the values held by transition staff and by administrators in a service system determine how the program operates and affects features of the program, such as support strategies, processes for establishing goals, focus of services, responsiveness to young people, involvement of parents, funding plans, hiring and training of staff, and support of staff and young people who are contributing. Based on an extensive review of community-based transition programs helping youth and young adults move into the world of adult responsibility, Clark, Unger, and Stewart (1993) identified program values that appeared to be essential in guiding quality transition programs.

These transition process values are similar, but not identical, to those underlying the children's system of care model (Stroul & Friedman, 1986) and the wraparound process (VanDenBerg, 1993). These transition values are infused throughout the TIP system guidelines. Thus, if personnel who are working with young people and their informal and formal key players are functioning in accordance with the TIP guidelines and the site's program managers, administrators, and policy makers are supporting and facilitating this work, the result should be an effective, quality TIP system.

JOB OPPORTUNITIES FOR YOUTH WITH EMOTIONAL AND BEHAVIOR DISORDERS

Students with behavior disorders are capable of working in a variety of jobs with help, training, and support (Smith, Belcher, & Juhrs, 1995). It is very important to focus on training for constructive and productive work activity with these students, as unstructured or empty time usually leads to inappropriate behavior. These individuals have done especially well in some industries, which include tasks that teachers should look for in forming functional curriculum (see Table 19.5).

Manufacturing Jobs

Workers with behavior disorders can work in a variety of jobs in the manufacturing field. They can assemble computer cables, air conditioning parts, electronic parts, venetian blinds, fuses, and dental supplies. They can also perform other manufacturing duties, such as laminating, rolling and labeling posters, and enlarging and copying microfiche. Manufacturing jobs typically have the advantages of providing spacious—sometimes isolated—work spaces, requiring little or no language, requiring little or no social skills, providing well-established routines, and involving repetitive jobs.

Retail Jobs

Workers with behavior disorders can be employed in various retail settings, including clothing stores, toy stores, hardware stores, housewares stores, department stores, and

Table 19.5.   Jobs for people with behavior disorders

Computer cable assembler

Job description	This job involves assembly line production of computer cables according to consumer specification.
Worksite description	This is a medium-size company that manufactures and installs computer cables and connections; the company employs about 15 workers to assemble cables.
Job tasks	• Measure and cut cable according to specifications.
	• Strip the ends of each cable with a razor blade.
	• Operate a crimping machine.
	• Place pins in the connection by matching a numbered slot to a colored wire.
	• Assemble hood over connection.
	• Label cable for length and assembler initials.
	• Test cable using a volt meter.

Equipment, machinery, and hand tools needed to complete job tasks
- Hand-operated cable measurement device
- Hydraulic crimping machine
- Volt meter
- Razor blade

Receiving clerk/stock clerk

Job description	This job involves working in the stockroom, preparing price tags, and pricing merchandise.
Worksite description	This job is with a large catalog discount store, which is part of a chain; the store employs approximately 30 workers, including one employee with autism.
Job tasks	• Make price tags.
	• Open boxes of merchandise.
	• Apply price tags to merchandise and repack boxes.
	• Price merchandise using a hand gun.
	• Pull up computer printouts of orders.
	• Fill orders by locating merchandise in stockroom.
	• Stock shelves with merchandise.

Equipment, machinery, and tools needed to complete job tasks
- Order forms
- Map used to locate items in warehouse
- Pricing gun

Warehouse worker

Job description	This job involves managing inventory for a lighting fixture warehouse.
Worksite description	The job is with a division of a large corporation that distributes lighting fixtures to retail stores; there are approximately 100 workers in the warehouse, 4 of whom work in the same area as the 2 with autism.
Job tasks	• Pull ordered items from shelves.
	• Pack items for shipping.
	• Price items.
	• Restock shelves.
	• Sweep and clean.
	• Assemble wheelbarrows and other items.

Equipment, machinery, and hand tools needed to complete job tasks
- Boxes
- Tape gun
- Box labels
- Pricing gun
- Screwdrivers
- Hammers

(continued)

drug stores. Job duties have involved stocking and restocking shelves, straightening displays, tagging merchandise, filling orders, retrieving merchandise from the stockroom, sorting merchandise, collecting damaged items, peeling stickers from incorrectly priced items, and organizing merchandise. Retail jobs can be found that require

Table 19.5.   *(continued)*

Bindery worker	
Job description	This job involves completing various steps in the assembly of books, booklets, pamphlets, and other printed matter.
Worksite description	This job is with a medium-size, family-owned printing company; there are 16 rooms in the company, 4 of which are used by employees. There are approximately 40 workers in the company—2 with autism who work with 4–8 other employees in the bindery performing similar jobs.
Job tasks	• Separate and pack books from the printer.
	• Collate inserts into brochures.
	• Punch holes in book covers.
	• Bind booklets.
	• Wrap books in plastic using a shrink-wrap machine.
	• Keep inventory of completed work.
	• Retrieve materials from storage.
	• Assemble cardboard boxes.
	• Sweep work area.

Equipment, machinery, and hand tools needed to complete job tasks
- Binding punch
- Tape gun
- Tape dispenser
- Jacks
- Binding machine
- Carts and skids for moving materials
- Razor blades and scissors
- Shrink-wrap machine

From Smith, M.D., Belcher, R.G., and Juhrs, P.D. (1995). *A guide to successful employment for individuals with autism* (pp. 110, 141, 179, 228). Baltimore: Paul H. Brookes Publishing Co.; reprinted by permission.

minimal or no interaction with the public so that emphasis on language or social skills competencies is not needed.

Delivery Jobs

Delivery jobs have the advantages of being outdoors and requiring a great deal of walking. They typically require no spoken language, few social skills, and no fine motor skills. If behavior problems do occur or if productivity slows for some reason, then there is no disruption to co-workers because these are relatively solitary jobs. People with behavior disorders have been successfully hired by companies to prepare items for delivery and to deliver the items to residents in the community such as advertisements for pizza delivery services and newspapers.

Jobs in Warehousing and Distribution

Workers with behavior disorders can work in numerous warehouses and distribution centers. Warehouse jobs include a variety of tasks, such as cleaning rental glassware, folding rental party linens, packaging items for display in vending machines, filling orders for music tapes and compact discs, filling orders for electronic parts, and doing inventory. These jobs allow students to focus on specific work tasks, thereby reducing the likelihood of inappropriate social behavior.

Jobs in Printing

Typically, jobs in printing companies are held by workers with spoken language abilities, although these abilities may not be necessary for some printing jobs. Work in printing companies often involves limited interaction with the public, and tasks are often done alone in an assembly-line fashion in spacious work areas with a high background noise level. Printing is a business that is becoming computer based, utilizing machines that people with behavior disorders can learn to operate. Although there might be a variety of job tasks for the worker to learn, each task is usually done in the same way each time, according to rigid routines. Work is usually precise and requires good visual and fine motor skills.

SUPPORTED EMPLOYMENT OUTCOMES FOR INDIVIDUALS WITH EMOTIONAL AND BEHAVIOR DISORDERS

As noted in earlier chapters, supported employment (SE) is one very successful way to help youth and adults enter the labor force. This is true for youth with significant psychiatric disorders as well. There have been many excellent studies to support these outcomes (Bond, 2004a; Drake et al., 2001).

What Is Effective in Supported Employment?[2]

Drake and Becker developed the Individual Placement and Support (IPS) model (Becker & Drake, 1993, 2003), which is a better defined and tested extension of the early work by Wehman (1981). The IPS model is now regarded as synonymous with evidence-based SE for individuals with psychiatric disabilities. This work and research has been groundbreaking and, along with Bond (2004a), has been extraordinarily well researched. Among the key principles defining IPS are the following (Becker & Bond, 2002; Bond, 1998, 2004a):

1. Services focused on competitive employment: The agency providing SE services is committed to competitive employment as an attainable goal for its consumers with psychiatric disorders, devoting its resources for rehabilitation services to this endeavor, rather than to intermediate activities, such as day treatment or sheltered work.

2. Eligibility based on consumer choice: No one is excluded who wants to participate.

3. Rapid job search: SE programs use a rapid job search approach to help consumers obtain jobs directly, rather than providing lengthy pre-employment assessment, training, and counseling.

4. Integration of rehabilitation and mental health: The SE program is closely integrated with the mental health treatment team.

5. Attention to consumer preferences: Services are based on consumers' preferences and choices, rather than providers' judgments. Staff and consumers find individualized job placements based on consumer preferences, strengths, and work experiences.

6. Time-unlimited and individualized support: Follow-along supports are individualized and continued indefinitely.

---

[2]Portions of this section were drawn from Bond, Wehman, and Wittenburg (2005).

7. Benefits counseling is provided: Consumers are given specific and timely guidance tailored to their unique circumstances.

Evidence-based SE (i.e., the IPS model) has been described in detail in a practice manual (Becker & Drake, 2003) and an implementation resource kit (Becker & Bond, 2002). A well-validated SE fidelity scale has been developed (Becker, Smith, Tanzman, Drake, & Tremblay, 2001; Bond, Becker, Drake, & Vogler, 1997; Bond, Vogler, et al., 2001). There are no shortage of excellent training materials for teachers and counselors who wish to provide SE services for youth with behavior disorders.

Using the most stringent requirements for level of evidence, all the reviews of SE for clients with psychiatric disabilities point to the conclusion that it should be considered an evidence-based practice (Bond, 2004a; Bond, Becker, et al., 2001; Bond, Drake, Mueser, & Becker, 1997; McLaren, 2004; Moll, Huff, & Detwiler, 2003; Ridgway & Rapp, 1998; Schneider, Heyman, & Turton, 2002; Twamley, Jeste, & Lehman, 2003). The studies cited are excellent examples of how research can be translated into practice to improve transition outcomes for youth who are significantly challenged with behavioral issues.

Day Treatment Conversion Studies   Four studies have been conducted examining the effectiveness of converting day treatment services to SE (Bailey, Ricketts, Becker, Xie, & Drake, 1998; Becker, Bond, et al., 2001; Drake et al., 1994; Drake, Becker, Biesanz, Wyzik, & Torrey, 1996; Gold & Marrone, 1998) in similar fashion to what was described in Chapter 12. These studies involved six different sites converting from day treatment to SE, five of which closed down their day treatment services altogether (Becker, Bond, et al., 2001; Drake et al., 1994; Drake, Becker, et al., 1996; Gold & Marrone, 1998) and one which curtailed its day treatment services (Bailey et al., 1998). The first study compared a day treatment program conversion with a center that did not initially convert its services (Drake et al., 1994), but later did (Drake, Becker, et al., 1996); the second compared a portion of their program that converted with a group of day treatment clients not involved in the conversion (Bailey et al., 1998); the third compared two centers undergoing conversions with one that did not (Becker, Bond, et al., 2001); and the fourth was a 1-year follow-up study of consumers enrolled in a day treatment program after its closing (Gold & Marrone, 1998). Altogether, these studies included 317 consumers in sites converting to SE and 184 consumers in the comparison sites. The pre/post time periods varied across studies, ranging from 3 to 12 months for baseline and from 3 to 24 months for follow-up. During the baseline period, while consumers were still attending day treatment, the employment rate was 13% in the conversion sites and 12% in the comparison sites. During follow-up, after the converting sites had switched to SE, 38% of the consumers in the SE sites worked competitively, compared with 15% of the consumers in the comparison sites. On average, then, the percentage of consumers obtaining competitive jobs nearly tripled after conversion of day treatment to SE, whereas competitive employment rates in nonconverting sites remained virtually static.

Randomized Controlled Trials   Bond (2004a) summarized the findings for nine randomized controlled trials (RCTs) comparing SE with a variety of traditional vocational services for people with severe psychiatric disorders (e.g., Bond, Dietzen, Mc-Grew, & Miller, 1995; Chandler, Meisel, Hu, McGowen, & Madison, 1997; Drake et al., 1999; Drake, McHugo, Becker, Anthony, & Clark, 1996; Gervey & Bedell, 1994; Mueser et al., 2004). Since that time, three more unpublished studies have been reported in professional conferences and other venues (Bond, 2004b; Latimer et al., 2004; Twamley, Bartels, Becker, & Jeste, 2004). These 12 studies have been conducted by nine different research teams (although Becker and Drake have been consultants on a number of these studies) in various geographic regions (New Hampshire, New York, Connecticut, Maryland, District of Columbia, South Carolina, Indiana, Illinois, California, and Québec), representing both rural and urban communities. Eight of the studies have compared IPS to some form of standard practice (Bond, 2004b; Drake et al., 1999; Drake, McHugo, et al., 1996; Gold et al., 2002; Latimer et al., 2004; Lehman et al., 2002; Mueser et al., 2004; Twamley et al., 2004). In every case, fidelity to the IPS model was ensured through intensive training and monitoring using the IPS Fidelity Scale (Bond, Becker, et al., 1997).

Most recently, conversion from a sheltered to integrated employment work environment has been empirically proven to be successful. In a major case report, Oldman, Thomson, Calsaferri, Luke, and Bond (2005) described the transformation of a sheltered workshop to evidence-based SE services provided in partnership with five community treatment teams. Over a 15-year period, a Canadian nonprofit agency providing employment services for people with severe mental illness made a series of programmatic changes to increase their effectiveness. The agency initially modified their facility-based sheltered workshop to include a prevocationally oriented work preparation program, later added brokered SE services, and finally completely transformed their organization by relocating their vocational rehabilitation (VR) counselors to five community mental health teams in order to implement an evidence-based SE program based on the IPS model. During the initial sheltered employment period, less than 5% of unemployed clients entering the workshop achieved competitive employment annually. The annual competitive employment rate did not materially increase during the prevocational phase; it increased during the brokered SE phase, but did not exceed 25%. By contrast, after shifting to evidence-based SE, 84 (50%) of 168 unemployed clients receiving between 6 and 29 months of IPS services achieved competitive employment. This report also documented the role of agency planning and commitment quality improvement in implementing change.

In conclusion, SE for people with severe mental illnesses is an evidence-based practice, based on converging findings from four studies of the conversion of day treatment to SE and nine randomized controlled trials comparing SE with a variety of alternative approaches. These two lines of research suggest that between 40% and 60% of consumers enrolled in SE obtain competitive employment, whereas less than 20% of similar consumers do so when not enrolled in SE. Consumers who hold competitive jobs for a sustained period of time show benefits such as improved self-esteem and better symptom control, although by itself, enrollment in SE has no systematic impact on nonvocational outcomes, either on undesirable outcomes, such as rehospitalization, or on valued outcomes, such as improved quality of life. The psychiatric rehabilitation field has achieved consensus on a core set of principles of SE, although efforts continue to develop enhancements. A review of the evidence suggests strong support for four of the seven principles of SE, whereas the evidence for the remaining three is relatively weak. Continued innovation and research on principles is recommended.

This rapidly growing body of research has given tremendous program validity to the material by Ford (1995, 2001) on designing employment programs for people with long-term mental illness. In this text, Ford provided a blueprint for effective SE outcomes, emphasizing the important integration of psychotherapeutic supports with practical behavioral supports in the workplace.

Rogers, MacDonald-Wilson, Danley, and Martin (1997) reported an analysis of SE services for people with mental illness. Their results included that best practices in SE programs

1. Involve participants in defining the type of job environment that is the best match not only for skills, job tasks, hours, and wages, but also for emotional support and personal preferences.

2. Discuss the advantages and disadvantages of disclosure prior to interviewing for jobs, before the student enters the "Getting" phase. This has implications for the involvement of the employment specialist in developing the job, for the length of time that the participant is in the Getting phase, and for the type of and amount of support needed to obtain the job.

3. Discuss with the participant the type, frequency, and location of emotional support needed during each phase of the SE process. Frequent but brief contacts to provide emotional support away from the jobsite (and often by telephone) may be just as effective as extended support on the jobsite. Contact may be helpful before going to work (i.e., a telephone call to help decrease anxiety), after returning from work (i.e., to discuss what happened at work), or on weekends. Employment specialists may initiate these contacts, especially just before a participant starts a job and within the first few weeks or months on a new job. Consider developing other resources and supports, including natural supports both on and off the job, to assist the participant in maintaining employment.

4. Develop an employment support plan (ESP) with the participant. Help the participant to identify possible indicators that symptoms are increasing or a crisis is looming. Consider involving the employer (if disclosure has occurred), other service providers, and family or friends in helping to recognize these indicators. Specify actions to be taken to manage symptoms, behaviors, or crises once they are recognized.

The transition plan can be merged with an ESP in order to gain the best benefits. Rogers and her associates (1997) reported that SE programs and staff must be extremely flexible, responsive, and accessible in terms of when and with whom contacts and interactions occur. Emotional support is the most frequent specific task required of SE staff, suggesting the need for staff to be highly skilled in counseling interventions and relationship building. Accessibility of supports on the individual's own terms,

EDWARD

Edward is a young man in his early 30s living in a small town in the Northwest. For more than a decade, between hospitalizations and stretches of unemployment, he worked for the three glass installation businesses in his home town of 15,000. His erratic behavior cost him all those jobs, but not before he learned the ins and outs of the trade. Most important, Edward recognized his former employers' lapses in customer service and set out to start a business that accommodated the symptoms of his bipolar disorder and addressed the needs of construction companies and homebuilders seeking high-quality windows and glazing.

Edward's state employment counselor rejected his business idea, but working with a U.S. Department of Labor–funded disability demonstration project and the local Small Business Development Center funded by the Small Business Administration, he secured grant money to launch his enterprise. After an initial investment of under $20,000, Edward's business grossed more than $100,000 each quarter after the first hard year and is projected to generate $800,000 during its second year of operation.

and in a variety of modalities, appears important for the success of programs providing services to people with psychiatric disabilities.

As educators, guidance counselors, and rehabilitation counselors work together to determine how to evaluate outcomes appropriately, several variables should be considered. First, does the student have a job? Having a job in which one works a minimum of 15 hours per week, receives at least minimum wage, and learns how to get along with co-workers should be a priority of any transition evaluation checklist. Second, what are the student's self-esteem, confidence, and happiness levels? Does he or she seem excited and motivated by the prospect of coming to school, participating in community-based training, and having a job? If not, then activities such as teaching self-management and exposing students to the positive consequences of work can be very beneficial. Third, what level of behavior is the student exhibiting daily? Are there periodic outbursts of frustration or frequent unpredictable and explosive outbursts? Clearly, the likelihood of a satisfactory level of confidence and self-esteem should be influential in reducing these types of negative behaviors. A fourth form of transition evaluation is an examination of how many important community living skills in which the student gains competence during a 1-year span.

As we close out this chapter, it is reasonable to examine how two young people with significant emotional disabilities developed their own business (see sidebars). They took the best of what we learned in Chapter 11 with what we know about how SE can work and overcome barriers to success.[3]

Edward and Jack, and thousands of others like James at the beginning of this chapter, can work, and work can help to manage behavioral problems and issues. The training technology is there—we need only to learn it and use it.

CONCLUSION

Work experience, paid work, self-employment, and high levels of activity at community-based instruction sites are very important vehicles for improving the quality of behavior in students with behavior disorders. This is how high levels of inappropriate behaviors are reduced. Establishing meaningful work behaviors provide an alternative way to manage these antisocial behaviors. New skills and activities are generated that provide

---

[3]Reprinted with permission from Griffin and Hammis (2001).

JACK

Jack is 22 years old and lives in a community of 50,000. He has several diagnostic labels. His strong psychotropic medicine slowed him down a bit. His local VR counselor recognized Jack's love of music and woodworking and sent him away to a community college that certified him as a violin repair professional. For the past 6 months, Jack has been marketing his services locally and refining his production methods. His long-term strategy is to carve a niche that includes intense attention to customer service. Typically, customers are high school and college music teachers who temporarily patch their student's broken instruments in order to get them through the school term. Violin repair shops are inundated with rush orders over Christmas break and during the summer because sending a broken instrument in during the academic year often means a student has no violin to use for weeks.

Jack's simple, yet elegant solution is to buy and repair an inventory of used violins and keep them as ready replacements for broken ones. He will advertise to music teachers and provide a loaned instrument, shipped overnight, to be used while he repairs the student's violin. This presents an immediate solution to the music teacher and the student and allows Jack to spread his work out over the year instead of creating high anxiety periods of production over the holidays and the summer. His unique customer service niche accommodates his disability perfectly.

important ways to reduce aberrant behavior therapeutically in this population, regardless of the level of behavior disorder, emotional disturbance, or autism. Self-management, self-control, self-reinforcement, and self-observation strategies are underutilized by educators. Students with behavior disorders must feel that they have control over their environments and help to choose what they want to do. They need choices as well as explicit structure. In addition, there are a number of important behaviors associated with job seeking and employment—travel, training, use of money, banking, and social and personal skills at the jobsite—that are important curriculum material for teachers who are responsive to individual transition needs.

STUDY QUESTIONS

1. What are the possible characteristics that indicate that a student may have an emotional or behavior disorder?

2. Describe some of the challenges youth with behavior disorders are faced with.

3. What challenges are educators and counselors faced with in working with students with emotional or behavior disorders?

4. What do educators need to consider when planning for transition for students with emotional or behavior disorders?

5. Describe five strategies for teaching self-control and self-management to students with emotional and behavior disorders.

6. Describe programs that teach social skills to students with emotional and behavior disorders.

7. What are some categories of jobs that youths with emotional and behavior disorders might be considered for?

8. Describe how effective SE can be for people with emotional or behavior disorders?

20

Applications for Youth with Autism Spectrum Disorders

Carol Schall, Elin Cortijo-Doval, Pam Sherron Targett, and Paul Wehman

AFTER COMPLETING THIS CHAPTER, THE READER WILL BE ABLE TO

○ Identify the characteristics of individuals with autism spectrum disorders

○ Identify the primary and secondary challenges associated with autism spectrum disorders

○ Identify the characteristics of autism spectrum disorders in adolescence and adulthood

○ Describe the process of completing a functional behavior assessment (FBA) and developing a positive behavior support plan for a person with an autism spectrum disorder

○ Describe specialized supports used when teaching individuals with autism spectrum disorders how to work

○ Discuss how self-determination and person-centered planning assist teams supporting individuals with autism spectrum disorders in developing transition plans

○ Discuss the importance of early transition planning

○ Discuss the importance of team collaboration and parental participation for an effective transition plan

○ Discuss the importance of job matching, coaching, support, and follow-along for a person with an autism spectrum disorder in the work force

Jenny is 20 years old and is preparing for graduation from her high school in a few months. She has a diagnosis of autism, an IQ score of 65, and secondary diagnoses of seizure disorder and mild mental retardation. Despite her cognitive and health impairment, she has accomplished a great deal in her academic career. She passed the state standardized test in the ninth grade, committed to memory more than 200 historical events from a history time line including the dates and years of passage of every amendment to the United States Constitution, and remembered the birthday of every person who has ever worked with her or taught her. She does not remember, however, to ask for help when she is frustrated or confused. Instead, she shakes her head, cries, whines, complains, and refuses to do what she has been asked to do. She often becomes frustrated by changes in her schedule and routine, by tasks that require her to write or use fine motor skills, and when she is corrected for an error. She also takes verbal cues and directions very literally. For example, when she was 18, her parents tried her out at a weekend respite camp. When she asked what time she had to go to bed, the staff told her she could go to bed whenever she wanted. By 2 A.M. the next day, they said, "Okay, time for bed now!" She whined, complained, and argued that they had lied about her bedtime. She went home the next morning at 6 A.M. because the staff could no longer handle the crying and complaining. When she was

Now that Jenny and Evan's (see sidebars, this page and p. 539) school careers are ending, what will they do? Will they be able to find a job and work, or will their routines and subsequent behavior challenges interfere with their independence? Will they be able to one day live on their own and manage their own financial affairs? These are the critical questions that Jenny, Evan, and their parents are facing as they prepare for their high school graduation. They, like so many other people with autism spectrum disorders, and their parents are facing one of the most difficult times in their lives. On one hand, Jenny and Evan seem to be able to do cognitive tasks beyond their predicted "profiles." On the other hand, they have significant communication and social skill deficits that present considerable challenges. This scattered profile, in which a person appears very skilled and competent in some areas and challenged in other areas, is very common for individuals across the autism spectrum. During such a transition, though, it is the challenges related to behavioral difficulties that can be most difficult for families and support providers. Despite these challenges, people with autism spectrum disorders are able to work successfully with the proper supports (Datlow Smith, Belcher, & Juhrs, 1995; Howlin, 1997).

This chapter explores the primary and secondary characteristics of autism spectrum disorders, particularly as they relate to transition from high school to the world of work and adult living. In addition, this chapter explores some of the specialized supports that are now being used to help individuals like Jenny and Evan cope with the social and personal demands of work and adult living. Finally, this chapter discusses the specific job supports that assist individuals with autism spectrum disorders adjust to life beyond the classroom.

CHARACTERISTICS OF YOUTH WITH AUTISM

Previous editions of this book did not include a chapter on autism spectrum disorders, yet this fourth edition does. This reflects a change in the professional community's understanding of autism. More specifically, there are three reasons for the increased interest in autism in the recent past. They include an apparent increase in the prevalence of autism spectrum disorders in the school-age population, an increased understanding that the challenges presented by the disorder are unique among other disabilities, and an emerging understanding of the specialized supports that individuals with autism require.

younger, such challenges sometimes resulted in hitting others and throwing things.

Jenny lives with her parents at home and has created routines for every aspect of her day, from about 4:00 in the morning when she wakes up and stands by the door to wave at the paper deliverer, to 8:30 at night when her father tells her, "About time, missy," which is her cue to go to bed. Jenny's routines sometimes result in frustration for her caregivers. She frequently refuses to alter a routine such as wearing particular clothes on particular days or going to church on any day other than Sunday. Because of her routines, she sometimes appears much younger than she is, particularly when her routines involve watching her favorite television shows, Mister Rogers and Sesame Street. Her parents worry that she will not find a job or live independently because of her behavior and her immaturity.

Jenny also has many behaviors that make her stand out from others in her school. When she walks, she shakes her head from side to side. She rocks back and forth in every chair she sits in. She does not like loud noises and will become upset at high school pep rallies and assemblies. Despite her dislike for loud noises, she talks very loud and does not alter her voice volume for the situation. For every task she does, she asks many questions before, during, and after the task is complete, exasperating those who support her. Her parents think back to the time when she did not talk at all and laugh about how the doctors encouraged them to teach

Prevalence of Autism Among Transition-Age Youth

The prevalence of autism spectrum disorders appears to be much higher than originally thought in the early 1990s. Prevalence rates have increased from 4 to 10 people per 10,000 births having autism to the current best estimate of 60–70 people per 10,000 births having an *autism spectrum disorder* (Fombone, 2003; Yeargin-Allsopp et al., 2003). The U.S. Department of Education (2002) presented evidence to Congress that the prevalence of autism increased by 1,354.3% between the 1991–1992 and the 2000–2001 school years. Although this astounding increase may be due in part to new reporting requirements between those years, it is still a very significant finding and suggests that the prevalence of autism has changed greatly during that period. The causes of this increase are not known, but there is strong evidence that increased awareness, increased diagnosis, diagnostic substitutions[1], and widening the disorder to include individuals with average or above average abilities are most likely driving the increase. Nevertheless, the majority of the increase in prevalence in the United States is found in children ages 5–11 (Fombone, 2003; U.S. Department of Education, 2000).

Although estimates of the prevalence of autism are changing dramatically, evidence continues to indicate that approximately 70% of individuals with autism also exhibit cognitive impairments. For example, a prevalence study in metropolitan Atlanta found that, overall, 68% of children with autism between the ages of 3 and 10 years also had mental retardation; with 20% exhibiting mild mental retardation, 11% exhibiting moderate mental retardation, 7% exhibiting severe mental retardation, 3% exhibiting profound mental retardation, and 9% exhibiting mental retardation of unknown severity (Yeargin-Allsopp et al., 2003). Although there is tremendous overlap between autism and mental retardation, autism differs from mental retardation in that its characteristic feature is not a delay in development, but a series of striking deviations in normal development patterns that generally become apparent by 3 years of age (American Psychiatric Association, 2000). In addition, unlike children with mental retardation who typically display delayed functioning in all

---

[1]A diagnostic substitution occurs when the greater medical and psychological community reclassify behaviors under different disability names. For example, prior to 1994, individuals who now have Asperger's syndrome were either not classified as having a disability or were classified as having an emotional disturbance.

her to talk. Now they sometimes wish they had not taught her to talk *so much!* Finally, Jenny is almost constantly in motion. Her parents report that they are very stressed trying to keep her engaged and busy. This high level of activity is sometimes very destructive. She can't seem to keep her hands off of things and often breaks the things she touches.

Jenny and her family met with a worker from the state vocational rehabilitation (VR) agency who reported that, on one hand, Jenny had many good skills, but on the other hand, had so many behavior challenges that they were not sure where the best job would be. They set up a placement for her at the local Goodwill where Jenny had many behavior challenges. On one occasion, the staff at the Goodwill arranged for a field trip to the bank and rearranged the schedule for the individuals they served. Jenny refused to rearrange her schedule and go on the field trip. When the rest of the workers took their break at 9:45 and got on the van at 10:00, Jenny continued working and took her break at 10:00 as she had done every other day. When the staff came in to get her ready for the field trip, she cried and yelled at them for changing her routine. She was fired from the placement for noncompliance and failure to respect authority.

areas, children with autism can have dramatic strengths that coexist with dramatic weakness. For example, children with autism tend to perform better on visual motor tasks than on verbal tasks. It is important to distinguish autism from mental retardation or other mental disorders because diagnostic confusion may result in referral to inappropriate and ineffective treatment techniques.

Given the dramatic increase in prevalence and the coexistence of other developmental and mental disorders, teachers and service personnel serving transition-age youth must be aware of two important implications. First, there is a very large group of children with autism spectrum disorders who will be entering transition services in the next few years. Second, it is likely that there are currently youth in transition programs with other diagnoses who might actually have an autism spectrum disorder but have not been diagnosed. Fombone (2003) estimated that between 55,602 and 121,324 youth between the ages of 15 and 19 have an autism spectrum disorder. Meanwhile, the U.S. Department of Education (2002) reported that the number of students ages 6–21 with autism served under the Individuals with Disabilities Education Act (IDEA) Amendments of 1997 (PL 105-17) was 78,749 in 2000–2001 school year. In other words, conservative estimates place the measured prevalence of the disorder in the entire group of school-age children and youth with autism spectrum disorders under the estimate expected for only those youth between the ages of 15 and 19. This indicates that regardless of better diagnosis, we could still be underdiagnosing autism spectrum disorders by about 50%.

DIAGNOSTIC AND BEHAVIORAL CHARACTERISTICS OF INDIVIDUALS WITH AUTISM SPECTRUM DISORDERS

Autism is a lifelong developmental disability that profoundly affects how an individual interacts with the world. Problems in communication and social skills make it difficult for the person to interact with those around him or her. Many individuals with autism do not speak and do not compensate for a lack of speech by using gestures, pantomime, or eye gaze to communicate. Those who speak may have great difficulty in initiating, maintaining, repairing, and ending conversations. They may respond to the initiations of others in unusual ways (e.g., repeat what the person has just said), repeat familiar phrases or songs (functional echolalia), or not speak at all. Even people with autism who do speak may not easily share accomplishments or enjoyment with others. These problems make having and keeping friends difficult, thus further isolating the individual. Compounding the situation, many people with autism have difficulty in

EVAN

Evan is the same age as Jenny and demonstrates many of the same characteristics, but he is unable to communicate using verbal language. Instead, he uses some sign language, pushes, pulls, and moves people to get his needs met. During a community-based vocational training experience at a fast-food pizza restaurant, Evan presented serious problems. He became easily upset, said "wooh, wooh, wooh," and pulled others from their workstation when his co-worker did not empty containers of cheese or pizza sauce at one time. He refused to wear different clothes and would not wear his uniform on the days he worked. If his parents, teachers, or support staff pushed him to comply, then he would hit, push, and attempt to bite them. He would grab food from the salad bar, put it in his mouth, and spit it out if he did not like it. Finally, when the restaurant became busy or noisy, he would run from the building and hide behind the dumpster in the parking lot. He too will end his school career in a few short months and the same challenges that are present with Jenny trouble Evan's family and team. Despite these challenges, Evan has incredible computer and puzzle skills given his profile. He enjoys quiet work on the computer or puzzle and will remain occupied for a long time when he is engaged in either activity.

processing sensory information, making it difficult for them to make sense of and react to the world around them. They may be hyper- or hyposensitive to touch, taste, smell, sight, and/or hearing. For example, some may find certain frequencies of sound painful, whereas others may have difficulty eating certain foods or wearing certain clothes. To cope with sensory problems, many engage in repetitive self-stimulatory behavior such as rocking or hand flapping (National Research Council, 2001; Wetherby & Prizant, 2000). Still others, like Jenny and Evan, may be extremely bound to routines making it difficult for them to cope with changes. In addition, they may be extremely anxious, especially in situations that are unpredictable. In the previous examples, many of the classic characteristics of autism are present in Jenny and Evan's inability to communicate with ease, their social skill deficits, and their demands that routines remain unchanged.

Although people with autism have some global characteristics in common, such as problems communicating and socializing, each person with autism is *unique*. They may have particular strengths and weaknesses that are very different from someone else with the same disability. In fact, autism is considered a spectrum disorder, which ranges in severity from very severe to extremely mild. Falling under the diagnostic category "Pervasive Developmental Disorders" in the *Diagnostic and Statistical Manual of Mental Disorders*, fourth edition, text revision (DSM-IV-TR; American Psychiatric Association, 2000), autism spectrum disorders include Autism, Pervasive Developmental Disorder-Not Otherwise Specified (PDD-NOS), Rett syndrome, Childhood Disintegrative Disorder (CDD), and Asperger syndrome. The five disorders that comprise autism spectrum disorders differ mainly by age of onset (CDD), severity of symptoms (PDD-NOS and Asperger syndrome), and course of disorder (Rett syndrome). All five of the disorders concur in requiring the presence of symptoms from "the triad": 1) social deficits, 2) communication impairments, and 3) restricted and repetitive repertoire of behaviors (Seltzer et al., 2003). The social deficits include decreased use of nonverbal behaviors such as body language and eye contact, difficulty developing peer relationships, difficulty sharing enjoyment with others, and lack of "social or emotional reciprocity" in which the person appears to be rather solitary versus interactive with others. The communication deficits are wide ranging and include every possible communication difficulty from those who do not talk at all to those who talk but fail to follow standard social communication conventions. Finally, the restricted and repetitive repertoire of behaviors describes a wide category of unusual characteristics. This category includes odd, repetitive, and persistent motor movements such as rocking, spinning objects, or hand flapping; a preoccupation with particular subjects or interests; and a preoccupation with parts of objects (e.g., the spinning wheels of a toy car instead of pretending to drive a toy car). Table 20.1 describes the differences between the five disorders within the autism spectrum in more detail.

In order for a diagnosis of autism, these behavioral characteristics must be present before the age of 3 years. Nevertheless, diagnosis may occur after the age of 3 because of a failure to recognize the complex pattern of behaviors that comprise the disorder. All of the disorders within the autism spectrum, except for Rett syndrome, are more prevalent among males, affecting four males to every female. Currently, the causes of autism are not well understood. Research is concentrating on the possibility of genetic influences and other medical conditions (e.g., prenatal exposure to viruses, metabolic disorders). It is possible to have autism co-occur with other disorders such as (but not limited to) Down syndrome, seizure disorders, cerebral palsy, depression, attention-deficit/hyperactivity disorder, and anxiety disorders.

Many early follow-up studies suggested that the long-term prognosis was poor for the majority of people with autism (Lockyer & Rutter, 1970; Lotter, 1974; Rutter, Greenfield, & Lockyer, 1967). These early studies consistently indicated some useful predictors for better outcomes, including some useful speech by age 6 and the ability to score at or above the mildly retarded range on nonverbal IQ tests. Later research has indicated better outcomes for those who are identified early and for whom early intensive treatment is provided, thus emphasizing the importance of early identification and education (Howlin, Goode, Hutton, & Rutter, 2004; Iovannone, Dunlap, Huber, & Kincaid, 2003; National Research Council, 2001; Odom et al., 2003).

In addition to the primary or core characteristics, individuals with autism spectrum disorders very often exhibit secondary symptoms that are particularly challenging. In Jenny's example, she exhibited some problem behaviors when her routine was changed. Specifically she would whine, cry, complain, and argue for a very long time, whereas Evan would push, pull, and become aggressive. In addition, Jenny would ask so many questions that her caregivers would frequently become frustrated with her constant talking, whereas Evan relied on behavior to communicate his needs. In other words, their communication deficits (Jenny's not being able to begin and end conversations gracefully, Evan's inability to talk) and their social skills difficulties (not being able to adjust their behavior based on the circumstances and social requirements of the situation) combined to create problem behaviors. Table 20.2 lists a number of behavioral characteristics of the disorder.

AUTISM AS A MULTIDIMENSIONAL DISORDER

We often think of disabilities in terms of one dimension and characterize the person by that dimension. When we describe someone as "high functioning," we generally mean that such a person has higher than average cognitive skills when compared with their peers with disabilities. Such discriminations do not seem to apply for people with autism spectrum disorders. In fact, autism spectrum disorder is multidimensional rather than reflecting a single dimension. Thus, in order to serve a person well, the

Table 20.1. Differences between the five diagnoses within the pervasive developmental disorders

Diagnosis	Social skills deficits	Communication deficits	Restricted repetitive repertoire of behaviors profile	Cognitive abilities and prognosis
Autism	Extreme difficulty orienting to others Sometimes "uses" other people's hands as mechanical objects Relies on behavior instead of communication to meet needs	Significant and severe deficits in ability to communicate using words When person is able to use words, many other disorders such as echolalia or pronoun reversal are frequently present. Frequently presents with grammatical and syntactical disorders when the ability to talk is present.	Odd and repetitive motor movements are frequently pervasive, such as rocking, spinning, flapping fingers or hands, and picking dust from the air.	This group appears to be more prone to cognitive impairments such as mental retardation and other significant learning disabilities. Many people with cognitive impairments have life-long needs for support. Although individuals with autism, as a group, require more support in adult life, many improve over time throughout their life.
Asperger syndrome	May seek out friends and orient to others, but have difficulty knowing and following social conventions of behavior. Social skills deficits are most apparent when person is communicating with others.	The ability to talk and develop appropriate grammar and syntax is present. In fact, many individuals appear to have exceptional language skills for their age. There are typically significant "pragmatic" communication disorders present. That is, although the person can talk well, he or she has an extremely difficult time communicating.	This tends to express itself in the form of excessive interests, in particular, fact-based topics. Odd motor movements may be present, but do not appear as pervasive as they are in autism.	Many, but not all, individuals have average to above-average intellectual abilities. Many individuals are able to live and function independently. Social skills deficits have significant impact on work skills and behaviors. Such individuals continue to improve throughout their life.
Pervasive developmental disorder–not otherwise specified	In order to qualify for this disorder, people demonstrate many, but not all, of the symptoms of either autism or Asperger syndrome.	In order to qualify for this disorder, people demonstrate many, but not all, of the symptoms of either autism or Asperger syndrome.	In order to qualify for this disorder, people demonstrate many, but not all, of the symptoms of either autism or Asperger syndrome.	In order to qualify for this disorder, people demonstrate many, but not all, of the symptoms of either autism or Asperger syndrome.

(continued)

Table 20.1.   *(continued)*

Diagnosis	Social skills deficits	Communication deficits	Restricted repetitive repertoire of behaviors profile	Cognitive abilities and prognosis
Childhood disintegrative disorder	May demonstrate any of the symptoms of either autism or Asperger syndrome	May demonstrate any of the symptoms of either autism or Asperger syndrome	May demonstrate any of the symptoms of either autism or Asperger syndrome	Such individuals appear to have developed typically and show marked loss of communication and social skills after the age of 3. Such individuals experience significant deterioration in their cognitive and motor abilities over time.
Rett syndrome	Typically demonstrates the symptoms of severe autism.	Typically demonstrates the symptoms of severe autism.	Typically demonstrates the symptoms of severe autism.	Significant and severe mental retardation is typically present. This group is overwhelmingly female (whereas all of the other disorders are overwhelmingly male). This group continues to show significant cognitive and motor skill deterioration over time.

teacher and support staff must understand the entire person from a multidimensional perspective.

Communication Skills and Abilities

Professionals must understand both the forms of communication (e.g., words, pictures, sign language, gestures) and the function of communication (e.g., getting one's needs met, engaging in conversation with others, adjusting conversations based on the social situation). Instead of observing the social cues that tell her that her communication partner is tired of talking, Jenny talks too much. As a result, she is not able to get her needs met with communication and is easily frustrated. However, Evan does not use words to talk at all.

Social Skills and Abilities

Professionals must understand the degree to which the person with autism is able to assess the social situation and select appropriate responses. In fact, challenging behaviors are often the result of deficit social skills. For example, Jenny did not know how to negotiate with her staff and resorted to arguing, complaining, and noncompliance.

Table 20.2. Behavioral characteristics across the major symptoms of the syndromes of autism spectrum disorder

Speech and communication deficits

Nonverbal; may use sounds, gestures, or pictorial cues

Limited ability to express self

Limited ability to understand the thoughts, beliefs, or feelings of others

Difficulty following instructions

Unable to follow lengthy conversations or participate in back-and-forth exchanges

Does not understand abstract concepts

Literally interprets speech

Poor pragmatic language skills (e.g., does not use eye contact, affect, or gestures when sharing experiences, fails to pick up on subtle nonverbal cues such as voice intonation, facial expressions, or body posture)

Trouble answering open-ended questions

Abnormal speech rhythm; may speak too fast or too slow

Monotone speech or flat affect

Repeatedly and persistently speaks about the same topic or asks the same question

Repeats back verbatim what was heard (e.g., may be current or previous conversation)

Mimics and synchronizes facial expressions, vocalizations, and movements with another person

Uses the pronoun *you* instead of using the pronoun *I*

May use behaviors (e.g., self-injury behavior, tantrum, aggression) to communicate (e.g., get attention, escape task, protest change, regulate social interaction in predictable manner)

Personal relationships and social skills deficits

Appears to have decided lack of interest in other people in the environment

Fails to make friends

Fails to engage in social interactions

Withdrawn from others and/or prefers to be alone

Does not know how to terminate conversation (e.g., many walk away while someone is talking to them)

Does not use certain social skills (e.g., walks in room and does not acknowledge others' presence, does not say hello or good-bye, interrupts others)

Does not use social amenities (e.g., please, thank you, you're welcome)

Invades other people's personal space (e.g., stands too close to others when communicating)

Acts immature

Talks loudly to self

Preservation on bizarre topics

Asks embarrassing personal questions (e.g., How old are you? Are you married? Why not?)

Incessant talking or questioning

Presence of abnormal verbalizations (e.g., scream, hoot, yell, hum)

Avoids eye contact and/or fails to orient body toward person speaking

Interrupts others

Displays unusual responses to sensory stimulation and repetitive motor movements

(continued)

Table 20.2. *(continued)*

Ignores important environmental events

Seeks out objects or activities that offer desired stimulation to the exclusion of other activities

Attends to unusual sensory stimuli (e.g., things that spin, shiny objects, certain textures)

Focuses on minute details and is oblivious to rest of the environment

Has difficulty attending to auditory and tactile input and prefers visual or vestibular channels

Engages in repetitive behaviors that provide sensory stimulation (e.g., repetitive noise making, hand flapping, rocking, pacing, finger flicking, tapping, spinning, jumping up and down)

Has averse or fearful reaction to certain stimuli (e.g., certain noises, food textures, fluctuations in lighting) that are not necessarily threatening

Reacts to certain sounds that others cannot hear

Fails to react to painful or uncomfortable stimuli

Engages in self-injurious behaviors (e.g., skin scratching, head banging, hits or bites self)

Note: Not all people with autism spectrum disorders exhibit all of the symptoms listed.

Evan did not know the social rules about salad bars. Tasting food is a reasonable response to the presence of food, except when that food is on a salad bar.

Cognitive Abilities

Professionals must carefully assess the cognitive skills and abilities of people with autism spectrum disorders, otherwise they may make errors about the person. Individuals with autism frequently have a "scattered" profile in which they have very high abilities in some areas and deficits in others. Jenny has some very strong cognitive abilities. Yet, she has significant skill needs. Likewise, Evan demonstrates some cognitive strengths that could be capitalized in a transition plan. A good transition program would address both strengths and needs.

Ability to Focus and Attend in Learning and Work Situations

Individuals with autism spectrum disorders across the spectrum frequently have difficulty attending and focusing on tasks in the presence of distractions. Professionals must understand each individual's response to various environmental conditions and make reasonable adjustments to increase the person's ability to attend. In Jenny's case, she has variable abilities to focus and attend. She would not be successful in an unstructured environment with frequent changes in her routine and noise. In fact, she would be very challenging in such a situation. Evan demonstrates some of the same challenges in the fast-food restaurant when it is busy or noisy, but is able to focus for a long period of time in certain situations, such as playing games on the computer or working on a puzzle.

Ability to Regulate Emotions in Stressful Situations

It is very important that professionals serving individuals with autism spectrum disorders understand the people's ability to regulate their emotional state. Both Jenny and Evan will resort to challenging behavior (e.g., tantrums, aggression) when they are pushed under stress. This does not mean that they cannot work or be in community places; rather, it means that support staff must understand the conditions that cause stress and methods for teaching the person to regulate his or her own emotional state. Very often, there are sensory and organizational supports that can be in place for people with autism. Both Jenny and Evan would do well with calming time after they have to be in a noisy and chaotic environment. They would be able to calm themselves if, for example, they were able to go for a brisk walk after a pep rally. Such calming activities must be understood and profiled for each individual.

In the previous examples, describing Jenny or Evan based on the arbitrary distinction of high or low functioning is not helpful in understanding their strengths and needs. Consequently, successful programs would begin with an analysis of a person's strengths and needs in each dimension. In fact, this multidimensional variability creates the greatest challenges and confusion for support staff. When we assume that a person's abilities are singular in dimension based on cognitive abilities, we make errors of intention. Support staff who assumed that Jenny was bright and, therefore, she was in perfect control of her behavior might blame her for her difficulties when her routine changes and she whines. Likewise, staff who assumed that Evan was low functioning because of his inability to talk using words might miss his abilities with computers and ignore the possibilities of office work or alternative communication systems. As a result, he might be plagued to work in fast-food restaurants and other such noisy environments to his and his support staff's detriment.

UNIQUE CHALLENGES OF TRANSITION-AGE YOUTH WITH AUTISM SPECTRUM DISORDERS

Adolescence is a time of major change for all of us. Physical, psychological, and social changes make this time both challenging and rewarding for the adolescent and those around him or her. People with autism face similar changes; however, difficulties in socialization and communication can make this an extremely demanding time for those with autism. Adolescents with autism change physically in ways similar to their peers, but the discrepancy between the complex social behavior of a typical adolescent and that of someone with autism may become quite large (Collier & Schall, 2003; McGovern & Sigman, 2005; Ruble & Dalrymple, 1993). The adolescent with autism may have a similar desire to have a girlfriend or boyfriend but may be faced with difficulties in developing and maintaining these relationships. In some cases, the adolescent may be increasingly aware of his or her differences, which may result in increasing his or her anxiety or lead to bouts of depression. As well, adolescents with autism may not be adequately prepared for the physical and social changes that they will face, thus furthering the challenge for them to cope with adolescence (Collier & Schall, 2003; Ruble & Dalrymple, 1993). Others may face additional problems. Some adolescents with autism and greater cognitive impairment may develop seizures during this time (Volkmar & Nelson, 1990).

Families frequently experience greater anxiety once their child with autism enters adolescence. The recognition that the child is now nearing adulthood and will likely require lifelong services, combined with the need to make arrangements for such services, creates increased stress on the family. Fong, Wilgosh, and Sobsey (1993) identified six areas that families report increased concerns regarding their adolescent with autism. They include

1. Behavioral concerns (obsessions, aggression, and tantrums)

2. Social and communicative concerns (inappropriate or inadequate social skills)

3. Family-related concerns (restriction in family life, need for constant supervision)

4. Education and related concerns (choosing integrated versus specialized services, gaining access to behavior management services)

5. Concerns about relationships with professionals (ineffective communication, criticism or blame from professionals)

6. Concerns about independence and future services (residential, vocational, and leisure services)

These concerns can and should be part of the overall planning related to transition services. In fact, the transition plan should include goals and activities that address each of the concerns directly through training and indirectly through linking the individual and family with community-based supports and services.

Although all of the autism spectrum disorders are lifetime disorders, there is evidence that some of the specific symptoms may improve or abate as the person ages. Seltzer et al. (2003) noted in a cross-sectional study that adolescents and adults with autism spectrum disorders appeared to improve in their communication and social skills, whereas their restricted and repetitive interests and stereotypic behaviors seemed to abate somewhat. This does not mean that improvement should nullify the need for services. Seltzer et al. noted,

> That the disorder changes in its manifestation over the life course does not, therefore, indicate that affected individuals have any less of a need for services and supports as they move through adolescence into adulthood and midlife than they did in childhood. Rather, developmentally appropriate services are needed for adolescents and adults with ASD diagnoses. (2003, p. 579)

Thus, it should be the goal of professionals serving individuals with autism spectrum disorders to develop and measure the effects of programs serving transition-age youth with autism spectrum disorders to ensure long-term success through adulthood.

Given the secondary concerns related to autism spectrum disorders, it is critical that professional staff have efficient and effective ways to assess and modify problem behavior. The next section will review the process of completing a FBA and developing a positive behavior support plan for an individual with an autism spectrum disorder.

BEHAVIOR CHALLENGES, FUNCTIONAL BEHAVIOR ASSESSMENT, AND BEHAVIOR INTERVENTION PLANS

Lonny's story is not unusual. One of the most challenging aspects of educating young men and women with autism is addressing these "secondary" behavior challenges. Frequently, it takes a team of people to assess and develop intervention plans to address such behavioral challenges. A team can consist of parents and siblings, special education teachers, paraprofessionals, related services professionals, school administrators,

Lonny has the ideal educational program. He is a 12-year-old young man with severe autism. He uses the "picture exchange communication system" (PECS; Bondy & Frost, 2001) to ask for items and activities he wants and needs. In the morning, he attends one of the best private applied behavior analysis schools with a one-to-one teacher. In the afternoon, he attends a public middle school with a one-to-one aide and a mixture of inclusion and special education services. He also has one-to-one home support services in the afternoon and on weekends. All of his team members are highly trained in applied behavior analysis, PECS, and the characteristics of autism.

Lonny is an engaging young man with a beautiful smile. His family is very supportive of him and has made significant sacrifices to meet his needs. Lonny is a creative communicator using pictures. His teacher told about a time when he wanted to go for a ride but could not find his PECS book. He got the telephone book, found a picture of a pizza delivery truck, and pointed to the truck to say, "I want to go in the car." They also talk at length about his sense of humor. He will often hide behind the door of his classroom to surprise his teacher when she enters the room

Despite his having the "Cadillac of services," Lonny also has severe challenging behaviors. Specifically, he will hit himself and others, scratch, pinch, bite, and scream. The severity of his behavior increases the most when one of his teachers has to deny an activity or item he requested. This resulted in the

in-home support professionals and paraprofessionals, and case managers. It is critical that all such people who serve a person with an autism spectrum disorder come together to complete a FBA. Each person's diverse perspective can add to a greater understanding of the problem behavior and will result in a proactive plan to address an individual's needs and change his or her behavior (Benninghof & Singer, 1992; Jensen & Kiley, 1998).

Functional Behavior Assessment

FBA is the process that helps teams move from reaction to proaction. The process of completing an FBA includes three essential steps (O'Neill et al., 1997).

1. Team interview and record review

2. Systematic observation of the behavior in natural and (sometimes) in contrived situations

3. Behavior hypothesis development

In this case, the term *functional* does not describe a person's abilities, as in understanding their "functioning level." Instead, the term refers to a description of how the behavior works in a given environment to achieve a specific purpose. Thus, the term in FBA is a description of how and how well a behavior works to assist a person in achieving his or her needs.

At the heart of an FBA is a problem-solving approach that includes multiple methods of team learning. When a team completes an FBA, they study the behavior in many different ways from understanding what the team currently knows about the behavior (team interviews), to studying the behavior in the natural environment (systematic observation), to sometimes studying the behavior in contrived or experimental environments. The team learns how to work together and learn from each other in a coordinated dance that is mutually supportive and informative. In addition, they are truly assessing the subtle environmental factors that trigger the challenging behavior. According to Tilly et al.,

> The process involved in [Functional Behavior Assessment], is not a procedural one. Indeed, FBA is not a set of procedures and protocols, but instead is an integrated problem-solving approach to creating educational supports and interventions with a high likelihood of success. The FBA process is flexible in that different procedures might be used under different circumstances (1998, p. 3).

The process of completing an FBA results in a clearer understanding of the behavior and that, in turn, leads to a co-

public school being unable to serve Lonny, and he began receiving homebound school services. It also resulted in his inability to use his PECS pictures to avoid the possibility that he might ask for something that will result in an aggressive behavior or restraint. His team was greatly concerned that they would not be able to continue this excellent educational program if he could not communicate with PECS. In addition, they wanted to understand his behavior and help him change it now while he is young and relatively small. If left unattended, then his behavior is likely to become more severe as he grows.

ordinated, multicomponent behavior intervention plan. In addition, those closest to the problem complete the process. This represents a departure from former ways of addressing problem behavior in which reactive strategies were developed by consultants or psychologists who did not "live with" the problem. In this case, the student's team completes the entire process. The five steps from FBA to behavior intervention plan development, evaluation, and revision are

- *Problem identification and definition:* The team moves from general descriptions of emotional states to specific, behaviorally defined definitions of challenging behaviors. For example, a team may move from referring to a behavior as "angry and disruptive" to a fine-grained description—"When Lonny is told 'no,' he will hit and grab others and fall to the floor."

- *Problem analysis:* The team completes interviews and observations so that they can understand the connection between the person, the environment where the behavior occurs, and the needs that the behavior meets for the person. For example, "When Lonny asks for a desired object or activity and is told 'no,' he will hit, bite, and scratch in order to get the object or activity he desires."

- *Intervention development:* Once the team identifies the connection between the person, behavior, and environment, they develop a multicomponent intervention plan. Such a plan uses individually tailored strategies to 1) prevent the problem from occurring, 2) teach the person a new way to get his or her needs met, and 3) respond to the problem behavior in a new way so that it becomes inefficient and unnecessary in meeting the person's original need.

- *Monitoring progress and evaluating outcomes:* This process is based on the large literature in applied behavior analysis. As such, it is critical to evaluate the success of the plan by tracking whether the problem behavior decreased, the new replacement behavior increased, and, finally, the person's quality of life is better.

- *Intervention revision as indicated by monitoring and evaluation:* Inevitably, the behavior plan will require revision as the person and environmental contexts change. If, for example, a team finds that the person has not decreased the frequency of challenging behavior, then the team would be required to revise the behavior intervention plan until they see a reduction in the problem behavior (Fox, Vaughn, Dunlap, & Bucy, 1997; Lohrmann-O'Rourke, Knoster, & Llewellyn, 1999; McConnell, Hilvitz, & Cox, 1998; Tilly et al., 1998; Vaughn, Dunlap, Fox, Clarke, & Bucy, 1997).

When an interdisciplinary team completes the process, it has the opportunity to learn more effective ways of teaching students with autism and coordinating varied and diverse services. Team members who are open to the process find that they have to change their own behavior in order to support the change of the student they are supporting (Kincaid, Chapman, Shannon, Schall, & Harrower, 2002).

In Lonny's case, the team did coordinate efforts to complete an FBA and develop a positive behavior support plan. In a moment of profound insight, with the support of the whole team, they realized the underlying need that Lonny was communicating with his behavior. That is, *when Lonny doesn't know what will happen next in his schedule and doesn't know how to ask, "What will happen next?" he will ask for something (usually something that he can't have) in order to increase his knowledge of what will happen. If he is told "no," he will bite, scratch, pinch, hit, or head bang in order to get what he asked for.* Although he had a visual schedule, it was not specific enough to help him predict what was actually going to happen next. He also had no way to identify when he could and could not ask for activities such as a car ride. When he tried to ask using PECS and was told no, he then resorted to the way he communicated as a young child (aggression). The team also discovered that Lonny's behavior did not have a singular function. *He also engaged in the problem behavior when he was asked to do a challenging task in order to avoid the task and when his head hurt.*

Developing a Behavior Intervention Plan

These findings were in direct opposition to the interventions that the team was using to suppress Lonny's behavior. When Lonny engaged in challenging behavior, sometimes his support staff would give him the activity that he requested, whereas other times they would not. In other words, they intermittently reinforced Lonny's behavior. They realized that they had spent the majority of the year reinforcing the very behavior that they wanted to stop. Their reactive strategies were effective in stopping the behavior in the short term but were actually causing more problem behavior to occur over the long term. Because of their work as a team, they developed a multicomponent positive behavior intervention plan (Carr, Horner, & Turnbull, 1999; see Table 20.3). There are four critical and required areas of intervention in multicomponent positive behavior support plans:

1. *Preventing strategies:* Such strategies are designed to change the environment so that the person does not have to use the behavior to get his or her needs met. Teams consider if they can change the environment so that they can eliminate, block, neutralize, or otherwise change the triggers or "antecedents" that lead to problem behavior.

2. *Teaching new behavior strategies:* These strategies are designed to replace the problem behavior with a new, more efficient and effective adaptive behavior. Instead of hitting, a team might develop a method to teach a person to ask for a break. The behaviors that a team must teach fall into three categories: 1) direct replacement behaviors that will replace the problem behavior, 2) general behaviors that will increase the person's success in the environment, and 3) coping and tolerance behaviors that will increase the person's ability to cope with frustrating or challenging times.

3. *Responding to new behavior strategies:* These strategies provide a road map for the team to reinforce and respond to the new behaviors. For example, in Lonny's case, the team discovered that some of his hitting was due to a desire to avoid tasks. A replacement behavior for hitting in that case is "asking for a break." His educational

Table 20.3.   Lonny's positive behavior intervention plan

Preventing strategies

Provide a detailed visual schedule with every single activity depicted (e.g., not just "work" but "count money," "read words").

When on a break, always offer him *deliverable* choices with pictures in a file folder.

Offer frequent sensory breaks (e.g., intense physical jumping on trampoline, rolling on the floor, taking walks).

When he requests something that you can't deliver, show him on his schedule when he can have the activity (e.g., "We can take a car ride tomorrow").

Give him access to a "different work" manila folder that has pictures of other work that he enjoys. Allow him to choose an alternative work session when he appears to be frustrated.

Use errorless learning to decrease the number of corrections you have to do.

Use a digital timer to let him know how long he has to wait for an activity or item.

Try a "migraine band" for his head when he requests pushing/pressing on his face.

Teaching new behavior strategies

Teach Lonny to make his own schedule by placing pictures of the activities that he has to do and offering choices on activities that he wants to do.

Teach Lonny to accept changes in his routine by changing his visual schedule with him.

Teach Lonny to request the "different work" folder when he appears frustrated by the work that he is doing.

Teach Lonny to make *deliverable* choices by offering him a choice from a manila folder with pictures of activities that he can have.

Teach Lonny to use sign language.

Teach Lonny to say "hurt" in words, sign language, or pictures when he rubs his head or requests pressing on his face.

Teach Lonny to accept a "no" response using videotapes of others accepting a "no" response and using social stories.

Responding to new behavior strategies

Have Lonny move the pictures from his schedule to the "done" envelope once he completes the activity.

Reinforce Lonny with a fun activity after accepting change in routine.

Offer the work that he selects.

Offer the activity that he selects.

Converse with him in sign language.

Offer the migraine band when he says "hurt."

Praise Lonny whenever he accepts a "no" response or makes an alternative choice of an activity.

Responding to problem behavior strategies, including a crisis management plan

At the earliest point that you recognize that Lonny is getting frustrated:

Offer him the "different work" folder.

Offer him a sensory break.

Show him when he can have a requested item on his schedule.

Offer him "squishy" toys to release frustration.

If he becomes aggressive:

Redirect him to his current work.

If you have enough staff support (two or more people), continue to stay with him until he gets back to work while protecting him and others in the area.

If working with Lonny alone and he continues to grab at you, leave the room.

Continue to redirect him back to his work or activity.

Once he is calm, offer him a sensory break.

Increasing quality-of-life strategies

Convene a person-centered planning meeting to identify long-term goals and redefine his current curriculum in line with the long-term goals.

Train all new team members to work with Lonny before they start working with him.

Hold a team meeting with all service parties to introduce new team members to Lonny's support team.

Continue to hold team meetings on at least a quarterly basis to discuss consistency across service providers.

Support for team member's strategies

Lonny will develop a "home" schedule with help from Paige and train Mom, Dad, and sister in using it.

Schedule all team meetings to discuss summer services as soon as possible.

Convene regular all-team meetings with all staff and family at least once every marking period.

Celebrate Lonny's success with whole team.

Train all staff working with Lonny how to correct errors without saying "no."

Convene an IEP meeting to plan for fall school services as soon as possible.

Develop a communication system that will go between all three service providers and will include information about successful strategies discovered, unsuccessful strategies tried, new triggers that lead to challenging behavior, and ideas for the other team members.

and home support team might be reluctant to give him a break, but if they don't, Lonny can resort to hitting again. This part of a behavior intervention plan directs the team specifically how to respond to Lonny's request for a break so that they reinforce his adaptive attempt to avoid tasks.

4. *Responding to challenging behaviors, including a crisis management plan:* If Lonny's team is trying to replace his hitting with the behavior of asking for a break, then they must also have a way to respond to his hitting that 1) does not result in a break and 2) reminds him that there is a better way to ask for a break. Thus, this section of a behavior intervention plan teaches the team how to respond to a person when the problem behavior does occur. In addition to responding to the challenging behavior, sometimes it is necessary to implement a crisis management plan that will keep the person and those around him or her safe. In the case of positive behavior support plans, the role of the crisis management plan is to keep the person and others around him or her safe, not to attempt to change behavior with punitive or reactive management.

The other two areas in Lonny's plan, increasing quality-of-life strategies and supporting team members' strategies, are important to help the team move beyond their current crisis and proactively plan for Lonny's future. In order to do that, the team has to help Lonny achieve a better quality of life and help each other implement the plan and communicate well across team members.

Positive behavior support is a critical support for many youth with and without disabilities. Given the unique secondary challenges associated with autism spectrum disorders, it is critical that teachers and support personnel supporting such youth be skilled in its use. In addition to positive behavior support, there are other unique supports that increase the successful transition and adaptation for youth with autism spectrum disorders. The next section will review those supports as they relate to transition in detail.

Jenny's and Evan's support teams had to implement some specialized supports to increase their success in traditional school-based activities and in community- and work-based training situations. First, they found that they had to get down to the most important goals and objectives as both their time in public school came to an end. Each team met with the individual, his or her parents, all of his or her teachers in the current schedule, and some community individuals who were involved in Jenny's and Evan's lives. They identified their vision for each person and developed an action plan to move closer toward that vision in the coming year. They also realized that they had to design specialized teaching methods. They implemented data-based instruction and decision-making protocols to guide them through the ups and downs of educating both individuals. They changed the way they communicated with each about their day. They developed a calendar for Evan, showing him what clothes he could wear on particular days. They also offered him more choices of breakfast foods on the days he had to wear his work uniform. For Jenny, they developed a daily schedule and would frequently change her break time to teach her that she could follow a schedule instead of demanding her break at the same time every day. Both Jenny and Evan had goals and objectives that addressed their social and communication skills. For Jenny, they worked on teaching her to address different individuals based on their relationship to her. For Evan, they worked on teaching him to use both sign language and pictures to communicate with others. Finally, both the family and educational team implemented consistent interventions. When they implemented a new schedule or choice menu for either Jenny or Evan, the family and teachers would write notes back and forth to describe how the plan was working. They met every 1–2 months to discuss changes to their interventions. Finally, they also held celebrations when great things happened for each person. They became a true support team for Jenny and Evan as well as each other.

CHARACTERISTICS OF PROGRAMS FOR INDIVIDUALS WITH AUTISM SPECTRUM DISORDERS

The majority of research, to date, has focused on successful intervention for young and elementary school children with autism spectrum disorders. Little of the research has focused on the program components that predict excellent outcomes for transition-age youth with autism spectrum disorders. As a result, some have made the error of assuming that intervention designed for very young children is equally successful for transition-age youth. There is currently no evidence that such models designed for early intervention result in better outcomes for transition-age youth with autism (Iovannone et al., 2003; National Research Council, 2001; Odom et al., 2003; Simpson, 2005). Finally, there are very few descriptions of excellent programs serving transition-age youth with autism spectrum disorder in the current literature (Datlow Smith, Belcher, & Juhrs, 1995; Keel, Mesibov & Woods, 1997; Mawhood & Howlin, 1999).

The issues related to the paucity of research in this important area are critical to consider in light of the No Child Left Behind (NCLB) Act of 2001 (PL 107-110). When considering the educational needs of transition-age youth, NCLB stipulates that schools receiving funding through federal sources use educational practices developed from scientifically based research (Simpson, 2005; Yell, Drasgow, & Lowrey, 2005). To date, few educational practices developed for students with autism meet these criteria (Simpson, 2005).

Nevertheless, a review across the literature of service types and models for treatment reveal that many models of services result in successful outcomes for individuals with autism spectrum disorders (Garcia-Villamisar, Wehman, & Navarro, 2002; Iovannone et al., 2003; Müller, Schuler, Burton, & Yates, 2003; National Research Council, 2001; Simpson, 2005). Thus, there is an emerging base of characteristics across treatment models that provide guidance in program development for teachers and staff providing transition services to youth with autism spectrum disorders. Iovannone et al. (2003) reviewed the literature in autism for individuals across the age range. They found six critical components of quality programs. Together, these program components provide the critical elements necessary to assist youth with autism spectrum disorders to acclimate to educational and work environments and to develop a supportive team necessary for successful integration in the community.

Individualized Supports and Services for Students and Their Families

Autism spectrum disorders are a complex constellation of disorders that includes the entire range of human abilities with many different symptoms. Two individuals with exactly the same disorder may present vastly different symptom profiles. Consequently, each individual's program must consider the preferences and goals for the person and his or her support network. As noted in Chapters 2 and 3, teaching self-determination and developing person-centered plans are the most logical way to develop such individualized supports for youth with autism spectrum disorders.

Systematic, Carefully Planned Instruction that Results in a High Degree of Student/Youth Engagement

The most debilitating core feature of autism appears to be the lack of engagement or stereotypic engagement that individuals with autism spectrum disorders display in most environments (Iovannone et al., 2003; Wetherby & Prizant, 2000). Instead of interacting with and learning from people, experiences, and environments, individuals with autism tend to rely on known and learned patterns and routines of interaction. Consequently, they may not have the ability to learn in novel situations. Thus, the single most important aspect of any transition plan must include guiding the person to increase his or her engagement with people, experiences, and environments. This is typically accomplished through the use of carefully structured and implemented teaching techniques. Many of these techniques rely on the application of behavior analytic principles to educational, work, and community-based environments. Chapter 7 described the process of designing units and lessons for transition-age youth in community-based settings. Without such structured experiences, youth with autism do not typically engage in exploration in such a way to lead to self-guided learning.

Comprehensible and/or Structured Environments

This particular program element is unique to programs that serve individuals with autism spectrum disorders. In order to serve individuals with autism spectrum disorders, specialized programs typically provide extensive environmental, written, and picture designs that result in visually clear expectations for individuals with autism spectrum disorders. Again, one of the core features of the autism spectrum is an inability to adjust behavior based on subtle environmental and social cues. For example, most workers learn to behave differently in the presence of their supervisor. A workplace where workers joke and cajole each other will snap to attention when the boss enters the scene. Across the entire spectrum and ability range, individuals with autism spectrum disorders do not typically change their behavior in the presence of such subtle social cues. Thus, those who serve individuals with autism spectrum disorders must design the environment to provide obvious cues to such behavior.

In work environments, individuals with autism spectrum disorders frequently work best in cubicle-like environments where there is decreased auditory and visual distraction, clear traffic patterns, clear patterns of where to get new work, where to complete work, where to place work when it is complete, and clearly designated areas for breaks and social interaction (Hagner & Cooney, 2005; Lattimore, Parsons, & Reid, 2003; Müller et al., 2003). In such an environment, the worker with an autism spectrum disorder can adjust his or her behavior purely by noting where he or she is located. Thus, such a worker learns that socialization occurs only in the break area, and work occurs only in the cubicle.

Educators use this same arrangement in classroom settings as well. Instead of the classic classroom design with desks in rows oriented toward the teacher, individuals with autism spectrum disorders frequently have classrooms in which their independent work spaces are desks in cubicle areas facing a wall, and group learning experiences are at large tables in the center of the room. Finally, break areas in such classrooms are usually separated from the educational environment with book shelves, dividers, and other tall furniture. Interestingly, the arrangements described here are, in fact, common in most workplaces. Most often, employees' workspaces are individualized and not centralized as in the classic classroom row design. Sometimes, individuals with severe autism do better in community-based work environments that support such individualized stations and clearly designated areas.

In addition to specialized environmental arrangements, autism-specific programs frequently have numerous picture and written ways for the person with an autism spectrum disorder to predict the daily schedule and transition between activities. Hodgdon (1995) described at least four ways in which picture and/or written information could be used to increase a person's understanding of the environment, increase his or her completion of required activities and behaviors, and decrease problem behaviors associated with transition between activities.

Giving Information to the Person with an Autism Spectrum Disorder Programs that use visual supports such as daily schedules, mini-schedules, calendars, and choice menus find that they have less challenges related to transitions between activities. When teachers use individual student schedules in classroom settings, individuals with autism spectrum disorders are learning important work skills related to making and changing a daily schedule. People in work environments are most often schedule driven and least often people directed. Thus, learning to use and follow a personal schedule is, in fact, a functional work behavior. (For more information on visual schedules, see Hodgdon, 1995.)

Giving Effective Directions to the Person with an Autism Spectrum Disorder

Because of the severe communication challenges across the ability range of the autism spectrum, individuals with autism spectrum disorders may have difficulty remembering long sequences of tasks described in verbal terms (Wetherby & Prizant, 2000). At the same time, most complex tasks in school are presented using words. By presenting long sequences with pictures or written words, people with autism spectrum disorders are better able to successfully complete such tasks with minimal challenges.

Organizing the Environment

When organizing an environment, visual supports are provided, including labeling and providing information about the expected behavior. Once the environment is appropriately designed, successful programs often provide further visual information in the form of a name for the area, (e.g., "Break Zone") and a list of the accepted behavior in the area (e.g., eat at the table, clean up your area, talk quietly). (For more information on environmental organization for students with autism spectrum disorders, see Chapman, 2004.)

Mediating Communication Between Environments

Again, the challenges associated with this disorder mean that the person will not likely know how to communicate with his or her family about his or her day and his or her needs for the next day. Teachers and support staff can address this by providing the person with picture or written lists of what he or she did or what he or she needs for the next day.

Each of these environmental and visual supports can be used in school, at home, or in the community. They are flexible and should be designed for easy transportation between school, work, community, and home. In addition, these types of supports are not limited to individuals with severe autism who have difficulty communicating. Even individuals who are able to communicate with verbal language use such supports to increase their success in school, work, and at home. In the case studies, both Jenny (who talks a lot) and Evan (who does not use words to communicate) benefited from the use of visual supports.

Specialized Curriculum Content that Specifically Addresses Communication and Social Skills

In all of the previous examples, Jenny, Evan, and Lonny have very specialized social and communication skill needs. Jenny does not understand the difference between communicating with people of various "ranks" in her life. She yells at her supervisor, teachers, and principal the same way she does at her parents. Evan thinks that all food is his to eat. Lonny has trouble using the PECS and needs retraining in how to use this system. Because communication and social skill deficits are core challenges in this disorder, communication and social skill goals and objectives must be embedded into every domain in the educational and vocational curriculum. In a vocational curriculum in which the person with an autism spectrum disorder will work in various community-based experiences, it is critical that trainers teach the communication and social skill needs of the job as well as the actual job tasks themselves. Such communication and social skills include

- Asking for more work
- Asking for help
- Taking a break in the break room
- Saying "excuse me" when bumping into someone
- Talking with co-workers about mutually interesting topics
- Talking with supervisors and co-workers with respect
- Asking for clarification when given conflicting jobs

There are a few published curricula that address the specific social and communication needs of individuals with autism spectrum disorders (Gutstein & Sheely, 2002; Moyes & Moreno, 2001; Quill, 2000). As in other areas of the curriculum, no published work will replace the knowledge of a skilled teacher. Thus, much of the specialized curriculum components related to communication and social skills must be developed in the context of the individualized and person-centered planning process.

Functional Approach to Problem Behavior

The functional approach described here is the same approach described earlier in this chapter as positive behavior support. In this context, it is important to note that teachers and staff who work in programs supporting individuals with autism spectrum disorders must be able to use FBA to develop positive behavior support plans.

Intensive Family Training and Involvement

Raising a person with an autism spectrum disorder is a lifelong endeavor. Parents and families are the most stable and enduring supports in the life of the person with an autism spectrum disorder. They frequently supersede their role as family member and become interpreters and translators for their child. Families often carry an amazing amount of intuitive and historical knowledge that helps teachers and staff understand the person with an autism spectrum disorder. Families frequently understand both the meaning and history of idiosyncratic responses to circumstances. They contribute to the team by interpreting the experiences of the person with autism. They also contribute to the success of the transition plan by implementing interventions at home. Finally, they translate the expectations of the school or work environment to the person by providing extra practice on relevant skills.

Successful programs fully involve families in planning by providing intensive individualized training about the disorder and the person's plan, including the family in all team meetings to help solve problems, and communicating with the family about day-to-day issues in the person's life. Without the full involvement of the person's family in the ongoing implementation of the transition plan, the transition team is likely to struggle a bit more.

DONALD

Donald is beginning high school this year. Throughout his education, he has been both very gifted (he took ninth-grade algebra in the sixth grade) and very challenging. In fact, during his sixth-grade year, his public school system considered out-of-district placement because he talked throughout class, ran in the halls, did not consistently do his homework, and frequently came to class disheveled and without the appropriate materials. His peers considered him eccentric and generally avoided him. His teachers became easily frustrated with his lack of attention to task and his constant loud talking. His science teacher told about a time when, after she changed the posters in the room for a new science unit, he spent the entire day staring at the posters and reading each one. He did not respond to any questions or class assignments. He and his seemingly purposeful behavior baffled them. After all, how could a student be so smart and have such a behavior problem at the same time.

In time, Donald's team learned about his disorder and how to work with him to provide him an excellent education in the public school setting. They completed a FBA on his most challenging behavior, provided him with sensory breaks between class changes, developed a positive reinforcement system to encourage better behavior, gave him a detailed schedule, and worked with his family to implement these changes in his program. Finally, his speech-language therapist, occupational therapist, and guidance counselor collaborated to provide Donald with an intensive social skill-training program.

This section has described the six characteristics of programs that serve individuals with autism spectrum disorders. In addition, we have provided examples of how these elements are implemented with transition-age youth. These general supports are important, but without excellent transition services, even these supports will fall short of the person's goals. The next section will review the specific characteristics of successful transition services for individuals with autism spectrum disorders.

TRANSITION SERVICES FOR INDIVIDUALS WITH AUTISM SPECTRUM DISORDERS

Early on, the treatment community of experts considered autism and its related disorders to be among the most severe. It was widely believed that individuals with autism were "too disabled" to work. Recently, however, programs such as Division TEACCH (Treatment and Education of Autistic and related Communication handicapped Children) at the University of North Carolina at Chapel Hill, and Community Services for Autistic Adults and Children (CSAAC) in Rockville, Maryland, have developed and written about their supported employment (SE) programs (Datlow Smith, Belcher, & Juhrs, 1995; Keel, Mesibov & Woods, 1997). These programs use a combination of autism-specific supports, and quality job support services that are universal for individuals with disabilities. As a result, more programs have demonstrated that individuals with autism spectrum disorders are successful in community employment settings (Mawhood & Howlin, 1999, Müller et al., 2003). Consequently, schools serving students with autism spectrum disorders must include the full array of transition services including community-based job exploration and training; community-based life skills instruction; instruction in personal management, hygiene, and leisure and recreation skills; and instruction in functional academic skills.

Transition Needs of Individuals with Asperger Syndrome

The cognitive abilities of individuals with Asperger syndrome may confuse some educators and service providers; they may assume that an individual who is able to participate fully in the general education curriculum does not need further specialized support. Yet, Donald (see sidebar) needed specific and individualized autism supports. In addition, when these supports were delivered in the context of his educational program, he achieved greater success in that program. Once more, the assumption that youth with minimal or no cognitive impairment have a milder form of autism spectrum disorder is a false one (Müller et al., 2003).

The next section of the chapter will review strategies that educators can use to identify the critical job and life skills for inclusion in the individualized education program (IEP) and transition plan for individuals with autism spectrum disorders. In addition, this section will review teaching, prompting, and job exploration strategies.

Planning, Implementing, and Evaluating a Functional Curriculum

Although the cognitive abilities of individuals within the autism spectrum vary greatly, many individuals need specific education in everyday survival skills. Such skills enable a person to function successfully with as much independence as is possible. A *functional curriculum* is developed when those skills are combined into an individualized plan for a person. A functional curriculum, coupled with sensitivity to the unique social, communicative, cognitive, and perceptual needs of the youth with autism, allows educators to obtain a reliable and valid assessment of skills and helps plan appropriate functional educational activities to promote independence in the community. This approach paves the way for the student and family to have the most productive and independent lifestyle as possible.

Students with autism have a great deal of potential, and a functional curriculum that places emphasis on optimizing independence in current and future environments is essential. An effective curriculum for students with autism spectrum disorders is based on the same key tenants used to design programs for other students with significant disabilities. The curriculum should be *person-centered, functional, and flexible* (Wehman, 1997a).

Person-Centered Curriculum   Each student should have a detailed set of goals and learning objectives specifically chosen to meet his or her particular needs. A *person-centered plan* is developed when teams who support a person with an autism spectrum disorder come together to determine the personalized dreams and goals for the person. Person-centered planning is one technique that can be used to help develop a long-term curriculum and help ensure that critical information on student abilities and future needs is communicated among educational staff year after year. In fact, it is the person-centered plan that should guide the transition activities. Considering the wide spectrum of autism, it is clear that there are many and varied paths that a person's life may take. Some individuals with lower cognitive impairments, such as Donald, may plan to attend college, whereas others similar to Jenny, Evan, and Lonny may seek vocational education. Regardless of their abilities, all people with autism require a person-centered approach that will maximize the effectiveness of their educational program in achieving their vision for their lives.

Functional Curriculum   The curriculum must also be practical (Clark, 1996). To design a functional curriculum, the teacher should ask about the skills the student needs to learn to be as independent as possible now and in the future. Even individuals with fewer cognitive impairments will have social impairments that, if ignored, will decrease their independent functioning as adults. Müller et al. (2003) found that individuals with Asperger syndrome report that, despite excellent academic preparation, as a group they are chronically unemployed or underemployed. They report that the social and functional aspects of jobs confuse them and lead to significant challenges at work. When considering this information for today's transition-age youth with autism spectrum disorder, it is critical that future skills needed must be considered across various environments (e.g., community, vocational, home living, leisure/recreational). For example, a student may currently live at home with his or her parents. But, if the goal is for person to eventually live independently or in a supervised apartment setting, then that student will need training or education in the skills necessary to be independent. Likewise, if the goal is for full and fulfilling employment, then the transition plan must include activities to achieve that goal.

One way to ensure the development of a functional or ecologically oriented curriculum is to conduct an ecological inventory (Brown, Nietupski, & Hamre-Nietupski, 1976; Snell, 1993). As previously mentioned, this involves identifying various environments where the student currently performs or would like to function in the future (e.g., live in an apartment, shop at the grocery store, work as a stocker, withdraw money from an ATM, eat in a restaurant, ride a bus). Once an environment is identified, then the subenvironments, various activities, and the skills needed to participate in each can be determined. Afterward, the educator evaluates the student's current skill level by observing him or her performing certain activities within the environment. The data provide valuable insight into possible areas for instruction and help the teacher, student, and family prioritize and individualize educational goals and objectives for the IEP.

When determining whether to teach a particular skill, the teacher should consider not only the functionality of the skill or behavior (both now and in the future), but also the feasibility of teaching a particular skill. As stated previously, if teaching the skill or behavior will increase the student's level of independence, now and in the future, it is functional. In addition, because there are literally thousands on thousands of skills that could be taught to a given student, thought must also be given to the feasibility or length of time required to teach a particular skill. Arguably, given the proper techniques and sufficient time, all individuals could learn most skills. However, the time that it would take may be so long that only a portion of a skill could be mastered in the year. Thus, it is entirely feasible that an alternative approach to performing the task could be identified to reduce instructional time. Browder and Snell (2000) described four possible curricula to consider for students with severe disabilities (see Table 20.4). Any given student could receive instruction in different curriculum for different subject areas. The student with an autism spectrum disorder who has strength in mathematics might receive instruction from the *general education curriculum with adaptations*, whereas that same student might receive instruction from the *embedded academic skills usable in specific life routines curriculum* for reading or language arts. The teacher should always be prepared to offer guidance on what skills and curricula are necessary to maximize future levels of independence. Sometimes, student preferences will be apparent; other times they will not. Regardless, attention to this will help ensure that student likes and preferences are considered in all areas of instruction and that the curriculum is flexible in meeting the needs and wants of the student and his or her family.

Table 20.4.   Four curriculum approaches to teaching functional academics

Curriculum	Learning outcome
General education curriculum with or without adaptations	Student will master grade-level material with outcomes similar to classmates
Functional, generalized skills usable across life routines	Student will master critical skills for use in home, community, school, and work settings. Students in this curriculum may perform between a second- and fifth-grade level.
Embedded academic skills usable in specific life routines	Student will acquire academic skills in the context of their daily routine (e.g., reading the menu choices at lunch, counting the coins to make a vending machine purchase).
Adaptations to bypass academic skills	Students will use community-based functional adaptations to academic skills (e.g., having money counted out by support people in bus envelope, using picture menus to order food at restaurants).

SNELL, MARTHA E.; BROWN, FREDDA, INSTRUCTION OF STUDENTS WITH SEVERE DISABILITIES, 5th Edition, © 2000. Adapted by permission of Pearson Education, Inc., Upper Saddle River, NJ.

Flexible Curriculum   The curriculum must also be flexible and adapted as needed. Goals and objectives are subject to change. If the task being taught is too difficult or too easy to perform, not preferred or not needed by the student, or has been mastered, or a more important goal has been identified, then the student's team should update their plan. Sometimes a revision will be necessary, at other times a change in instruction may be warranted (e.g., increase reinforcement, task analysis may need more steps). No matter what the final outcome, it is essential to update the IEP and individual transition plan (ITP) as needed, rather than only on an annual basis or according to a predetermined schedule.

Process for Developing a Functional Curriculum

In order to begin development of a functional curriculum, the IEP objectives must be appropriate for a particular student. This means that the objectives should address skills that are relevant to the student's daily activities that are currently necessary or will be required in the future. Student's goals and objectives should span across instructional domains. Therefore, the first phase of development involves identifying the curriculum domains. These generally include community, home living, vocational, and leisure/recreational domains. These domain areas are representative of major life skills, lead to the selection of practical skills, and emphasize the functional goal of self-sufficiency.

Next, the teacher works closely with the student and the family to identify settings where the student presently functions within various domains. The team also considers and plans for future environments to determine the skills needed for successful transition to an adult life. As noted earlier, the team derives the future plan from the person-centered plan itself. For example, in the home living domain, the student lives with his or her parents in a single-family dwelling. In the future, the parents plan for the student to live in a supervised apartment setting. In the vocational domain, the student's parents provide transportation to the local mall for shopping, but in the future, the student will need to ride the subway, catch a bus, or get a taxi cab to travel to work or other destinations. These areas are important areas to consider when selecting settings to analyze for a student's individual curriculum.

Once the team has identified the critical settings for a student to receive instruction, then the team explores the subenvironments within each previously identified environment. For example, within the home living domain, the family residence is made up of various subenvironments such as the kitchen, laundry room, bedroom, living room, and yard. A vocational domain, such as a retail store, is made up of various subenvironments such as a workstation, restroom, store floor, and break room.

When the subenvironments are identified, the team inventories each subenvironment to identify the relevant activities performed there. For instance, kitchen activities include cleaning, preparing food, and storing food. Activities within the retail store's workstation include setting up the workstation, unloading the truck, processing merchandise, and cleaning the workstation. For people with autism spectrum disorders, it is critical, at this point in the planning, to inventory the communication and social skills needed in each subenvironment as well. Again, the social and communication behavior that is acceptable in the break room is vastly different than that which is acceptable on the store floor. This analysis leads to an identification of possible IEP goal and objective areas within the various environments and subenvironments; yet, it does not finalize the process of selecting goals and objectives. The next step will provide the necessary prioritization of skills for inclusion in the person's individual plan.

After the subenvironments inventory, the team identifies the most relevant activities to current and future independence and isolates the various skills to teach. Finally, the team identifies relevant skills to teach to the student based on the functional criteria discussed previously (e.g., practical, suitable to student's age, can be taught within reasonable time frame). Again, because there are so many skills that could be taught, it is important to prioritize those for immediate instruction. The basic rule here is twofold: 1) select those skills that the student requires most often to function more independently in current environments and 2) select those skills that will enhance functioning and optimize his or her independence in the least restrictive environment in the future. Thus, the team prioritizes critical skills at the top of the list. Table 20.5 demonstrates an example of a partial ecological inventory for dining in a restaurant. Keep in mind that the team will then review these skills and prioritize those that are most critical to an individual student.

In order to teach the skills that the team prioritized for inclusion in the IEP, those skills are task analyzed into sequences of behaviors. The task analysis is useful for providing instruction and measuring the student's progress. It is important to remember that there are various skills involved in completing an activity. Thus, the student must receive instruction on all skills to eventually be able to complete the entire sequence of skills necessary to successfully perform a particular activity.

Once the important skills have been identified and prioritized for instruction, then the transition team can establish long- and short-term goals. The Appendix at the end of the chapter provides examples of objectives across different domains for Quinton in his ITP. Most goals and objectives will relate to either learning new skills or generalizing those already learned.

Table 20.5.   Partial ecological inventory for a restaurant

Domain: Community
Environment: Happy Family Grill

Subenvironment	Activity	Skill(s) (including social and communication skills
Parking lot	Walking to front entrance	Getting in and out of the vehicle, walking safely through the parking lot, talking in conversational voice tone to companions
Front entrance/ hostess station	Being seated at an empty table	Waiting in line, greeting the hostess, following the hostess to be seated
	Using a pay telephone	Locating the telephone, dialing home, leaving a message, asking for assistance
Seating area	Ordering food	Looking at a menu, greeting wait staff, making a food selection, placing an order, waiting for food, saying "thank you" when food arrives, leaving a tip
	Socializing with others	Commenting on food, talking about topics of shared interests, requesting assistance
	Eating the meal	Using eating utensils, using condiments, using napkin, drinking, chewing with mouth shut
Public restroom	Washing and drying hands	Locating restroom, washing hands, drying hands with automatic hand dryer, returning to table
	Toileting	Finding empty bathroom stall, locking door, flushing toilet
	Maintaining a good personal appearance	Locating comb, combing hair, returning comb to purse or pocket, straightening clothes, washing face if needed
Cashier's workstation	Paying the check	Locating cashier's station, giving cashier the check, giving the cashier money, receiving change, using a credit card, signing name to receipt, returning change or card to purse or wallet, saying "thank you," saying "good-bye"

INTERVENTION STRATEGIES

The astute teacher will keep in mind that there is no one specific set of guidelines that encapsulates every learner because each student with an autism spectrum disorder is different and comes to the classroom with unique abilities and challenges (Case-Smith, Allen, & Pratt, 1996). However, there are some best practices that can be used to assist students with the most severe disabilities, including autism, with learning new skills. It is beyond the scope of this chapter to review all of the possible intervention strategies aimed at increasing behavior, so our focus will be on systematic instruction. Table 20.6 offers a brief explanation of some of the most common instructional meth-

Table 20.6. Instructional methods

Verbal instruction

Preferred method (if person can hear/use it; least intrusive method)

Use even if person has no speech (because receptive language is often better than expressive language; over time the person may learn to respond)

Instructions should be very specific (vague instructions may elicit no or wrong response)

Keep language concrete and realistic (avoid abstract terms, analogies or metaphors)

Note: Some students will only need verbal instruction; but in most cases, verbal instruction alone will not be sufficient for teaching new skills.

Demonstration

Necessary to teach most new tasks

Show the person what to do step by step

Pair demonstration with step-by-step verbal instructions

Allow opportunities to practice

Be sure to demonstrate the correct way to complete task the first time because individuals with autism may have difficulty with changing repertoire

Note: Some students may learn a task after one or a few demonstrations; others may need weeks to learn the skill.

Graduated guidance

Use if the student needs more than verbal instruction paired with demonstration

Involves giving physical assistance to complete a task

Begin with full hand-over-hand assistance paired with verbal instruction (teacher puts hands over student's hands and guides his or her hands through the correct motion while telling him or her what he or she is doing)

Fade full manual guidance to partial guidance with verbal instruction (teacher moves to partial guidance by gently guiding hands using thumb and forefinger while giving specific verbal instruction)

Fade partial guidance to shadowing (teacher holds his or her hand several inches above the student's as he or she performs the correct movement while telling him or her what he or she is doing)

Fade shadowing to independent performance with no assistance from the teacher

ods used to teach individuals with autism in community-based settings (e.g., home, work, store, restaurant).

An important goal of instruction is to teach the student to respond to natural environmental cues. However, this cannot be left to chance; instead, educators must systematically plan for learning. The complexity of many of the tasks taught necessitates a systematic approach to instruction, and the use of task analysis is central to such an approach (Cuvo, Leaf, & Borakove, 1978). Therefore, educators who teach students with autism spectrum disorders should be skilled at using systematic instruction. Systematic teaching is defined, replicable, and uses performance data to make modifications. This approach also ensures that instruction proceeds through the stages of learning (e.g., acquisition, fluency, maintenance, generalization). Effective teachers know not only how to use these specific procedures, but also when, under what conditions,

Table 20.7.   Types of prompts

Nonspecific verbal prompts give a student the least amount of information and are easier to fade. Some examples include statements such as, What do you do next? How do you get started? What else should you do?

Verbal prompts give the student specific information on what to do next. Some examples include turn on the water, pick up the soap, lather up your hands, rinse your hands, dry your hands.

Gestural prompts are motions that direct the student's attention toward specific materials or an area. This may involve pointing or motioning the student to attend to something.

In modeling, the teacher demonstrates how to perform a step in the task and then allows the student to try it.

Physical prompts may be partial or full physical guidance to the student. This is considered the most intensive type of prompt and is usually more difficult to fade.

Examples may include hand-over-hand guidance to expose the learner to new movements or guiding hands to where they need to be by touching and pushing the elbow.

and in what combination to use them. Coupled with knowledge about and experience with teaching people with autism, this strategy can enhance learning.

A major component of a systematic instructional program is the application of specific prompting procedures that maximize the student's independence while minimizing errors (Smith & Belcher, 1995; Snell, 1993). An *instructional cue* or *prompt* is a form of information that a teacher provides before a response to help the student correctly complete an activity. For example, a teacher may say, "Pick up the book," point to a book that a student needs to pick up, or may physically guide the student's hand toward a book to pick up. In some instances, prompts may be combined to give extra stimulus to facilitate the correct response. For example, the teacher may say, "Pick up the book" while pointing to the book that needs to be picked up. In both instances, the teacher is simply giving the student extra information, or prompting the student to make the correct response.

Prompts may be used singularly, in combination, or as part of a hierarchy of prompts (see Table 20.7). Effective instructional prompts will vary from person to person and task to task. The basic rule is to select the least intrusive prompt that will allow the student to emit the correct response. These various types or combinations of prompts can be arranged into a hierarchy, or an ordered sequence for delivery. This allows the teacher to systematically provide assistance to the student and allows for subsequent fading of prompts. The teacher should begin with the least intensive prompt (one or a combination that provides the least amount of information) and then proceed to use more intensive prompts (one or combination that provides the most information) if needed until the desired student response occurs. Prompt hierarchies consist of a sequence of two or more prompts that are arranged from the least to most or most to least intrusive order. An example of a least prompts procedure is offered in Table 20.8.

Systems of least prompts have been used to effectively train people with severe disabilities. Adults with autism have learned to perform a number of self-care, domestic, and vocational tasking using this approach. These procedures help ensure that too much assistance is not provided by allowing the student time to respond with some degree of independence. Using this approach, the teacher must wait before providing assistance. Often, during this time, the person with autism will respond correctly. It also

Table 20.8. System of least prompts strategy

Get the student's attention.

If you have the student's attention, then give the instructional cue.

If you do not have the student's attention, then repeat Step 1 and proceed.

Teacher gives the student initial verbal cue to begin the task.

Wait/allow 5 seconds for independent response.

If correct, then provide reinforcement and proceed.

If incorrect or no response, then provide a verbal prompt on a specific step and allow 5 seconds for a response.

If incorrect or no response, then provide a gestural prompt with the verbal prompt on a specific step. Allow 5 seconds for response.

If incorrect or no response, then model the step while delivering the verbal prompt. Allow 5 seconds for response.

If incorrect or no response, then give physical guidance while delivering the verbal prompt.

offers a way to redirect the off-task learner back to the task at hand without unduly rewarding off-task behavior. If teachers follow the procedure for least prompting carefully, then the more intrusive prompts will naturally be faded out. Although this helps prevent the teacher from providing too much assistance and creating a student who is dependent on prompting, there are no guarantees. If a student becomes prompt dependent, then it may be difficult to correct the problem. Thus, the teacher should review data on an ongoing and regular basis to determine if the student is becoming more or less independent. For example, if less prompting is required or the type of prompt needed to elicit the correct response is less intrusive, then it is unlikely that the student is becoming dependent.

Time delay is a prompting procedure that is especially useful for promoting errorless learning by immediately prompting the correct response and reinforcing it. In the progressive time delay approach, the length of time between the cue and the prompts increases by small increments of time. Progressive time delay has been effective in teaching a variety of skills including sign language to students with autism and other severe disabilities (Browder, Morris, & Snell, 1981; Browder, Snell, & Wildonger, 1988; Snell, 1982; Snell & Gast, 1981). The advantage of progressive time delay is that it prevents errors and increases the likelihood that the student will respond to the most important cues. In addition, because there are fewer errors, the student is more likely to be reinforced for the correct response; thereby increasing the chances of making the right response more often. Students with autism may insist on doing a task exactly the same way every time and may be resistant to doing something a new or different way. Therefore, it is very important to teach the task the correct and most efficient way the first and every time.

One of the most troublesome aspects of educating students with autism is the frequent lack of spontaneous generalization and retention of skills learned (Gast, Collins, Wolery, & Jones, 1993; Haring, Kennedy, Adams, & Pitts-Conway, 1987). Most of the time, skills taught in the traditional classroom setting will not transfer to or occur in other environments (e.g., home, community) and are not maintained over time (Carr,

1980; Smith, 1991; Strain, 1980). To help students transfer or use skills learned in different environments, teachers should arrange for the student to have multiple opportunities to learn and practice the skills in different settings and with different people. For example, when a student is taught to order something to eat and drink at a fast-food drive-through window, at a restaurant, and in a movie theater, they are more likely to be successful when ordering food. In addition, using multiple instructors across environments can also improve generalization of skills. For example, a student can practice greetings in school (taught by teachers or peers), at work (taught by job coach or work personnel) and at home (taught by parents, siblings, or neighbors).

Teaching the skill directly in the environment where it is used also strengthens generalization. For example, teaching social skills in a classroom is not likely to generalize over in to the workplace. Thus, friendly work behaviors could be taught on the job and the problem of generalization becomes less critical. Although teaching the skill in the actual environment does not eliminate generalization concerns, it does increase the likelihood that the skill will be used in that particular place.

APPLYING THE PRINCIPLES FOR FUNCTIONAL CURRICULUM TO COMMUNICATION AND SOCIAL SKILLS TEACHING

Very often, teachers supporting individuals with an autism spectrum disorder have difficulty identifying the specific social and communication skills that the person needs. There are two basic ways to identify those skills. First, and best, teachers can use the principles for developing a functional academic curriculum and apply that to social and communication skill environments using the same domain/subenvironment/activity analysis approach described previously. The second method, an "after the fact" method, is more frequently used when a problem behavior has occurred. Each method is discussed next using social and communication skill identification.

Using the Domain/Subenvironment Approach to Identify Social Skill Needs

Teachers should use the general rules for functional curriculum when determining which social and communication skills to teach (e.g., useful for the student now or in the foreseeable future, age appropriate, valued by parents or the person him- or herself). Consider Donald, the student discussed earlier who has Asperger syndrome. As his team prepares for his transition to college, they should think about all the environments in which Donald will need new social skills. Their list of environments includes the cafeteria, dorm, library, classroom, and so forth. Subenvironments in the dorm include Donald's room, (there are myriad social skills Donald will need to learn to get along with a roommate), the common area or living room, and the lobby/entry way. These subenvironments are ripe for an analysis of activities that require social and communication skills that Donald may not currently exhibit. A way to identify the social skills needed in these environments requires that Donald and his teachers observe people interacting in the dorm, for example. When completing such an analysis for social skill development, Donald and his teachers should watch the activities in the subenvironments and answer the following six questions:

1. How do people in this environment communicate with each other (e.g., talking, gesturing, writing notes)?

2. What are the typical interactions that occur in this environment (e.g., typical topics of conversation, how people greet each other, how loudly they talk with each other, how they handle disagreements or conflicts)?

3. How do people in this subenvironment take a break?

4. How do people get the things they need in this subenvironment during this activity?

5. When and how do people in this subenvironment maintain their focus?

6. How do they get attention when they need it during this activity?

Once they have developed this social and communication skills list for activities in each of the subenvironments, then they have a list of the basic social and communication skills needed for college life for Donald.

Next, they have to consider Donald's current skills. For example, Donald, like many people with Asperger syndrome, does not know how and when to talk about personal information. He is likely to discuss highly personal information in the lobby of his dorm while greeting other dorm mates. Donald has difficulty monitoring his voice volume and tends to talk very loudly. Finally, he may push past people he knows without saying hello to them. Comparing Donald's current social skills with the list of needed social skills and identifying the discrepancies provides the list of skills that Donald needs to learn. At this point, the teacher needs to develop a teaching plan for each needed skill. Such an analysis, during any transition, increases the likelihood that the student will be socially successful in the new environment.

Analyzing Problem Behavior to Identify Social Skill Needs

Students may be taught social skills using a basic behavioral approach, which was described previously (e.g., least prompts, time delay). In order to elicit information that may be useful when developing individual social goals and teaching objectives, ask all team members, including the student's parents, to describe social situations where the student behaves appropriately and situations where the student does not behave appropriately. It is important to get details related to the behavior people present, and consider environmental factors that may affect the behavior. Then analyze the relevant factors in each environment and consider the social skills that the student may be missing. In fact, it is often helpful to think about behavior challenges as the tip of an ice berg. What you see in the environment is the problem behavior. However, underneath the water line is a number of missing social skills. Figure 20.1 provides an example of this concept in a graphic form.

Evan's problems related to eating food off the salad bar indicate a lack of understanding of how to get food from a salad bar. Instead of simply suppressing Evan's behavior, his team will be more successful when they teach him when and how to get food from a salad bar.

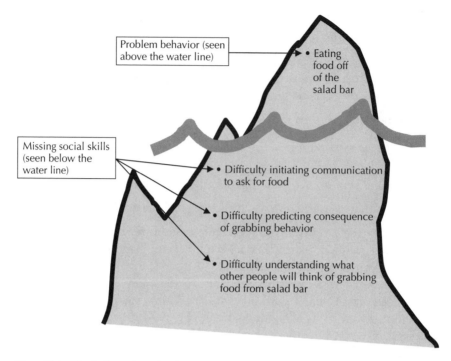

Figure 20.1. The "iceberg relationship" between social skill needs and problem behavior.

TRANSITION TO WORK

It was previously thought that the employment prospects for people with autism were bleak; however, experience has shown that, with the proper intervention and supports, individuals with autism spectrum disorders can work in a variety of businesses for minimum wage or better. SE is a concept that has been used to assist people with severe disabilities such as autism with gaining and maintaining employment. It was founded on the belief that all people, regardless of the severity of their disability, should have the opportunity to work. Often perceived as too disabled to work, people with severe disabilities such as autism were relegated to work in sheltered workshops or day activity center.

SE was designed to give these individuals, or those who are viewed as too disabled to work, tailored assistance that can make going to work a reality. Using SE, the person with a severe disability is assisted by a VR specialist or designated school personnel with identifying vocational strengths and potential support needs, locating a real job for real pay in the community, receiving one-to-one on-the-job support and skills training, and obtaining long-term follow-up and job retention services. If best practices have been followed, then the student will be employed when he or she leaves school and the transition should be a simple handoff from one set of support providers to another (school to adult vocational service provider). Garcia-Villamisar, Wehman, and Navarro (2002) found that SE resulted in greater quality of life for people with autism across a 4-year period of time than employment for individuals in sheltered environments. Thus, community-based vocational training programs can and should be developed to assist students with exploring jobs and creating a vision for future employment, learning work values and skills in actual work settings, and becoming employed before leaving school.

Very often, individuals with autism require special job matching that takes into account the effects of the disability on the person in varied environments. Given Evan's sensitivities to chaotic environments and his obsession with empty pizza sauce and cheese containers, he is more likely to have difficulties in the food industry. Careful matching would indicate the need for a different type of job. When Evan switched to working in a recycling plant where he sorted colored paper and glass, he did much better. Likewise, Jenny enjoyed working in a library where she could set her own break schedule much better than at Goodwill where she had to take a break with everyone else at the same time. Donald will likely acquire the skills to work in a more complex job, but would not be successful in the customer service industry. Thus, it is critical to consider the strengths and interests as well as the work environment needs of each person with autism. Division TEACCH identifies appropriate vocational settings as those that have jobs that are predictable, have potential for clearly defined work tasks, and can be adapted to the individual's need for structure. They seek employers and co-workers who are receptive to training and who are willing to create an environment where an individual is more likely to succeed. Finally, they identify job settings in which there is potential to utilize individual strengths (Chapman, 2004). Careful consideration of all of these components has lead to a highly successful SE program for individuals with autism spectrum disorders.

A few sources have addressed the needs of individuals with autism spectrum disorders when seeking and engaging in community-based paid employment (Datlow Smith, Belcher, & Juhrs, 1995; Hagner & Cooney, 2005; Hawkins, 2004; Lattimore, Parsons, & Reid, 2003; Meyer, 2001). They identified very specific steps that are necessary to ensure successful employment for individuals with autism:

- Assessing job and task preferences carefully before placement: As a group, individuals with autism are much more likely to be successful when they engage in preferred tasks regularly in their job. In fact, many sources recommended that jobs be modified to address the people's work preferences (Hagner & Cooney, 2005; Hawkins, 2004; Lattimore, Parsons, & Reid, 2003).

- Assessing social, communication, and job skill needs: This is the one area where people with autism struggle most. Müller et al. (2003) found that people with autism spectrum disorders were frequently fired from jobs because of social and communication difficulties, not an inability to perform job skills.

- Making a careful match between the job, the person's preferences, the social and communication demands in the environment, and the tolerance of co-workers for diversity: This step is critical to developing a successful job placement. Frequently, people with autism spectrum disorders have difficulty with jobs that require a high degree of interaction with others. Nevertheless, they may be able to tolerate such interaction better with training and matching with a supportive environment. Thus, this is a critical step when seeking employment opportunities for people with autism spectrum disorders (Datlow Smith, Belcher, & Jurhs, 1995; Meyer, 2001).

- Teaching the social and communication skills required in the job, in addition to the actual job skills: The "hard skills" in a job (e.g., how to do the job itself) are frequently not difficult for most people with autism spectrum disorders. The "soft skills" in a job (e.g., how to interact with the supervisor and co-workers, how to tolerate change, how to make requests in the environment, how to take a break) are frequently areas that cause great stress and discord for people with autism spectrum disorders. Thus, teaching these skills is as important, if not slightly more important, than teaching the job skills themselves (Müller et al., 2003).

- Preparing employers and co-workers for the diverse behaviors that a person with autism may display, if necessary: At times, it may be necessary to prepare co-workers and employers for some of the nonharmful but odd behavior or movements in which a person with autism may engage. Not every case requires such intervention; nevertheless, it is possible that when placing a person with an autism spectrum disorder in a work environment, the support provider may have to educate co-workers and employers about the person and his or her different behavior (Howlin et al., 2004).

- Teaching co-worker/employee/employer relationship behaviors to the person with an autism spectrum disorder: The communication and social skill deficits in people with autism spectrum disorders across the entire spectrum are such that they may not understand differences in how to interact with friends, co-workers, or supervisors. In the modern workplace, a simple social error, such as hugging a co-worker, could result in termination of employment. A person with an autism spectrum disorder may unknowingly engage in forbidden behavior and not understand the resulting consequence. Thus, it is essential that the person receive support from job placing professionals in understanding acceptable and unacceptable behavior (Datlow Smith, Belcher, & Juhrs, 1995; Meyer, 2001).

- Making modifications and adaptations in the job environment to meet the social and communication needs of the worker: People with autism spectrum disorders may require that jobs be modified to meet their individual communication, social, and sensory needs. Such modifications and adaptations may include

  - Providing a consistent schedule

  - Decreasing or developing predictable social interactions

  - Providing visual organizers for job tasks

  - Providing direct supervisory feedback instead of subtle communication about job expectations and performance

  - Explaining and preparing the person for changes at the worksite before they occur

  - Encouraging co-workers to initiate interactions with the person

  - Explaining that the failure to say hello is not an intentional slight, but a disability-specific oversight

  - Providing job coach contact and follow-along during the entire tenure of employment

Such support make the challenges of autism spectrum disorder less of an issue in work environments (Hagner & Cooney, 2005; Müller et al., 2003).

- Supporting the person through job challenges and crises: All people who work have bad days at work. For the average person without a disability, such days are measured against the many good days that a person has. For the person with an autism spectrum disorder who tends to have great difficulty maintaining perspective and insight, a bad day at the office can become a crisis. Consequently, people with autism spectrum disorders frequently need support from co-workers, friends, family, and paid support providers in balancing and coping with everyday work challenges (Müller et al., 2003).

CONCLUSION

As noted before, people with autism spectrum disorders present unique challenges and, as such, require specific supports in work environments. Very often, people with autism spectrum disorders are very successful in completing the skills for jobs but have difficulty managing the social environment for work. Nevertheless, mindful implementation of supports and services frequently result in highly successful employment for people with autism spectrum disorders.

The critical steps to achieving employment are early exposure to the world of work and training in a variety of community-based job experiences. In order to achieve steady and successful employment, people with autism spectrum disorders need a combination of specialized services tailored to meet the challenges of the disorder, universal services designed to assist the person in acquiring the necessary job skills, and involvement from the person's team. Experience has demonstrated that individuals with autism spectrum disorders are successful in adult life when their educational team, family, and community service providers collaborate to plan early, consider the person through person-centered planning, and match the educational curriculum to meet the person's needs.

STUDY QUESTIONS

1. How does the dramatic increase in the prevalence of children and youth with autism affect transition programs for youth with disabilities?

2. What are the three primary characteristics of autism spectrum disorders?

3. List some examples of the behaviors associated with autism spectrum disorders.

4. What are some of the secondary characteristics of autism spectrum disorders?

5. Describe the multidimensional perspective of autism and list and describe the five dimensions that must be considered when serving a person with an autism spectrum disorder.

6.   What are the five steps a team must execute when completing a FBA and developing a behavior intervention plan?

7.   What are the six characteristics of excellent programs for individuals with autism spectrum disorders?

8.   What is the process for developing a functional curriculum?

9.   Give examples of how to implement three different prompting and instructional strategies.

10. What are two ways that transition teams can use to identify the necessary communication and social skills a person with autism spectrum disorders may need to learn?

11. Describe the types of experiences that are necessary to prepare a person with an autism spectrum disorder for life after school.

12. List and describe the eight critical steps that ensure successful job placement for a person with an autism spectrum disorder.

Appendix

Individualized Transition Plan for a Student with Autism

I. Career and economic self-sufficiency

1. Employment goal	Quinton will be employed full time.
Level of present performance	Quinton has interests in drawing and watching sports on television. He participated in three situational assessments this past year (retail/stocker, restaurant/food prep, and processor/industrial setting). The assessments revealed that Quinton learned best with visual cues and modeling, can remain on task for up to 20 minutes, and worked at a slow to moderate pace. He seemed to enjoy working with food but did not care to get his hands dirty. Some of the sounds in the industrial setting were distracting and caused Quinton to cover his ears, which impeded his ability to pace himself.
	Quinton has a history of severe behavior problems. A functional assessment of his behavior has revealed that he has trouble handling changes in his environment, including changes in staff or the normal routine. He did very well in a structured work environment that presented few changes. A behavioral plan was successfully implemented to assist Quinton with exhibiting acceptable social behaviors at work, with a decrease in self-injury and destruction of property.
Steps needed to accomplish goal (person[s] responsible)	Quinton needs to get job experience prior to exiting school and needs to 1. Enroll in SE, meet with a state VR counselor to apply for SE services (school transition coordinator and VR counselor to contact parents and Quinton). 2. Choose a SE provider (VR counselor, Quinton, and his parents). 3. Investigate the use of Social Security work incentives (VR counselor, parents, and Social Security benefits assistance representative). 4. Determine availability of transportation options for getting to and from work (parents and VR counselor).
Date of completion	
2. Vocational education/training goal	Quinton will participate in the community-based vocational training program and a paid work experience this year.
Level of present performance	Quinton prefers to work in an environment that is void of extremely loud noises (e.g., beeping forklifts, ringing alarms). He will do well in a setting where he can watch others performing the work he needs to do. Changes in tasks from day to day may cause aggressive behavior to emerge or destruction to property.
Steps needed to accomplish goal (person[s] responsible)	Enroll Quinton in the community-based vocational training site located at the market distribution center 5 hours per day, 5 days per week (teacher and Quinton). Assist Quinton with locating a paid work opportunity (transition coordinator and/or a job coach). Interview for job (transition coordinator and/or job coach, and Quinton). Coordinate transportation to and from work (parents). Provide on-the-job training (transition coordinator or job coach). Arrange or facilitate necessary supports on and off the job (transition coordinator or job coach and parents).
Date of completion	

3. Postsecondary education goal	N/A
Level of present performance	N/A
Steps needed to accomplish goal (person[s] responsible)	N/A
Date of completion	
4. Financial/income needs goal	Quinton will open a savings account.
Level of present performance	Quinton's parents take care of his finances. They have concerns about his needs being met after their deaths. They would like to investigate establishing a trust and having the majority of his future earnings deposited there.
Steps needed to accomplish goal (person[s] responsible)	Learn about trusts and Social Security benefits (parents, attorney, Social Security department).
	Determine best way to secure/build future finances for Quinton (parents).
Date of completion	

II. Community integration and participation

5. Independent living goal	Quinton will live in a supervised apartment with peers.
Level of present performance	Quinton is independent in basic self-care. He can use the microwave to prepare a simple meal. He helps his parents with some general yard work, takes out the trash, and is learning how to do his own laundry.
Steps needed to accomplish goal (person[s] responsible)	Apply for residential services
	Enroll in the center for independent living
	Continue training at home to do his laundry (parents and Quinton)
	Learn how to make a bed (parents)
Date of completion	
6. Transportation/mobility goal	Quinton will take the city bus to work.
Level of present performance	Quinton travels to some places on the school campus independently. There is a bus stop one block from his house.
Steps needed to accomplish goal (person[s] responsible)	Find a volunteer or (if in paid employment) job coach to teach Quinton how to ride the bus to work.
	Identify destination (trainer).
	Get bus pass for Quinton and trainer (trainer).
Date of completion	
7. Social relationships goal	Quinton will greet others with a handshake and a smile.
Level of present performance	Quinton does not initiate greetings with strangers. If someone says "Hello" to him, he usually walks away. His parents indicate that he sometimes greets people he has seen on a regular basis, such as his neighbors and cousins.
Steps needed to accomplish goal (person[s] responsible)	Teach Quinton to greet others with a handshake and a smile (teacher and parents).
Date of completion	
8. Recreation/leisure goal	Quinton will attend school sporting events and be the bat boy for the school's varsity baseball team.
Level of present performance	Quinton enjoys sporting events but rarely attends school sports functions.
Steps needed to accomplish goal (person[s] responsible)	Provide parents with schedule of school sporting events (teacher).
	Provide information on car pooling options to after-school sports events (teacher).
	Meet with the varsity boys coach to discuss having Quinton serve as bat boy for the upcoming season (teacher).
Date of completion	

III. Personal competence

9. Health/safety goal	Quinton will improve his personal hygiene.
Level of present performance	Quinton's personal hygiene is inadequate. Although he showers three times per week, he fails to wear deodorant on a regular basis. He also has bad breath on the days that he forgets to brush his teeth. His clothes are well matched and hair is groomed in the mornings, but he does not take steps to improve his appearance (e.g., straighten disheveled clothing, comb hair) during the day. He does properly wash his hands after going to the restroom. Sometimes he has to be prompted to stop washing his hands and dry them.
Steps needed to accomplish goal (person[s] responsible)	Provide training on how to properly apply deodorant to underarms (teacher). Store deodorant, toothbrush, and toothpaste at school (use as needed). Provide training on how to groom appearance during the day (brush hair and adjust clothing; teacher).

Date of completion

10. Self-advocacy/future planning goal	Quinton will be able to let others know when he is feeling stressed by something in his environment.
Level of present performance	Quinton will most likely require case management and advocacy services for his adult life. He has become more attentive to stimuli in the environment that he finds aversive. However, he reacts aggressively rather than removing himself or telling others about the problem.
Steps needed to accomplish goal (person[s] responsible)	Identify type(s) of stimuli that Quinton finds aversive by interviewing his parents (teacher). Develop picture cues that Quinton can show to others to explain the problem (teacher). Avoid work environments that have aversive stimuli (transition coordinator or job coach).

Date of completion

Student career preference

Student's major transition needs

Employment

Increase endurance and stamina for job that requires standing most of the day

Increase recreation with peers

Supported living arrangement

21

Applications for Youth with Orthopedic and Other Health Impairments

PAUL WEHMAN AND MICHAEL D. WEST

AFTER COMPLETING THIS CHAPTER, THE READER WILL BE ABLE TO

○ List five orthopedic impairments and five other health impairments

○ Understand potential implications of orthopedic and other health impairments on transition planning in functional areas

○ Describe three potential postschool employment or educational environments and the implications of each for transition planning

○ Describe at least four strategies for adapting or supporting work tasks or work-related activities of students with orthopedic or other health impairments

○ Develop an evaluation plan for transition services for youth with orthopedic and other health impairments

LINDA

Linda was diagnosed with cerebral palsy soon after birth. She learned to walk with the assistance of a walker but uses a wheelchair for long distances. Her speech is difficult to understand, and she has only limited use of her hands. She received her early education in a special school operated by a private service organization. When she was 14, she asked her parents if she could go to the general high school in her neighborhood, and they agreed. Her first year there was difficult; the counselors, principal, and teachers had little experience with students who have physical impairments and the school building itself, built prior to the Americans with Disabilities Act (ADA) of 1990 (PL 101-336), was not very accessible for students with mobility issues.

Over the next few years, the school made accommodations for Linda: adjusting classes so that she wouldn't have to encounter many stairs or long walks, modifying classroom setups so that she could move about more easily, modifying her classwork and examinations to better suit her abilities, and working with Linda to locate and train peer assistants. Overall it was a positive experience, and Linda was able to complete the requirements for a diploma and made a few close friends along the way.

Unfortunately, the school didn't adequately plan for Linda's adjustment from high school to adulthood. She graduated and had no place to go. Employment seemed an impossible goal, and she did not feel that she could handle the

Since the 1970s, adult services providers and education organizations serving people with disabilities have attempted to design programs around certain values, among them inclusion in a variety of community settings and activities, normalized lifestyles, enhanced quality of life, productive employment with meaningful wages, and, most recently, choice and empowerment. Education personnel are becoming increasingly aware of the need to prepare youth with disabilities for the same goals as youth without disabilities: the advancement of students' own educational and employment goals and goals to live, work, and participate as independently as possible in their home communities after leaving school. School systems often fail to meet this obligation adequately, as shown by the case of Linda and many others.

Helping Linda (see sidebar) and others is challenging yet absolutely essential. A health impairment is an ongoing long-term problem, but it is not and should not be an insurmountable barrier to work, successful school experiences, community living, and adult adjustment. Like all other special needs that most children and youth face, each barrier must be brainstormed for a solution that can work.

This chapter discusses issues and guidelines related to school-to-work transitions and postsecondary education for youth with orthopedic and other health impairments, presenting examples of the transition process in action.

BEHAVIOR AND LEARNING CHARACTERISTICS OF YOUTH WITH ORTHOPEDIC AND OTHER HEALTH IMPAIRMENTS

By statutory definition, *orthopedic impairments* are severe physical or motor disabilities caused by disease, congenital anomalies, or trauma (excluding brain trauma, which is a distinct educational classification that adversely affect a student's educational performance). *Other health impairments* are acute or chronic health problems that limit a student's strength, vitality, or alertness. Some common orthopedic and health impairments are listed in Table 21.1, although not all students with any of these types of problems are automatically considered to have educational disabilities. The determination of disability depends on the degree to which the impairment affects learning or performance.

In the education literature, students with orthopedic and other health impairments are frequently considered together because the physical manifestations and educational implications of their disabilities tend to be similar. These manifestations frequently include impaired movement and

physical and mental demands of college. It was not until 5 years after graduation that she enrolled in community college, taking classes in computer programming. With adaptations, she was able to use a keyboard and joy-stick mouse. She later transferred to a 4-year college and received services and accommodations related to her disabilities. She earned her degree in information systems over a longer period of time than most students because her physical limitations prevented her from taking a full class load. After graduation, it took her another 3 years to land her first job. In all, the time from high school graduation to her first job amounted to 15 years. At the time that Linda's peers were well along in their careers and building their earning capacity, Linda was just beginning.

mobility, fatigue, tendencies for injury and illness, and secondary visual or auditory impairments (DePaepe, Garrison-Kane, & Doelling, 2002).

According to the Twenty-Third Annual Report to Congress (U.S. Department of Education, 2001) on the Implementation of Individuals with Disabilities Education Act, 254,110 students were classified as eligible under the *other health impairment* category in 1999–2000. This number represents a 351% increase from the total number of students eligible in that category during 1990–1991. The increase in percentage of students who have health problems that adversely affect their educational performance has been greater than any other eligibility category since 1990.

Students diagnosed with various health conditions who attend public schools may require some degree of accommodations to allow them equal access to educational services. Some students with health conditions determined to adversely affect their educational performance may be found to be eligible for special education and related services under the Individuals with Disabilities Education Act (IDEA) Amendments of 1997 (PL 105-17) and IDEA 2004 (PL 108-446) eligibility category *other health impairment.* These students have:

> Limited strength, vitality or alertness, including a heightened alertness to environmental stimuli, that results in limited alertness with respect to the educational environment, that (i) is due to chronic or acute health problems such as asthma, attention deficit disorder or attention deficit hyperactivity disorder, diabetes, epilepsy, a heart condition, hemophilia, lead poisoning, leukemia, hephritis, rheumatic fever, and sickle cell anemia; and (ii) adversely affects a child's educational performance (IDEA final Regulations 34 C.F.R. § 300.7 [b] [9], p. 3)

UNIQUE CHALLENGES PRESENTED BY YOUTH WITH ORTHOPEDIC AND OTHER HEALTH IMPAIRMENTS

Students with orthopedic and other health impairments present many unique challenges for transition planning teams. Two major challenges for these students are 1) the need for personal assistance services in postschool environments and 2) the need for assistive technology (AT) and rehabilitation engineering in postschool environments. In addition, student self-advocacy is necessary for an effective transition.

Personal Assistance Services and Transition

Personal assistance services are broadly defined by Nosek (1991) as "assistance from another person with activities of daily living to compensate for a functional limitation" (p. 2) and include assistance with personal hygiene, meal preparation, housekeeping and other household chores, and community mobility. In the words of Litvak, Zukas, and Heumann (1987), these services are "tasks . . . that individuals would normally do for themselves if they did not have a disability" (p. 1).

Table 21.1.   Common orthopedic impairments and other health impairments

Orthopedic impairments	Other health impairments
Cerebral palsy	Tuberculosis
Spasticity	Rheumatic fever
Athetosis	Nephritis
Rigidity	Asthma
Dystonia	Sickle cell anemia
Hypotonia	Hemophilia
Mixed	Epilepsy
Spina bifida	Lead poisoning
Traumatic brain injury	Leukemia and other childhood cancers
Spinal cord injury	Cardiac defects
Curvatures of the spine	Ventricular septal defects
Scoliosis	Atrial septal defects
Kyphosis	Pulmonary valve stenosis
Lordosis	Aortic valve stenosis
Congenital limb absence	Metabolic disorders
Hip conditions	Hurler syndrome
Legg-Perthes disease	Phenylketonuria (PKU)
Congenital dislocation	Cystic fibrosis
Poliomyelitis	Diabetes mellitus
Rheumatoid arthritis	Acquired immunodeficiency syndrome (AIDS)
Muscular dystrophy	
Bone tuberculosis	
Amputation	
Contractures	
Club foot	

Source: Umbreit (1983).

The primary value of personal assistance services is that they allow people with severe physical or health impairments to participate more fully in community settings and activities, including employment. A personal assistant can fill in the gaps between the requirements or demands of a particular setting and the functional limitations of the individual.

Historically, personal assistance services have been viewed as an essential way of supporting individuals with physical disabilities in their independent living. The use of personal assistance services has been an important extension of empowering individuals with disabilities to live at home and to move about the community with a greater degree of independence. Without personal assistance services, thousands of people with physical and other significant disabilities would be confined to institutionalized nursing home environments or other segregated living situations that were predicated on the need for group care. Fortunately, since the 1980s, there has been both a philosophical and programmatic move away from institutional living arrangements and an understanding that a personal assistant can play a critically vital role in allowing for improved quality of community living for many people with significant disabilities.

Unfortunately, a myriad of problems is holding back the expansion of personal assistance services. First, there is a scarcity of personnel who are willing and able to fulfill this personal care attendant role. Remember, personal assistants have responsibilities for the lives in their hands, and if they are indifferent or not trained properly in how to perform their duties, particularly in a crisis situation, it can be the difference between life and death. The second problem is that there are very few well-developed training programs for guiding people who wish to become competent personal assistants. The third and perhaps the most significant obstacle has been the lack of a clear stream of funding from the state or federal government in helping to underwrite the costs of personal care services as a genuine long-term support priority. It is reasonable to argue that if the federal government is going to pay for wheelchairs, respirators, cochlear implants, job coaches, and other types of long-term support services and devices, then public funding for the use of personal assistants to help people enjoy a better quality of life and reduce institutionalization would also be a good investment. To date, this critical shortage of skilled personal care attendants, the lack of quality training resources, and the limited funding available for personal care services are primary obstacles that have made independent living more difficult for people with significant disabilities.

Although modern medicine and contemporary rehabilitation, as well as families and friends, have helped individuals with disabilities become individually empowered at home, transition and employment must not be left out. In fact, one could very reasonably argue that returning to a previous job, entering new employment, starting a business, or telecommuting are all important elements of closing the rehabilitation loop for people who have suffered serious injuries or experienced significant and/or life-changing disabilities. Living with independence at home is vital. Moving about the community is essential, but productive work provides that final stage of fulfillment and meaningfulness that home living by itself cannot provide. This is especially true for younger Americans with disabilities, full of energy and excitement and looking forward to making an impact on the world around them.

Consider, for example, the young man in the movie *Remember the Titans* who was a star defensive linebacker and larger than life in many of his actions as he struggled to overcome discrimination and improve his athletic prowess. When this young man was in a severe care accident that left him paralyzed, he was the same person—but was he? In reality, he was very much the same person except that he had lost the use of his legs and needed the aid of a personal assistant for him to extend his life in a similar way but with different outcomes. This young man was able to go on and become a star in the Olympics, despite the fact that he used a wheelchair and the services of a personal assistant.

During childhood and adolescence, the personal assistance needs of students with orthopedic and health impairments are typically filled by parents and other family members; in school, teachers, aides, or other students provide assistance. During the transition process, personal assistance needs as they relate to the workplace and other community-based environments are of prime interest to the student and his or her family (Nehring, 1990; Newacheck et al., 1998).

The transition individualized education program (IEP) team should identify the anticipated personal assistance needs of the student, as well as the available resources, formal and informal, for meeting those needs. For many daily functions, family, friends, or volunteers can provide work-related assistance without stigmatizing the student. For example, transportation to and from work can be provided by a family member or co-worker. In many, if not most, workplaces, supportive co-workers can be found who will assist the student with getting from one area to another or with eating; however, it is unusual to find co-workers willing to assist with toileting at work, to clean up after toileting accidents, to administer injections, or to take care of other personal and medical needs. A paid assistant is a viable option for those students who would feel stigmatized by having a family member come to the workplace for these purposes (Racino, 1995). Although the use of a personal assistant in the workplace may initially seem unusual to co-workers, the arrangement should eventually become accepted, particularly if the student hires, trains, and pays the assistant.

Assistive Technology, Rehabilitation Engineering, and Transition

Students with severe orthopedic and health impairments are frequently described as being *technology supported* or *technology assisted* (Flippo, Inge, & Barcus, 1995; Knight & Wadsworth, 1994). These terms describe their use of specialized equipment and procedures to gain more control, independence, and efficiency in day-to-day activities and to participate more fully in community-based vocational and social activities (Johanson, 1997). When technology is used by people with disabilities, it is termed *assistive technology* (Franklin, 1991). When AT is used in education, employment, or independent living settings, it is frequently termed *rehabilitation engineering*. In most states, this is a service offered by vocational rehabilitation (VR) agencies (Flippo, Inge, & Barcus, 1995; Langston, Coker, & Smith, 1989).

Examples of technological support for students with health impairments are ventilators to aid respiration, intravenous nutrition, mobility aids, and artificial or transplanted organs. For students with orthopedic impairments, technology can include an array of assistive devices, from very simple pointing devices to motorized wheelchairs, robotic limbs, and voice and eye gaze–activated computer programs that help users to achieve greater independence in communication and environmental control.

Blackhurst, Lahm, Harrison, and Chandler (1999), adapting Melichar's (1978) listing of seven functional areas, have presented a framework for decision making regarding the areas in which AT might be needed and the types of technology to try. Table 21.2 summarizes the areas that a transition planning team needs to explore to assess the need for technology.

Independence and efficiency are important factors in today's workplace. Many of the accommodations made on the job are aimed at increasing autonomy and productivity. AT is a viable complement and/or alternative to a personal assistant for many who are seeking to become more efficient and independent in completing their job requirements. Although AT certainly will not replace the personal assistant, it can sometimes serve to reduce the number of hours that the personal assistant is needed on the jobsite.

The following example shows how AT can complement the workplace personal assistant. John worked for a heat exchange manufacturing plant and was responsible for assembling three types of sales binders. The material used for the binders was located on an 8-foot high shelving unit, and John was unable to gain access to much of the material on his own because it was stacked above his reach. To rectify this problem, John asked his personal assistant to aid him in identifying the most frequently used material. This information was placed on a "lazy Susan" file added to the corner of John's desk. Material that was used less frequently was placed within his reach on the shelving unit; infrequently used material was placed on the higher shelves. John could not perform many of the functions of the binding task independent of his personal assistant. In this situation, John utilizes his personal assistant on the job and a

Table 21.2. Functional areas and assistive technology needs

Functional domain	Functional skill area	Illustrative assistive technology
Existence	Personal health care	Built-up handle on hair brush
	Food preparation	Food chopper
Communication	Receptive understanding	Vocabulary tutor
	Expressive understanding	Talk board
	Interactive skills	E-mail
Body support, alignment, and posturing	Knowledge of support options	Armrests, rigid pelvic stabilizer, and so forth
Travel and mobility	Walking	Folding cane
	Using public transportation	Step lift
	Bicycling	Hand cycle
Environmental support	Time management	Memory aids
	Safety procedures	Picture-based signs
	Street crossing	Voice or visual crosswalk signals
Learning, education, and rehabilitation	Note-taking	Tape recorder
	Reading	Page turner
	Writing	Ribbed writing pen
Sports, leisure, and recreation	Attending scheduled events	Electronic calendar
	Hobbies	One-handed aids
	Group interactions	Internet chat groups

Source: Blackhurst et al. (1999).

simple assistive accommodation (the lazy Susan) to increase his autonomy and productivity on the job. John continued to use his personal assistant for other job tasks.

Students must have an understanding of AT to apply it effectively in the classroom, home, or workplace. According to the Technology-Related Assistance for Individuals with Disabilities Act of 1988 (PL 100-407), the legal definition of *assistive technology* is "any device, piece of equipment, or product system, whether acquired commercially or off the self, modified, or customized, that is used to increase, maintain or improve functional capabilities of individuals with disabilities" (2[b] [1]). This broad definition is appropriate because of the varied nature of AT applications. AT can be "high tech," which refers to equipment that is expensive and frequently has a computer component. Examples of such equipment include a voice-activated software system, an augmentative communication device, and an electric wheelchair. "Low technology" is generally more easily obtained and less expensive. The range of low-tech devices includes everything from Velcro to an electric stapler.

As consumers of AT, it is important to have an idea of the types of equipment that are available in today's marketplace. Often times, creativity plays a large role in the equipment selected for any given situation. Sometimes the simplest interventions can make a world of difference. For example, Andy, who was responsible for opening mail and entering billing information into a computer, found it extremely difficult to turn on his equipment in the morning. To turn on an electric letter opener, a computer, and a monitor took him about 10 minutes. A simple solution was identified: a power strip was added that all devices were plugged into. The power strip was fastened with Velcro inside a top drawer; he only had to pull open the drawer and flip one switch, reducing the time for completing this task from 10 minutes to 1 minute. Thinking outside of the box allowed Andy to become more efficient and effective in this seem-ingly simple task for the cost of about $10.

Researching AT is an important step in the identification of a piece of AT. In any given situation where a technological intervention may be beneficial, there may be many solutions. If the prospective user has a clear understanding of the options avail-able, then he or she is able to choose the device(s) that best fits the situation. Perceived stigmas associated with using AT may play a lead role in guiding a person's decision. A user must be comfortable with the technology selected or it will be abandoned.

Student Empowerment and Choice Making

Historically, recipients of education and human services have not been given much of a voice in what services are offered, how services are administered, or what the outcomes of services should be. The prevailing attitude on both sides of the provider–recipient fence seems to have been that "beggars can't be choosers." However, in recent years, we have witnessed a growing belief that consumers should gain some power over human services and, in the process, gain or regain power over their own lives. *Empowerment* can be broadly defined as the transfer of power and control over the values, decisions, choices, and directions of human services from external entities (e.g., government, agencies, service providers, social forces) to the consumers of services. The likely effects of the transfer of choice making to consumers would be increased independence, greater motivation to participate and succeed, and a greater degree of dignity.

Choice is defined as "the act of an individual's selection of a preferred alternative from among several familiar options" (Shevin & Klein, 1984, p. 160). This implies that choice making involves two parts—identifying one's preferences and then expressing those choices. Individuals with severe disabilities may have difficulty with one or both of these skills due to a lack of training on how to make choices, inexperience with choice making, little knowledge about possible alternatives, limitations with commu-nication, or frustration over not having choices respected in the past. People who have communication difficulties may express preferences through overt actions, whose meanings are not easily interpretable. Individuals with disabilities frequently respond positively to a question or answer in a manner they feel the questioner would prefer, because often they do not understand what is being asked, are not aware of the given alternatives, or do not want to jeopardize their chance to receive employment services. Unfortunately, these "choices" often translate into service delivery with little regard to whether the response reflects what the individual actually wants. It is likely that indi-viduals with severe disabilities will require additional assistance, support, or time in order to make and express their preferred choices.

In the past, individuals with severe disabilities were not given a choice regarding vocational services. An individual either met the eligibility criteria for rehabilitation work adjustment to "get ready" to go to work, or was denied services or relegated to sheltered workshops or day activity centers. With supported employment (SE), indi-viduals are not excluded or prepared; rather, the delivery of services is built around his or her current skills, abilities, interests, and preferences. The foundation of this model is the provision of individualized supports that will assist a person who has a severe dis-ability participate in the roles and settings that he or she prefers and chooses. Flexible, individualized supports allow an individual to rely on personal skills and resources to

Table 21.3.   Empowering consumers in supported employment

- Provide opportunities to choose from a variety of interesting, motivating, and socially and personally valued career areas. It is in these areas that job development or job tryout activities should be concentrated.

- Provide opportunities for expressing preferences and making choices between specific jobs based on such factors as pay, work hours, work expectations, compatibility with the supervisor or co-workers, and the degree to which the consumer feels comfortable interacting with co-workers or customers.

- In the areas in which there are multiple providers of employment services, provide the opportunity to express a preference for a particular provider based on personal experience or track record.

- Provide opportunities to express a preference for particular job coaches, again based on prior experience or track record.

- Provide opportunities for expressing preferences in training methods, adaptive devices, or compensatory strategies, based on ease of use, comfort or discomfort, stigmatizing effects, or any other factor.

- Allow consumers choice in either keeping a position, changing job responsibilities, or resigning and seeking a more compatible position.

From West, M.D., and Parent, W. (1992). Consumer choice and empowerment in supported employment. In P. Wehman, P. Sale, and W. Parent (Eds.), *Supported employment: Strategies for integration of workers with disabilities* (p. 32). Stoneham, MA: Andover Medical Publishers.

achieve his or her chosen lifestyle. For example, SE extends the right of choice to those people who typically have had few opportunities to choose how they want to live their life, where they want to work, and the services they would like to receive.

The opportunity to choose where one wants to work and the chance to change one's mind when that choice is no longer desirable has been shown to have a significant effect on the degree of job satisfaction that an individual experiences. Studies investigating job satisfaction of workers without disabilities have reported that the meaning of the concept is very individualized and factors such as the amount of pay, the personal relationships on the job, the amount of autonomy, the challenge of the work, the prestige of the position, or the steadiness of employment all vary depending on the individual. The factors associated with job satisfaction are no different for workers with a disability and will vary in importance, depending on the individual. Within all SE services, there are ample opportunities to empower all consumers (see Table 21.3).

ASSESSMENT OF YOUTH WITH ORTHOPEDIC AND OTHER HEALTH IMPAIRMENTS

Regardless of a student's academic skills and educational goals, assessment for transition needs should take a very functional approach. School- and community-based work experience programs are ideal for assessing functional abilities and limitations in work environments. This section briefly describes assessment questions that should be addressed by transition IEP teams (Thies & McAllister, 2001). These assessment areas are discussed in detail by Sowers (1991) and Sowers and Powers (1991).

Bathroom use: Many students with orthopedic and other health impairments have problems with incontinence, accidents, catheterization, transferring to toilets, and using handheld urinals and require assistance with toileting and other personal needs. Those who use wheelchairs also require accessible bathrooms. Transition planning, therefore, involves assessing future bathroom needs and planning for their provision.

Work endurance: Students with orthopedic and other health impairments often experience fatigue. During school-based work experiences, a student's endurance can be assessed on a multitude of tasks, which drive job placement decisions and adaptation needs.

Eating and drinking: The amount of assistance required for eating and drinking must be assessed. This includes time requirements, messiness, special diets, and any implications of these factors in transition to work or postsecondary education.

Communication: Meeting communication needs requires an assessment of the means of communication the student uses and the student's proficiency in receptive and expressive communication. Secondary communication modes may need to be developed if those within the student's repertoire are not functional in work settings.

Grooming: Grooming includes the student's personal hygiene and the type and appearance of clothing. Grooming can be problematic for some students because of limited use of hands and arms, visual or perceptual problems, or simply lack of experience with taking care of one's appearance. Because drooling or toileting accidents can occur, assessment should be conducted at the beginning of and throughout the work period.

Hand use: Hand use assessment includes the ability to grasp and manipulate objects, hand and arm strength, and amount of control over hands and arms.

Medical needs: For many students with health impairments, and to some extent those with orthopedic impairments, health limitations and the ongoing need for medical monitoring may be issues in future employment. For example, a student with a seizure disorder who experiences tonic-clonic seizures may need to have a place at the job where he or she can go to rest following a seizure or work-time adjustments for unpredictable "breaks" due to seizures. School personnel should include plans to bridge the gap between pediatric and adult health services and financing as a part of the transition IEP process (Bauer, 1994; Rinehart, 1994).

Mobility: Mobility assessment areas include the means that the student uses; distances that can be safely or independently traversed; and needs for accessible entrances, elevators, and so forth. Mobility assessment should also include the need for assistance from others and the need for adaptations to work areas due to limited range of motion or other motor impairments.

Transportation: Getting to and from work is a critical issue for students with orthopedic and, to a lesser degree, health impairments, particularly if the student uses a wheelchair or walker or lives in an area with limited or no public transportation. The transition IEP team may need to develop creative solutions to transportation problems, such as ride-sharing.

Social interaction: Assessment of social interaction includes appropriate and inappropriate social behaviors and responses to stress, criticism, pressure to perform, and so forth. Social assessment should occur in a variety of community-based environments, not just in educational settings.

Academic skills: An assessment of reading, writing, and mathematics skills leads the transition IEP team in targeting jobs and adaptation strategies. Academic assessments should also help the transition IEP team to identify appropriate postsecondary education or training needs and goals.

Tom is a 19-year-old student with severe cerebral palsy and mild mental retardation. He is nonambulatory and has very limited use of his hands. His speech is very difficult to understand, but he can recognize 30–40 sight words and can add and subtract using a calculator. He uses augmentative communication and can operate his motorized wheelchair.

Tom lives in a small house with his parents. His father is retired, and his mother has never worked outside the house. Tom's parents have difficulty in caring for his personal needs because of Tom's size and their ages. They depend on Tom's older, married brother to take Tom to appointments and on occasional recreational outings. A transition IEP was developed specifically for Tom (see Figure 21.1).

TEACHING STRATEGIES FOR YOUTH WITH ORTHOPEDIC AND OTHER HEALTH IMPAIRMENTS

As with assessment, teaching strategies for students with orthopedic and other health impairments in transition should take a very functional approach. Sharpton and West (1991) summarized this approach: "If a work skill or task can be taught, teach it; if it can't be taught, adapt it; if it can't be taught or adapted, support it" (p. 16).

For students with orthopedic and health impairments, jobsite interventions focus less on training in specific job tasks and more on adaptations of the work environment or job duties and support for the student/worker, the supervisor, and co-workers (Mast, West, & Johnson, 1996; West, Callahan, Lewis, Mast, & Sleight, 1991). The use of adaptations and support strategies in work settings for students with physical limitations has been labeled *jobsite enabling* (Sowers & Powers, 1991; Wood, 1988), a term that captures the importance of adaptation and support for future employment success.

For problems or performance impairments in each of the functional areas described in the preceding section, the transition IEP team members should explore the feasibility of the following adaptation and support strategies suggested by Sowers and Powers (1991):

- Redesign the sequence of the task or activity to eliminate difficult steps.

- Determine alternative means of performing the task or activity that are within the student's physical capacity.

- Rearrange the environment to permit easier access to work areas and materials.

- Position the equipment or materials to make the job easier for the individual to reach or manipulate.

- Enhance existing cues (e.g., signs, buttons, instructions) or develop alternative types of cues that the student can discriminate.

- Make or purchase assistive devices that alleviate difficulties with mobility, movement, discrimination, work speed, visual acuity, and so forth.

- Have a co-worker or other support person complete tasks that the student cannot.

DESIGNING AND IMPLEMENTING INDIVIDUALIZED TRANSITION PLANS FOR YOUTH WITH ORTHOPEDIC AND OTHER HEALTH IMPAIRMENTS

Although the transition planning process is generally perceived as focusing on the move from school to work, it is important to recognize that transition planning

Description of Student's Future Vision

Tom would like to be employed full time in a career in computers, data entry, or programming and live independently with personal assistance.

Individualized Transition Plan

Student's Name *Tom*

Birthdate _____

Student's Identification Number _____

School *Smithville*

ITP Conference Date _____

Participants:

Name	Position
Tom	*Student*
Claire	*Parent*
Lauren	*Teacher*
Sue	*Service coordinator*

Career and Economic Self-Sufficiency

Employment Goal *Tom will work full time in a computer data entry position in the Department of Motor Vehicles.*

Level of present performance: *Tom has a strong desire to be employed. He utilizes a computer in class using a head pointer.*

Steps needed to accomplish goal: *1. Tom will take computer classes. 2. Tom will be referred to VR. 3. Arrangements will be made for Tom to take STAR. 4. Tom will apply for Personal Assistance Service. 5. Tom will be evaluated for equipment modification needs.*

Date of completion: *June 1, 2005*

Person(s) responsible for implementation: *Teacher and service coordinator*

Vocational Education/Training Goal *Tom will complete computer training courses.*

Level of present performance: *Tom has used a computer for academics and recreation but has not taken any occupation-related courses.*

Steps needed to accomplish goal: *1. Review course/program options at community high school. 2. Enroll in classes. 3. Arrange for transportation and classroom assistance as needed.*

Date of completion: *December 2005*

Person(s) responsible for implementation: *Teacher and service coordinator*

Figure 21.1.   Tom's transition IEP. (From Wehman, P. [1995]. *Individual transition plans: The teacher's curriculum guide for helping youth with special needs* [pp. 243–248]. Austin, TX: PRO-ED; adapted by permission.)

Postsecondary Education Goal   *Tom will take computer courses related to his job at the community college.*

Level of present performance: *Tom's position will be at the entry level. He will need to keep up with computer technology advances.*

Steps needed to accomplish goal: *1. Identify course options (i.e., in-service training, community college course). 2. Meet with admissions officer at community college. 3. Budget for course and transportation. 4. Budget for personal assistance as needed.*

Date of completion: *December 2004*

Person(s) responsible for implementation: *Service coordinator, guidance counselor, and community college admissions*

Financial/Income Needs Goal   *Tom will be financially independent of his parents.*

Level of present performance: *Tom is dependent upon his parents for basic needs. He rarely obtains cash from his Social Security income to make purchases.*

Steps needed to accomplish goal: *1. Assist Tom in opening bank accounts. 2. Place SSI and wages in his personal accounts. 3. Teach Tom budgeting skills. 4. Identify computer software to help him manage funds.*

Date of completion: *March 2005*

Person(s) responsible for implementation: *Service coordinator, teacher, and Tom*

Career and Economic Self-Sufficiency

Independent Living Goal   *Tom will live with a roommate without disabilities in an accessible apartment.*

Level of present performance: *Tom wants to live independently. He requires assistance for all daily living activities.*

Steps needed to accomplish goal: *1. Arrange for residential services. 2. Arrange for personal assistance services for designated times daily. 3. Modify appliances for safety and increased independence. 4. Train Tom to use adaptations for self-care and safety.*

Date of completion: *August 2004*

Person(s) responsible for implementation: *Service coordinator and Center for Independent Living*

Transportation/Mobility Goal   *Tom will travel safely in his wheelchair in the community.*

Level of present performance: *Tom has had limited experience traveling on sidewalks or crossing streets. He can travel to familiar destinations on the school campus.*

Steps needed to accomplish goal: *1. Provide community-based instruction on safe travel in traffic areas. 2. Teach Tom, roommate, and personal assistant basic wheelchair maintenance.*

(continued)

Figure 21.1. *(continued)*

Date of completion: *March 2005*

Person(s) responsible for implementation: *Teacher and service coordinator*

Social Relationships Goal *Tom will functionally use an appropriate augmentative communication device.*

Level of present performance: *Tom has used a variety of devices to communicate, some of which were cumbersome and inflexible for various environments.*

Steps needed to accomplish goal: *1. Determine Tom's communication needs in different environments. 2. Schedule assistive technology evaluation at Cerebral Palsy Center. 3. Acquire funding for needed equipment. 4. Train Tom to use communication equipment.*

Date of completion: *January 2005*

Person(s) responsible for implementation: *Teacher and speech therapist*

Recreation/Leisure Goal *Tom will use the public library weekly.*

Level of present performance: *Tom enjoys videos, music, and books on tape. He does not have a CD or DVD player at home. Tom does not live close to a library.*

Steps needed to accomplish goal: *1. Assist Tom in obtaining library card from area library. 2. Budget funds for tape player and/or VCR. 3. Teach Tom how to use library. 4. Arrange transportation to library. 5. Teach Tom how to use tape player/VCR with adaptations.*

Date of completion: *April 2005*

Person(s) responsible for implementation: *Teacher and service coordinator*

Personal Competence

Health/Safety Goal *Tom will receive regular dental care.*

Level of present performance: *Tom has difficulty maintaining proper dental hygiene and rarely sees a dentist.*

Steps needed to accomplish goal: *1. Teach Tom methods for daily dental care. 2. Locate appropriate dentist. 3. Determine source of funding for dental care fees. 4. Maintain regular dental appointments.*

Date of completion: *November 2004*

Person(s) responsible for implementation: *Service coordinator and teacher*

Self-Advocacy/Future Planning   *Guardianship by Tom's parents will be transferred to limited guardianship by Tom's brother.*

Level of present performance: *Tom's brother has maintained close contact with him. Tom's parents are elderly and depend on Tom's brother for assistance in legal and financial affairs.*

Steps needed to accomplish goal: *1. Obtain legal services. 2. Document Tom's choices/desires for employment and independent living. 3. Transfer guardianship.*

Date of completion: *August 2005*

Person(s) responsible for implementation: *Family and service coordinator*

Student Career Preference

Working with computers

Student's Major Transition Needs

1. Employment
2. Residential services
3. Transportation
4. Assistance with self-care
5. Self-advocacy

Additional Notes

Judith has congenital spastic diplegia cerebral palsy but is mobile with Canadian crutches or a scooter. She has a learning disability and a visual impairment that causes her to walk looking down at all times, resulting in a severe problem with balance and frequent falls. Judith attended school at a special education center until she reached high school age, at which point she was mainstreamed into general education classes with resource help provided as needed.

Judith had some difficulty adjusting to life in high school. The size of the school itself, with more than 1,200 students, overwhelmed her. She had difficulty maneuvering around the building and was frequently late for classes, which tended to upset her more than her teachers. Judith was initially reluctant to ask for help from the resource staff but did when she found it was necessary to do so in order to keep up with other students in her classes. She was able to maintain average grades.

Judith's high school has two types of transition program options. One option is special education in a self-contained classroom in which students work on required subjects for graduation as well as job readiness and life skills. Frequently, students from this program make transitions to day programs or workshop facilities; sometimes, they enter SE programs.

The second option is JOBS, a program that includes general high school classes in addition to a job readiness class. Students begin JOBS in their junior year and frequently work

involves not only the student's future job and work environment but also his or her living situation, recreational and social activities, community mobility, and use of community services.

Transition from School to Competitive Employment

In many cases, individuals with even severe orthopedic or health impairments are able to locate, obtain, and maintain employment without specialized services or through time-limited vocational education or VR services that teach job-seeking and interviewing skills and provide career exploration, work experience, or work adjustment training. Individuals with orthopedic and health impairments may also need occasional assistance from co-workers, friends, and general employee assistance programs to complete tasks and solve work-related problems.

Outcomes-Based Planning Although models range from the practical to the esoteric, transition planning typically focuses on finding and obtaining employment, not necessarily achieving quality-of-life outcomes (e.g., reduced financial dependence, friendships, increased self-esteem and self-direction). Steere, Wood, Pancsofar, and Butterworth (1990) presented an outcomes-based planning model of transition for students with disabilities—based on a career planning model—that can be useful in identifying and achieving quality of life outcomes for all students with disabilities.

The outcomes-based model has three appealing features for students with orthopedic and health impairments. First, this model does not assume that employment is an end in itself but that it is instead a means of achieving a happy and productive adulthood for the student. Second, with the outcomes-based planning model, transition IEP goals and processes are consumer driven, based on the desired outcomes of the student and his or her family. Third, this planning process encourages the transition IEP team to explore transition creatively to achieve an array of potential postsecondary outcomes. The six-step approach to outcome-based planning is as follows:

1. During an orientation session, the team members are introduced, along with the student and family members, and a team leader is named to coordinate the efforts of the group. The steps of outcomes-based planning and a rationale for integrated employment are given during this orientation.

a portion of each day by their senior year. Transition options are supported by the VR system, and students are served by a VR counselor.

During her junior year, at age 17, Judith was referred to the transition program and the VR agency. She worked with the VR counselor to establish a program that would result in employment after graduation. She was enrolled in the JOBS program that met at 7:30 A.M. (Judith eventually came to hate the early morning and initially wanted a job that began at noon.) During Judith's junior year, the JOBS class included exploring types of jobs and careers and preparing mentally and physically for work. A transition team, which met quarterly during the year, was established that included Judith, her parents, the VR counselor, her JOBS teacher, and her high school guidance counselor.

Each spring, the VR agency sponsored a transition fair for students and their parents to learn about available programs. Included in this fair are representatives from workshops, skills training programs, residential programs, day training, and SE programs. After attending the fair, Judith and her parents were enthusiastic about a clerical skills training program that teaches entry-level clerical skills to people with disabilities and places them in clerical jobs. They discussed this option with the transition team, and another meeting was arranged with a representative from the training program. The program includes 6 months of individualized training, meeting every day for 6 hours. The next session began in July, but Judith

2. A brief biographical sketch of the student is presented that details his or her noteworthy characteristics and achievements. This may also include likes and dislikes, special interests, and support needs. The intent is not necessarily to identify skill limitations, but to focus on ways of building competencies.

3. A brainstorming session is initiated for generating possible quality-of-life outcomes with input from the student. This may involve some interpretations of the student's communication abilities and behaviors and possibly some preconference discussions with the student. From this brainstorming, a priority list of outcomes and definition statements, or descriptors, is generated through team consensus.

4. A measurement system is then identified for determining whether desired outcomes are being or have been attained.

5. The list of outcomes, descriptors, and standards is then used for initial compatibility screening with potential employment situations as they become available. As each is considered, team members also consider possible barriers and challenges that impede movement to the position. Possible solutions and action plans may be developed to serve as a framework for achieving optimum employment experiences.

6. The members of the team continue to meet to follow up on progress in the completion of action plans and meeting desired outcomes. The process can be repeated as deemed necessary to accommodate the student's growth and changing needs.

This method of planning can be used in conjunction with both the transition IEP and the IEP (Steere et al., 1990). It can also serve as a guide for selecting postschool employment.

Transition Between School and Hospital

Students with multiple disabilities have higher rates of illness and hospitalization than do other children (Caldwell & Sirvis, 1991; Surgeon General, 2001). Because of these special health care needs, students with multiple disabilities may be more likely to be absent from school than others. Anecdotal reports suggest students with multiple disabilities who require hospitalization may miss weeks or even months of school each academic year (e.g., Kenndy & Thompson, 2000;

still had 1 year of school left before graduation. After several meetings with the program staff, it was arranged that Judith would begin full-time training with the class in July until school began in September. Then, she would attend the training for a half-day during the entire school year. She would attend training during the morning and be back at the high school for afternoon classes. She would continue to attend the 7:30 A.M. JOBS class at the school. A school bus would be provided to get her to the training by 9:00 A.M.

Judith spent the summer with her VR counselor learning to ride the bus. She also attended a cooking class at the local United Cerebral Palsy Association (UCP) affiliate and learned to prepare her own meals so that her mother no longer had to come home to make lunch for her. In July, Judith began the training program with 12 other people. She was very enthusiastic and enjoyed the contact with others in the class. Her courses included filing, basic bookkeeping, typing, word processing, and receptionist techniques.

In September, Judith started her senior year in high school. She attended JOBS class from 7:30 A.M. to 8:30 A.M. at the school, then took a school bus to the clerical training program at 9:00 A.M., which picked her up again at noon to return to school. She had lunch and at 12:45 P.M. began her afternoon classes. Because of the structure of the training, it was decided that the process should be reversed during the second semester.

Monthly meetings were held with the transition IEP team,

Thompson & Guess, 1989). This is a concern because extended absences from school have been associated with skill regression and decreases in academic and social functioning (Browder, Lentz, Knoster, & Wilansky, 1988; House of Representatives, 1996; Rothman, 2001). Because of this concern, IDEA 2004 requires that explicit support strategies be developed for students who have IEPs and are hospitalized. These plans include the identification of a team to implement the IEP while the student is out of school and the specifications of what will be taught by whom during the absence.

A prevalent approach for preventing academic and social regression associated with hospitalization is the use of transition plans to specify and coordinate the types of educational services a student will receive during his or her absence. Recommended practices for school-to-hospital transition plans include: 1) specifying services to be provided at the hospital and/or home, 2) integrating those services into the student's existing IEP, 3) using a transdisciplinary, family-centered approach to decision making, 4) explicitly identifying individuals in different settings who are responsible for implementing the IEP and transition plan, 5) training those involved in implementing the IEP and transition plan, and 6) ongoing monitoring of the implementation of the IEP and transition plan (Graff & Ault, 1993; Parette & Barlett, 1996; Stuart & Goodsitt, 1996).

In a further look at the issue of transition, Borgioli and Kennedy (2003) studied the causes, educational continuity, and parental perceptions associated with students with multiple disabilities making the transition from school to hospital. A sample from the Southeastern United States was obtained for students who had been hospitalized during the previous 5 years. Interviews were conducted with the families of those students to collect information relating to their hospitalization and educational programming. A series of closed-ended questions revealed that 61% of all hospitalizations were for emergencies and that students were absent from school longer when hospitalizations were scheduled (38 versus 23 days). Only 1 in 46 hospitalizations actually had a transition plan to deliver education services while students were absent from school. Open-ended questions revealed two general patterns. First, parents were concerned about the absence of educational services and attempted to improve service delivery. Second, parents were not concerned regarding the absence of educational services and noted the severity of their child's disability as the reason. Their findings suggest that active efforts to provide transition services are needed for students with multiple disabilities when they are hospitalized.

which now included the training instructor from the clerical program. As graduation and completion of the clerical program approached, the focus shifted to finding jobs. The job developer from the training program worked with the VR counselor, the JOBS teacher, and Judith in selecting types of employment situations appropriate for her skills. Judith did very well at filing and receptionist tasks. Her typing was slow as a result of the spasticity in her hands, but it was very accurate. They made a list of employers who could possibly use Judith's skills and made appointments with several of the employers on the list. The job developer from the training program made the initial contacts with the employers. After 2 months of searching, a job was found for Judith as a receptionist with a large agency. She would be the first person encountered by visitors, signing them in and out, and monitoring people entering and leaving the building. In addition, she would answer incoming calls to the general information number, switch callers to extension numbers, and take messages on a computer.

The starting date was set for September 1. This provided some time to work on another of the family's requests—helping Judith to move out of her parents' home. Judith had been associated with an agency that provided residential services, and she qualified for a community independent-living program. She and a roommate moved into their own apartment in August. Together they were able to take care of most of their needs, requiring an aide only 3–4 hours per day.

Transition to Work for Youth with Physical Impairments

Individuals with physical disabilities have motor impairments related to a variety of diagnoses including cerebral palsy, muscular dystrophy, multiple sclerosis, rheumatoid arthritis, traumatic brain injury, and spinal cord injury. In addition, many individuals have secondary disabilities of perceptual or cognitive deficits and concomitant disabilities, such as sensory or medical conditions. Individuals with physical disabilities may have multiple needs and frequently require assistance in mobility, communication, learning, self-care, or decision making.

Employment issues for individuals with physical disabilities can be quite different from those of people with severe cognitive impairments. The term *jobsite enabling* (Sowers & Powers, 1991; Wood, 1988) is frequently used, which focuses less on jobsite training and more on modifications, adaptations, and compensatory strategies to assist an individual with functioning more independently. Other services from an occupational therapist, physical therapist, or speech-language therapist may be needed to assist with positioning, mobility, adaptive equipment, and communication needs. Due to the lack of a single agency being assigned responsibility for the coordination of services for individuals with physical disabilities, employment specialists may find themselves identifying and gaining access to services from other agencies or service providers, normally the role of a service coordinator. Similarly, not having an agency responsible for the delivery of services has created additional limitations with funding, administering, and staffing ongoing, follow-along services essential for SE. Transportation problems can further restrict employment options because specialized services or lift-equipped buses are often necessary.

Decisions regarding employment choices are also affected by the same issues confronted during service delivery. Communication, motor, and sensory impairments can make it difficult for an individual to express his or her preferences and be accurately understood by another person. The use of augmented communication systems and adaptive equipment can enhance one's ability to express choices and participate in the ongoing decision-making process. Emphasizing the physical environment (e.g., calm, comfortable, free of stress) and providing ample time (e.g., not rushing, waiting during pauses) are critical for valid choice making. Slow or uncontrolled motor movement and unclear speech should not be interpreted as an inability to choose, but rather as a signal to the employment specialist to utilize adaptations, modifications, or

When Judith began work, several adaptations were needed: very simple additions to the computer, a telephone headset, and an enlarged office directory. The job developer from the training program made weekly visits to help Judith to make a smooth transition to work. After several months, visits were reduced to one per month. This visiting schedule continues.

SANDY

Sandy has cerebral palsy that causes unsteady movement in both hands and arms. She was offered a position at a university student identification center as a customer service representative and camera operator. The camera is operated through a computer, which Sandy had never used. She spent the first week learning to operate the computer, while the job coach performed the other functions of the job. After that week, she was comfortable enough to begin adding other tasks to her repertoire.

Several accommodations had to be made to ensure that Sandy could perform her job independently. The first accommodation was to extend the focus knobs on the camera. This reduced her need to reach and made them easier for Sandy to manipulate. Next, an office chair that swiveled was purchased to make getting up and down easier. The chair also had arms to increase her stability. Finally, fine motor skills such as writing take Sandy a great deal of time to complete. In order to increase her speed in keeping track of who she photographed, a typewriter was obtained. Finally, a trackball was purchased to replace the standard mouse.

other techniques to make communication easier for the individual. Often just spending time together, listening to how an individual speaks, and observing his or her mannerisms of expression can eliminate the need to utilize additional supplemental aids.

The planning process for transition to work is similar to planning for the transition to unsupported competitive employment. Planning for these needs is critical because the level of support needed for the student to obtain and keep employment is high. Sowers (1991) recommended a three-step process for developing an employment support plan:

1. A student's work skills, experiences, and anticipated support needs in the areas of toileting assistance or bathroom accessibility, work endurance, eating and drinking, communication, grooming, hand use, vision and hearing, medical needs, mobility, transportation to and from work, social interactions and behaviors, and academic skills are summarized.

2. During a transition planning meeting attended by the student, his or her family, educational staff, and adult services agency representatives, the student's available resources are identified, including both formal and informal support mechanisms.

3. The transition planning team develops a plan for identifying appropriate employment options, the types and minimum amounts of supports to be provided, and the providing and funding entities.

It often happens that an individual who has severe functional limitations cannot perform some of the tasks that an employer expects of his or her employees. For example, an employee with mobility impairments may be able to complete work at a computer or copier, but not deliver finished products or visit customers. One technique that is often used in this type of situation is called *job carving* (see Chapter 11), which entails selecting a supported employee's work duties based on his or her strengths and abilities and reassigning those tasks that are too difficult or impossible. Job carving does not create a new position for the employee with a disability but allows an employer to reshuffle job duties to accommodate the worker with disabilities and, in the process, make operations more efficient.

Transition from School to Postsecondary Education and Training

Students with disabilities are enrolling in postsecondary schools in increasing numbers, although the exact propor-

Sandy used cheat sheets to remind her how to operate the office machinery, such as the encoder and the cash register. She also received a great deal of support from her co-workers. Sandy had problems manipulating money. She used a small tray to assist in carrying money back and forth to the register. This worked especially well when large amounts of change were involved. She also had to balance her drawer both before and after her work shifts. She was able to complete this without AT, but it was very hard on her muscles. In order to make the job less cumbersome, the job coach arranged for the donation of a surplus currency counter from a local bank. This technology made all the difference in Sandy's confidence on her job.

CARY

Cary is a 19-year-old man with sickle cell anemia, resulting in jaundice, fatigue, infections, and occasional vaso-occlusive episodes requiring medical care and even hospitalization. Despite periodic absences during relapses and treatments, he maintained good grades in high school and wanted to attend college to pursue a business degree. Cary's parents were supportive of his goals and willing to finance his education to the extent they were able.

During Cary's junior year, his high school guidance counselor convened a transition IEP team to help him and his family select a university. During the first meeting, the team members established three criteria: 1) the university they select should offer a business program up to the graduate level in case Cary decides to pursue

Table 21.4. Postsecondary education and training for youth with orthopedic and other health impairments

Educational institution	Orthopedic impairments (%)	Other health impairments (%)
Postsecondary vocational program	12.6	33.9
Two-year college	32.3	28.4
Four-year college	12.9	21.9

Source: Fairweather and Shaver (1991).

tion is not known because disability disclosure is voluntary. Students with disabilities continue to lag far behind those without disabilities in terms of participation in postsecondary education and training, however. Table 21.4 summarizes data about the participation of students with orthopedic and other health impairments in different types of postsecondary settings.

Section 504 of the Rehabilitation Act of 1973 (PL 93-112) prohibits discrimination on the basis of disabilities by programs and activities receiving or benefiting from federal financial assistance—a protection that was extended to all citizens with disabilities through the ADA. Subpart E of the rules and regulations for Section 504 of the Rehabilitation Act ("Nondiscrimination on Basis of Handicap," 1977) addresses postsecondary educational services and specifically prohibits discrimination in recruitment and admissions, academic and athletic programs and activities, student examinations and evaluations, housing, financial aid, counseling, and career planning and placement. In addition, schools are required to make modifications to academic requirements and other rules that discriminate against students with disabilities; to provide auxiliary aids, such as recorded texts and readers, to students with disabilities; and to ensure that social organizations supported by the school do not discriminate on the basis of disability.

The transition planning process includes decisions about which educational institutions the student will apply for admission—decisions made on the basis of physical accessibility, available accommodations, and the student's educational goals and abilities. The student and his or her family should be encouraged to arrange visits to schools to meet with service coordinators, tour the campus and buildings in which the student will have classes, and talk with instructors and other students with disabilities. If student housing will be needed, then the accessibility of rooms and the availability of domestic assistance can be assessed. These site visits provide more valid information than any college catalog.

After acceptance at a postsecondary school, the coordinator of services for students with disabilities at that school

a master's of business admin-istration, 2) it should be de-signed so that Cary could get around without excessive fa-tigue, and 3) the faculty should be willing to make allowances for Cary's periodic absences from class. Cary also stated during the meeting that he wanted to attend an out-of-town university. When ques-tioned, he stated that he felt overprotected by his parents and wanted to gain more inde-pendence. Although surprised by his request, his parents agreed to consider not only the two universities in their city but also any other state-supported schools as well.

Over the course of his junior year, Cary and his parents vis-ited four universities, meeting with business faculty and ser-vice coordinators. The fourth university they visited, located approximately 2 hours from his hometown, seemed ideal, and they decided to concentrate their efforts on getting Cary en-rolled there. Several factors led them to choose this university. Although the campus was large, it had an extensive bus system that connected the residence halls, library, and most of the buildings in which Cary would have classes. The university had comprehensive student health services with on-campus clinics. Faculty members of the school of business met with Cary and his parents and assured them that they would accommodate Cary's absences and would help him to keep up with his courses. The disability services coordina-tor impressed them with her knowledge of sickle cell anemia and its implications for Cary's educational career. She also as-sured them that she could arrange for notetakers or other

should be invited to become a member of the transition plan-ning team so that proactive planning can occur, even if ser-vices will not be sought immediately upon admission. If the student's health or physical condition worsens and problems with attendance or classwork arise, then prior knowledge of the student and his or her disability will help the service co-ordinator to make arrangements with the student's instruc-tors before the student's grades are affected.

EVALUATION OF TRANSITION OUTCOMES FOR YOUTH WITH ORTHOPEDIC AND OTHER HEALTH IMPAIRMENTS

Evaluating transition programs includes process and outcome evaluation. Process evaluation involves determining whether individual students are participating in transition planning and are meeting transition objectives. Outcome evaluation involves conducting follow-up or follow-along studies of stu-dents who have been through the program. There are four purposes of conducting outcome evaluations:

1. To assess the postsecondary employment or educational status of students who have received transition services

2. To assess adaptive behavior competence of students who have made transitions

3. To evaluate the degree of coordination of different agen-cies in the community and their effects on the adjustment of special education graduates

4. To evaluate the satisfaction of students and their families with the transition services they have received and to so-licit their suggestions for improving transition

These evaluations help to determine how students are per-forming and whether the school and family network are help-ing them on their journey to work and community adjustment.

CONCLUSION

In sum, students with disabilities are making transitions into an economic and social climate that is equally favorable or inhospitable to students with and without disabilities. Sur-veying representative samples of students without disabilities is suggested as another desirable feature for outcome studies. For students with orthopedic and health impairments, pri-mary questions for follow-along surveys include student mo-bility within the workplace and the community, use of and need for AT and rehabilitation engineering services, use of

assistance on short notice when Cary would have to miss class or could not get out to do library research or other class requirements. She had also made arrangements prior to their visit for them to talk with a student with a coronary disorder who had received similar services.

During Cary's senior year, the other members of the transition IEP team helped him and his family with the application process by planning for unforeseen contingencies. The disability services coordinator joined the transition IEP team and was instrumental in identifying problems they might encounter. For instance, Cary had applied for on-campus housing, but the service coordinator informed them that there are never enough dormitory rooms to meet the demand. In case on-campus housing was unavailable, their contingency plan was that Cary and his family would find an apartment on a bus route and advertise for a roommate to share expenses. Fortunately, Cary was accepted for a residence hall, and the contingency plan was not needed.

Another problem area was finances. Cary's parents could afford his tuition, housing, and meal plan, but not much else. The service coordinator brought financial aid applications to the transition IEP meeting for Cary to complete and Cary applied for scholarships and work-study. Between transition IEP meetings, the service coordinator met with the university's work-study coordinator and identified available jobs that would not fatigue Cary and were flexible enough to allow for periodic absences. Cary's transition went very smoothly, thanks to the thorough troubleshooting

and need for personal assistants or volunteer assistants on the job, involvement in postsecondary education and training, and satisfaction with transition services and the quality of adult life. Answers to these questions allow transition programs to individualize services for their communities and students.

This chapter has reviewed issues and strategies for successful transitions for students with orthopedic and other health impairments to postschool work, educational, and training environments. Key issues include the need for AT and personal assistants, self-advocacy, and the identification of appropriate postschool environments. In addition, students with orthopedic and health impairments and their families should learn the rights and assurances provided to them under IDEA 2004 and other disability-related legislation, such as the Rehabilitation Act and the ADA, and effective means of advocating for those rights. Functional assessment, primarily of mobility, endurance, medical needs, transportation, and physical assessment needs, helps to ensure smoother transitions.

STUDY QUESTIONS

1. What are the common manifestations of orthopedic and other health impairments?

2. Why is it challenging for many youth with orthopedic or other health impairments to have access to personal assistance services? What can be done during the transition process in order to make sure personal assistant needs are met after graduating from high school?

3. How can AT help youth with orthopedic and other health impairments in a workplace? Describe by using an example.

4. Why is empowerment and choice making important in transition planning?

5. What are the 10 areas of functional assessment for students with orthopedic and other health impairments?

6. Describe the adaptation and support strategies that can be used for youth with orthopedic and other health impairments?

and contingency planning of the transition IEP team. Cary is now in his sophomore year and is still in the business program. He works 15–20 hours per week in a computer lab, helping other students learn to use word processing, graphics, and spreadsheet programs. His health has been relatively stable, and he has not missed many classes for health reasons; his 7:30 A.M. classes, however, are another story.

7. What are the six steps to outcome-based transition planning?

8. Describe the process for developing an employment support plan.

9. What are some special considerations for students with orthopedic and other health impairments who are making the transition to postsecondary education?

22

Applications for Youth
with Traumatic Brain Injury

Pam Sherron Targett, Satoko Yasuda, and Paul Wehman

AFTER COMPLETING THIS CHAPTER, THE READER WILL BE ABLE TO

○ Describe traumatic brain injury (TBI), including information about its incidence and prevalence

○ Understand at least five unique challenges and difficulties faced by young people with TBI

○ Discuss the transition from the hospital and rehabilitation back to the school

○ Discuss the strategies necessary for conducting employment assessments

○ Be aware of ways in which compensatory strategies can help youth with TBI to enter the workplace

Preparation of this chapter was supported in part by Cooperative Agreement No. H133B9800036 from the National Institute on Disability and Rehabilitation Research (NIDRR), U.S. Department of Education. This support does not constitute official endorsement of the information or views presented here.

ROBERTO
AND JOSE

On a cold, late, winters afternoon, 15-year-old Roberto,
twin brother Jose, mother
Rose, and father John were
traveling home from their annual pilgrimage to the boys'
grandmother's house when it
began to sleet and snow. Because they were only about an
hour's drive from home, John
decided to keep traveling, but
to substantially slow down the
pace. About 1 hour later, and
only 10 minutes from their final
destination, visibility became
extremely poor as the weather
deteriorated and nighttime approached. Everyone in the car
was quiet and tense as they
continued on their journey
home. Suddenly, there was a
severe impact from behind.
The light blue sedan careened
off the road and crash-landed
upside down at the bottom of a
steep embankment. In the previous moments, a truck traveling at a high rate of speed had
suddenly swerved from the
passing lane into the other one
in an attempt to miss a fast
braking vehicle. Unfortunately,
although this prevented one
accident, it caused another.

The truck's driver pulled over
and called 911 for help. It took
about 20 minutes for the rescue
team to arrive. Rose and John
were released from the hospital
later that evening with minor injuries, but the twins were not so
fortunate. Roberto had experienced a broken leg and collar
bone as well as minor TBI. He
had lost consciousness for 1
hour. He spent 4 days in the
hospital and returned to school
a couple of weeks later. Prior to
his injury, Roberto was an average student with plans to attend
a technical institute to pursue a
career as a computer program-

Unfortunately, there are many school-age children who are
experiencing situations similar to those of Roberto and Jose
(see sidebar). Many individuals with mild brain injuries, like
Roberto, recover quickly and return to school with no immediate evidence of complications. However, problems may develop, even after mild brain injuries. Problems with academic
achievement may not be apparent for a year or more after injury. When problems are detected, they may not initially be associated with the injury, or patients and families may deny the
presence of mild impairments until more severe problems develop (Clark, 1996; Johnston, Goverover, & Dijkers, 2005).
Often, students with mild brain injuries find that fatigue and
attention deficits contribute to failure in the classroom.

Although some students with mild injury will need help,
most with moderate to severe TBI, like Jose, will require ongoing educational assistance. It is reported that between 9%
and 13% of students with TBI are referred to special education (Agency for Health Care Policy and Research, 1999). In
order to help each student reach his or her fullest potential
and enhance the quality of his or her future life, educators
should be familiar with TBI and best practices for transition.
This chapter provides an overview of TBI; examines some of
the common changes that a student may experience postinjury; and offers some insight into effective teaching, transition, and other support strategies.

WHO ARE INDIVIDUALS WITH TRAUMATIC BRAIN INJURY?

TBI, also called craniocerebral trauma, is the most common
cause of death and disability of children in the United States.
Each year, more than 1 million children sustain TBI and
more than 30,000 experience lifelong disability (National Information Center for Children and Youth with Disabilities,
2003). Advances in medical technology have improved the
survival rates and thus more people are recovering and eventually being discharged from the hospital back into their
communities to get on with their lives.

Brain injury differs from other types of disabilities in a
number of important ways. First, unlike many developmental
disabilities, TBI occurs suddenly. Because of the immediate
onset of injury, family members and survivors alike need time
and support to adjust to the reality of and effects of the injury.
Second, individuals who experience physical disabilities may
have their cognitive abilities intact, thereby allowing them to
compensate for lost physical function. However, TBI usually
affects intellectual and emotional functions, which limits the
person's ability to compensate. Third, TBI may initially go

mer. When discharged from the hospital, the doctor instructed Roberto to contact him if he had any problems and to follow up in 3 months. Soon after returning to school, Roberto experienced many problems such as frequent headaches, fatigue, and lapses in memory. His grades dropped. He also experienced significant depression as he began to do poorly, lose touch with his friends, and worry about his brother's recovery.

Jose was less fortunate. He experienced a punctured lung, damage to his spleen, and a severe TBI. He was in a coma for 6 weeks and afterward began intensive rehabilitation. Spring came and went, but Jose had not returned to school. Prior to his injury, Jose was an above-average student with plans to attend the local university to pursue a career as an architectural engineer. That summer he was discharged from the hospital to day rehabilitation where he continued to receive services until the insurance company would no longer authorize payment. On the last day of rehabilitation, the staff gave Jose a small going-away party and reminded him to use the various compensatory memory strategies he had learned. Jose returned to school that Fall and experienced a multitude of problems. Specifically, he lacked the ability to initiate activities and had a poor memory that affected his ability to retain information and learn. He also experienced extreme emotional outbursts on a regular basis over seemingly trivial matters. In addition, he did not use the strategies he had been taught in the rehabilitation environment because he was not able to generalize their use to this "real life" setting.

unnoticed to those who are not familiar with the person or unaware of the injury. Although people might notice visible disabilities, such as paraplegia, cognitive impairments may go undetected until some time is spent with the person.

TBI can lead to a variety of physical, cognitive, and psychosocial/behavioral changes. Examples of postinjury physical and sensory changes may include loss of motor speed coordination or balance, disruption in normal movements, changes in endurance and stamina, problems with vision and perception, or difficulties with speech (Gagnon, Forget, Swaine, & Friedman, 2002; Greenwald et al., 2001). Cognitive deficits may include short-term memory loss, limited attention and concentration, problems with processing abstract information, or inability to initiate and plan daily activities or solve problems (Flashman & McAillister, 2002; Hart, Sherer, Whyte, Polansky, & Novack, 2004; McDonald, Flashman, & Saykin, 2002). Psychosocial and behavioral changes may include irritability, impulsivity, depression (Starkstein & Lischinsky, 2002), a loss of identity and self-esteem, exhibiting socially unacceptable behaviors, and problems associated with changes in mood or emotional state (Bloom et al., 2001; Hayman-Abello, Rourke, & Fuerst, 2003; Jorge & Robinson, 2002; Kim, 2002; Taylor et al., 2002; Volgenthaler, 1987a, 1987b).

Prior to 1994, any trauma to the head or brain was called a *head injury*. In 1994, the World Health Organization adapted the term *acquired brain injury* (ABI) to describe any damage to the brain that is not present at birth. TBI, a type of ABI, includes any damage to the brain caused by an external acting force. These changes led the National Head Injury Association to change its name to Brain Injury Association (BIA) in 1995. The definition of TBI, according to BIA and the Individuals with Disabilities Education Improvement Act (IDEA) of 2004 (PL 108-446) are offered in Table 22.1.

There are other sources of acquired injury to the brain that are not traumatic in nature, brain damage due to birth trauma, stroke, anoxia, infections, and degenerative processes. This chapter, however, focuses on traumatic, not nontraumatic, brain injury.

Incidence and Prevalence

TBI is sometimes referred to as the "silent epidemic" because of the staggering number of people who sustain and survive injury each year. Annually, an estimated 1.4 million Americans sustain TBI (Centers for Disease Control and Prevention [CDC], 2001). This means someone sustains a TBI in

Table 22.1.   Definition of traumatic brain injury

Brain Injury Association (BIA)

Traumatic brain injury is an insult to the brain not a degenerative or congenital nature, which is caused by an external physical force that may produce a diminished or altered state of consciousness, and which results in an impairment of cognitive abilities or physical functioning. It can also result in the disturbance of behavioral or emotional functioning.

Individuals with Disabilities Education Improvement Act (IDEA) of 2004

An acquired injury to the brain caused by an external physical force, resulting in total or partial functional disability or psychosocial impairment, or both, that adversely affects a child's educational performance. The term applies to open or closed head injuries resulting in impairments in one or more, such as cognition; language; memory; attention; reasoning; abstract thinking; judgment; problem-solving; sensory, perceptual, and motor abilities; psycho-social behavior; physical functions; information processing; and speech. The term does not apply to brain injuries that are congenital or degenerative, or to brain injuries induced by birth trauma." [34 Code of Federal Regulations § 300.7(c)(12)]

the United States approximately every 15 seconds. As a result, an estimated 5.3 million men, women, and children are living with a permanent disability due to TBI (Thurman, Alverson, Dunn, Guerrero, & Sniezek, 1999).

TBI is the leading cause of disability and death in children and youth age birth to 14 in the United States (CDC, 2003). Each year an estimated 3,000 children or youth die as a result of injury, 29,000 are hospitalized, and 400,000 are treated in hospital emergency departments (Langlois & Gotsch, 2001). To put this into perspective, consider the following comparisons. The annual total number of individuals sustaining a TBI is eight times higher than the number of women diagnosed with breast cancer and 34 times more than the number of new cases of HIV/AIDS (CDC, 2003). The incidence of a TBI is 12 times greater than spinal cord injury in children and adolescents (Savage, 2000).

Cost Associated with Injury

In addition to the physical and emotional costs with which individuals with TBI and their families cope, they must also deal with new financial demands. Costs to society also exist in the forms of medical costs, lost wages, and insurance administrative expenses (Johnstone, Mount, & Schopp, 2003; Johnstone, Schopp, Harper, & Koscuilet, 1999; Wehman, Kregel, et al., 2003).

The additional burden of financial difficulties at a time when family members are grieving the loss of the person that their child once was can often lead to decreased family functioning. The costs of medical and rehabilitative care, as well as the increased amount of time needed to care for the injured child, often result in financial and work-related problems in families. Subsequently, it is not surprising that the occurrence of TBI has been strongly associated with increases in incidences of child neglect and abuse, divorce, loss of home, and loss of work in families (Sander & Kreutzer, 1999).

Determining Severity of Injury

TBIs are classified according to severity: mild, moderate, and severe. There are a number of methods that are used to determine the severity of injury. One of the first re-

Table 22.2.   Duration of posttraumatic amnesia (PTA) and injury severity

PTA duration	Severity
Less than 5 minutes	Very mild
5–60 minutes	Mild
1–24 hours	Moderate
1–7 days	Severe
1–4 weeks	Very severe
More than 4 weeks	Extremely severe

Source: Jennett & Teasdale (1981).

ported and perhaps most valid measure of severity is the duration of posttraumatic amnesia (PTA). Russell (1932) first correlated PTA with outcome and produced an assessment scale that he based on his findings; the scale was subsequently expanded by Jennett and Teasdale (1981; see Table 22.2). This duration has proved to be a valid indicator of the person's future outcomes in terms of independent living, productivity, and rehabilitative potential (Blumbergs, Jones, & North, 1989; Jennett & Teasdale, 1981).

Jennett and Teasdale (1977) also devised their own assessment scale—the Glasgow Coma Scale—on the basis of the level of responsiveness in eye opening, motor response, and verbal performance (see Table 22.3). Individuals are rated in each area, and the com-

Table 22.3.   Glasgow Coma Scale

Area of responsiveness	Examiner's test	Injured person's response	Score
Eye opening	Spontaneous	Opens eyes independently	4
	Speech	Opens eyes when asked in a loud voice	3
	Pain	Opens eyes when pinched	2
	Pain	Does not open eyes	1
Best motor response	Commands	Follows simple commands	6
	Pain	Pulls examiner's hand away when pinched	5
	Pain	Pulls a part of body away when pinched	4
	Pain	Flexes body inappropriately to pain (decorticate posturing)	3
	Pain	Body becomes rigid in an extended position when examiner flinches (decerebrate posturing)	2
	Pain	Has no motor response to pinch	1
Verbal response	Speech	Carries on a conversation well and tells examiner where he or she is, who he or she is, and the month and year	5
	Speech	Seems confused or disoriented	4
	Speech	Talks so examiner can understand but makes no sense	3
	Speech	Makes sounds that examiner cannot understand	2
	Speech	Makes no noise	1

Summed scores
Vegetative state = 3
Severe disability = 4–8
Moderate disability = 9–11
Good recovery = 12 or greater

Source: Jennett & Teasdale (1977).

bined score is used to determine a level of severity. This scale has produced consistent and reliable ratings of levels of responsiveness and consciousness across settings and raters (Teasdale, Knill-Jones, & Van der Sande, 1978), a formidable feat considering that *coma* is often a loosely defined term that can refer to various levels of consciousness.

Other formal and informal means of assessing injury severity include focal neurological signs, cognitive functioning, neurological complications from the injury (e.g., epilepsy, hematoma), and physical and behavioral sequelae (Jennett, 1976; Jennett & Teasdale, 1981; Ylvisaker, Hartwick, Ross, & Nussbaum, 1994). However, duration of PTA and the Glasgow Coma Scale remain the most commonly cited means and are frequently described as the most reliable indicators of severity of injury and potential for recovery (Jennett & Teasdale, 1981; Kraus & McArthur, 1999).

Course of Recovery

Recovery from TBI depends on a number of factors, including the severity and location of the injury, the preinjury personality and coping strength of the individual, and the types of resultant medical and psychological problems. Recovery from TBI is variable and may range from days to weeks to years (Wehman, Kregel, et al., 2003). Although recovery from severe injury is often slow and incomplete, many students will be able to resume preinjury activities with rehabilitation and the right supports.

Individuals who sustain minor injuries and mild TBI may experience mild complications, such as nausea, dizziness, or headaches, and may not seek or receive treatment. Others are sent home from the emergency department with instructions to take aspirin, rest, and call back under certain circumstances. This has helped attribute to the long-held assumption that people with mild injury experience no permanent damage or long-term effects (Vogenthaler, 1987a); however, evidence has shown that some individuals continue to have sensory, motor, cognitive, or psychological difficulties that inhibit the return to their preinjury lifestyle (e.g., Barth, Diamond, & Errico, 1996; Ponsford et al., 2000). Teachers should be on the lookout for students who show a sudden decrease in school performance or increase in behavior problems that did not previously exist. If changes are noted in the student's ability to process information, memory and concentration difficulties arise, or headaches and/or dizziness are noted, then it may signal problems stemming from a mild TBI. The teacher can communicate such observations to the family so appropriate action can be taken at home and within the school.

Even after returning home and to school, many students will need to continue to receive therapies to improve functioning and meet the new demands associated with return to community and to school (Hanley, Ward, Magnay, & Mychalkin, 2004). The functional capacities and limitations of a student with TBI are different for each person and can change over time. Because of the changing picture, it is important for educators to be flexible in their approach. Educators need knowledge of the nature of the disability because, unlike people with other disabilities, individuals with TBI often have multiple areas of functioning affected.

CHARACTERISTICS OF YOUTH WITH TRAUMATIC BRAIN INJURY

Those with severe brain injury are likely to have diffuse or widespread brain damage due to shearing and tearing of brain cells that result in impairment in all areas of function, whereas damage in a specific area of the brain will result in more localized problems. Youth who sustain a TBI may experience changes in their physical, cognitive, social, and behavioral functions (see Table 22.4).

TBI results in a unique combination of changes for each person and most individuals will have some residual skills and areas of strength. This can also mislead educators and family members to think that the student can easily perform at areas both below and beyond that level. Also, cognitive difficulties may not become readily apparent until the student reaches a new developmental stage or is required to learn more complex information (Savage, DePompei, Tyler, & Lash, 2005).

Although all of the effects of TBI present significant challenges, the cognitive deficits are often the most difficult for the individuals as well as for family members and educators to address (Johnstone, Vessell, Bounds, Hoskins, & Sherman, 2003; National Institutes of Health, 1998; Sherer et al., 2002, 2003). One reason relates to the fact that an individual with a mild or moderate head injury may have no immediate or outward signs of disability. For example, a person may not have any noticeable behavioral changes and appear "normal." Later, when the individual begins to exhibit problems such as not being able to remember or acts inappropriately, others may not understand the reasons why this is happening because the person looks "normal" and should act and behave in a "normal" manner. A number of factors will ultimately influence how well a student functions postinjury, including residual or preinjury skills and abilities; age at injury; severity of injury; medical treatment and rehabilitation; emotional or social adjustment; and support at home, in the classroom, and in the community.

ENHANCING ACADEMIC REENTRY AND INCLUSION

Savage and his colleagues (2005) are leading writers in the area of educational identification and classification of children with TBI (see also Savage & Wolcott, 1994), and have noted two major issues that are related to classification. The first issue concerns the usefulness and validity of medical classifications such as mild, moderate, and severe TBI. The second issue concerns classification of educational services versus rehabilitation therapy (e.g., occupational, physical, speech-language) that schools are required to provide under IDEA 2004. Physicians usually make clinical evaluations in the emergency room that may have very little or no utility in classifying and placing a student into educational arrangements. It is important for educators and families to understand the nature and severity of the injury (Kraemer & Blacher, 1997). The definition of TBI presented in this chapter provides a necessary starting point for an interdisciplinary team to make an initial determination of the nature of the disability. However, this information is descriptive at best and, along with the problematic issues surrounding classification, makes an impending placement very difficult.

It is critical for local hospitals and schools to develop policies and procedures that promote effective communication and discharge planning because medical services are the beginning of an array of long-term services that children with TBI will need (Bedell, 2004; Savage, Pearson, McDonald, Potoczny-Gray, & Marcgese, 2001). Lack of communication creates referral gaps when children are discharged to home or school (Christensen, 1997; Savage, 1997). Research examining the educational outcomes of

Table 22.4.   Changes after a traumatic brain injury (TBI)

Physical and motor changes	Mobility
	Balance
	Coordination
	Fluid movements
	Range of motion
	Swallowing
	Strength
	Endurance
Regulatory changes	Body temperature
	Eating habits
	Bladder control
	Sleep patterns
	Stamina and energy
Sensory and perceptual changes	Touching
	Hearing
	Tasting
	Smelling
	Vision and visual interpretation
Visual perceptual changes	Understanding relationships among objects in space
	Perception of how far away something is
	Recognition of familiar things
Communication	Understanding what is said or read
	Use of verbal or written skills to express thoughts
	Use or interpretation of body language
	Speech
Thinking and learning	Attention
	Concentration
	Memory
	Self-awareness
	Solving problems
	Planning and organizing
	Initiating and sustaining actions
	Monitoring and adjusting actions
Personal and social behavior changes	Impulse control
	Maturity level
	Conformance to social norms
	Emotional control
	Emotional expression
	Personality
	Perception of social actions
	Judgment
	Cooperation
	Use of alcohol
	Patience
	Happiness

Note: Changes in abilities may have been observed in a student who has experienced a TBI. Changes range from those that are readily observable to those that are not recognized by the casual observer. Individuals may also experience headaches, chronic pain, seizure activity, and side effects from medications.

students with TBI found that the time for students to return to school varied from 3 to 24 months postinjury (Stewart, Jacinta, & Douglas, 1998). Many students with TBI return to school while still requiring ongoing medication and rehabilitation services and their individualized education programs (IEPs) need to incorporate ongoing medical needs. For example, in a study that compared 50 students with autism and 50 students with TBI, whereas students with autism required 1–4 hours of consultative physical, occupational, and speech-language therapies every month, students with TBI required 1–4 hours of direct therapy each week. In addition, students with autism were prescribed a total of 12 medications averaging one dose a day, whereas students with TBI were prescribed 108 medications with 312 doses per day (Savage, 1991). This reality requires the school system to have a program that combines rehabilitation therapies with the traditional special education programs (Kaufman & Blanchon, 1996).

Teachers and peers need to be educated about the student who is returning to school (Savage et al., 2001, 2005), and support plans should already be in place (Tyler & Wilkerson, 1999; Ylvisaker, Szekers, & Haarbauer-Krupa, 1998). Upon return to the classroom, students may experience a number of academic changes, including enrollment in different courses, a reduction in courseload to part-time study, altered educational and vocational goals, and an increased need to use study-skills strategies. Many of the services that students will need can be managed through the student's IEP (Savage et al., 2001).

Inclusion in the general classroom is a preferred placement, but other placement options for returning students include mainstreaming with part-time specialized classroom or therapy services, self-contained classrooms, or residential placement. The development of the IEP, amid the recommendations of the interdisciplinary team, should lead to an appropriate placement. In making the placement decision, it is also helpful for the school personnel to observe the student during therapy session while still in the hospital and attend predischarge meetings. Information acquired from these observations and meetings, together with evaluation results, will help to determine what is best for the student.

To a large extent, the appropriateness of the placement depends on the flexibility with which the teachers and therapists are willing to provide services. Students with TBI should be given every opportunity to be included in as many general education activities as possible, academic as well as extracurricular. But continuing failure can lead to frustration, aggression, and greatly lowered self-esteem.

In helping the IEP team make an appropriate placement, it may be helpful to determine whether the child can 1) follow simple directions, 2) function within a group of two or more students, 3) engage in some type of meaningful communication, 4) tolerate 20–30 minutes of general classroom stimulation, and 5) attend to a task for at least 10–15 minutes. In a review of the numerous issues related to placement in different educational arrangements that may be offered by the school system, Savage (1991) suggested that the following points should be considered:

1. Does the school know the definition of TBI?

2. Does the school know what the child can do now?

3. Does the school know what the child needs to do next?

4. What environmental program changes does the child need in school?

5. Who will be responsible for the child's educational program?

6. How will the family know that the educational program is working for the child?

Savage et al. (2005) further noted that children with traumatic brain injury (TBI), regardless of the severity of the injury, often face challenges when living at home, in school, and in the community. Their needs are often overlooked and recognition of the long-term consequences is not always central to the management of the child in the school or community. Savage et al. provide references to pertinent literature and suggestions for intervention from the clinical experiences of four individuals with extensive experience of the family stresses and educational, cognitive-communicative, and behavioral challenges that occur after TBI in children. Savage et al. also provide information regarding these issues, particularly educational situations, and suggest methods that may be useful for service providers and family members. See Table 22.5, for tips for enhancing learning after TBI.

The challenges of identifying, classifying, and placing students with disabilities are only further compounded when a child sustains a moderate or severe TBI. Special education personnel know very little about TBI, and it is not surprising that these children are somewhat lost in the public education system. Because TBI is the primary cause of pediatric morbidity, however, it is essential for special educators to improve their knowledge base. Thus, in-service training for educators is a crucial component of academic reentry.

Table 22.5.   Problems and solutions for a student with TBI

Problem	Solution
Mary is unable to utilize emergency assistance via telephone.	A Duo/Speaker Phone is preprogrammed with emergency numbers (e.g., police, fire, ambulance) so that Mary can call them with the push of a button. Each word is paired with a symbol (i.e., "fire" and a flame). Her mother's work number is also programmed so that Mary can contact her at any time.
Mary opens the door indiscriminately because she cannot see who is there.	A surveillance camera allows Mary to turn on the television set to identify visitors visually. If Mary does not recognize the visitor, she is not to open the door, unless the individual provides appropriate identification.
Mary is unable to safely use appliances in her home.	Electronic buzzers installed on the stove and microwave alert Mary when an appliance has not been turned off.
Mary has difficulty remembering time and date.	A digital calendar watch helps Mary keep track of the date, month, and time.
Mary is unable to keep appointments, pay bills on time, or meet other deadlines.	Mary consults an electronic calendar daily to obtain information about appointments and deadlines. The calendar is programmed monthly, and instructions are listed sequentially. For example, the day before a medical appointment, the electronic calendar instructs Mary to call the taxi company to arrange transportation; the next day, the calendar informs her of the arrival time of the taxi as well as the time of the appointment.

Managing the Transition from Hospital to School

One important decision that individuals with the TBI, their families, educators, and medical professionals will be involved in is whether the student is ready to return to school and, if so, what supports and academic assistance are necessary. Not all students with TBI require special education; however, for those who do need assistance, it can vary from minor accommodations in the general classroom setting to home-based instruction or residential placements (Clark, 1997; Savage & Mishkin, 1994). Therefore, individualizing the educational planning is critical to meet each student's unique needs.

An increasing number of individuals are staying at in- and out-patient health care facilities for a shorter length of time. In addition, rehabilitation services may not be available due to a lack of financial resources or inadequate insurance coverage. This means that the student may be returning to school while continuing in or in need of additional rehabilitation. Differing degrees of support and assistance are available through federal legislation.

Meeting the student's needs in the least restrictive environment may be accomplished in different educational settings. For example, the student may be in a resource program with accommodation if needed for certain subjects and in special class placement when more support is needed. Summer programs may also be useful to help students stay abreast of and/or make up some of their academic losses.

Because students with brain injury and their family members typically have had no prior experience with special education or accommodations, they need information about IDEA and Section 504 of the Rehabilitation Act of 1973 (PL 93-112). Students who are covered under IDEA are eligible for 504, but those covered under 504 are not always covered by IDEA. To qualify for IDEA, an evaluation is required. Both require written plans (i.e., 504 committee develops a 504 plan, IEP team develops IEP) that give legal protection of rights. Accommodations are provided in regular education under 504 and special education under IDEA. Federal funding is available under IDEA, but not under 504. Finally, IDEA only covers individuals with disabilities through age 21, whereas 504 covers adults with disabilities as well.

Savage et al. (2005) and Hawley (2005) have indicated that a number of points need to be understood during the all-important school reentry process:

1. Initial reentry planning

2. Reentry activities through the rehabilitation admission

3. Reentry activities shortly before discharge

4. Transitional classrooms

5. Support to general classrooms

Much of the frustration and confusion experienced by family, school personnel, peers, and the reentering student can be avoided by reentry planning. Reentry planning consists of conducting a thorough student assessment, determining the appropriate school and classroom placement, and developing an appropriate education program well before the student returns to school. This means that the hospital service coordinator, social worker, or other outreach coordinator must immediately communicate with school personnel.

Educating Staff and Peers

Even if the special education teacher is familiar with TBI, it is unlikely that other school personnel will be familiar with the disability and the best ways to create a valuable and successful educational experience for the returning student. In-service training for key school personnel should include general information about brain injury and its impact on behavioral, cognitive, and physical function and specific information about the particular student's deficits and educational needs. The purpose of in-service training is to provide educators with information regarding strategies to assist students as they return to the classroom (e.g., environmental modifications) and enable them to identify subtle difficulties before more severe problems develop (Glang et al., 2004).

Peer education is a valuable tool that helps classmates understand brain injury. Peer education usually involves simple in-class presentations about TBI in general or specifically related to circumstances involving the returning student and can be enhanced through peer mentoring (Dopp & Block, 2004). This may help other students to understand the need for accommodation and may also increase the returning student's self-esteem.

To gather better insight into student functioning in the classroom, teachers may want to use an observational checklist such as the one presented in Table 22.6. Later, the information can be analyzed to try and determine patterns and effectiveness of strategies.

Using the Interdisciplinary Team Approach

Educators have found that using an interdisciplinary team approach is an effective way to assist students with TBI to accomplish their goals. Members of the team work together, communicate frequently, and set mutual goals for recovery and optimal performance. An advantage of the team approach is that each member has a unique set of skills to contribute to the treatment and intervention plan.

Team composition varies depending on the individual's needs and phase of recovery. Following are brief descriptions of each member of an educational and treatment team who may be involved in assisting the student with TBI with regaining the ability to function as independently as possible:

- The teacher is the leader of the educational team and helps the student and family make choices about transition goals, curriculum, and types of community placement.

- Employment specialists, also known as a job coaches, are knowledgeable about the employment challenges of individuals with TBI and provide specialized and individualized assistance in gaining and maintaining employment.

- The vocational rehabilitation (VR) counselor is a specially trained professional who offers career counseling and coordinates services that can lead to employment (Goodall, Lawyer, & Wehman, 1994). For example, the counselor is involved in counseling the individual and the family regarding work-related and independent living needs.

- A neuropsychologist understands how problems with the brain and nervous system affect emotions and intelligence and performs evaluations to diagnose emotional

Table 22.6. Observational checklist to identify problems that impede learning

Attention and concentration	☐ Does not follow teacher's instructions
	☐ Repeatedly asks teacher to repeat instructions
	☐ Fails to complete tasks or assignments
	☐ Does not attend to speaker and loses track of conversations
	☐ Switches from one topic to another
	☐ Switches from performing one task to another
	☐ Complains of difficulties understanding
	☐ Cannot maintain eye contact with speaker and gazes about classroom
	☐ Immediately attends to any slightly unusual occurrence (e.g., people moving)
Communication	☐ Cannot find the "right" word
	☐ Writing difficulties (e.g., spelling, sentence structure)
	☐ Slurred or very slow speech
	☐ Unable to read
	☐ Uses the wrong or nonsense word
	☐ Expresses frustration with inability to communicate thoughts
	☐ Becomes angry when interrupted during speech
Executive functioning	☐ Fails to follow agreed-upon plan of action
	☐ Although appears to understand, fails to initiate first step of task
	☐ Difficulty or inability to organize environment
	☐ Difficulty making plans to complete a task
	☐ Changes in routine cause confusion and anger
	☐ Lacks personal insight into difficulties experienced
Memory	☐ Does not follow instructions
	☐ Does not turn in assignments
	☐ Cannot remember how to perform simple tasks
	☐ Cannot remember locker combination or how to get from one area of the building to another
	☐ Loses assignments and books
	☐ Forgets names
	☐ Does not remember earlier events
Other	_____

problems as well as intellectual problems involving memory, learning ability, and arithmetic reasoning (Atchison et al., 2004; Boake et al., 2001).

- Occupational therapists are specially trained professionals who help individuals to regain their ability to carry out activities of daily living. Therapeutic exercises provided by occupational therapists improve the strength and the coordination skills required for eating, dressing, toileting, and bathing.

- Physiatrists are physicians who specialize in the field of rehabilitation. They typically have primary responsibility for managing the individual's day-to-day care after discharge from neurosurgical care.

- Social workers are trained to recognize financial and daily living needs. A social worker is likely to be involved in arranging for insurance coverage and placement for an individual after discharge.

- Speech-language pathologists have special knowledge regarding communication and language and help with basic problems in oral comprehension and expression. A speech-language pathologist may teach exercises for mouth and tongue muscles so the individual can develop better control in speech and eating.

DESIGNING SCHOOL-TO-WORK TRANSITION
PROGRAMS FOR YOUTH WITH TRAUMATIC BRAIN INJURY

The process for arranging and determining the most appropriate educational supports and services for a student with TBI is complex. When planning a transition program for youth with TBI, especially those who are 18–21 years of age, the transition team must extensively examine a future career. Specifically, those youth who are not attending postsecondary education should experience work in real employment settings (Clark, 1996). Therefore, the transition program presented in the following section emphasizes how to support youth with TBI in competitive work environments.

Research Related to Return to Work

Much of the research relates to return to work for adults with TBI. However, a review of it can provide some insight into problems that youth may face. Yasuda, Wehman, Targett, Cifu, and West (2001) reviewed the literature related to return to work for people with TBI. There are contradicting studies regarding the effect of severity of injury on returning to work depending on the measure used. The relationship between returning to work and duration of posttraumatic amnesia has not been identified (Brookes, Campsie, Symington, Beattie, & McKinley, 1987; Rao et al., 1990). Those who returned to work were likely to have shorter duration of coma (Dikmen et al., 1994; Rao et al., 1990) and better scores on the Glasgow Coma Scale at admission (Cifu, Craig, & Rowland, 1996). Despite the varying results, it is important to note that some individuals sustaining very severe injuries are able to return to employment relatively unhindered (McMordie, Barker, & Paolo, 1990; Rao et al., 1990), and not all investigators have found a relationship between injury severity and return to work (Brookes et al., 1987; Gollaher et al., 1998; Ip, Dornan, & Schentag, 1995).

The specific types of cognitive, physical, and psychosocial impairments associated with an individual's TBI may be more predictive of his or her return to work than the measure of injury severity (Sander, Kreutzer, Rosenthal, Delmonico, & Young, 1996). For example, significant physical disability, psychosocial impairment, memory/reasoning deficits, and history of alcohol abuse have all been linked to poor work outcomes. Acquired deficits in areas of social behavior, cognitive functioning, and personality, all of which can result from TBI, also are barriers for people with TBI in becoming successfully employed (Kreutzer et al., 2003). In addition, lack of diagnosis or identification of TBI-related problems and late diagnosis or identification of problems have been indicated as primary barriers to employment after TBI (Prigatano, 1995).

MARCUS

Marcus is an attractive 18-year-old student with a diagnosis of TBI. He speaks in complete sentences but has difficulty finding certain words. His speech is slurred. Marcus reads at an eighth-grade level. He has a poor short-term memory and has difficulty engaging in social interactions. He also tends to be socially inappropriate and hugs everyone he meets. Marcus, like many 18-year-olds, is interested in girls and cars. He indicates that he would like to be an automobile mechanic or airline pilot, like his dad.

Age is a significant predictor for people with TBI and employment outcome. People who were over the age 40 at the time of injury were less likely to return to work (Dikmen et al., 1994; Keyser-Marcus et al., 2002; Ponsford, Oliver, Curran, & Ng, 1995; Sander et al., 1996). Other factors that are reported to negatively affect returning to work include low educational attainment (Ip et al., 1995; Keyser-Marcus et al., 2002) and low level of social support.

Supported Employment

There are a number of VR programs for people with TBI, such as the New York University Head Trauma program (Ezrachi, Ben-Yishay, Kay, Diller, & Rattok, 1991) and the Work Reentry Program (Haffey & Abrams, 1991). However, very few studies compare current rehabilitation strategies in terms of their vocational outcomes. The supported employment (SE) model is an alternative approach that has been used to enhance return to work following TBI (Wehman & Kreutzer, 1990). It has been reported to be both successful as well as cost effective (Wehman, Kregel, et al., 2003). It is different from other models in that it attempts to enhance regaining work by providing vocational intervention, which includes training, counseling, and ongoing support, at the jobsite while the individual is already engaged in competitive employment. This allows employment specialists to help individuals overcome their inability to generalize or retain skills, as well as help with other social, behavioral, and physical impairments that traditionally have impeded them from maintaining employment (Wehman, Bricout, Targett, & Johns, 2001). The major characteristics of a SE model are 1) job placement made after an analysis of potential work environments, as well as the individual's abilities and support needs; 2) on-the-job training and advocacy efforts individually determined for each worker; 3) ensuring employer performance standards related to quality and quantity of work are achieved daily; and 4) after the individual reaches competence, ongoing monitoring of work performance and social adjustment with additional intervention as needed (Wehman, Kreutzer, et al., 1988, 1989).

The value of supportive work environments and financial rewards in long-term job retention has been empirically established for members of the general work force and, to a limited extent, other disability groups; yet, this work factor for people with TBI has only begun to receive attention (Keyser-Marcus et al., 2002). A prospective study by West (1994) found that individuals with TBI who experienced positive SE outcomes had been placed in positions that offered more opportunities for socialization with co-workers, more company-sponsored supports such as employee assistance programs, and other types of natural supports (Curl, Fraser, Cook, & Clemmons, 1996). In addition, work outcomes were enhanced by placement in jobs that offered fringe benefits, particularly medical insurance and regular reviews for raises and advancement. No other factors, including preinjury variables, injury-related variables, or postinjury services or work histories, appeared to influence SE outcomes.

The evidence is overwhelming that TBI severity has a clear and powerful effect on return to work (Wehman, Targett, West, & Kregel, 2005). Research literature supports this finding and is useful for practitioners planning on the amount of time and effort that will need to be expended in return-to-work interventions. Similarly, severe neuropsychological impairments influence work outcome. Those with the most severe cognitive impairments are less likely to reenter the work force successfully than those with mild dysfunctions. This is not to suggest, however, that return to work is unlikely and intervention is ineffectual. Emerging technologies, including SE, assistive technology, job carving, and workplace accommodations, can mitigate the effects of cognitive, physical, and psychosocial impairments resulting from TBI.

EMPLOYMENT SUPPORTS

Community-based work experiences—paid or unpaid, part time or full time—are extremely valuable activities that should be provided as early as possible during the postacute phase. Engaging regularly in productive community work experiences helps students discover their work preferences, ambitions, and needs (Wehman, Kregel, et al., 2003).

The first step is to assist the student with exploring various career options and develop a better understanding of what career path he or she wants to pursue. Next, on-the-job supports are arranged or provided to assist the student with learning a job. Finally, if using SE, long-term, ongoing job retention services are offered. This section will review some strategies related to vocational assessment, on-the-job support, and long-term follow up.

Most quality school-to-work transition programs for students with TBI concentrate on an individual's interests and preferences because people work most effectively in jobs they like, a particularly relevant assumption for people with TBI who often feel a need to gain control over at least some aspects of their lives (Fraser, 2000). In determining vocational goals and expectations for students with TBI, the following should be considered:

- What type of work is the individual interested in doing?

- What type of work at home or in the community, if any, has the person done preinjury? Postinjury?

- What are the family's work expectations for the individual?

- What are the person's existing skills and support needs?

- What supports does the individual use now?

- What is the individual's ability to learn new skills?

- What teaching strategies seem to work best?

If these issues are not considered before the job search, job seekers may repeatedly refuse potential employment interviews or accept jobs in which they are unhappy, which affect retention (Wehman, Bricout, & Targett, 2000).

Unfortunately, many individuals hold unrealistic vocational expectations because brain injury itself can cause diminished self-sight and lower ability to solve problems and perceive situations correctly (Sherer et al., 2003). Families contribute to denial by

Table 22.7. Developing community-based vocational assessment sites

1. Identify a variety of businesses in the community that make up the local labor market and will offer students options from which to choose.

2. Contact the appropriate business representative (e.g., human resources representative, CEO) and schedule an appointment to visit the organization.

3. During the visit, describe the purpose of situational assessment and the responsibilities of the employer, school personnel, and student during an assessment. If the company agrees to participate in a situational assessment, then schedule an appointment to meet with department supervisors.

4. Meet with department supervisors and identify tasks suitable for situational assessment. Arrange to observe workers performing the targeted work and develop task analyses and other data collection tools.

5. Identify students to participate in the assessment, schedule times, arrange transportation, and get necessary releases signed. Depending on the tasks performed, the amount of information desired, and the needs of the student and employer, the length of time required for an assessment might range from hours to several days and possibly longer under some circumstances.

6. Complete the assessment and record observations and work-related skills, abilities, interests, and support needs.

7. Provide verbal feedback on the experience to the student, family members, and other staff.

8. Plan next steps (e.g., additional assessments, community-based training, paid employment).

Note: Prior to establishing sites, staff should be familiar with the U.S. Department of Labor standards.

predicting a complete recovery in which the individual will return to preinjury employment (Kreutzer, Wehman, Morton, & Stonnington, 1988; Sander & Kreutzer, 1999). Intervention through education or counseling may be necessary if the desires and work expectations of the individual and family conflict with the professional opinions of the transition staff.

Situational Assessment

Actual work settings are used in situational assessments to enable students to test their interests in job duties and work environments, to observe students' responses to training strategies, and to identify needs for support. Because a real worksite offers characteristics that are common to most work environments (e.g., interruptions in routine, distractions), this approach to assessment has a greater likelihood of yielding information relevant to a job placement than assessments performed in an office or facility-based setting. Table 22.7 outlines the basic steps for developing situational assessment sites.

Career Search Exercise

Numerous tools, such as standardized career interest inventories and computerized vocational assessment programs, are available. Consider, though, that many of these tools were not specifically developed for people with physical or cognitive disabilities associated with TBI. Nonetheless, working through a career search exercise with a student can yield valuable assessment information in addition to helping the student to identify potential jobs.

Writing a Functional Résumé

The process of writing a résumé can be useful to students with TBI and program staff in clarifying and defining vocational goals. Depending on the type and level of position to be pursued, an employer may require a résumé instead of, or in addition to, a job application. Although a traditional chronological résumé can be utilized, sometimes a functional résumé is more useful. A functional résumé portrays an individual's broad skill areas developed as a result of employment, volunteer, recreational, and educational experiences and is ideal for individuals who have limited pre- and/or postinjury work experience or for those who have not retained many of their preinjury cognitive, academic, or physical skills.

Setting Vocational Transition Goals

Once assessments are completed, the transition goals need to be established (Condeluci, 1994; DePompei & Blosser, 1999; Savage & Wolcott, 1994). The student, family, and other team members must confer to identify next steps. The transition team can then take this information and form a job search and support plan.

Many individuals with severe injury will benefit from job coach assistance. This involves having an employment specialist or job coach facilitating or providing jobsite support and training and continually monitoring and assessing an individual's employment situation and corresponding needs. The goal of providing on-the-job supports is to close the gap between the new employee's ability on the first day of work and the employer's ultimate requirements for maintaining and retaining a job.

On-the-Job Skills Training

Sometimes a student with a TBI will need additional skills training on how to perform various job functions and particularly on how to use specific compensatory strategies. Sometimes this instruction will need to be provided by a job coach or employment specialist because the employer will not have the resources to allow for the additional time needed. The employment specialist will also make sure all the work is complete, if possible. Thus, the newly hired student will receive the additional help needed to learn how to get the job done, and the employer's work is completed in a timely manner. A number of instructional strategies have been used to teach employees with TBI on the job and help them gain access to various supports (see Table 22.8). The most important thing to keep in mind is that instructional strategies must be individualized to the learner and the work setting as well as to the task being taught.

Implementation Strategies, Adaptations, Modifications, and Restructuring

The implementation of compensatory strategies, adaptations, and modifications, in addition to restructuring the work environment, can enhance a student's learning and promote the ability to perform independently at a jobsite. As mentioned previously, adjustments can be cognitively oriented, providing the individual with effective ways to remember what to do and how to do it (e.g., a worksheet outlining the steps needed to balance a cash drawer, a map that outlines a route to follow when cleaning apartment grounds, detailed written instructions to follow when cleaning plants). Other im-

Table 22.8.   Instructional strategy

Strategy	Possible uses	Examples
Modeling: Trainer provides the learner with a correct and positive model to follow.	Training series of steps in task Training physical skills Training behaviors difficult to explain or describe with words	Greeting customers Folding boxes Arranging a reservation with a specialized transportation provider for a ride to work
Role playing: Trainer explains how a situation should be handled and gives learner a chance to practice the correct response. (Trainer and learner take turns/switch roles).	Developing face-to-face interactions Developing verbal interactions with others	Meeting co-workers Responding to supervisory feedback Answering the telephone
Least prompts: Trainer provides the least amount to most amount of assistance in the form of a prompt, using a prompting hierarchy.	Training series of steps in a task	Filing medical charts Using a cash register Learning to use a map to orient to various work areas

plementations may be used to compensate for physical limitations (e.g., providing a lapboard for individuals involved in data entry to reduce ataxia, use of a stand to reduce unsteadiness in upright positions while an individual sorts mail). Development and implementation of strategies usually occur when an individual encounters difficulty in learning a new task, shows great variability in task performance, or is unable to meet the required production standard. A review of probe data reveals where difficulties arise.

To increase their effectiveness, compensatory strategies must be functional and unobtrusive in work settings, and they should be developed in conjunction with family members and the individual who will be using them. Family members are especially resourceful because they know about compensatory strategies that have been used successfully in the home. As students with TBI go to work, their independence and productivity can be enhanced through the development of effective compensatory strategies and physical adaptations. Here are some additional examples of strategies that can be used in employment settings to help foster independence:

- *Use lists to compensate for memory problems.* Information can be written in a pocket notebook or an appointment book or listings posted where a particular task or behavior is to occur. Checklists can be used to remind the student that certain activities have been completed.

- *Use individual auditory or visual cues.* Tape-recorded messages or instructions are excellent auditory cues. Different colored containers can serve as visual cues for specific items. Structure the environment to enhance functioning. Accommodate endurance levels and stress tolerance by sequencing tasks (e.g., schedule more difficult tasks first to alleviate fatigue). Change the environment, if possible, to decrease stress that may result from excessive noise or temperatures.

- *Use physical adaptations.* Trays or jigs can help students to keep materials in place and improve work speed. Materials such as electric staplers, rubber band holders, rubber fingertips, and laminated work materials increase work efficiency.

JOE

Joe is a 15-year-old who sustained a TBI in a serious car accident. He was in a coma for more than 2 months and was hospitalized for 5 months. Since the injury, Joe uses a leg brace and walks with a cane. He has little control over the tremors in his right hand and has difficulty seeing out of his left eye. Prior to his injury, Joe worked part-time as a grocery clerk and animal care attendant during the summers. After returning to school, Joe indicated a desire for a part-time job that took advantage of his numerical acumen.

A 20-hour-per-week job as an auditor at a large accounting firm was located. The job involved processing expense and merchandise checks and digitally storing documents. Joe, with help from a job coach, learned all of his jobs within 40 days.

Despite Joe's rapid skill acquisition, problems with work quality and skill maintenance occurred during the first 4 months of employment. These problems included forgetting the steps involved in the job, slow production rate, difficulty in operating the equipment, and sequencing and addition errors. The following job modifications and adaptations helped to improve Joe's job performance:

1. The worktable was elevated using two wooden two-by-fours.

2. Written notes related to missed steps were posted as visual cues.

3. A keyguard was used to help prevent hitting incorrect keys.

4. Large paper clips were substituted for small ones.

5. An electric stapler replaced the manual one.

Joe also had problems outside of work, including periodic drinking binges and poor nutrition. Therefore, an off-site intervention plan was put into place to help address these problems.

Joe continued to work 20-hour weeks. When he left school, he was offered a full-time job with benefits. Today, Joe lives independently. He has purchased a stereo and a new car. He still goes out socially, but much less frequently than he did before. His work quality remains stable, and a job coach continues to visit him periodically.

- *Rearrange the immediate work area.* To save time, reduce confusion, and compensate for specific limitations, arrange the workspace, the sequence of job tasks, and the overall workday so that the majority of time on the job is productive. For example, place work materials on the left if the student has problems with the right visual field or situate an individual apart from other workers if distractibility is a concern.

The three case studies (see sidebars) illustrate how effective supports can be provided to assist individuals with TBI with going to work.

It is important that the student perceive the usefulness of compensatory strategies and participate in the planning process. The guidelines listed in Table 22.9 may be useful when discussing the development of a compensatory strategy, adaptation, modification, or job restructuring with a student.

Long-Term Support and Service Coordination

If using SE, the employment specialist fades his or her presence from the employment site as the new employee successfully and independently demonstrates the ability to perform the job requirements. This is referred to as *fading*, and, once the person reaches stabilization, the follow-along or long-term support phase of SE begins. From a funding point of view, this is the point of time when time-limited funding is terminated and extended service funding starts. The guidelines for determining stabilization and funding will differ from state to state.

During this job retention phase of SE, the employment specialist continues to monitor how the employee is doing from both the worker's and employer's perspectives. As warranted, additional support services are arranged or delivered by the employment specialist. Some reasons for intervention may include the need to learn a new job duty, the arrival of a new supervisor, the need to develop interpersonal relations, and the diminishment of good work

STAN

Stan is a 24-year-old who experienced TBI after falling asleep while driving and crashing his car. He was not discovered for nearly 12 hours. Stan was in a coma for 21 days. Following the injury, Stan had decreased short-term memory, difficulty following instructions, poor concentration, occasional confusion, and reduced physical mobility on the left side.

Prior to the accident, Stan wrote for his school newspaper and planned to pursue a degree in journalism as a sportswriter. He returned to school 8 months after his injury. Through the transition to work program, he became employed at a law firm as a document copier. He quit the job 1 month later because he could not meet the firm's high-paced production standards.

A position as an activities aide at a retirement home became available. The job involved 20 hours of work per week at $6.50 per hour. Job duties involved one-to-one visitations with residents who were unable to leave their rooms independently. The job also required documentation of these visits on a patient interaction report for funding purposes.

Stan's interest in working with people, his good communication skills, and his preference for nonrepetitive work made him a good candidate for the position. In addition, the job duties placed minimal demands on his visual and motor skills. The work environment was fairly quiet, which increased Stan's ability to concentrate on job tasks.

A job coach played a major role in structuring and organiz-

Table 22.9.   Guidelines for developing compensatory strategies

1. Determine student's strengths and preferred learning style.

2. Commend performance to date in areas in which the individual does well.

3. Ask student to describe performance in certain areas to gauge insight into a knowledge of areas that are not presenting difficulties. If student recognizes a problem area, then solicit ideas on possible ways to improve and go to Step 7.

4. If student does not recognize a problem, then set up an opportunity for problem to present itself. When it occurs, bring it to the student's attention and go to next step.

5. Have student state concerns and identify ways to enhance performance.

6. Review data, indicate the individual's current performance, and explain the importance of accomplishing task/improving performance.

7. Brainstorm ideas on potential strategies to use in order to enhance performance.

8. Reinforce student's ideas. If ideas are unrealistic, then guide the individual through a decision-making process that will lead to the agreed-upon objective.

9. Whenever possible, give the student control (e.g., what size the checklist should be, what color notebook it should be, what words are used).

10. Commend the student for selecting a strategy and explain that strategies may be removed at some point in time.

11. Discuss the positive aspects of using the strategy (e.g., continued employment and independence) with the student and reinforce.

12. Train the student to use the strategy (if tangible, item training should include where to store it and a back-up strategy if it is lost).

habits. The goal is to keep tabs on how the employee-employer relationship is developing and provide either party with additional support to make this a mutually beneficial experience.

During this time, the employment specialist will continue to collect data and make observations to document performance. Some areas that the employment specialist will want to remain aware of include the following: dependability, job performance, use of and effectiveness of compensatory strategies, jobsite relationships, satisfaction with work, and any other factors outside of work that may adversely affect job performance if left unattended (Wehman, Bricout, & Targett, 2000). It is very important that the employment specialist use techniques that do not interrupt the natural flow of business to accumulate data or make observations. The best and most unobtrusive way to do this will vary from business to business, and the employee should be involved in determining the techniques to be used. Many companies will have set schedules for

ing the work so Stan could accomplish it independently. In addition, the job coach modeled appropriate ways to interact during visits and gave Stan feedback on his performance.

Today, a job coach contacts Stan and the employer twice a month to ensure all is well. Stan, the coach, and the activities director meet quarterly to update the visitation schedule. Stan has been employed for 15 months and expresses a strong desire to work in this field full time when he exists school next year.

RUFUS

Rufus is employed part time as an order entry operator for a pizza company. His duties include taking incoming calls from customers, ordering pizza, and routing orders to the appropriate distribution centers via computer terminal. Rufus had minimal problems learning the necessary skills for his job. In fact, he learned how to do the job by the second week of employment. However, because of physical and cognitive limitations (i.e., left-hand ataxia; right-side hemiplegia; slowed, disorganized thinking), he was unable to consistently work fast enough to meet the employer's production standard. Factors contributing to his slow speed were his inability to press the SHIFT key and other keys simultaneously and difficulty turning the pages of a

evaluating employees' performance that can also be used to validate the finding of the employment specialist.

CONCLUSION

TBI affects thousands of youth each year. The physical, cognitive, and psychological/ behavioral changes experienced by people with TBI range from mild to severe and have varying impacts on return to school and eventual employment. The role of transition planning is central in that the unique challenges of these young people are formidable and may include distorted vocational aspirations, serious cognitive and psychological problems, and ongoing physical disabilities. Work is an important medium for therapeutically overcoming many of the obstacles they face and with which they will need to learn to live. A combination of work and school (e.g., a part-time job and participation in the community college) is often an effective bridge from school into the world of work. The combined efforts of family, education, and intervention team members play an important role in this process.

Table 22.10.   Rufus's workplace supports

Problem	Possible solutions
Inability to press shift key and other keys simultaneously (Rufus types with his left hand due to right-hand paralysis.)	Use a computer accessory Use a SHIFT key device Program the computer to allow sequential pressing of certain keys
Slow rate of data entry due to periods of increased extraneous movement caused by left-hand ataxia	Use a lapboard to give arm stability Raise the surface on the keyboard using double-sided tape to give hand stability
Difficulty turning pages of city map due to left-hand ataxia and right-hand hemiplegia	Use an automatic page turner Laminate pages of map in a binder and use tabs Laminate map and hang it on a wall
Inability to remember exceptions to basic routine	Program computer to flag special exception orders
Frequent inapproprate requests (e.g., requests for longer lunch break because of his disability)	Provide counseling on appropriate versus inappropriate requests Encourage Rufus to discuss appropriate requests with his employer

city map used to locate customer delivery areas. This was due to increased extraneous movement caused by left-hand ataxia and poor fine motor skills.

In addition, at times Rufus could not recall procedures for exceptions to the basic routine (e.g., remembering to calculate a 10% discount if a customer ordered 10 or more pizzas). Finally, Rufus made frequent requests for special considerations. A physical therapist and job coach went in to assist him. Some modifications, adaptations, and interventions that were effective in alleviating these issues and are listed in Table 22.10.

STUDY QUESTIONS

1. What is TBI? What are some of its causes, and how does it affect the individual, the family, and the community?

2. How is severity of TBI assessed?

3. How does TBI affect a youth's life?

4. Who are typically involved in the IEP planning team for students with TBI, and what are their roles?

5. Why is using the interdisciplinary team approach especially important for students with TBI?

6. What should be taken into consideration when determining vocational goals and expectations for students with TBI?

7. What are some examples of compensatory strategies and physical adaptation that can be used to accommodate injury-related disability?

8. What factors typically enhance the likelihood of successful vocational outcomes for individuals who have sustained TBI?

References

Abbott, M., Walton, C., Tapia, Y., & Greenwood, C.R. (1999). Research to practice: A "blueprint" for closing the gap in local schools. *Exceptional Children, 65,* 339–352.

AbleLink Technologies, Inc. (2005). Visual Assistant [Computer software]. Retrieved April 21, 2003, from http://www.ablelinktech.com/_handhelds/productview.asp?ID=19

Agency for Health Care Policy and Research. (1999). *Rehabilitation for traumatic brain injury in children and adolescents. Summary, evidence reports/technology assessment: Number 2, Supplement.* Rockville, MD: Author. Available on-line at http://www.ahrq.gov/clinic/epcsums/tbisum2.htm

Agran, M. (1997). *Student directed learning: Teaching self-determination skills.* Pacific Grove, CA: Brooks/Cole.

Agran, M., Alper, S., & Wehmeyer, M. (2002). Access to the general curriculum for students with significant disabilities: What it means to teachers. *Education and Training in Mental Retardation and Developmental Disabilities, 37*(2), 123–133.

Agran, M., Blanchard, C., & Wehmeyer, M.L. (2000). Promoting transition goals and self-determination through student self-directed learning: The Self-Determined Learning Model of Instruction. *Education and Training in Mental Retardation and Developmental Disabilities, 35*(4), 351–364.

Agran, M., Fodor-Davis, J., & Moore, S. (1986). The effects of self-instructional training on job-task sequencing: Suggesting a problem-solving strategy. *Education and Training in Mental Retardation, 21,* 273–281.

Agran, M., King-Sears, M., Wehmeyer, M.L., & Copeland, S.R. (2003). *Teachers' guides to inclusive practices: Student-directed learning.* Baltimore: Paul H. Brookes Publishing Co.

Agran, M., Martin, J.E., & Mithaug, D.E. (1989). Achieving transition through adaptability instruction. *TEACHING Exceptional Children, 21,* 4–7.

Agran, M., & Moore, S.C. (1994). *How to teach self-instruction of job skills.* Washington, DC: American Association on Mental Retardation.

Agran, M., Salzberg, C.L., & Stowitschek, J.J. (1987). An analysis of the effects of a social skills training program using self-instructions on the acquisition and generalization of two social behaviors in a work setting. *Journal of The Association for Persons with Severe Handicaps, 12,* 131–139.

Agran, M., Sinclair, T., Alper, S., Cavin, M., Wehmeyer, M., & Hughes, C. (2005). Using self-monitoring to increase following-direction skills of students with moderate to severe disabilities in general education. *Education and Training in Developmental Disabilities, 40*(1), 3–13.

Al Otaiba, S., & Hosp, M.K. (2004). Providing effective literacy instruction to students with down syndrome. *TEACHING Exceptional Children, 36*(4), 28–34.

Alberto, P.A., Taber, T.A., & Fredrick, L.D. (1999). Use of self-operated auditory prompts to decrease aberrant behaviors in students with moderate mental retardation. *Research in Developmental Disabilities, 20*(6), 429–439.

Algozzine, B., Browder, D., Karvonen, M., Test, D.W., & Wood, W.M. (2001). Effects of intervention to promote self-determination for individuals with disabilities. *Review of Educational Research, 71,* 219–277.

Algozzine, B., & Ysseldyke, J.E. (1986). The future of the LD field: Screening and diagnosis. *Journal of Learning Disabilities, 19*(7), 394–398.

Allen, S.K., Smith, A.C., Test, D.W., Flowers, C., & Wood, W.M. (2001). The effects of "self-directed IEP" on student participation in IEP meetings. *Career Development for Exceptional Individuals, 4,* 107–120.

Allen, T.E., Rawlings, B.W., & Schildroth, A.N. (1989). *Deaf students and the school-to-work transition.* Baltimore: Paul H. Brookes Publishing Co.

Almond, P.J., Lehr, C., Thurlow, M.L., & Quenemoen, R. (2002). Participation in large-scale state assessment and accountability systems. In T.M. Haladyna (Ed.), *Large-scale assessment programs for all students: Validity, technical adequacy, and implementation* (pp. 341–370). Mahwah, NJ: Lawrence Erlbaum Associates.

American Association on Mental Retardation. (2002). *Mental retardation: Definition, classification and systems of support.* Washington, DC: Author.

American Association on Mental Retardation. (2003). *Supports Intensity Scale (SIS).* Washington, DC: Author.

American Foundation for the Blind. (2005). Retrieved October 21, 2005, from http://www.afb.org

American Medical Association. (2002, May). *Educational forum on adolescent health: Youth bullying.* Chicago: Author.

American Psychiatric Association. (2000). *Diagnostic and statistical manual of mental disorders* (4th ed., text revision). Washington, DC: Author.

American Youth Policy Forum. (2000). *High schools of the millennium: Report of the work group.* Washington, DC: Author.

Americans with Disabilities Act of 1990, PL 101-336, 42 U.S.C. §§ 12101 *et seq.*

Anderson, P.L. (2000). Using literature to teach social skills to adolescents with LD. *Intervention in School and Clinic, 35,* 271–279.

Anderson, S., Yilmaz, O., & Washburn-Moses, L. (2004). Middle and high school students with learning disabilities: Practical academic interventions for general education teachers—A review of literature. *American Secondary Education, 32*(2), 19–38.

Ansell, S.E. (2004, January). *Put to the test.* Retrieved February 12, 2003, from http://www.edweek.org/sreports/qc04/reports/17teaching-t1b.cfm

Architectural and Transportation Barriers Compliance Board. (1994). *Americans with Disabilities Act: Accessibility guidelines for buildings and facilities, transportation facilities, and transportation vehicles.* Washington, DC: Author.

Armstrong, T. (2000). *Multiple intelligences in the classroom* (2nd ed.). Alexandria, VA: Association of Supervision and Curriculum Development.

Armstrong, T. (2003). *The multiple intelligences of reading and writing: Making the words come alive.* Alexandria, VA: Association of Supervision and Curriculum Development.

ASK v. Oregon State Board of Education, No. CV 99-263 KI (D. Or. Jan. 30, 2001).

Aspel, N., Bettis, G., Test, D., & Wood, W. (1998). An evaluation of a comprehensive system of transition services. *Career Development for Exceptional Individuals, 21,* 203–222.

Asselin, S.B., Todd-Allen, M., & deFur, S. (1998). Transition coordinators: Define yourselves. *TEACHING Exceptional Children, 30*(3), 11–15.

Atchison, T.B., Sander, A.M., Struchen, M.A., High, W.M., Roebuck, T.M., Contant, C.F., et al. (2004). Relationship between neuropsychological test performance and productivity at 1-year following traumatic brain injury. *Clinical Neuropsychologist, 18,* 249–265.

Aune, E. (1991). A transition model for postsecondary-bound students with learning disabilities. *Learning Disabilities Research and Practice, 6,* 177–187.

Austin, V.L. (2001). Teachers' beliefs about co-teaching. *Remedial and Special Education, 22*(4), 245–255.

Babbitt, C.E., & Burbach, H.J. (1990). Note on the perceived occupational future of physically disabled college students. *Journal of Employment Counseling, 27,* 98–103.

Bader, B.A. (2003). Identification of best practices in One Stop Career Centers that facilitate use by people with disabilities seeking employment (Doctoral dissertation, Virginia Commonwealth University, 2003). *Dissertation Abstracts International,* AAT 3091823.

Baer, R., & Rumrill, P. (2001). Coordinating transition services. In R. Flexer, T. Simmons, P. Luft, & R. Baer (Eds.), *Transition strategies for secondary students with disabilities* (pp. 364–384). Upper Saddle River, NJ: Merrill/Prentice Hall.

Bailey, E., Ricketts, S., Becker, D.R., Xie, H., & Drake, R.E. (1998). Conversion of day treatment to supported employment: One-year outcomes. *Psychiatric Rehabilitation Journal, 22*(1), 24–29.

Baird, P.A., & Everson, J.M. (1999, August). *Person-centered planning: A guide for facilitators and participants.* New Orleans: Louisiana State University Health Science Center, Human Development Center.

Balanced Budget Act of 1997, PL 105-33, 111 Stat. 329.

Bambara, L.M., & Ager, C. (1992). Using self-scheduling to promote self-directed leisure activity in home and community settings. *Journal of The Association for Persons with Severe Handicaps, 17*(2), 67–76.

Bambara, L., & Cole, C. (1997). Permanent antecedent prompts. In M. Agran (Ed.), *Student directed learning: Teaching self-determination skills.* Pacific Grove, CA: Brooks/Cole.

Bandura, A. (1977). Self-efficacy: Toward a unifying theory of behavioral change. *Psychological Review, 84*(2), 191–215.

Bandura, A., & Cervone, D. (2000). Self-evaluative and self-efficacy mechanisms of governing the motivational effects of goal systems. In E.T. Higgins & A.W. Kruglanski (Eds.), *Motivational science: Social and personality perspectives. Key reading in social psychology* (pp. 202–214). Philadelphia: Psychology Press.

Baron, J., & Brown, R.V. (Eds.). (1991). *Teaching decision making to adolescents.* Mahwah, NJ: Lawrence Erlbaum Associates.

Barr, R.D. (1981). Alternatives for the eighties: A second decade of development. *Phi Delta Kappan, 62*(8), 570–573.

Barth, J.T., Diamond, R., & Errico, A. (1996). Mild head injury and post concussion syndrome: Does anyone really suffer? *Clinical Electroencephalogram, 27,* 183.

Bateman, B. (1994). Toward better identification of learning disabilities. *Learning Disabilities, 5*(2), 95–99.

Batshaw, M.L. (Ed.). (2002). *Children with disabilities* (5th ed.). Baltimore: Paul H. Brookes Publishing Co.

Bauer, A.M., & Brown, G.M. (2001). *Adolescents and inclusion: Transforming secondary schools.* Baltimore: Paul H. Brookes Publishing Co.

Bauer, A.M., & Ulrich, M.E. (2002). "I've got my palm in my pocket." Using handheld computers in an inclusive classroom. *TEACHING Exceptional Children, 35*(2), 18–22.

Bauer, D.K. (1994). School health services: Supporting students with special health needs. *Impact, 7*(2), 8–9.

Baugh, T. (2003). *Bystander Focus Groups: Bullying—Roles, rules, and coping tools to break the cycle.* Washington, DC: The George Washington University.

Bauwens, J., & Hourcade, J. (1995). *Cooperative teaching.* Austin, TX: PRO-ED.

Beaulieu, L.J. (2002). *Mapping the assets of your community: A key component to building local capacity.* Starkville: Mississippi State University, Southern Rural Development Center.

Becker, D.R., & Bond, G.R. (Eds.). (2002). *Supported employment implementation resource kit.* Rockville, MD: Center for Mental Health Services, Substance Abuse and Mental Health Services Administration.

Becker, D.R., Bond, G.R., McCarthy, D., Thompson, D., Xie, H., McHugo, G.J., & Drake, R.E. (2001). Converting day treatment centers to supported employment programs in Rhode Island. *Psychiatric Services, 52,* 351–357.

Becker, D.R., & Drake, R.E. (1993). *A working life: The Individual Placement and Support (IPS) Program.* Concord, NH: New Hampshire-Dartmouth Psychiatric Research Center.

Becker, D.R., & Drake, R.E. (2003). *A working life for people with severe mental illness.* New York: Oxford Press.

Becker, D.R., Smith, J., Tanzman, B., Drake, R.E., & Tremblay, T. (2001). Fidelity of supported employment programs and employment outcomes. *Psychiatric Services, 52*, 834–836.

Bedell, G.M. (2004). Developing a follow-up focused on participation of children and youth with acquired brain injuries after discharge from inpatient rehabilitation. *NeuroRehabilitation, 19*(3), 191–205.

Bender, W.N., Marshall, R., & Wehman, P. (1997). Learning disabilities. In P. Wehman (Ed.), *Exceptional individuals in school, community, and work* (pp. 175–205). Austin, TX: PRO-ED.

Bender, W.N., & McLaughlin, P.J. (1997). Violence in the classroom: Where we stand. *Intervention in School and Clinic, 32*, 196–198.

Beninghof, A. (1993). *Ideas for inclusion: The classroom teacher's guide.* Longmont, CO: Sopris West.

Beninghof, A.M., & Singer, A.L. (1992). Transdisciplinary teaming: An inservice training activity. *TEACHING Exceptional Children, 24*, 56–61.

Benz, M.R., Lindstrom, L., & Halpern, A.S. (1995). Mobilizing local communities to improve transition services. *Career Development for Exceptional Individuals, 18*, 21–32.

Benz, M.R., Lindstrom, L., & Latta, T. (1999). Improving collaboration between schools and vocational rehabilitation: The youth transition program model. *Journal of Vocational Rehabilitation, 13*, 55–63.

Benz, M.R., Lindstrom, L., & Yovanoff, P. (2000). Improving graduation and employment outcomes of students with disabilities: Predictive factors and student perspectives. *Exceptional Children, 66*, 509–529.

Bergen County Vocational-Technical High School, Hackensack, NJ; Cornell University, Ithaca, NY, Food Industry Training Div.; Wakefern Food Corp., Elizabeth, NJ, ShopRite Div. (1990). *Supermarket careers: A partnership in training. Final Report.* Ithaca, NY: Cornell University.

Bernard-Opitz, V., Sriram, N., & Nakhoda-Sapuan, S. (2001). Enhancing social problem solving in children with autism and normal children through computer-assisted instruction. *Journal of Autism and Developmental Disorders, 31*(4), 377–398.

Berry, H.G. (2000). The supplemental security income program and employment for young adults with disabilities: An analysis of the National Health Interview Survey on Disability. *Focus on Autism and Other Developmental Disabilities, 15*, 176–181.

Beyth-Marom, R., Fischhoff, B., Quadrel, M.J., & Furby, L. (1991). Teaching decision making to adolescents: A critical review. In J. Baron & R.V. Brown (Eds.), *Teaching decision making to adolescents* (pp. 19–59). Mahwah, NJ: Lawrence Erlbaum Associates.

Biehl, J. (1996, July/August). I am hard of hearing, but I can see fine: Coping with hearing and vision loss. *Hearing Loss*, 8–11.

Bissonnette, D. (1994). *Beyond traditional job development* Chatsworth, CA: Milt Wright and Associates.

Black, R.S., Mrasek, K.D., & Ballinger, R. (2003). Individualist and collectivist values in transition planning for culturally diverse students with special needs. *The Journal for Vocational Special Needs Education, 25*(2, 3), 20–29.

Black, S. (2004). Teachers can engage disengaged students. *The Education Digest, 69*, 39–44.

Blackhurst, A.E., Lahm, E.A., Harrison, E.M., & Chandler, W.G. (1999). A framework for aligning technology with transition competencies. *Career Development for Exceptional Individuals, 22*, 153–183.

Blackorby, J., & Wagner, M. (1996). Longitudinal postschool outcomes of youth with disabilities: Findings from the National Longitudinal Transition Study. *Exceptional Children, 62*(5), 399–413.

Blanck, P., Hill, E., Siegal, C.D., & Waterstone, M. (2004). *Disability civil rights law and policy.* St. Paul, MN: Thomson West.

Block, N., & Dworkin, G. (Eds.). (1976). *The I.Q. controversy.* New York: Random House.

Block, S.R. (1997). Closing the sheltered workshop: Toward competitive employment opportunities for persons with development disabilities. *Journal of Vocational Rehabilitation, 9*, 267–275.

Bloom, D.R., Levin, H.S., Ewing-Cobbs, L., Saunders, A.E., Song, J., Fletcher, J.M., & Kowatch, R.A. (2001). Lifetime and novel psychiatric disorders after pediatric traumatic brain injury. *Journal of American Academy of Child and Adolescent Psychiatry, 40*, 572–579.

Blumbergs, P.C., Jones, N.R., & North, J.B. (1989). Diffuse axonal injury in head trauma. *Journal of Neurology, Neurosurgery, and Psychiatry, 52*, 838.

Boake, C., Millis, S.R., High, W.M., Delmonico, R.L., Kreutzer, J.S., Rosenthal, M., et al. (2001). Using early neuropsychologic testing to predict long-term productivity outcome from traumatic brain injury. *Archives of Physical Medicine and Rehabilitation, 82*, 761–768.

Board for Rights of Virginians with Disabilities Technical Assistance Project (BRVD-TAP). (1991). *Results from the Board for Rights of Virginians with Disabilities' survey of the needs, concerns, and satisfaction with services of Virginia's postsecondary students with disabilities.* Richmond: Virginia Commonwealth University (VCU), Virginia Institute for Developmental Disabilities.

Board of Education v. Ambach, 436 N.Y.S.2d 564 (N.Y. Sup. 1981).

Bolles, R.N., & Brown, D.S. (2001). *Job hunting for the so-called handicapped or people who have disabilities.* Berkley, CA: Ten Speed Press.

Bolton, B., & Roessler, R. (1986, December). *Work personality profile.* Fayetteville: Arkansas Research and Training Center in Vocational Rehabilitation.

Bond, G.R. (1992). Vocational rehabilitation. In R.P. Liberman (Ed.), *Handbook of psychiatric rehabilitation* (pp. 244–275). New York: Macmillan.

Bond, G.R. (1998). Principles of the Individual Placement and Support model: Empirical support. *Psychiatric Rehabilitation Journal, 22*(1), 11–23.

Bond, G.R. (2004a). Supported employment: Evidence for an evidence-based practice. *Psychiatric Rehabilitation Journal, 27*, 345–359.

Bond, G.R. (2004b, March 26). *The thresholds study of individual placement and support: Progress report on a randomized controlled trial.* Paper presented at the Research Seminar of New Hampshire-Dartmouth Psychiatric Research Center, Lebanon.

Bond, G.R., Becker, D.R., Drake, R.E., Rapp, C.A., Meisler, N., Lehman, A.F., Bell, M.D., & Blyler, C.R. (2001). Implementing supported employment as an evidence-based practice. *Psychiatric Services, 52*, 313–322.

Bond, G.R., Becker, D.R., Drake, R.E., & Vogler, K.M. (1997). A fidelity scale for the Individual Placement and Support model of supported employment. *Rehabilitation Counseling Bulletin, 40*, 265–284.

Bond, G.R., Dietzen, L.L., McGrew, J.H., & Miller, L.D. (1995). Accelerating entry into supported employment for persons with severe psychiatric disabilities. *Rehabilitation Psychology, 40*, 91–111.

Bond, G.R., Drake, R.E., Becker, D.R., & Mueser, K.T. (1999). Effectiveness of psychiatric rehabilitation approaches for employment of people with severe mental illness. *Journal of Disability Policy Studies, 10*(1), 18–52.

Bond, G.R., Drake, R.E., Mueser, K.T., & Becker, D.R. (1997). An update on supported employment for people with severe mental illness. *Psychiatric Services, 48*, 335–346.

Bond, G.R., Vogler, K.M., Resnick, S.G., Evans, L.J., Drake, R.E., & Becker, D.R. (2001). Dimensions of supported employment: Factor structure of the IPS Fidelity Scale. *Journal of Mental Health, 10*, 383–393.

Bond, G.R., Wehman, P., & Wittenburg, D. (2005). *Evidence-based practices that promote employment of people with disabilities.* Richmond, VA: Rehabilitation Research and Training Center on Workplace Supports and Retention, Virginia Commonwealth University.

Bondy, A., & Frost, L. (2001). The picture exchange communication system. *Behavior Modification, 25*, 725–744.

Borgioli, J.A., & Kennedy, C.H. (2003). Transitions between school and hospital for students with multiple disabilities: A survey of causes, educational continuity, and parental perceptions. *Research and Practice for Persons with Severe Disabilities, 28*(1), 1–6.

Bosch, H. (1991). Postsecondary issues for adults with learning disabilities. *Postsecondary LD Network News, 13*(5), 37–39.

Bouck, E.C. (2004). State of curriculum for secondary students with mild mental retardation. *Education and Training in Developmental Disabilities, 39*(2), 169–176.

Boudah, D.J., Knight, S.L., Kostohryz, C., Welch, N., Laughter, D., & Branch, R. (2000). Collaborative research in inclusive classrooms: An investigation with reflections by teachers and researchers. *Teacher Education and Special Education, 23*(3), 241–252.

Boutot, E.A., & Bryant, D.P. (2005). Social integration of students with autism in inclusive settings. *Education and Training in Developmental Disabilities, 40*(1), 14–23.

Bove, M.E., Nevin, A., Paolucci-Whitcomb, P., & McNeil, M.E. (1991). What have we accomplished in the education of persons with severe challenges? *Teacher Education and Special Education, 14*, 110–115.

Bowe, F.G. (2000). *Universal design in education: Teaching nontraditional students.* Westport, CT: Bergin & Garvey.

Boyles, S. (2005, March 30). *Half of kids are bullied, study suggests. Bullied children more likely to report emotional problems and physical symptoms.* WebMD Health. Available on-line at http://webcenter.health.webmd.netscape.com

Bracey, G.W. (2000). *Bail me out! Handling difficult data and tough questions about public schools.* Thousand Oaks, CA: Corwin Press.

Braddock, D., Hemp, R., Rizzolo, M., Coulter, D., Haffer, L., & Thompson, M. (2005). *The state of the states in developmental disabilities: 2005 study summary.* Boulder: University of Colorado, Coleman Institute for Cognitive Disabilities and Department of Psychiatry.

Braddock, D., Rizzolo, M.C., & Hemp, R. (2004). Most employment services growth in developmental disabilities during 1988–2002 was in segregated settings. *Mental Retardation, 42*(4), 317–320.

Bradfield A.L. (1992). Environmental assessment and job site modifications for people who are visually impaired. *Journal of Vocational Rehabilitation, 2,* 39–45.

Branham, R.S., Collins, B.C., Schuster, J.W., & Kleinert, H. (1999). Teaching community skills to students with moderate disabilities: Comparing combined techniques of classroom simulation, videotape modeling, and community-based instruction. *Education and Training in Mental Retardation and Developmental Disabilities, 34*(2), 170–181.

Bremer, C., Kachgal, M., & Schoeller, K. (2003). *Self-determination: Supporting successful transition.* Retrieved April 2, 2005, from http://www.ncset.org/publications/viewdesc.asp?id=962

Brentro, L., Brokenleg, M., & Van Bockern, S. (1990). *Reclaiming youth at risk: Our hope for the future.* Bloomington, IN: National Educational Services.

Briel, L.W., & Getzel, E.E. (2001). Internships in higher education: Promoting success for students with disabilities. *Disability Studies Quarterly, 21*(1), 38–48.

Briel, L.W., & Wehman, P. (2005). Career planning and placement. In E.E. Getzel & P. Wehman (Eds.), *Going to college: Expanding opportunities for people with disabilities* (pp. 291–305). Baltimore: Paul H. Brookes Publishing Co.

Brinckerhoff, L.C., McGuire, J.M., & Shaw, S.F. (2002). *Postsecondary education and transition for students with learning disabilities* (2nd ed.). Austin, TX: PRO-ED.

Brinckerhoff, L.C., Shaw, S.F., & McGuire, J.M. (1993). *Promoting postsecondary education for students with learning disabilities: A handbook for practitioners.* Austin, TX: PRO-ED.

Brooke, V. (1999). It's up to us: Practice and attitudes cannot be legislated [Editorial]. *Journal of Vocational Rehabilitation, 12*(1), 1–5.

Brooke, V., Inge, K.J., Armstrong, A.J., & Wehman, P. (1997). *Supported employment handbook: A customer-driven approach for persons with significant disabilities.* Richmond: Virginia Commonwealth University, Rehabilitation Research and Training Center.

Brooke, V., & O'Mara, S. (2001). Social Security work incentives: Issues and implementation. In P. Wehman (Ed.), *Supported employment in business: Expanding the capacity of workers with disabilities* (pp. 227–238). St. Augustine, FL: Training Resource Network.

Brookes, D.N., Campsie, L., Symington, C., Beattie, A., & McKinley, W. (1987). The effects of severe head injury on patient and relatives within seven years of injury. *Journal of Head Trauma Rehabilitation, 2*(3), 1–13.

Brookhart v. Illinois State Department of Education, 697 F.2d 179 (7th Circuit 1983).

Brooks-Lane, N., Butterworth, J., Ghiloni, C., & Revell, G. (2004). *Customized employment Q & A: Creating a diversified funding base.* Richmond, VA: Training and Technical Assistance for Providers (T-TAP). Available at http://www.t-tap.org/strategies/factsheet/diversifiedfunding. html

Brooks-Lane, N., Hutcheson, S., & Revell, G. (2005). Supporting consumer-directed employment outcomes. *Journal of Vocational Rehabilitation, 23*(2), 123–134.

Brotherson, M.J., Cook, C.C., Cunconon-Lehr, R., & Wehmeyer, M. (1995). Policy supporting self-determination in the environments of children with disabilities. *Education and Training in Mental Retardation and Developmental Disabilities, 30*(1), 3–12.

Browder, D., Lentz, F., Knoster, T., & Wilansky, C. (1988). Determining extended school year eligibility: From esoteric to explicit criteria. *Journal of The Association for Persons with Severe Handicaps, 13*, 235–243.

Browder, D.M., & Minarovic, T.J. (2000). Utilizing sight words in self-instruction training for employees with moderate mental retardation in competitive jobs. *Education and Training in Mental Retardation and Developmental Disabilities, 35*, 78–89.

Browder, D.M., Morris, W.W., & Snell, M.E. (1981). The use of time delay to teach manual signs to a severely retarded student. *Education and Training of the Mentally Retarded, 16*, 252–258.

Browder, D., & Snell, M.E. (2000). Teaching functional academics. In M.E. Snell, & D. Browder (Eds.), *Instruction of students with severe disabilities* (5th ed., pp. 493–542). Upper Saddle River, NJ: Prentice Hall.

Browder, D., Snell, M., & Wildonger, B. (1988). Simulation and community-based instruction of vending machines with time delay. *Education and Training in Mental Retardation, 23*, 175–185.

Browder, D.M., & Spooner, F. (2003). Potential benefits of the adequate yearly progress provision of NCLB for students with significant disabilities. *TASH Connections*, 12–17.

Browder, D., Spooner, F., Ahlgrim-Delzell, L., Flowers, C., & Karvonen, M. (2003). What we know and need to know about alternate assessment. *Exceptional Children, 70*(1), 45–61.

Brown v. Board of Education, 347 U.S. 483 (1954).

Brown, D. (1982). Rehabilitating the learning disabled adult. *American Rehabilitation, 7*(3), 17–22.

Brown, F., Appel, C., Corsi, L., & Wenig, B. (1993). Choice diversity for people with severe disabilities. *Education and Training in Mental Retardation, 28*(4), 318–326.

Brown, L., Farrington, K., Suomi, J., & Ziegler, M. (1999). Work–wage relationships and individuals with disabilities. *Journal of Vocational Rehabilitation, 13*(1), 5–13.

Brown, L., Long, E., Udvari-Solner, A., Davis, L., Van Deventer, P., Ahlgren, C., Johnson, F., Gruenewald, L., & Jorgensen, J. (1989). The home school: Why students with severe intellectual disabilities must attend the schools of their brothers, sisters, friends, and neighbors. *Journal of the Association for Persons with Severe Handicaps, 14*(1), 1–7.

Brown, L., Nietupski, J., & Hamre-Nietupski, S. (1976). The criterion of ultimate functioning. In M.A. Thoma (Ed.), *Hey, don't forget about me! New directions for serving the handicapped* (pp. 2–15). Reston, VA: Council for Exceptional Children.

Brown, L., & York, R. (1974). Developing programs for severely handicapped students: Teacher training and classroom instruction. *Focus on Exceptional Children, 6*(2), 1–11.

Brownell, K.D., Colletti, G., Ersner-Hershfield, R., Hershfield, S.M., & Wilson, G.T. (1977). Self-control in school children: Stringency and leniency in self-determined and externally imposed performance standards. *Behavior Therapy, 8*, 442–455.

Bryan, T. (1990, Spring). Social vulnerability of students with learning disabilities [Special issue]. *The Lantern, 6*.

Bryant, B., Bryant, D., & Reith, H. (2002). The use of assistive technology in postsecondary education. In L. Brinckerhoff, J. McGuire, & S. Shaw (Eds.), *Postsecondary education and transition for students with learning disabilities* (pp. 389–429). Austin, TX: PRO-ED.

Buckley, J., & Bellamy, G.T. (1985). *National survey of day and vocational programs for adults with severe disabilities: A 1984 profile.* Unpublished manuscript, The Johns Hopkins University, Baltimore.

Bullis, M., Davis, C., Bull, B., & Johnson, B. (1995). Transition achievement among young adults with deafness: What variables relate to success? *Rehabilitation Counseling Bulletin, 39*, 130–151.

Bullis, M., & Fredericks, H.D. (2002). *Vocational and transition services for adolescents with emotional and behavioral disorders: Strategies and best practices.* Champaign, IL: Research Press.

Bullis, M., Morgan, T., Benz, M.R., Todis, B., & Johnson, M.D. (2002). Description and evaluation of the ARIES project: Achieving rehabilitation, individualized education, and employment success for adolescents with emotional disturbance. *Career Development for Exceptional Individuals, 25*(1), 41.

Burgstahler, S. (2003). The role of technology in preparing youth with disabilities for postsecondary education and employment. *Journal of Special Education Technology, 18*(4), 7–21.

Burkhauser, R.V., & Stapleton, D.C. (2004). The decline in the employment rate for people with disabilities: Bad data, bad health, or bad policy? *Journal of Vocational Rehabilitation, 20*(3), 185–201.

Burkhauser, R.V., & Wittenburg, D.C. (1996). *How current disability transfer policies discourage work: Analysis of the 1990 SIPP.* Syracuse, NY: Syracuse University.

Bursuck, W., & Rose, E. (1992). Community college options for students with mild disabilities. In F.R. Rusch, L. DeStefano, J. Chadsey-Rusch, A. Phelps, & E. Szymanski (Eds.), *Transition from school to adult life: Models, linkages, and policy* (pp. 71–92). Sycamore, IL: Sycamore Publishing.

Butera, G., Belcastro, R., Friedland, B., Henderson, J., Jackson, C., Klein, H., et al. (1996). Suspension discipline and disabilities: Perspectives from practice. *The Special Education Leadership Review, 3*(1), 77–89.

Buxton, V.S. (2004, Summer). Customized employment makes dreams come true. *Making a Difference,* 21.

Caldwell, T.H., & Sirvis, B. (1991). Students with special health care conditions: An emerging population presents new challenges. *Preventing School Failure, 35,* 13–18.

Callahan, M.J., & Garner, J.B. (1997). *Keys to the workplace: Skills and supports for people with disabilities.* Baltimore: Paul H. Brookes Publishing Co.

Cameto, R. (2005). The transition planning process. *National Longitudinal Transition Study 2, 4*(1). Minneapolis: National Center on Secondary Education and Transition, University of Minnesota.

Campbell, K. (1988). Learning: A struggle and a challenge. *Their World, 67,* 42–43.

Carey, A.C., DelSordo, V., & Goldman, A. (2004). Assistive technology for all: Access to alternative financing for minority populations. *Journal of Disability Policy Studies, 14*(4), 194–203.

Carey, A.C., Potts, B.B., Bryen, D.N., & Shankar, J. (2004). Networking towards employment: Experiences of people who use augmentative and alternative communication. *Research and Practice for Persons with Severe Disabilities, 29*(1), 40–52.

Carnine, D. (1981). High and low implementation of direct instruction teaching techniques. *Education and Treatment of Children, 4,* 43–51.

Carnine, D., Silbert, J., & Kameenui, E. (1997). *Direct instruction reading* (3rd ed). Columbus, OH: Charles E. Merrill.

Carr, E.G. (1980). Generalization of treatment effects following educational intervention with autistic children and youth. In B. Wilcox & A. Thompson (Eds.), *Critical issues in educating autistic children and youth* (pp. 118–134). Washington, DC: U.S. Department of Education.

Carr, E.G., Dunlap, G., Horner, R.H., Koegel, R.L., Turnbull, A.P., Sailor, W., et al. (2002). Positive behavior support: Evolution of an applied science. *Journal of Positive Behavior Interventions, 4,* 4–16.

Carr, E.G., Horner, R.H., & Turnbull, A.P. (1999). *Positive behavior support for people with developmental disabilities: A research synthesis.* Washington, DC: American Association on Mental Retardation.

Carr, E.G., Levin, L., McConnachie, G., Carlson, J.I., Kemp, D.C., & Smith, C.E. (1994). *Communication-based intervention for problem behavior: A user's guide for producing positive change.* Baltimore: Paul H. Brookes Publishing Co.

Cartledge, G., & Kiarie, M.W. (2001). Learning social skills through literature for children and adolescents. *TEACHING Exceptional Children, 34*(2), 40–47.

Cartledge, G., & Milburn, J.F. (1995). *Teaching social skills to children and youth: Innovative approaches* (3rd ed.). Boston: Allyn & Bacon.

Cartwright, G.P., Cartwright, C.A., & Ward, M.E. (1989). *Educating special learners* (3rd ed.). Belmont, CA: Wadsworth.

Case-Smith, J., Allen, A., & Pratt, P. (1996). *Occupational therapy for children.* St. Louis: Mosby-Year Book.

Cassam, D. (1995). Telework: Enabling the disabled. *Search, 26*(7), 201–202.

Causton-Theoharis, J., & Malmgren, K. (2005). Building bridges: Strategies to help paraprofessionals promote peer interaction. *TEACHING Exceptional Children, 37*(6), 18–24.

Cawley, J.F., Foley, T.E., & Doan, T. (2003). Giving students with disabilities a voice in the selection of arithmetical content. *TEACHING Exceptional Children, 36*(1), 8–16.

Center for Workforce Preparation. (2004). *Dispelling the myths: How people with disabilities can meet employer needs.* Washington, DC: United States Chamber of Commerce.

Centers for Disease Control and Prevention. (2001). *Injury fact book 2001–2002.* Atlanta, GA: Author.

Centers for Disease Control and Prevention. (2003). *Traumatic brain injury in the United States: A report to Congress.* Atlanta, GA: Author.

Certo, N.J., Mautz, D., Pumpian, I., Sax, C., Smalley, K., Wade, H.A., et al. (2003). Review and discussion of a model for seamless transitions to adulthood. *Education and Training in Developmental Disabilities, 38*(1), 3–17.

Chadsey-Rusch, J., DeStefano, L., O'Reilly, M., Gonzalez, P., & Collet-Klingenberg, L. (1992). Assessing the loneliness of workers with mental retardation. *Mental Retardation, 30*(2), 5–92.

Chadsey-Rusch, J., & Gonzalez, P. (1996). Analysis of directions, responses, and consequences involving persons with mental retardation in employment and vocational settings. *American Journal on Mental Retardation, 100*(5), 481–492.

Chambers, C.R., Hughes, C., & Carter, E.W. (2004). Parent and sibling perspectives on the transition to adulthood. *Education and Training in Developmental Disabilities, 39*(2), 79–94.

Chanda Smith v. Los Angeles Unified School District, No. CV 93-7044-LEW(GHKx).

Chandler, D., Meisel, J., Hu, T., McGowen, M., & Madison, K. (1997). A capitated model for a cross-section of severely mentally ill clients: Employment outcomes. *Community Mental Health Journal, 33,* 501–516.

Chandler, S.K., & Pankaskie, S.C. (2004). Socialization, peer relationships, and self-esteem. In P. Wehman & J. Kregel (Eds.), *Functional curriculum for elementary, middle, and secondary age students with special needs* (2nd ed., pp. 165–189). Austin, TX: PRO-ED.

Chapman v. California Department of Education, No. C 01-01780 CRB (N.D. California, February 21, 2002).

Chapman, M. (2004). *Philosophy and overview of supported employment program.* Retrieved January 26, 2004, from http://www.teacch.com/teacchsu.htm

Charles, K.K. (2004). The extent and effect of employer compliance with the accommodations mandates of the Americans with Disabilities Act. *Journal of Disability Policy Studies, 15*(2), 86–96.

Cheney, D., Hagner, D., Malloy, J., Cormier, G., & Bernstein, S. (1998). Transition to adulthood for students with serious mental illness: Initial results of project RENEW. *Career Development for Exceptional Individuals, 21,* 17–32.

Chiron, R., & Gerken, K. (1983). The effects of a self-monitoring technique on the locus of control orientation of educable mentally retarded children. *School Psychology Review, 3,* 87–92.

Choate, J.S. (Ed.). (1993). *Successful inclusive teaching: Proven ways to detect and correct special needs* (4th ed.). Boston: Pearson Allyn & Bacon.

Christensen, J. (1997). Pediatric traumatic brain injury rehabilitation: Challenges in care delivery. *NeuroRehabilitation, 9*(2), 105–112.

Cifu, D., Craig, E., & Rowland, T. (1996). Neuromedical considerations affecting return to work in the brain injured adult. *Journal of Vocational Rehabilitation, 7,* 257–265.

Cimera, R.E. (1998). Are individuals with severe mental retardation and multiple disabilities cost-efficient to serve via supported employment programs. *Mental Retardation, 36*(4), 280–292.

Cimera, R.E. (2001). Utilizing co-workers as natural supports. *Journal of Disability Policy Studies, 11,* 194–201.

Cimera, R., & Rusch, F. (2000). Transition and youth with mental retardation: Past, present and future. In M. Wehmeyer & J. Patton (Eds.), *Mental retardation in the 21st century* (pp. 59–89). Austin, TX: PRO-ED.

Clark, E. (1997). Children and adolescents with traumatic brain injury: Reintegration challenges in educational settings. In E.D. Bigler & E. Clark (Eds.), *Childhood traumatic brain injury: Diagnosis, assessment, and intervention* (pp. 191–211). Austin, TX: PRO-ED.

Clark, G.M. (1996). Transition planning assessment for secondary-level students with learning disabilities. *Journal of Learning Disabilities, 29*(1), 79–92.

Clark, G.M. (1998). *Assessment for transitions planning: Transition series.* Austin, TX: PRO-ED.

Clark, H.B. (1993). Transition to independence process (TIP) system: Definition. In H.B. Clark, E.S. Stewart, C. Roberts-Friedman, & L.K. Armstrong (Eds.), *Navigating rough waters: Facilitating transition into adulthood for individuals with emotional/behavioral disturbances.* Tampa, FL: Preconference Institute, The Conference on Rehabilitation of Children, Youth, and Adults with Psychiatric Disabilities.

Clark, H.B. (1995). *Operating procedures for a transition to independence process system.* Tampa: University of South Florida, Florida Mental Health Institute.

Clark, H.B. (2004). *TIP system development and operations manual.* Tampa: University of South Florida, Florida Mental Health Institute.

Clark, H.B., & Davis, M. (2000). *Transition to adulthood: A resource for assisting young people with emotional or behavioral difficulties.* Baltimore: Paul H. Brookes Publishing Co.

Clark, H.B., Deschenes, N., & Jones, J. (2000). A framework for the development and operation of a transition system. In H.B. Clark & M. Davis (Eds.), *Transition to adulthood: A resource for assisting young people with emotional or behavioral difficulties* (pp. 29–51). Baltimore: Paul H. Brookes Publishing Co.

Clark, H.B., & Foster-Johnson, L. (1996). Serving youth in transition to adulthood. In B.A. Stroul (Ed.), *Children's mental health: Creating systems of care in a changing society* (pp. 553–551). Baltimore: Paul H. Brookes Publishing Co.

Clark, H.B., Pschorr, O., Wells, P., Curtis, M., & Tighe, T. (2004). Transition into community roles for young people with emotional/behavioral difficulties: Collaborative systems and program outcomes. In D. Cheney (Ed.), *Transition issues and strategies for youth and young adults with emotional and/or behavioral difficulties to facilitate movement in to community life.* Arlington, VA: Council for Exceptional Children.

Clark, H.B., Unger, K.V., & Stewart, E.S. (1993). Transition of youth and young adults with emotional/behavioral disorders into employment, education, and independent living. *Community Alternatives: International Journal of Family Care, 5*(2), 19–46.

Cleaver, J. (1999). Willing and able: Telecommuters with physical impairments. *Home Office Computing, 17*(12), 112.

Colby, C.R. (1987). Developing a positive learning environment. *Journal for Vocational Needs and Special Education, 12,* 33.

Cole, C.M., Waldron, N., & Majd, M. (2004). Academic progress of students across inclusive and traditional settings. *Mental Retardation, 42*(2), 136–144.

Collier, V., & Schall, C. (2003). Adolescence and autism: What you can expect. *The Advocate 35*(4), 20–23.

Collins, M.E., Bybee, D., & Mowbry, C.T. (1998). Effectiveness of supported education for individuals with psychiatric disabilities: Results from an experimental study. *Community Mental Health Journal, 34*(6), 595–613.

Condeluci, A. (1991). *Interdependence: The route to community.* Orlando, FL: Paul TTM Deutsch Press.

Condeluci, A. (1994). Transition to employment. In R.C. Savage & G.F. Wolcott (Eds.), *Educational dimensions of acquired brain injury* (pp. 519–542). Austin, TX: PRO-ED.

Condeluci, A. (1996). *Beyond difference.* Delray Beach, FL: St. Lucie Press.

Condon, C., Enein-Donovan, L., Gilmore, M., & Jordan, M. (2004). *When existing jobs don't fit: A guide to job creation.* Boston: Institute of Community Inclusion.

Condon, E., & Brown, K. (2005). *It takes a village (or at least several partners) to transition a student from school to work* [Monograph]. Missoula, MT: The University of Montana Rural Institute.

Condon, E., Moses, L., Brown, K., & Jurica, J. (2003). *PASS the bucks: Increasing consumer choice and control in transition planning through the use of SSA work incentives.* Missoula: Rural Institute, University of Montana.

Conley, R.W. (2003). Supported employment in Maryland: Success and issues. *Mental Retardation, 41*(4), 237–249.

Connell, R., Jones, M., Mace, R., Mueller, J., Mullick, A., Ostroff, E., et al. (1997). *The principles of universal design.* Center for Universal Design. Retrieved July 1, 2005, from www.design.ncsu.edu/cud/univ_design/principles/udprinciples.htm

Cook, B.G., Landrum, T.J., Tankersley, M., & Kauffman, J.M. (2003). Bringing research to bear on practice: Effecting evidence-based instruction for students with emotional or behavioral disorders. *Education and Treatment of Children, 26,* 345–361.

Cook, B.G., & Rumrill, P. (2000). Inclusion and transition in special education: Partners in progress or policy paradox? *Work, 14*(1), 13–21.

Cook, J.A., Solomon, M.L., Farrell, D., & Koziel, M. (1997). Vocational initiatives for transition-age youths with severe mental illness. In S.W. Henggeler & A.B. Santos (Eds.), *Innovative approaches for difficult-to-treat populations* (pp. 139–163). Washington, DC: American Psychiatric Press.

Coombs-Richardson, R., & Mead, J. (2001). Supporting general educators' inclusive practices. *Teacher Education and Special Education, 24*(4), 383–390.

Cooney, B. (2002). Exploring perspectives on transition of youth with disabilities: Voices of young adults, parents, and professionals. *Mental Retardation, 40*(6), 425–435.

Cooper, K.J., & Browder, D.M. (1998). Enhancing choice and participation for adults with severe disabilities in community-based instruction. *Journal of The Association for Persons with Severe Handicaps, 23,* 252–260.

Copeland, S.R., & Hughes, C. (2002). Effects of goal setting on task performance of persons with mental retardation. *Education and Training in Mental Retardation and Developmental Disabilities, 37*(1), 40–54.

Corey H. v. Board of Education of the City of Chicago, et al., 995 F. Supp. 900 (N.D. Ill 1998).

Corn, A. (1980). *Development and assessment of an in-service training program for teachers of the visually handicapped: Optical aids in the classroom.* Unpublished doctoral dissertation, Columbia University Teachers College, New York.

Council for Exceptional Children. (1993). CEC policy on inclusive schools and community settings. *TEACHING Exceptional Children, 25*(4) (Supplement).

Council for Exceptional Children. (2003a). Advocacy in action: CEC members speak out against No Child Left Behind. *CEC Today, 10*(4), 4, 7.

Council for Exceptional Children. (2003b). *No Child Left Behind Act of 2001: Reauthorization of the Elementary and Secondary Education Act: A technical assistance resource.* Arlington, VA: Author.

Craddock, G., & Scherer, M.J. (2002). Assessing individual needs for assistive technology. In C.L. Sax & C.A. Thoma (Eds.), *Transition assessment: Wise practices for quality lives* (pp. 87–101). Baltimore: Paul H. Brookes Publishing Co.

Crane, K., & Skinner, B. (2003). Community resource mapping: A strategy for promoting successful transition for youth with disabilities. *National Center on Secondary Education and Transition (NCSET) Information Brief, 2*(1), 1–5.

Crimmins, D.B., & Woolf, S.B. (1997). *Positive strategies: Training teams in positive behavior support.* Valhalla, NY: Westchester Institute for Human Development.

Crites, S.A., & Dunn, C. (2004). Teaching social problem solving to individuals with mental retardation. *Education and Training in Developmental Disabilities, 39*(4), 301–309.

Crone, E.A., Vendel, I., & van der Molen, M.W. (2003). Decision-making in disinhibited adolescents and adults: Insensitivity to future consequences or driven by immediate reward? *Personality and Individual Differences, 35*(7), 1625–1641.

Cronin, M.S., & Patton, J.R. (1993). *Life skills across the curriculum for youths with special needs.* Austin, TX: PRO-ED.

Cross, T., Cooke, N.L., Wood, W.M., & Test, D.W. (1999). Comparison of the effects of MAPS and ChoiceMaker on students' self-determination skills. *Education and Training in Mental Retardation and Developmental Disabilities, 34,* 499–510.

Curl, R.M., Fraser, R.T., Cook, R.G., & Clemmons, D. (1996). Traumatic brain injury vocational rehabilitation: Preliminary findings for the coworker as trainer project. *Journal of Head Trauma Rehabilitation, 11,* 75–85.

Cuvo, A.J., Leaf, R.B., & Borakove, L.S. (1978). Teaching janitorial skills to the mentally retarded: Acquisition, generalization, and maintenance. *Journal of Applied Behavior Analysis, 11,* 345–355.

Czarnecki, E., Rosko, D., & Fine, E. (1998). How to call up note taking skills. *TEACHING Exceptional Children, 31*(6), 14–19.

D'Amico, R. (1995). *The early work experiences of youth with disabilities: Trends in employment rates and job characteristics.* [A Report from the National Longitudinal Transition Study of Special Education Students]. Washington, DC: Office of Special Education and Rehabilitative Services, U.S. Department of Education.

Dannhauser, C.L. (1999). Who's in the home office? *American Demographics, 21*(6), 50–56.

Darch, C., & Gersten, R. (1986). Direction setting in reading comprehension: A comparison of two approaches. *Learning Disabilities Quarterly, 9,* 235–243.

Datlow Smith, M., Belcher, R.G., & Juhrs, P.D. (1995). *A guide to successful employment for individuals with autism.* Baltimore: Paul H. Brookes Publishing Co.

Dattilo, J. (1991). Recreation and leisure: A review of the literature and recommendations for future directions. In L.H. Meyer, C.A. Peck, & L. Brown (Eds.), *Critical issues in the lives of people with severe disabilities* (pp. 126–137). Baltimore: Paul H. Brookes Publishing Co.

Dattilo, J., & Hoge, G. (1999). Effects of a leisure education program on youth with mental retardation. *Education and Training in Mental Retardation and Developmental Disabilities, 34,* 20–34.

Dattilo, J., & Schleien, S.J. (1994). Understanding leisure services for individuals with mental retardation. *Mental Retardation, 32,* 43–52.

Davies, D., Stock, S., & Wehmeyer, M. (2002). Enhancing independent task performance for individuals with mental retardation through the use of a handheld self-directed visual and audio prompting system. *Education and Training in Mental Retardation and Developmental Disabilities, 37*(2), 209–218.

Davies, D.K., Stock, S.E., & Wehmeyer, M.L. (2003). A palmtop computer-based intelligent aid for individuals with intellectual disabilities to increase independent decision making. *Research and Practice for Persons with Severe Disabilities, 28*(4), 182–193.

Davis, P.K., & Pancsofar, E.L. (1999). Living in the community. In P. Wehman & P. Sherron-Targett (Eds.), *Vocational curriculum for individual with special needs: Transition from school to adulthood* (pp. 111–130). Austin, TX: PRO-ED.

de la Garza, D., & Erin, J. (1993). Employment status and quality of life of graduates of a state residential school. *Journal of Visual Impairment and Blindness, 87*(6), 229–233.

DeBoer, A., & Fister, S. (1995). *Working together: Tools for collaborative teaching.* Longmont, CO: Sopris West.

Debra P. v. Turlington, 654 F 2d 1079 (5th Cir., 1981).

deFur, S.H., Getzel, E.E., & Kregel, J. (1994). Individual transition plans: A work in progress. *Journal of Vocational Rehabilitation, 4*(2), 139–145.

deFur, S.H., Getzel, E.E., & Trossi, K. (1996). Making the postsecondary education match: A role for transition planning. *Journal of Vocational Rehabilitation, 6,* 231–241.

deFur, S.H., & Taymans, J. (1995). Competencies needed for transition specialists in vocational rehabilitation, vocational education, and special education. *Exceptional Children, 62,* 38–51.

deFur, S., Todd-Allen, M., & Getzel, E. (2001). Parent participation in the transition planning process. *Career Development for Exceptional Individuals, 24,* 71–88.

Denning, C.B., Chamberlain, J.A., & Polloway, E.A. (2000). An evaluation of state guidelines for mental retardation: Focus on definition and classification practices. *Education and Training in Mental Retardation and Developmental Disabilities, 35*(2), 226–232.

Dennis, R.E., & Ryan, S.M. (2000). Experiences and perceptions of rural Alaskan general educators: Implications for preparation in inclusive practices. *Rural Education Quarterly, 19*, 30–43.

DePaepe, P., Garrison-Kane, L., & Doelling, J. (2002). Supporting students with health needs in schools: An overview of selected health conditions. *Focus on Exceptional Children, 35*(1), 1–24.

DePompei, R., & Blosser, J.L. (1999). Managing transitions for education. In M. Rosenthal, E.R. Griffith, J.S. Kreutzer, & B. Pentland (Eds.), *Rehabilitation of the adult and child with traumatic brain injury* (3rd ed., pp. 393–409). Philadelphia: F.A. Davis.

Derer, K., Polsgrove, L., & Rieth, H. (1996). A survey of assistive technology applications in schools and recommendations for practice. *Journal of Special Education Technology, 13*(2), 62–80.

Desch, L.W. (2000). Visual and hearing impairments. In R.E. Nickel & L.W. Desch (Eds.), *The physician's guide to caring for children with disabilities and chronic conditions* (pp. 265–320). Baltimore: Paul H. Brookes Publishing Co.

Deschamps, A. (2004). Traveling the road from high school to college: Tips for the journey. *Transition Voice, 8*(1), 6–7.

Deschenes, N., Gomez, A., & Clark, H.B. (1999). *TIP case study protocol for continuing system improvement.* Tampa: University of South Florida, Florida Mental Health Institute, Department of Child and Family Studies.

Deshler, D., Ellis, E.S., & Lenz, B.K. (1996). *Teaching adolescents with learning disabilities: Strategies and methods.* Denver, CO: Love Publishing.

Deshler, D., Schumaker, J., Lenz, B., Bulgren, J., Hock, M., Knight, J., & Ehren, B. (2001). Ensuring content-area learning by secondary students with learning disabilities. *Learning Disabilities Research and Practice, 16*(2), 96–108.

Desktop Reference Guide for SSA Youth Transition Waivers. (2005). Richmond: Virginia Commonwealth University Rehabilitation Research and Training Center on Workplace Supports and Job Retention. (Draft not for Distribution).

Dettmer, P., Thurston, L.P., & Dyck, N. (2002). *Consultation, collaboration and teamwork for students with special needs.* Boston: Allyn & Bacon.

Developmental Disabilities Assistance and Bill of Rights Act of 1984, PL 98-527, 42 U.S.C. §§ 6000 *et seq.*

Dikmen, S.S., Temkin, N.R., Machamer, J.E., Holubkov, A.L., Fraser, R.T., & Winn, H.R. (1994). Employment following traumatic head injuries. *Archives of Neurology, 51*, 177–186.

DiLeo, D., Rogan, P., & Geary, T. (2000). APSE's position statement on segregated services: A background paper for advocates. *Advance, 10*(4), 1–2.

Dillion, M. (1997, October). *Preparation: A key to college success.* Paper presented at the meeting of the Division of Career Development and Transition International Conference, Overland Park, KS.

Disability Rights Advocates. (2001). *Do no harm: High stakes testing and students with learning disabilities.* Oakland, CA: Author.

Dixon, K., Kruse, D., & Van Horn, C. (2003). Employer survey: Misconceptions still an obstacle to job seekers with disabilities. *InfoLines, 14*(7), 1, 3, 6.

Doll, B., & Sands, D.J. (1998). Student involvement in goals setting and educational decision making: Foundations for effective instruction. In M.L. Wehmeyer & D.J. Sands (Eds.), *Making it happen: Student involvement in education planning, decision making, and instruction.* Baltimore: Paul H. Brookes Publishing Co.

Dopp, J., & Block, T. (2004). High school peer mentoring that works! *TEACHING Exceptional Children, 37*(1), 56–62.

Dorn, S., & Fuchs, D. (2004). Trends in placement issues. In A.M. Sorrells, H.J. Rieth, & P.T. Sindelar (Eds.), *Critical issues in special education: Access, diversity, and accountability* (pp. 57–69). Boston: Pearson Education.

Dowler, D., Batiste, L., & Whidden, E. (1998). Accommodating workers with spinal cord injury. *Journal of Vocational Rehabilitation, 10*, 115–122.

Downing, J.E. (2005). *Teaching literacy to students with significant disabilities: Strategies for the K–12 inclusive classroom.* Thousand Oaks, CA: Corwin Press.

Downing, J.E., & Eichinger, J. (2003). Creating learning opportunities for students with severe disabilities in inclusive classrooms. *TEACHING Exceptional Children, 36*(1), 26–31.

Drake, R.E., Becker, D.R., Biesanz, J.C., Torrey, W.C., McHugo, G.J., & Wyzik, P.F. (1994). Rehabilitation day treatment vs. supported employment: I. Vocational outcomes. *Community Mental Health Journal, 30,* 519–532.

Drake, R.E., Becker, D.R., Biesanz, J.C., Wyzik, P.F., & Torrey, W.C. (1996). Day treatment versus supported employment for persons with severe mental illness: A replication study. *Psychiatric Services, 47,* 1125–1127.

Drake, R.E., Goldman, H.H., Leff, H.S., Lehman, A.F., Dixon, L., Mueser, K.T., & Torrey, W.C. (2001). Implementing evidence-based practices in routine mental health service settings. *Psychiatric Services, 52,* 179–182.

Drake, R.E., McHugo, G.J., Bebout, R.R., Becker, D.R., Harris, M., Bond, G.R., & Quimby, E. (1999). A randomized clinical trial of supported employment for inner-city patients with severe mental illness. *Archives of General Psychiatry, 56,* 627–633.

Drake, R.E., McHugo, G.J., Becker, D.R., Anthony, W.A., & Clark, R.E. (1996). The New Hampshire study of supported employment for people with severe mental illness: Vocational outcomes. *Journal of Consulting and Clinical Psychology, 64,* 391–399.

Dreilinger, D., Gilmore, D.S., & Butterworth, J. (2001). National day and employment service trends in MR/DD agencies. *Research to Practice, 7*(3), 1.

Dreilinger, D., & Timmons, J. (2001). *From stress to success: Making Social Security work for your young adult (tools for inclusion).* Boston: Children's Hospital, Institute for Community Inclusion.

Dunlap, G., Kern-Dunlap, L., Clarke, S., & Robbins, F.R. (1994). Some characteristics of nonaversive intervention for severe behavior problems. In E. Schopler & G.B. Mesibov (Eds.), *Behavioral issues in autism* (pp. 227–245). New York: Plenum.

Dunn, C. (1996). A status report on transition planning for individuals with learning disabilities. In J.R. Patton & G. Blalock (Eds.), *Transition and students with learning disabilities: Facilitating the movement from school to adult life* (pp. 19–41). Austin, TX: PRO-ED.

Durlak, C.M. (1992). *Preparing high school students with learning disabilities for the transition to postsecondary education: Training for self-determination.* Unpublished doctoral dissertation, Northern Illinois University, DeKalb.

Dymond, S. (2004). Community participation. In P. Wehman & J. Kregel (Eds.), *Functional curriculum for elementary, middle, and secondary age students with special needs* (2nd ed., pp. 259–291). Austin, TX: PRO-ED.

D'Zurilla, T.J., & Goldfried, M.R. (1971). Problem solving and behavior modification. *Journal of Abnormal Psychology, 8,* 107–126.

D'Zurilla, T.J., & Nezu, A. (1980). A study of the generation-of-alternatives process in social problem solving. *Cognitive Therapy and Research, 4*(1), 67–72.

Eaton, H. (1998, August). Can telecommuting close disability-related employment gaps? *High Tech Careers Magazine* [online serial]. Available at http://www.hightechcareers.com

Eaton, H., & Coull, L. (1999). *Transitions to postsecondary learning: Self-advocacy handbook for students with learning disabilities and/or attention deficit disorder.* Vancouver, British Columbia, Canada: Eaton Coull Learning Group.

Education Commission of the States. (2002). *State performance indicators.* Denver, CO: Author.

Education for All Handicapped Children Act of 1975, PL 94-142, 20 U.S.C. §§ 1400 *et seq.*

EEOC v. Dollar General, U.S. Court, Middle District of NC. (2003, March). Raleigh, NC.

EEOC v. Home Depot, U.S. District Court, ED, NY, Civil Action No. 03-4880, New York City, NY.

Eisenberg, D. (2002, May 6). The coming job boom. *Time,* 41–42.

Elementary and Secondary Education Act of 1965, PL 89-10, 20 U.S.C. §§ 241 *et seq.*

El-Khiami, A. (1993). Employment transitions and establishing careers by postsecondary alumni with hearing loss. *Volta Review, 95*, 357–366.

Epstein, M.H., & Sharma, J.M. (1998). *Behavioral and emotional rating scale: A strength-based approach to assessment.* Austin, TX: PRO-ED.

Ettinger, J. (1995). Towards a better understanding of the career development of individuals with disabilities. In J. Ettinger & N. Wysong (Eds.), *Career development for individuals with disabilities: Providing effective services* (Vol. 1, pp. 2–39). Madison, WI: Center on Education and Work.

Everson, J. (1995). *Supporting young adults who are deaf-blind in their communities: A transition planning guide for service providers, families, and friends.* Baltimore: Paul H. Brookes Publishing Co.

Everson, J.M., Filce, H.G., Zhang, D., Guillory, J., & Kimbrel, M. (1999, September). *Defining the roles and responsibilities of transition personnel in Louisiana: A systems change response.* New Orleans: Louisiana State University Health Sciences Center, Human Development Center.

Everson, J.M., Rachal, P., & Michael, M.C. (1992). *Interagency collaboration for young adults with deaf-blindness: Toward a common transition goal.* Sands Point, NY: Helen Keller National Center-Technical Assistance Center.

Everson, J.M., & Reid, D.H. (1999). *Person-centered planning and outcome management: Maximizing organizational effectiveness in supporting quality lifestyles among people with disabilities.* Morganton, NC: Habilitative Management Consultants.

Ezrachi, O., Ben-Yishay, Y., Kay, T., Diller, L., & Rattok, J. (1991). Predicting employment in traumatic brain injury following neuropsychological rehabilitation. *Journal of Head Trauma Rehabilitation, 6*(3), 71–84.

Fabian, E.S., & Luecking, R.G. (1991). Doing it the company way: Using internal company supports in the workplace. *Journal of Applied Rehabilitation Counseling, 22*(2), 32–35.

Faherty, C. (2000). *What does it mean to me? A workbook explaining self awareness and life lessons to the child or youth with high functioning autism or Asperger's.* Arlington, TX: Future Horizons.

Fair Labor Standards Act of 1938, PL 75-718, 29 U.S.C. §§ 201 *et. seq.*

Fairweather, J.S., & Shaver, D.M. (1991). Making the transition to post-secondary education and training. *Exceptional Children, 57*(2), 264–268.

Falvey, M.A. (1989). *Community-based curriculum: Instructional strategies for students with severe handicaps* (2nd ed.). Baltimore: Paul H. Brookes Publishing Co.

Falvey, M.A. (2005). *Believe in my child with special needs!: Helping children achieve their potential in school.* Baltimore: Paul H. Brookes Publishing Co.

Falvey, M.A., Eshilian, L., Miller, C., Zimmerman, F., Russell, R., & Rosenberg, R. (1997). Developing a community of learners at Whittier High School. In D. Sage (Ed.), *Inclusion in secondary schools: Bold initiatives challenging change* (pp. 45–74). Port Chester, NY: National Professional Resources.

Falvey, M., Forest, M., Pearpoint, J., & Rosenberg, R. (1998). *All my life's a circle: Using the tools—circles, MAPS, & PATH.* Toronto: Inclusion Press.

Farley, R.C., Bolton, P., & Parkerson, R. (1992). Effects of client involvement in assessment on vocational development. *Rehabilitation Counseling Bulletin, 35*(3), 146–153.

Federal Register. (2000). *Americans with Disabilities Act (ADA): Accessibility guidelines for buildings and facilities.* Washington, DC: U.S. Government Printing Office.

Federal Register. (2001, January 17). *State vocational rehabilitation services program: Final rules.* Washington, DC: U.S. Government Printing Office.

Felce, D., & Perry, J. (1995). Quality of life: Its definition and measurement. *Research in Developmental Disabilities, 16*(1), 51–74.

Ferguson, D. (1995). *Developmental disabilities: A handbook for interdisciplinary practice.* Cambridge, MA: Brookline Books.

Ferguson, P., Hibbard, M., Leinen, J., & Schaff, S. (1990). Supporting community life: Disability policy and the renewal of mediating structures. *Journal of Disability Policy Studies, 1*(1), 10–35.

Fialka, J. (n.d.). *Opening new doors: What's new in transition.* Transition Services Project. Retrieved July 20, 2003, from http://www.cenmi.org/tspmi/articleID=2.asp

Fichten, C.S., Barile, M., & Asuncion, J.V. (1999). *Learning technologies: Adaptech project: Students with disabilities in postsecondary education.* Montreal, Quebec, Canada: Dawson College, Office of Learning Technologies Human Resources Development.

Field, S., & Hoffman, A. (1994). Development of a model for self-determination. *Career Development for Exceptional Individuals, 17,* 159–169.

Field, S., & Hoffman, A. (1996). *Steps to self-determination.* Austin, TX: PRO-ED.

Field, S., Martin, J., Miller, R., Ward, M., & Wehmeyer, M. (1998). Self-determination in career and transition programming: A position statement of the Council for Exceptional Children. *Career Development for Exceptional Individuals, 21*(2), 113–128.

Fiscus, R.S., Schuster, J.W., Morse, T.E., & Collins, B.C. (2002). Teaching elementary students with cognitive disabilities food preparation skills while embedding instructive feedback in the prompt and consequent event. *Education and Training in Mental Retardation and Developmental Disabilities, 37*(1), 55–69.

Fisher, D. (2000, March). Curriculum and instruction for all abilities and intelligences. *High School Magazine, 7*(7), 22.

Fisher, D., & Frey, N. (Eds.). (2003). *Inclusive urban schools.* Baltimore: Paul H. Brookes Publishing Co.

Fisher, D., & Pumpian, I. (1998). Parent and caregiver impressions of different educational models. *Remedial and Special Education, 19*(3), 173–180.

Fisher, D., & Sax, C.L. (2002). For whom the test is scored: Assessments, the school experience, and more. In C.L. Sax & C.A. Thoma (Eds.), *Transition assessment: Wise practices for quality lives* (pp. 1–12). Baltimore: Paul H. Brookes Publishing Co.

Fisher, D., Sax, C.L., & Pumpian, I. (1999). *Inclusive high schools: Learning from contemporary classrooms.* Baltimore: Paul H. Brookes Publishing Co.

Fisher, S., & Eskow, K.G. (2004). Getting together in college: An inclusion program for young adults with disabilities. *TEACHING Exceptional Children, 36*(3), 26–32.

Flannery, K.B., Newton, S., Horner, R.H., Slovic, R., Blumberg, R., & Ard, W.R. (2000). The impact of person centered planning on the content and organization of individual supports. *Career Development for Exceptional Individuals, 23*(2), 123–137.

Flashman, L.A., & McAllister, T.W. (2002). Lack of awareness and its impact in traumatic brain injury. *NeuroRehabilitation, 17*(4), 285–296.

Flippo, K.F., Inge, K.J., & Barcus, J.M. (Eds.). (1995). *Assistive technology: A resource for school, work, and community.* Baltimore: Paul H. Brookes Publishing Co.

Florida Inclusion Network. (2004). *Student's course selection and services worksheet.* Tallahassee: Florida Department of Education, Bureau of Instructional Services and Community Support.

Foley, S., Butterworth, J., & Heller, A. (1999). A profile of Vocational Rehabilitation interagency activity improving supported employment for people with disabilities. In G. Revell, K. Inge, D. Mank, & P. Wehman (Eds.), *The impact of supported employment for people with significant disabilities: Preliminary findings from the National Supported Employment Consortium* (pp. 89–99). Richmond: Virginia Commonwealth University Rehabilitation Research and Training Center on Workplace Supports.

Foley, S., & Green, J. (1999). Interagency agreements encouraging supported employment for people with disabilities: Preliminary report on exemplary practices. In G. Revell, K. Inge, D. Mank, & P. Wehman (Eds.), *The impact of supported employment for people with significant disabilities: Preliminary findings from the National Supported Employment Consortium* (pp. 99–107). Richmond: Virginia Commonwealth University Rehabilitation Research and Training Center on Workplace Supports.

Fombone, E. (2003). Epidemiological surveys of autism and other pervasive developmental disorders: An update. *Journal of Autism and Developmental Disorders, 23,* 365–382.

Fong, L., Wilgosh, L., & Sobsey, D. (1993). The experience of parenting an adolescent with autism. *International Journal of Disability, Development, and Education, 40,* 105–113.

Ford, L.H. (1995). *Providing employment support for people with long-term mental illness: Choices, resources, and practical strategies.* Baltimore: Paul H. Brookes Publishing Co.

Ford, L. (2001). Supported employment for people with psychiatric disabilities. In P. Wehman (Ed.), *Supported employment in business: Expanding the capacity of workers with disabilities* (pp. 133–151). St. Augustine, FL: Training Resource Network.

Foreman, P., Arthur-Kelly, M., Pascoe, S., & King, B.S. (2004). Evaluating the educational experiences of students with profound and multiple disabilities in inclusive and segregated classroom settings: An Australian perspective. *Research and Practice for Persons with Severe Disabilities 29*(3), 183–193.

Forest, M., & Lusthaus, E. (1987). The kaleidoscope: Challenge to the cascade. In M. Forest (Ed.), *More education/integration* (pp. 1–16). Downsview, Ontario: G. Allan Roeher Institute.

Forgan, J.W., & Gonzalez-DeHass, A.R. (2004). How to infuse social skills training into literacy instruction. *TEACHING Exceptional Children, 36*(6), 24–30.

Forness, S.R., Walker, H.M., & Kavale, K.A. (2003, November/December). Psychiatric disorders and treatments: A primer for teachers. *TEACHING Exceptional Children*, 42–49.

Foster, S.K., Paulk, A., & Dastoor, B.R. (1999). Can we really teach test-taking skills? *New Horizons in Adult Education, 13*(1), 14.

Fox, L., Vaughn, B.V., Dunlap, G., & Bucy, M. (1997). Parent–professional partnership in behavioral support: A qualitative analysis of one family's experience. *Journal of The Association for Persons with Severe Handicaps, 22*, 198–207.

Frank, A.R., & Sitlington, P.L. (1993). Graduates with mental disabilities: The story three years later. *Education and Training in Mental Retardation, 28*, 30–37.

Frank, A.R., & Sitlington, P.L. (2000). Young adults with mental disabilities: Does transition planning make a difference? *Education and Training in Mental Retardation and Developmental Disabilities, 35*(2), 119–134.

Frank, A.R., Sitlington, P.L., & Carson, R.R. (1995). Young adults with behavioral disorders: A comparison with peers with mild disabilities. *Journal of Emotional and Behavioral Disorders, 3*, 154–156.

Frank, A.R., Sitlington, P., Cooper, L., & Cool, V. (1990). Adult adjustment of recent graduates of Iowa mental disabilities programs. *Education and Training in Mental Retardation, 25*, 62–75.

Frank, J.J. (2003). *The impact of the Americans with Disabilities Act (ADA) on the employment of individuals who are blind or have severe visual impairments.* Starkville: Mississippi State University, Rehabilitation Research and Training Center on Blindness and Low Vision.

Frankie, P., Levine, P., Mowbray, C.T., Shriner, W., Conklin, C., & Thomas, E. (1996). Supported education for persons with psychiatric disabilities: Implementation in an urban environment. *Journal of Mental Health Administration, 23*(4), 406–417.

Franklin, K.S. (1991). Assistive technology: Where are we? Where are we going? *Journal of Vocational Rehabilitation, 1*(2), 6–7.

Fraser, R.T. (2000). The basis of the placement approach: Vocational evaluation. In R.T. Fraser & D.C. Clemmons (Eds.), *Traumatic brain injury rehabilitation* (pp. 163–171). Boca Raton, FL: CRC Press.

Friend, M. (2000). Myths and misunderstandings about professional collaboration. *Remedial and Special Education, 21*(3), 130–132.

Friend, M., & Cook, L. (2003). *Interactions: Collaboration skills for school professionals* (4th ed.). Boston: Allyn & Bacon.

Froschi, M., Rousso, H., & Rubin, E. (2001). Nothing to do after school: More of an issue for girls. In H. Rousso & M.L. Wehmeyer (Eds.), *Double jeopardy: Addressing gender equity in special education* (pp. 313–337). Albany: State University of New York Press.

Fuchs, D., & Fuchs, L. (1991). Framing the REI debate: Abolitionists versus conservationists. In J.W. Lloyd, N.N. Singh, & A.C. Repp (Eds.), *The regular education initiative: Alternative perspectives on concepts, issues, and models* (pp. 241–255). Sycamore, IL: Sycamore Publishing.

Fuchs, D., & Fuchs, L.S. (1994). Inclusive schools movement and the radicalization of special education reform. *Exceptional Children, 60*(4), 294–309.

Fuchs, D., & Fuchs, L.S. (1998a). Competing visions for educating students with disabilities: Inclusion versus full inclusion. *Childhood Education, 74*, 309–316.

Fuchs, D., & Fuchs, L.S. (1998b). Researchers and teachers working together to adapt instruction for diverse learners. *Learning Disabilities Research and Practice, 13*, 126–137.

Fuchs, L.S., Fuchs, D., Hamlett, C.L., Philips, N.B., & Karns, K. (1995). General educators' specialized adaptation for students with learning disabilities. *Exceptional Children, 61*(5), 440–459.

Fuhrman, S.H. (1999). *The new accountability* (Policy brief: Reporting issues in education reform). Philadelphia: Consortium for Policy in Research in Education.

Fujiura, G.T. (2003). Continuum of intellectual disability: Demographic evidence for the "forgotten generation." *Mental Retardation, 41*(6), 420–429.

Fuller, W.E., & Wehman, P. (2003). College entrance exams for students with disabilities: Accommodations and testing guidelines. *Journal of Vocational Rehabilitation, 18*(3), 191–197.

Fullerton, A. (1995). Promoting self-determination for adolescents and young adults with autism. *Journal of Vocational Rehabilitation, 5*(4), 337–346.

Furlong, M., Jonikes, J., Cook, J.A., Hathaway, L., & Goode, S.C. (1994). *Providing vocational services: Job coaching and ongoing support for persons with severe mental illness.* Chicago: Thresholds National Research and Training Center on Rehabilitation and Mental Illness.

Furney, K.S., Hasazi, S.B., Clark/Keefe, K., & Hartnett, J. (2003). A longitudinal analysis of shifting policy landscapes in special and general education reform. *Exceptional Children, 70*(1), 81–94.

Furney, K.S., Hasazi, S.B., & DeStefano, L. (1997). Transition policies, practices, and promises: Lessons from three states. *Exceptional Children, 63*(3), 343–355.

Gable, R. (1999). Functional assessment in school settings. *Behavior Disorders, 24*(3), 246–248.

Gable, R.A., & Warren, S.F. (1993). *Strategies for teaching students with mild to severe mental retardation.* Baltimore: Paul H. Brookes Publishing Co.

Gagnon, I., Forget, R., Swaine, B., & Friedman, D. (2002). Balance findings after a mild head injury in children [abstract]. *Neurorehabilitation and Neural Repair, 16*, 22–23.

Gagnon, J.C., McLaughlin, M.J., Rhim, L.M., & Davis, G.A. (2002). Standards-driven reform policies at the local level: Report on a survey of local special education directors in large-districts. *Journal of Special Education Leadership, 15*(1), 3–9.

Gajar, A., Goodman, L., & McAfee, J. (1993). *Secondary schools and beyond: Transition of individuals with mild disabilities.* New York: Macmillan.

Gallagher, J. (1994). The pull of societal forces on special education. *Journal of Special Education, 27*, 521–530.

Galvin, J., & Phillips, B. (1994). *How to evaluate and select assistive technology: What is appropriate technology?* Washington, DC: The Arc of the United States.

Garay, S.V. (2003). Listening to the voices of the deaf. *TEACHING Exceptional Children, 35*(4), 44–48.

Garcia-Villamisar, D., Ross, D., & Wehman, P. (2000). Clinical differential analysis of persons with autism in a work setting: A follow-up study. *Journal of Vocational Rehabilitation, 14*, 183–185.

Garcia-Villamisar, D., Wehman, P., & Navarro, M.D. (2002). Changes in the quality of autistic people's life that work in supported and sheltered employment. A 5-year follow-up study. *Journal of Vocational Rehabilitation, 17*, 309–312.

Gardner, H. (1983). *Frames of mind: The theory of multiple intelligences.* New York: Basic Books.

Gartin, B., Rumrill, P., & Serebrini, R. (1998). The higher education transition model: Guidelines for facilitating college transition among college-bound students with disabilities. In D. Podell (Ed.), *Perspectives: Educating exceptional learners* (pp. 92–96). Chicago: Coursewise Publishing.

Gaskin v. Pennsylvania Department of Education, No. 94-CV-4048.

Gast, D.L., Collins, B.C., Worley, M., & Jones, R. (1993). Teaching preschool children with disabilities to respond to the lures of strangers. *Exceptional Children, 59*, 301–311.

Gast, D.L., & Worley, M. (1986). Severe maladaptive behaviors. In M.E. Snell (Ed.), *Systematic instruction of persons with severe handicaps* (3rd ed., pp. 300–332). Columbus, OH: Charles E. Merrill.

Gaumer, A.S., Morningstar, M.E., & Clark, G.M. (2004). Status of community-based transition programs: A national database. *Career Development for Exceptional Individuals, 27*(2), 131–149.

Gavin, M., Tindall, L.W., & Gugerty, J.J. (1990). *Still puzzled about educating students with disabilities? Vocational preparation of students with disabilities.* Madison: University of Wisconsin–Madison, The Vocational Studies Center.

Gayler, T., Chudowsky, N., Hamilton, H., Kober, N., & Yeager, M. (2004). *State exit exams: A maturing reform.* Washington, DC: Center for Education Policy.

Gee, K., Graham, N., Sailor, W., & Goetz, L. (1995). Use of integrated, general education, and community settings as primary contexts for skill instruction for students with severe, multiple disabilities. *Behavior Modification, 19,* 33–58.

Geenen, S., Powers, L., Vasquez, A.L., & Bersani, H. (2003). Understanding and promoting the transition of minority adolescents. *CDEI, 26*(1), 27–46.

Geisthardt, C.L., Brotherson, M.J., & Cook, C.C. (2002). Friendship of children with disabilities in the home environment. *Education and Training in Mental Retardation and Developmental Disabilities, 37*(3), 235–252.

George, N.L., George, M.P., Gersten, R., & Grosenick, J.K. (1995). To leave or stay? An exploratory study of teachers with emotional and behavioral disorders. *Remedial and Special Education, 16,* 227–236.

Gerber, P.J., & Price, L. (2003). Persons with learning disabilities in the workplace: What we know so far in the Americans with disabilities act era. *Learning Disabilities Research and Practice, 18*(2), 132–136.

Gerber, P.J., Schnieders, C.A., Paradise, L.V., Reiff, H.B., Ginsberg, R.J., & Popp, P.A. (1990). Persisting problems of adults with learning disabilities: Self-reported comparisons from their local school age and adult years. *Journal of Learning Disabilities, 23*(9), 570–573.

Gerry, M. (2002). *State of the art for SSA and employment support services.* March 2002, SPI Conference, Los Angeles.

Gervey, R., Gao, N., & Rizzo, D. (2004). Gloucester county one-stop project: Baseline level of access and satisfaction of one-stop customers with disabilities. *Journal of Vocational Rehabilitation, 21*(2), 103–115.

Gervey, R., & Kowal, H. (2005). The job developer's presence in the job interview: Is it helpful or harmful to persons with psychiatric disabilities seeking employment? *Psychiatric Rehabilitation Journal, 29*(2), 128–131.

Getzel, E.E., Briel, L.W., & Kregel, J. (2000). Comprehensive career planning: The VCU career connections program. *Journal of Work, 14,* 41–49.

Getzel, E.E., & Finn, D.E. (2005). Training university faculty and staff. In E.E. Getzel & P. Wehman (Eds.), *Going to college: Expanding opportunities for people with disabilities* (pp. 199–216). Baltimore: Paul H. Brookes Publishing Co.

Getzel, E.E., Flippo, K.F., Wittig, K.M., & Russell, D.L. (1997). Beyond high school: Postsecondary education as a transition outcome. In S. Pueschel & M. Sustrova (Eds.), *Adolescents with Down syndrome: Toward a more fulfilling life* (pp. 199–213). Baltimore: Paul H. Brookes Publishing Co.

Getzel, E.E., & Kregel, J. (1996). Transitioning from the academic to the employment setting: The employment connection program. *Journal of Vocational Rehabilitation, 6,* 273–287.

Getzel, E.E., McManus, S., & Briel, L.W. (2004). *An effective model for college students with learning disabilities and attention deficit hyperactivity disorders.* Retrieved January 20, 2004, from www.ncset.org/publications/researchtopractice/NCSETResearchBrief_3.1.pdf

Getzel, E.E., & Wehman, P. (2005). *Going to college: Expanding opportunities for people with disabilities.* Baltimore: Paul H. Brookes Publishing Co.

Giangreco, M.F., Cloninger, C.J., & Iverson, V.S. (1998). *Choosing outcomes and accommodations for children (COACH): A guide to educational planning for students with disabilities* (2nd ed.). Baltimore: Paul H. Brookes Publishing Co.

Giangreco, M.F., Dennis, R., & Edelman, S. (1991). Common professional practices that interfere with the integrated delivery of related services. *Remedial and Special Education, 12*(2), 16–24.

Giangreco, M., & Ruelle, K. (1998). *Ants in his pants: Absurdities and realities of special education.* Minnetonka, MN: Peytral Publications.

Gilberts, G.H., Agran, M., Hughes, C., & Wehmeyer, M. (2001). The effects of peer-delivered self-monitoring strategies on the participation of students with severe disabilities in general education classrooms. *Journal of The Association for Persons with Severe Handicaps, 26,* 25–36.

Gilmore, D.S., Schuster, J.L., Timmons, J.C. & Butterworth, J. (2000). An analysis of trends for people with MR, cerebral palsy, and epilepsy receiving services from state vocational rehabilitation agencies: Ten years of progress. *Rehabilitation Counseling Bulletin, 44*(1), 30–39.

Gilmore, L., Campbell, J., & Cuskelly, M. (2003). Developmental expectations, personality stereotypes, and attitudes towards inclusive education: Community and teacher views of Down syndrome. *International Journal of Disability, Development, and Education, 50*(1), 65–76.

Gilson, B.B., & Gilson, S.F. (1998). Making friends and building relationships. In P. Wehman & J. Kregel (Eds.), *More than a job: Securing satisfying careers for people with disabilities* (pp. 301–318). Baltimore: Paul H. Brookes Publishing Co.

Gilson, S.F. (1996). Students with disabilities: An increasing voice and presence on college campuses. *Journal of Vocational Rehabilitation, 6,* 263–272.

Girard, S., & Willing, K. (1996). *Partnerships for classroom learning: From reading buddies to pen palls to the community and the world beyond.* Portsmouth, NH: Heinemann.

Glang, A., Tyler, J., Pearson, S., Todis, B., & Morvant, M. (2004). Improving educational services for students with TBI through state-wide consulting teams. *NeuroRehabilitation, 19*(3), 219–231.

Goals 2000: Educate America Act of 1994, PL 103-227, 20 U.S.C. §§ 5801 *et seq.*

Gold, M., & Mann, D. (1984). *Expelled to a friendlier place: A study of effective alternative schools.* Ann Arbor: University of Michigan Press.

Gold, M., & Marrone, J. (1998). Mass Bay Employment Services (a service of Bay Cove Human Services, Inc.): A story of leadership, vision, and action resulting in employment for people with mental illness. *Roses and Thorns from the Grassroots* (Vol. Spring). Boston: Institute for Community Inclusion.

Gold, P.B., Meisler, N., Santos, A.B., Williams, O.H., Kelleher, J., & Carnemolla, M.A. (2002). *A randomized, clinical trial of integrated supported employment and assertive community treatment for rural Southern patients with severe mental illness.* Manuscript submitted for publication.

Goldberg, M. (1991, September). Choices—A parent's view [Special issue]. *The PACESETTER,* 10.

Golden, T.P. (1999). Overview of Social Security Administration disability programs. *Directions in Rehabilitation Counseling, 10*(4), 1–4.

Golden, T., O'Mara, S., Ferrell, C., & Sheldon, J. (2000). A theoretical construct for benefits planning and assistance in the Ticket to Work and Work Incentive Improvement Act. *Journal of Vocational Rehabilitation, 14*(3), 147–152.

Goldstein, A.P., Sprafkin, R.P., Gershew, R., & Cline, T. (1980). *Social skills curriculum.* New York: Yeshiva University.

Gollaher, K., High, W., Shere, M., Bergloff, P., Boake, C., Young, M., & Ivanhoe, C. (1998). Prediction of employment outcome one to three years following traumatic brain injury. *Brain Injury, 12*(4), 255–263.

Goodall, P., Lawyer, H., & Wehman, P. (1994). Vocational rehabilitation of TBI: A legislative public policy perspective. *Journal of Head Trauma Rehabilitation, 9*(2), 62–81.

Goodman, C.R. (1988). Learning how to work. *Their World, 67,* 82–94.

Goodson, L.A. (1995). Roles for success in community living: A report on the development of self-determination. *Journal of Vocational Rehabilitation, 5*(4), 347–356.

Gordon, M., & Keiser, S. (1998). Underpinnings. In M. Gordon & S. Keiser (Eds.), *Accommodations in higher education under the Americans with Disabilities Act* (pp. 3–19). De Witt, NY: GSI Publications.

Gordon, M., Lewandowski, L., & Keiser, S. (1999). The LD label for relatively well-functioning students: A critical analysis. *Journal of Learning Disabilities, 32*(6), 485–490.

Gore, M.C. (2004). *Successful inclusion strategies for secondary and middle school teachers.* Thousand Oaks, CA: Corwin Press.

Gowdy, E.A., Carlson, L.S., & Rapp, C.A. (2004). Organizational factors differentiating high performing from low performing supported employment programs. *Psychiatric Rehabilitation Journal, 28*(2), 150–156.

Goyette, C.H., & Washburn, C. (1984). *Vocational rehabilitation of learning disabled adults, participants manual.* Pittsburgh, PA: Vocational Rehabilitation Center of Allegheny County.

Graff, J.C., & Ault, M.M. (1993). Guidelines for working with students having special health care needs. *Journal of School Health, 63,* 335–338.

Graham, S., & Harris, K.R. (1989). Improving learning disabled students' skills at composing essays: Self-instructional strategy training. *Exceptional Children, 56,* 231–214.

Graham, S., Harris, K., & Reid, R. (1990). Learning disabilities. In E.L. Meyen (Ed.), *Exceptional children in today's schools* (2nd ed., pp. 207–217). Denver, CO: Love Publishing.

Graves, T.B., Collins, B.C., Schuster, J.W., & Kleinert, H. (2005). Using video prompting to teach cooking skills to secondary students with moderate disabilities. *Education and Training in Developmental Disabilities, 40*(1), 34–46.

Green, J.H., & Brooke, V. (2001). Recruiting and retaining the best from America's largest untapped talent pool. *Journal of Vocational Rehabilitation, 16,* 83–88.

Greenbaum, B., Graham, S., & Seeles, W. (1995). Adults with learning disabilities: Education, social experiences during college. *Exceptional Children, 61*(5), 460–471.

Greene, G., & Kochhar-Bryant, C.A. (2003). *Pathways to successful transition for youth with disabilities.* Upper Saddle River, NJ: Prentice Hall.

Greene, J.P., & Winters, M.A. (2004). *Pushed out or pulled up? Exit exams and dropout rates in public high schools.* New York: Manhattan Institute.

Greenwald, B.D., Cifu, D.X., Marwitz, J.H., et al. (2001). Factors associated with balance deficits on admission to rehabilitation after traumatic brain injury: A multicenter analysis. *Journal of Head Trauma Rehabilitation, 16,* 238–252.

Gregg, N., & Scott, S.S. (2000). Definition and documentation: Theory, measurement, and the courts. *Journal of Learning Disabilities, 33*(1), 5–13.

Gregg, N., Scott, S., McPeek, D., & Ferri, B. (1999). Definitions and eligibility criteria applied to the adolescent and adult population with learning disabilities across agencies. *Learning Disability Quarterly, 22*(3), 213–222.

Gregory, M.W. (1994). *How to provide accommodations for students with learning disabilities.* Columbia, MO: University of Missouri–Columbia, Department of Special Education.

Griffin, C.C., & Hammis, D. (1994). *The Northern Colorado Corporate Partnership Initiative.* Project proposal submitted to Colorado Vocational Rehabilitation.

Griffin, C., & Hammis, D. (2001). Choose-launch-grow: Self-employment for individuals with psychiatric disabilities. *The Rural Exchange: Addressing the Diversity of Rural Life, 14*(1), 1–2.

Griffin, C.C., & Hammis, D. (2002). Job carving: Finding goodness of fit. In C.C. Griffin & D. Hammis (Eds.), *The training connection series for employment specialists* (pp. 20–22). Missoula, MT: The Rural Institute and The Job Training Placement Report.

Griffin, C.C., & Hammis, D. (2003). *Making self-employment work for people with disabilities.* Baltimore: Paul H. Brookes Publishing Co.

Griffin, C.C., & Hammis, D. (2005). Big sign syndrome: The job developer's small business advantage. *TASH Connections, 31*(5/6), 16–17.

Griffin, C.C., Hammis, D., & Geary, T. (2004). *The job developer's handbook: Practical tactics for customized employment.* Baltimore: Paul H. Brookes Publishing Co.

Grigal, M., & Neubert, D.A. (2004). Parents' in-school values and post-school expectations for transition-aged youth with disabilities. *Career Development for Exceptional Individuals, 27,* 65–85.

Grigal, M., Neubert, D.A., & Moon, M.S. (2001). Public school programs for students with significant disabilities in post-secondary settings. *Education and Training in Mental Retardation and Developmental Disabilities, 36,* 244–254.

Grigal, M., Neubert, D.A., & Moon, M.S. (2002). Postsecondary options for students with significant disabilities. *TEACHING Exceptional Children, 35*(2), 68–73.

Grigal, M., Test, D., Beattie, J., & Wood, W. (1997). An evaluation of transition components of individualized education programs. *Exceptional Children, 63*(3), 357–372.

Grossi, T.A. (1998). Using a self-operated auditory prompting system to improve the work performance of two employees with severe disabilities. *Journal of The Association for Persons with Severe Handicaps, 23*(2), 149–154.

Grossi, T.A., & Heward, W.L. (1998). Using self-evaluation to improve the work productivity of trainees in a community-based restaurant training program. *Education and Training in Mental Retardation and Developmental Disabilities, 33*, 248–263.

Guetzloe, E. (1999a). What can we do to stop students killing students? *CEC Today, 5*(7), 14–15.

Guetzloe, E. (1999b). With IDEA reauthorized, what do we do now? *Council for Children with Behavior Disorders, 11*(4), 1, 6, 8.

Gugerty, J.J., & Gavin, M.K. (1991). *Designated vocational instruction: A cooperative process for change.* Unpublished manuscript, Wisconsin Department of Public Instruction, Madison.

Gugerty, J.J., Tindall, L.W., Gavin, M.K., & Gribbon-Fago, B. (1993). *Serving students with learning or cognitive disabilities effectively in two-year colleges: Seven exemplary approaches.* Madison: University of Wisconsin–Madison, Center on Education and Work.

Gumpel, T.P., Tappe, P., & Araki, C. (2000). Comparison of social problem-solving abilities among adults with and without developmental disabilities. *Education and Training in Mental Retardation and Developmental Disabilities, 35*, 259–268.

Gutstein, S.E., & Sheely, R.K. (2002). *Relationship development with young children: Social and emotional development activities for Asperger's syndrome, Autism, PDD, and NLD.* London: Jessica Kingsley Publishing.

Haager, D. (1997). Learning disabilities. In J.W. Wood & A.M. Lazzari (Eds.), *Exceeding the boundaries: Understanding exceptional lives* (pp. 116–159). Orlando, FL: Harcourt Brace & Company.

Haffey, W., & Abrams, D. (1991). Employment outcomes for participants in brain injury work reentry program: Preliminary findings. *Journal of Head Trauma Rehabilitation, 6*(3), 24–34.

Hagborg, W.J. (1996). Self-concept and middle school students with learning disabilities: A comparison of scholastic competence subgroups. *Learning Disability Quarterly, 19*(2), 117–126.

Hagenbaugh, B. (2004, December 9). More temps getting permanent gigs: Hiring recession may be over, but caution remains. *USA Today,* p. B.1.

Hagner, D. (2000). *Coffee breaks and birthday cakes: Evaluating workplace cultures to develop natural supports for employees with disabilities.* St. Augustine, FL: Training Resource Network.

Hagner, D., Butterworth, J., & Keith, G. (1995). Strategies and barriers in facilitating natural supports for employment of adults with severe disabilities. *Journal of The Association for Persons with Severe Handicaps, 20*, 110–120.

Hagner, D., & Cooney, B.F. (2005). "I do that for everybody": Supervising employees with autism. *Focus on Autism and Other Developmental Disabilities, 20*, 91–97.

Hagner, D., & Davies, T. (2002). Doing my own thing: Supported self-employment for individuals with cognitive disabilities. *Journal of Vocational Rehabilitation, 17*(2), 65–74.

Hagner, D., & DiLeo, D. (1996). *Working together: Workplace culture, supported employment and people with disabilities.* Cambridge, MA: Brookline Press.

Hagner, D., Helm, D.T., & Butterworth, J. (1996, June). "This is your meeting": A qualitative study of person-centered planning. *Mental Retardation, 34*(3), 159–171.

Halloran, W.D., & Simon, M.Y. (1995). The transition services requirement: A federal perspective on issues, implications, and challenges. *Journal for Vocational Special Needs Education, 17*, 94–97.

Halpern, A.S. (1994). The transition of youth with disabilities to adult life: A position statement of the Division on Career Development and Transition, the Council for Exceptional Children. *Career Development for Exceptional Individuals, 17*, 115–124.

Halpern, A.S., Herr, C.M., Wolf, N.K., Doren, B., Johnson, M.D., & Lawson, J.D. (1997). *Next S.T.E.P.: Student transition and educational planning.* Austin, TX: PRO-ED.

Hammill, D.D. (1990). On defining learning disabilities: An emerging consensus. *Journal of Learning Disabilities, 23*(2), 74–84.

Hammill, D.D., & Bartel, N. (1986). *Teaching students with learning and behavior problems* (4th ed.). Boston: Allyn & Bacon.

Hammis, D. (1994). Ask another question. *The Field Report, 4,* 3. (Available from the Center for Technical Assistance and Training, University of Minnesota, Minneapolis.)

Hammis, D., & Griffin, C. (1998). Employment for anyone, anywhere, anytime. *The Rural Exchange, 11*(1), 28.

Hammis, D., & Miller, L. (2005). Parent-to-child deeming. In L. Miller & V. Brooke (Eds.), *Benefits Assistance Resource Center.* Richmond: Virginia Commonwealth University Rehabilitation Research and Training Center on Workplace Supports and Job Retention.

Hanley, C.A., Ward, A.B., Magnay, A.R., & Mychalkin, W. (2004). Return to school after brain injury. *Archives of Disease in Childhood, 89*(2), 136–142.

Hanley-Maxwell, C., & Millington, M. (1992). Enhancing independence in supported employment: Natural supports in business and industry. *Journal of Vocational Rehabilitation, 2,* 51–58.

Hanley-Maxwell, C., & Szymanski, E.M. (1995). School to work transition and supported employment. In R.M. Parker & E.M. Szymanski (Eds.), *Rehabilitation counseling: Basics and beyond* (2nd ed., pp. 327–355). Austin, TX: PRO-ED.

Hanushek, E.A., & Raymond, M.E. (2002). The confusing world of educational accountability. *National Tax Journal, LIV,* 365–384.

Haring, T.G., Kennedy, C.H., Adams, M.J., & Pitts-Conway, V. (1987). Teaching generalization of purchasing skills across community settings to autistic youth using videotape modeling. *Journal of Applied Behavior Analysis, 20,* 89–96.

Harrison, P.L., & Oakland, T. (2003). *Adaptive behavior assessment system* (2nd ed.). San Antonio, TX: Harcourt Assessment.

Harry, B., Grenot-Scheyer, M., Smith-Lewis, M., Park, H.S., Xin, F., & Schwartz, I. (1995). Developing culturally inclusive services for individuals with severe disabilities. *Journal of The Association for Persons with Severe Handicaps, 20*(2), 99–109.

Hart, D., Zafft, C., & Zimbrich, K. (2001). Creating access to college for all students. *Journal for Vocational Special Needs Education, 23*(2), 19–31.

Hart, T., Sherer, M., Whyte, J., Polansky, M., & Novack, T.A. (2004). Awareness of behavioral, cognitive, and physical deficits in acute traumatic brain injury. *Archives of Physical Medicine and Rehabilitation, 85,* 1450–1456.

Hartnett, J.T., Collins, M., & Tremblay, T. (2002). Longitudinal outcomes in Vermont's Consumer Choice Demonstration Project (1993–1999). *Journal of Vocational Rehabilitation, 17*(3), 145–154.

Hartz, D. (2000). Literacy leaps as blind students embrace technology. *English Journal, 90*(2), 52–59.

Hasazi, S.B., Gordon, L., & Roe, C.A. (1985). Factors associated the employment status of handicapped youth exiting high school from 1979 to 1983. *Exceptional Children, 51*(6), 455–469.

Hawkins, G. (2004). *How to find work that works for people with Asperger's syndrome: The ultimate guide for getting people with Asperger's syndrome into the workplace (and keeping them there).* London: Jessica Kingsley Publishing.

Hawley, C.A. (2005). Saint or sinner? Teacher perceptions of a child with traumatic brain injury. *Pediatric Rehabilitation, 8*(2), 117–129.

Hayden, M., & Abery, B. (Eds.). (1994). *Challenges for a service system in transition: Ensuring quality community experiences for persons with developmental disabilities.* Baltimore: Paul H. Brookes Publishing Co.

Hayman-Abello, S.E., Rourke, B.P., & Fuerst, D.R. (2003). Psychosocial status after pediatric traumatic brain injury: A subtype analysis using Child Behavior Checklist. *Journal of the International Neuropsychological Society, 9,* 887–898.

Hayward, B. (1998). *Third interim report: Characteristics and outcomes of former VR consumers with an employment outcomes.* Submitted by the Research Triangle Institute to the Rehabilitation Services Administration of the U.S. Department of Education. Available at http://www.rti.org/publications/pubs.cfm?pub cat id=19

Hayward, B., & Schmidt-Davis, H. (2000). *Fourth Interim Report: Characteristics and outcome of transitional youth in VR. A longitudinal study of the vocational rehabilitation program.* Submitted by the

Research Triangle Institute to the Rehabilitation Services Administration of the U.S. Department of Education. Available at http://www.rti.org/publications/pubs.cfm?pub cat id=19

Hayward, B., & Tashjian, M. (1995). *First interim report.* Submitted by the Research Triangle Institute to the Rehabilitation Services Administration of the U.S. Department of Education. Available at http://www.rti.org/publications/pubs.cfm?pub cat id=19

Hayward, B., & Tashjian, M. (1996). *Second interim report: Characteristics and perspectives of vocational rehabilitation consumers.* Submitted by the Research Triangle Institute to the Rehabilitation Services Administration of the U.S. Department of Education. Available at http://www.rti.org/publications/pubs.cfm?pub cat id=91

Health Resource Center. (2005). *2005 summer pre-college programs for students with disabilities.* Retrieved April 1, 2005, from http://www.heath.gwu.edu/PDFs/Summer%20Pre-College%202005.pdf

Heaviside, S., Rowand, C., Williams, C., & Farris, E. (1998). *Violence and discipline problems in U.S. Public Schools: 1996–1997* (Report No. NCES 98-030). Washington, DC: U.S. Department of Education, National Center for Education Statistics. (ERIC Document Reproduction Service No. ED417257)

Held, M.F., Thoma, C.A., & Thomas, K. (2004). The John Jones show: How one teacher pulled it all together to facilitate self-determined transition planning for a young man with autism. *Focus on Autism and Developmental Disabilities, 19*(3), 177–188.

Helen Keller National Center. (1994). *Guidelines for identifying, selecting, creating, and evaluating assistive technology.* New York: Author.

Henderson, C. (1999). *College freshmen with disabilities: A biennial statistical profile.* Washington, DC: Heath Resource Center of the American Council on Education.

Henderson, C. (2001). *College freshmen with disabilities: A biennial statistical profile.* Washington, DC: Heath Resource Center of the American Council on Education.

Herman, J.L., Ashbacher, P.R., & Winters, L. (1992). *A practical guide to alternative assessment.* Alexandria, VA: Association for Supervision and Curriculum Development.

Herman, R., Oliva, T., & Gioia, J. (2002). *Impending crisis.* Akron, OH: Oakhill Press.

Hernandez, B., Keys, C., & Balcazar, F. (2000). Employer attitudes toward workers with disabilities and their ADA employment rights: A literature review. *Journal of Rehabilitation, 66,* 4–16.

Heron, E., & Jorgensen, C.M. (1995). Addressing learning differences right from the start. *Educational Leadership, 52*(4), 56–58.

Hershenson, D.B., & Szymanski, E.M. (1992). Career development of people with disabilities. In R.M. Parker & E.M. Szymanski (Eds.), *Rehabilitation counseling: Basics and beyond* (2nd ed., pp. 273–303). Austin, TX: PRO-ED.

Hess, C., Kregel, J., & Wehman, P. (1991). *Houston area post-21 follow-up study.* Houston, TX: Region IV Education Service Center.

Hesse, B.W. (1995). Curb cuts in the virtual community: Telework and persons with disabilities. *Proceedings of the 28th Annual Hawaii International Conference on Systems Sciences, IEEE, 36*(6), 418–425.

Heubert, J.P., & Hauser, R.M. (Eds.). (1999). *High-stakes: Testing for tracking, promotion and graduation.* Washington, DC: National Academy Press.

Heward, W.L. (2003). Ten faulty notions about teaching and learning that hinder the effectiveness of special education. *The Journal of Special Education, 36*(4), 186–205.

Hickson, L., Blackman, L.S., & Reis, E.M. (1995). *Mental retardation: Foundations of educational programming.* Boston: Allyn & Bacon.

Hildreth, B.L. (1995). The comprehensive calendar: An organizational tool for college students with learning disabilities. *Intervention in School and Clinic, 30*(5), 306–308.

Hocutt, A.M., McKinney, J.D., & Montague, M. (2002). The impact of managed care of efforts to prevent development of serious emotional disturbance in young children. *Journal of Disability Policy Studies, 13*(1), 51–60.

Hodgdon, L. (1995). *Visual strategies for improving communication: Practical supports for home and school.* Troy, MI: QuirkRoberts Publishing.

Hoff, D., Gandolfo, C., Gold, M., & Jordan, M. (2000). *Demystifying job development.* St. Augustine, FL: Training Resource Network.

Hoffman, A., & Field, S. (1995). Self-determination through effective curriculum development. *Intervention in School and Clinic, 30,* 134–141.

Holburn, S. (2002). How science can evaluate and enhance person-centered planning. *Research and Practice for Persons with Severe Disabilities, 27*(4), 250–260.

Holburn, S., & Vietze, P.M. (2002). *Person-centered planning: Research, practice, and future directions.* Baltimore: Paul H. Brookes Publishing Co.

Honey, A. (2000). Psychiatric vocational rehabilitation: Where are the customers' views? *Psychiatric Rehabilitation Journal, 23,* 270–279.

Hoover, J., & Stenhjem, P. (2003). Bullying and teasing of youth with disabilities: Creating positive school environments for effective inclusion. *National Center on Secondary Education and Transition, 2*(3). Available at http://www.ncset.org/publications/print-resource.asp?id=1332

Horner, R.H., Dunlap, G., Koegel, R.L., Carr, E.G., Sailor, W., Anderson, J., et al. (1990). Toward a technology of nonaversive behavioral support. *Journal of The Association for Persons with Severe Handicaps, 15,* 125–132.

Horner, R.H., & McDonald, R. (1982). A comparison of single instance and general case instruction in teaching a generalized vocational skill. *Journal of The Association for Persons with Severe Handicaps, 7,* 7–20.

Horvath-Rose, A.E., Stapleton, D.C., & O'Day, B. (2004). Trends in outcomes for young people with work disabilities: Are we making progress? *Journal of Vocational Rehabilitation, 21,* 175–187.

House of Representatives Standing Committee on Employment, Education and Training. (1996). *Truancy and exclusion from school.* AGPS, Canberra, P3.

Housing Act of 1959, PL 86-372, 42 U.S.C. § 1400 *et seq.*

Housing and Community Development Act of 1974, PL 93-383, 42 U.S.C. § 5300 *et seq.*

Howlin, P. (1997). Prognosis in autism: Do specialist treatments affect long-term outcome? *European Child and Adolescent Psychiatry, 6,* 55–72.

Howlin, P., Goode, S., Hutton, J., & Rutter, M. (2004). Adult outcome for children with autism. *Journal of Child Psychology and Psychiatry, 45,* 212–229.

Hughes, B. (2004, November 19). *Major change: Many American students use college as way to pick careers.* Retrieved April 4, 2005, from http://www.decaturdaily.com/decaturdaily/news/041119/majors.shtml

Hughes, C. (2001). Transition to adulthood: Supporting young adults to access social, employment, and civic pursuits. *Mental Retardation and Developmental Disabilities Research Reviews, 7,* 84–90.

Hughes, C., & Carter, E.W. (2000). *The transition handbook: Strategies high school teachers use that work!* Baltimore: Paul H. Brookes Publishing Co.

Hughes, C., & Carter, E.W. (2002). Informal assessment procedures. In C.L. Sax & C.A. Thoma (Eds.), *Transition assessment: Wise practices for quality lives* (pp. 51–69). Baltimore: Paul H. Brookes Publishing Co.

Hughes, C., Copeland, S.R., Agran, M., Wehmeyer, M.L., Rodi, M.S., & Presley, J.A. (2002). Using self-monitoring to improve performance in general education high school classes. *Education and Training in Mental Retardation and Developmental Disabilities, 37,* 262–271.

Hughes, C., Guth, C., Hall, S., Presley, J., Dye, M., & Byers, C. (1999). "They are my best friends": Peer buddies promote inclusion in high school. *TEACHING Exceptional Children, 31*(5), 32–37.

Hughes, C., & Rusch, F.R. (1989). Teaching supported employees with mental retardation to solve problems. *Journal of Applied Behavior Analysis, 22,* 365–372.

Hunt, P., & Goetz, L. (1997). Research on inclusive educational programs, practices, and outcomes for students with severe disabilities. *Journal of Special Education, 31*(1), 3–29.

Idol, L., Paolucci-Whitcomb, P., & Nevin, A. (1986). *Collaborative consultation.* Austin, TX: PRO-ED.

Imada, D., Doyle, B.A., Brock, B., & Goddard, A. (2002, September/October). Developing leadership skills in students with mild disabilities. *TEACHING Exceptional Children*, 48–54.

Improving America's Schools Act of 1994, PL 103-382, 20 U.S.C. §§ 630 *et seq.*

Individuals with Disabilities Education Act Amendments of 1997, PL 105-17, 20 U.S.C. §§ 1400 *et seq.*

Individuals with Disabilities Education Act of 1990, PL 101-476, 20 U.S.C. §§ 1400 *et seq.*

Individuals with Disabilities Education Improvement Act of 2004, PL 108-446, 20 U.S.C. §§ 1400 *et seq.*

Inestroza, R.A. (1990). Integrating basic skills for IEPs in vocational education. *Journal for Vocational Special Needs Education*, *13*(1), 41.

Inge, K. (1991, Fall). *Bridges from school to work: Marriott Foundation for People with Disabilities.* Richmond: Virginia Commonwealth University Rehabilitation Research and Training Center of Workplace Supports Newsletter.

Inge, K. (1999, Spring). *Who's providing the support? Job-site training issues and strategies.* Richmond: Virginia Commonwealth University.

Inge, K.J. (2001). Supported employment for individuals with physical disabilities. In P. Wehman (Ed.), *Supported employment in business: Expanding the capacity of workers with disabilities* (pp. 153–180). St. Augustine, FL: Training Resource Network.

Inge, K.J., & Dymond, S. (1994). Challenging behaviors in the workplace: Increasing a student's access to community-based vocational instruction. *Journal of Vocational Rehabilitation*, *4*, 272–284.

Inge, K., Dymond, S., & Wehman, P. (1996). Community based vocational training. In P. McLaughlin & P. Wehman (Eds.), *Mental retardation and developmental disabilities* (pp. 297–316). Austin, TX: PRO-ED.

Inge, K.J., & Shepherd, J. (1995). Assistive technology applications and strategies for school system personnel. In K.F. Flippo, K.J. Inge, & J.M. Barcus (Eds.), *Assistive technology: A resource for school, work, and community* (pp. 133–166). Baltimore: Paul H. Brookes Publishing Co.

Institute on Community Integration. (2003). Feature issue on social inclusion through recreation for persons with disabilities. *Impact*, *16*(2), 1–34.

Interstate New Teacher Assessment and Support Consortium. (2001, May). *Model standards for licensing general and special education teachers of students with disabilities: A resource for state dialogue.* Washington, DC: Council of Chief State School Officers. Retrieved November 18, 2004, from http://www.ccsso.org/intasc.html

Iovannone, R., Dunlap, G., Huber, H., & Kincaid, D. (2003). Effective educational practices for students with autism spectrum disorders. *Focus on Autism and Other Developmental Disabilities*, *18*(3), 150–165.

Ip, R., Dornan, J., & Schentag, C. (1995). Traumatic brain injury: Factors predicting return to work or school. *Brain Injury*, *9*, 517–532.

Ispen, C., Arnold, N.L., & Colling, K. (2005). Self-employment for people with disabilities: Enhancing services through interagency linkages. *Journal of Disability Policy Studies*, *15*(4), 231–239.

Izzo, M.V., Johnson, J.R., Levitz, M., & Aaron, J.H. (1998). Transition from school to adult life: New roles for educators. In P. Wehman & J. Kregel (Eds.), *More than a job: Securing satisfying careers for people with disabilities* (pp. 249–286). Baltimore: Paul H. Brookes Publishing Co.

Izzo, M.V., Pritz, S.G., & Ott, P. (1990). Teaching problem-solving skills: A ticket to a brighter future. *Journal for Vocational Special Needs Education*, *13*(1), 23–26.

Izzo, M.V., & Schumate, R. (1991). *Transition planning guide.* Columbus: Ohio Department of Education.

Jackson, L., & Panyan, M.V. (2004). *Positive behavioral support in the classroom: Principles and practices.* Baltimore: Paul H. Brookes Publishing Co.

Janney, R.E., Snell, M.E., Beers, M.K., & Raynes, M. (1995). Integrating students with moderate and severe disabilities into general education classes. *Exceptional Children*, *61*(5), 425–439.

Jennett, B. (1976). Assessment of severity of head injury. *Journal of Neurology, Neurosurgery, and Psychiatry*, *39*, 647–655.

Jennett, B., & Teasdale, G. (1977). Aspects of coma after severe head injury. *Lancet*, *1*, 878–881.

Jennett, B., & Teasdale, G. (1981). *Management of severe head injuries.* Philadelphia: F.A. Davis.

Jensen, R.A., & Kiley, T.J. (1998). *Teams or torture?: Creating a climate for collaboration.* (ERIC Document Reproduction Service No. ED419344)

Job Accommodation Network. (1999). *Accommodation benefit cost data.* Retrieved July 30, 1999, from http://jan.wvu.edu/media/Stats/BenCosts0799.html

Job Accommodation Network. (2000). *Discover the facts about job accommodations.* Retrieved March 7, 2000, from http://janweb.icdi.wvu.edu/english/accfact.htm

Job Accommodation Network. (n.d.). *Low cost accommodation solutions.* Accessed October 21, 2005, at http://www.jan.wvu.edu/media/LowCostSolutions.html

Job Training Partnership Act of 1982, PL 97-300, 29 U.S.C. §§ 1501 *et seq.*

Johanson, J. (1997). *Technology in education: A case for change.* Macomb: Western Illinois University. (ERIC Document Reproduction Service No. ED410740)

Johnson, D.R. (2004). Supported employment trends: Implications for transition-age youth. *Research and Practice for Persons with Severe Disabilities, 29*(4), 243–247.

Johnson, D. (2005). Key provisions of transition: A comparison of IDEA 1997 and IDEA 2004. *Career Development for Exceptional Individuals, 28*(1), 60–68.

Johnson, D., & Emanuel, E. (2000). *Issues influencing the future of transition programs and services in the United States.* Minneapolis: National Transition Network, Institute on Community Integration, University of Minnesota.

Johnson, D.R., Stodden, P.A., Emanuel, E.J., Luecking, R., & Mack, M. (2002). Current challenges facing secondary education and transition services: What research tells us. *Exceptional Children, 68,* 419–531.

Johnson, D.R., & Thurlow, M.L. (2003). *A national study on graduation requirements and diploma options for youth with disabilities.* Retrieved February 4, 2004, from http://education.umn.edu/NCEO/OnlinePubs/Technical36.htm

Johnson, D.W., & Johnson, R.T. (1989). *Cooperation and competition: Theory and research.* Edina, MN: Interaction Books.

Johnson, D.W., & Johnson, R.T. (2000). Cooperative learning, values, and culturally plural classrooms. In M. Leicester, S. Modgill, & C. Modgill (Eds.), *Classroom issues: Practice, pedagogy, and curriculum* (Vol. 3, pp. 15–29). London: Falmer Press.

Johnson, D.W., & Johnson, R.T. (2003). Ensuring diversity is positive: Cooperative community, constructive conflict, and civic values. In J.S. Thousand, R.A. Villa, & A.I. Nevin (Eds.), *Creativity and collaborative learning: A practical guide to empowering students, teachers, and families* (2nd ed., pp. 271–283). Baltimore: Paul H. Brookes Publishing Co.

Johnson, R.D., & Sharpe, N.M. (2000). Analysis of local education agency efforts to implement the transition services requirements of IDEA of 1990. In D.R. Johnson & E.J. Emanuel (Eds.), *Issues influencing the future of transition programs and services in the United States* (pp. 31–48). Minneapolis: University of Minnesota.

Johnston, M.V., Goverover, Y., & Dijkers, M. (2005). Community activities and individuals' satisfaction with them: Quality of life in the first year after traumatic brain injury. *Archives of Physical Medicine and Rehabilitation, 86,* 735–745.

Johnstone, B., Mount, D., & Schopp, L.H. (2003). Financial and vocational outcomes one year after traumatic brain injury. *Archives of Physical Medicine and Rehabilitation, 84,* 238–241.

Johnstone, B., Schopp, L.H., Harper, J., & Koscuilek, J. (1999). Neuropsychological impairments, vocational outcomes, and financial costs for individuals with traumatic brain injury receiving state vocational rehabilitation services. *Journal of Head Trauma Rehabilitation, 143,* 220–232.

Johnstone, B., Vessell, R., Bounds, T., Hoskins, S., & Sherman, A. (2003). Predictors of success for state vocational rehabilitation clients with traumatic brain injury. *Archives of Physical Medicine and Rehabilitation, 84,* 283–241.

Jorge, R., & Robinson, R.G. (2002). Mood disorders following traumatic brain injury. *NeuroRehabilitation, 17*(4), 311–324.

Joyce, B., & Weil, M. (1980). *Models of teaching* (2nd ed.). Upper Saddle River, NJ: Prentice Hall.

Kameenui, E.J., & Darch, C.B. (1995). *Instructional classroom management.* White Plains, NY: Longman Publishers.

Kamens, M.W., Loprete, S.J., & Slostad, F.A. (2000). Classroom teachers' perceptions about inclusion of students with disabilities. *Teacher Education, 11,* 147–158.

Kapadia, S., & Fantuzzo, J.W. (1988). Training children with developmental disabilities and severe behavior problems to use self-management procedures to sustain attention to preacademic/academic tasks. *Education and Training in Mental Retardation, 23,* 59–69.

Karger, J., & Pullin, D. (2002). *Exit documents and students with disabilities: Legal issues* (Issue Brief 2). College Park: University of Maryland, Educational Policy Research Reform Institute, Institute for the Study of Exceptional Children and Youth.

Karpur, A., Clark, H.B., Caproni, P., & Sterner, H. (2005). Transition to adult roles for students with emotional/behavioral disturbances: A follow-up study of student exiters from steps-to-success. *Career Development for Exceptional Individuals, 28*(1), 36–46.

Karpur, A., Clark, H.B., Caproni, P., Sterner, H., & Whitfield, D. (2003). *Transition to adult roles for students with EBD: A follow-up study of student exiters from a transition program.* Tampa: Florida Mental Health Institute, University of South Florida.

Katsiyannis, A., deFur, S., & Conderman, G. (1998). Transition services: Systems change for youth with disabilities? A review of state practices. *Journal of Special Education, 32*(1), 55–61.

Katsiyannis, A., & Yell, M.L. (2004). Critical issues and trends in the education of students with emotional or behavioral disorders. *Behavioral Disorders, 29*(3), 209–210.

Katsiyannis, A., Zhang, D., Woodruff, N., & Dixon, A. (2005). Transition supports to students with mental retardation: An examination of data from the national longitudinal Transition Study 2. *Education and Training in Developmental Disabilities, 40*(2), 109–116.

Kauffman, J., & Hallahan, D. (1995). *The illusion of full inclusion.* Austin, TX: PRO-ED.

Kauffman, J., Mostert, M., Trent, S., & Hallahan, D. (1998). *Managing classroom behavior: A reflective case-based approach.* Boston: Allyn & Bacon.

Kaufman, J., & Blanchon, D. (1996). Managed care for children with special need: A care coordination model. *Journal of Care Management, 2*(2), 46–59.

Kaye, H. (2000). *Computer and internet use among people with disabilities. Disability Statistics Report 13.* Washington, DC: U.S. Department of Education, National Institute on Disability and Rehabilitation Research.

Kazdin, A.E. (1980). *Behavior modification in applied settings* (2nd ed.). Homewood, IL: Dorsey Press.

Keefe, E.B., Moore, V., & Duff, F. (2004). The four "knows" of collaborative teaching. *TEACHING Exceptional Children, 36*(5), 36–41.

Keel, J.H., Mesibov, G.B., & Woods, A.V. (1997). TEACCH-supported employment program. *Journal of Autism and Developmental Disorders, 27,* 3–9.

Keenan, S. (2004). Bullying: A culture of fear and disrespect. *The Council for Children with Behavioral Disorders, 18*(2), 1, 2, 4.

Kennedy, C.H., & Fisher, D. (2001). *Inclusive middle schools.* Baltimore: Paul H. Brookes Publishing Co.

Kennedy, C.H., Long, T., Jolivette, K., Cox, J., Tang, J.C., & Thompson, T. (2001). Facilitating general education participation for students with behavior problems by linking positive behavior supports and person-centered planning. *Journal of Emotional and Behavioral Disorders, 9*(3), 161–171.

Kennedy, C.H., & Thompson, T. (2000). Health conditions contributing to problem behavior among people with mental retardation and developmental disabilities. In M. Wehmeyer & J. Patten (Eds.), *Mental retardation in the 21st century* (pp. 211–231). Austin, TX: PRO-ED.

Kennedy, M.J. (1996). Self-determination and trust: My experiences and thoughts. In D.J. Sands & M.L. Wehmeyer (Eds.), *Self-determination across the life span: Independence and choice for people with disabilities* (pp. 37–49). Baltimore: Paul H. Brookes Publishing Co.

Kennedy, M.J. (2004). Living outside the system: The ups and downs of getting on with out lives. *Mental Retardation, 42*(3), 229–231.

Keogh, B.K. (2003). *Temperament in the classroom: Understanding individual differences.* Baltimore: Paul H. Brookes Publishing Co.

Kerr, M.M., & Nelson, C.M. (1998). *Strategies for managing problem behaviors in the classroom* (2nd ed.). Columbus, OH: Charles E. Merrill.

Keyes, M.W., & Owens-Johnson, L. (2003). Developing person-centered IEPs. *Intervention in School and Clinic, 38*(3), 145–152.

Keyser-Marcus, L., Bricout, J., Wehman, P., Campbell, L., Cifu, D., Englander, J., et al. (2002). Acute predictors of return to employment after traumatic brain injury: A longitudinal follow-up. *Archives of Physical Medicine and Rehabilitation, 83,* 635–641.

Khemka, I. (2000). Increasing independent decision-making skills of women with mental retardation in simulated interpersonal situations of abuse. *American Journal on Mental Retardation, 105,* 387–401.

Kiernan, W. (2000). Where are we now: Perspectives on employment of persons with mental retardation. *Focus on Autism and Other Developmental Disabilities, 15*(2), 90–96.

Kim, E. (2002). Agitation, aggression, and disinhibition syndromes after traumatic brain injury. *NeuroRehabilitation, 17*(4), 297–310.

Kim, K-H., & Turnbull, A. (2004). Transition to adulthood for students with severe intellectual disabilities: Shifting toward person-family interdependent planning. *Research and Practice for Persons with Severe Disabilities, 29*(1), 53–57.

Kincaid, D., Chapman, C., Shannon, P., Schall, C., & Harrower, J.K. (2002). Families and the Tri-State Consortium for positive behavior support: A unique collaboration for people with challenging behavior. In J.M. Lucyshyn, G. Dunlap, & R.W. Albin (Eds.), *Families and positive behavior support: Addressing problem behaviors in family contexts* (pp. 309–328). Baltimore: Paul H. Brookes Publishing Co.

Klein, J. (1992). Get me the hell out of here: Supporting people with disabilities to live in their own homes. In J. Nisbet (Ed.), *Natural supports in school, at work, and in the community for people with severe disabilities* (pp. 277–339). Baltimore: Paul H. Brookes Publishing Co.

Kleinwaks, L.E. (1996). Considerations and practices in the vocational evaluation of high school students who are deaf. *Vocational Evaluation and Work Adjustment Bulletin, 29,* 102–107.

Kline, F.M., & Silver, L.B. (2004). *The educator's guide to mental health issues in the classroom.* Baltimore: Paul H. Brookes Publishing Co.

Knight, D., & Wadsworth, D.E. (1994). Guidelines for educating students who are technology-dependent. *Physical Disabilities: Education and Related Services, 13*(1), 1–8.

Knitzer, J., Steinberg, Z., & Fleisch, B. (1990). *At the schoolhouse door.* New York: Bank Street College.

Knott, L., & Asselin, S.B. (1999). Transition competencies: Perception of secondary special education teachers. *Teacher Education and Special Education, 22,* 55–65.

Koch, L.C. (2001). Vocational assessment in the Americans with Disabilities Act era. In P.D. Rumrill, J.L. Bellini, & L.C. Koch (Eds.), *Emerging issues in rehabilitation counseling: Perspectives on the new millennium* (pp. 89–126). Springfield, IL: Charles C Thomas.

Kochhar, C.A., West, L.L., & Taymans, J.M. (2000). *Successful inclusion: Practical strategies for a shared responsibility.* Upper Saddle River, NJ: Prentice Hall.

Koegel, L.K., Koegel, R.L., & Dunlap, G. (1996). *Positive behavioral support: Including people with difficult behavior in the community.* Baltimore: Paul H. Brookes Publishing Co.

Kohler, P.D., & Field, S. (2003). Transition-focused education: Foundation for the future. *Journal of Special Education, 37*(3), 174–183.

Kohn, A. (2004). *What does it mean to be well educated?* Portsmouth, NH: Heinemann.

Kraemer, B.R., & Blacher, J. (1997). An overview of educationally relevant effects, assessment, and school reentry. In A. Glang, G.H.S. Singer, & B. Todis (Eds.), *Students with acquired brain injury* (pp. 3–31). Baltimore: Paul H. Brookes Publishing Co.

Kraemer, B.R., & Blacher, J. (2001). Transition for young adults with severe mental retardation: School preparation, parent expectations, and family involvement. *Mental Retardation, 39*(6), 423–435.

Kraemer, B.R., McIntyre, L.L., & Blacher, J. (2003). Quality of life for young adults with mental retardation during transition. *Mental Retardation, 41*(4), 250–262.

Kraus, J.F., & McArthur, D.L. (1999). Incidence and prevalence of, and costs associated with, traumatic brain injury. In M. Rosenthal, E.R. Griffith, J.S. Kreutzer, & B. Pentland (Eds.), *Rehabilitation of the adult and child* (3rd ed., pp. 3–18). Philadelphia: F.A. Davis.

Kregel, J., & Dean, D.H. (2002). Sheltered work vs. supported employment: A direct comparison of long-term earnings outcomes for individuals with cognitive disabilities. In J. Kregel, D.H. Dean, & P. Wehman (Eds.), *Achievements and challenges in employment services for people with disabilities: The longitudinal impact of workplace supports* (Monograph). Richmond: Virginia Commonwealth University, Rehabilitation Research and Training Center on Workplace Supports.

Kregel, J., & Dean, D. (2003). Sheltered work vs. supported employment: A direct comparison of long-term earnings. *InfoLines, 14*(6), 1, 3.

Kreutzer, J.S., Marwitz, J.H., Walker, W., Sander, A., Sherer, M., Bogner, J., et al. (2003). Moderating factors in return to work and job stability after traumatic brain injury. *Journal of Head Trauma Rehabilitation, 18*, 128–138.

Kreutzer, J.S., Wehman, P., Morton, M.V., & Stonnington, H. (1988). Supported employment and cognitive compensatory strategies for enhancing vocational outcome following traumatic brain injury. *Brain Injury, 2*(3), 205–223.

Krom, D.M., & Prater, M.A. (1993). IEP goals for intermediate-aged students with mild mental retardation. *Career Development for Exceptional Individuals, 16*(1), 87–95.

Krupa, T. (2004). Employment, recovery, and schizophrenia: Integrating health and disorder work. *Psychiatric Rehabilitation Journal, 28*(1), 8–15.

Kruse, D., Krueger, K., & Drastal, S. (1996). Legal forum: Computer use, computer training, and employment. *Spine, 21*, 891–896.

Ladd, H.F. (2002). School based accountability systems: The promise and the pitfalls. *New Tax Journal, 54*, 385–400.

Lagomarcino, T.R., & Rusch, F.R. (1989). Utilizing self-management procedures to teach independent performance. *Education and Training in Mental Retardation, 24*, 297–305.

Lahm, E.A., & Nickels, B.L. (1999). Assistive technology competencies for special educators. *TEACHING Exceptional Children, 32*(1), 56–63.

Lane, H., Hoffmeister, R., & Bahan, B. (1996). *A journey into the Deaf world.* San Diego: Dawn Sign Press.

Lane, K.L., Wehby, J.H., Little, M.A., & Cooley, C. (2005a). Academic, social, and behavioral profiles of students with emotional and behavioral disorders educated in self-contained classrooms and self-contained schools: Part I. Are they more alike then different? *Behavior Disorders, 30*(4), 349–361.

Lane, K.L., Wehby, J.H., Little, M.A., & Cooley, C. (2005b). Students educated in self-contained classrooms and self-contained schools: Part II. How do they progress over time? *Behavioral Disorders, 30*(4), 363–374.

Langdon, C.A. (1999). The fifth Phi Delta Kappa poll of teachers' attitudes toward the public schools. *Phi Delta Kappan, 80*, 611–618.

Lange, C.M., & Sletten, S.J. (2002). *Alternative education: A brief history and synthesis.* Alexandria, VA: Project Forum at National Association of State Directors of Special Education.

Langlois, J., & Gotsch, K. (2001). *Traumatic brain injury in the United States: Assessing outcomes in children.* Atlanta, GA: National Center for Injury Prevention and Control, Centers for Disease Control and Prevention.

Langone, J. (2000). Technology for individuals with severe and physical disabilities. In D. Lindsey (Ed.), *Technology and exceptional individuals* (pp. 327–351). Austin, TX: PRO-ED.

Langston, A., Coker, C.C., & Smith, C.A. (1989). A descriptive study of rehabilitation technology utilization in state vocational rehabilitation agencies. *Journal of Rehabilitation Administration, 13*(5), 45–50.

Langton, A.J., & Ramseur, H. (2001). Enhancing employment outcomes through job accommodation and assistive technology resources and services. *Journal of Vocational Rehabilitation, 16*(1), 27–37.

Larkin, C., & Gaylord, V. (2003). Medicaid home and community-based services: The first 20 years. *Policy Research Brief, 14*(3).

Larkin, C., Prouty, P., & Coucouvanis, K. (2005). Long-term service and support expenditures for persons with ID/DD within the overall Medicaid Program. *Mental Retardation, 43*(1), 68–72.

Larson, R.W. (2000). Towards a psychology of positive youth development. *American Psychologist, 55*(1), 170–183.

Latham, G.P., & Locke, E.A. (1991). Self-regulation through goal setting. *Organizational Behavior and Human Decision Processes, 50*(2), 212–247.

Latimer, E., Becker, D., Drake, R.E., Lecomte, T., Duclos, I., & Piat, P. (2004). *Individual placement and support to help people with severe mental illness find and maintain competitive employment: Preliminary results of the first Canadian randomized trial.* Poster presented at the 21st annual Pittsburgh Schizophrenia Conference.

Lattimore, L.P., Parsons, M.B., & Reid, D.H. (2003). Assessing preferred work among adults with autism beginning supported jobs: Identification of constant and alternating task preferences. *Behavioral Interventions, 18*, 161–177.

Lattin, D., & Wehmeyer, M.L. (2003). *The role of Centers for Independent Living in transition services for youth with disabilities: A national survey.* Manuscript submitted for publication.

Lavin, D. (2000). *Reach for the stars!* Spring Lake Park, MN: RISE.

Lawhead, R.A. (2005). *Hearing on Opportunity for Too Few? Oversight of federal employment programs for people with disabilities.* Testimony before the Health, Education, Labor & Pensions Committee, U.S. Senate, October 20, 2005.

Lawrence-Brown, D. (2004). Differentiated instruction: Inclusive strategies for standards-based learning that benefit the whole class. *American Secondary Education, 32*(2), 34–62.

Lazarus, B.B. (1996). Flexible skeletons guided notes for adolescents. *TEACHING Exceptional Children, 28*(3), 36–40.

LD Online. (2000). *Tell me the facts about learning disabilities* [on-line]. Available at http://www.ldonline.org/ccldinfo/l.html

Lee, M., Storey, K., Anderson, J.L., Goetz, L., & Zivolich, S. (1996). The effect of mentoring versus job coach instruction on integration in supported employment settings. *Journal of The Association of Persons with Severe Handicaps, 22*(3), 151–158.

Lehman, A.F., Goldberg, R.W., Dixon, L.B., McNary, S., Postrado, L., Hackman, A., et al. (2002). Improving employment outcomes for persons with severe mental illness. *Archives of General Psychiatry, 59*, 165–172.

Lehr, C., & Thurlow, M. (2003). *Putting it all together: Including students with disabilities in assessment and accountability systems* (Policy Directions No. 16). Retrieved July 28, 2004, from http://education.umn.edu/NCEO/OnlinePubs/Synthesis47.html

Leiter, V., Wood, M.L., & Bell, S.H. (1997). Case management at work for SSA disability beneficiaries: Process results of Project NetWork return-to-work demonstration. *Social Security Bulletin, 60*(1), 1–8.

Lemke, A. (1991). Keeping them on the job: Ways to assist employees with LD in upgrading their skills. *Puzzle People News, 4*(4), 10–13.

Leone, P.E., Mayer, M.J., Malmgren, K., & Meisel, S.M. (2000). School violence and disruption; Rhetoric, reality, and reasonable balance. *Focus on Exceptional Children, 33*(1), 1–20.

Lerner, J. (2003). *Learning disabilities: Theories, diagnosis, and teaching practices.* Boston: Houghton Mifflin Company.

Levine, M.D. (1989). Learning disabilities at 25: The early adulthood of a maturing concept. *Learning Disabilities, 1*(1), 1–11.

Levine, M.D. (1990). *Keeping ahead in school.* Cambridge, MA: Educator's Publishing Service.

Levy, S., & Vaughn, S. (2002). An observational study of teacher's reading instruction for students with emotional or behavioral disorders. *Behavioral Disorders, 27,* 215–235.

Lewis, R.B. (1998). Assistive technology and learning disabilities: Today's realities and tomorrow's promises. *Journal of Learning Disabilities, 31*(1), 16–26, 54.

Lewis, R.B., & Doorlag, D.H. (1999). *Teaching special students in general classrooms* (5th ed.). Upper Saddle River, NJ: Prentice Hall.

Lichtenstein, S. (1993). Transition from school to adulthood: Case studies of adults with learning disabilities who dropped out of school. *Exceptional Children, 59*(4), 336–347.

Lieberman, L.M. (1985). Special education and regular education: A merger made in heaven? *Exceptional Children, 51*(6), 513–516.

Lieshout, R.V. (2001). Increasing the employment of people with disabilities through the Business Leadership Network. *Journal of Vocational Rehabilitation, 16,* 77–81.

Lilly, M.S. (1979). *Children with exceptional needs.* New York: Holt, Rinehart & Winston.

Lindstrom, J., Moberg, A., & Rapp, B. (1997). On the classification of telework. *European Journal of Information Systems, 6*(4), 243–255.

Linn, R.L. (2000). Assessments and accountability. *Educational Researcher, 29*(2), 1–15.

Linn, R.L. (2001). *The design and evaluation of educational assessment and accountability systems.* Los Angeles: National Center for Research on Evaluation, Standards, and Student Testing (CRESST).

Litvak, S., Zukas, H., & Heumann, J.E. (1987). *Attending to America: Personal assistance for independent living: A survey of attendant service programs in the United States for people of all ages with disabilities.* Berkeley: University of California at Berkeley, World Institute on Disability.

Lockyer, L., & Rutter, M. (1970). A five to fifteen year follow-up study of infantile psychosis: IV. Patterns of cognitive abilities. *British Journal of Social and Clinical Psychology, 9,* 152–163.

Lohrmann-O'Rourke, S., Knoster, T., & Llewellyn, G. (1999). Screening for understanding: An initial line of inquiry for school-based settings. *Journal of Positive Behavior Interventions, 1,* 35–42.

Lohrmann-O'Rourke, S., & Zirkel, P.A. (1998). The case law on aversive interventions for students with disabilities. *Exceptional Children, 65*(1), 101–123.

Lotter, B. (1974). Factors related to outcome in autistic children. *Journal of Autism and Childhood Schizophrenia, 4,* 263–277.

Louis Harris and Associates. (2000). *The N.O.D./Harris survey program on participation and attitudes: Survey of Americans with disabilities.* New York: Author.

Loveland, T., McLeskey, J., So, T.H., Swanson, K., & Waldron, L. (2001). Perspectives of teachers toward inclusive school programs. *Teacher Education and Special Education, 24*(2), 108–127.

Lovett, D.L., & Haring, K.A. (1989). The effects of self-management training on the daily living of adults with mental retardation. *Education and Training in Mental Retardation, 24,* 306–307.

Lovitt, T.C., Cushing, S.S., & Stump, C.S. (1994). High school students rate their IEPs: Low opinions and lack of ownership. *Intervention in School and Clinic, 30*(1), 34–37.

Luckasson, R., Borthwick-Duffy, S., Buntinx, W.H.E., Coulter, D.L., Craig, E.M., Reeve, A., et al. (2002). *Mental retardation: Definition, classification, and systems of supports* (10th ed.). Washington, DC: American Association on Mental Retardation.

Luckasson, R., Coulter, D.L., Polloway, E.A., Reiss, S., Schalock, R.L., Snell, M.E., et al. (1992). *Mental retardation: Definition, classification, and systems of supports* (9th ed.). Washington, DC: American Association on Mental Retardation.

Luckasson, R., & Spitalnik, D. (1994). Political and programmatic shifts of the 1992 AAMR definition of mental retardation. In V.J. Bradley, J.W. Ashbaugh, & B.C. Blaney (Eds.), *Creating individual supports for people with developmental disabilities: A mandate for change at many levels* (pp. 81–95). Baltimore: Paul H. Brookes Publishing Co.

Lucyshyn, J.M., Dunlap, G., & Albin, R.W. (2002). *Families and positive behavior support: Addressing problem behavior in family contexts.* Baltimore: Paul H. Brookes Publishing Co.

Lueck, A.H., Dote-Kwan, J., Senge, J.C., & Clarke, L. (2001). Selecting assistive technology for greater independence. *RE:View, 33*(1), 21–33.

Luecking, R.G., & Certo, N.J. (2005). Integrating service systems at the point of transition for youth with significant support needs: A model that works. In E. Condon & K. Brown (Eds.), *It takes a village (or at least several partners) to transition a student from school to work* (pp. 71–86). Missoula: Transition Institute at The Rural Institute: Center for Excellence in Disability Education, Research and Service, University of Montana.

Luecking, R.G., & Crane, K. (2002). Addressing the transition needs of youth with disabilities through the WIA System. *Information Brief, 1*(6), 2.

Luecking, R.G., Fabian, E.S., & Tilson, G.P. (2004). *Working relationships: Creating career opportunities for job seekers with disabilities through employer partnerships.* Baltimore: Paul H. Brookes Publishing Co.

Luecking, R., & Gramlich, M. (2003). Quality work-based learning and postschool employment success. *Issue Brief: Examining Current Challenges in Secondary Education and Transition, 2*(2), 1–5.

Luft, P. (2000). Communication barriers for deaf employees: Needs assessment and problem-solving strategies. *Work, 14*, 51–59.

Luft, P., & Koch, L. (1998). Transition of adolescents with chronic illness: Overlooked needs and rehabilitation considerations. *Journal of Vocational Rehabilitation, 10*(3), 205–217.

Luft, P., Rumrill, P., Snyder, J., & Hennessey, M. (2001). Transition strategies for youths with sensory impairments. *Work: A Journal of Prevention, Assessment, and Rehabilitation, 17*(2), 123–134.

Luiselli, J.K., & Cameron, M.J. (1998). *Antecedent control: Innovative approaches to behavioral support.* Baltimore: Paul H. Brookes Publishing Co.

Lynch, R., & Gussel, L. (1996). Disclosure and self-advocacy regarding disability-related need: Strategies to maximize integration in post-secondary education. *Journal of Counseling and Development, 74*, 352–357.

MacDuff, G.S., Krantz, P., & McClannahan, L.E. (1993). Teaching children with autism to use photographic activity schedules: Maintenance and generalization of complex response chains. *Journal of Applied Behavior Analysis, 26*, 89–97.

Mace, F.C., Shapiro, E.S., West, B.J., Campbell, C., & Altman, J. (1986). The role of reinforcement in reactive self-monitoring. *Applied Research in Mental Retardation, 7*, 315–327.

MacMillan, D.L. (1977). *Mental retardation in school and society.* Boston: Little, Brown.

MacMillan, D.L., & Reschly, D.J. (1998). Overrepresentation of minority students: The case for greater specificity or reconsideration of the variables examined. *Journal of Special Education, 32*(1), 15–24.

Madaus, J.W. (2003). What high school students with learning disabilities need to know about college foreign language requirements. *TEACHING Exceptional Children, 36*(2), 62–66.

Madaus, J.W. (2005, January/February). Navigating the college transition maze: A guide for students with learning disabilities. *TEACHING Exceptional Children, 37*(3), 32–37.

Manganello, R. (1994). Time management instruction for older students with learning disabilities. *TEACHING Exceptional Children, 26*, 60–62.

Mank, D. (1994). The underachievement of supported employment: A call for reinvestment. *Journal of Disability Policy Studies, 5*(2), 1–24.

Mank, D., Cioffi, A., & Yovanoff, P. (1998). Employment outcomes for people with severe disabilities: Opportunities for improvement. *Mental Retardation, 36*(3), 205–216.

Mank, D., Cioffi, A., & Yovanoff, P. (2003). Supported employment outcomes across a decade: Is there evidence of improvement in the quality of implementation? *Mental Retardation, 41*(3), 188–197.

Mank, D., O'Neill, C., & Jansen, R. (1998). Quality in supported employment: A new demonstration of the capabilities of people with severe disabilities. *Journal of Vocational Rehabilitation, 11*(1), 83–95.

Mank, D., Rhodes, L., & Bellamy, G.T. (1986). Four supported employment alternatives. In W.E. Kiernan & J.A. Stark (Eds.), *Pathways to employment for adults with developmental disabilities* (pp. 139–155). Baltimore: Paul H. Brookes Publishing Co.

Mann, W.C., & Lane, J.P. (1991). *Assistive technology for persons with disabilities: The role of occupational therapy.* Rockville, MD: American Occupational Therapy Association.

Manski, C. (1993). Adolescent econometricians: How do youth infer the returns to schooling? In C.T. Clotfelter & M. Rothschild (Eds.), *Studies of supply and demand in higher education* (pp. 43–57). Chicago: University of Chicago Press.

Marks, S., & Feeley, D. (1995). Transition in action: Michigan's experience. *Journal of Visual Impairment and Blindness, 89*(3), 272–275.

Martin, J.E., & Marshall, L.H. (1994). *ChoiceMaker self-determination transition curriculum matrix.* Colorado Springs: University of Colorado at Colorado Springs, Center for Educational Research.

Martin, J.E., & Marshall, L.H. (1995). ChoiceMaker: A comprehensive self-determination transition program. *Intervention in School and Clinic, 30*, 147–156.

Martin, J.E., Marshall, L.H., & Sale, P. (2004). A 3-year study of middle, junior high, and high school IEP meetings. *Exceptional Children, 70*, 285–297.

Martin, J.E., Mithaug, D.E., Cox, P., Peterson, L.Y., Van Dycke, J.L., & Cash, M.E. (2003). Increasing self-determination: Teaching students to plan, work, evaluate, and adjust. *Exceptional Children, 69*(4), 431–447.

Marzano, R.J. (2000). *Transforming classroom grading.* Alexandria, VA: Association for Supervision and Curriculum Development.

Mason, C., Field, S., & Sawilowsky, S. (2004). Implementation of self-determination activities and student participation in IEPs. *Exceptional Children, 70*, 441–451.

Mason, C., McGahee-Kovac, M., Johnson, L., & Stillerman, S. (2002). Implementing student-led IEPs: Student participation and student and teacher reactions. *Career Development for Exceptional Individuals, 25*, 171–192.

Mast, M., West, M., & Johnson, A. (1996). Results from the Research and Demonstration Project on Supported Employment for People with Severe Physical Disabilities. *Advance, 7*(3), 1–4.

Mastropieri, M.A., & Scruggs, T.E. (2000). *The inclusive classroom: Strategies for effective instruction.* Upper Saddle River, NJ: Prentice Hall.

Mastropieri, M.A., & Scruggs, T.E. (2001). Promoting inclusion in secondary schools. *Learning Disability Quarterly, 24*, 265–274.

Mawhood, L., & Howlin, P. (1999). The outcome of a supported employment scheme for high functioning adults with autism or Asperger's syndrome. *Autism, 3*, 229–254.

McAfee, J. (2001). *Navigating the social world: A curriculum for individuals with Asperger's syndrome, high functioning autism and related disorders.* Arlington, TX: Future Horizons.

McCarl, J.J., Svobodny, L., & Beare, P.L. (1991). Self-recording in a classroom for students with mild to moderate mental handicaps: Effects on productivity and on-task behavior. *Education and Training in Mental Retardation, 26*, 79–88.

McConnell, M.E., Hilvitz, P.B., & Cox, C.J. (1998). Functional assessment: A systematic process for assessment and intervention in general and special education classrooms. *Intervention in School and Clinic, 34*, 10–20.

McDermott, S., Martin, M., & Butkus, S. (1999). What individual, provider, and community characteristics predict employment of individuals with mental retardation? *American Journal on Mental Retardation, 104*(4), 346–355.

McDonald, B.C., Flashman, L.A., & Saykin, A.J. (2002). Executive dysfunction following traumatic brain injury: Neural substrates and treatment strategies. *Neurorehabilitation, 17*(4), 333–334.

McDonnell, J. (1998). Instruction for students with severe disabilities in general education settings. *Education and Training in Mental Retardation and Developmental Disabilities, 33*(3), 199–215.

McDonnell, J., Hardman, M., Hightower, J., Keifer-O'Donnell, R., & Drew, C. (1993). Impact of community-based instruction on the development of adaptive behavior of secondary-level students with mental retardation. *American Journal of Mental Retardation, 97*(5), 575–584.

McDonnell, J., Mathot-Buckner, C., & Ferguson, B. (1996). *Transition programs for students with moderate/severe disabilities.* Pacific Grove, CA: Brooks/Cole.

McDonnell, L.M., McLaughlin, M.J., & Morison, P. (1997). *Educating one and all: Students with disabilities and standards-based reform.* Washington, DC: National Academies Press.

McEachin, J.J., Smith, T., & Lovaas, O.I. (1993). Long-term outcome for children with autism who received early intensive behavioral treatment. *American Journal of Mental Retardation, 97,* 359–372.

McGahee, M., Mason, C., Wallace, T., & Jones, B. (2001). *Student-led IEPs: A guide for student involvement.* Alexandria, VA: Council for Exceptional Children.

McGaughey, M.J., Kiernan, W.E., McNally, L.C., Gilmore, D.S., & Keith, G.R. (1995). Beyond the workshop: National trends in integrated and segregated day and employment services. *Journal of The Association for Persons with Severe Handicaps, 20,* 270–284.

McGlashing-Johnson, J., Agran, M., Sitlington, P., Cavin, M., & Wehmeyer, M.L. (2003). Enhancing the job performance of youth with moderate to severe cognitive disabilities using the self-determined learning model of instruction. *Research and Practice for Persons with Severe Disabilities, 28*(4), 194–204.

McGovern, C.W., & Sigman, M. (2005). Continuity and change from early childhood to adolescence in autism. *Journal of Child Psychology and Psychiatry, 46,* 401–408.

McGregor, G., & Vogelsberg, R.T. (1998). *Inclusive schooling practices: Pedagogical and research foundations.* Baltimore: Paul H. Brookes Publishing Co.

McLaren, K. (2004). *Work in practice.* Wellington, New Zealand: Platform.

McLaughlin, M.J. (2002). *Issues for consideration in the reauthorization of Part B of the Individuals with Disabilities Education Act. A timely IDEA: Rethinking federal education programs for children with disabilities.* Washington, DC: Center on Education Policy.

McLaughlin, M.J., Henderson, K., & Rhim, L.M. (1997). *Snapshots of reform: A report of reform in five local school districts.* Alexandria, VA: National Association of State Boards of Education, Center for Policy Research on the Impact of General and Special Education Reform.

McLaughlin, M.J., & Thurlow, J. (2003). Educational accountability and students with disabilities: Issues and challenges. *Journal of Educational Policy, 17*(4), 431–451.

McLaughlin, M.W., & Shepard, L.A. (1995). *Improving education through standards-based reform: A report of the National Academy of Education panel on standards-based reform.* Stanford, CA: The National Academy of Education.

McLeskey, J., Henry, D., & Axelrod, M.I. (1999). Inclusion of students with learning disabilities: An examination of data from reports to congress. *Exceptional Children, 66*(1), 55–66.

McMahon, B.T., Edwards, R., Rumrill, P.D., & Hursh, N. (2005). An overview of the national EEOC ADA research project [Guest editorial]. *Journal of Vocational Rehabilitation, 25*(1), 1–7.

McMahon, B., Wehman, P., Brooke, V., Habeck, R., Green, H., & Fraser, R. (2004). *Business, disability and employment: Corporate models of success: A collection of successful approaches reported from 20 employers* [Monograph]. Richmond, VA: Rehabilitation Research and Training Center on Workplace Supports.

McMahon, B.T., West, S.L., Shaw, L.R., Waid-Ebbs, K., & Belongia, L. (2005). Workplace discrimination and traumatic brain injury: The national EEOC ADA research project. *Journal of Vocational Rehabilitation, 25*(1), 67–75.

McMillan, A.F. (2000). *Employment options have improved for people with developmental disabilities.* New York: CNN America.

McMordie, W.R., Barker, S.L., & Paolo, T.M. (1990). Return to work (RTW) after head injury. *Brain Injury, 4,* 57–69.

McMorris, F.A. (2000, March 10). Discrimination is hard to prove if a book treats everyone badly. *Wall Street Journal,* pp. B1, B4.

Mechling, L.C., Pridgen, L.S., & Cronin, B.A. (2004). Computer-based video instruction to teach students with intellectual disabilities to verbally respond to questions and make purchases in fast food restaurants. *Education and Training in Developmental Disabilities, 40*(1), 47–59.

Melichar, J.F. (1978). ISAARE: A description. *AAESPH Review, 3,* 259–268.

Meyer, R.N. (2001). *Asperger's syndrome employment workbook: An employment workbook for adults with Asperger's syndrome.* London: Jessica Kingsley Publishing.

Michaels, C.A., Pollack Prezant, F., Morabito, S.M., & Jackson, K. (2002). Assistive and instructional technology for college students with disabilities: A national snapshot of postsecondary service providers. *Journal of Special Education Technology, 17*(1), 5–14.

Miller, D. (1997). Encouraging an adolescent daughter who is blind and learning disabled to read and write. *Journal of Visual Impairment and Blindness, 91*(3), 213–218.

Miller, J.L. (1990). Apocalypse or renaissance or something in between? Toward a realistic appraisal of the learning mystique. *Journal of Learning Disabilities, 23*(2), 86–91.

Miller, K.J., Wienke, W.D., & Savage, L.B. (2000). Elementary and middle/secondary educator's pre and post training perceptions of ability to instruct students with disabilities. *Rural Education Quarterly, 19*, 30–43.

Miller, L., & Newbill, C. (2005). *Section 504 in the classroom.* Austin, TX: PRO-ED.

Miller, L., O'Mara, S., & Ferrell, C. (2005). 2005 student earned income exclusion. In L. Miller & V. Brooke (Eds.), *Benefits Assistance Resource Center.* Richmond: Virginia Commonwealth University Rehabilitation Research and Training Center on Workplace Supports and Job Retention.

Miller, P.S. (1999). The Equal Employment Opportunity Commission and people with mental retardation. *Mental Retardation, 37*(2), 162–165.

Mills v. Board of Education, DC, 348 F. Supp. 866 (D. DC 1972). Retrieved October 12, 2005, from http://www.faculty.piercelaw.edu/redfield/library/case-mills.boe.htm

Miner, C.A., & Bates, P.E. (1997, June). The effect of person-centered planning activities on the IEP/transition planning process. *Education and Training in Mental Retardation and Developmental Disabilities*, 105–112.

Minnesota Department of Children, Families and Learning. (2002). *Five step process.* St. Paul: Author.

Mirenda, P., Wilk, D., & Carson, P. (2000). A retrospective analysis of technology use patterns of students with autism over a five-year period. *Journal of Special Education Technology, 15*(3), 5–15.

Mithaug, D.E., Martin, J.E., Agran, M., & Rusch, F.R. (1988). *Why special education graduates fail.* Colorado Springs, CO: Ascent Publications.

Mithaug, D.E., Mithaug, D., Agran, M., Martin, J., & Wehmeyer, M.L. (Eds.). (2003). *Self-determined learning theory: Construction, verification, and evaluation.* Mahwah, NJ: Lawrence Erlbaum Associates.

Mithaug, D.E., Wehmeyer, M.L., Agran, M., Martin, J.E., & Palmer, S. (1998). The Self-Determined Learning Model of Instruction: Engaging students to solve their learning problems. In M.L. Wehmeyer & D.J. Sands (Eds.), *Making it happen: Student involvement in education planning, decision making, and instruction* (pp. 299–328). Baltimore: Paul H. Brookes Publishing Co.

Moll, S., Huff, J., & Detwiler, L. (2003). Supported employment: Evidence for a best practice model in psychosocial rehabilitation. *Canadian Journal of Occupational Therapy, 70*, 298–310.

Moon, M.S. (Ed.). (1994). *Making school and community recreation fun for everyone: Places and ways to integrate.* Baltimore: Paul H. Brookes Publishing Co.

Moon, M.S., & Inge, K. (2000). Vocational preparation and transition. In M. Snell & F. Brown (Eds.), *Instruction of students with severe disabilities* (5th ed., pp. 591–628). Upper Saddle River, NJ: Prentice Hall.

Moon, M.S., Inge, K.J., Wehman, P., Brooke, V., & Barcus, J.M. (1990). *Helping persons with severe mental retardation get and keep employment: Supported employment issues and strategies.* Baltimore: Paul H. Brookes Publishing Co.

Moon, M.S., Kiernan, W., & Holloway, W. (1990). School-based vocational programs and labor laws: A 1990 update. *Journal of The Association for Persons with Severe Handicaps, 15*(3), 177–185.

Mooney, P., Denny, R.K., & Gunter, P.L. (2004). The impact of NCLB and the reauthorization of IDEA on academic instruction of students with emotional or behavior disorders. *Behavior Disorders, 29*(3), 237–247.

Moore, C.L., Alston, R.J., Donnell, C.M., & Hollis, B. (2003). Correlates of rehabilitation success among African American and Caucasian SSDI recipients with mild mental retardation. *Journal of Applied Rehabilitation Counseling, 34*(3), 25–32.

Moore, C.L., Flowers, D.R., & Taylor, D. (2000). Vocational rehabilitation services: Indicators of successful rehabilitation for persons with mental retardation. *Journal of Applied Rehabilitation Counseling, 31*(2), 36–40.

Moore, J.E., Graves, W., & Patterson, J.B. (1997). *Foundations of rehabilitation counseling with persons who are blind or visually impaired.* New York: American Foundation for the Blind Press.

Moore, S.C., Agran, M., & Fodor-Davis, J. (1989). Using self-management strategies to increase the production rates of workers with severe handicaps. *Education and Training in Mental Retardation, 24,* 324–332.

Moores, D.F. (2001). *Educating the deaf: Psychology, principles, and practices* (5th ed.). Boston: Houghton Mifflin.

Morgan, R.L. (2003). Test-retest reliability and criterion validity of a motion video, CD-ROM program designed to allow youth with disabilities to select preferred jobs. *Career Development for Exceptional Individuals, 26*(1), 67–84.

Morgan, R.L., & Alexander, M. (2005). The employer's perception: Employment of individuals with developmental disabilities. *Journal of Vocational Rehabilitation, 23*(1), 39–49.

Morgan, R.L., & Ellerd, D.A. (2005). Development and evaluation of a video CD-ROM program for individuals with developmental disabilities to determine job preferences. *Journal of Vocational Rehabilitation, 23,* 1–10.

Morgan, R.L., Gerity, B.P., & Ellerd, D.A. (2000). Using video and CD-ROM technology in a job preference inventory for youth with severe disabilities. *Journal of Special Education Technology, 15*(3), 25–33.

Morley, R. (1991). *Alternative education.* Clemson, SC: National Dropout Prevention Center.

Morningstar, M.E., Turnbull, A.P., & Turnbull, H.R., III. (1995, December). What do students with disabilities tell us about the importance of family involvement in the transition from school to adult life? *Exceptional Children, 62*(3), 249–260.

Mount, B. (1989). *Making futures happen: A manual for facilitators of personal futures planning.* St. Paul, MN: Governor's Planning Council on Developmental Disabilities.

Mount, B. (1991). *Person-centered planning: A source book of values, ideals, and methods to encourage person-centered development.* New York: Graphic Features.

Mount, B. (1994). Benefits and limitations of Persons Futures Planning. In V.J. Bradley, J.W. Ashbaugh, & B.C. Blaney (Eds.), *Creating individual supports for people with developmental disabilities: A mandate for change at many levels* (pp. 97–108). Baltimore: Paul H. Brookes Publishing Co.

Mount, B. (1995). *Capacity works: Finding windows for change using personal futures planning.* Manchester, CT: Communitas.

Mount, B. (1997). *Person-centered planning: Finding director for change using personal futures planning* (2nd ed.). New York: Graphic Futures.

Mount, B., & O'Brien, C.L. (2002). *Building new worlds: A sourcebook for students with disabilities in transition from high school to adult life.* Armenia, NY: Capacity Works.

Mount, B., & Zwernik, K. (1988). *It's never too early, it's never too late: An overview of personal futures planning.* St. Paul, MN: Governor's Planning Council on Developmental Disabilities.

Moyes, R.A., & Moreno, S.J. (2001). *Incorporating social goals in the classroom: A guide for teachers and parents of children with high functioning autism and Asperger's syndrome.* London: Jessica Kingsley Publishers.

Mueser, K.T., Clark, R.E., Haines, M., Drake, R.E., McHugo, G.J., Bond, G.R., et al. (2004). The Hartford study of supported employment for persons with severe mental illness. *Journal of Consulting and Clinical Psychology, 72,* 479–490.

Mull, C.A., & Sitlington, P.L. (2003). The role of technology in the transition to postsecondary education of students with learning disabilities: A review of the literature. *Journal of Special Education, 37*(1), 26–32.

Mull, C., Sitlington, P.L., & Alper, S. (2001). Postsecondary education for students with learning disabilities: A synthesis of the literature. *Exceptional Children, 68*(1), 97–118.

Müller, E., Schuler, A., Burton, B.A., & Yates, G.B. (2003). Meeting the vocational needs of individuals with Asperger's syndrome and other autism spectrum disabilities. *Journal of Vocational Rehabilitation, 18,* 163–175.

Murawski, W.W., & Dieker, L.A. (2004). Tips and strategies for co-teaching at the secondary level. *TEACHING Exceptional Children, 36*(5), 52–58.

Murphy, S.T., Rogan, P.M., Handley, M., Kincaid, C., & Royce-Davis, J. (2002). People's situations and perspectives eight years after workshop conversion. *Mental Retardation, 40,* 30–40.

Myers, A., & Eisenman, L. (2005). Student-led IEPs: Take the first step. *TEACHING Exceptional Children, 37*(4), 52–58.

Nagle, K.M. (2001). Transition to employment and community life for youths with visual impairments: Current status and future directions. *Journal of Visual Impairment and Blindness, 95*(12), 725–739.

Nagle, K.M. (2004). *Topical review 4: Emerging state-level themes: Strengths and stressors in educational accountability reform.* College Park: University of Maryland, Educational Policy Reform Research Institute.

National Alliance of Business. (1996, Summer). *Workforce development trends.* Washington, DC: Author.

National Association of Counselors and Employers. (2004, January 14). *Employers identify the skills, qualities of the "ideal candidate"* [Web press release]. Retrieved February 7, 2004, from http://www.naceweb.org/press/display.asp?year=2004&prid=184

National Benefits Planning, Assistance, and Outreach (BPAO) Data Collection Report. (2005). *National report through May 31, 2005.* Richmond: Virginia Commonwealth University Benefits Assistance Resource Center (VCU-BARC). Retrieved from http://www.vcu-barc.org/Nat Report/53105.html

National Center for Education Statistics. (2000). *Schools and staffing survey.* Retrieved July 15, 2005, from http://nces.ed.gov/surveys/SASS/OVERVIEW

National Center for Education Statistics. (2002). *Public high school dropouts and completers from the common core data: School year 2000–2001.* Washington, DC: Institute of Education Sciences, U.S. Department of Education.

National Center for Learning Disabilities. (2002). *Students with learning disabilities: A national review.* Washington, DC: Author.

National Center for Research in Vocational Education. (1998, October). The role of the community partnerships in school-to-work programs. *Centerfocus, 20,* 1–4.

National Center on Secondary Education and Transition. (2005). *Key provisions on transition: IDEA 1997 compared to H.R. 1315 (IDEA 2004).* Minneapolis: University of Minnesota Institute on Community Integration.

National Commission on Excellence in Education. (1983). *A nation at risk: The imperative for educational reform.* Washington, DC: U.S. Department of Education.

National Council on Disability. (1997). Removing barriers to work: Action proposals for the 105th Congress and beyond. *Pacesetter,* 8–9.

National Council on Disability. (2000, November 1). *Transition and post-school outcomes for youth with disabilities: Closing the gaps to post-secondary education and employment.* Retrieved July 15, 2005, from http://www.ncd.gov/newsroom/publications/transition11-1-00.html#1

National Council on Disability. (2004). *Improving educational outcomes for students with disabilities.* Retrieved July 23, 2004, from http://www.ncd.gov/newsroom/publications/2004/ publications. htm

National Council on Disability. (2005, February 10). *National Council on Disability government performance and results act annual report to the president and congress fiscal year 2003.* Retrieved July 15, 2005, from http://www.ncd.gov/newsroom/publications/2005/pdf/government_performance. pdf

National Employer Leadership Council. (1996). *The Employer Participation Model.* Washington, DC: Author.

National Information Center for Children and Youth with Disabilities. (2003). *Fact sheet number 18: Traumatic brain injury.* Washington, DC: Author. Available on-line at http://www.nichcy. org/pubs/factshe/fs18.pdf

National Institutes of Health. (1998). Rehabilitations of persons with traumatic brain injury. *NIH Consensus Statement, 16*(1), 1–41.

National Joint Committee on Learning Disabilities (NJCLD). (1990). *Letter to NJCLD member organizations.* Austin, TX: PRO-ED.

National Organization on Disability. (2001). *The top ten reasons to hire people with disabilities.* Retrieved June 28, 2001, from http://www.nod.org

National Organization on Disability. (2004). *N.O.D./Harris Survey of Americans with Disabilities: Landmark survey finds pervasive disadvantages.* Washington, DC: Author. Available at http://www.nod.org/content.cfm?id=1537

National Research Council. (2001). *Educating children with autism.* Washington, DC: National Academy Press.

Natriello, G., McDill, E., & Pallas, A. (1990). *Schooling disadvantaged children: Racing against catastrophe.* New York: Teachers College Press.

Natural supports: The emerging role of business in employment of people with moderate and severe disabilities. (1997). Minneapolis, MN: Pacer Center.

Nehring, W.M. (1990, April). *Transition needs for children with chronic illness into adulthood: Alleviating the concerns of families with information and knowledge.* Paper presented at the 11th Annual International Conference on Developmental Disabilities, Young Adult Institute, New York.

Nelson, J.R., Roberts, M., Mathurs, S., & Rutherford, R. (1999). Has public policy exceeded our knowledge base? A review of the functional behavioral assessment literature. *Behavior Disorders, 24*(2), 169–179.

Nerney, T. (2005). Self-determination after a decade. *TASH Connections, 31*(3/4), 3–4.

Ness, J., & Price, L.A. (1990). Meeting the psychosocial needs of adolescents and adults with learning disabilities. *Intervention in School and Clinic, 26*(1), 16–21.

Neubert, D., Moon, S., & Grigal, M. (2002). Post-secondary education and transition services for students ages 18–21 with significant disabilities. *Focus on Exceptional Children, 34*(8), 1–9.

Newacheck, P.W., Strickland, B., Shonkoff, J.P., Perrin, J.M., McPherson, M., McManus, M., et al. (1998). An epidemiologic profile of children with special health care needs. *Pediatrics, 102*(1), 117–123.

Newman, L. (2001). Montana/Wyoming careers through partnerships. In C. Griffin, M. Flaherty, D. Hammis, M. Katz, N. Maxson, & R. Shelley (Eds.), *People who own themselves* (pp. 57–61). Missoula: University of Montana, Rural Institute.

Newton, J.S., Horner, R.H., Ard, W., LeBaron, N., & Sappington, G. (1994). A conceptual model for improving a social life of individuals with mental retardation. *Mental Retardation, 32*(6), 393–402.

Newton, J.S., Olson, D., Horner, R.H., & Ard, W. (1996). Social skills of the stability of social relationships between individuals with intellectual disabilities and other community members. *Research in Developmental Disabilities, 17*(1), 15–26.

Nietupski, J., & Hamre-Nietupski, S. (2000). A systematic process for carving supported employment positions for people with severe disabilities. *Journal of Developmental and Physical Disabilities, 12*(2), 103–119.

Nietupski, J., & Hamre-Nietupski, S. (2001). A business approach to finding and restructuring supported employment opportunities. In P. Wehman (Ed.), *Supported employment in business* (pp. 59–74). St. Augustine, FL: Training Resource Network.

Nietupski, J., Hamre-Nietupski, S., Donder, D., Houselog, M., & Anderson, R. (1988). Proactive administration strategies for implementing community-based programs for students with moderate/severe handicaps. *Education and Training in Mental Retardation, 23*(2), 138–146.

Nietupski, J., Hamre-Nietupski, S., VanderHart, N.S., & Fishback, K. (1996). Employer perceptions of the benefits and concerns of supported employment. *Education and Training in Mental Retardation and Developmental Disabilities, 31*(4), 310–323.

Nietupski, J., Verstegen, D., Reilly, J., Hutson, J., & Hamre-Nietupski, S. (1997). A pilot investigation into the effectiveness of cold call and referred job development models in supported employment. *Journal of Vocational Rehabilitation, 8*, 89–98.

Nilles, J. (1998). *Managing telework: Strategies for managing the virtual workplace.* New York: John Wiley & Sons.

Nirje, B. (1972). The right to self-determination. In W. Wolfensberger (Ed.), *The principle of normalization in human services* (pp. 176–193). Toronto: National Institute on Mental Retardation.

Nisbet, J., Clark, M., & Covert, S. (1991). Living it up! An analysis of research on community living. In L.H. Meyer, C.A. Peck, & L. Brown (Eds.), *Critical issues in the lives of people with severe disabilities* (pp. 115–144). Baltimore: Paul H. Brookes Publishing Co.

No Child Left Behind Act of 2001, PL 107-110, 115 Stat. 1425, 20 U.S.C. §§ 6301 *et seq.*

Nolet, V., & McLaughlin, M.J. (2005). *Accessing the general curriculum: Including students with disabilities in standards-based reform* (2nd ed.). Thousand Oaks, CA: Corwin Press.

Noon v. Alaska State Board of Education, No. A04-0057 (U.S. District Court 2004).

Nosek, M.A. (1991). Personal assistance services: A review of the literature and analysis of policy implications. *Journal of Disability Policy Studies, 2*(2), 1–17.

Nougaret, A.A. (2002). *The impact of licensure status on the pedagogical competence of first-year special education teachers.* Unpublished doctoral dissertation, George Mason University, Fairfax, VA.

Novak, J. Rogan, P., Mank, D., & DiLeo, D. (2003). Supported employment and systems change: Findings from a national survey of state vocational rehabilitation agencies. *Journal of Vocational Rehabilitation, 19*(3), 157–166.

Noyes, D.A., & Sax, C.L. (2004). Changing systems for transition: Students, families, and professionals working together. *Education and Training in Developmental Disabilities, 39*(1), 35–44.

Nozoki, K., & Mochizuki, A. (1995). Assessing choice making of a person with profound disabilities. *Journal of The Association for Persons with Severe Handicaps, 20*(3), 173–175.

Nuehring, M.L., & Sitlington, P.L. (2003). Transition as a vehicle: Moving from high school to an adult vocational service provider. *Journal of Disability Policy Studies, 14*(1), 25–35.

O'Brien, D., Revell, G., & West, M. (2003). The impact of the current employment policy environment on self-determination of individuals with disabilities. *Journal of Vocational Rehabilitation, 19*(2), 105–118.

O'Brien, J. (1987). A guide to lifestyle planning: Using the activities catalogue to integrate services and natural support systems. In G.T. Bellamy & B. Wilcox (Eds.), *A comprehensive guide to the activities catalogue: An alternative curriculum for youth and adults with severe disabilities* (pp. 175–189). Baltimore: Paul H. Brookes Publishing Co.

O'Brien, J. (1992). *Getting the job done: Learning to expand the social resources available to people with severe disabilities at work.* Syracuse, NY: Syracuse University, Center on Community Living.

O'Brien, J. (1994). Down stairs that are never your own: Supporting people with developmental disabilities in their own homes. *Mental Retardation, 32,* 1–6.

O'Brien, J. (2002). Person-centered planning as a contributing factor in organizational and social change. *Research and Practice for Persons with Severe Disabilities, 27*(4), 261–264.

O'Brien, J., & O'Brien, C.L. (1992). Members of each other: Perspectives on social support for people with severe disabilities. In J. Nisbet (Ed.), *Natural supports in school, at work, and in the community for people with severe disabilities* (pp. 17–63). Baltimore: Paul H. Brookes Publishing Co.

O'Connor, S., & Racino, J.A. (1993). A home of my own: Community housing options and strategies. In J.A. Racino, P. Walker, S. O'Connor, & S.J. Taylor (Eds.), *Housing, support, and community: Choices and strategies for adults with disabilities* (pp. 137–160). Baltimore: Paul H. Brookes Publishing Co.

O'Day, B. (1999). Policy barriers for people with disabilities who want to work. *American Rehabilitation, 25*(1), 17–24.

O'Hara, B. (2004). Twice penalized: Employment discrimination against women with disabilities. *Journal of Disability Policy Studies, 15*(1), 27–34.

O'Neill, R., Horner, R., Albin, R., Sprague, J., Storey, K., & Newton, S. (1997). *Functional assessment and program development for problem behavior: A practical handbook* (2nd ed.). Pacific Grove, CA: Brooks/Cole.

O'Reilly, M.F., Lancioni, G.E., & O'Kane, N. (2000). Using a problem solving approach to teach social skills to workers with brain injuries in supported employment settings. *Journal of Vocational Rehabilitation, 14,* 187–194.

Oberti v. Board of Education of the Borough of Clemington School District, 995 F.2d 1204 (3rd Cir. 1993).

Odom, S.L., Brown, W.H., Frey, T., Karasu, N., Smith-Canter, L.L., & Strain, P.S. (2003). Evidence-based practice for young children with autism: Contributions from single-subject design research. *Focus on Autism and Other Developmental Disabilities, 18*, 166–175.

Ohtake, Y., & Chadsey, J.G. (2001). Continuing to describe the natural support process. *Journal of The Association for Persons with Severe Handicaps, 26*, 87–95.

Ohtake, Y., & Chadsey, J.G. (2003). Facilitation strategies used by job coaches in supported employment settings: A preliminary investigation. *Research and Practice for Persons with Severe Disabilities, 28*(4), 214–227.

Oldman, J., Thomson, L., Calsaferri, K., Luke, A., & Bond, G.R. (2005). A case report of the conversion of sheltered employment to evidence-based supported employment. *Psychiatric Services, 56*(11), 1436–1440.

Ollendick, T.H., Green, R., Francis, G., & Baum, C.G. (1991). Sociometric status: Its stability and validity among neglected, rejected and popular children. *Journal of Child Psychology and Psychiatry, 32*, 525–534.

Olson, D., Cioffi, M.A., Yovanoff, P., & Mank, D. (2001). Employer's perceptions of employees with mental retardation. *Journal of Vocational Rehabilitation, 16*(2), 125–133.

Olson, J.F., Jones, I.A., & Bond, L.A. (2001). *State student assessment programs: Annual survey.* Washington, DC: Council of Chief State School Officers.

Olweus, D. (1993). *Bullying at school: What we know and what we can do.* Cambridge, MA: Blackwell Publishers.

Orkwis, R., & McLane, K. (1998, Fall). *A curriculum every student can use: Design principles for student access.* ERIC/OSEP Topical Brief. Reston, VA: Council for Exceptional Children.

Oseroff, A., Oseroff, C.E., Westling, D., & Gessner, L.J. (1999). Teachers' beliefs about maltreatment of students with emotional/behavioral disorders. *Behavioral Disorders, 24*(3), 197–209.

Owens, L., & Kieker, L.A. (2003). How to spell success for secondary students labeled EBD: How students define effective teachers. *Beyond Behavior, 3.*

Owens-Johnson, L., & Hanley-Maxwell, C. (1999). Employer views on job development strategies for marketing supported employment. *Journal of Vocational Rehabilitation, 12*(2), 113–123.

Owens-Johnson, L., & Johnson, J. (1999). The local employer survey project: An effective school-to-work curriculum. *TEACHING Exceptional Children, 31*(5), 18–23.

P.J. v. State of Connecticut, Board of Education, 788 F. Supp. 673, 679 (D.Conn. 1992).

Palmer, S.B., Wehmeyer, M.L., Gipson, K., & Agran, M. (2004). Promoting access to the general curriculum by teaching self-determination skills. *Exceptional Children, 70*, 427–439.

Palomar College. (1992). *Partnerships for employing students with disabilities.* San Marcos, CA: Author.

Pamenter, F. (1999). Recruitment management. *Ivey Business Journal, 14*, 61–66.

Parent, W., Gibson, K., Unger, D., & Clements, C. (1994). The role of the job coach. Orchestrating community and workplace supports. In P. Wehman & J. Kregel (Eds.), *New directions in supported employment* (pp. 12–18). Richmond: Virginia Commonwealth University, Rehabilitation Research and Training Center on Supported Employment, Natural Supports Transition Project.

Parent, W., Kregel, J., & Wehman, P. (1992). *Vocational integration index: A guide for rehabilitation and special education professionals.* Austin, TX: PRO-ED.

Parent, W., Kregel, J., Wehman, P., & Metzler, H. (1991). Measuring the social integration of supported employment workers. *Journal of Vocational Rehabilitation, 1*(1), 35–58.

Parent, W., Unger, D., Gibson, K., & Clements, C. (1994). The role of job coach: Orchestrating community and workplace supports. *American Rehabilitation, 20*(3), 2–11.

Parent, W., Unger, D., & Inge, K.J. (1997). Customer profile. In V. Brooke, K.J. Inge, A.J. Armstrong, & P. Wehman (Eds.), *Supported employment handbook: A customer-driven approach for persons with significant disabilities* (Monograph). Richmond: Virginia Commonwealth University, Rehabilitation Research and Training Center on Supported Employment.

Parent, W., Wehman, P., & Bricout, J. (2001). Supported employment and natural supports. In P. Wehman (Ed.), *Supported employment in business: Expanding the capacity of workers with disabilities* (pp. 93–112). St. Augustine, FL: Training Resource Network.

Parette, H.P. (1997). Assistive technology devices and services. *Education and Training in Mental Retardation and Developmental Disabilities, 32*(4), 267–280.

Parette, H.P., & Bartlett, C.S. (1996). Collaboration and ecological assessment: Bridging the gap between medical and educational environments for students who are medically fragile. *Physical Disabilities: Education and Related Services, 15*, 33–47.

Parette, P., & Scherer, M. (2004). Assistive technology use and stigma. *Education and Training in Developmental Disabilities, 39*(3), 217–226.

Patton, J.M. (1998). The disproportionate representation of African Americans in special education: Looking behind the curtain for understanding and solutions. *Journal of Special Education, 32*(1), 25–31.

Patton, J.R. (1999). Basic concepts of the transition process. In S.H. deFur & J.R. Patton (Eds.), *Transition and school-based services interdisciplinary perspectives for enhancing the transition process* (pp. 3–13). Austin, TX: PRO-ED.

Patton, J.R., Cronin, M.E., & Wood, S.J. (1999). *Infusing real-life topics into existing curricula: Recommended procedures and instructional examples for the elementary, middle, and high school levels.* Austin, TX: PRO-ED.

Patton, P.L., de la Garza, B., & Harmon, C. (1997). Employability skills + adult agency support + family support + on-the-job support = successful employment. *TEACHING Exceptional Children, 29*,(3), 4–10.

Pearman, E., Elliott, T., & Aborn, L. (2004). Transition services model: Partnership for student success. *Education and Training in Developmental Disabilities, 39*(1), 26–34.

Peck, B., & Kirkbride, L.T. (2001). Why businesses don't employ people with disabilities. *Journal of Vocational Rehabilitation, 16*, 71–75.

Peniston, L.C. (1994, November). *Strategies on time management for college students with learning disabilities.* Paper presented at the meeting of annual meeting of the Center for Academic Support Programs, Lubbock, TX.

Pennsylvania Association for Retarded Citizens (PARC) v. Commonwealth of Pennsylvania, 343 F. Supp. 279 (1972). Retrieved October 12, 2005, from http://www.faculty.piercelaw.edu/redfield/library/case-parc.htm

Perske, R. (1972). The dignity of risk and the mentally retarded. *Mental Retardation, 10*, 24–27.

Perske, R. (2004). Nirje's eight planks. *Mental Retardation, 42*(2), 147–150.

Personal Responsibility and Work Opportunity Reconciliation Act of 1996, PL 104-193, 42 U.S.C. §§ 211 *et seq.*

Peterson, J.M., & Hittie, M.M. (2003). *Inclusive teaching: Creating effective schools for all learners.* Boston: Pearson Education.

Peterson, M., Tamor, L., Feen, H., & Silagy, M. (2002). *Learning well together: Lessons about connecting inclusive education to whole school improvement.* Whole Schooling Research Project Final Report. Detroit: Whole School Consortium, Wayne State University.

Phillips, B. (1993). Technology abandonment from the consumer point of view. *National Rehabilitation Information Center (NARIC) Quarterly, 3*(2, 3), 4–91.

Piepmeier, J.M. (1992). *The outcome following traumatic spinal cord injury.* Mount Kisco, NY: Futura.

Pierangelo, R., & Guiliani, G.A. (2004). *Transition services in special education: A practical approach.* Boston: Pearson Education.

Pitonyak, D. (2004). The importance of belonging. Circle of friends: Acceptance, belonging & community. *Community Opportunities, Inc. Newsletter, 2*(1), 1.

Pitt-Catsouphes, M., & Butterworth, J. (1995). *Different perspectives: Workplace experience with the employment of individuals with disabilities.* Boston: Institute for Community Inclusion at Children's Hospital Center on Work and Family at Boston University.

Polloway, E.A. (2004). Eulogy for "mild" retardation? *Division on Developmental Disability Express, 14*(3), 1,8.

Polloway, E.A., Smith, J.D., Chamberlain, J., Denning, C.B., & Smith, T.E.C. (1999). Levels of deficits or supports in the classification of mental retardation: Implementation practices. *Education and Training in Mental Retardation and Developmental Disabilities, 34*(2), 200–206.

Ponsford, J., Oliver, J., Curran, C., & Ng, K. (1995). Prediction of employment status 2 years after traumatic brain injury. *Brain Injury, 9,* 11–20.

Ponsford, J.L., Willmott, C., Rothwell, A., et al. (2000). Factors influencing outcome following mild traumatic brain injury in adults. *Journal of International Neuropsychological Society, 6,* 568–579.

Posner, G.J., & Rudnitsky, A.N. (1997). *Course design: A guide to curriculum development for teachers* (5th ed.). New York: Longman.

Post, M., & Storey, K. (2002). Review of using auditory prompting systems with persons who have moderate to severe disabilities. *Education and Training in Mental Retardation and Developmental Disabilities, 37*(3), 317–327.

Post, M., Storey, K., & Karabin, M. (2002). Supporting students and adults in work and community environments. *TEACHING Exceptional Children, 34*(3), 60–65.

Poteet, J.A., Choate, J.S., & Stewart, S.C. (1993). Performance assessment and special education: Practices and prospects. *Focus on Exceptional Children, 26*(1), 1–20.

Pottie, C., & Sumarah, J. (2004). Friendships between persons with and without developmental disabilities. *Mental Retardation, 42*(1), 55–66.

Powell, T.H., Pancsofar, E.L., Steere, D.E., Butterworth, J., Itzkowitz, J.S., & Rainforth, B. (1991). *Supported employment: Providing integrated employment opportunities for persons with disabilities.* New York: Longman.

Powers, L.E., Sowers, J., Turner, A., Nesbitt, M., Knowles, E., & Ellison, R. (1996). TAKE CHARGE! A model for promoting self-determination among adolescents with challenges. In L.E. Powers, G.H.S. Singer, & J. Sowers (Eds.), *On the road to autonomy: Promoting self-competence in children and youth with disabilities* (pp. 291–332). Baltimore: Paul H. Brookes Publishing Co.

Powers, L.E., Turner, A., Matuszewski, J., Wilson, R., & Phillips, A. (2001). TAKE CHARGE for the future: A controlled field-test of a model to promote student involvement in transition planning. *Career Development for Exceptional Individuals, 24,* 89–103.

Powers, L.E., Turner, A., Westwood, D., Loesch, C., Brown, A., & Rowland, C. (1998). TAKE CHARGE for the future: A student-directed approach to transition planning. In M.L. Wehmeyer & D.J. Sands (Eds.), *Making it happen: Student involvement in education planning, decision making, and instruction* (pp. 187–210). Baltimore: Paul H. Brookes Publishing Co.

Pratt, J. (1999). Cost/benefits of teleworking to manage work/life responsibilities. *1999 Telework America National Telework Survey,* 1–8.

Pratt, J.H. (2000). Asking the right questions about telecommuting: Avoiding pitfalls in surveying home based work. *Transportation, 27,* 99–116.

President's Committee on Intellectual Disabilities. (2004). *A charge we have to keep: A road map to personal and economic freedom for people with intellectual disabilities in the 21st century.* Washington, DC: U.S. Department of Health and Human Services.

Price, L. (1990). *A selective literature review concerning the psychosocial issues of LD individuals.* Minneapolis, MN: The LD Transition Project. (ERIC Document Reproduction Service No. ED315956)

Price, L. (1997). Psychosocial issues of workplace adjustment. In P.J. Gerber & D.S. Brown (Eds.), *Learning disabilities and employment* (pp. 275–306). Austin, TX: PRO-ED.

Prigatano, G.P. (1995). Senior lectureship: The problem of lost normality after brain injury. *Head Trauma Rehabilitation, 10,* 87.

Pugach, M.C., & Johnson, L.J. (1989). The challenge of implementing collaboration between general and special education. *Exceptional Children, 56*(3), 232–235.

Pugach, M.C., & Johnson, L.J. (1995). *Collaborative practitioners: Collaborative schools.* Denver: Love Publishing.

Putnam, R., & Feldstein, L. (2003). *Better together: Restoring the American community.* New York: Simon & Schuster.

Quality Counts. (2004). Count me in: Special education in an era of standards [Special issue]. *Education Week, 23*(7).

Quality Housing and Work Responsibility Act of 1998, PL 105-276, 42 U.S.C. § 1437 *et seq.*

Quenemoen, R., Thompson, S., & Thurlow, M. (2003). *Measuring academic achievement of students with significant cognitive disabilities: Building understanding of alternate assessment scoring criteria* (Synthesis Report 50). Retrieved July 29, 2004, from http://education.umn.edu/NCEO/OnlinePubs/Synthesis50.html

Quill, K.A. (2000). *Do-Watch-Listen-Say: Social communication intervention for children with autism.* Baltimore: Paul H. Brookes Publishing Co.

Racino, J.A. (1995). *Personal assistance services (PAS): Toward universal access to support: Annotated bibliography.* Berkeley: University of California at Berkeley, World Institute on Disability. (ERIC Document Reproduction Service No. ED405705)

Racino, J.A., & Taylor, S.M. (1993). People first: Approaches to housing and support. In J.A. Racino, P. Walker, S. O'Connor, & S.J. Taylor (Eds.), *Housing, support, and community: Choices and strategies for adults with disabilities* (pp. 33–56). Baltimore: Paul H. Brookes Publishing Co.

Rackham, N., Friedman, L., & Ruff, R. (1997). *Getting partnering right: How market leaders are creating long-term competitive advantage.* New York: McGraw-Hill.

Rainforth, B., & England, J. (1997). Collaborations for inclusion. *Education and Treatment of Children, 20,* 85–104.

Rao, N., Rosenthal, M., Cronin-Stubbs, D., Lambert, R., Barnes, P., & Swanson, B. (1990). Return to work after rehabilitation following traumatic brain injury. *Brain Injury, 4,* 49–56.

Rappaport, J. (1981). In praise of a paradox: A social policy of empowerment over prevention. *American Journal of Community Psychology, 9,* 1–25.

Raskind, M.H. (1994). Assistive technology for adults with learning disabilities: A rationale for use. In P.J. Gerber & H.B. Reiff (Eds.), *Learning disabilities in adulthood: Persisting problems and evolving issues* (pp. 152–162). Boston: Andover Medical Publishers.

Raskind, M.H., Gerber, P.J., Goldberg, R.J., Higgins, E.L., & Herman, K.L. (1998). Longitudinal research in learning disabilities: Report on an international symposium. *Journal of Learning Disabilities, 31*(3), 266–277.

Rea, P.J., McLaughlin, B., & Walther-Thomas, C. (2002). Outcomes for students with learning disabilities in inclusive and pullout programs. *Exceptional Children, 68*(2), 203–222.

Regan, K.S. (2003, November/December). Using dialogue journals in the classroom: Forming relationships with students with emotional disturbance. *TEACHING Exceptional Children, 36*–41.

Rehabilitation Act Amendments of 1986, PL 99-506, 29 U.S.C. §§ 701 *et seq.*

Rehabilitation Act Amendments of 1992, PL 102-569, 29 U.S.C. §§ 701 *et seq.*

Rehabilitation Act Amendments of 1998, PL 105-220, 29 U.S.C. §§ 701 *et seq.*

Rehabilitation Act of 1973, PL 93-112, 29 U.S.C. §§ 701 *et seq.*

Reid, D.H., Everson, J.M., & Green, C.W. (1999). A systematic evaluation of preferences identified through person-centered planning for people with multiple disabilities. *Journal of Applied Behavior Analysis, 32*(4), 467–477.

Reid, D.H., & Parsons, M.B. (2003). *Positive behavior support training curriculum: Supervisory edition.* Washington, DC: American Association on Mental Retardation.

Reiff, H., Ginsberg, R., & Gerber, P.J. (1995). New perspectives on teaching from successful adults with learning disabilities. *Remedial and Special Education, 16*(1), 29–37.

Reiling, C. (1990). *How significant is "significant"? A personal glimpse of life with a learning disability.* Columbus, OH: Association of Handicapped Student Service Programs in Postsecondary Education.

Reitman, D., Drabman, R.S., Speaks, L.V., Burkley, S., & Rhode, P.C. (1998). Problem social behavior in the workplace: An analysis of social behavior problems in a supported employment setting. *Research in Developmental Disabilities, 20*(3), 215–228.

Repetto, J.B., & Webb, K.W. (1999). A model for guiding the transition process. In S.H. deFur & J.R. Patton (Eds.), *Transition and school-based services: Interdisciplinary perspectives for enhancing the transition process* (pp. 421–442). Austin, TX: PRO-ED.

Revell, G., Inge, K.J., Mank, D., & Wehman, P. (1999). *The impact of supported employment for people with significant disabilities: Preliminary findings from the national supported employment consortium.* Richmond: Virginia Commonwealth University.

Revell, G., Wehman, P., Kregel, J., West, M., & Rayfield, R. (1994). Funding supported employment: Are there better ways? In P. Wehman, J. Kregel, & M. West (Eds.), *Supported employment research: Expanding competitive employment opportunities for persons with significant disabilities.* Richmond: Virginia Commonwealth University Rehabilitation Research and Training Center on Supported Employment.

Review & Outlook: America works [Editorial]. (2003, August 29). *Wall Street Journal*, p. A8.

Reyes, D.A. (1993, July-December). Access to context: A basic need for deafblind people. *Deafblind Education*, 5–9.

Richards, S., Taylor, R., Ramasamy, R., & Richards, R. (1999). *Single subject research applications in educational and clinical settings.* San Diego: Singular Publishing Group.

Richardson, B.G., & Shupe M.J. (2003, November/December). The importance of teacher self-awareness in working with students with emotional and behavioral disorders. *TEACHING Exceptional Children*, 8–13.

Richmond Times-Dispatch. (2004, November 7). Coalition for Juvenile Justice.

Ridgway, P., & Rapp, C. (1998). *The active ingredients in achieving competitive employment for people with psychiatric disabilities: A research synthesis.* Lawrence: University of Kansas School of Social Welfare.

Rinehart, P.M. (1994). Moving on: Transition from pediatric to adult health care. *Connections: The Newsletter of the National Center for Youth with Disabilities*, 5(1), 1–5.

Rispens, J., van Yperen, T.A., & van Duijn, G.A. (1991). The irrelevance of IQ to the definition of learning disabilities: Some empirical evidence. *Journal of Learning Disabilities*, 24(7), 434–438.

Rizzolo, M.C., Hemp, R., Braddock, D., & Pomeranz-Essley, A. (2004). *The state of the states in developmental disabilities.* Boulder: University of Colorado, Coleman Institute for Cognitive Disabilities and Department of Psychiatry.

Roberts, K.D., & Stodden, R.A. (2005). The use of voice recognition software as a compensatory strategy for post secondary education students receiving services under the category of learning disabled. *Journal of Vocational Education*, 22(1), 49–64.

Rogan, P., Banks, B., & Howard, M. (2000, Spring). Workplace supports in practice: As little as possible, as much as necessary. *Focus on Autism and Other Developmental Disabilities*, 15(1), 2–11.

Rogan, P., Grossi, T., Mank, D., Haynes, D., Thomas, F., & Majd, C. (2002). What happens when people leave the workshop? Outcomes of workshop participants now in supported employment. *InfoLines*, 13(4), 1, 3, 6.

Rogan, P., Hagner, D., & Murphy, S. (1993). Natural supports: Reconceptualizing job coach roles. *Journal of The Association for Persons with Severe Handicaps*, 18, 275–281.

Rogan, P., & Walker, P. (2003, November/December). What's taking so long? The slow pace of organizational change from congregate services to integrated supports. *TASH Connections*, 10–11.

Rogers, E.S. (2000, October 13). *A randomized controlled study of psychiatric vocational rehabilitation services.* Paper presented at the 4th Biennial Research Seminar on Work (Matrix Research Institute), Philadelphia.

Rogers, E.S., MacDonald-Wilson, K., Danley, K., & Martin, R. (1997). A process analysis of supported employment services for persons with serious psychiatric disability: Implications for program design. *Journal of Vocational Rehabilitation*, 8(3), 233–242.

Rogers, J. (1993). *The inclusion revolution.* Bloomington, IN: Phi Delta Kappan, Center for Evaluation, Development, and Research.

Rojewski, J.W. (1996). Educational and occupational aspirations of high school students with learning disabilities. *Exceptional Children*, 62(5), 463–476.

Rose, D., & Meyer, A. (2000). Universal design for individual differences. *Educational Leadership*, 58(3), 39–43.

Rose, D.H., Meyer, A., & Hitchcock, C. (2005). *The universally-designed classroom: Accessible curriculum and digital technologies.* Cambridge, MA: Harvard University Press.

Rosenberg, M.S., Sindelar, P.T., & Hardman, M.L. (2004). Preparing highly qualified teachers for students with emotional or behavioral disorders: The impact of NCLB and IDEA. *Behavioral Disorders*, 29(3), 266–278.

Rothman, S. (2001). School absence and student background factors: A multilevel analysis. *International Education Journal, 2*(1), 59–68.

Rotter, J.B. (1954). *Social learning and clinical psychology*. Upper Saddle River, NJ: Prentice Hall.

Rotter, J.B. (1966). Generalized expectancies for internal versus external control of reinforcement. *Psychological Monographs, 80*(1), 244–248.

Rubin, S., & Roessler, R. (2000). *Foundations of the vocational rehabilitation process* (5th ed.). Austin, TX: PRO-ED.

Ruble, L.A., & Dalrymple, N.J. (1993). Social/sexual awareness of persons with autism: A parental perspective. *Archives of Sexual Behavior, 22*(3), 229–240.

Ruef, M.B., & Turnbull, A.P. (2002). The perspectives of individuals with cognitive disabilities and/or autism on their lives and their problem behavior. *Research and Practice for Persons with Severe Disabilities, 27*(2), 125–140.

Rumrill, P. (1999). Effects of a social competence training program on accommodation request activity, situational self-efficacy, and Americans with Disabilities Act knowledge among employed people with visual impairments and blindness. *Journal of Vocational Rehabilitation, 12*(1), 25–31.

Rumrill, P. (2001). Contemporary issues in postsecondary education for students with disabilities: Roles and responsibilities for educators and rehabilitation professionals. *Journal of Vocational Rehabilitation, 16*(3, 4), 143–144.

Rumrill, P., Roessler, R., Battersby, J., & Schuyler, B. (1998). Situational assessment of the accommodation needs of employees who are visually impaired. *Journal of Visual Impairment and Blindness, 92*(1), 42–54.

Rumrill, P., & Scheff, C. (1997). Impact of the Americans with Disabilities Act on the employment and promotion of persons who are visually impaired. *Journal of Visual Impairment and Blindness, 91*(5), 460–466.

Rupp, K., & Scott, C.G. (1995, July). *Determinants of duration on the disability rolls and program trends*. Paper presented at the Social Security Administration/Association for Persons in Supported Employment conference on the Social Security Administration's Disability Programs, Washington, DC.

Rusch, F.R., & Braddock, D. (2004). Adult day programs versus supported employment (1988–2002): Spending and service practices of mental retardation and developmental disabilities state agencies. *Research and Practice for Persons with Severe Disabilities, 29*(4), 237–242.

Rusch, F.R., & Chadsey, J.C. (1998). *Beyond high school: Transition from school to work*. Albany, NY: Wadsworth.

Russell, W.R. (1932). Cerebral involvement in head trauma: A study based on the examination of 200 cases. *Brain Injury, 55*, 549–603.

Rust, K.L., & Smith, R.O. (2005). Assistive technology in the measurement of rehabilitation and health outcomes: A review and analysis of instruments. *American Journal of Physical Medicine and Rehabilitation, 84*(10), 780–793.

Rutter, M., Greenfield, D., & Lockyer, L. (1967). A five to fifteen year follow-up study of infantile psychosis: II. Social and behavioural outcome. *British Journal of Psychiatry, 113*, 1183–1199.

Ryan, D. (2000). *Networking and mentors: Job search handbook for people with disabilities*. Indianapolis, IN: JIST Works.

Rylance, B.J. (1997). Predictors of high school graduation or dropping out for youths with severe emotional disturbances. *Behavioral Disorders, 23*, 5–17.

Sacks, S.Z., & Wolffe, K. (1992). The importance of social skills in the transition process for students with visual impairments. *Journal of Vocational Rehabilitation, 2*(1), 46–55.

Sacramento Unified School District v. Rachel H., 14 F.3rd 1398 (9th Cir. 1994).

Salend, S.J., Duhaney, D., Anderson, D.J., & Gottschalk, C. (2004). Using the Internet to improve homework communication and completion. *TEACHING Exceptional Children, 36*(3), 64–73.

Salisbury, C., & Chambers, A. (1994). Instructional costs of inclusive schooling. *Journal of The Association for Persons with Severe Handicaps, 19*(3), 215–222.

Sampson, M., Hermanson, J., Griffin, C.C., & Morton, M.V. (2000). Connecting with the community. In M.S.E. Fishbaugh (Ed.), *The collaboration guide for early career educators* (pp. 79–116). Baltimore: Paul H. Brookes Publishing Co.

Sander, A.M., & Kreutzer, J.S. (1999). A holistic approach to family assessment after brain injury. In M. Rosenthal, E.R. Griffith, J.S. Kreutzer, & B. Pentland (Eds.), *Rehabilitation of the adult and child with traumatic brain injury* (3rd ed., pp. 199–215). Philadelphia: F.A. Davis.

Sander, A.M., Kreutzer, J.S., Rosenthal, M., Delmonico, R., & Young, M. (1996). A multicenter longitudinal investigation of return to work and community integration following traumatic brain injury. *Journal of Head Trauma Rehabilitation, 11*(5), 70–84.

Sandlund, C. (2001, July 26). Untapped talent. *Fortune Small Business.*

Sands, D. (1999). *Best practices in transition.* Denver: University of Colorado at Denver.

Sapon-Shevin, M. (1994). Celebrating diversity, creating community: Curriculum that honors and builds on differences. In S. Stainback & W. Stainback (Eds.), *Inclusion: A guide for educators* (pp. 255–270). Baltimore: Paul H. Brookes Publishing Co.

Sarkees-Wircenski, M.D., & Scott, J.L. (1995). *Vocational special needs.* Homewood, IL: American Technical Publishers.

Sarkees-Wircenski, M.D., & Wircenski, J. (1994). Transition planning: Developing a career portfolio for students with disabilities. *Career Development for Exceptional Individuals, 17*(2), 203–214.

Savage, R.C. (1991). Identification, classification, and placement issues for students with traumatic brain injuries. *Journal of Head Trauma Rehabilitation, 6*(1), 1–9.

Savage, R.C. (1997). Integrating rehabilitation and special education services for school-age children with brain injuries. *Journal of Head Trauma and Rehabilitation, 12*(2), 11–20.

Savage, R.C. (2000, August). *An analysis of 15,024 children with TBI.* Paper presented at the Brain Injury Association 20th Symposium, Chicago.

Savage, R.C., DePompei, R., Tyler, J., & Lash, M. (2005). Paediatric traumatic brain injury: A review of pertinent issues. *Pediatric Rehabilitation, 8*(2), 92–103.

Savage, R.C., & Mishkin, L. (1994). A neuroeducational model for teaching students with acquired brain injury. In R.C. Savage & G.F. Wolcott (Eds.), *Educational dimensions of acquired brain injury* (pp. 393–412). Austin, TX: PRO-ED.

Savage, R.C., Pearson, S., McDonald, H., Potoczny-Gray, A., & Marcgese, N. (2001). After hospital: Working with schools and families to support the long term needs of children with brain injuries. *NeuroRehabilitation, 16*, 49–58.

Savage, R.C., & Wolcott, G. (1994). *An educator's manual: What educators need to know about students with traumatic brain injury.* Washington, DC: Brain Injury Association.

Sax, C.L. (2002). Person-centered planning: More than a strategy. In C.L. Sax & C.A. Thoma (Eds.), *Transition assessment: Wise practices for quality lives* (pp. 15–31). Baltimore: Paul H. Brookes Publishing Co.

Sax, C.L., & Thoma, C.A. (2002). *Transition assessment: Wise practices for quality lives.* Baltimore: Paul H. Brookes Publishing Co.

Scanlon, D., Deshler, D., & Schumaker, J. (1996). Can a strategy be taught and learned in secondary inclusive classrooms? *Learning Disabilities Research and Practice, 11*(1), 41–57.

Schalock, R.L. (2004). The emerging disability paradigm and its implications for policy and practice. *Journal of Disability Policy Studies, 14*(4), 204–215.

Schalock, R.L., Stark, J., Snell, M., Coulter, D., Polloway, E., Luckasson, R., et al. (1994). The changing conception of mental retardation: Implications for the field. *Mental Retardation, 32*(3), 181–193.

Schiller, E., Bobronnikov, E., Brown-Lyons, M., Burnaska, K., Burstein, N., & Fritts, J. (2004). *The study of state and local implementation and impact of the Individuals with Disabilities Education Act: Draft—2nd interim report.* Bethesda, MD: Abt Associates Inc.

Schleien, S.J., Meyer, L.H., Heyne, L.A., & Brandt, B.B. (1995). *Lifelong leisure skills and lifestyles for persons with developmental disabilities.* Baltimore: Paul H. Brookes Publishing Co.

Schloss, P.J., & Smith, M.A. (1998). *Applied behavior analysis in the classroom.* Boston: Allyn & Bacon.

Schmidt, P. (2005, February 22). Students with mental retardation are knocking on college doors, and colleges are responding. *The Chronicle of Higher Education: Today's News*.

Schneider, J., Heyman, A., & Turton, N. (2002). *Occupational outcomes: from evidence to implementation*. Durham, England: University of Durham, Centre for Applied Social Studies. Available online at http://www.dur.ac.uk/CASSS/Research/papers/ETP%20abridged.pdf

Schneider, M. (1999). Achieving greater independence through assistive technology, job accommodation and supported employment. *Journal of Vocational Rehabilitation, 12*(3), 159–164.

Schoen, S.F., & Nolen, J. (2004, September/October). Action research: Decreasing acting-out behavior and increasing learning. *TEACHING Exceptional Children*, 26–29.

Schriner, K., Rumrill, P., & Parlin, R. (1995). Rethinking disability policy: Equity in the ADA era and the meaning of specialized services for people with disabilities. *Journal of the Health and Human Services Administration, 17*(4), 478–500.

Schunk, D.H. (1981). Modeling and attributional effects on children's achievement: A self-efficacy analysis. *Journal of Educational Psychology, 73*, 93–105.

Schuster, J.L., Timmons, J.C., & Moloney, M. (2003). Barriers to successful transition for young adults who receive SSI and their families. *Career Development for Exceptional Individuals, 26*(1), 47–66.

Schwartz, A.A., Holburn, S.C., & Jacobson, J.W. (2000). Defining person-centeredness: Results of two consensus methods. *Education and Training in Mental Retardation and Developmental Disabilities, 35*(3), 235–249.

Schwartz, D.B. (1992). *Crossing the river: Creating a conceptual revolution in community and disability*. Cambridge, MA: Brookline.

Schwartzman, L., Martin, G.L., Yu, C.T., & Whiteley, J. (2004). Choice, degree of preference, and happiness indices with persons with intellectual disabilities: A surprising finding. *Education and Training in Developmental Disabilities, 39*(3), 265–269.

Schwier, K.M., & Hingsburger, D. (2000). *Sexuality: Your sons and daughters with intellectual disabilities*. Baltimore: Paul H. Brookes Publishing Co.

Scott, S.S. (1996). Understanding colleges: An overview of college support services and programs available from transition planning through graduation. *Journal of Vocational Rehabilitation, 6*, 217–230.

Scott, T.M., McIntyre, J., Liaupsin, C., Nelson, C.M., & Conroy, M. (2004). An examination of functional behavior assessment in public school settings: Collaborative teams, experts, and methodology. *Behavior Disorders, 29*(4), 384–395.

Scruggs, T.E., & Mastropiero, M.A. (1995). What makes special education special? Evaluating inclusion programs with the PASS variables. *Journal of Special Education, 28*(2), 224–233.

Seltzer, M.M., Krauss, M.W., Shattuck, P.T., Orsmond, G., Swe, A., & Lord, C. (2003). The symptoms of autism spectrum disorders in adolescence and adulthood. *Journal of Autism and Developmental Disorders, 33*, 565–581.

Sergiovanni, T.J. (1994). *Building community in schools*. San Francisco: Jossey-Bass.

Shafer, M.S., Wehman, P., Kregel, J., & West, M. (1990). National supported employment initiative: A preliminary analysis. *American Journal of Mental Retardation, 95*(3), 316–327.

Sharpe, M.N., & Hawes, M.E. (2003). Collaboration between general and special education: Making it work. *Issue Brief: Examining Current Challenges in Secondary Education and Transition, 2*(1), 1–6.

Sharpe, M.N., Johnson, D.R., Izzo, M., & Murray, A. (2005). An analysis of instructional accommodations and assistive technologies used by postsecondary graduates with disabilities. *Journal of Vocational Rehabilitation, 22*(1), 3–11.

Sharpton, W.R., & West, M. (1991). Severe and profound mental retardation. In P. McLaughlin & P. Wehman (Eds.), *Handbook of developmental disabilities: A guide to best practices* (pp. 16–29). Austin, TX: PRO-ED.

Sherer, M., Hart, T., Nick, T.G., Whyte, J., Thompson, R.N., & Yablon, S.A. (2003). Early impaired self-awareness after traumatic brain injury. *Archives of Physical Medicine and Rehabilitation, 84*, 168–176.

Sherer, M., Sander, A.M., Nick, T.G., High, W.M., Jr., Malec, J.F., & Rosenthal, M. (2002). Early cognitive status and productivity outcome after traumatic brain injury: Findings from the TBI Model Systems. *Archives of Physical Medicine and Rehabilitation, 83*, 183–192.

Shevin, M., & Klein, N.K. (1984). The importance of choice-making skills for students with severe disabilities. *Journal of The Association for Persons with Severe Handicaps, 9*, 159–166.

Shilling, D. (1998). *The complete guide to human resources and the law.* Upper Saddle River, NJ: Prentice Hall.

Shogren, K.A., Faggella-Luby, M., Bae, S.J., & Wehmeyer, M.L. (2004). The effect of choice-making as an intervention for problem behavior: A meta-analysis. *Journal of Positive Behavior Interventions, 6*, 228–237.

Shoultz, B., & Lakin, K.C. (2001). Volunteer and service opportunities for people with developmental disabilities. *Impact, 14*(2), 2–3.

Shriner, J.G., & DeStefano, L. (2001). *Curriculum access and state assessment for students with disabilities: A research update.* Paper presented at the annual conference of the Council for Exceptional Children, Kansas City, MO.

Siegel, L.S. (1999). Issues in the definition of and diagnosis of learning disabilities: A perspective on Guckenberger v. Boston University. *Journal of Learning Disabilities, 32*(4), 304–319.

Simon, M., Cobb, B., Norman, M., & Bourexix, P. (1994). *Meeting the needs of youth with disabilities: Handbook for implementing community-based vocational education programs according to the Fair Labor Standards Act.* Minneapolis, MN: National Transition Network.

Simon, M., & Halloran, W. (1994). Community-based vocational education: Guidelines for complying with the Fair Labor Standards Act. *Journal of The Association for Persons with Severe Handicaps, 19*(1), 52–60.

Simpson, A., Langone, J., & Ayres, K.M. (2004). Embedded video and computer based instruction to improve social skills for students with autism. *Education and Training in Developmental Disabilities, 39*(3), 240–252.

Simpson, R.L. (2004). Inclusion of students with behavior disorders in general education settings: Research and measurement issues. *Behavior Disorders, 30*(1), 19–31.

Simpson, R. (2005). Evidence-based practices and students with autism spectrum disorders. *Focus on Autism and Other Developmental Disabilities, 20*, 140–149.

Sinclair, M.F., Christenson, S.L., Evelo, D.L., & Hurley, C.M. (1998). Dropout prevention for youth with disabilities: Efficacy of a sustained school engagement procedure. *Exceptional Children, 65*(1), 7–21.

Singh, D.K. (2002). Regular educators and students with physical disabilities. *Education, 123*(2), 236–245.

Siperstein, G.N., Reed, D., Wolraich, M., & O'Keefe, P. (1990). Capabilities essential for adults who are mentally retarded to function in different residential settings. *Education and Training in Mental Retardation, 25*, 45–51.

Siperstein, G.N., Romano, N., Mohler, A. & Parker, R. (2006). A national survey of consumer attitudes towards companies that hire people with disabilities. *Journal of Vocational Rehabilitation, 24*(1), 3–9.

Sitlington, P.L., & Clark, G.M. (2006). *Transition education and services for students with disabilities* (4th ed.). Boston: Allyn & Bacon.

Sitlington, P.L., Clark, G.M., & Kolstoe, O.P. (2000). *Transition education and services for adolescents with disabilities* (3rd ed.). Boston: Allyn & Bacon.

Sitlington, P.L., & Frank, A.R. (1990). Are adolescents with learning disabilities successfully crossing the bridge into adult life? *Learning Disability Quarterly, 113*, 97–111.

Sitlington, P.L., & Frank, A.R. (1998). *Follow-up studies: A practitioner's handbook.* Austin, TX: PRO-ED.

Sitlington, P.L., Frank, A.R., & Carson, R. (1992). Adult adjustment among high school graduates with mild disabilities. *Exceptional Children, 39*(3), 221–233.

Sitlington, P.L., & Neubert, D.A. (2004). Preparing youth with emotional and behavioral disorders for transition to adult life: Can this be done under No Child Left Behind and Individuals with Disabilities Education Act priorities? *Behavior Disorders, 9*(3), 279–288.

Sitlington, P.L., Neubert, D.A., Begun, W., Lombard, R.C., & Leconte, P.J. (1996). *Assess for success: Handbook on transition assessment.* Reston, VA: Council for Exceptional Children, Division on Career Development and Transition.

Sizer, T.R. (1992). *Horace's school: Redesigning the American high school.* Boston: Houghton Mifflin.

Skiba, R. (2002). Special education and school discipline: A precarious balance. *Behavior Disorders, 27,* 81–97.

Skiba, R.J., & Peterson, R.L. (2000). School discipline at a crossroads: From zero tolerance to early response. *Exceptional Children, 66*(3), 335–347.

Skinner, B.F. (1953). *Science and human behavior.* New York: Macmillan.

Smith, C.R. (1991). *Learning disabilities: The interaction of learner, task, and setting* (2nd ed.). Boston: Allyn & Bacon.

Smith, C.R. (2000). Behavioral and discipline provisions of IDEA '97: Implicit competencies yet to be confirmed. *Exceptional Children, 66*(3), 403–412.

Smith, M.D., & Belcher, R. (1995). Teaching life skills to adults disabled by autism. *Journal of Autism and Developmental Disorders, 15*(2), 163–178.

Smith, M.D., Belcher, R.G., & Juhrs, P.D. (1995). *A guide to successful employment for individuals with autism.* Baltimore: Paul H. Brookes Publishing Co.

Smith, S. (1997, Winter). Embracing inclusion: Examining fears and solutions. *Children Our Concern, 22,* 27–29.

Smith, S.W. (1990). Individualized education programs (IEPs) in special education: From intent to acquiescence. *Exceptional Children, 57,* 6–14.

Smith, S.W., & Brownell, M.T. (1995). Individualized education program: Considering the broad context of reform. *Focus on Exceptional Children, 28*(1), 1–10.

Smith, S.W., & Daunic, A.P. (2004). Research on preventing behavior problems using a cognitive-behavioral intervention: Preliminary findings, challenges, and future directions. *Behavioral Disorders, 30*(1), 72–76.

Smith, T.E.C., Polloway, E.A., Patton, J.R., & Dowdy, C.A. (2005). *Teaching children with special needs in inclusive settings.* Boston: Allyn & Bacon.

Smith, T.E.C., & Puccini, I.K. (1995). Position statement: Secondary curricula and policy issues for students with mental retardation. *Education and Training in Mental Retardation and Developmental Disabilities, 30*(4), 275–281.

Smull, M., & Harrison, B. (1992). *Supporting people with severe reputations in the community.* Alexandria, VA: National Association of State Mental Retardation Program Directors.

Snell, M.E. (1982). Analysis of time delay procedures in teaching daily living skills to retarded adults. *Analysis and Intervention in Developmental Disabilities, 2,* 139–156.

Snell, M. (1993). *Systematic instruction for individuals with severe disabilities* (4th ed.). New York: Merrill.

Snell, M., & Brown, F. (2000). *Instruction of students with severe disabilities* (5th ed.). Upper Saddle River, NJ: Merrill/Prentice Hall.

Snell, M.E., & Gast, D.L. (1981). Applying delay procedure to the instruction of the severely handicapped. *Journal of The Association of the Severely Handicapped, 5*(4), 3–14.

Snell, M.E., & Janney, R.E. (2005). *Collaborative teaming* (2nd ed.). Baltimore: Paul H. Brookes Publishing Co.

Snyder, E.P. (2002). Teaching students with combined behavioral disorders and mental retardation to lead their own IEP meetings. *Behavioral Disorders, 27,* 340–357.

Snyder, E.P., & Shapiro, E.S. (1997). Teaching students with emotional/behavioral disorders the skills to participate in the development of their own IEPs. *Behavioral Disorders, 22,* 246–259.

Snyder, M.C., & Bambara, L.M. (1997). Teaching secondary students with learning disabilities to self-manage classroom survival skills. *Journal of Learning Disabilities, 30*(5), 534–543.

Social Security Act Amendments of 1972, PL 92-603, 42 U.S.C. 402, §§ 413 *et seq.*

Social Security Administration, Government Accountability Office. (2005, March). *Better planning could make the ticket program more effective. Report to Congressional Committees*, Washington, DC: Author.

Social Security Independence and Program Improvements Act of 1994, PL 103-296, 42 U.S.C. 1382, §§ 202 *et seq.*

Southwest Educational Development Laboratory. (1995). *Inclusion: The pros and cons.* Retrieved August 25, 2001, from http://www.sedl.org/change/issues

Sowers, J.A. (1991). Transitioning students with physical and multiple disabilities to supported employment. *Journal of Vocational Rehabilitation, 1*(4), 25–37.

Sowers, J.A., McLean, D., & Owens, C. (2003). Self-directed employment: Changes needed to put people with disabilities in charge. *InfoLines, 14*(5), 1, 3, 7.

Sowers, J.A., & Powers, L. (1991). *Vocational preparation and employment of students with physical and multiple disabilities.* Baltimore: Paul H. Brookes Publishing Co.

Sowers, J., & Powers, L. (1995). Enhancing the participation and independence of students with severe physical and multiple disabilities in performing community activities. *Mental Retardation, 33*, 209–220.

Sowers, J., Verdi, M., Bourbeau, P., & Sheehan, M. (1985). Teaching job independence and flexibility to mentally retarded students through the use of a self-control package. *Journal of Applied Behavior Analysis, 18*, 81–85.

Spooner, F., & Wood, W.M. (2004). Teaching personal care and hygiene skills. In P. Wehman & J. Kregel (Eds.), *Functional curriculum for elementary, middle, and secondary age students with special needs* (2nd ed.). Austin, TX: PRO-ED.

Sprague, J., & Walker, H. (2000). Early identification and intervention for youth with antisocial and violent behavior. *Exceptional Children, 66*(3), 367–379.

Stainback, S.B., Stainback, W.C., & Harris, K.C. (1989). Support facilitation: An emerging role for special educators. *Teacher Education and Special Education, 12*(4), 148–153.

Stainback, W., & Stainback, S. (1985). *Integration of students with severe handicaps into regular schools.* Reston, VA: Council for Exceptional Children.

Stancliffe, R.J., & Wehmeyer, M.L. (1995). Variability in the availability of choice to adults with mental retardation. *Journal of Vocational Rehabilitation, 5*, 319–328.

Stanovich, K.E. (1999). The sociopsychometrics of learning disabilities. *Journal of Learning Disabilities, 32*(4), 350–361.

Stapleton, D.C., O'Day, B., Livermore, G.A., & Imparato, A.J. (2005). *Dismantling the poverty trap: Disability policy for the 21st century.* Washington, DC: Cornell University Institute for Policy Research.

Starkstein, S.E., & Lischinsky, A. (2002). The phenomenology of depression after brain injury, *NeuroRehabilitation, 17*(2), 105–113.

State Vocational Rehabilitation Services Program, Final Rule, 66 Fed. Reg. 7249-7258 (Jan. 22, 2001, codified at 34 C.F.R. § 361).

Steere, D.E., & Cavaiuolo, D. (2002). Connecting outcomes, goals, and objectives in transition planning. *TEACHING Exceptional Children, 34*(6), 54–59.

Steere, D.E., Wood, R., Pancsofar, E.L., & Butterworth, J. (1990). Outcome-based school-to-work transition planning for students with severe disabilities. *Career Development for Exceptional Individuals, 13*, 57–69.

Sternberg, L. (Ed.) (1994). *Individuals with profound disabilities instructional and assistive strategies* (3rd ed.). Austin, TX: PRO-ED.

Stewart, A.M., Jacinta, S., & Douglas, M. (1998). Educational outcome for secondary and postsecondary students following traumatic brain injury. *Brain Injury, 12*(4), 317.

Stock, S.E., Davies, D.K., Secor, R.R., & Wehmeyer, M.L. (2003). Self-directed career preference selection for individual with intellectual disabilities: Using computer technology to enhance self-determination. *Journal of Vocational Rehabilitation, 19*, 95–103.

Stodden, R.A., Brown, S.E., Galloway, L.M., Myrazek, S., & Noy, L. (2004). *Essential tools: Interagency transition team development and facilitation.* Minneapolis: University of Minnesota, Institute on Community Integration, National Center on Secondary Education and Transition.

Stodden, R.A., Conway, M.A., & Chang, K.B.T. (2003). Findings from the study of transition, technology and postsecondary supports for youth with disabilities: Implications for secondary school educators. *Journal of Special Education Technology, 18*(4), 29–44.

Stodden, R.A., & Dowrick, P.W. (2000). The present and future of postsecondary education for adults with disabilities. *Impact, 13,* 4–5.

Stodden, R.A., & Dowrick, P.W. (2001). *The present and future of postsecondary education for adults with disabilities.* Honolulu: University of Hawaii, Rehabilitation Research and Training Center.

Stodden, R., Whelley, T., Chang, C., & Harding, T. (2001). Current status of educational support provision to students with disabilities in postsecondary education. *Journal of Vocational Rehabilitation, 16*(3, 4), 189–198.

Storey, K. (2002). Strategies for increasing interactions in supported employment settings: An updated review. *Journal of Vocational Rehabilitation, 17,* 231–237.

Storms, J., O'Leary, E., & Williams, J. (2000). *The Individuals with Disabilities Education Act of 1997 transition requirements: A guide for states, districts, schools, universities and families.* Eugene, OR: Western Regional Resource Center.

Stout, H. (1999, November 15). Scoop on summer jobs: Even the menial ones will pay off in the end. *Wall Street Journal,* p. B1.

Strain, P.S. (1980). Social behavior programming with severely handicapped and autistic children. In B. Wilcox & A. Thompson (Eds.), *Critical issues in educating autistic children and youth* (pp. 179–206). Washington, DC: U.S. Department of Education.

Strauss, H. (1999). The future of the web, intelligent devices, and education. *Educom Review, 34*(4), 16–19, 52–54.

Stroul, B., & Friedman, R.A. (1986). *A system of care for severely emotionally disturbed children and youth.* Washington, DC: Georgetown University Child Development Center, CASSP Technical Assistance Center.

Strully, J., & Strully, C. (1985). Friendship and our children. *Journal of The Association for Persons with Severe Handicaps, 10,* 224–227.

Stuart, J., & Goodsitt, J.L. (1996). From hospital to school: How transition liaison can help. *TEACHING Exceptional Children, 4,* 58–62.

Sugai, G., Horner, R.H., & Sprague, J.R. (1999). Functional-assessment-based behavior support planning: Research to practice to research. *Behavioral Disorders, 24*(3), 253–257.

Sutherland, K.S., Alder, N., & Gunter, P.L. (2003). The effect of varying rates of opportunities to respond to academic requests on the classroom behavior of students with E/BD. *Journal of Emotional and Behavioral Disorders, 11,* 239–248.

Szymanski, D., Gugerty, J.J., Tindall, L., & Schmidt, G. (1989). *Successful vocational rehabilitation of persons with learning disabilities: Best practices.* Madison: University of Wisconsin, Wisconsin Association for Children and Adults with Learning Disabilities and Vocational Studies Center.

Szymanski, E.M., & Hershenson, D.B. (1998). Career development of people with disabilities: An ecological model. In R.M. Parker & E.M. Szymanski (Eds.), *Rehabilitation counseling: Basics and beyond* (3rd ed., pp. 327–378). Austin, TX: PRO-ED.

Taber, T.A., Alberto, P.A., Hughes, M., & Seltzer, A. (2002). A strategy for students with moderate disabilities when lost in the community. *Research and Practice for Persons with Severe Disabilities, 27*(2), 141–152.

Taber, T.A., Alberto, P.A., Seltzer, A., & Hughes, M. (2003). Obtaining assistance when lost in the community using cell phones. *Research and Practice for Persons with Severe Disabilities, 28*(3), 105–116.

Tallal, P. (1999, May). Understanding of learning disabilities grows, but so do numbers of students. *Disability Funding News,* 4.

Tanchak, T.L., & Sawyer, C. (1995). Augmentative communication. In K. Flippo, K. Inge, & J.M. Barcus (Eds.), *Assistive technology: A resource for school, work, and community* (pp. 57–79). Baltimore: Paul H. Brookes Publishing Co.

Targett, P., & Wehman, P. (2002). Supported employment: The challenges of staff recruitment, selection, and retention. *Education and Training in Mental Retardation and Developmental Disabilities, 37*(4), 434–446.

Targett, P., & Wehman, P. (2003). Successful work supports for persons with spinal cord injury. *Official Journal of the American Association of Spinal Cord Injury Psychologists and Social Workers, 16*(1), 6–11.

Targett, P., Wehman, P., & Young, C. (2004). Return to work for persons with spinal cord injury: Designing work supports. *Neurorehabilitation, 19*(2), 131–140.

Targett, P.S., Yasuda, S., & West, M. (2001). Lessons in RTW following TBI: Case studies in long-term job retention. *Brain Injury Source, 5*(1), 28–30.

Taunt, H.M., & Hastings, R.P. (2002). Positive impact of children with developmental disabilities on their families: A preliminary study. *Education and Training in Mental Retardation, 37*(4), 410–420.

Tax Reform Act of 1986, PL 99-514, 26 U.S.C. § 1 *et seq.*

Taylor, H.G., Yeates, K.O., Wade, S.L., Drotar, D., Stancin, T., & Minich, N. (2002). A prospective study of short-and long-term outcomes after traumatic brain injury in children: Behavior and achievement. *Neuropsychology, 16*, 15–27.

Taylor, L., Adelman, H.S., & Kaser Boyd, N. (1983). Perspectives of children regarding their participation in psychoeducational decisions. *Professional Psychology: Research and Practice, 14*(6), 882–894.

Taylor, P., Collins, B.C., Schuster, J.W., & Kleinert, H. (2002). Teaching laundry skills to high school students with disabilities: Generalization of targeted skills and nontargeted information. *Education and Training in Mental Retardation and Developmental Disabilities, 37*(2), 172–183.

Taylor, S.J. (1988). Caught in the continuum: A critical analysis of the principle of least restrictive environment. *Journal of The Association for Persons with Severe Handicaps, 13*, 41–53.

Teasdale, G., Knill-Jones, R., & Van der Sande, J. (1978). Observer variability in assessing impaired consciousness and coma. *Journal of Neurology, Neurosurgery, and Psychiatry, 41*, 603–610.

Technology-Related Assistance for Individuals with Disabilities Act Amendments of 1994, PL 103-218, 29 U.S.C. §§ 2201 *et seq.*

Technology-Related Assistance for Individuals with Disabilities Act of 1988, PL 100-407, 29 U.S.C. §§ 2201 *et seq.*

Test, D.W., Browder, D.M., Karvonen, M., Wood, W., & Algozzine, B. (2002). Writing lesson plans for promoting self-determination. *TEACHING Exceptional Children, 35*(1), 8–14.

Test, D.W., Fowler, C.H., & Wood, W.M. (2005). A conceptual framework of self-advocacy for students with disabilities. *Remedial and Special Education, 26*(1), 43–54.

Test, D.W., Karvonen, M., Wood, W.M., Browder, D., & Algozzine, B. (2000). Choosing a self-determination curriculum: Plan for the future. *TEACHING Exceptional Children, 33*(2), 48–54

Test, D.W., Mason, C., Hughes, C., Konrad, M., Neale, M., & Wood, W. (2004). Student involvement in individualized education program meetings. *Exceptional Children, 70*, 391–412.

Test, D.W., & Wood, W.M. (1996). Natural supports in the workplace: The jury is still out. *Journal of The Association for Persons with Severe Handicaps, 21*(4), 155–173.

Thakker, D.A. (1997). Employers and the Americans with Disabilities Act: Factors influencing manager adherence with the ADA, with specific reference to individuals with psychiatric disabilities (Doctoral dissertation, University of Pennsylvania, 1997). *Dissertation Abstracts International, 58-03A*, 1116.

Thies, K.M., & McAllister, J.W. (2001). The health and education leadership project: A school initiative for children and adolescents with chronic health conditions. *Journal of School Health, 71*(5), 167–172.

Thoma, C.A. (1999). Supporting student voice in transition planning. *TEACHING Exceptional Children, 31*(5), 4–9.

Thoma, C.A., & Getzel, E.E. (2005). "Self-determination is what it's all about": What Postsecondary students with disabilities tell us are important considerations for success. *Education and Training in Developmental Disabilities, 40*(3), 234–242.

Thoma, C.A., & Held, M.F. (2002). Measuring what's important: Using alternative assessments. In C.L. Sax & C.A. Thoma (Eds.), *Transition assessment: Wise practices for quality lives* (pp. 71–85). Baltimore: Paul H. Brookes Publishing Co.

Thoma, C.A., & Wehmeyer, M.L. (2005). Self-determination and the transition to postsecondary education. In E.E. Getzel & P. Wehman (Eds.), *Going to college: Expanding opportunities for people with disabilities* (pp. 49–68). Baltimore: Paul H. Brookes Publishing Co.

Thomas, S.B. (2000). College students and disability law. *Journal of Special Education, 33*(4), 248–257.

Thompson, A.R., & Bethea, L. (1996). *College students with disabilities: A desk reference guide for faculty and staff.* Mississippi State: Mississippi State University, Department of Counselor Education and Educational Psychology.

Thompson, B., & Guess, D. (1989). Students who experience the most profound disabilities: Teacher perspectives. In F. Brown & D.H. Lehr (Eds.), *Persons with disabilities who challenge the system* (pp. 3–41). Baltimore: Paul H. Brookes Publishing Co.

Thompson, J.R., Hughes, C., Schalock, R.L., Silverman, W., Tasse, M.J., Bryant, B., et al. (2002). Integrating supports in assessment and planning. *Mental Retardation, 40,* 390–405.

Thompson, S., & Thurlow, M.M. (2003). *2003 state special education outcomes: Marching on.* Retrieved July 28, 2004, from http://education.umn.edu/NCEO/OnlinePubs/2003State Report.htm/

Thottam, J. (2003, November 24). Health kick: Why one industry always has more good jobs than it can fill. *Time,* 54–55.

Thousand, J.S., Rosenberg, R.L., Bishop, K.D., & Villa, R.A. (1997). The evolution of secondary inclusion. *Remedial and Special Education, 18,* 270–284.

Thurlow, M.L. (2004). Biting the bullet: Including special-needs students in accountability systems. In R. Elmore (Ed.), *Redesigning accountability systems for education* (pp. 115–137). New York: Teachers College Press.

Thurlow, M.L., Lazarus, S., Thompson, S., & Robey, J. (2002). *2001 state policies on assessment participation and accommodations* (Synthesis Report 46). Retrieved July 24, 2003, from http://education. umn.edu/NCEO/OnlinePubs/Synthesis46.html

Thurlow, M.L., Nelson, J.R., Teelucksingh, E., & Ysseldyke, J.E. (2000). *Where's Waldo? A third search for students with disabilities in state accountability reports* (Technical Report No. 25). Minneapolis: University of Minnesota, National Center on Educational Outcomes.

Thurman, D.J., Alverson, C.A., Dunn, K.A., Guerrero, J., & Sniezek, J.E. (1999). Traumatic brain injury in the United States: A public health perspective. *Journal of Head Trauma Rehabilitation, 14*(6), 602–615.

Ticket to Work and Work Incentive Improvement Act of 1999, PL 106-170, 42 U.S.C. §§ 1305 *et seq.*

Tilly, W.D., Knoster, T.P., Kovaleski, J., Bambara, L., Dunlap, G., & Kincaid, D. (1998). *Functional behavior assessment: Policy development in light of emerging research and practice.* Alexandria, VA: National Association of State Directors of Special Education.

Tilson, G.P., Luecking, R.G., & Donovan, M.R. (1994). Involving employers in transition: The Bridges Model. *Career Development for Exceptional Individuals, 17*(1), 77–89.

Timmons, J.D., McIntyre, J.P., Whitney-Thomas, J., Butterworth, J., & Allen, D. (1998). Barriers to transition planning for parents of adolescents with special health care needs. *Research to Practice, 4*(7), 7–16.

Toch, T. (2003). *High schools on a human scale.* Boston: Beacon Press.

Tomblin, M. (1999, March). *Trials and tribulations of employment trends for students with learning disabilities.* Paper presented at the "Rural Special Education for the New Millennium" Conference Proceedings of the American Council on Rural Special Education (ACRES), Albuquerque, NM. (ERIC Document Reproduction Service No. ED429784)

Tomlinson, C. (2001). *How to differentiate instruction in mixed-ability classrooms* (2nd ed.). Alexandria, VA: Association for Supervision and Curriculum Development.

Torgesen, J.K. (1982). The learning disabled child as an inactive learner: Educational implications. *Topics in Learning and Learning Disabilities, 2,* 45–51.

Turnbull, A.P., & Turnbull, H.R. (1996). Group Action Planning as a strategy for providing comprehensive family support. In L.K. Koegel, R.L. Koegel, & G. Dunlap (Eds.), *Community, school, family, and social inclusion through positive behavioral support: Including people with difficult behavior in the community* (pp. 99–114). Baltimore: Paul H. Brookes Publishing Co.

Turnbull, R., Turnbull, A., Shank, M., Smith, S., & Leal, D. (2001). Severe and multiple disabilities. In R. Turnbull, A. Turnbull, M. Shank, S. Smith, & D. Leal (Eds.), *Exceptional lives: Special education in today's schools* (3rd ed., pp. 300–334). Upper Saddler River, NJ: Prentice Hall.

Twamley, E.W., Bartels, S.J., Becker, D., & Jeste, D.V. (2004, May 18–21). *Individual placement and support for middle-aged and older clients with schizophrenia.* Paper presented at the International Association of Psychosocial Services, San Diego.

Twamley, E.W., Jeste, D.V., & Lehman, A.F. (2003). Vocational rehabilitation in schizophrenia and other psychotic disorders: A literature review and meta-analysis of randomized controlled trials. *Journal of Nervous and Mental Disease, 191,* 515–523.

Tyler, J., & Wilkerson, L. (1999). Planning school transitions for students with TBI. In Brain Injury Association (Ed.), *Brain injury source* (pp. 14–16). Alexandria, VA: Brain Injury Association.

U.S. Census Bureau. (2003, March). *Disability status: 2000: Census brief.* Retrieved July 19, 2005, from http://www.census.gov/prod/2003pubs/c2kbr-17.pdf

U.S. Department of Education, National Center for Education Statistics. (2002). *Characteristics of the 100 largest public elementary and secondary school districts in the United States: 2000–2001.* Washington, DC: Author.

U.S. Department of Education, Office of Special Education Programs. (2000). *History: Twenty-five years of progress in educating children with disabilities through IDEA.* Retrieved July 19, 2005, from http://www.ed.gov/policy/speced/leg/idea/history.pdf

U.S. Department of Education, Office of Special Education Programs. (2004a). *Child Count 2003.* Retrieved July 19, 2005, from http://www.ideadata.org/index.html

U.S. Department of Education, Office of Special Education Programs. (2004b, April). *National longitudinal studies: Standardized testing among secondary school students with disabilities.* Menlo Park, CA: SRI International. Available at http://www.nlts2.org/pdfs/fact_sheet4 _05_04.pdf

U.S. Department of Education. (1996). *To assure the free appropriate public education of all children with disabilities: Eighteenth annual report to Congress on the implementation of the Individuals with Disabilities Education Act.* Washington, DC: Author.

U.S. Department of Education. (2000). *To assure the free and appropriate public education of all children with disabilities: Twenty-second annual report to Congress on the implementation of the Individuals with Disabilities Education Act.* Washington, DC: Author.

U.S. Department of Education. (2001). *Twenty-third annual report to Congress on implementation of the Individuals with Disabilities Education Act.* Washington, DC: Author.

U.S. Department of Education. (2002). *To assure the free and appropriate public education of all children with disabilities: Twenty-fourth annual report to Congress on the implementation of the Individuals with Disabilities Education Act.* Washington, DC: Author.

U.S. Department of Education. (2005). *25th annual (2003) report to Congress on the implementation of IDEA, Volume 2.* Washington, DC: Office of Special Education and Rehabilitative Services, Office of Special Education Programs.

U.S. Department of Labor. (1998, July). *One-stop disability initiative draft memo.* Washington, DC: Author.

U.S. Department of Labor. (2005, November 3). *Employment report provided for U.S., November, 2005.* Washington, DC: Author.

U.S. employment rates of people with disabilities. (2004, December/2005, January). *InfoLines, 15*(10), 1, 3, 6.

U.S. General Accounting Office. (1996, April). *SSA disability: Program redesign necessary to encourage return to work.* Washington, DC: Author.

U.S. General Accounting Office. (2003, June). *Workforce Investment Act: One-stop centers implemented strategies to strengthen services and partnerships, but more research and information sharing is needed.* Washington, DC: Author.

U.S. Senate, Committee on Health, Education, Labor, and Pensions. (2005, October 20). Opening statements by Senators Enzi and Kennedy: "Opportunities for Too Few? Oversight of Federal Employment Programs for Persons with Disabilities." Washington, DC.

U.S. Surgeon General. (2001). *National meeting on health and health care needs of individuals with mental retardation.* Washington, DC: Surgeon General's Office.

Udvari-Solner, A., & Thousand, J.S. (1996). Creating a responsive curriculum for inclusive schools. *Remedial and Special Education, 17*(3), 182–193.

Umbreit, J. (Ed.). (1983). *Physical disabilities and health impairments: An introduction.* Columbus, OH: Charles E. Merrill.

Unger, D. (2001a). Employers' attitudes toward persons with disabilities in the workforce: Myths or realities? *Focus on Autism and Other Developmental Disabilities, 16*(1), 67–75.

Unger, D. (2001b). *National study of employers' experiences with workers with disabilities and their knowledge and utilization of accommodations.* Unpublished doctoral dissertation, Virginia Commonwealth University, Richmond.

Unger, D.D. (2002). Employers' attitudes toward persons with severe disabilities in the workforce: Myths or realities? *Focus on Autism and Other Developmental Disabilities, 17*(1), 2–11.

Unger, D.D., Campbell, L.R., & McMahon, B.T. (2005). Workplace discrimination and mental retardation: The national EEOC ADA Research Project. *Journal of Vocational Rehabilitation, 23*(3), 145–154.

Unger, D., Kregel, J., Wehman, P., & Brooke, V. (2002). *Employers' view of workplace supports: Virginia Commonwealth University Charter Business Roundtable's national study of employers' experiences with workers with disabilities.* Richmond: Virginia Commonwealth University, Rehabilitation Research and Training Center.

Unger, K. (2005). Working with students who have psychiatric disabilities. In E.E. Getzel & P. Wehman (Eds.), *Going to college: Expanding opportunities for people with disabilities.* Baltimore: Paul H. Brookes Publishing Co.

United States Equal Employment Opportunity Commission. (1997a). *The Americans with Disabilities Act: Questions and answers.* Available on-line at http://www.eeoc.gov/facts/adaqu1.html

United States Equal Employment Opportunity Commission. (1997b). *The Americans with Disabilities Act: Your rights as an individual with a disability.* Available on-line at http://www.eeoc.gov/facts/ada18.html

Usiak, D.J., Stone, V.I., House, R.B., & Montgomery, M.E. (2004). Stakeholder perceptions of an effective CIL. *Journal of Vocational Rehabilitation, 20*(1), 35–43.

Uttermohlen, T., & Miller, L. (2004). Special Medicaid beneficiaries. In L. Miller & V. Brooke (Eds.), *Benefits Assistance Resource Center.* Richmond: Virginia Commonwealth University Rehabilitation Research and Training Center on Workplace Supports and Job Retention.

Vail, P. (1992). *Learning styles.* Rosemont, NJ: Modern Learning Press.

Van Reusen, A.K., & Bos, C.S. (1990). I Plan: Helping students communicate in planning conferences. *TEACHING Exceptional Children, 22*(4), 30–32.

Van Reusen, A.K., Bos, C.S., Schumaker, J.B., & Deshler, D.D. (2002). *The self-advocacy strategy for education and transition planning.* Lawrence, KS: Edge Enterprises.

Van Reusen, A.K., Deshler, D.D., & Schumaker, J.B. (1989). Effects of a student participation strategy in facilitating the involvement of adolescents with learning disabilities in individualized education program planning process. *Learning Disabilities, 1*, 23–34.

VanDenBerg, J. (1993). Integration of individualized mental health services into the system of care for children and adolescents. *Administration and Policy in Mental Health, 20*(4).

Vandercook, T., & York, J. (1990). A team approach to program development and support. In W. Stainback & S. Stainback (Eds.), *Support network for inclusive schooling* (pp. 117–118). Baltimore: Paul H. Brookes Publishing Co.

Vandercook, T., York, J., & Forest, M. (1989). The McGill Action Planning System (MAPS): A strategy for building the vision. *Journal of The Association for Persons with Severe Handicaps, 14*(3), 205–215.

Vanderwood, M., McGrew, K.S., & Ysseldyke, J.E. (1998). Why we can't say much about students with disabilities during education reform. *Exceptional Children, 64*(3), 359–370.

Vaughn, B.J., Dunlap, G., Fox, L., Clarke, S., & Bucy, M. (1997). Parent–professional partnership in behavioral support: A case study of community based intervention. *The Journal of The Association for Persons with Severe Handicaps, 22*, 186–197.

Vaughn, S., Bos, C., & Schumm, J.S. (1997). *Teaching mainstreamed, diverse and at risk students in the general classroom.* Boston: Allyn & Bacon.

Vaughn, S., Bos, C.S., & Schumm J.S. (2003). *Teaching exceptional, diverse, and at-risk students in the general education classroom* (2nd ed.). Boston: Allyn & Bacon.

Vaughn, S., Klingner, J.K., & Hughes, M.T. (2004). Sustainability of research based practices: Implications for students with disabilities. In A.M. Sorrells, H.J. Reith, & P.J. Sindelar (Eds.), *Critical issues in special education* (pp. 135–153). Boston: Allyn & Bacon.

Vaughn, S., & La Greca, A. (1993). Social skills training: Why, who, what, and how. In W.N. Bender (Ed.), *Learning disabilities: Best practices for professionals* (pp. 251–271). Austin, TX: PRO-ED.

Vaughn, S., Moody, S.W., & Schumm, J.S. (1998). Broken promises: Reading instruction in the resource room. *Exceptional Children, 64*, 211–225.

Viadero, D. (1989, November). Side by side. *Teacher Magazine Reader, 1–5.*

Villa, R.A., & Thousand, J.S. (1992). Restructuring public school systems: Strategies for organizational change and progress. In R.A. Villa, J.S. Thousand, W. Stainback, & S. Stainback (Eds.), *Restructuring for caring and effective education: An administrative guide to creating heterogeneous schools* (pp. 109–140). Baltimore: Paul H. Brooks Publishing Co.

Villa, R.A., Thousand, J.S., & Nevin, A.I. (1996). Instilling collaboration for inclusive schooling as a way of doing business in public schools. *Remedial and Special Education, 17*, 169–181.

Villa, R.A., Thousand, J.S., & Nevin, A.I. (2004). *A guide to co-teaching: Practical tips for facilitating student learning.* Thousand Oaks, CA: Corwin Press.

Virginia Commonwealth University. (2004). *Self-determination skills needed for college students with disabilities: Summary of state-wide focus group results.* Richmond: Virginia Commonwealth University, Rehabilitation Research and Training Center on Workplace Supports.

Virginia Department of Education. (2003). *Virginia's college guide for students with disabilities: You know you can do it! Here's how!* Richmond: Virginia Department of Education Division of Special Education and Student Services.

Virginia Higher Education Leadership Partners. (2005). *Requirements of the Individuals with Disabilities Education Act (IDEA), Section 504 of the Rehabilitation Act (Section 504), and the Americans with Disabilities Act (ADA).* Unpublished document. Virginia Commonwealth University at Richmond.

Vogel, S. (1997). Ways that students can help themselves. *College students with learning disabilities: A handbook for college students with LD, faculty and staff, administrators, and disability support service providers.* Available on-line at http://www.ldonline.com/ld_indepth/postsecondary/vogel_tips.html

Vogenthaler, D.R. (1987a). An overview of head injury: Its consequences and rehabilitation. *Brain Injury, 1*, 113–127.

Vogenthaler, D.R. (1987b). Rehabilitation after closed head injury: A primer. *Journal of Rehabilitation, 53*(4), 15–21.

Volkmar, F.R., & Nelson, D.S. (1990). Seizure disorders in autism. *Journal of the American Academy of Child and Adolescent Psychiatry, 29*, 127–129.

Wacker, D.P., & Berg, W.K. (1993). Effects of picture prompts on the acquisition of complex vocational tasks by mentally retarded adolescents. *Journal of Applied Behavior Analysis, 16,* 417–443.

Wagner, M., Cameto, R., & Newman, L. (2003). *Youth with disabilities: A changing population: A report of findings from the National Longitudinal Transition Study (NLTS) and the National Longitudinal Transition Study-2 (NLTS2).* Menlo Park, CA: SRI International.

Wagner, M., Newman, L., D'Amico, R., Jay, D., Butler-Nalin, P., Marder, C., & Cox, R. (1991). *Youth with disabilities: How are they doing?* Washington, DC: US Department of Education, Office of Special Programs.

Waldron, N.L., & McLeskey J. (1998). The effects of an inclusive school program on students with mild and severe learning disabilities. *Exceptional Children, 64,* 395–405.

Walker, D.K., Singer, J.D., Palfrey, J.S., Orza, M., Wenger, M., & Butler, J.A. (1988). Who leaves and who stays in special education: A 2-year follow-up study. *Exceptional Children, 54*(5), 393–402.

Walker, H.M., & Gresham, E.M. (1997). Making schools safer and violence free. *Intervention in School and Clinic, 32,* 199–204.

Walker, H., McConnell, S., Holmes, D., Todis, B., Walker, J., & Golden, N. (1983). *Walker Social Skills Curriculum.* Austin, TX: PRO-ED.

Walker, J.L. (1988). Young American Indian children. *TEACHING Exceptional Children, 20*(4), 45–51.

Wallace, J., & Neal, S. (1993). *Special topic report: Funding assistive technology.* Richmond, VA: Virginia Assistive Technology System.

Wallis, C. (2004, May 10). What makes teens tick. *Time, 163*(19), 57–65.

Walsh, J.M., & Jones, B. (2004, May/June). New models of cooperative teaching. *Exceptional Children, 36*(5), 14–20.

Walther-Thomas, C., & Bryant, M. (1996). Planning for effective co-teaching. *Remedial and Special Education, 17*(4), 255–266.

Ward, M.J. (1991, September). *Self-determination revisited: Going beyond expectations.* NICHCY Transition Summary. Washington, DC: National Information Center for Children and Youth with Disabilities and HEATH Resource Center.

Ward, M.J. (1996). Coming of age in the age of self-determination: A historical and personal perspective. In D.J. Sands & M.L. Wehmeyer (Eds.), *Self-determination across the life span: Independence and choice for people with disabilities* (pp. 1–16). Baltimore: Paul H. Brookes Publishing Co.

Ward, M.J., & Kohler, P.D. (1996). Promoting self-determination for individuals with disabilities: Content and process. In L.E. Powers, G.H.S. Singer, & J. Sowers (Eds.), *On the road to autonomy: Promoting self-competence in children and youth with disabilities* (pp. 275–290). Baltimore: Paul H. Brookes Publishing Co.

Watanabe, M., & Sturmey, P. (2003). The effect of choice-making opportunities during activity schedules on task engagement of adults with autism. *Journal of Autism and Developmental Disorders, 33,* 535–538.

Weaver, C.L. (1994). Privatizing vocational rehabilitation: Options for increasing individual choice and enhancing competition. *Journal of Disability Policy Studies, 5*(1), 53–76.

Webber, J. (1997). Comprehending youth violence: A practicable perspective. *Remedial and Special Education, 18,* 94–104.

Wehby, J.H., Lane, K.L., & Falk, K.B. (2003). Academic instruction for students with emotional and behavioral disorders. *Journal of Emotional and Behavioral Disorders, 11,* 194–197.

Wehman, P. (1981). *Competitive employment: New horizons for severely disabled individuals.* Baltimore: Paul H. Brookes Publishing Co.

Wehman, P. (1992). Transition for young people with disabilities: Challenges for the 1990s. *Education and Training in Mental Retardation, 27,* 112–118.

Wehman, P. (1996). *Life beyond the classroom: Transition strategies for young people with disabilities* (2nd ed.). Baltimore: Paul H. Brookes Publishing Co.

Wehman, P. (1997a). Curriculum design. In P. Wehman & J. Kregel (Eds.), *Functional curriculum for elementary, middle, and secondary age students with special needs, 1,* 1–17.

Wehman, P. (1997b). *Exceptional individuals in school, community, and work.* Austin, TX: PRO-ED.

Wehman, P. (2001a). *Life beyond the classroom: Transition strategies for young people with disabilities* (3rd ed.). Baltimore: Paul H. Brookes Publishing Co.

Wehman, P. (2001b). *Supported employment in business: Expanding the capacity of workers with disabilities.* St. Augustine, FL: Training Resource Network.

Wehman, P. (2002a). *Individual transition plans: The teacher's curriculum guide for helping youth with special needs* (2nd ed.). Austin, TX: PRO-ED.

Wehman, P. (2002b). A new era: Revitalizing special education for children and their families. *Focus on Autism and Other Developmental Disabilities, 17*(4), 194–197.

Wehman, P. (2003). Workplace inclusion: Persons with disabilities and coworkers working together. *Journal of Vocational Rehabilitation, 18*(2), 131–141.

Wehman, P. (2005). Students with low incidence disabilities. In J. Wood (Ed.), *Adapting instruction in accommodating students in inclusive settings* (5th ed., pp. 56–87). Upper Saddle River, NJ: Prentice Hall.

Wehman, P., & Bricout, J. (2001). Supported employment: New directions for the new millennium In P. Wehman (Ed.), *Supported employment in business: Expanding the capacity of workers with disabilities* (pp. 3–22). St. Augustine, FL: Training Resource Network.

Wehman, P., Bricout, J., & Kregel, J. (2000). Supported employment in 2000: Changing the locus of control from agency to consumer. In M.L. Wehmeyer & J.R. Patton (Eds.), *Mental retardation in the 21st century* (pp. 115–150). Austin, TX: PRO-ED.

Wehman, P., Bricout, J., & Targett, P. (2000). Supported employment for persons with traumatic brain injury: A guide for implementation. In R.T. Fraser & D.C. Clemmons (Eds.), *Traumatic brain injury: Practical vocational, neuropsychological, and psychotherapy interventions* (pp. 201–240). Boca Raton, FL: CRC Press.

Wehman, P., Bricout, J., Targett, P., & Johns, J. (2001). Traumatic brain injury and return to work. In P. Wehman (Ed.), *Supported employment in business: Expanding the capacity of workers with disabilities.* St. Augustine, FL: Training Resource Network.

Wehman, P., Brooke, V., & Green, H. (2004). *Public-private partnerships: A model for success.* Richmond: Virginia Commonwealth University Rehabilitation Research and Training Center on Workplace Supports and Job Retention.

Wehman, P., & Getzel, E.E. (2005). *Going to college: Expanding opportunities for people with disabilities.* Baltimore: Paul H. Brookes Publishing Co.

Wehman, P., Gibson, K., Brooke, V., & Unger, D. (1998). Transition from school to competitive employment: Illustrations of competence for two young women with severe mental retardation. *Focus on Autism and Other Developmental Disabilities, 13*(3), 130–143.

Wehman, P., Hewett, M., Tipton, M., Brooke, V., & Green, H. (2005). *Business and the public sector working together to promote employment for persons with developmental disabilities: Preliminary results.* (Unpublished paper). Richmond: Virginia Commonwealth University, Rehabilitation Research and Training Center.

Wehman, P., Inge, K.J., Revell, W.G., & Brooke, V.A. (in press). *Real work for real pay: Inclusive employment for people with disabilities.* Baltimore: Paul H. Brookes Publishing Co.

Wehman, P., & Kregel, J. (1995). At the crossroads: Supported employment a decade later. *Journal of The Association for Persons with Severe Handicaps, 20,* 286–299.

Wehman, P., & Kregel, J. (1998). *More than a job: Securing satisfying careers for people with disabilities.* Baltimore: Paul H. Brookes Publishing Co.

Wehman, P., & Kregel, J. (2004). *Functional curriculum for elementary, middle, secondary age students with special needs* (2nd ed.). Austin, TX: PRO-ED.

Wehman, P., Kregel, J., & Barcus, M. (1985). From school to work: A vocational transition model for handicapped students. *Exceptional Children, 52*(1), 25–37.

Wehman, P., Kregel, J., Keyser-Marcus, L., Sherron-Targett, P., Campbell, L., West, M., et al. (2003). Supported employment for persons with traumatic brain injury: A preliminary investigation of long-term follow-up cost and program efficiency. *Archives of Physical Medicine and Rehabilitation, 84,* 192–196.

Wehman, P., Kregel, J., & Revell, G. (1991). *National analysis of supported employment implementation: FY 1986-FY 1990.* Richmond: Virginia Commonwealth University, Rehabilitation Research and Training Center.

Wehman, P., Kregel, J., & Seyfarth, J. (1985). Transition from school to work for youth with severe handicaps: A follow-up study. *Journal of The Association for Persons with Severe Handicaps, 10*(3), 132–136.

Wehman, P., & Kreutzer, J. (Eds.). (1990). *Vocational rehabilitation for persons with traumatic brain injury.* Baltimore: Aspen Publishers.

Wehman, P., Kreutzer, J.S., Stonnington, H.H., Wood, W., Sherron, P., Diambra, J., et al. (1988). Supported employment for persons with traumatic brain injury: A preliminary report. *Journal of Head Trauma Rehabilitation, 3*(4), 82–90.

Wehman, P., Kreutzer, J.S., West, M., Sherron, P., Diambra, J., Fry, R., et al. (1989). Employment outcomes of persons following traumatic brain injury: Pre-injury, post-injury, and supported employment. *Brain Injury, 3*(12), 397–412.

Wehman, P., Moon, M.S., Everson, J.M., Wood, W., & Barcus, J.M. (1988). *Transition from school to work: New challenges for youth with severe disabilities.* Baltimore: Paul H. Brookes Publishing Co.

Wehman, P., & Revell, G. (1996). Supported employment from 1986–1993: A national program that works. *Focus on Autism and Developmental Disabilities, 11*, 235–242.

Wehman, P., & Revell, G. (1997). Transition from school to adulthood: Looking ahead. In P. Wehman (Ed.), *Exceptional individuals in school and work* (pp. 597–648). Austin, TX: PRO-ED.

Wehman, P., & Revell, G. (2002). *Lessons learned from the provision and funding of employment services for the MR/DD population: Implications for assessing the adequacy of the SSA ticket to work program.* Washington, DC: Urban Institute.

Wehman, P., Revell, G., & Brooke, V. (2003). Competitive employment: Has it become the "first choice" yet? *Journal of Disability Policy Studies, 14*(3), 163–173.

Wehman, P., Revell, G., & Kregel, J. (1998). Supported employment: A decade of rapid growth and impact. *American Rehabilitation, 24*(1), 31–43.

Wehman, P., & Targett, P. (2002, December). Supported employment: The challenges of new staff recruitment, selection and retention. *Education and Training in Mental Retardation and Developmental Disabilities, 37*(4), 434–446.

Wehman, P., & Targett, P. (2004). Principles of curriculum design: Road to transition from school to adulthood. In P. Wehman & J. Kregel (Eds.), *Functional curriculum for elementary, middle and high school age students with special needs* (pp. 1–26). Austin, TX: PRO-ED.

Wehman, P., Targett, P.S., West, M.D., Eltzeroth, H., Green, J.H., & Brooke, V. (2001). Corporate initiated workplace supports. In A.J. Tymchuk, K.C. Lakin, & R. Luckasson (Eds.), *The forgotten generation: The status and challenges of adults with mild cognitive limitations* (pp. 99–118). Baltimore: Paul H. Brookes Publishing Co.

Wehman, P., Targett, P., West, M., & Kregel, J. (2005). Productive work and employment for persons with TBI: What have we learned after 20 years? *Journal of Head Trauma Rehabilitation, 20*(2), 115–127.

Wehman, P., Wittig, K., & Dowdy, V. (2002). Transition plans for youth with intellectual disabilities. In P. Wehman (Ed.), *Individual transition plans: The teacher's curriculum guide for helping youth with special needs* (2nd ed., pp. 161–166). Austin, TX: PRO-ED.

Wehmeyer, M. (1992). Self-determination and the education of students with mental retardation. *Education and Training in Mental Retardation, 27*, 302–314.

Wehmeyer, M.L. (1996). Self-determination as an educational outcome: Why is it important to children, youth, and adults with disabilities? In D.J. Sands & M.L. Wehmeyer (Eds.), *Self-determination across the life span: Independence and choice for people with disabilities* (pp. 17–36). Baltimore: Paul H. Brookes Publishing Co.

Wehmeyer, M.L. (1998). Self-determination and individuals with significant disabilities: Examining meanings and misinterpretations. *Journal of The Association for Persons with Severe Handicaps, 23*(1), 5–16.

Wehmeyer, M.L. (1999). A functional model of self-determination: Describing development and implementing instruction. *Focus on Autism and Other Developmental Disabilities, 14*(1), 53–61.

Wehmeyer, M.L. (2001a). Self-determination and mental retardation. In L.M. Glidden (Ed.), *International review of research in mental retardation* (Vol. 24, pp. 1–48). San Diego: Academic Press.

Wehmeyer, M.L. (2001b). Self-determination and mental retardation: Assembling the puzzle pieces. In H. Switzky (Ed.), *Personality and motivational differences in persons with mental retardation* (pp. 147–198). Mahwah, NJ: Lawrence Erlbaum Associates.

Wehmeyer, M.L. (2002). *Providing access to the general curriculum: Teaching students with mental retardation.* Baltimore: Paul H. Brookes Publishing Co.

Wehmeyer, M.L., Abery, B., Mithaug, D.E., & Stancliffe, R.J. (2003). *Theory in self-determination: Foundations for educational practice.* Springfield, IL: Charles C Thomas.

Wehmeyer, M.L., Agran, M., & Hughes, C. (1998). *Teaching self-determination to students with disabilities: Basic skills for successful transition.* Baltimore: Paul H. Brookes Publishing Co.

Wehmeyer, M.L., Agran, M., & Hughes, C. (2000). A national survey of teachers' promotion of self-determination and student-directed learning. *Journal of Special Education, 34*, 58–68.

Wehmeyer, M.L., Field, S., Doren, B., Jones, B., & Mason, C. (2004). Self-determination and student involvement in standards-based reform. *Exceptional Children, 70*(4), 413–425.

Wehmeyer, M.L., Garner, N., Lawrence, M., Yeager, D., & Davis, A.K. (in press). Infusing self-determination into 18–21 services: A multistage model. *Education and Training in Developmental Disabilities.*

Wehmeyer, M.L., & Gragoudas, S. (2004). Centers for independent living and transition-age youth: Empowerment and self-determination. *Journal of Vocational Rehabilitation, 20*(1), 53–58.

Wehmeyer, M.L., & Kelchner, K. (1995a). *The Arc's self-determination scale.* Arlington, TX: The Arc.

Wehmeyer, M.L., & Kelchner, K. (1995b). Measuring the autonomy of adolescents and adults with mental retardation. *Career Development for Exceptional Individuals, 18*(1), 3–20.

Wehmeyer, M.L., Lance, G.D., & Bashinski, S. (2002). Promoting access to the general curriculum for students with mental retardation: A multi-level model. *Education and Training in Mental Retardation and Developmental Disabilities, 37*(3), 223–234.

Wehmeyer, M.L., Lattimore, J., Jorgensen, J.D., Palmer, S.B., Thompson, E., & Schumaker, K.M. (2003). The self-determined career development model: A pilot study. *Journal of Vocational Rehabilitation, 19*, 79–89.

Wehmeyer, M.L., Lattin, D., & Agran, M. (2001). Promoting access to the general curriculum for students with mental retardation: A decision-making model. *Education and Training in Mental Retardation and Developmental Disabilities, 36*, 329–344.

Wehmeyer, M.L., & Lawrence, M. (1995). Whose future is it anyway? Promoting student involvement in transition planning. *Career Development for Exceptional Individuals, 18*, 69–83.

Wehmeyer, M.L., & Lawrence, M. (in press). A national replication of a student-directed transition planning process: Impact on student knowledge of and perceptions about transition planning. *Treatment of Exceptional Children.*

Wehmeyer, M.L., Lawrence, M., Kelchner, K., Palmer, S., Garner, N., & Soukup, J. (2004). *Whose future is it anyway? A student-directed transition planning process* (2nd ed.). Lawrence, KS: Beach Center on Disability.

Wehmeyer, M.L., & Palmer, S.B. (2003). Adult outcomes for students with cognitive disabilities three years after high school: The impact of self-determination. *Education and Training in Developmental Disabilities, 38*, 131–144.

Wehmeyer, M.L., Palmer, S.B., Agran, M., Mithaug, D.E., & Martin, J.E. (2000). Promoting causal agency: The Self-Determined Learning Model of Instruction. *Exceptional Children, 66*(4), 439–453.

Wehmeyer, M.L., & Sands, D.J. (Eds.). (1998). *Making it happen: Student involvement in education planning, decision making, and instruction.* Baltimore: Paul H. Brookes Publishing Co.

Wehmeyer, M.L., & Schwartz, M. (1997). Self-determination and positive adult outcomes: A follow-up study of youth with mental retardation or learning disabilities. *Exceptional Children*, *63*(2), 245–255.

Wehmeyer, M.L., & Schwartz, M. (1998). The relationship between self-determination and quality of life for adults with mental retardation. *Education and Training in Mental Retardation and Developmental Disabilities*, *33*(1), 3–12.

Wehmeyer, M.L. (with Sands, D.J., Knowlton, H.E., & Kozleski, E.B.). (2002). Achieving access to the general curriculum. In *Teaching students with mental retardation: Providing access to the general curriculum* (pp. 50–68). Baltimore: Paul H. Brookes Publishing Co.

Wehmeyer, M.L. (with Sands, D.J., Knowlton, H.E., & Kozleski, E.B.). (2002). *Teaching students with mental retardation: Providing access to the general curriculum.* Baltimore: Paul H. Brookes Publishing Co.

Wehmeyer, P., & Patten, J. (Eds.). (2000). *Mental retardation in the 21st century.* Austin, TX: PRO-ED.

Weiner, H.M. (2003). Effective inclusion: professional development in the context of the classroom. *TEACHING Exceptional Children*, *35*(6), 12–18.

Weiner, J.S., & Zivolich, S. (1995). If not now, when?: The case against waiting for sheltered workshop changeover. *Journal of The Association for Persons with Severe Handicaps*, *20*, 311–312.

Weiner, J.S., & Zivolich, S. (1998). Universal access: A natural support corporate initiative at universal studios Hollywood. *Journal of Vocational Rehabilitation*, *10*, 5–14.

Weiner, J.S., & Zivolich, S. (2003). A longitudinal report for three employees in a training consultant model of natural support. *Journal of Vocational Rehabilitation*, *18*, 199–202.

Weiss, M.P., & Lloyd, J. (2003). Conditions for co-teaching: Lessons from a case study. *Teacher Education and Special Education*, *26*(1), 27–41.

Weller, B. (1994). Unmet needs for developmental disabilities services: Population and environment *Journal of Interdisciplinary Services*, *15*(4), 279–302.

Wertheimer, A. (1995). *Circle of support: Building inclusive communities.* Bristol, England: Circles Network UK.

Wessel, D. (2004, February 12). Barbell effect: The future of jobs—New ones arise, wage gap widens. *Wall Street Journal*, p. A1.

West, L.L., Corbey, S., Boyer-Stephens, A., Jones, B., Miller, R.J., & Sarkees-Wircenski, M. (1999). *Transition and self-advocacy: Integrating transition planning into the IEP process* (Monograph). Reston, VA: Council for Exceptional Children.

West, M. (1994). Aspects of brain injury in the workplace. *Brain Injury*, *8*(4), 232–234.

West, M. (1995). Choice, self-determination, and VR services: Systematic barriers for consumers with severe disabilities. *Journal of Vocational Rehabilitation*, *5*(4), 281–290.

West, M., & Anderson, J. (2005). Telework and employees with disabilities: Accommodations and funding options. *Journal of Vocational Rehabilitation*, *23*(2), 115–122.

West, M., Barcus, M., Brooke, V., & Rayfield, R.G. (1995). An exploratory analysis of self-determination of persons with disabilities. *Journal of Vocational Rehabilitation*, *5*(4), 357–369.

West, M., Callahan, M., Lewis, M.B., Mast, M., & Sleight, L. (1991). Supported employment and assistive technology for individuals with physical impairments. *Journal of Vocational Rehabilitation*, *1*(2), 29–39.

West, M., Hill, J., Revell, G., Smith, G., Kregel, J., & Campbell, L. (2002). Medicaid HCBS waivers and supported employment: Pre-and post-Balanced Budget Act of 1997. *Mental Retardation*, *40*(2), 142–147.

West, M.D., Hock, T., Wittig, K.M., & Dowdy, V.Z. (1998). Getting to work: Personal and public transportation. In P. Wehman (Ed.), *More than a job: Securing satisfying careers for people with disabilities* (pp. 287–299). Baltimore: Paul H. Brookes Publishing Co.

West, M., Kregel, J., Getzel, E.E., Zhu, M., Ipsen, S., & Martin, E.D. (1993). Beyond Section 504: Satisfaction and empowerment of students with disabilities in higher education. *Exceptional Children*, *59*, 456–467.

West, M.D., & Parent, W. (1992). Consumer choice and empowerment in supported employment. In P. Wehman, P. Sale, & W. Parent (Eds.), *Supported employment: Strategies for integration of workers with disabilities* (pp. 29–48). Stoneham, MA: Andover Medical Publishers.

West, M.D., & Parent, W.S. (1995). Community and workplace supports for individuals with severe mental illness in supported employment. *Psychosocial Rehabilitation Journal, 18*(4),13–24.

West, M., Rayfield, R.G., Clements, C., Unger, D., & Thornton, T. (1994). An illustration of positive behavioral support in the workplace for individuals with severe mental retardation. *Journal of Vocational Rehabilitation, 4*(4), 265–271.

West, M.D., Wehman, P.B., & Wehman, P.H. (2005). Competitive employment outcomes for persons with intellectual and developmental disabilities: The national impact of the Best Buddies Job Program. *Journal of Vocational Rehabilitation, 23,* 51–63.

West, M.D., Wittig, K., & Dowdy, V. (2004). Travel and mobility training. In P. Wehman & J. Kregel (Eds.), *Functional curriculum for elementary, middle, & secondary age students with special needs* (2nd ed., pp. 245–258). Austin, TX: PRO-ED.

Westling, D.L., & Fox, L. (2000). *Teaching students with severe disabilities* (2nd ed.). Upper Saddle River, NJ: Merrill/Prentice Hall.

Wetherby, A.M., & Prizant, B.M. (2000). Introduction to autism spectrum disorders. In A.M. Wetherby & B.M. Prizant (Eds.), *Autism spectrum disorders: A transactional developmental perspective.* Baltimore: Paul H. Brookes Publishing Co.

Whelley, T.A., Radtke, R., Burgstahler, S., & Christ, T.W. (2003). Mentors, advisers, role models, and peer supporters: Career development relationships and individuals with disabilities. *American Rehabilitation, 27*(1), 42–49.

White, J., & Weiner, J.S. (2004). Influence of least restrictive environment and community based training on integrated employment outcomes for transitioning students with severe disabilities. *Journal of Vocational Rehabilitation, 21,* 149–156.

Whitman, T.L. (1990). Self-regulation and mental retardation. *American Journal on Mental Retardation, 94*(4), 347–362.

Whitney-Thomas, J., Shaw, D., Honey, K., & Butterworth, J. (1998). Building a future: A study of student participation in person-centered planning. *Journal of The Association for Persons with Severe Handicaps, 23*(2), 119–133.

Whittenburg, D., & Maag, E. (2002). School to where? A literature review on economic outcomes of youth with disabilities. *Journal of Vocational Rehabilitation, 17,* 265–280.

Wiggins, G. (1993). *Assessing student performance: Exploring the purpose and limits of testing.* San Francisco: Jossey-Bass.

Will, M.C. (1984). *OSERS programming for the transition of youth with disabilities: Bridges from school to working life.* Washington, DC: Office of Special Education and Rehabilitative Services, U.S. Department of Education.

Wille-Gregory, M., Graham, J.W., & Hughes, C. (1995, Spring). Preparing students with learning disabilities for success in postsecondary education. *Transition Linc,* 1–6.

Williams, I.J., Petty, D.M., & Verstegen, D. (1998). The business approach to job development. *Journal of Vocational Rehabilitation, 10,* 23–29.

Williams, J. (2004, July). *The role of standards-based education in transition.* Paper presented at Texas Association of Vocational Adjustment Counselors, Austin, TX.

Williams, J.M., & Martin, S.M. (2001). Implementing the Individuals with Disabilities Education Act of 1997: The consultant's role. *Journal of Educational and Psychological Consultation, 12*(1), 59–81.

Williams, J.M., & O'Leary, E. (2001). What we've learned and where we go from here. *Career Development of Exceptional Individuals, 24*(1), 51–71.

Williard, E., & Dotson, D. (2005). Self-determination in Maryland takes a new direction. *TASH Connections, 31*(3/4), 16–17.

Wilson, K.E. (1998). Centers for independent living in support of transition. *Focus on Autism and Other Developmental Disabilities, 13*(4), 246–252.

Wilson, K., Getzel, E., & Brown, T. (2000). Enhancing the post-secondary campus climate for students with disabilities. *Journal of Vocational Rehabilitation, 14*(1), 37–50.

Wilson, K.E., Kregel, J.J., & Getzel, E.E. (1999, February 22). *External review final report services for students with disabilities.* Richmond: Virginia Commonwealth University Rehabilitation Research and Training Center and School of Education.

Wisconsin Division of Vocational Rehabilitation Counselors, Wisconsin Association of Children and Adults with Learning Disabilities, and Vocational Studies Center. (1988). *Best practices: Successful vocational rehabilitation of persons with learning disabilities.* Madison: University of Wisconsin–Madison.

Wittenburg, D.C., Golden, T., & Fishman, M. (2002). Transition options for youth with disabilities: An overview of the programs and polices that affect the transition from school. *Journal of Vocational Rehabilitation, 17,* 195–206.

Wittenburg, D.C., & Maag, E. (2002). School to where? A literature review on economic outcomes of youth with disabilities. *Journal of Vocational Rehabilitation, 17,* 265–280.

Woelders, H.J. (1990). Telework: New opportunities for the handicapped unemployed workers. *International Journal of Sociology and Social Policy, 10*(4–6), 176–180.

Wolfensberger, W. (Ed.). (1972). *The principle of normalization in human services.* Toronto: National Institute on Mental Retardation.

Wood, J.W. (2006). *Teaching students in inclusive settings: Adapting and accommodating instruction.* Upper Saddle River, NJ: Prentice Hall.

Wood, W. (1988). Supported employment for persons with physical and disabilities. In P. Wehman & M.S. Moon (Eds.), *Vocational rehabilitation and supported employment* (pp. 341–363). Baltimore: Paul H. Brookes Publishing Co.

Wood, W.M., Karvonen, M., Test, D.W., Browder, D., & Algozzine, B. (2004). Promoting student self-determination skills in IEP planning. *TEACHING Exceptional Children, 36*(3), 8–16.

Woods, L.L., & Martin, J.E. (2004). Improving supervisor evaluations through the use of self-determination contracts. *Career Development for Exceptional Individuals, 27,* 207–220.

Workforce Investment Act Implementation Taskforce Office. (1998, November 12). *Implementing the Workforce Investment Act of 1998.* Available on-line at http://usworkforce.org/wpaper3.htm

Workforce Investment Act of 1998, PL 105-220, 29 U.S.C. §§ 2801 *et seq.*

Wynn, B. (1995, February). *Introduction to deafblindness.* Presentation at the Institute on Deafness, In-Service Training on Deaf-Blindness, Orientation to Blindness for the Deafness Professional, Northern Illinois University, DeKalb.

Yasuda, S., Wehman, P., Targett, P., Cifu, D., & West, M. (2001). Return to work for persons with traumatic brain injury. *American Journal of Physical Medicine and Rehabilitation, 80*(11), 852–864.

Yates, J. (1980). *Program design sessions.* Stoughton, MA: Author.

Yeargin-Allsopp, M., Rice, C., Karapurkar, T., Doernbert, N., Boyle, C., & Murphy, C. (2003). Prevalence of autism in a U.S. metropolitan area [Electronic version]. *Journal of the American Medical Association, 289,* 49–55.

Yell, M.L., Drasgow, E., & Lowrey, K.A. (2005). No Child Left Behind and students with autism spectrum disorders. *Focus on Autism and Other Developmental Disabilities, 20,*(3), 130–139.

Ylvisaker, M., Hartwick, P., Ross, B., & Nussbaum, N. (1994). Cognitive assessment. In R. Savage & D. Wolcott (Eds.), *Educational dimensions of acquired brain injury* (pp. 311–347). Austin, TX: PRO-ED.

Ylvisaker, M., Szekers, S.F., & Haarbauer-Krupa, J. (1998). Cognitive rehabilitation: Organization, memory, and language. In M. Ylvistaker (Ed.), *Traumatic brain injury rehabilitation: Children and adolescents* (pp. 181–220). Boston: Butterworth-Heinemann.

Young, T. (1990). *Public alternative education: Options and choice for today's schools.* New York: Teachers College Press.

Ysseldyke, J., & Bielinski, J. (2000). *Interpreting trends in the performance of special education students.* Minneapolis: MN: National Center on Education Outcomes.

Ysseldyke, J., & Bielinski, J. (2002). Effect of different methods of reporting and reclassification on trends in test scores for students with disabilities. *Exceptional Children, 68*(2), 189–200.

Ysseldyke, J., Nelson, J.R., Christenson, S., Johnson, D.R., Dennison, A., Triezenberg, H., et al. (2004). What we know and need to know about the consequences of high-stakes testing for students with disabilities. *Exceptional Children, 71*(1), 75–94.

Zhang, D. (1998). *The effect of self-determination instruction on high school students with mild disabilities.* Unpublished doctoral dissertation. University of New Orleans, Department of Special Education, New Orleans.

Zhang, D. (2001). The effect of 'Next S.T.E.P.' instruction on the self-determination skills of high school students with learning disabilities. *Career Development for Exceptional Individuals, 24,* 121–132.

Zhang, D., Katsiyannis, A., & Herbst, M. (2004). Disciplinary exclusions in special education: A 4-year analysis. *Behavioral Disorders, 29*(4), 337–347.

Zigmond, N. (1995). An exploration of the meaning and practice of special education in the context of full inclusion of students with learning disabilities. *Journal of Special Education, 29*(2), 109–115.

Zigmond, N. (2003). Where should students with disabilities receive special education services? Is one place better than another? *Journal of Special Education, 37*(3), 193–199.

Zuna, N., & McDougall, D. (2004, September/October). Using positive behavior support to manage avoidance of academic tasks. *TEACHING Exceptional Children, 37* 18–24.

Index

Page numbers followed by *f* indicate figures; those followed by *t* indicate tables.